Skip·Beat!

Shojo Beat

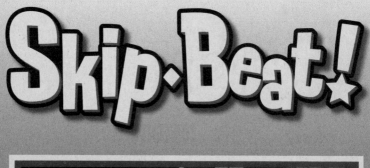

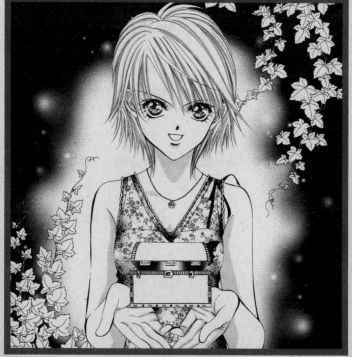

Vol. 1

Story & Art by Yoshiki Nakamura

Skip·Beat!
Volume 1

CONTENTS

SKIP BEAT 1

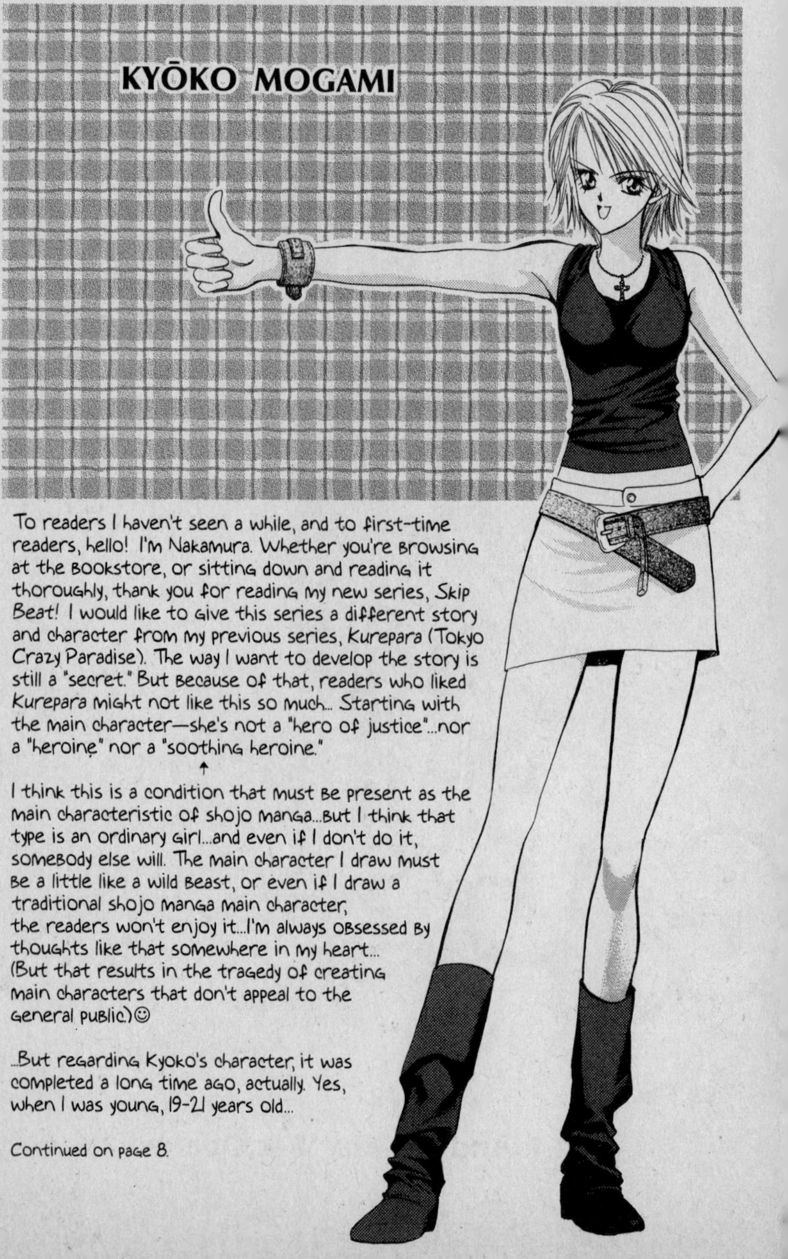

KYŌKO MOGAMI

To readers I haven't seen a while, and to first-time readers, hello! I'm Nakamura. Whether you're browsing at the bookstore, or sitting down and reading it thoroughly, thank you for reading my new series, *Skip Beat!* I would like to give this series a different story and character from my previous series, *Kurepara* (*Tokyo Crazy Paradise*). The way I want to develop the story is still a "secret." But because of that, readers who liked *Kurepara* might not like this so much... Starting with the main character—she's not a "hero of justice"...nor a "heroine," nor a "soothing heroine."

I think this is a condition that must be present as the main characteristic of shojo manga...But I think that type is an ordinary girl...and even if I don't do it, somebody else will. The main character I draw must be a little like a wild beast, or even if I draw a traditional shojo manga main character, the readers won't enjoy it...I'm always obsessed by thoughts like that somewhere in my heart... (But that results in the tragedy of creating main characters that don't appeal to the general public.)☺

...But regarding Kyoko's character, it was completed a long time ago, actually. Yes, when I was young, 19-21 years old...

Continued on page 8.

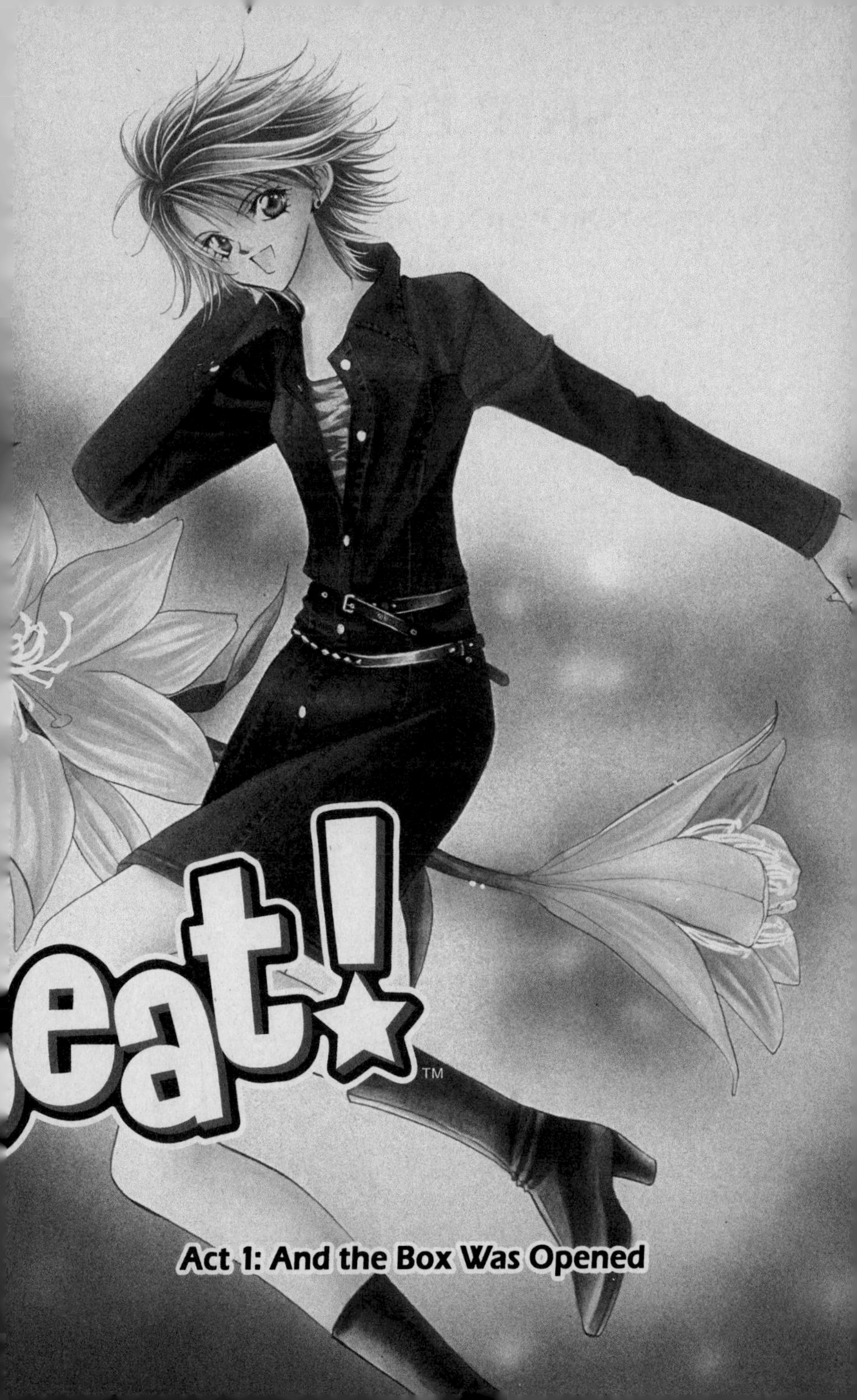
eat!™
Act 1: And the Box Was Opened

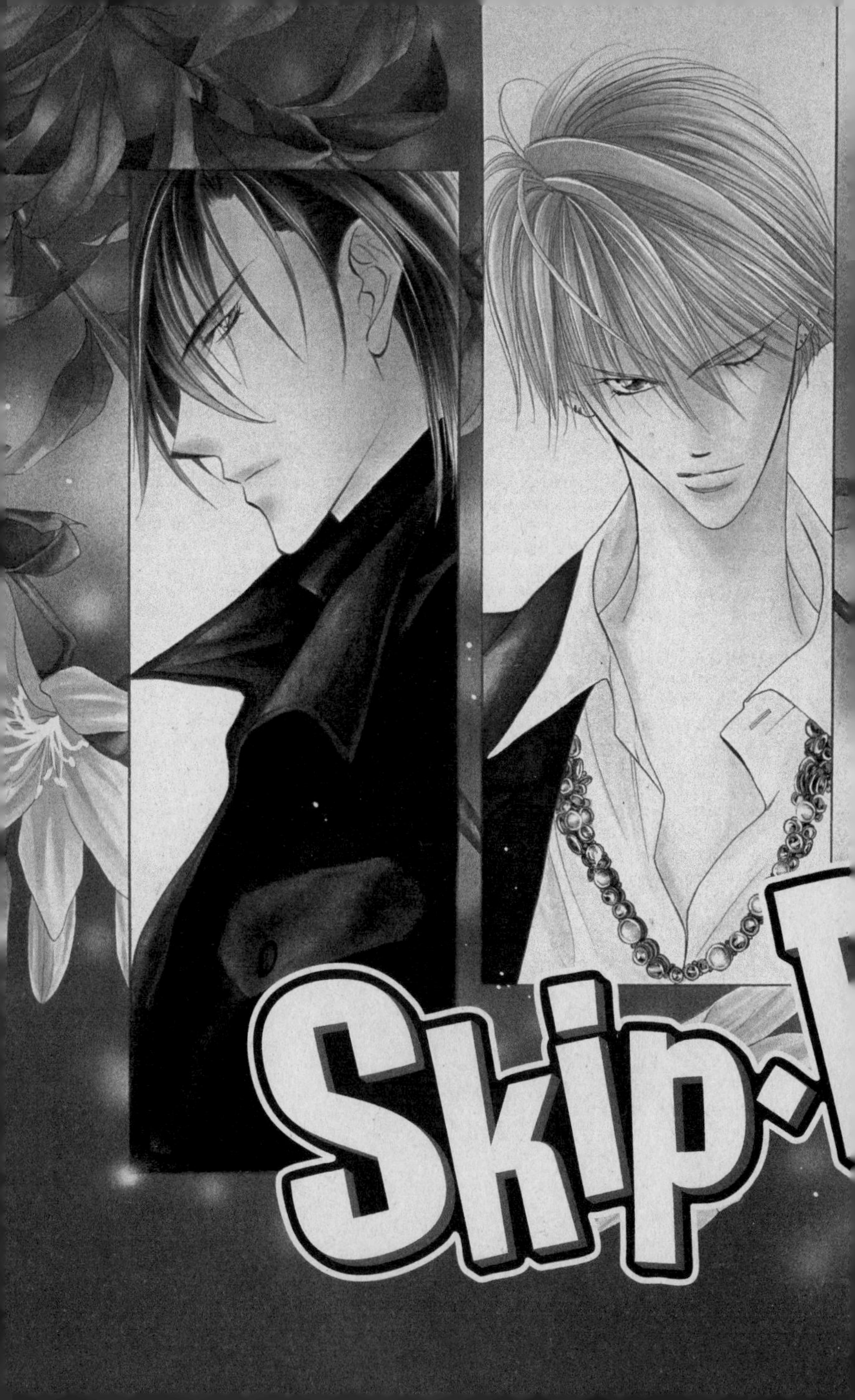
Skip

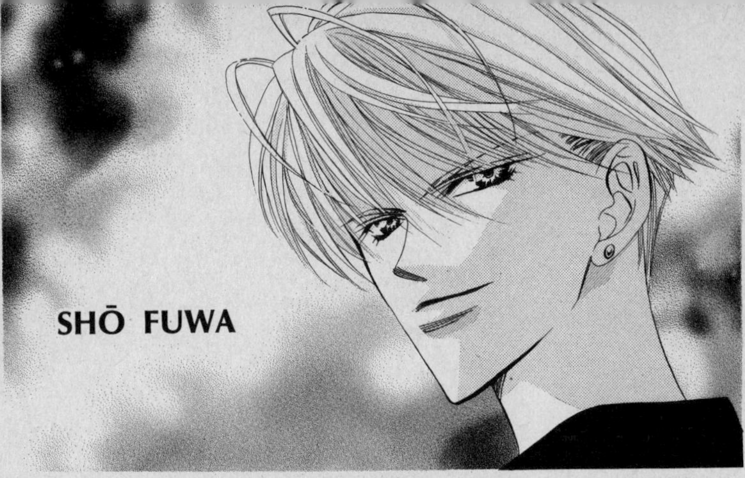
SHŌ FUWA

At my first job, a very depressing Kyoko character was created, who reflected my gray life (she could see spirits, and was good at witchcraft and making straw dolls for cursing people, so she was always a vengeful-spirit Kyoko). But although she could curse people, the curses usually failed. A silly character... Then I quit my first job and before I went to my second job, Kyoko's appearance changed a little (the changed Kyoko is on page 88), and after I made my debut as a mangaka, I drew a 30-page storyboard for a one-shot story with that Kyoko appearing as a side character.

↑ The antagonist's younger sister, an extremely evil personality.

...But before I could show it to my editor, I found out that my debut work would be a series. So I didn't show it to anybody, and it was put to sleep. But because I didn't use it then, I think I was able to use it now...Well, she has been changed for the series to be a little more cheerful than before. But the dark side is part of Kyoko's individuality, so she always has to be dark here and there. Because I have the image of the original Kyoko inside me, I have to be careful about the amount of darkness... It has to be in the range that is acceptable for a shojo manga heroine. By the way, when I was asked by my editor about ideas for the new series, I had in mind a simple school-based story... The main character was a beautiful, angel-like girl hiding Kyoko inside...so there was a wide gap between her looks and her real personality, a character with poison. But at that time I was doing a school-based story in *Hana to Yume*...

Continued on page 25.

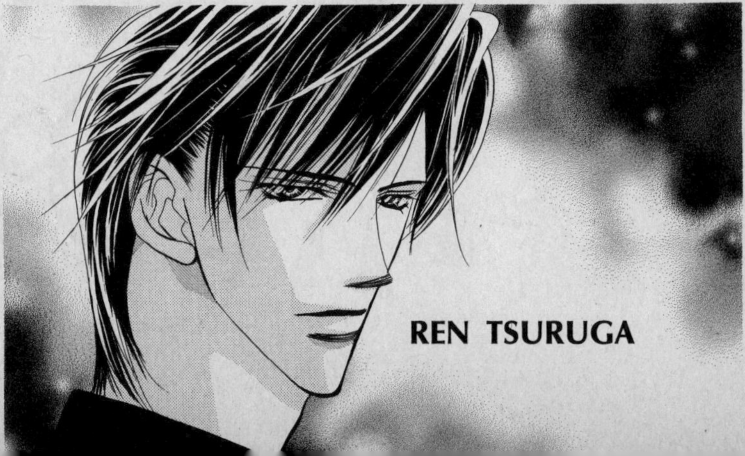
REN TSURUGA

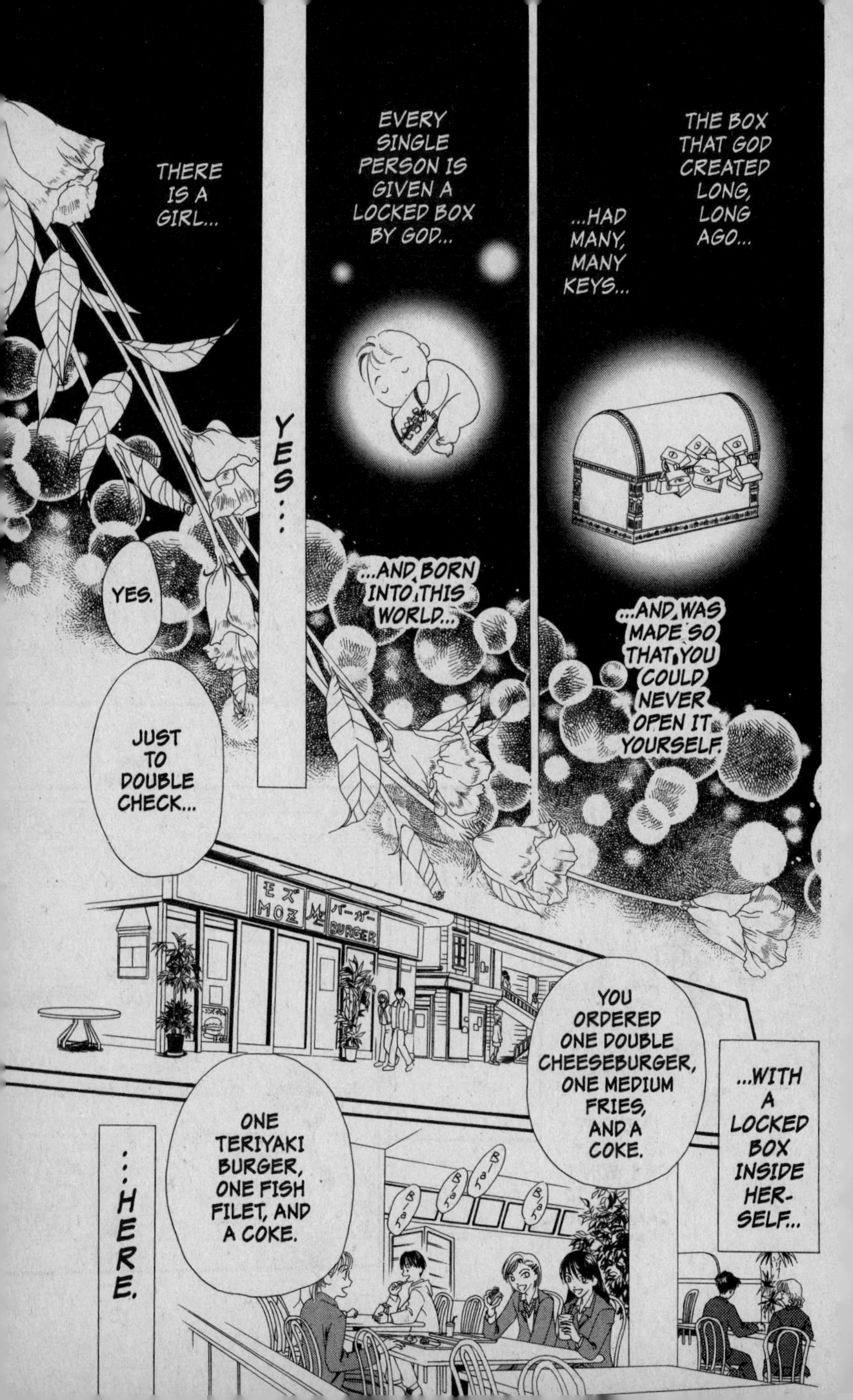
THE BOX THAT GOD CREATED LONG, LONG AGO...
...HAD MANY, MANY KEYS...
...AND WAS MADE SO THAT YOU COULD NEVER OPEN IT YOURSELF.
EVERY SINGLE PERSON IS GIVEN A LOCKED BOX BY GOD...
...AND BORN INTO THIS WORLD...
YES...
THERE IS A GIRL...
YES.
JUST TO DOUBLE CHECK...
モズ MOZ
バーガー BURGER
...WITH A LOCKED BOX INSIDE HERSELF...
YOU ORDERED ONE DOUBLE CHEESEBURGER, ONE MEDIUM FRIES, AND A COKE.
ONE TERIYAKI BURGER, ONE FISH FILET, AND A COKE.
...HERE.

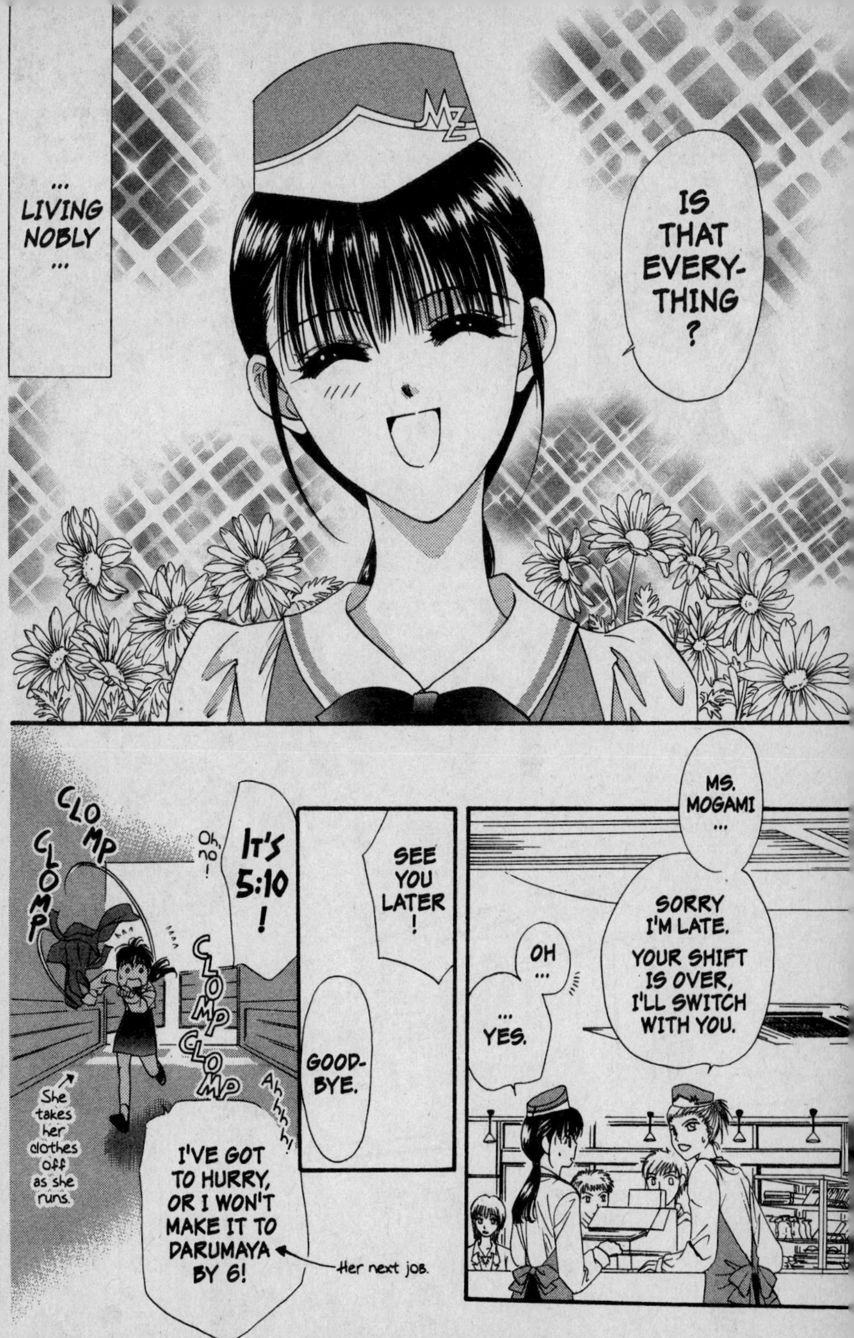
IS THAT EVERY-THING?
... LIVING NOBLY ...
MS. MOGAMI ...
SORRY I'M LATE.
YOUR SHIFT IS OVER, I'LL SWITCH WITH YOU.
OH ...
... YES.
SEE YOU LATER!
GOOD-BYE.
CLOMP
CLOMP
Oh, no!
It's 5:10!
CLOMP CLOMP
Ahhhh!
I'VE GOT TO HURRY, OR I WON'T MAKE IT TO DARUMAYA BY 6!
Her next job.
She takes her clothes off as she runs.

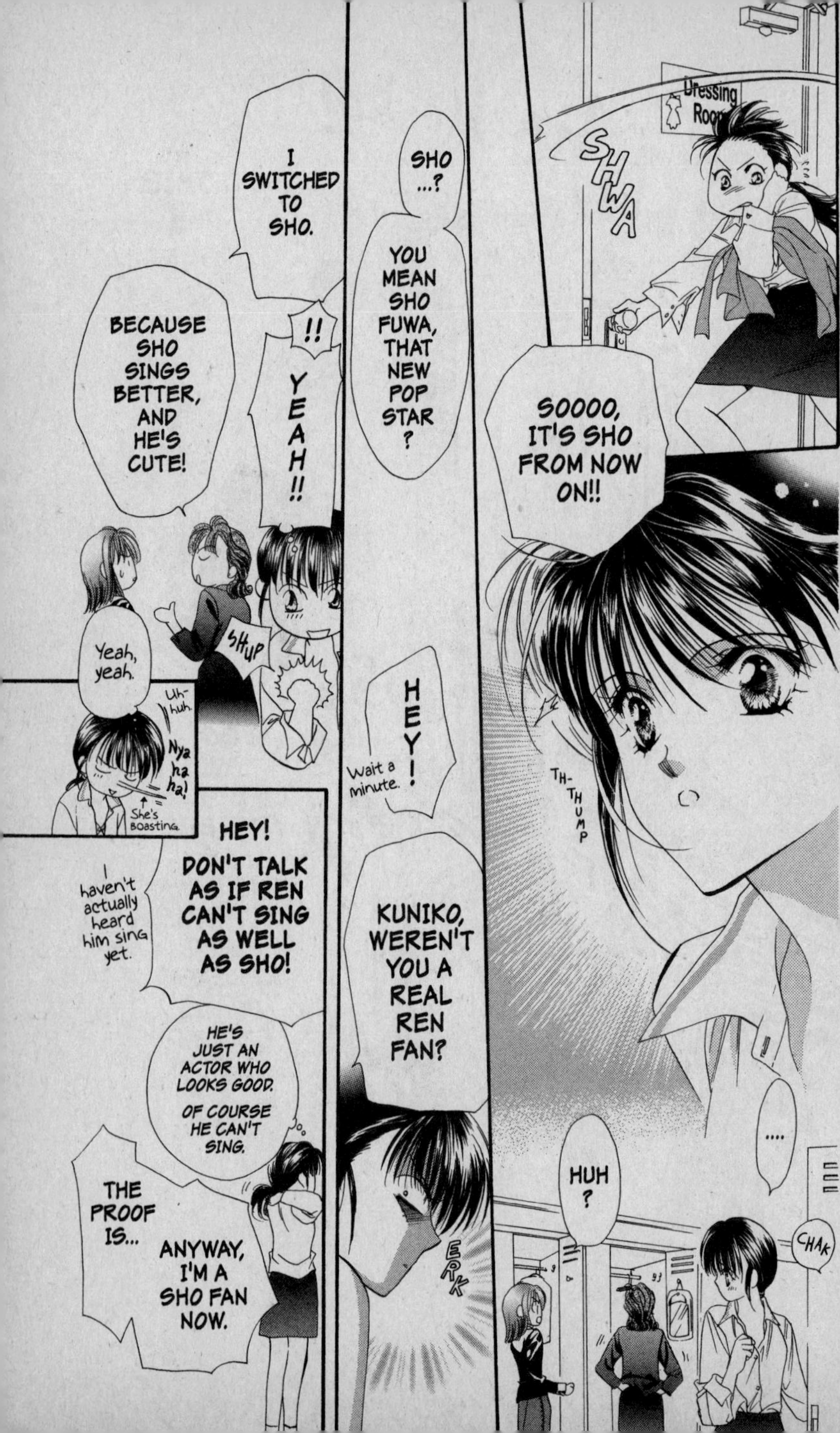
Dressing Room
SHWA
SOOOO, IT'S SHO FROM NOW ON!!
TH-THUMP
....
HUH?
CHAK
SHO ...?
YOU MEAN SHO FUWA, THAT NEW POP STAR?
HEY!
Wait a minute.
KUNIKO, WEREN'T YOU A REAL REN FAN?
ERK
I SWITCHED TO SHO.
!!
YEAH!!
BECAUSE SHO SINGS BETTER, AND HE'S CUTE!
SHUP
Yeah, yeah.
Uh-huh.
Nya ha ha!
She's boasting.
HEY! DON'T TALK AS IF REN CAN'T SING AS WELL AS SHO!
I haven't actually heard him sing yet.
HE'S JUST AN ACTOR WHO LOOKS GOOD. OF COURSE HE CAN'T SING.
THE PROOF IS...
ANYWAY, I'M A SHO FAN NOW.

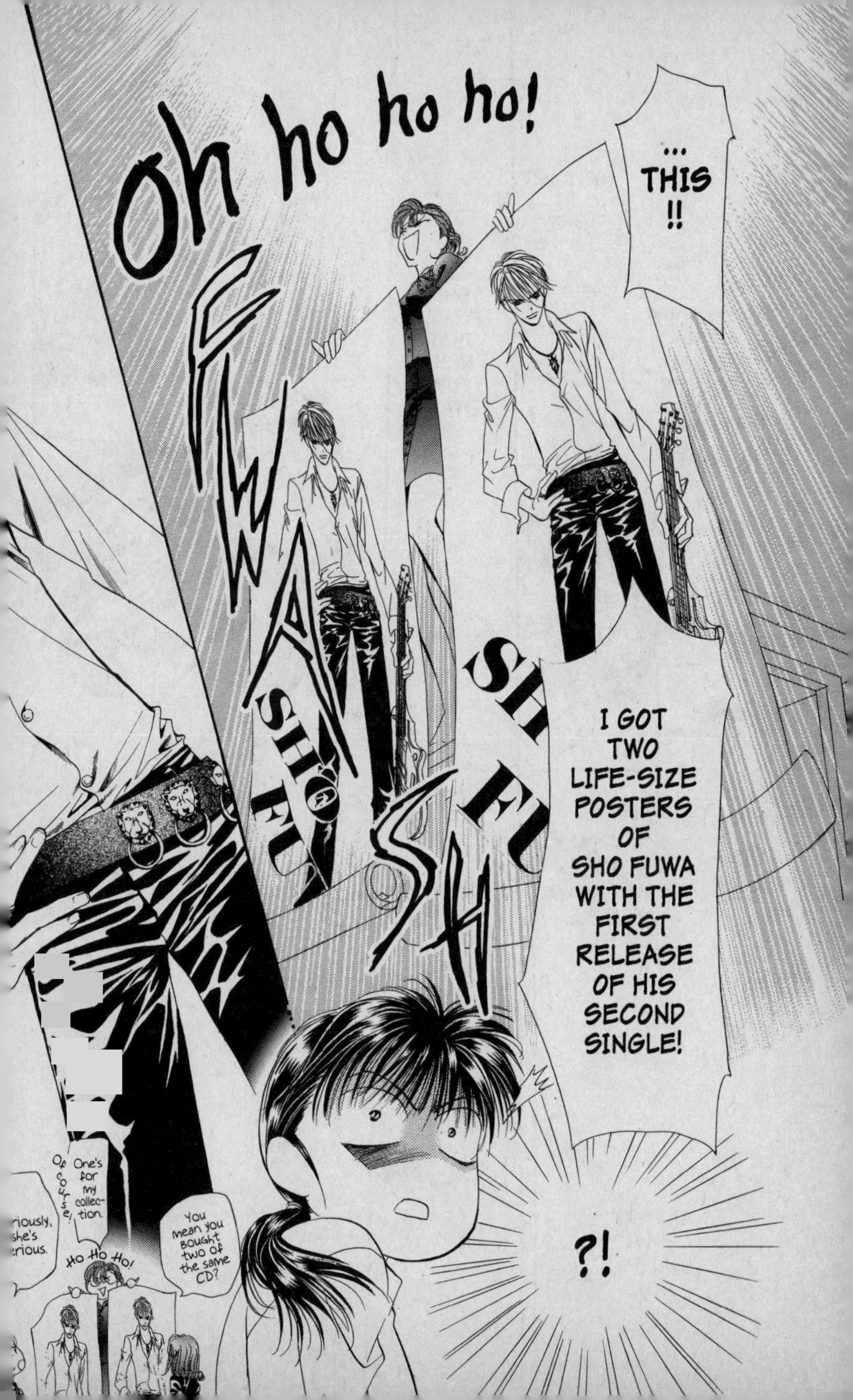

... THIS !!
Oh ho ho ho!
FLASH
SHO FU
SHO FU
I GOT TWO LIFE-SIZE POSTERS OF SHO FUWA WITH THE FIRST RELEASE OF HIS SECOND SINGLE!
?!
You mean you bought two of the same CD?
One's for my collection.
Of course!
Ho Ho Ho!
riously, she's rious.

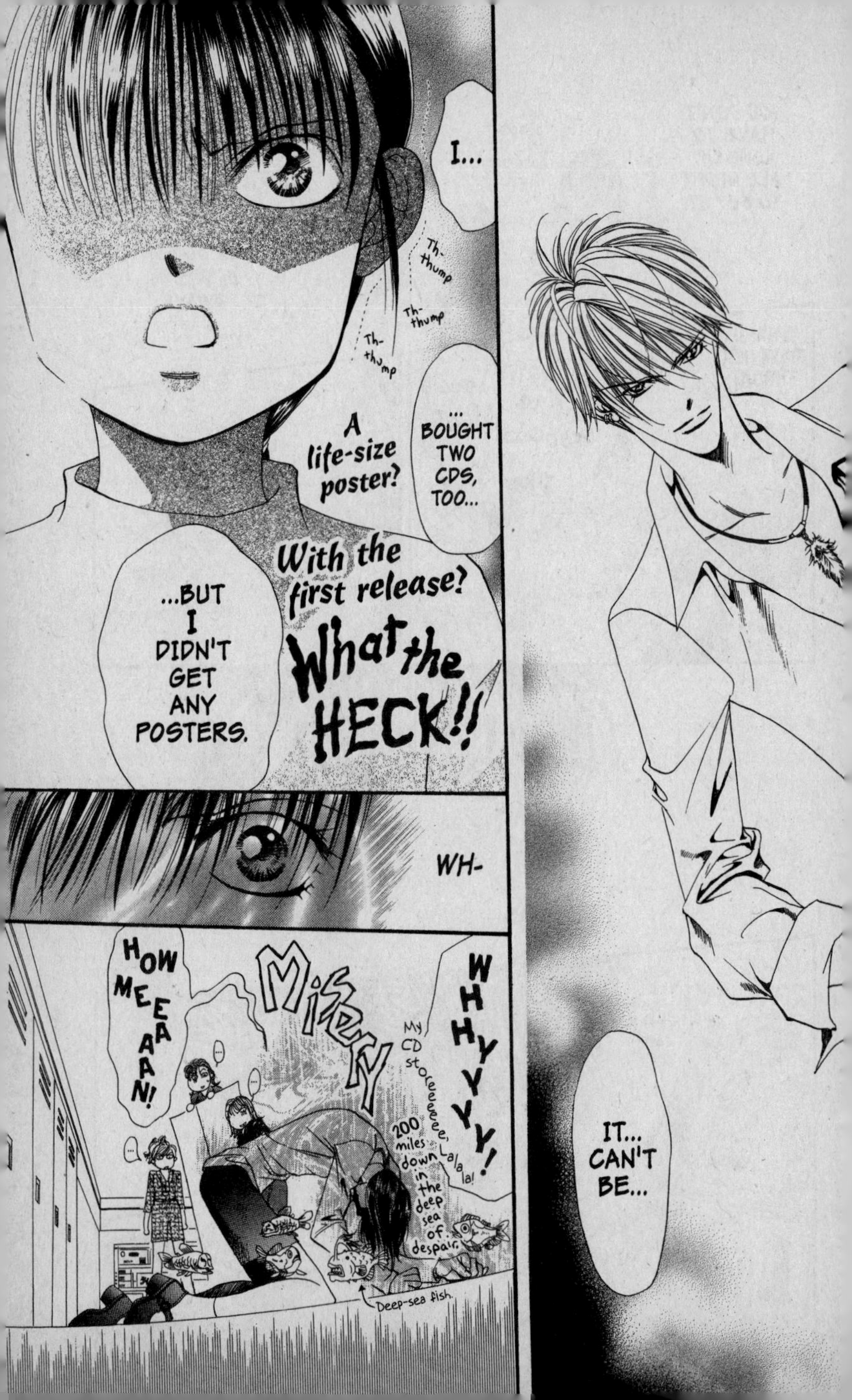
IT... CAN'T BE...
I...
...BOUGHT TWO CDS, TOO...
A life-size poster?
Th-thump
Th-thump
Th-thump
With the first release? What the HECK!!
...BUT I DIDN'T GET ANY POSTERS.
WH-
WHHYYYY!
My CD storeeeeee, Lalala!
200 miles down in the deep sea of despair.
MISERY
HOW MEEAAAN!
...
...
...
Deep-sea fish.

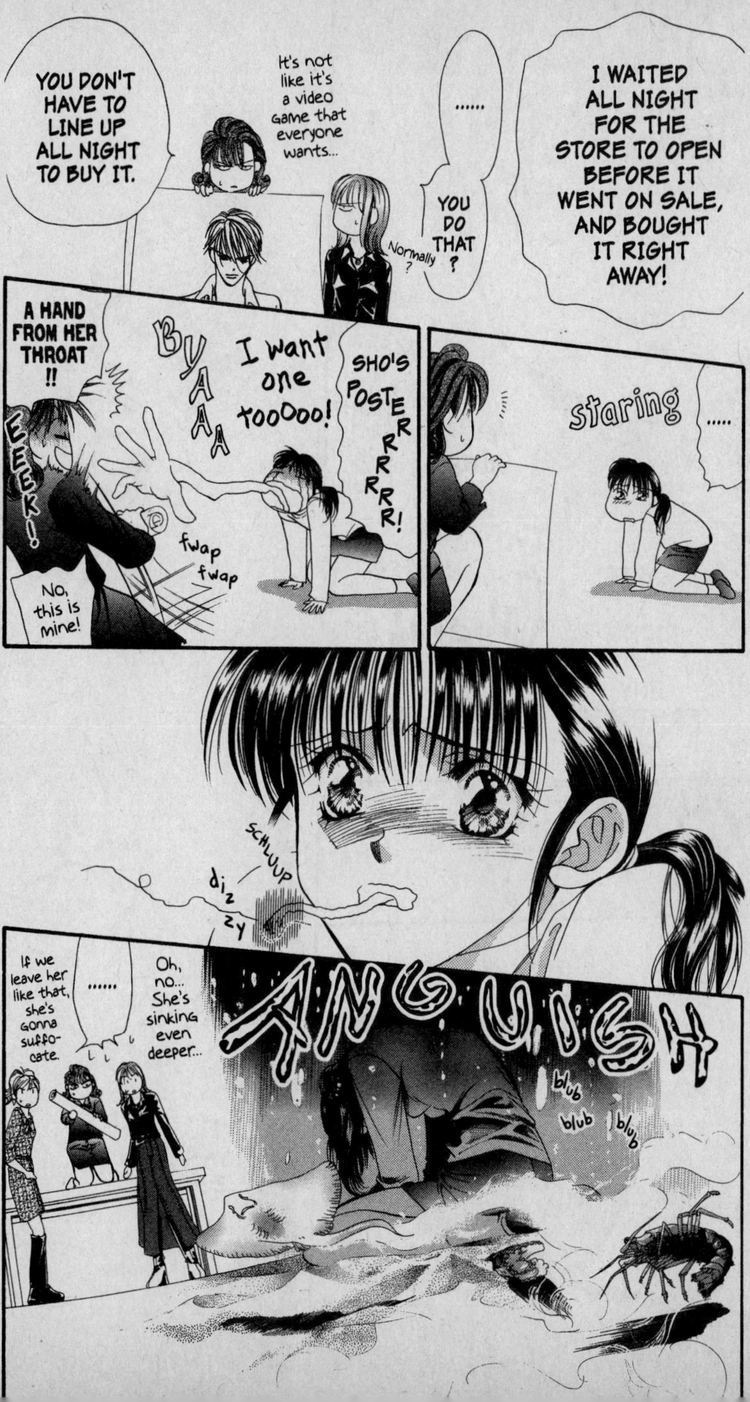
I WAITED ALL NIGHT FOR THE STORE TO OPEN BEFORE IT WENT ON SALE, AND BOUGHT IT RIGHT AWAY!
......
YOU DO THAT?
Normally?
It's not like it's a video game that everyone wants...
YOU DON'T HAVE TO LINE UP ALL NIGHT TO BUY IT.
staring
.....
SHO'S POSTERRRRRR!
I want one tooOoo!
BYAAAA
A HAND FROM HER THROAT !!
EEEK!
fwap fwap
No, this is mine!
SCHLUUP
dizzy
ANGUISH
blub blub blub
Oh, no... She's sinking even deeper...
......
If we leave her like that, she's gonna suffocate.

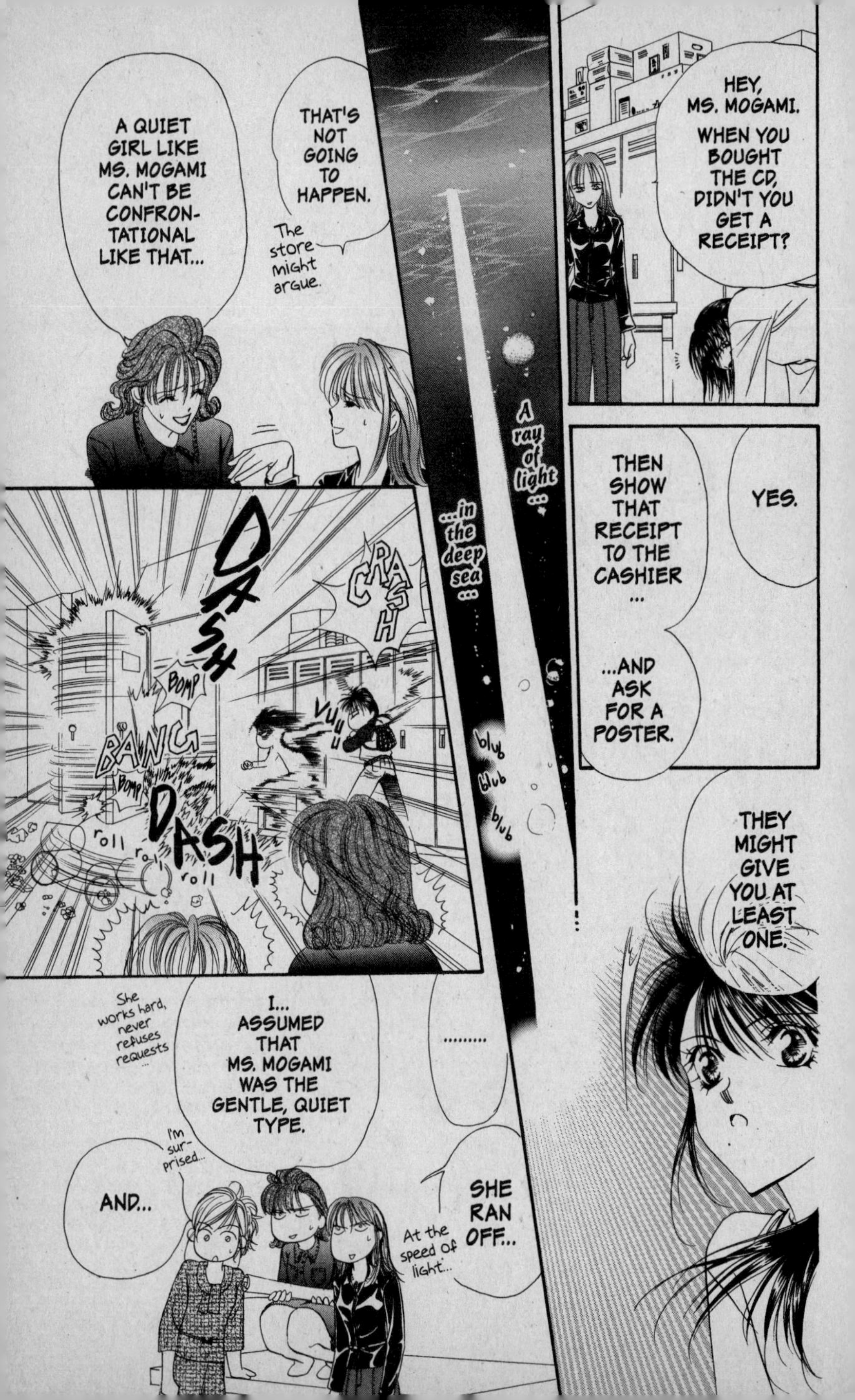
HEY, MS. MOGAMI. WHEN YOU BOUGHT THE CD, DIDN'T YOU GET A RECEIPT?
YES.
THEN SHOW THAT RECEIPT TO THE CASHIER ...
...AND ASK FOR A POSTER.
THEY MIGHT GIVE YOU AT LEAST ONE.
A ray of light ...
...in the deep sea ...
blub
blub
blub
THAT'S NOT GOING TO HAPPEN.
The store might argue.
A QUIET GIRL LIKE MS. MOGAMI CAN'T BE CONFRON-TATIONAL LIKE THAT...
CRASH
DASH
BOMP
VUUU
BANG
BOMP
DASH
roll
roll
roll
....
I... ASSUMED THAT MS. MOGAMI WAS THE GENTLE, QUIET TYPE.
She works hard, never refuses requests ...
SHE RAN OFF...
At the speed of light...
AND...
I'm sur-prised...

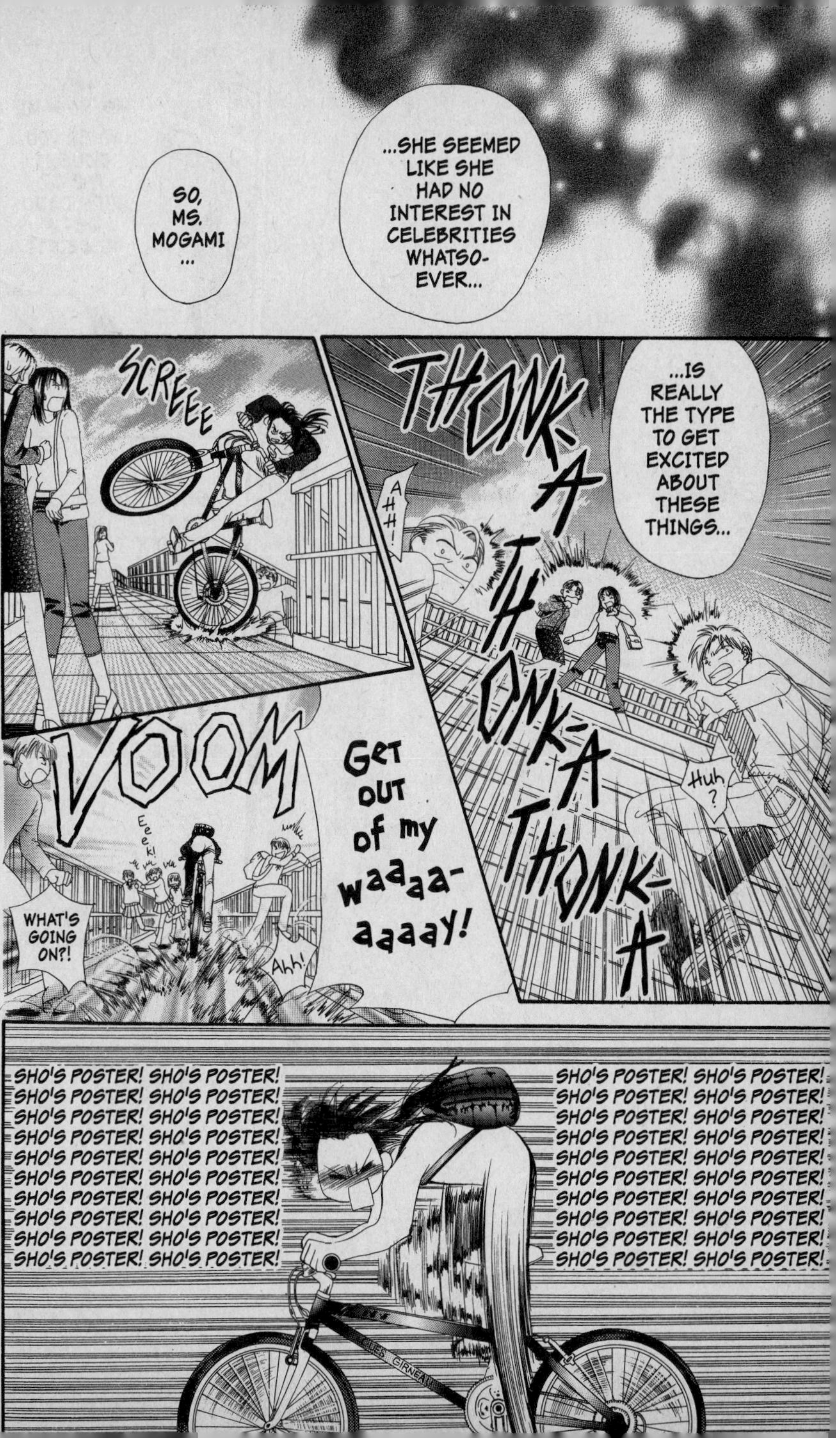
...SHE SEEMED LIKE SHE HAD NO INTEREST IN CELEBRITIES WHATSO-EVER...
SO, MS. MOGAMI...
...IS REALLY THE TYPE TO GET EXCITED ABOUT THESE THINGS...
THONK-A THONK-A THONK-A
AHH!
Huh?
SCREEEE
Get OUT of my waaaa-aaaay!
VOOM
Eeek!
WHAT'S GOING ON?!
Ahh!
SHO'S POSTER! SHO'S POSTER! SHO'S POSTER! SHO'S POSTER! SHO'S POSTER! SHO'S POSTER! SHO'S POSTER! SHO'S POSTER! SHO'S POSTER! SHO'S POSTER! SHO'S POSTER! SHO'S POSTER! SHO'S POSTER! SHO'S POSTER! SHO'S POSTER! SHO'S POSTER! SHO'S POSTER! SHO'S POSTER! SHO'S POSTER! SHO'S POSTER!
SHO'S POSTER! SHO'S POSTER! SHO'S POSTER! SHO'S POSTER! SHO'S POSTER! SHO'S POSTER! SHO'S POSTER! SHO'S POSTER! SHO'S POSTER! SHO'S POSTER! SHO'S POSTER! SHO'S POSTER! SHO'S POSTER! SHO'S POSTER! SHO'S POSTER! SHO'S POSTER! SHO'S POSTER! SHO'S POSTER! SHO'S POSTER! SHO'S POSTER!

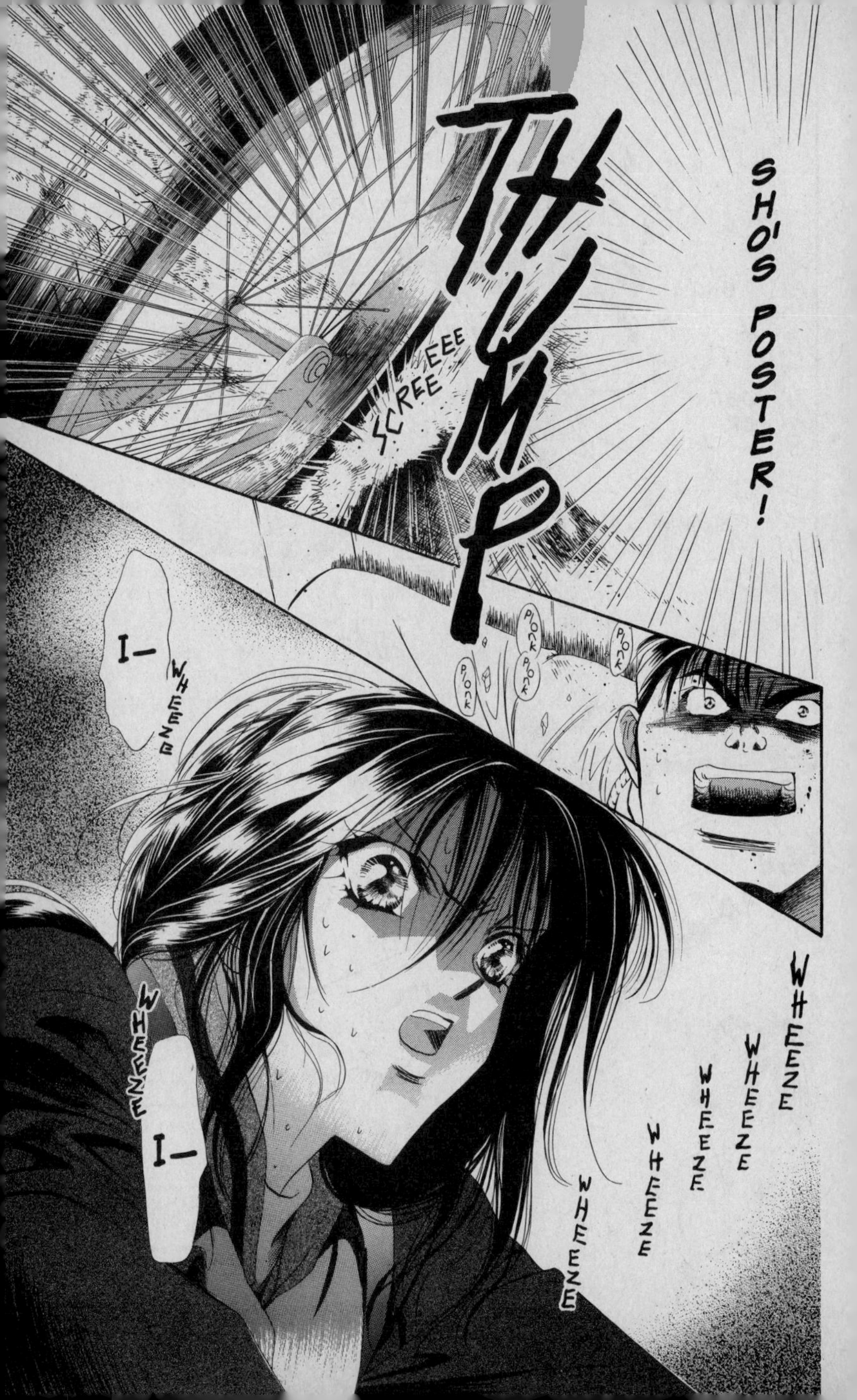

SHO'S POSTER!
THUMP
SCREEEE
PLONK
PLONK
PLONK
PLONK
WHEEZE
WHEEZE
WHEEZE
WHEEZE
WHEEZE
I—
WHEEZE
I—
WHEEZE

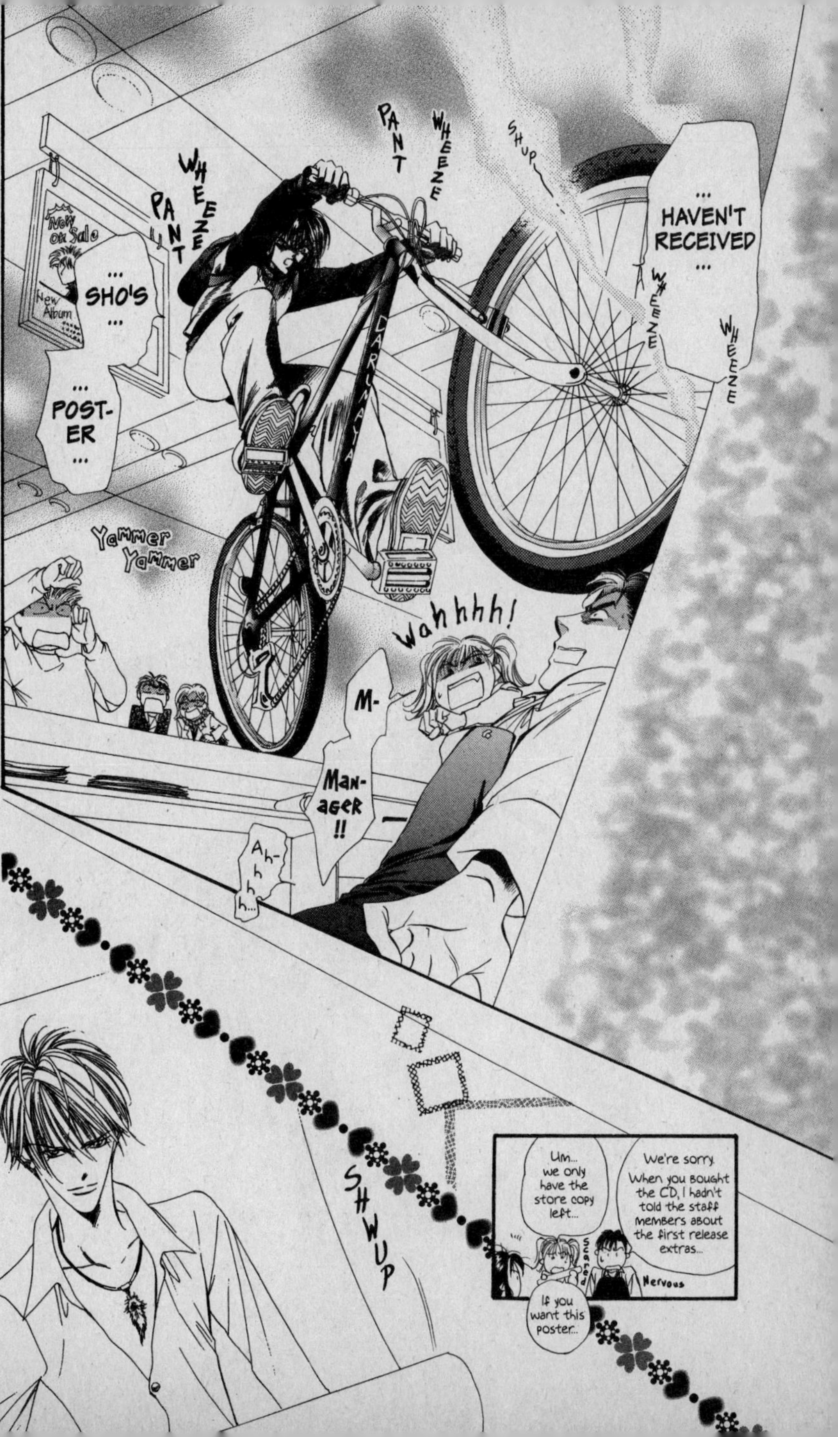
... HAVEN'T RECEIVED ...
WHEEZE
WHEEZE
SHUP
PANT
WHEEZE
PANT
WHEEZE
... SHO'S ...
... POSTER ...
Now on Sale
New Album
Yammer Yammer
Wahhhh!
M-
Manager!!
Ah-h h h...
SHWUP
We're sorry. When you bought the CD, I hadn't told the staff members about the first release extras...
Um... we only have the store copy left...
Scared
Nervous
If you want this poster...

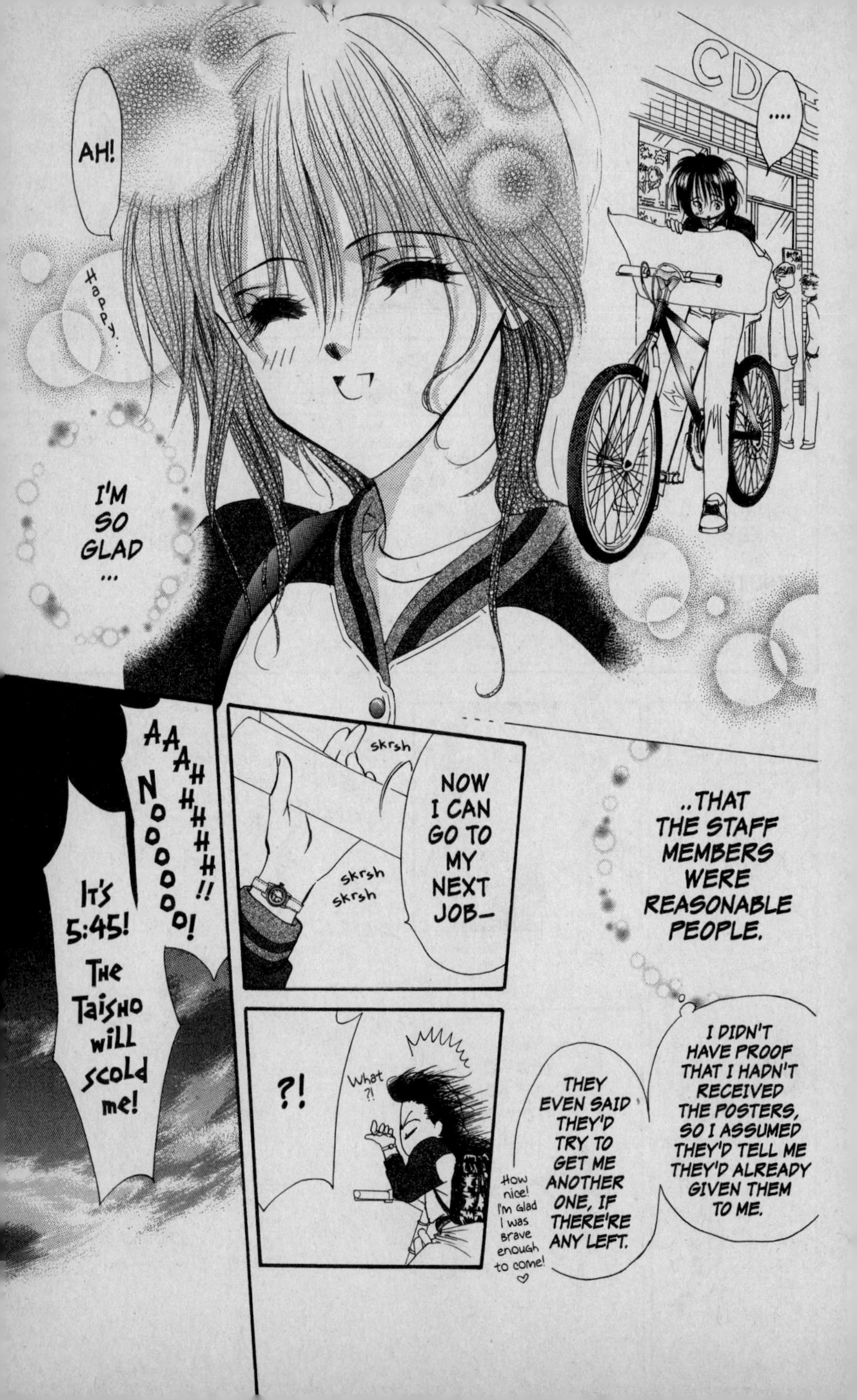
....
AH!
Happy...
I'M SO GLAD ...
..THAT THE STAFF MEMBERS WERE REASONABLE PEOPLE.
I DIDN'T HAVE PROOF THAT I HADN'T RECEIVED THE POSTERS, SO I ASSUMED THEY'D TELL ME THEY'D ALREADY GIVEN THEM TO ME.
THEY EVEN SAID THEY'D TRY TO GET ME ANOTHER ONE, IF THERE'RE ANY LEFT.
How nice! I'm Glad I was Brave enough to come! ♡
NOW I CAN GO TO MY NEXT JOB—
skrsh
skrsh skrsh
?!
What ?!
AAAHHHHH!!
NOOOOOO!
It's 5:45! The Taisho will scold me!

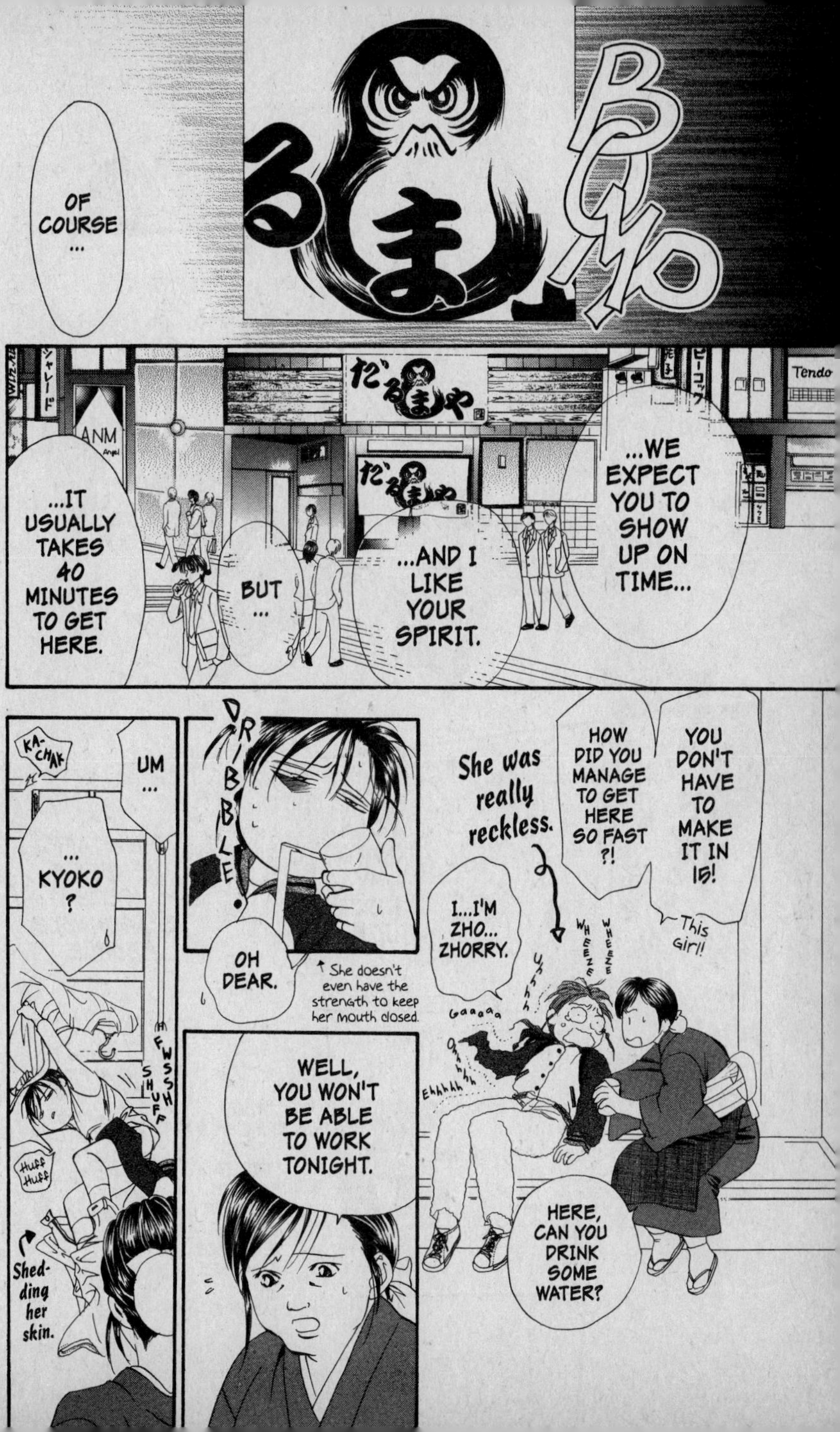
OF COURSE ...
...WE EXPECT YOU TO SHOW UP ON TIME...
...AND I LIKE YOUR SPIRIT.
BUT ...
...IT USUALLY TAKES 40 MINUTES TO GET HERE.
Tendo
ANM Angel
YOU DON'T HAVE TO MAKE IT IN 15!
This Girl!
HOW DID YOU MANAGE TO GET HERE SO FAST?!
She was really reckless.
WHEEZE WHEEZE
I...I'M ZHO... ZHORRY.
Uhhhh
Gaaaaa
Ohhhhh
Ehhhhh
HERE, CAN YOU DRINK SOME WATER?
DRIBBLE
OH DEAR.
She doesn't even have the strength to keep her mouth closed.
WELL, YOU WON'T BE ABLE TO WORK TONIGHT.
KA-CHAK
UM ...
... KYOKO ?
FWSSH
SHUFF
Huff Huff
Shedding her skin.

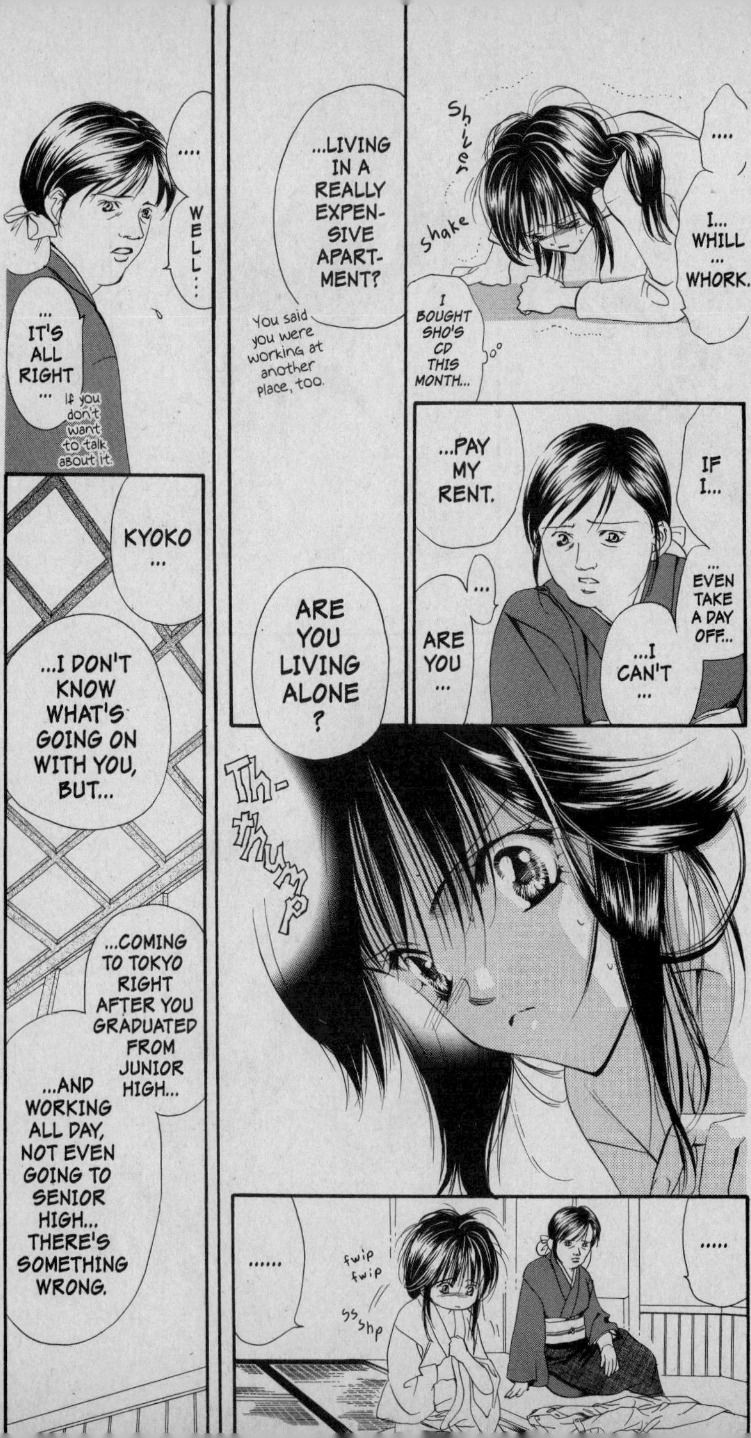

....
I... WHILL ... WHORK.
Shiver
Shake
I BOUGHT SHO'S CD THIS MONTH...
IF I...
... EVEN TAKE A DAY OFF...
...I CAN'T ...
...PAY MY RENT.
ARE YOU ...
...LIVING IN A REALLY EXPEN-SIVE APART-MENT?
You said you were working at another place, too.
ARE YOU LIVING ALONE ?
Th-thump
.....
......
fwip fwip
ss shp
....
WELL...
... IT'S ALL RIGHT ...
If you don't want to talk about it.
KYOKO ...
...I DON'T KNOW WHAT'S GOING ON WITH YOU, BUT...
...COMING TO TOKYO RIGHT AFTER YOU GRADUATED FROM JUNIOR HIGH...
...AND WORKING ALL DAY, NOT EVEN GOING TO SENIOR HIGH... THERE'S SOMETHING WRONG.

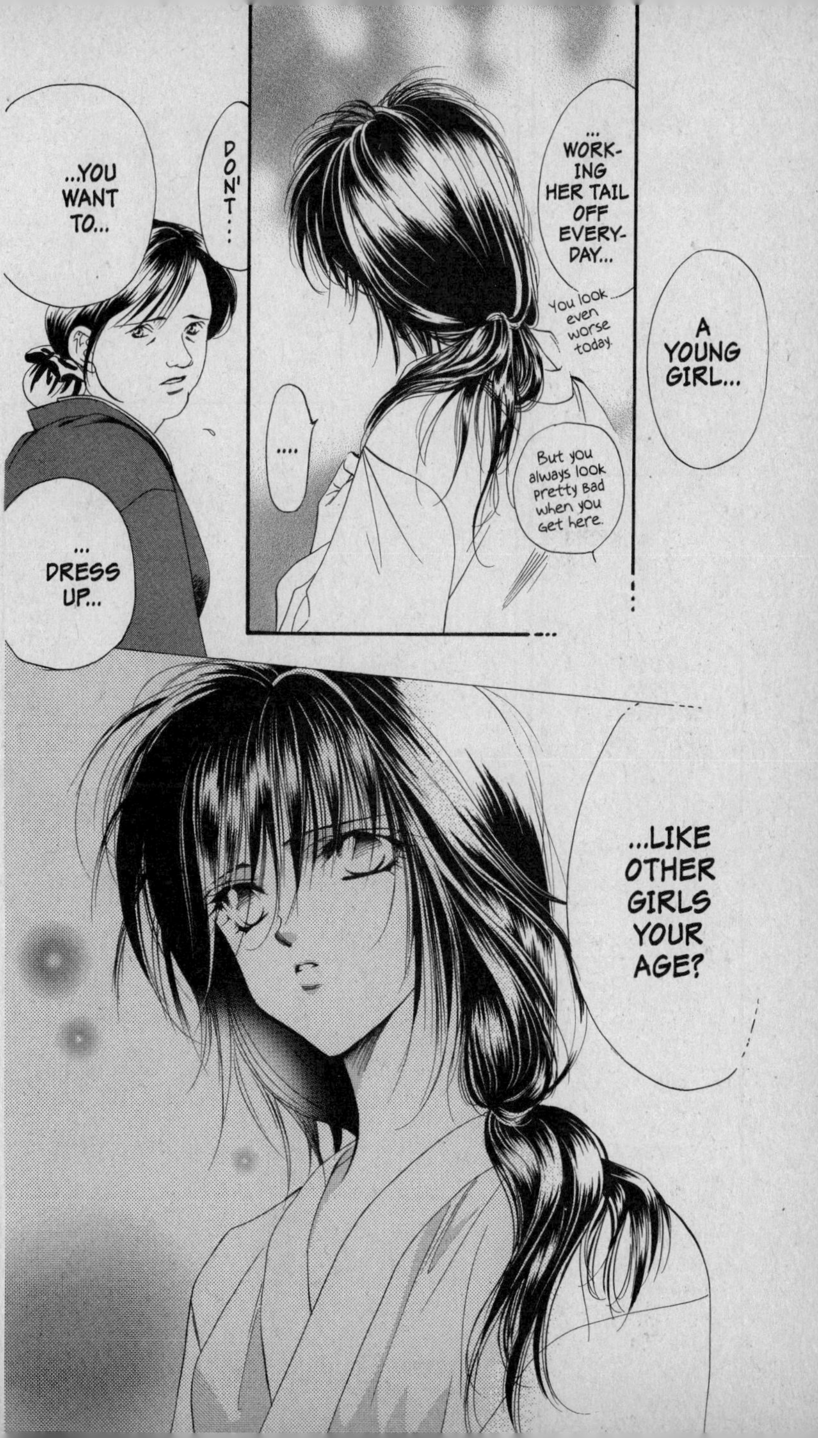
A YOUNG GIRL...
...WORKING HER TAIL OFF EVERY-DAY...
You look... even worse today.
But you always look pretty bad when you get here.
....
DON'T...
...YOU WANT TO...
...DRESS UP...
...LIKE OTHER GIRLS YOUR AGE?

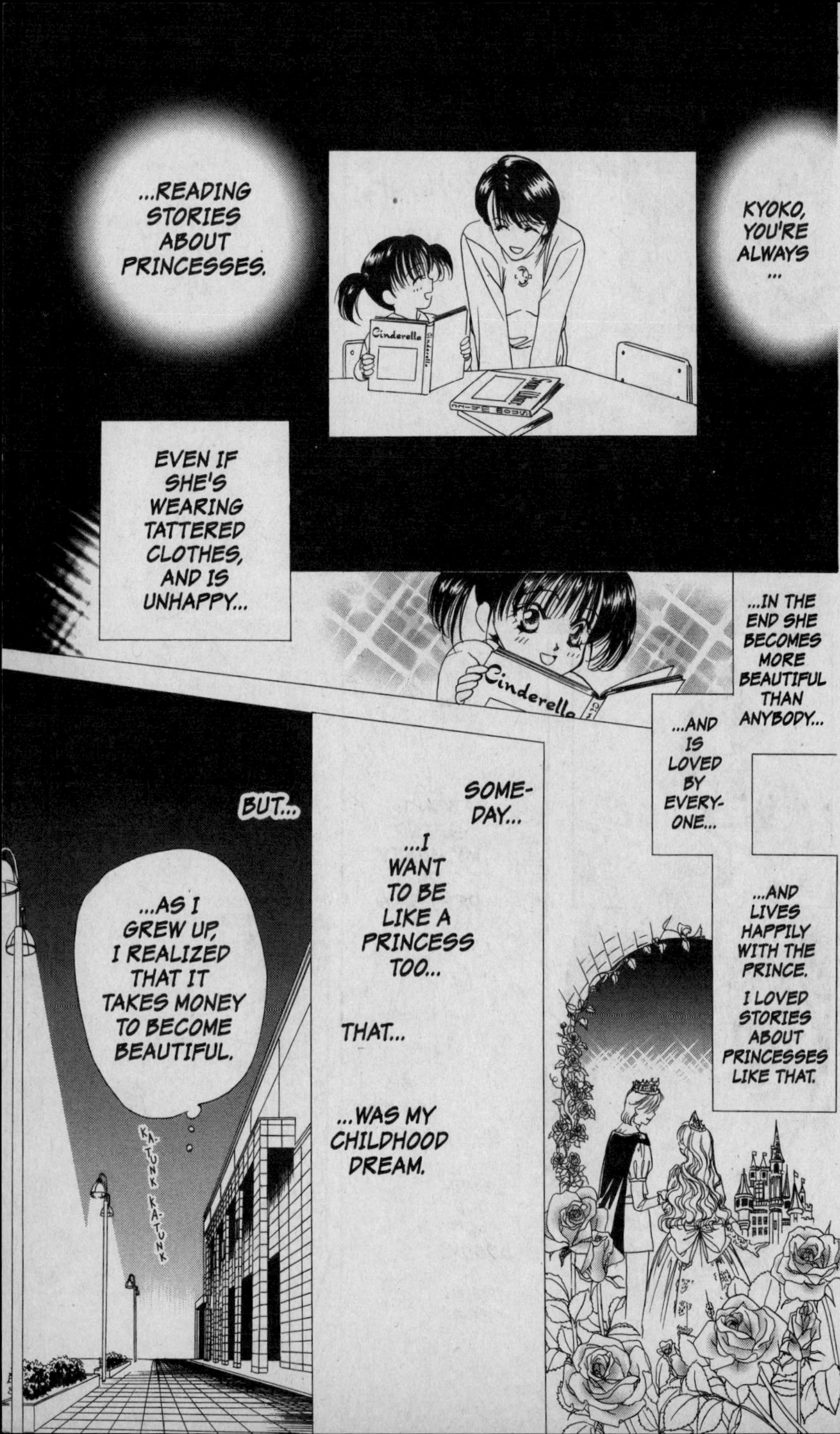
KYOKO, YOU'RE ALWAYS ...
...READING STORIES ABOUT PRINCESSES.
EVEN IF SHE'S WEARING TATTERED CLOTHES, AND IS UNHAPPY...
...IN THE END SHE BECOMES MORE BEAUTIFUL THAN ANYBODY...
...AND IS LOVED BY EVERY-ONE...
...AND LIVES HAPPILY WITH THE PRINCE.
I LOVED STORIES ABOUT PRINCESSES LIKE THAT.
SOME-DAY...
...I WANT TO BE LIKE A PRINCESS TOO...
THAT...
...WAS MY CHILDHOOD DREAM.
BUT...
...AS I GREW UP, I REALIZED THAT IT TAKES MONEY TO BECOME BEAUTIFUL.
KA-TUNK KA-TUNK

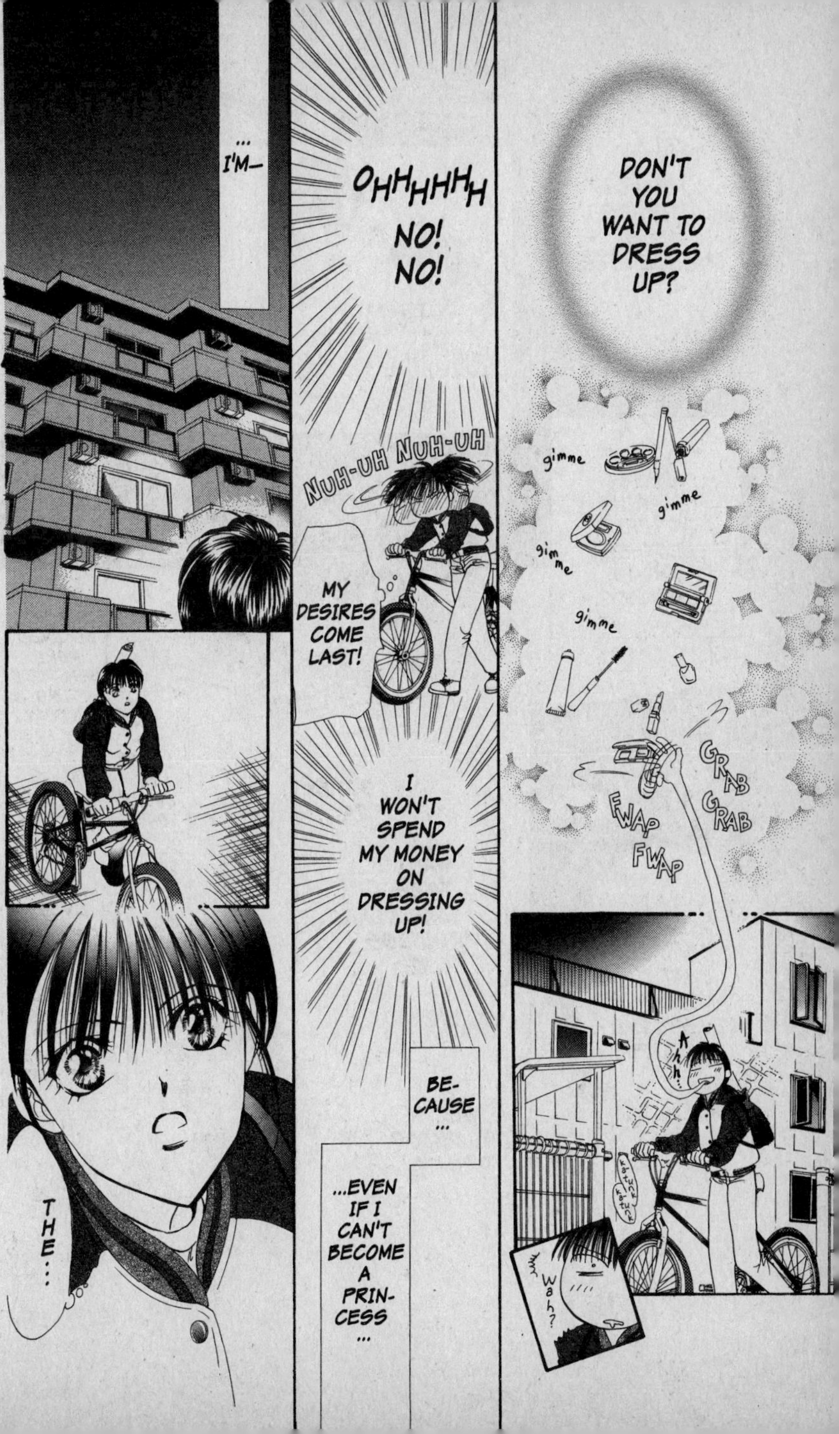
DON'T YOU WANT TO DRESS UP?
gimme
gimme
gimme
gimme
GRAB GRAB
FWAP FWAP
Ahh...
Wah?
OHHHHHH
NO! NO!
NUH-UH NUH-UH
MY DESIRES COME LAST!
I WON'T SPEND MY MONEY ON DRESSING UP!
BE-CAUSE ...
...EVEN IF I CAN'T BECOME A PRIN-CESS ...
... I'M—
THE...

Sidebar 1
Oh no!

Something came up that could have been a problem. Well, there was a manga with a very similar poignant story... I thought, "Oh no!! Someone did it first!!" How about the rough school-based story that I had written down as an idea for a one-shot when I was still doing Kurepara? There weren't any other ideas I could do as a series... (Actually, there were, but they weren't suited for Hana to Yume... and there were even ideas that the editor-in-chief told me were "not in style, so wait 5 more years"... So, the school-based story was the one that looked as if it would work for Hana to Yume...But I didn't have the courage or spirit to do that story at that time. I was stuck, so I consulted the editor-in-chief, and received the advice "Why don't you change the setting?" When I took the school-based story's good parts (a school with a performance arts course and the settings for each character), and thought of an interesting "setting," I could only think up a showbiz-based story... I don't have that much interest in showbiz, and don't become a passionate fan of celebrities...

Continued on page 33.

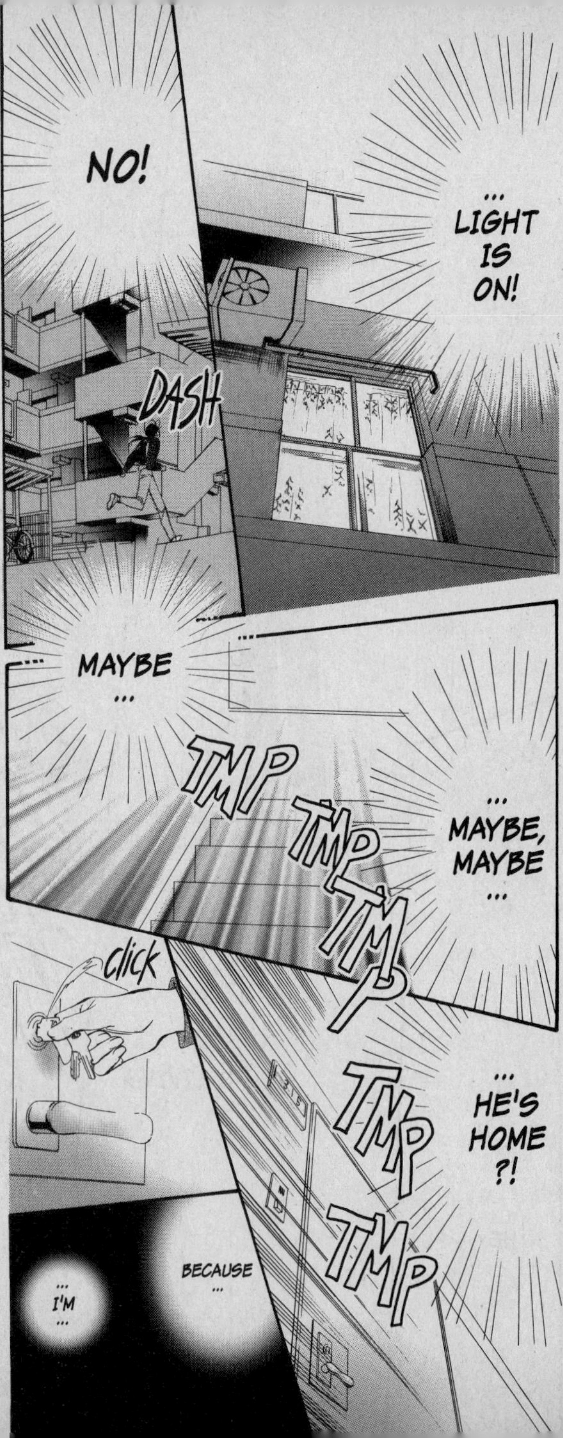
... LIGHT IS ON!
NO!
DASH
... MAYBE, MAYBE ...
... MAYBE ...
TMP TMP TMP
... HE'S HOME ?!
TMP TMP
click
BECAUSE ...
... I'M ...

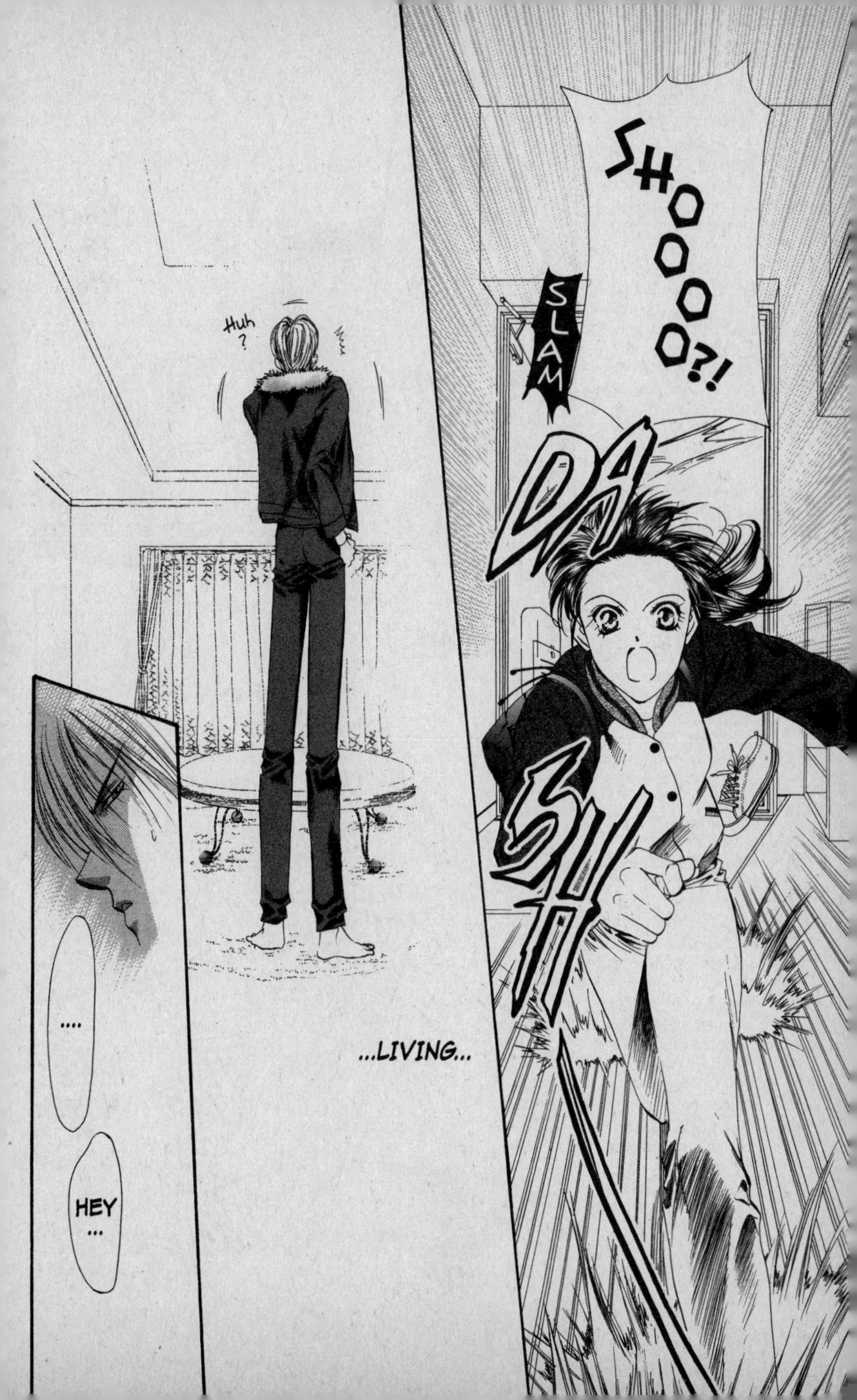
SHOOOO?!
SLAM
DASH
Huh ?
...LIVING...
....
HEY ...

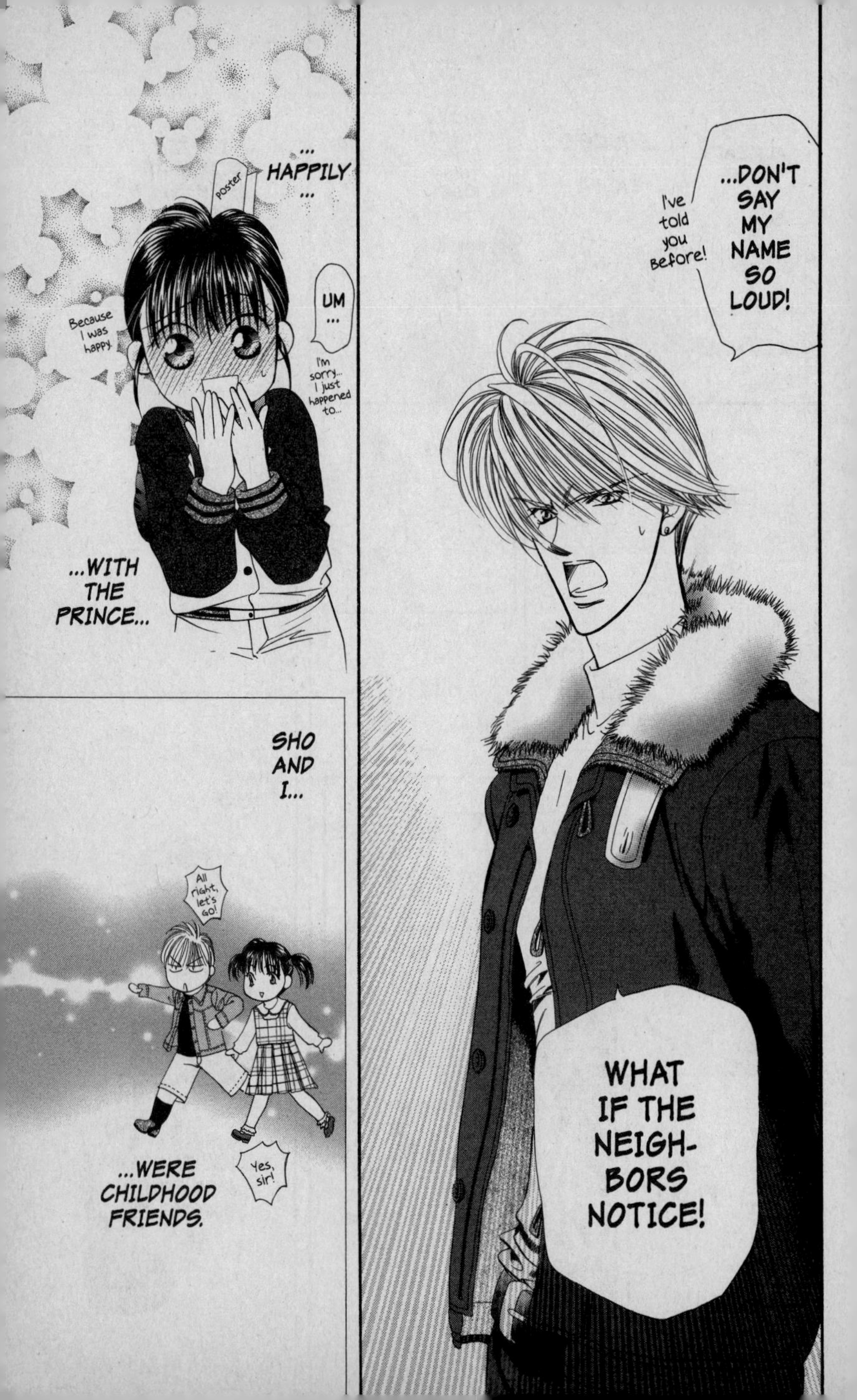
...DON'T SAY MY NAME SO LOUD!
I've told you before!
WHAT IF THE NEIGHBORS NOTICE!
...HAPPILY...
poster
UM...
I'm sorry... I just happened to...
Because I was happy.
...WITH THE PRINCE...
SHO AND I...
All right, let's GO!
Yes, sir!
...WERE CHILDHOOD FRIENDS.

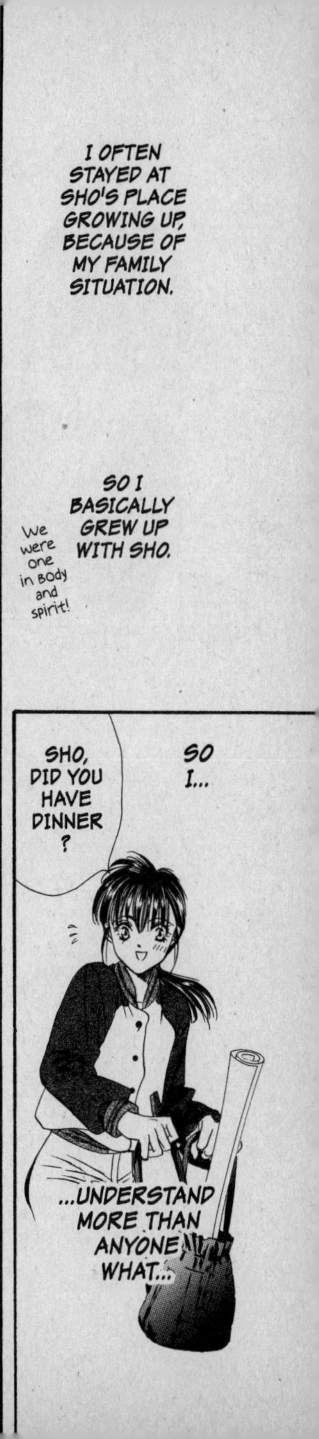
I OFTEN STAYED AT SHO'S PLACE GROWING UP, BECAUSE OF MY FAMILY SITUATION.
SO I BASICALLY GREW UP WITH SHO.
We were one in body and spirit!
SO I...
SHO, DID YOU HAVE DINNER?
...UNDERSTAND MORE THAN ANYONE WHAT...

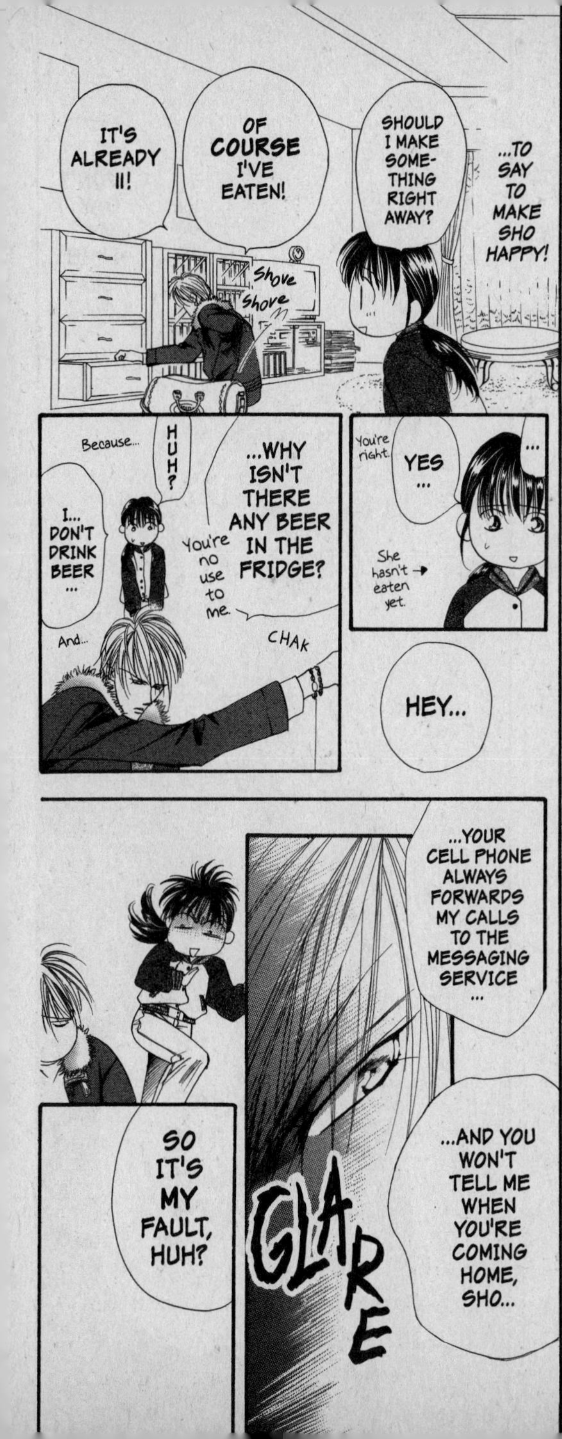
...TO SAY TO MAKE SHO HAPPY!
SHOULD I MAKE SOMETHING RIGHT AWAY?
OF COURSE I'VE EATEN!
IT'S ALREADY 11!
Shove
Shove
...
YES...
You're right.
She hasn't eaten yet.
...WHY ISN'T THERE ANY BEER IN THE FRIDGE?
HUH?
Because...
I... DON'T DRINK BEER...
You're no use to me.
And...
CHAK
HEY...
...YOUR CELL PHONE ALWAYS FORWARDS MY CALLS TO THE MESSAGING SERVICE...
...AND YOU WON'T TELL ME WHEN YOU'RE COMING HOME, SHO...
GLARE
SO IT'S MY FAULT, HUH?

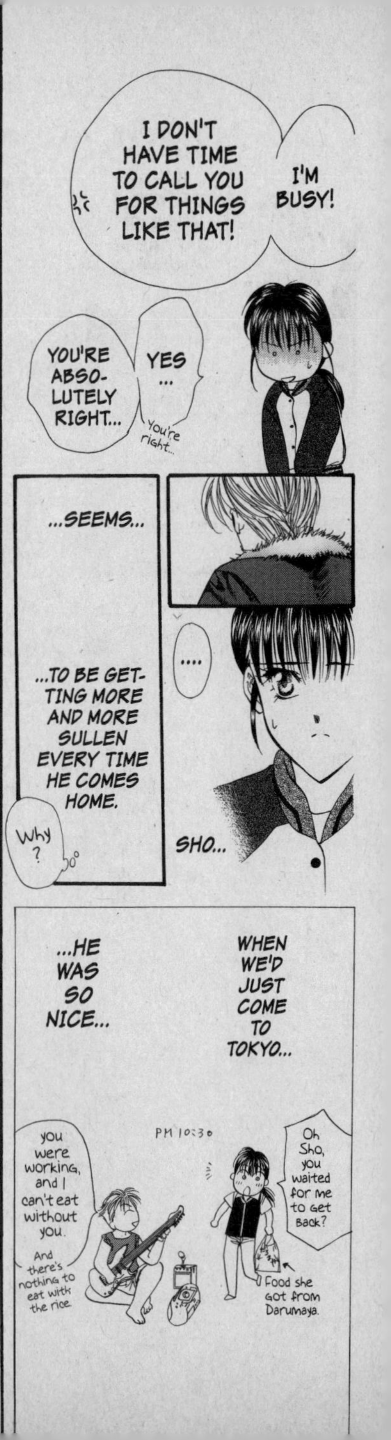
I'M BUSY!
I DON'T HAVE TIME TO CALL YOU FOR THINGS LIKE THAT!
YES ...
YOU'RE ABSOLUTELY RIGHT...
You're right...
....
SHO...
...SEEMS...
...TO BE GETTING MORE AND MORE SULLEN EVERY TIME HE COMES HOME.
Why?
WHEN WE'D JUST COME TO TOKYO...
...HE WAS SO NICE...
PM 10:30
Oh Sho, you waited for me to get back?
Food she got from Darumaya.
you were working, and I can't eat without you.
And there's nothing to eat with the rice

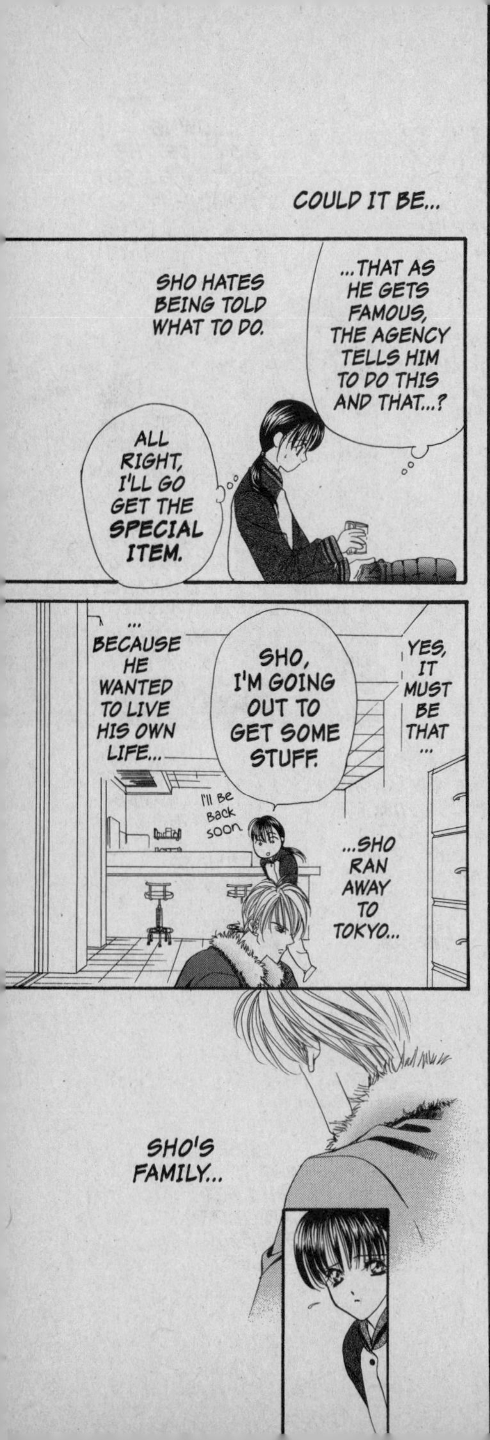
COULD IT BE...
...THAT AS HE GETS FAMOUS, THE AGENCY TELLS HIM TO DO THIS AND THAT...?
SHO HATES BEING TOLD WHAT TO DO.
ALL RIGHT, I'LL GO GET THE SPECIAL ITEM.
YES, IT MUST BE THAT ...
SHO, I'M GOING OUT TO GET SOME STUFF.
... BECAUSE HE WANTED TO LIVE HIS OWN LIFE...
I'll be back soon.
...SHO RAN AWAY TO TOKYO...
SHO'S FAMILY...

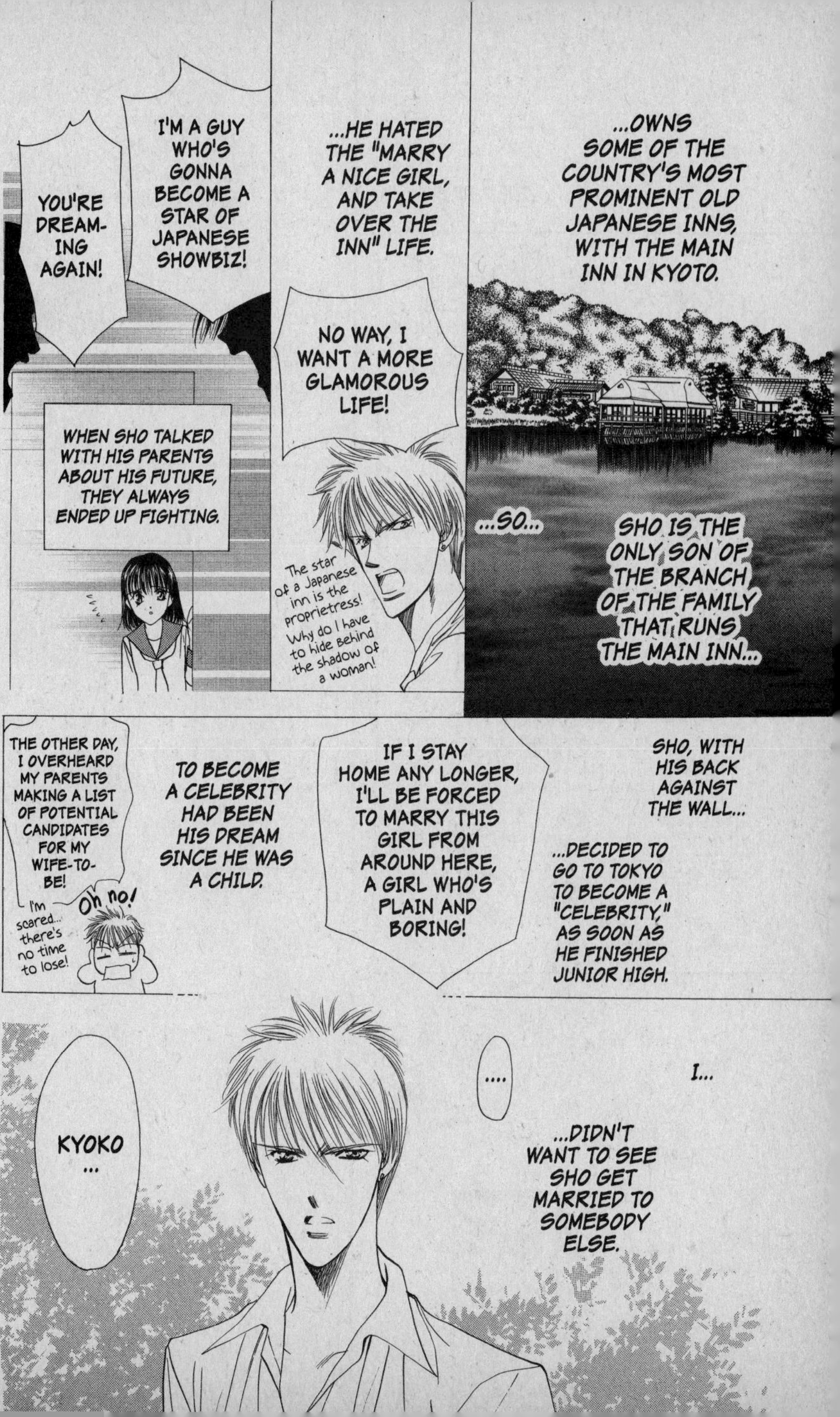
...OWNS SOME OF THE COUNTRY'S MOST PROMINENT OLD JAPANESE INNS, WITH THE MAIN INN IN KYOTO.
SHO IS THE ONLY SON OF THE BRANCH OF THE FAMILY THAT RUNS THE MAIN INN...
...SO...
...HE HATED THE "MARRY A NICE GIRL, AND TAKE OVER THE INN" LIFE.
NO WAY, I WANT A MORE GLAMOROUS LIFE!
The star of a Japanese inn is the proprietress! Why do I have to hide behind the shadow of a woman!
I'M A GUY WHO'S GONNA BECOME A STAR OF JAPANESE SHOWBIZ!
YOU'RE DREAM-ING AGAIN!
WHEN SHO TALKED WITH HIS PARENTS ABOUT HIS FUTURE, THEY ALWAYS ENDED UP FIGHTING.
SHO, WITH HIS BACK AGAINST THE WALL...
...DECIDED TO GO TO TOKYO TO BECOME A "CELEBRITY," AS SOON AS HE FINISHED JUNIOR HIGH.
IF I STAY HOME ANY LONGER, I'LL BE FORCED TO MARRY THIS GIRL FROM AROUND HERE, A GIRL WHO'S PLAIN AND BORING!
TO BECOME A CELEBRITY HAD BEEN HIS DREAM SINCE HE WAS A CHILD.
THE OTHER DAY, I OVERHEARD MY PARENTS MAKING A LIST OF POTENTIAL CANDIDATES FOR MY WIFE-TO-BE!
Oh no!
I'm scared... there's no time to lose!
I...
...DIDN'T WANT TO SEE SHO GET MARRIED TO SOMEBODY ELSE.
....
KYOKO...

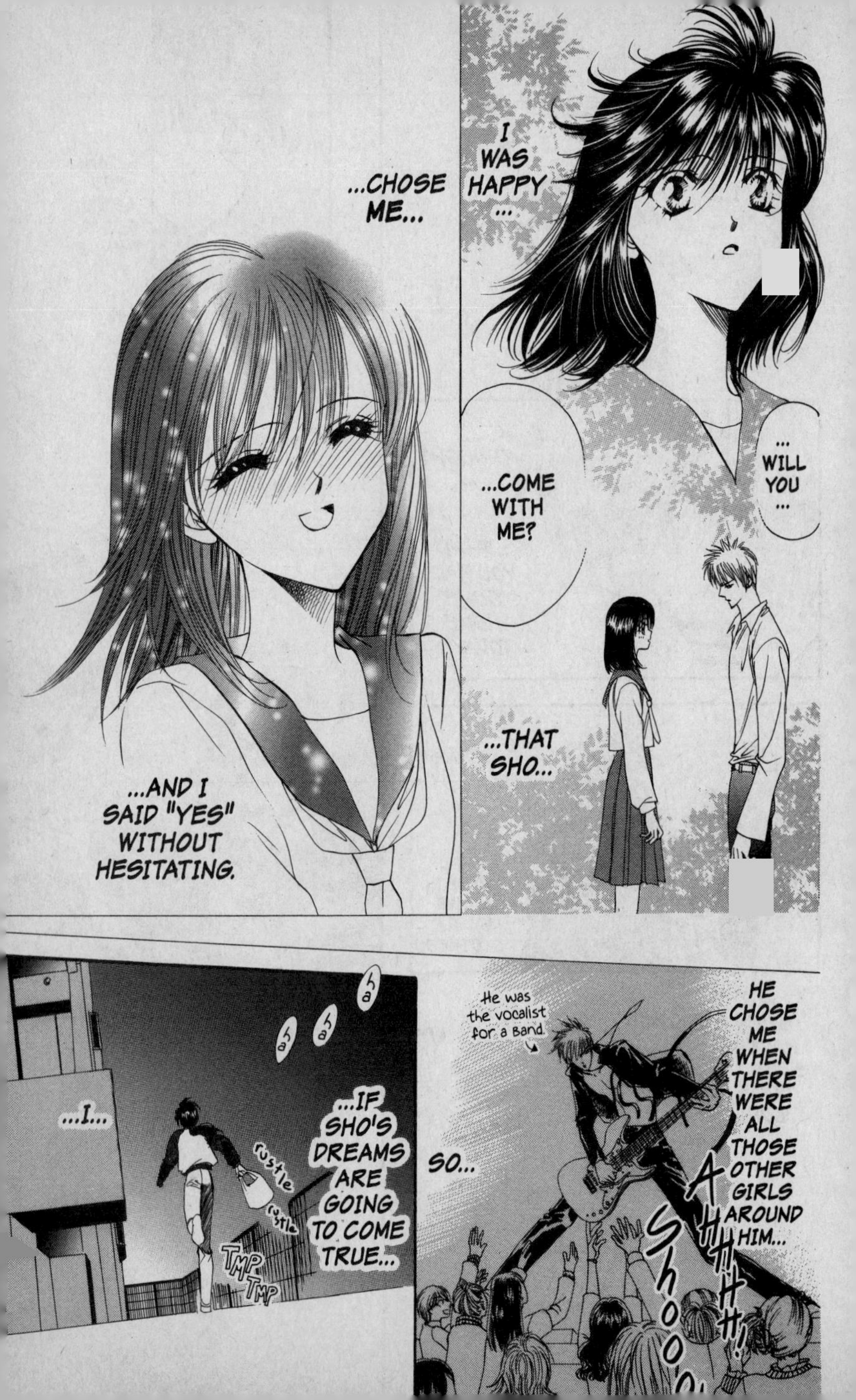
I WAS HAPPY...
...WILL YOU...
...COME WITH ME?
...THAT SHO...
...CHOSE ME...
...AND I SAID "YES" WITHOUT HESITATING.
He was the vocalist for a Band.
HE CHOSE ME WHEN THERE WERE ALL THOSE OTHER GIRLS AROUND HIM...
AHHHH!
SHOOO
SO...
...IF SHO'S DREAMS ARE GOING TO COME TRUE...
ha ha ha
...I...
rustle rustle
TMP TMP

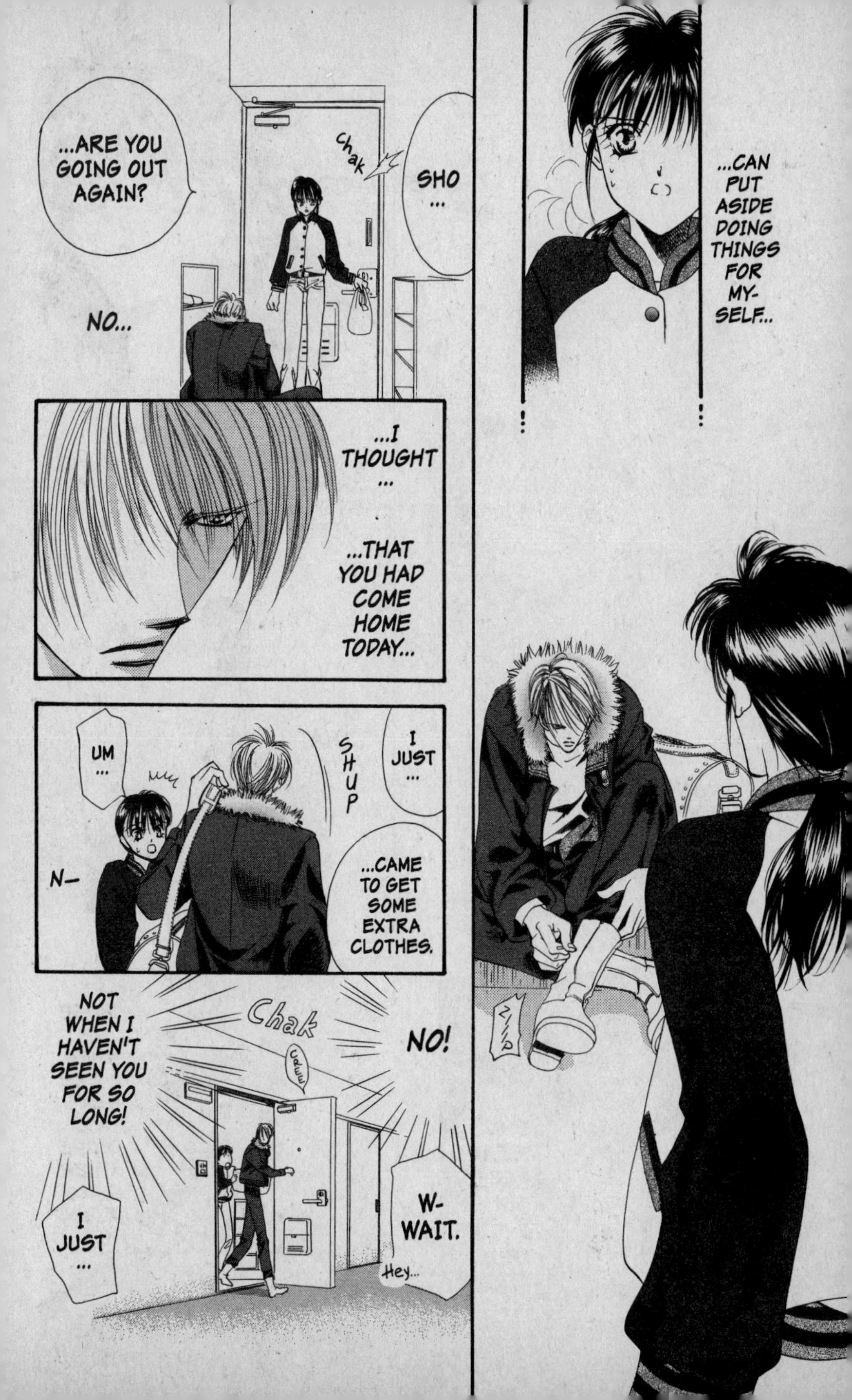
...CAN PUT ASIDE DOING THINGS FOR MY-SELF...
SHO ...
Chak
...ARE YOU GOING OUT AGAIN?
NO...
...I THOUGHT ...
...THAT YOU HAD COME HOME TODAY...
I JUST ...
...CAME TO GET SOME EXTRA CLOTHES.
SHUP
UM ...
N—
NO!
Chak
NOT WHEN I HAVEN'T SEEN YOU FOR SO LONG!
W-WAIT.
Hey...
I JUST ...

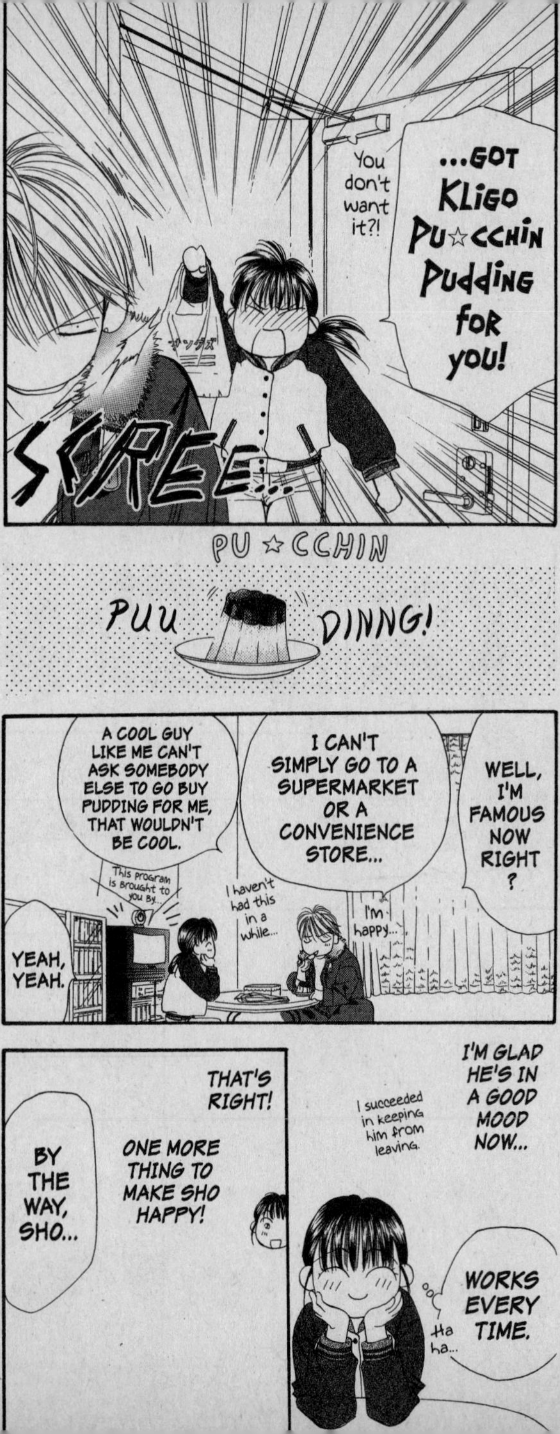
...GOT KLIGO PU☆CCHIN PUDDING FOR YOU!
You don't want it?!
SKREE...
PU☆CCHIN
PUU DINNG!
WELL, I'M FAMOUS NOW RIGHT?
I CAN'T SIMPLY GO TO A SUPERMARKET OR A CONVENIENCE STORE...
A COOL GUY LIKE ME CAN'T ASK SOMEBODY ELSE TO GO BUY PUDDING FOR ME, THAT WOULDN'T BE COOL.
I'm happy...
I haven't had this in a while...
This program is brought to you by...
YEAH, YEAH.
I'M GLAD HE'S IN A GOOD MOOD NOW...
I succeeded in keeping him from leaving.
WORKS EVERY TIME.
Ha ha...
THAT'S RIGHT!
ONE MORE THING TO MAKE SHO HAPPY!
BY THE WAY, SHO...

2

I have no desire to keep up with the latest trends, thus I don't have any taste in fashion. A show-biz story... I was very worried whether I would be all right going boldly in that direction? But if I was going to draw it, I didn't want to draw a Cinderella-type story where "One day, due to some chance, someone debuts as a celebrity." I do believe that those types of stories grab the hearts of girls more easily, though...

...So I'm writing as if I'm a know-it-all. Although I made up my mind to write a showbiz-based story, I'm having a very hard time drawing. The storyboards take even more time than Kurepara did. (Although it definitely doesn't look that way...) I'd assumed that the new series would be easier to do, both the storyboards and drawing the series itself... I'm a real fool, so I'm struggling to have people enjoy reading *Skip Beat!* each time. Please enjoy it!

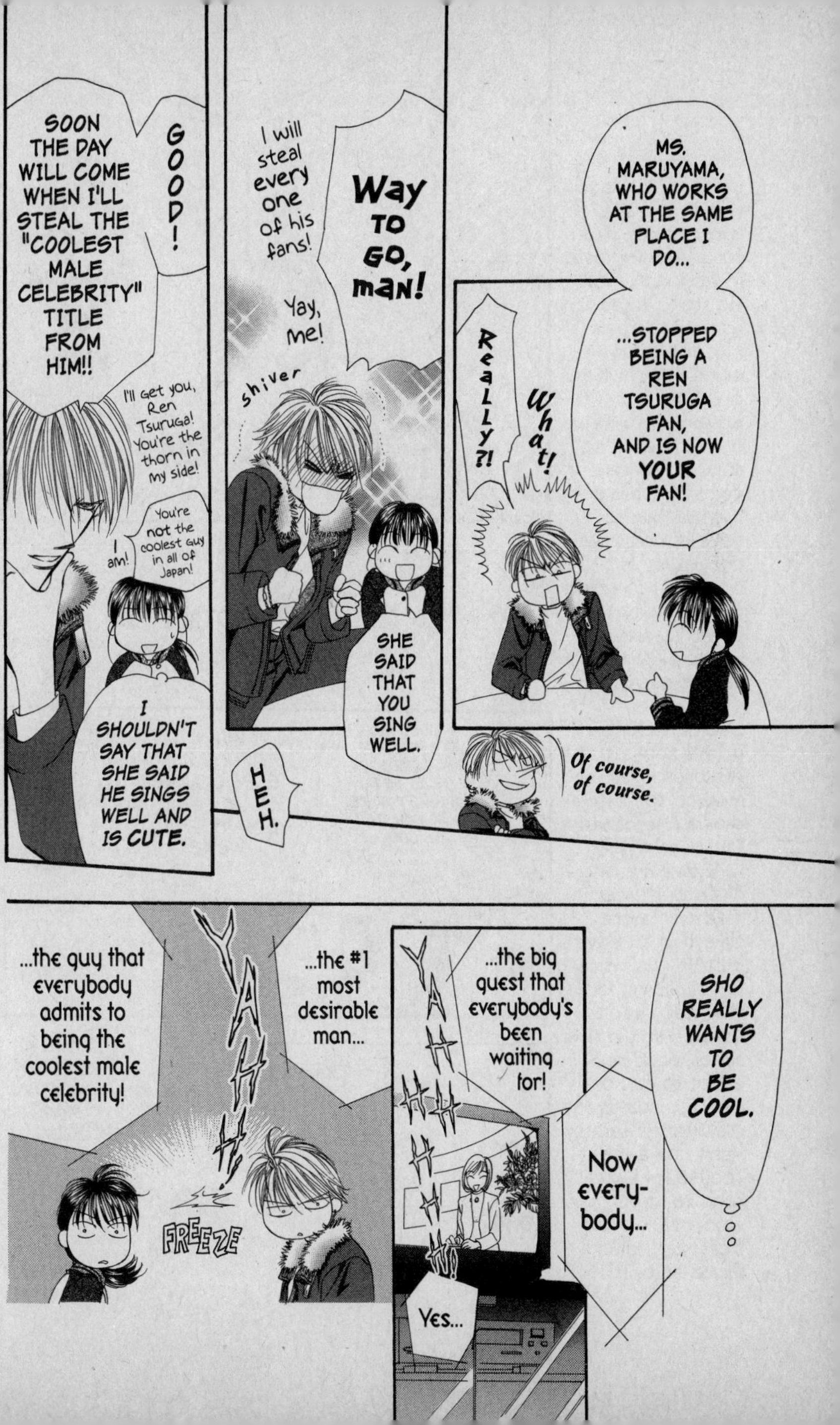
MS. MARUYAMA, WHO WORKS AT THE SAME PLACE I DO...
...STOPPED BEING A REN TSURUGA FAN, AND IS NOW YOUR FAN!
What!
Really?!
Way to go, man!
I will steal every one of his fans!
Yay, me!
shiver
SHE SAID THAT YOU SING WELL.
Of course, of course.
GOOD!
SOON THE DAY WILL COME WHEN I'LL STEAL THE "COOLEST MALE CELEBRITY" TITLE FROM HIM!!
I'll get you, Ren Tsuruga! You're the thorn in my side!
You're not the coolest guy in all of Japan!
I am!
I SHOULDN'T SAY THAT SHE SAID HE SINGS WELL AND IS CUTE.
HEH.
SHO REALLY WANTS TO BE COOL.
Now every-body...
YAHHHHHH!
Yes...
...the big guest that everybody's been waiting for!
...the #1 most desirable man...
YAHHH!
...the guy that everybody admits to being the coolest male celebrity!
FREEZE

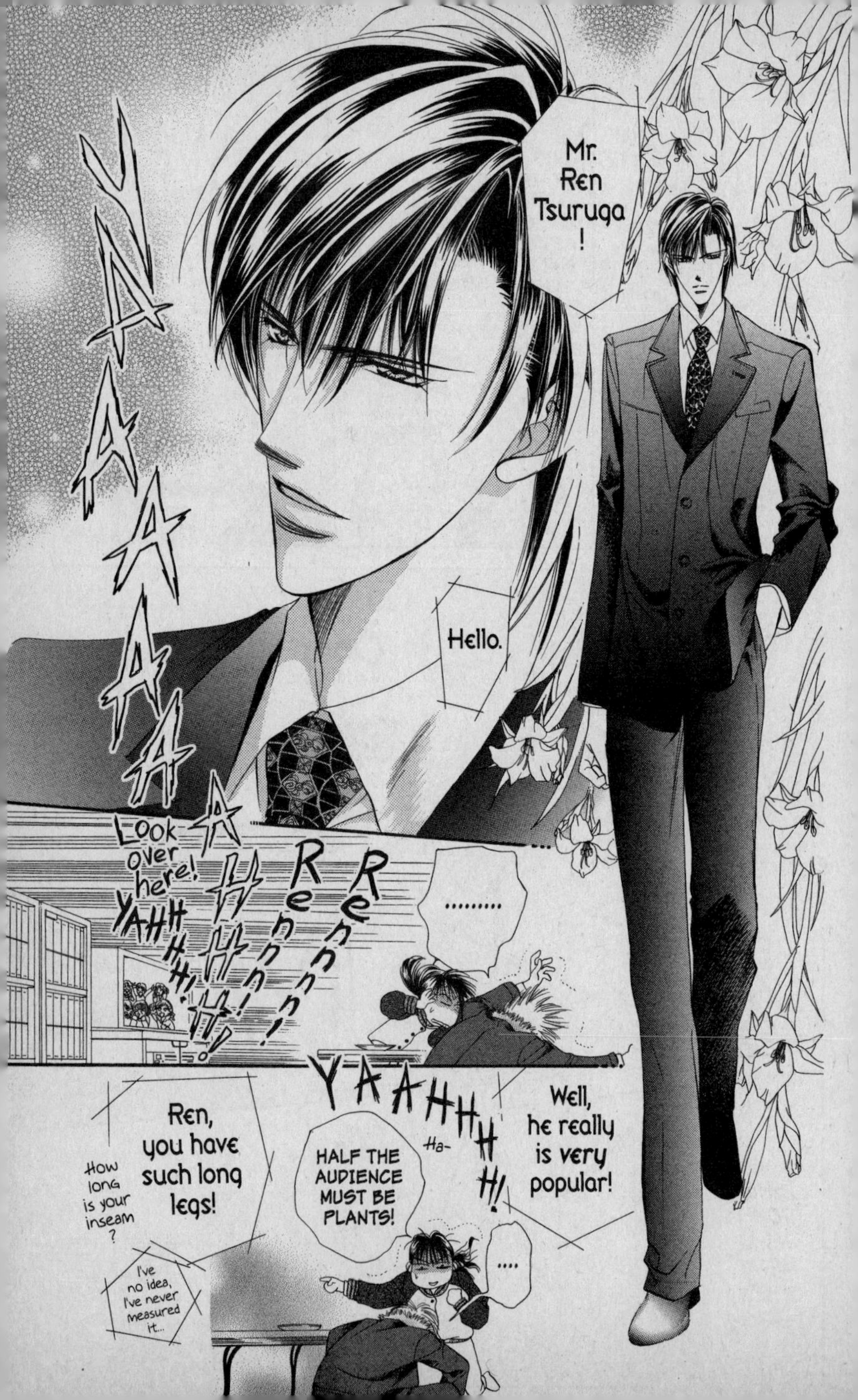
Mr. Ren Tsuruga!
Hello.
YAAAAAA
AHHHHH!
Renn!
Rennn!
Look over here!
YAHHH!
....
YAAHHHH!
Well, he really is very popular!
....
Ha-
HALF THE AUDIENCE MUST BE PLANTS!
Ren, you have such long legs!
How long is your inseam?
I've no idea, I've never measured it...

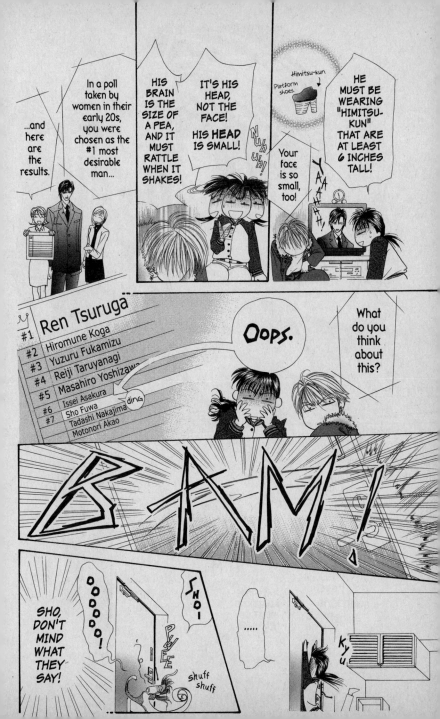

...and here are the results.

In a poll taken by women in their early 20s, you were chosen as the #1 most desirable man...

HIS BRAIN IS THE SIZE OF A PEA, AND IT MUST RATTLE WHEN IT SHAKES!

IT'S HIS HEAD, NOT THE FACE! HIS **HEAD** IS SMALL!

Nuh uh!

Your face is so small, too!

YAAAHH!

Himitsu-kun

Platform shoes.

HE MUST BE WEARING "HIMITSU-KUN" THAT ARE AT LEAST 6 INCHES TALL!

#1	Ren Tsuruga
#2	Hiromune Koga
#3	Yuzuru Fukamizu
#4	Reiji Taruyanagi
#5	Masahiro Yoshizawa
#6	Issei Asakura
#7	Sho Fuwa
	Tadashi Nakajima
	Motonori Akao

Oops.

ding

What do you think about this?

B AM!

OOOOO!

SHO-

shuff shuff

.....

Kyu

SHO, DON'T MIND WHAT THEY SAY!

3
Title

Readers close to my age will think of the same thing if they heard the words "Skip Beat." Actually, I rejected the title many times, as well as the character designs, and when I was thinking about the Nth title, I felt that I wanted to put "Skip" in the title, like "Skip something" or "Something Skip." It sounds fun and foreign. A smart kid "skips" from being a grade-schooler or a junior high-schooler to becoming a college student all of a sudden. Like Kyoko says in the story, becoming a star instantaneously, without experiencing periods of obscurity. I wanted to put "Skip" in the title no matter what... and if "Skip" is there, the next thing is "Beat"... My editor and I brainstormed about whether there was another word to use. The word "beat" has the springing meaning, to "hit, drum" (my personal impression) and to "win against the other party or an opponent"...

Continued on page 61.

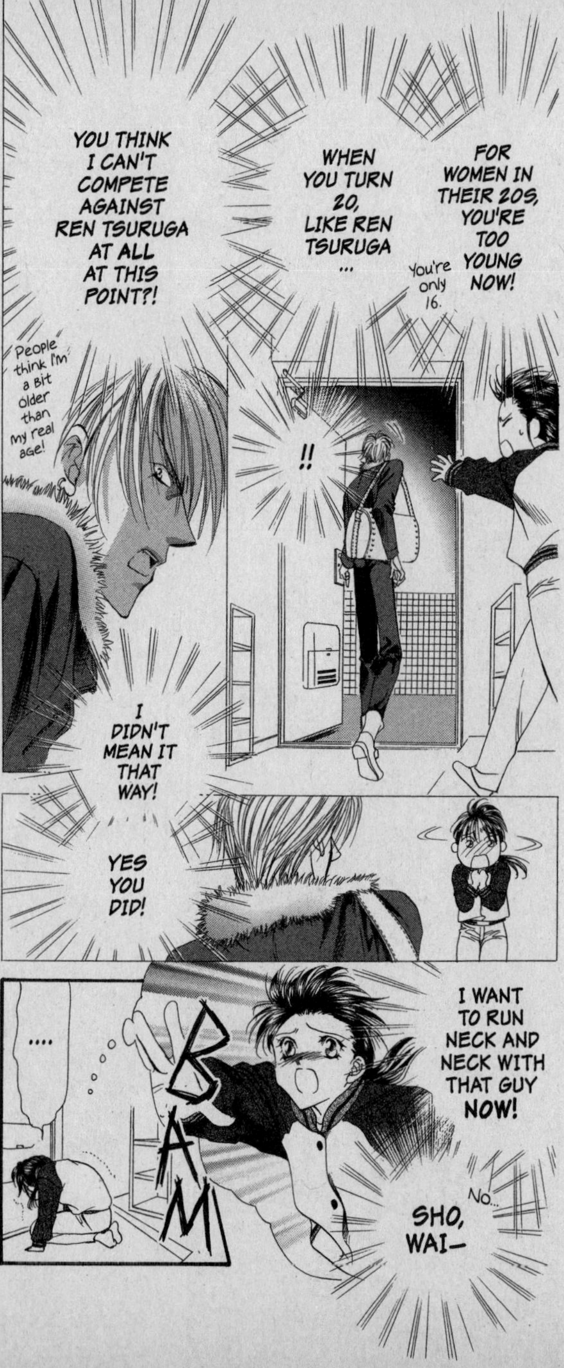
FOR WOMEN IN THEIR 20S, YOU'RE TOO YOUNG NOW!
You're only 16.
WHEN YOU TURN 20, LIKE REN TSURUGA ...
YOU THINK I CAN'T COMPETE AGAINST REN TSURUGA AT ALL AT THIS POINT?!
People think I'm a bit older than my real age!
!!
I DIDN'T MEAN IT THAT WAY!
YES YOU DID!
I WANT TO RUN NECK AND NECK WITH THAT GUY NOW!
BAM
No...
SHO, WAI—
....

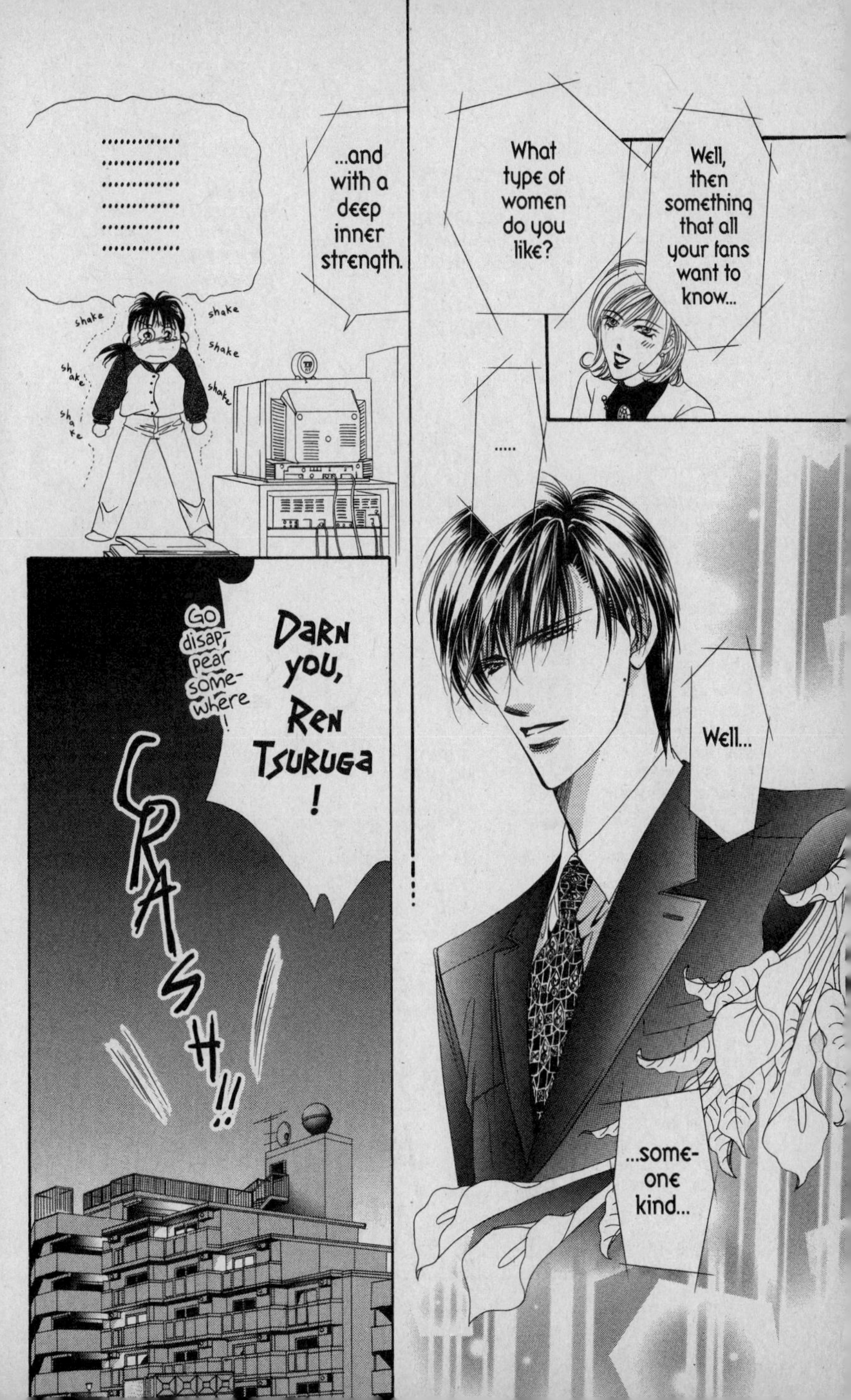

Well, then something that all your fans want to know...
What type of women do you like?
.....
Well...
...some-one kind...
...and with a deep inner strength.
....
....
....
....
....
....
shake
shake
shake
shake
shake
shake
Darn you, Ren Tsuruga!
Go disap-pear some-where!
CRASH!!

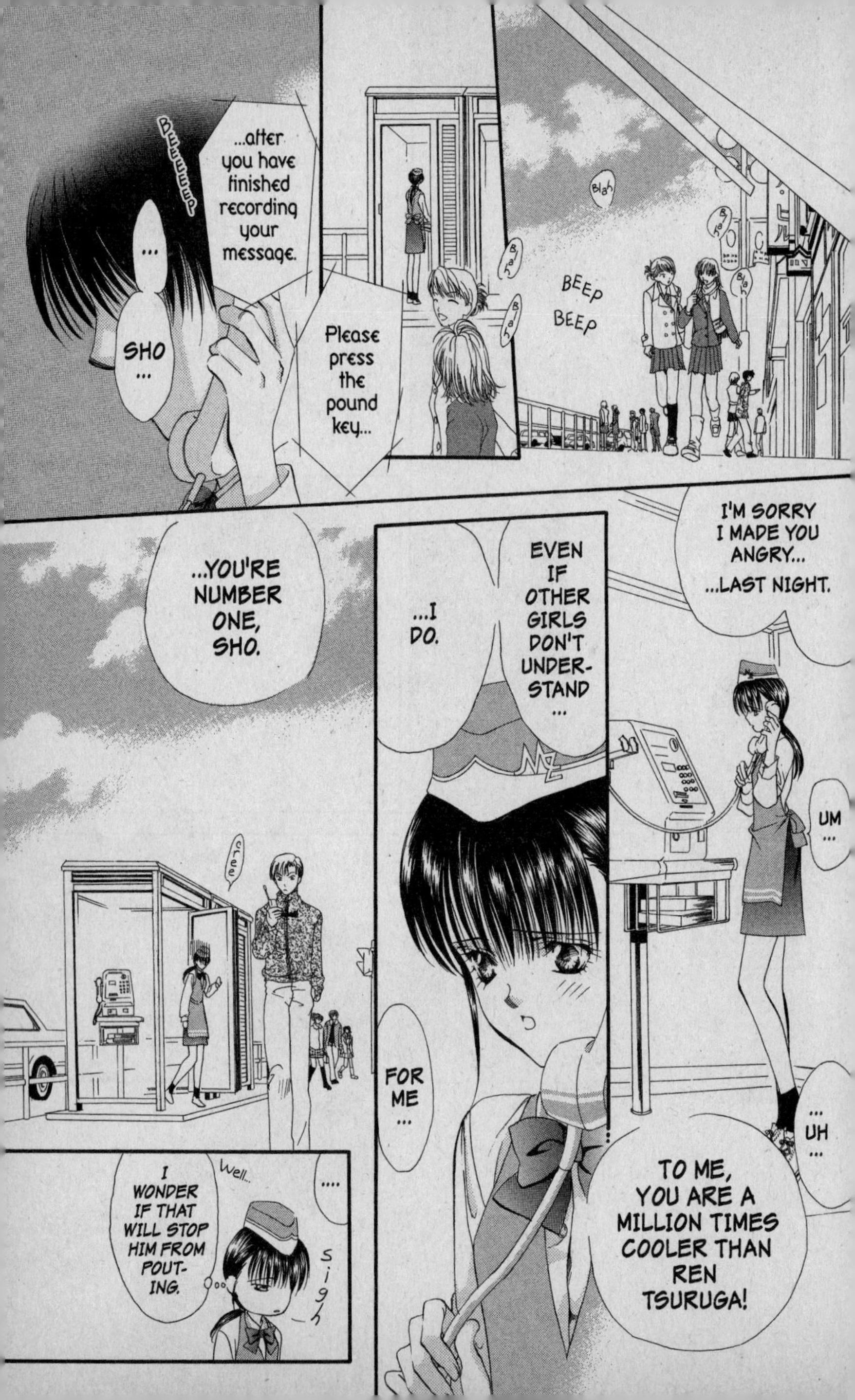
Blah
Blah
Blah
BEEP
BEEP
Blah
Blah
Please press the pound key...
...after you have finished recording your message.
BEEEEEP
...
SHO ...
I'M SORRY I MADE YOU ANGRY... ...LAST NIGHT.
UM ...
... UH ...
TO ME, YOU ARE A MILLION TIMES COOLER THAN REN TSURUGA!
EVEN IF OTHER GIRLS DON'T UNDERSTAND ...
...I DO.
FOR ME ...
...YOU'RE NUMBER ONE, SHO.
cree
....
Well..
I WONDER IF THAT WILL STOP HIM FROM POUT-ING.
sigh

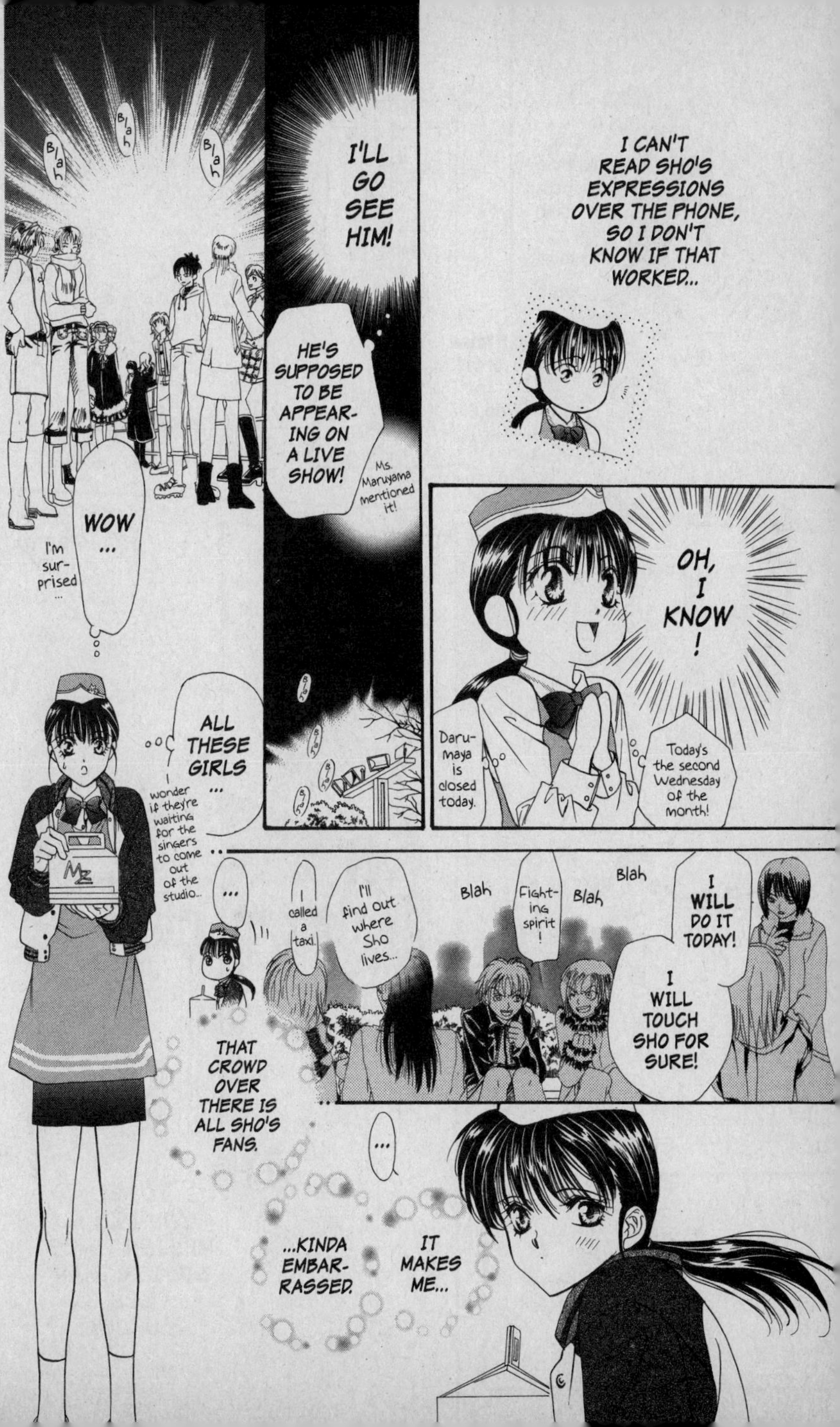

I CAN'T READ SHO'S EXPRESSIONS OVER THE PHONE, SO I DON'T KNOW IF THAT WORKED...
OH, I KNOW!
Today's the second Wednesday of the month!
Daru-maya is closed today.
I'LL GO SEE HIM!
HE'S SUPPOSED TO BE APPEAR-ING ON A LIVE SHOW!
Ms. Maruyama mentioned it!
Blah
Blah
Blah
Blah
Blah
Blah
Blah
WOW...
I'm sur-prised...
ALL THESE GIRLS...
I wonder if they're waiting for the singers to come out of the studio...
...
I WILL DO IT TODAY!
Blah
Blah
Fight-ing spirit!
Blah
I'll find out where Sho lives...
I called a taxi.
I WILL TOUCH SHO FOR SURE!
THAT CROWD OVER THERE IS ALL SHO'S FANS.
...
IT MAKES ME...
...KINDA EMBAR-RASSED.

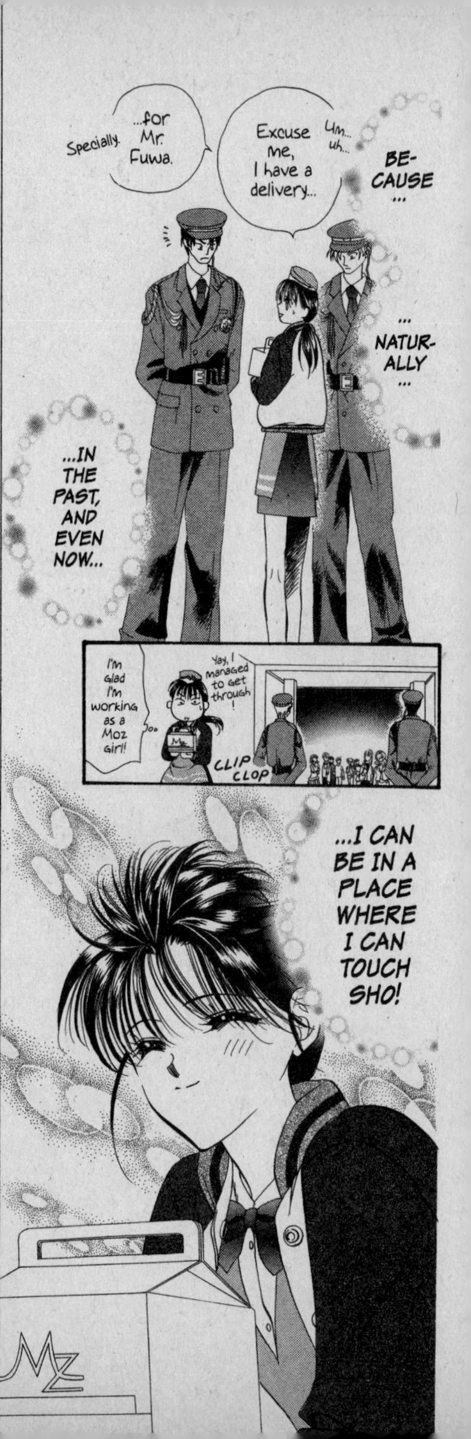
BE-CAUSE ...
Um... uh...
Excuse me, I have a delivery...
...for Mr. Fuwa.
Specially.
... NATUR-ALLY ...
...IN THE PAST, AND EVEN NOW...
Yay, I managed to get through!
I'm glad I'm working as a Moz Girl!
CLIP CLOP
...I CAN BE IN A PLACE WHERE I CAN TOUCH SHO!
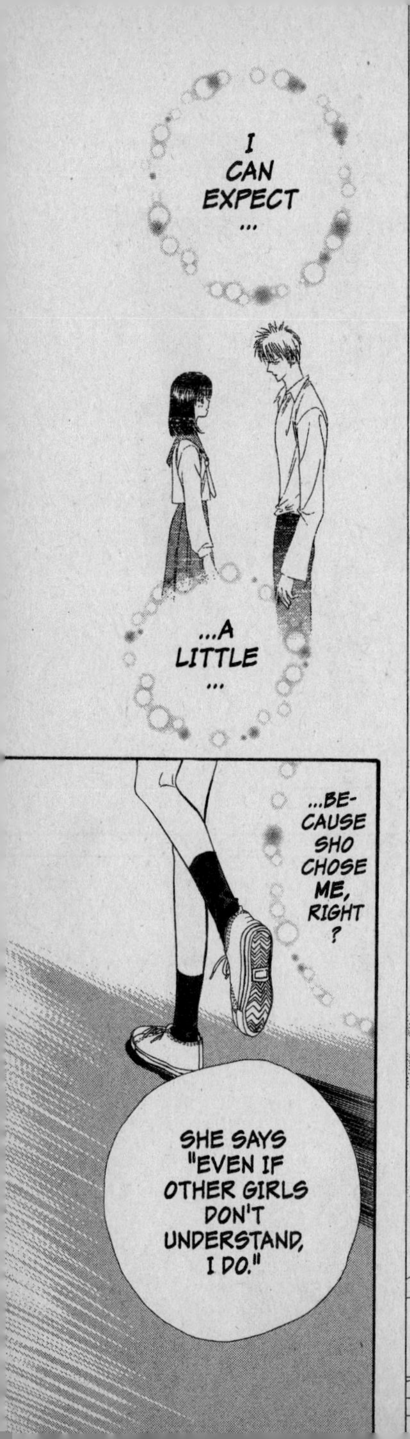
I CAN EXPECT ...
...A LITTLE ...
...BE-CAUSE SHO CHOSE ME, RIGHT ?
SHE SAYS "EVEN IF OTHER GIRLS DON'T UNDERSTAND, I DO."

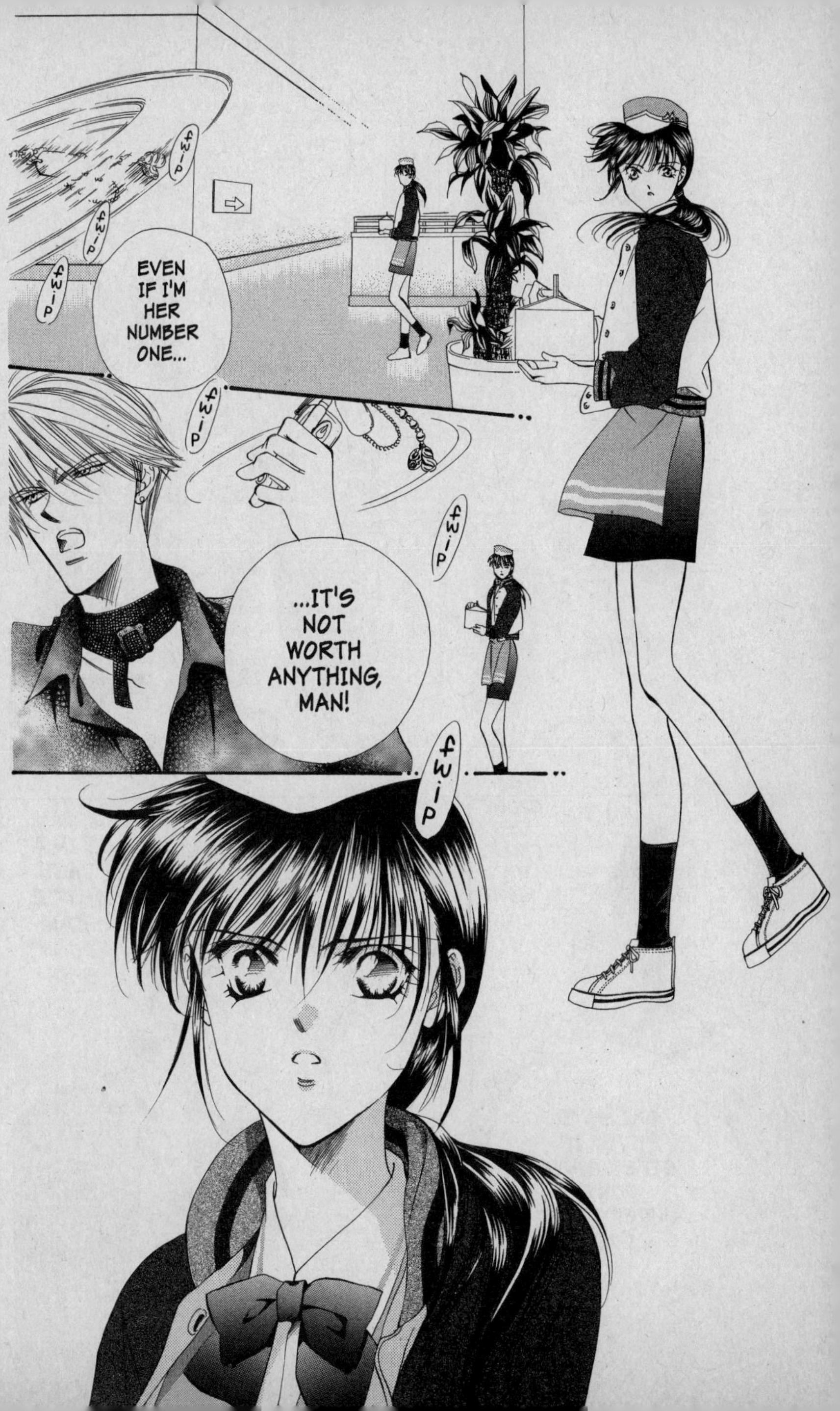
fwip
fwip
fwip
EVEN IF I'M HER NUMBER ONE...
fwip
fwip
...IT'S NOT WORTH ANYTHING, MAN!
fwip

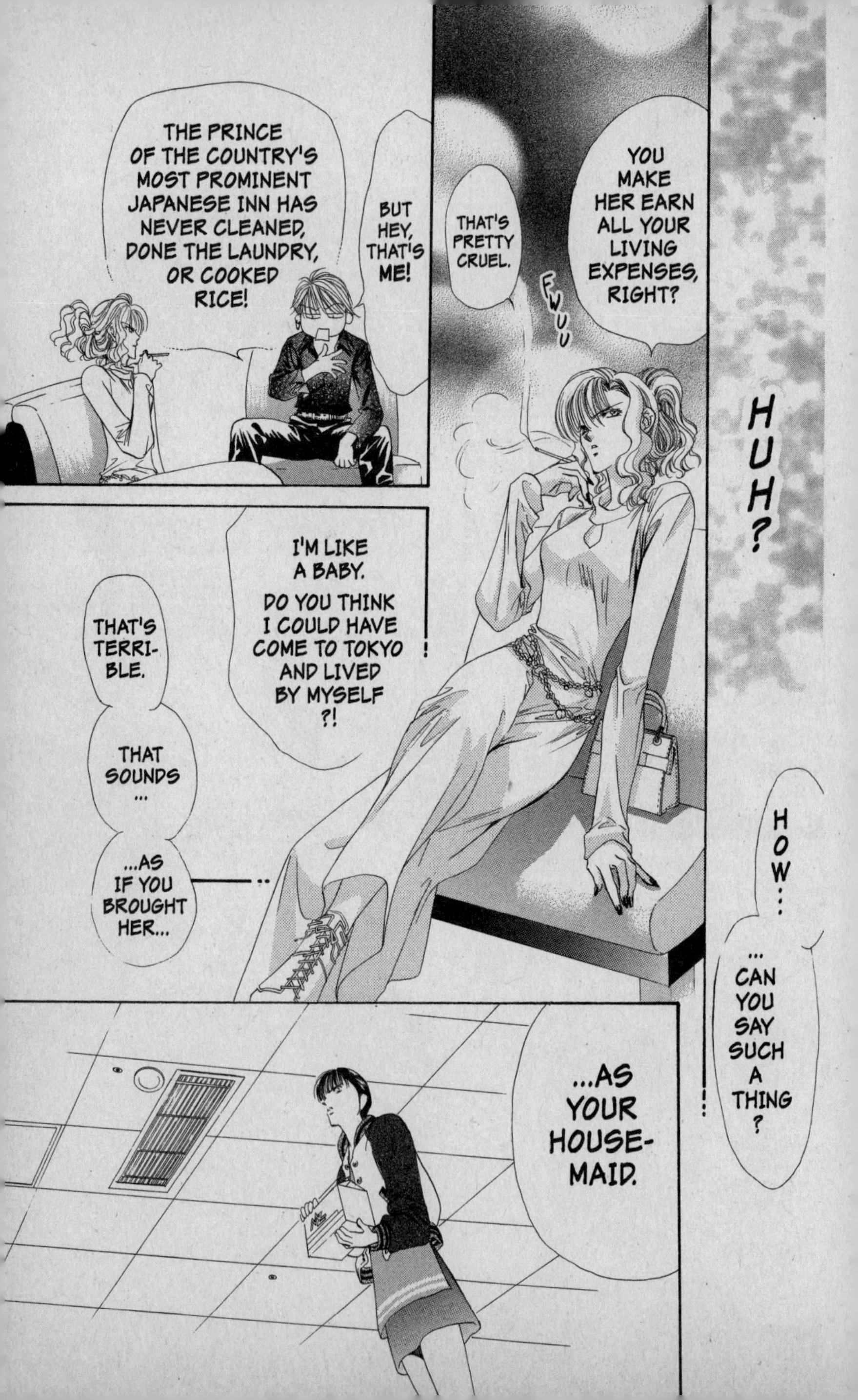
YOU MAKE HER EARN ALL YOUR LIVING EXPENSES, RIGHT?
THAT'S PRETTY CRUEL.
FWUU
HUH?
BUT HEY, THAT'S ME!
THE PRINCE OF THE COUNTRY'S MOST PROMINENT JAPANESE INN HAS NEVER CLEANED, DONE THE LAUNDRY, OR COOKED RICE!
I'M LIKE A BABY.
DO YOU THINK I COULD HAVE COME TO TOKYO AND LIVED BY MYSELF ?!
THAT'S TERRI-BLE.
THAT SOUNDS ...
...AS IF YOU BROUGHT HER...
HOW...
...CAN YOU SAY SUCH A THING?
...AS YOUR HOUSE-MAID.

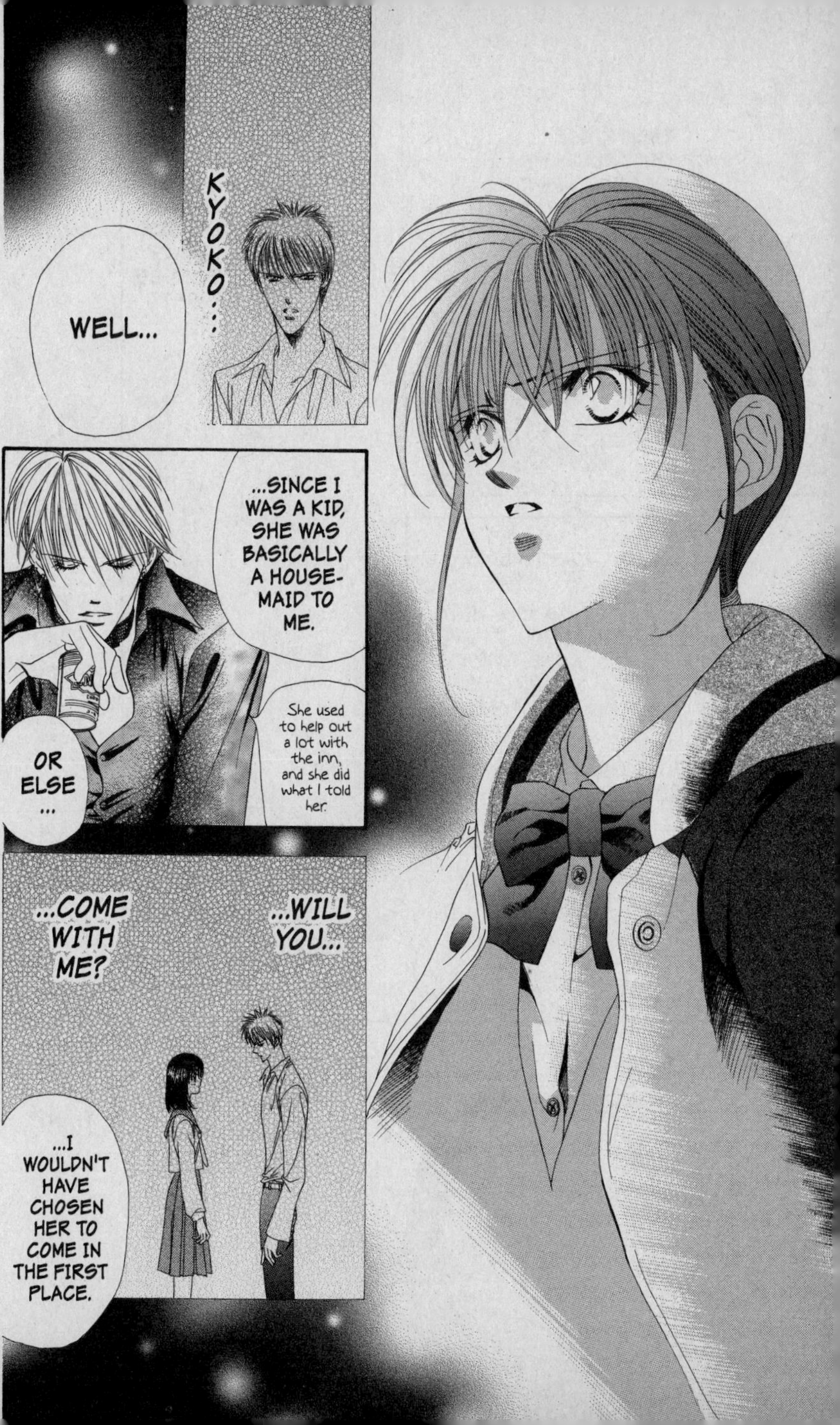
KYOKO...
WELL...
...SINCE I WAS A KID, SHE WAS BASICALLY A HOUSE-MAID TO ME.
She used to help out a lot with the inn, and she did what I told her.
OR ELSE...
...WILL YOU...
...COME WITH ME?
...I WOULDN'T HAVE CHOSEN HER TO COME IN THE FIRST PLACE.

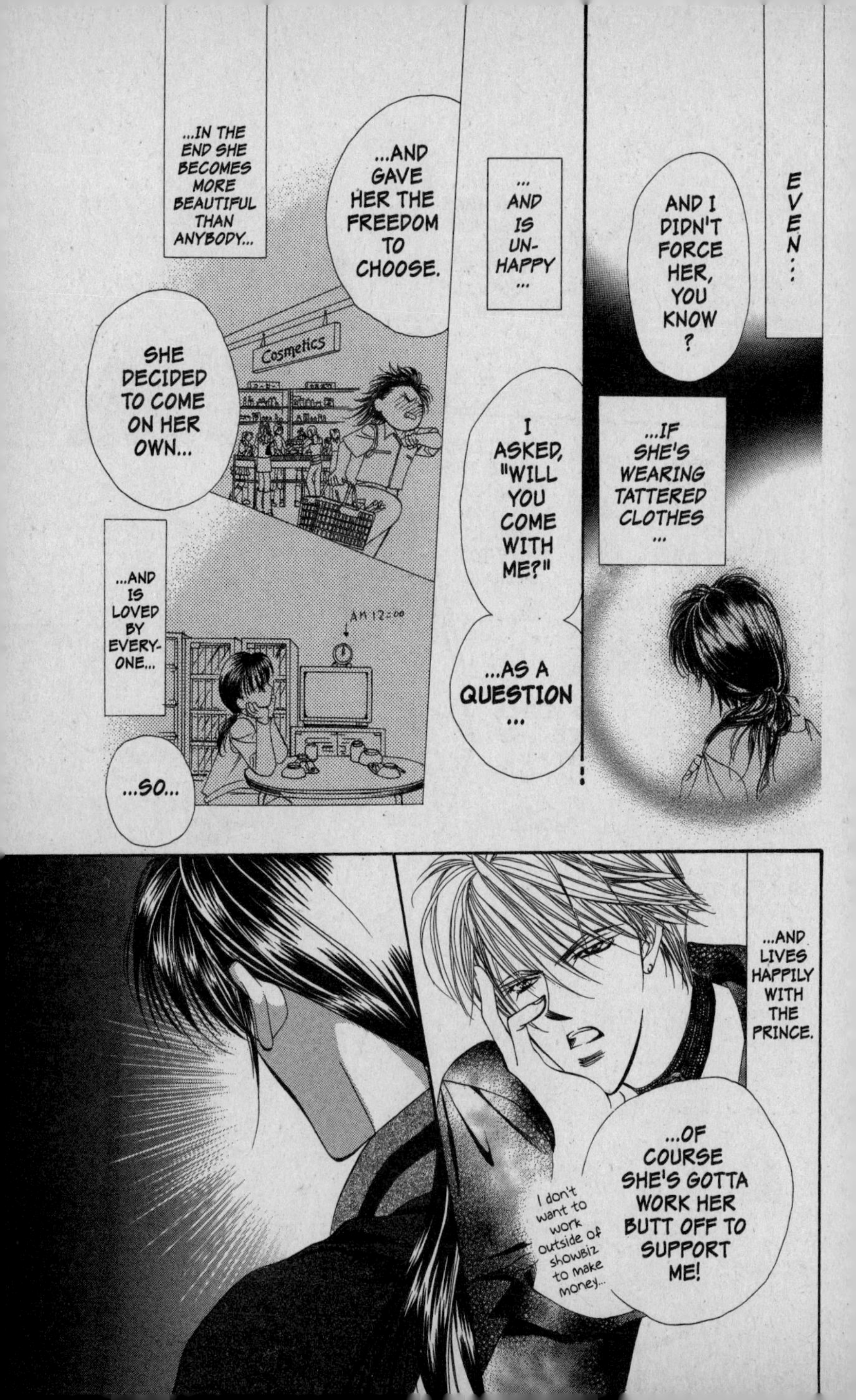
EVEN...
AND I DIDN'T FORCE HER, YOU KNOW?
...IF SHE'S WEARING TATTERED CLOTHES...
...AND IS UN-HAPPY...
I ASKED, "WILL YOU COME WITH ME?"
...AS A QUESTION...
...AND GAVE HER THE FREEDOM TO CHOOSE.
...IN THE END SHE BECOMES MORE BEAUTIFUL THAN ANYBODY...
SHE DECIDED TO COME ON HER OWN...
Cosmetics
...AND IS LOVED BY EVERY-ONE...
AM 12:00
...SO...
...AND LIVES HAPPILY WITH THE PRINCE.
...OF COURSE SHE'S GOTTA WORK HER BUTT OFF TO SUPPORT ME!
I don't want to work outside of showbiz to make money...

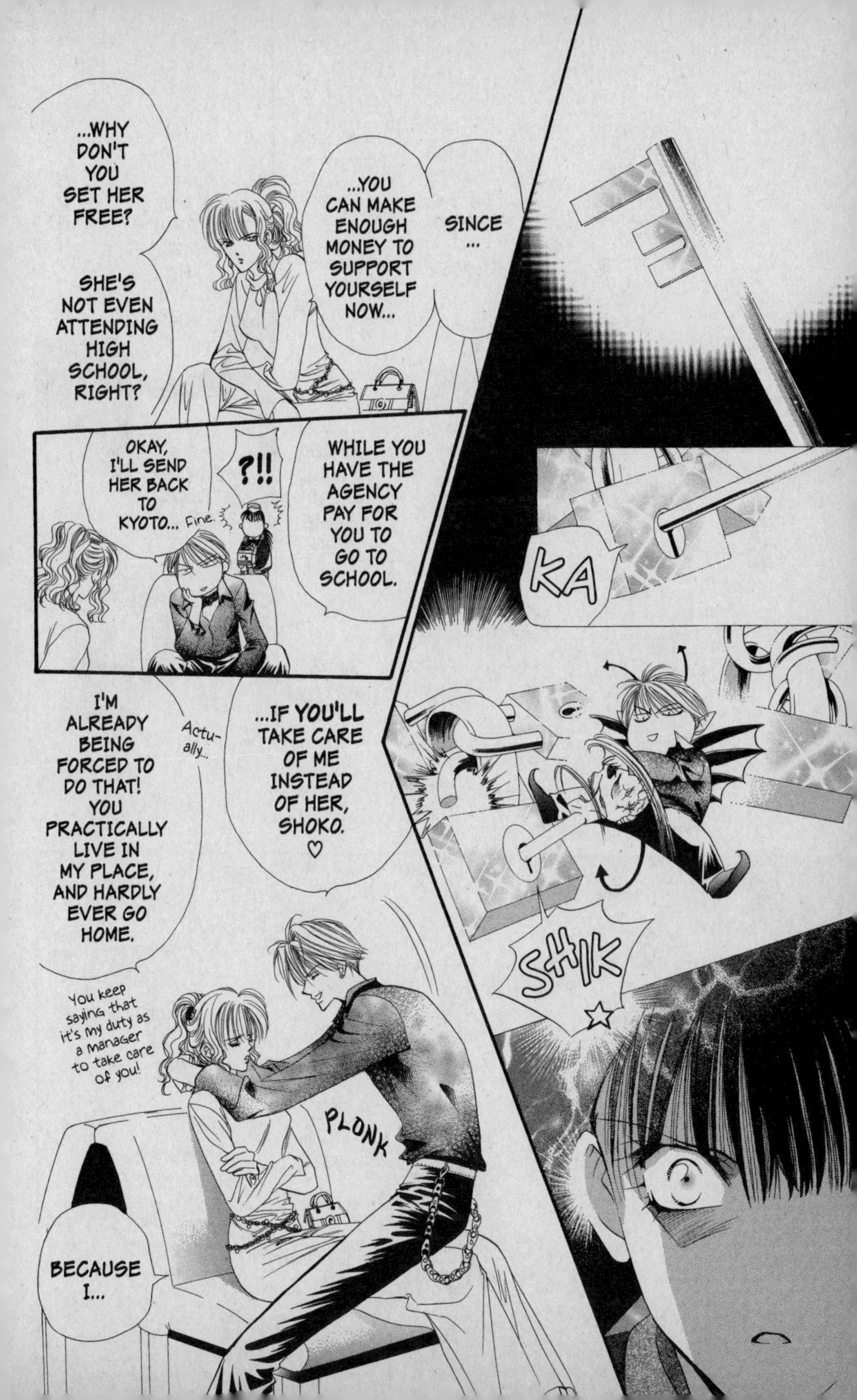
SINCE ...
...YOU CAN MAKE ENOUGH MONEY TO SUPPORT YOURSELF NOW...
...WHY DON'T YOU SET HER FREE?
SHE'S NOT EVEN ATTENDING HIGH SCHOOL, RIGHT?
KA
WHILE YOU HAVE THE AGENCY PAY FOR YOU TO GO TO SCHOOL.
?!!
OKAY, I'LL SEND HER BACK TO KYOTO... Fine.
SHIK
...IF YOU'LL TAKE CARE OF ME INSTEAD OF HER, SHOKO. ♡
Actu-ally...
I'M ALREADY BEING FORCED TO DO THAT! YOU PRACTICALLY LIVE IN MY PLACE, AND HARDLY EVER GO HOME.
You keep saying that it's my duty as a manager to take care of you!
PLONK
BECAUSE I...

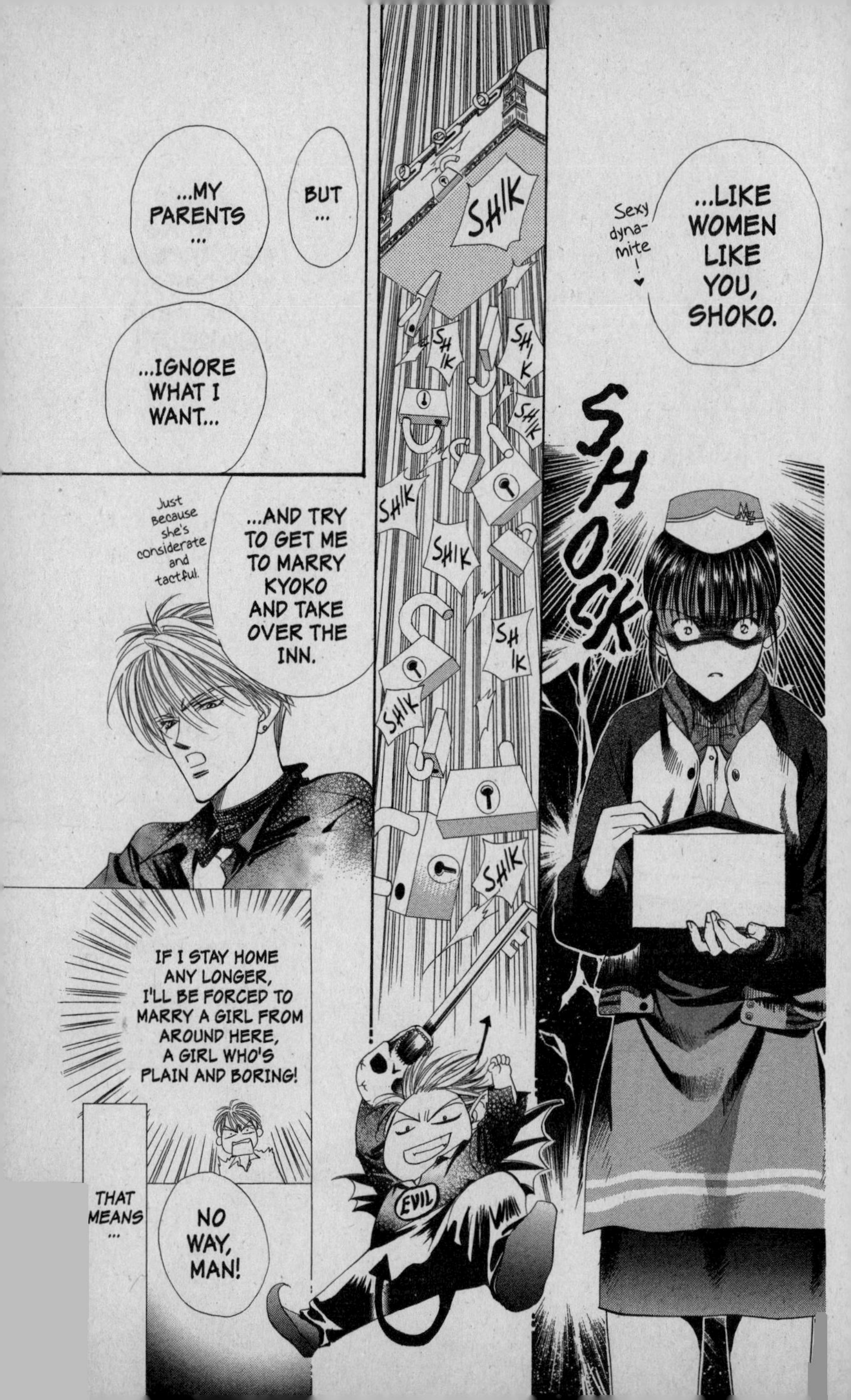
...LIKE WOMEN LIKE YOU, SHOKO.
Sexy dyna-mite! ♥
SHOCK
SHIK
SHIK
SHIK
SHIK
SHIK
SHIK
SHIK
SHIK
SHIK
EVIL
BUT...
...MY PARENTS...
...IGNORE WHAT I WANT...
...AND TRY TO GET ME TO MARRY KYOKO AND TAKE OVER THE INN.
Just because she's considerate and tactful.
IF I STAY HOME ANY LONGER, I'LL BE FORCED TO MARRY A GIRL FROM AROUND HERE, A GIRL WHO'S PLAIN AND BORING!
NO WAY, MAN!
THAT MEANS...

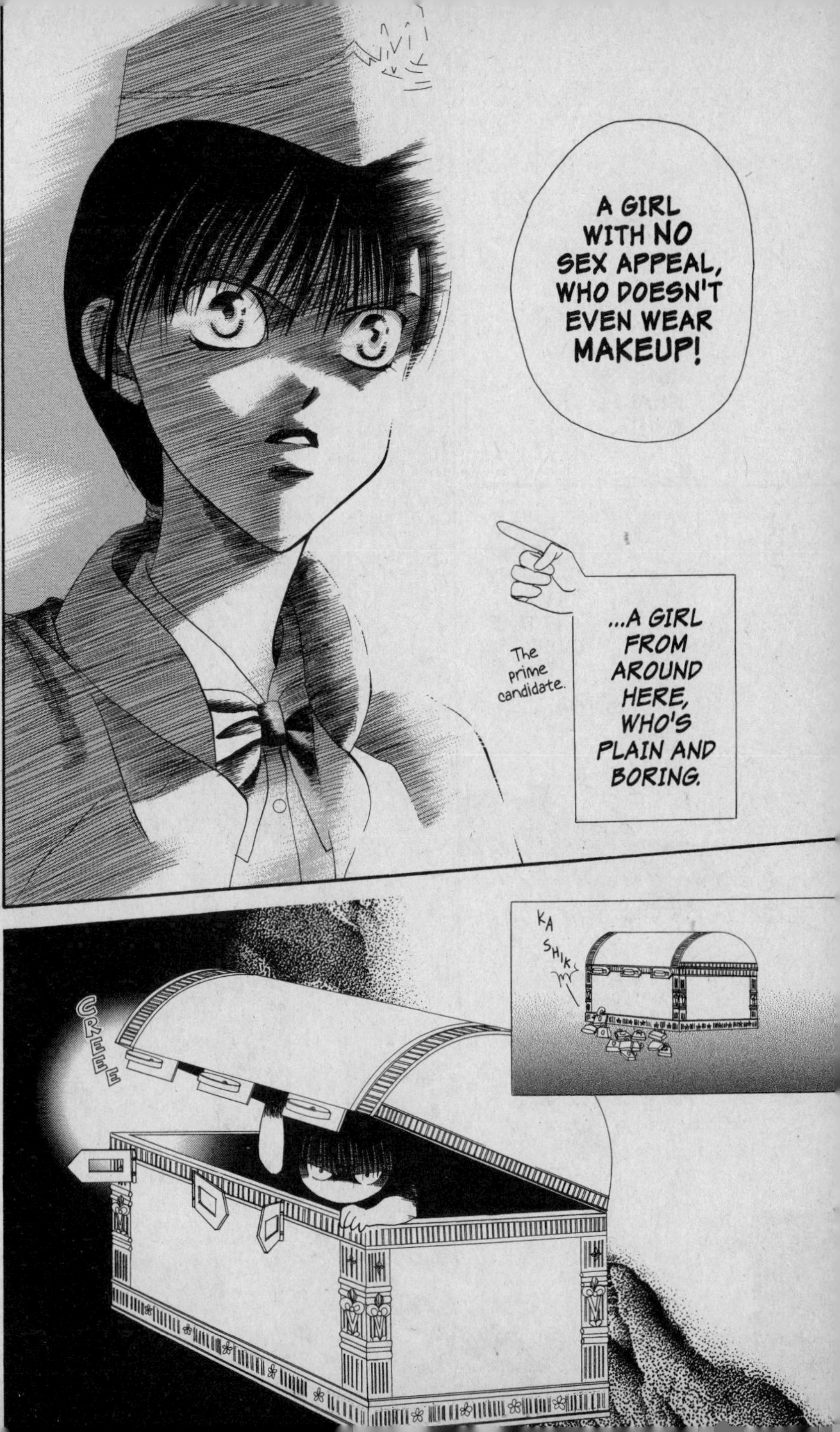
A GIRL WITH NO SEX APPEAL, WHO DOESN'T EVEN WEAR MAKEUP!
...A GIRL FROM AROUND HERE, WHO'S PLAIN AND BORING.
The prime candidate.
KA SHIK
CREEE

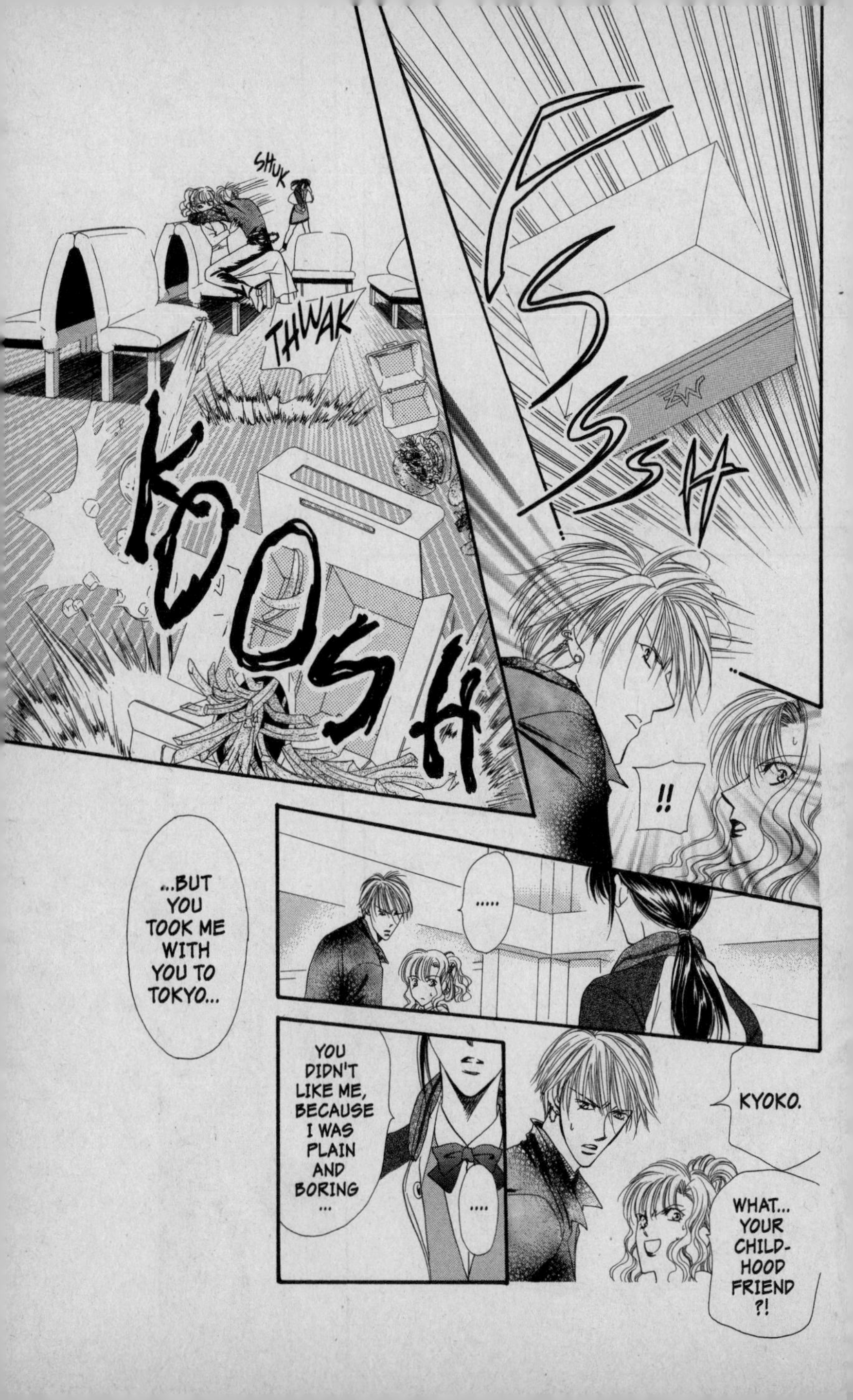

FSSSH
...
!!
SHUK
THWAK
KDOSH
.....
...BUT YOU TOOK ME WITH YOU TO TOKYO...
KYOKO.
WHAT... YOUR CHILDHOOD FRIEND?!
....
YOU DIDN'T LIKE ME, BECAUSE I WAS PLAIN AND BORING...

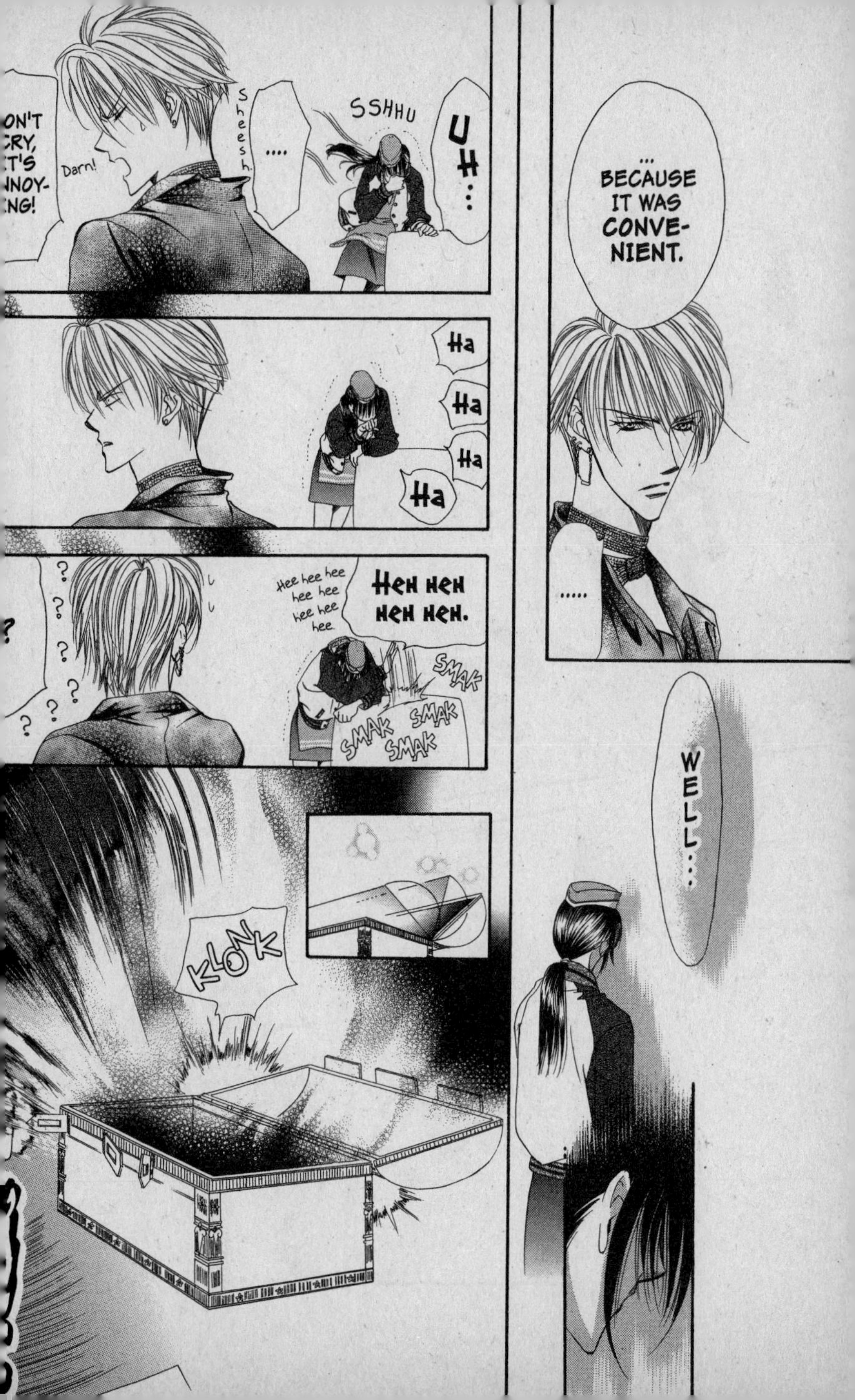
... BECAUSE IT WAS CONVENIENT.
.....
WELL...
UH...
SSHHU
....
Sheesh.
Darn!
ON'T CRY, T'S NNOY-NG!
Ha
Ha
Ha
Ha
HEH HEH HEH HEH.
Hee hee hee hee hee hee hee hee hee.
SMAK
SMAK
SMAK
SMAK
KLONK

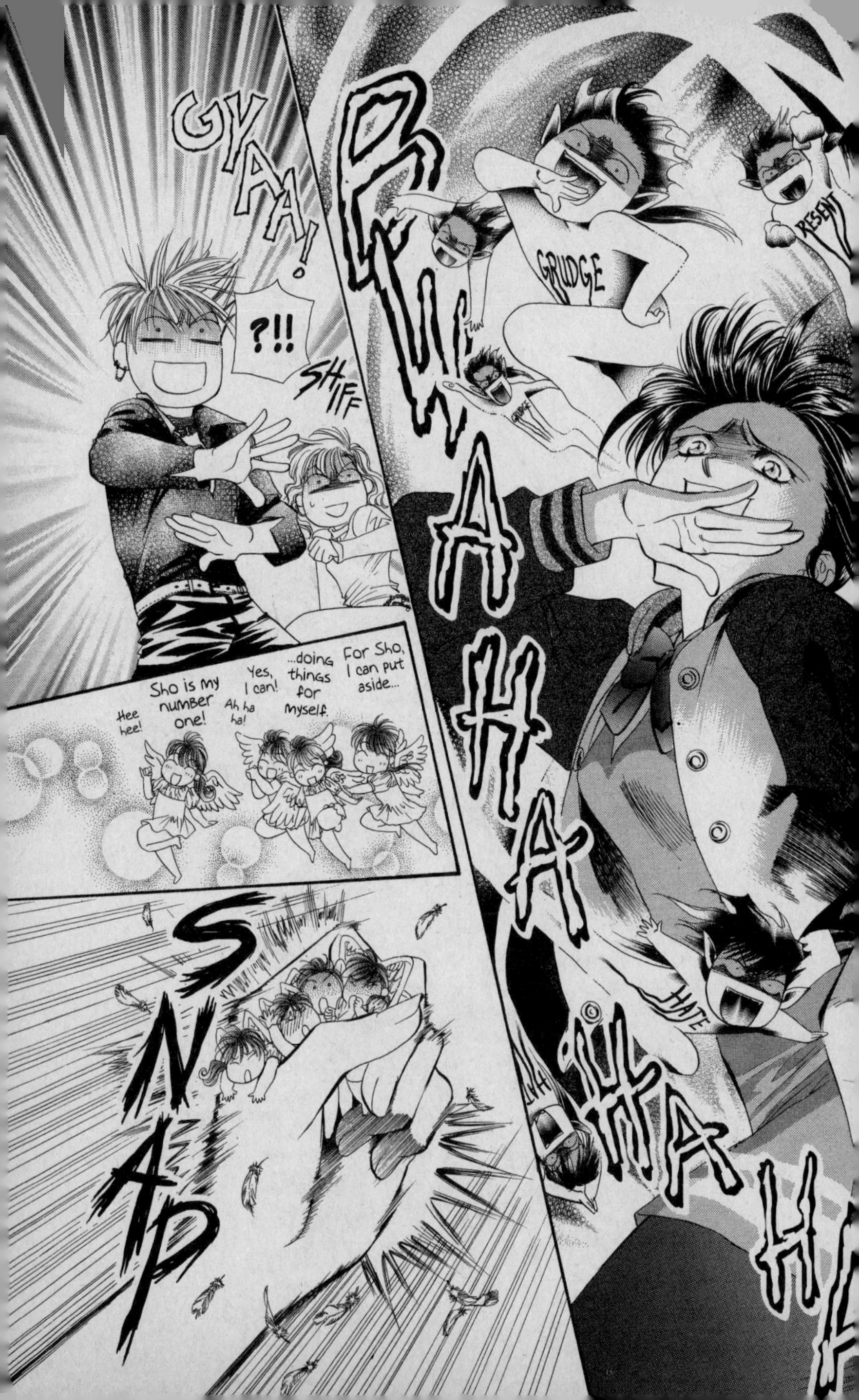
BWAHAHA
GRUDGE
RESENT
GRUDGE
HATE
HAHAHA
GYAA!
?!!
SHIFF
For Sho, I can put aside...
...doing things for myself.
Yes, I can!
Ah ha ha!
Sho is my number one!
Hee hee!
SNAP

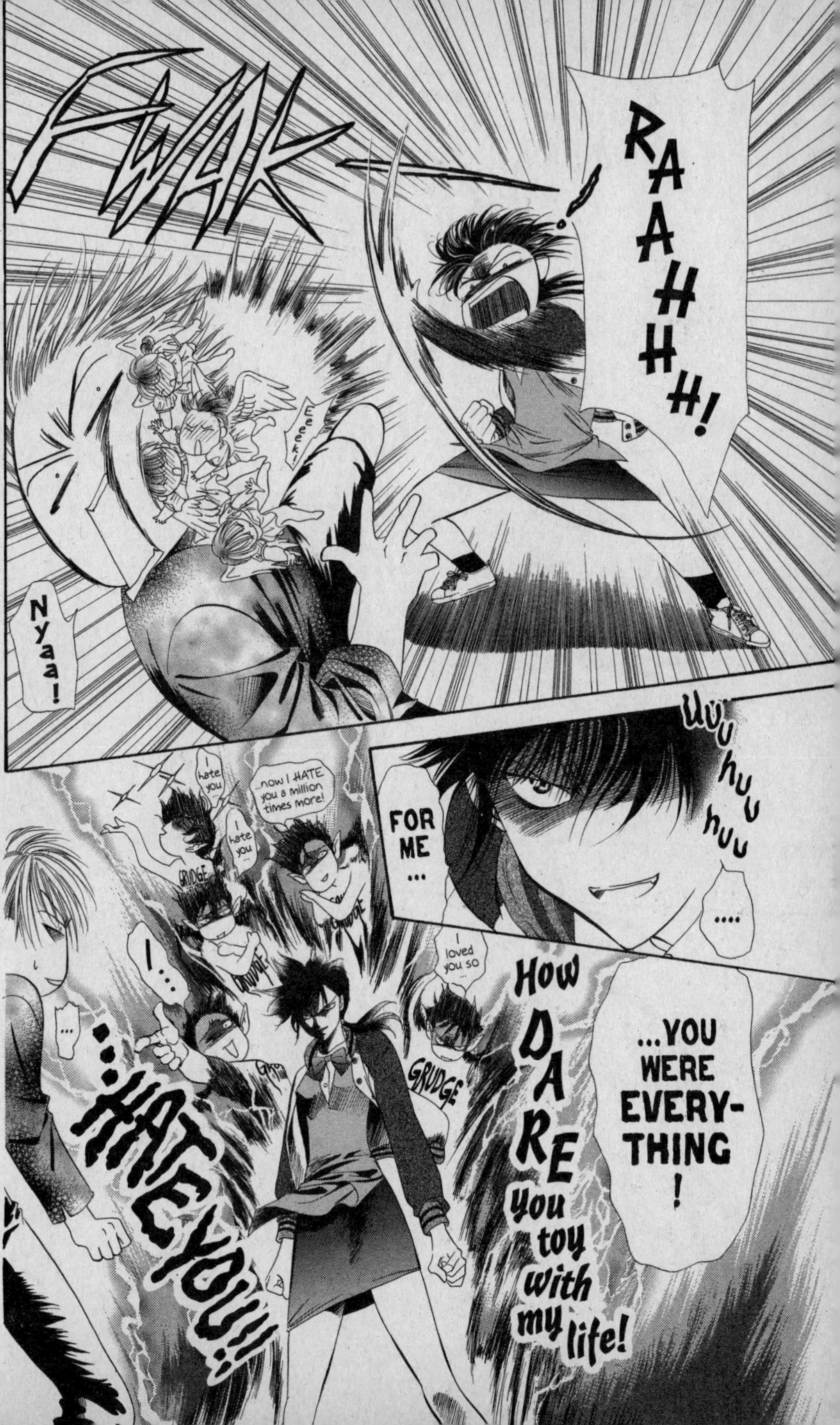
RAAHHHH!
PWAK
Eeeek!
Nyaa!
Uuu huu huu
....
FOR ME ...
...YOU WERE EVERYTHING!
How DARE you toy with my life!
I loved you so ...
...now I HATE you a million times more!
I hate you ...
I hate you ...
GRUDGE
GRUDGE
GRUDGE
GRUDGE
I...
...HATE YOU!!
....

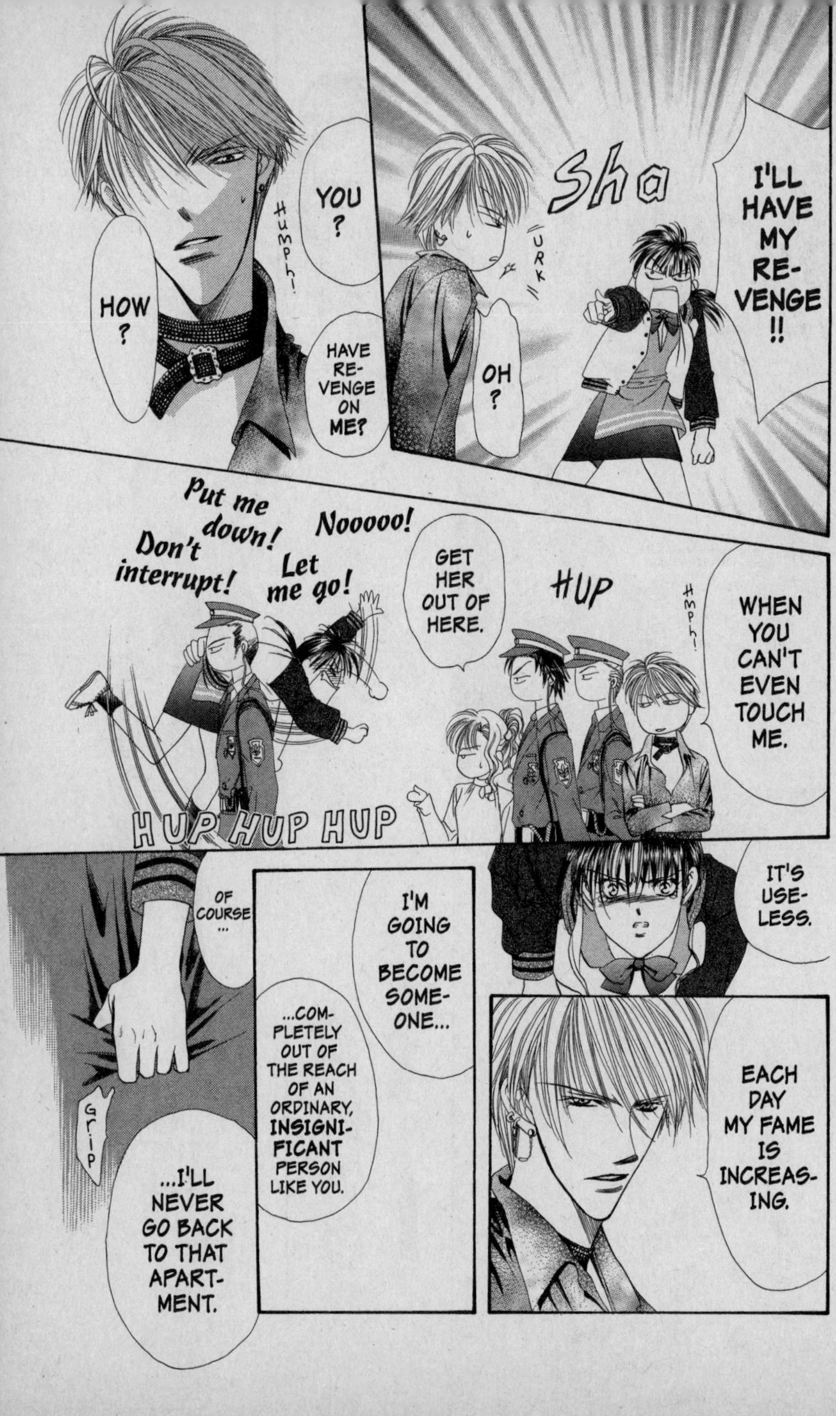
I'LL HAVE MY RE-VENGE!!
Sha
URK
OH?
YOU?
HAVE RE-VENGE ON ME?
Humph!
HOW?
WHEN YOU CAN'T EVEN TOUCH ME.
Hmph!
HUP
GET HER OUT OF HERE.
Nooooo!
Put me down!
Let me go!
Don't interrupt!
HUP HUP HUP
IT'S USE-LESS.
EACH DAY MY FAME IS INCREAS-ING.
I'M GOING TO BECOME SOME-ONE...
...COM-PLETELY OUT OF THE REACH OF AN ORDINARY, INSIGNIFICANT PERSON LIKE YOU.
OF COURSE...
Grip
...I'LL NEVER GO BACK TO THAT APARTMENT.

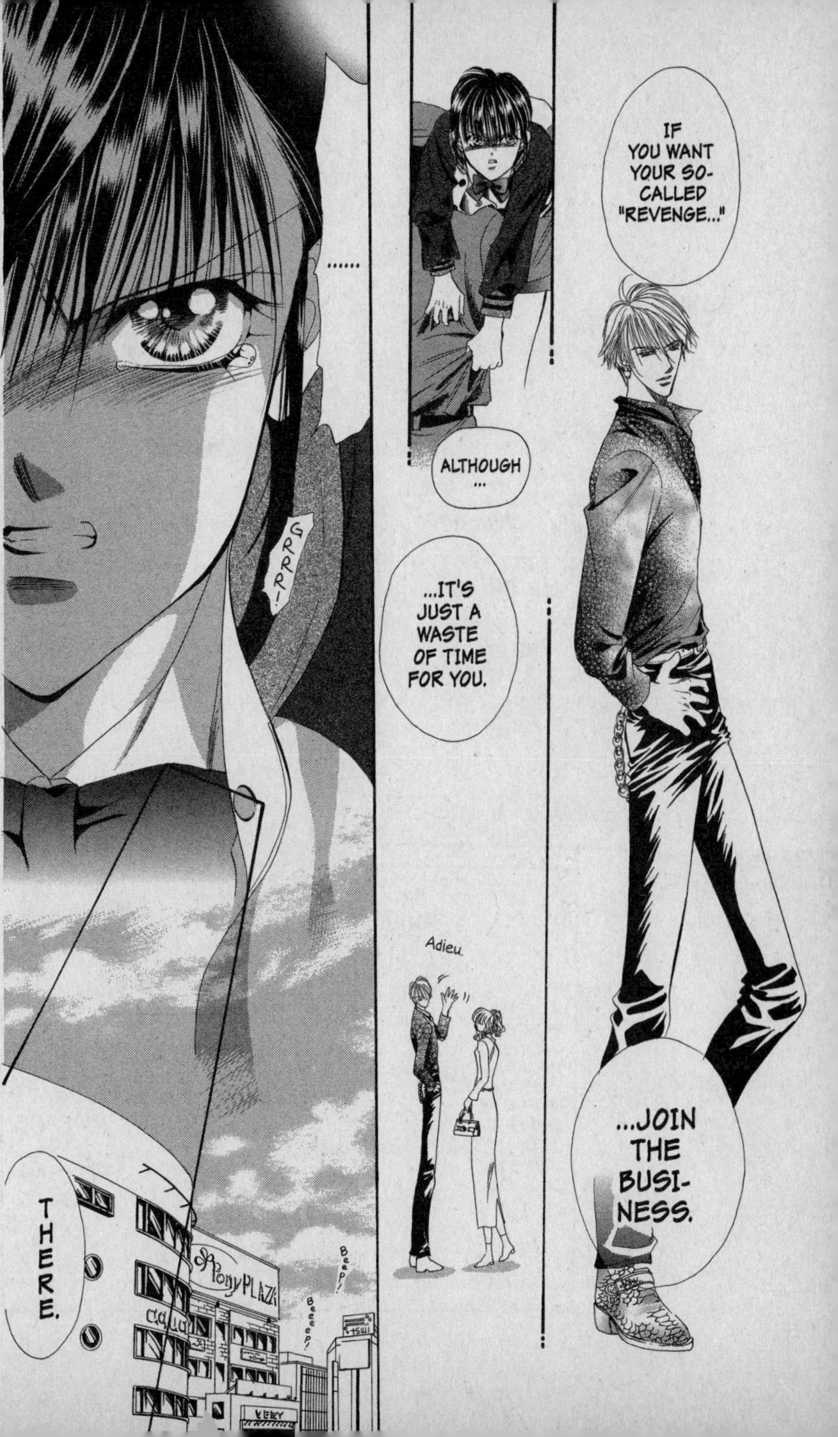
IF YOU WANT YOUR SO-CALLED "REVENGE..."
...JOIN THE BUSI-NESS.
ALTHOUGH ...
...IT'S JUST A WASTE OF TIME FOR YOU.
Adieu.
......
GRRR!
THERE.
Beep!
Beeeep!
PonyPLAZA

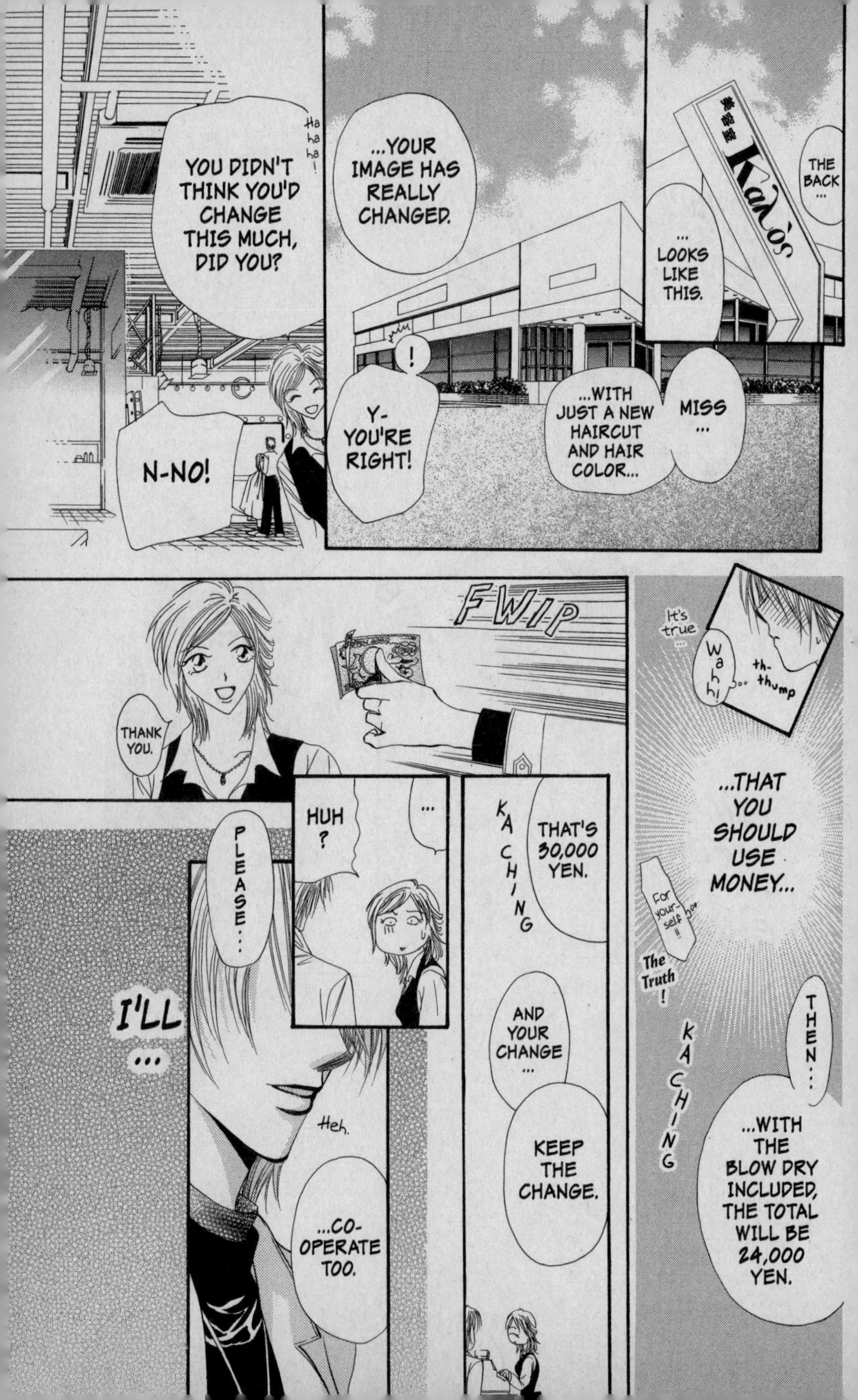
THE BACK...
Kano's
...LOOKS LIKE THIS.
...YOUR IMAGE HAS REALLY CHANGED.
MISS...
...WITH JUST A NEW HAIRCUT AND HAIR COLOR...
!
Y-YOU'RE RIGHT!
Ha ha ha!
YOU DIDN'T THINK YOU'D CHANGE THIS MUCH, DID YOU?
N-NO!
It's true...
Wahh!...
th-thump
...THAT YOU SHOULD USE MONEY...
For your-self!!
hoo
The Truth!
THEN...
KA CHING
...WITH THE BLOW DRY INCLUDED, THE TOTAL WILL BE 24,000 YEN.
FWIP
THANK YOU.
KA CHING
THAT'S 30,000 YEN.
AND YOUR CHANGE...
KEEP THE CHANGE.
...
HUH?
PLEASE...
I'LL...
Heh.
...CO-OPERATE TOO.

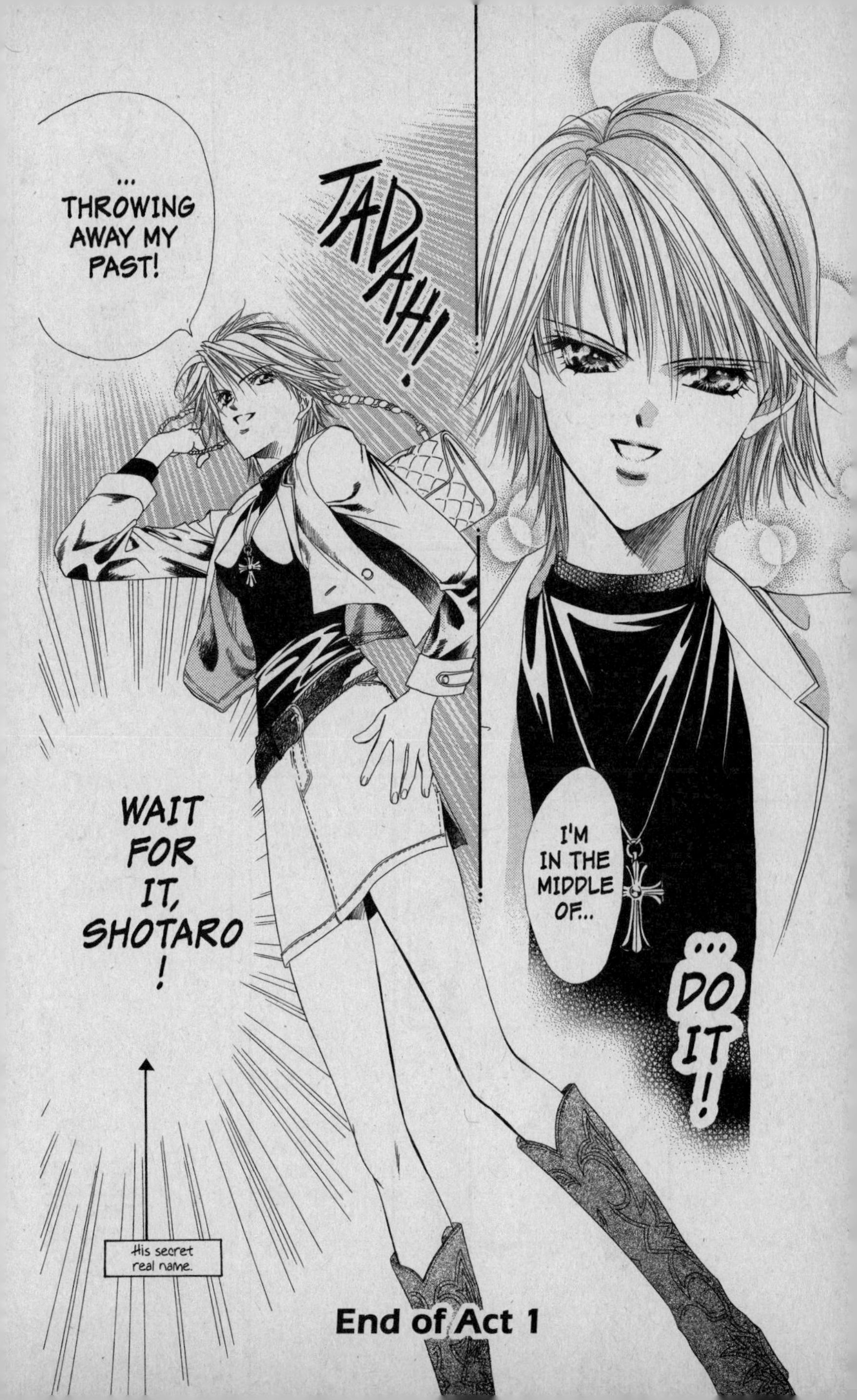
I'M IN THE MIDDLE OF...
...DO IT!
TADAH!
...THROWING AWAY MY PAST!
WAIT FOR IT, SHOTARO!
His secret real name.

End of Act 1

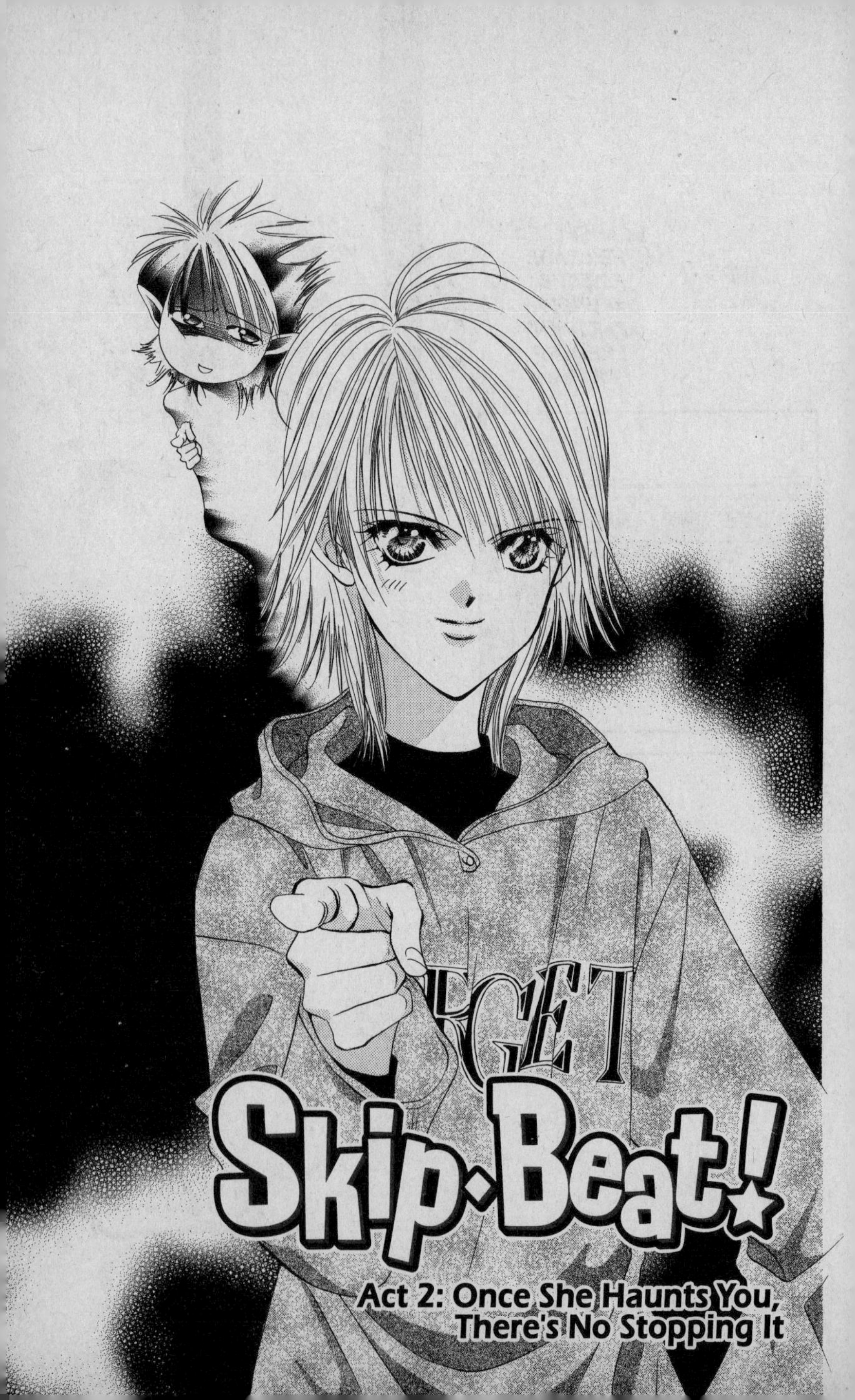
Skip·Beat!
Act 2: Once She Haunts You, There's No Stopping It

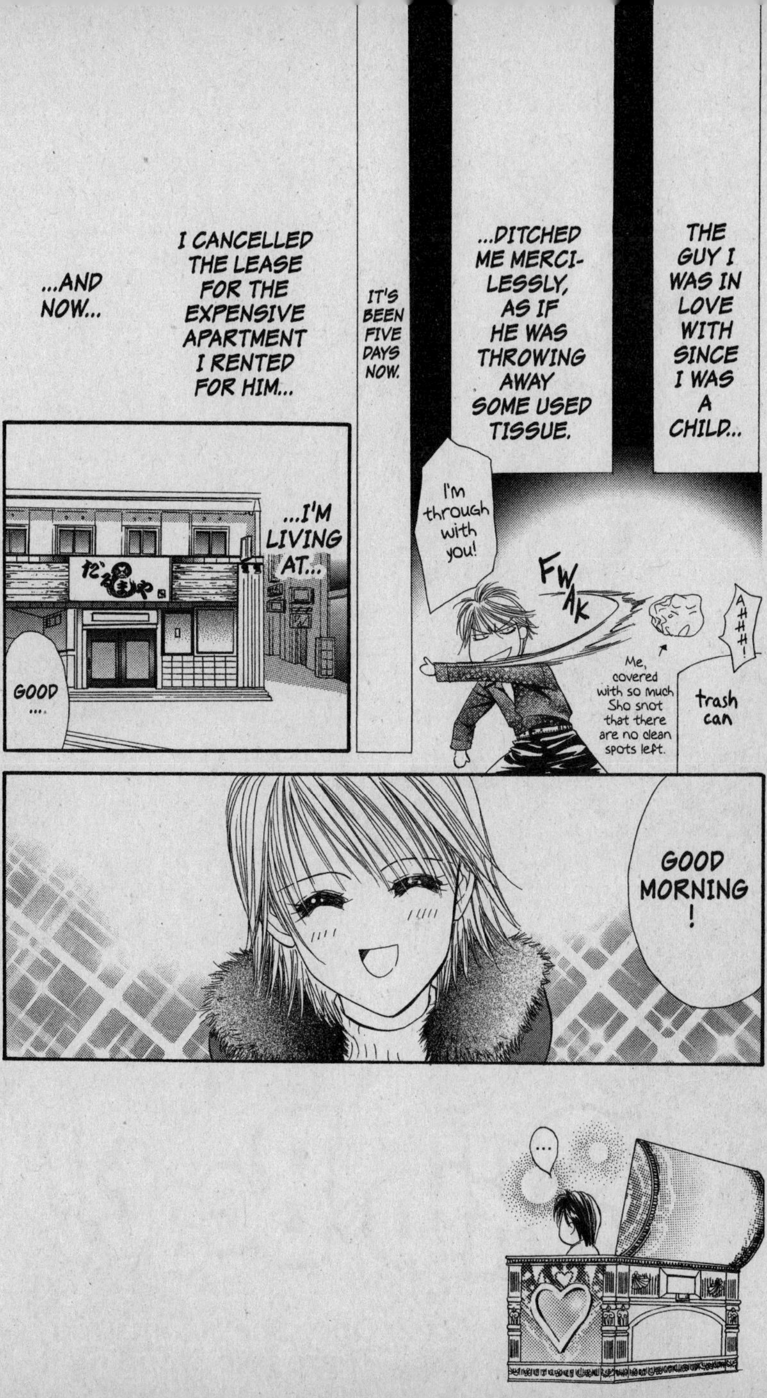
THE GUY I WAS IN LOVE WITH SINCE I WAS A CHILD...
...DITCHED ME MERCILESSLY, AS IF HE WAS THROWING AWAY SOME USED TISSUE.
I'm through with you!
FWAK
AHHH!
Me, covered with so much Sho snot that there are no clean spots left.
trash can
IT'S BEEN FIVE DAYS NOW.
I CANCELLED THE LEASE FOR THE EXPENSIVE APARTMENT I RENTED FOR HIM...
...AND NOW...
...I'M LIVING AT...
GOOD ....
GOOD MORNING!
...

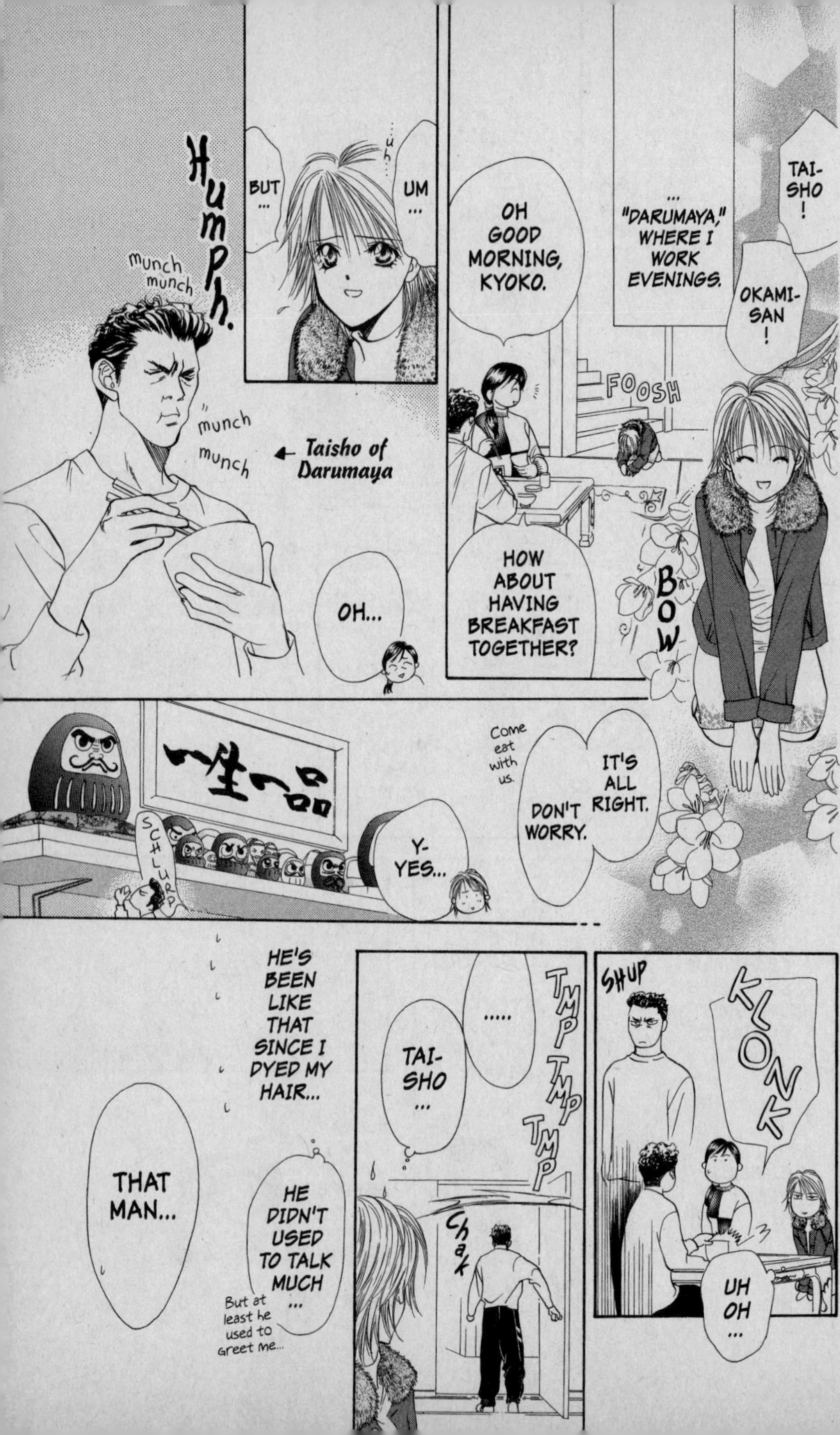
TAI-SHO!
OKAMI-SAN!
... "DARUMAYA," WHERE I WORK EVENINGS.
FOOSH
BOW
OH GOOD MORNING, KYOKO.
HOW ABOUT HAVING BREAKFAST TOGETHER?
UM ...
...uh
BUT ...
Humph.
munch munch
munch munch
Taisho of Darumaya
OH...
IT'S ALL RIGHT.
DON'T WORRY.
Come eat with us.
Y-YES...
SCHLURRP
SHUP
KLONK
UH OH ...
TMP TMP TMP
.....
TAI-SHO ...
Chak
HE'S BEEN LIKE THAT SINCE I DYED MY HAIR...
HE DIDN'T USED TO TALK MUCH ...
But at least he used to greet me...
THAT MAN...

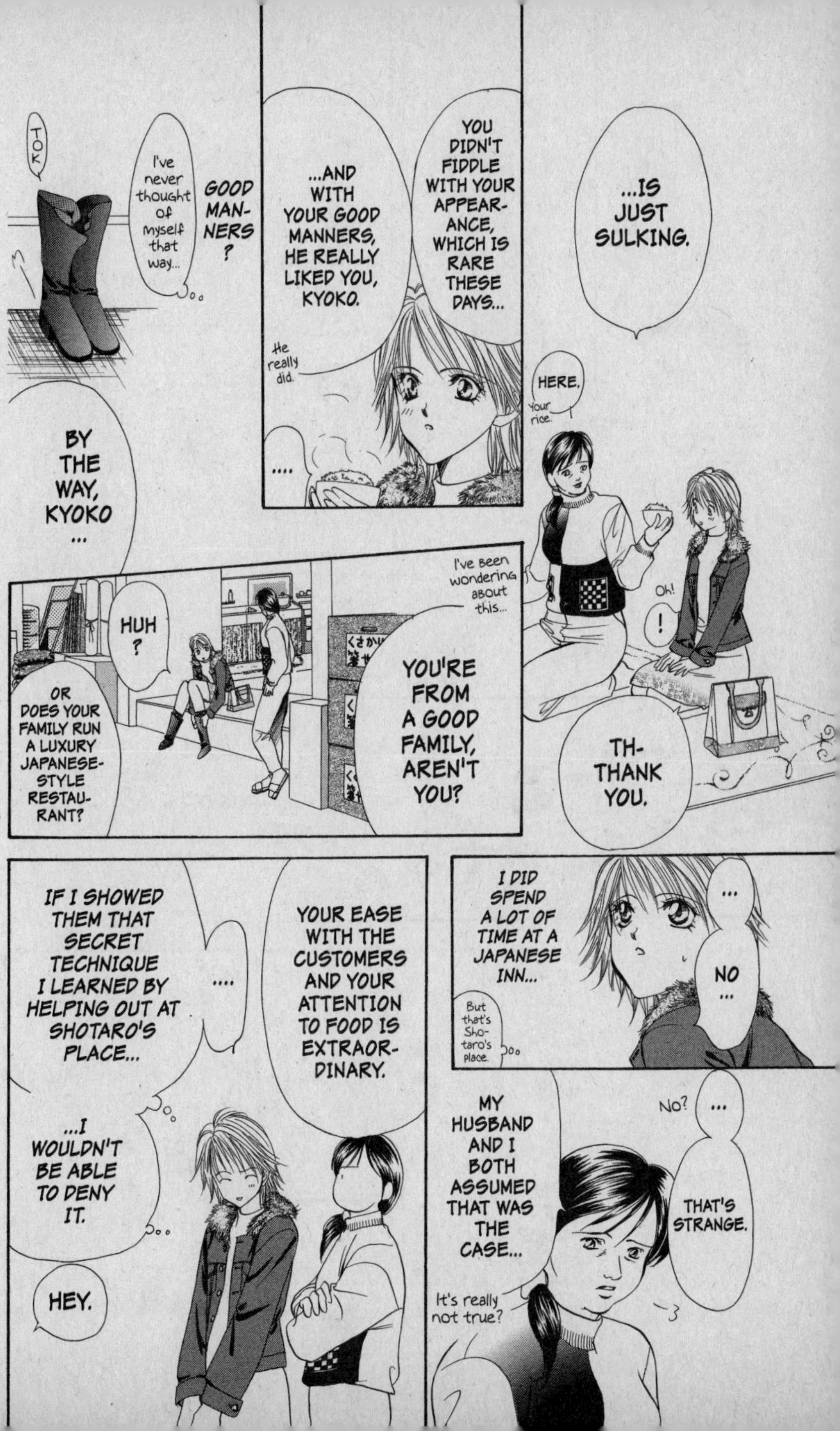
...IS JUST SULKING.
HERE.
Your rice.
Oh!
!
TH-THANK YOU.
YOU DIDN'T FIDDLE WITH YOUR APPEARANCE, WHICH IS RARE THESE DAYS...
...AND WITH YOUR GOOD MANNERS, HE REALLY LIKED YOU, KYOKO.
He really did.
....
GOOD MANNERS?
I've never thought of myself that way...
TOK
BY THE WAY, KYOKO...
I've been wondering about this...
YOU'RE FROM A GOOD FAMILY, AREN'T YOU?
HUH?
OR DOES YOUR FAMILY RUN A LUXURY JAPANESE-STYLE RESTAURANT?
...
NO...
I DID SPEND A LOT OF TIME AT A JAPANESE INN...
But that's Shotaro's place.
...
No?
THAT'S STRANGE.
MY HUSBAND AND I BOTH ASSUMED THAT WAS THE CASE...
It's really not true?
YOUR EASE WITH THE CUSTOMERS AND YOUR ATTENTION TO FOOD IS EXTRAORDINARY.
....
IF I SHOWED THEM THAT SECRET TECHNIQUE I LEARNED BY HELPING OUT AT SHOTARO'S PLACE...
...I WOULDN'T BE ABLE TO DENY IT.
HEY.

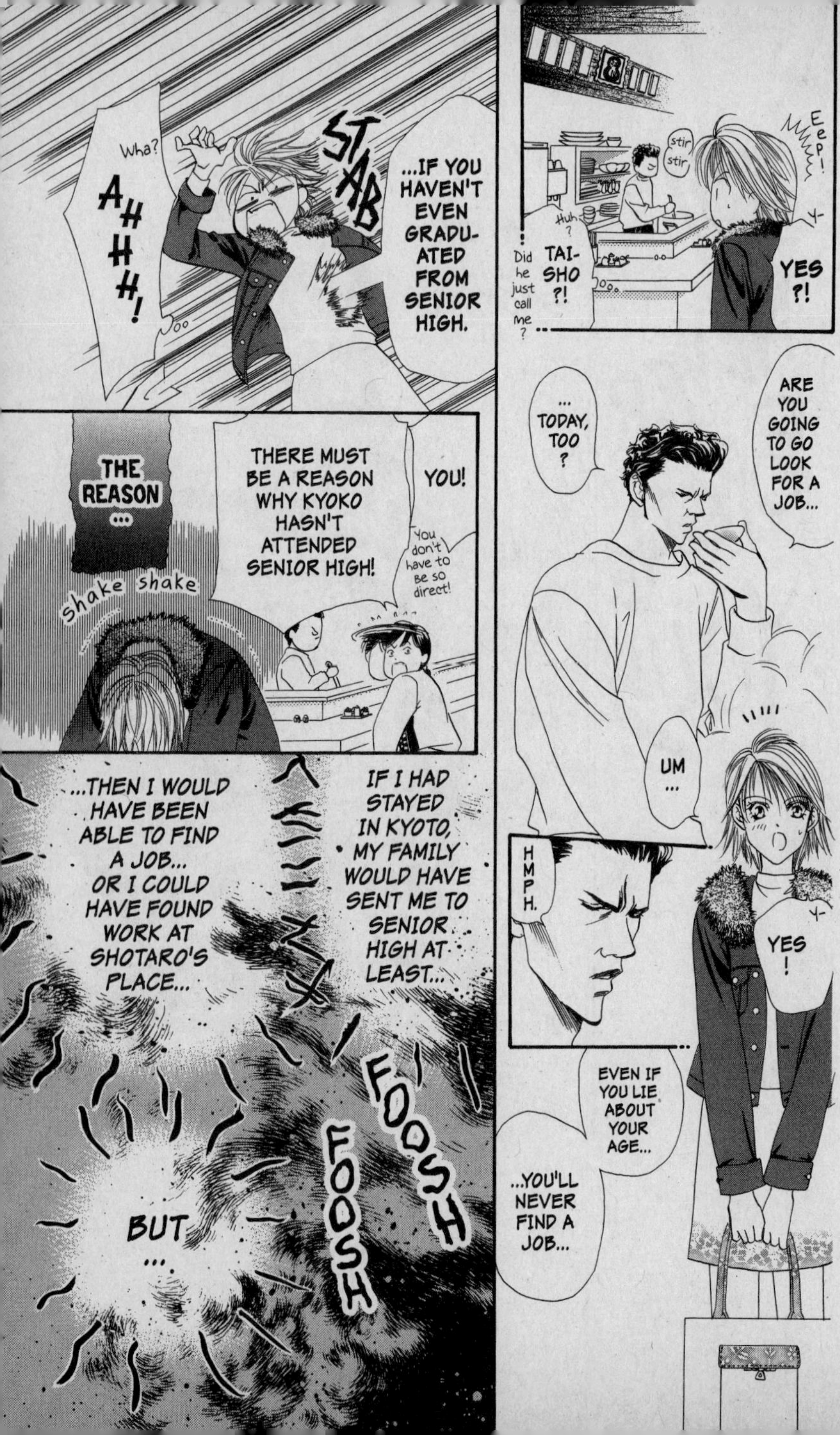

Eep!
Y-
YES ?!
stir stir
Huh ?
TAI-SHO ?!
Did he just call me ?
ARE YOU GOING TO GO LOOK FOR A JOB...
... TODAY, TOO ?
UM ...
HMPH.
Y-
YES !
EVEN IF YOU LIE ABOUT YOUR AGE...
...YOU'LL NEVER FIND A JOB...
...IF YOU HAVEN'T EVEN GRADUATED FROM SENIOR HIGH.
STAB
Wha?
AHHH!
YOU!
THERE MUST BE A REASON WHY KYOKO HASN'T ATTENDED SENIOR HIGH!
You don't have to be so direct!
THE REASON ...
shake shake
IF I HAD STAYED IN KYOTO, MY FAMILY WOULD HAVE SENT ME TO SENIOR HIGH AT LEAST...
...THEN I WOULD HAVE BEEN ABLE TO FIND A JOB... OR I COULD HAVE FOUND WORK AT SHOTARO'S PLACE...
FOOSH
FOOSH
BUT ...

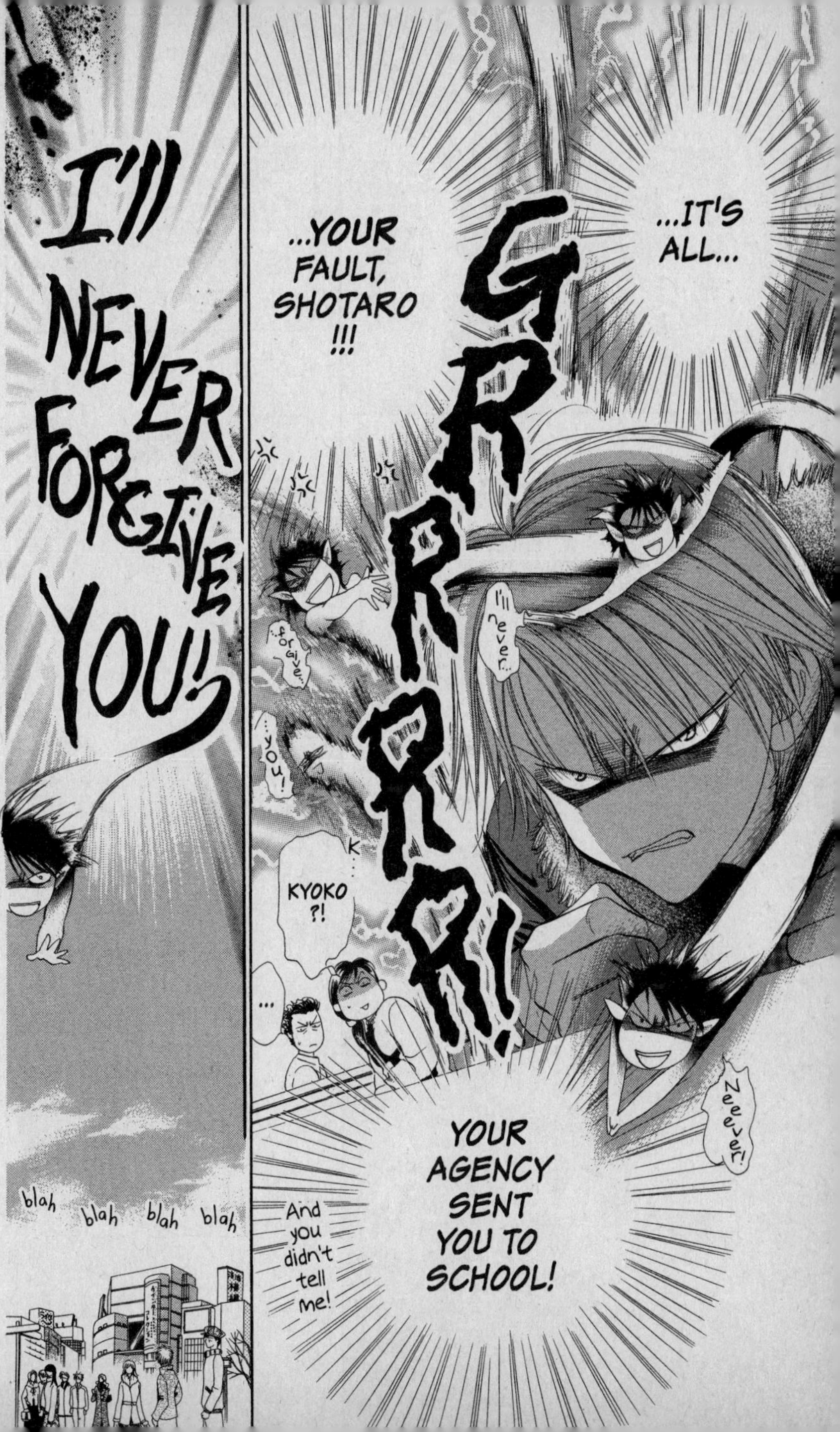
...IT'S ALL...
...YOUR FAULT, SHOTARO!!!
GRRRRR!
I'll never...
...forgive...
...you!
K...
KYOKO?!
...
Neeever!
YOUR AGENCY SENT YOU TO SCHOOL!
And you didn't tell me!
I'LL NEVER FORGIVE YOU!!
blah blah blah blah

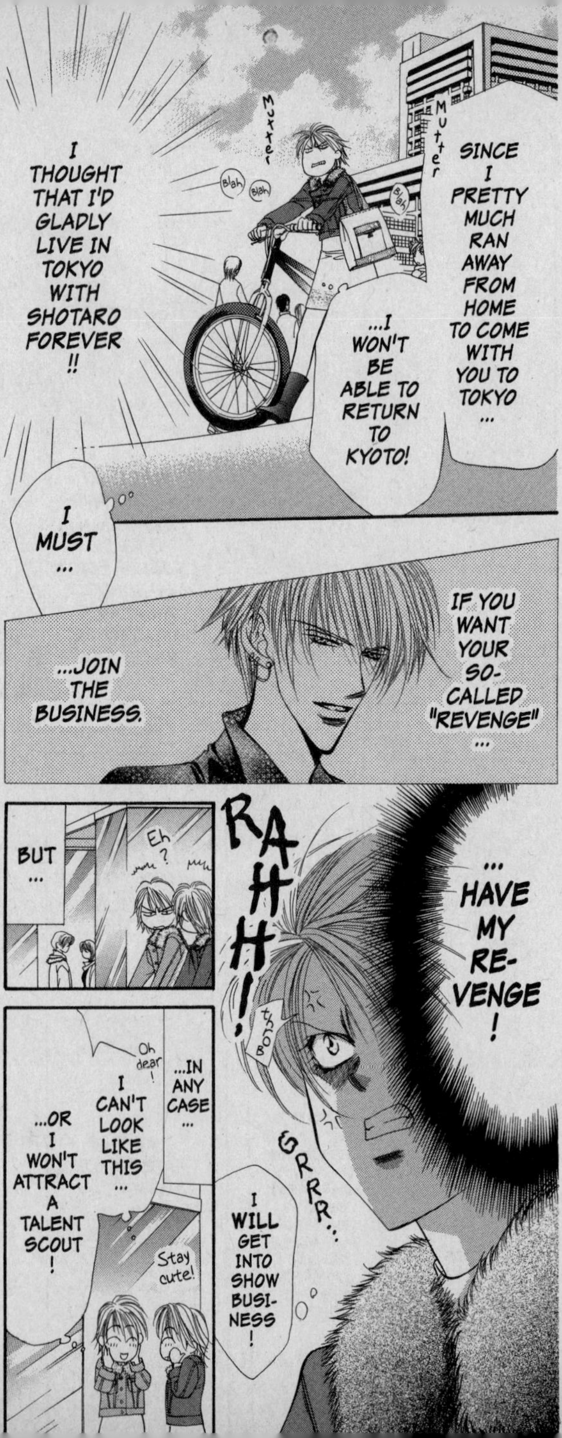
SINCE I PRETTY MUCH RAN AWAY FROM HOME TO COME WITH YOU TO TOKYO...
...I WON'T BE ABLE TO RETURN TO KYOTO!
Mutter
Blah
Blah
Blah
Mutter
I THOUGHT THAT I'D GLADLY LIVE IN TOKYO WITH SHOTARO FOREVER!!
I MUST...
IF YOU WANT YOUR SO-CALLED "REVENGE"...
...JOIN THE BUSINESS.
RAHH!
...HAVE MY REVENGE!
throb
GRRR...
I WILL GET INTO SHOW BUSINESS!
BUT...
Eh?
...IN ANY CASE...
Oh dear!
I CAN'T LOOK LIKE THIS...
...OR I WON'T ATTRACT A TALENT SCOUT!
Stay cute!

4

It's perfect for Kyoko!! My heart throbbed, and the title became "Skip Beat!" Regarding the title—for a long time and up until the last moment, I was thinking about it. So I feel I inconvenienced my editor a lot... The first title I submitted was kinda depressing, and after that I submitted ones that didn't have much effect, or ones people couldn't figure out the meanings of, and they got rejected. And unlike an adult, I complained... (shame) My character designs kept getting rejected too (actually, Ren was rejected, too), and I complained, "Then, what kind of stuff IS acceptable?!" I apologize for being short-tempered. But you, the editor who patiently dealt with me when I had a short fuse, you're a real role model for editors. Thank you so very much.

I will try to watch myself, but I don't know when I may turn out to be a wild horse. So, when that happens, please rein me in.

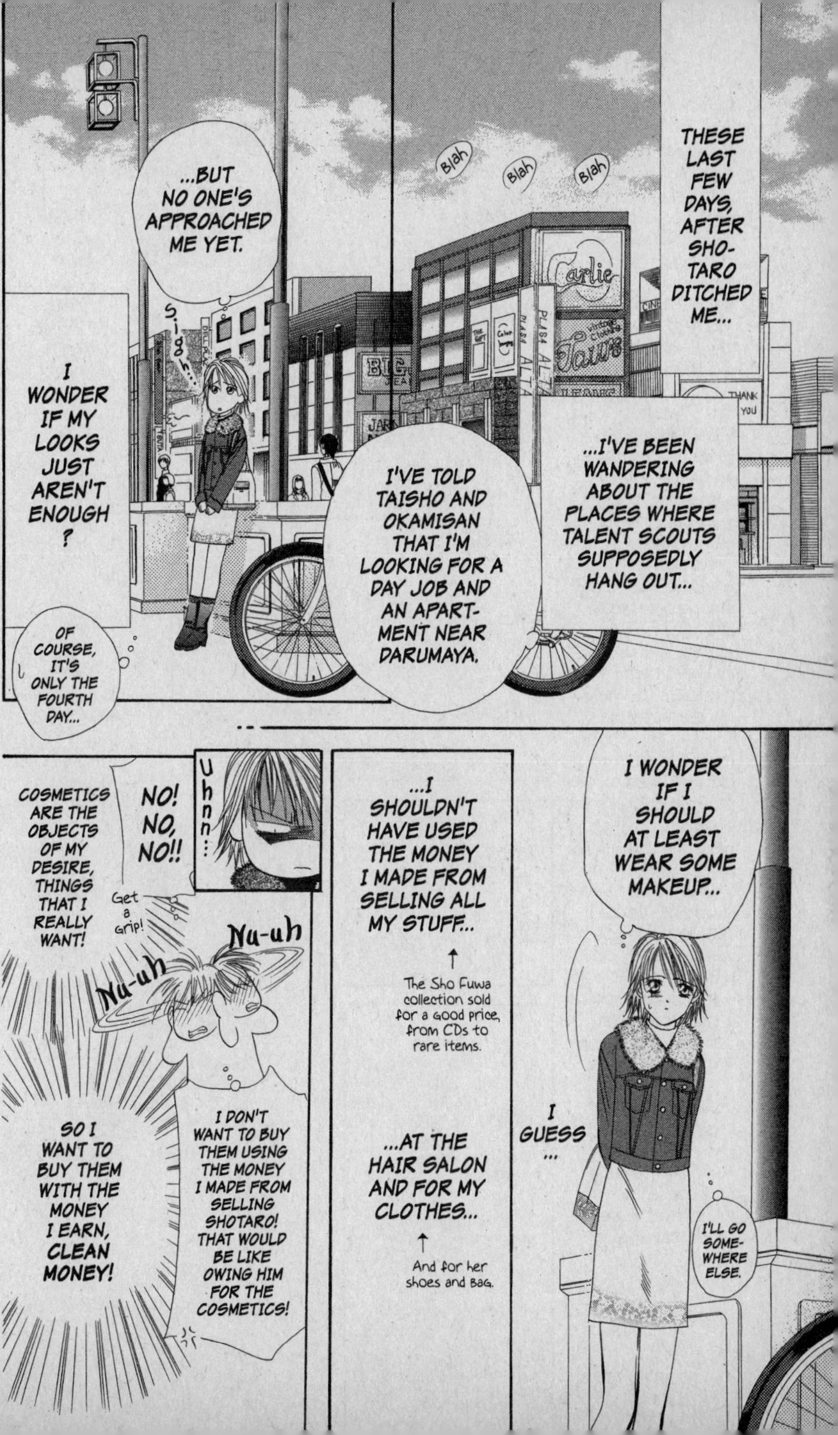
THESE LAST FEW DAYS, AFTER SHO-TARO DITCHED ME...
...I'VE BEEN WANDERING ABOUT THE PLACES WHERE TALENT SCOUTS SUPPOSEDLY HANG OUT...
I'VE TOLD TAISHO AND OKAMISAN THAT I'M LOOKING FOR A DAY JOB AND AN APART-MENT NEAR DARUMAYA.
Blah
Blah
Blah
...BUT NO ONE'S APPROACHED ME YET.
Sigh...
I WONDER IF MY LOOKS JUST AREN'T ENOUGH?
OF COURSE, IT'S ONLY THE FOURTH DAY...
I WONDER IF I SHOULD AT LEAST WEAR SOME MAKEUP...
I GUESS...
I'LL GO SOME-WHERE ELSE.
...I SHOULDN'T HAVE USED THE MONEY I MADE FROM SELLING ALL MY STUFF...
The Sho Fuwa collection sold for a good price, from CDs to rare items.
...AT THE HAIR SALON AND FOR MY CLOTHES...
And for her shoes and bag.
Uhnn...
NO! NO, NO!!
COSMETICS ARE THE OBJECTS OF MY DESIRE, THINGS THAT I REALLY WANT!
Get a grip!
Nu-uh
Nu-uh
I DON'T WANT TO BUY THEM USING THE MONEY I MADE FROM SELLING SHOTARO! THAT WOULD BE LIKE OWING HIM FOR THE COSMETICS!
SO I WANT TO BUY THEM WITH THE MONEY I EARN, CLEAN MONEY!

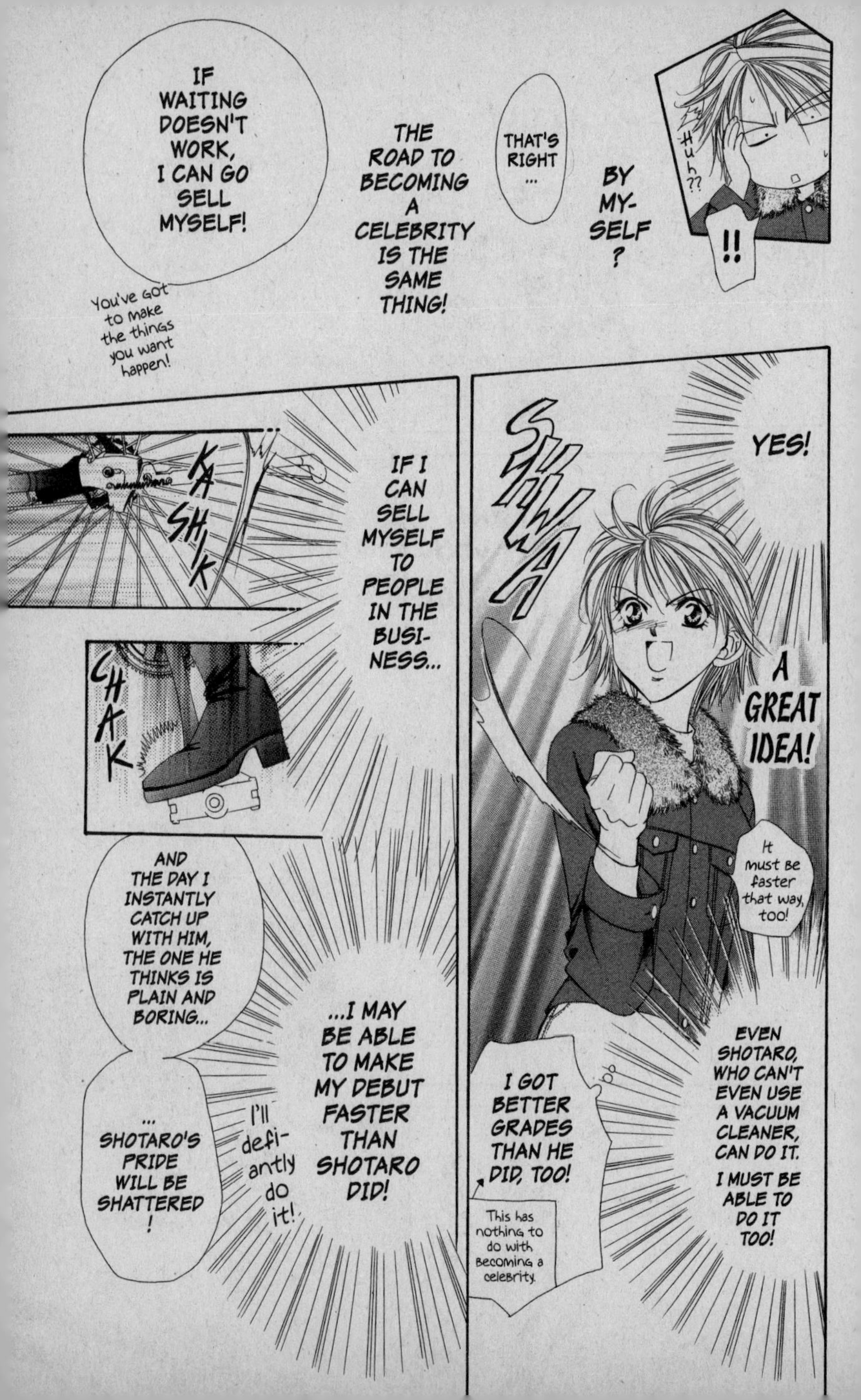
Huh??
!!
BY MYSELF?
THAT'S RIGHT...
THE ROAD TO BECOMING A CELEBRITY IS THE SAME THING!
IF WAITING DOESN'T WORK, I CAN GO SELL MYSELF!
You've got to make the things you want happen!
SHWA
YES!
A GREAT IDEA!
It must be faster that way, too!
EVEN SHOTARO, WHO CAN'T EVEN USE A VACUUM CLEANER, CAN DO IT.
I MUST BE ABLE TO DO IT TOO!
I GOT BETTER GRADES THAN HE DID, TOO!
This has nothing to do with becoming a celebrity.
KASHIK
IF I CAN SELL MYSELF TO PEOPLE IN THE BUSINESS...
CHAK
...I MAY BE ABLE TO MAKE MY DEBUT FASTER THAN SHOTARO DID!
AND THE DAY I INSTANTLY CATCH UP WITH HIM, THE ONE HE THINKS IS PLAIN AND BORING...
...SHOTARO'S PRIDE WILL BE SHATTERED!
I'll defiantly do it!

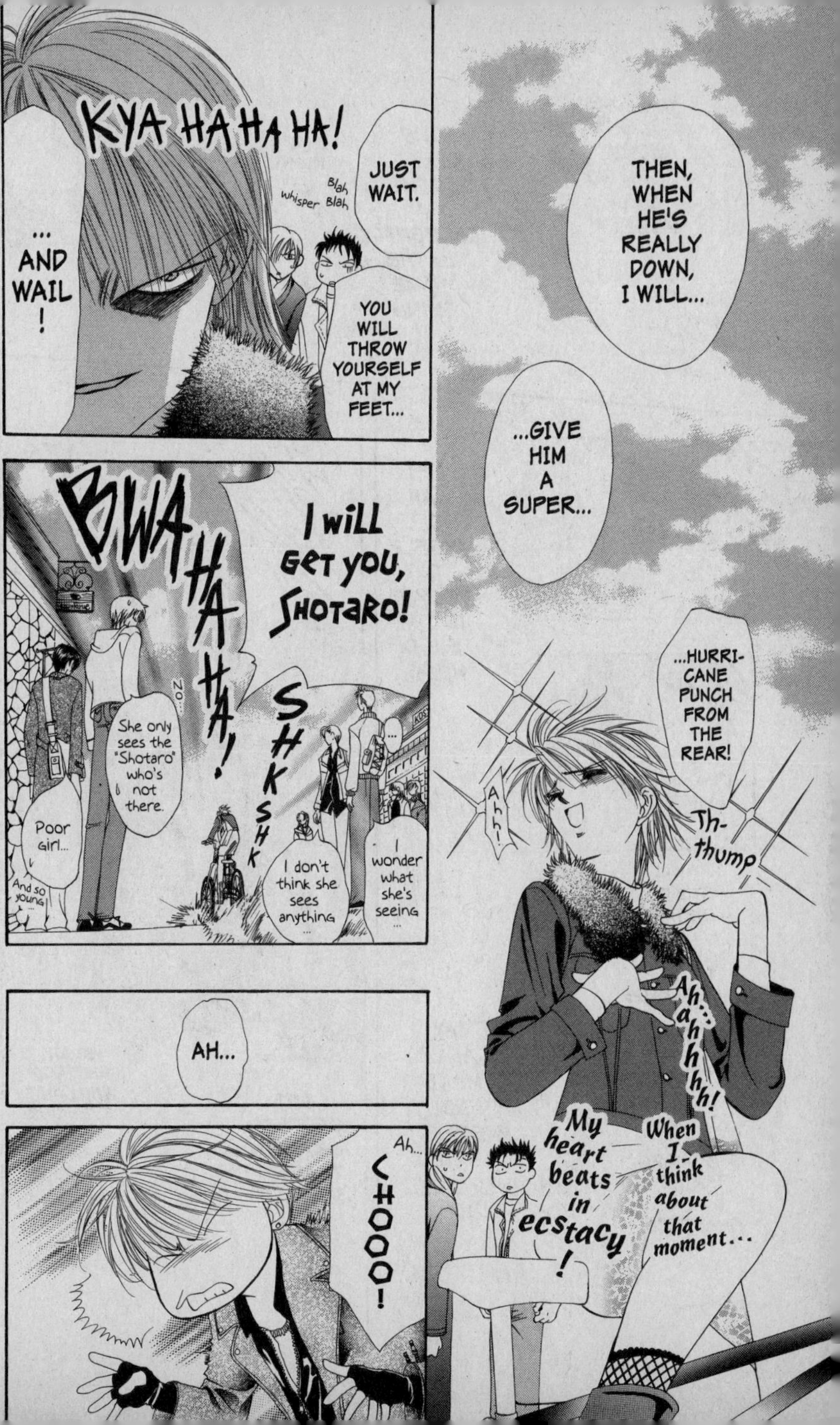
THEN, WHEN HE'S REALLY DOWN, I WILL...
...GIVE HIM A SUPER...
...HURRICANE PUNCH FROM THE REAR!
Ahh!
Th-thump
Ah...ahhhhhh!
When I think about that moment...
My heart beats in ecstacy!
JUST WAIT.
Blah whisper Blah
YOU WILL THROW YOURSELF AT MY FEET...
...AND WAIL!
KYA HA HA HA HA!
BWAHAHAHA!
I will get you, Shotaro!
SHKSHK
...
I wonder what she's seeing...
I don't think she sees anything...
No...
She only sees the "Shotaro" who's not there.
Poor girl...
And so young...
AH...
Ah...
CHOOO!

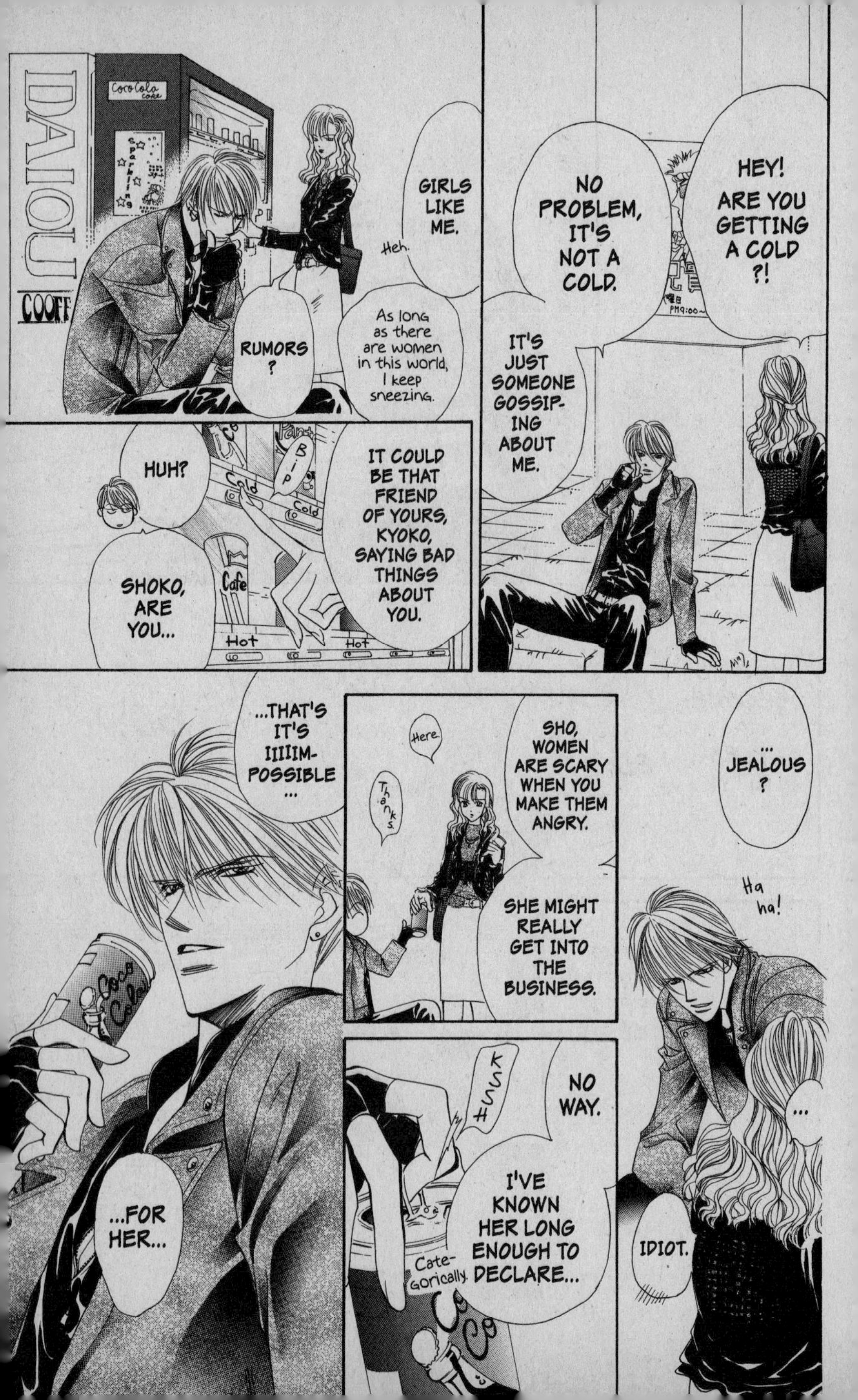
HEY! ARE YOU GETTING A COLD ?!
NO PROBLEM, IT'S NOT A COLD.
IT'S JUST SOMEONE GOSSIP-ING ABOUT ME.
GIRLS LIKE ME.
Heh.
As long as there are women in this world, I keep sneezing.
RUMORS ?
IT COULD BE THAT FRIEND OF YOURS, KYOKO, SAYING BAD THINGS ABOUT YOU.
BIP
HUH?
SHOKO, ARE YOU...
... JEALOUS ?
Ha ha!
...
IDIOT.
SHO, WOMEN ARE SCARY WHEN YOU MAKE THEM ANGRY.
Here.
Thanks.
SHE MIGHT REALLY GET INTO THE BUSINESS.
NO WAY.
KSSH
I'VE KNOWN HER LONG ENOUGH TO DECLARE...
Cate-Gorically.
...THAT'S IT'S IIIIIM-POSSIBLE ...
...FOR HER...

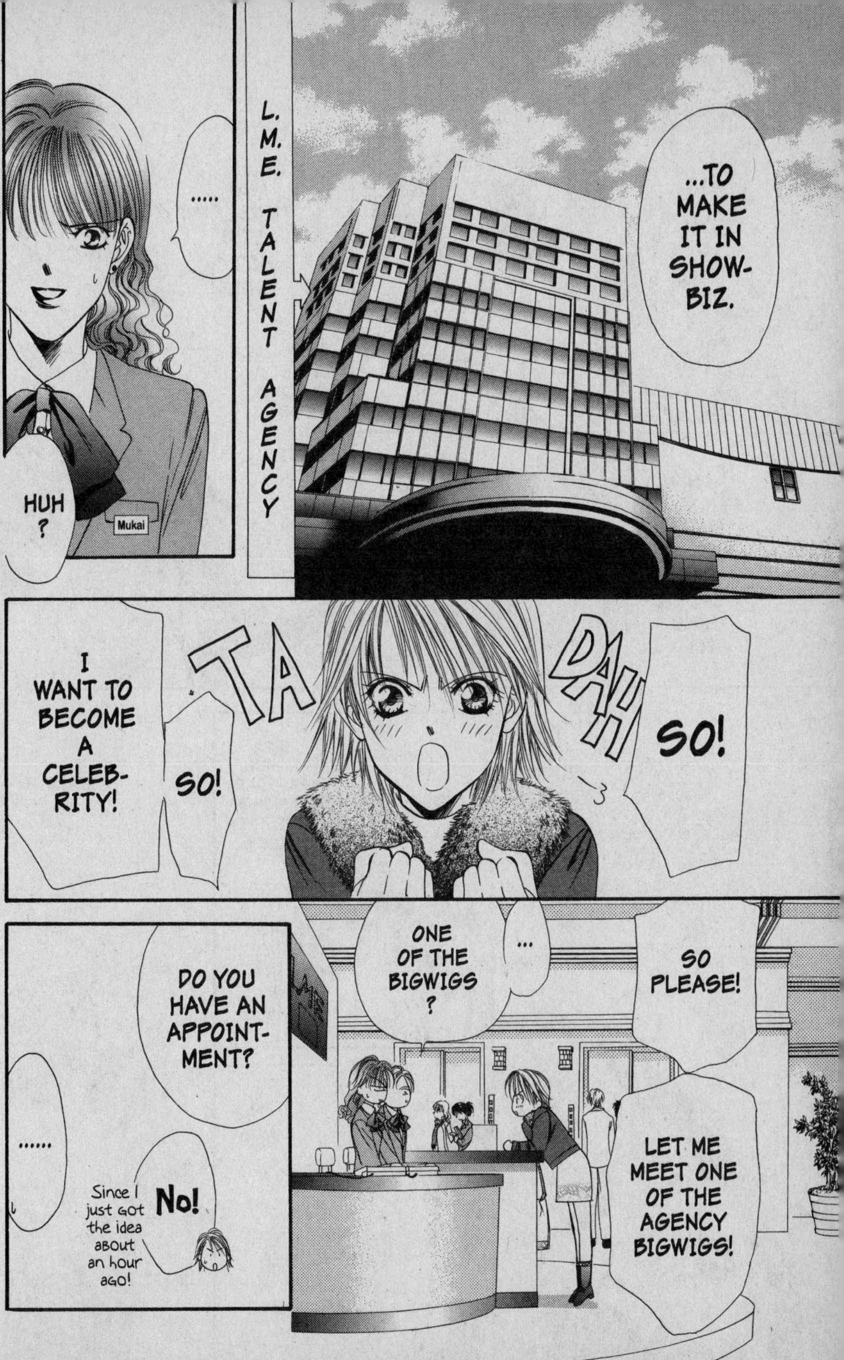
...TO MAKE IT IN SHOW-BIZ.
L.M.E. TALENT AGENCY
.....
HUH?
Mukai
SO!
TA DAH
SO!
I WANT TO BECOME A CELEBRITY!
SO PLEASE!
LET ME MEET ONE OF THE AGENCY BIGWIGS!
...
ONE OF THE BIGWIGS?
DO YOU HAVE AN APPOINTMENT?
......
No!
Since I just got the idea about an hour ago!

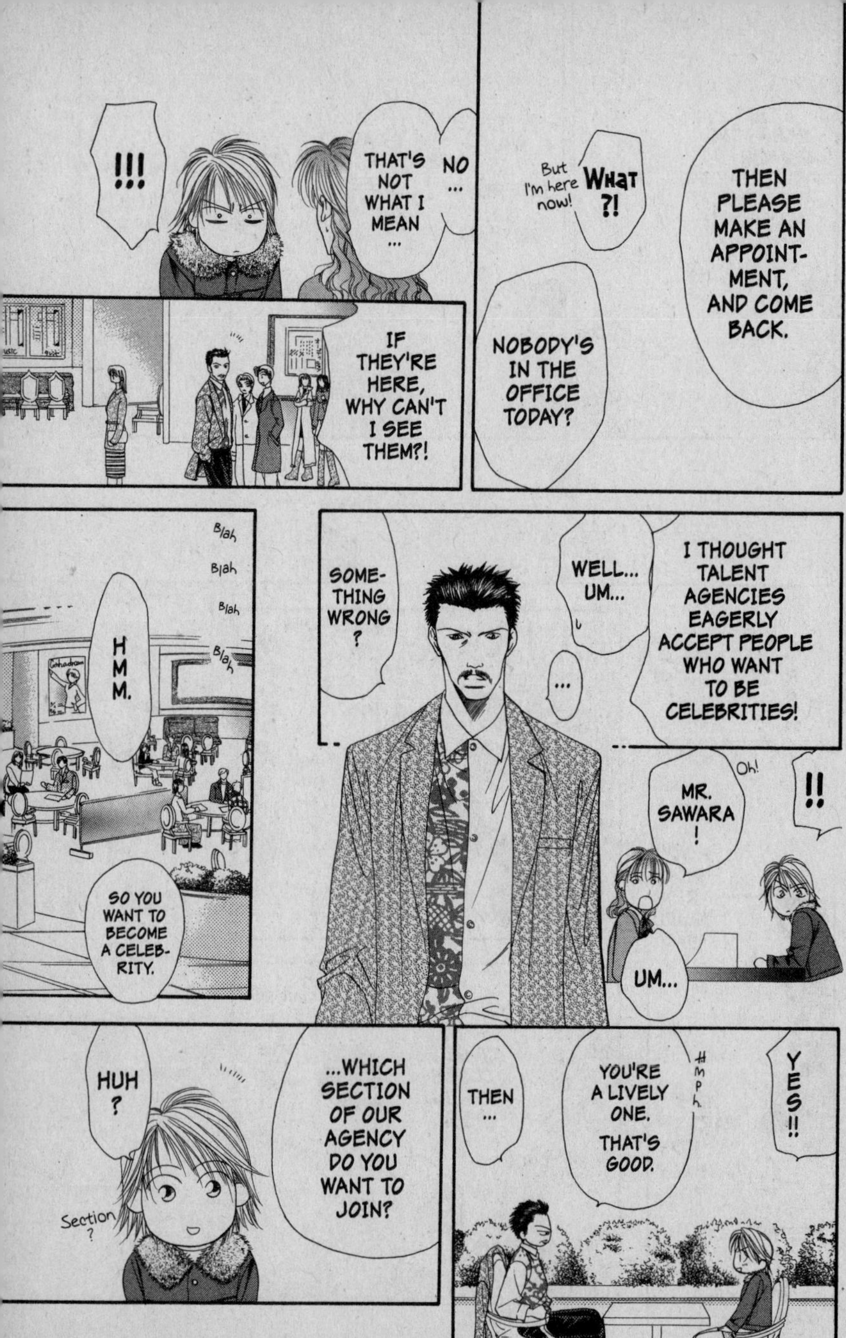
THEN PLEASE MAKE AN APPOINTMENT, AND COME BACK.
WHAT?!
But I'm here now!
NOBODY'S IN THE OFFICE TODAY?
NO ...
THAT'S NOT WHAT I MEAN ...
!!!
IF THEY'RE HERE, WHY CAN'T I SEE THEM?!
I THOUGHT TALENT AGENCIES EAGERLY ACCEPT PEOPLE WHO WANT TO BE CELEBRITIES!
WELL... UM...
...
SOMETHING WRONG?
!!
Oh!
MR. SAWARA!
UM...
Blah
Blah
Blah
Blah
HMM.
SO YOU WANT TO BECOME A CELEBRITY.
YES!!
Hmph.
YOU'RE A LIVELY ONE. THAT'S GOOD.
THEN ...
...WHICH SECTION OF OUR AGENCY DO YOU WANT TO JOIN?
HUH?
Section?

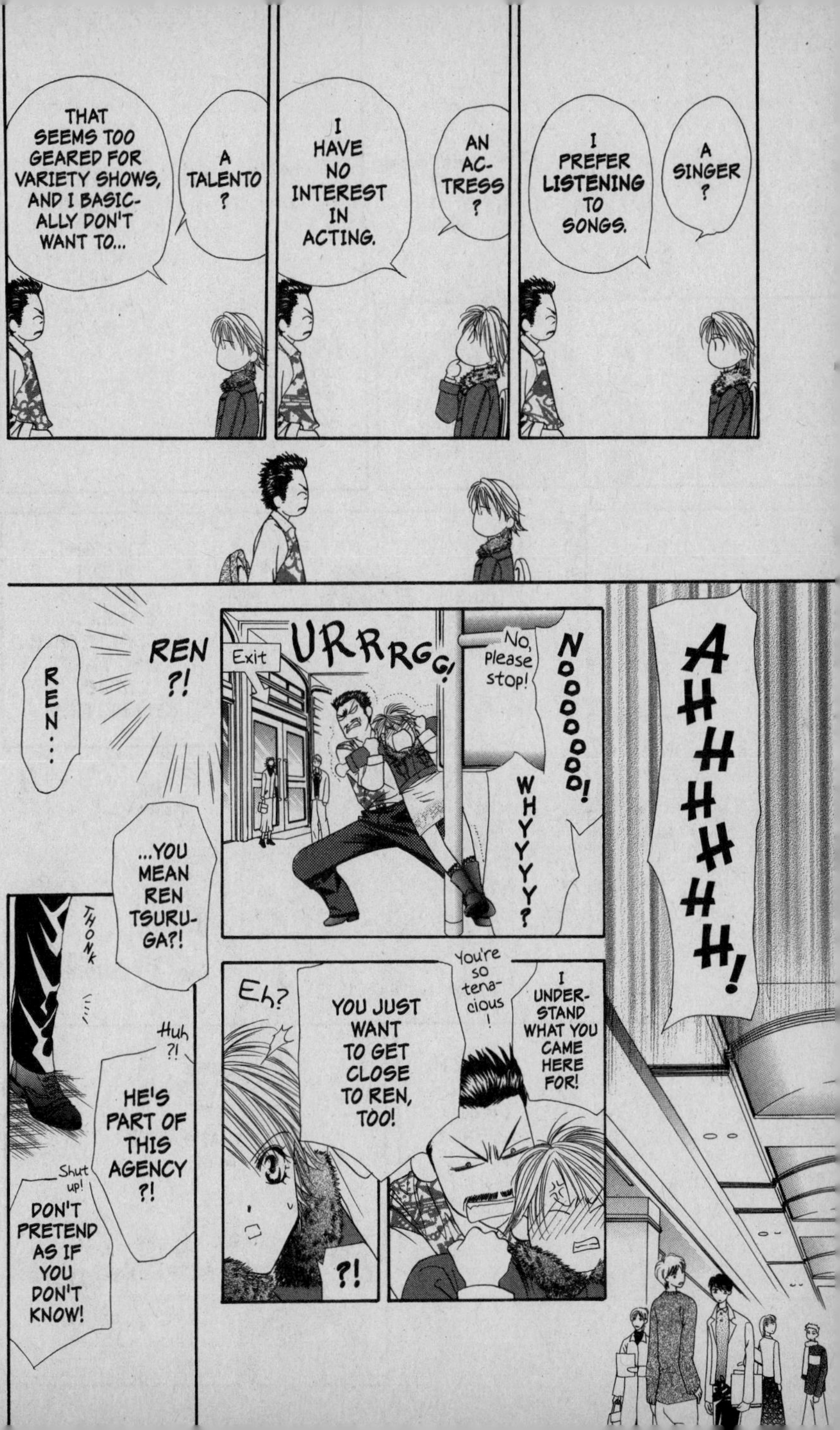

A SINGER?
I PREFER LISTENING TO SONGS.
AN ACTRESS?
I HAVE NO INTEREST IN ACTING.
A TALENTO?
THAT SEEMS TOO GEARED FOR VARIETY SHOWS, AND I BASICALLY DON'T WANT TO...
AHHHHHHH!
NOOOOOOOO!
No, please stop!
WHYYYY?
URRRGG!
Exit
REN?!
REN...
...YOU MEAN REN TSURUGA?!
I UNDERSTAND WHAT YOU CAME HERE FOR!
You're so tenacious!
YOU JUST WANT TO GET CLOSE TO REN, TOO!
Eh?
?!
THONK
...
Huh?!
HE'S PART OF THIS AGENCY?!
Shut up!
DON'T PRETEND AS IF YOU DON'T KNOW!

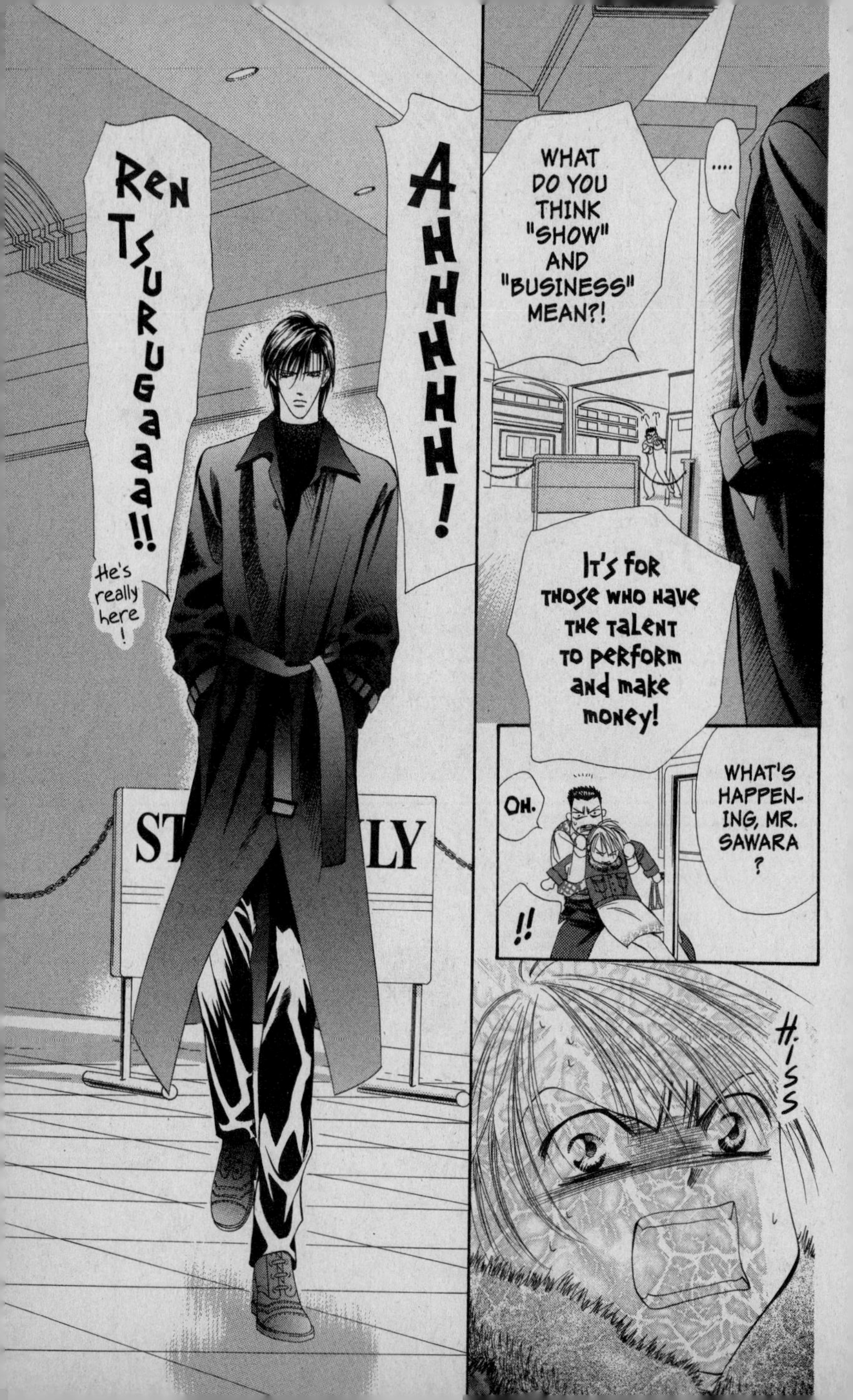
....
WHAT DO YOU THINK "SHOW" AND "BUSINESS" MEAN?!
It's for those who have the talent to perform and make money!
WHAT'S HAPPEN-ING, MR. SAWARA ?
OH.
!!
HISS
AHHHHH!
REN TSURUGaaa!!
He's really here!
ST LY

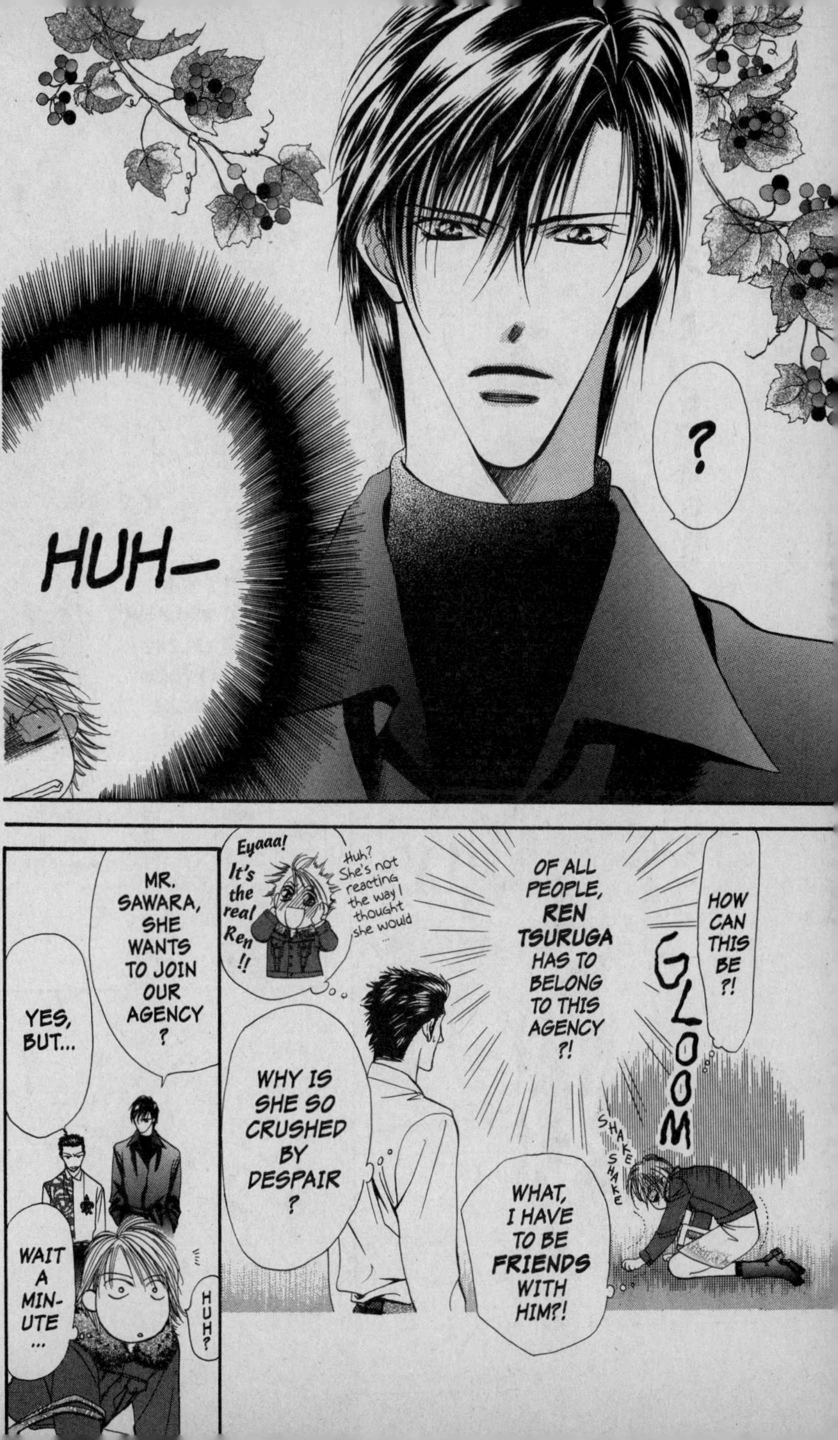
?
HUH—
HOW CAN THIS BE ?!
GLOOM
OF ALL PEOPLE, REN TSURUGA HAS TO BELONG TO THIS AGENCY ?!
SHAKE SHAKE
Huh? She's not reacting the way I thought she would ...
Eyaaa! It's the real Ren !!
WHY IS SHE SO CRUSHED BY DESPAIR ?
WHAT, I HAVE TO BE FRIENDS WITH HIM?!
MR. SAWARA, SHE WANTS TO JOIN OUR AGENCY ?
YES, BUT...
HUH?
WAIT A MIN-UTE ...

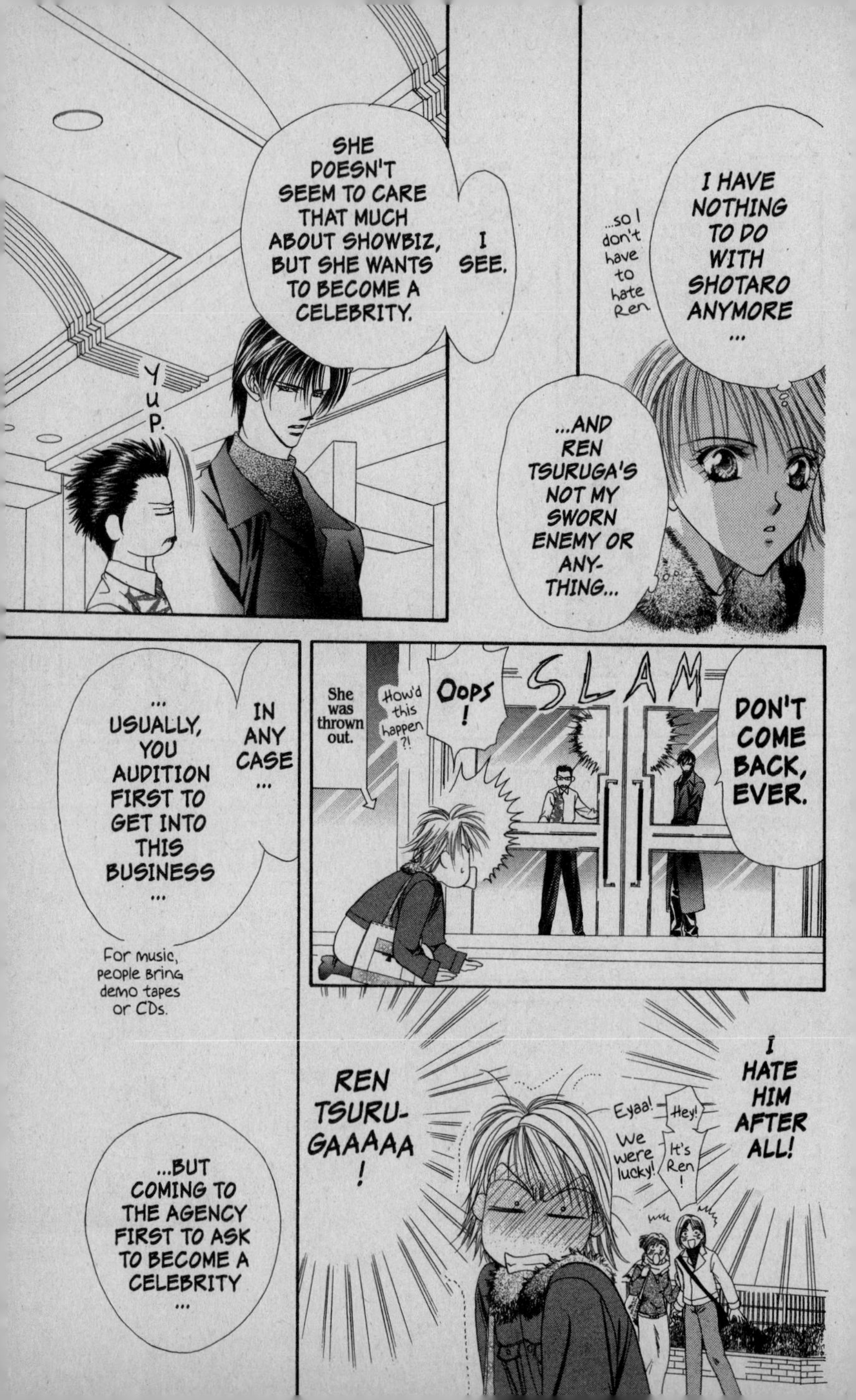
I HAVE NOTHING TO DO WITH SHOTARO ANYMORE...
...so I don't have to hate Ren.
...AND REN TSURUGA'S NOT MY SWORN ENEMY OR ANY-THING...
SHE DOESN'T SEEM TO CARE THAT MUCH ABOUT SHOWBIZ, BUT SHE WANTS TO BECOME A CELEBRITY.
I SEE.
YUP.
DON'T COME BACK, EVER.
SLAM
OOPS!
How'd this happen?!
She was thrown out.
I HATE HIM AFTER ALL!
Hey!
It's Ren!
Eyaa!
We were lucky!
REN TSURU-GAAAAA!
IN ANY CASE...
...USUALLY, YOU AUDITION FIRST TO GET INTO THIS BUSINESS...
For music, people bring demo tapes or CDs.
...BUT COMING TO THE AGENCY FIRST TO ASK TO BECOME A CELEBRITY...

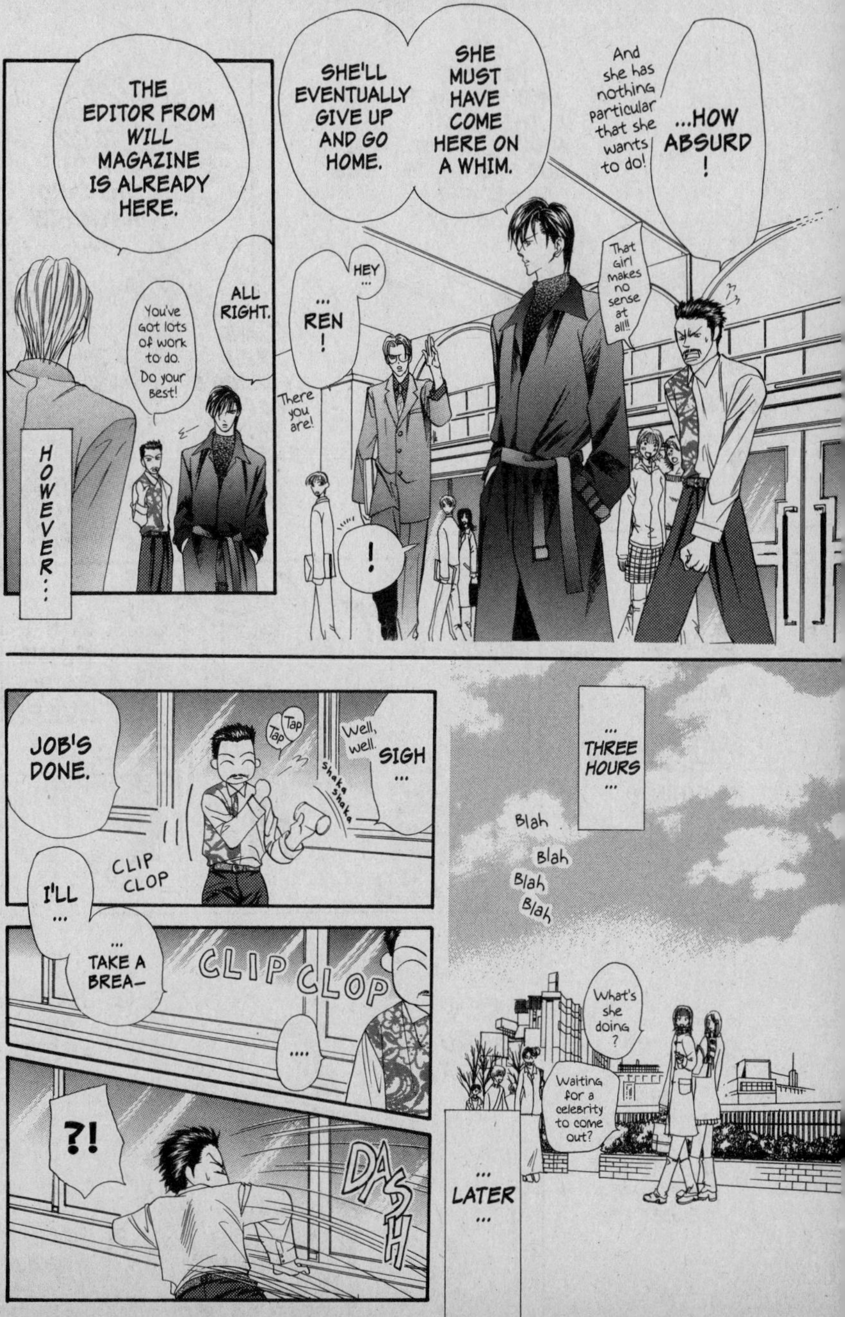
...HOW ABSURD!
And she has nothing particular that she wants to do!
SHE MUST HAVE COME HERE ON A WHIM.
SHE'LL EVENTUALLY GIVE UP AND GO HOME.
That Girl makes no sense at all!!
HEY ...
... REN !
There you are!
!
THE EDITOR FROM WILL MAGAZINE IS ALREADY HERE.
ALL RIGHT.
You've Got lots of work to do. Do your best!
HOWEVER...
... THREE HOURS ...
Blah
Blah
Blah
Blah
What's she doing?
Waiting for a celebrity to come out?
... LATER ...
Well, well.
SIGH ...
Tap
Tap
Shaka shaka
JOB'S DONE.
CLIP CLOP
I'LL ...
... TAKE A BREA—
CLIP CLOP
....
DASH
?!

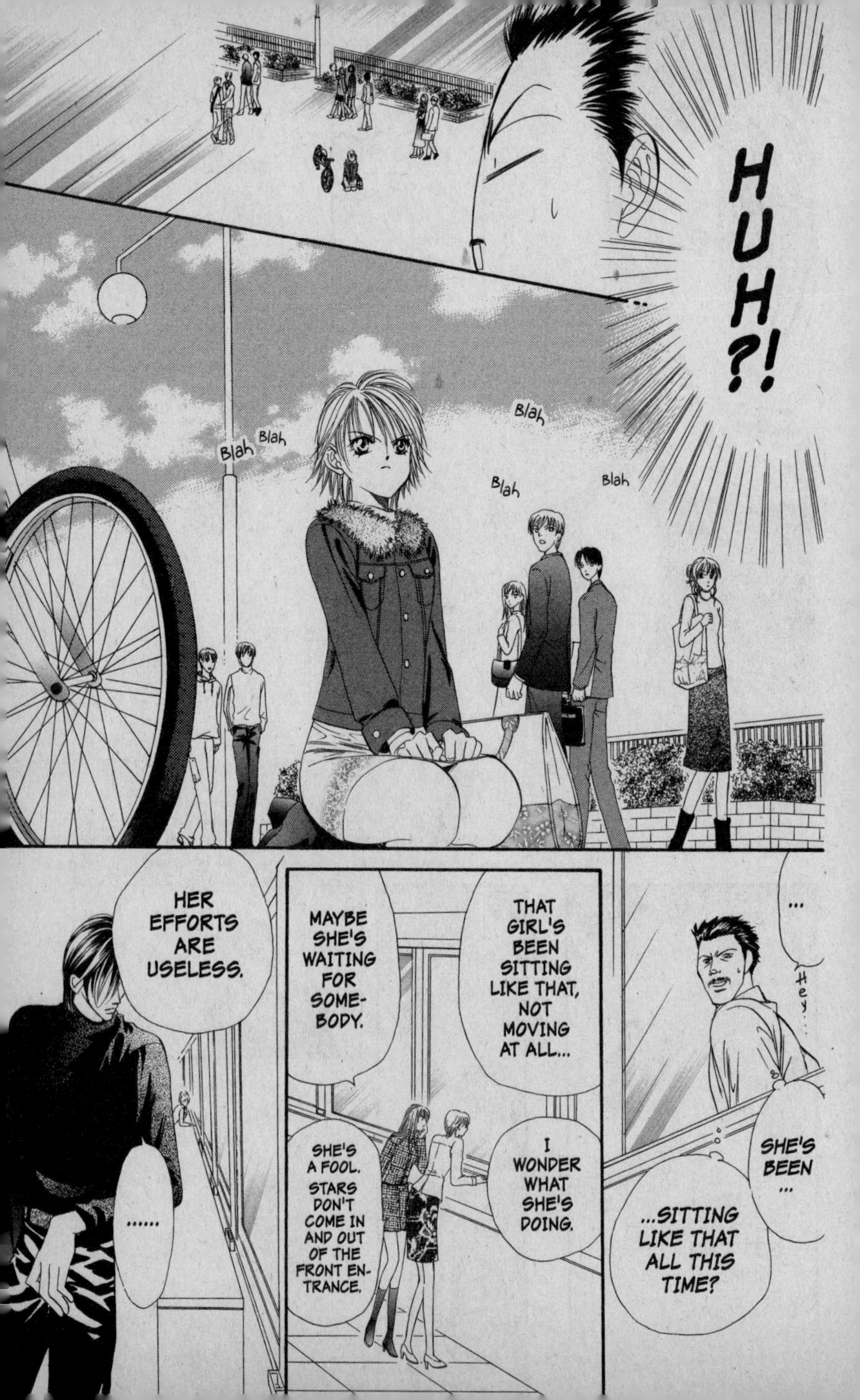
HUH?!
Blah
Blah
Blah
Blah
Blah
...
Hey...
SHE'S BEEN...
...SITTING LIKE THAT ALL THIS TIME?
THAT GIRL'S BEEN SITTING LIKE THAT, NOT MOVING AT ALL...
MAYBE SHE'S WAITING FOR SOMEBODY.
I WONDER WHAT SHE'S DOING.
SHE'S A FOOL. STARS DON'T COME IN AND OUT OF THE FRONT ENTRANCE.
HER EFFORTS ARE USELESS.
......

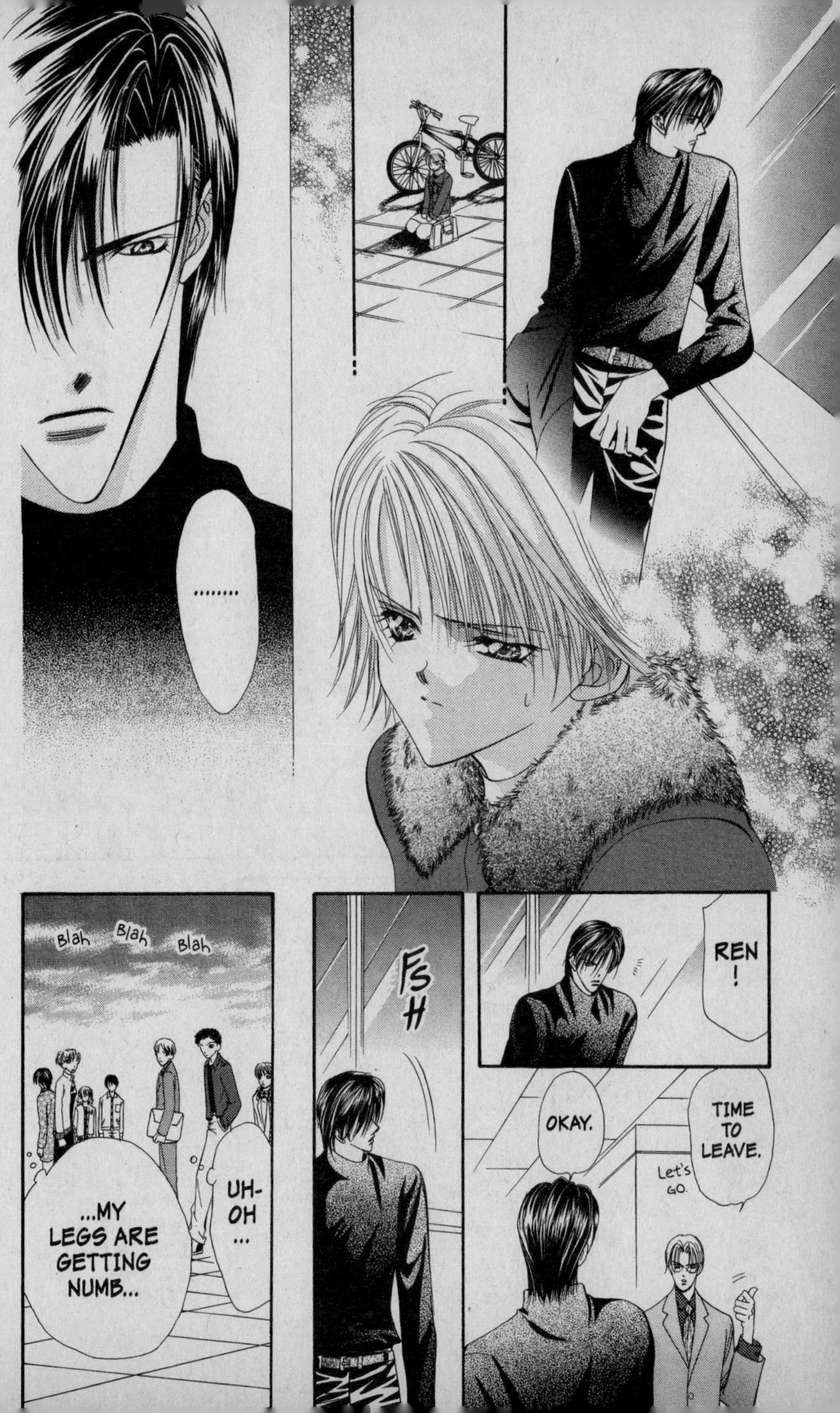
....
REN!
TIME TO LEAVE.
Let's GO.
OKAY.
FSH
Blah Blah Blah
UH-OH...
...MY LEGS ARE GETTING NUMB...

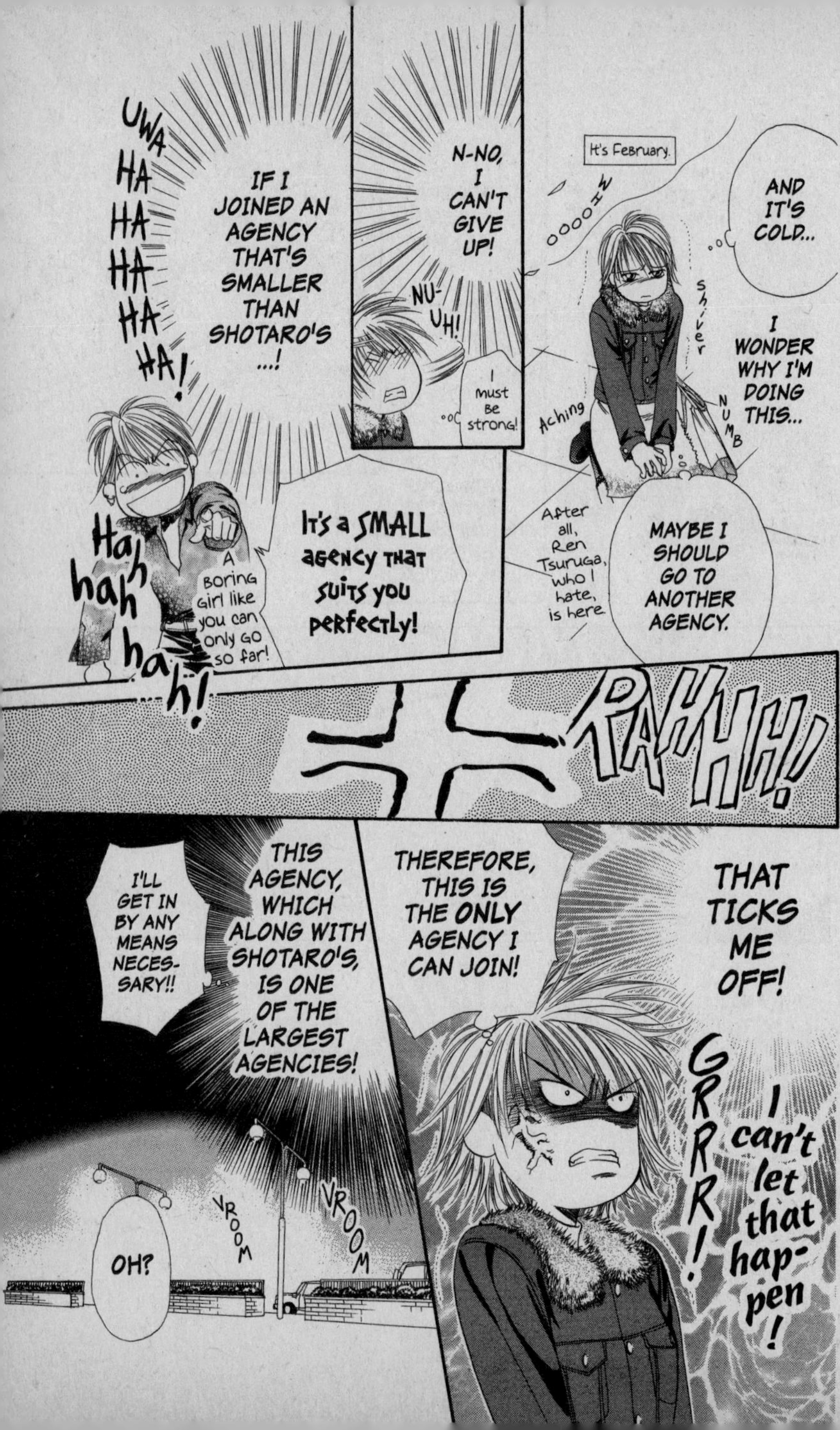
It's February.
WHOOOOO
AND IT'S COLD...
Shiver
I WONDER WHY I'M DOING THIS...
NUMB
Aching
MAYBE I SHOULD GO TO ANOTHER AGENCY.
After all, Ren Tsuruga, who I hate, is here.
N-NO, I CAN'T GIVE UP!
NU-UH!
I must be strong!
IF I JOINED AN AGENCY THAT'S SMALLER THAN SHOTARO'S ...!
UWAHAHAHAHAHA!
It's a SMALL agency that suits you perfectly!
A boring girl like you can only go so far!
Hah hah hah hah!
RAHHH!
THAT TICKS ME OFF!
GRRR!
I can't let that hap-pen!
THEREFORE, THIS IS THE ONLY AGENCY I CAN JOIN!
THIS AGENCY, WHICH ALONG WITH SHOTARO'S, IS ONE OF THE LARGEST AGENCIES!
I'LL GET IN BY ANY MEANS NECES-SARY!!
VROOM
VROOM
OH?

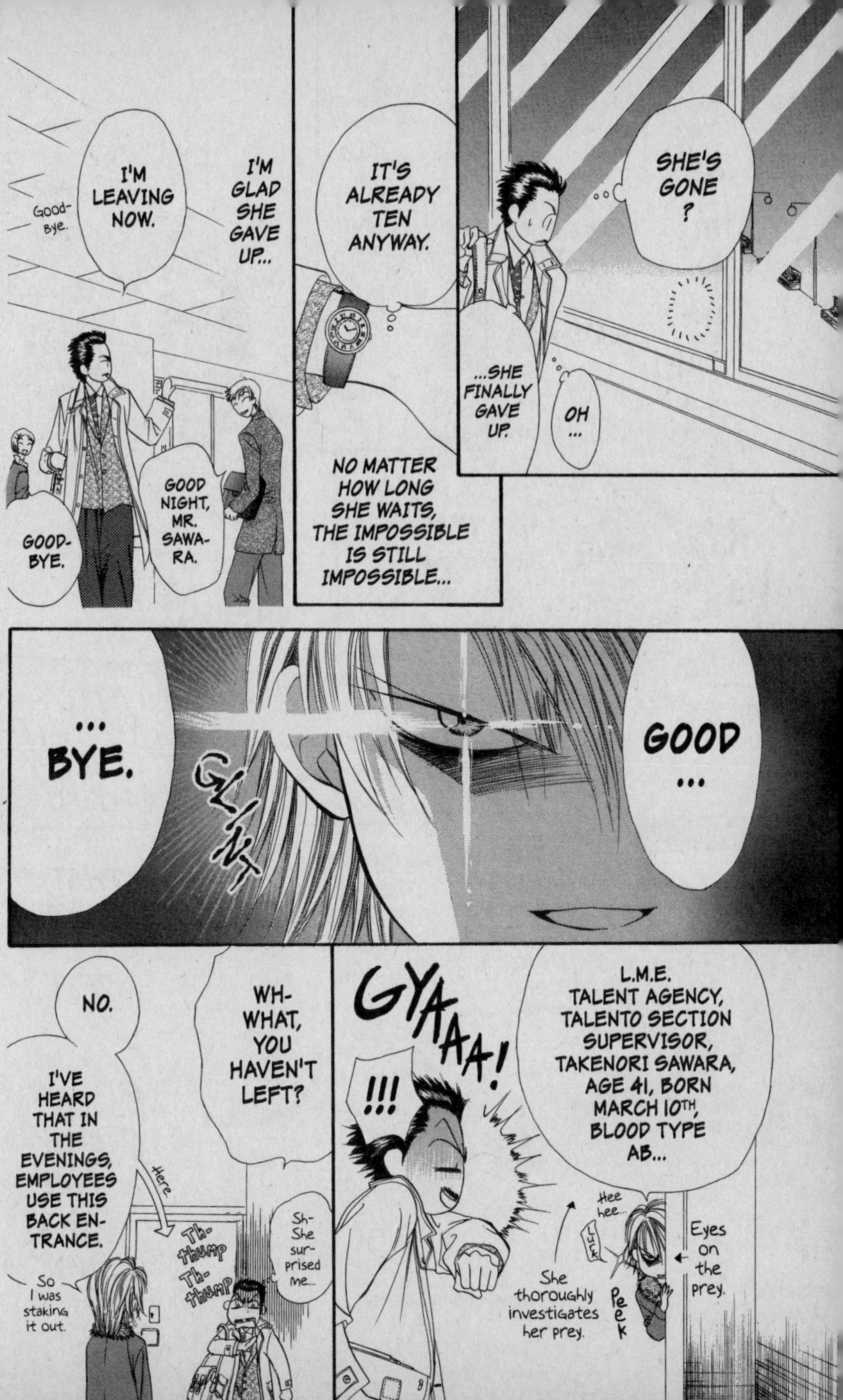
SHE'S GONE ?
OH ...
...SHE FINALLY GAVE UP.
IT'S ALREADY TEN ANYWAY.
NO MATTER HOW LONG SHE WAITS, THE IMPOSSIBLE IS STILL IMPOSSIBLE...
I'M GLAD SHE GAVE UP...
I'M LEAVING NOW.
Good-bye.
GOOD NIGHT, MR. SAWARA.
GOOD-BYE.
GOOD ...
GLINT
... BYE.
L.M.E. TALENT AGENCY, TALENTO SECTION SUPERVISOR, TAKENORI SAWARA, AGE 41, BORN MARCH 10TH, BLOOD TYPE AB...
GYAAAA!
!!!
Hee hee...
Lurk
Eyes on the prey.
Peek
She thoroughly investigates her prey.
WH-WHAT, YOU HAVEN'T LEFT?
NO.
Sh-She surprised me...
Th-thump
Th-thump
I'VE HEARD THAT IN THE EVENINGS, EMPLOYEES USE THIS BACK ENTRANCE.
Here.
So I was staking it out.

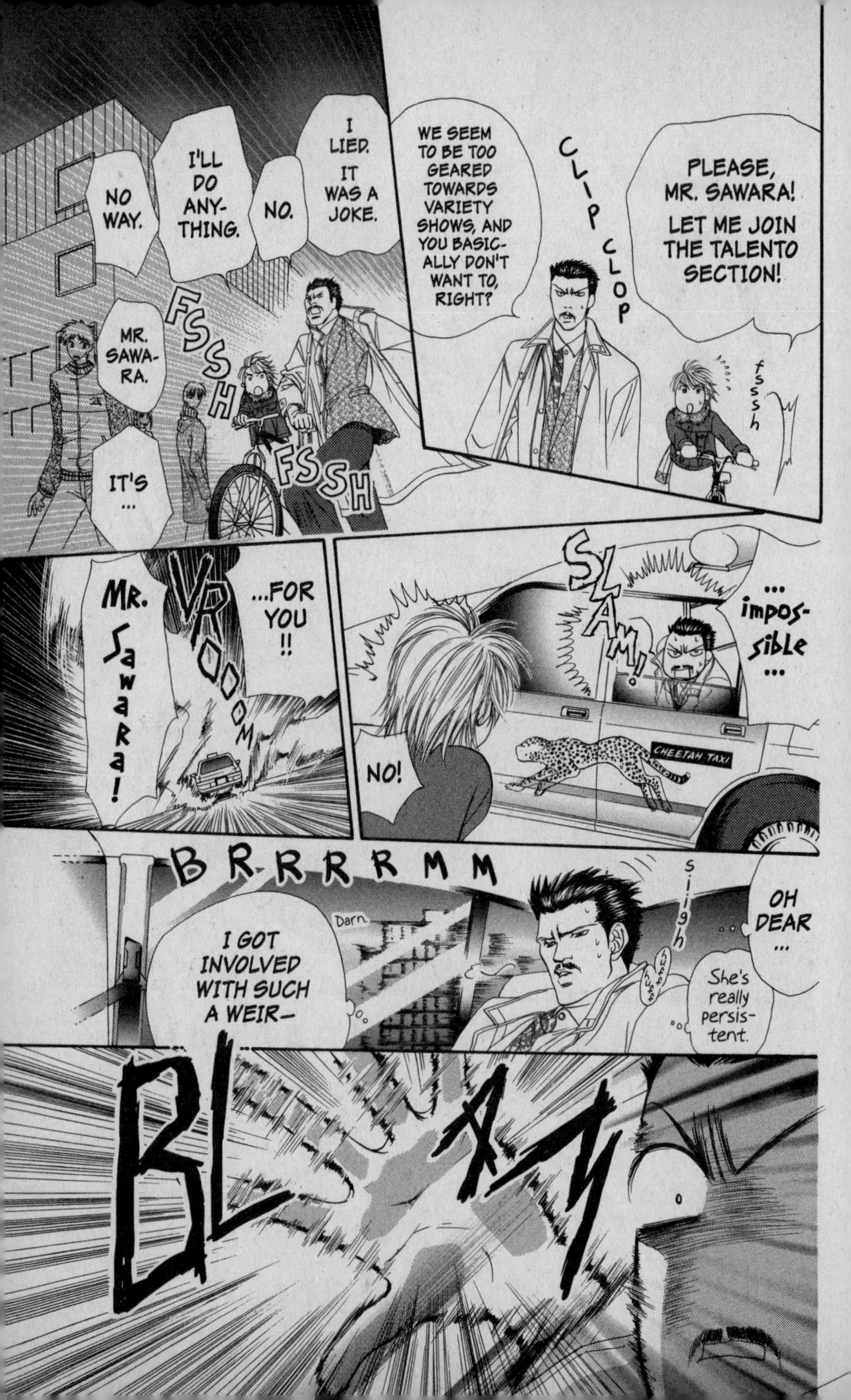
PLEASE, MR. SAWARA!
LET ME JOIN THE TALENTO SECTION!
fsssh
CLIP CLOP
WE SEEM TO BE TOO GEARED TOWARDS VARIETY SHOWS, AND YOU BASIC-ALLY DON'T WANT TO, RIGHT?
I LIED.
IT WAS A JOKE.
NO.
I'LL DO ANY-THING.
NO WAY.
FSSH
FSSH
MR. SAWA-RA.
IT'S ...
... impos-sible ...
SLAM!
NO!
...FOR YOU !!
VROOOOM
Mr. Sawara!
CHEETAH TAXI
OH DEAR ...
She's really persis-tent.
sigh
BRRRRRMM
Darn.
I GOT INVOLVED WITH SUCH A WEIR—
BLAM

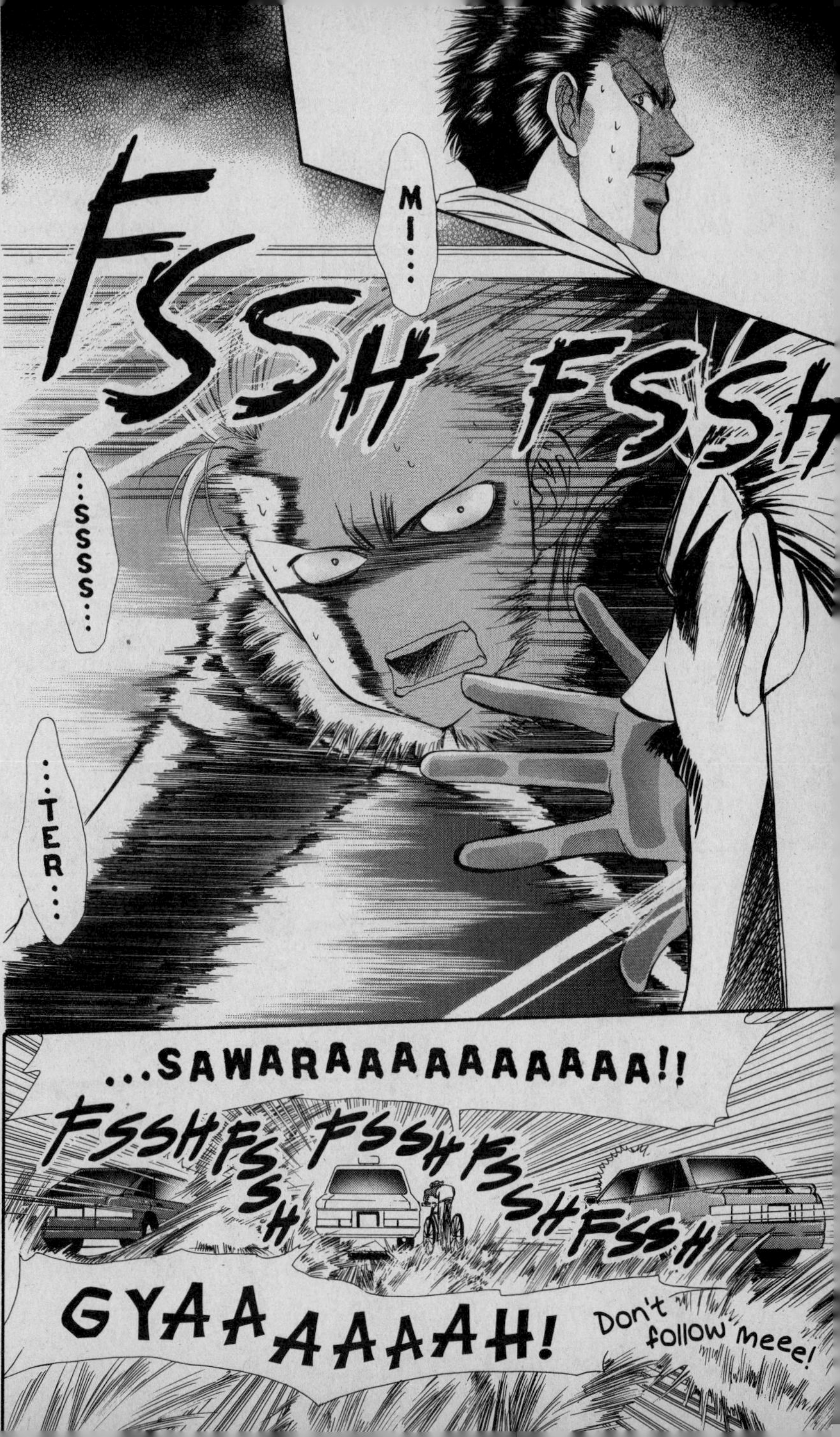
MI...
FSSH FSSH
...SSSS...
...TER...
...SAWARAAAAAAAAAAAA!!
FSSHFSSH FSSHFSSHFSSH
Don't follow meee!
GYAAAAAAAH!

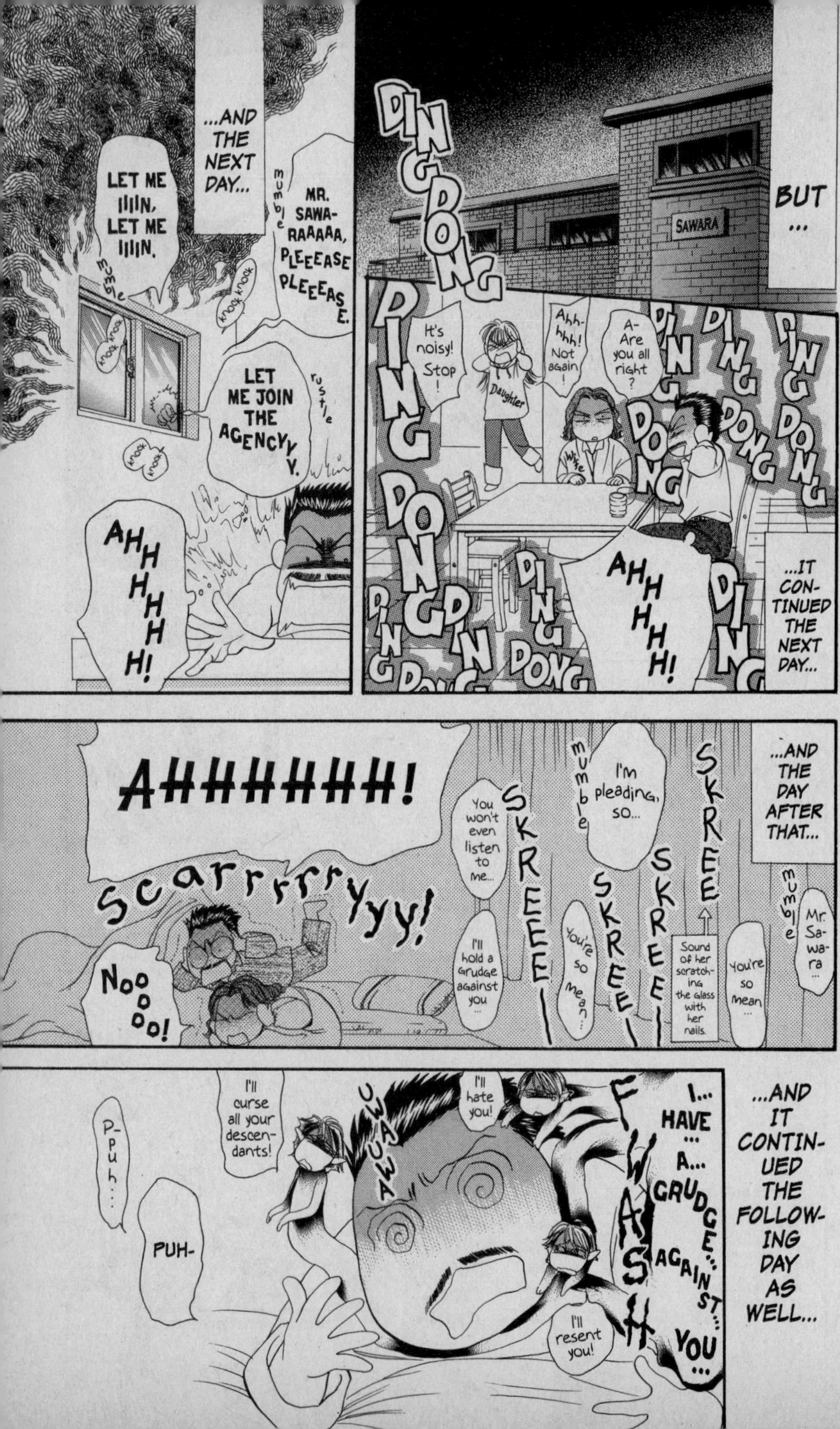
BUT ...
SAWARA
DING DONG
...IT CONTINUED THE NEXT DAY...
DING DONG DING DONG DING DONG
A- Are you all right?
Ahh-hhh! Not again!
Wife
It's noisy! Stop!
Daughter
DING DONG DING DONG DING DONG
AHHHHH!
...AND THE NEXT DAY...
MR. SAWA-RAAAAAA, PLEEEASE PLEEEASE.
mumble
LET ME IIIIN, LET ME IIIIN.
mumble
knock knock
knock knock
LET ME JOIN THE AGENCYYYY.
rustle
knock knock
AHHHHHH!
...AND THE DAY AFTER THAT...
mumble
Mr. Sawara...
You're so mean...
SKREE
Sound of her scratching the glass with her nails.
SKREE
mumble
I'm pleading, so...
SKREE
You're so mean...
SKREE
You won't even listen to me...
I'll hold a grudge against you...
AHHHHHHH!
Scarrrrrryyy!
Noooooo!
...AND IT CONTINUED THE FOLLOWING DAY AS WELL...
I... HAVE... A... GRUDGE... AGAINST... YOU...
FWASH
I'll hate you!
I'll resent you!
UWAWA
I'll curse all your descendants!
P-puh...
PUH-

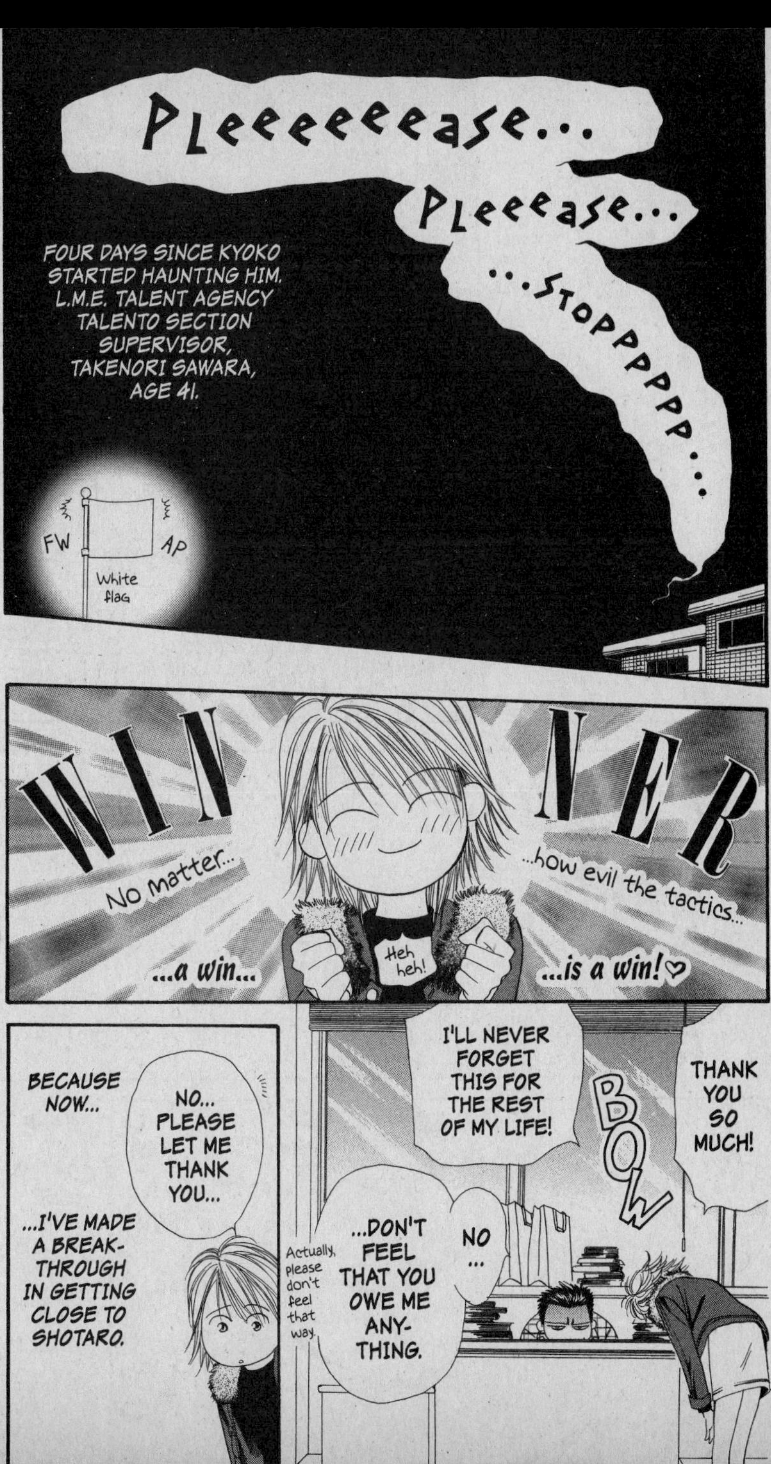
Pleeeeeease...
Pleeease...
...Stopppppp...
FOUR DAYS SINCE KYOKO STARTED HAUNTING HIM. L.M.E. TALENT AGENCY TALENTO SECTION SUPERVISOR, TAKENORI SAWARA, AGE 41.
FW
White flag
AP
WINNER
No matter...
...how evil the tactics...
...a win...
...is a win!♡
Heh heh!
THANK YOU SO MUCH!
I'LL NEVER FORGET THIS FOR THE REST OF MY LIFE!
BOW
NO...
...DON'T FEEL THAT YOU OWE ME ANYTHING.
Actually, please don't feel that way.
NO... PLEASE LET ME THANK YOU...
BECAUSE NOW...
...I'VE MADE A BREAK-THROUGH IN GETTING CLOSE TO SHOTARO.

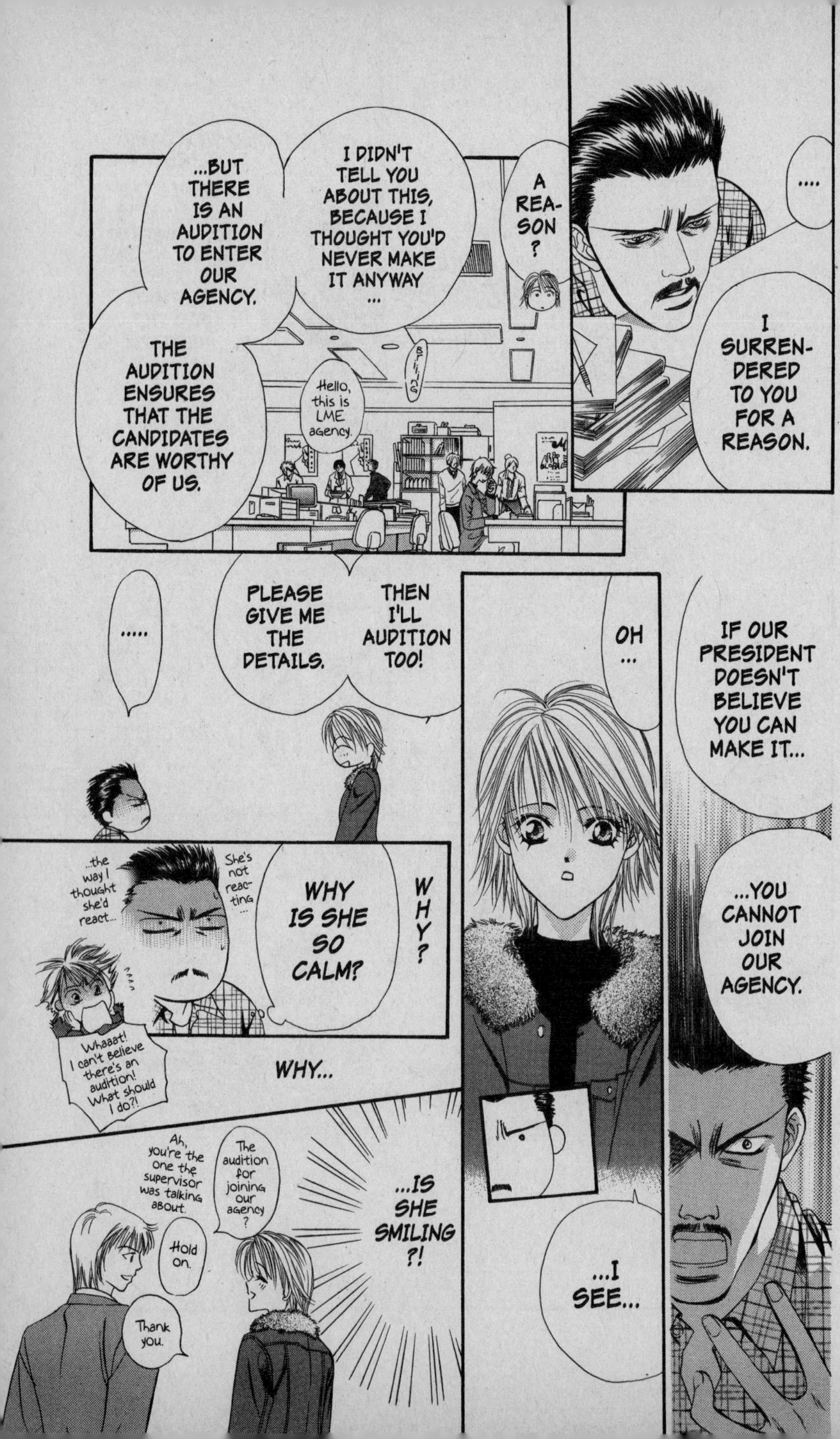
....
I SURRENDERED TO YOU FOR A REASON.
A REASON?
I DIDN'T TELL YOU ABOUT THIS, BECAUSE I THOUGHT YOU'D NEVER MAKE IT ANYWAY...
...BUT THERE IS AN AUDITION TO ENTER OUR AGENCY.
THE AUDITION ENSURES THAT THE CANDIDATES ARE WORTHY OF US.
Hello, this is LME agency.
IF OUR PRESIDENT DOESN'T BELIEVE YOU CAN MAKE IT...
...YOU CANNOT JOIN OUR AGENCY.
OH...
...I SEE...
THEN I'LL AUDITION TOO!
PLEASE GIVE ME THE DETAILS.
.....
WHY?
WHY IS SHE SO CALM?
She's not reacting...
...the way I thought she'd react...
Whaaat! I can't believe there's an audition! What should I do?!
WHY...
...IS SHE SMILING?!
The audition for joining our agency?
Ah, you're the one the supervisor was talking about.
Hold on.
Thank you.

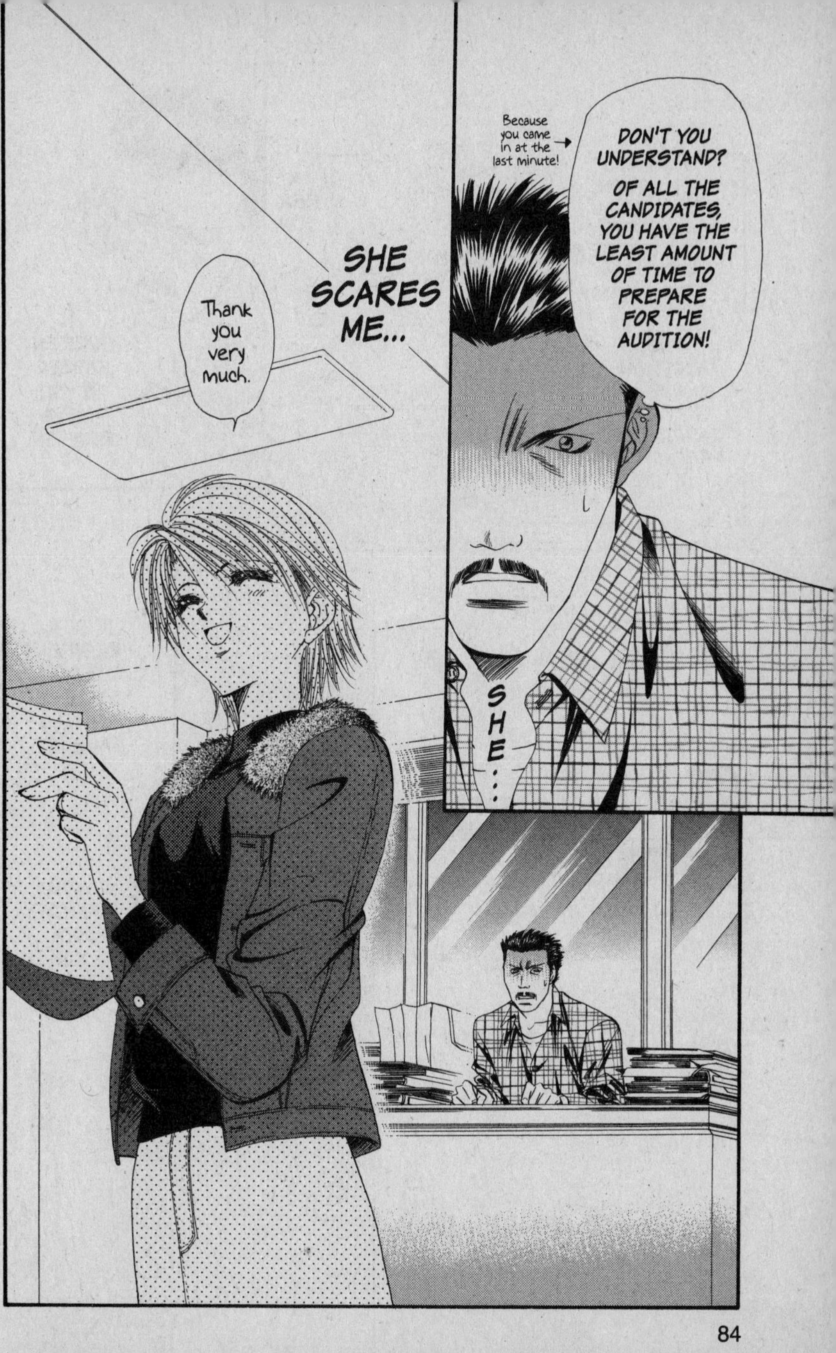
DON'T YOU UNDERSTAND?
OF ALL THE CANDIDATES, YOU HAVE THE LEAST AMOUNT OF TIME TO PREPARE FOR THE AUDITION!
Because you came in at the last minute!
SHE...
SHE SCARES ME...
Thank you very much.

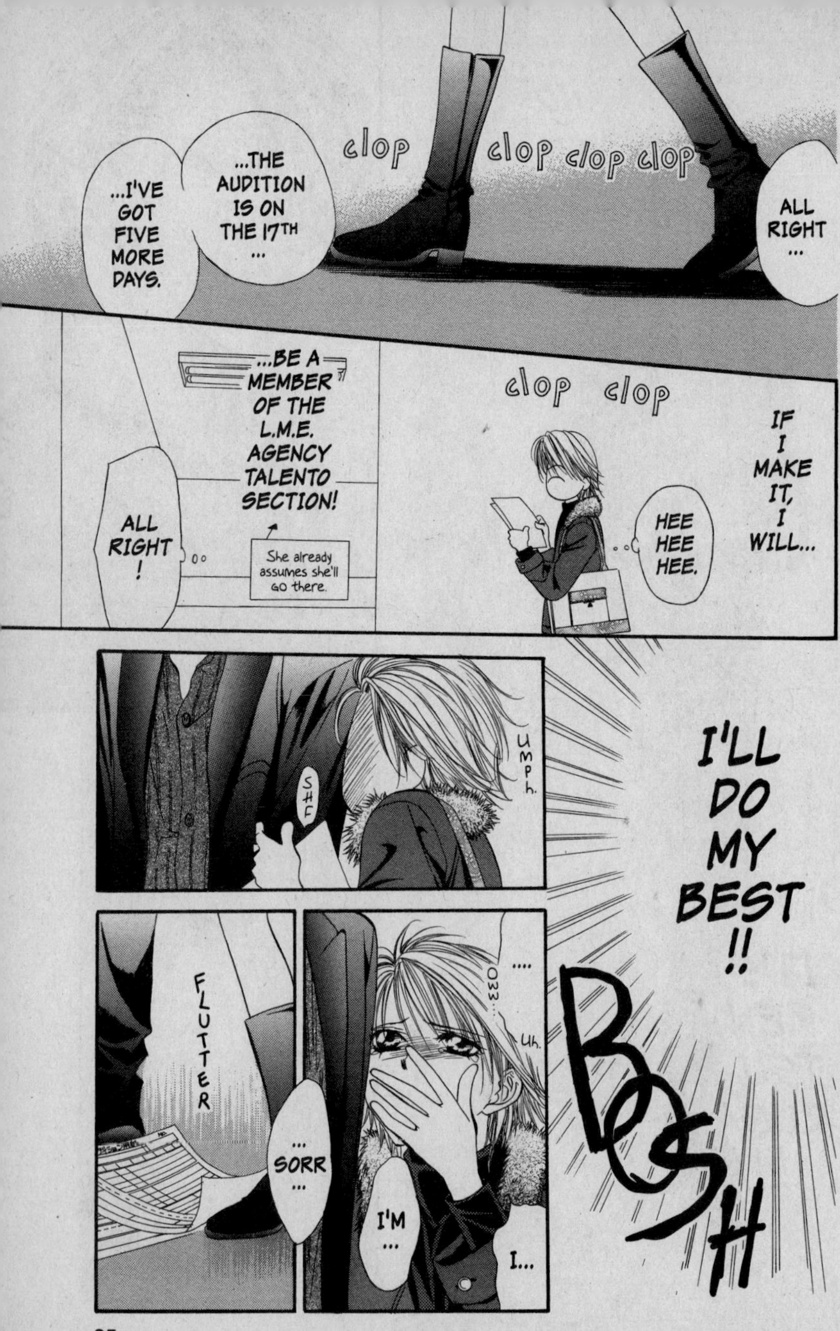

ALL RIGHT ...
clop clop clop
clop
...THE AUDITION IS ON THE 17TH ...
...I'VE GOT FIVE MORE DAYS.
IF I MAKE IT, I WILL...
clop clop
HEE HEE HEE.
...BE A MEMBER OF THE L.M.E. AGENCY TALENTO SECTION!
ALL RIGHT!
She already assumes she'll GO there.
I'LL DO MY BEST!!
Umph.
SHF
BOSH
....
Oww...
Uh.
I...
I'M ...
... SORR ...
FLUTTER

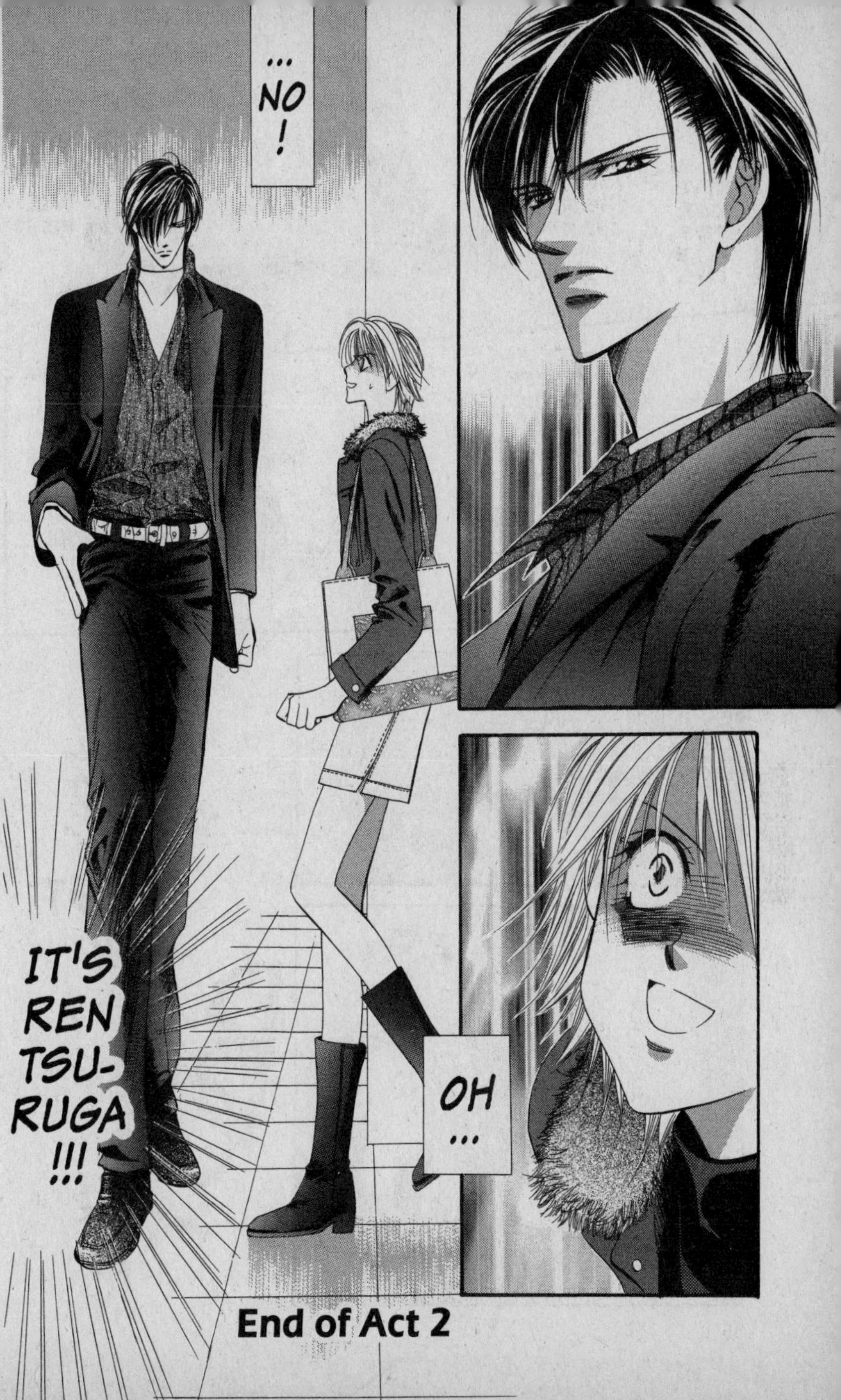
OH ...
... NO !
IT'S REN TSU-RUGA !!!

End of Act 2

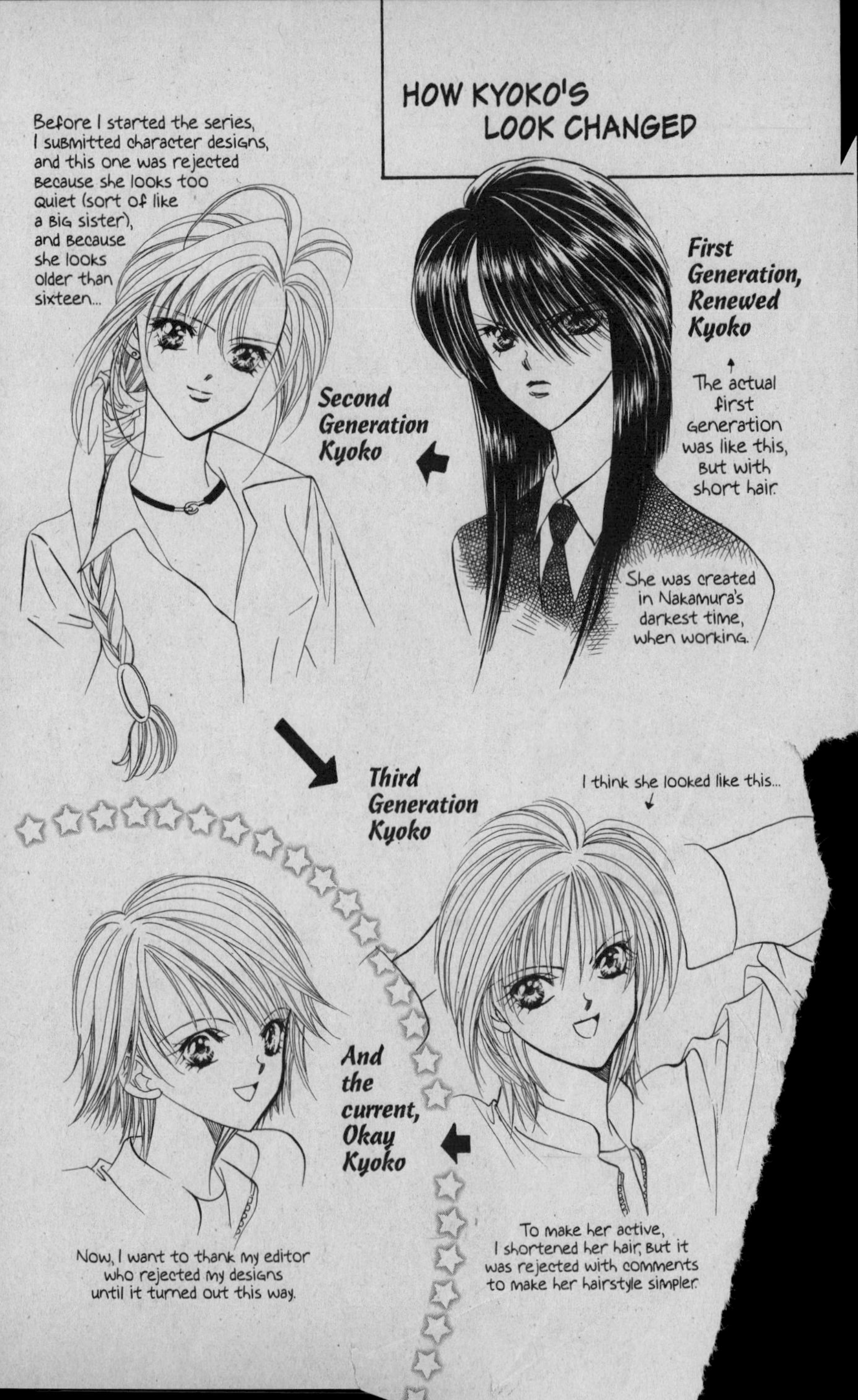
HOW KYOKO'S LOOK CHANGED
First Generation, Renewed Kyoko
The actual first generation was like this, but with short hair.
She was created in Nakamura's darkest time, when working.
Second Generation Kyoko
Before I started the series, I submitted character designs, and this one was rejected because she looks too quiet (sort of like a big sister), and because she looks older than sixteen...
Third Generation Kyoko
I think she looked like this...
To make her active, I shortened her hair, but it was rejected with comments to make her hairstyle simpler.
And the current, Okay Kyoko
Now, I want to thank my editor who rejected my designs until it turned out this way.

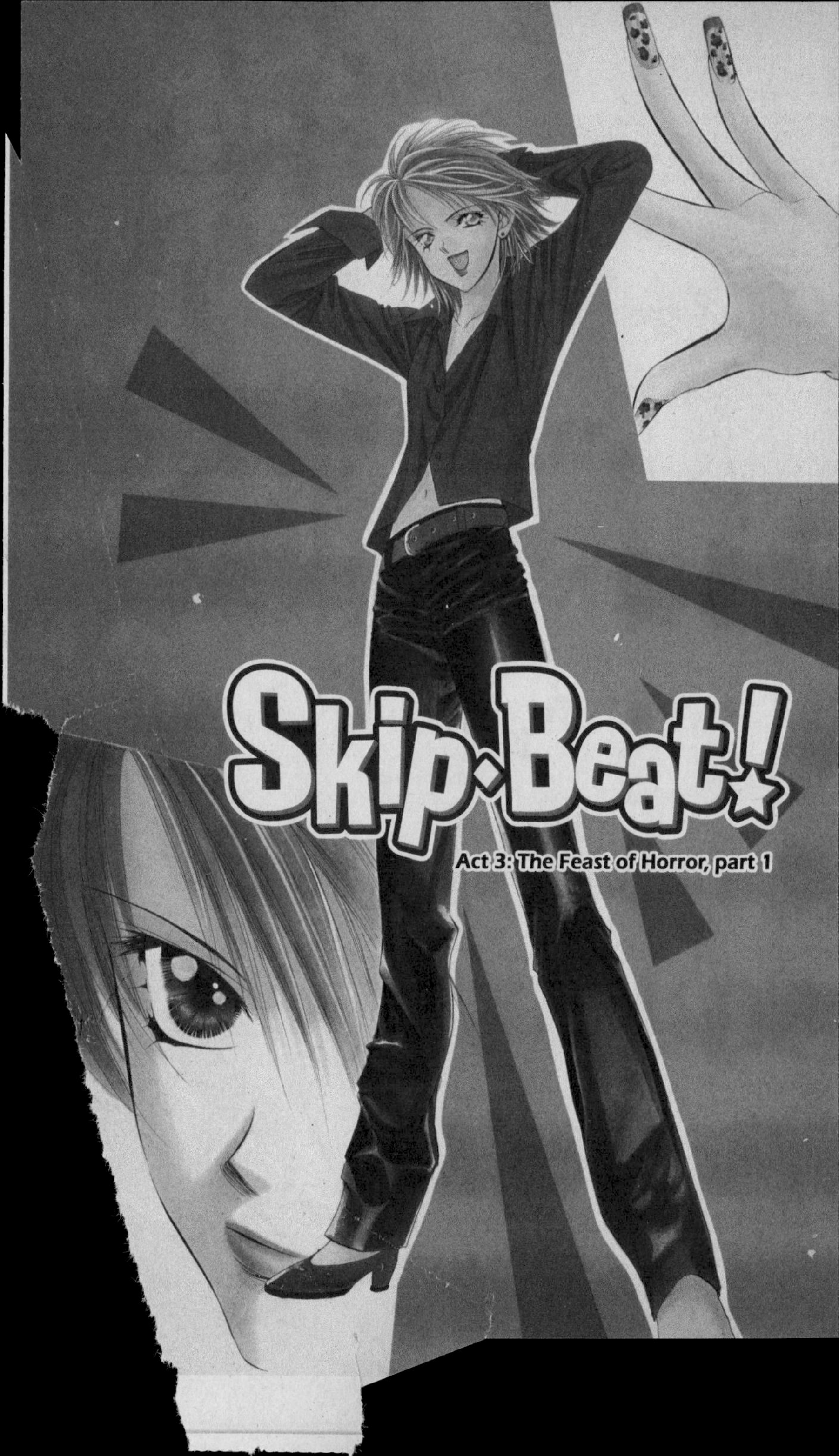
Skip·Beat!
Act 3: The Feast of Horror, part 1

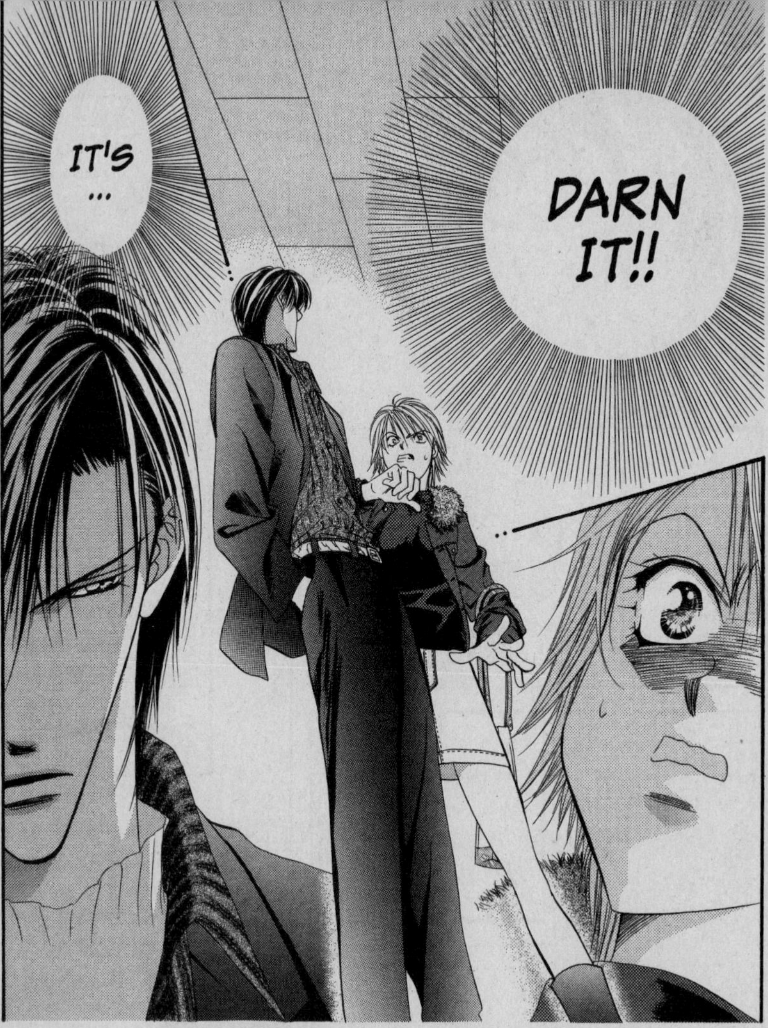
DARN IT!!
IT'S ...

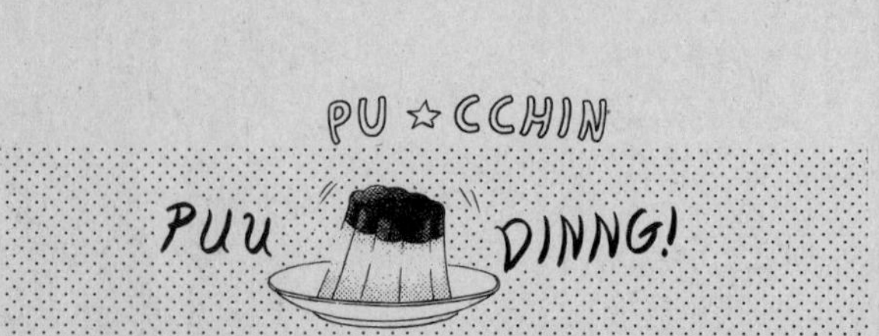
PU☆CCHIN
PUU
DINNG!

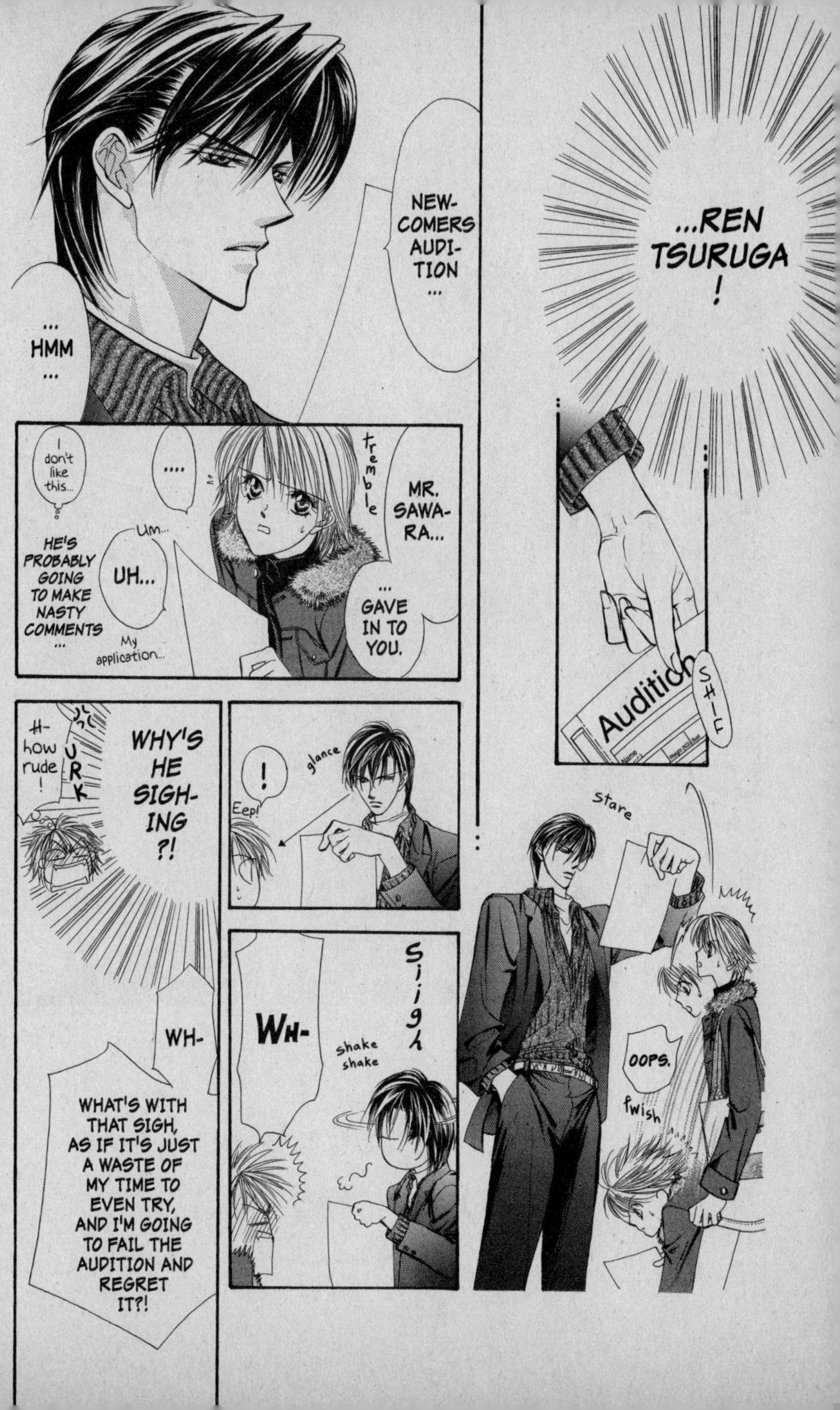
...REN TSURUGA!
Audition
SHIF
stare
OOPS.
fwish
NEW-COMERS AUDITION...
...HMM...
MR. SAWARA...
tremble
...GAVE IN TO YOU.
....
Um...
UH...
I don't like this...
HE'S PROBABLY GOING TO MAKE NASTY COMMENTS...
My application...
glance
!
Eep!
Sigh
shake shake
WH-
URK
H-how rude!
WHY'S HE SIGHING?!
WH-
WHAT'S WITH THAT SIGH, AS IF IT'S JUST A WASTE OF MY TIME TO EVEN TRY, AND I'M GOING TO FAIL THE AUDITION AND REGRET IT?!

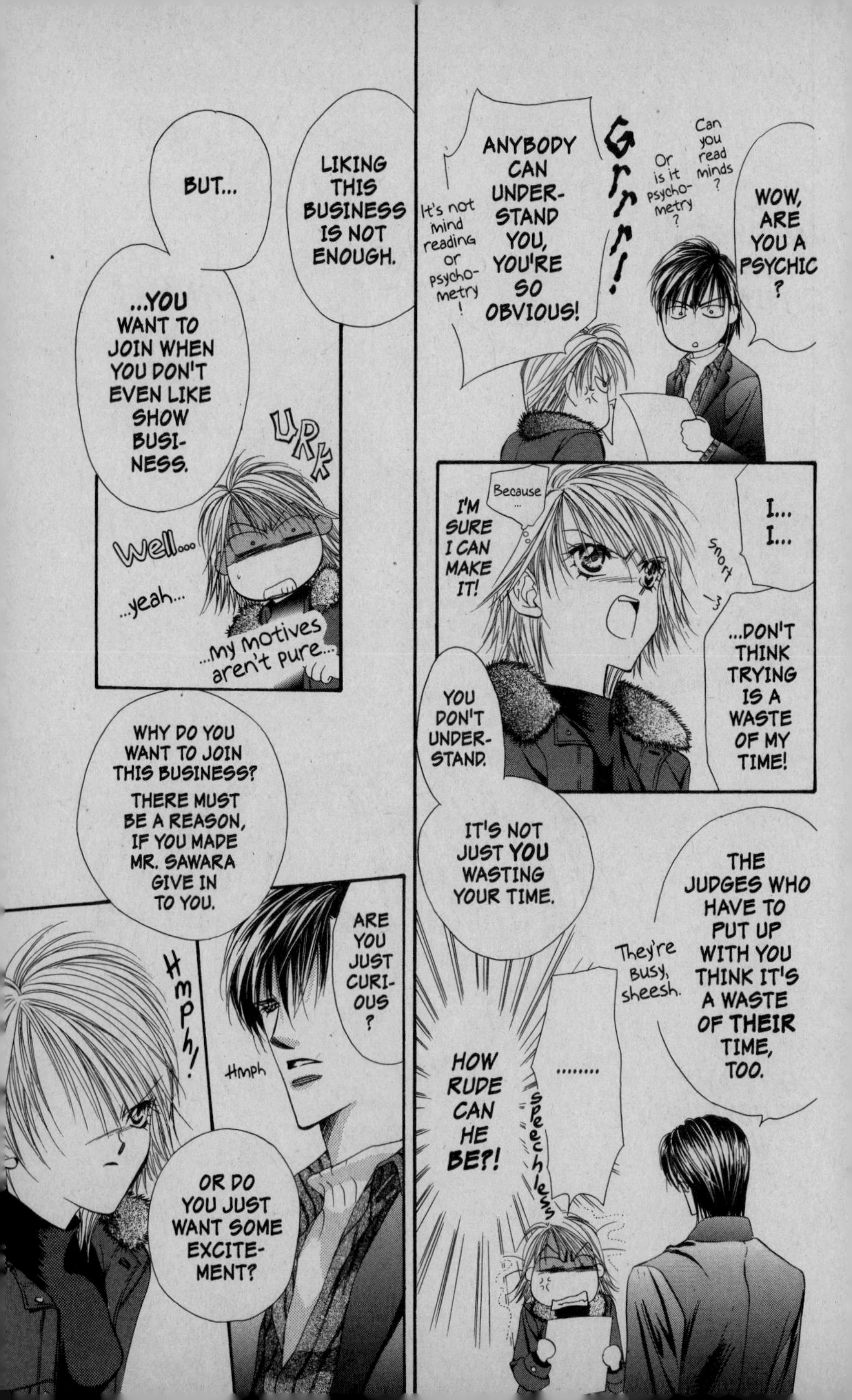
WOW, ARE YOU A PSYCHIC?
Can you read minds?
Or is it psychometry?
Grrr!
ANYBODY CAN UNDERSTAND YOU, YOU'RE SO OBVIOUS!
It's not mind reading or psychometry!
I... I...
snort
...DON'T THINK TRYING IS A WASTE OF MY TIME!
Because...
I'M SURE I CAN MAKE IT!
YOU DON'T UNDERSTAND.
IT'S NOT JUST YOU WASTING YOUR TIME.
THE JUDGES WHO HAVE TO PUT UP WITH YOU THINK IT'S A WASTE OF THEIR TIME, TOO.
They're busy, sheesh.
....
HOW RUDE CAN HE BE?!
speechless
LIKING THIS BUSINESS IS NOT ENOUGH.
BUT...
...YOU WANT TO JOIN WHEN YOU DON'T EVEN LIKE SHOW BUSINESS.
URK
Well...
...yeah...
...my motives aren't pure...
WHY DO YOU WANT TO JOIN THIS BUSINESS? THERE MUST BE A REASON, IF YOU MADE MR. SAWARA GIVE IN TO YOU.
ARE YOU JUST CURIOUS?
Hmph
Hmph!
OR DO YOU JUST WANT SOME EXCITEMENT?

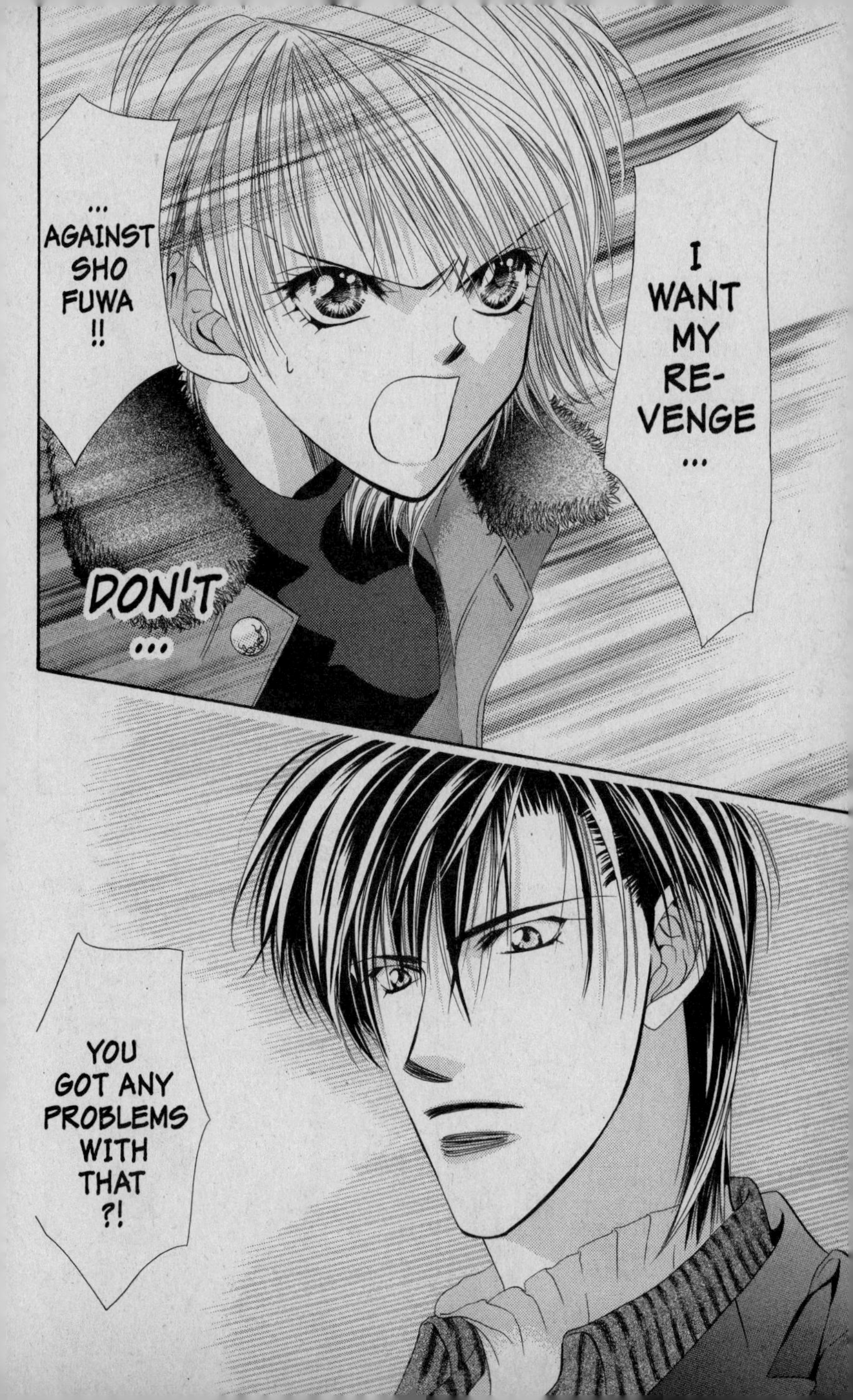
I WANT MY RE-VENGE...
...AGAINST SHO FUWA!!
DON'T ...
YOU GOT ANY PROBLEMS WITH THAT?!

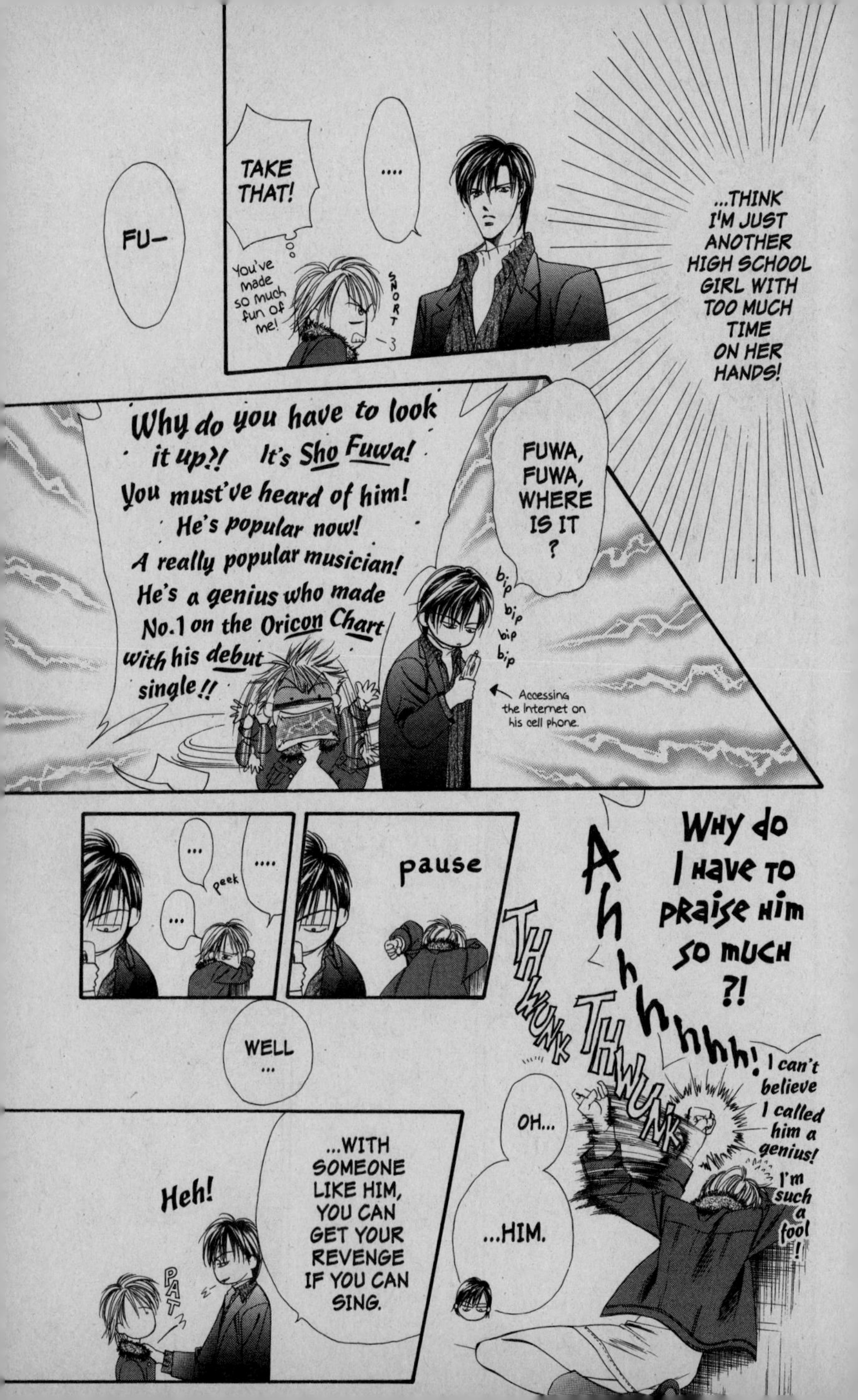
...THINK I'M JUST ANOTHER HIGH SCHOOL GIRL WITH TOO MUCH TIME ON HER HANDS!
....
TAKE THAT!
SNORT
You've made so much fun of me!
FU–
FUWA, FUWA, WHERE IS IT?
bip bip bip bip
Accessing the Internet on his cell phone.
Why do you have to look it up?! It's Sho Fuwa! You must've heard of him! He's popular now! A really popular musician! He's a genius who made No.1 on the Oricon Chart with his debut single!!
Why do I have to praise him so much?!
Ahhhhhh!
THWUNK THWUNK
I can't believe I called him a genius! I'm such a fool!
OH...
...HIM.
pause
....
...
peek
...
WELL ...
...WITH SOMEONE LIKE HIM, YOU CAN GET YOUR REVENGE IF YOU CAN SING.
Heh!
PAT

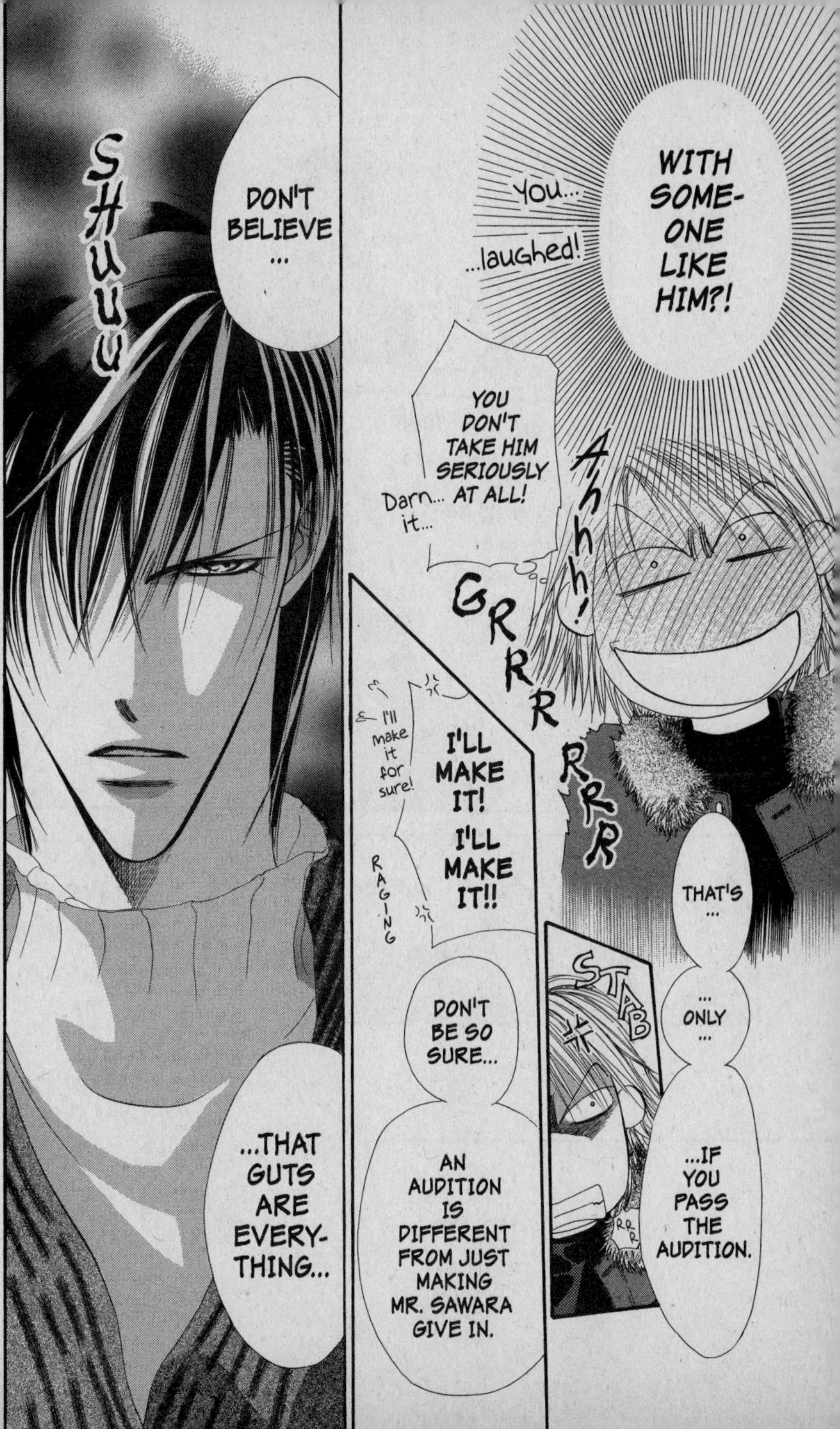
WITH SOME-ONE LIKE HIM?!
You...
...laughed!
YOU DON'T TAKE HIM SERIOUSLY AT ALL!
Darn... it...
Ahhh!
GRRRRRRR
I'LL MAKE IT! I'LL MAKE IT!!
I'll make it for sure!
RAGING
THAT'S...
...ONLY...
...IF YOU PASS THE AUDITION.
STAB
RRR
DON'T BE SO SURE...
AN AUDITION IS DIFFERENT FROM JUST MAKING MR. SAWARA GIVE IN.
DON'T BELIEVE...
...THAT GUTS ARE EVERYTHING...
SHUUU

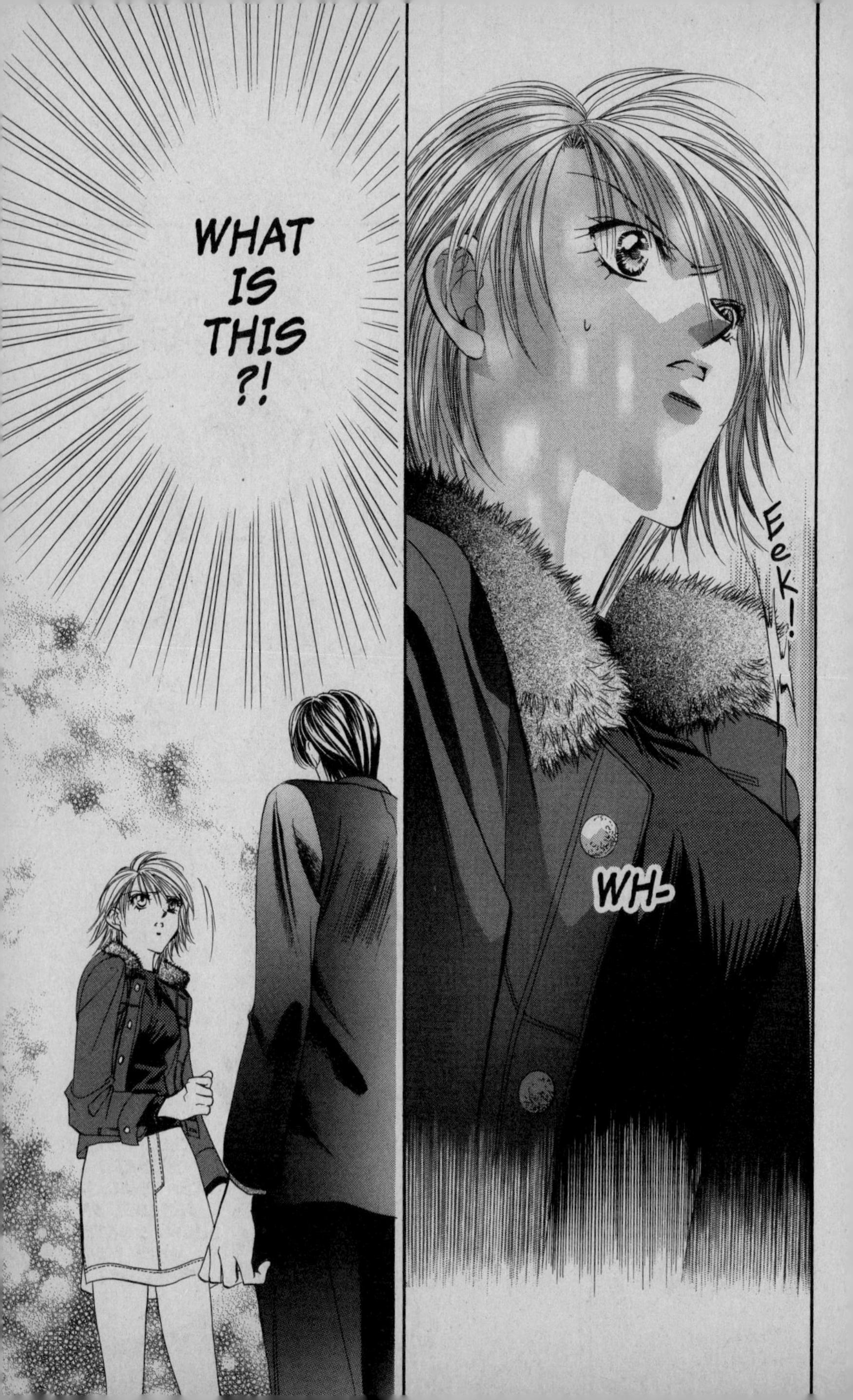
Eek!
WH-
WHAT IS THIS ?!

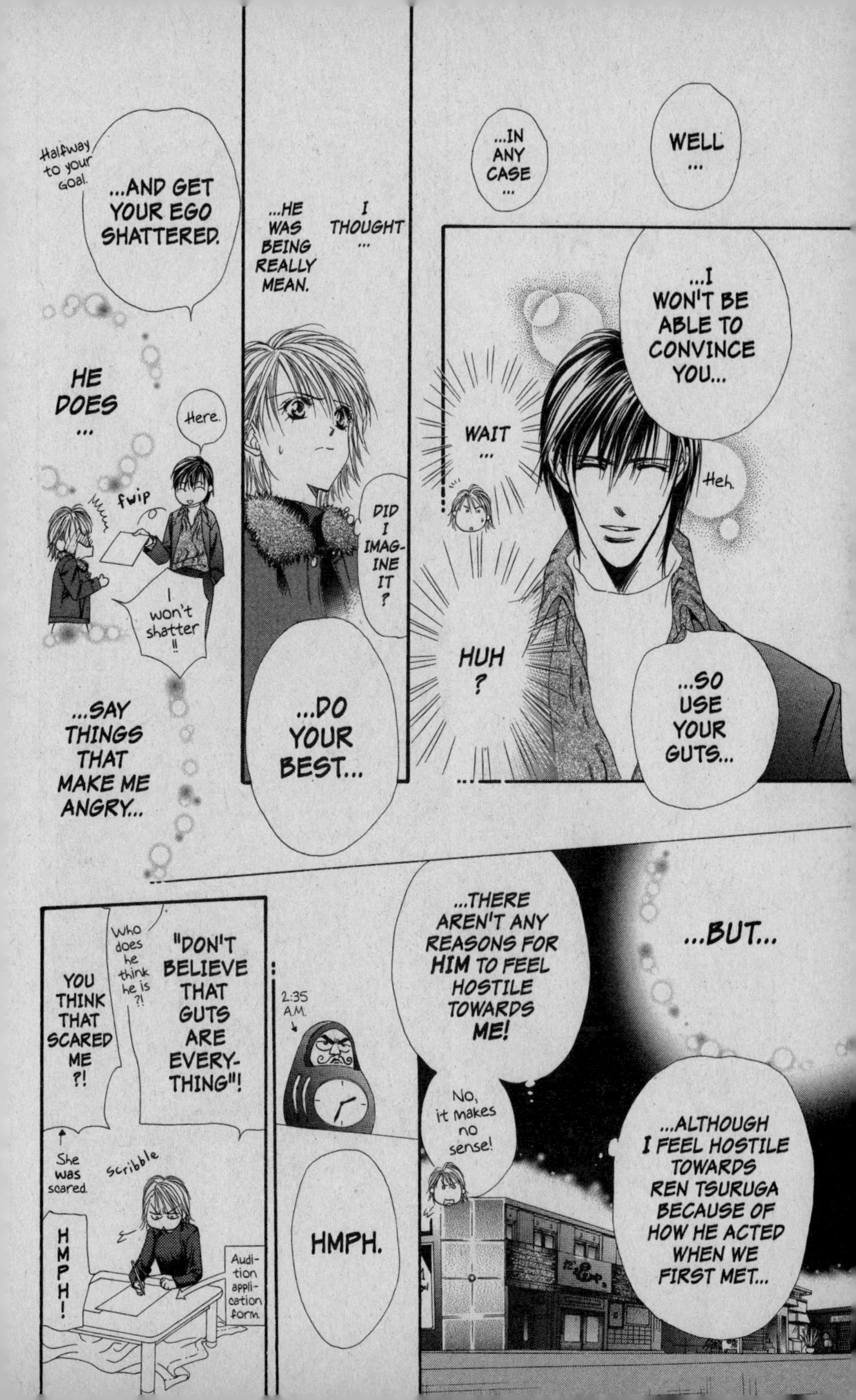
WELL...
...IN ANY CASE...
...I WON'T BE ABLE TO CONVINCE YOU...
Heh.
WAIT...
...SO USE YOUR GUTS...
HUH?
I THOUGHT...
...HE WAS BEING REALLY MEAN.
DID I IMAGINE IT?
...DO YOUR BEST...
...AND GET YOUR EGO SHATTERED.
Halfway to your goal.
HE DOES...
Here.
fwip
I won't shatter!!
...SAY THINGS THAT MAKE ME ANGRY...
...BUT...
...THERE AREN'T ANY REASONS FOR HIM TO FEEL HOSTILE TOWARDS ME!
...ALTHOUGH I FEEL HOSTILE TOWARDS REN TSURUGA BECAUSE OF HOW HE ACTED WHEN WE FIRST MET...
No, it makes no sense!
2:35 A.M.
HMPH.
"DON'T BELIEVE THAT GUTS ARE EVERYTHING"!
Who does he think he is?!
YOU THINK THAT SCARED ME?!
She was scared.
scribble
HMPH!
Audition application form

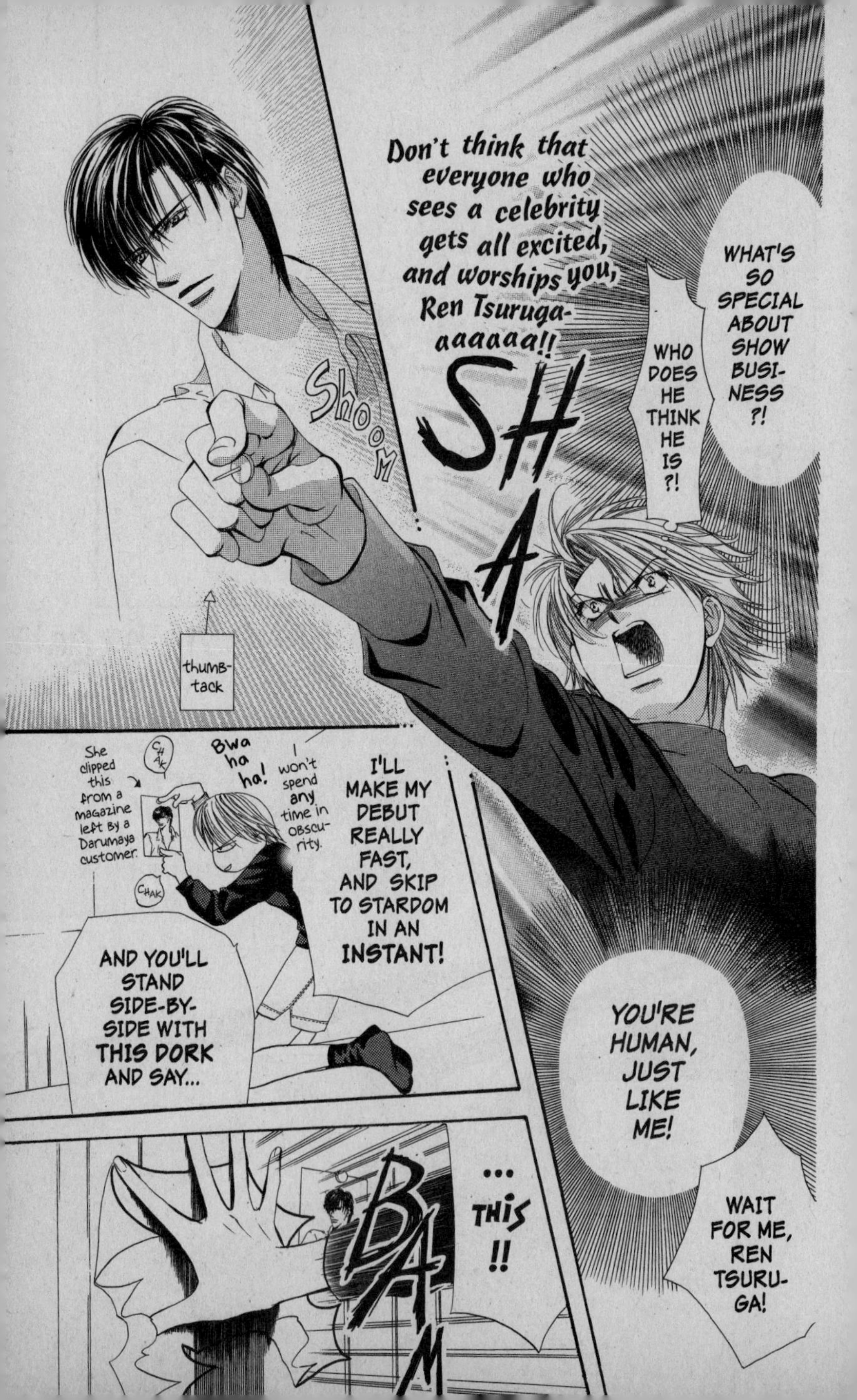
WHAT'S SO SPECIAL ABOUT SHOW BUSINESS?!
WHO DOES HE THINK HE IS?!
Don't think that everyone who sees a celebrity gets all excited, and worships you, Ren Tsuruga-aaaaaa!!
SHA
YOU'RE HUMAN, JUST LIKE ME!
WAIT FOR ME, REN TSURUGA!
Shoom
thumb-tack
I'LL MAKE MY DEBUT REALLY FAST, AND SKIP TO STARDOM IN AN INSTANT!
I won't spend any time in obscurity.
Bwa ha ha!
CHAK
She clipped this from a magazine left by a Darumaya customer.
CHAK
AND YOU'LL STAND SIDE-BY-SIDE WITH THIS DORK AND SAY...
...THIS!!
BAM

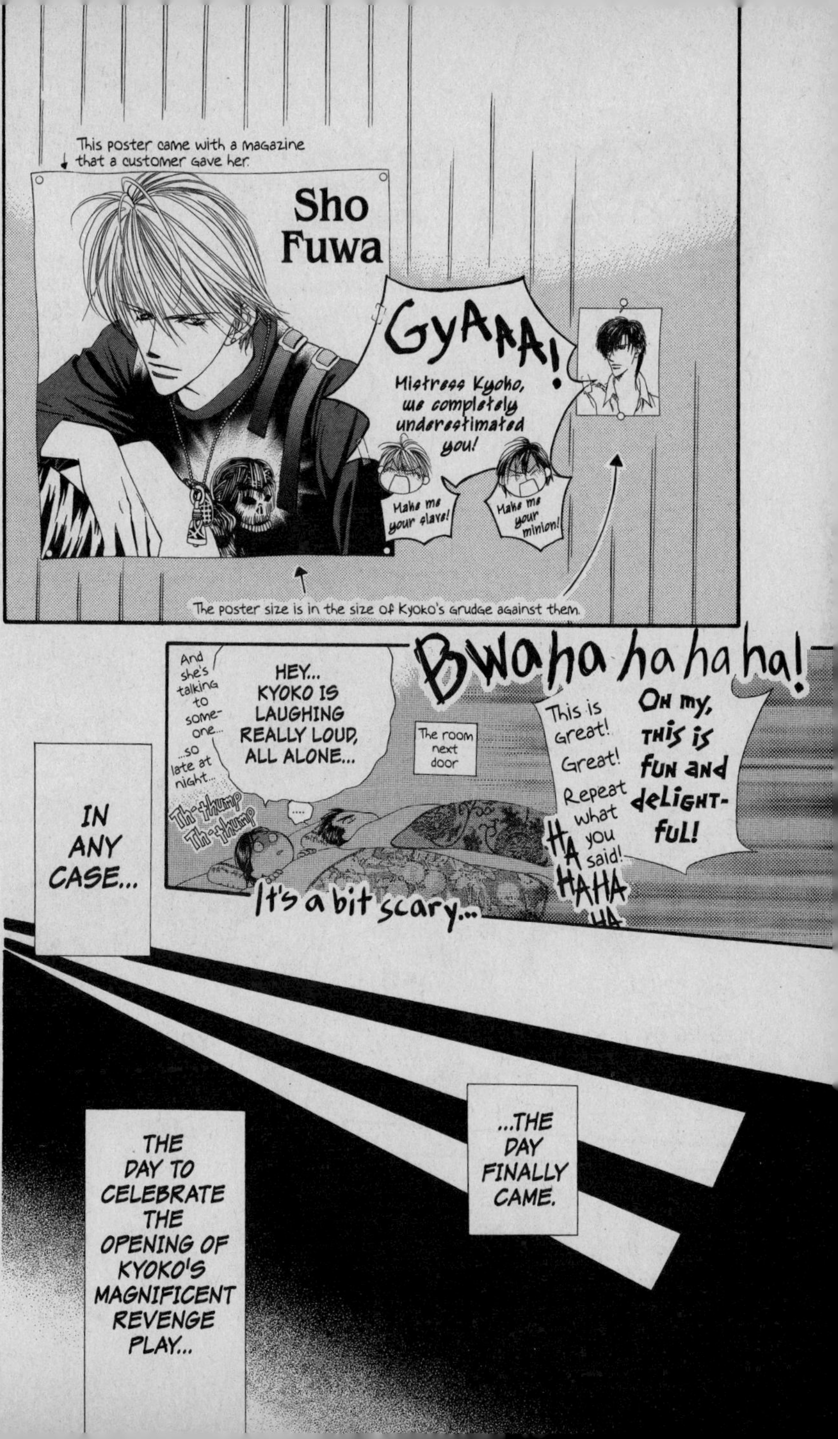

GYAAA!
Mistress Kyoko, we completely underestimated you!
Make me your minion!
Make me your slave!
Sho Fuwa
This poster came with a magazine that a customer gave her.
The poster size is in the size of Kyoko's grudge against them.
Bwaha ha ha ha!
Oh my, this is fun and delightful!
This is great! Great! Repeat what you said!
HA HA HA HA HA
The room next door
HEY... KYOKO IS LAUGHING REALLY LOUD, ALL ALONE...
And she's talking to someone... ...so late at night...
Th-thump Th-thump
....
It's a bit scary...
IN ANY CASE...
THE DAY TO CELEBRATE THE OPENING OF KYOKO'S MAGNIFICENT REVENGE PLAY...
...THE DAY FINALLY CAME.

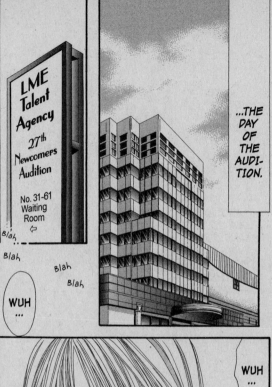

...THE DAY OF THE AUDITION.
LME Talent Agency
27th Newcomers Audition
No. 31-61 Waiting Room
Blah
Blah
Blah
Blah
WUH...
WUH...
WOW...!

5
I will not make any excuses.

Usually, when drawing manga, you have the editor check your penciling, then you do the inking (But...most mangakas probably do the inking without waiting for editors to respond...Because there's no time. 6)

I have Been doing that for many years since I've Become a mangaka, and that day, I sent in my penciled pages as usual. They were the penciling for the last story in this volume, "Act 5: The Emotion She Lacks." My editor looked at it, and phoned me as usual. And after we talked about the things he had checked, he suddenly said, "Ms. Nakamura, who's your favorite *Skip Beat!* character?"

...I'm not the type to "love" my characters, and being asked my favorite when I've just started a series (only Kyoko and Sho have some personality...) I don't dislike Kyoko as a female character, so I can say I like her. As a reader, Sho is someone I definitely...

Continued on page 129

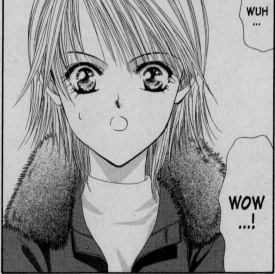

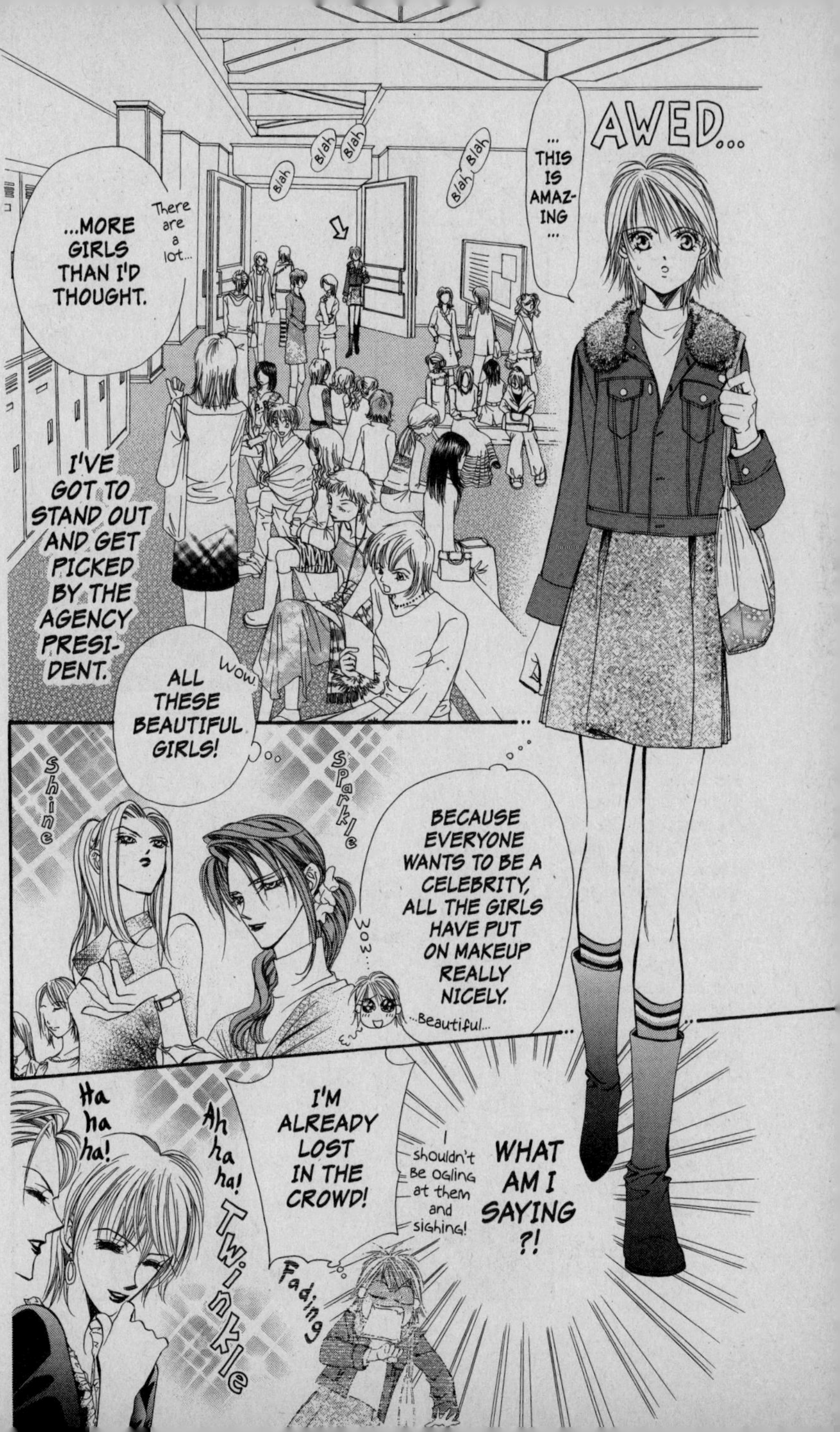
AWED...
...THIS IS AMAZING...
Blah Blah
Blah
Blah
Blah
There are a lot...
...MORE GIRLS THAN I'D THOUGHT.
I'VE GOT TO STAND OUT AND GET PICKED BY THE AGENCY PRESIDENT.
Wow.
ALL THESE BEAUTIFUL GIRLS!
BECAUSE EVERYONE WANTS TO BE A CELEBRITY, ALL THE GIRLS HAVE PUT ON MAKEUP REALLY NICELY.
Sparkle
Shine
Wow...
...Beautiful...
WHAT AM I SAYING?!
I shouldn't be ogling at them and sighing!
I'M ALREADY LOST IN THE CROWD!
Fading
Twinkle
Ah ha ha!
Ha ha ha!

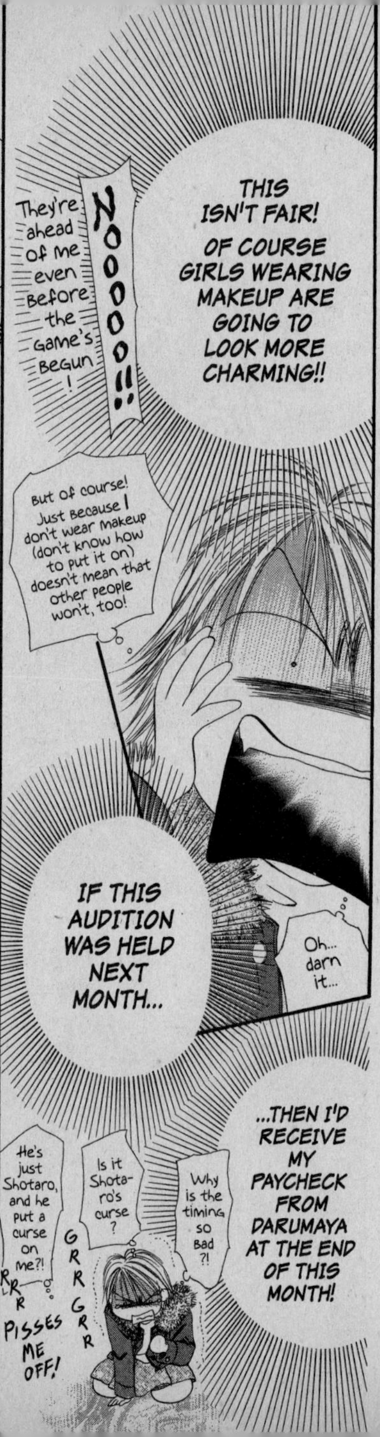
THIS ISN'T FAIR! OF COURSE GIRLS WEARING MAKEUP ARE GOING TO LOOK MORE CHARMING!!
NOOOOO!!
They're ahead of me even before the game's begun!
But of course! Just because I don't wear makeup (don't know how to put it on) doesn't mean that other people won't, too!
IF THIS AUDITION WAS HELD NEXT MONTH...
Oh... darn it...
...THEN I'D RECEIVE MY PAYCHECK FROM DARUMAYA AT THE END OF THIS MONTH!
Why is the timing so bad?!
Is it Shotaro's curse?
He's just Shotaro, and he put a curse on me?!
GRRR GRRR
RRR
PISSES ME OFF!
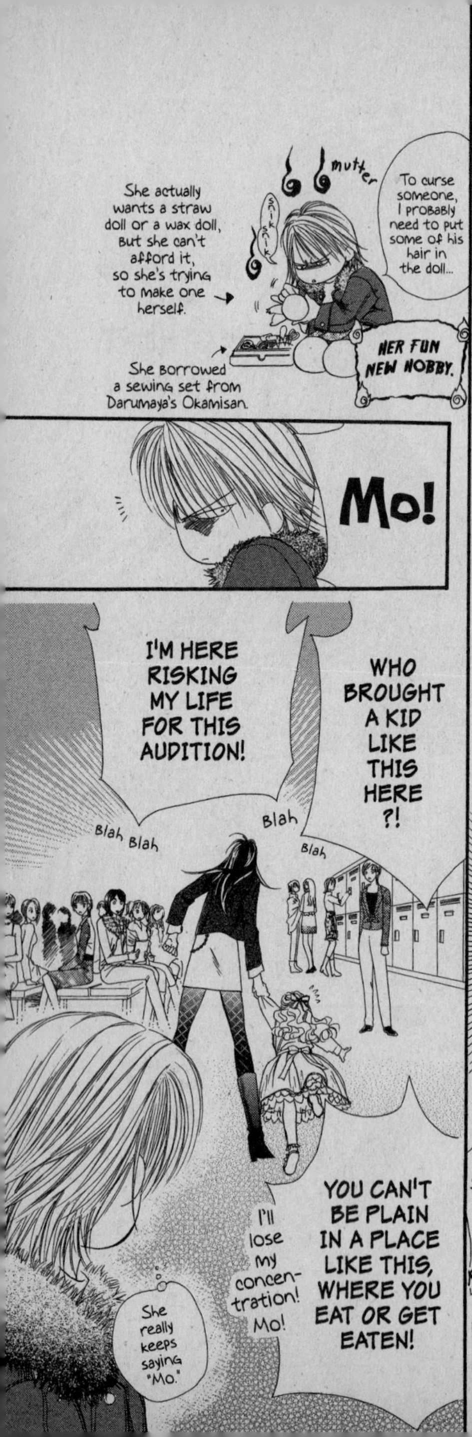
To curse someone, I probably need to put some of his hair in the doll...
mutter
snik snik
She actually wants a straw doll or a wax doll, but she can't afford it, so she's trying to make one herself.
HER FUN NEW HOBBY.
She borrowed a sewing set from Darumaya's Okamisan.
Mo!
WHO BROUGHT A KID LIKE THIS HERE?!
I'M HERE RISKING MY LIFE FOR THIS AUDITION!
Blah
Blah Blah
Blah
YOU CAN'T BE PLAIN IN A PLACE LIKE THIS, WHERE YOU EAT OR GET EATEN!
I'll lose my concentration! Mo!
She really keeps saying "Mo."

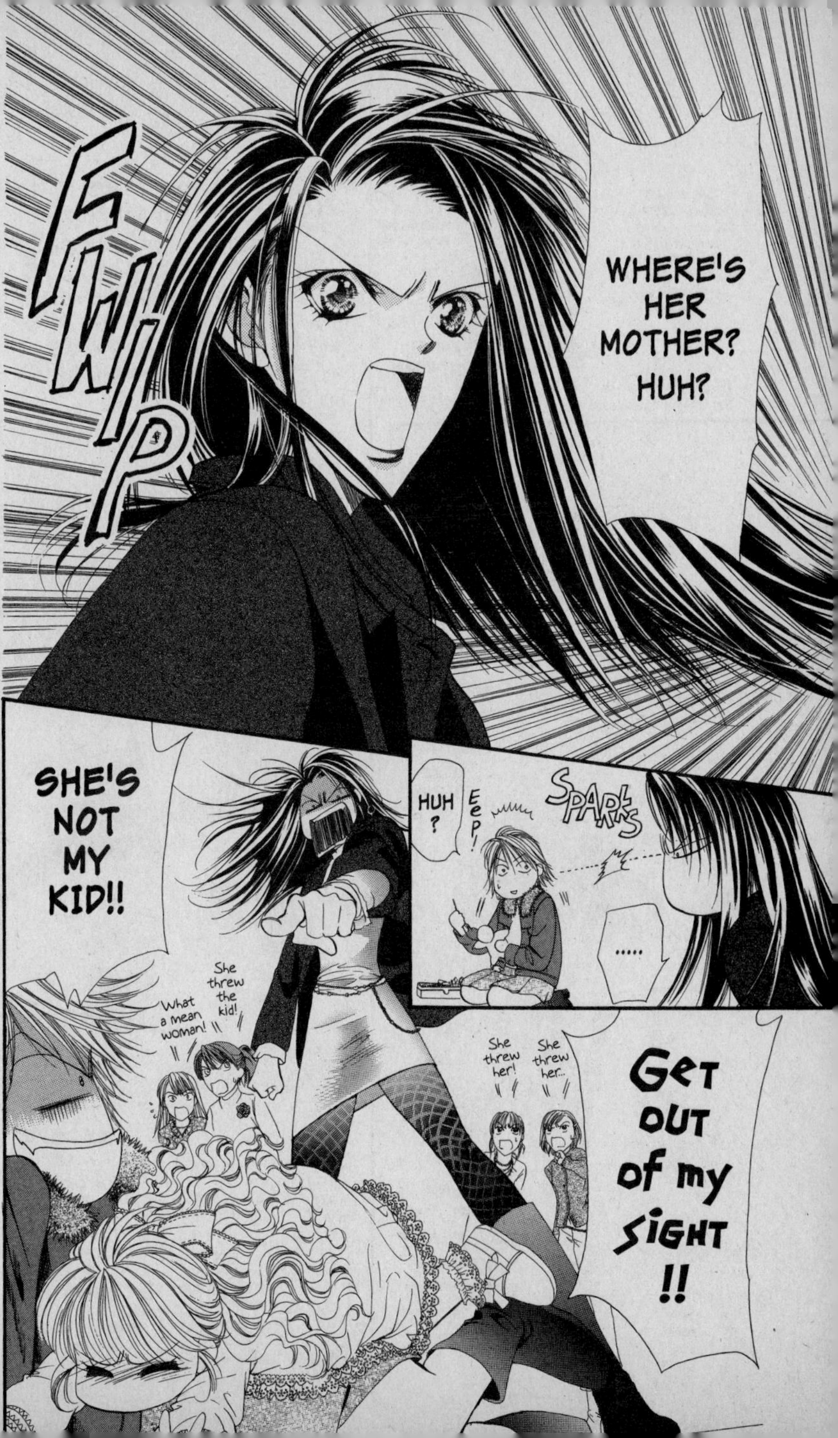
WHERE'S HER MOTHER? HUH?
FWIP
HUH?
Eep!
SPARKS
.....
SHE'S NOT MY KID!!
Get out of my sight!!
She threw her!
She threw her...
She threw the kid!
What a mean woman!

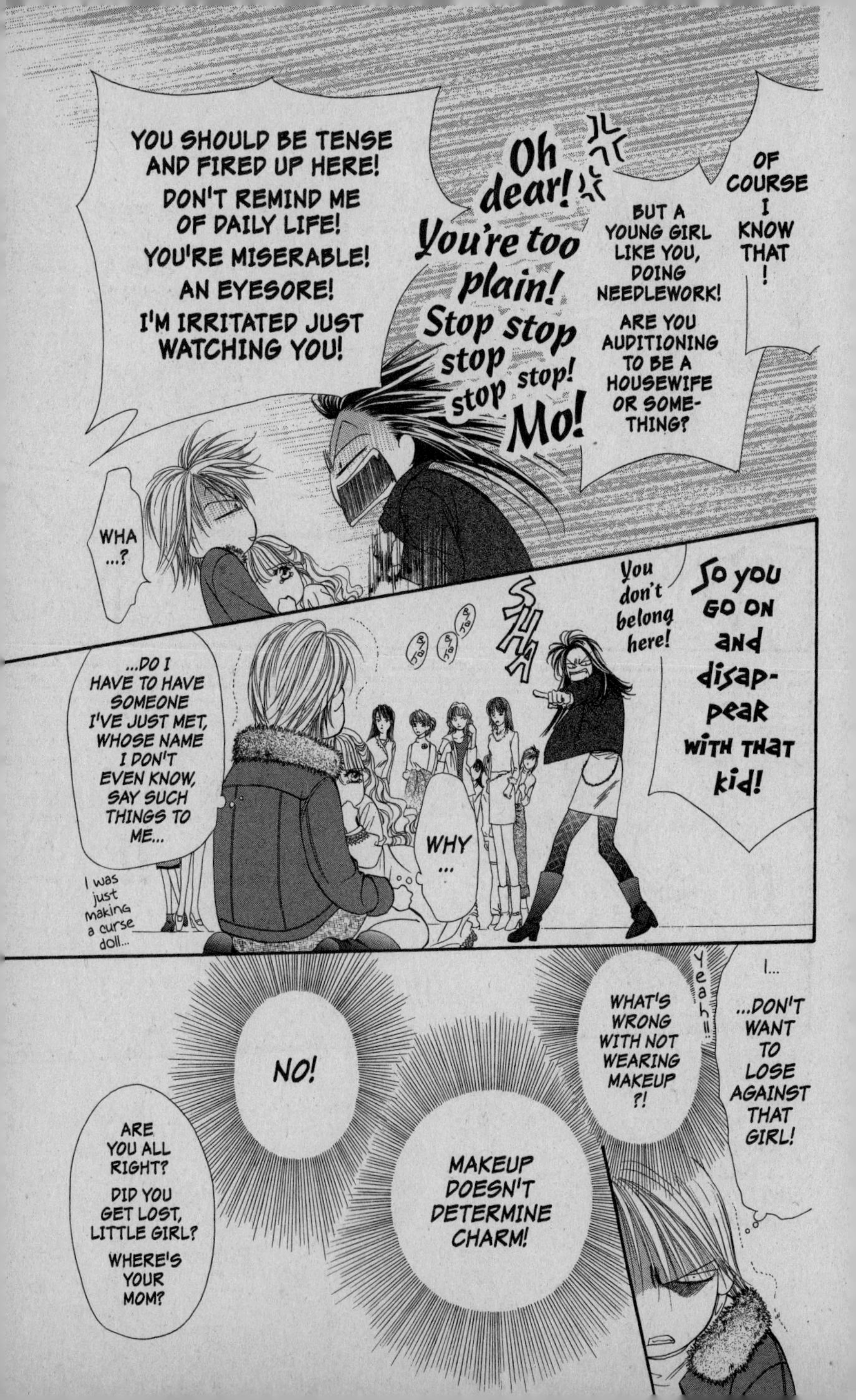
OF COURSE I KNOW THAT!
BUT A YOUNG GIRL LIKE YOU, DOING NEEDLEWORK! ARE YOU AUDITIONING TO BE A HOUSEWIFE OR SOME-THING?
Oh dear! You're too plain! Stop stop stop stop stop! Mo!
YOU SHOULD BE TENSE AND FIRED UP HERE! DON'T REMIND ME OF DAILY LIFE! YOU'RE MISERABLE! AN EYESORE! I'M IRRITATED JUST WATCHING YOU!
WHA...?
So you go on and disap-pear with that kid!
You don't belong here!
SHA
WHY...
...DO I HAVE TO HAVE SOMEONE I'VE JUST MET, WHOSE NAME I DON'T EVEN KNOW, SAY SUCH THINGS TO ME...
I was just making a curse doll...
I... ...DON'T WANT TO LOSE AGAINST THAT GIRL!
Yeah!!
WHAT'S WRONG WITH NOT WEARING MAKEUP?!
NO!
MAKEUP DOESN'T DETERMINE CHARM!
ARE YOU ALL RIGHT? DID YOU GET LOST, LITTLE GIRL? WHERE'S YOUR MOM?

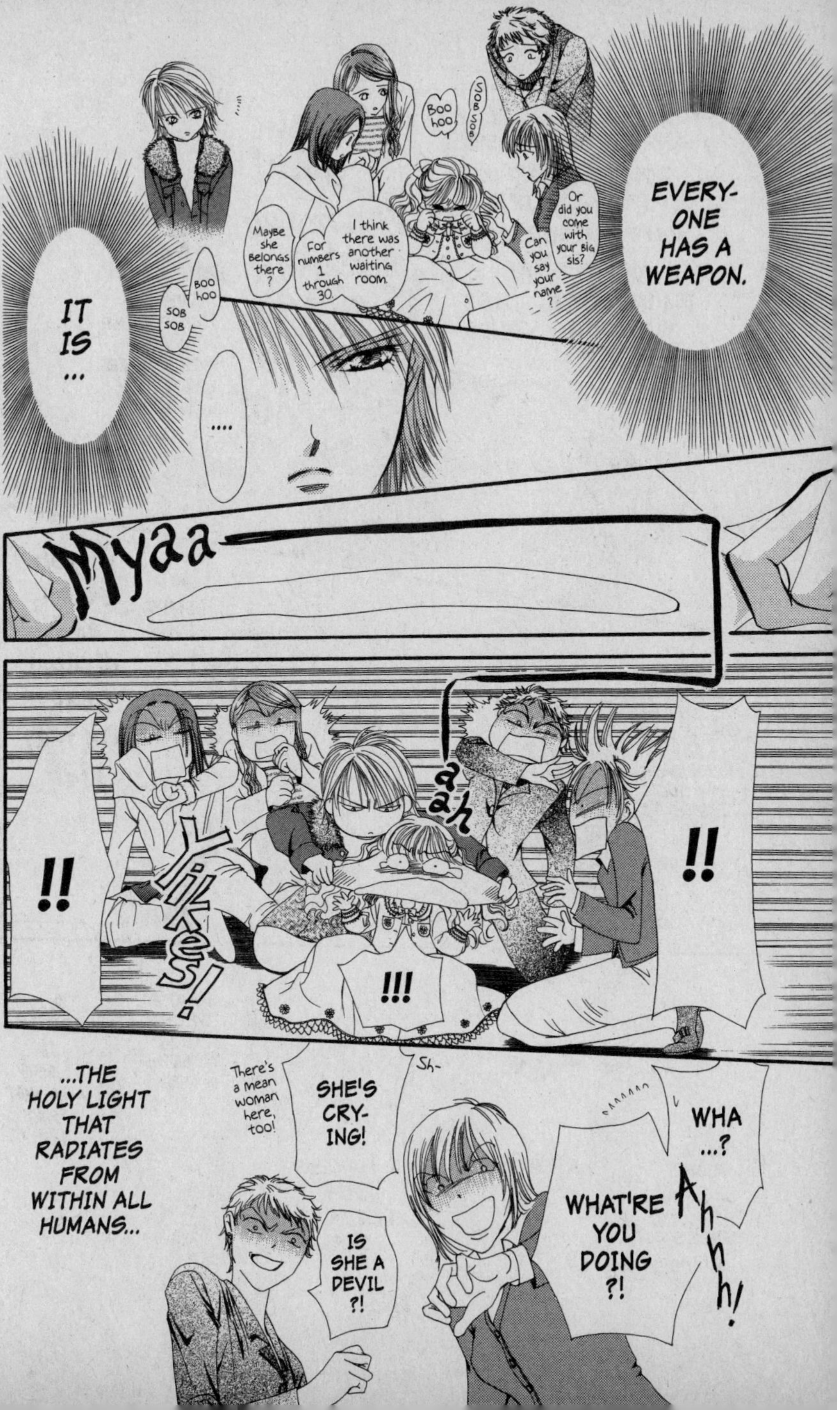

EVERY-ONE HAS A WEAPON.
SOB SOB
BOO HOO
Or did you come with your big sis?
Can you say your name?
I think there was another waiting room.
For numbers 1 through 30.
Maybe she belongs there?
BOO HOO
SOB SOB
IT IS...
....
Myaa
!!
aah
!!!
Yikes!
!!
Sh-
SHE'S CRY-ING!
There's a mean woman here, too!
...THE HOLY LIGHT THAT RADIATES FROM WITHIN ALL HUMANS...
WHA...?
Ahhh!
WHAT'RE YOU DOING?!
IS SHE A DEVIL?!

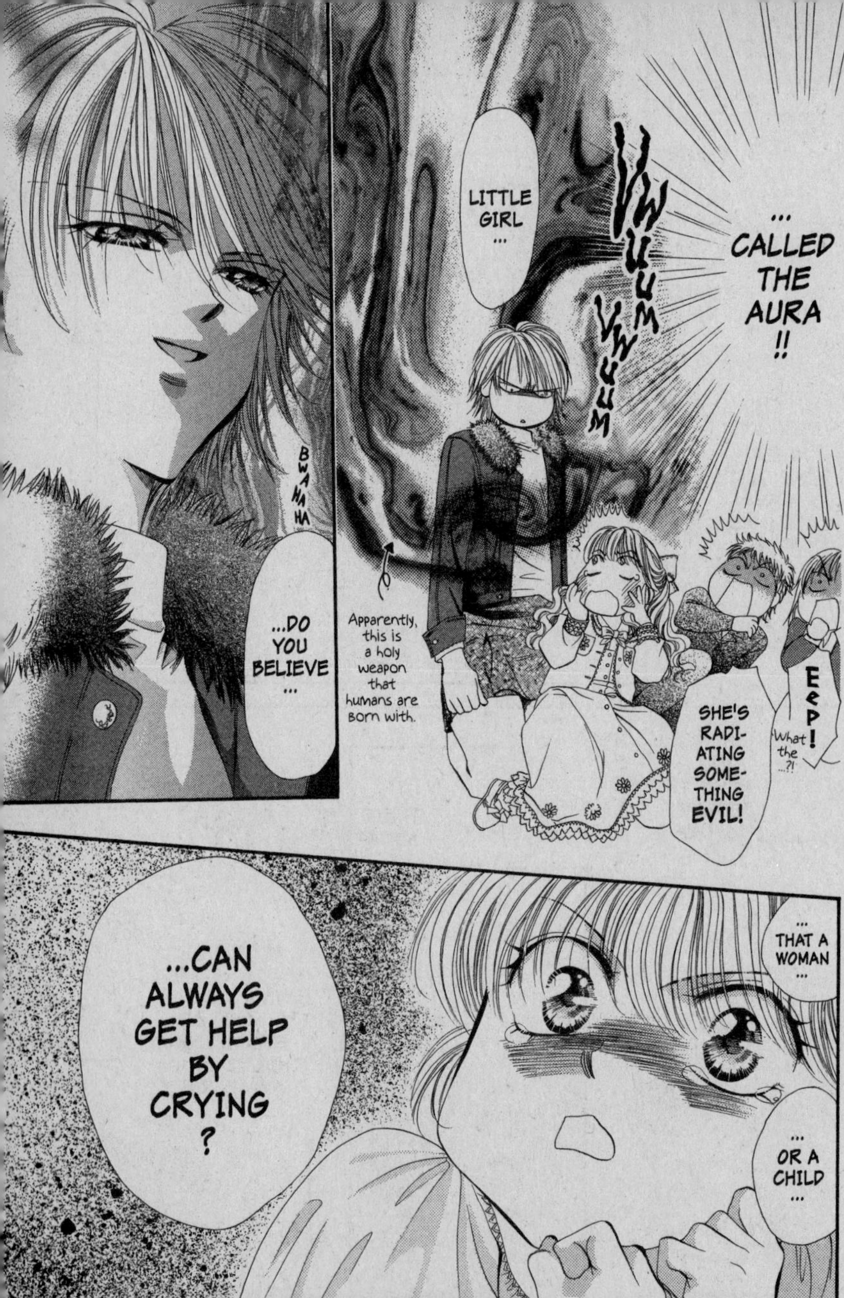
... CALLED THE AURA !!
VWUUM VWUUM
LITTLE GIRL ...
Eep!
What the ...?!
SHE'S RADIATING SOMETHING EVIL!
Apparently, this is a holy weapon that humans are born with.
BWA HA HA
...DO YOU BELIEVE ...
... THAT A WOMAN ...
... OR A CHILD ...
...CAN ALWAYS GET HELP BY CRYING ?

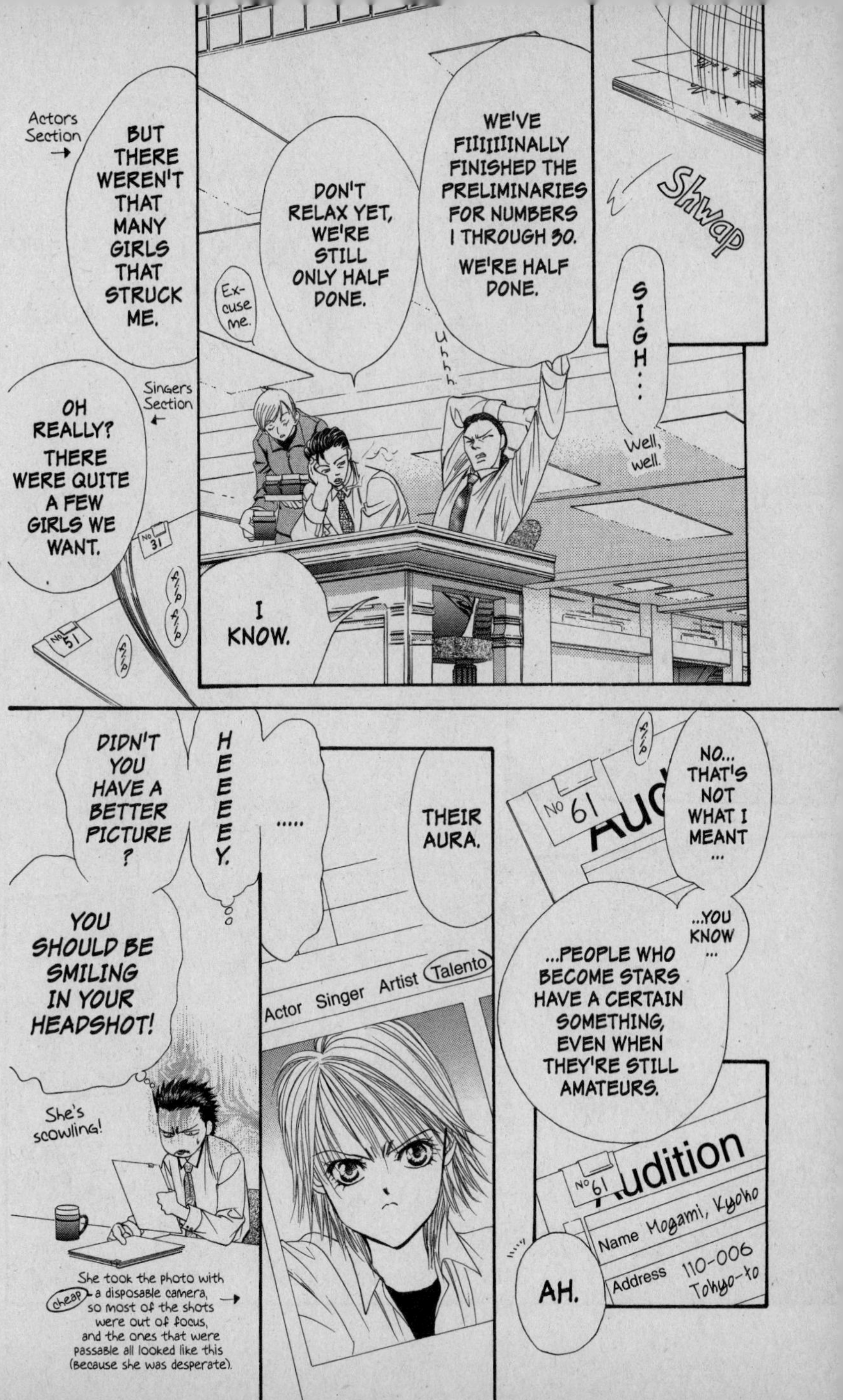

Shwap
SIGH...
Well, well.
WE'VE FIIIIIINALLY FINISHED THE PRELIMINARIES FOR NUMBERS 1 THROUGH 30.
WE'RE HALF DONE.
Uhhh.
DON'T RELAX YET, WE'RE STILL ONLY HALF DONE.
Ex-cuse me.
Actors Section →
BUT THERE WEREN'T THAT MANY GIRLS THAT STRUCK ME.
Singers Section ←
OH REALLY? THERE WERE QUITE A FEW GIRLS WE WANT.
I KNOW.
No 31
flip flip
No 51
flip
flip
No 61
NO... THAT'S NOT WHAT I MEANT...
...YOU KNOW...
...PEOPLE WHO BECOME STARS HAVE A CERTAIN SOMETHING, EVEN WHEN THEY'RE STILL AMATEURS.
Audition
No 61
Name Mogami, Kyoko
Address 110-006 Tokyo-to
AH.
THEIR AURA.
.....
Actor Singer Artist Talento
HEEEEEY.
DIDN'T YOU HAVE A BETTER PICTURE?
YOU SHOULD BE SMILING IN YOUR HEADSHOT!
She's scowling!
She took the photo with a (cheap) disposable camera, so most of the shots were out of focus, and the ones that were passable all looked like this (because she was desperate). →

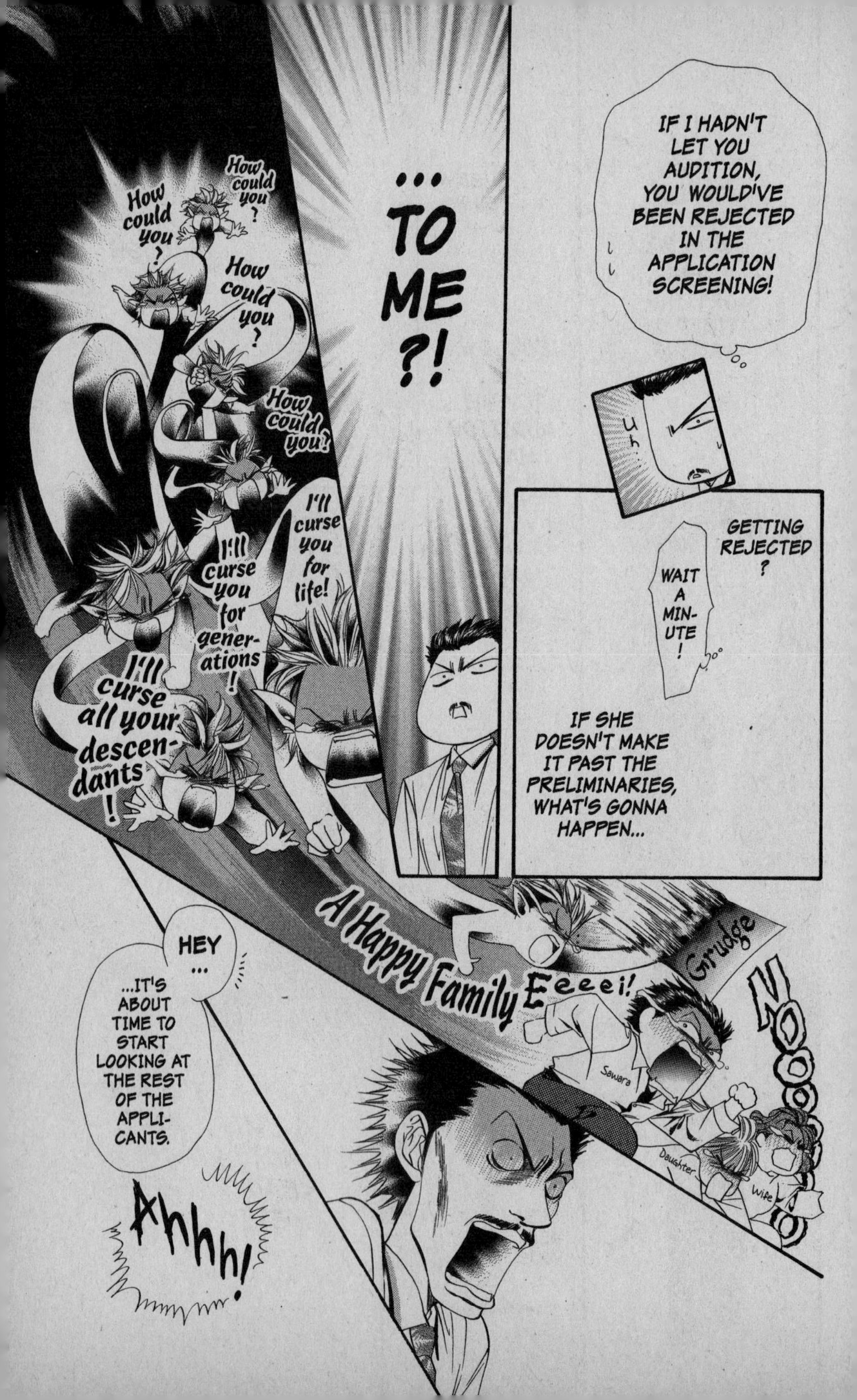
IF I HADN'T LET YOU AUDITION, YOU WOULD'VE BEEN REJECTED IN THE APPLICATION SCREENING!
Uh...
GETTING REJECTED?
WAIT A MIN-UTE!
IF SHE DOESN'T MAKE IT PAST THE PRELIMINARIES, WHAT'S GONNA HAPPEN...
...TO ME?!
How could you?
How could you?
How could you?
How could you!
I'll curse you for life!
I'll curse you for gener-ations!
I'll curse all your descen-dants!
A Happy Family Eeeei!
Grudge
NOOOOOO
Sawara
Daughter
Wife
HEY...
...IT'S ABOUT TIME TO START LOOKING AT THE REST OF THE APPLI-CANTS.
Ahhh!

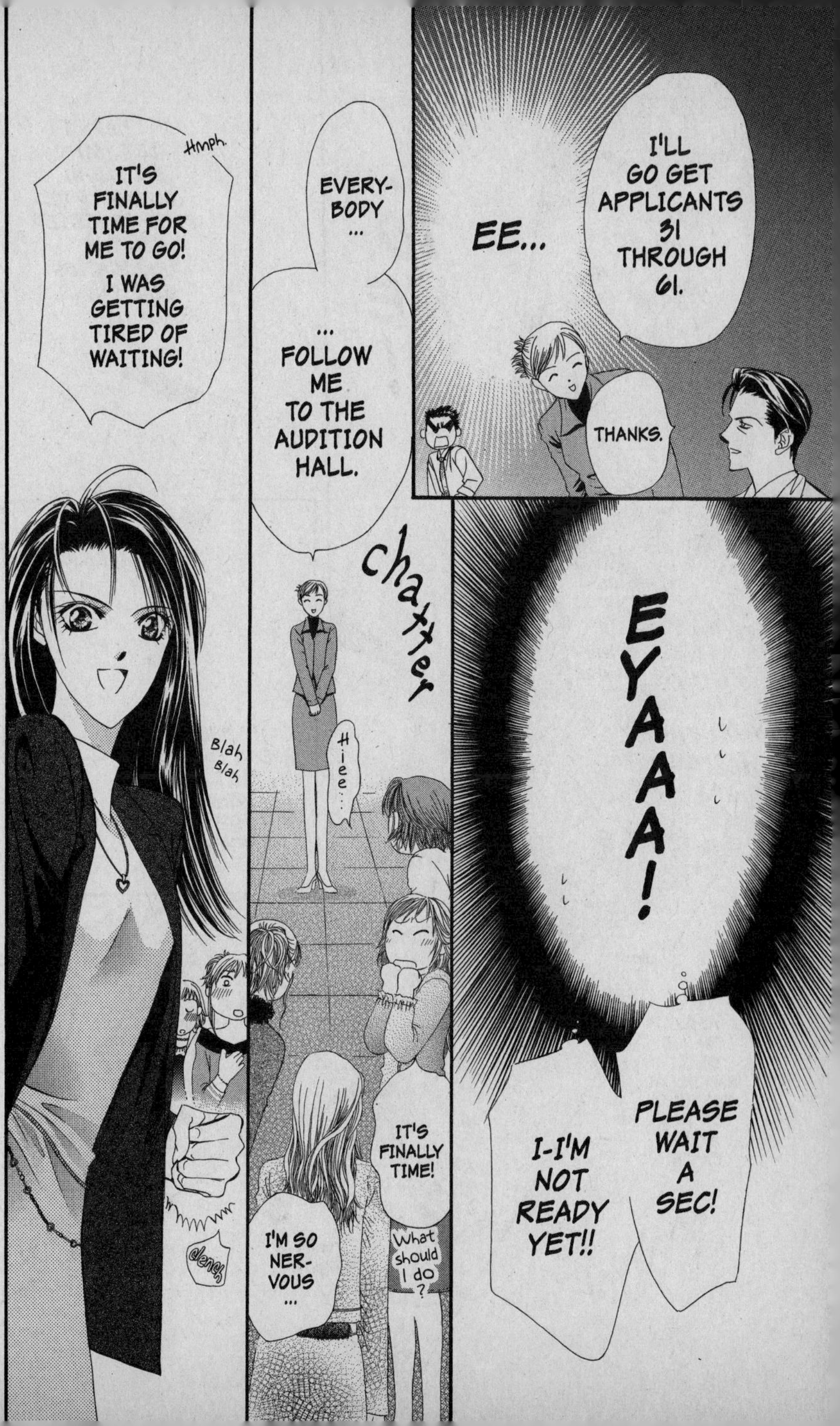
I'LL GO GET APPLICANTS 31 THROUGH 61.
EE...
THANKS.
EYAAA!
PLEASE WAIT A SEC!
I-I'M NOT READY YET!!
EVERYBODY...
... FOLLOW ME TO THE AUDITION HALL.
chatter
Hiee...
IT'S FINALLY TIME!
What should I do?
I'M SO NERVOUS...
Hmph.
IT'S FINALLY TIME FOR ME TO GO!
I WAS GETTING TIRED OF WAITING!
Blah Blah
clench

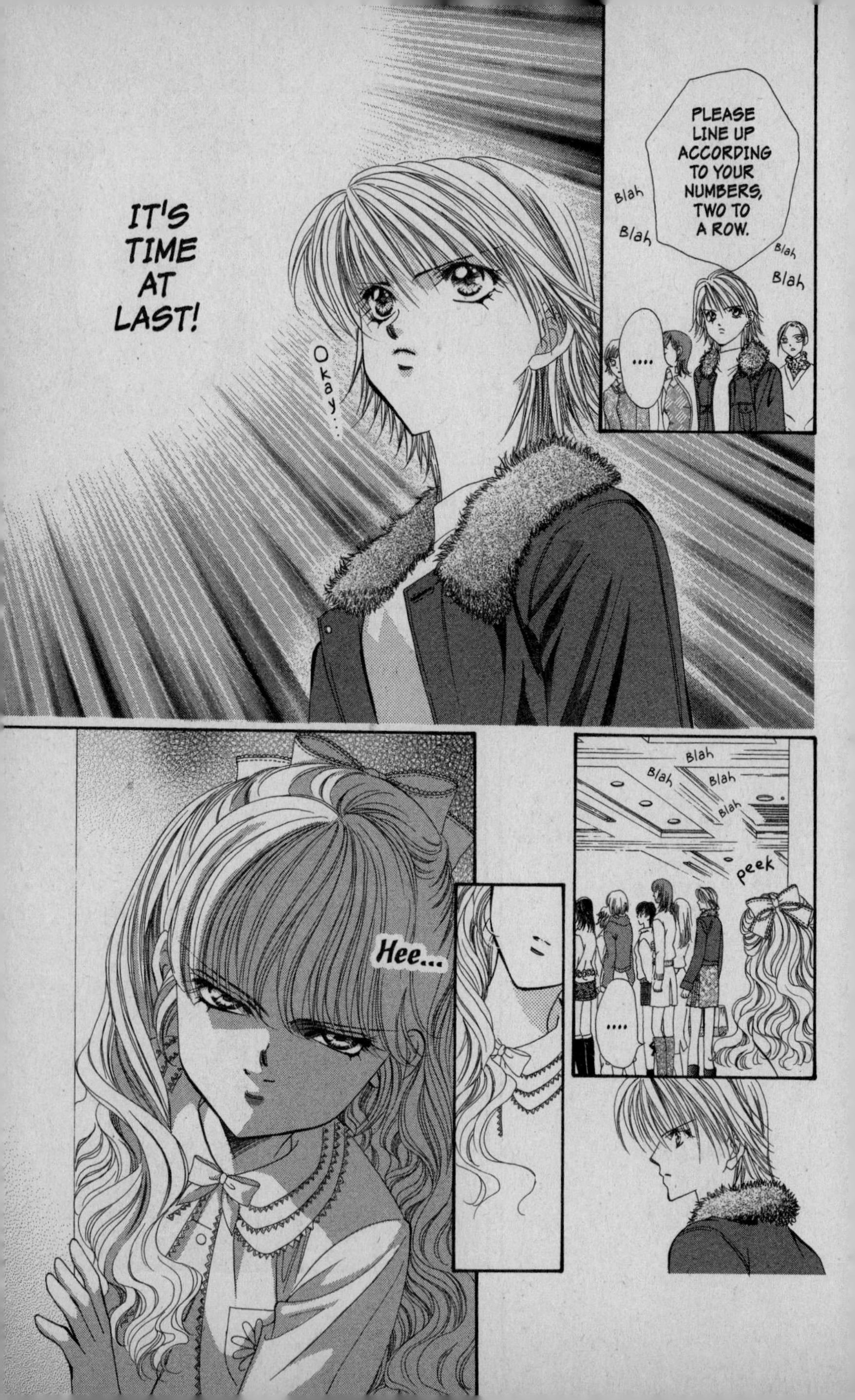
PLEASE LINE UP ACCORDING TO YOUR NUMBERS, TWO TO A ROW.
Blah
Blah
Blah
Blah
....
IT'S TIME AT LAST!
Okay...
Blah
Blah
Blah
Blah
peek
....
Hee...

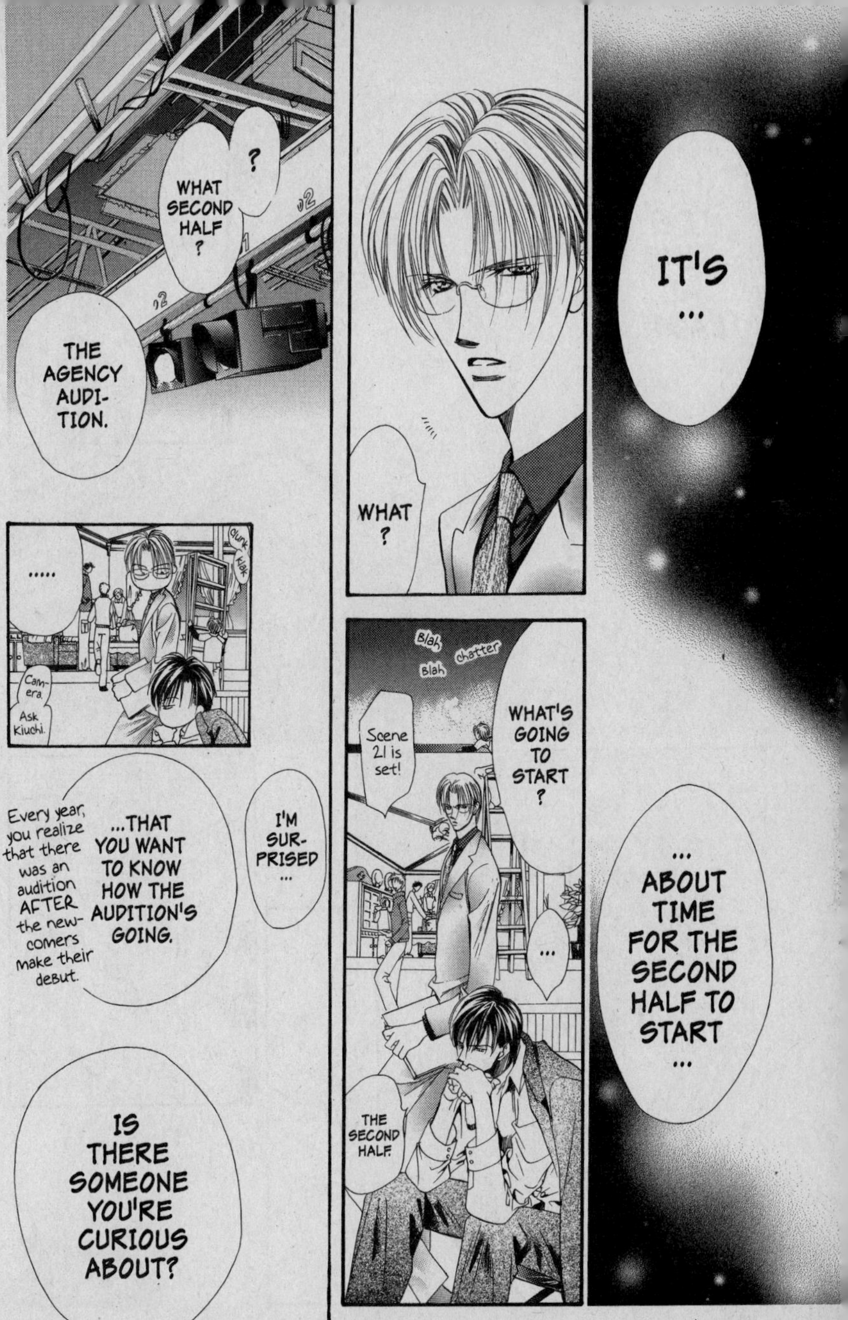
IT'S ...
... ABOUT TIME FOR THE SECOND HALF TO START ...
WHAT ?
Blah
Blah
chatter
WHAT'S GOING TO START ?
Scene 21 is set!
...
THE SECOND HALF.
?
WHAT SECOND HALF ?
THE AGENCY AUDITION.
.....
Clunk
klak
Camera.
Ask Kiuchi.
I'M SURPRISED ...
...THAT YOU WANT TO KNOW HOW THE AUDITION'S GOING.
Every year, you realize that there was an audition AFTER the new-comers make their debut.
IS THERE SOMEONE YOU'RE CURIOUS ABOUT?

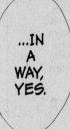

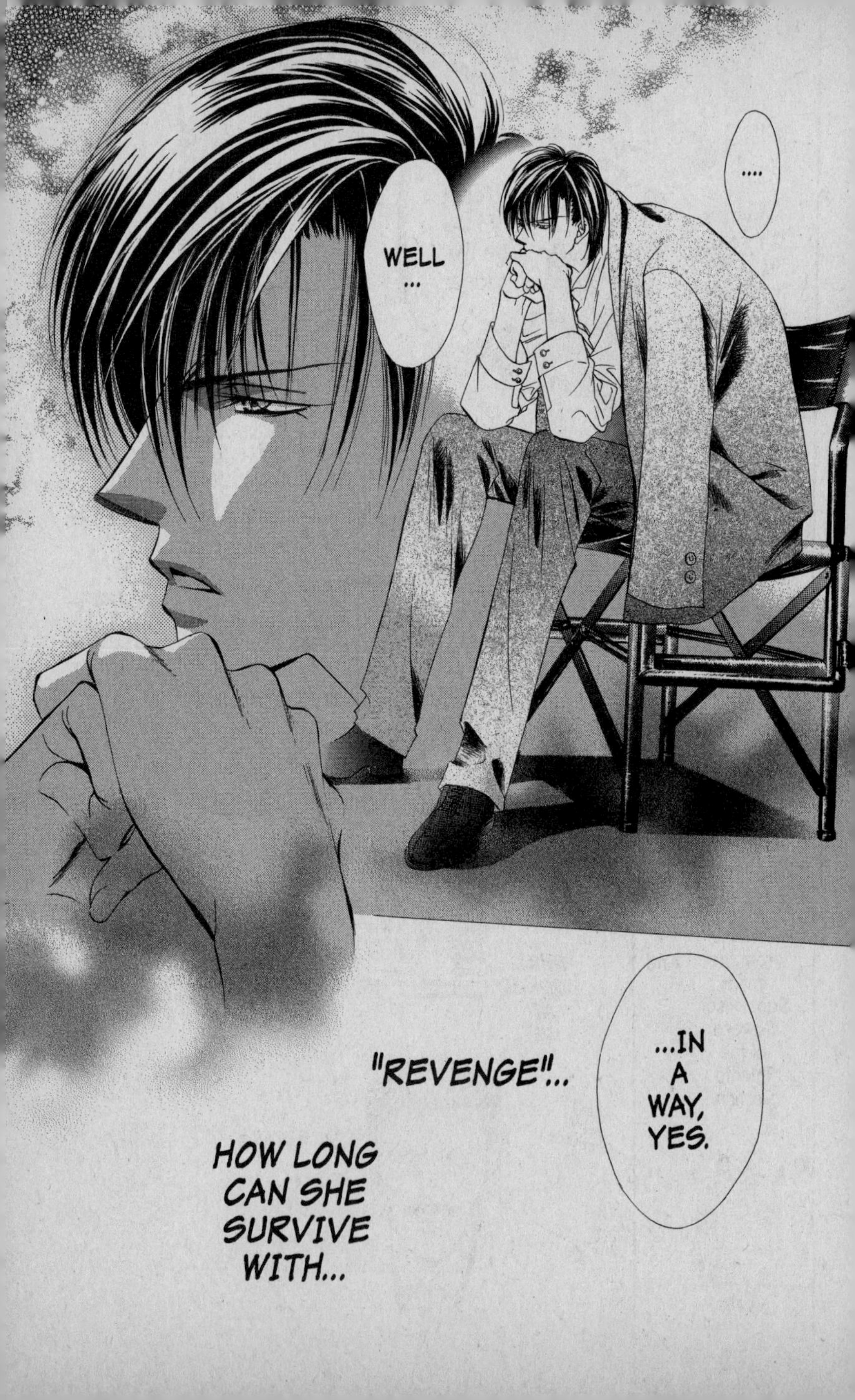

WELL ...

....

"REVENGE"...

...IN A WAY, YES.

HOW LONG CAN SHE SURVIVE WITH...

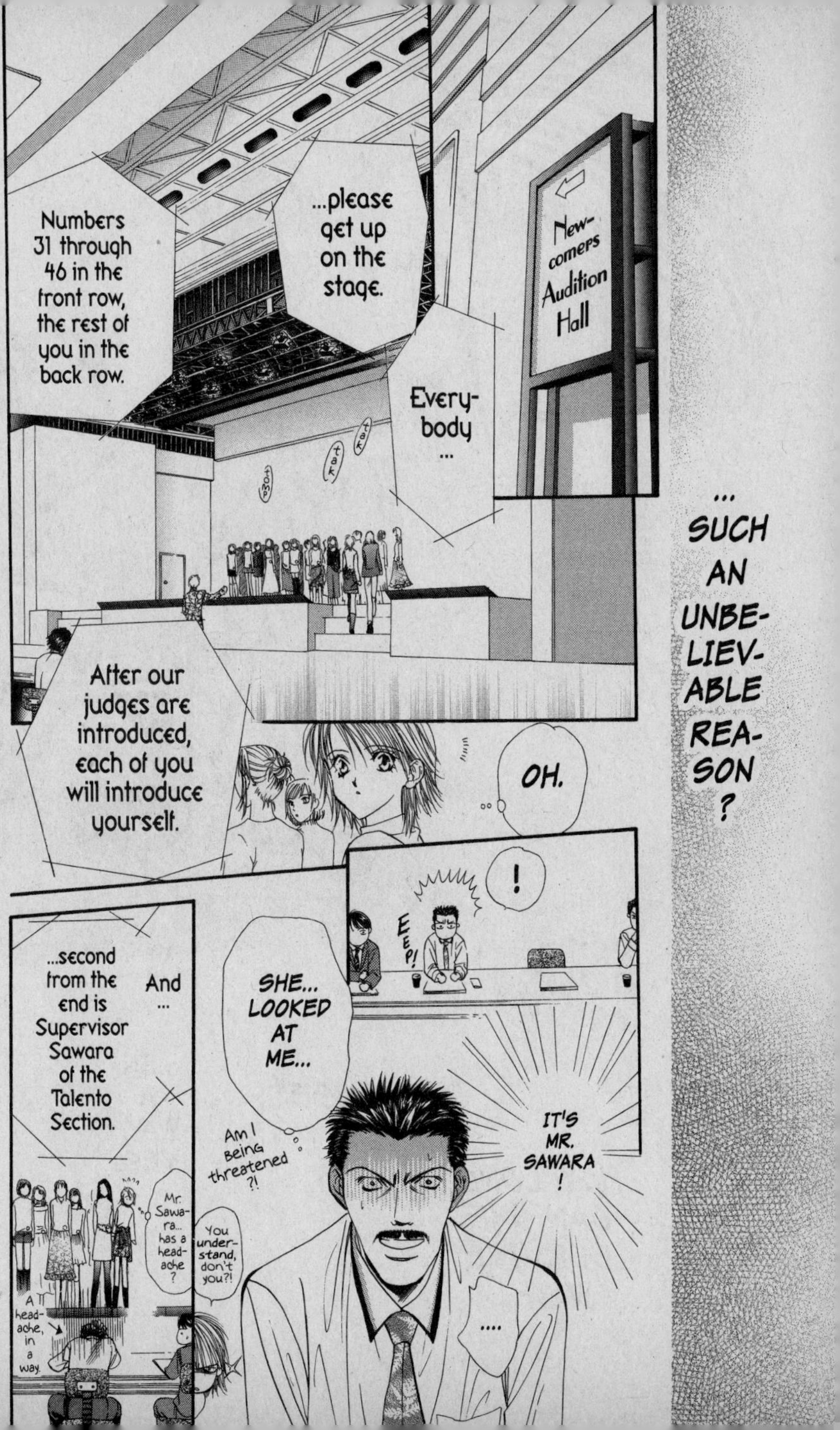

...SUCH AN UNBE-LIEV-ABLE REA-SON?
New-comers Audition Hall
Every-body...
...please get up on the stage.
Numbers 31 through 46 in the front row, the rest of you in the back row.
tak
tak
tomp
After our judges are introduced, each of you will introduce yourself.
OH.
!
EEP!
SHE... LOOKED AT ME...
IT'S MR. SAWARA!
....
Am I being threatened?!
And...
...second from the end is Supervisor Sawara of the Talento Section.
Mr. Sawa-ra... has a head-ache?
You under-stand, don't you?!
A head-ache, in a way.

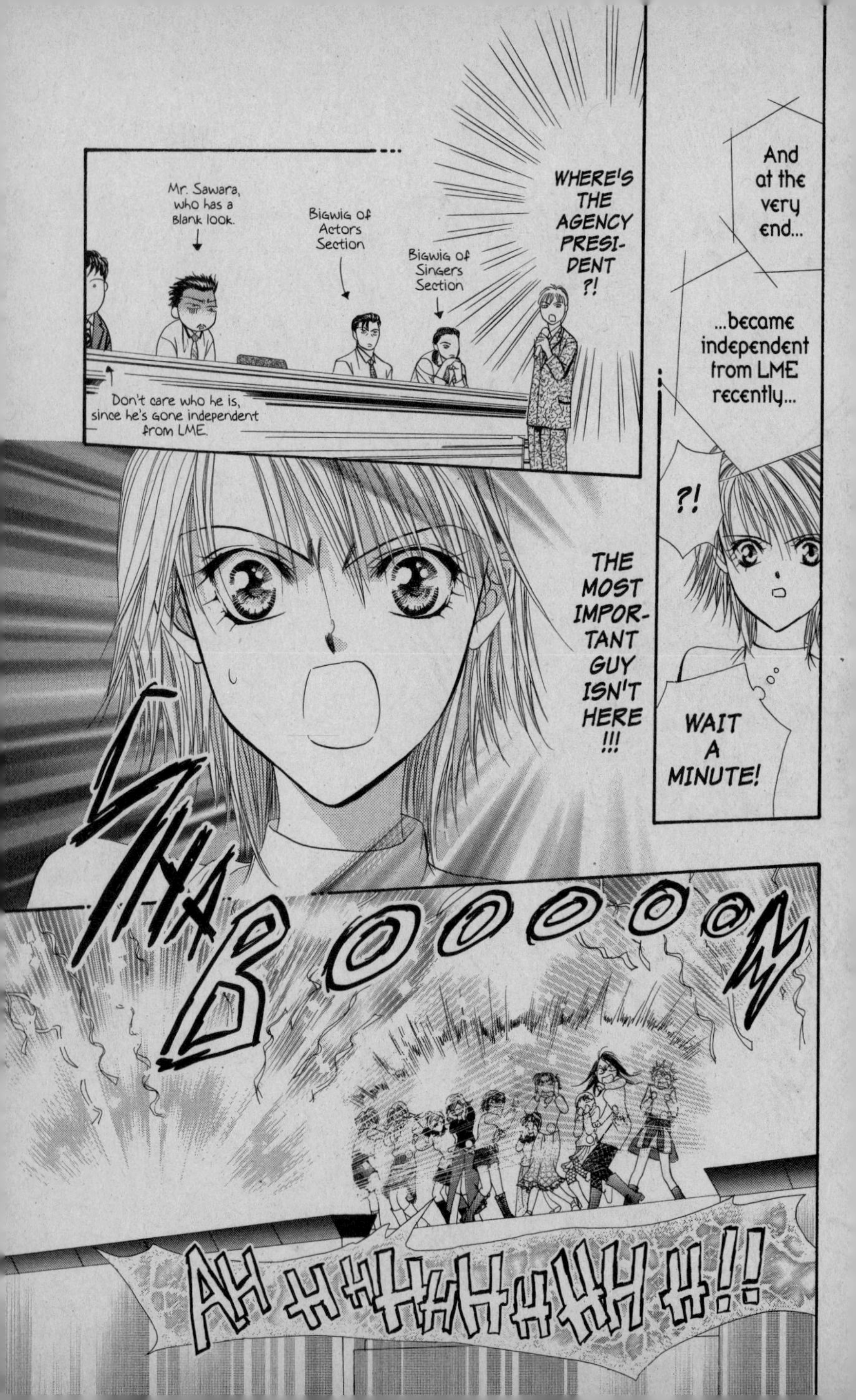
And at the very end...
...became independent from LME recently...
?!
WAIT A MINUTE!
WHERE'S THE AGENCY PRESIDENT ?!
Bigwig of Singers Section
Bigwig of Actors Section
Mr. Sawara, who has a blank look.
Don't care who he is, since he's gone independent from LME.
THE MOST IMPORTANT GUY ISN'T HERE !!!
SHABOOOOOM
AHHHHHHHHHH!!

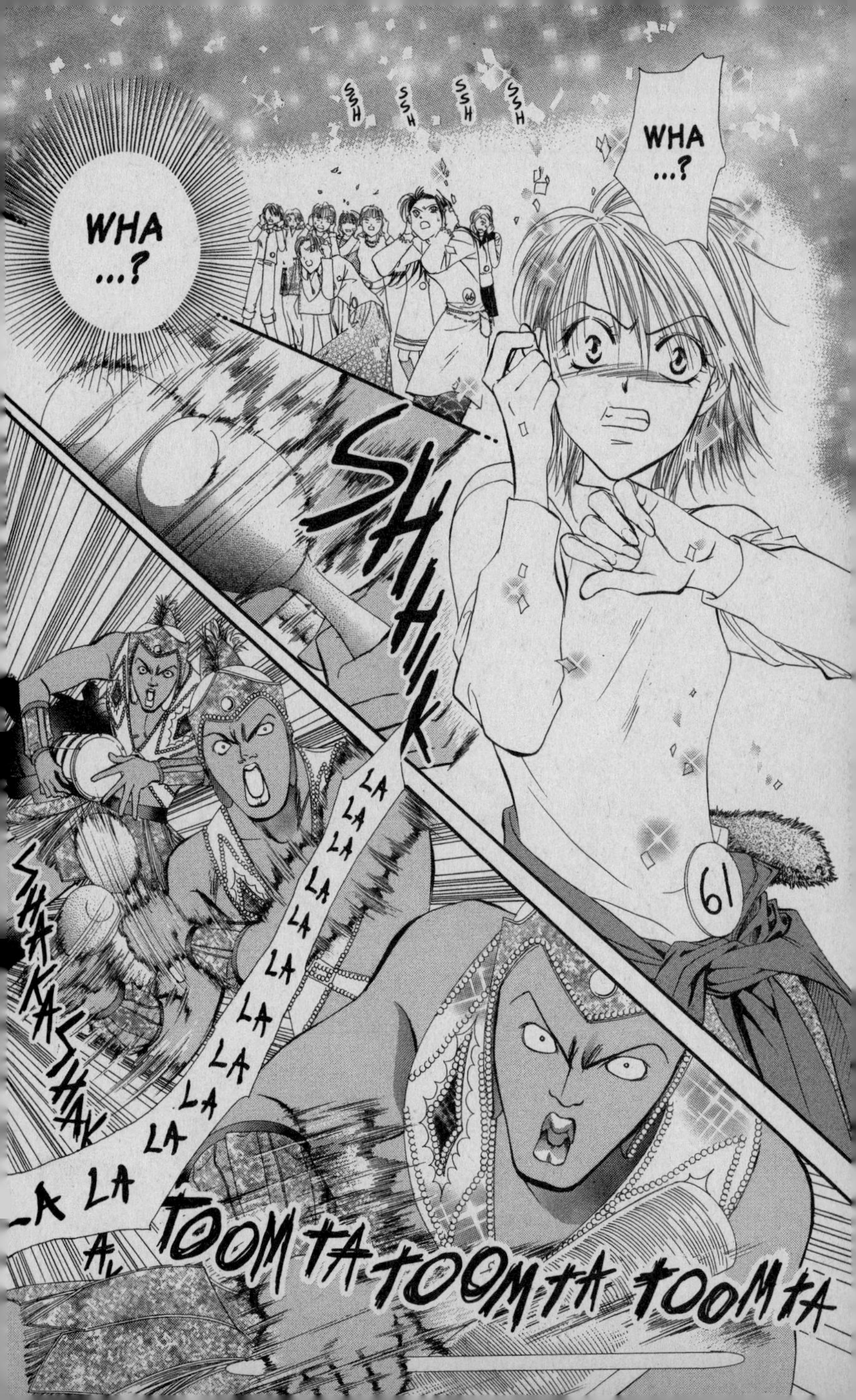
WHA ...?
SSH SSH SSH SSH
WHA ...?
SHHIK
LA LA LA LA LA LA LA LA LA LA LA LA LA LA LA LA -A A
SHAKA SHAKA
TOOM TA TOOM TA TOOM TA

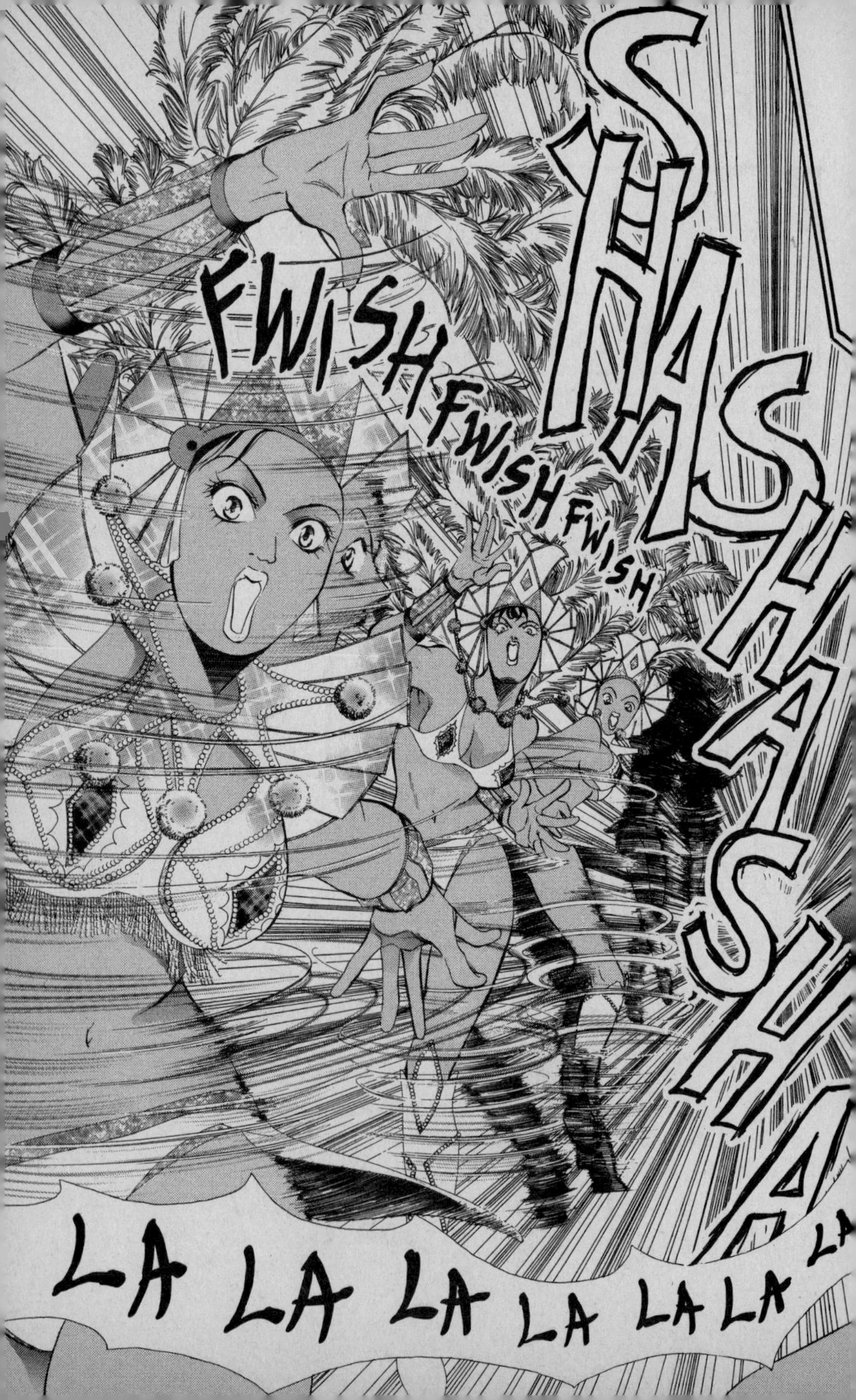
SHASHASHASHA
FWISH FWISH FWISH FWISH
LA LA LA LA LA LA LA

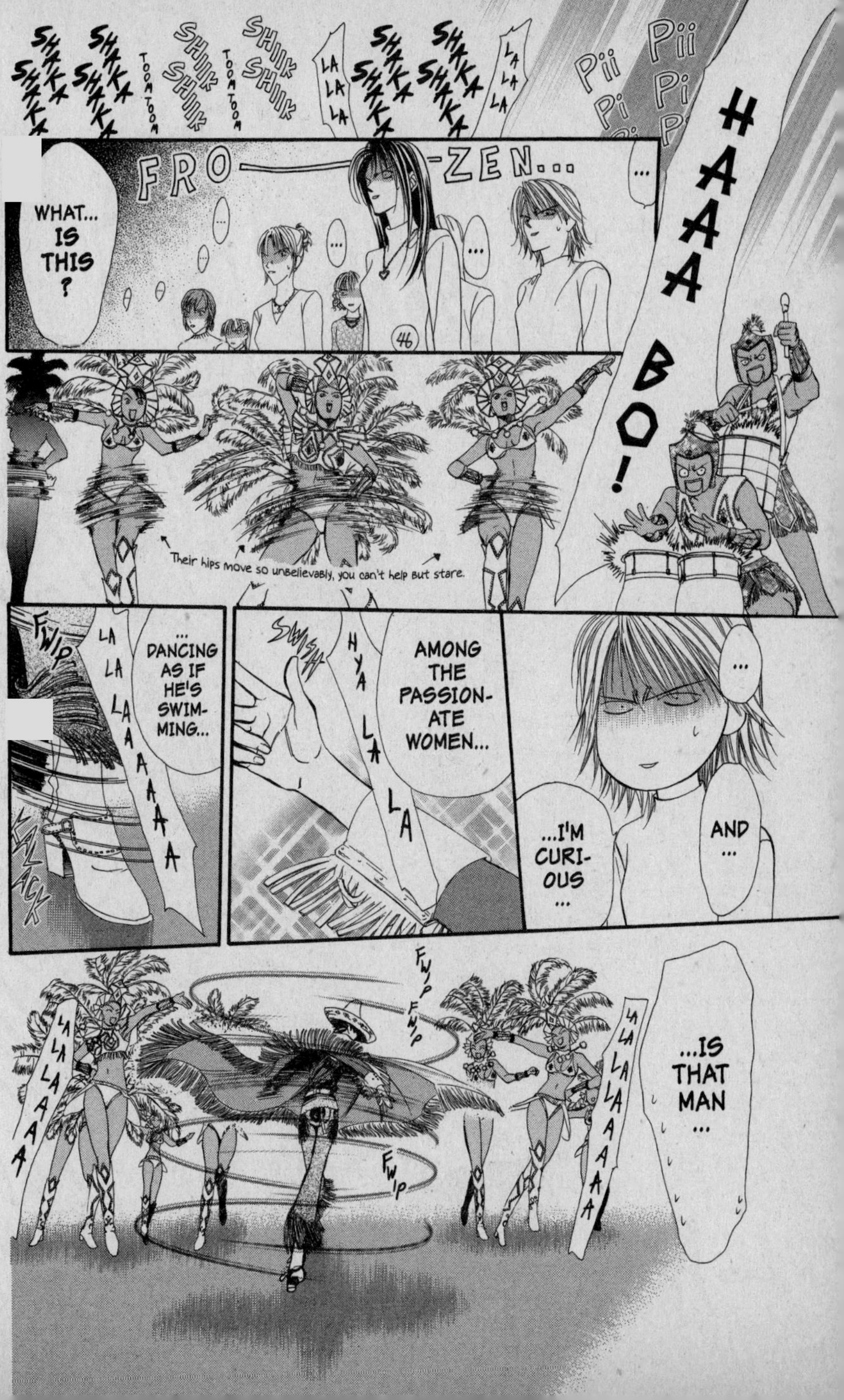
Pii Pi Pi
Pii Pi Pi
LA LA LA
SHAKA SHAKA
SHAKA SHAKA
LA LA LA
SHIIK SHIIK
TOOM TOOM
SHIIK SHIIK
TOOM TOOM
SHAKA SHAKA
SHAKA SHAKA
HAAAA BO!
...
FRO—ZEN...
...
...
...
WHAT... IS THIS?
Their hips move so unbelievably, you can't help but stare.
...
AND...
...I'M CURIOUS...
AMONG THE PASSION-ATE WOMEN...
HYA LA LA
SWISH
...DANCING AS IF HE'S SWIMMING...
LA LA LAAAAAAA
FWIP
KALACK
...IS THAT MAN...
LA LA LA LA LAAAAA
FWIP FWIP
FWIP
LA LA LA LAAAA

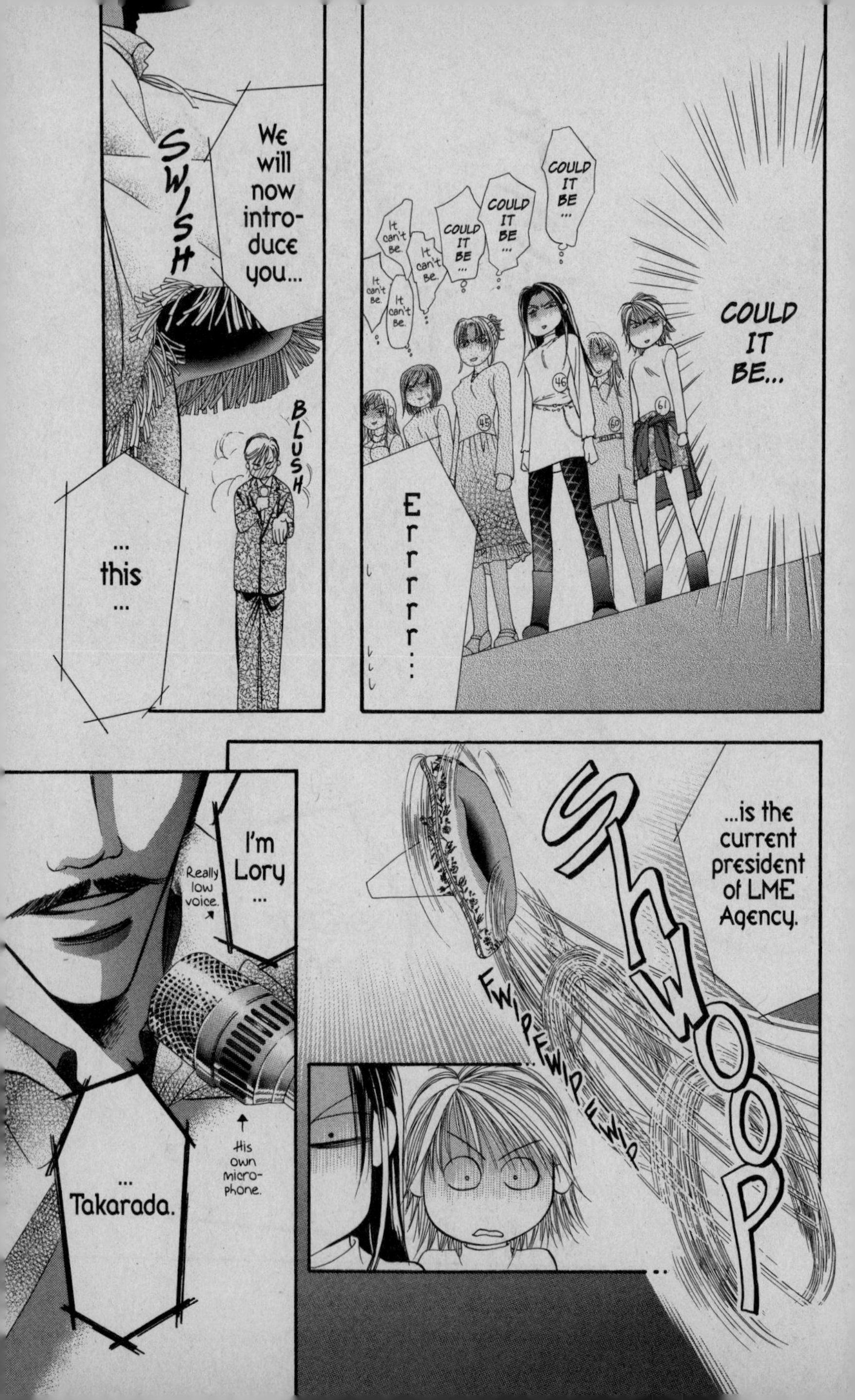
COULD IT BE...
COULD IT BE...
COULD IT BE...
COULD IT BE...
It can't Be.
It can't Be.
It can't Be.
It can't Be.
Errrrr...
SWISH
We will now introduce you...
BLUSH
...this...
...is the current president of LME Agency.
SHWOOP
FWIP FWIP FWIP FWIP...
...
I'm Lory...
Really low voice.
His own microphone.
...Takarada.

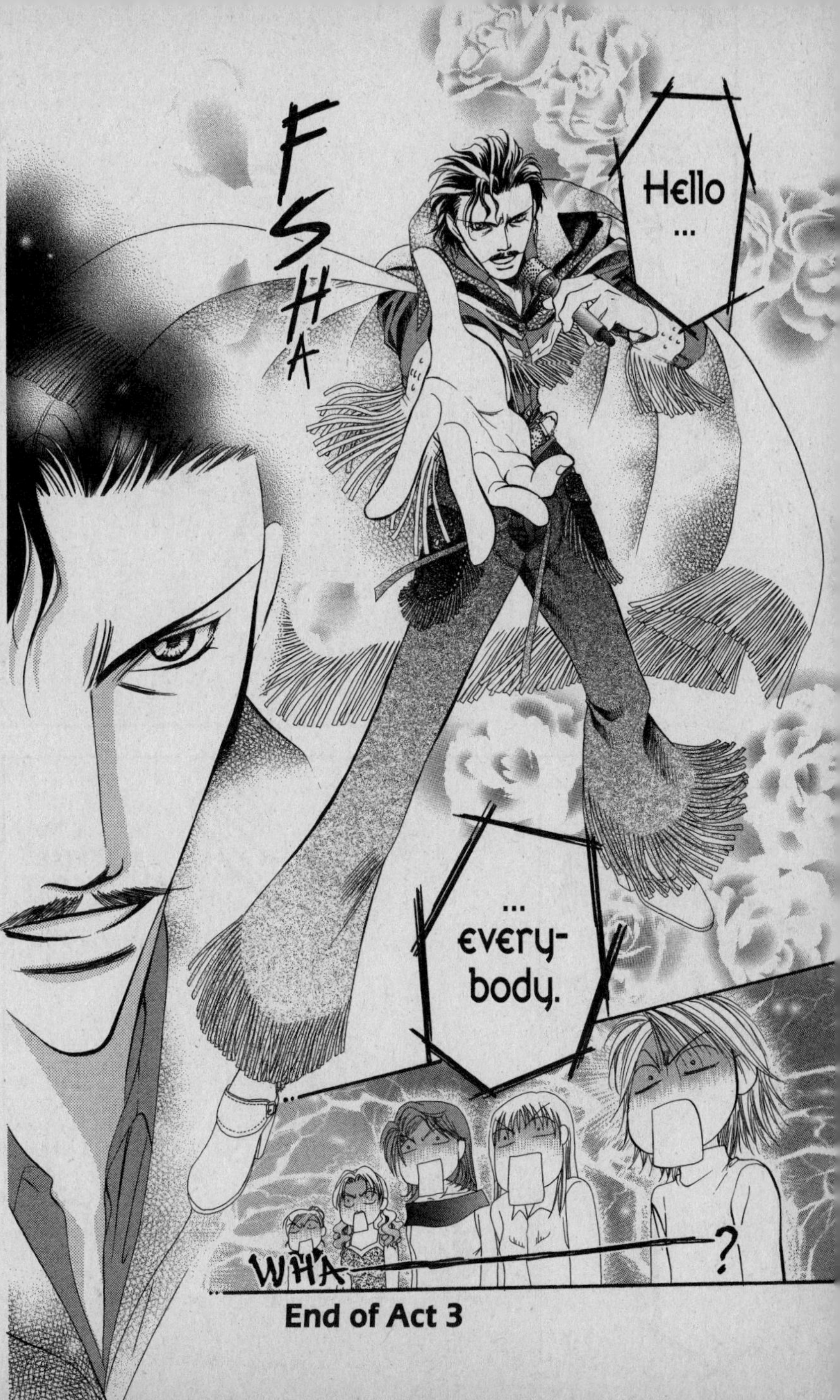
Hello ...
FSHA
... every-body.
...
WHA?

End of Act 3

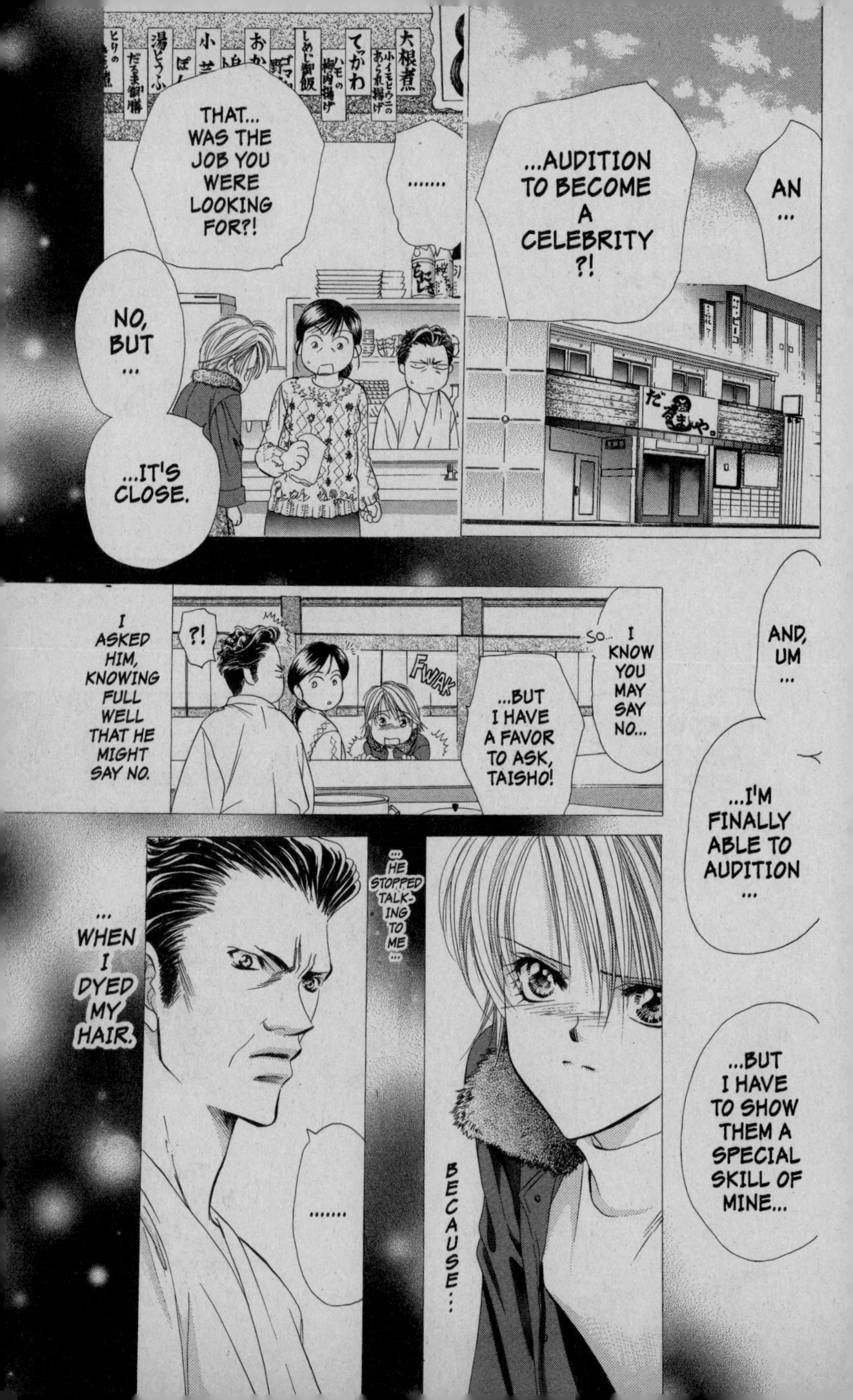
AN...
...AUDITION TO BECOME A CELEBRITY?!
だるまや
大根煮
小イモとウニのあられ揚げ
てっかわ
ハモの梅肉揚げ
しめじ御飯
湯どうふ
だるま御膳
....
THAT... WAS THE JOB YOU WERE LOOKING FOR?!
NO, BUT...
...IT'S CLOSE.
AND, UM...
SO... I KNOW YOU MAY SAY NO...
...BUT I HAVE A FAVOR TO ASK, TAISHO!
FWAK
?!
I ASKED HIM, KNOWING FULL WELL THAT HE MIGHT SAY NO.
...I'M FINALLY ABLE TO AUDITION...
...BUT I HAVE TO SHOW THEM A SPECIAL SKILL OF MINE...
BECAUSE...
...HE STOPPED TALKING TO ME...
...WHEN I DYED MY HAIR.
....

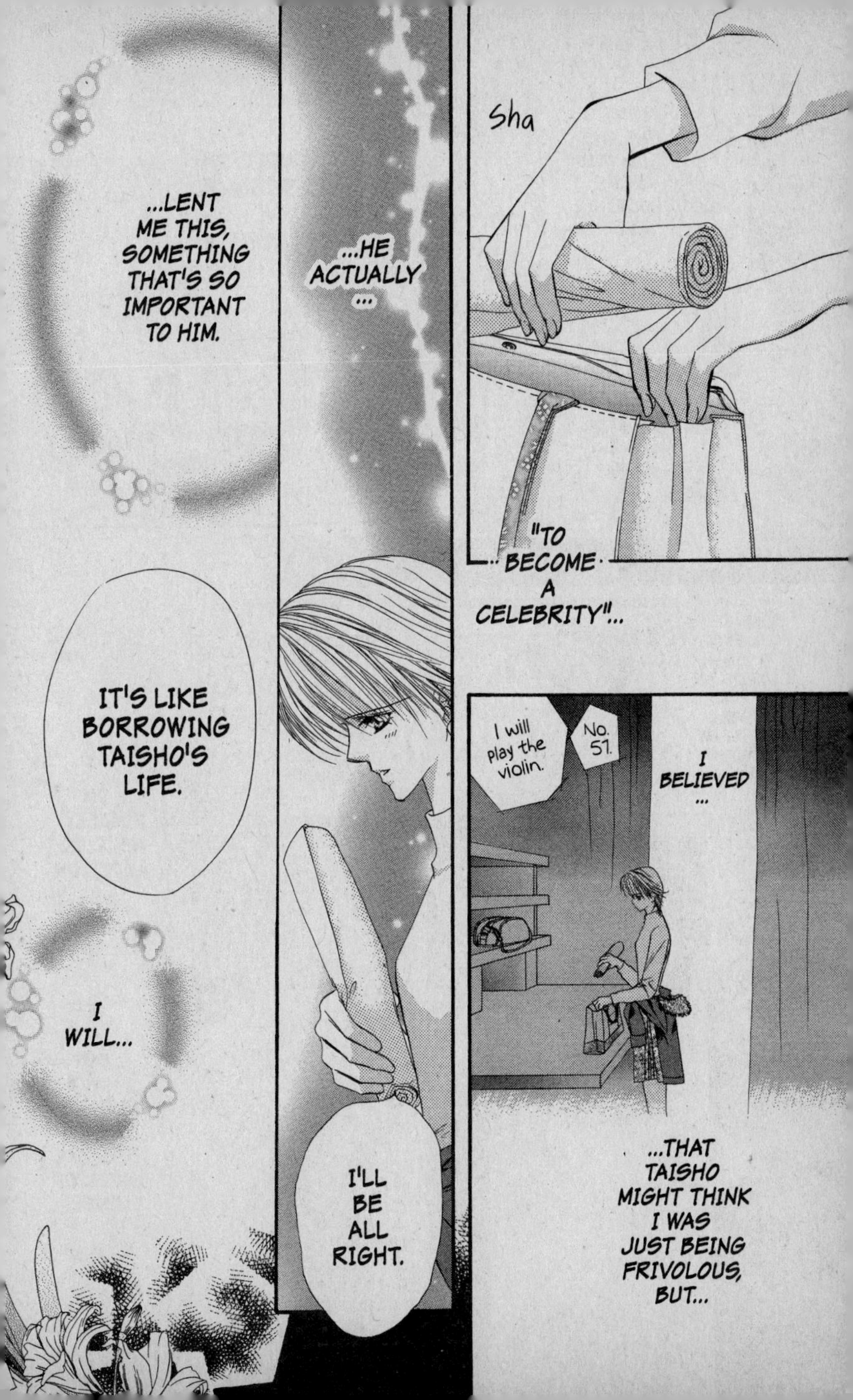
Sha
"TO BECOME A CELEBRITY"...
No. 51.
I will play the violin.
I BELIEVED...
...THAT TAISHO MIGHT THINK I WAS JUST BEING FRIVOLOUS, BUT...
...HE ACTUALLY...
I'LL BE ALL RIGHT.
...LENT ME THIS, SOMETHING THAT'S SO IMPORTANT TO HIM.
IT'S LIKE BORROWING TAISHO'S LIFE.
I WILL...

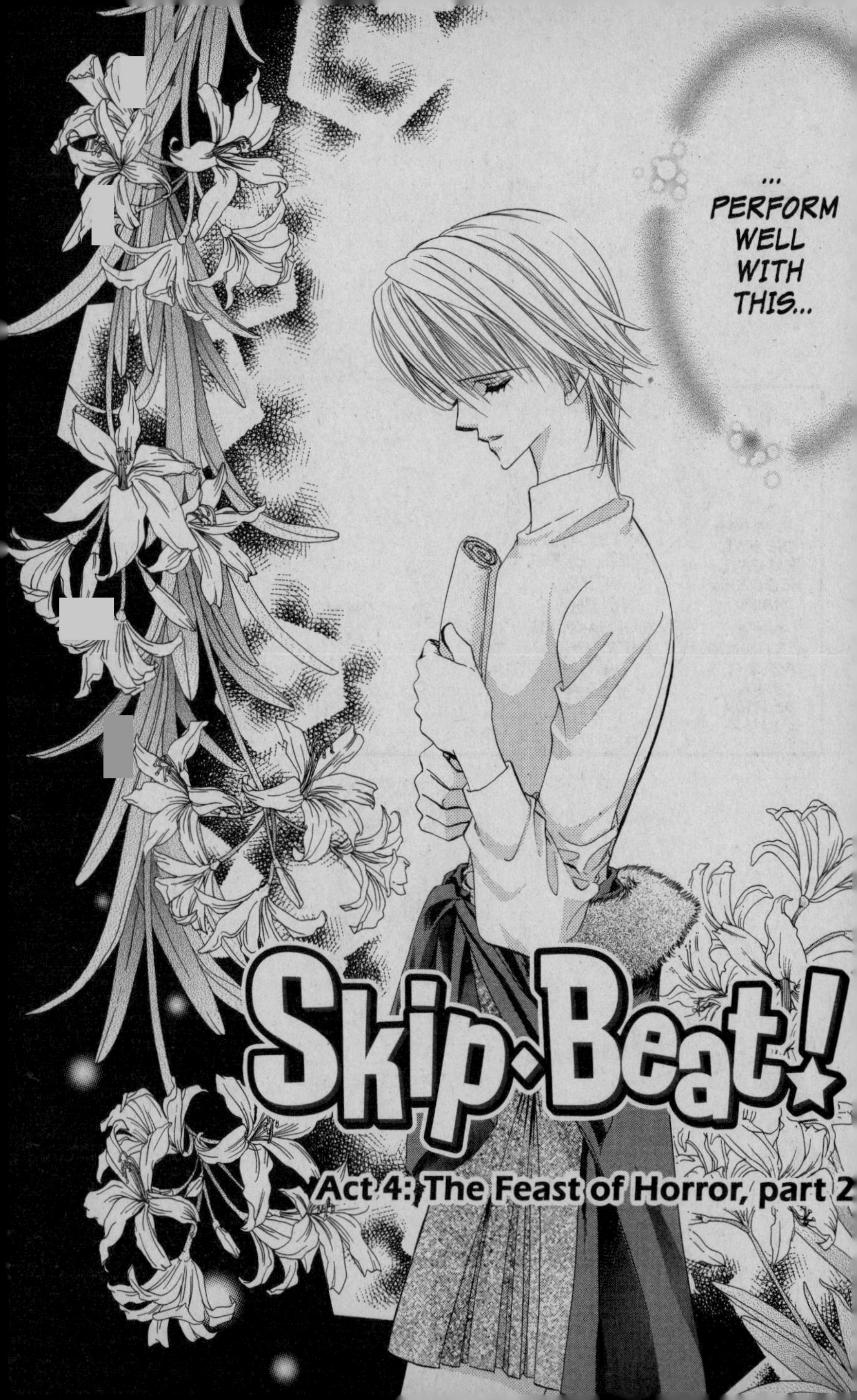
... PERFORM WELL WITH THIS...
Skip·Beat!
Act 4: The Feast of Horror, part 2

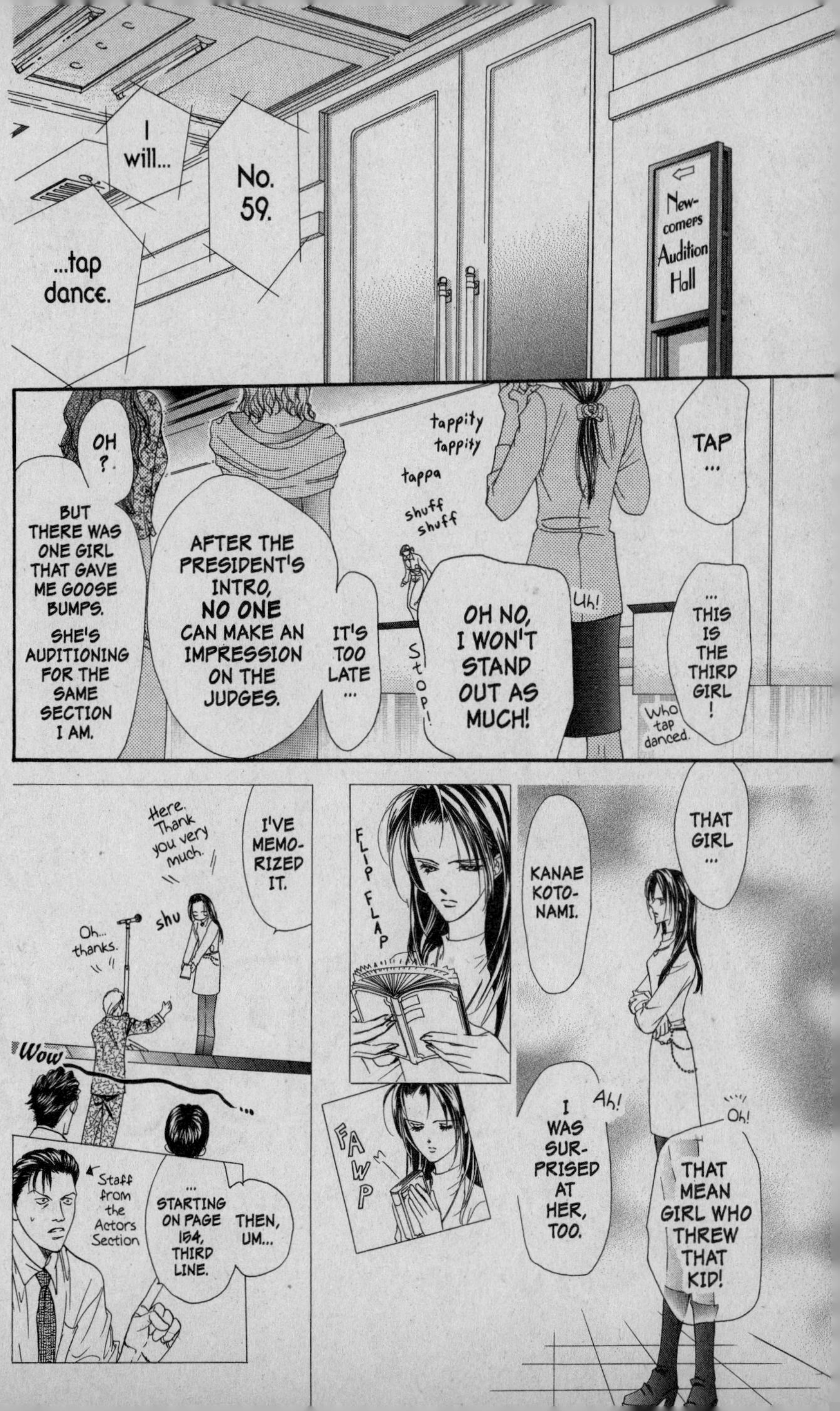
Newcomers Audition Hall
No. 59.
I will...
...tap dance.
TAP...
...THIS IS THE THIRD GIRL!
Who tap danced.
Uh!
OH NO, I WON'T STAND OUT AS MUCH!
STOP!
tappity tappity
tappa
shuff shuff
IT'S TOO LATE...
AFTER THE PRESIDENT'S INTRO, NO ONE CAN MAKE AN IMPRESSION ON THE JUDGES.
OH?
BUT THERE WAS ONE GIRL THAT GAVE ME GOOSE BUMPS.
SHE'S AUDITIONING FOR THE SAME SECTION I AM.
THAT GIRL...
Oh!
THAT MEAN GIRL WHO THREW THAT KID!
KANAE KOTONAMI.
Ah!
I WAS SURPRISED AT HER, TOO.
FLIP FLAP
FAWP
I'VE MEMORIZED IT.
Here. Thank you very much.
shu
Oh... thanks.
Wow...
THEN, UM...
...STARTING ON PAGE 154, THIRD LINE.
Staff from the Actors Section

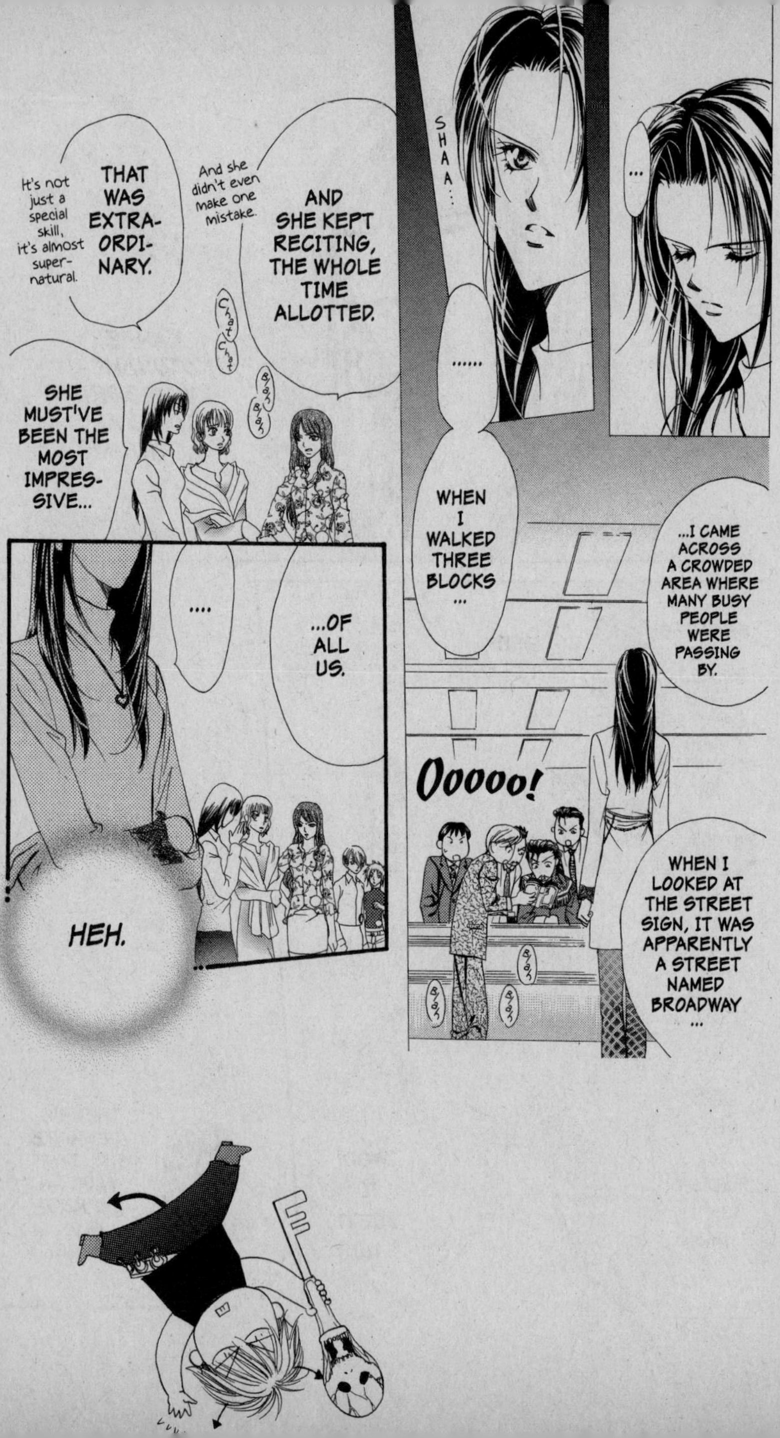
...
SHAA...
......
WHEN I WALKED THREE BLOCKS...
...I CAME ACROSS A CROWDED AREA WHERE MANY BUSY PEOPLE WERE PASSING BY.
Ooooo!
Blah Blah Blah
WHEN I LOOKED AT THE STREET SIGN, IT WAS APPARENTLY A STREET NAMED BROADWAY...
AND SHE KEPT RECITING, THE WHOLE TIME ALLOTTED.
And she didn't even make one mistake.
THAT WAS EXTRA-ORDINARY.
It's not just a special skill, it's almost super-natural.
Chat Chat
Blah Blah
SHE MUST'VE BEEN THE MOST IMPRES-SIVE...
...OF ALL US.
....
HEH.

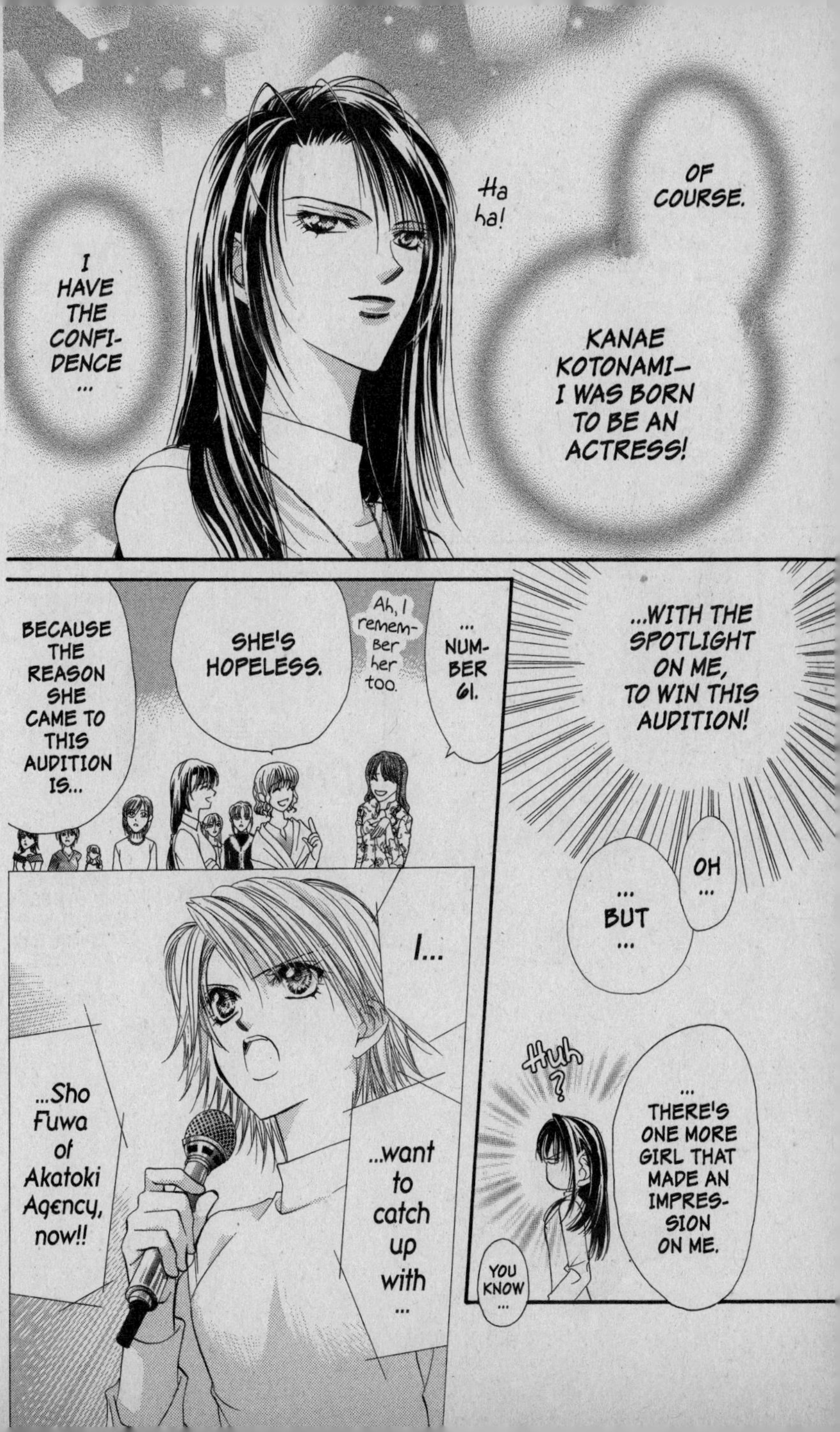
OF COURSE.
Ha ha!
KANAE KOTONAMI— I WAS BORN TO BE AN ACTRESS!
I HAVE THE CONFIDENCE...
...WITH THE SPOTLIGHT ON ME, TO WIN THIS AUDITION!
OH...
...BUT...
Huh?
...THERE'S ONE MORE GIRL THAT MADE AN IMPRESSION ON ME.
YOU KNOW...
...NUMBER 61.
Ah, I remember her too.
SHE'S HOPELESS.
BECAUSE THE REASON SHE CAME TO THIS AUDITION IS...
I...
...want to catch up with...
...Sho Fuwa of Akatoki Agency, now!!

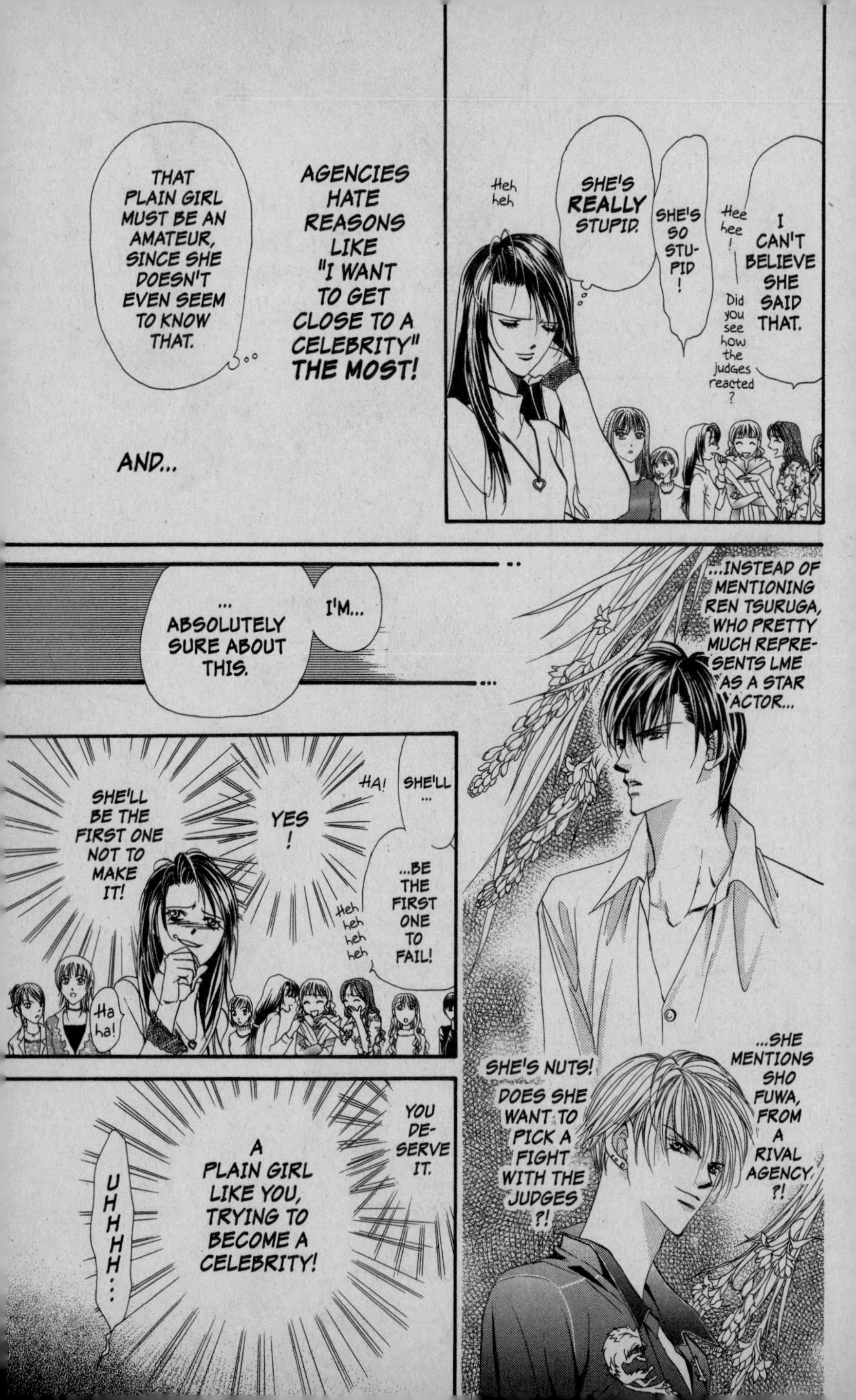
I CAN'T BELIEVE SHE SAID THAT.
Hee hee! Did you see how the judges reacted?
SHE'S SO STUPID!
SHE'S REALLY STUPID.
Heh heh
AGENCIES HATE REASONS LIKE "I WANT TO GET CLOSE TO A CELEBRITY" THE MOST!
THAT PLAIN GIRL MUST BE AN AMATEUR, SINCE SHE DOESN'T EVEN SEEM TO KNOW THAT.
AND...
...INSTEAD OF MENTIONING REN TSURUGA, WHO PRETTY MUCH REPRESENTS LME AS A STAR ACTOR...
...SHE MENTIONS SHO FUWA, FROM A RIVAL AGENCY?!
SHE'S NUTS! DOES SHE WANT TO PICK A FIGHT WITH THE JUDGES?!
I'M...
...ABSOLUTELY SURE ABOUT THIS.
SHE'LL...
HA!
...BE THE FIRST ONE TO FAIL!
Heh heh heh heh
YES!
SHE'LL BE THE FIRST ONE NOT TO MAKE IT!
Ha ha!
YOU DESERVE IT.
A PLAIN GIRL LIKE YOU, TRYING TO BECOME A CELEBRITY!
UHHHH...

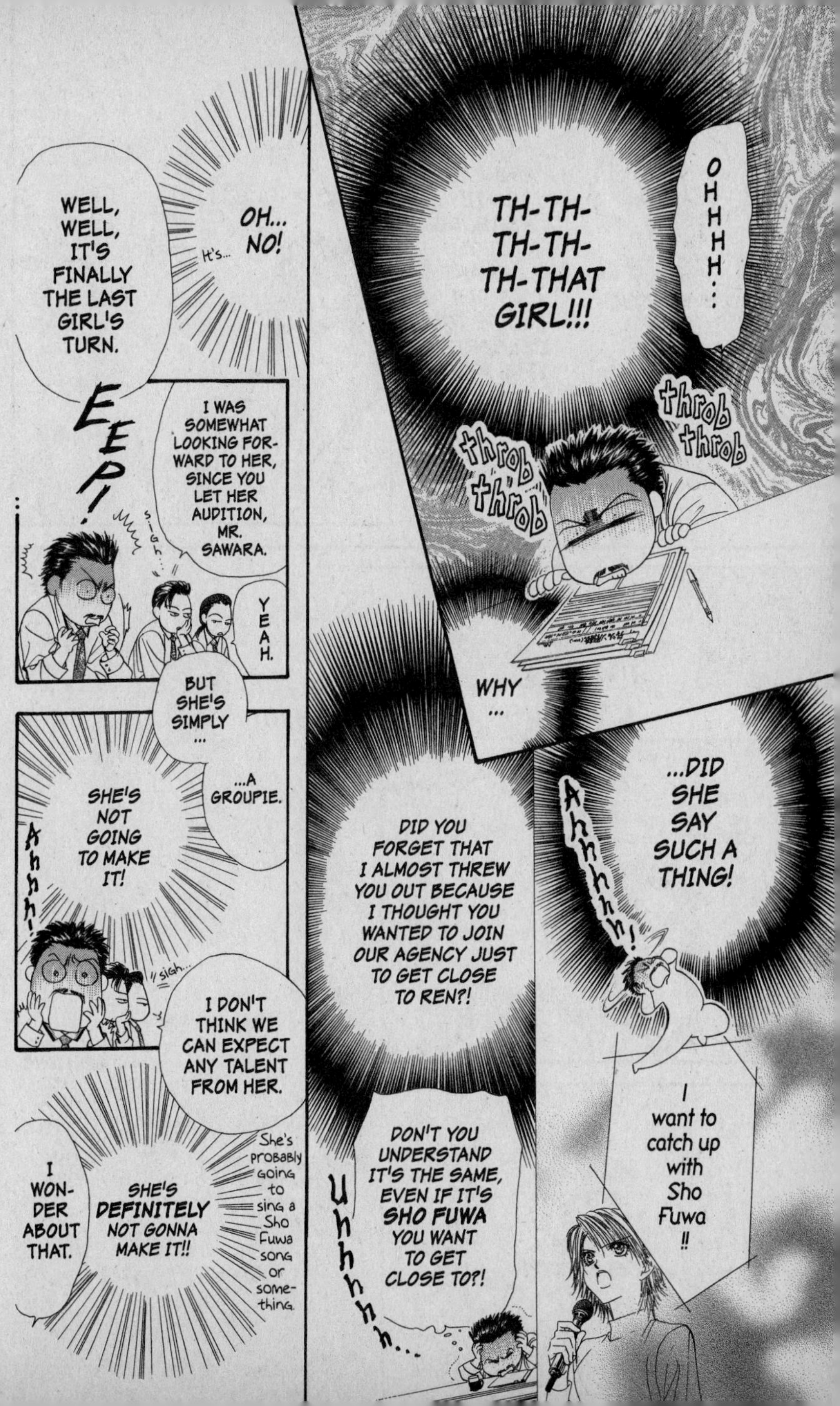
OHHHH...
TH-TH-TH-TH-TH-THAT GIRL!!!
throb throb
throb throb
WHY...
...DID SHE SAY SUCH A THING!
Ahhhhhh!
I want to catch up with Sho Fuwa!!
DID YOU FORGET THAT I ALMOST THREW YOU OUT BECAUSE I THOUGHT YOU WANTED TO JOIN OUR AGENCY JUST TO GET CLOSE TO REN?!
DON'T YOU UNDERSTAND IT'S THE SAME, EVEN IF IT'S **SHO FUWA** YOU WANT TO GET CLOSE TO?!
Uhhhhhh...
It's...
OH... NO!
WELL, WELL, IT'S FINALLY THE LAST GIRL'S TURN.
EEP!
I WAS SOMEWHAT LOOKING FORWARD TO HER, SINCE YOU LET HER AUDITION, MR. SAWARA.
sigh...
YEAH.
BUT SHE'S SIMPLY...
...A GROUPIE.
SHE'S NOT GOING TO MAKE IT!
Ahhh!
sigh...
I DON'T THINK WE CAN EXPECT ANY TALENT FROM HER.
She's probably going to sing a Sho Fuwa song or something.
SHE'S **DEFINITELY** NOT GONNA MAKE IT!!
I WONDER ABOUT THAT.

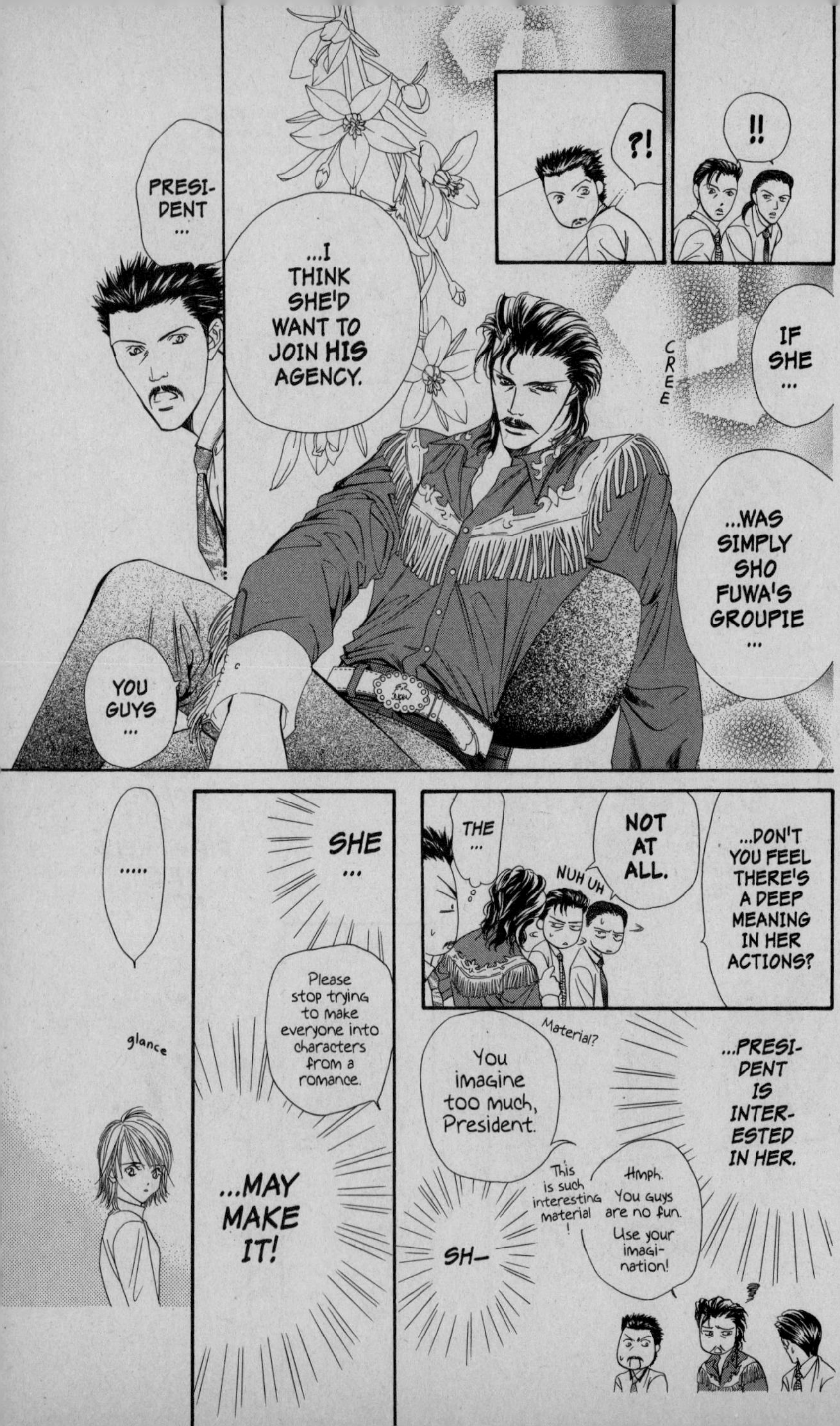

!!
?!
IF SHE...
...WAS SIMPLY SHO FUWA'S GROUPIE...
CREE
...I THINK SHE'D WANT TO JOIN HIS AGENCY.
PRESI-DENT...
YOU GUYS...
...DON'T YOU FEEL THERE'S A DEEP MEANING IN HER ACTIONS?
NOT AT ALL.
NUH UH
THE...
...PRESI-DENT IS INTER-ESTED IN HER.
Material?
You imagine too much, President.
Hmph. You guys are no fun. Use your imagi-nation!
This is such interesting material!
SH—
SHE...
Please stop trying to make everyone into characters from a romance.
...MAY MAKE IT!
.....
glance

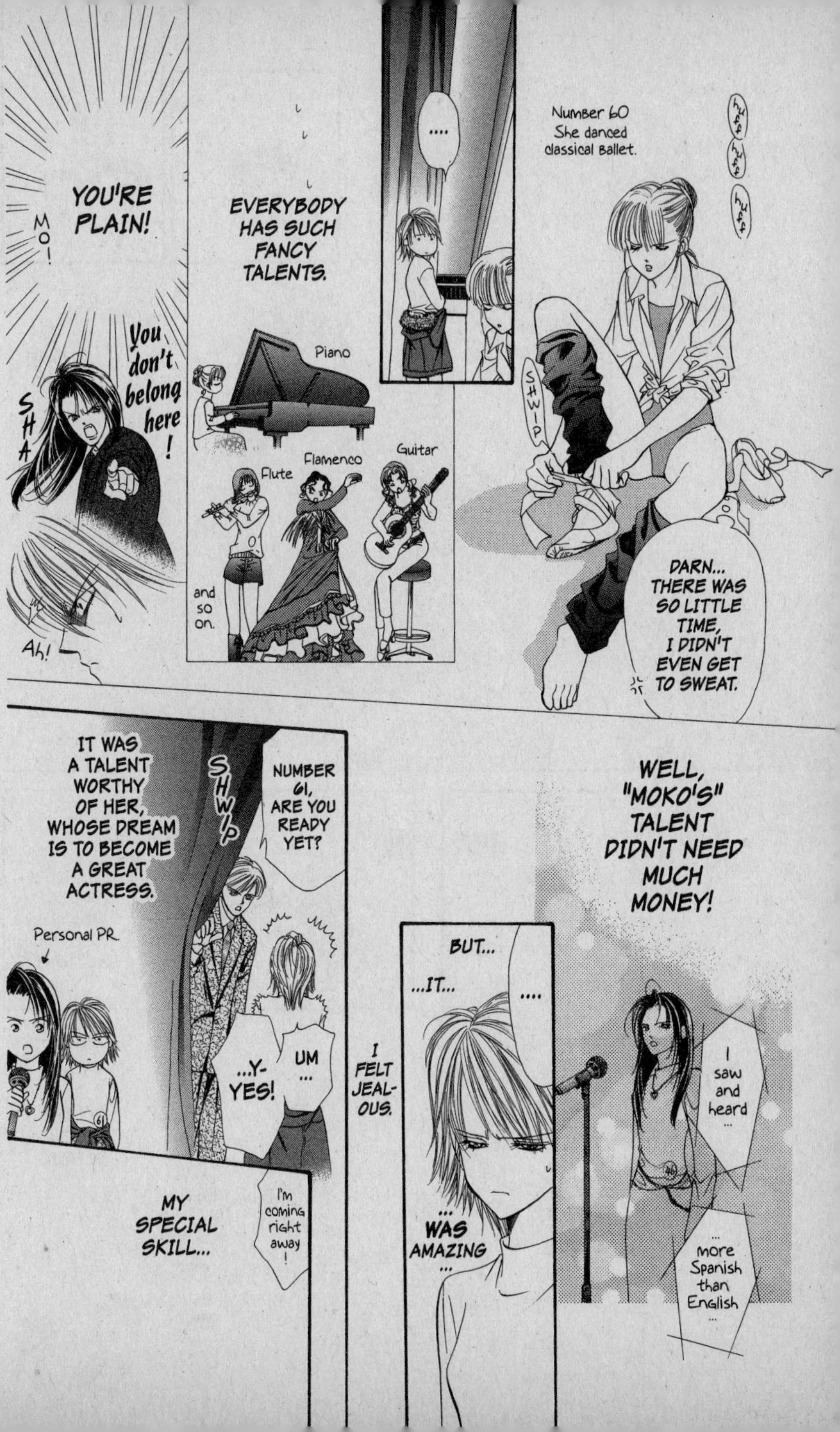
Number 60 She danced classical Ballet.
huff huff huff
SHWIP
DARN... THERE WAS SO LITTLE TIME, I DIDN'T EVEN GET TO SWEAT.
....
EVERYBODY HAS SUCH FANCY TALENTS.
Piano
Guitar
Flamenco
Flute
and so on.
YOU'RE PLAIN!
MO!
You don't belong here!
SHA
Ah!
WELL, "MOKO'S" TALENT DIDN'T NEED MUCH MONEY!
I saw and heard ...
... more Spanish than English ...
BUT...
....
...IT...
... WAS AMAZING ...
I FELT JEAL-OUS.
NUMBER 61, ARE YOU READY YET?
SHWIP
IT WAS A TALENT WORTHY OF HER, WHOSE DREAM IS TO BECOME A GREAT ACTRESS.
UM ...
...Y-YES!
Personal PR.
I'm coming right away!
MY SPECIAL SKILL...

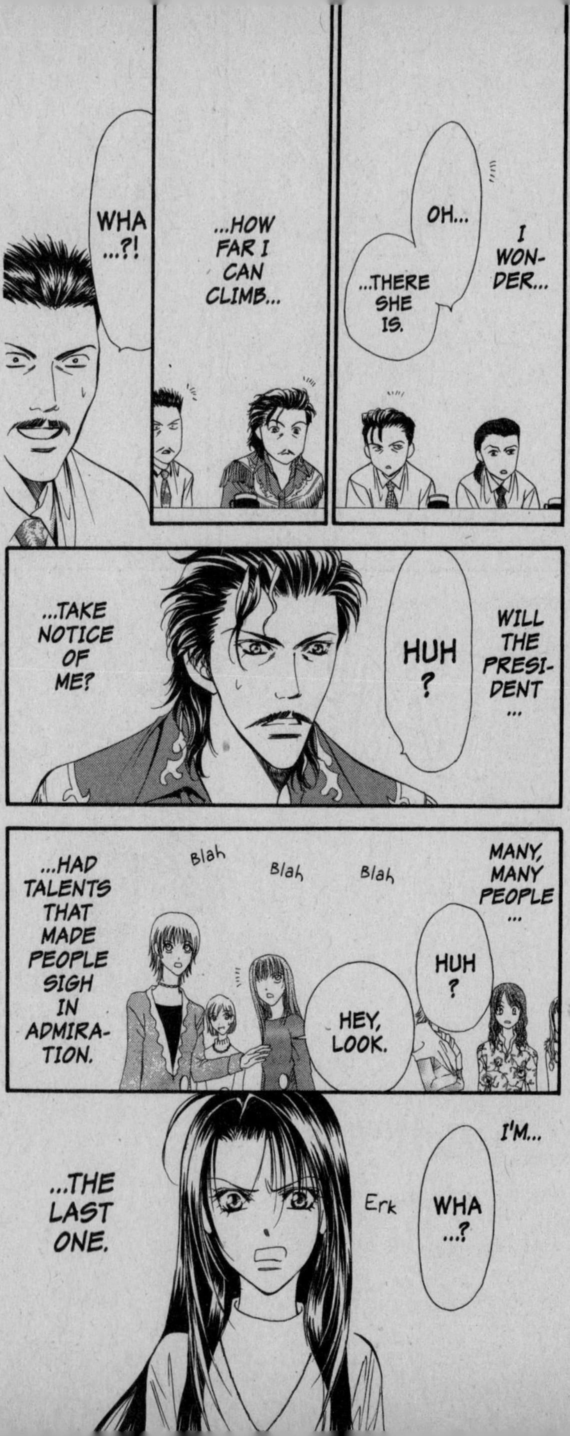
I WONDER...
OH...
...THERE SHE IS.
...HOW FAR I CAN CLIMB...
WHA...?!
WILL THE PRESIDENT...
HUH?
...TAKE NOTICE OF ME?
MANY, MANY PEOPLE...
HUH?
HEY, LOOK.
Blah
Blah
Blah
...HAD TALENTS THAT MADE PEOPLE SIGH IN ADMIRATION.
I'M...
WHA...?
Erk
...THE LAST ONE.

6

...wouldn't be into, but I can't hate him. I don't dislike him. With Ren, I haven't been able to put forward a firm personality for him, so he's out... Those were the things I was thinking, when the editor answered for me.

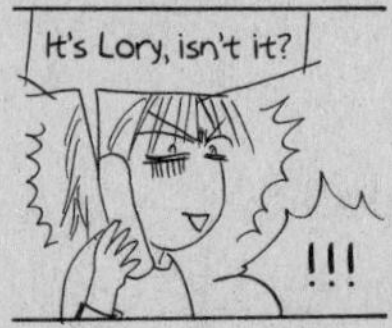
It's Lory, isn't it?
!!!

Well, in Act 3, although my schedule was tight, I drew his appearance in great detail, and I did enjoy it a bit. I enjoyed him in Act 4. And in Act 5, towards the very end, although he only appears in three panels, I stopped my hands and pondered many minutes to decide his costume...but...I'd kept it a secret...I'd kept it a secret...!! I thought I'd kept it hidden that I secretly (?) love him!!! (I don't "love" characters I draw?! Geez... And...it's a middle-aged man again...!!) Oh dear (tears).

...It was embarrassingly obvious... Something's wrong. I had declared that I'd refrain from drawing middle-aged guys...

Continued on page 163

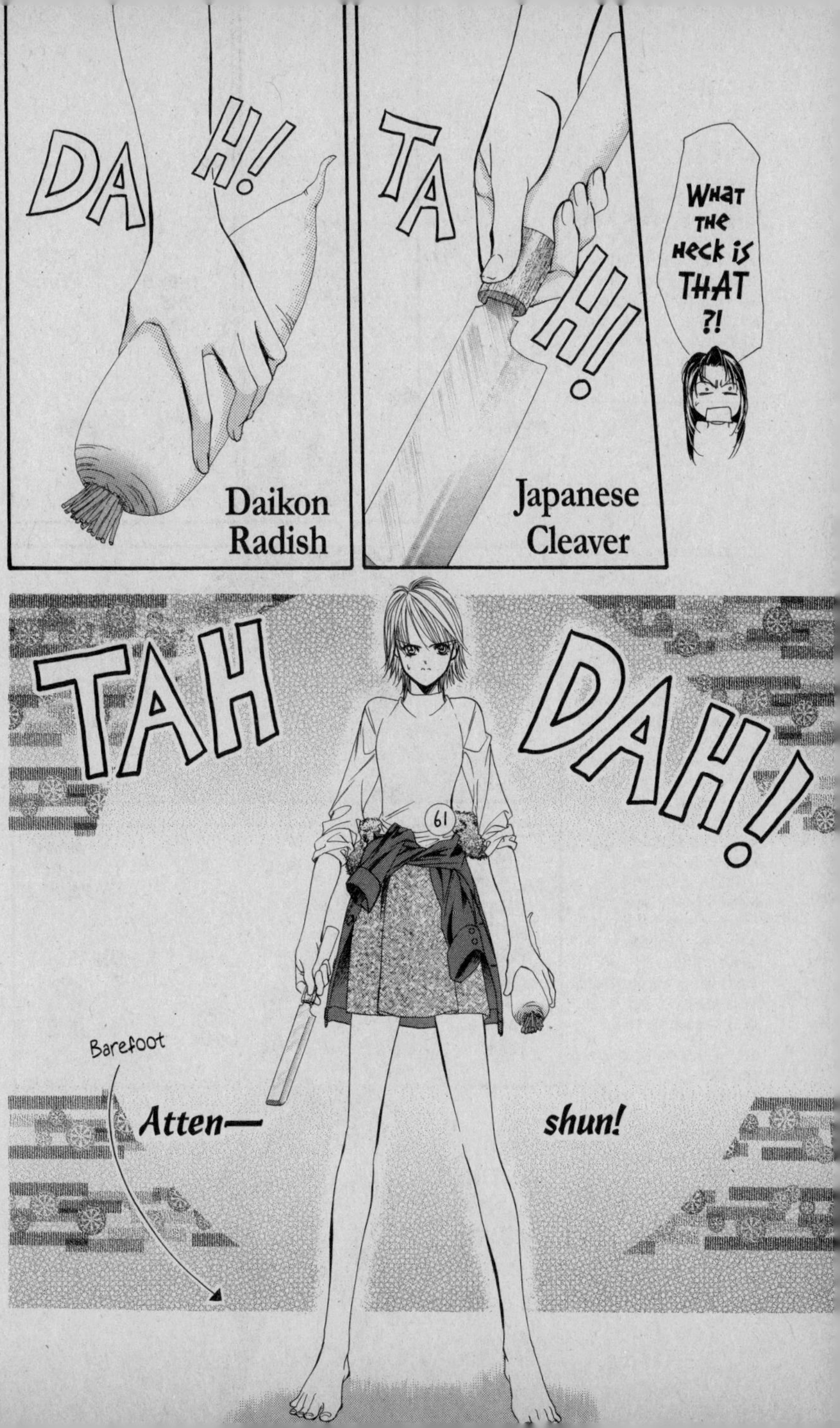
WHAT THE HECK IS THAT?!
TA H!
Japanese Cleaver
DA H!
Daikon Radish
TAH DAH!
61
Atten— shun!
Barefoot

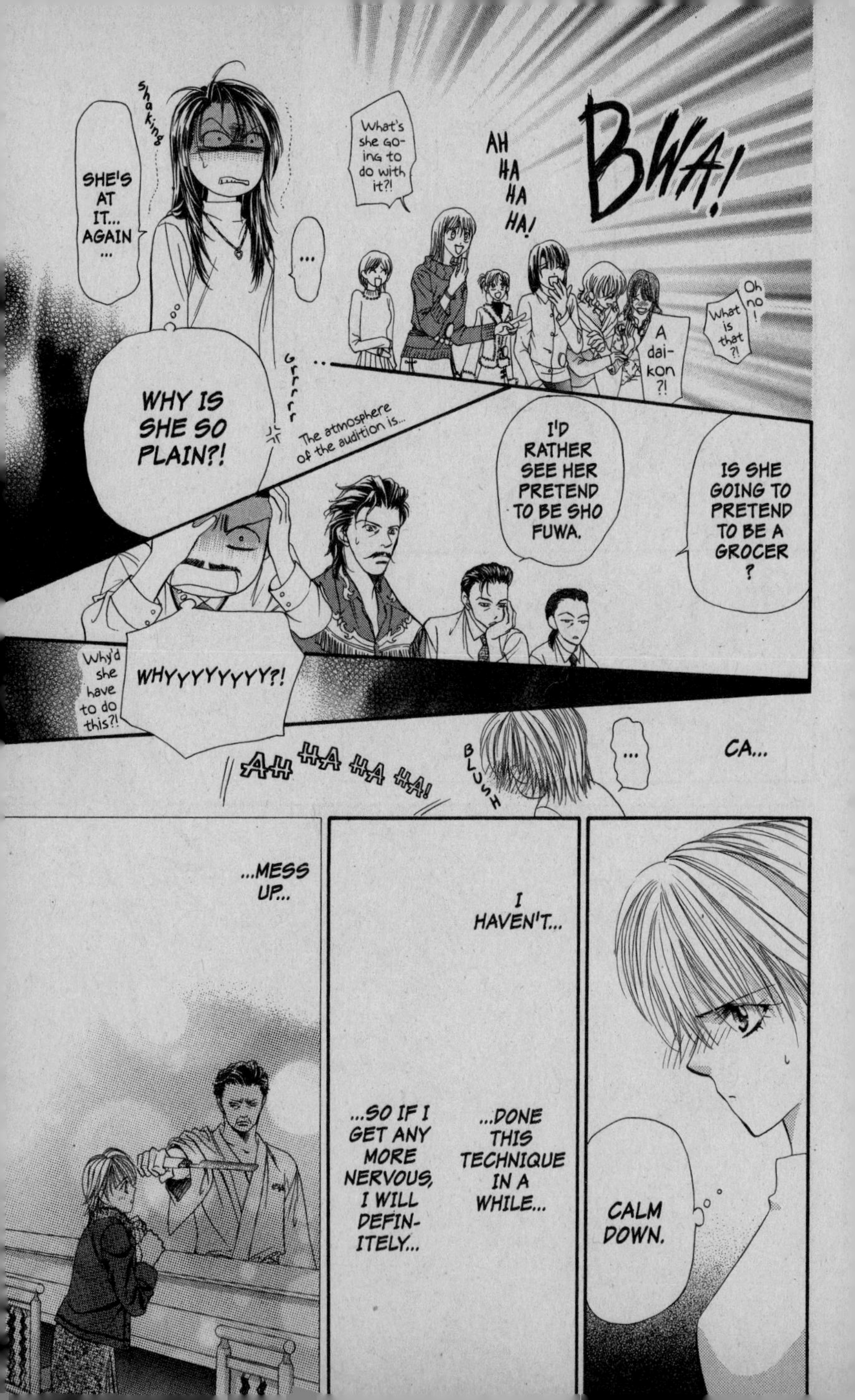
BWA!
Oh no!
What is that?!
A daikon?!
AH HA HA HA!
What's she going to do with it?!
...
Shaking
SHE'S AT IT... AGAIN...
WHY IS SHE SO PLAIN?!
Grrrr...
The atmosphere of the audition is...
IS SHE GOING TO PRETEND TO BE A GROCER?
I'D RATHER SEE HER PRETEND TO BE SHO FUWA.
WHYYYYYYYY?!
Why'd she have to do this?!
CA...
...
BLUSH
AH HA HA HA!
CALM DOWN.
I HAVEN'T...
...DONE THIS TECHNIQUE IN A WHILE...
...SO IF I GET ANY MORE NERVOUS, I WILL DEFINITELY...
...MESS UP...

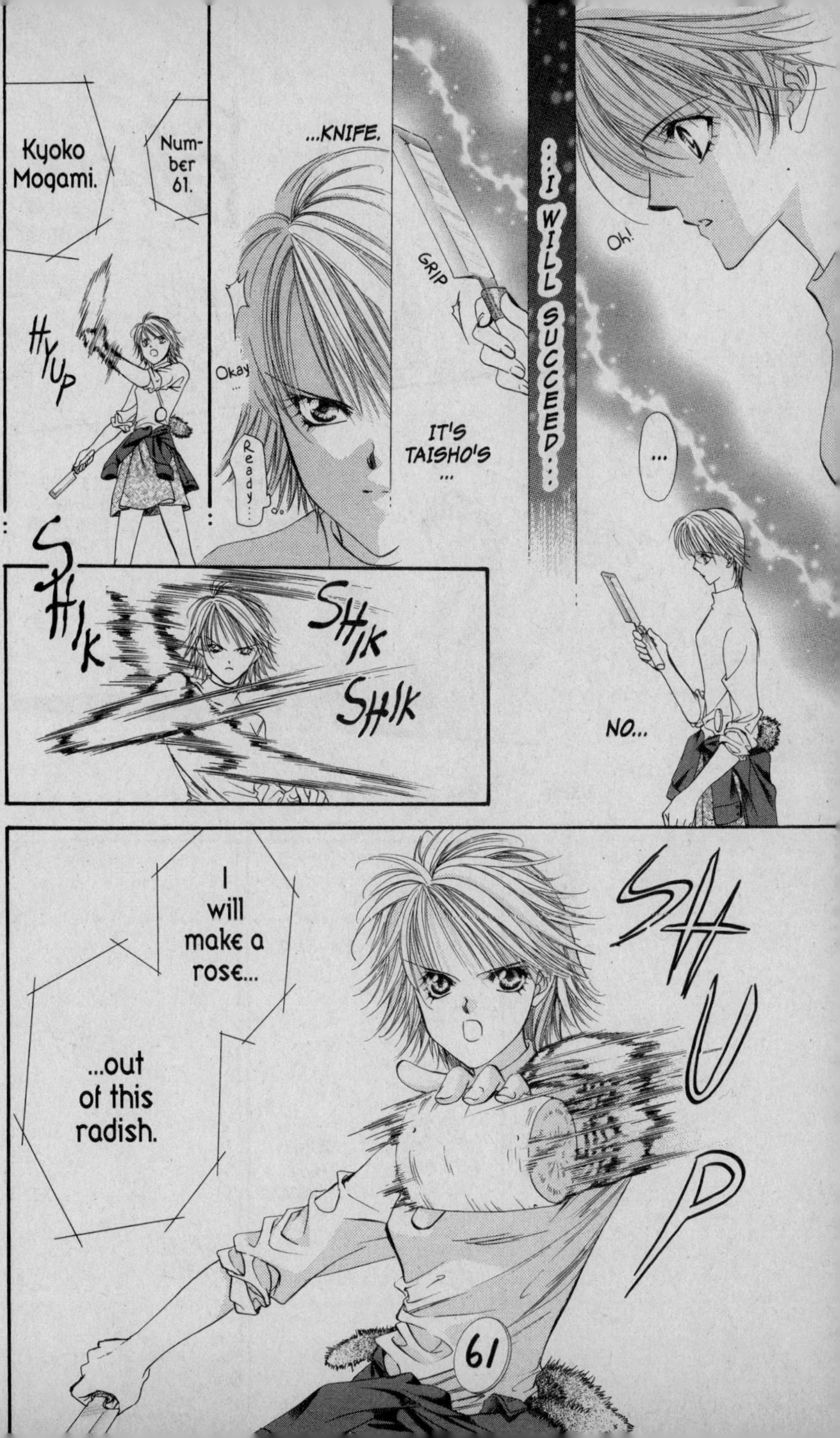
Oh!
...
NO...
...I WILL SUCCEED...
GRIP
IT'S TAISHO'S ...
...KNIFE.
Okay...
Ready...
Number 61.
Kyoko Mogami.
HYUP
SHIK
SHIK
SHIK
SHUP
I will make a rose...
...out of this radish.
61

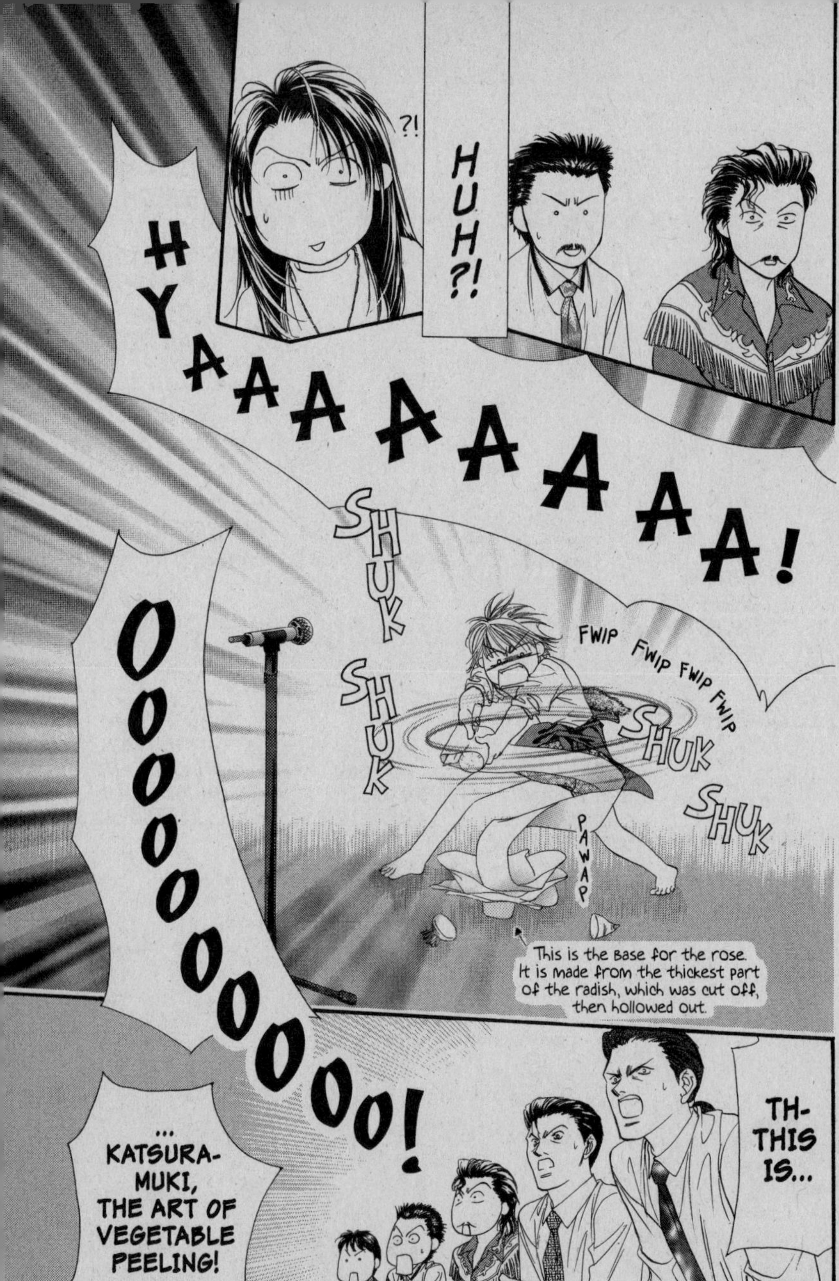
HUH?!
?!
HYAAAAAAAAAA!
SHUK SHUK
SHUK SHUK
FWIP FWIP FWIP FWIP
PAWAP
This is the base for the rose. It is made from the thickest part of the radish, which was cut off, then hollowed out.
OOOOOOOOOO!
TH-THIS IS...
...KATSURA-MUKI, THE ART OF VEGETABLE PEELING!

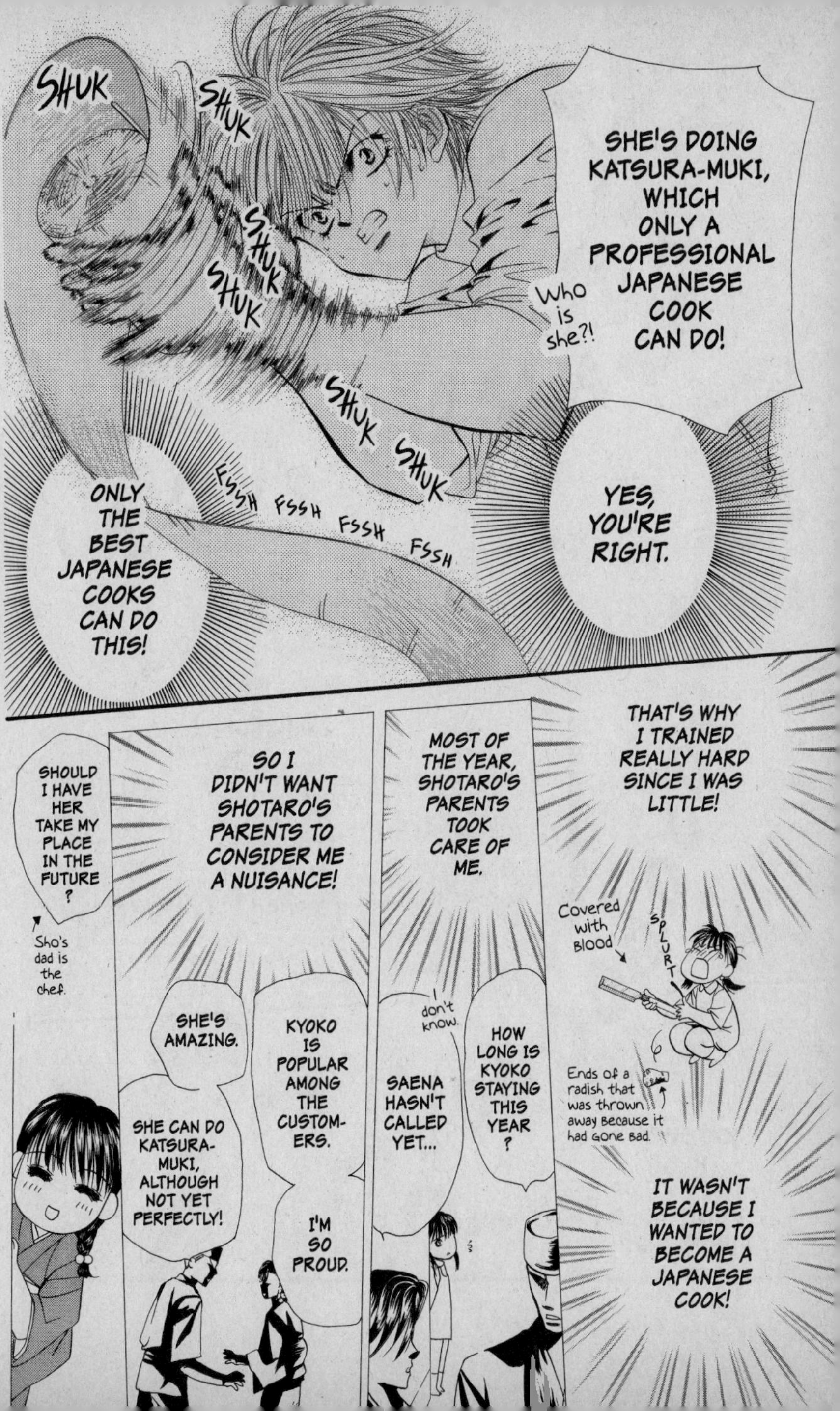
SHE'S DOING KATSURA-MUKI, WHICH ONLY A PROFESSIONAL JAPANESE COOK CAN DO!
Who is she?!
SHUK
SHUK
SHUK
SHUK
SHUK
SHUK
YES, YOU'RE RIGHT.
FSSH FSSH FSSH FSSH
ONLY THE BEST JAPANESE COOKS CAN DO THIS!
THAT'S WHY I TRAINED REALLY HARD SINCE I WAS LITTLE!
Covered with Blood
SPLURT
Ends of a radish that was thrown away Because it had Gone Bad.
IT WASN'T BECAUSE I WANTED TO BECOME A JAPANESE COOK!
MOST OF THE YEAR, SHOTARO'S PARENTS TOOK CARE OF ME.
HOW LONG IS KYOKO STAYING THIS YEAR?
I don't know.
SAENA HASN'T CALLED YET...
SO I DIDN'T WANT SHOTARO'S PARENTS TO CONSIDER ME A NUISANCE!
KYOKO IS POPULAR AMONG THE CUSTOMERS.
SHE'S AMAZING.
I'M SO PROUD.
SHE CAN DO KATSURA-MUKI, ALTHOUGH NOT YET PERFECTLY!
SHOULD I HAVE HER TAKE MY PLACE IN THE FUTURE?
Sho's dad is the chef.

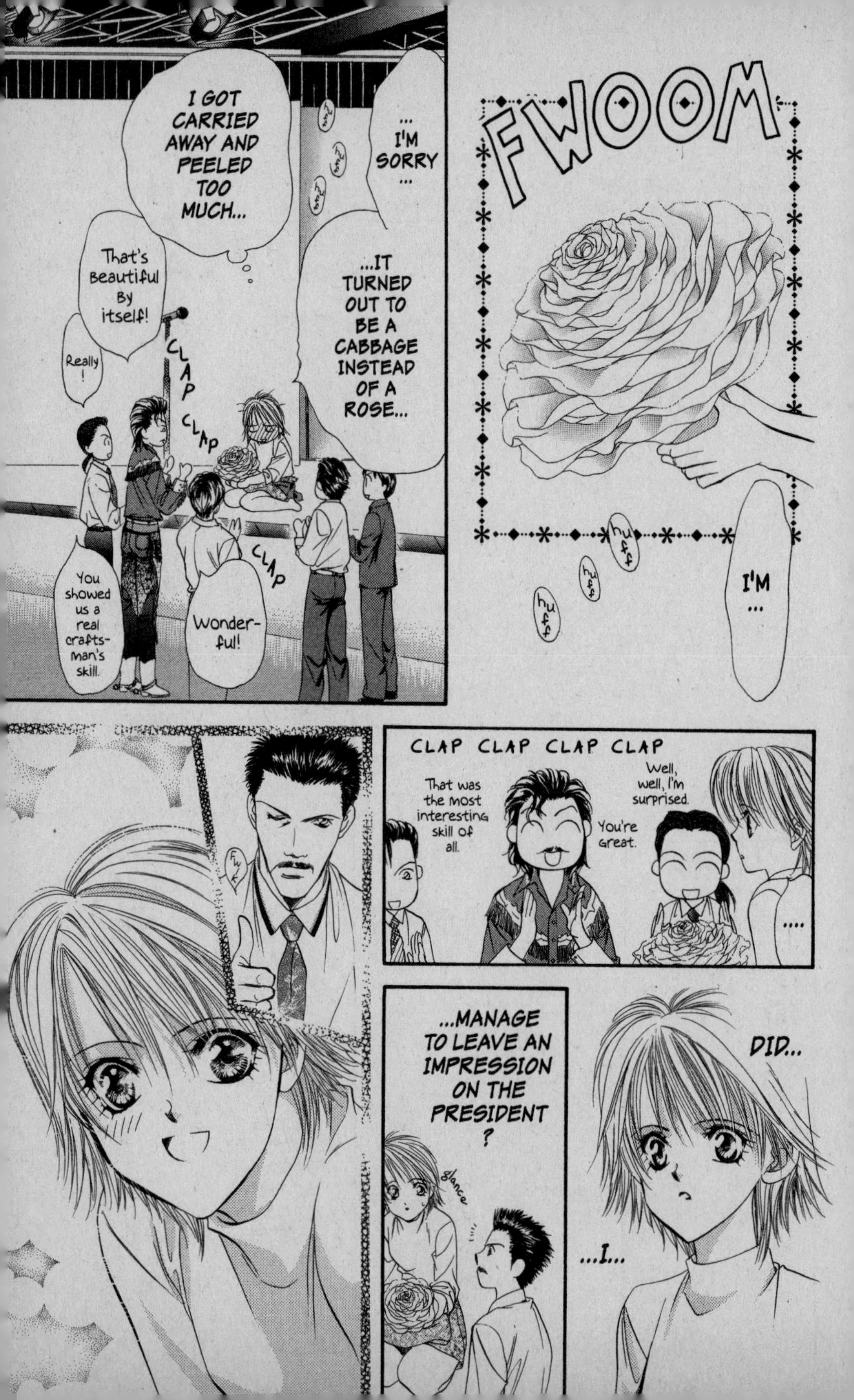
FWOOM
huff
huff
huff
I'M...
... I'M SORRY ...
I GOT CARRIED AWAY AND PEELED TOO MUCH...
...IT TURNED OUT TO BE A CABBAGE INSTEAD OF A ROSE...
That's Beautiful By itself!
Really!
CLAP CLAP
CLAP
Wonderful!
You showed us a real craftsman's skill.
CLAP CLAP CLAP CLAP
Well, well, I'm surprised.
You're Great.
That was the most interesting skill of all.
....
DID...
...I...
...MANAGE TO LEAVE AN IMPRESSION ON THE PRESIDENT?
glance
Fwk

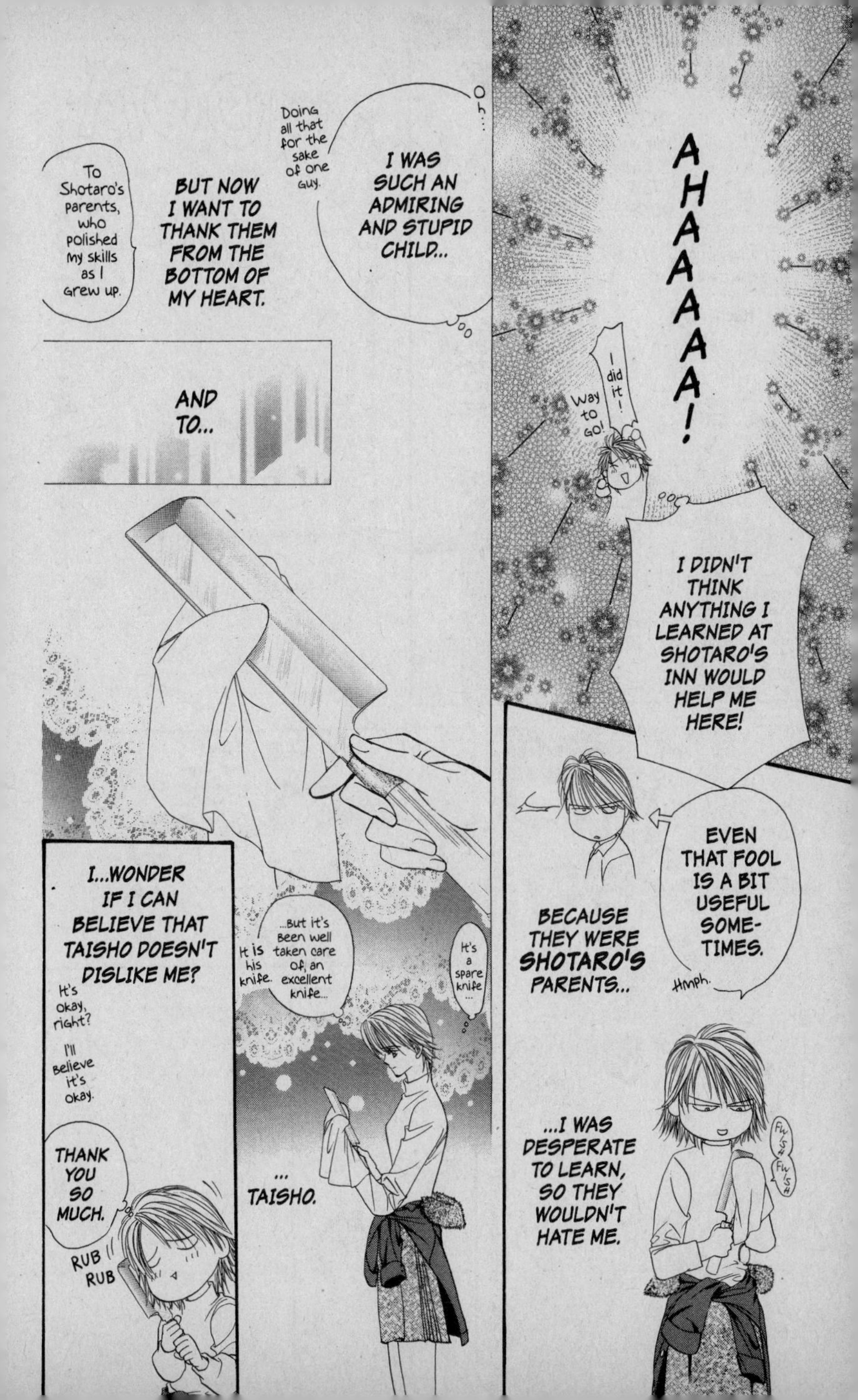

AHAAAAA!
I did it!
Way to go!
I DIDN'T THINK ANYTHING I LEARNED AT SHOTARO'S INN WOULD HELP ME HERE!
EVEN THAT FOOL IS A BIT USEFUL SOME-TIMES.
Hmph.
BECAUSE THEY WERE SHOTARO'S PARENTS...
...I WAS DESPERATE TO LEARN, SO THEY WOULDN'T HATE ME.
FWISH FWISH
Oh...
I WAS SUCH AN ADMIRING AND STUPID CHILD...
Doing all that for the sake of one guy.
BUT NOW I WANT TO THANK THEM FROM THE BOTTOM OF MY HEART.
To Shotaro's parents, who polished my skills as I grew up.
AND TO...
It's a spare knife...
...But it's been well taken care of, an excellent knife...
It is his knife.
... TAISHO.
I...WONDER IF I CAN BELIEVE THAT TAISHO DOESN'T DISLIKE ME?
It's okay, right?
I'll believe it's okay.
THANK YOU SO MUCH.
RUB RUB

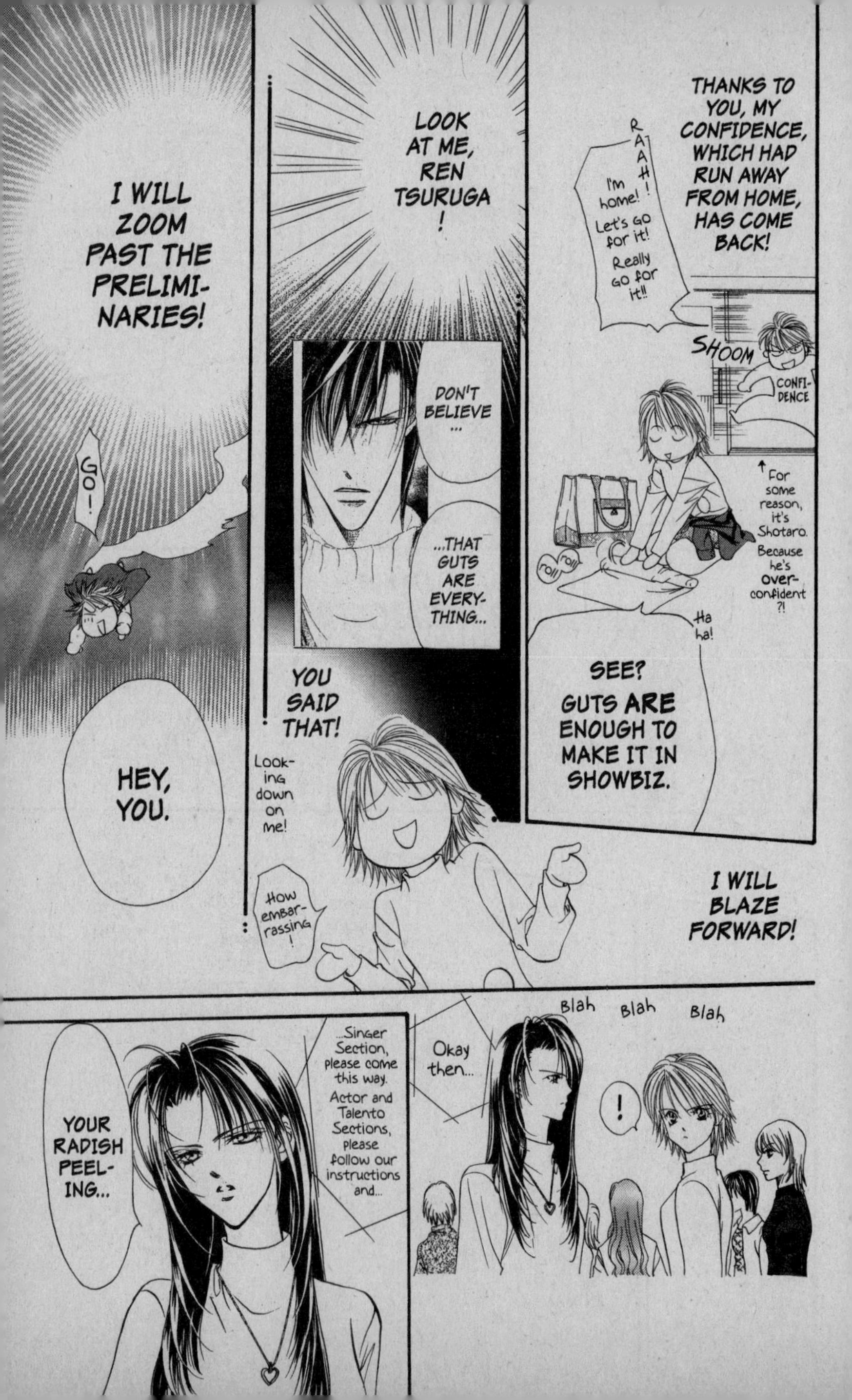
THANKS TO YOU, MY CONFIDENCE, WHICH HAD RUN AWAY FROM HOME, HAS COME BACK!
RAAH!
I'm home! Let's go for it! Really go for it!!
SHOOM
CONFIDENCE
↑ For some reason, it's Shotaro. Because he's over-confident?!
roll roll
Ha ha!
SEE? GUTS ARE ENOUGH TO MAKE IT IN SHOWBIZ.
I WILL BLAZE FORWARD!
LOOK AT ME, REN TSURUGA!
DON'T BELIEVE...
...THAT GUTS ARE EVERYTHING...
YOU SAID THAT!
Looking down on me!
How embarrassing!
I WILL ZOOM PAST THE PRELIMINARIES!
GO!
HEY, YOU.
Blah Blah Blah
!
Okay then...
...Singer Section, please come this way. Actor and Talento Sections, please follow our instructions and...
YOUR RADISH PEELING...

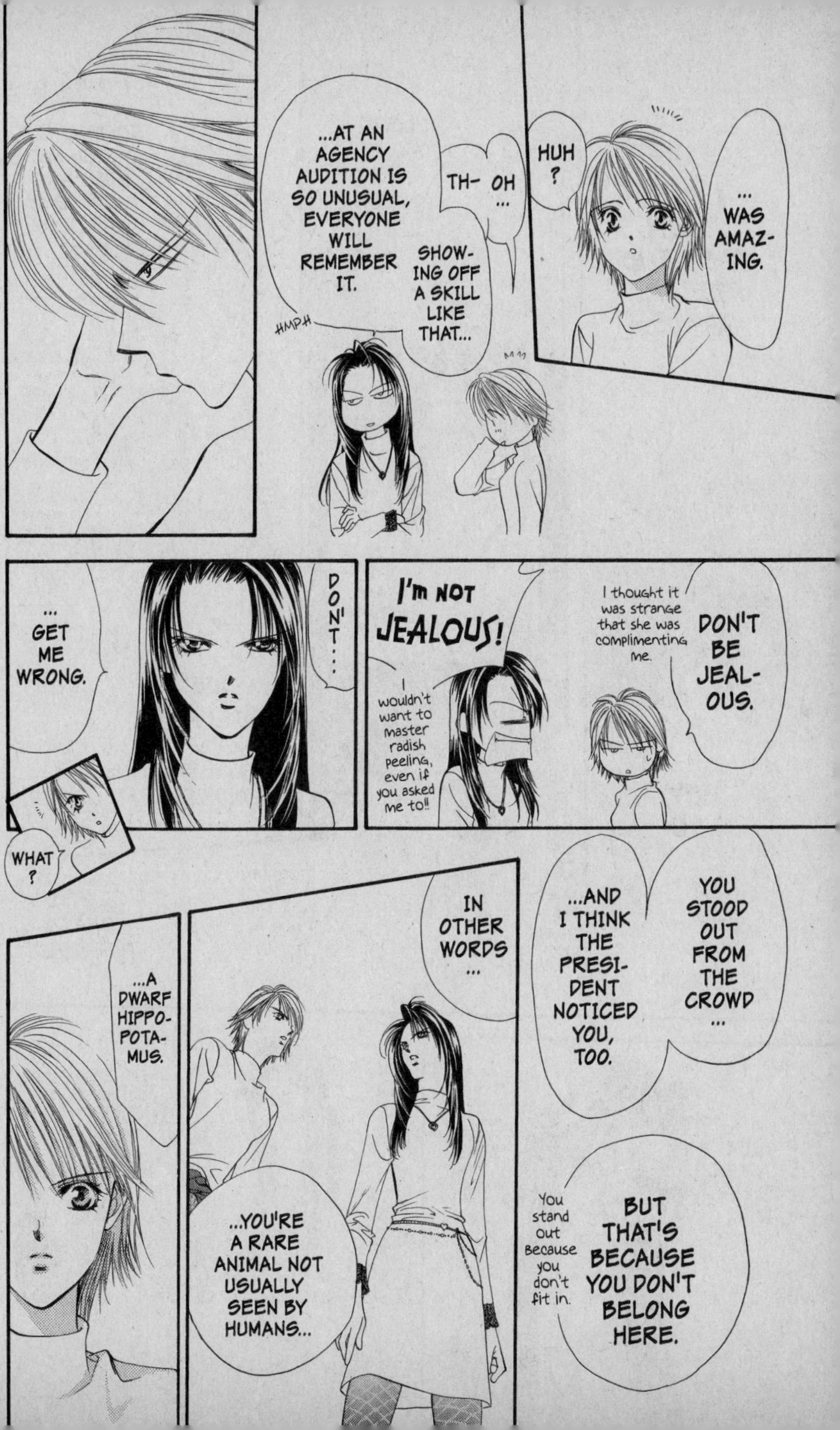
... WAS AMAZING.
HUH ?
TH- OH ...
SHOWING OFF A SKILL LIKE THAT...
...AT AN AGENCY AUDITION IS SO UNUSUAL, EVERYONE WILL REMEMBER IT.
HMPH
DON'T BE JEALOUS.
I thought it was strange that she was complimenting me.
I'm NOT JEALOUS!
I wouldn't want to master radish peeling, even if you asked me to!!
DON'T...
... GET ME WRONG.
WHAT ?
YOU STOOD OUT FROM THE CROWD ...
...AND I THINK THE PRESIDENT NOTICED YOU, TOO.
BUT THAT'S BECAUSE YOU DON'T BELONG HERE.
You stand out because you don't fit in.
IN OTHER WORDS ...
...YOU'RE A RARE ANIMAL NOT USUALLY SEEN BY HUMANS...
...A DWARF HIPPOPOTAMUS.

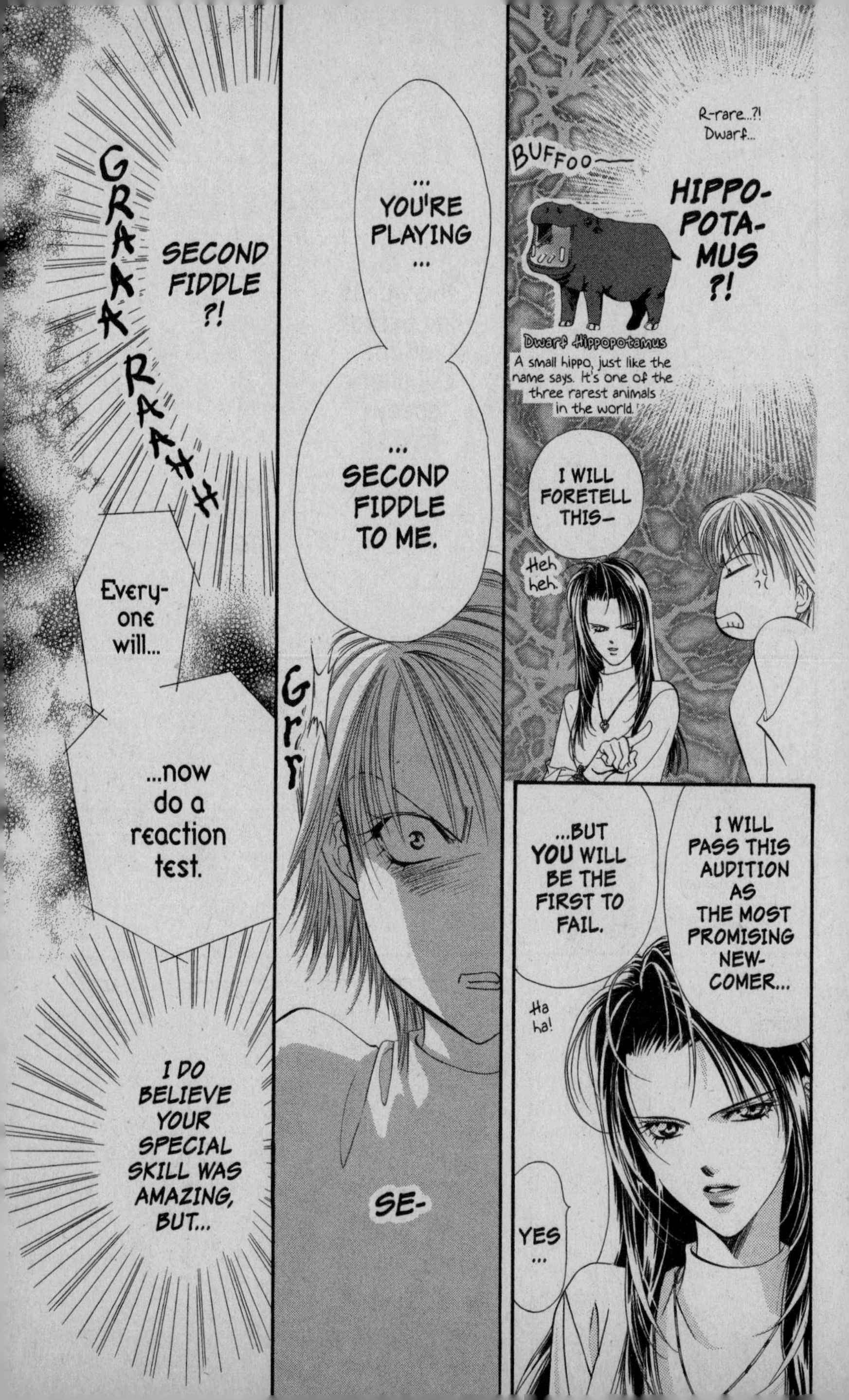
R-rare...?! Dwarf...
HIPPO-POTA-MUS?!
BUFFOO—
Dwarf Hippopotamus
A small hippo, just like the name says. It's one of the three rarest animals in the world.
I WILL FORETELL THIS—
Heh heh.
I WILL PASS THIS AUDITION AS THE MOST PROMISING NEW-COMER...
...BUT YOU WILL BE THE FIRST TO FAIL.
Ha ha!
YES...
... YOU'RE PLAYING ...
... SECOND FIDDLE TO ME.
Grr
SE-
SECOND FIDDLE ?!
GRAAA RAAHH
Every-one will...
...now do a reaction test.
I DO BELIEVE YOUR SPECIAL SKILL WAS AMAZING, BUT...

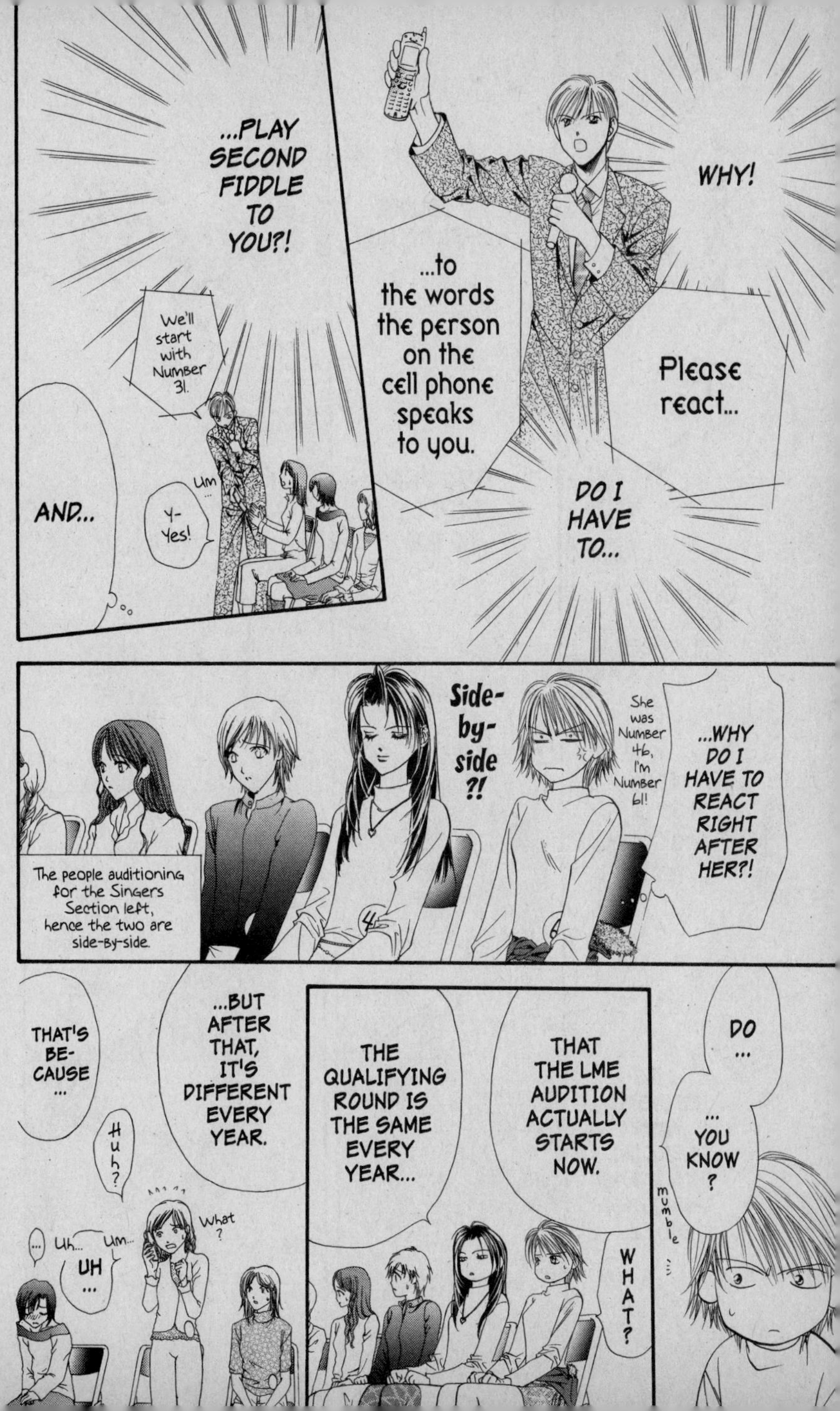
WHY!
Please react...
...to the words the person on the cell phone speaks to you.
DO I HAVE TO...
...PLAY SECOND FIDDLE TO YOU?!
We'll start with Number 31.
Um...
Y-Yes!
AND...
...WHY DO I HAVE TO REACT RIGHT AFTER HER?!
She was Number 46, I'm Number 61!
Side-by-side?!
The people auditioning for the Singers Section left, hence the two are side-by-side.
DO... ...YOU KNOW?
mumble...
THAT THE LME AUDITION ACTUALLY STARTS NOW.
THE QUALIFYING ROUND IS THE SAME EVERY YEAR...
WHAT?
...BUT AFTER THAT, IT'S DIFFERENT EVERY YEAR.
THAT'S BE-CAUSE...
Huh?
What?
Um...
Uh...
...
UH...

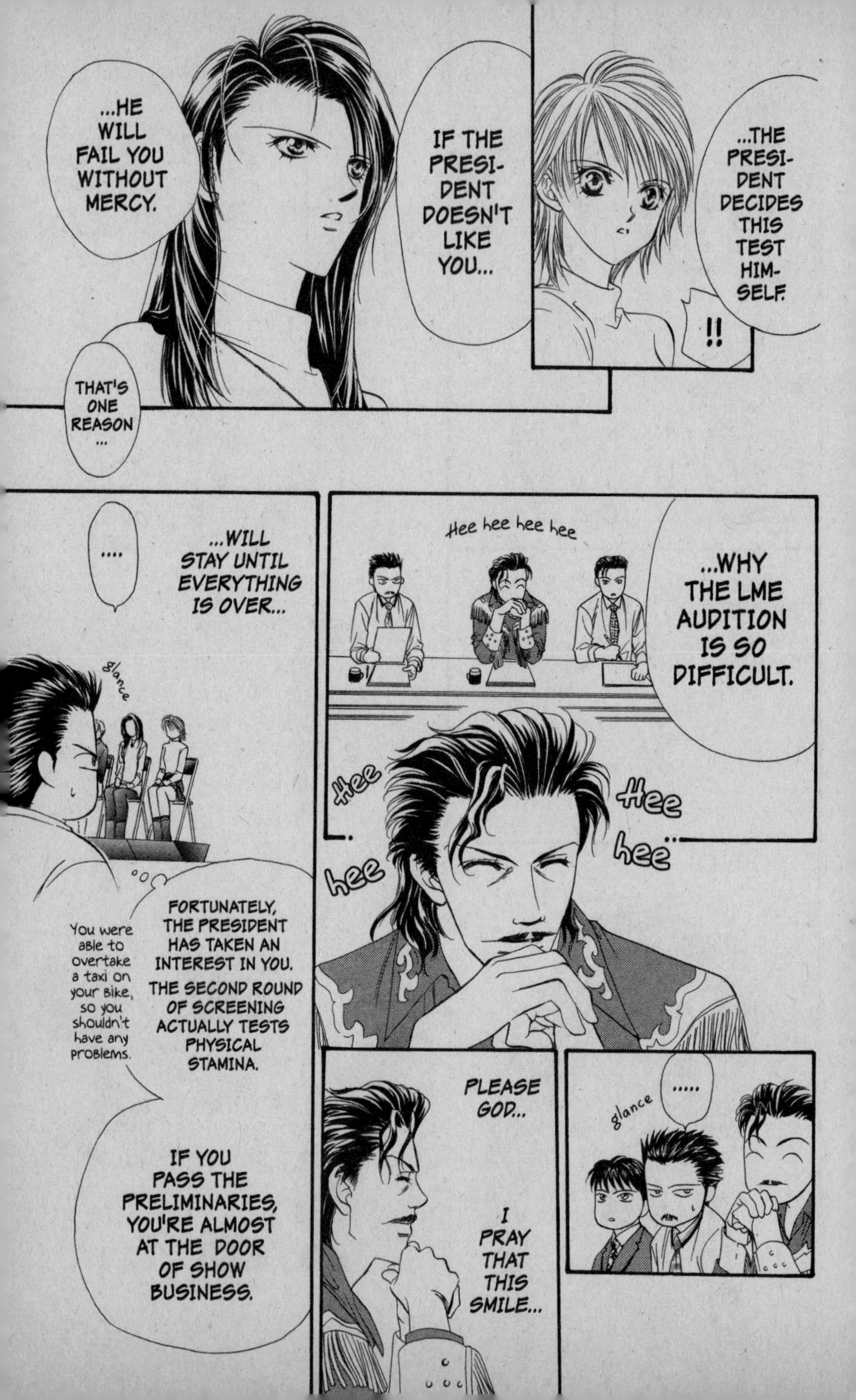
...THE PRESIDENT DECIDES THIS TEST HIMSELF.
!!
IF THE PRESIDENT DOESN'T LIKE YOU...
...HE WILL FAIL YOU WITHOUT MERCY.
THAT'S ONE REASON...
Hee hee hee hee
...WHY THE LME AUDITION IS SO DIFFICULT.
Hee
Hee
hee
hee
.....
glance
PLEASE GOD...
I PRAY THAT THIS SMILE...
....
...WILL STAY UNTIL EVERYTHING IS OVER...
glance
FORTUNATELY, THE PRESIDENT HAS TAKEN AN INTEREST IN YOU. THE SECOND ROUND OF SCREENING ACTUALLY TESTS PHYSICAL STAMINA.
You were able to overtake a taxi on your bike, so you shouldn't have any problems.
IF YOU PASS THE PRELIMINARIES, YOU'RE ALMOST AT THE DOOR OF SHOW BUSINESS.

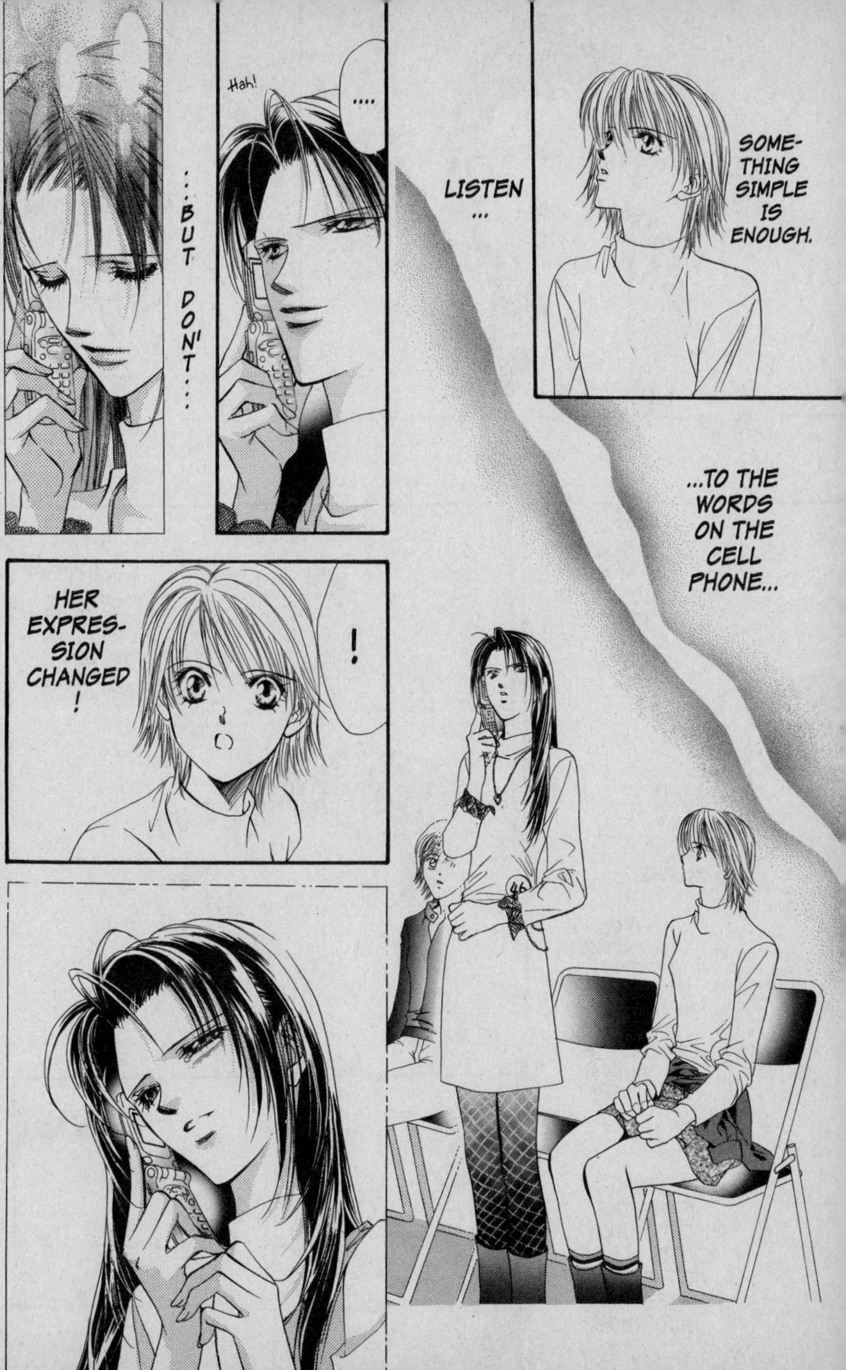

SOMETHING SIMPLE IS ENOUGH.
LISTEN ...
...TO THE WORDS ON THE CELL PHONE...
....
Hah!
...BUT DON'T...
!
HER EXPRESSION CHANGED!

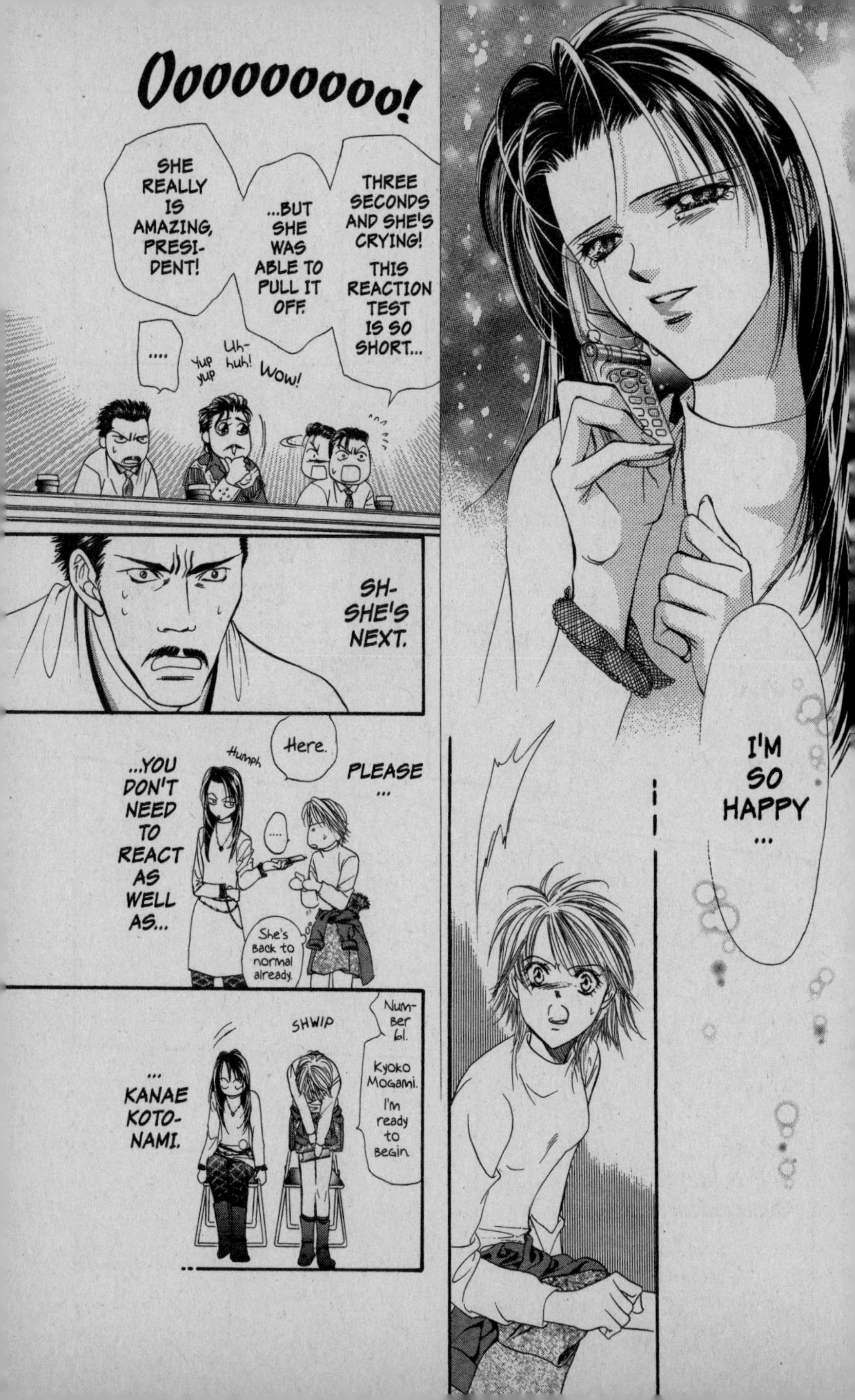
I'M SO HAPPY...
Oooooooo!
THREE SECONDS AND SHE'S CRYING! THIS REACTION TEST IS SO SHORT...
...BUT SHE WAS ABLE TO PULL IT OFF.
SHE REALLY IS AMAZING, PRESI-DENT!
Wow!
Uh-huh!
Yup yup
....
SH-SHE'S NEXT.
PLEASE...
Here.
Humph
...YOU DON'T NEED TO REACT AS WELL AS...
....
She's back to normal already.
Num-ber 61. Kyoko Mogami. I'm ready to begin.
SHWIP
...KANAE KOTO-NAMI.

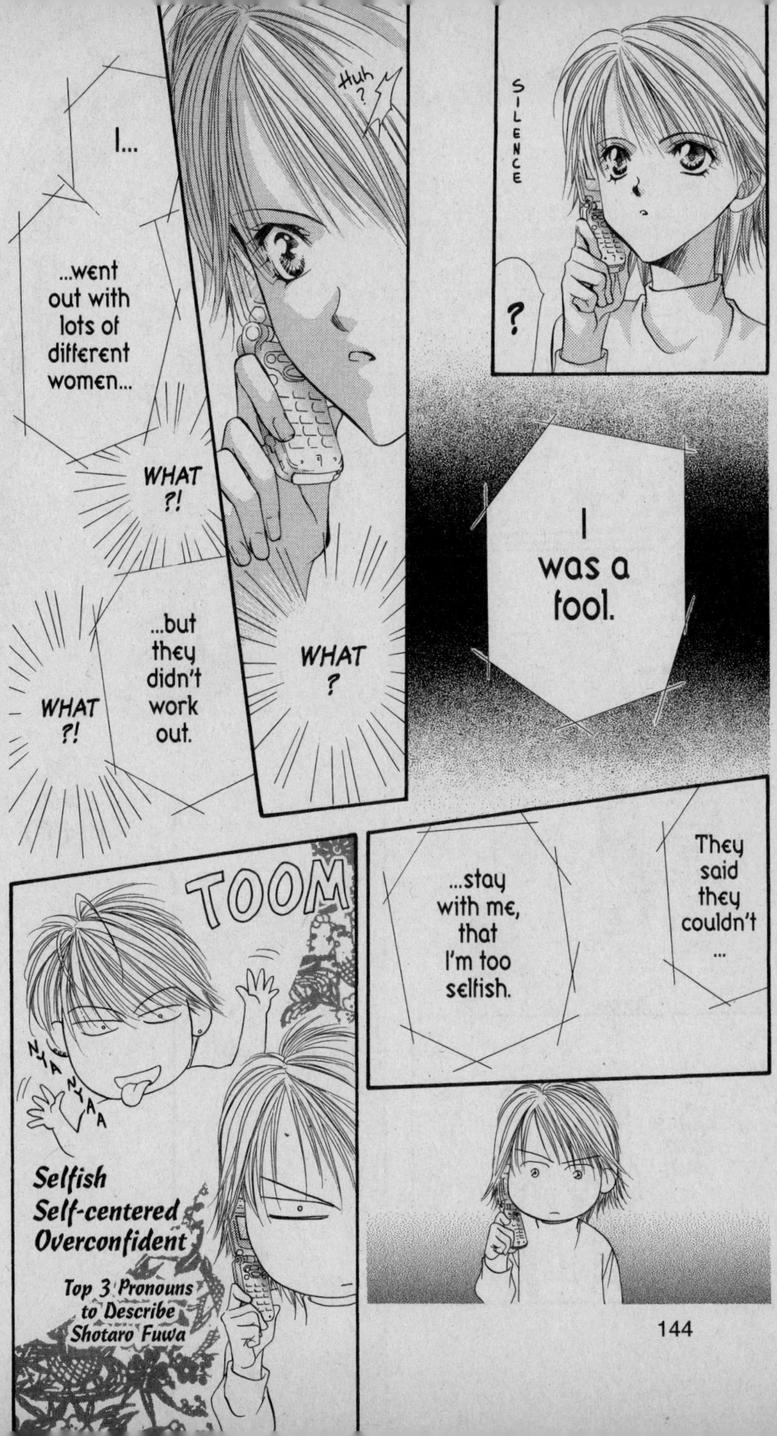
SILENCE
?
I was a tool.
Huh?
I...
...went out with lots of different women...
WHAT?!
...but they didn't work out.
WHAT?
WHAT?!
They said they couldn't...
...stay with me, that I'm too selfish.
TOOM
NYA NYA NYAA
Selfish
Self-centered
Overconfident
Top 3 Pronouns to Describe Shotaro Fuwa

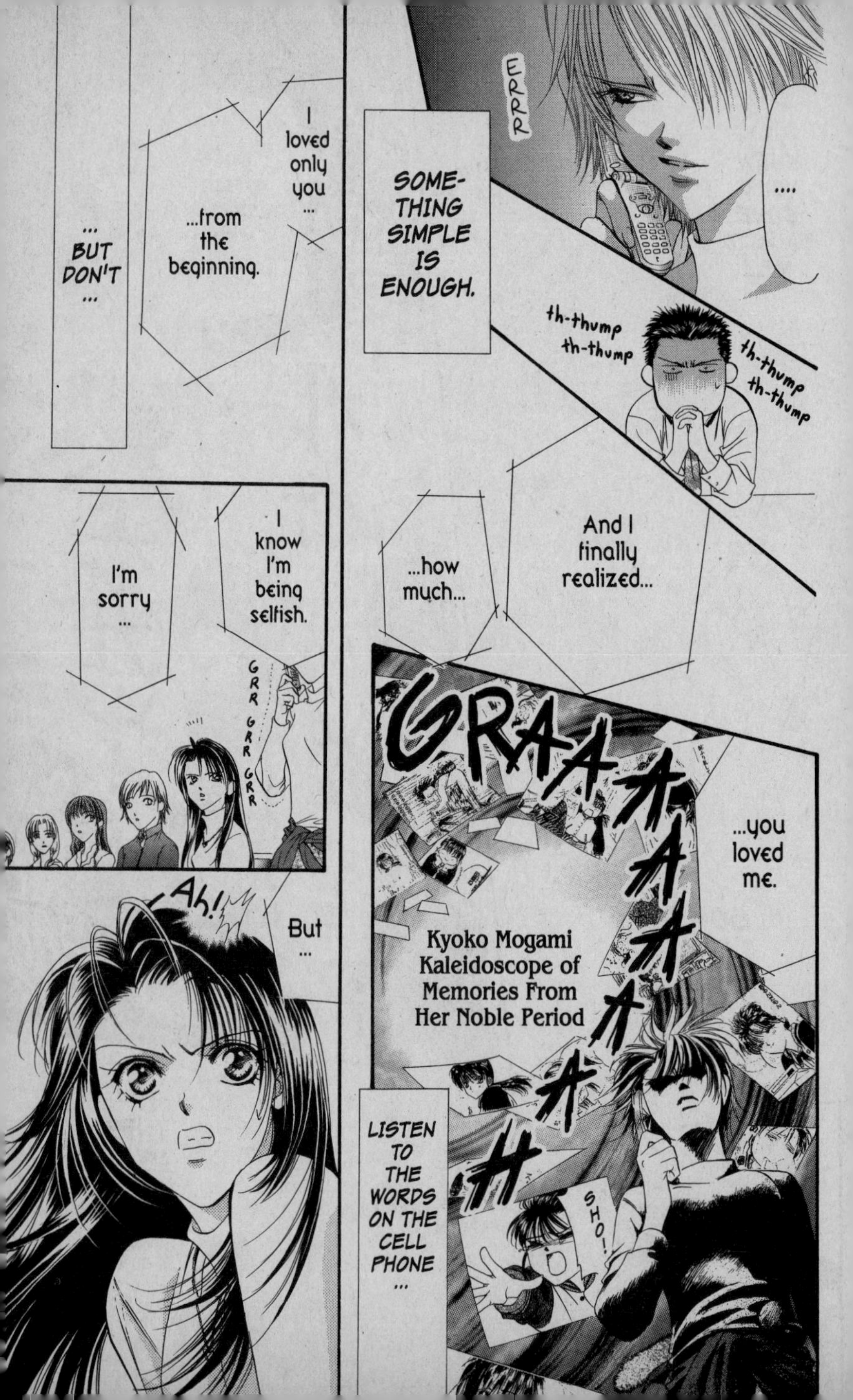
ERRR
....
SOME-THING SIMPLE IS ENOUGH.
th-thump th-thump
th-thump th-thump
And I finally realized...
...how much...
GRAAAAAAAAH
...you loved me.
Kyoko Mogami Kaleidoscope of Memories From Her Noble Period
LISTEN TO THE WORDS ON THE CELL PHONE ...
SHO!
I loved only you ...
...from the beginning.
... BUT DON'T ...
I know I'm being selfish.
I'm sorry ...
GRR GRR GRR
But ...
Ah!

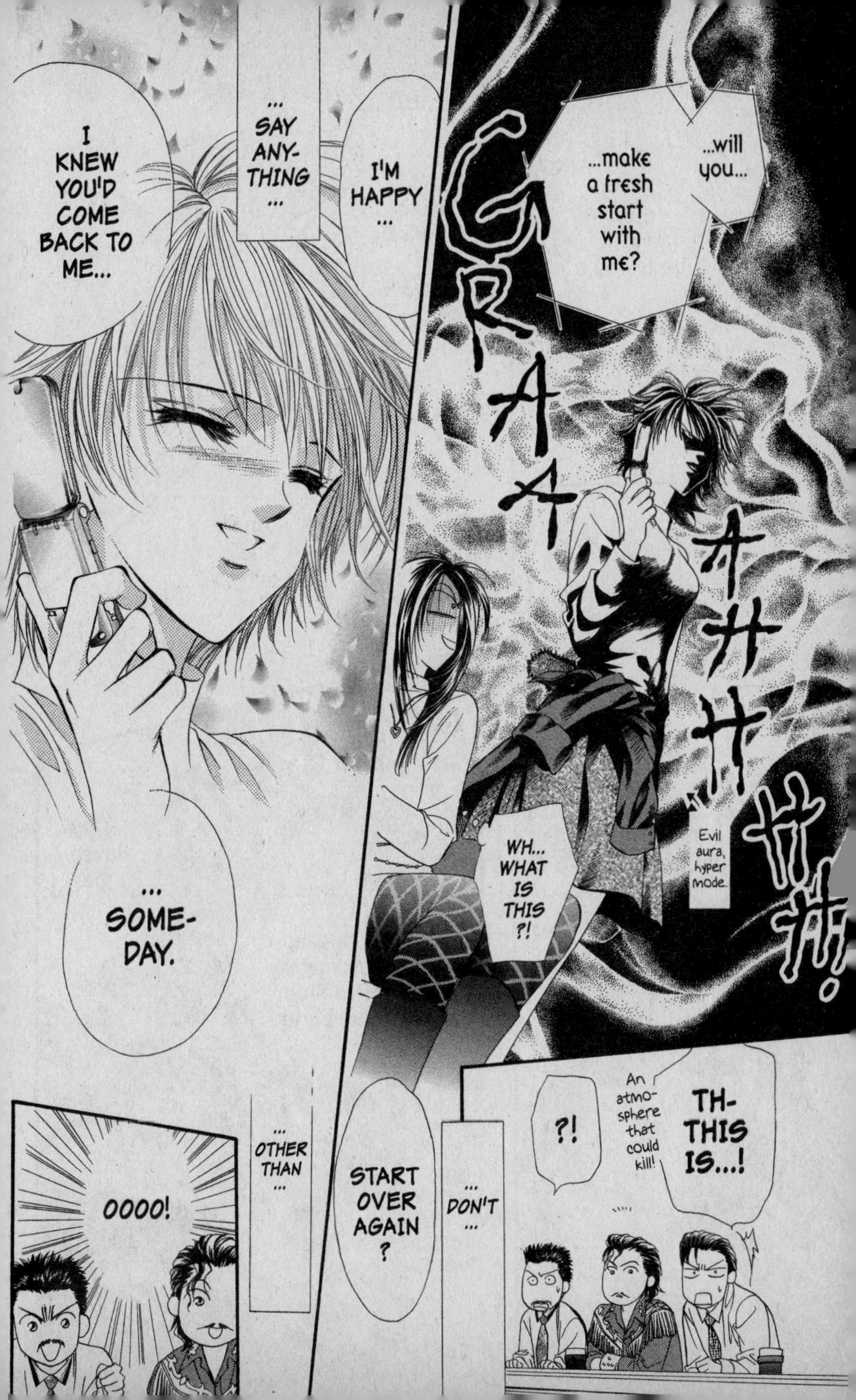
...will you...
...make a fresh start with me?
GRAAAHHHH!
Evil aura, hyper mode.
WH... WHAT IS THIS ?!
I'M HAPPY...
...SAY ANY-THING...
I KNEW YOU'D COME BACK TO ME...
...SOME-DAY.
TH-THIS IS...!
An atmo-sphere that could kill!
?!
...DON'T...
START OVER AGAIN?
...OTHER THAN...
OOOO!

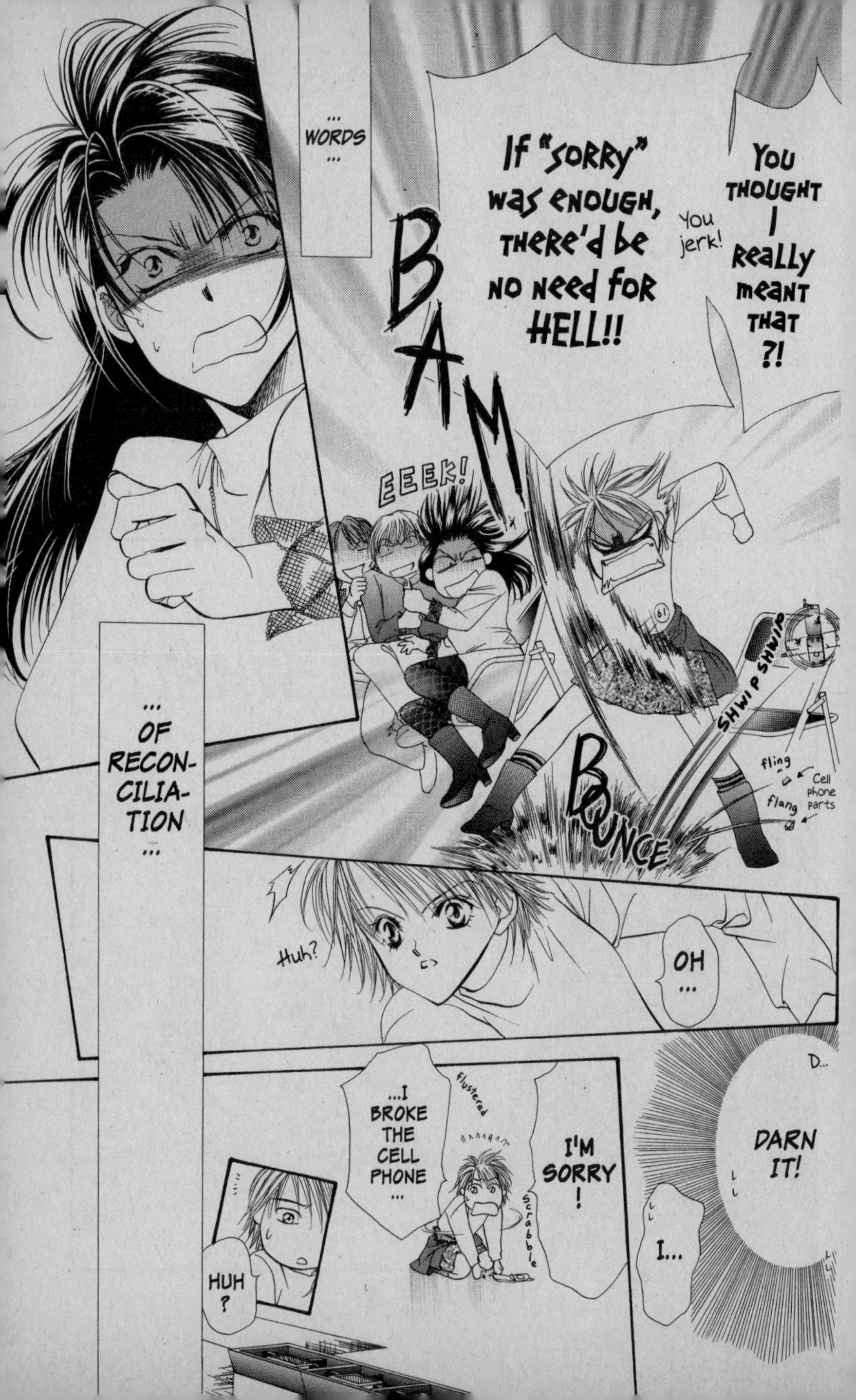
YOU THOUGHT I REALLY MEANT THAT?!
You jerk!
If "sorry" was enough, there'd be no need for HELL!!
BAM
EEEK!
SHWIP SHWIP
fling
flang
Cell phone parts
BOUNCE
...WORDS...
...OF RECONCILIATION...
OH...
Huh?
D...
DARN IT!
I...
I'M SORRY!
scrabble
...I BROKE THE CELL PHONE...
flustered
HUH?

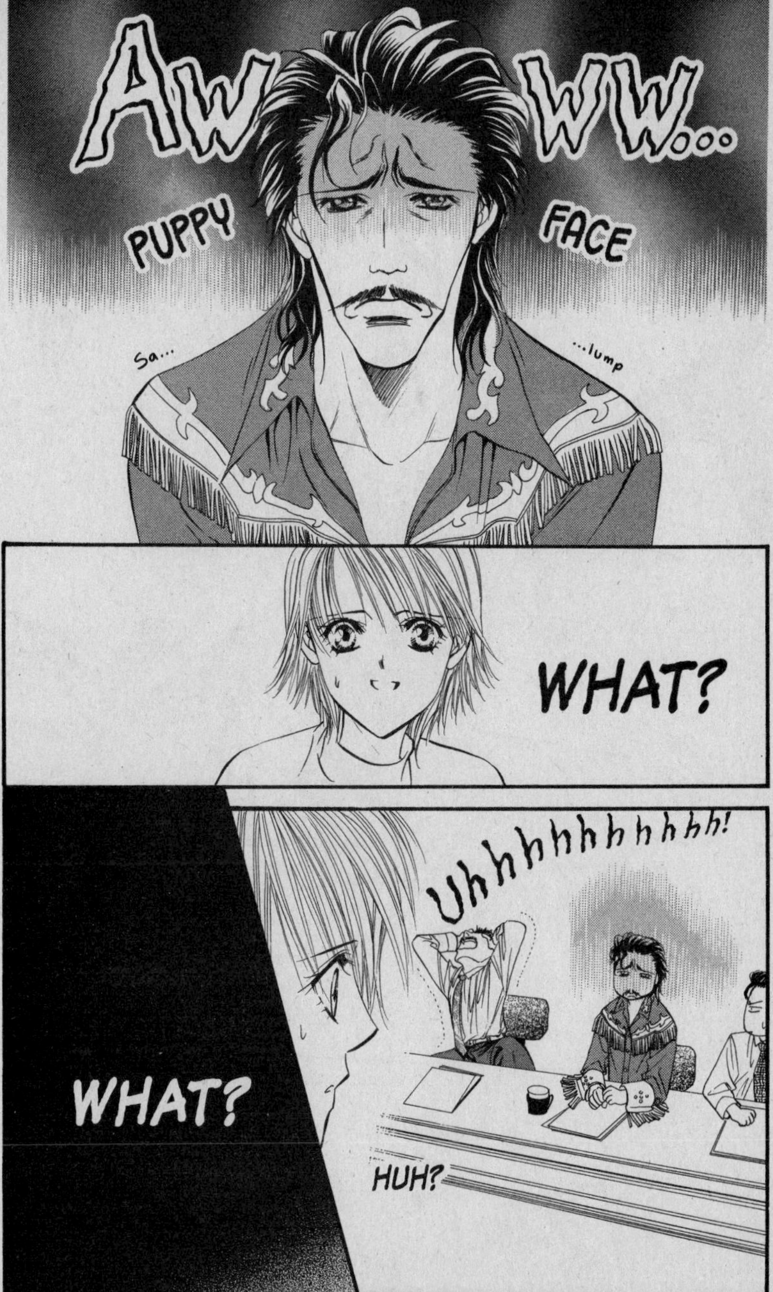
AWWWW...
PUPPY
FACE
Sa...
...lump
WHAT?
Uhhhhhhhhhhh!
HUH?
WHAT?

End of Act 4

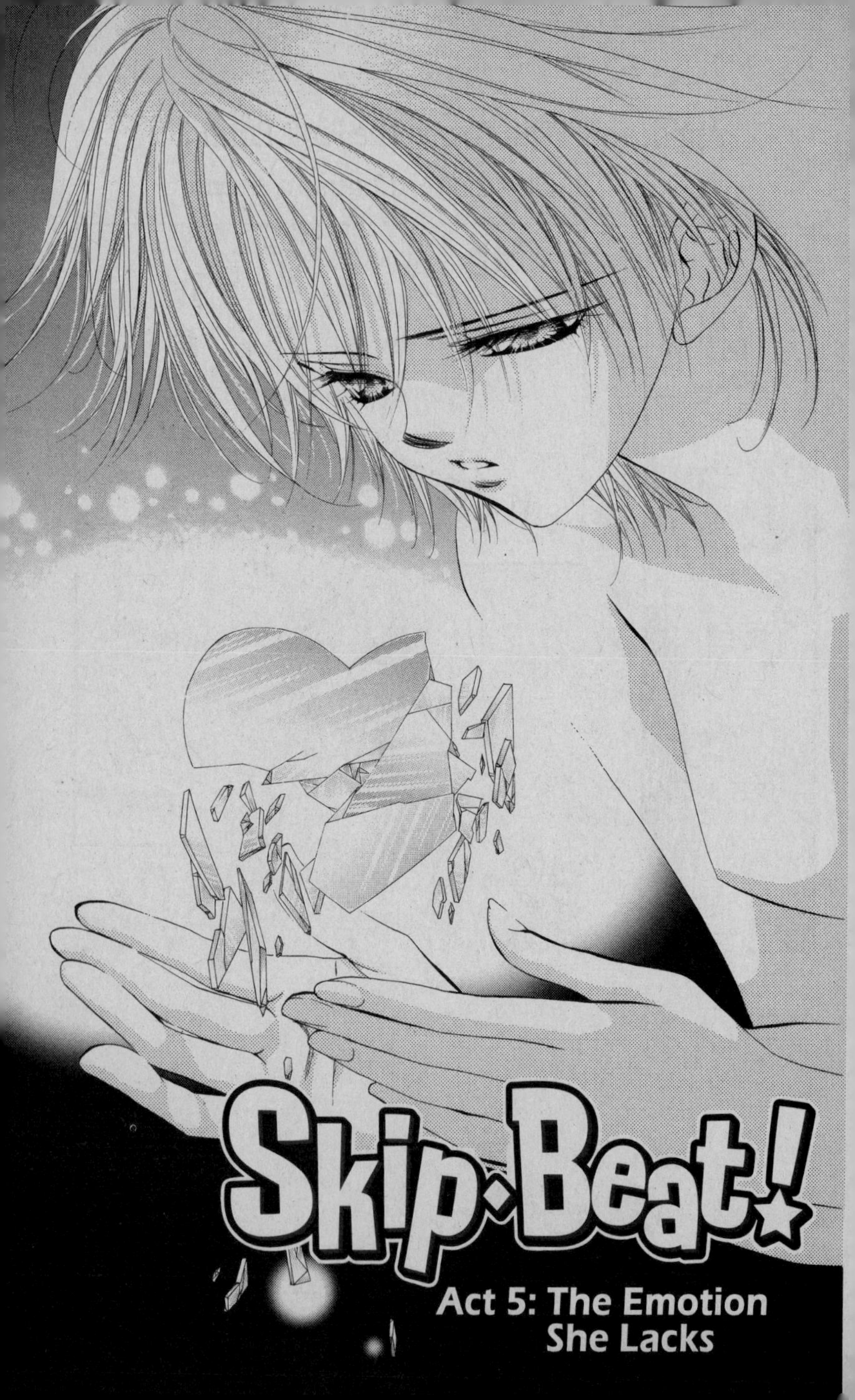
Skip·Beat!
Act 5: The Emotion She Lacks

Applicants Who Passed the First Round

(In the Acting and Talento divisions)

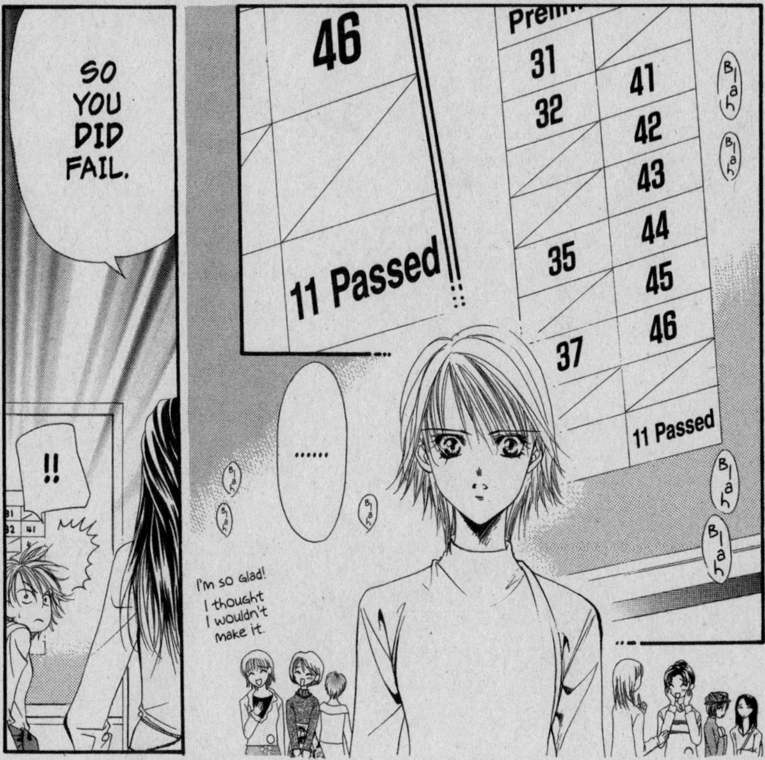
46
11 Passed
31
32
41
42
43
44
35
45
46
37
11 Passed
Blah
Blah
Blah
Blah
......
Blah
Blah
Blah
I'm so Glad! I thought I wouldn't make it.
SO YOU DID FAIL.
!!

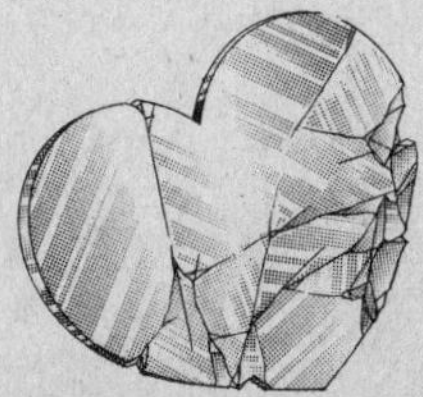

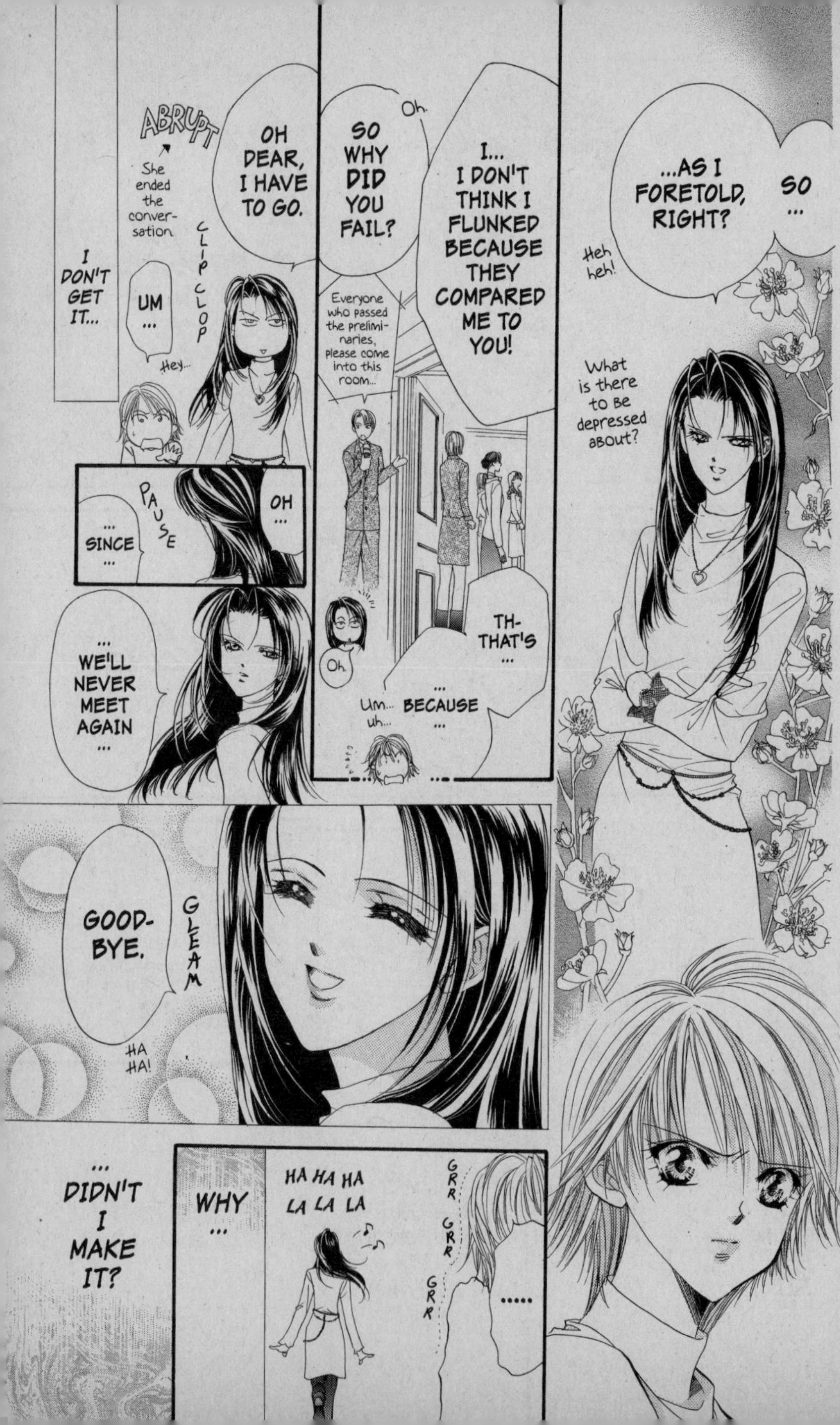

SO ...
...AS I FORETOLD, RIGHT?
Heh heh!
What is there to be depressed about?
I... I DON'T THINK I FLUNKED BECAUSE THEY COMPARED ME TO YOU!
Oh.
SO WHY DID YOU FAIL?
Everyone who passed the prelimi-naries, please come into this room...
TH- THAT'S ...
... BECAUSE ...
Um... uh...
Oh.
OH DEAR, I HAVE TO GO.
ABRUPT
She ended the conver-sation.
CLIP CLOP
UM ...
Hey...
I DON'T GET IT...
OH ...
PAUSE
... SINCE ...
... WE'LL NEVER MEET AGAIN ...
GOOD-BYE.
GLEAM
HA HA!
GRR GRR GRR
.....
HA HA HA LA LA LA
WHY ...
... DIDN'T I MAKE IT?

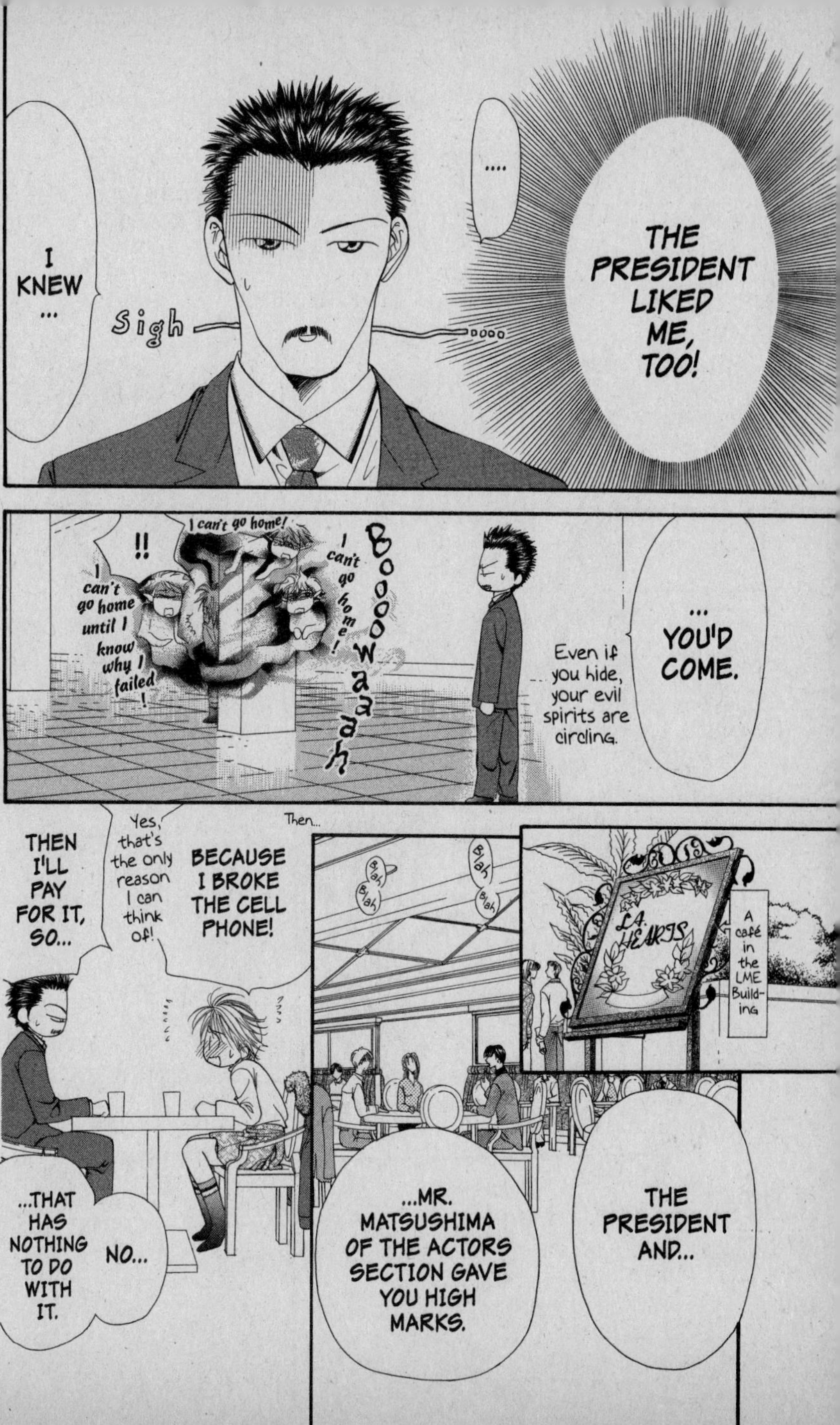
THE PRESIDENT LIKED ME, TOO!
....
Sigh
I KNEW ...
... YOU'D COME.
Even if you hide, your evil spirits are circling.
Booooowaaah
I can't go home!
I can't go home!
!!
I can't go home until I know why I failed!
LA HEARTS
A café in the LME Building
Then...
Blah Blah
Blah Blah
THE PRESIDENT AND...
...MR. MATSUSHIMA OF THE ACTORS SECTION GAVE YOU HIGH MARKS.
BECAUSE I BROKE THE CELL PHONE!
Yes, that's the only reason I can think of!
THEN I'LL PAY FOR IT, SO...
NO...
...THAT HAS NOTHING TO DO WITH IT.

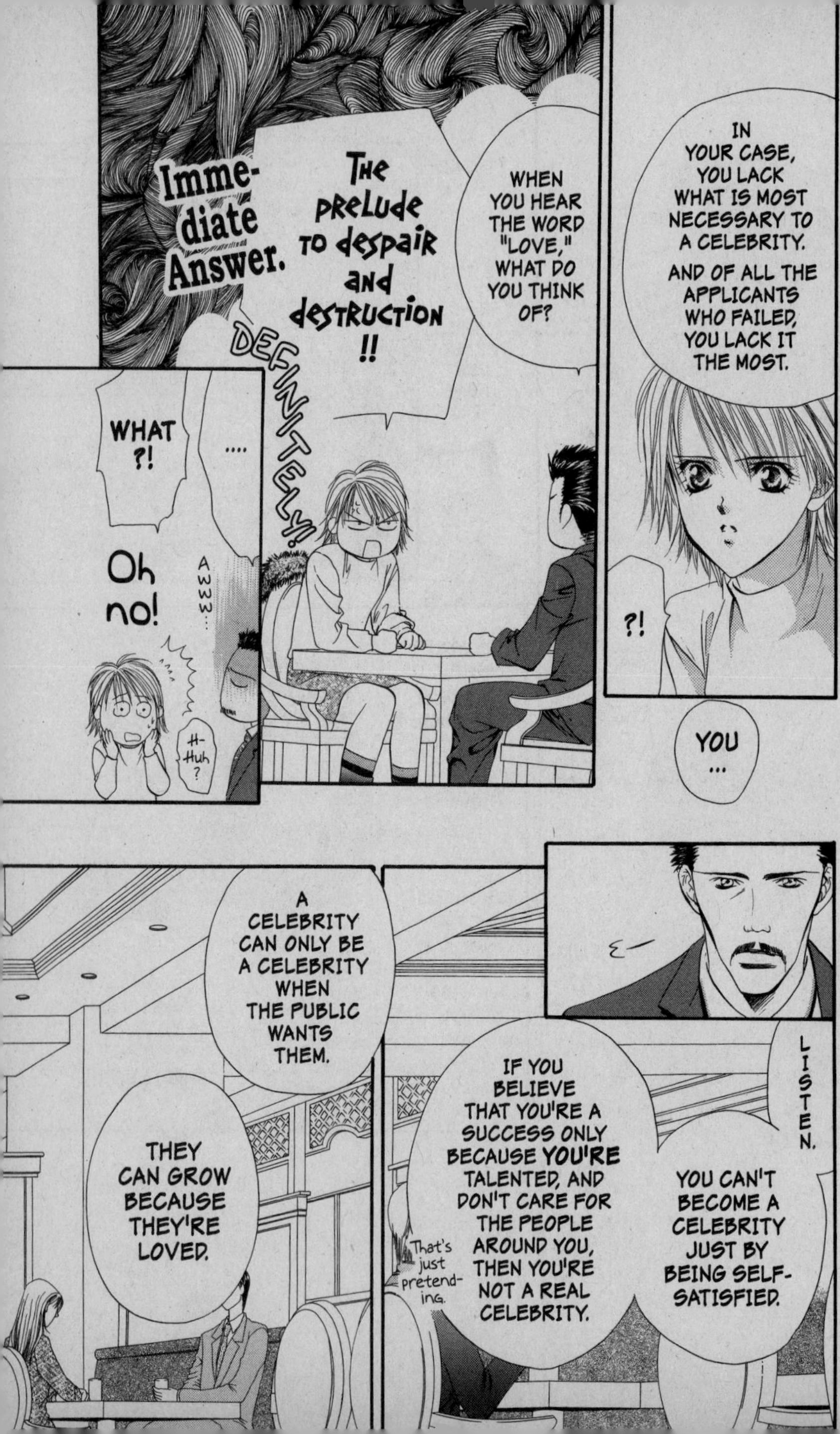
WHEN YOU HEAR THE WORD "LOVE," WHAT DO YOU THINK OF?
DEFINITELY!!
The prelude to despair and destruction!!
Immediate Answer.
WHAT?!
....
Oh no!
AWWW...
H-Huh?
IN YOUR CASE, YOU LACK WHAT IS MOST NECESSARY TO A CELEBRITY.
AND OF ALL THE APPLICANTS WHO FAILED, YOU LACK IT THE MOST.
?!
YOU...
ε—
LISTEN.
YOU CAN'T BECOME A CELEBRITY JUST BY BEING SELF-SATISFIED.
IF YOU BELIEVE THAT YOU'RE A SUCCESS ONLY BECAUSE YOU'RE TALENTED, AND DON'T CARE FOR THE PEOPLE AROUND YOU, THEN YOU'RE NOT A REAL CELEBRITY.
That's just pretend-ing.
A CELEBRITY CAN ONLY BE A CELEBRITY WHEN THE PUBLIC WANTS THEM.
THEY CAN GROW BECAUSE THEY'RE LOVED.

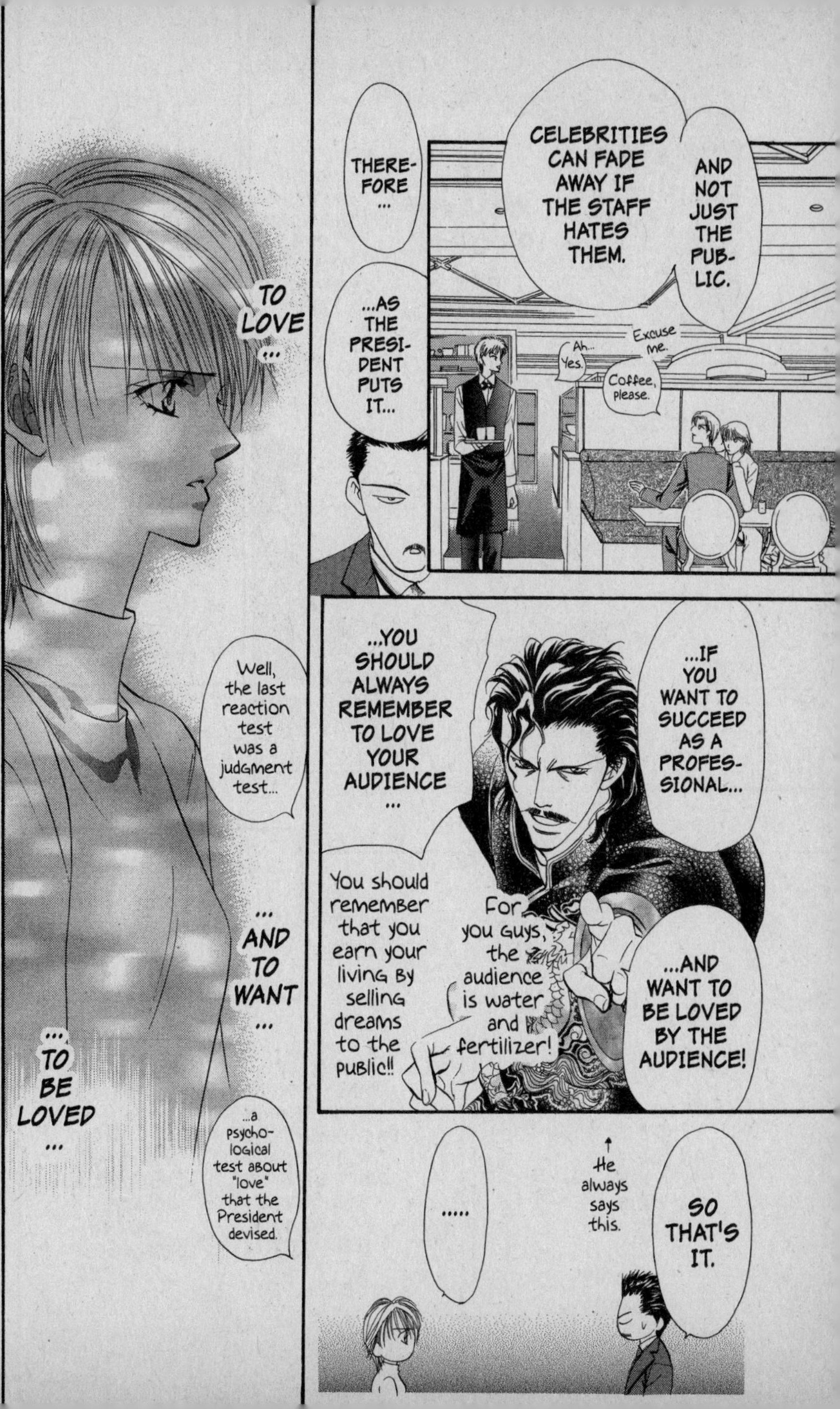
CELEBRITIES CAN FADE AWAY IF THE STAFF HATES THEM.
AND NOT JUST THE PUBLIC.
THEREFORE...
...AS THE PRESIDENT PUTS IT...
Excuse me.
Coffee, please.
Ah... Yes.
...IF YOU WANT TO SUCCEED AS A PROFESSIONAL...
...YOU SHOULD ALWAYS REMEMBER TO LOVE YOUR AUDIENCE...
...AND WANT TO BE LOVED BY THE AUDIENCE!
For you guys, the audience is water and fertilizer!
You should remember that you earn your living by selling dreams to the public!!
SO THAT'S IT.
↑ He always says this.
.....
TO LOVE...
Well, the last reaction test was a judgment test...
...AND TO WANT...
...TO BE LOVED...
...a psychological test about "love" that the President devised.

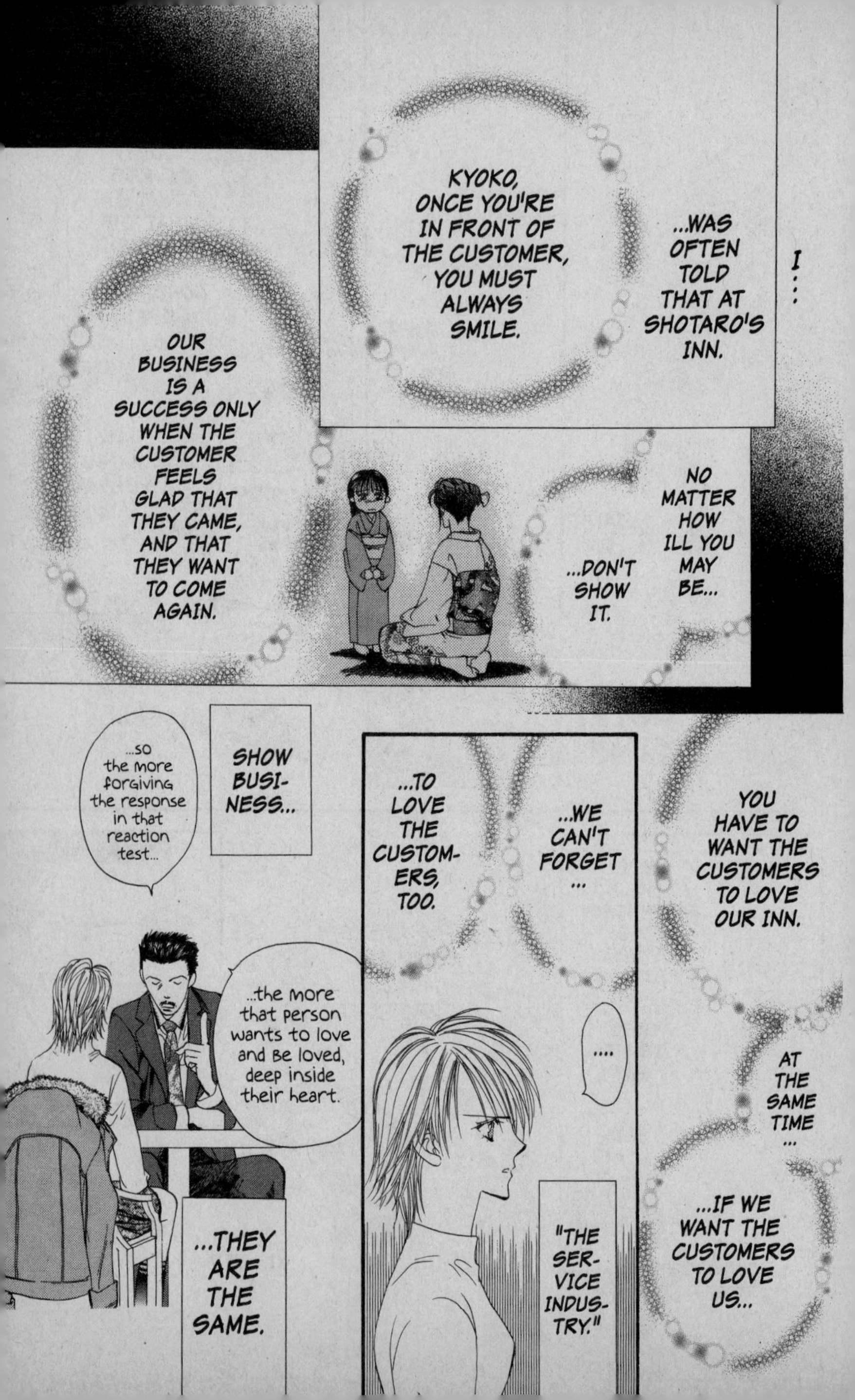
I...
...WAS OFTEN TOLD THAT AT SHOTARO'S INN.
KYOKO, ONCE YOU'RE IN FRONT OF THE CUSTOMER, YOU MUST ALWAYS SMILE.
NO MATTER HOW ILL YOU MAY BE...
...DON'T SHOW IT.
OUR BUSINESS IS A SUCCESS ONLY WHEN THE CUSTOMER FEELS GLAD THAT THEY CAME, AND THAT THEY WANT TO COME AGAIN.
YOU HAVE TO WANT THE CUSTOMERS TO LOVE OUR INN.
AT THE SAME TIME...
...IF WE WANT THE CUSTOMERS TO LOVE US...
...WE CAN'T FORGET...
...TO LOVE THE CUSTOMERS, TOO.
....
"THE SERVICE INDUSTRY."
SHOW BUSINESS...
...so the more forgiving the response in that reaction test...
...the more that person wants to love and be loved, deep inside their heart.
...THEY ARE THE SAME.

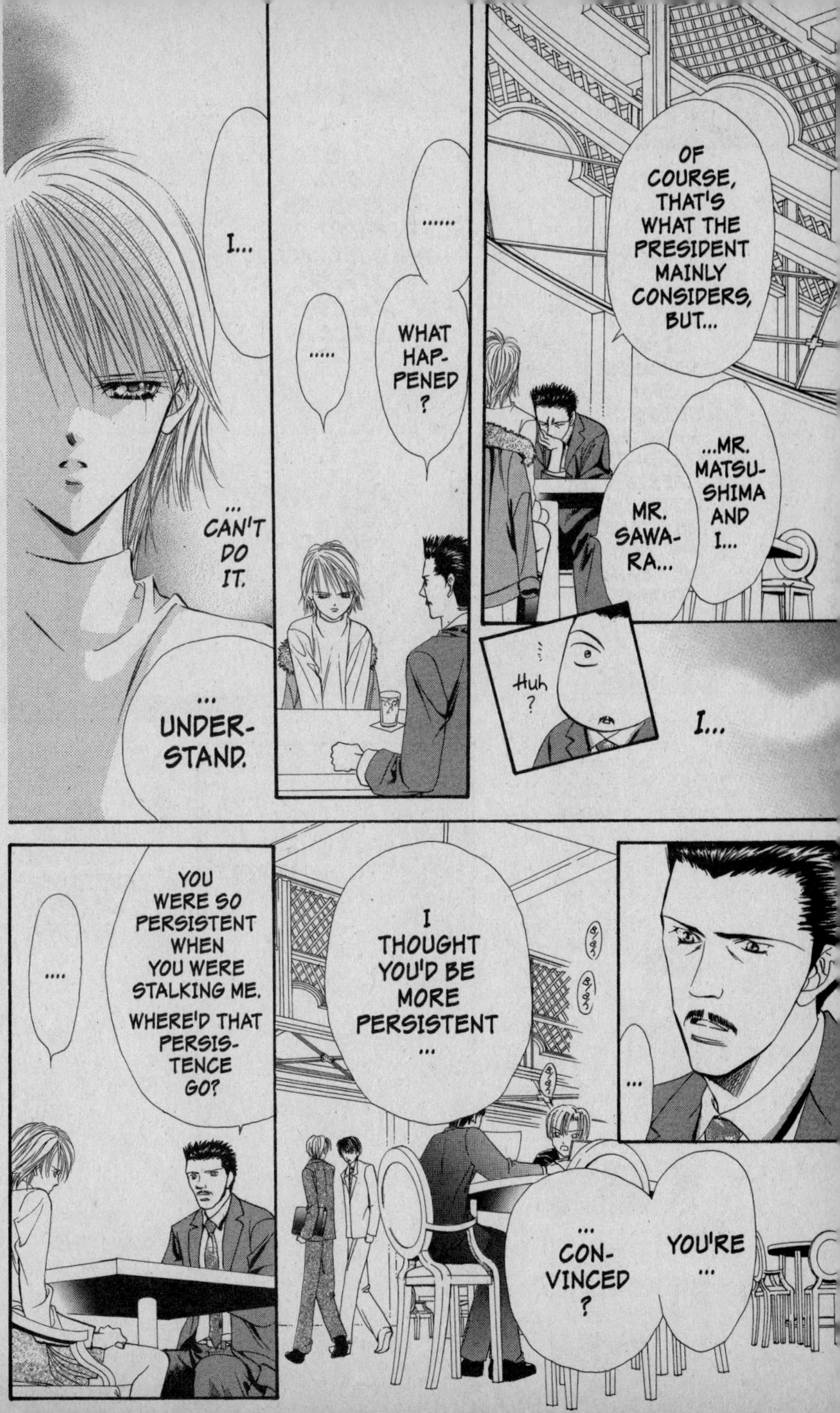
OF COURSE, THAT'S WHAT THE PRESIDENT MAINLY CONSIDERS, BUT...
...MR. MATSUSHIMA AND I...
MR. SAWARA...
I...
Huh?
......
WHAT HAPPENED?
.....
I...
...CAN'T DO IT.
...UNDERSTAND.
...
I THOUGHT YOU'D BE MORE PERSISTENT...
YOU'RE...
...CONVINCED?
YOU WERE SO PERSISTENT WHEN YOU WERE STALKING ME.
WHERE'D THAT PERSISTENCE GO?
....

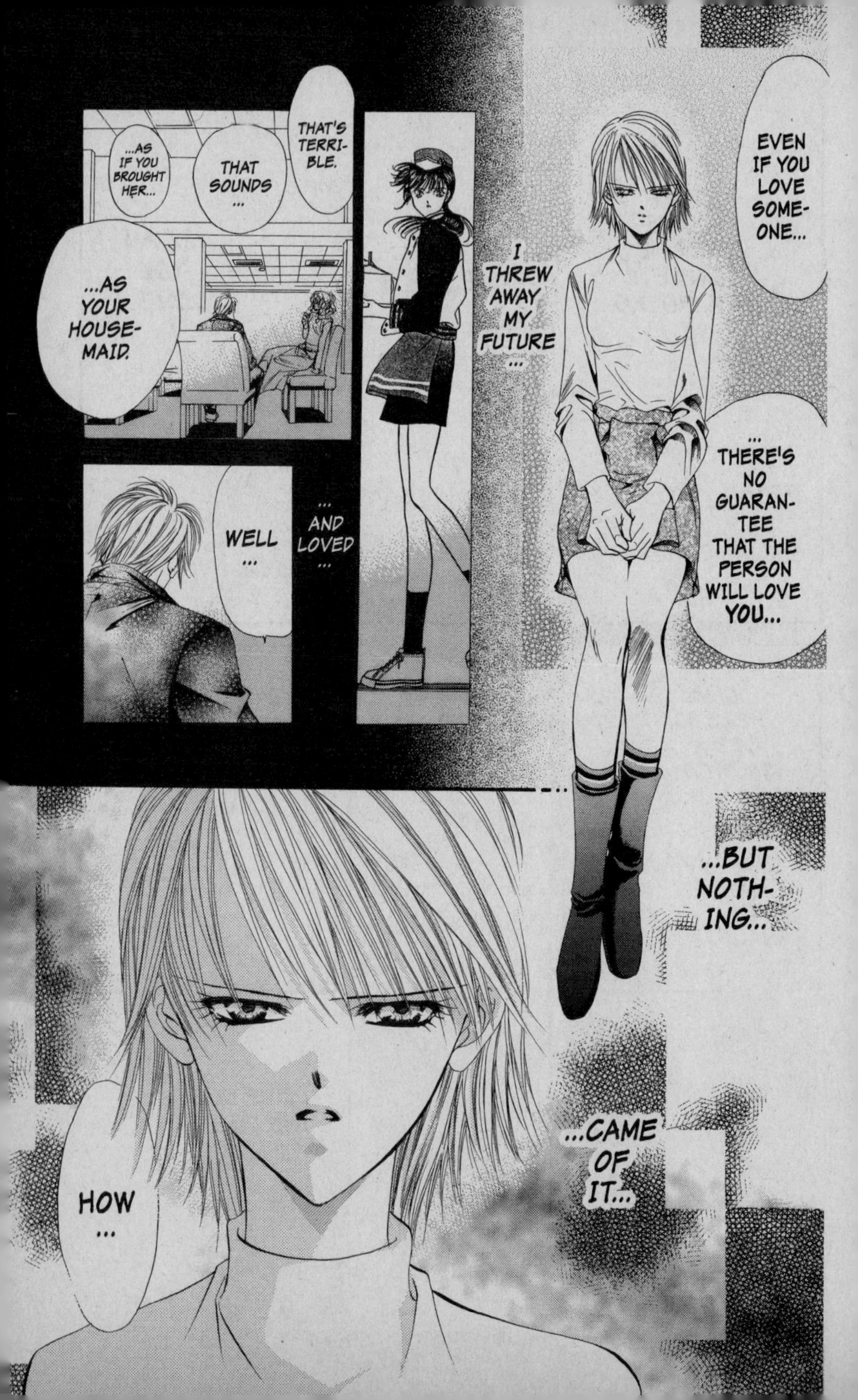
EVEN IF YOU LOVE SOME-ONE...
...THERE'S NO GUARAN-TEE THAT THE PERSON WILL LOVE YOU...
I THREW AWAY MY FUTURE...
THAT'S TERRI-BLE.
...AND LOVED...
THAT SOUNDS...
...AS IF YOU BROUGHT HER...
...AS YOUR HOUSE-MAID.
WELL...
...BUT NOTH-ING...
...CAME OF IT...
HOW...

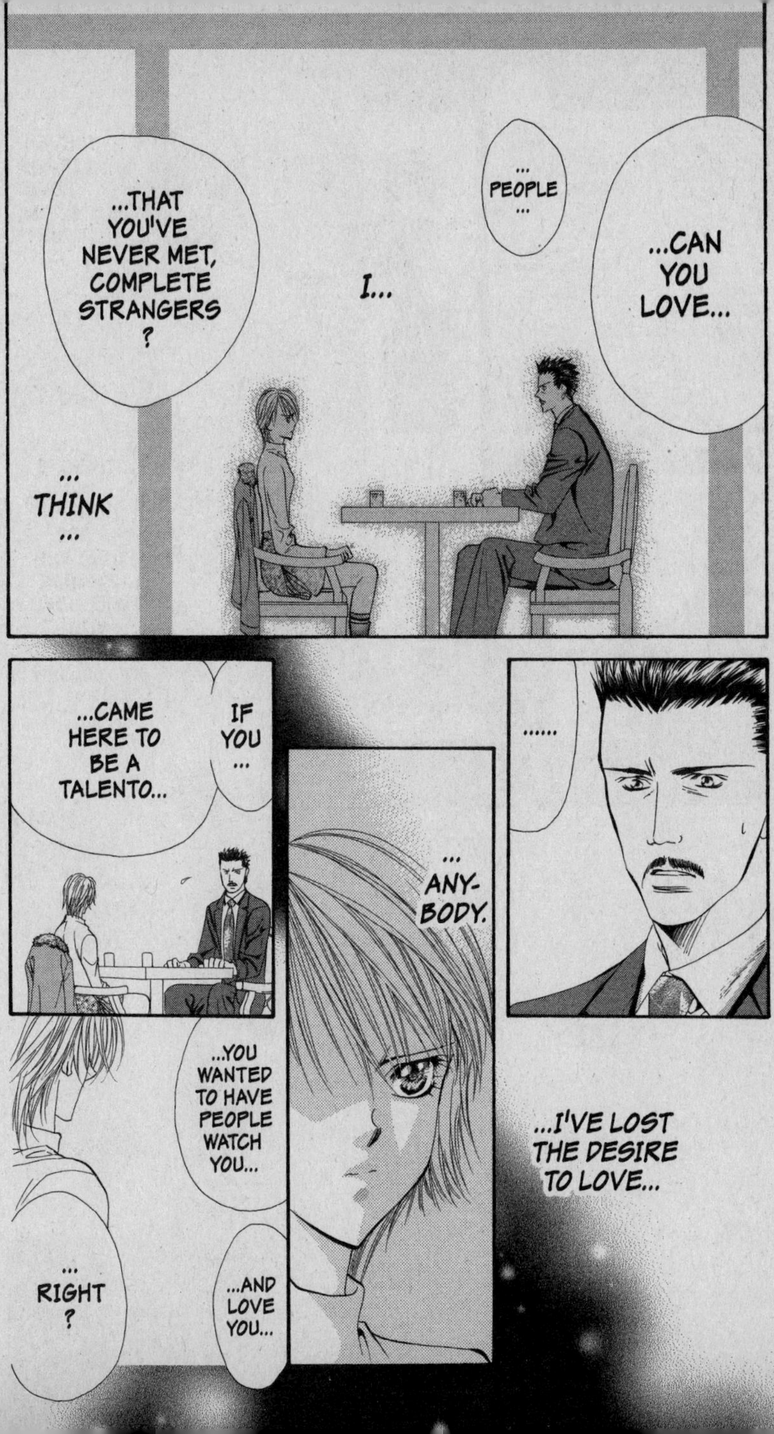
...CAN YOU LOVE...
...PEOPLE...
I...
...THAT YOU'VE NEVER MET, COMPLETE STRANGERS?
...THINK...
......
...ANY-BODY.
IF YOU...
...CAME HERE TO BE A TALENTO...
...I'VE LOST THE DESIRE TO LOVE...
...YOU WANTED TO HAVE PEOPLE WATCH YOU...
...AND LOVE YOU...
...RIGHT?

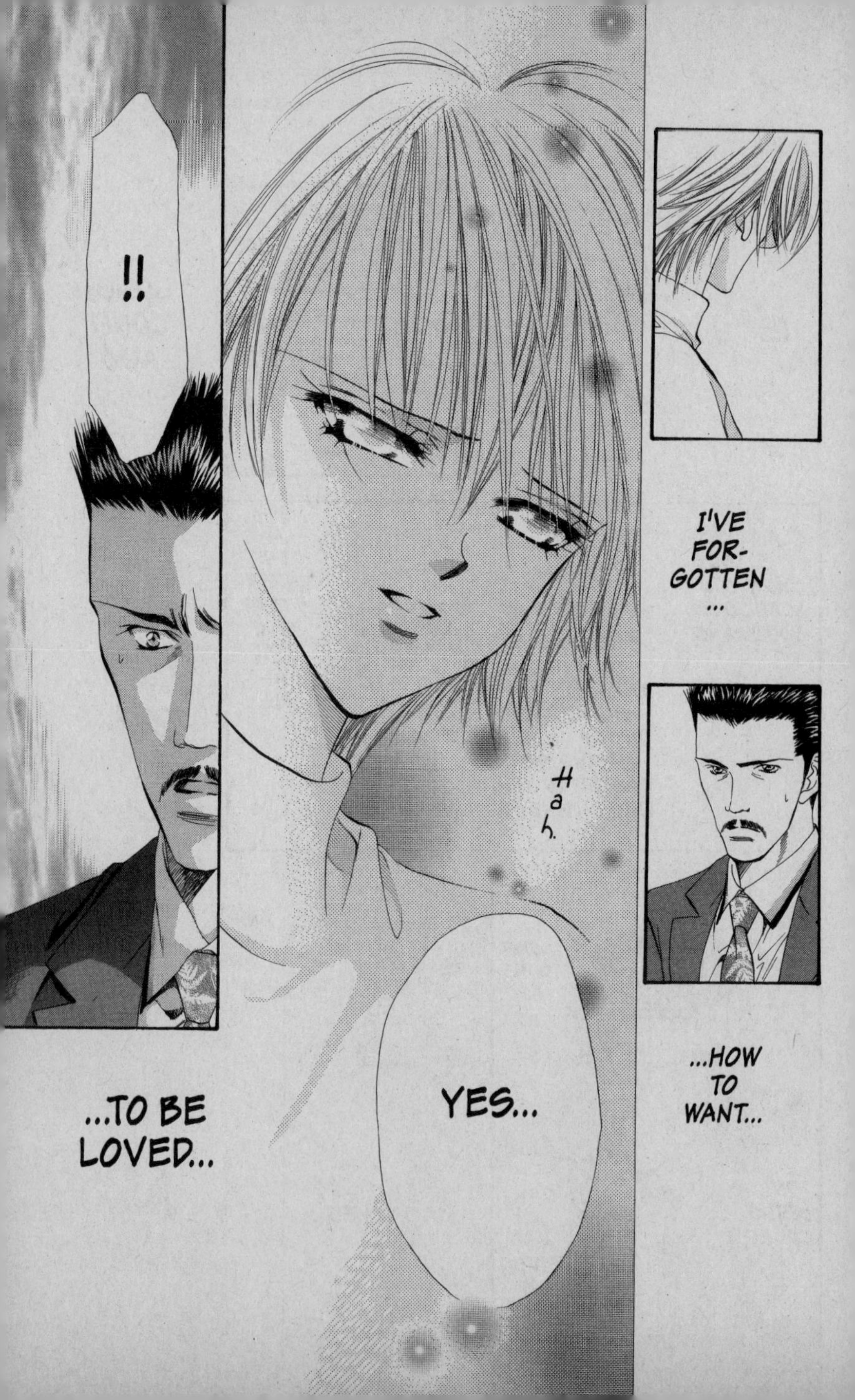
I'VE FOR-GOTTEN ...
...HOW TO WANT...
Hah.
YES...
!!
...TO BE LOVED...

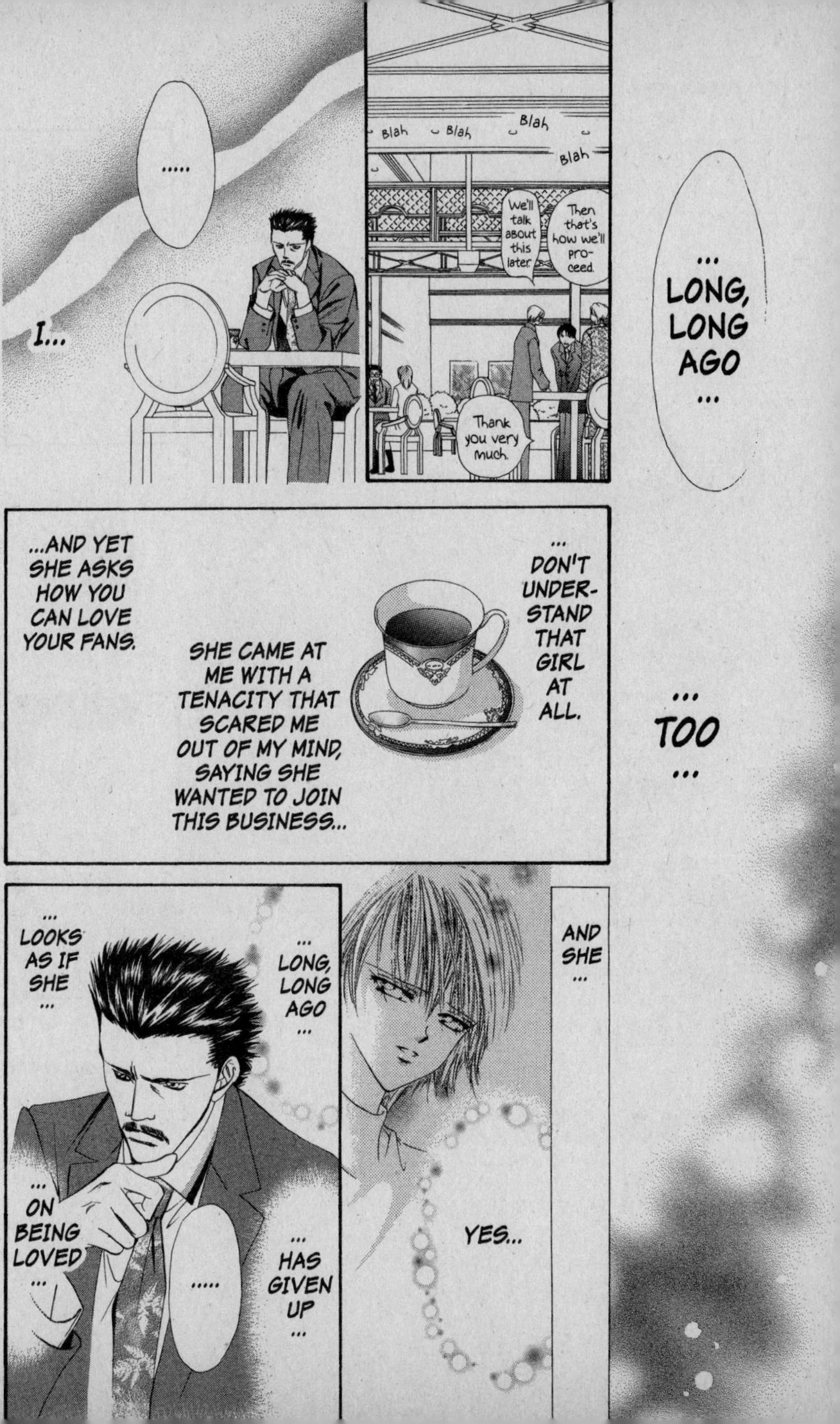
... LONG, LONG AGO ...
Blah
Blah
Blah
Blah
Then that's how we'll proceed.
We'll talk about this later.
Thank you very much.
.....
I...
... TOO ...
... DON'T UNDERSTAND THAT GIRL AT ALL.
SHE CAME AT ME WITH A TENACITY THAT SCARED ME OUT OF MY MIND, SAYING SHE WANTED TO JOIN THIS BUSINESS...
...AND YET SHE ASKS HOW YOU CAN LOVE YOUR FANS.
AND SHE ...
YES...
... LOOKS AS IF SHE ...
... LONG, LONG AGO ...
... HAS GIVEN UP ...
... ON BEING LOVED ...
.....

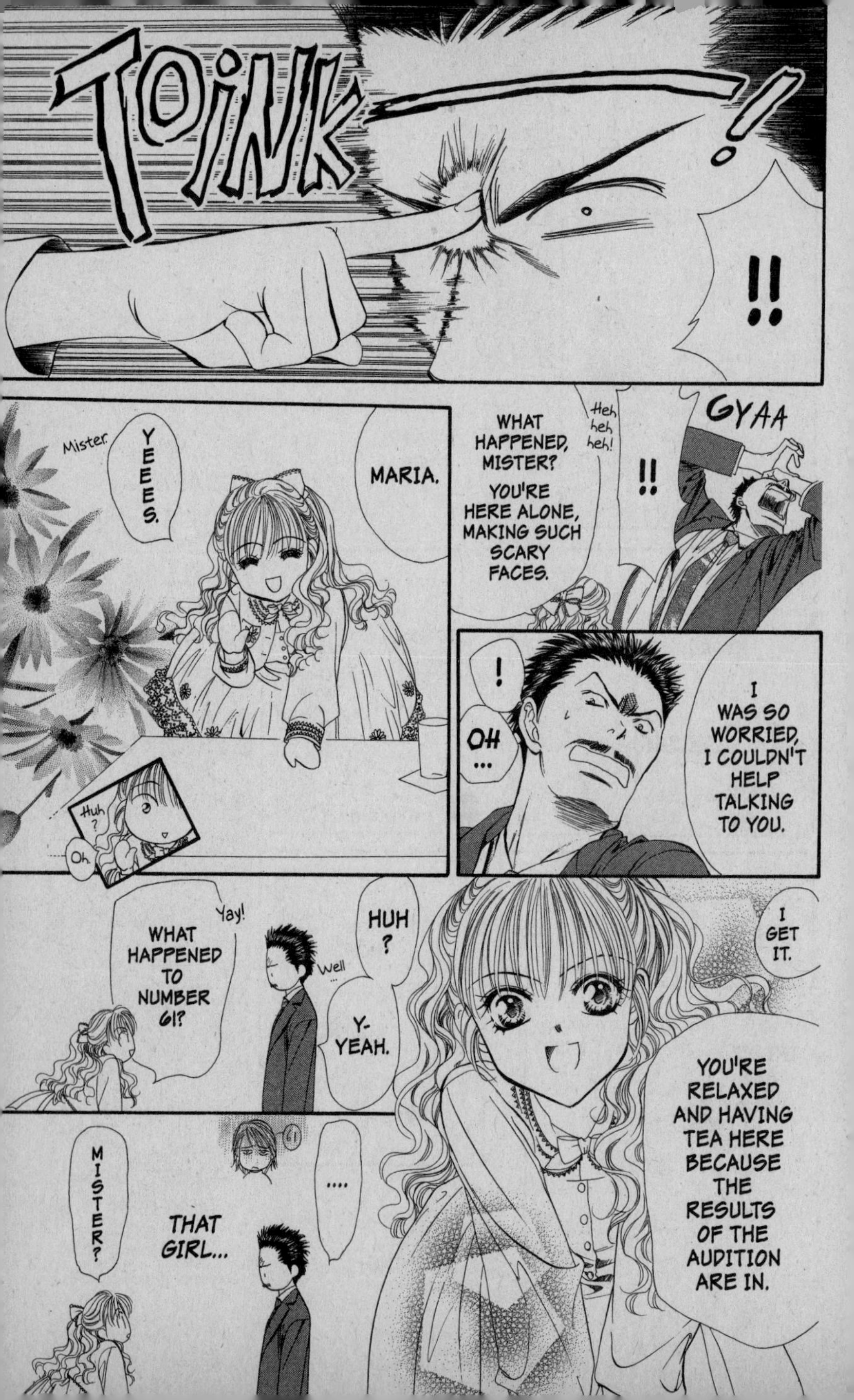
TOINK
!
!!
GYAA
!!
Heh heh heh!
WHAT HAPPENED, MISTER?
YOU'RE HERE ALONE, MAKING SUCH SCARY FACES.
I WAS SO WORRIED, I COULDN'T HELP TALKING TO YOU.
!
OH ...
MARIA.
YEEEES.
Mister.
Huh?
Oh.
I GET IT.
YOU'RE RELAXED AND HAVING TEA HERE BECAUSE THE RESULTS OF THE AUDITION ARE IN.
HUH?
Well ...
Y-YEAH.
Yay!
WHAT HAPPENED TO NUMBER 61?
....
61
THAT GIRL...
MISTER?

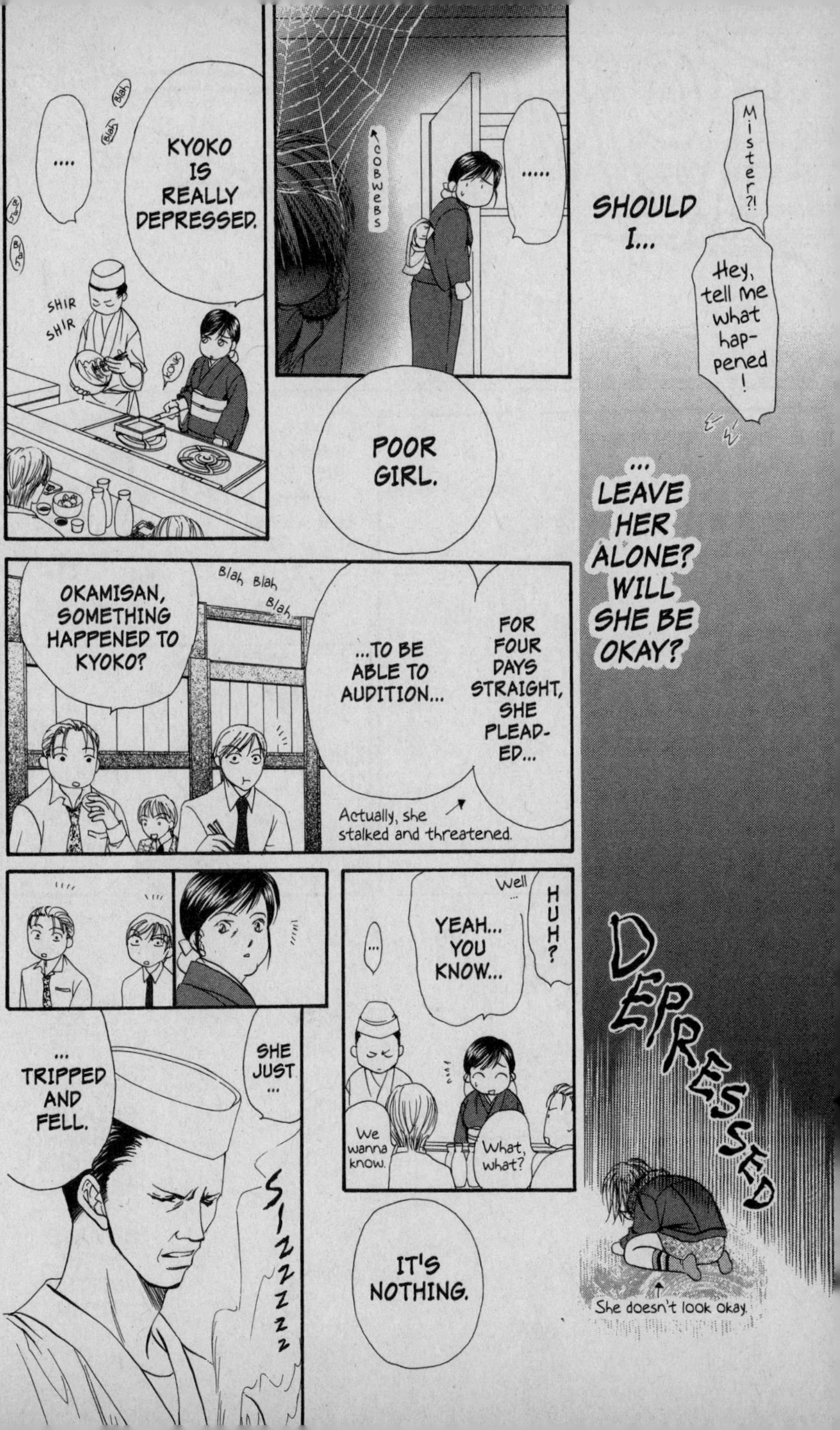
Mister?!
Hey, tell me what happened!
SHOULD I...
...LEAVE HER ALONE? WILL SHE BE OKAY?
DEPRESSED
She doesn't look okay.
COBWEBS
.....
Blah
Blah
Blah
Blah
KYOKO IS REALLY DEPRESSED.
....
SHIR SHIR
KONK
POOR GIRL.
FOR FOUR DAYS STRAIGHT, SHE PLEADED...
...TO BE ABLE TO AUDITION...
Actually, she stalked and threatened.
Blah Blah Blah
OKAMISAN, SOMETHING HAPPENED TO KYOKO?
HUH?
Well...
YEAH... YOU KNOW...
...
What, what?
We wanna know.
IT'S NOTHING.
SHE JUST...
...TRIPPED AND FELL.
SIZZZZZ

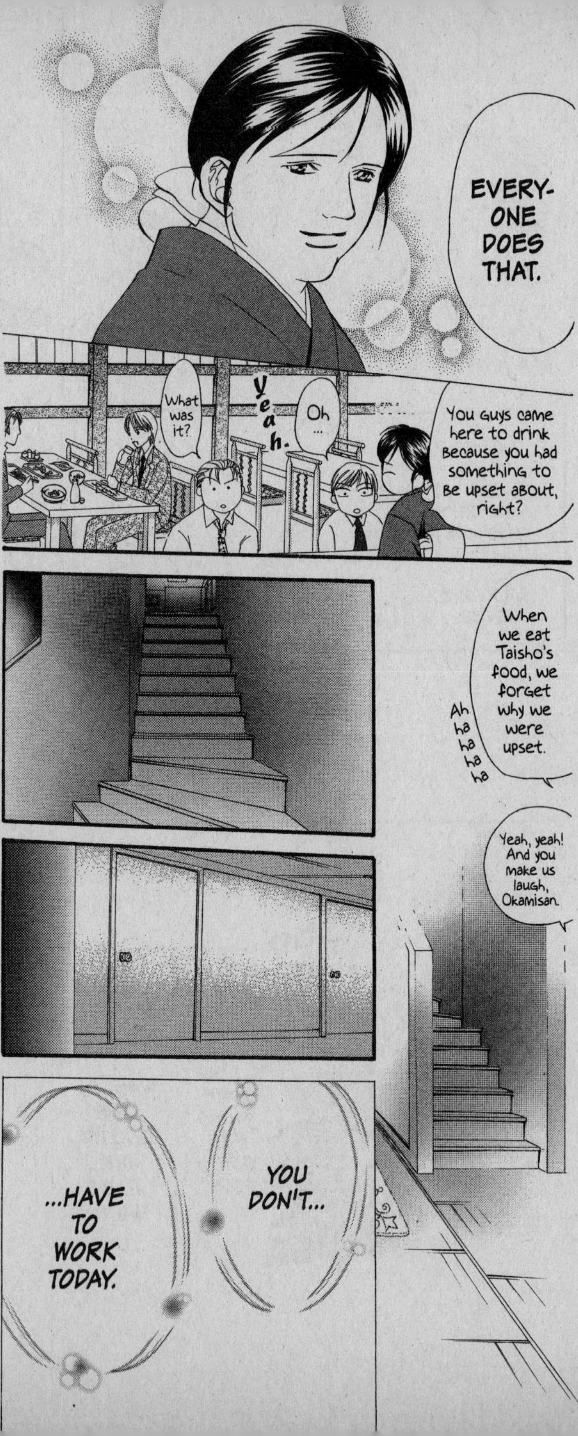
EVERY-ONE DOES THAT.
You guys came here to drink because you had something to be upset about, right?
Oh...
Yeah.
What was it?
When we eat Taisho's food, we forget why we were upset.
Ah ha ha ha ha ha
Yeah, yeah! And you make us laugh, Okamisan.
YOU DON'T...
...HAVE TO WORK TODAY.

7

When I realized that compared to the main, young characters, the ratio of middle-aged guys was going up... Oh nooooooo!! This is becoming like Kurepara!! I'm sorry!! I'm sorry!! I'll stop!! I'll really stop drawing middle-aged guys!! I will try to control myself...waaah!... It's not too late to start now...no more middle-aged guys!! ...But as I say this, I've added a scene where Lory ponders about Kyoko...this is not convincing at all...

I wanted to put this scene when the story was printed in the magazine too, and I couldn't... But... even if I could've put that scene in the magazine, I don't know whether he'd have been dressed like that, and pondering like that...well...in the end, I must love Lory...

...I definitely do not...

...deny it...

Ahhh!

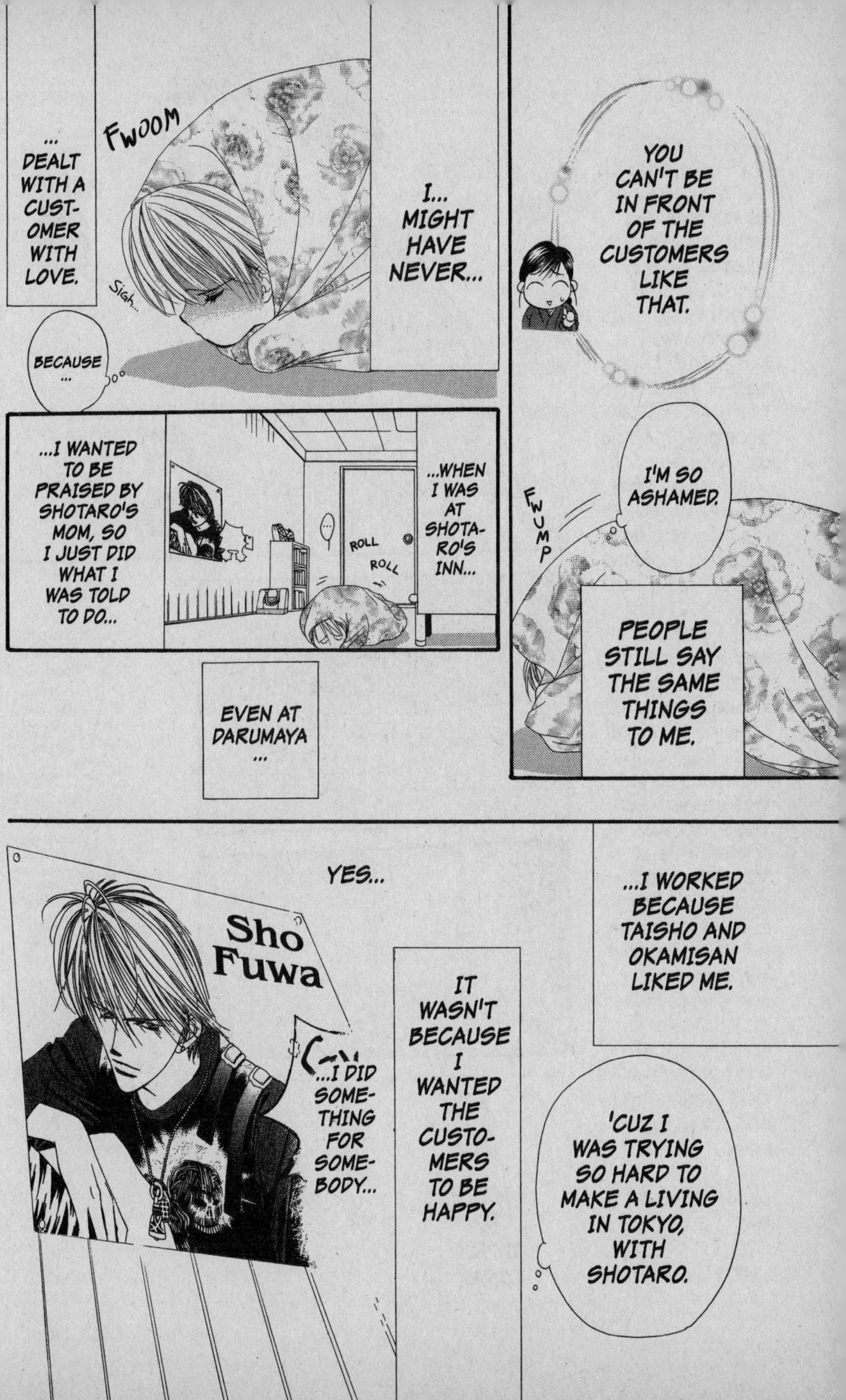
YOU CAN'T BE IN FRONT OF THE CUSTOMERS LIKE THAT.
FWUMP
I'M SO ASHAMED.
PEOPLE STILL SAY THE SAME THINGS TO ME.
I... MIGHT HAVE NEVER...
FWOOM
... DEALT WITH A CUST-OMER WITH LOVE.
Sigh...
BECAUSE ...
...WHEN I WAS AT SHOTA-RO'S INN...
ROLL
ROLL
...
...I WANTED TO BE PRAISED BY SHOTARO'S MOM, SO I JUST DID WHAT I WAS TOLD TO DO...
EVEN AT DARUMAYA ...
...I WORKED BECAUSE TAISHO AND OKAMISAN LIKED ME.
'CUZ I WAS TRYING SO HARD TO MAKE A LIVING IN TOKYO, WITH SHOTARO.
YES...
IT WASN'T BECAUSE I WANTED THE CUSTO-MERS TO BE HAPPY.
...I DID SOME-THING FOR SOME-BODY...
Sho Fuwa

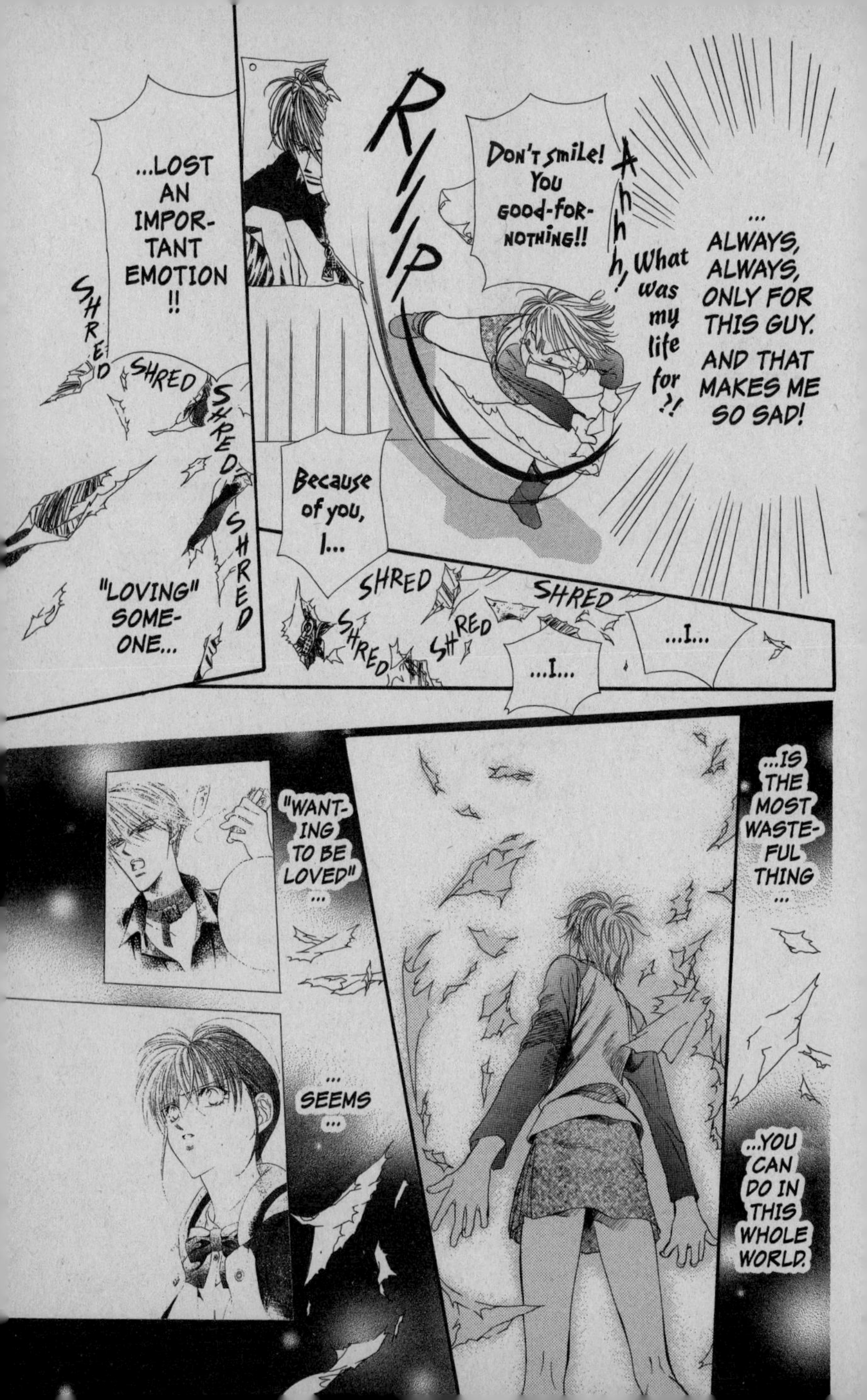
...ALWAYS, ALWAYS, ONLY FOR THIS GUY.
AND THAT MAKES ME SO SAD!
Ahhh!
What was my life for?!
Don't smile! You good-for-nothing!!
RIP
Because of you, I...
SHRED
SHRED
SHRED
SHRED
...I...
...I...
...LOST AN IMPORTANT EMOTION!!
SHRED
SHRED
SHRED
SHRED
"LOVING" SOMEONE...
...IS THE MOST WASTEFUL THING...
...YOU CAN DO IN THIS WHOLE WORLD.
"WANTING TO BE LOVED"...
...SEEMS...

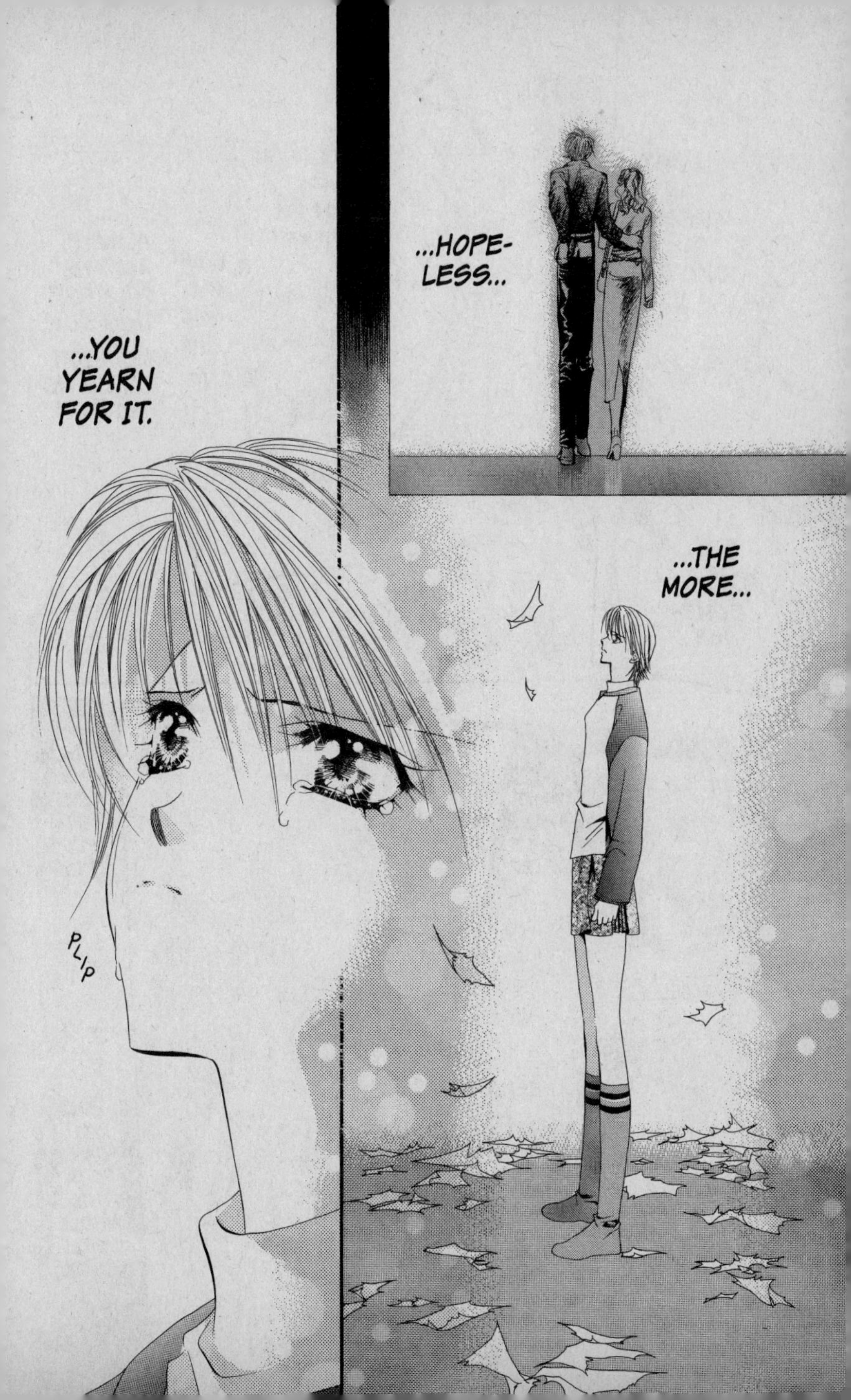
...HOPE-LESS...
...THE MORE...
...YOU YEARN FOR IT.
PLIP

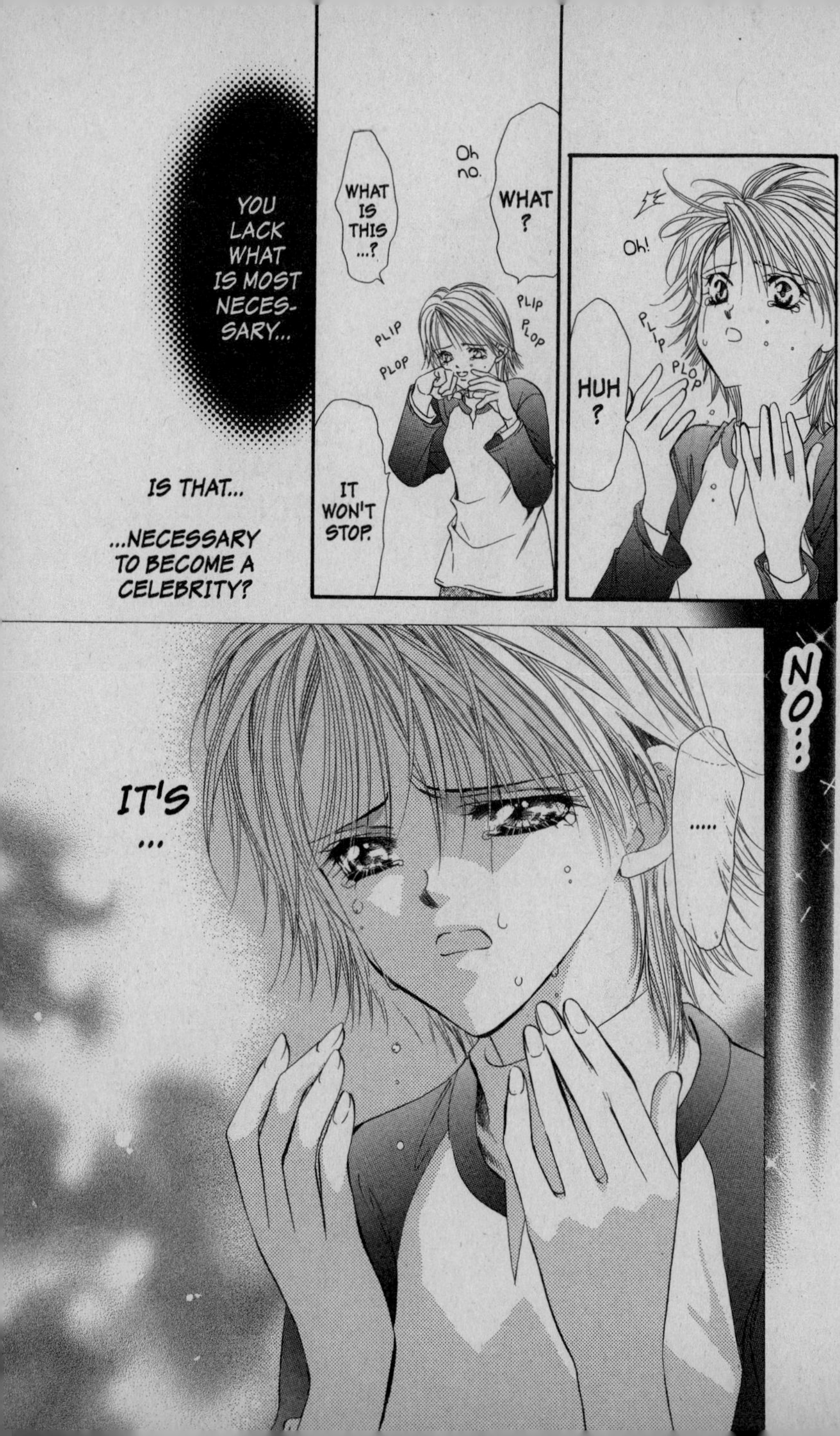
Oh!
PLIP PLOP
HUH?
Oh no.
WHAT?
WHAT IS THIS ...?
PLIP PLOP
PLIP PLOP
IT WON'T STOP.
YOU LACK WHAT IS MOST NECES-SARY...
IS THAT...
...NECESSARY TO BECOME A CELEBRITY?
NO...
.....
IT'S ...

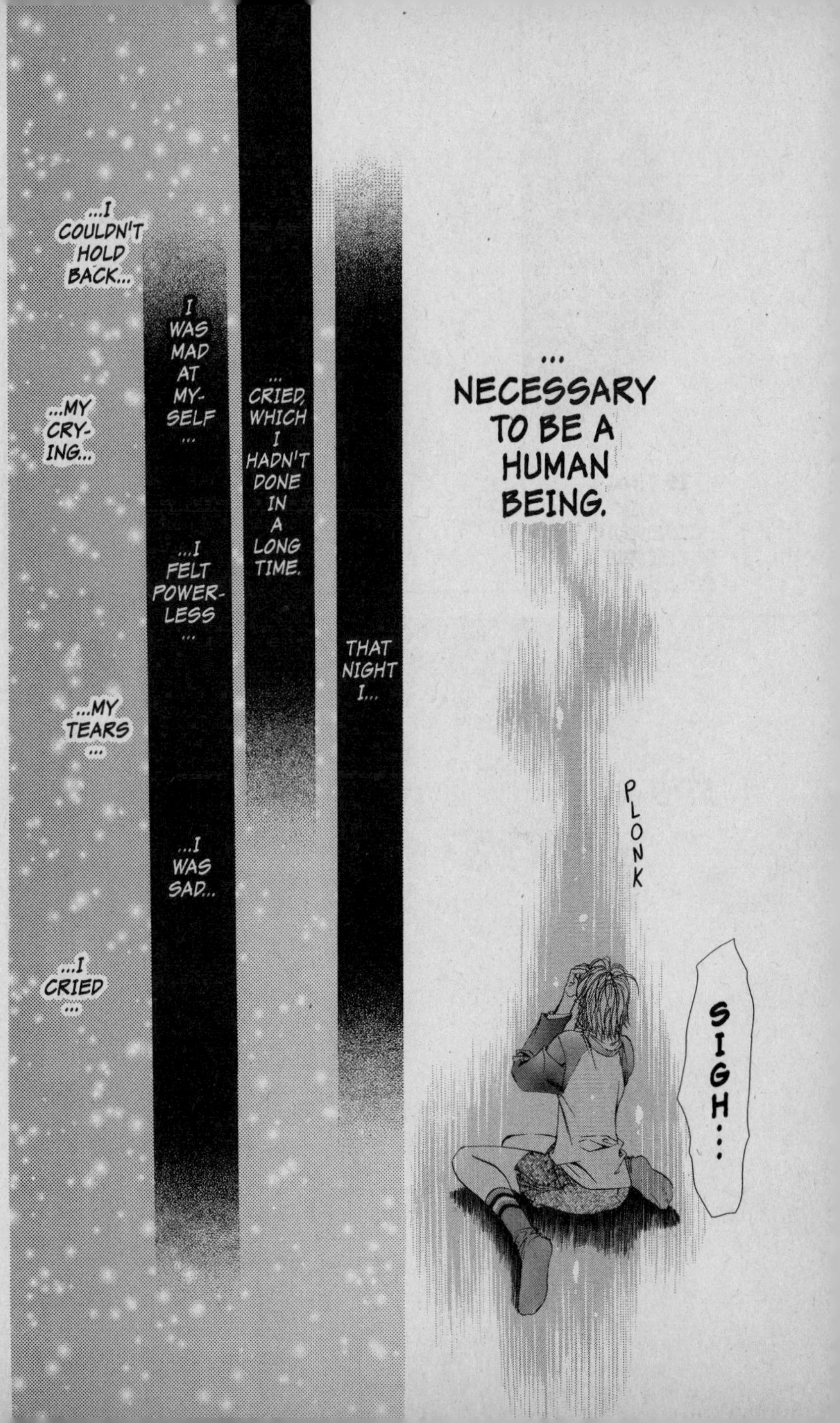

... NECESSARY TO BE A HUMAN BEING.
PLONK
SIGH...
THAT NIGHT I...
...CRIED, WHICH I HADN'T DONE IN A LONG TIME.
I WAS MAD AT MY-SELF...
...I FELT POWER-LESS...
...I WAS SAD...
...I COULDN'T HOLD BACK...
...MY CRY-ING...
...MY TEARS...
...I CRIED...

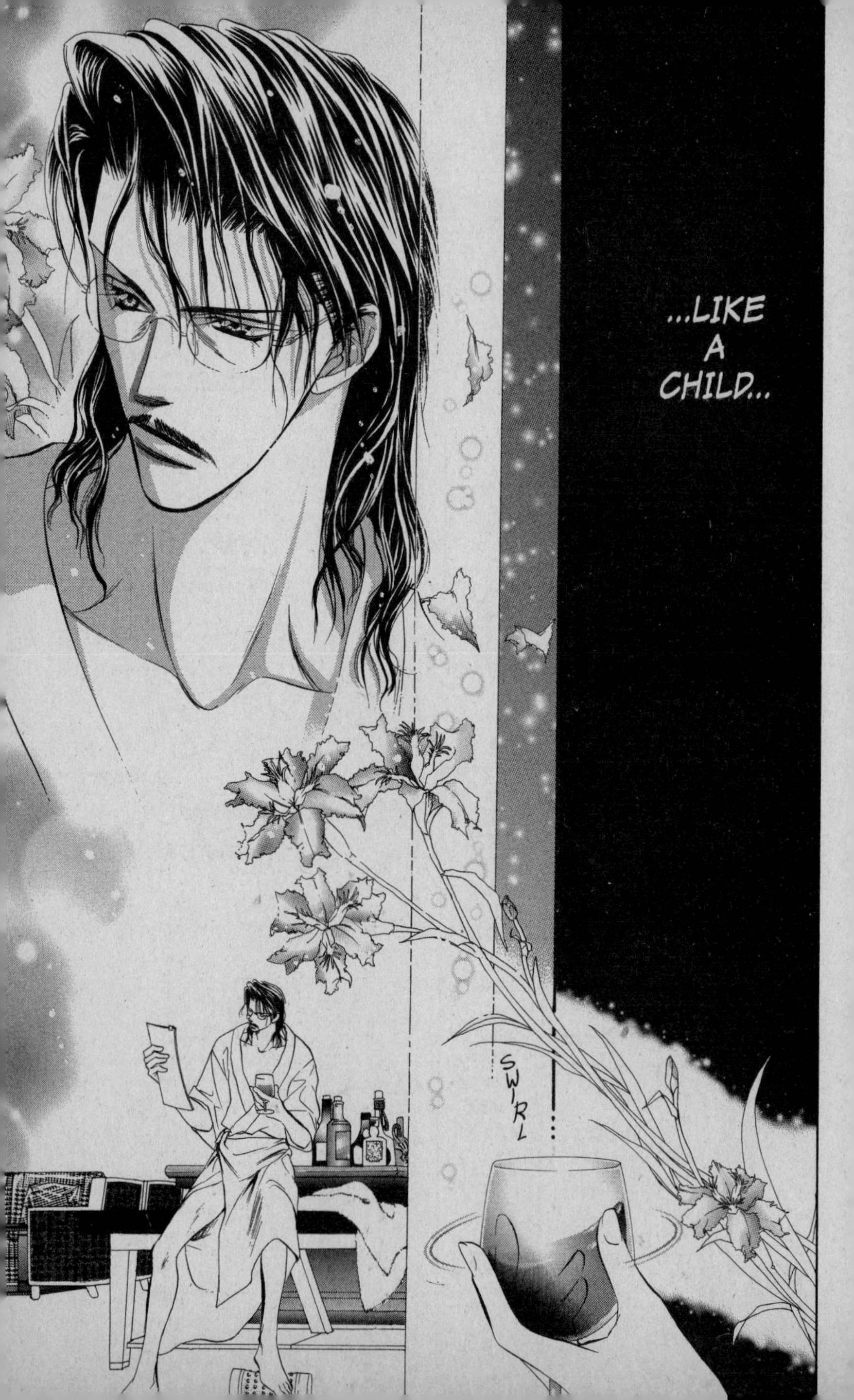
...LIKE A CHILD...
SWIRL

Objective: Actor Singer Artist Talento

Hmmm...

ROLL ROLL

ROLL ROLL

H
M
M
M.

....

Hmmm...

....

R
O
L
L

He's massaging the pressure points of his feet.

Special Skill	I can cut, peel, and take apart anything.
Favorite Word	Fugutaiten ←

She had to pick this word...

...

The feeling of hatred so great, you don't even want to let the person live.

THAT GIRL...

....

IF SHE GOES OUT INTO THE WORLD AS A TALENTO, I'M CURIOUS...

THE PEOPLE WHO RAISED ME WITHOUT SHUNNING ME.

THE PEOPLE WHO GAVE ME A PLACE TO SLEEP, WITHOUT BEGRUDGING IT.

THE PEOPLE I RESPECT.

↑
Shotaro's parents and Darumaya's owners.

...WILL NOT BE ABLE TO GROW...

....

...WHAT SHE'LL DO.

LOOKING AT COSMETICS.

HOBBY.

...

...EVEN IF SHE MAKES HER DEBUT.

BUT...

I watched her reaction test, and my instincts screamed out.

Briiiing

BUT...

Of all the girls I've seen so far...

THIS ISN'T RIGHT...

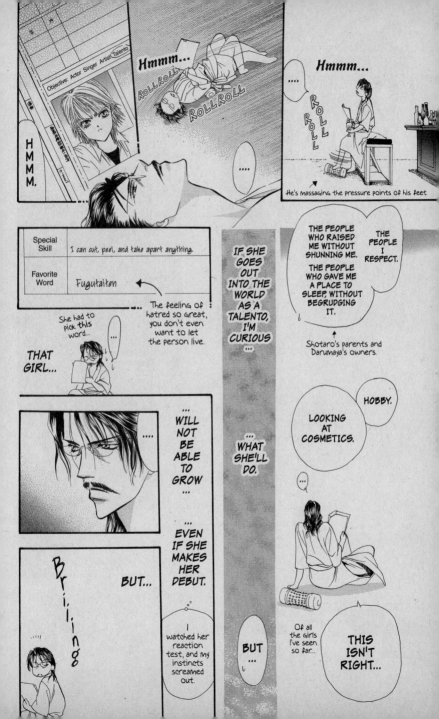

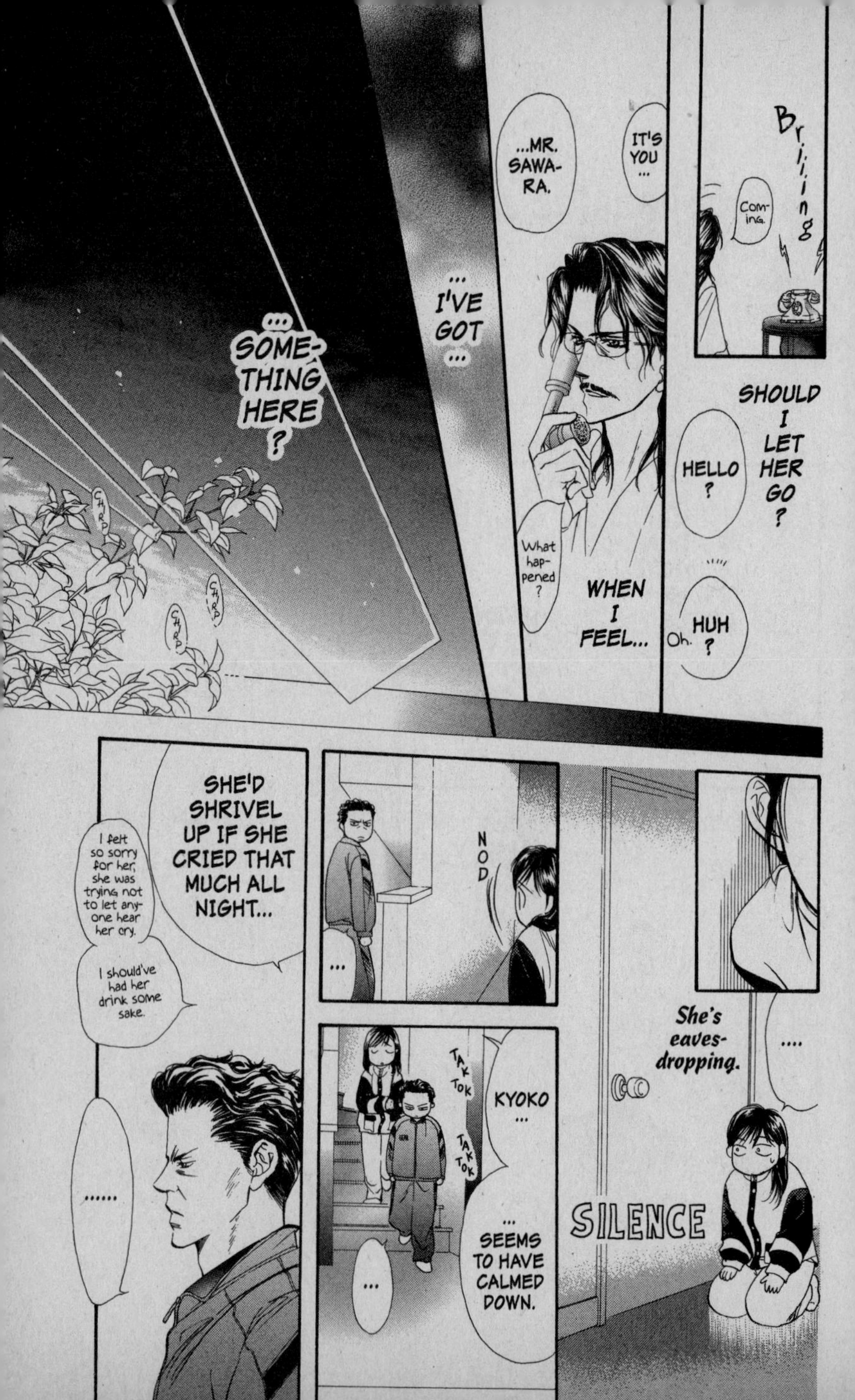
Briiiing
Com-ing.
SHOULD I LET HER GO?
HELLO?
HUH?
Oh.
IT'S YOU...
...MR. SAWARA.
What happened?
WHEN I FEEL...
...I'VE GOT...
...SOMETHING HERE?
CHIRP
CHIRP
CHIRP
She's eavesdropping.
....
SILENCE
NOD
...
KYOKO...
TAK TOK
TAK TOK
...SEEMS TO HAVE CALMED DOWN.
...
SHE'D SHRIVEL UP IF SHE CRIED THAT MUCH ALL NIGHT...
I felt so sorry for her, she was trying not to let anyone hear her cry.
I should've had her drink some sake.
......

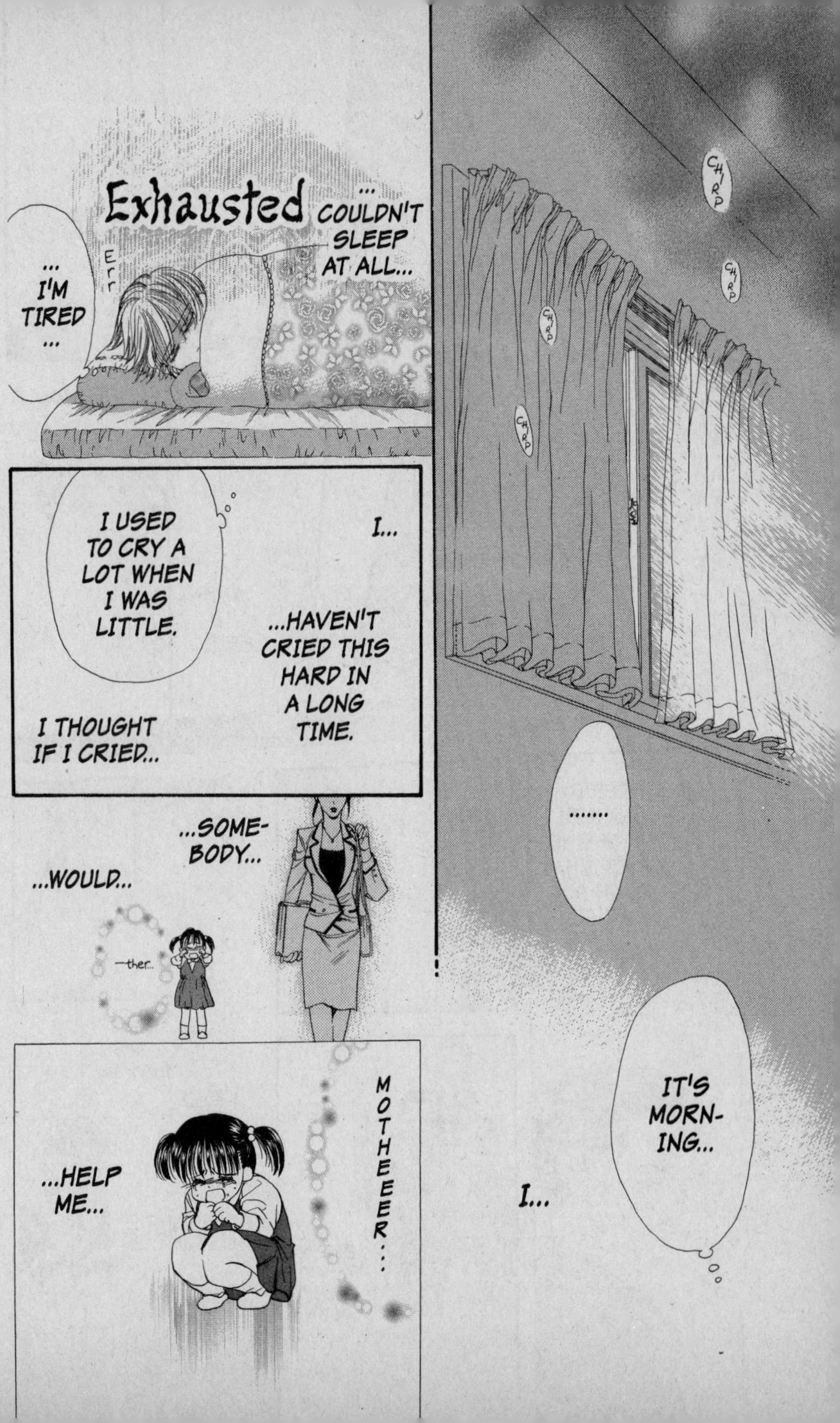
CHIRP
CHIRP
CHIRP
CHIRP
....
IT'S MORNING...
I...
Exhausted
...COULDN'T SLEEP AT ALL...
Err
...I'M TIRED...
I...
...HAVEN'T CRIED THIS HARD IN A LONG TIME.
I USED TO CRY A LOT WHEN I WAS LITTLE.
I THOUGHT IF I CRIED...
...SOMEBODY...
...WOULD...
—ther...
MOTHEEER...
...HELP ME...

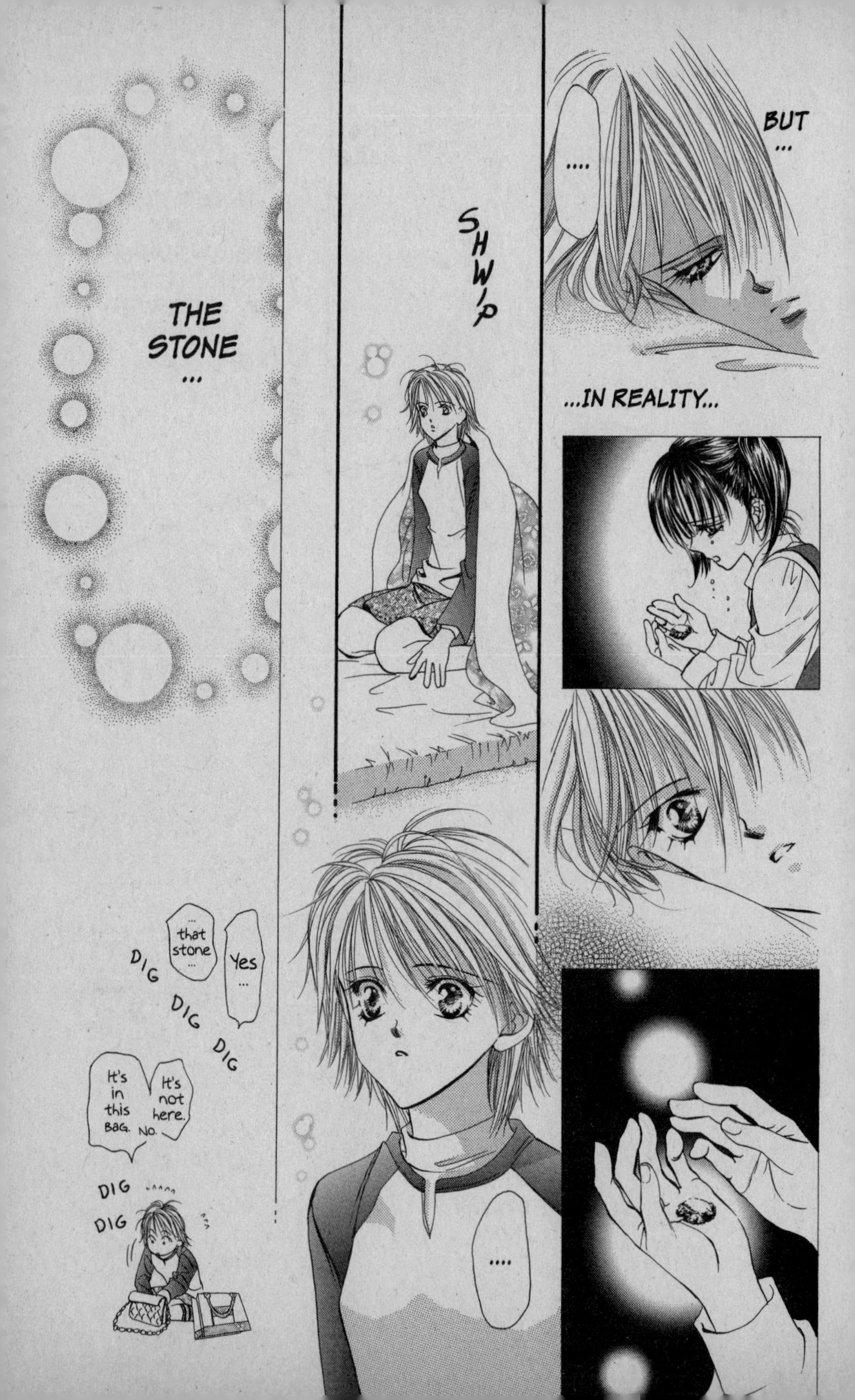
BUT ...
....
...IN REALITY...
SHWIP
....
THE STONE ...
... that stone ...
Yes ...
DIG DIG DIG
It's not here.
It's in this BAG. NO.
DIG DIG

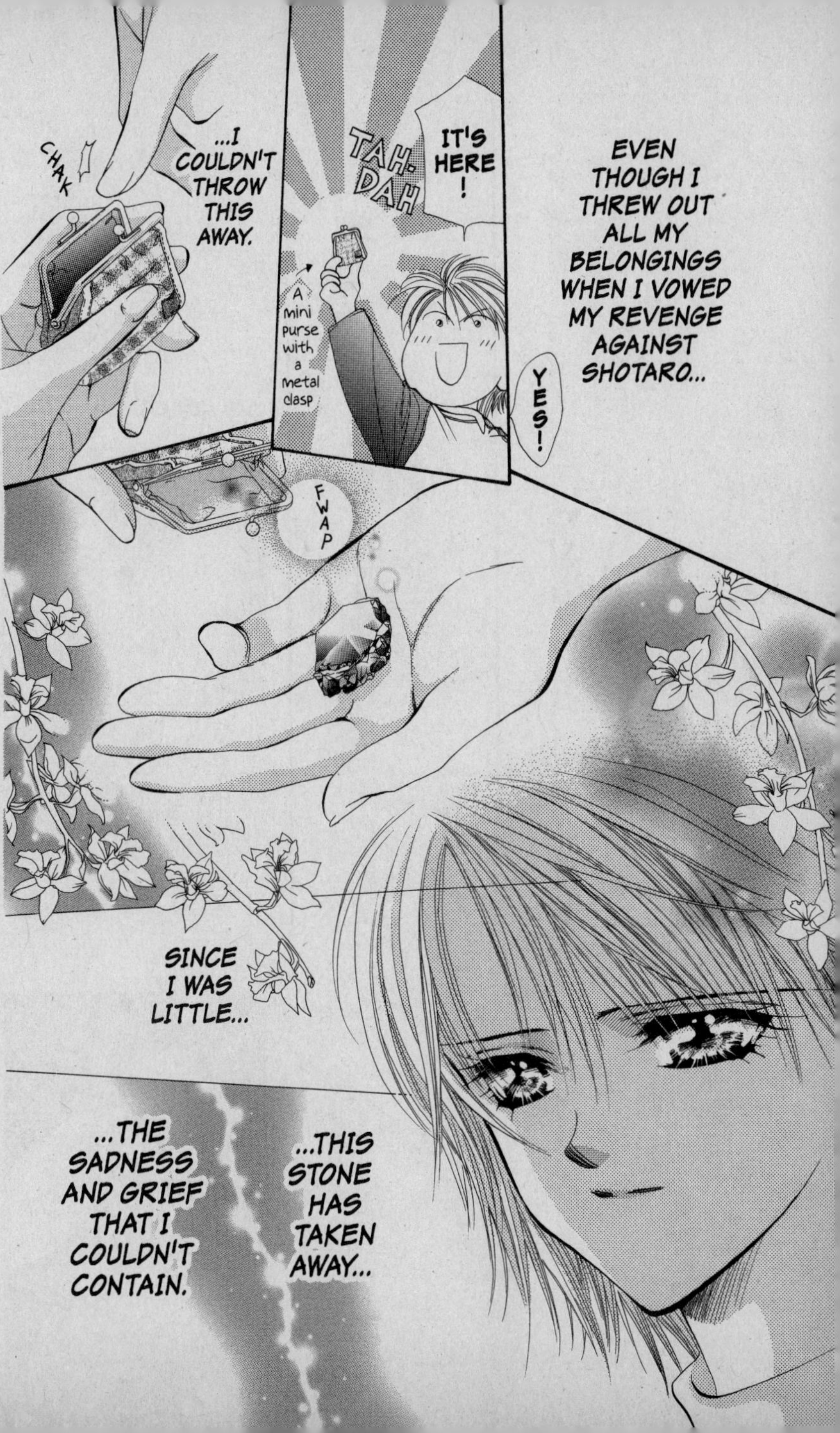
EVEN THOUGH I THREW OUT ALL MY BELONGINGS WHEN I VOWED MY REVENGE AGAINST SHOTARO...
IT'S HERE!
TAH-DAH
YES!
A mini purse with a metal clasp
...I COULDN'T THROW THIS AWAY.
CHAK
FWAP
SINCE I WAS LITTLE...
...THIS STONE HAS TAKEN AWAY...
...THE SADNESS AND GRIEF THAT I COULDN'T CONTAIN.

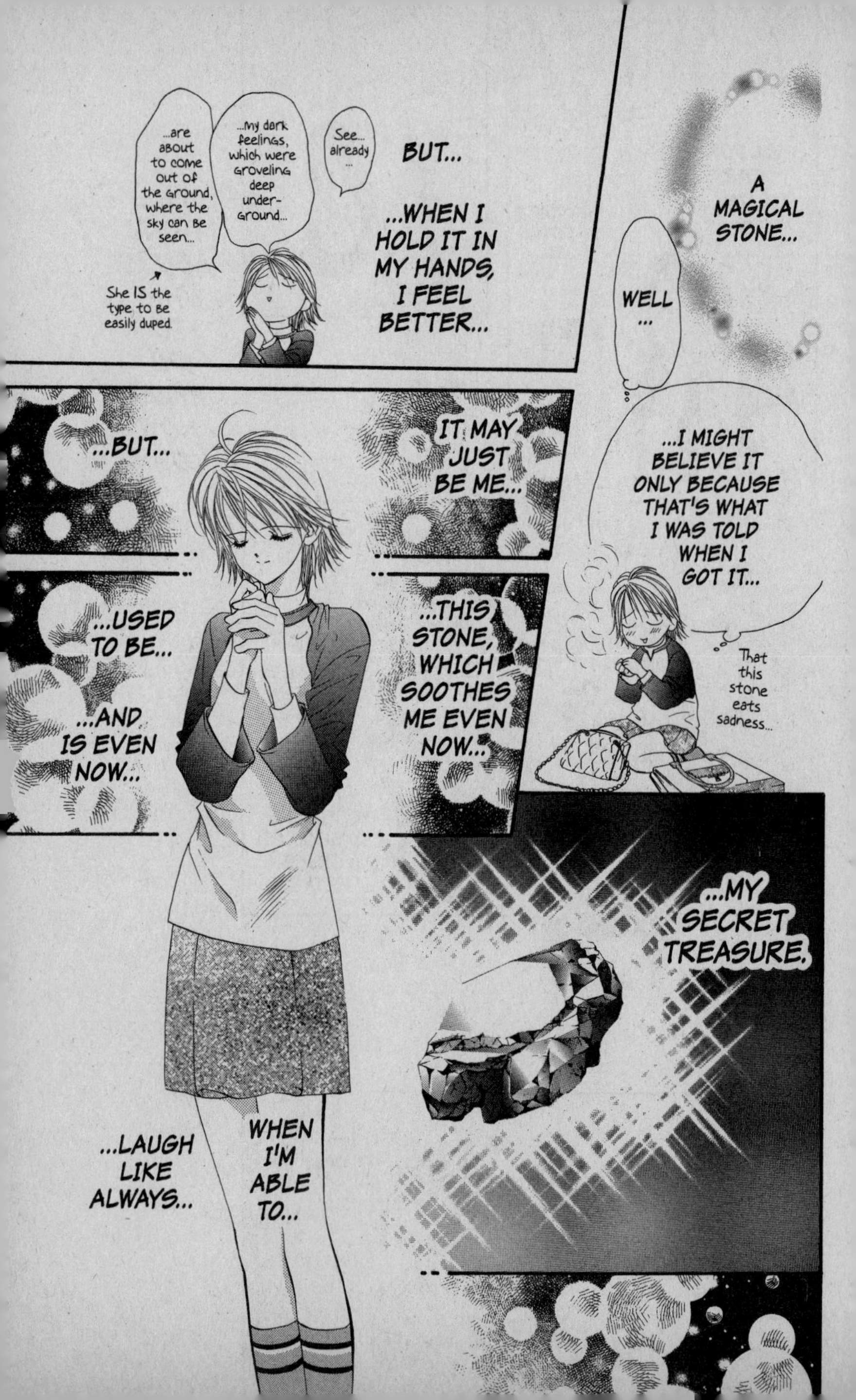
A MAGICAL STONE...
WELL...
...I MIGHT BELIEVE IT ONLY BECAUSE THAT'S WHAT I WAS TOLD WHEN I GOT IT...
That this stone eats sadness...
BUT...
...WHEN I HOLD IT IN MY HANDS, I FEEL BETTER...
See... already...
...My dark feelings, which were groveling deep underground...
...are about to come out of the ground, where the sky can be seen...
She IS the type to be easily duped.
IT MAY JUST BE ME...
...BUT...
...THIS STONE, WHICH SOOTHES ME EVEN NOW...
...USED TO BE...
...AND IS EVEN NOW...
...MY SECRET TREASURE.
WHEN I'M ABLE TO...
...LAUGH LIKE ALWAYS...

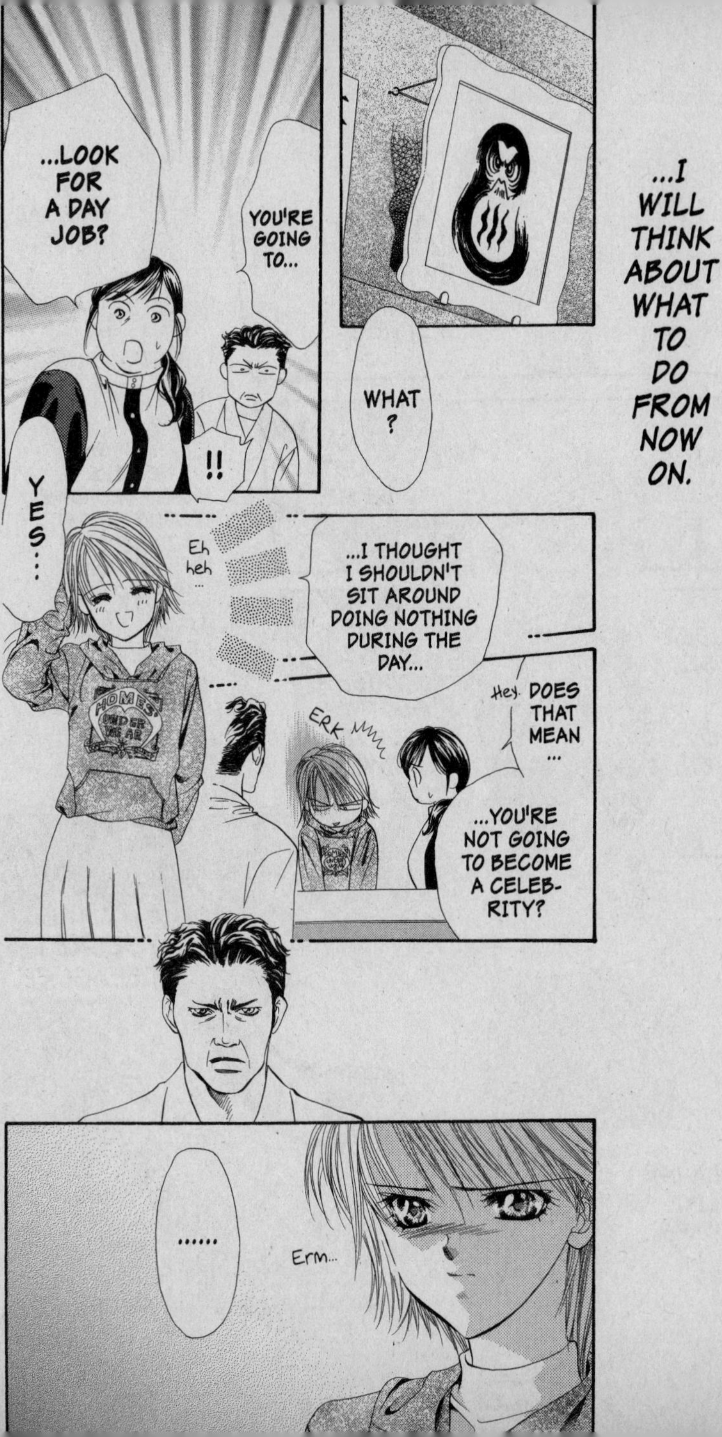
...I WILL THINK ABOUT WHAT TO DO FROM NOW ON.
WHAT?
YOU'RE GOING TO...
...LOOK FOR A DAY JOB?
!!
YES...
Eh heh...
...I THOUGHT I SHOULDN'T SIT AROUND DOING NOTHING DURING THE DAY...
Hey. DOES THAT MEAN...
ERK
...YOU'RE NOT GOING TO BECOME A CELEBRITY?
Erm...
......

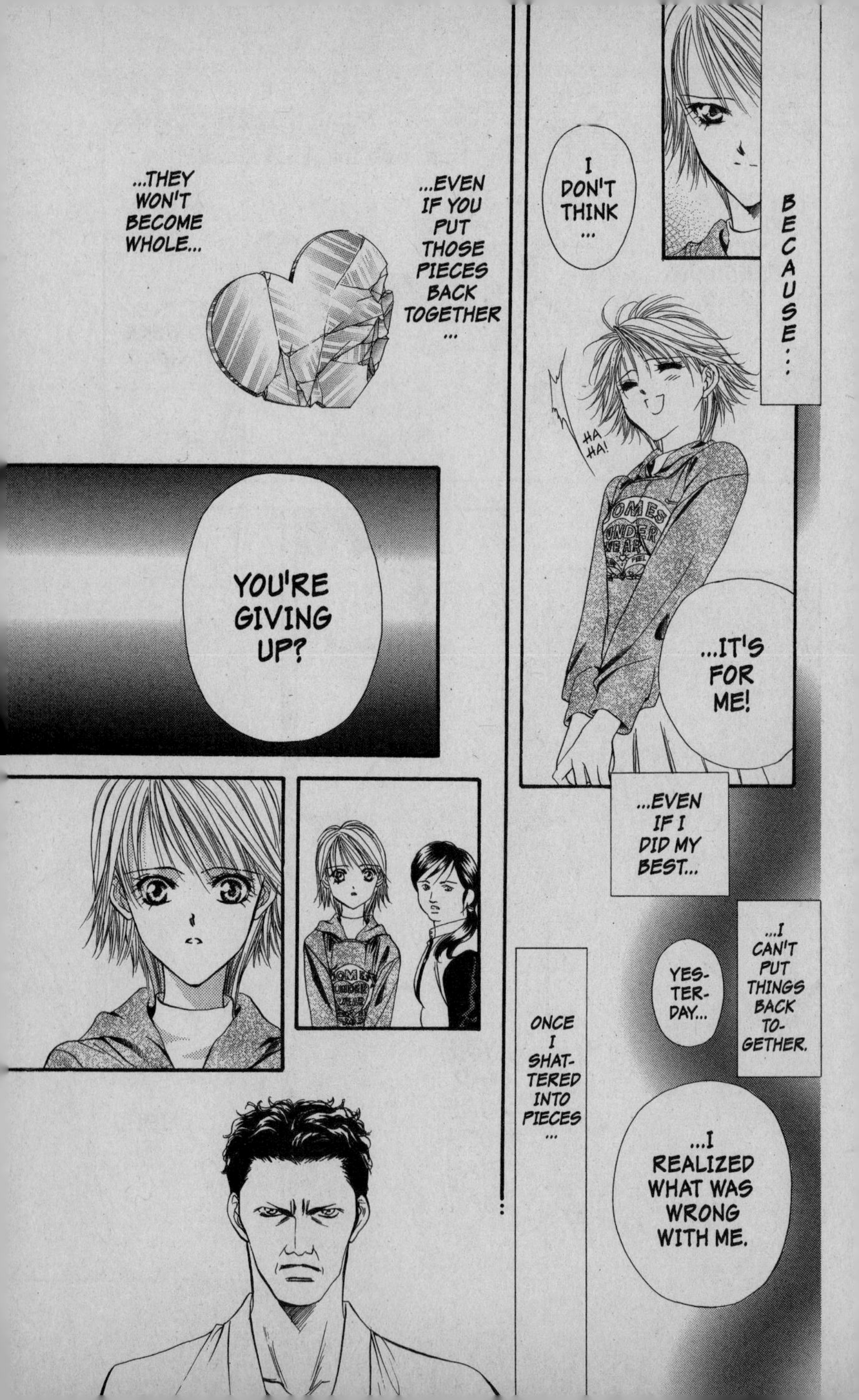
BECAUSE...
I DON'T THINK...
HA HA!
...IT'S FOR ME!
...EVEN IF I DID MY BEST...
...I CAN'T PUT THINGS BACK TOGETHER.
YESTERDAY...
ONCE I SHATTERED INTO PIECES...
...I REALIZED WHAT WAS WRONG WITH ME.
...EVEN IF YOU PUT THOSE PIECES BACK TOGETHER...
...THEY WON'T BECOME WHOLE...
YOU'RE GIVING UP?

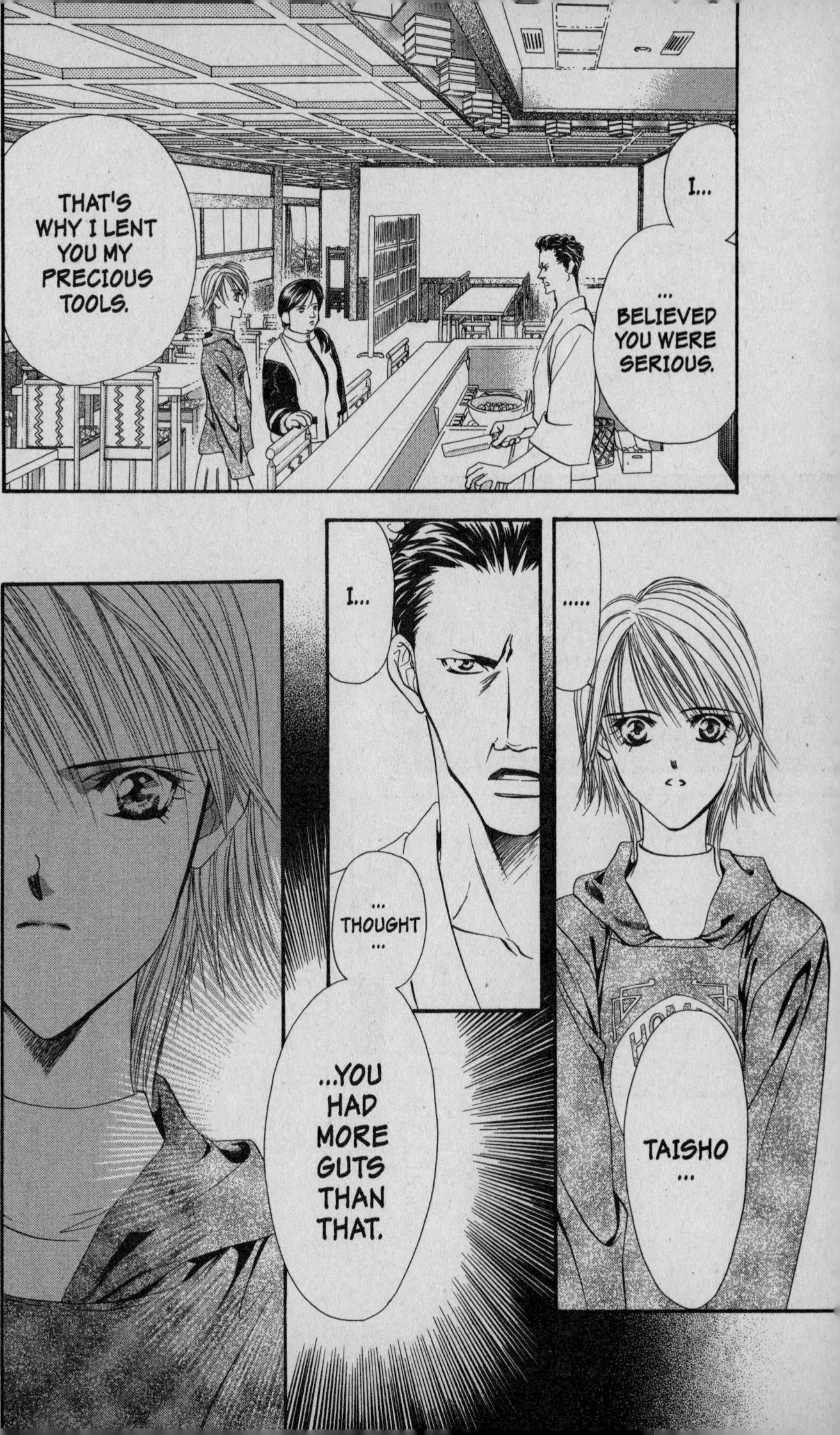
I...
...BELIEVED YOU WERE SERIOUS.
THAT'S WHY I LENT YOU MY PRECIOUS TOOLS.
.....
I...
...THOUGHT...
...YOU HAD MORE GUTS THAN THAT.
TAISHO...

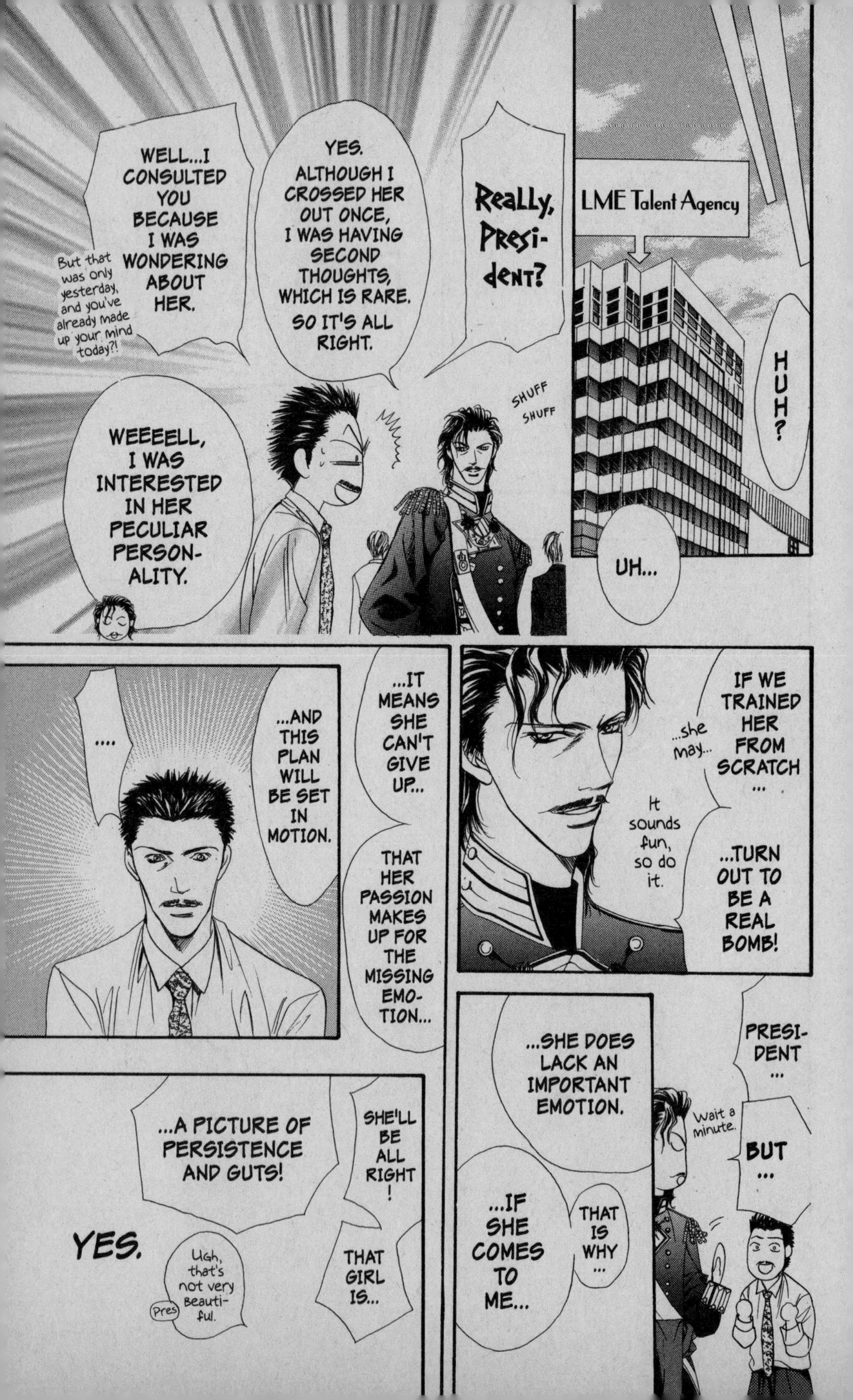
LME Talent Agency
HUH?
Really, President?
UH...
YES. ALTHOUGH I CROSSED HER OUT ONCE, I WAS HAVING SECOND THOUGHTS, WHICH IS RARE. SO IT'S ALL RIGHT.
SHUFF SHUFF
WELL...I CONSULTED YOU BECAUSE I WAS WONDERING ABOUT HER.
But that was only yesterday, and you've already made up your mind today?!
WEEEELL, I WAS INTERESTED IN HER PECULIAR PERSONALITY.
IF WE TRAINED HER FROM SCRATCH...
...she may...
...TURN OUT TO BE A REAL BOMB!
It sounds fun, so do it.
...IT MEANS SHE CAN'T GIVE UP...
THAT HER PASSION MAKES UP FOR THE MISSING EMOTION...
...AND THIS PLAN WILL BE SET IN MOTION.
....
PRESIDENT...
BUT...
Wait a minute.
...SHE DOES LACK AN IMPORTANT EMOTION.
THAT IS WHY...
...IF SHE COMES TO ME...
SHE'LL BE ALL RIGHT!
...A PICTURE OF PERSISTENCE AND GUTS!
THAT GIRL IS...
YES.
Ugh, that's not very Beautiful.
Pres

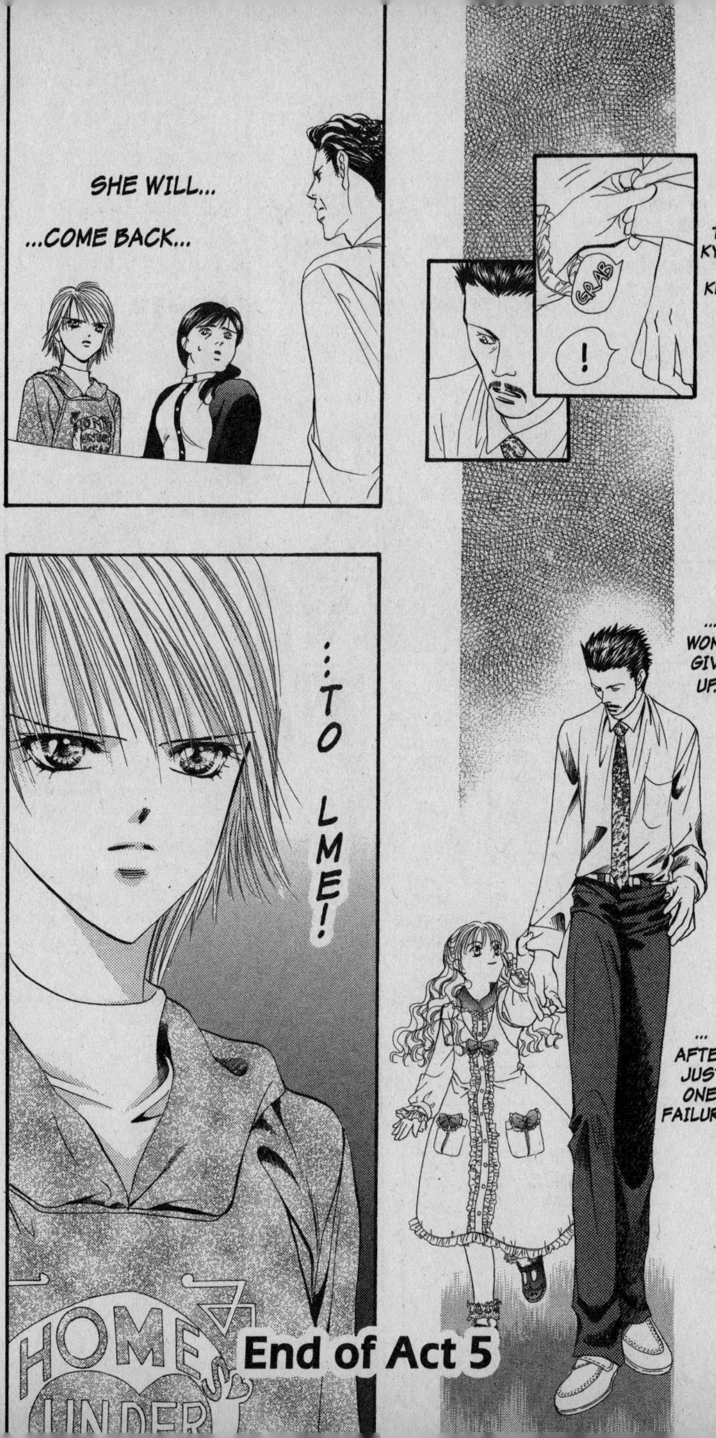
THE KYOKO I KNOW ...
GRAB
!
... WON'T GIVE UP...
... AFTER JUST ONE FAILURE.
SHE WILL...
...COME BACK...
...TO LME!
End of Act 5

Skip·Beat! End Notes
Everyone knows how to be a fan, but sometimes cool things
from other cultures need a little help crossing the language barrier.

Page 11, panel 5: Kyoko's long nose
In Japanese, someone who's very boastful or vain is described as being
a tengu. A tengu is a mountain spirit who has wings and a long nose.

Page 14, panel 3: The hand coming from Kyoko's throat
In Japanese, there's an expression "to want so much that a hand comes
out of the throat." This is a visual representation of that expression.

Page 19, panel 5: The Taisho
In traditional Japanese restaurants, the master is called "Taisho" and
his wife is called "Okami-san." The employees call them by their title,
as do the customers.

Page 21, panel 7: Kyoko isn't going to high school
Compulsory education in Japan is only up to ninth grade, so Kyoko
doesn't have to finish high school.

Page 30, panel 2: Inn proprietress
In Japanese inns, the "face" of the inn is the proprietress (*okami-san*),
who greets guests and takes care of the customers. The husband stays
in the background, taking care of management duties.

Page 33, panel 1: Kligo Pu★cchin Pudding
In Japan, there is a Glico product called "Pucchin Purin." The "pucchin"
describes popping a pin on the bottom on the container, which lets air in
and makes the pudding drop out.

Page 59, panel 1: Kyoko's bow
This is a formal way to greet a person, called "Mitsuyubi," where three fingers of each hand rest on the tatami mat. Mitsuyubi literally means "three fingers."

Page 66, panel 4: The big sneeze
In Japan, sneezing is a sign that people are talking about you. Sneeze once and you are being praised, twice and you are being criticized, three times and you are being laughed at (or admired or scolded), and four times means you will catch a cold.

Page 70, panel 3: Talento
Talentos, or talents, in Japan usually appear on various TV shows as regulars, but they may also appear in dramas/movies/commercials, MC a show, sing and put out CDs, write magazine columns/essays/books, etc.

Page 93, panel 3: Oricon
Oricon is the Japanese equivalent of the Billboard Music Chart.

Page 101, panel 2: Straw doll
In Japan straw dolls can be used, much like voodoo dolls, to put a curse on someone.

Page 101, panel 3: Mo!
A Japanese exclamation similar to "geez."

Page 133, panel 3: Katsura-muki
A technique for peeling daikon radish (and other vegetables, like cucumber and carrot) into paper-thin strips, which then are used in food presentation and preparation.

Shojo Beat

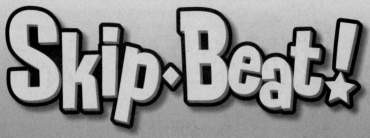

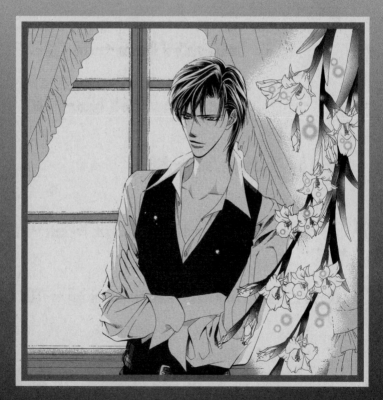

Vol. 2

Story & Art by Yoshiki Nakamura

Skip·Beat!

Volume 2

CONTENTS

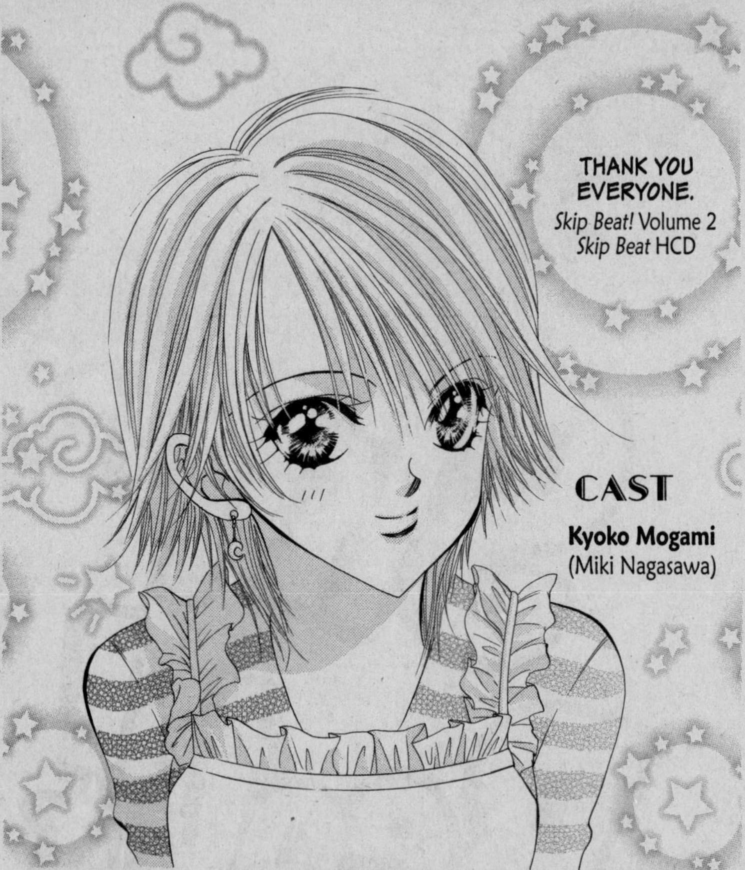
THANK YOU EVERYONE.
Skip Beat! Volume 2
Skip Beat HCD
CAST
Kyoko Mogami
(Miki Nagasawa)

Hello. I'm Nakamura. This is the second volume of the *Skip Beat!* manga. I started a series about "showbiz," and I was pretty worried. But I was able to bring the story this far, and I'm relieved. No, not about Kyoko's barging into showbiz... Her revenge against Shotaro has just started, but *Skip Beat!* itself wasn't originally a showbiz story, so it I hadn't decided specifically how Kyoko would join showbiz (we later decided on Kyoko failing the first audition and joining the Love Me Section). After that, now I go with whatever I think up in the moment. I know that doesn't sound like a good thing to say, and I'm having trouble effectively developing and bringing together the story I just thought up. Doing my storyboards is taking so much time, I feel like I'm in a crisis, and I feel a little disgusted with myself. What am I doing? The longer I am a mangaka, the longer it takes me to do storyboards!

I've been doing storyboards slowly, like a snail, and *Skip Beat!* has still managed to come this far... Amazingly, thankfully, HCD put out a *Skip Beat!* drama CD!!

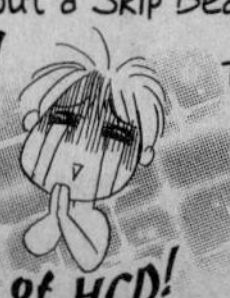
I'm happy!
Finally!
A member of HCD!
Tokyo Crazy Paradise wasn't an HCD, so it wasn't even included in the list of HCD advertisements!

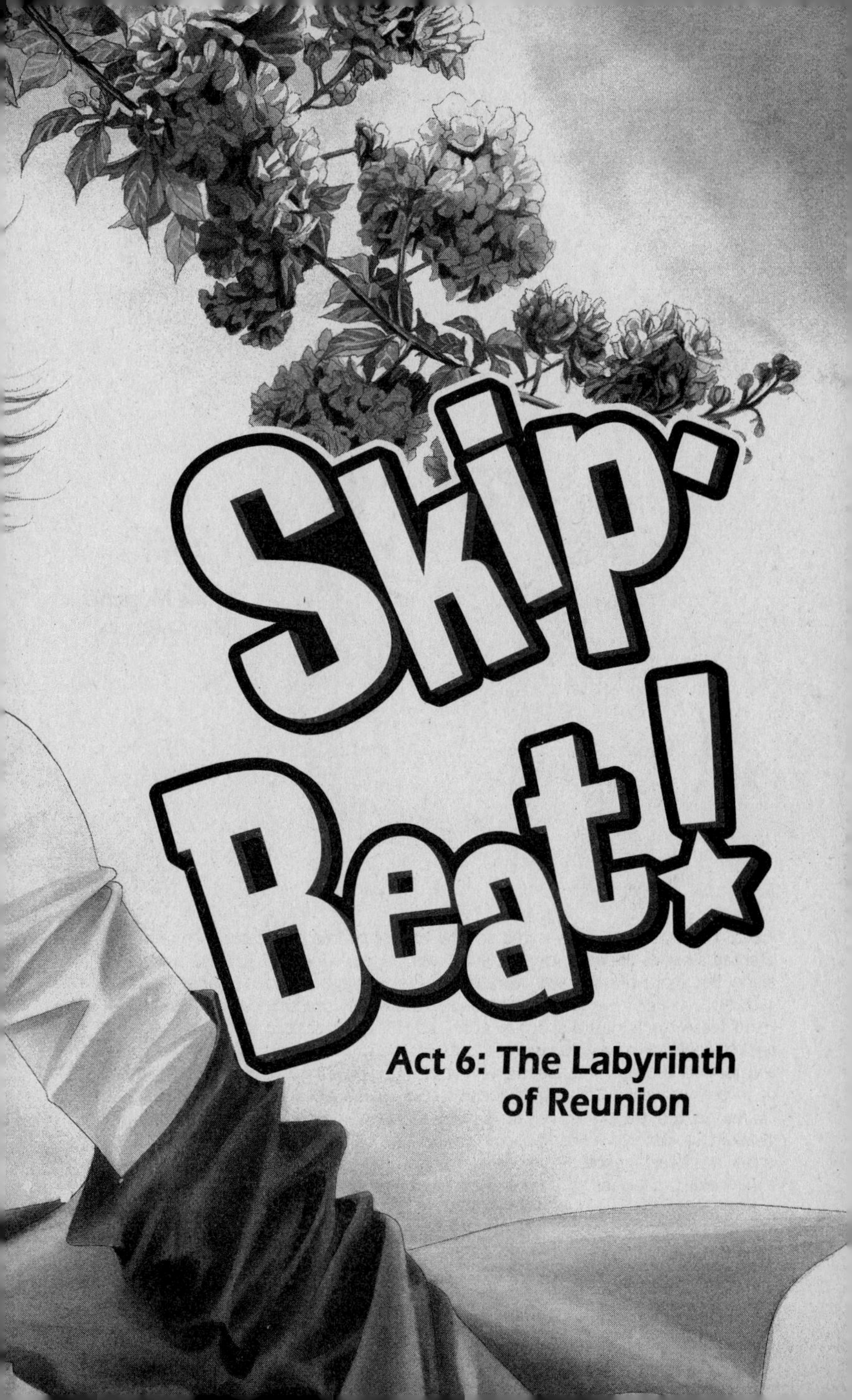
Skip Beat!
Act 6: The Labyrinth of Reunion

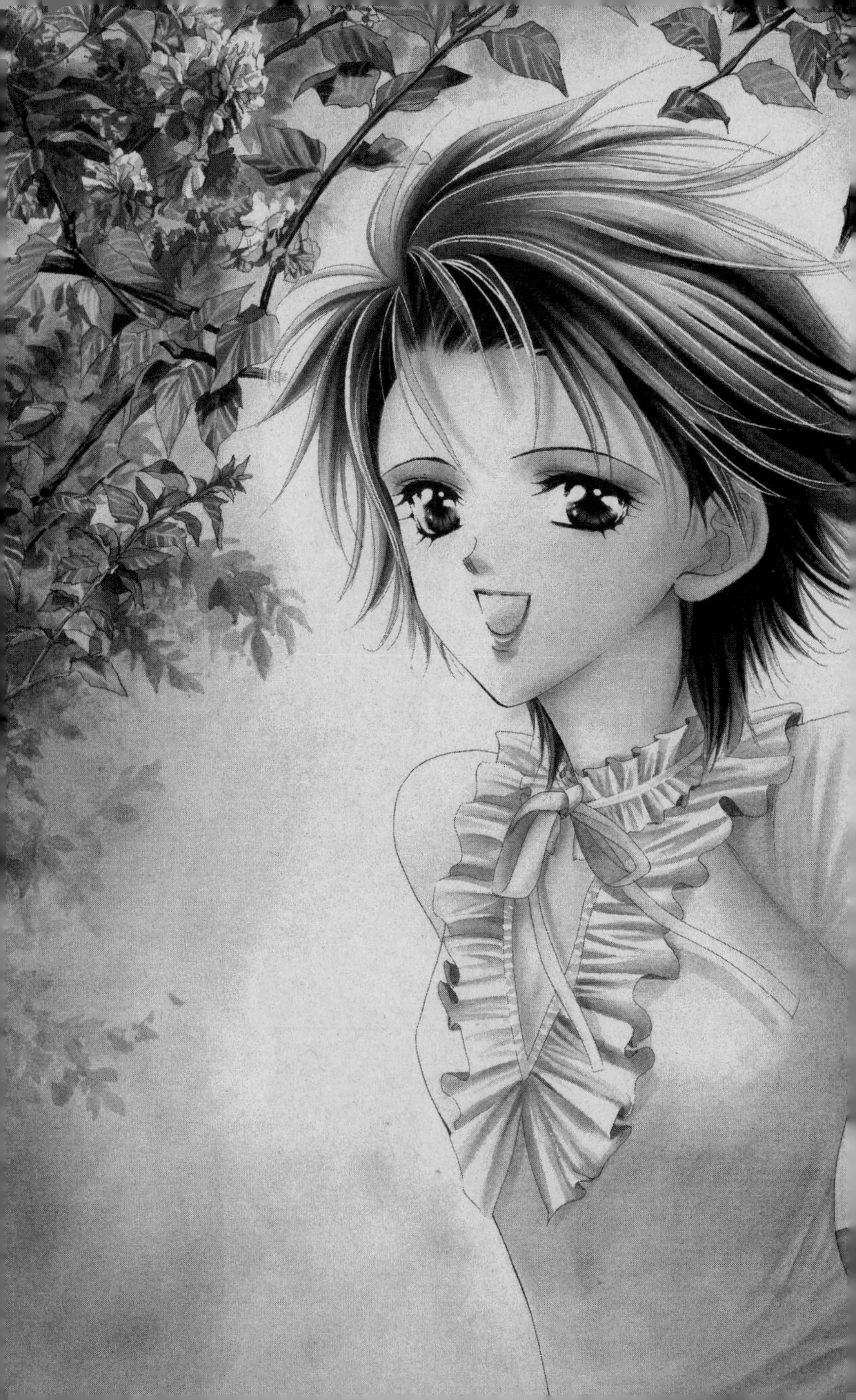

I heard about making *Skip Beat!* into an HCD in June. Volume 1 of the manga hadn't even come out yet (since it was coming out in July.) I was thankful for the offer, but I was very worried... The contents of the CD was going to be the volume 1 story, and there are no scenes to soften the hearts of shojo manga readers, like Sho and Kyoko being lovey-dovey, or Ren and Kyoko being lovey-dovey... (Since it just started, it can't be helped.) Moreover, the personalities of the characters other than Kyoko haven't been delved into yet (Both Sho and Ren don't appear enough...) What is really fatal is that *Skip Beat!* isn't known widely enough... So even if an HCD comes out, it might not sell. I understand that, but I decided to go with Hakusensha's generous offer.

...Because, if I refused the offer, another might never come...

I have no confidence...

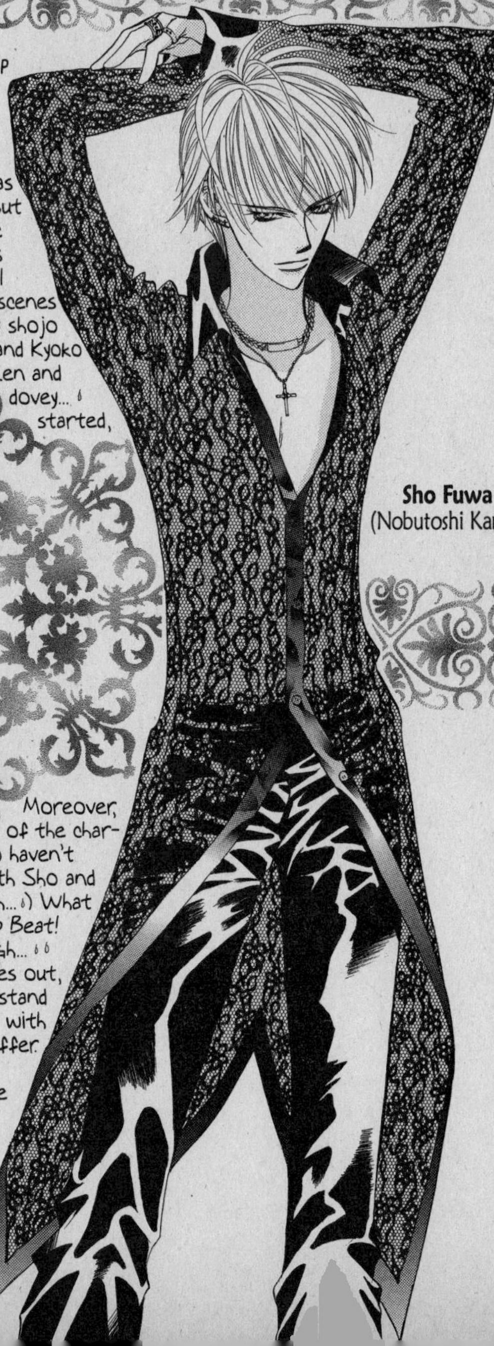

Sho Fuwa
(Nobutoshi Kanna)

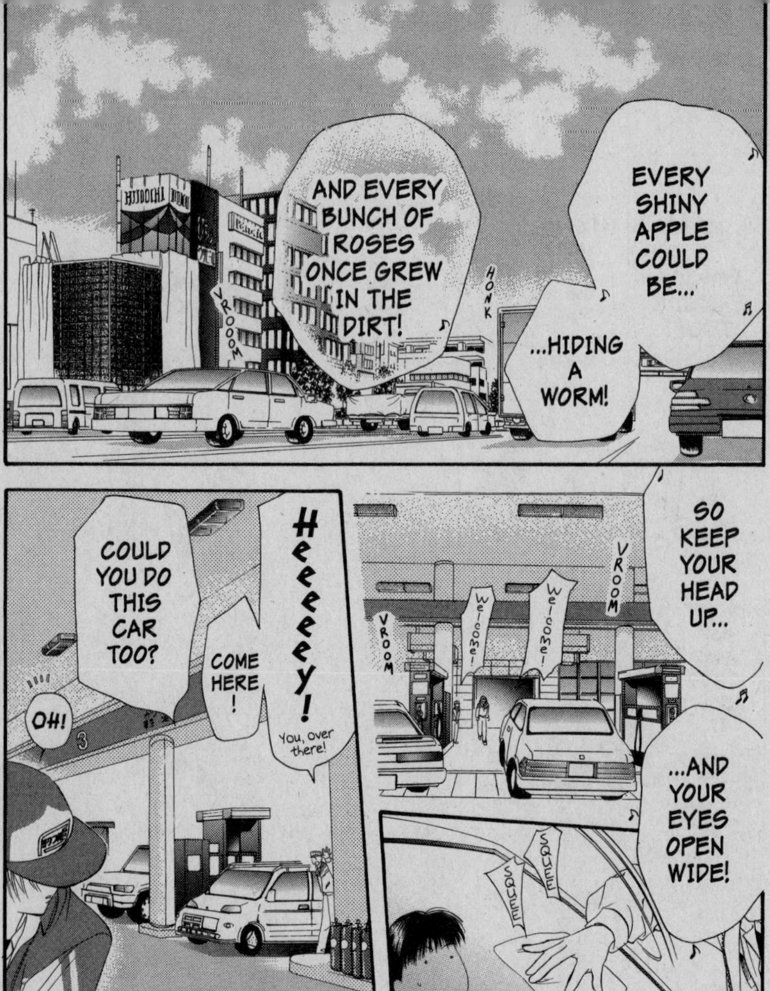
EVERY SHINY APPLE COULD BE...
...HIDING A WORM!
AND EVERY BUNCH OF ROSES ONCE GREW IN THE DIRT!
HONK
VROOOM
SO KEEP YOUR HEAD UP...
VROOM
Welcome!
Welcome!
VROOM
...AND YOUR EYES OPEN WIDE!
SQUEE
SQUEE
Heeeeey!
You, over there!
COME HERE!
COULD YOU DO THIS CAR TOO?
OH!

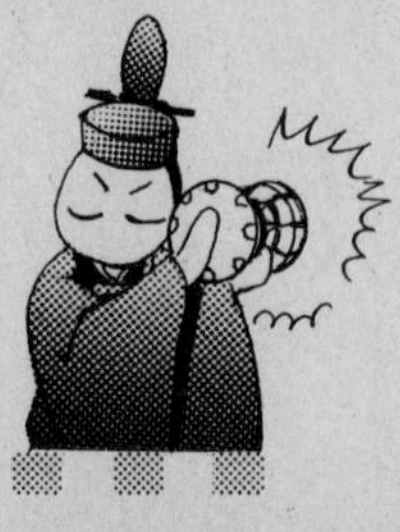

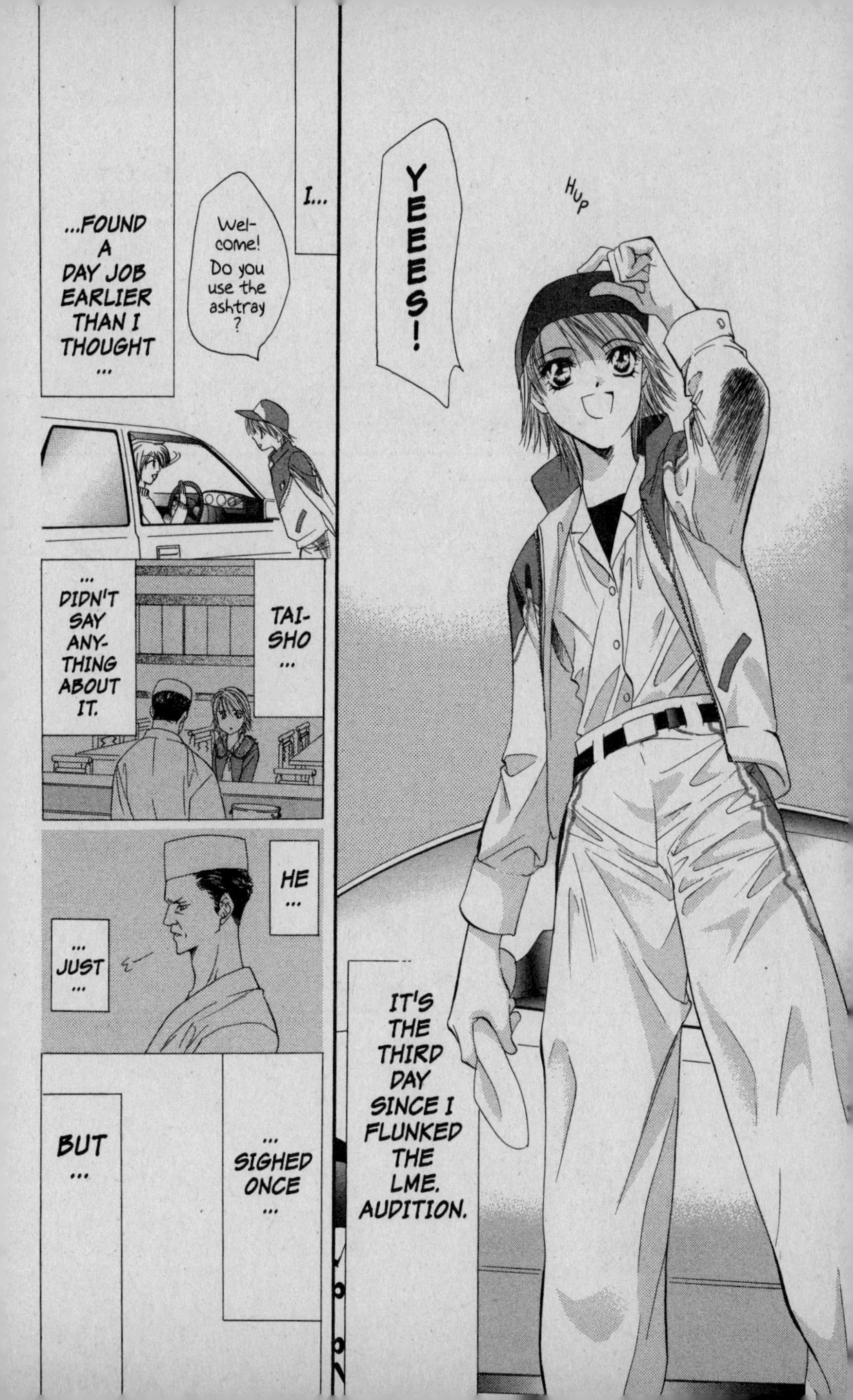
HUP
YEEES!
IT'S THE THIRD DAY SINCE I FLUNKED THE LME. AUDITION.
I...
Wel-come! Do you use the ashtray?
...FOUND A DAY JOB EARLIER THAN I THOUGHT...
TAI-SHO...
...DIDN'T SAY ANY-THING ABOUT IT.
HE...
...JUST...
...SIGHED ONCE...
BUT...

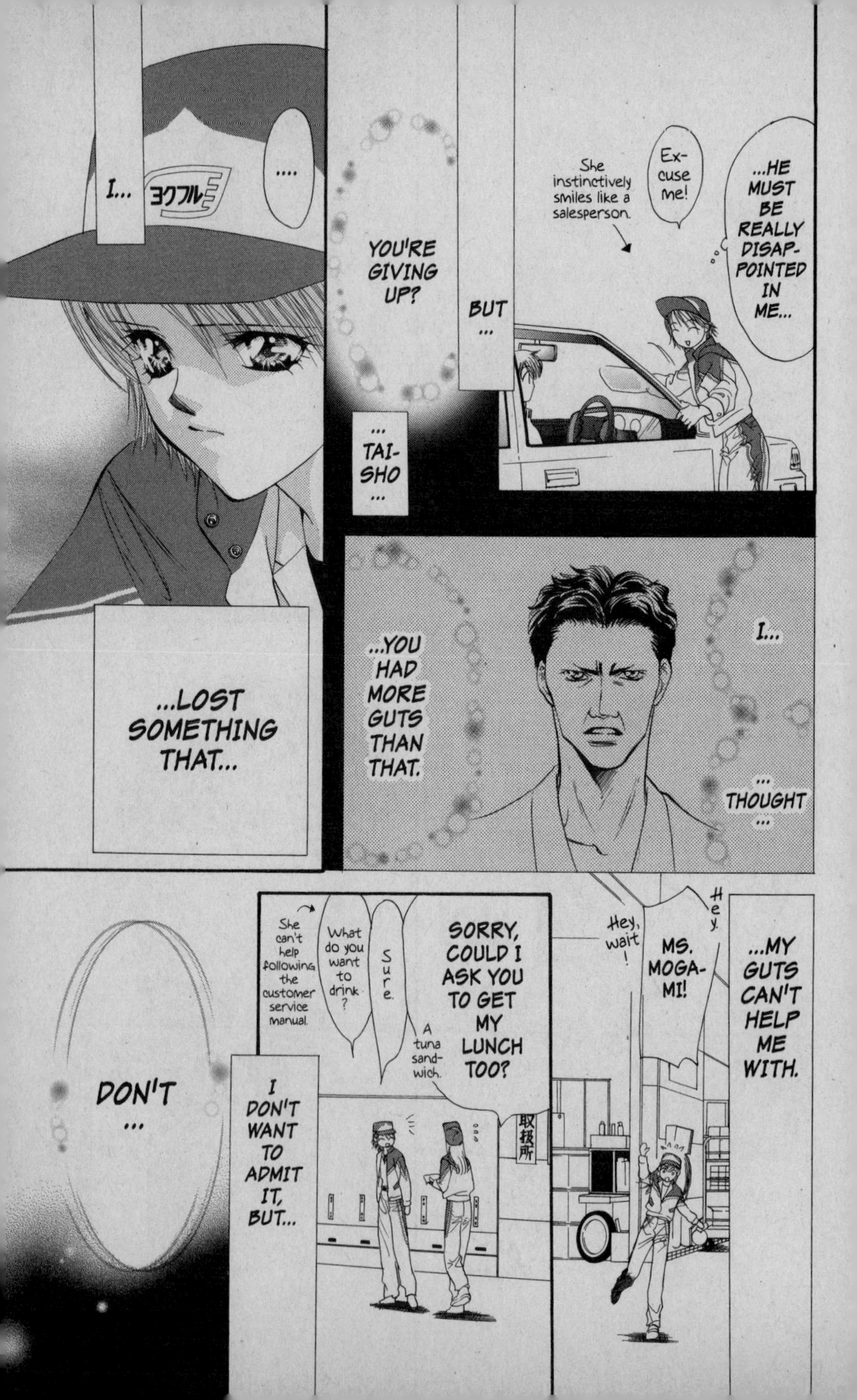
...HE MUST BE REALLY DISAPPOINTED IN ME...
Ex-cuse me!
She instinctively smiles like a salesperson.
BUT...
YOU'RE GIVING UP?
...TAI-SHO...
I...
...THOUGHT...
...YOU HAD MORE GUTS THAN THAT.
I...
ヨクフル
....
...LOST SOMETHING THAT...
Hey.
...MY GUTS CAN'T HELP ME WITH.
MS. MOGA-MI!
Hey, wait!
取扱所
SORRY, COULD I ASK YOU TO GET MY LUNCH TOO?
A tuna sand-wich.
Sure.
What do you want to drink?
She can't help following the customer service manual.
I DON'T WANT TO ADMIT IT, BUT...
DON'T...

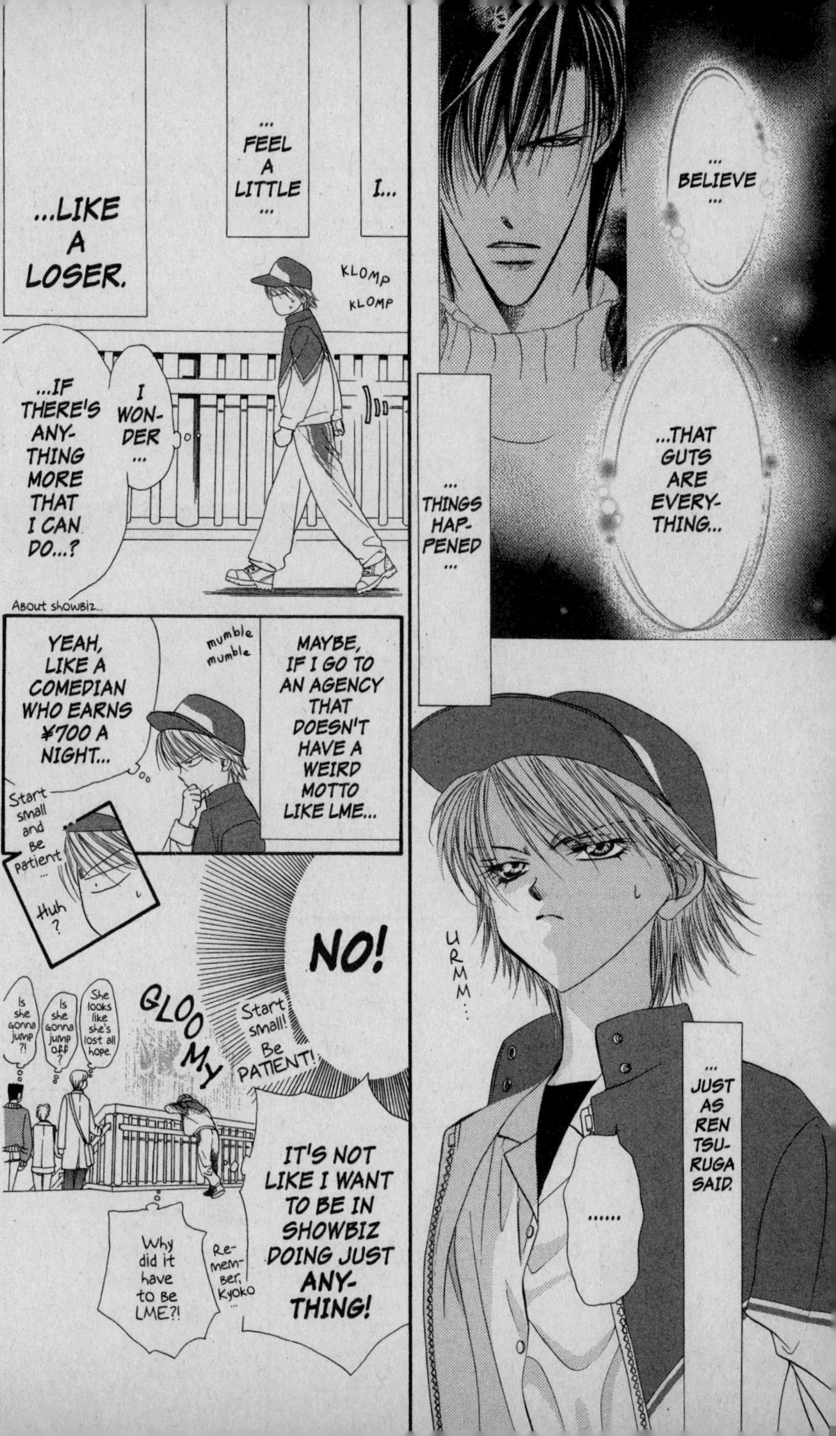

...BELIEVE...
...THAT GUTS ARE EVERYTHING...
...THINGS HAPPENED...
...JUST AS REN TSURUGA SAID.
URMM...
......
I...
...FEEL A LITTLE...
...LIKE A LOSER.
KLOMP
KLOMP
I WONDER...
...IF THERE'S ANYTHING MORE THAT I CAN DO...?
About showbiz...
MAYBE, IF I GO TO AN AGENCY THAT DOESN'T HAVE A WEIRD MOTTO LIKE LME...
mumble mumble
YEAH, LIKE A COMEDIAN WHO EARNS ¥700 A NIGHT...
Start small and be patient...
Huh?
NO!
Start small! Be PATIENT!
GLOOMY
She looks like she's lost all hope.
Is she gonna jump off
Is she gonna jump?!
IT'S NOT LIKE I WANT TO BE IN SHOWBIZ DOING JUST ANYTHING!
Remember, Kyoko...
Why did it have to be LME?!

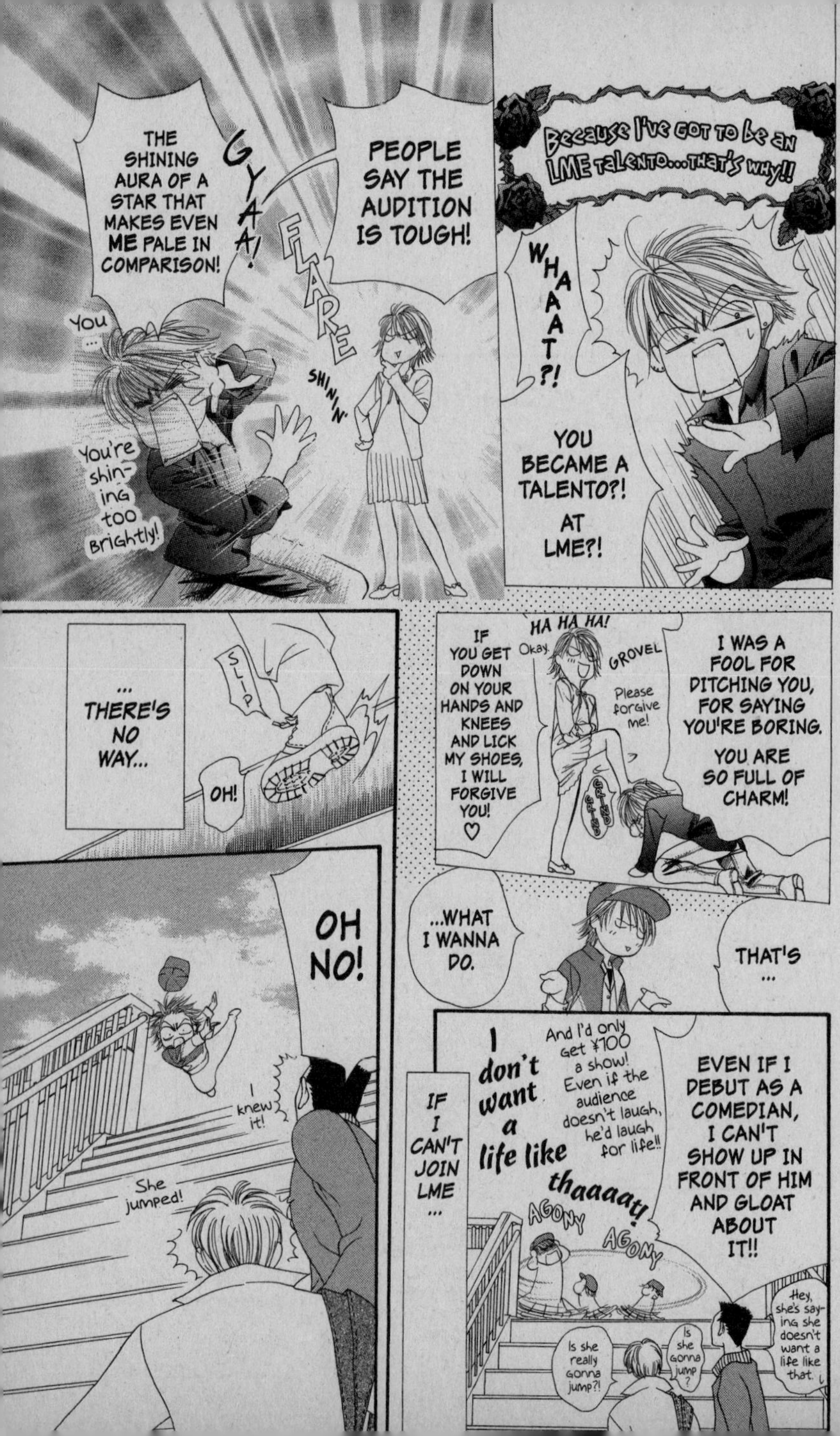
Because I've got to be an LME talento...that's why!!
WHAAAT?!
YOU BECAME A TALENTO?!
AT LME?!
PEOPLE SAY THE AUDITION IS TOUGH!
FLARE
GYAA!
THE SHINING AURA OF A STAR THAT MAKES EVEN ME PALE IN COMPARISON!
You...
You're shining too brightly!
SHININ'
I WAS A FOOL FOR DITCHING YOU, FOR SAYING YOU'RE BORING.
YOU ARE SO FULL OF CHARM!
HA HA HA!
GROVEL
Please forgive me!
Okay.
IF YOU GET DOWN ON YOUR HANDS AND KNEES AND LICK MY SHOES, I WILL FORGIVE YOU! ♡
GRIND GRIND
... THERE'S NO WAY...
SLIP
OH!
THAT'S ...
...WHAT I WANNA DO.
EVEN IF I DEBUT AS A COMEDIAN, I CAN'T SHOW UP IN FRONT OF HIM AND GLOAT ABOUT IT!!
And I'd only get ¥100 a show! Even if the audience doesn't laugh, he'd laugh for life!!
I don't want a life like thaaaat!
IF I CAN'T JOIN LME ...
AGONY
AGONY
Hey, she's saying she doesn't want a life like that.
Is she gonna jump?
Is she really gonna jump?!
OH NO!
I knew it!
She jumped!

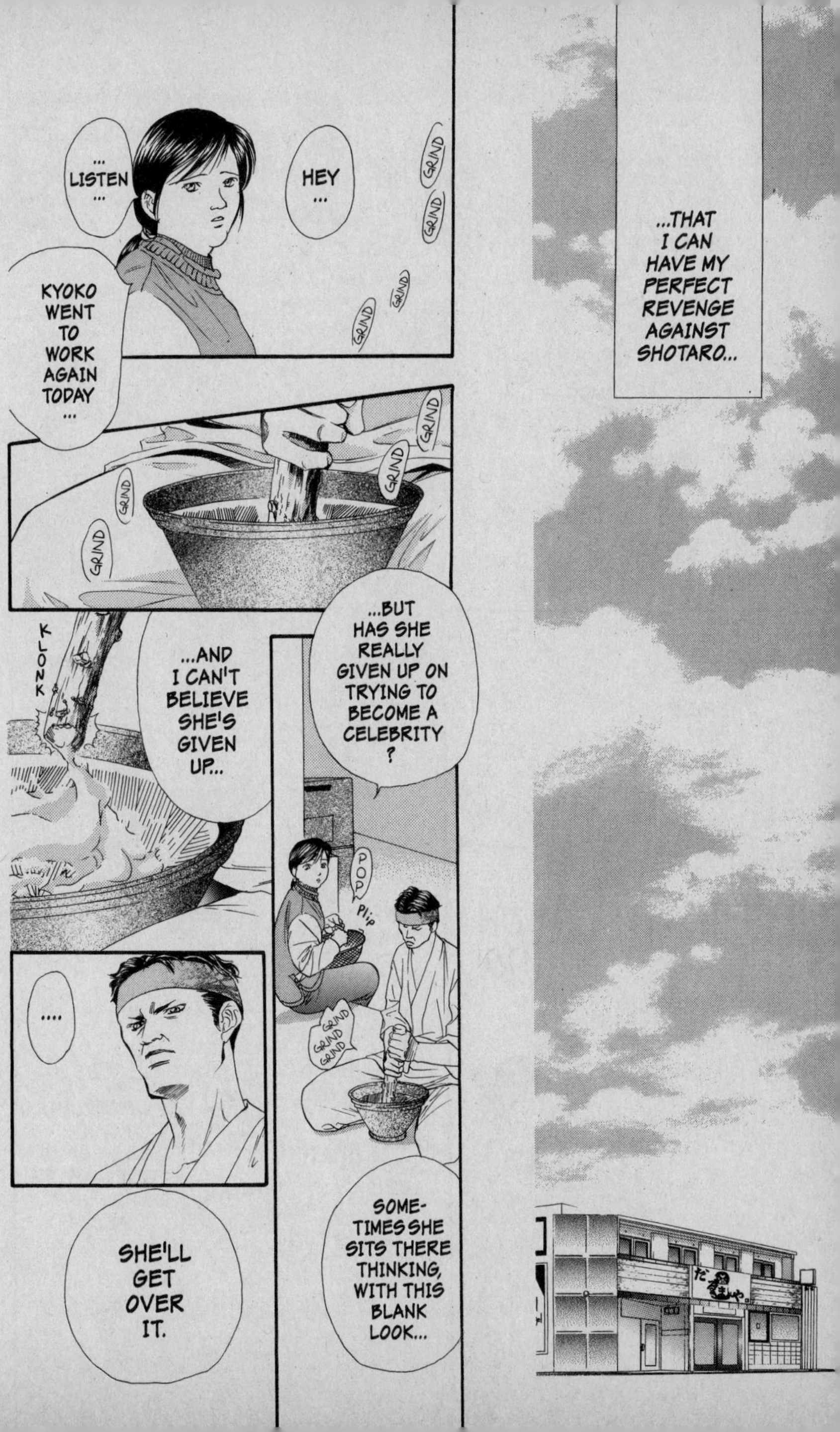
...THAT I CAN HAVE MY PERFECT REVENGE AGAINST SHOTARO...
GRIND GRIND
GRIND GRIND
HEY...
...LISTEN...
KYOKO WENT TO WORK AGAIN TODAY...
GRIND GRIND GRIND GRIND
KLONK
...AND I CAN'T BELIEVE SHE'S GIVEN UP...
...BUT HAS SHE REALLY GIVEN UP ON TRYING TO BECOME A CELEBRITY?
POP
Plip
GRIND GRIND GRIND
SOME-TIMES SHE SITS THERE THINKING, WITH THIS BLANK LOOK...
....
SHE'LL GET OVER IT.

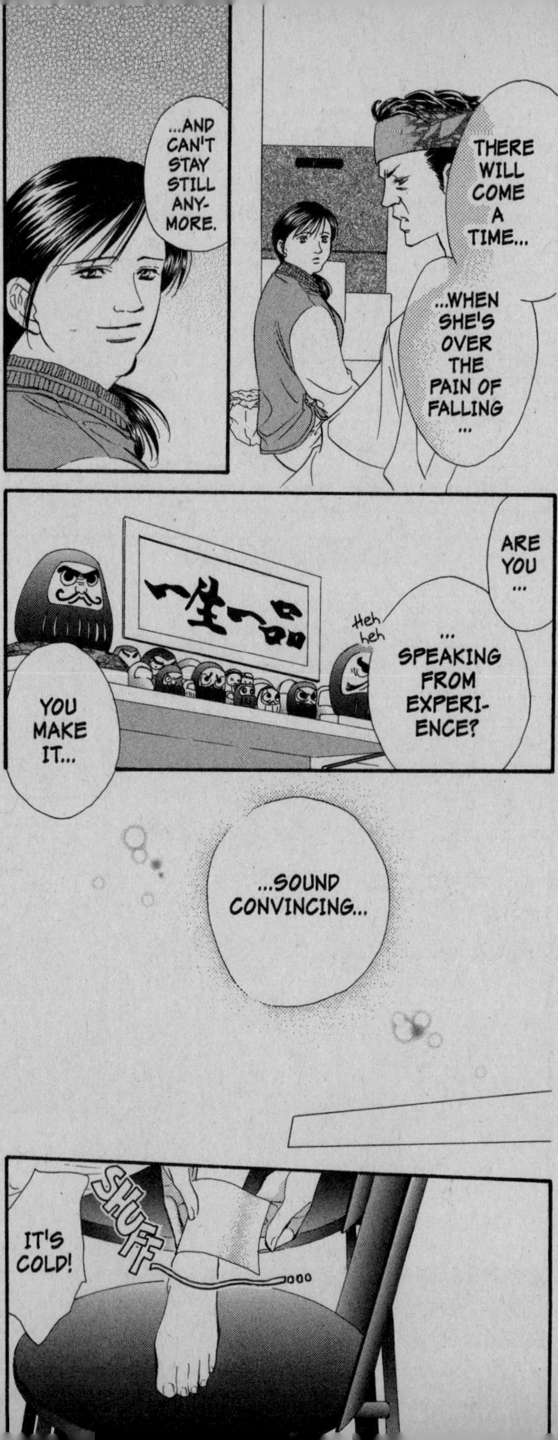
THERE WILL COME A TIME...
...WHEN SHE'S OVER THE PAIN OF FALLING...
...AND CAN'T STAY STILL ANYMORE.
ARE YOU...
Heh heh
...SPEAKING FROM EXPERIENCE?
一生一品
YOU MAKE IT...
...SOUND CONVINCING...
SHUFF
IT'S COLD!

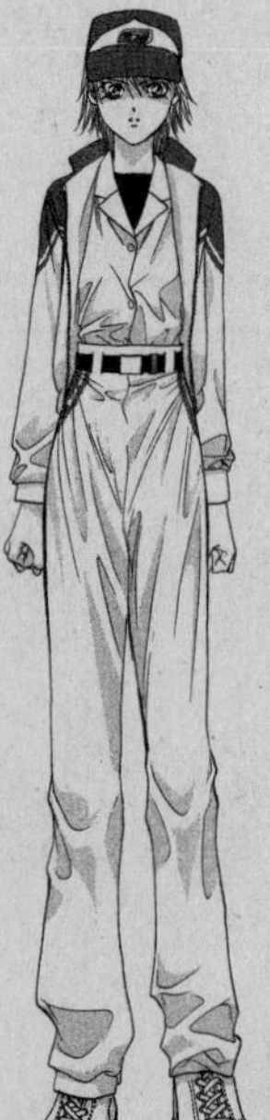

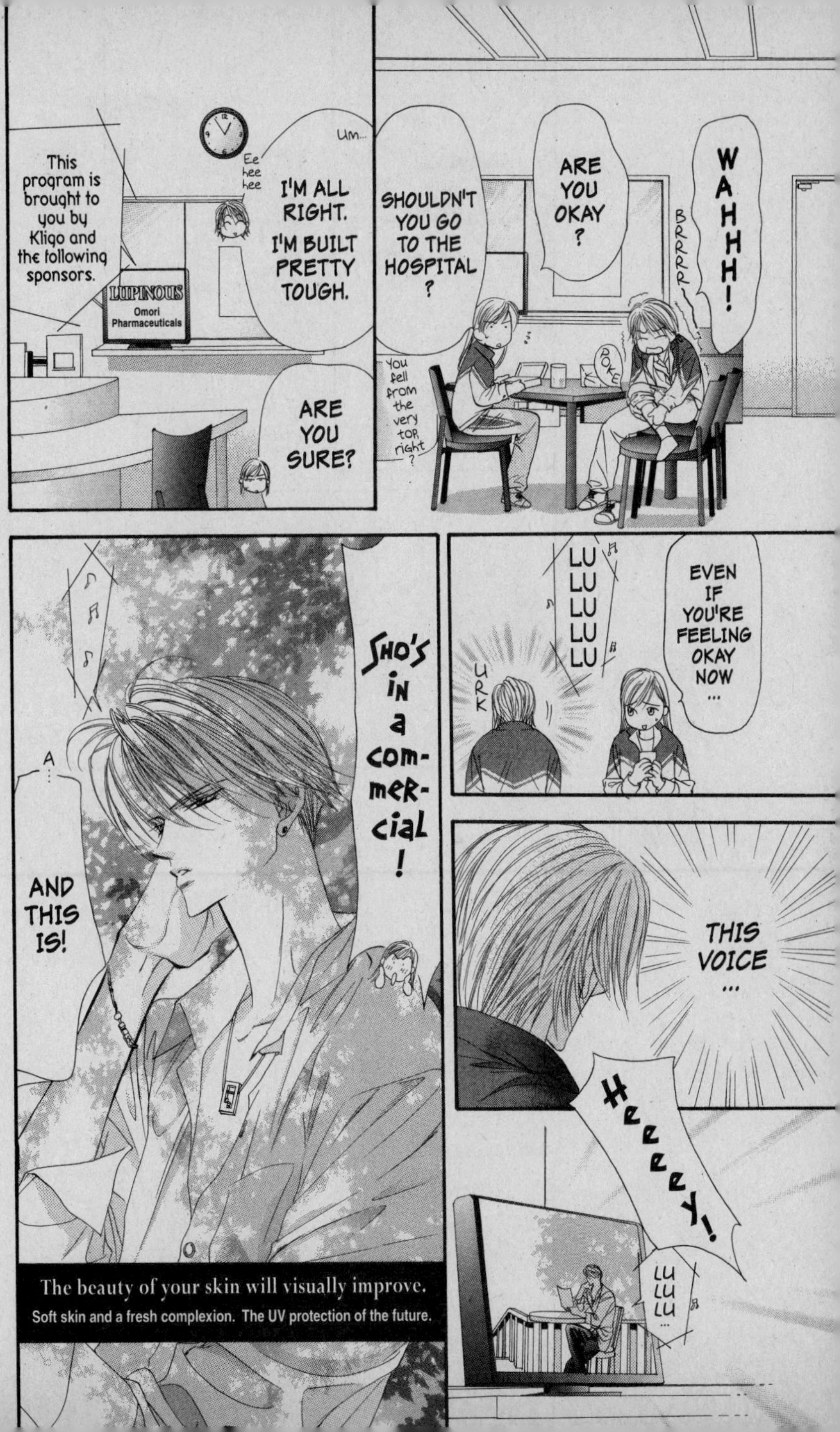
WAHHH!
BRRRRR
ARE YOU OKAY?
SHOULDN'T YOU GO TO THE HOSPITAL?
POKE
You fell from the very top, right?
Um...
I'M ALL RIGHT. I'M BUILT PRETTY TOUGH.
Ee hee hee
ARE YOU SURE?
This program is brought to you by Kligo and the following sponsors.
LUPINOUS
Omori Pharmaceuticals
EVEN IF YOU'RE FEELING OKAY NOW...
LU LU LU LU LU
URK
THIS VOICE...
Heeeey!
LULULU...
SHO's in a commercial!
A...
AND THIS IS!
The beauty of your skin will visually improve.
Soft skin and a fresh complexion. The UV protection of the future.

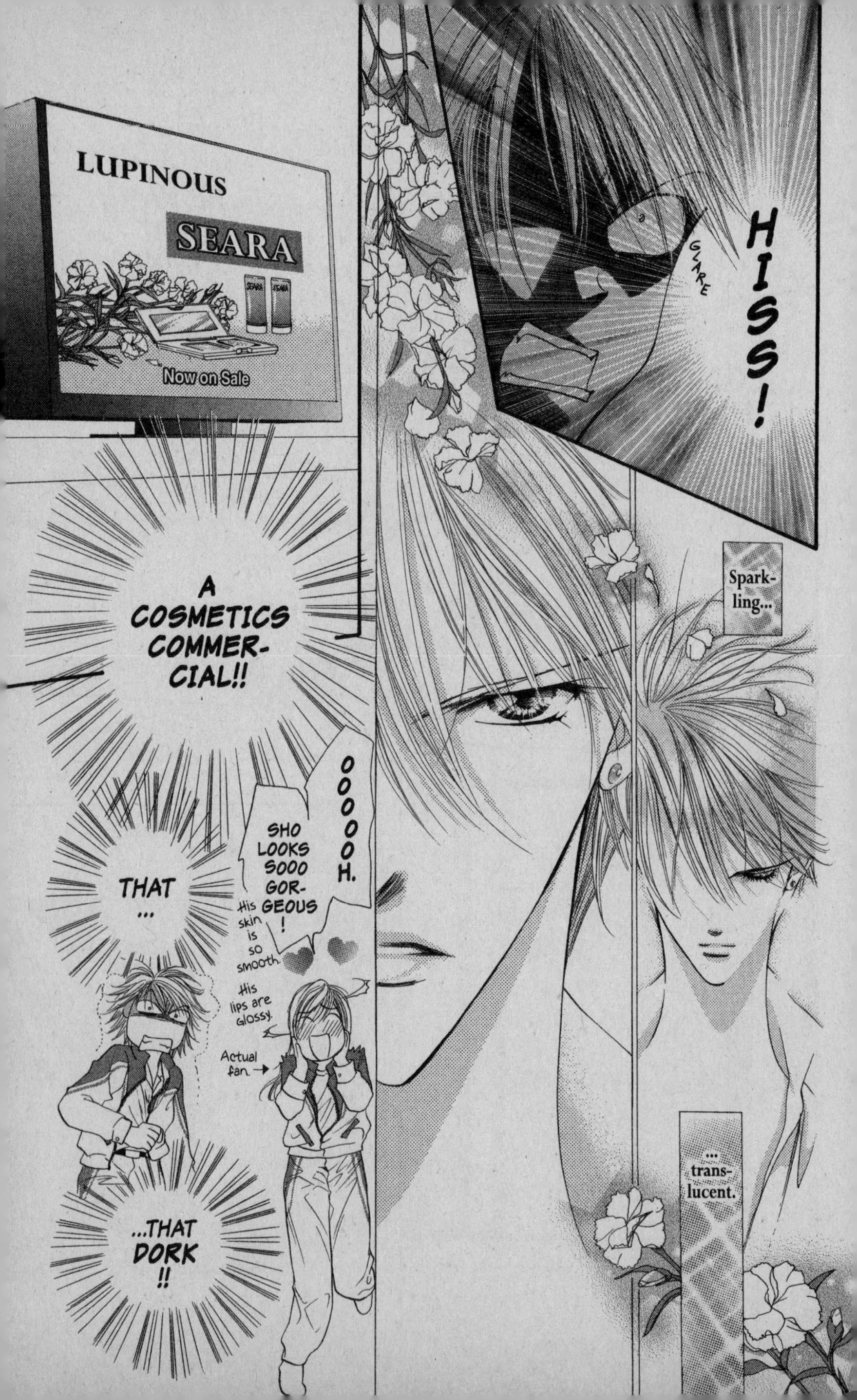
HISS!
GLARE
Sparkling...
... translucent.
LUPINOUS
SEARA
SEARA SEARA
Now on Sale
A COSMETICS COMMERCIAL!!
OOOOOOH.
SHO LOOKS SOOO GORGEOUS!
His skin is so smooth.
His lips are glossy.
Actual fan.
THAT...
...THAT DORK!!

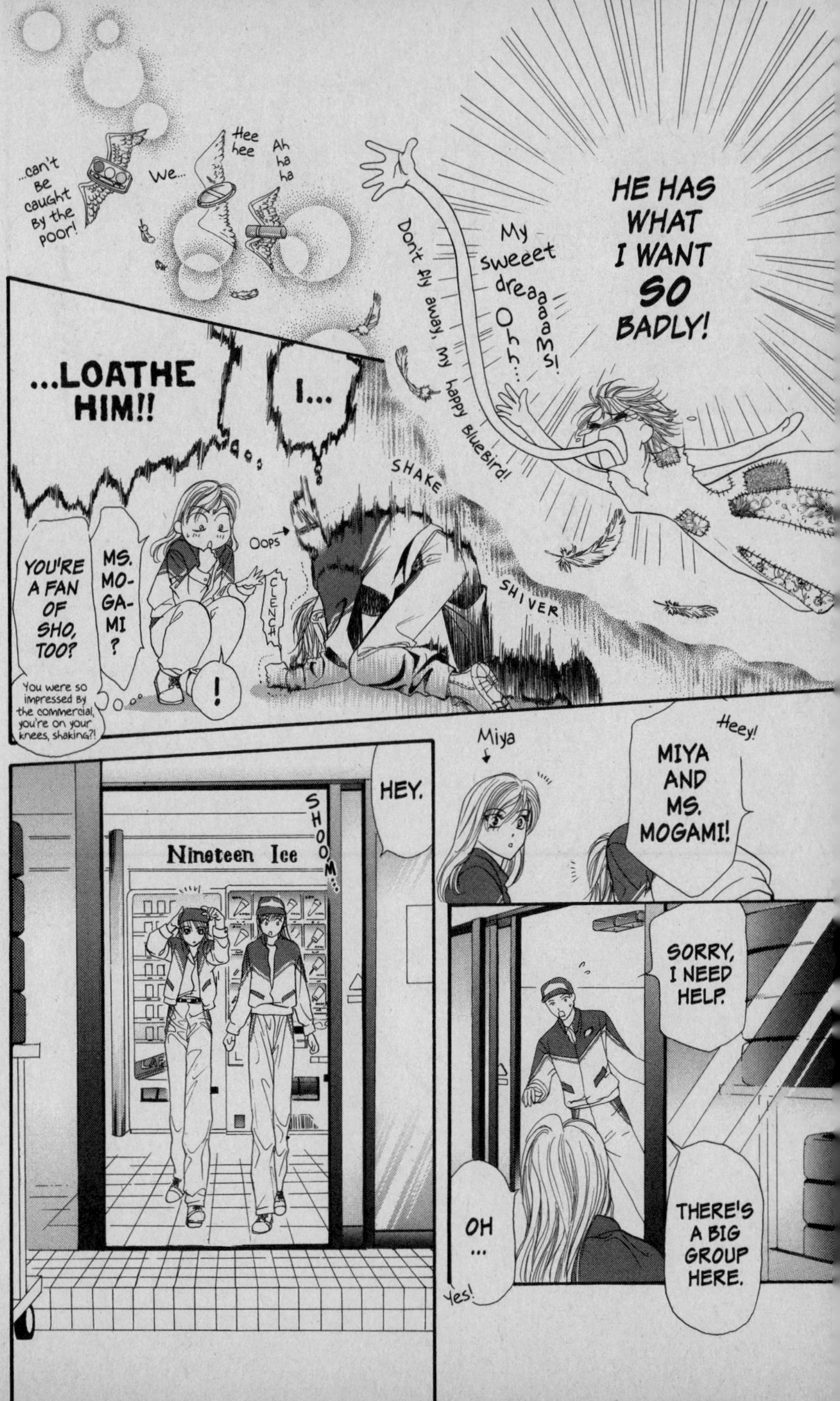
HE HAS WHAT I WANT SO BADLY!
My sweeet dreaaaaams! Ohhh...
Don't fly away, my happy BlueBird!
Hee hee
Ah ha ha
We...
...can't be caught By the poor!
I...
...LOATHE HIM!!
SHAKE
SHIVER
Oops
CLENCH
!
MS. MOGAMI?
YOU'RE A FAN OF SHO, TOO?
You were so impressed By the commercial, you're on your knees, shaking?!
Heey!
MIYA AND MS. MOGAMI!
Miya
SORRY, I NEED HELP.
THERE'S A BIG GROUP HERE.
OH ...
Yes!
HEY.
SHOOOM...
Nineteen Ice

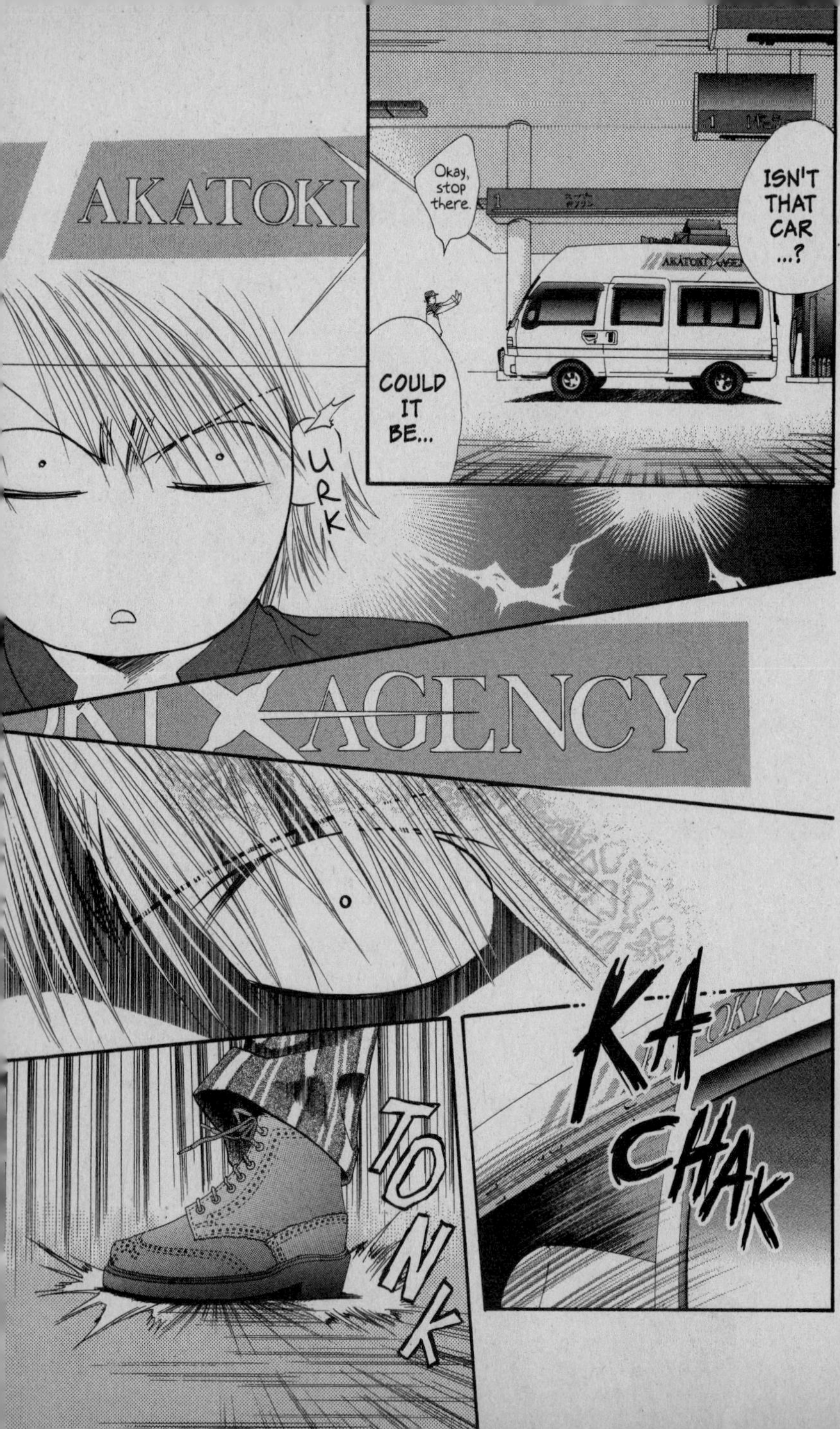
ISN'T THAT CAR ...?
Okay, stop there.
COULD IT BE...
AKATOKI
URK
AGENCY
KA CHAK
TONK

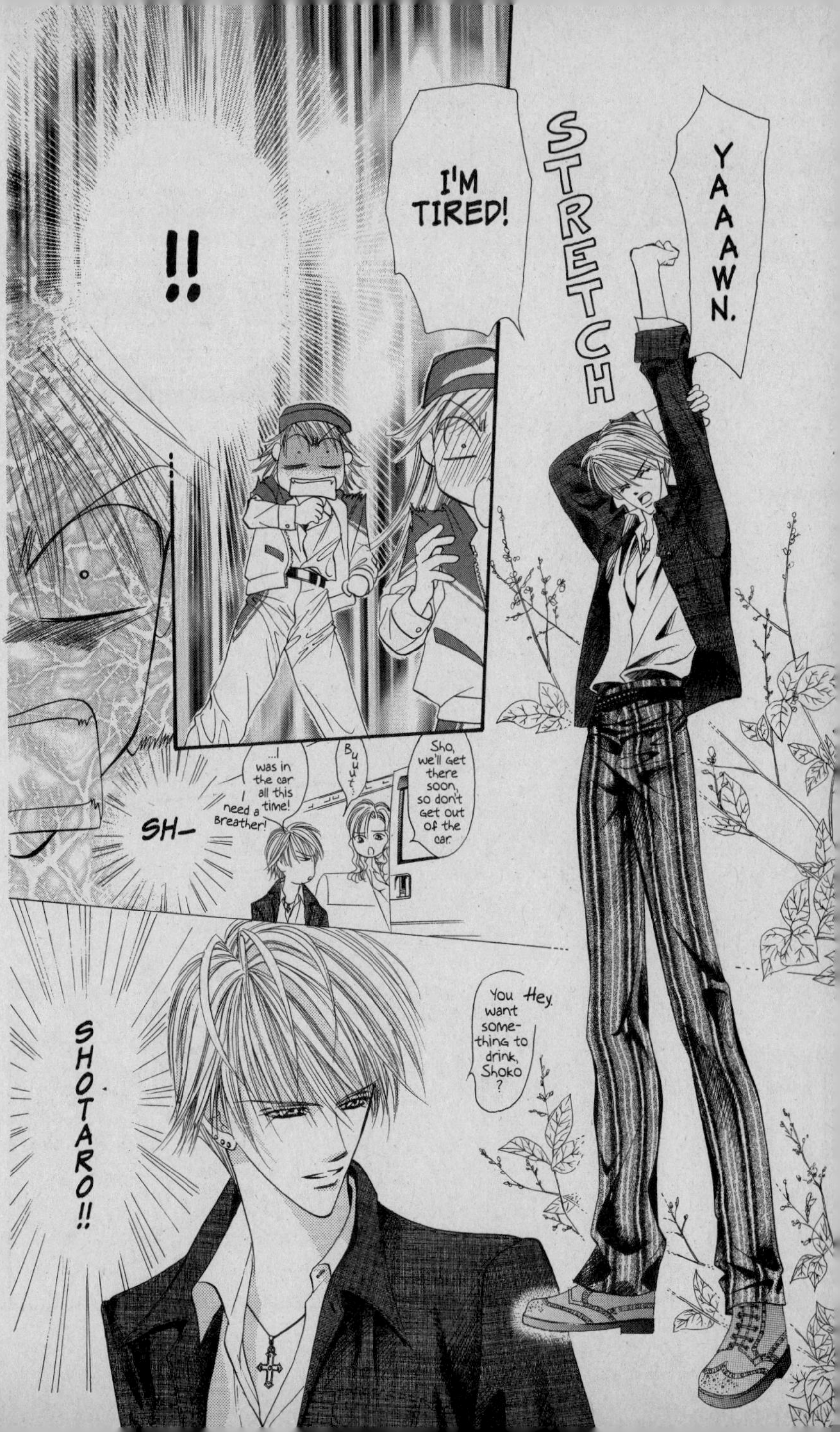

YAAAWN.
STRETCH
I'M TIRED!
Hey. You want something to drink, Shoko?
!!
Sho, we'll get there soon, so don't get out of the car.
Buuut...
...I was in the car all this time! I need a breather!
SH-
SHOTARO!!

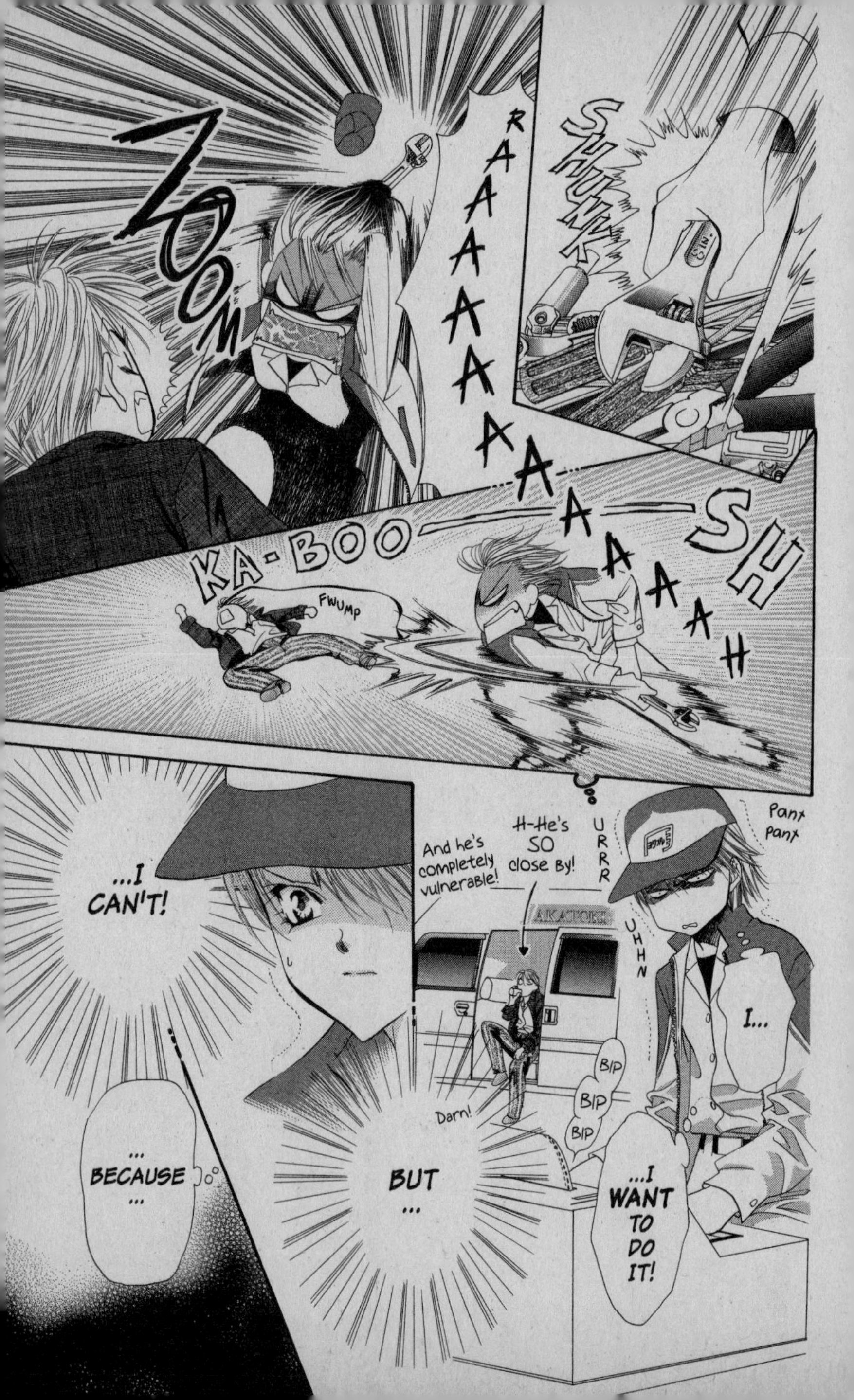
SHUHNK
ZOOM
RAAAAAAAAAAAAAH
KA-BOOSH
FWUMP
Pant pant
URRR
H-He's SO close by!
And he's completely vulnerable!
UHHN
I...
BIP
BIP
BIP
...I WANT TO DO IT!
Darn!
...I CAN'T!
BUT ...
... BECAUSE ...

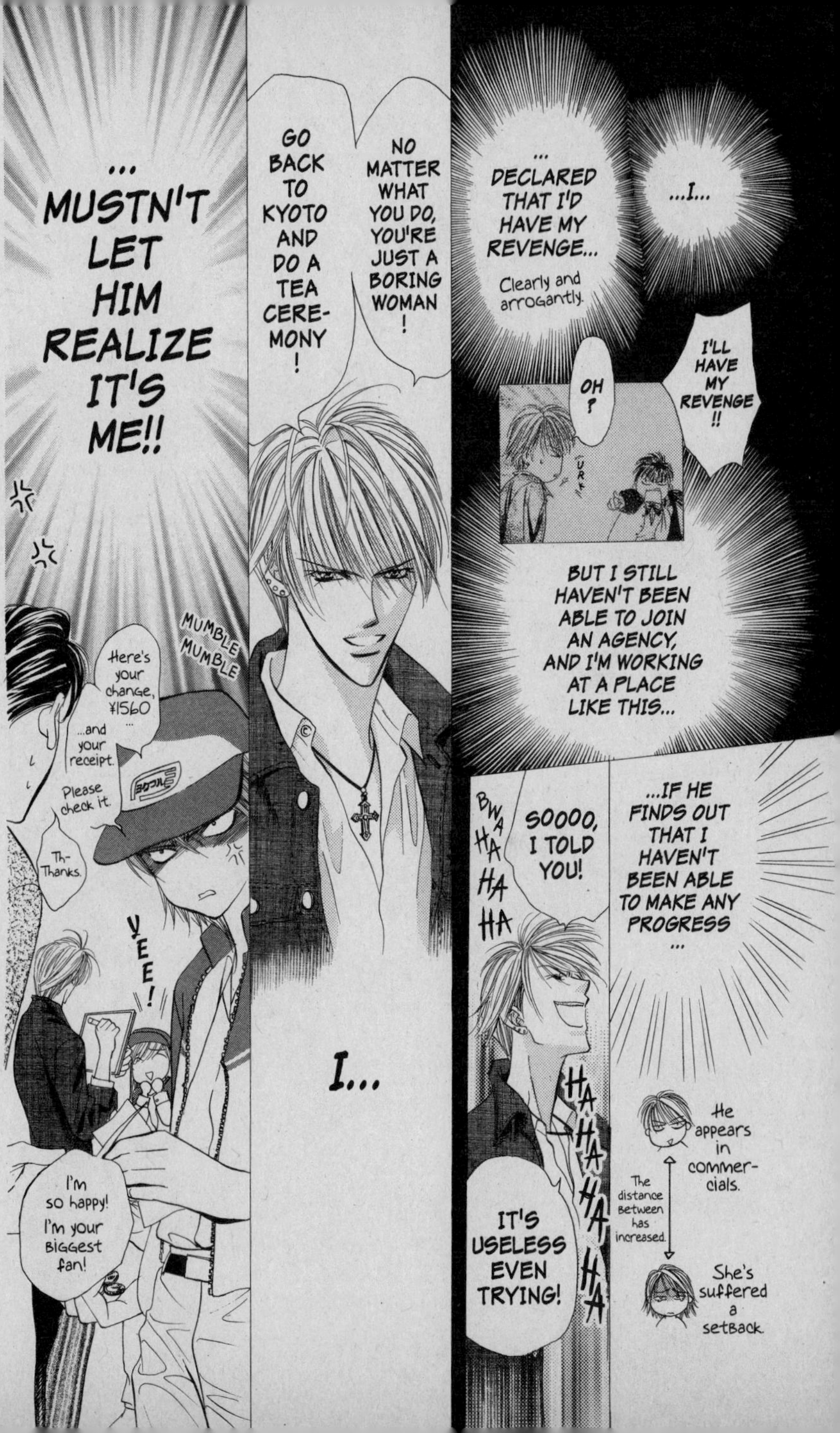

...I...
...DECLARED THAT I'D HAVE MY REVENGE...
Clearly and arrogantly.
I'LL HAVE MY REVENGE!!
OH?
URK
BUT I STILL HAVEN'T BEEN ABLE TO JOIN AN AGENCY, AND I'M WORKING AT A PLACE LIKE THIS...
...IF HE FINDS OUT THAT I HAVEN'T BEEN ABLE TO MAKE ANY PROGRESS...
He appears in commercials.
The distance between has increased.
She's suffered a setback.
BWAHAHAHAHA
SOOOO, I TOLD YOU!
HAHAHAHAHAHA
IT'S USELESS EVEN TRYING!
NO MATTER WHAT YOU DO, YOU'RE JUST A BORING WOMAN!
GO BACK TO KYOTO AND DO A TEA CEREMONY!
I...
...MUSTN'T LET HIM REALIZE IT'S ME!!
MUMBLE MUMBLE
Here's your change, ¥1560...
...and your receipt. Please check it.
Th-Thanks.
VEEE!
I'm so happy! I'm your biggest fan!

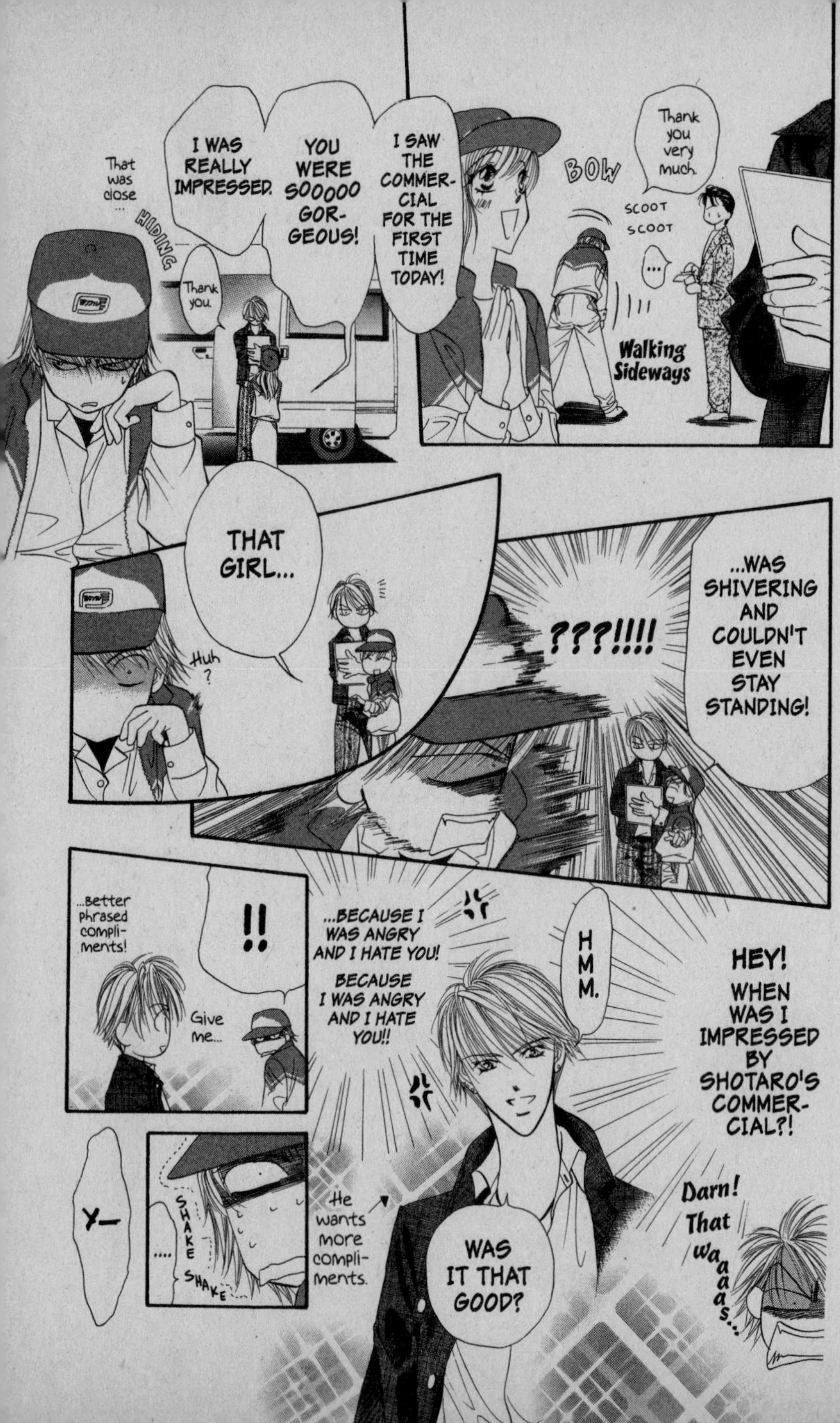
Thank you very much.
BOW
SCOOT SCOOT
...
Walking Sideways
I SAW THE COMMERCIAL FOR THE FIRST TIME TODAY!
YOU WERE SOOOOO GORGEOUS!
I WAS REALLY IMPRESSED.
Thank you.
That was close...
HIDING
...WAS SHIVERING AND COULDN'T EVEN STAY STANDING!
???!!!!
THAT GIRL...
Huh?
HEY! WHEN WAS I IMPRESSED BY SHOTARO'S COMMERCIAL?!
HMM.
...BECAUSE I WAS ANGRY AND I HATE YOU!
BECAUSE I WAS ANGRY AND I HATE YOU!!
!!
Give me...
...Better phrased compliments!
Darn! That waaaaas...
WAS IT THAT GOOD?
He wants more compliments.
SHAKE SHAKE
....
Y—

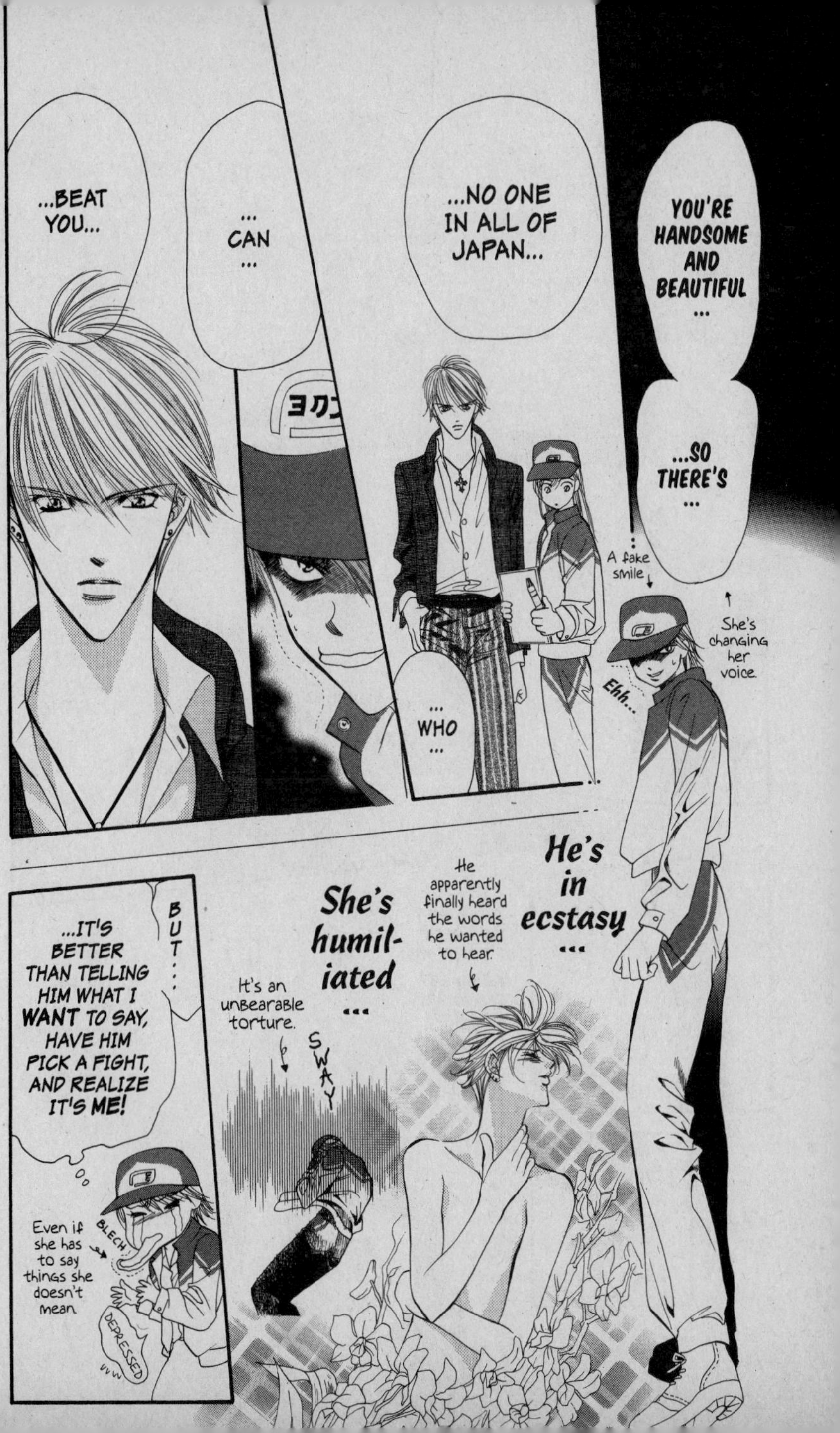
YOU'RE HANDSOME AND BEAUTIFUL ...
...SO THERE'S ...
A fake smile
She's changing her voice.
Ehh...
...NO ONE IN ALL OF JAPAN...
... WHO ...
... CAN ...
...BEAT YOU...
He's in ecstasy ...
He apparently finally heard the words he wanted to hear.
She's humil-iated ...
It's an unbearable torture.
SWAY
BUT...
...IT'S BETTER THAN TELLING HIM WHAT I WANT TO SAY, HAVE HIM PICK A FIGHT, AND REALIZE IT'S ME!
Even if she has to say things she doesn't mean.
BLECH
DEPRESSED

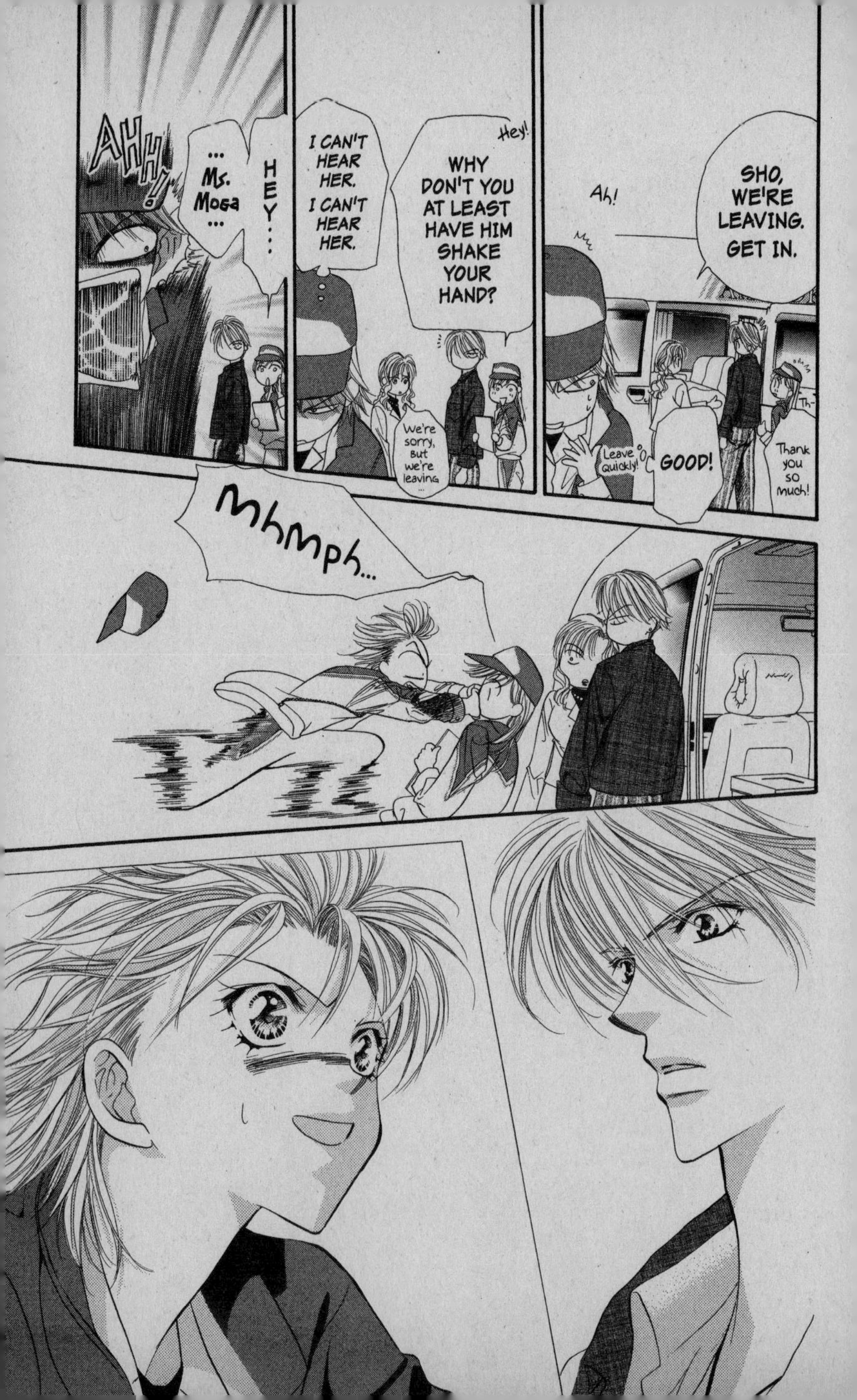
SHO, WE'RE LEAVING. GET IN.
Ah!
Th-
Thank you so much!
GOOD!
Leave quickly!
Hey!
WHY DON'T YOU AT LEAST HAVE HIM SHAKE YOUR HAND?
I CAN'T HEAR HER. I CAN'T HEAR HER.
We're sorry, but we're leaving...
HEY...
... Ms. Moga ...
AHH!
Mhmph...

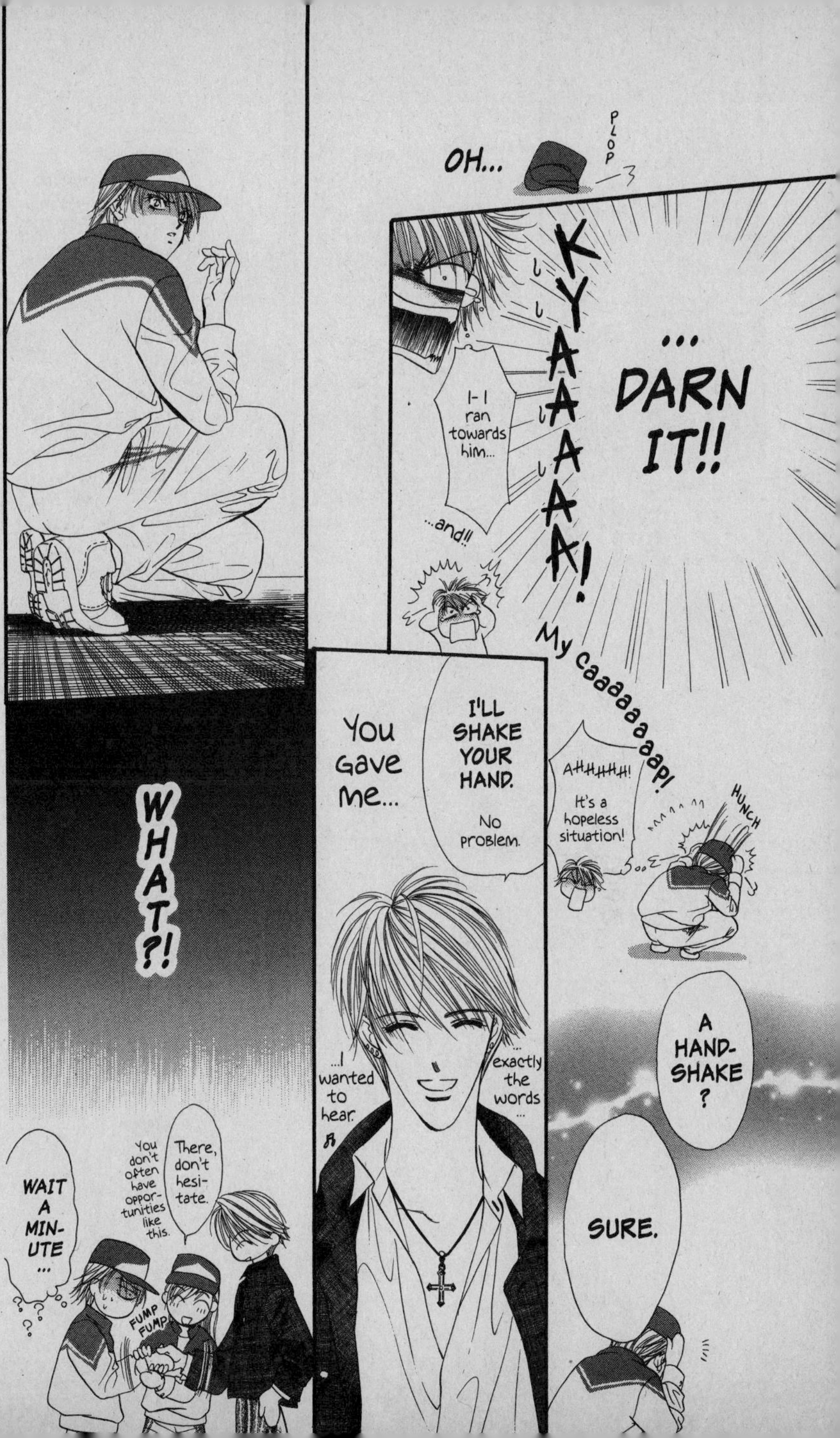

OH...
PLOP
KYAAAAA!
... DARN IT!!
I-I ran towards him...
...and!!
My caaaaaaaap!
AHHHHH!
It's a hopeless situation!
HUNCH
A HAND-SHAKE?
SURE.
I'LL SHAKE YOUR HAND.
No problem.
You Gave me...
...exactly the words...
...I wanted to hear.
WHAT?!
WAIT A MIN-UTE...
There, don't hesi-tate.
You don't often have oppor-tunities like this.
FUMP FUMP

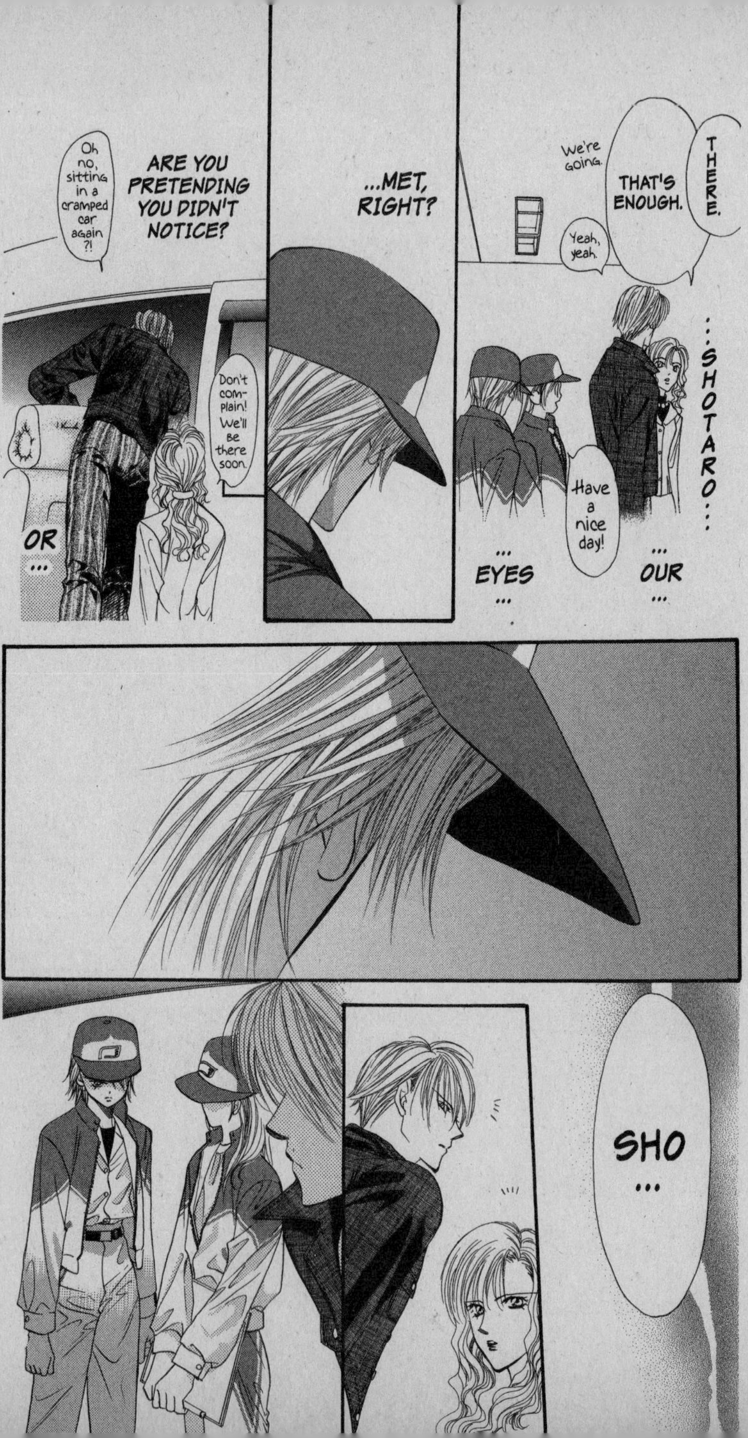
THERE.
THAT'S ENOUGH.
We're going.
Yeah, yeah.
...SHOTARO...
...OUR...
Have a nice day!
...EYES...
...MET, RIGHT?
ARE YOU PRETENDING YOU DIDN'T NOTICE?
Oh no, sitting in a cramped car again?!
Don't com-plain! We'll be there soon.
OR...
SHO...

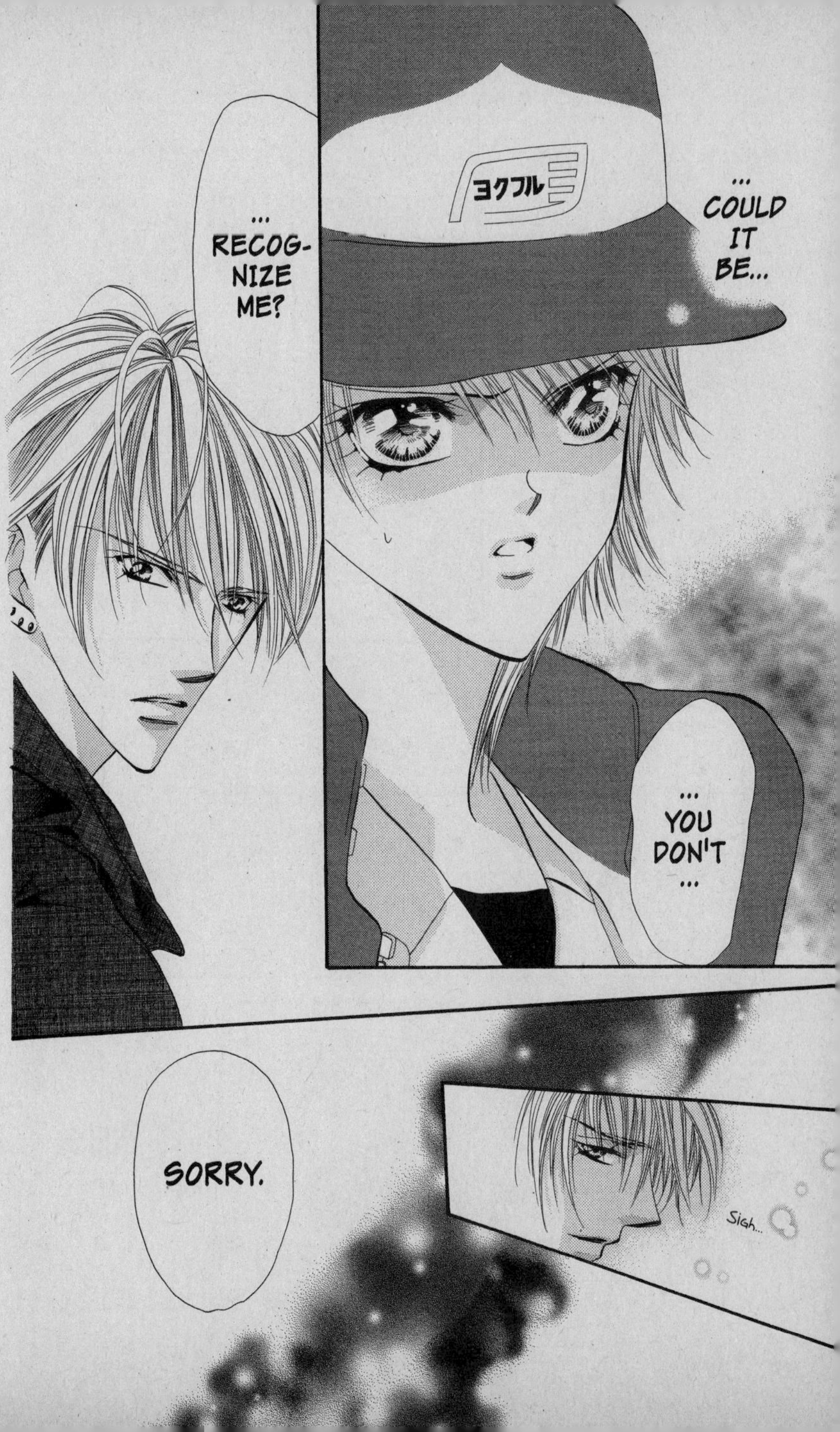
ヨクフル
... COULD IT BE...
... YOU DON'T ...
... RECOG- NIZE ME?
Sigh...
SORRY.

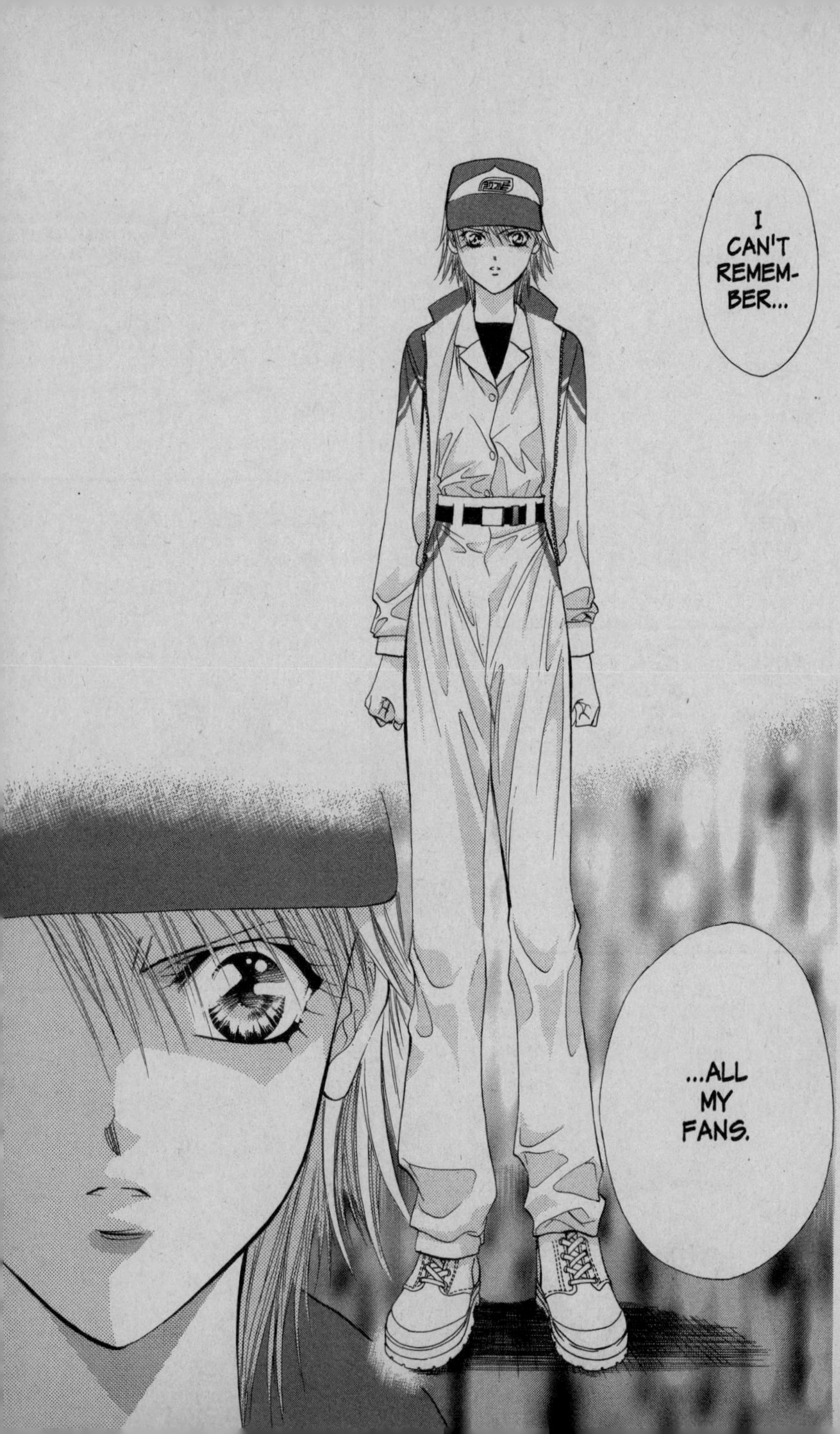
I CAN'T REMEMBER...
...ALL MY FANS.

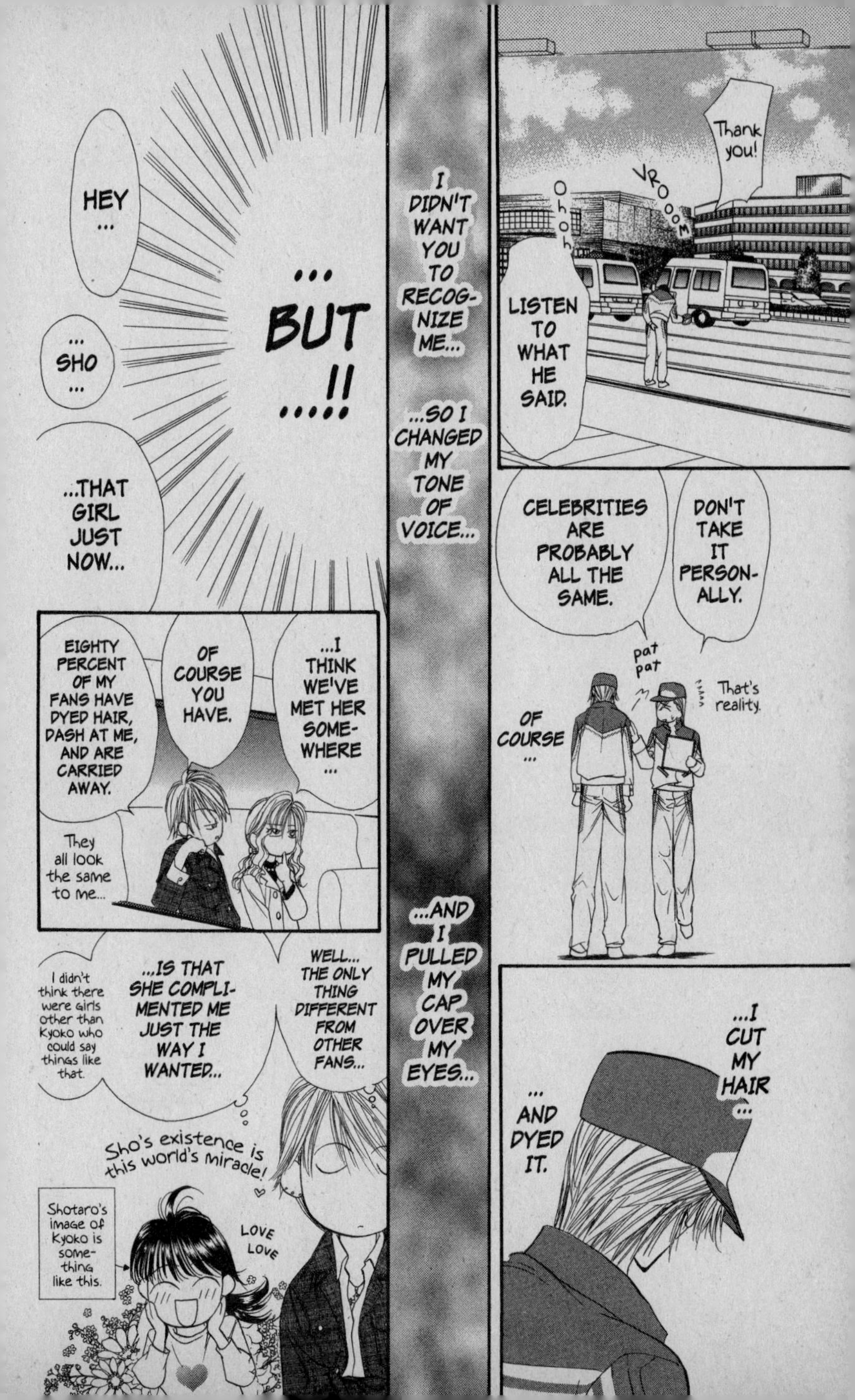
Thank you!
VROOOOM
Ohoh
LISTEN TO WHAT HE SAID.
DON'T TAKE IT PERSONALLY.
CELEBRITIES ARE PROBABLY ALL THE SAME.
pat pat
That's reality.
OF COURSE...
...I CUT MY HAIR...
...AND DYED IT.
I DIDN'T WANT YOU TO RECOGNIZE ME...
...SO I CHANGED MY TONE OF VOICE...
...AND I PULLED MY CAP OVER MY EYES...
...BUT!!
......!!
HEY...
...SHO...
...THAT GIRL JUST NOW...
...I THINK WE'VE MET HER SOMEWHERE...
OF COURSE YOU HAVE.
EIGHTY PERCENT OF MY FANS HAVE DYED HAIR, DASH AT ME, AND ARE CARRIED AWAY.
They all look the same to me...
WELL... THE ONLY THING DIFFERENT FROM OTHER FANS...
...IS THAT SHE COMPLIMENTED ME JUST THE WAY I WANTED...
I didn't think there were girls other than Kyoko who could say things like that.
Sho's existence is this world's miracle!
LOVE LOVE
Shotaro's image of Kyoko is something like this.

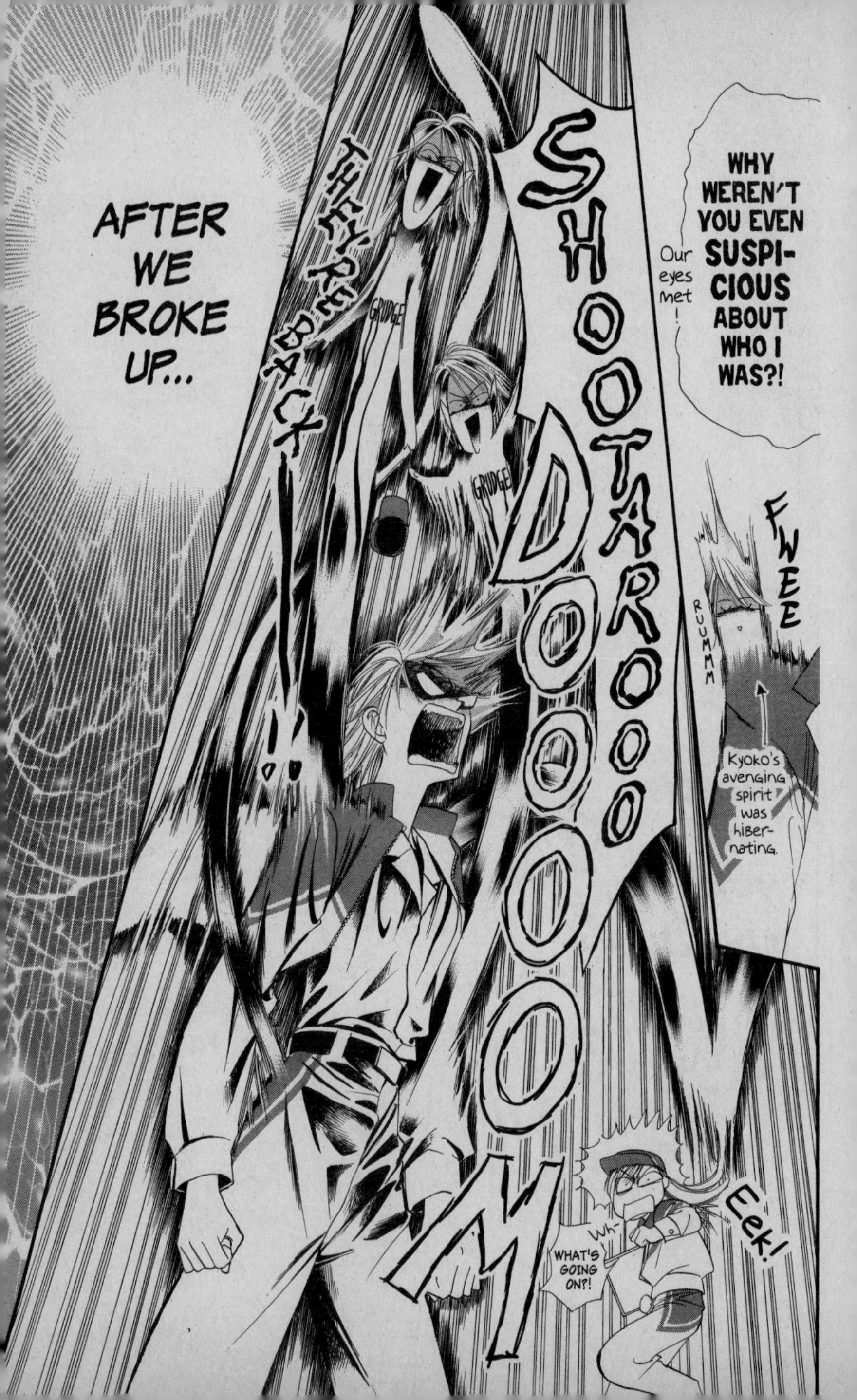
WHY WEREN'T YOU EVEN SUSPICIOUS ABOUT WHO I WAS?!
Our eyes met!
FWEEE
RUUMMM
Kyoko's avenging spirit was hibernating.
SHOOOTAROOOO
THEY'RE BACK!!
GRUDGE
GRUDGE
DOOOOOOOM
AFTER WE BROKE UP...
Eek!
Wh-
WHAT'S GOING ON?!

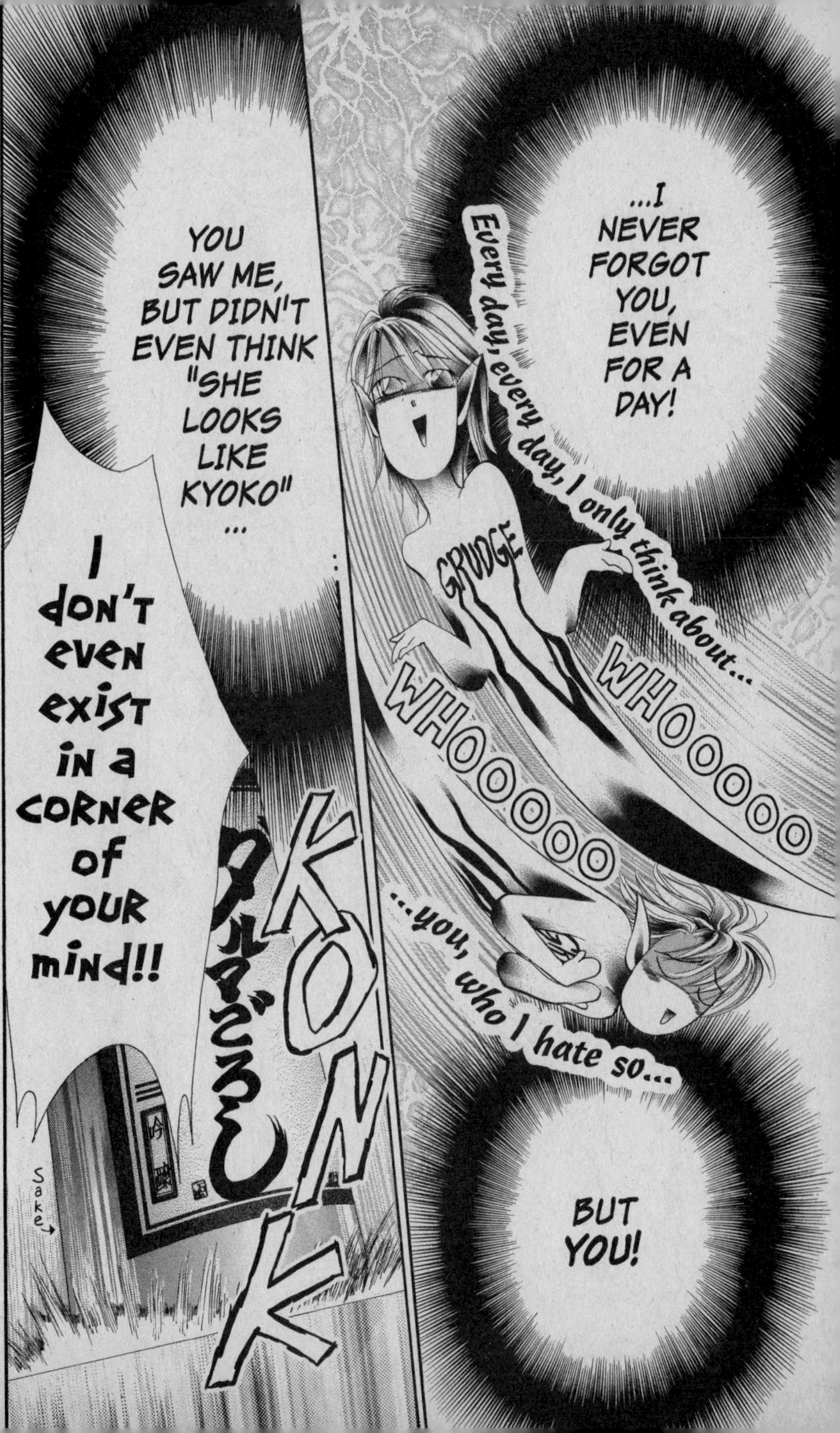
...I NEVER FORGOT YOU, EVEN FOR A DAY!
Every day, every day, I only think about...
GRUDGE
WHOOOOOO
WHOOOOOO
...you, who I hate so...
BUT YOU!
YOU SAW ME, BUT DIDN'T EVEN THINK "SHE LOOKS LIKE KYOKO"...
I don't even exist in a corner of your mind!!
KONK
Sake

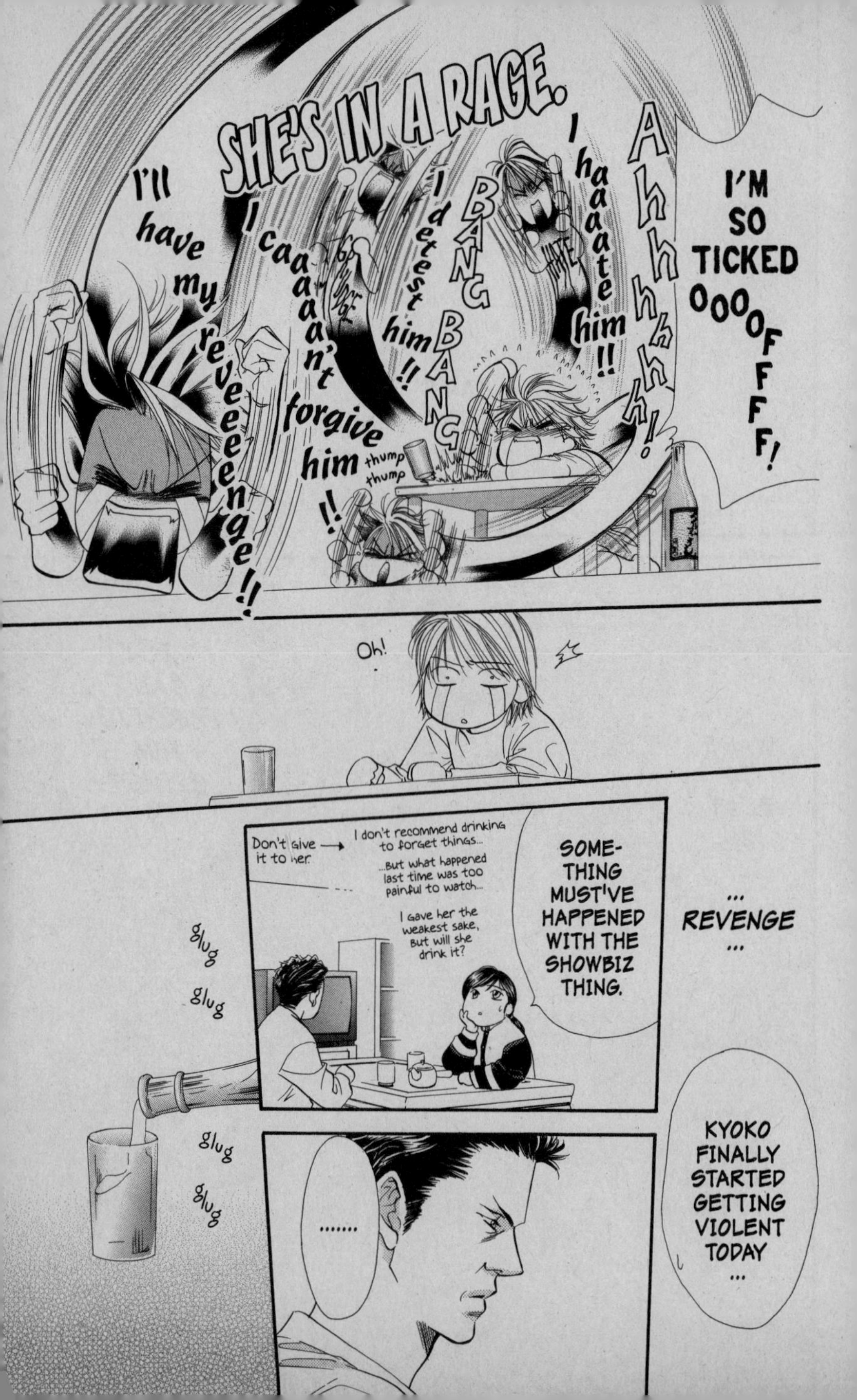
I'M SO TICKED OOOOFFFFF!
Ahhhhhh!
I haaaate him!!
SHE'S IN A RAGE.
BANG
BANG
I detest him!!
I caaaaaan't forgive him!!
thump thump
I'll have my reveeeeenge!!
Oh!
...REVENGE...
SOME-THING MUST'VE HAPPENED WITH THE SHOWBIZ THING.
I don't recommend drinking to forget things...
...but what happened last time was too painful to watch...
I gave her the weakest sake, but will she drink it?
Don't give it to her.
glug
glug
KYOKO FINALLY STARTED GETTING VIOLENT TODAY...
....
glug
glug

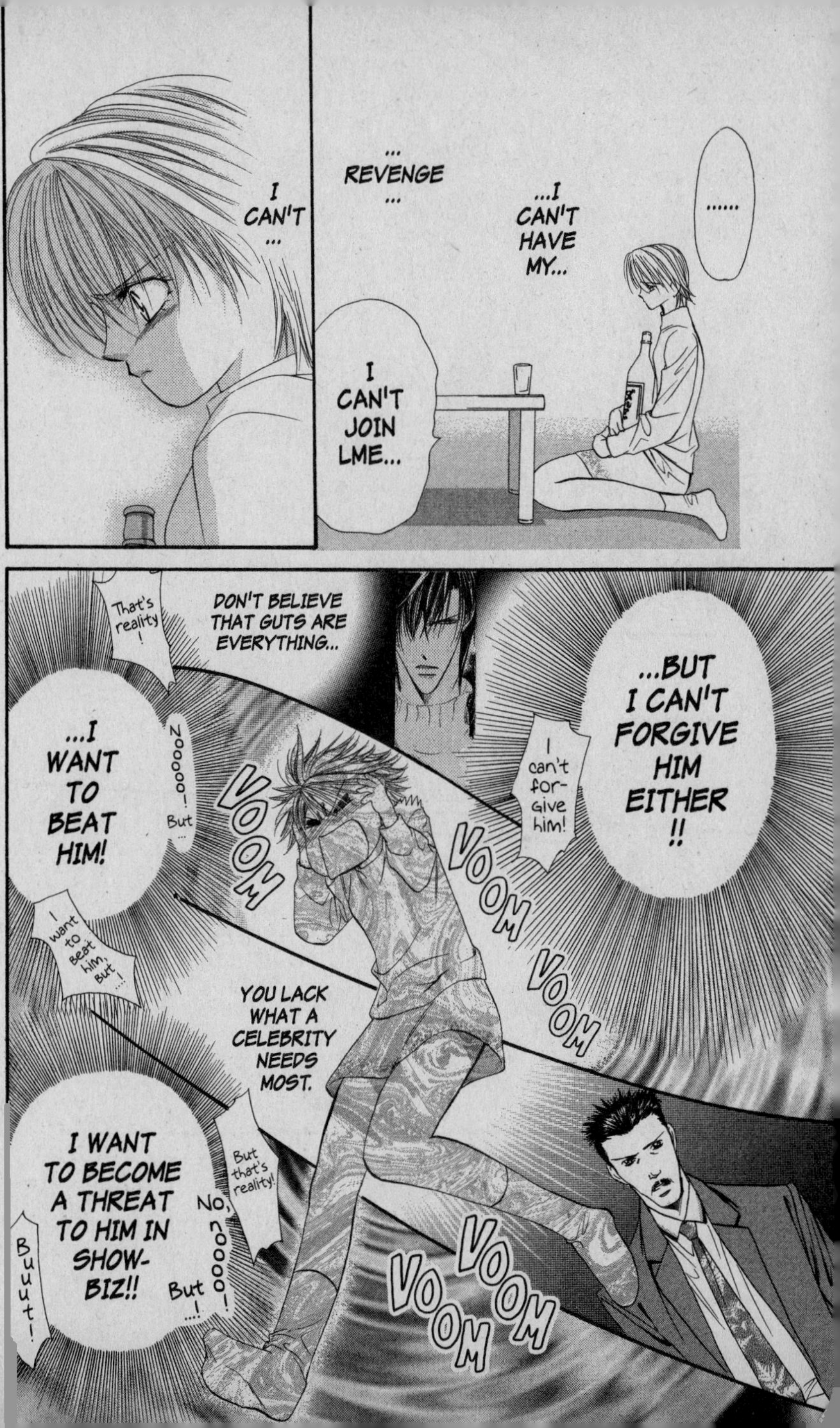
......
...I CAN'T HAVE MY...
...REVENGE...
I CAN'T JOIN LME...
I CAN'T...
...BUT I CAN'T FORGIVE HIM EITHER!!
I can't for-give him!
DON'T BELIEVE THAT GUTS ARE EVERYTHING...
VOOM
That's reality!
Noooo! But...
...I WANT TO BEAT HIM!
VOOM VOOM VOOM
I want to beat him, but...!
YOU LACK WHAT A CELEBRITY NEEDS MOST.
But that's reality!
VOOM VOOM
No, noooo! But...!
I WANT TO BECOME A THREAT TO HIM IN SHOW-BIZ!!
Buuut!

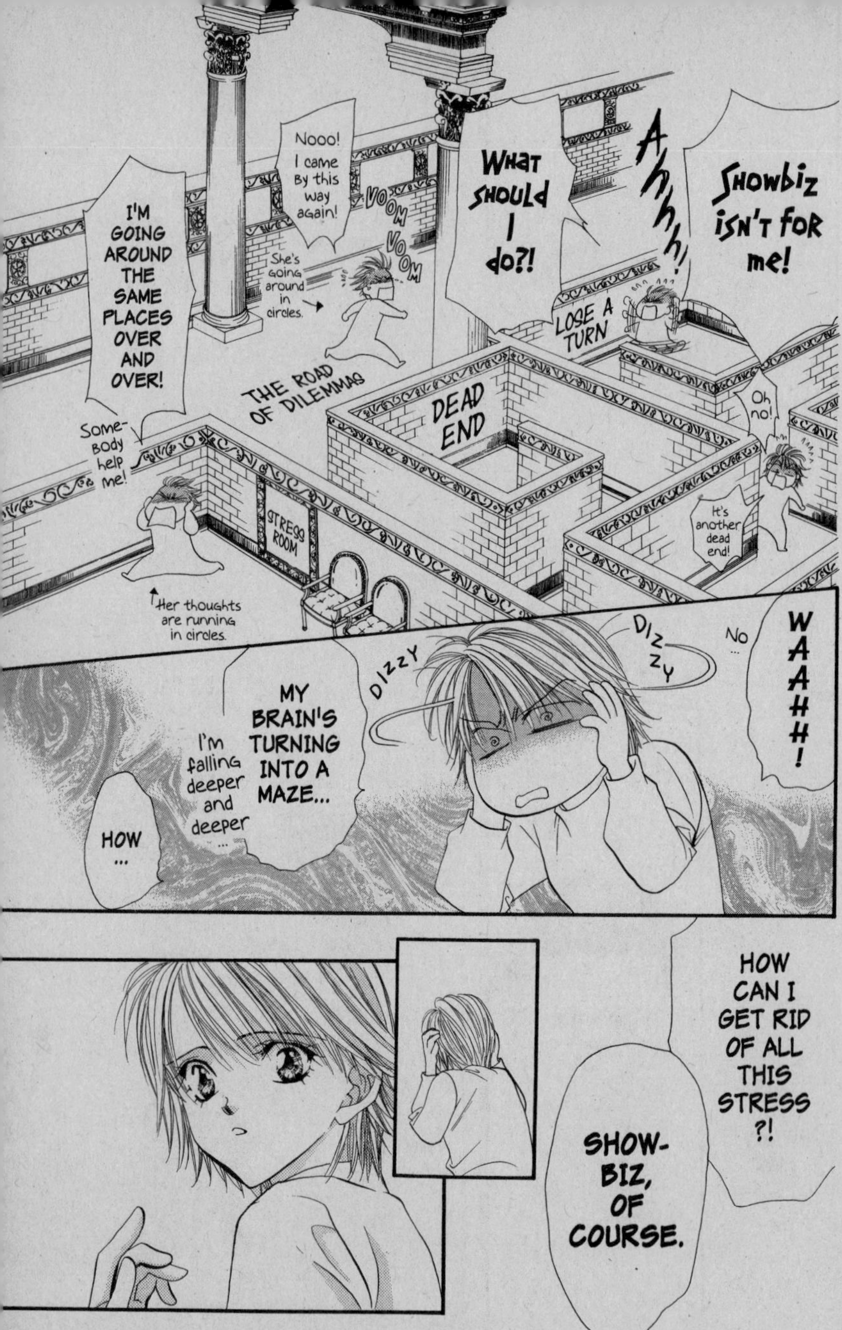
Showbiz isn't for me!
Ahhhh!
What should I do?!
LOSE A TURN
Nooo! I came by this way again!
VOOM VOOM
She's going around in circles.
I'M GOING AROUND THE SAME PLACES OVER AND OVER!
Oh no!
It's another dead end!
DEAD END
THE ROAD OF DILEMMAS
Somebody help me!
STRESS ROOM
Her thoughts are running in circles.
WAAAHH!
No...
DIZZY
DIZZY
MY BRAIN'S TURNING INTO A MAZE...
I'm falling deeper and deeper...
HOW...
HOW CAN I GET RID OF ALL THIS STRESS?!
SHOW-BIZ, OF COURSE.

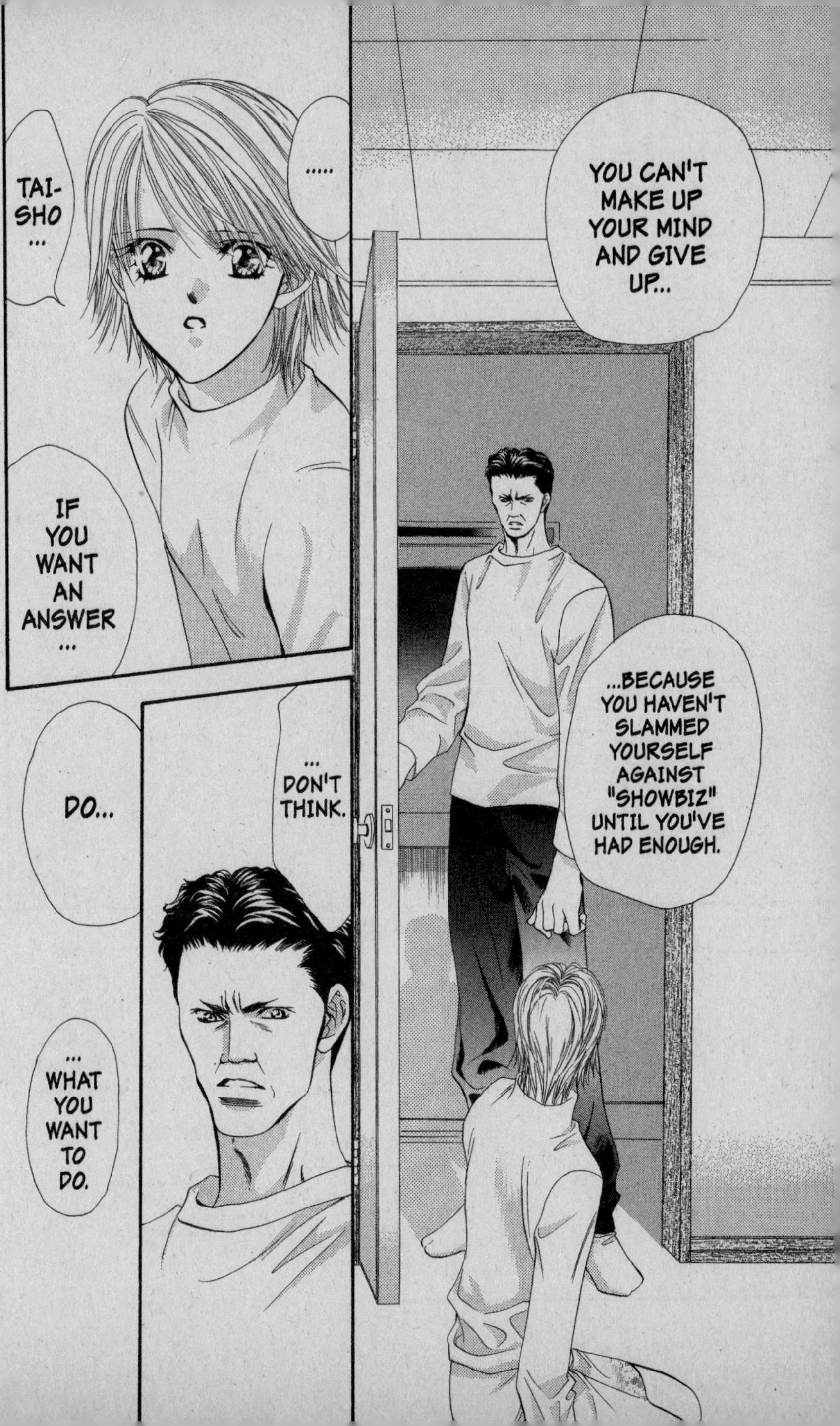
YOU CAN'T MAKE UP YOUR MIND AND GIVE UP...
...BECAUSE YOU HAVEN'T SLAMMED YOURSELF AGAINST "SHOWBIZ" UNTIL YOU'VE HAD ENOUGH.
.....
TAI-SHO...
IF YOU WANT AN ANSWER...
...DON'T THINK.
DO...
...WHAT YOU WANT TO DO.

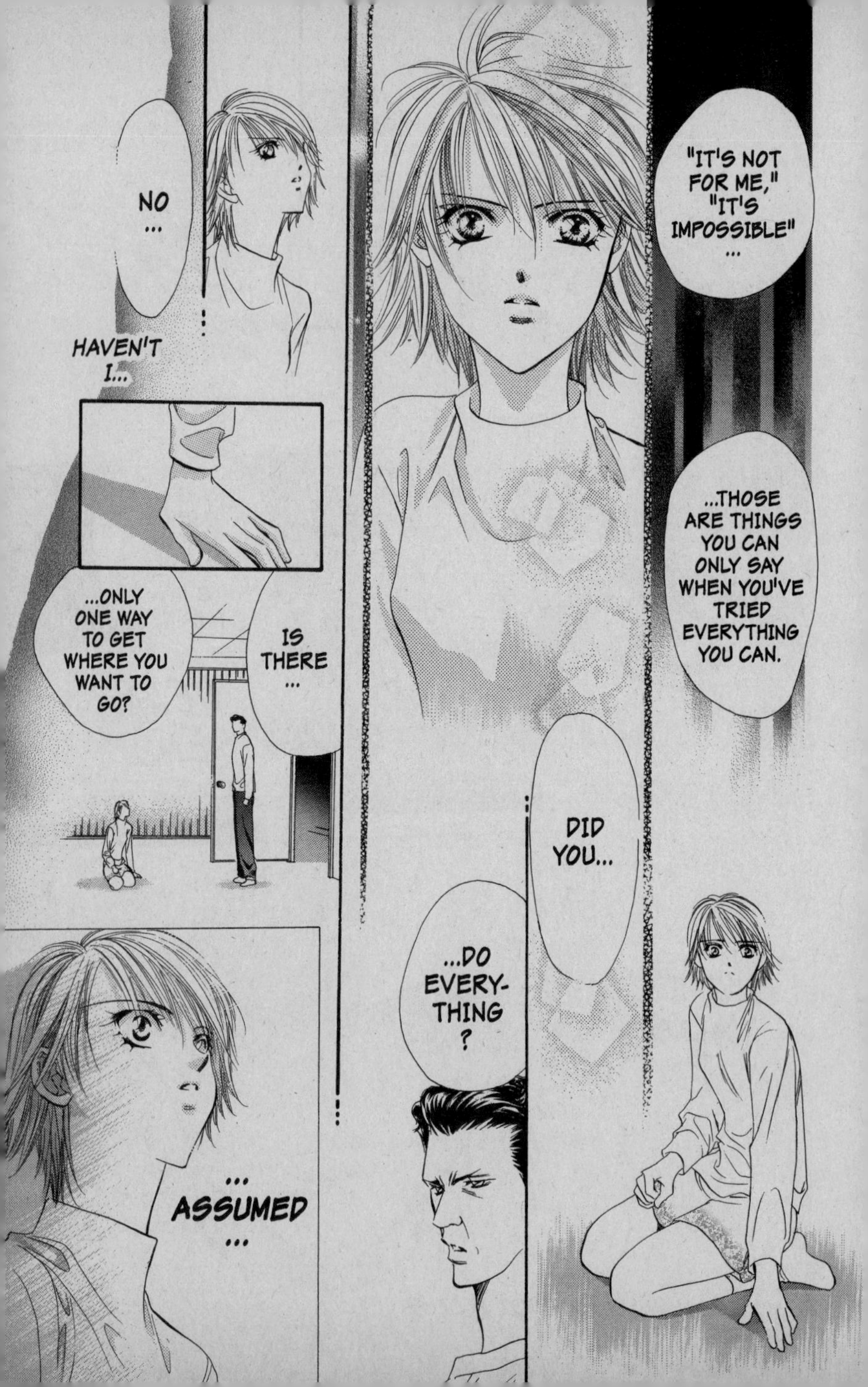

"IT'S NOT FOR ME," "IT'S IMPOSSIBLE" ...
...THOSE ARE THINGS YOU CAN ONLY SAY WHEN YOU'VE TRIED EVERYTHING YOU CAN.
DID YOU...
...DO EVERYTHING?
NO ...
HAVEN'T I...
IS THERE ...
...ONLY ONE WAY TO GET WHERE YOU WANT TO GO?
... ASSUMED ...

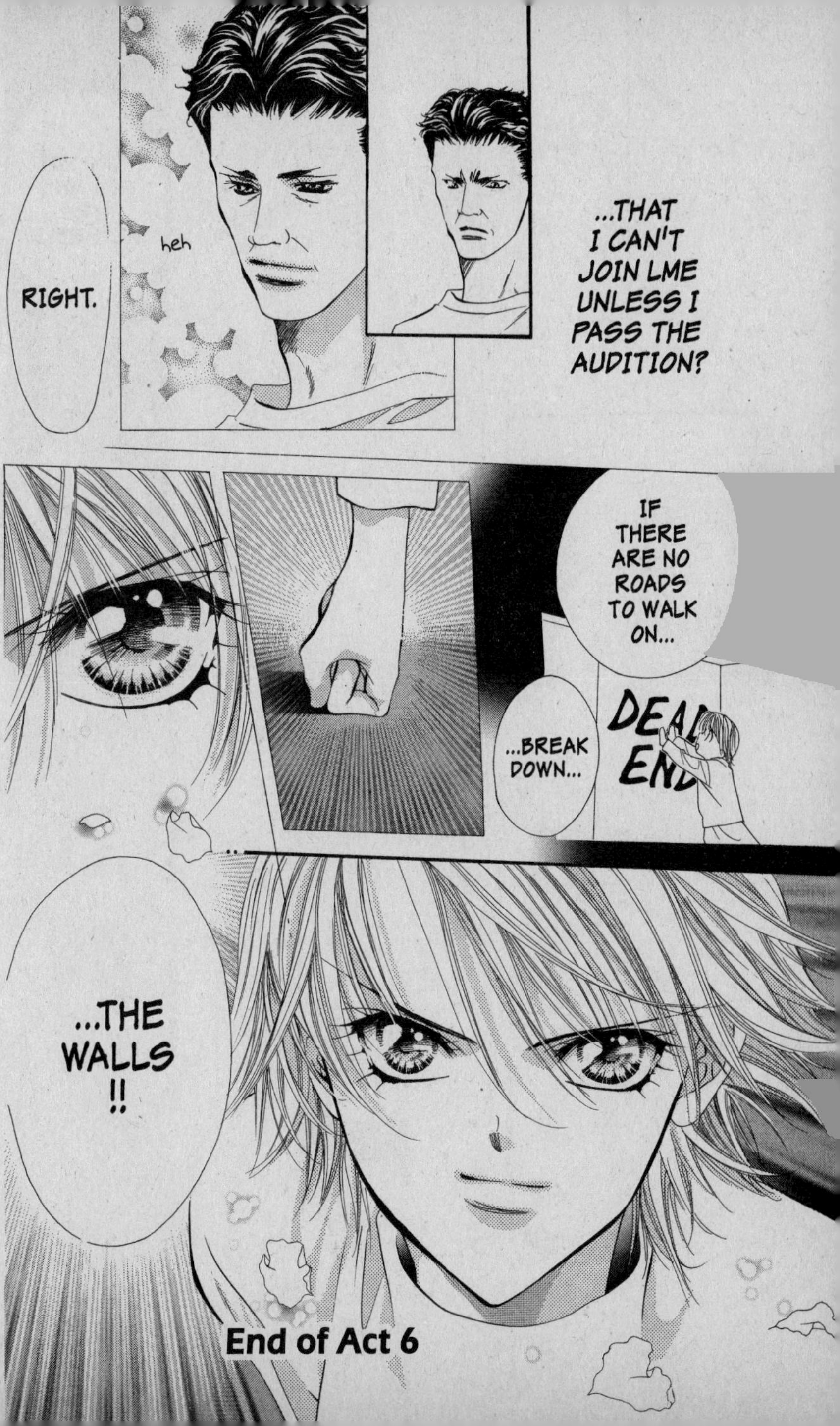
...THAT I CAN'T JOIN LME UNLESS I PASS THE AUDITION?
heh
RIGHT.
IF THERE ARE NO ROADS TO WALK ON...
DEAD END
...BREAK DOWN...
...THE WALLS !!
End of Act 6

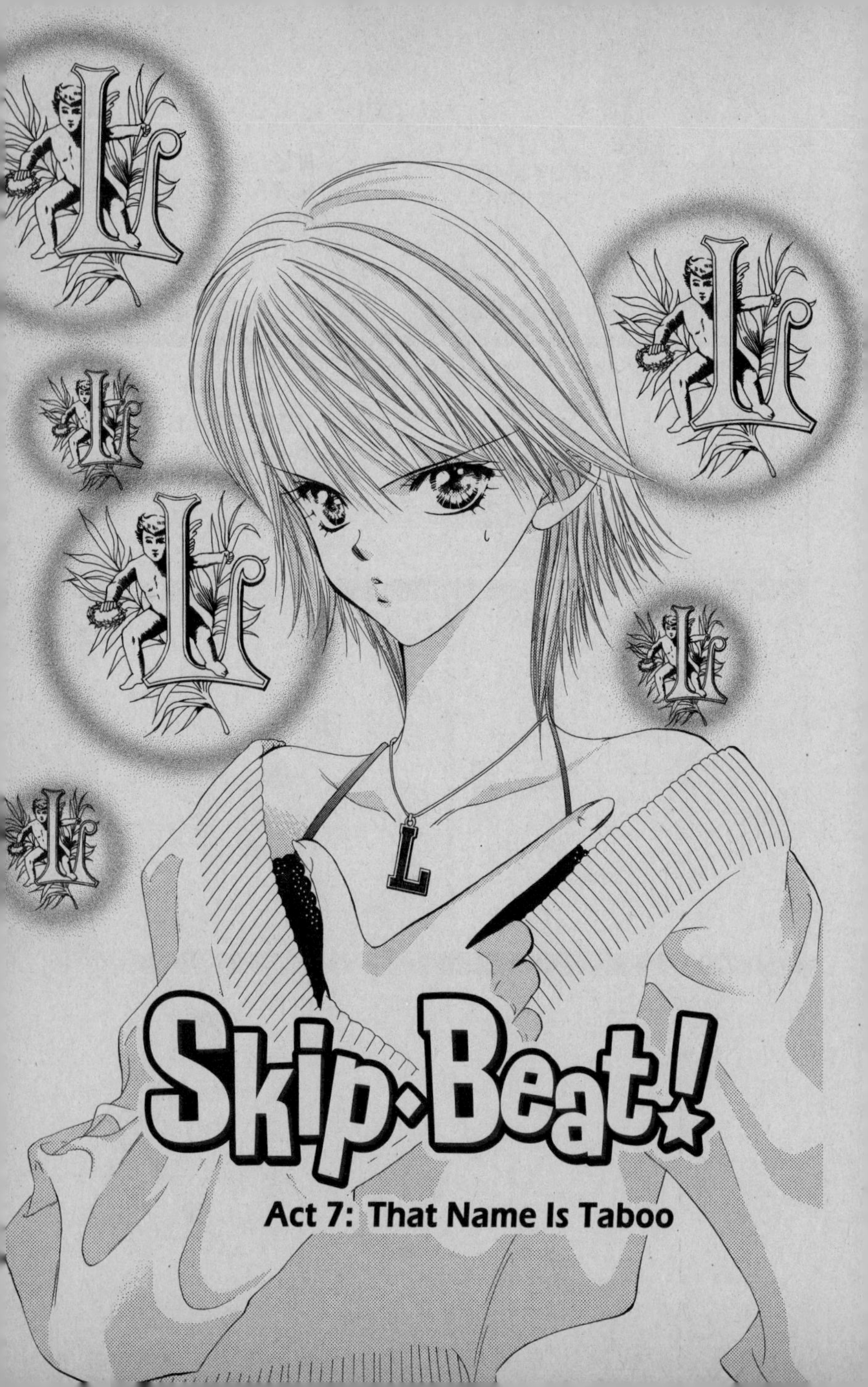
Skip·Beat!
Act 7: That Name Is Taboo

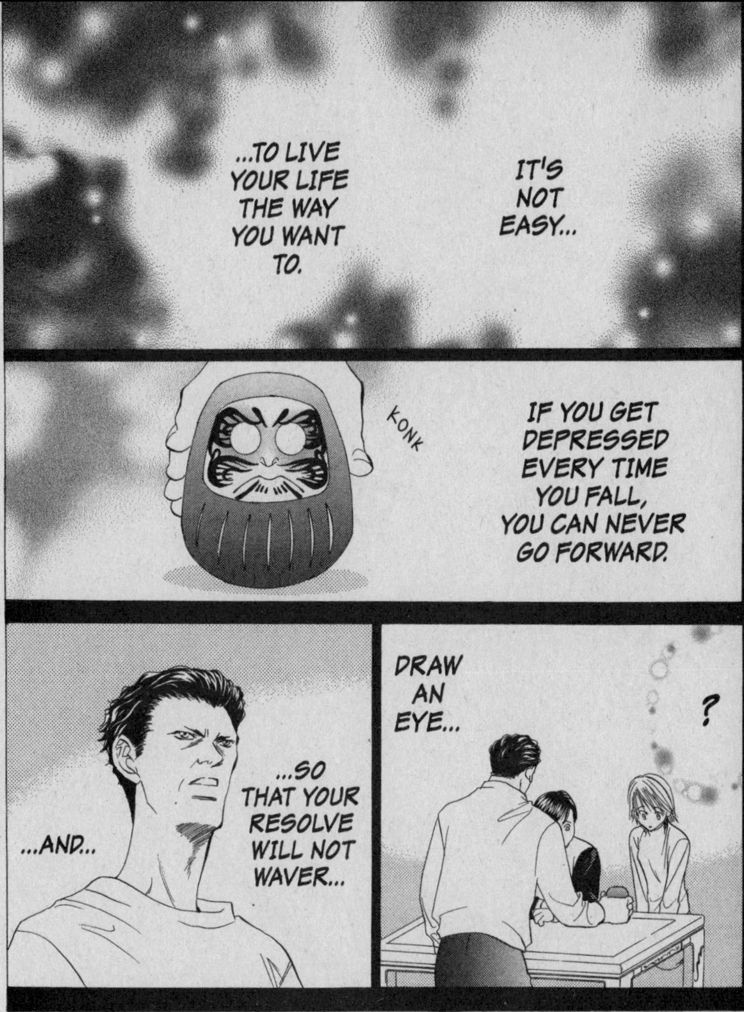
IT'S NOT EASY...
...TO LIVE YOUR LIFE THE WAY YOU WANT TO.
IF YOU GET DEPRESSED EVERY TIME YOU FALL, YOU CAN NEVER GO FORWARD.
KONK
?
DRAW AN EYE...
...SO THAT YOUR RESOLVE WILL NOT WAVER...
...AND...

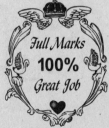

Full Marks
100%
Great Job

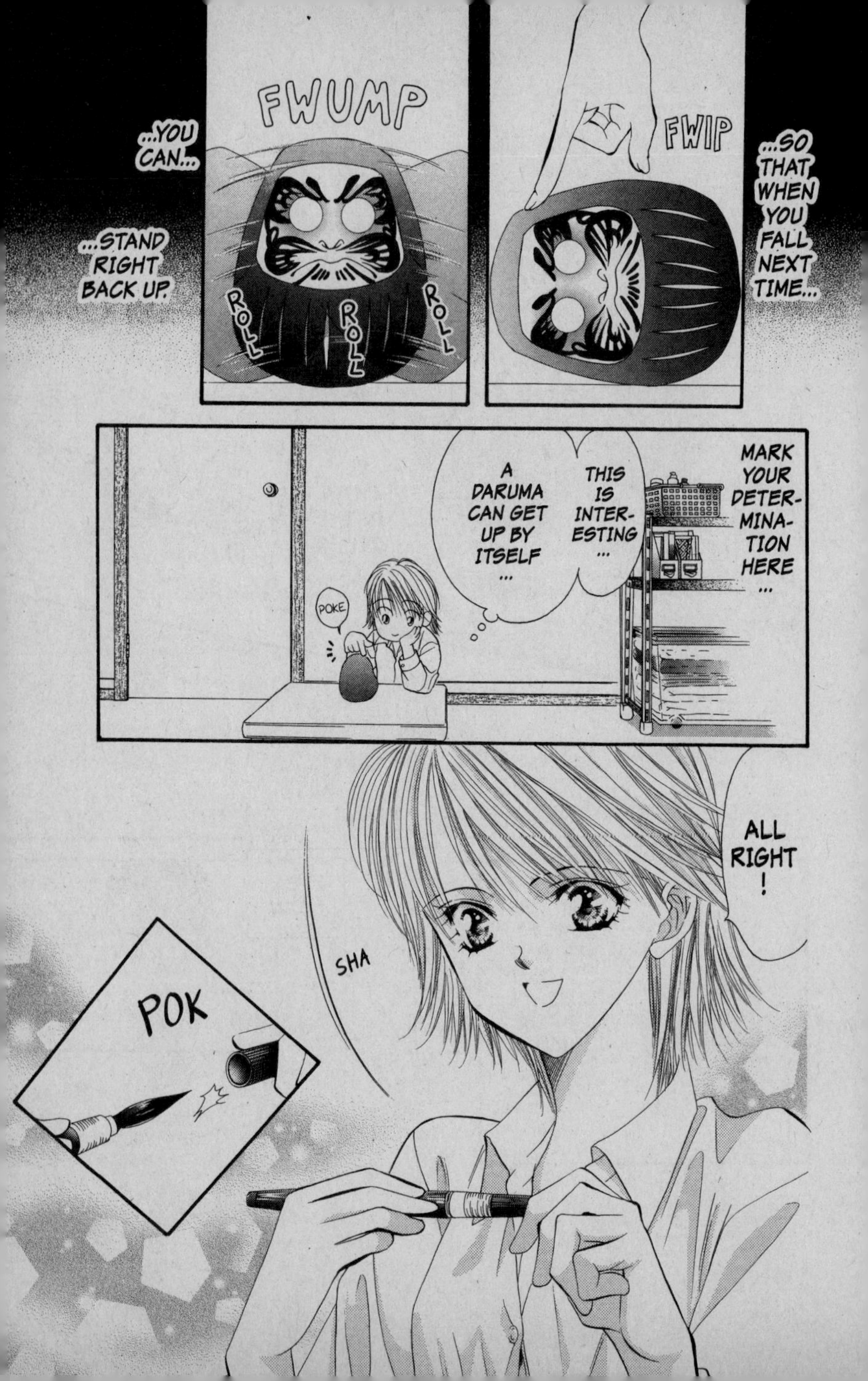
FWIP
...SO THAT WHEN YOU FALL NEXT TIME...
FWUMP
...YOU CAN...
...STAND RIGHT BACK UP.
ROLL
ROLL
ROLL
MARK YOUR DETERMINATION HERE...
THIS IS INTERESTING...
A DARUMA CAN GET UP BY ITSELF...
POKE
ALL RIGHT!
SHA
POK

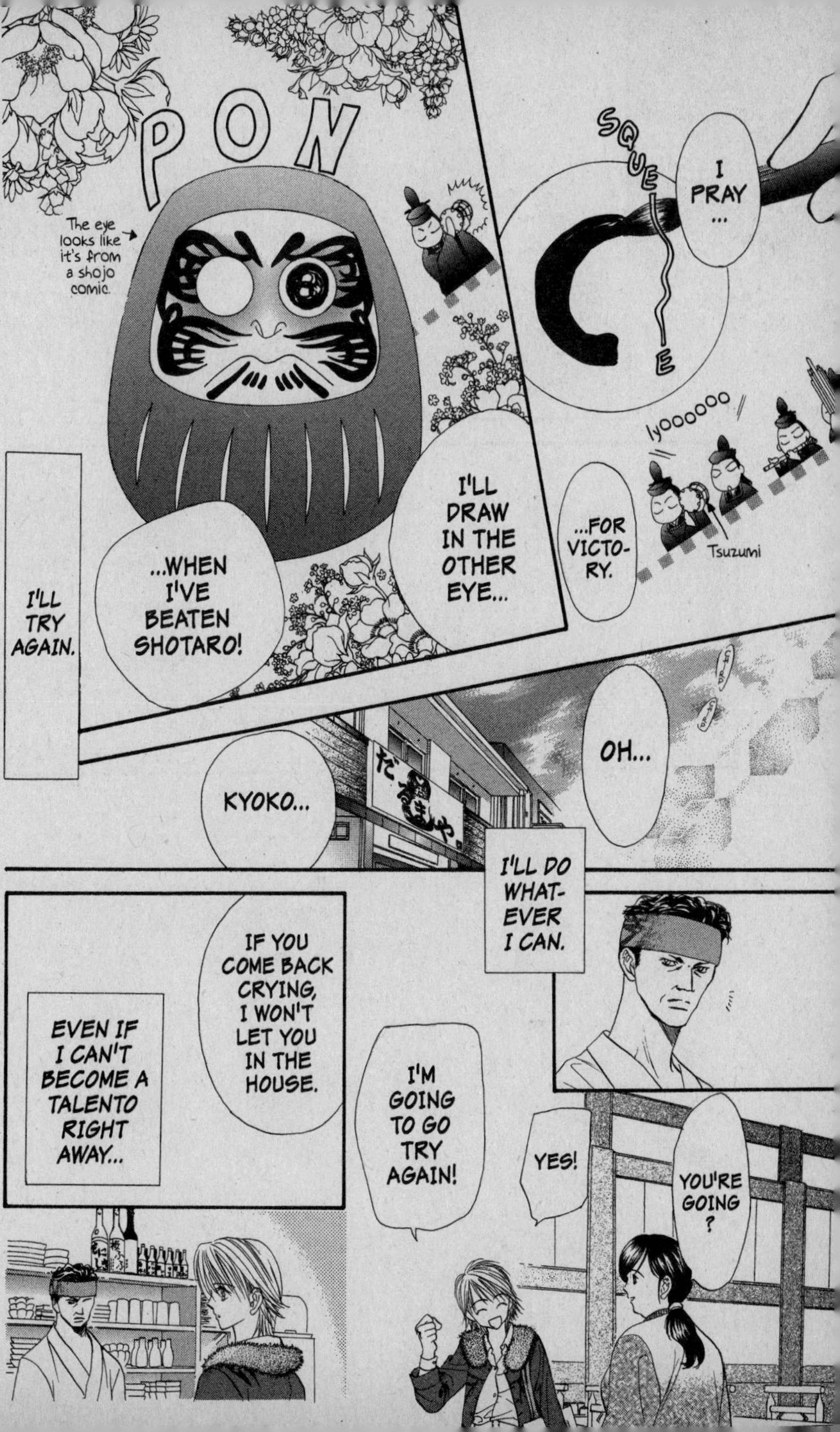
I PRAY...
SQUEE
Iyoooooo
...FOR VICTORY.
Tsuzumi
PON
The eye looks like it's from a shojo comic.
I'LL DRAW IN THE OTHER EYE...
...WHEN I'VE BEATEN SHOTARO!
I'LL TRY AGAIN.
OH...
KYOKO...
だるまや
I'LL DO WHATEVER I CAN.
IF YOU COME BACK CRYING, I WON'T LET YOU IN THE HOUSE.
EVEN IF I CAN'T BECOME A TALENTO RIGHT AWAY...
YOU'RE GOING?
YES!
I'M GOING TO GO TRY AGAIN!

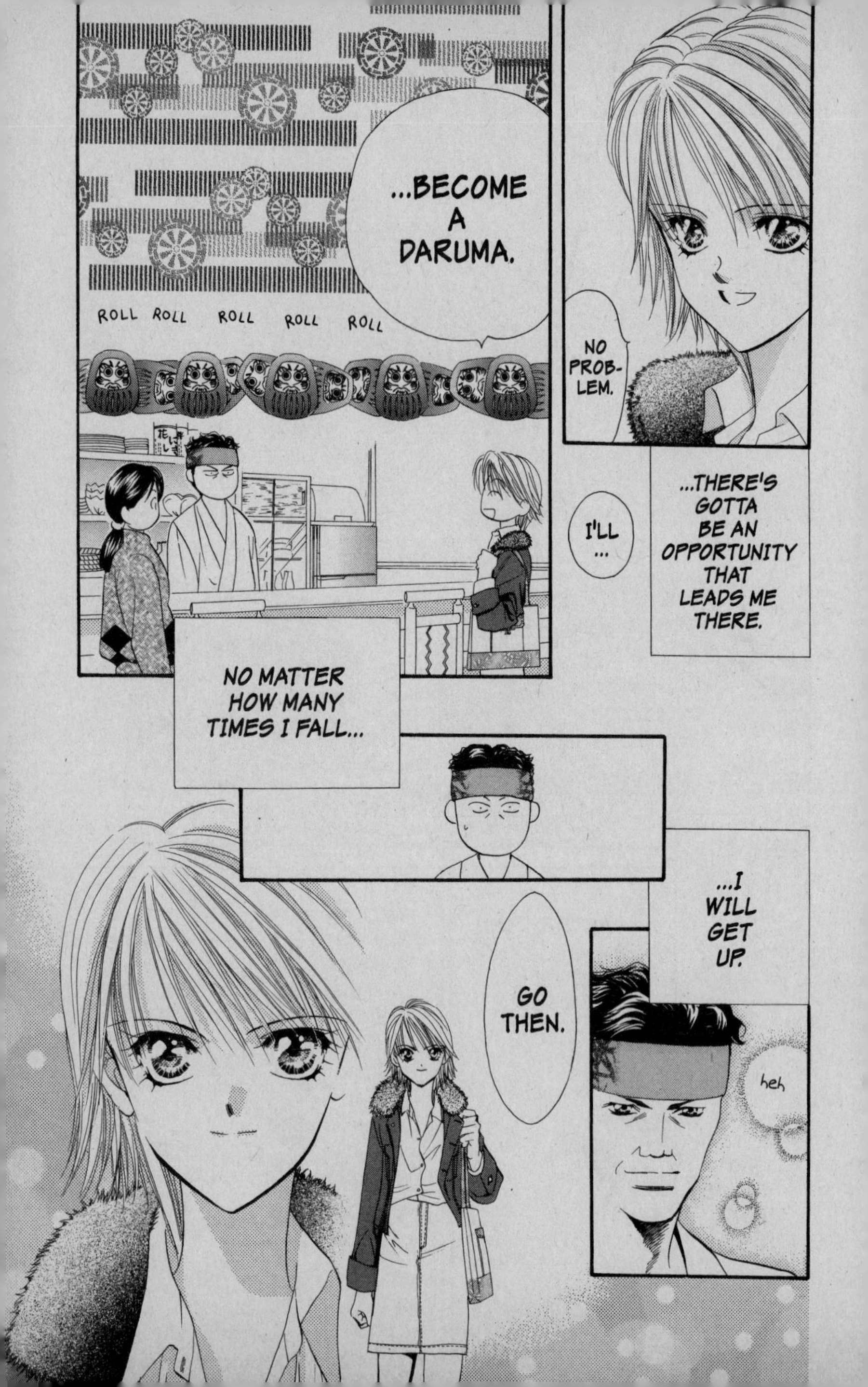
NO PROB-LEM.
I'LL ...
...BECOME A DARUMA.
ROLL ROLL ROLL ROLL ROLL
...THERE'S GOTTA BE AN OPPORTUNITY THAT LEADS ME THERE.
NO MATTER HOW MANY TIMES I FALL...
...I WILL GET UP.
GO THEN.
heh

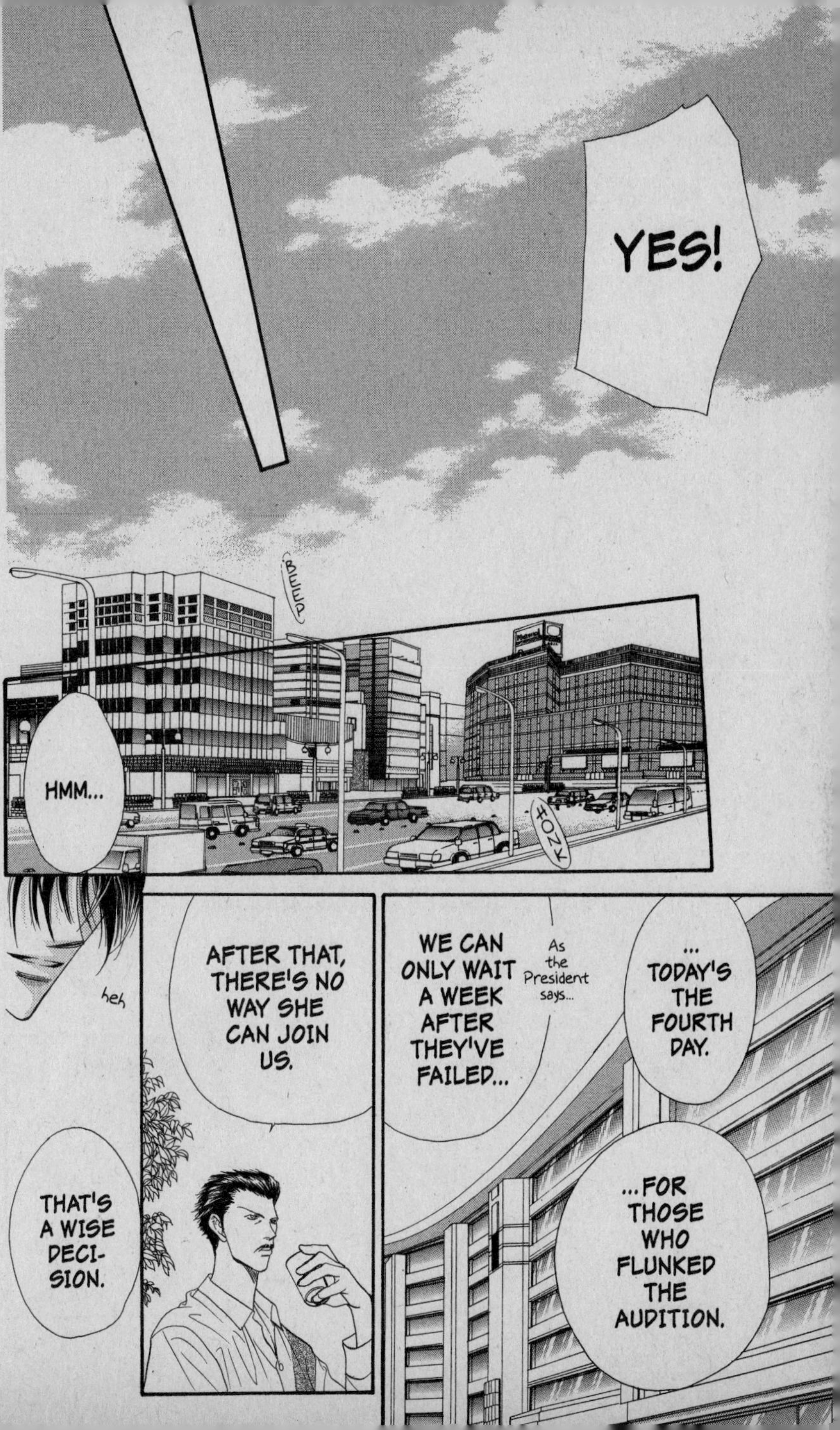
YES!
BEEP
HONK
HMM...
...TODAY'S THE FOURTH DAY.
...FOR THOSE WHO FLUNKED THE AUDITION.
WE CAN ONLY WAIT A WEEK AFTER THEY'VE FAILED...
As the President says...
AFTER THAT, THERE'S NO WAY SHE CAN JOIN US.
heh
THAT'S A WISE DECI-SION.

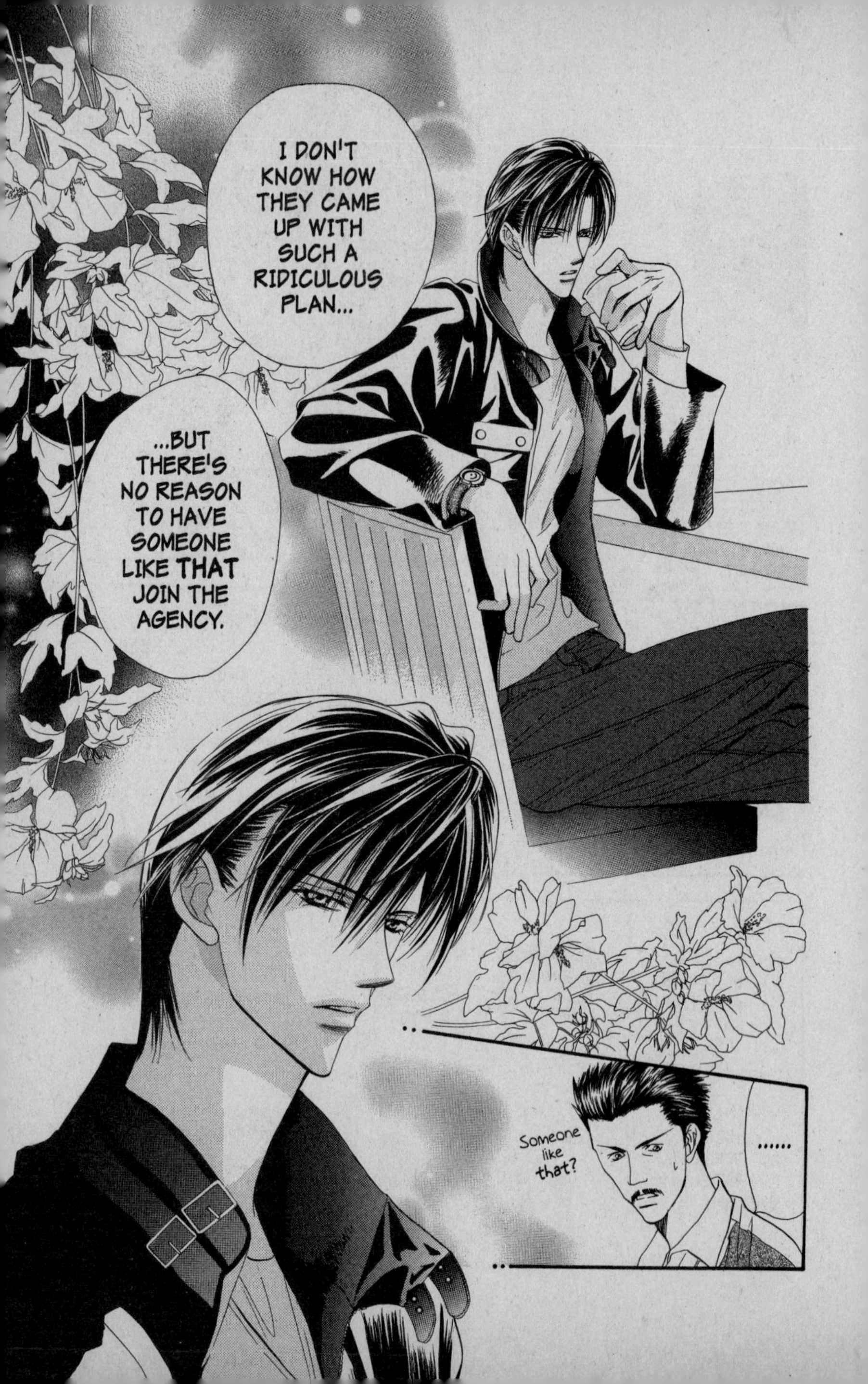
I DON'T KNOW HOW THEY CAME UP WITH SUCH A RIDICULOUS PLAN...
...BUT THERE'S NO REASON TO HAVE SOMEONE LIKE THAT JOIN THE AGENCY.
......
Someone like that?

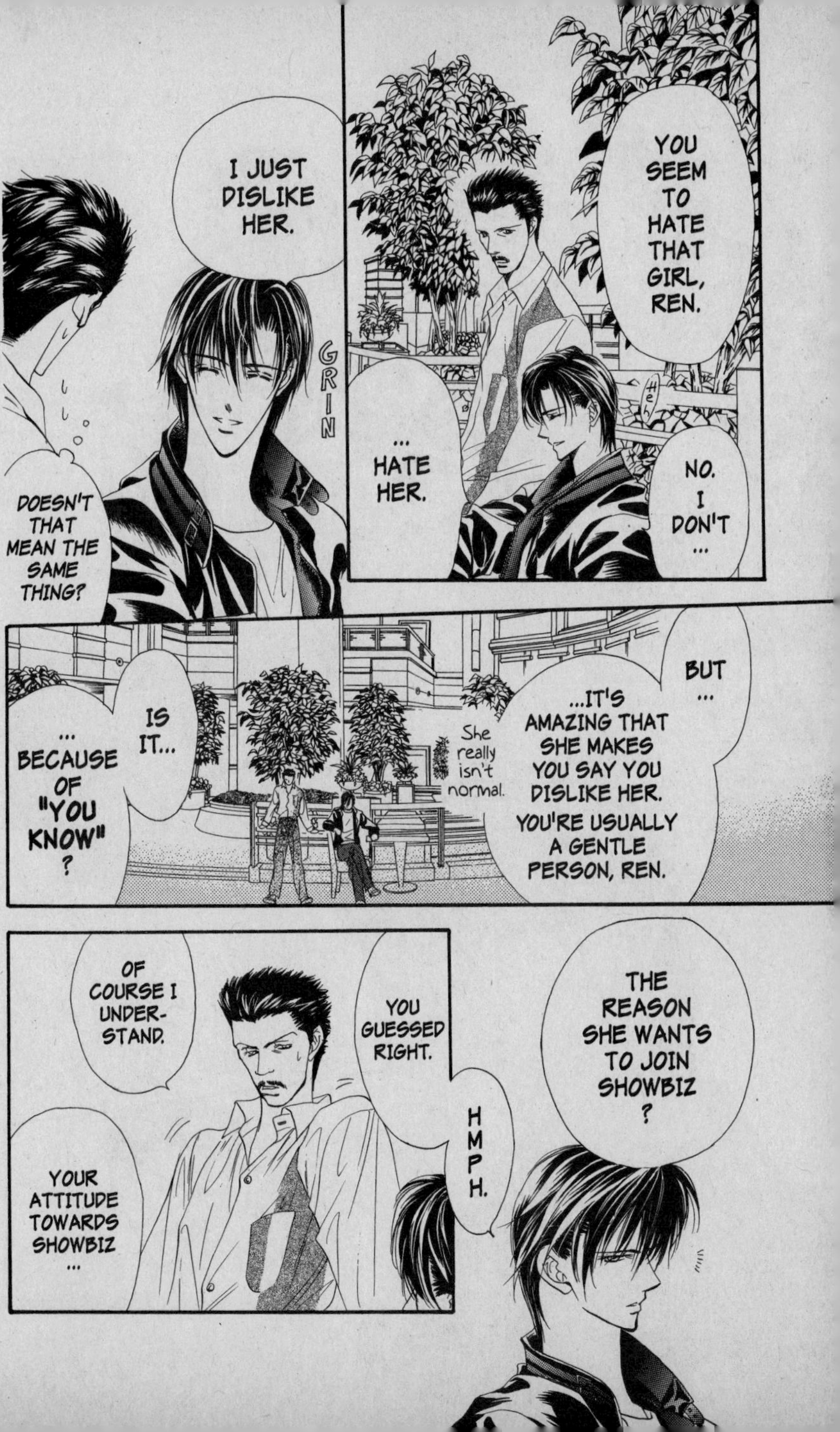
YOU SEEM TO HATE THAT GIRL, REN.
Heh
NO. I DON'T ...
... HATE HER.
I JUST DISLIKE HER.
GRIN
DOESN'T THAT MEAN THE SAME THING?
BUT ...
...IT'S AMAZING THAT SHE MAKES YOU SAY YOU DISLIKE HER. YOU'RE USUALLY A GENTLE PERSON, REN.
She really isn't normal.
IS IT...
... BECAUSE OF "YOU KNOW" ?
THE REASON SHE WANTS TO JOIN SHOWBIZ ?
HMPH.
YOU GUESSED RIGHT.
OF COURSE I UNDER-STAND.
YOUR ATTITUDE TOWARDS SHOWBIZ ...

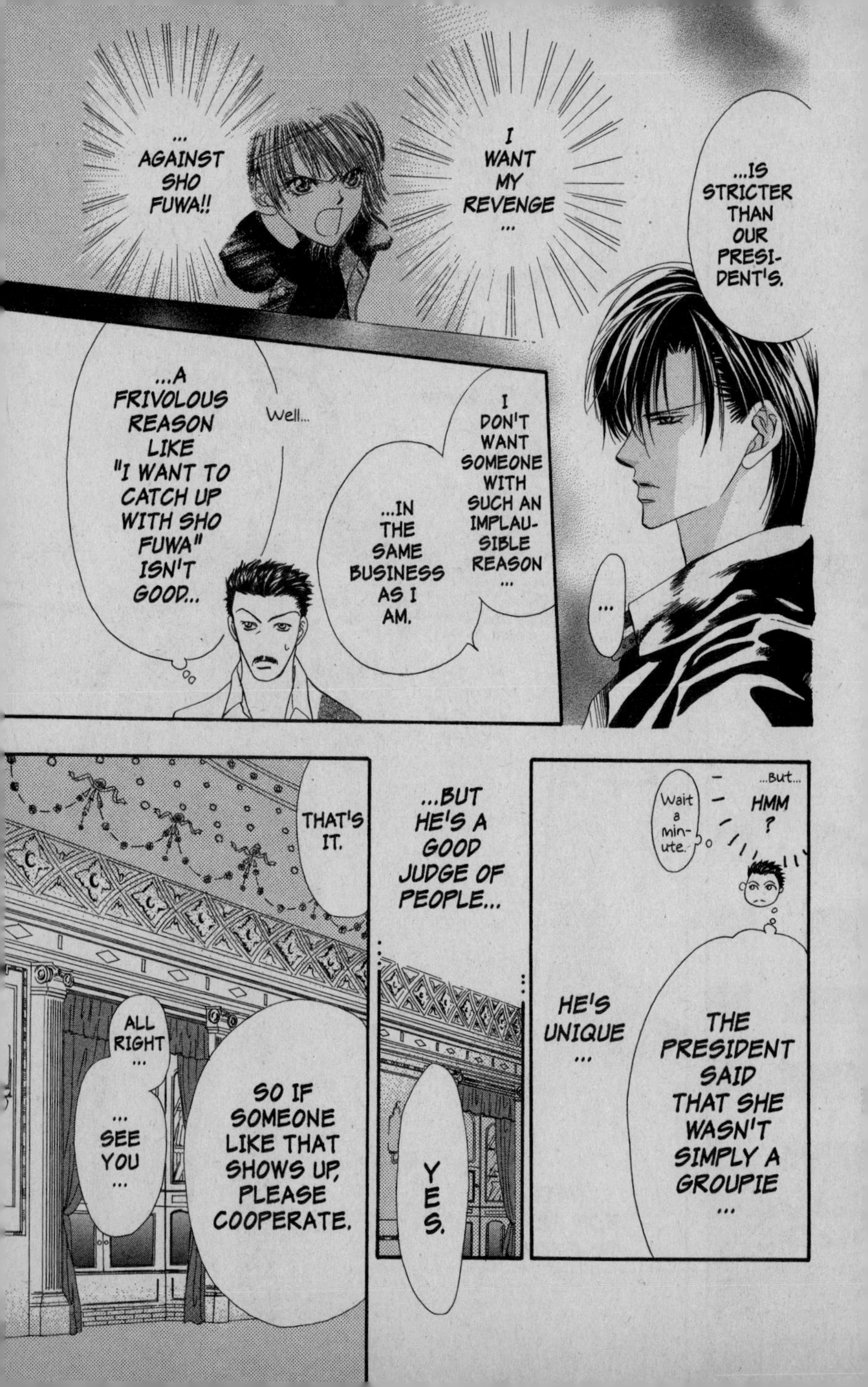
...IS STRICTER THAN OUR PRESIDENT'S.
I WANT MY REVENGE...
...AGAINST SHO FUWA!!
I DON'T WANT SOMEONE WITH SUCH AN IMPLAUSIBLE REASON...
...IN THE SAME BUSINESS AS I AM.
Well...
...A FRIVOLOUS REASON LIKE "I WANT TO CATCH UP WITH SHO FUWA" ISN'T GOOD...
...
...But...
HMM?
Wait a minute.
THE PRESIDENT SAID THAT SHE WASN'T SIMPLY A GROUPIE...
HE'S UNIQUE...
...BUT HE'S A GOOD JUDGE OF PEOPLE...
YES.
THAT'S IT.
SO IF SOMEONE LIKE THAT SHOWS UP, PLEASE COOPERATE.
ALL RIGHT...
...SEE YOU...

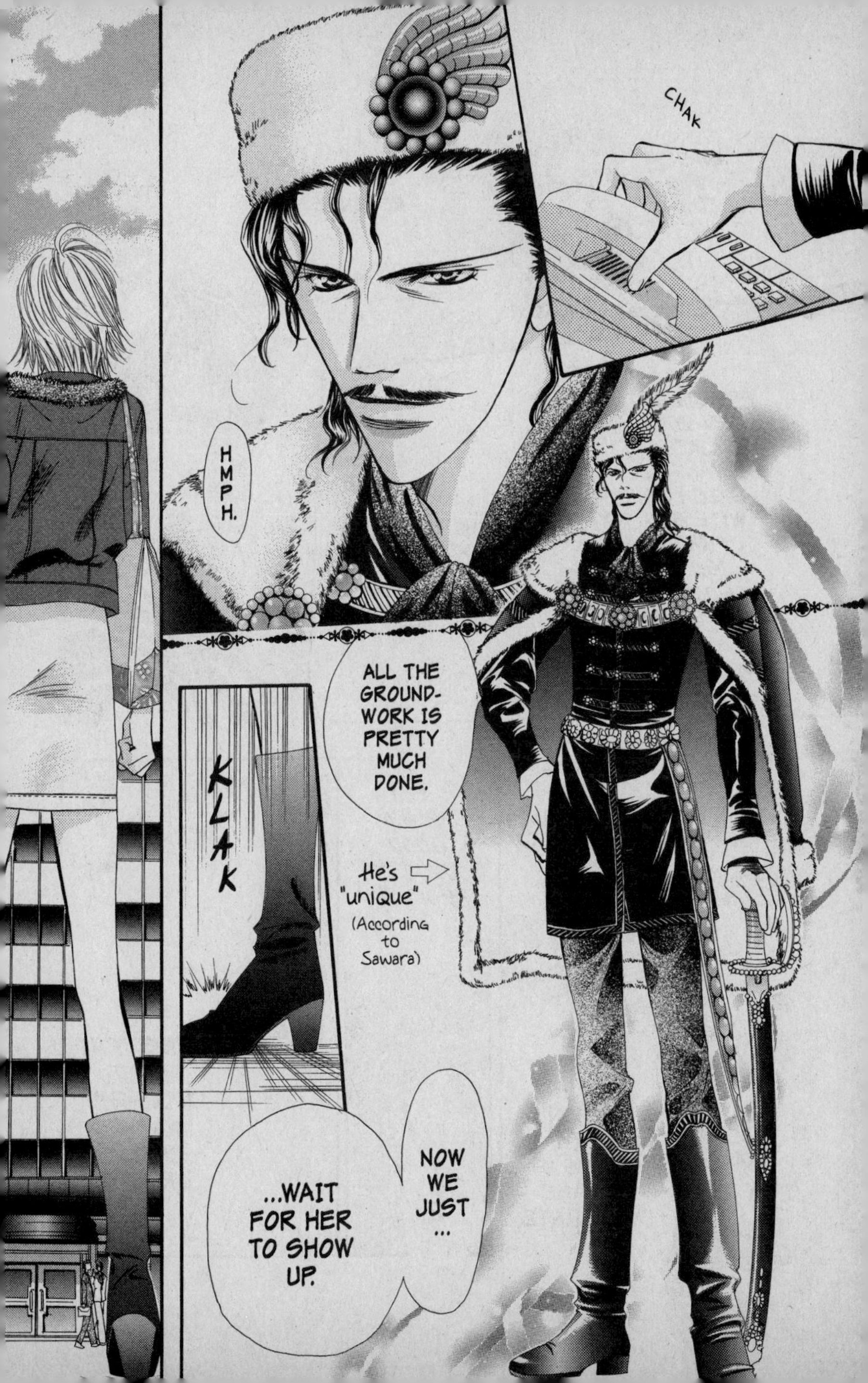
CHAK
HMPH.
ALL THE GROUND-WORK IS PRETTY MUCH DONE.
He's "unique" (According to Sawara)
KLAK
NOW WE JUST ...
...WAIT FOR HER TO SHOW UP.

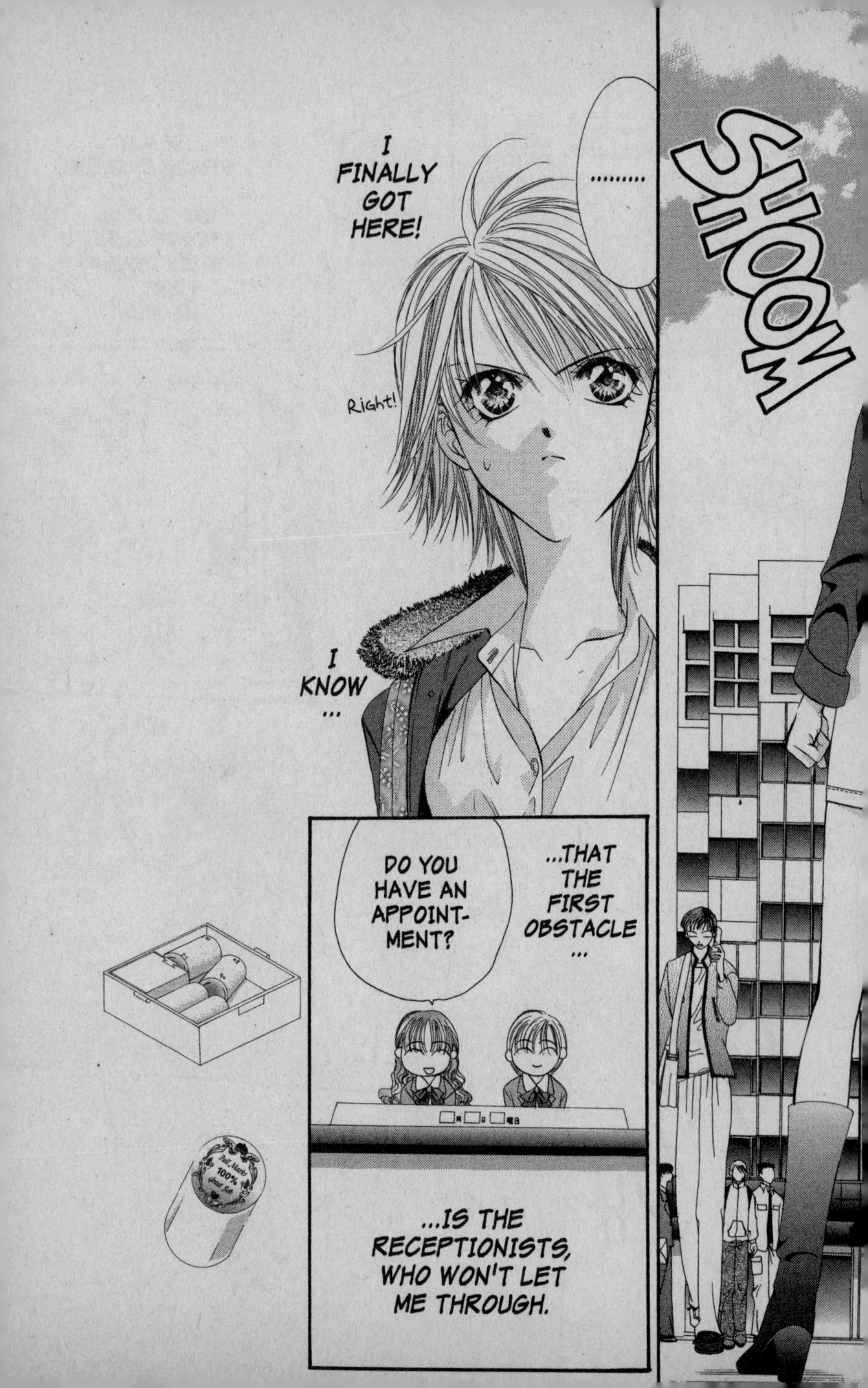
SHOOM
....
I FINALLY GOT HERE!
Right!
I KNOW ...
...THAT THE FIRST OBSTACLE ...
DO YOU HAVE AN APPOINTMENT?
...IS THE RECEPTIONISTS, WHO WON'T LET ME THROUGH.

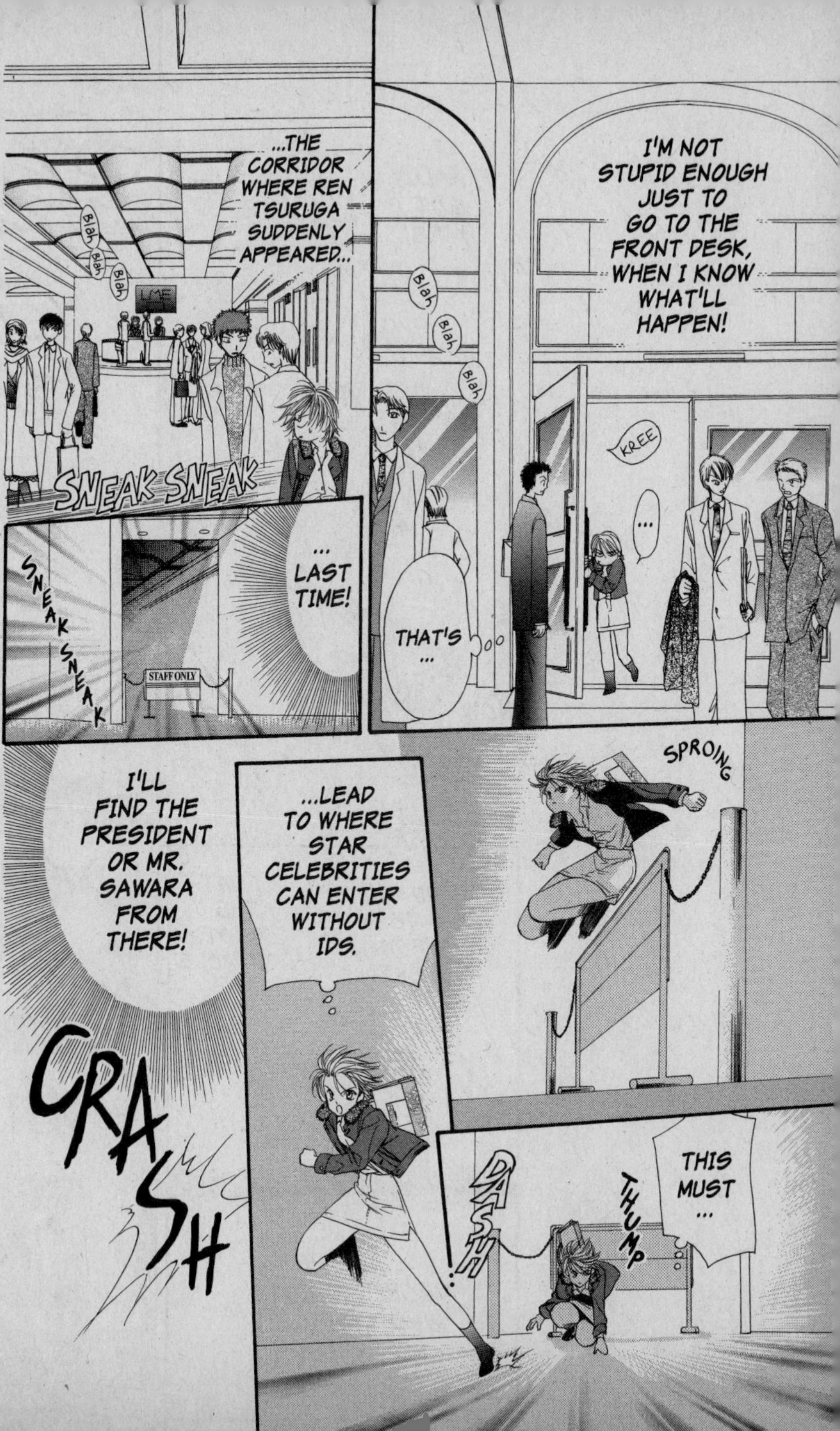
I'M NOT STUPID ENOUGH JUST TO GO TO THE FRONT DESK, WHEN I KNOW WHAT'LL HAPPEN!
Blah
Blah
Blah
KREE
...
THAT'S ...
...THE CORRIDOR WHERE REN TSURUGA SUDDENLY APPEARED...
Blah
Blah
Blah
SNEAK SNEAK
... LAST TIME!
SNEAK SNEAK
STAFF ONLY
SPROING
THIS MUST ...
THUMP
DASH
...LEAD TO WHERE STAR CELEBRITIES CAN ENTER WITHOUT IDS.
I'LL FIND THE PRESIDENT OR MR. SAWARA FROM THERE!
CRASH

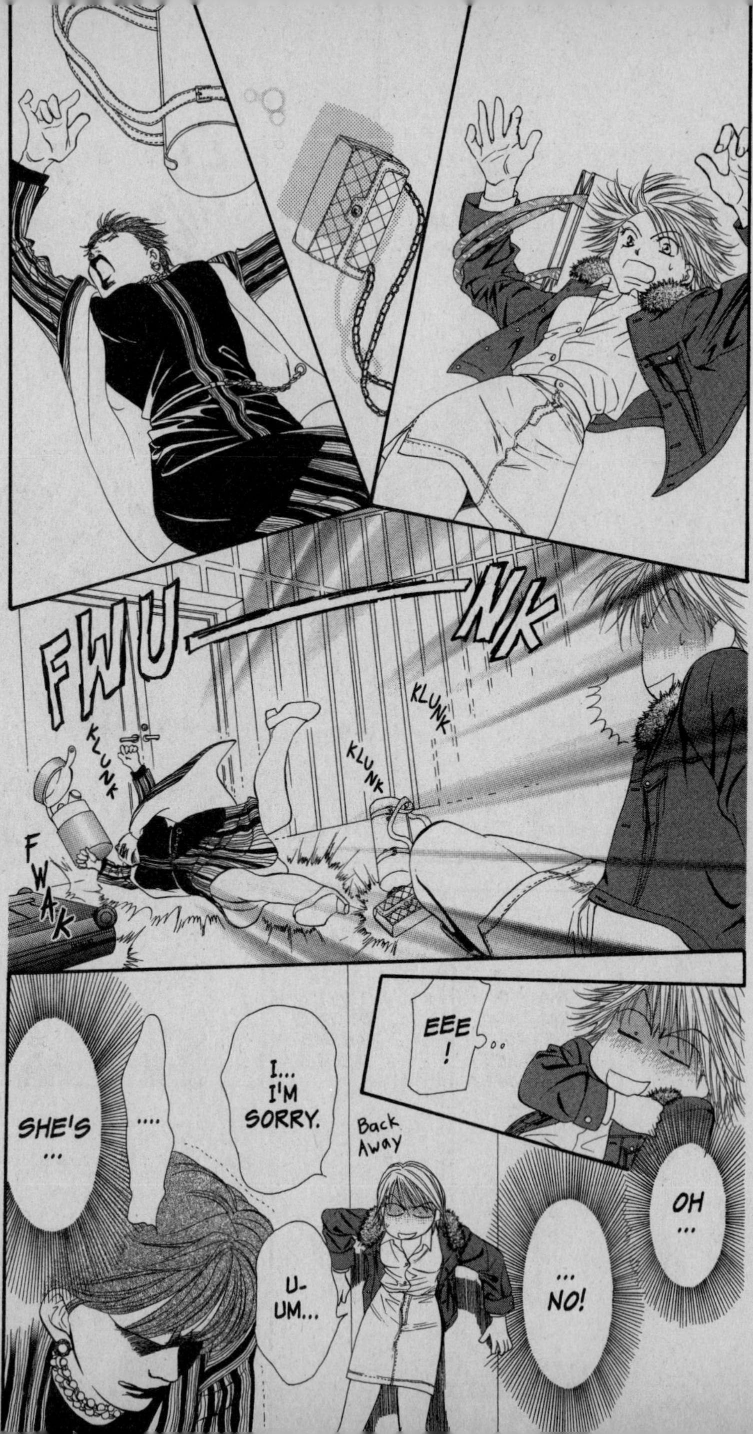
FWU—NK
KLUNK
KLUNK
KLUNK
FWAK
EEE! ...
OH ...
... NO!
Back Away
I... I'M SORRY.
U-UM...
....
SHE'S ...

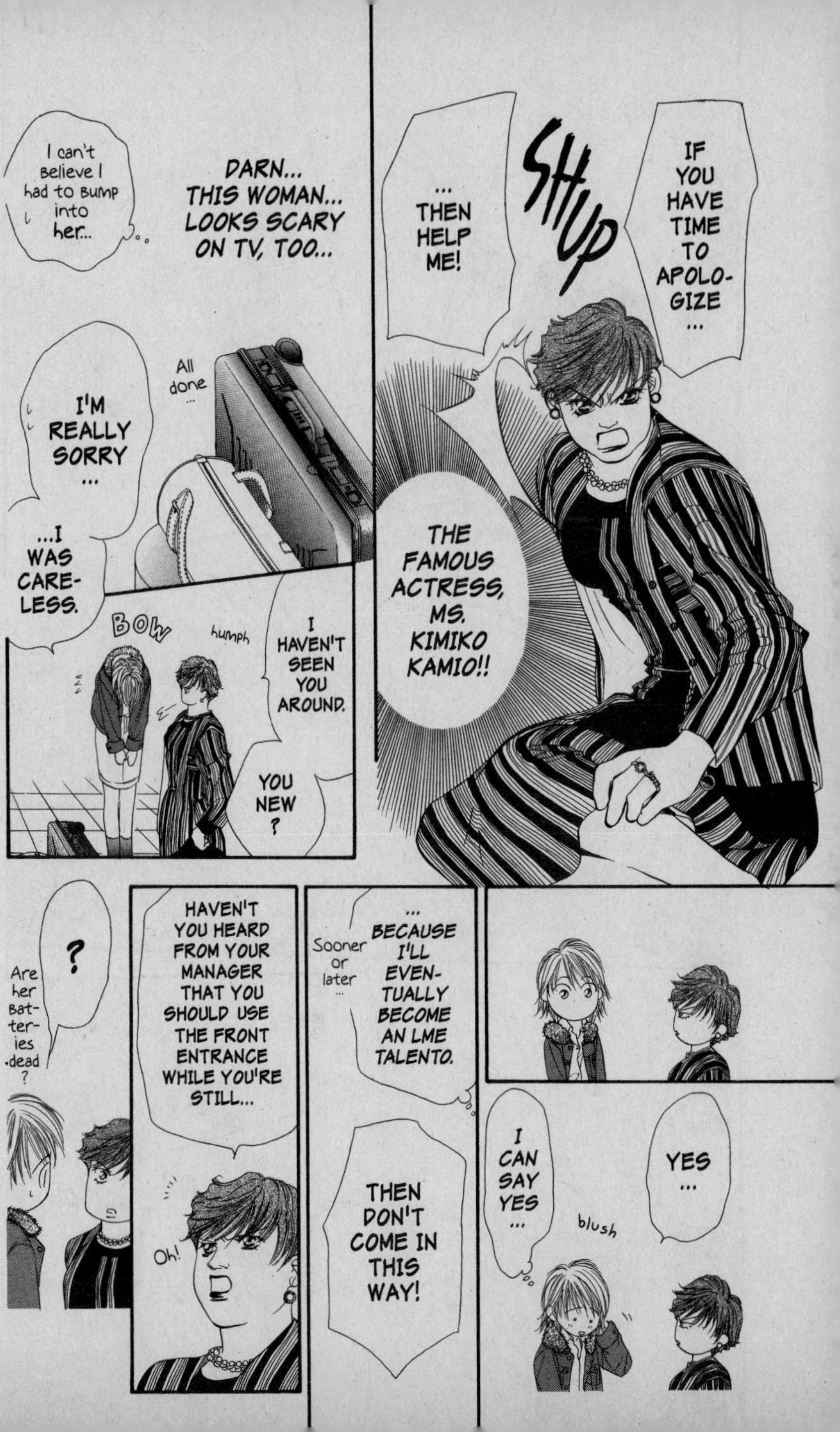
IF YOU HAVE TIME TO APOLOGIZE...
SHUP
...THEN HELP ME!
THE FAMOUS ACTRESS, MS. KIMIKO KAMIO!!
I can't believe I had to bump into her...
DARN... THIS WOMAN... LOOKS SCARY ON TV, TOO...
All done...
I'M REALLY SORRY...
...I WAS CARELESS.
BOW
humph
I HAVEN'T SEEN YOU AROUND.
YOU NEW?
YES...
I CAN SAY YES...
blush
...BECAUSE I'LL EVENTUALLY BECOME AN LME TALENTO.
Sooner or later...
THEN DON'T COME IN THIS WAY!
HAVEN'T YOU HEARD FROM YOUR MANAGER THAT YOU SHOULD USE THE FRONT ENTRANCE WHILE YOU'RE STILL...
Oh!
?
Are her batteries dead?

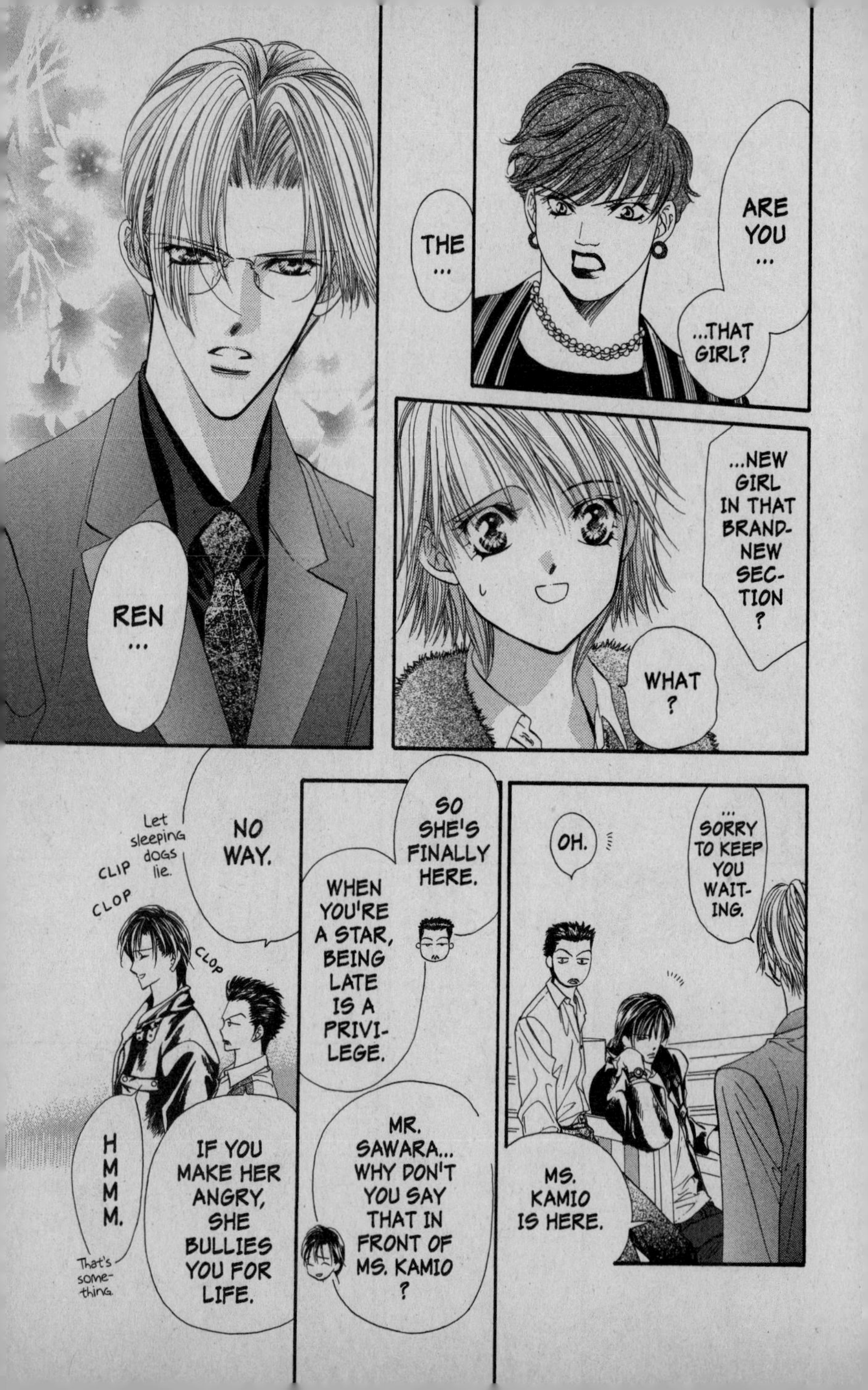
ARE YOU ...
...THAT GIRL?
THE ...
...NEW GIRL IN THAT BRAND-NEW SECTION?
WHAT?
REN ...
... SORRY TO KEEP YOU WAITING.
OH.
MS. KAMIO IS HERE.
SO SHE'S FINALLY HERE.
WHEN YOU'RE A STAR, BEING LATE IS A PRIVILEGE.
MR. SAWARA... WHY DON'T YOU SAY THAT IN FRONT OF MS. KAMIO?
NO WAY.
Let sleeping dogs lie.
CLIP
CLOP
CLOP
IF YOU MAKE HER ANGRY, SHE BULLIES YOU FOR LIFE.
HMMM.
That's some-thing.

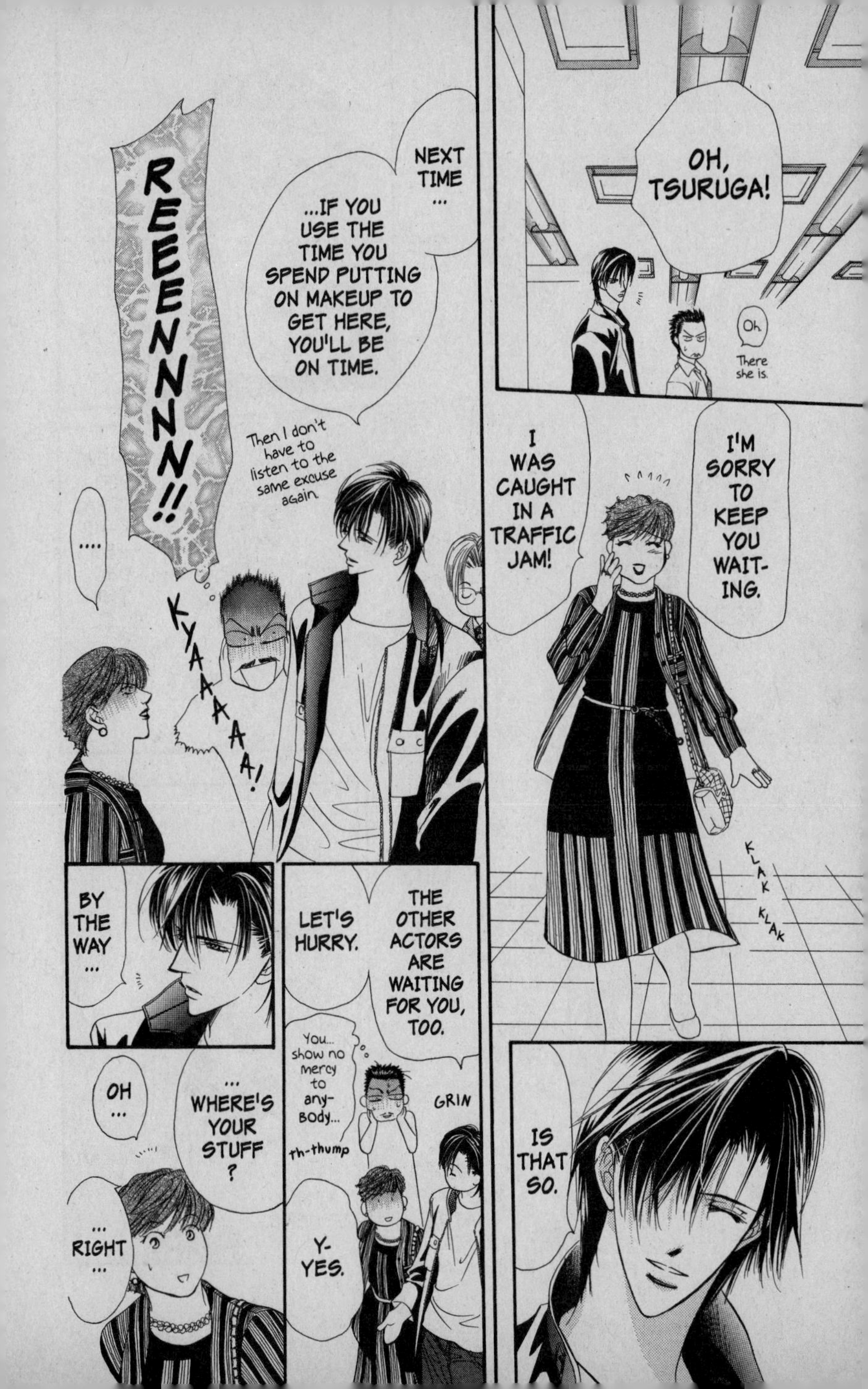
OH, TSURUGA!
Oh.
There she is.
I'M SORRY TO KEEP YOU WAIT-ING.
I WAS CAUGHT IN A TRAFFIC JAM!
KLAK KLAK
IS THAT SO.
NEXT TIME ...
...IF YOU USE THE TIME YOU SPEND PUTTING ON MAKEUP TO GET HERE, YOU'LL BE ON TIME.
Then I don't have to listen to the same excuse again.
REEENNNN!!
KYAAAAAA!
....
THE OTHER ACTORS ARE WAITING FOR YOU, TOO.
LET'S HURRY.
BY THE WAY ...
GRIN
You... show no mercy to any-body...
th-thump
... WHERE'S YOUR STUFF ?
OH ...
Y-YES.
... RIGHT ...

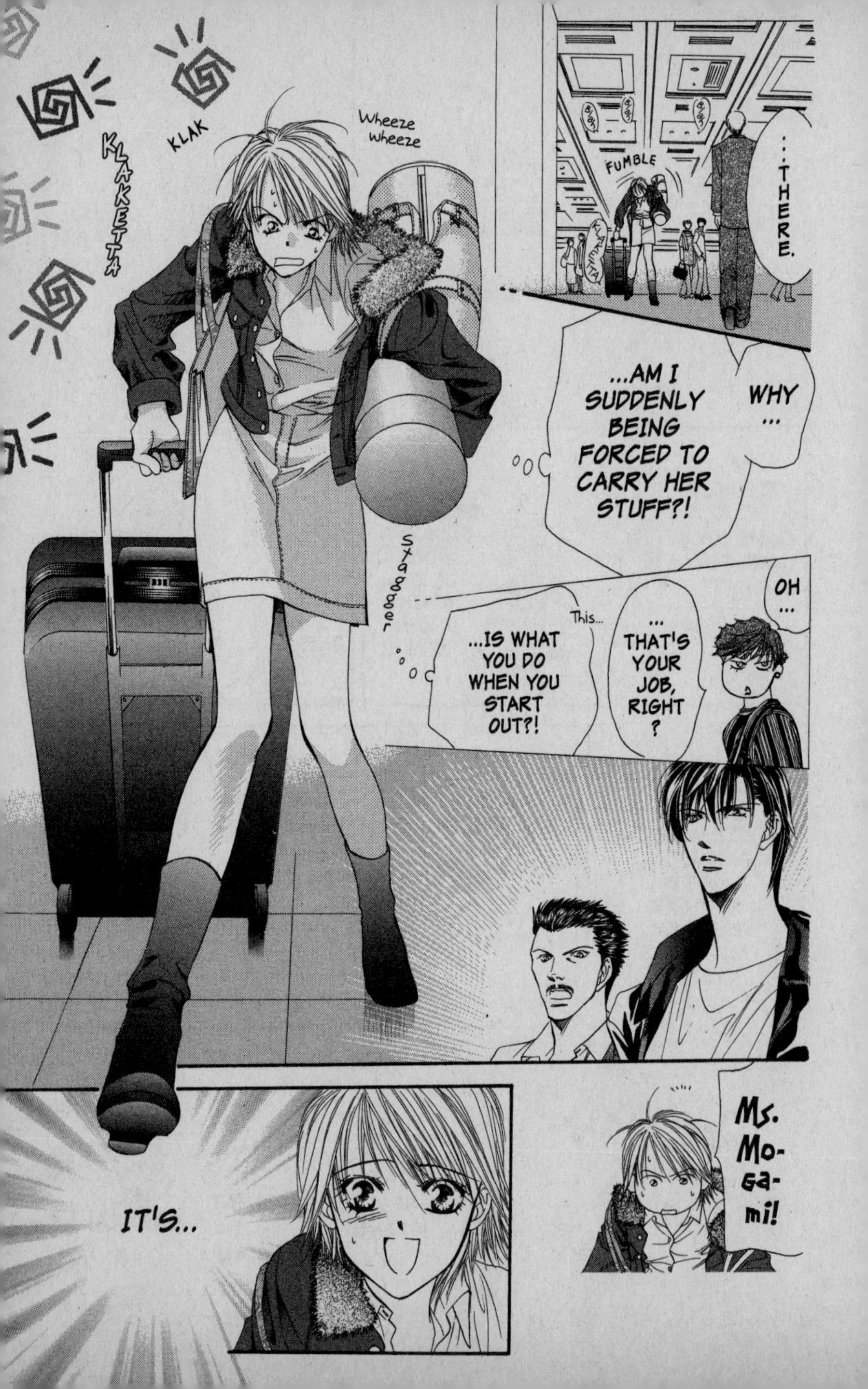
FUMBLE
KLAKETTA
...THERE.
WHY...
...AM I SUDDENLY BEING FORCED TO CARRY HER STUFF?!
OH...
...THAT'S YOUR JOB, RIGHT?
This...
...IS WHAT YOU DO WHEN YOU START OUT?!
Wheeze wheeze
KLAK
KLAKETTA
Stagger
Ms. Mo-ga-mi!
IT'S...

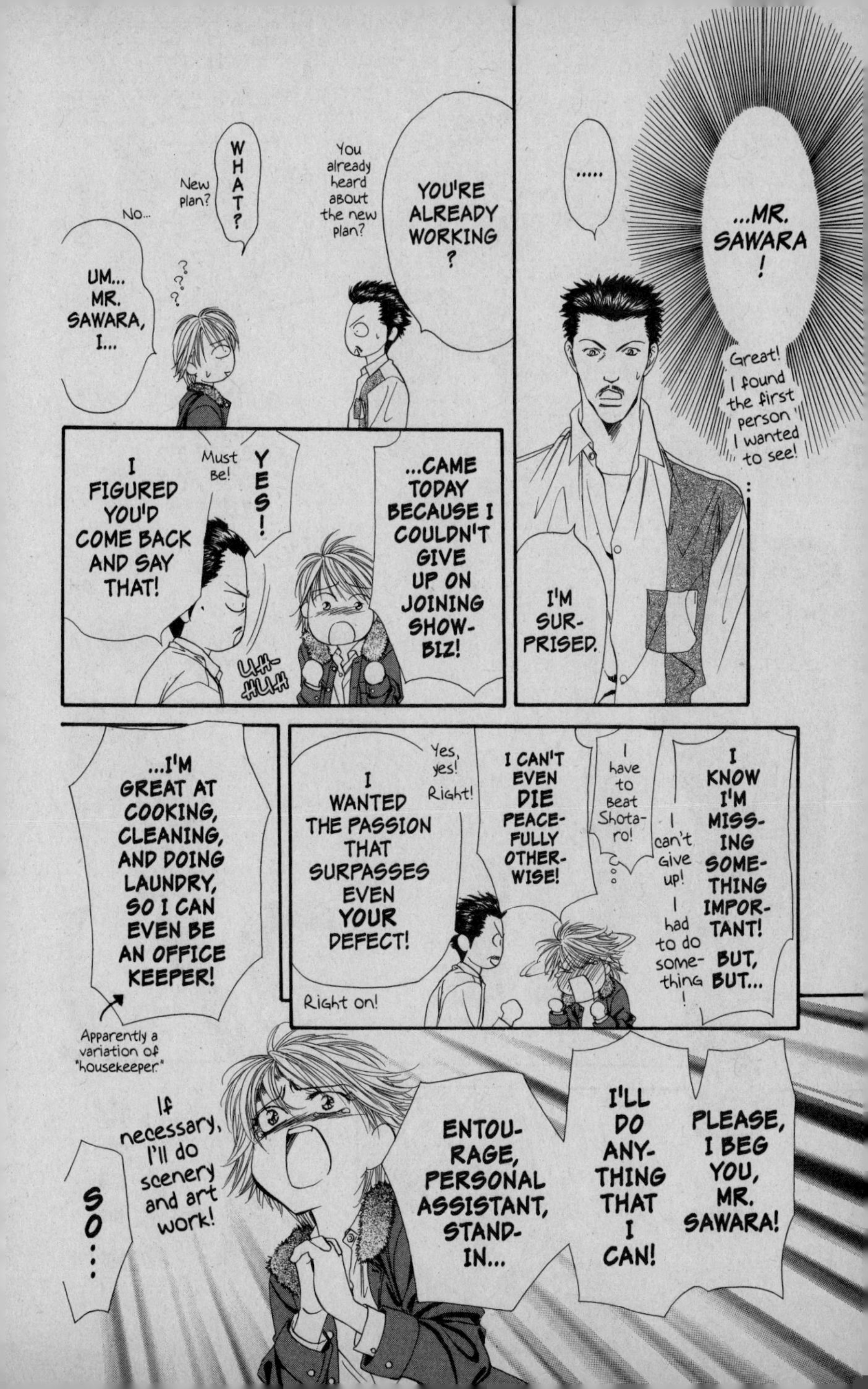
.....
...MR. SAWARA!
Great! I found the first person I wanted to see!
I'M SURPRISED.
YOU'RE ALREADY WORKING?
You already heard about the new plan?
WHAT?
New plan?
No...
UM... MR. SAWARA, I...
...CAME TODAY BECAUSE I COULDN'T GIVE UP ON JOINING SHOW-BIZ!
YES!
Must be!
I FIGURED YOU'D COME BACK AND SAY THAT!
UH-HUH
I KNOW I'M MISSING SOMETHING IMPORTANT! BUT, BUT...
I can't give up! I had to do something!
I have to beat Shotaro!
I CAN'T EVEN DIE PEACEFULLY OTHERWISE!
Yes, yes! Right!
I WANTED THE PASSION THAT SURPASSES EVEN YOUR DEFECT!
Right on!
...I'M GREAT AT COOKING, CLEANING, AND DOING LAUNDRY, SO I CAN EVEN BE AN OFFICE KEEPER!
Apparently a variation of "housekeeper."
PLEASE, I BEG YOU, MR. SAWARA!
I'LL DO ANYTHING THAT I CAN!
ENTOURAGE, PERSONAL ASSISTANT, STAND-IN...
If necessary, I'll do scenery and art work!
SO...

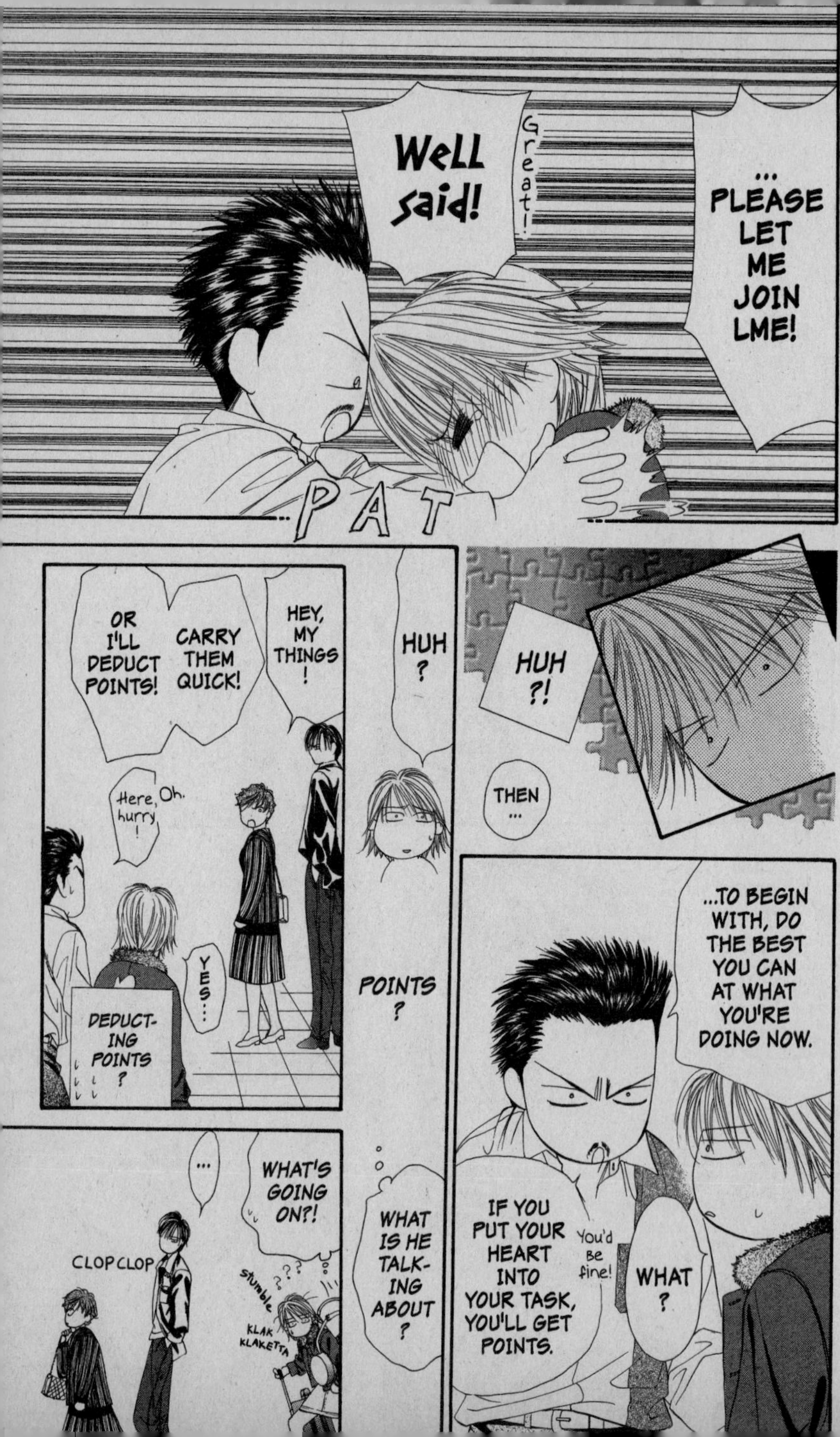
...PLEASE LET ME JOIN LME!
Great!
Well said!
PAT
HUH ?!
THEN ...
...TO BEGIN WITH, DO THE BEST YOU CAN AT WHAT YOU'RE DOING NOW.
WHAT ?
You'd be fine!
IF YOU PUT YOUR HEART INTO YOUR TASK, YOU'LL GET POINTS.
HUH ?
POINTS ?
WHAT IS HE TALKING ABOUT ?
HEY, MY THINGS !
CARRY THEM QUICK!
OR I'LL DEDUCT POINTS!
Oh.
Here, hurry !
YES...
DEDUCTING POINTS ?
WHAT'S GOING ON?!
...
CLOP CLOP
stumble
KLAK KLAKETTA

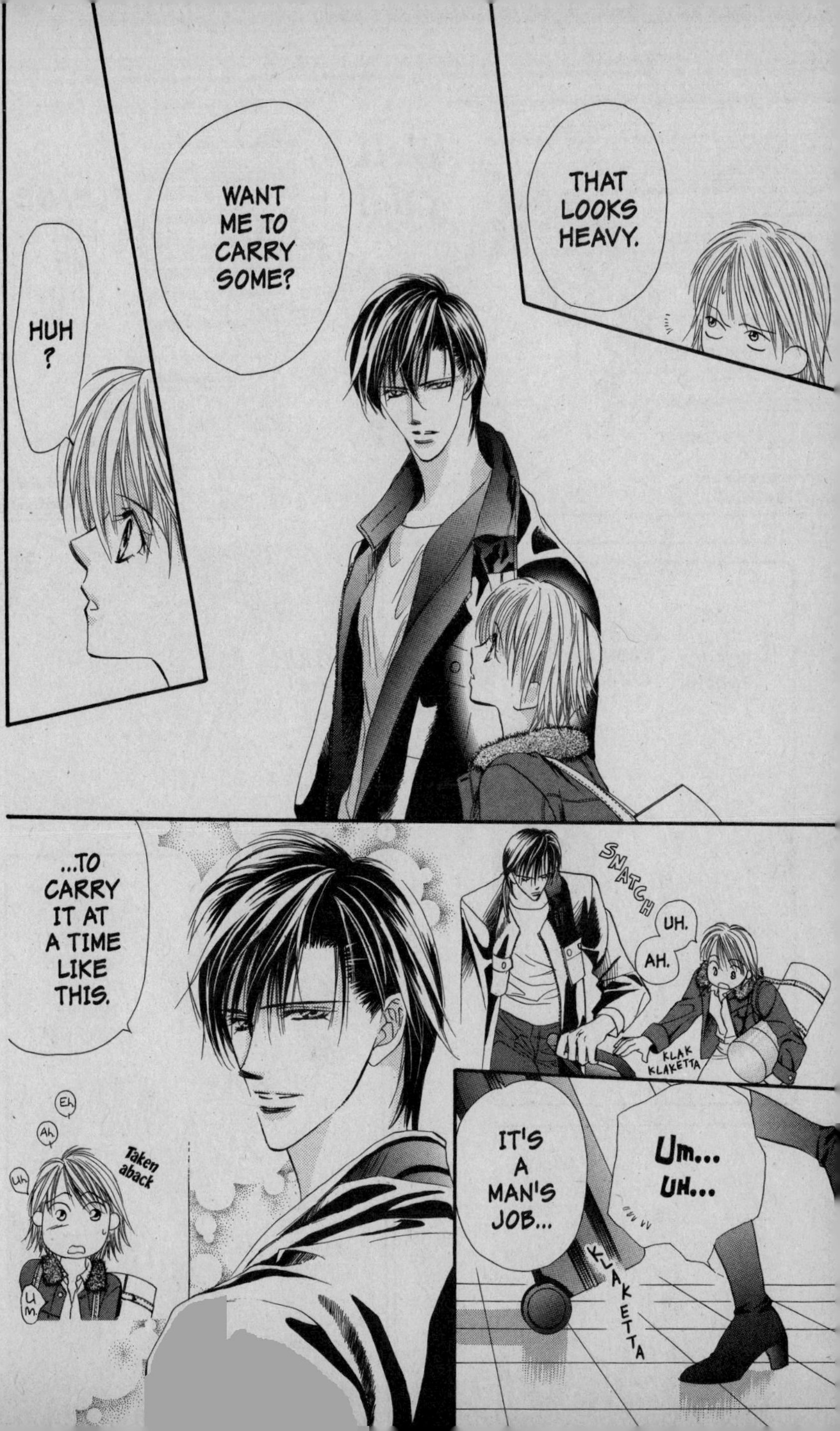
THAT LOOKS HEAVY.
WANT ME TO CARRY SOME?
HUH ?
SNATCH
UH.
AH.
KLAK KLAKETTA
Um... UH...
IT'S A MAN'S JOB...
KLAKETTA
...TO CARRY IT AT A TIME LIKE THIS.
Taken aback
Eh
Ah
Uh
Um.

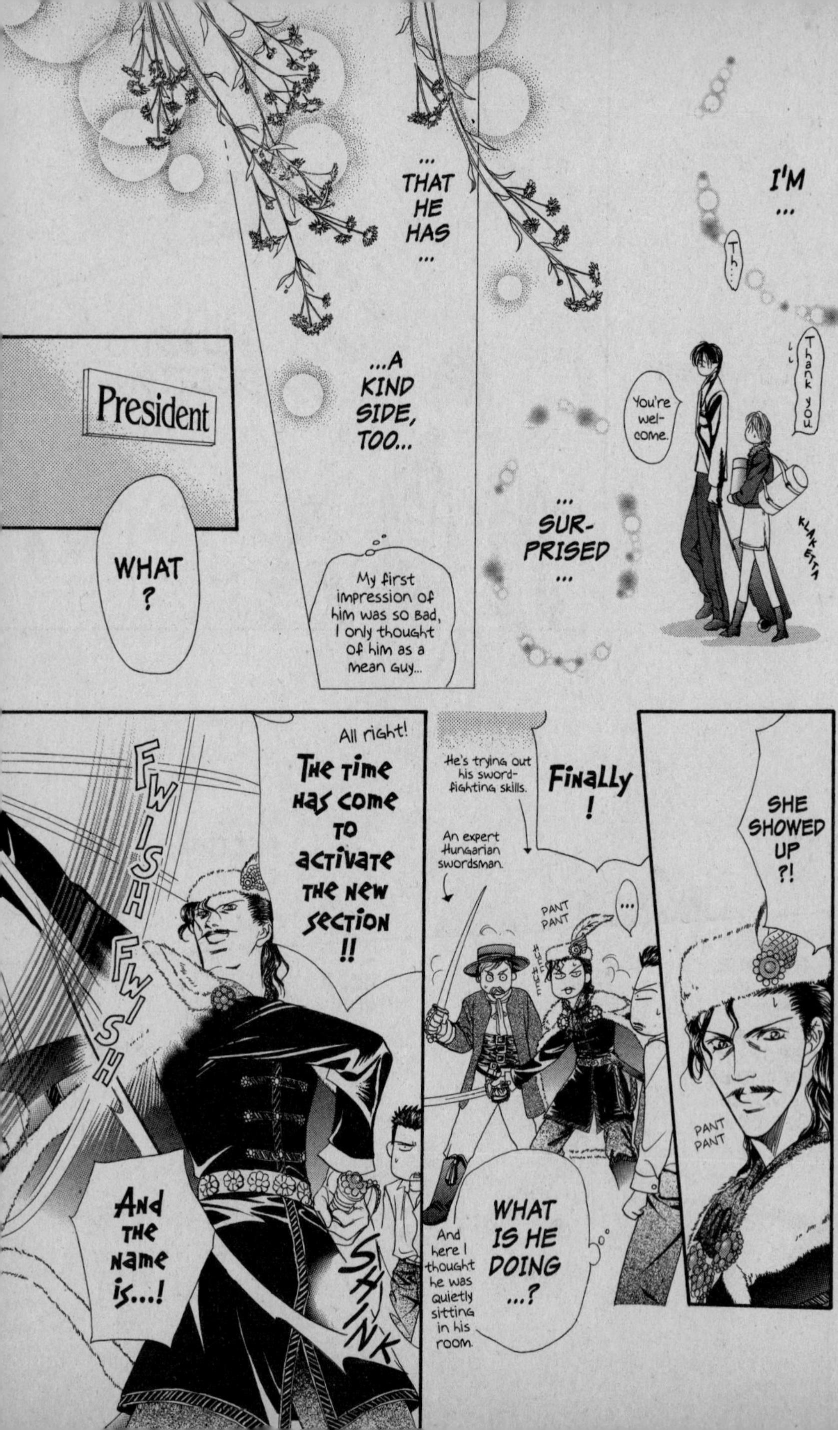
I'M ...
Th...
Thank you.
You're wel-come.
KLAKETTA
... SUR-PRISED ...
... THAT HE HAS ...
...A KIND SIDE, TOO...
My first impression of him was so bad, I only thought of him as a mean guy...
President
WHAT?
SHE SHOWED UP ?!
PANT PANT
Finally !
He's trying out his sword-fighting skills.
An expert Hungarian swordsman.
...
PANT PANT
HUFF HUFF
WHAT IS HE DOING ...?
And here I thought he was quietly sitting in his room.
All right!
The time has come to activate the new section !!
FWISH
FWISH
And the name is...!
SHINK

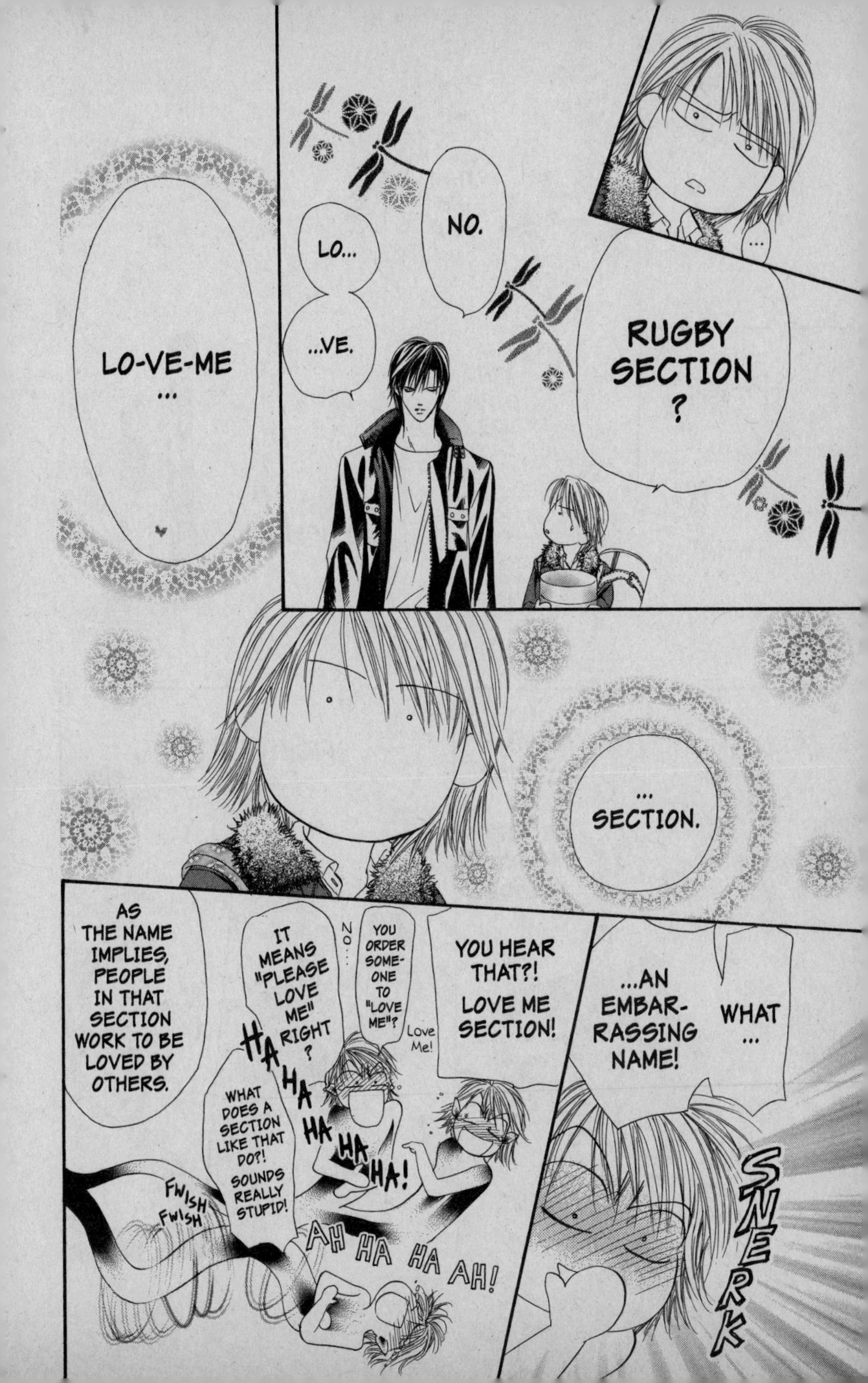
...
RUGBY SECTION ?
NO.
LO...
...VE.
LO-VE-ME ...
... SECTION.
WHAT ...
...AN EMBAR-RASSING NAME!
SNERK
YOU HEAR THAT?! LOVE ME SECTION!
YOU ORDER SOME-ONE TO "LOVE ME"?
Love Me!
NO...
IT MEANS "PLEASE LOVE ME" RIGHT ?
HA HA HA HA HA!
AS THE NAME IMPLIES, PEOPLE IN THAT SECTION WORK TO BE LOVED BY OTHERS.
WHAT DOES A SECTION LIKE THAT DO?! SOUNDS REALLY STUPID!
AH HA HA AH!
FWISH FWISH

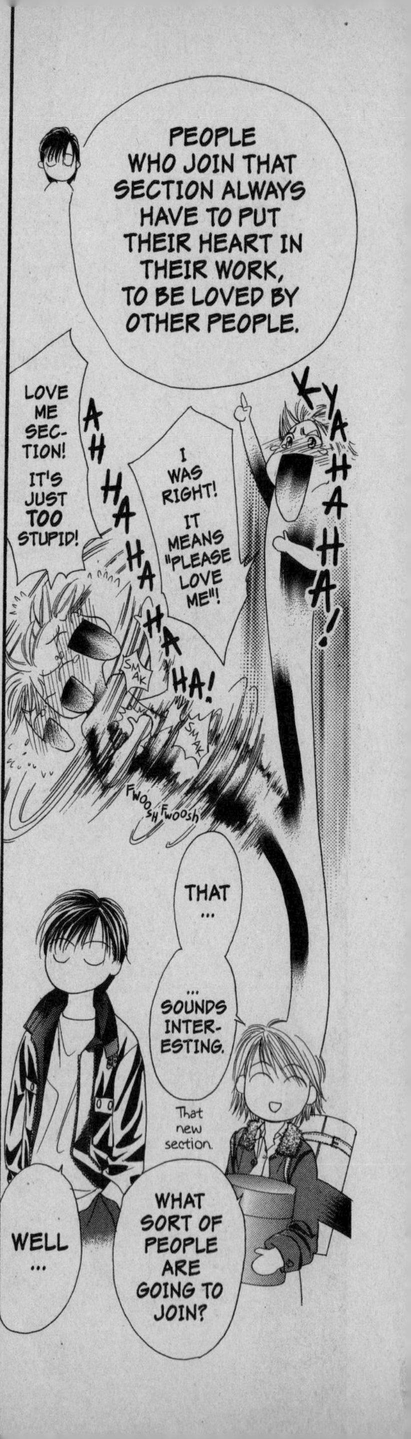
PEOPLE WHO JOIN THAT SECTION ALWAYS HAVE TO PUT THEIR HEART IN THEIR WORK, TO BE LOVED BY OTHER PEOPLE.
KYAHAHAHA!
I WAS RIGHT! IT MEANS "PLEASE LOVE ME"!
AHAHAHAHAHA!
LOVE ME SEC-TION! IT'S JUST TOO STUPID!
SMAK
SMAK
FWOOSH FWOOSH
THAT ...
... SOUNDS INTER-ESTING.
That new section.
WHAT SORT OF PEOPLE ARE GOING TO JOIN?
WELL ...
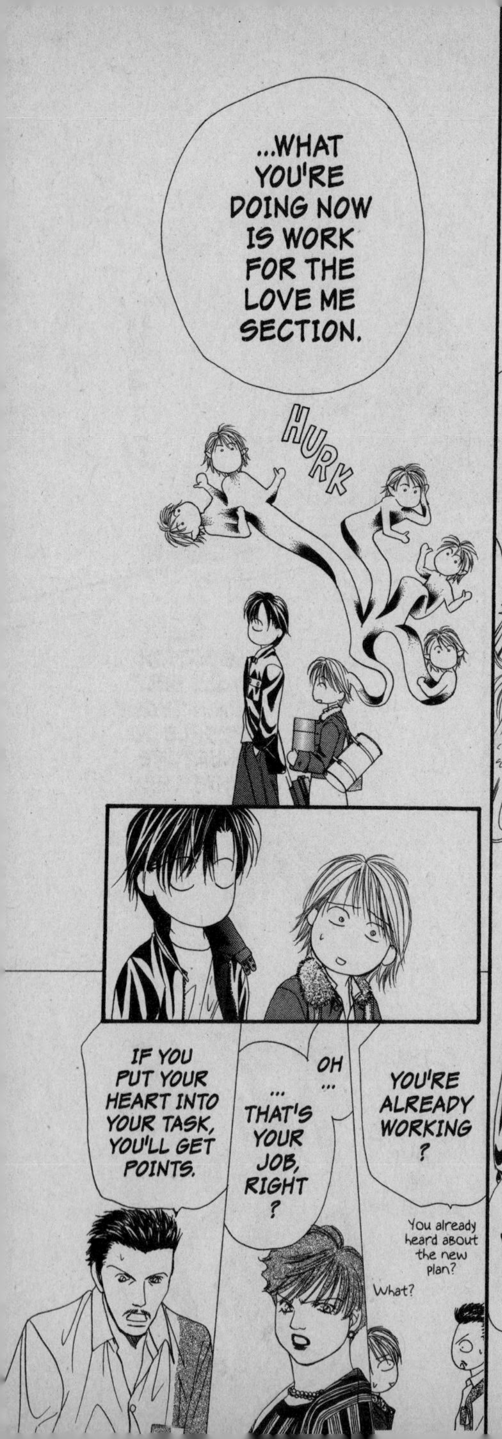
...WHAT YOU'RE DOING NOW IS WORK FOR THE LOVE ME SECTION.
HURK
YOU'RE ALREADY WORKING?
OH ... THAT'S YOUR JOB, RIGHT?
IF YOU PUT YOUR HEART INTO YOUR TASK, YOU'LL GET POINTS.
You already heard about the new plan?
What?

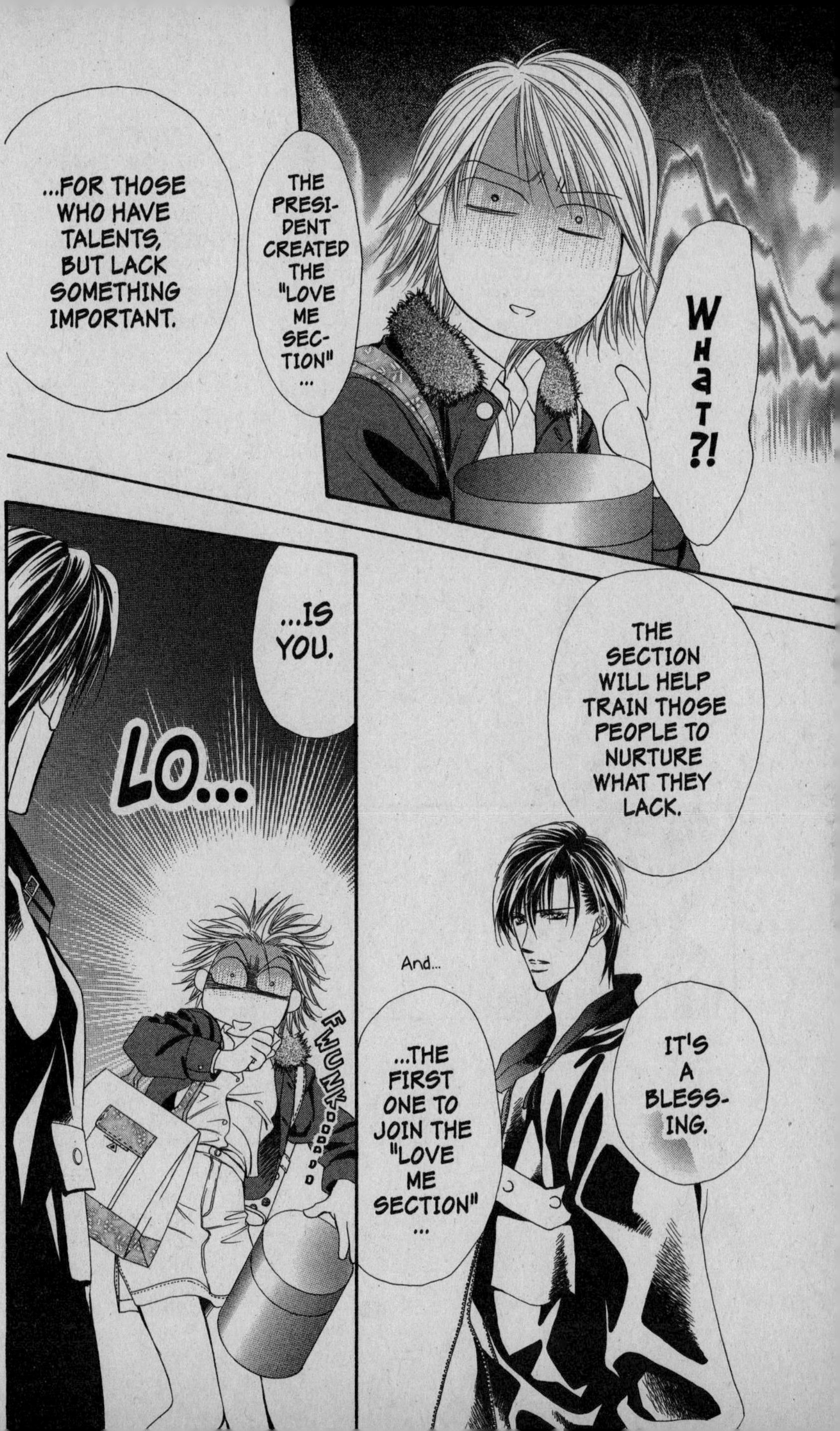
WHAT?!
THE PRESIDENT CREATED THE "LOVE ME SECTION"...
...FOR THOSE WHO HAVE TALENTS, BUT LACK SOMETHING IMPORTANT.
THE SECTION WILL HELP TRAIN THOSE PEOPLE TO NURTURE WHAT THEY LACK.
IT'S A BLESSING.
And...
...THE FIRST ONE TO JOIN THE "LOVE ME SECTION"...
...IS YOU.
LO...
FWUNKDDDDDD

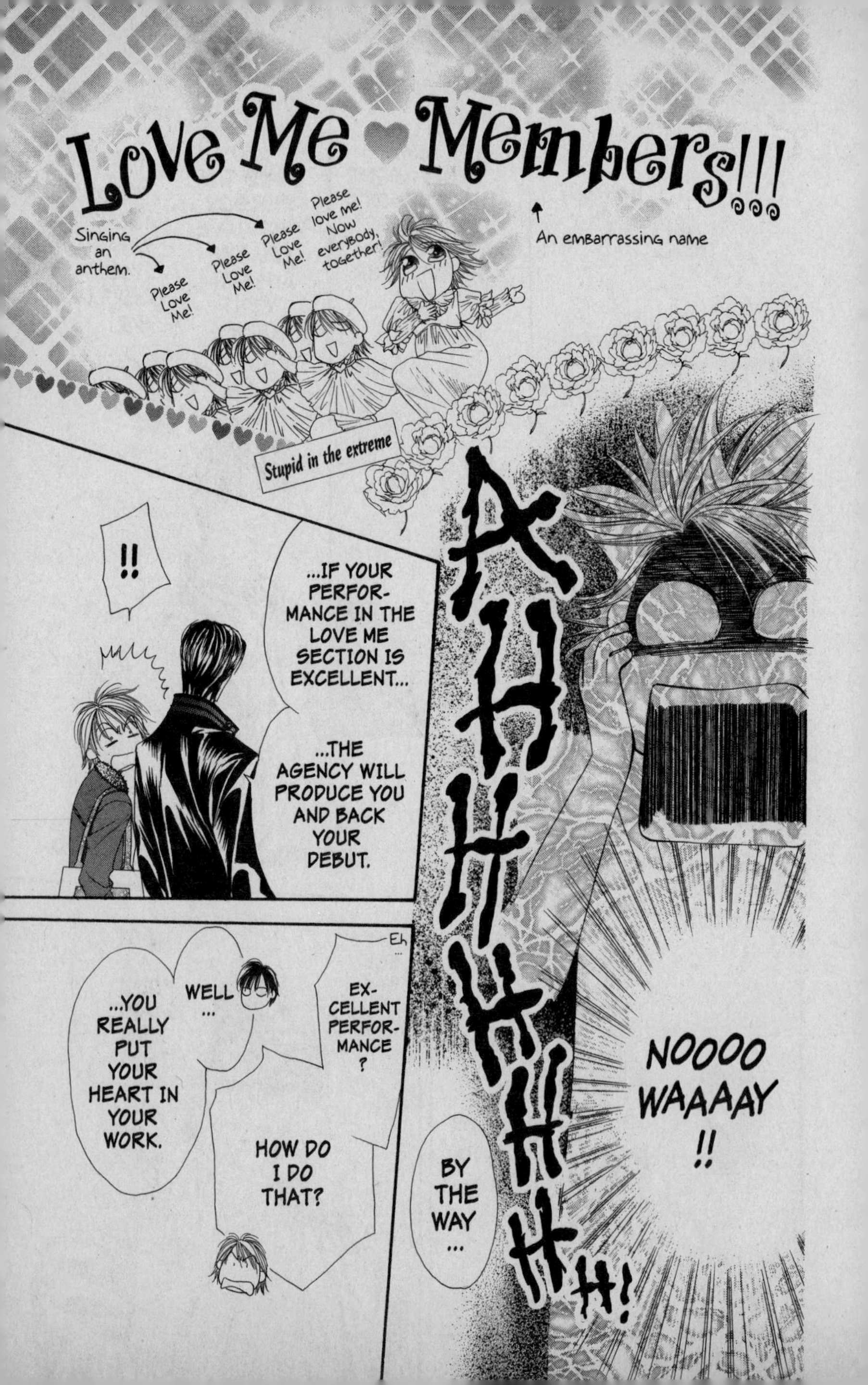

Love Me ♥ Members!!!
An embarrassing name
Singing an anthem.
Please Love Me!
Please Love Me!
Please Love Me!
Please love me! Now everybody, together!
Stupid in the extreme
AHHHHHHHHH!
NOOOO WAAAAY!!
!!
...IF YOUR PERFORMANCE IN THE LOVE ME SECTION IS EXCELLENT...
...THE AGENCY WILL PRODUCE YOU AND BACK YOUR DEBUT.
Eh...
EXCELLENT PERFORMANCE?
BY THE WAY...
WELL...
...YOU REALLY PUT YOUR HEART IN YOUR WORK.
HOW DO I DO THAT?

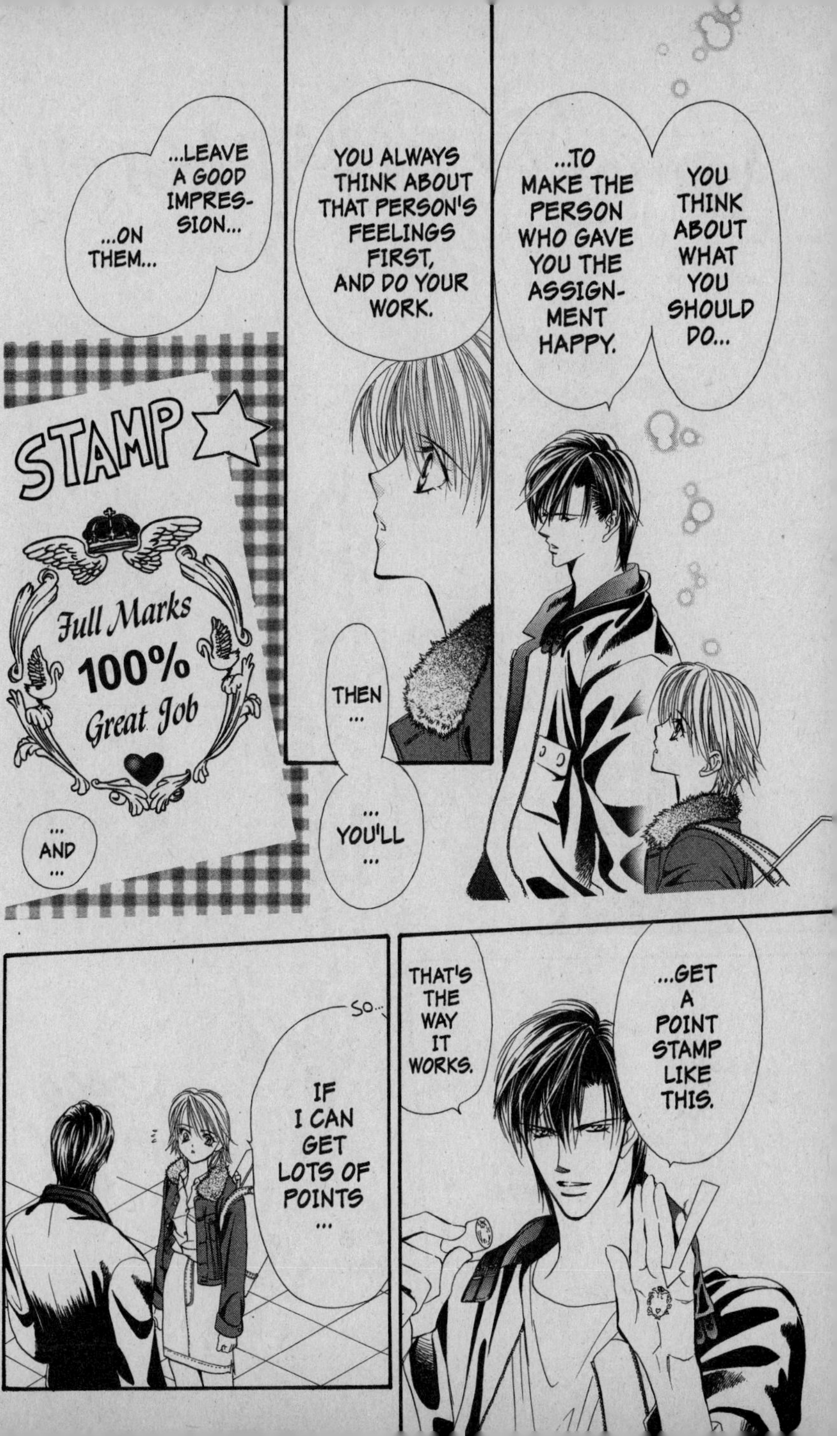
YOU THINK ABOUT WHAT YOU SHOULD DO...
...TO MAKE THE PERSON WHO GAVE YOU THE ASSIGNMENT HAPPY.
YOU ALWAYS THINK ABOUT THAT PERSON'S FEELINGS FIRST, AND DO YOUR WORK.
THEN...
...YOU'LL...
...LEAVE A GOOD IMPRESSION...
...ON THEM...
STAMP
Full Marks 100% Great Job
...AND...
...GET A POINT STAMP LIKE THIS.
THAT'S THE WAY IT WORKS.
SO...
IF I CAN GET LOTS OF POINTS...

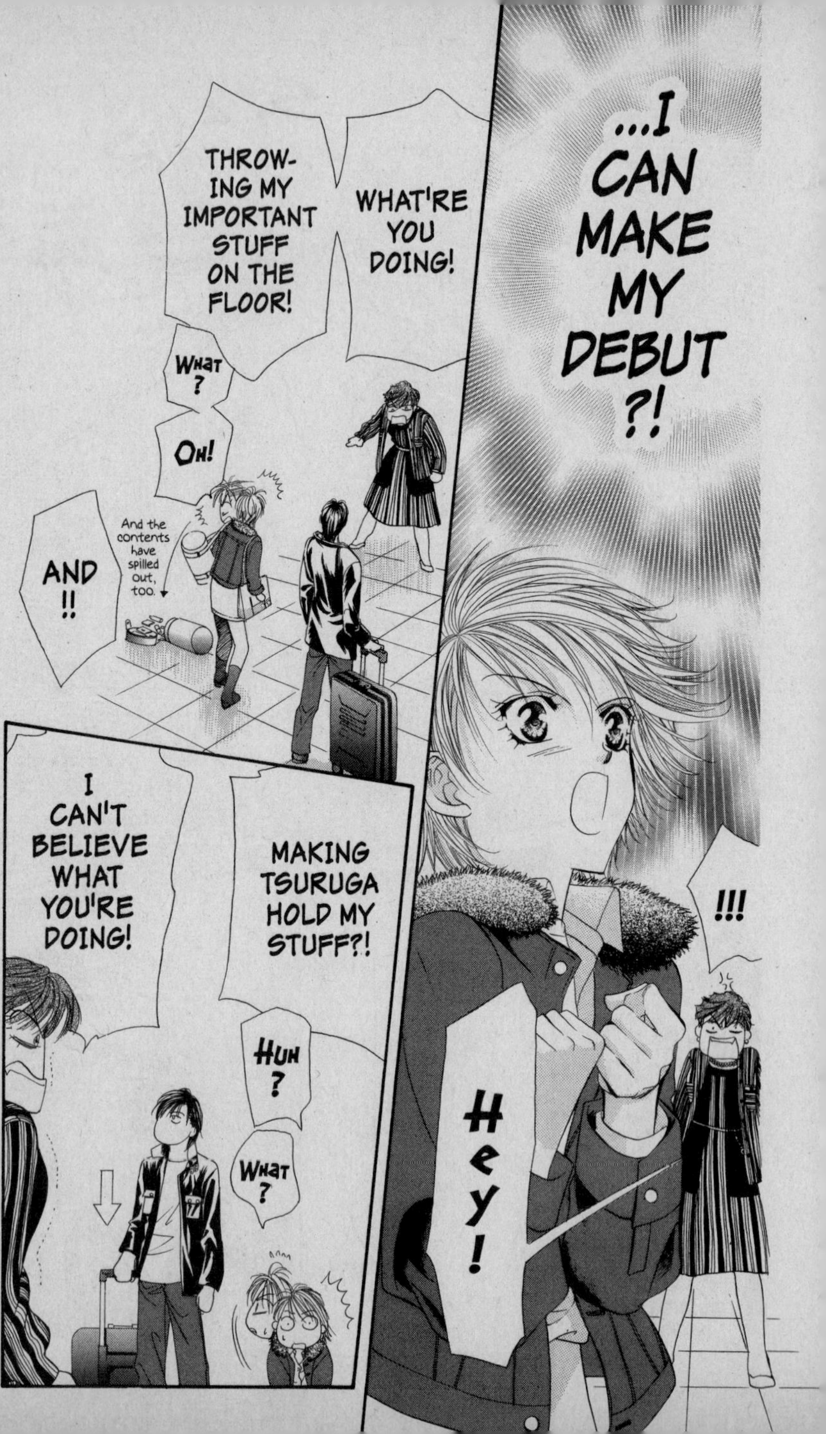
...I CAN MAKE MY DEBUT?!
!!!
Hey!
WHAT'RE YOU DOING!
THROWING MY IMPORTANT STUFF ON THE FLOOR!
WHAT?
OH!
And the contents have spilled out, too.
AND !!
MAKING TSURUGA HOLD MY STUFF?!
I CAN'T BELIEVE WHAT YOU'RE DOING!
HUH?
WHAT?

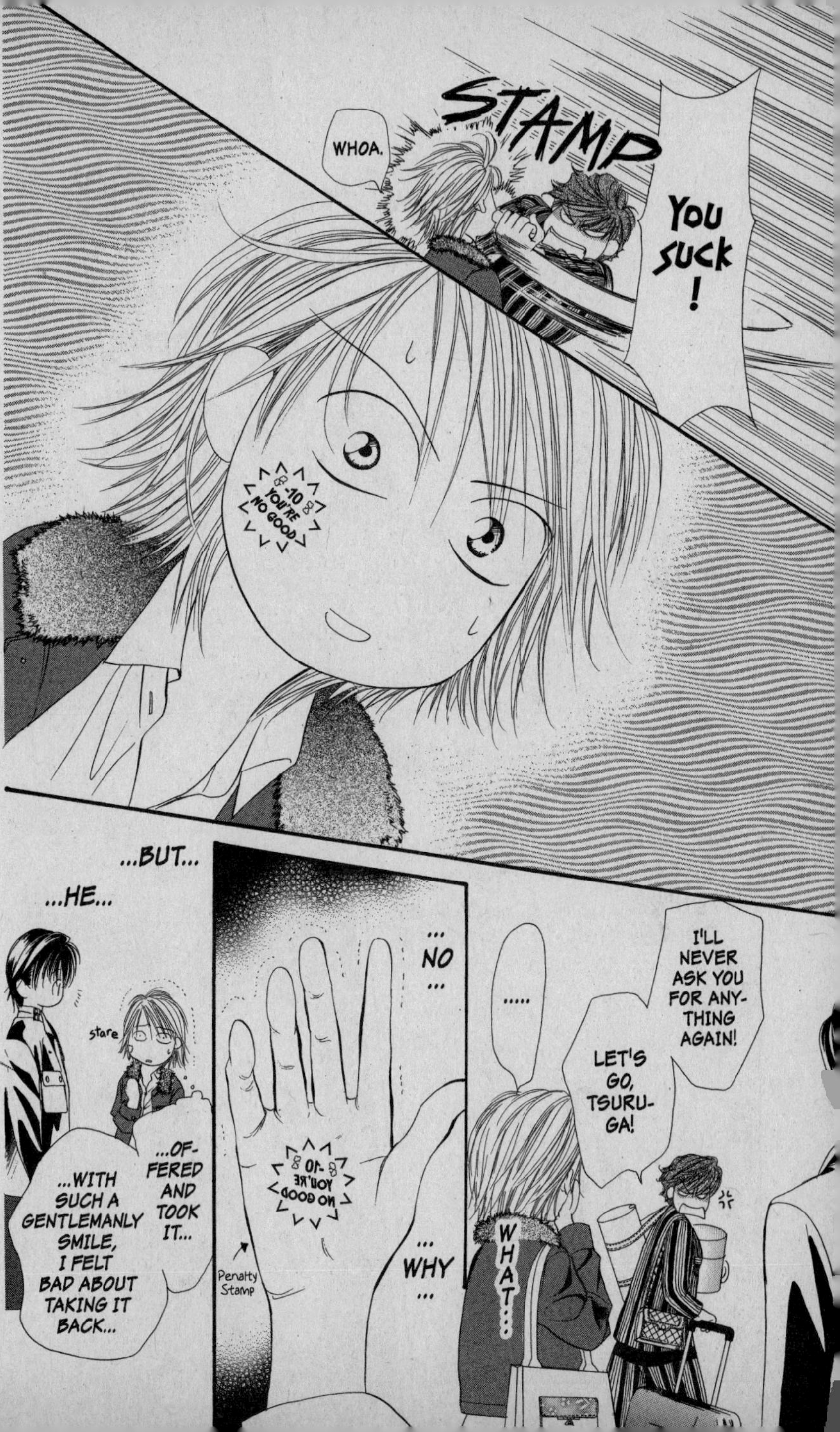
YOU SUCK!
STAMP
WHOA.
-10 YOU'RE NO GOOD
I'LL NEVER ASK YOU FOR ANYTHING AGAIN!
LET'S GO, TSURUGA!
.....
WHAT...
...NO...
...WHY...
-10 YOU'RE NO GOOD
Penalty Stamp
...BUT...
...HE...
stare
...OFFERED AND TOOK IT...
...WITH SUCH A GENTLEMANLY SMILE, I FELT BAD ABOUT TAKING IT BACK...

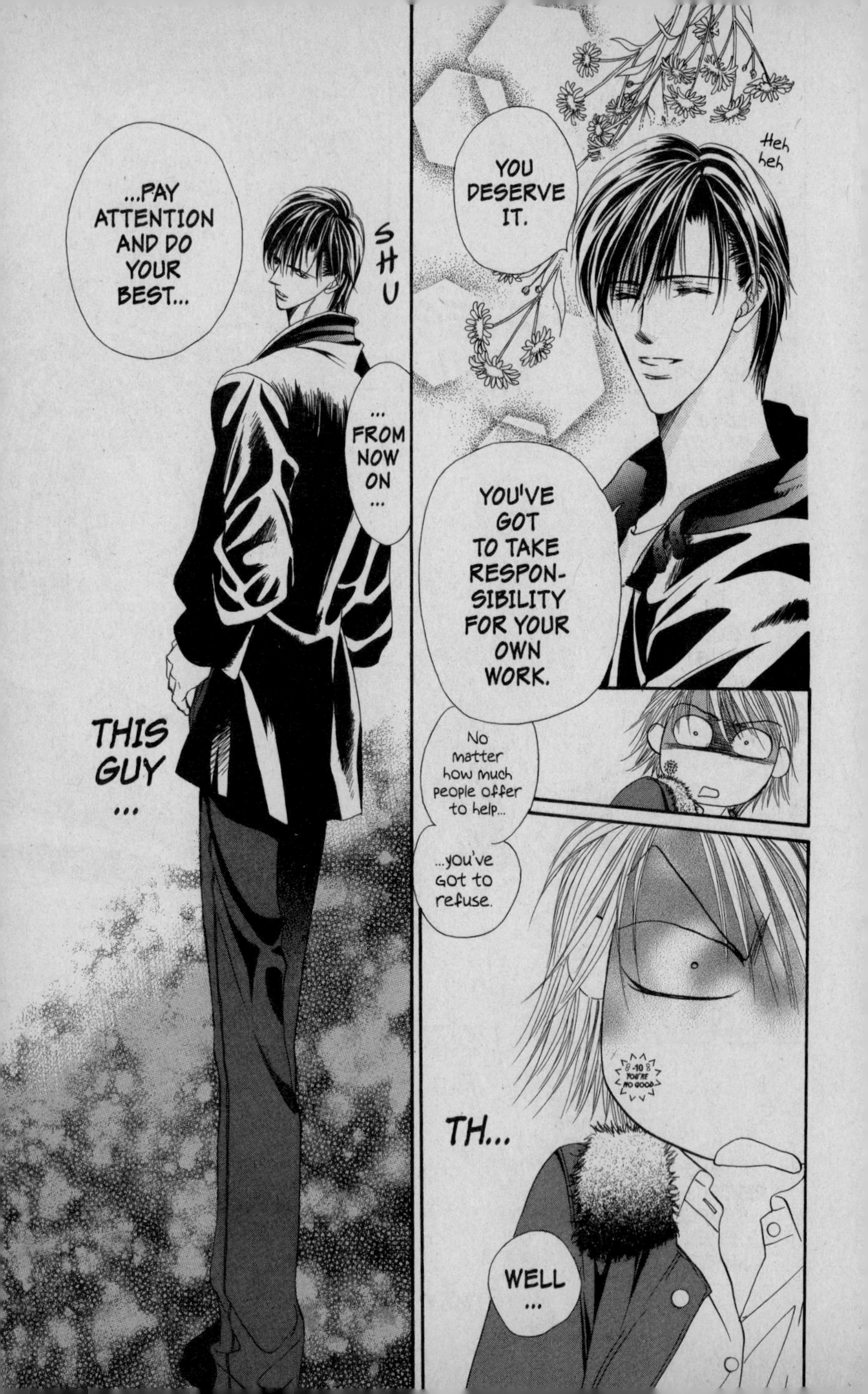
Heh heh
YOU DESERVE IT.
YOU'VE GOT TO TAKE RESPON-SIBILITY FOR YOUR OWN WORK.
No matter how much people offer to help...
...you've got to refuse.
YOU'RE NO GOOD
TH...
WELL ...
SHU
... FROM NOW ON ...
...PAY ATTENTION AND DO YOUR BEST...
THIS GUY ...

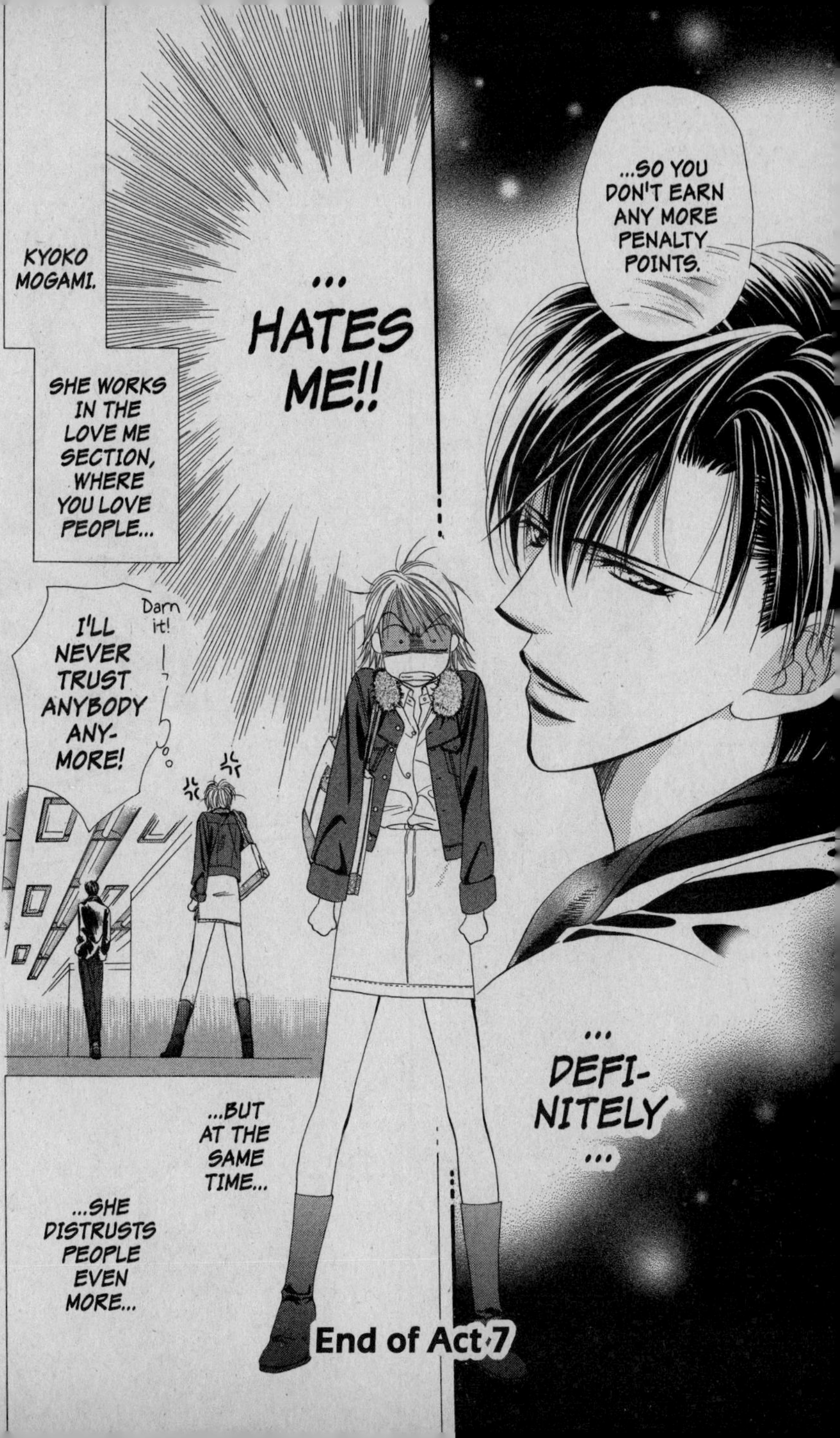
...SO YOU DON'T EARN ANY MORE PENALTY POINTS.
... DEFI-NITELY ...
KYOKO MOGAMI.
... HATES ME!!
SHE WORKS IN THE LOVE ME SECTION, WHERE YOU LOVE PEOPLE...
I'LL NEVER TRUST ANYBODY ANY-MORE!
Darn it!
...BUT AT THE SAME TIME...
...SHE DISTRUSTS PEOPLE EVEN MORE...

End of Act 7

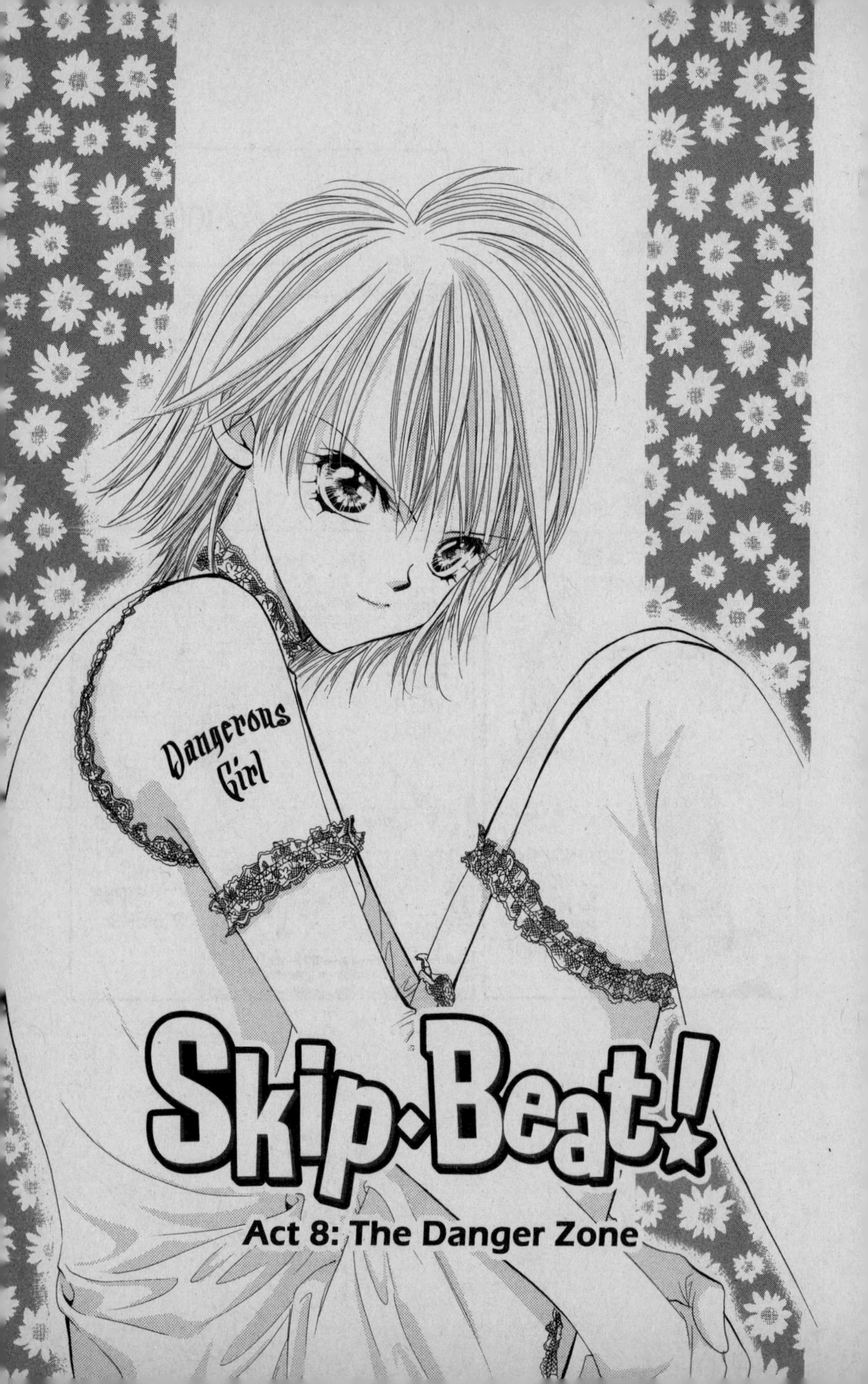
Dangerous Girl
Skip·Beat!
Act 8: The Danger Zone

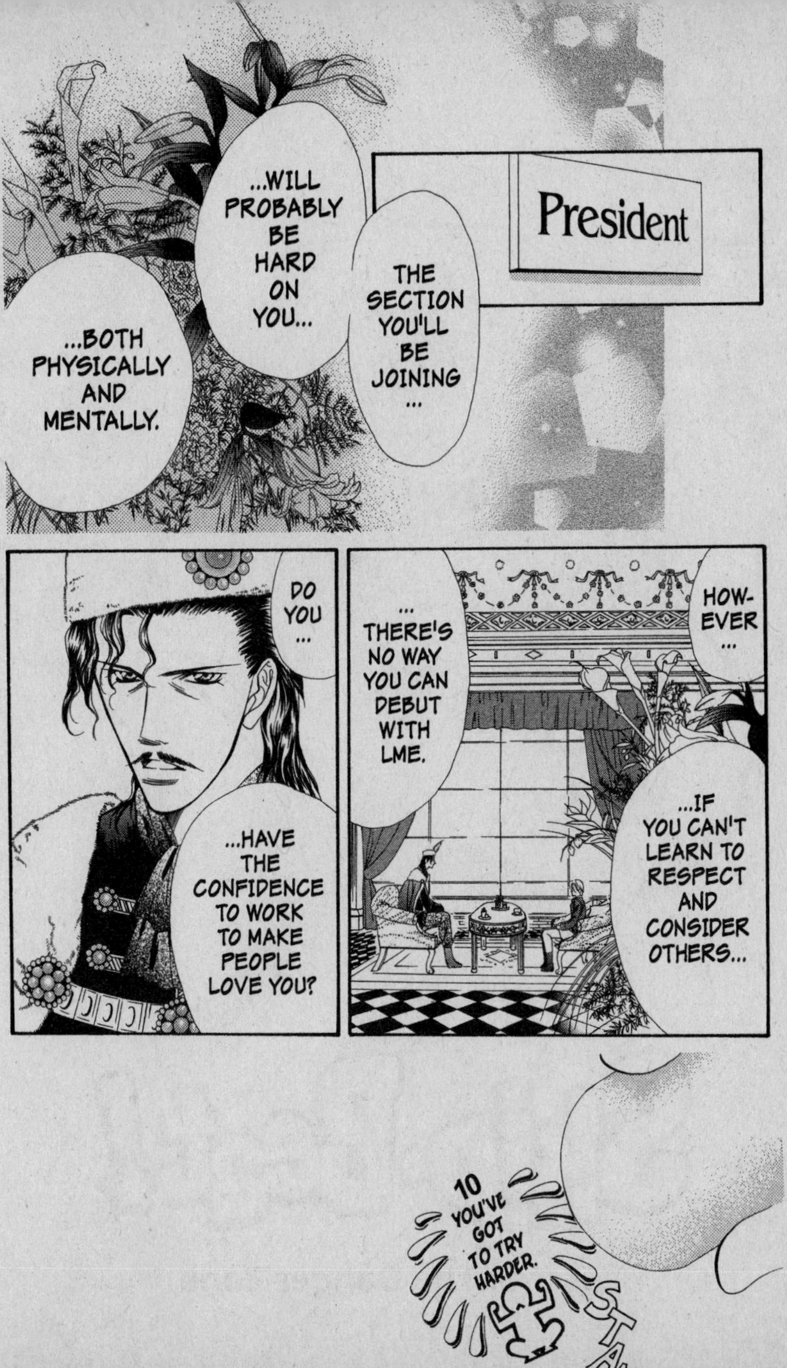
President
THE SECTION YOU'LL BE JOINING...
...WILL PROBABLY BE HARD ON YOU...
...BOTH PHYSICALLY AND MENTALLY.
HOW-EVER...
...IF YOU CAN'T LEARN TO RESPECT AND CONSIDER OTHERS...
...THERE'S NO WAY YOU CAN DEBUT WITH LME.
DO YOU...
...HAVE THE CONFIDENCE TO WORK TO MAKE PEOPLE LOVE YOU?
10 YOU'VE GOT TO TRY HARDER.
STAMP

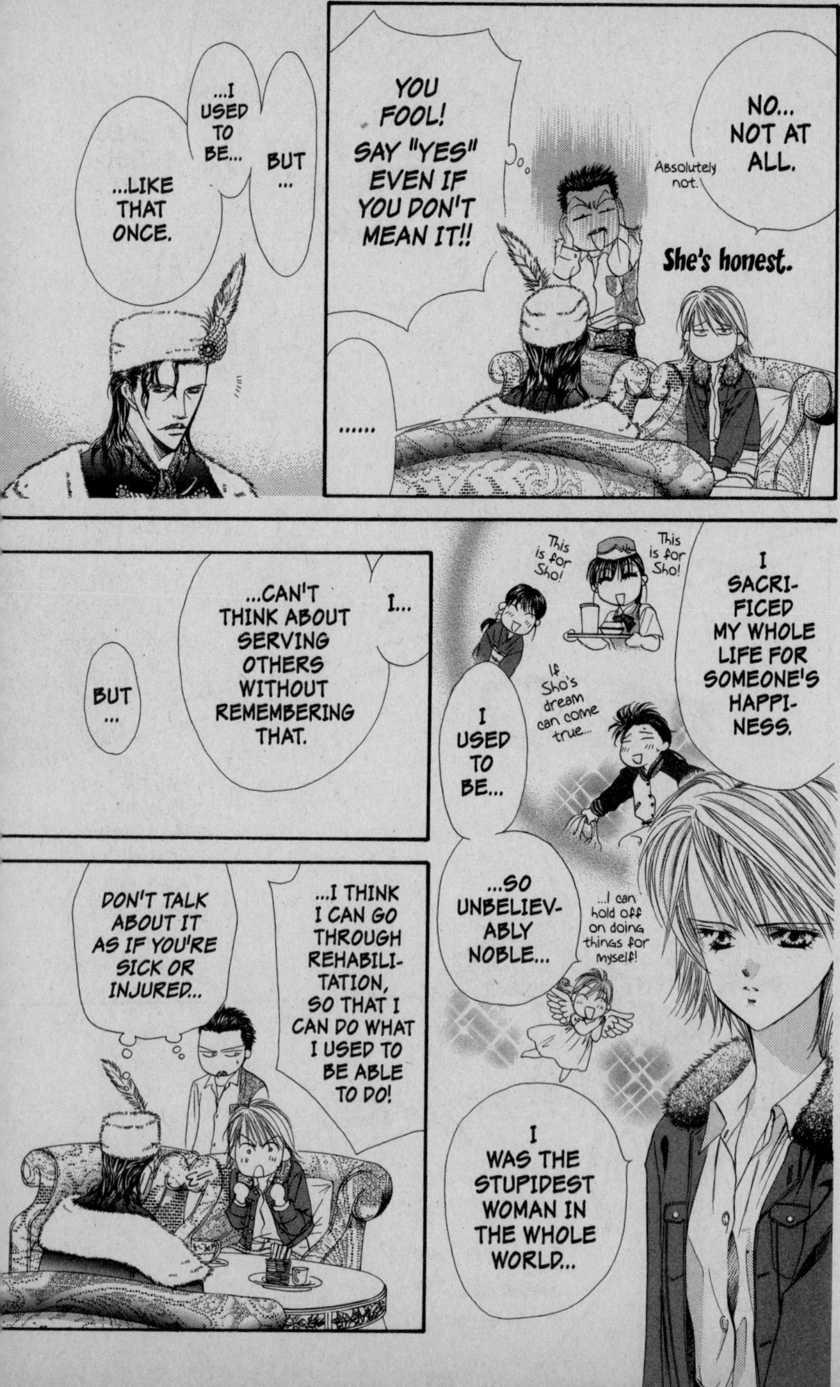
NO... NOT AT ALL.
Absolutely not.
She's honest.
YOU FOOL! SAY "YES" EVEN IF YOU DON'T MEAN IT!!
......
...I USED TO BE...
...LIKE THAT ONCE.
BUT ...
I SACRIFICED MY WHOLE LIFE FOR SOMEONE'S HAPPINESS.
This is for Sho!
This is for Sho!
I USED TO BE...
If Sho's dream can come true...
...SO UNBELIEVABLY NOBLE...
...I can hold off on doing things for myself!
I WAS THE STUPIDEST WOMAN IN THE WHOLE WORLD...
I...
...CAN'T THINK ABOUT SERVING OTHERS WITHOUT REMEMBERING THAT.
BUT ...
...I THINK I CAN GO THROUGH REHABILITATION, SO THAT I CAN DO WHAT I USED TO BE ABLE TO DO!
DON'T TALK ABOUT IT AS IF YOU'RE SICK OR INJURED...

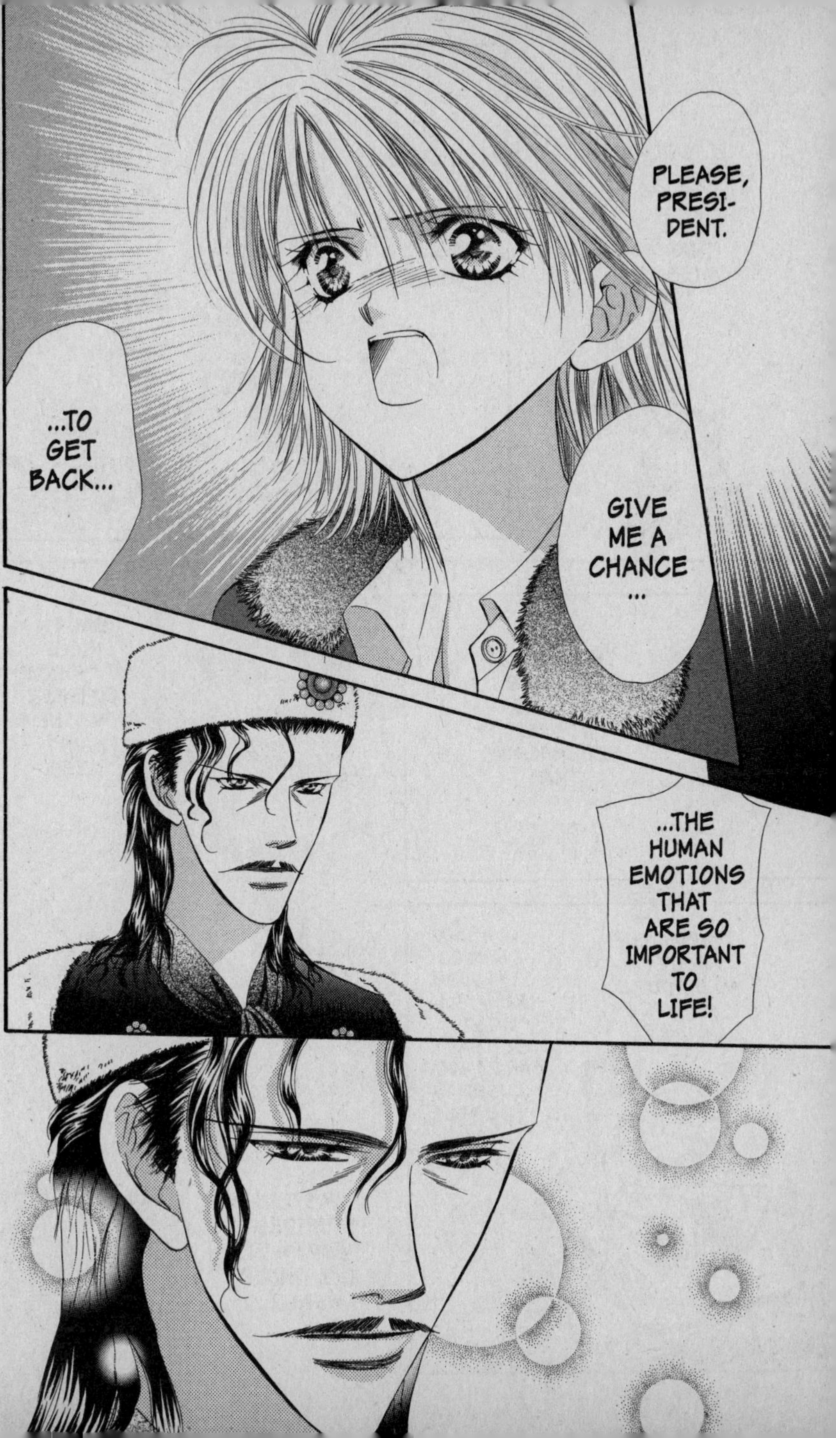
PLEASE, PRESIDENT.
GIVE ME A CHANCE ...
...TO GET BACK...
...THE HUMAN EMOTIONS THAT ARE SO IMPORTANT TO LIFE!

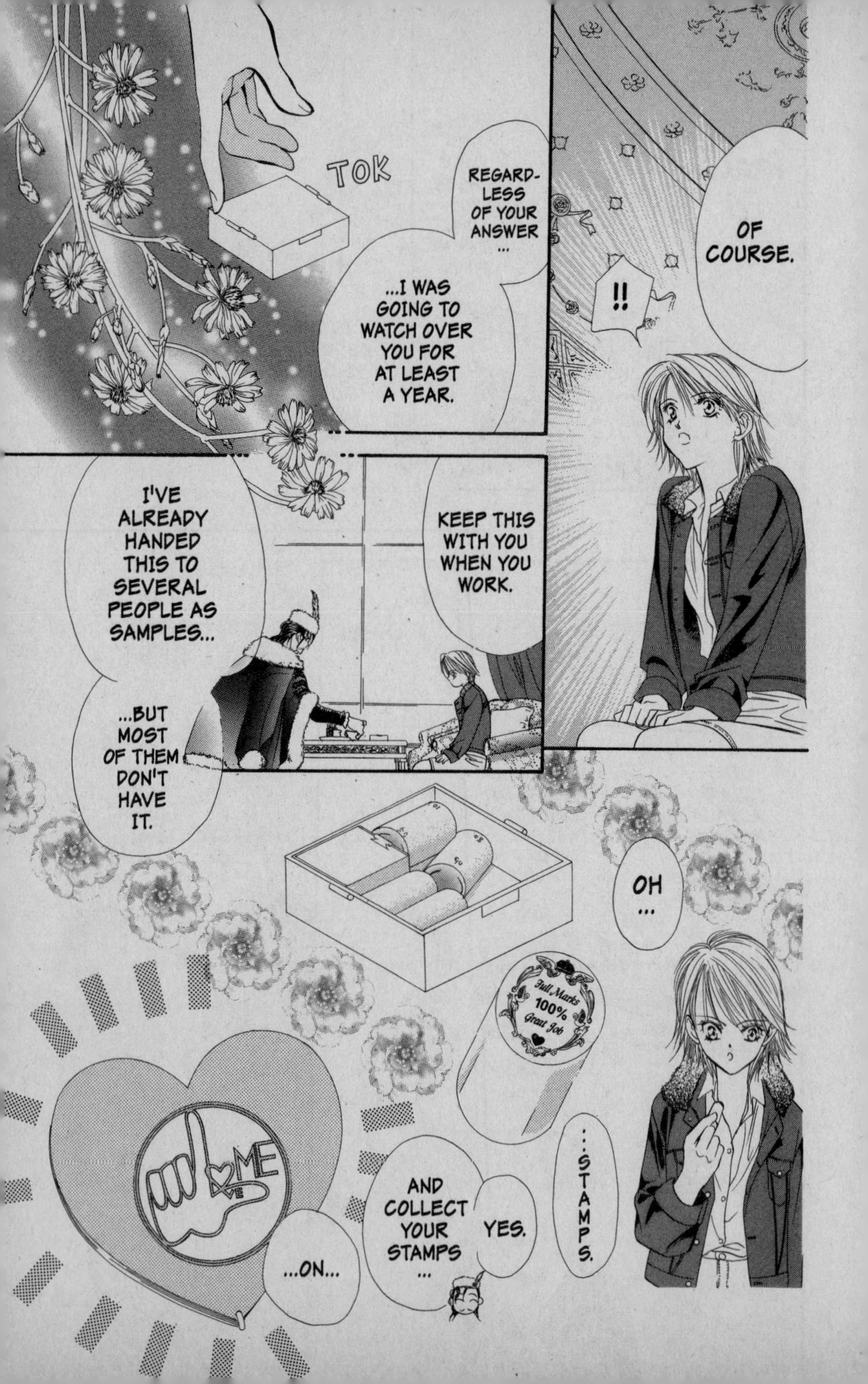
OF COURSE.
!!
TOK
REGARDLESS OF YOUR ANSWER...
...I WAS GOING TO WATCH OVER YOU FOR AT LEAST A YEAR.
KEEP THIS WITH YOU WHEN YOU WORK.
I'VE ALREADY HANDED THIS TO SEVERAL PEOPLE AS SAMPLES...
...BUT MOST OF THEM DON'T HAVE IT.
OH...
Full Marks 100% Great Job
...STAMPS.
YES.
AND COLLECT YOUR STAMPS...
...ON...
ME

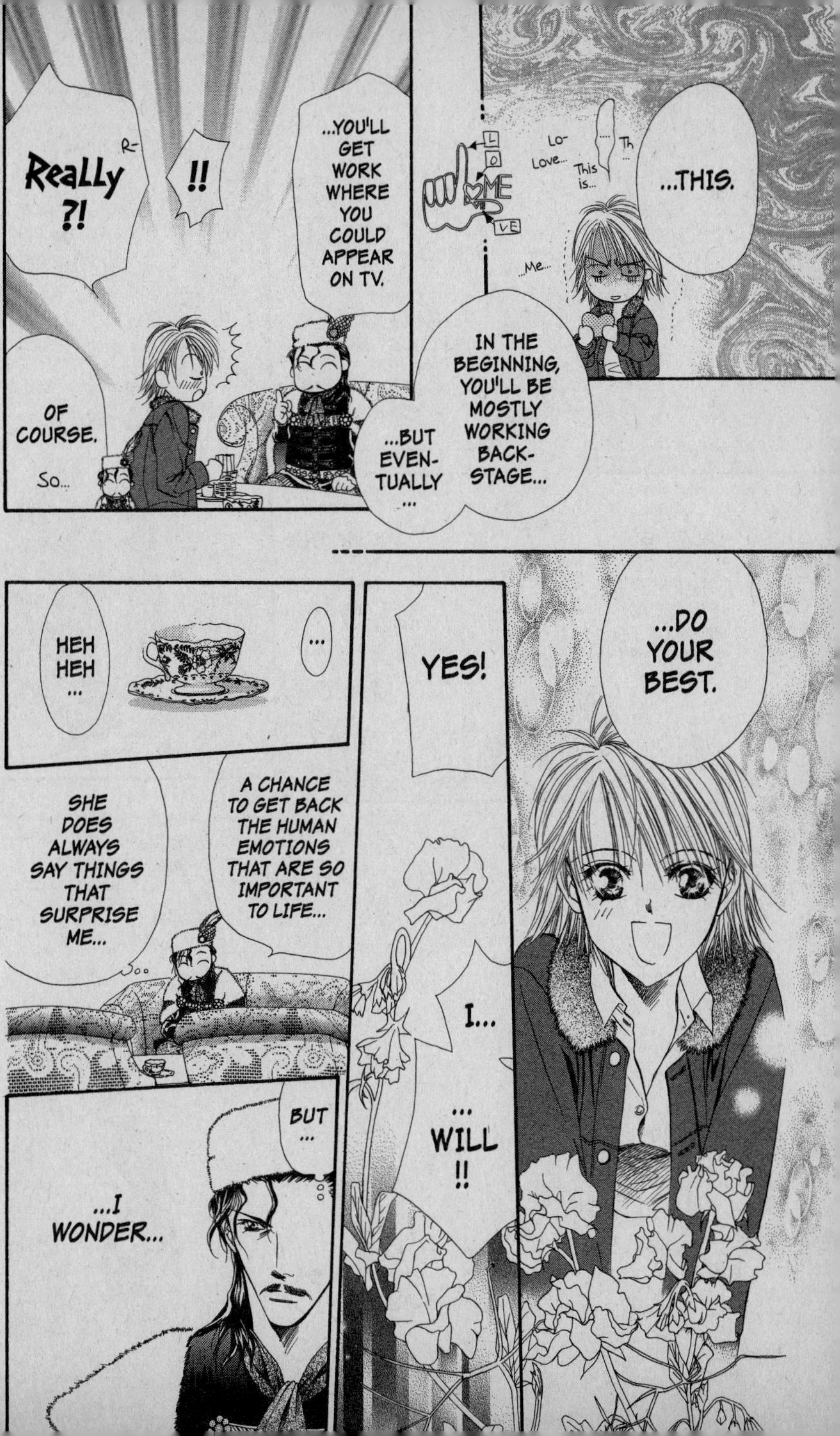
...THIS.
Th...
This is...
Lo- Love...
L
O
ME
VE
...Me...
IN THE BEGINNING, YOU'LL BE MOSTLY WORKING BACK-STAGE...
...BUT EVEN-TUALLY...
...YOU'LL GET WORK WHERE YOU COULD APPEAR ON TV.
!!
R-
Really ?!
OF COURSE.
So...
...DO YOUR BEST.
YES!
I...
...WILL !!
...
HEH HEH ...
A CHANCE TO GET BACK THE HUMAN EMOTIONS THAT ARE SO IMPORTANT TO LIFE...
SHE DOES ALWAYS SAY THINGS THAT SURPRISE ME...
BUT ...
...I WONDER...

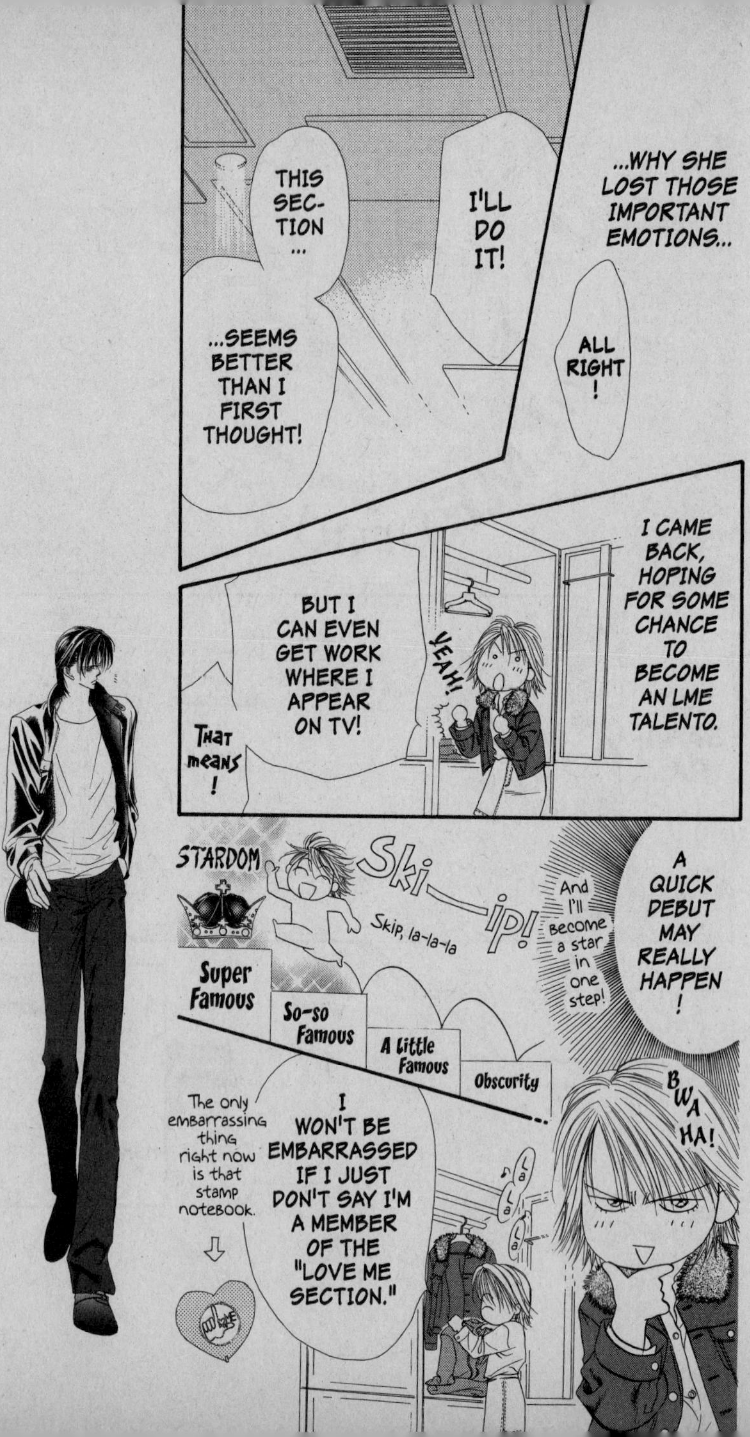
...WHY SHE LOST THOSE IMPORTANT EMOTIONS...
ALL RIGHT!
I'LL DO IT!
THIS SECTION...
...SEEMS BETTER THAN I FIRST THOUGHT!
I CAME BACK, HOPING FOR SOME CHANCE TO BECOME AN LME TALENTO.
YEAH!
BUT I CAN EVEN GET WORK WHERE I APPEAR ON TV!
That means!
A QUICK DEBUT MAY REALLY HAPPEN!
And I'll become a star in one step!
Ski—ip!
Skip, la-la-la
STARDOM
Super Famous
So-so Famous
A Little Famous
Obscurity
BWAHA!
La La La La
I WON'T BE EMBARRASSED IF I JUST DON'T SAY I'M A MEMBER OF THE "LOVE ME SECTION."
The only embarrassing thing right now is that stamp notebook.

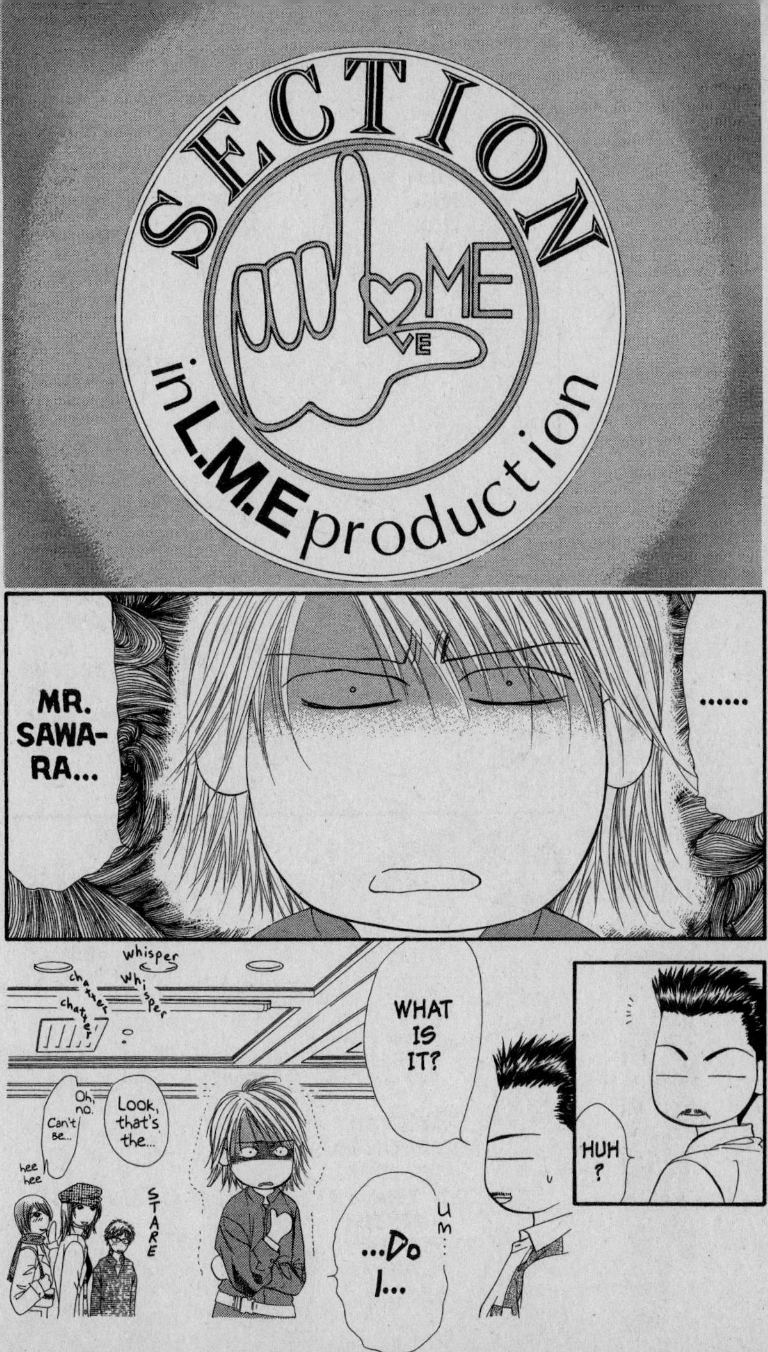
SECTION
LoME
in L.M.E production
......
MR. SAWARA...
...
HUH?
WHAT IS IT?
UM...
...DO I...
whisper whisper
chatter chatter
Look, that's the...
Oh, no. Can't be...
hee hee
STARE

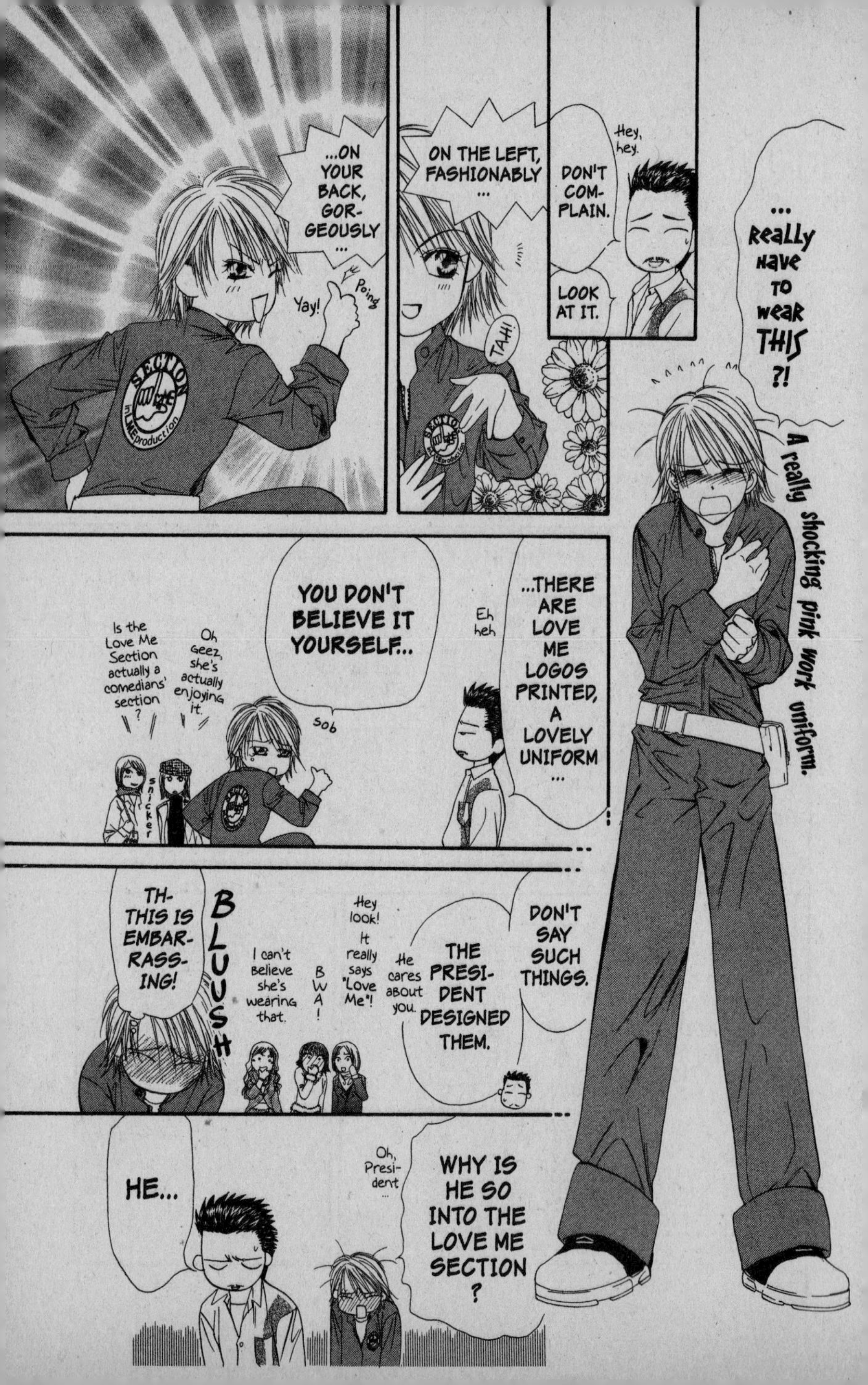

...Really have to wear THIS?!
A really shocking pink work uniform.
Hey, hey.
DON'T COMPLAIN.
LOOK AT IT.
ON THE LEFT, FASHIONABLY...
TAH!
...ON YOUR BACK, GORGEOUSLY...
Poing
Yay!
...THERE ARE LOVE ME LOGOS PRINTED, A LOVELY UNIFORM...
Eh heh
YOU DON'T BELIEVE IT YOURSELF...
sob
Oh Geez, she's actually enjoying it.
Is the Love Me Section actually a comedians' section?
snicker
DON'T SAY SUCH THINGS.
THE PRESIDENT DESIGNED THEM.
He cares about you.
Hey look! It really says "Love Me"!
BWA!
I can't believe she's wearing that.
BLUUSH
TH-THIS IS EMBARRASSING!
WHY IS HE SO INTO THE LOVE ME SECTION?
Oh, President...
HE...

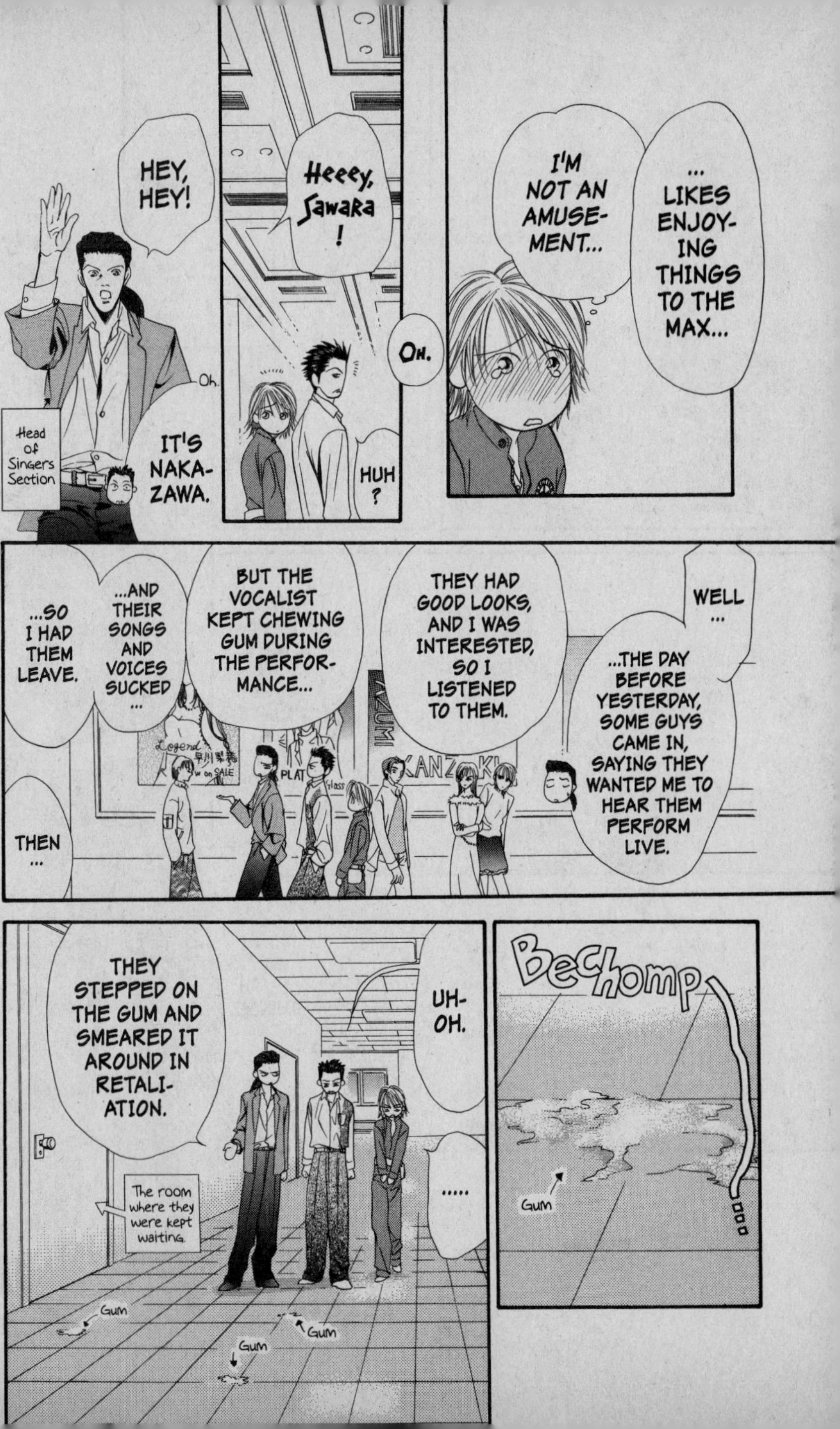
...LIKES ENJOYING THINGS TO THE MAX...
I'M NOT AN AMUSEMENT...
Heeey, Sawara!
OH.
HUH?
HEY, HEY!
Oh.
IT'S NAKAZAWA.
Head of Singers Section
WELL...
...THE DAY BEFORE YESTERDAY, SOME GUYS CAME IN, SAYING THEY WANTED ME TO HEAR THEM PERFORM LIVE.
THEY HAD GOOD LOOKS, AND I WAS INTERESTED, SO I LISTENED TO THEM.
BUT THE VOCALIST KEPT CHEWING GUM DURING THE PERFORMANCE...
...AND THEIR SONGS AND VOICES SUCKED...
...SO I HAD THEM LEAVE.
THEN...
Bechomp
Gum
UH-OH.
THEY STEPPED ON THE GUM AND SMEARED IT AROUND IN RETALIATION.
.....
The room where they were kept waiting
Gum
Gum
Gum

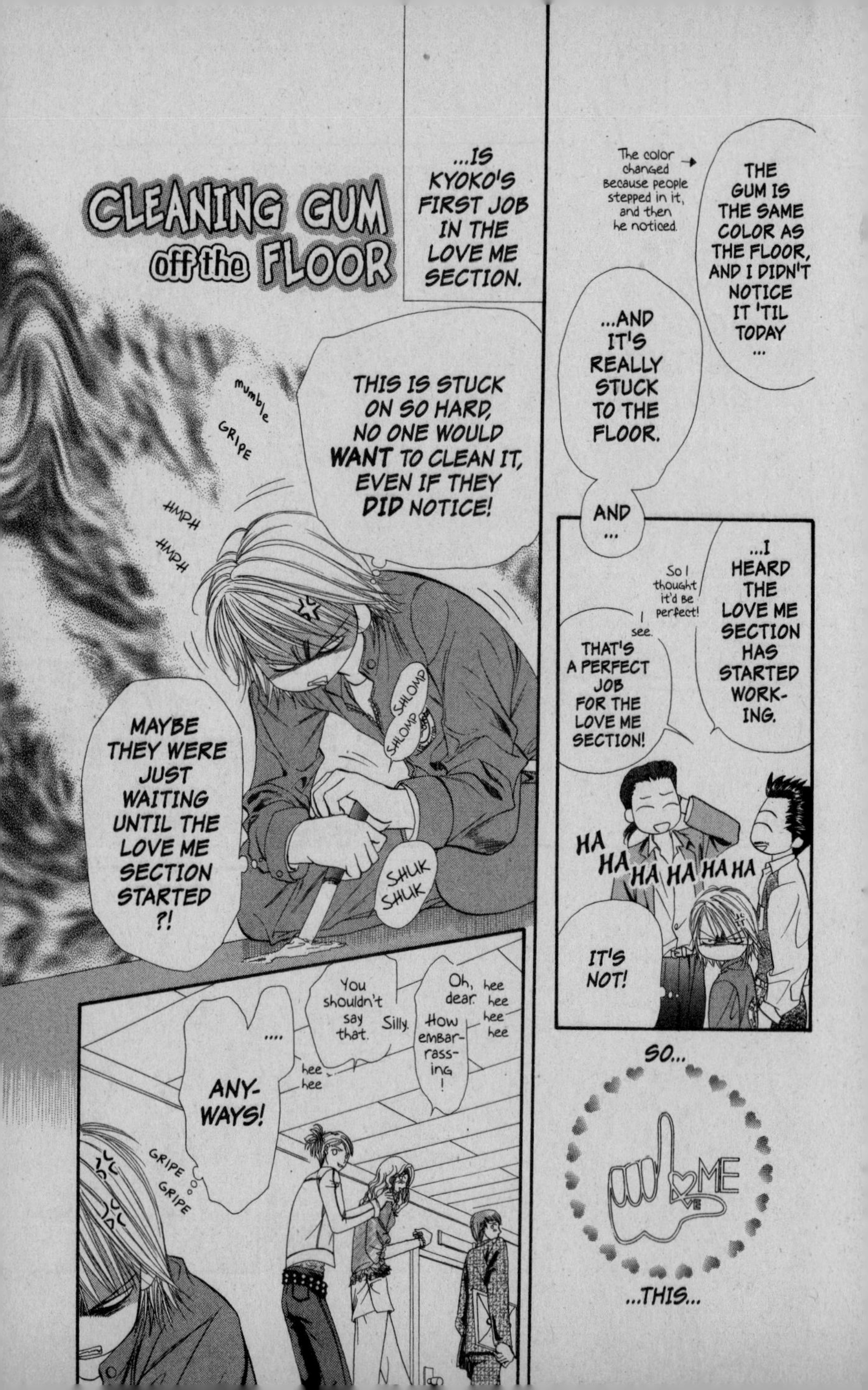
The color changed because people stepped in it, and then he noticed.
THE GUM IS THE SAME COLOR AS THE FLOOR, AND I DIDN'T NOTICE IT 'TIL TODAY ...
...AND IT'S REALLY STUCK TO THE FLOOR.
AND ...
...I HEARD THE LOVE ME SECTION HAS STARTED WORKING.
So I thought it'd be perfect!
I see.
THAT'S A PERFECT JOB FOR THE LOVE ME SECTION!
HA HA HA HA HA HA
IT'S NOT!
SO...
...THIS...
CLEANING GUM off the FLOOR
...IS KYOKO'S FIRST JOB IN THE LOVE ME SECTION.
THIS IS STUCK ON SO HARD, NO ONE WOULD WANT TO CLEAN IT, EVEN IF THEY DID NOTICE!
mumble
GRIPE
HMPH
HMPH
SHLOMP SHLOMP
SHUK SHUK
MAYBE THEY WERE JUST WAITING UNTIL THE LOVE ME SECTION STARTED ?!
Oh, dear. How embarrassing!
hee hee hee hee
You shouldn't say that.
Silly.
hee hee
....
ANY-WAYS!
GRIPE GRIPE

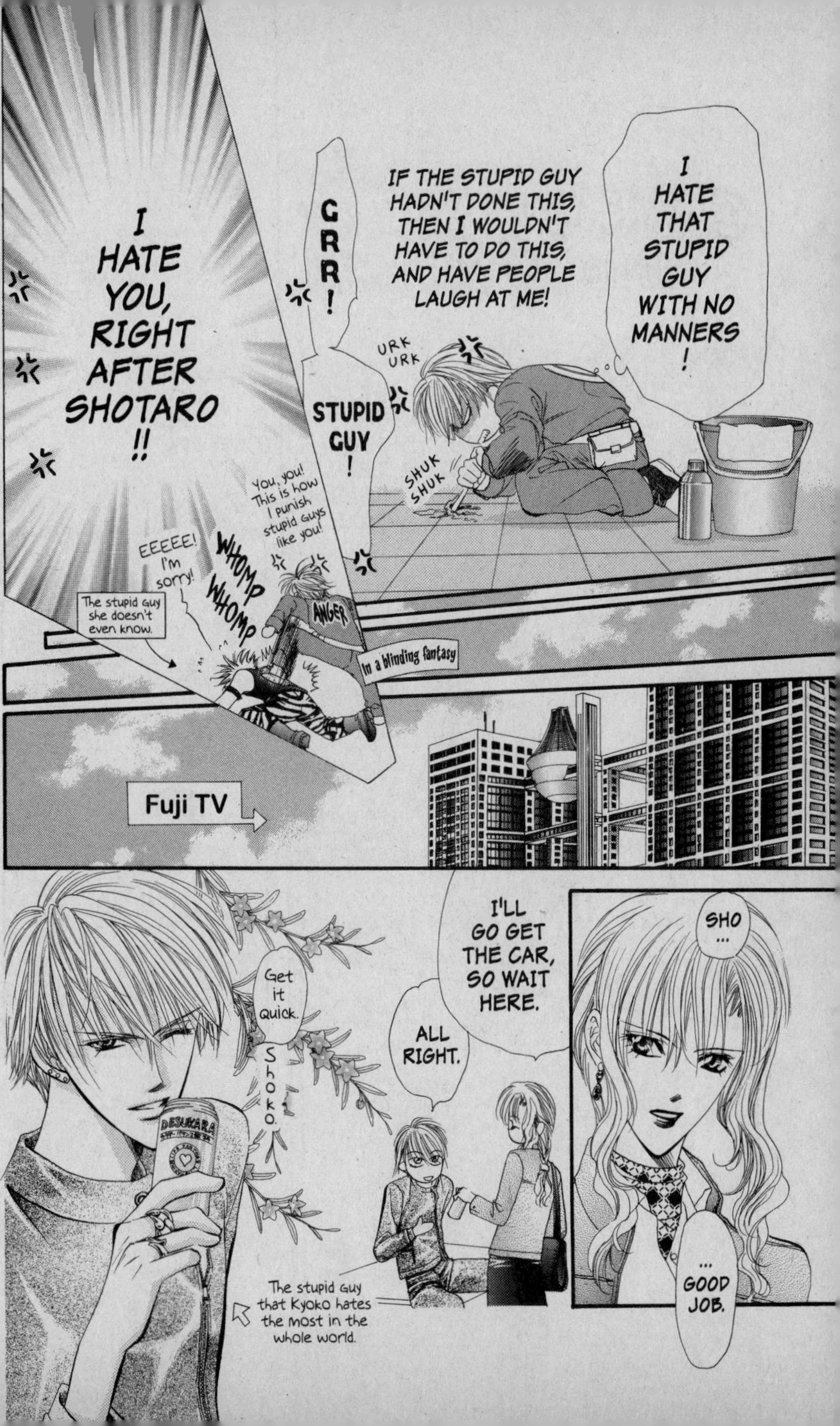
I HATE THAT STUPID GUY WITH NO MANNERS!
IF THE STUPID GUY HADN'T DONE THIS, THEN I WOULDN'T HAVE TO DO THIS, AND HAVE PEOPLE LAUGH AT ME!
GRR!
URK URK
SHUK SHUK
STUPID GUY!
I HATE YOU, RIGHT AFTER SHOTARO!!
You, you! This is how I punish stupid guys like you!
WHOMP WHOMP
ANGER
EEEEE! I'm sorry!
The stupid guy she doesn't even know.
In a blinding fantasy
Fuji TV
SHO...
...GOOD JOB.
I'LL GO GET THE CAR, SO WAIT HERE.
ALL RIGHT.
Get it quick.
Shoko.
DESUKARA
The stupid guy that Kyoko hates the most in the whole world.

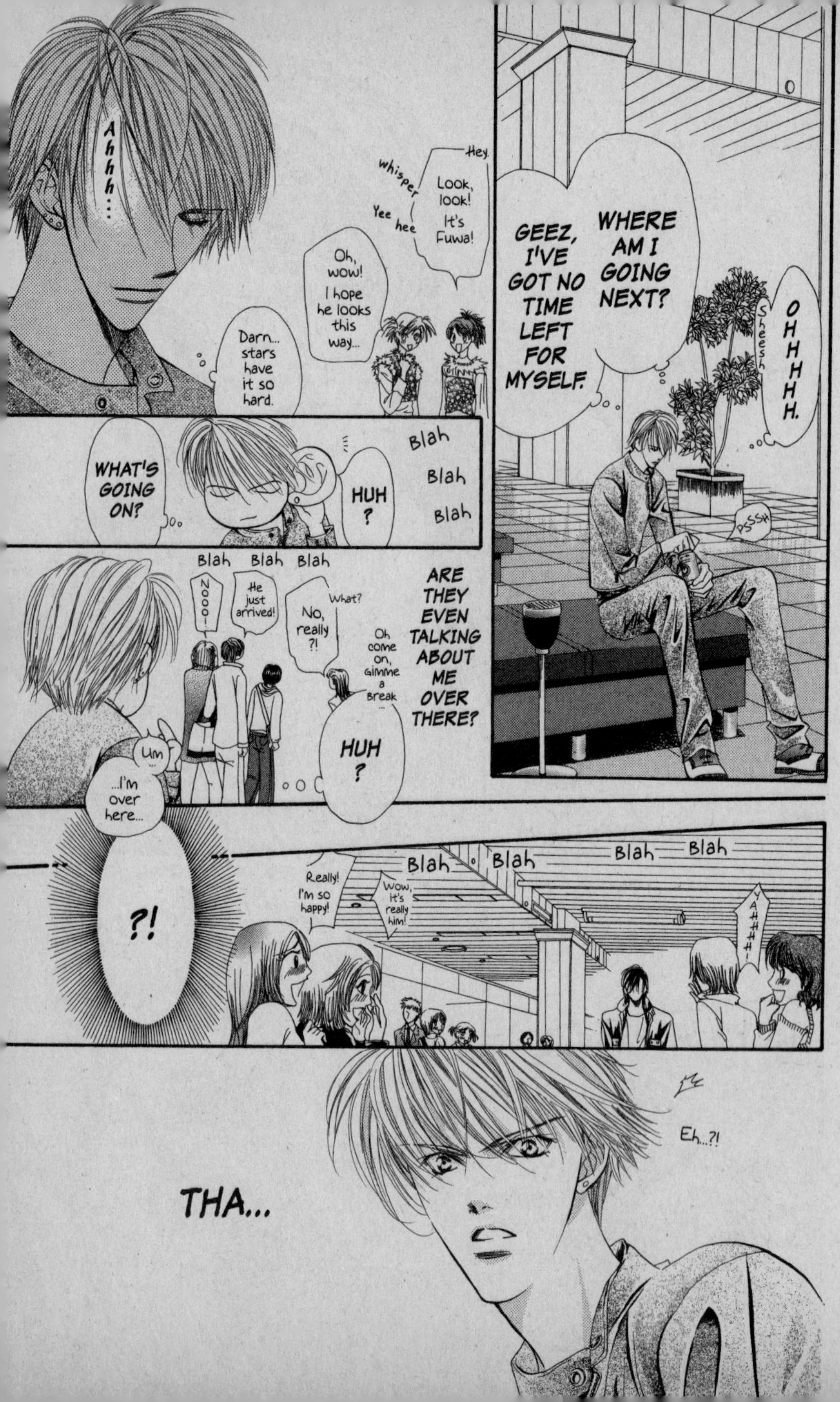
OHHHHH.
Sheesh
WHERE AM I GOING NEXT?
GEEZ, I'VE GOT NO TIME LEFT FOR MYSELF.
PSSSH
Hey.
Look, look! It's Fuwa!
whisper
Yee hee
Oh, wow! I hope he looks this way...
Darn... stars have it so hard.
Ahhh...
Blah
Blah
Blah
HUH?
WHAT'S GOING ON?
ARE THEY EVEN TALKING ABOUT ME OVER THERE?
Oh come on, Gimme a break...
What?
No, really?!
He just arrived!
Noooo!
Blah Blah Blah
HUH?
Um...
...I'm over here...
Blah Blah Blah Blah
YAHHHH!
Wow, it's really him!
Really! I'm so happy!
?!
Eh...?!
THA...

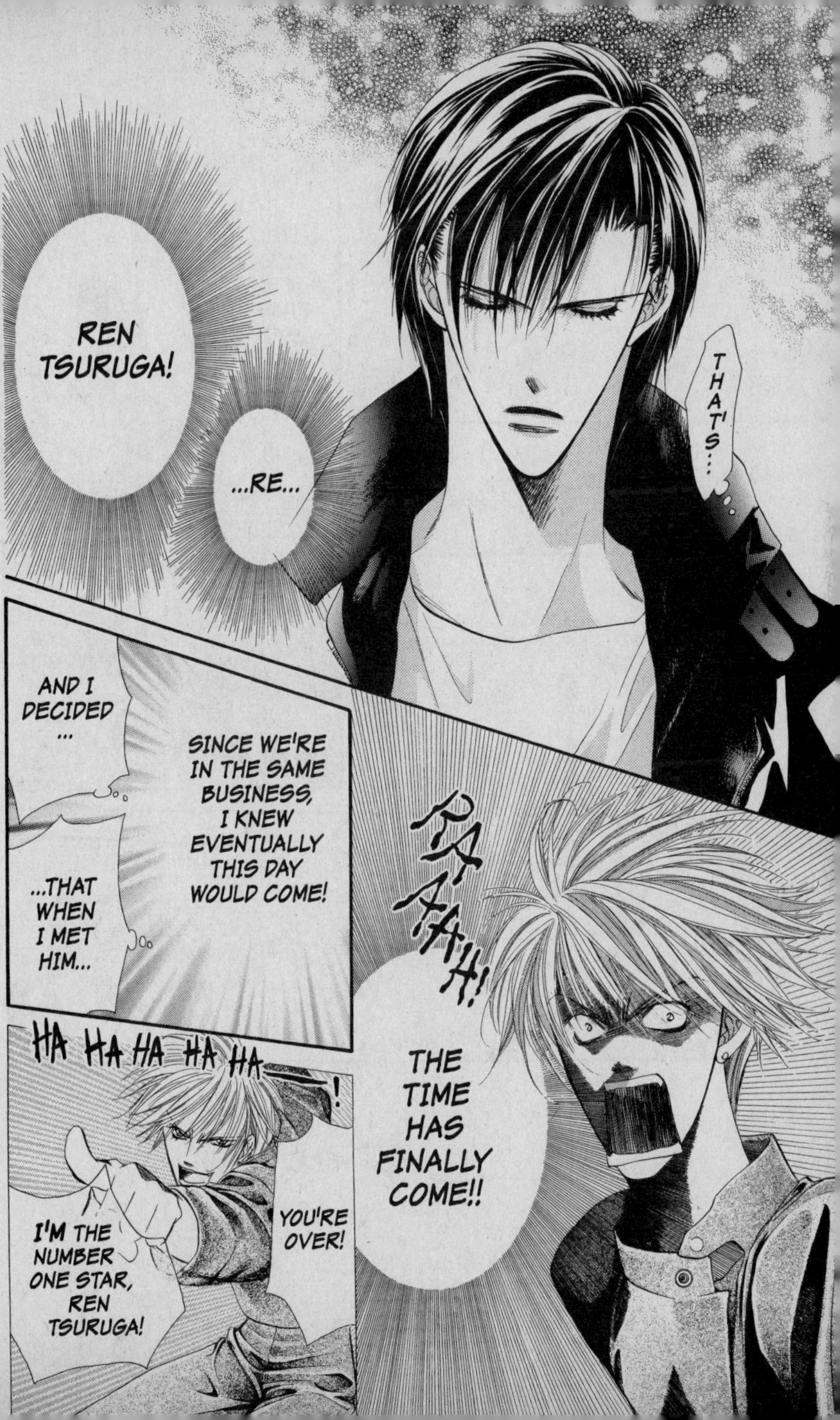
THAT'S...
...RE...
REN TSURUGA!
RAAAHH!
THE TIME HAS FINALLY COME!!
SINCE WE'RE IN THE SAME BUSINESS, I KNEW EVENTUALLY THIS DAY WOULD COME!
AND I DECIDED...
...THAT WHEN I MET HIM...
HA HA HA HA HA!
YOU'RE OVER!
I'M THE NUMBER ONE STAR, REN TSURUGA!

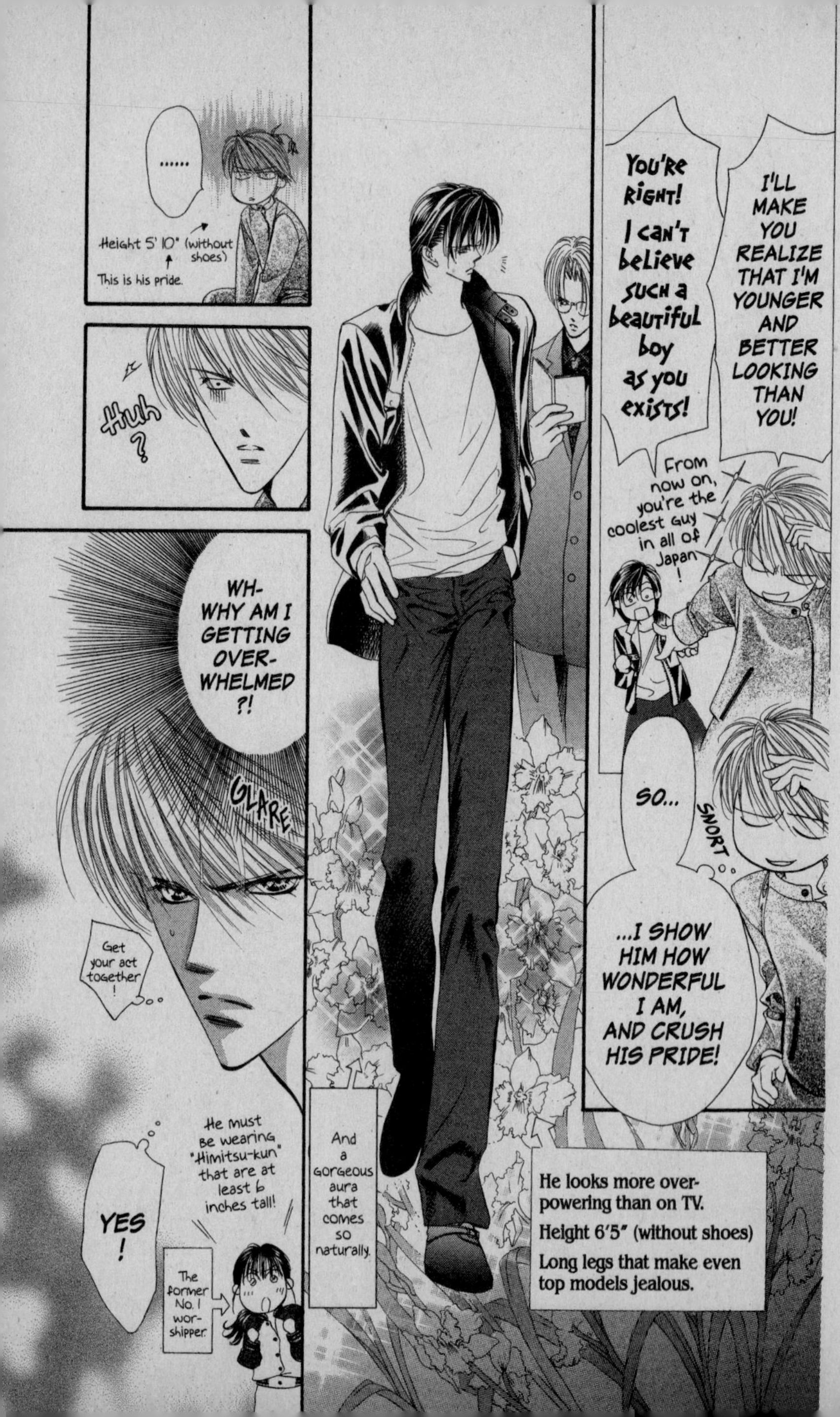

I'LL MAKE YOU REALIZE THAT I'M YOUNGER AND BETTER LOOKING THAN YOU!
You're right! I can't believe such a beautiful boy as you exists!
From now on, you're the coolest guy in all of Japan!
SO...
SNORT
...I SHOW HIM HOW WONDERFUL I AM, AND CRUSH HIS PRIDE!
He looks more over-powering than on TV.
Height 6'5" (without shoes)
Long legs that make even top models jealous.
And a gorgeous aura that comes so naturally.
......
Height 5' 10" (without shoes)
This is his pride.
Huh?
WH-WHY AM I GETTING OVER-WHELMED?!
GLARE
Get your act together!
He must be wearing "Himitsu-kun" that are at least 6 inches tall!
YES!
The former No. 1 wor-shipper.

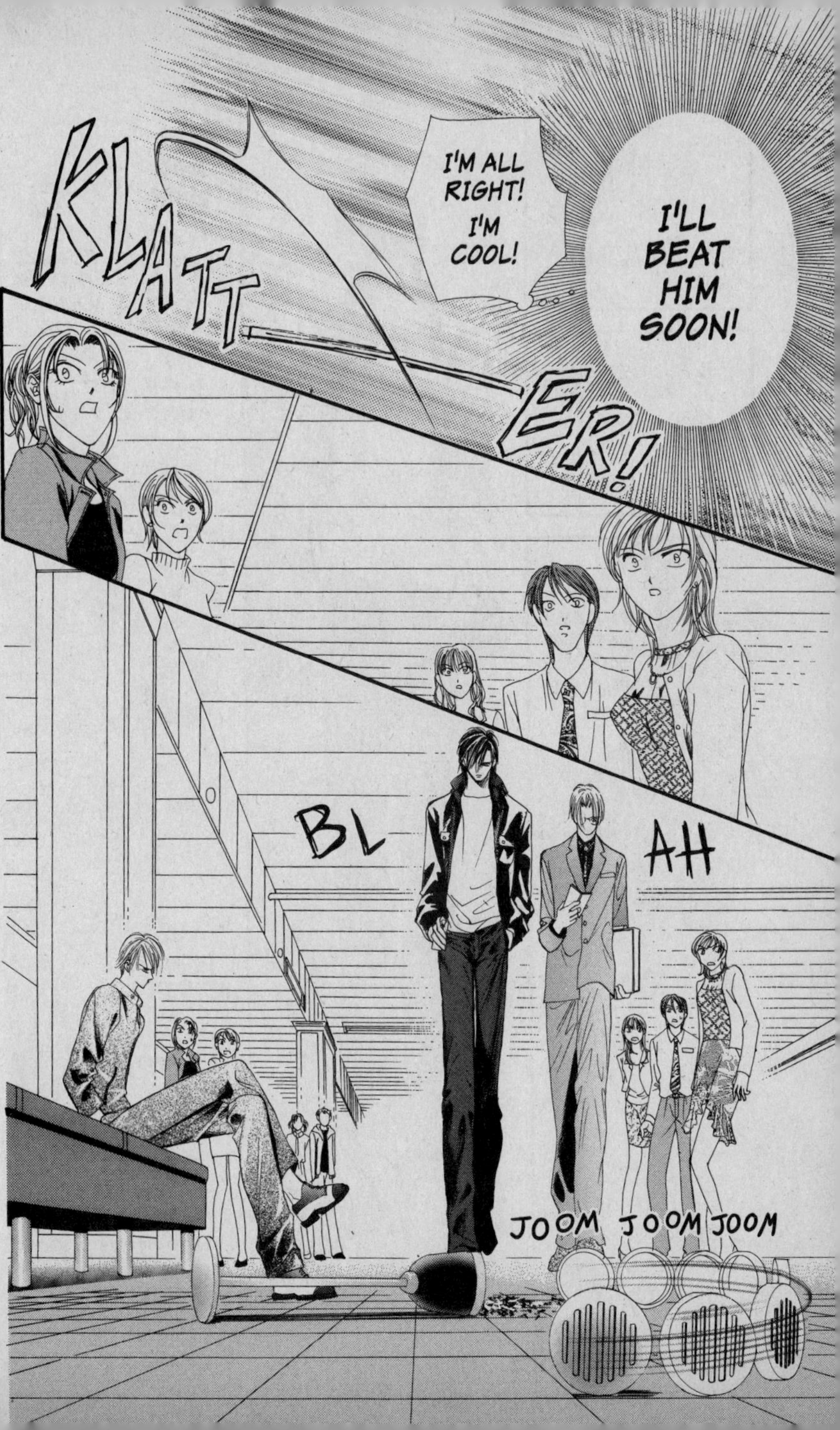
I'LL BEAT HIM SOON!
I'M ALL RIGHT! I'M COOL!
KLATTER!
BLAH
JOOM JOOM JOOM

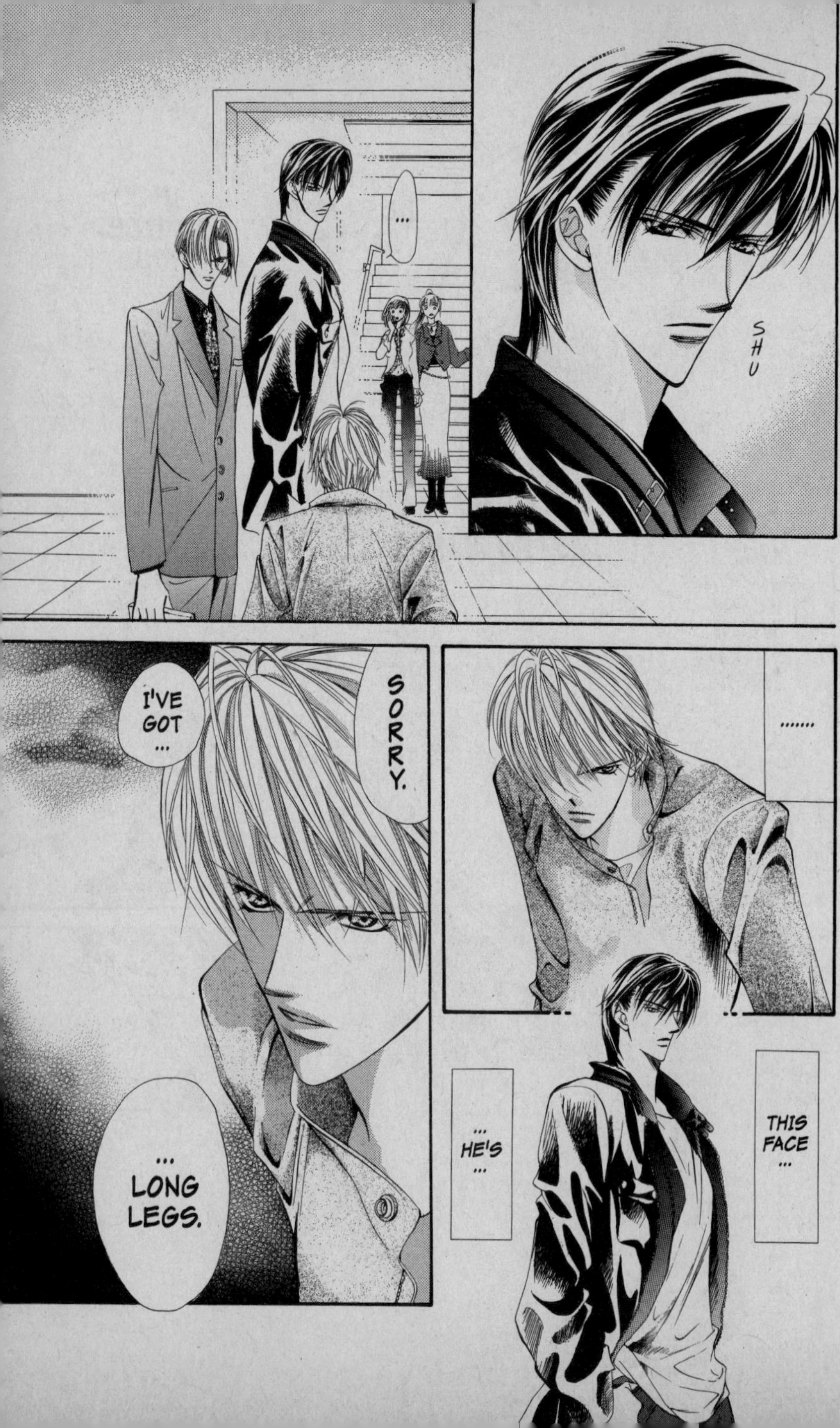
SHU
...
....
THIS FACE ...
... HE'S ...
SORRY.
I'VE GOT ...
... LONG LEGS.

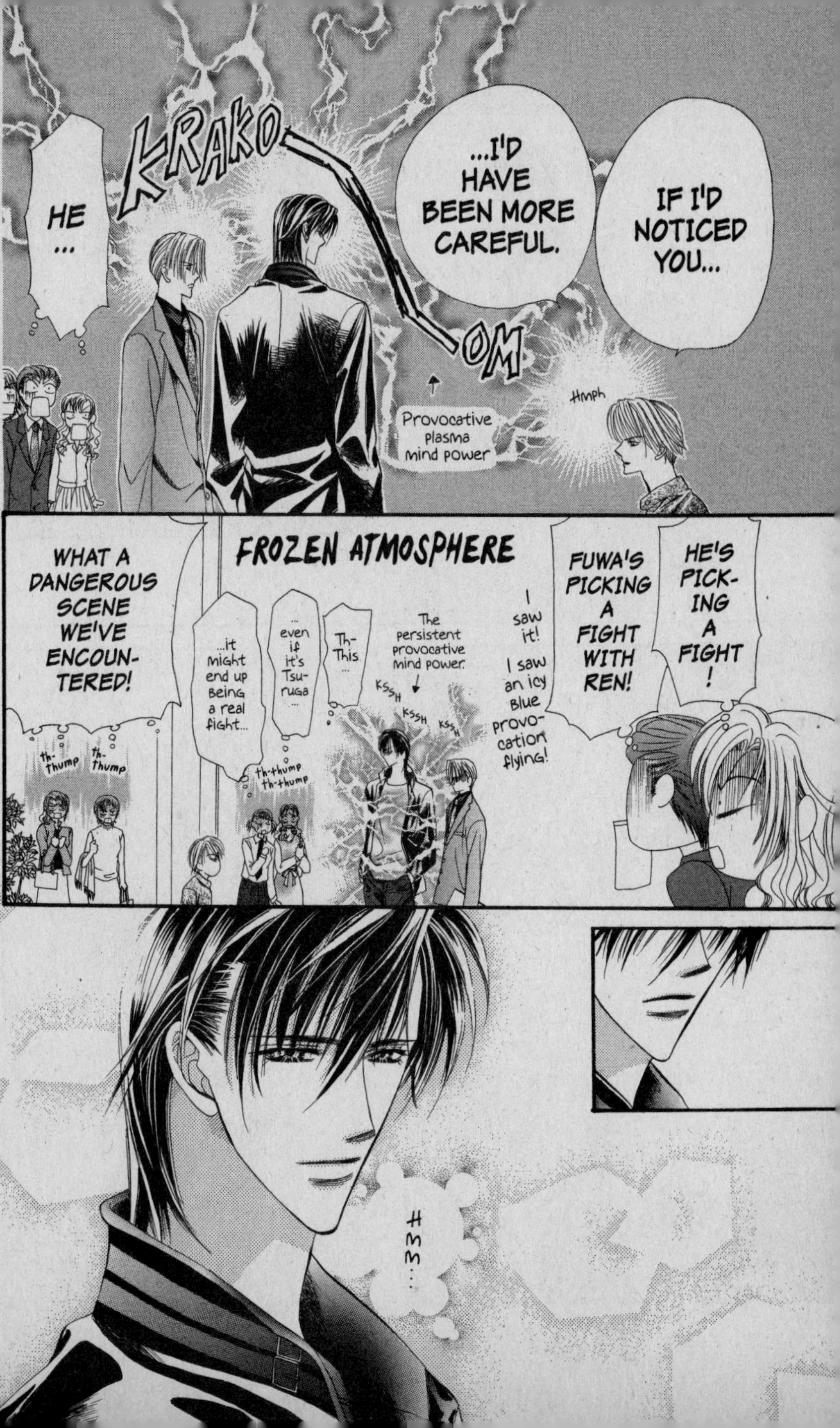
IF I'D NOTICED YOU...
...I'D HAVE BEEN MORE CAREFUL.
KRAKO-OM
Hmph
Provocative plasma mind power
HE ...
HE'S PICKING A FIGHT!
FUWA'S PICKING A FIGHT WITH REN!
I saw it! I saw an icy Blue provocation flying!
The persistent provocative mind power.
KSSH KSSH KSSH
Th- This ...
... even if it's Tsuruga ...
...it might end up being a real fight...
th-thump th-thump
FROZEN ATMOSPHERE
WHAT A DANGEROUS SCENE WE'VE ENCOUNTERED!
th-thump th-thump
HMM...

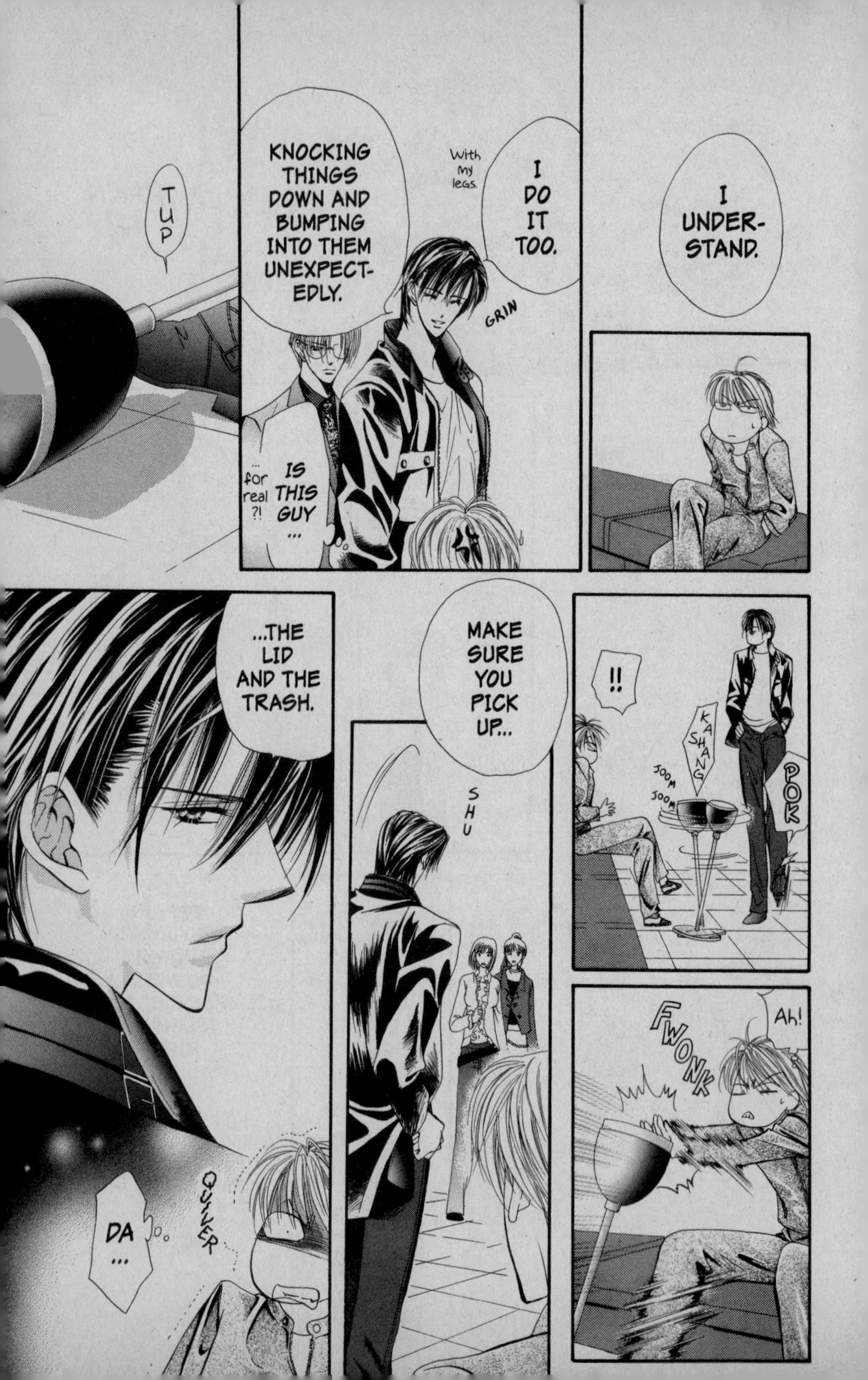
I UNDER-STAND.
I DO IT TOO.
With my legs.
GRIN
KNOCKING THINGS DOWN AND BUMPING INTO THEM UNEXPECTEDLY.
IS THIS GUY ...
... for real ?!
TUP
!!
KA SHANG
JOOM JOOM
POK
Ah!
FWONK
MAKE SURE YOU PICK UP...
SHU
...THE LID AND THE TRASH.
QUIVER
DA ...

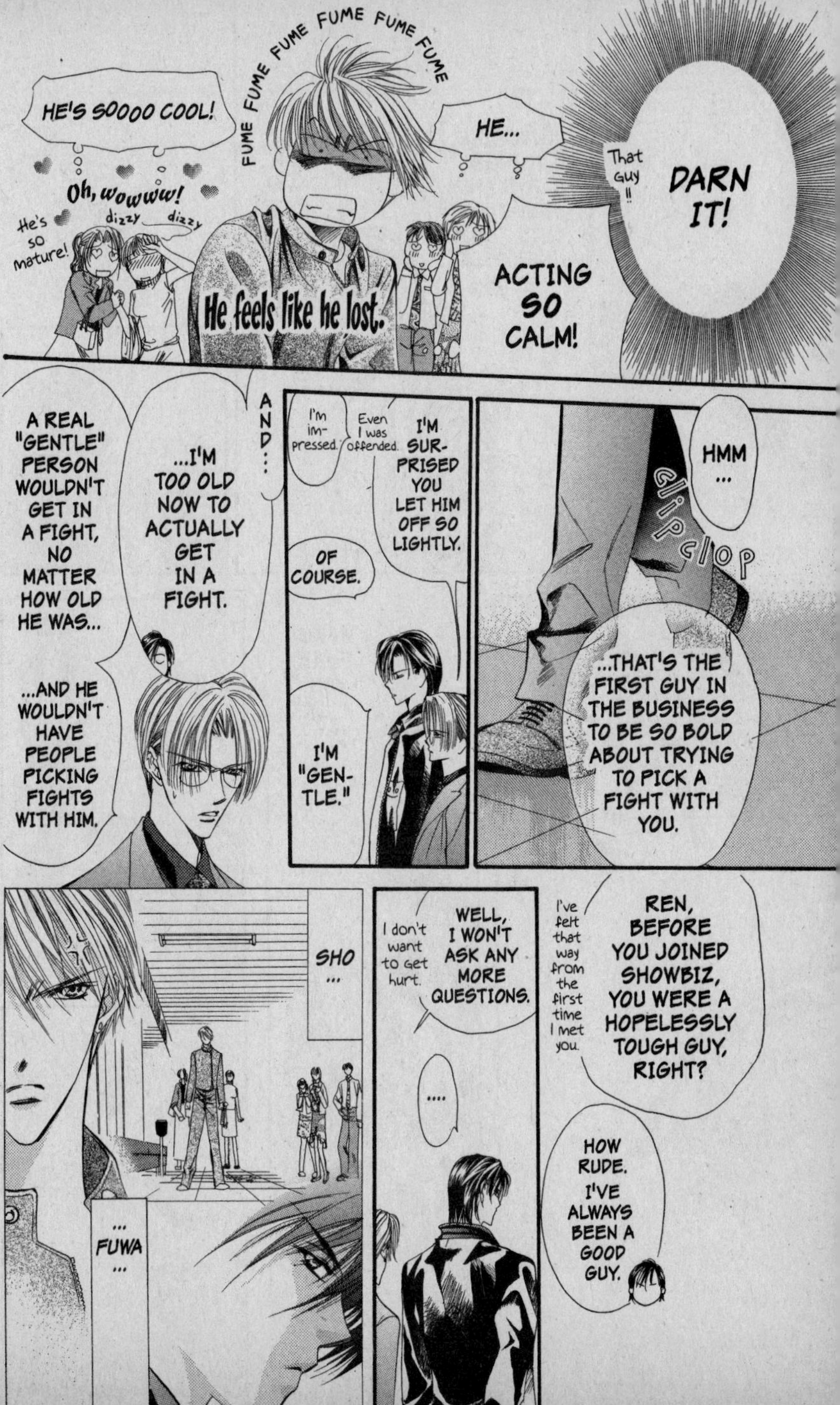
DARN IT!
That Guy !!
ACTING SO CALM!
HE...
FUME FUME FUME FUME FUME FUME FUME
HE'S SOOOO COOL!
Oh, wowww!
dizzy dizzy
He's so mature!
He feels like he lost.
HMM ...
clip clop
...THAT'S THE FIRST GUY IN THE BUSINESS TO BE SO BOLD ABOUT TRYING TO PICK A FIGHT WITH YOU.
I'M SUR-PRISED YOU LET HIM OFF SO LIGHTLY.
Even I was offended.
I'm im-pressed.
OF COURSE.
I'M "GEN-TLE."
AND...
...I'M TOO OLD NOW TO ACTUALLY GET IN A FIGHT.
A REAL "GENTLE" PERSON WOULDN'T GET IN A FIGHT, NO MATTER HOW OLD HE WAS...
...AND HE WOULDN'T HAVE PEOPLE PICKING FIGHTS WITH HIM.
REN, BEFORE YOU JOINED SHOWBIZ, YOU WERE A HOPELESSLY TOUGH GUY, RIGHT?
I've felt that way from the first time I met you.
HOW RUDE. I'VE ALWAYS BEEN A GOOD GUY.
WELL, I WON'T ASK ANY MORE QUESTIONS.
I don't want to get hurt.
....
SHO ...
... FUWA ...

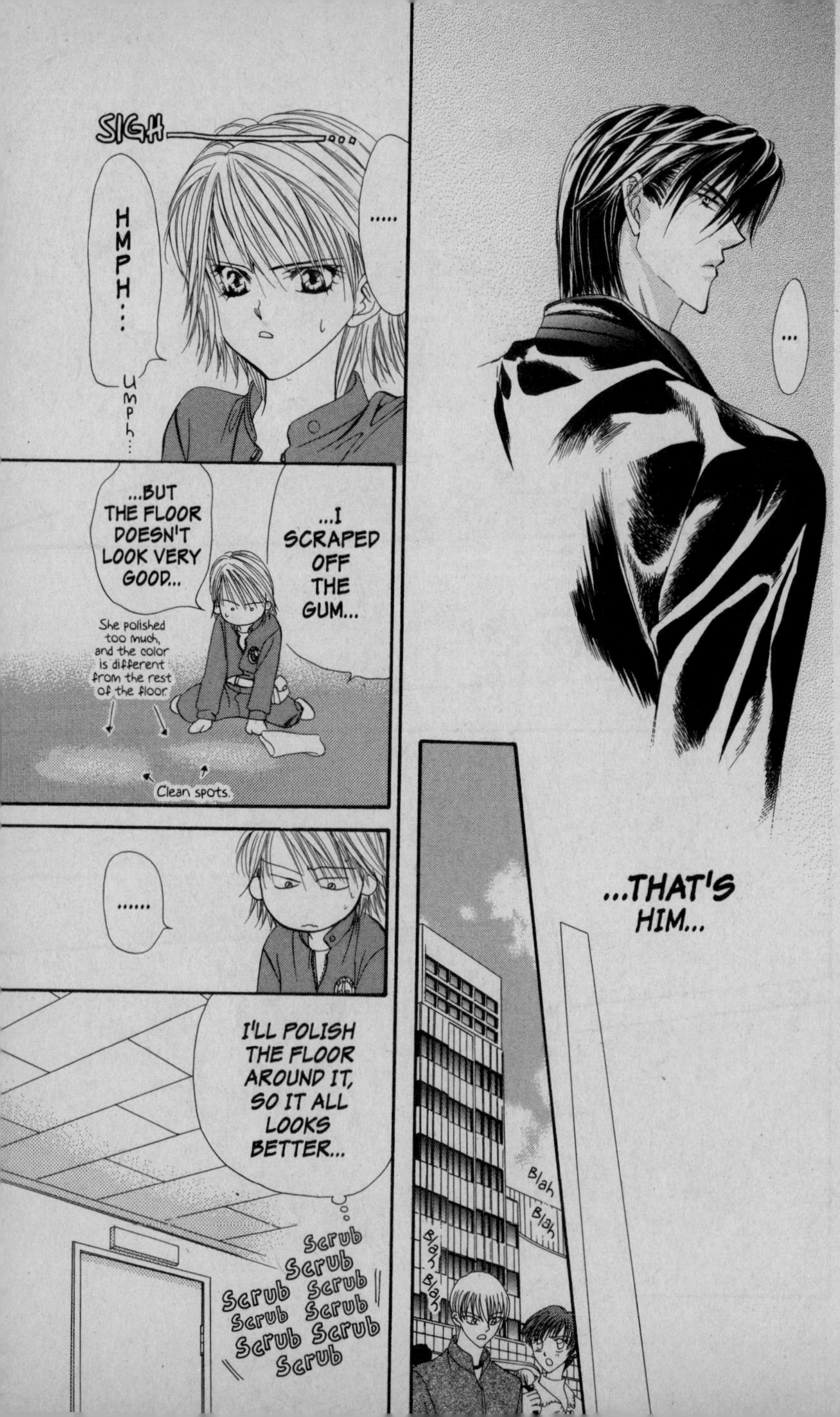
...
...THAT'S HIM...
Blah
Blah
Blah
Blah
.....
SIGH———...
HMPH...
Umph...
...I SCRAPED OFF THE GUM...
...BUT THE FLOOR DOESN'T LOOK VERY GOOD...
She polished too much, and the color is different from the rest of the floor.
Clean spots.
......
I'LL POLISH THE FLOOR AROUND IT, SO IT ALL LOOKS BETTER...
Scrub Scrub Scrub Scrub Scrub Scrub Scrub Scrub Scrub

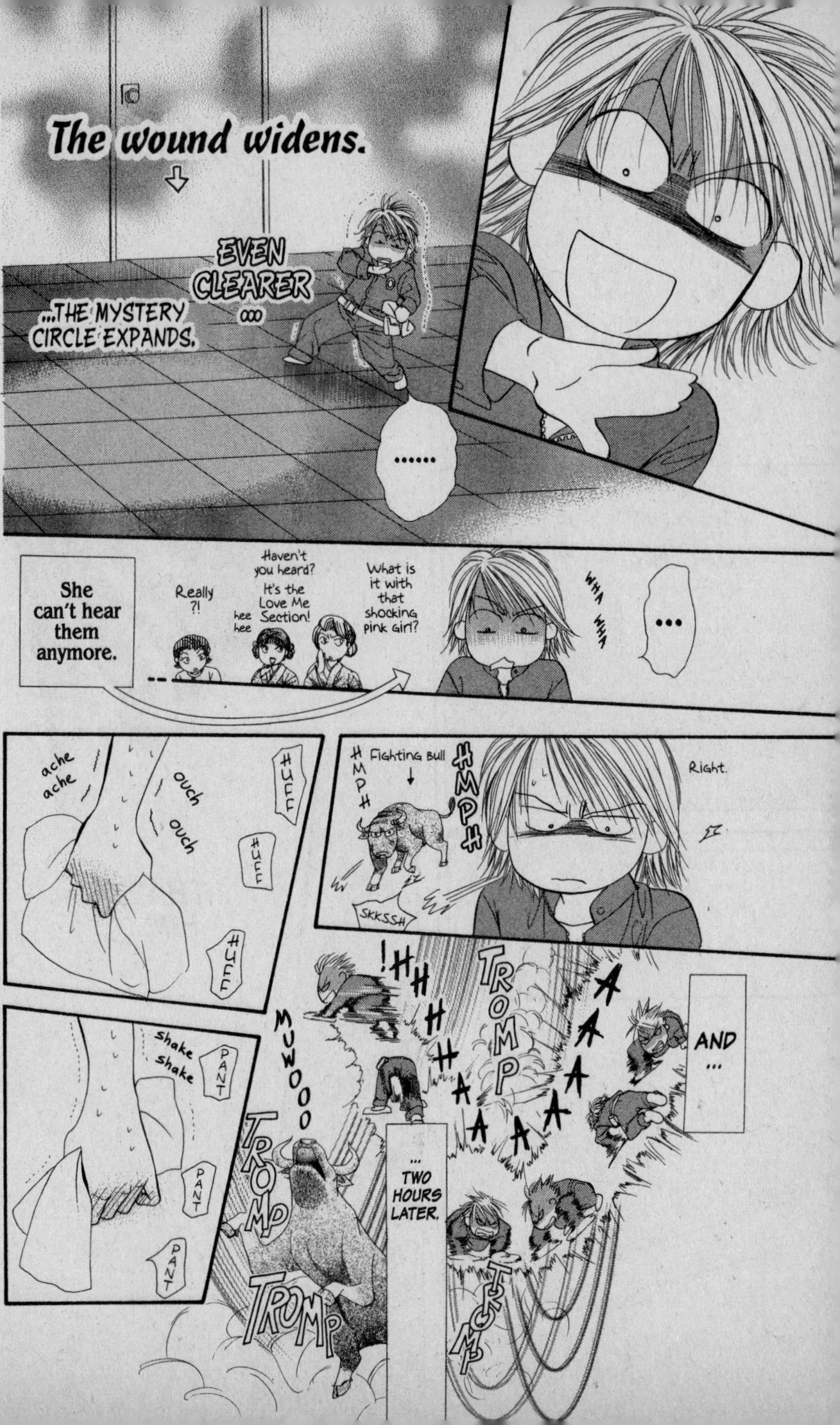
The wound widens.
EVEN CLEARER
ooo
...THE MYSTERY CIRCLE EXPANDS.
......
...
WHA WHA
What is it with that shocking pink girl?
Haven't you heard? It's the Love Me Section!
hee hee
Really?!
She can't hear them anymore.
Right.
HMPH
Fighting Bull
HMPH
SKKSSH
HUFF
HUFF
HUFF
ouch ouch
ache ache
AND ...
AAAAAAAAHHHHH!
TROMP
TROMP
... TWO HOURS LATER.
MUWOOOO
TROMP
TROMP
PANT
PANT
PANT
shake shake

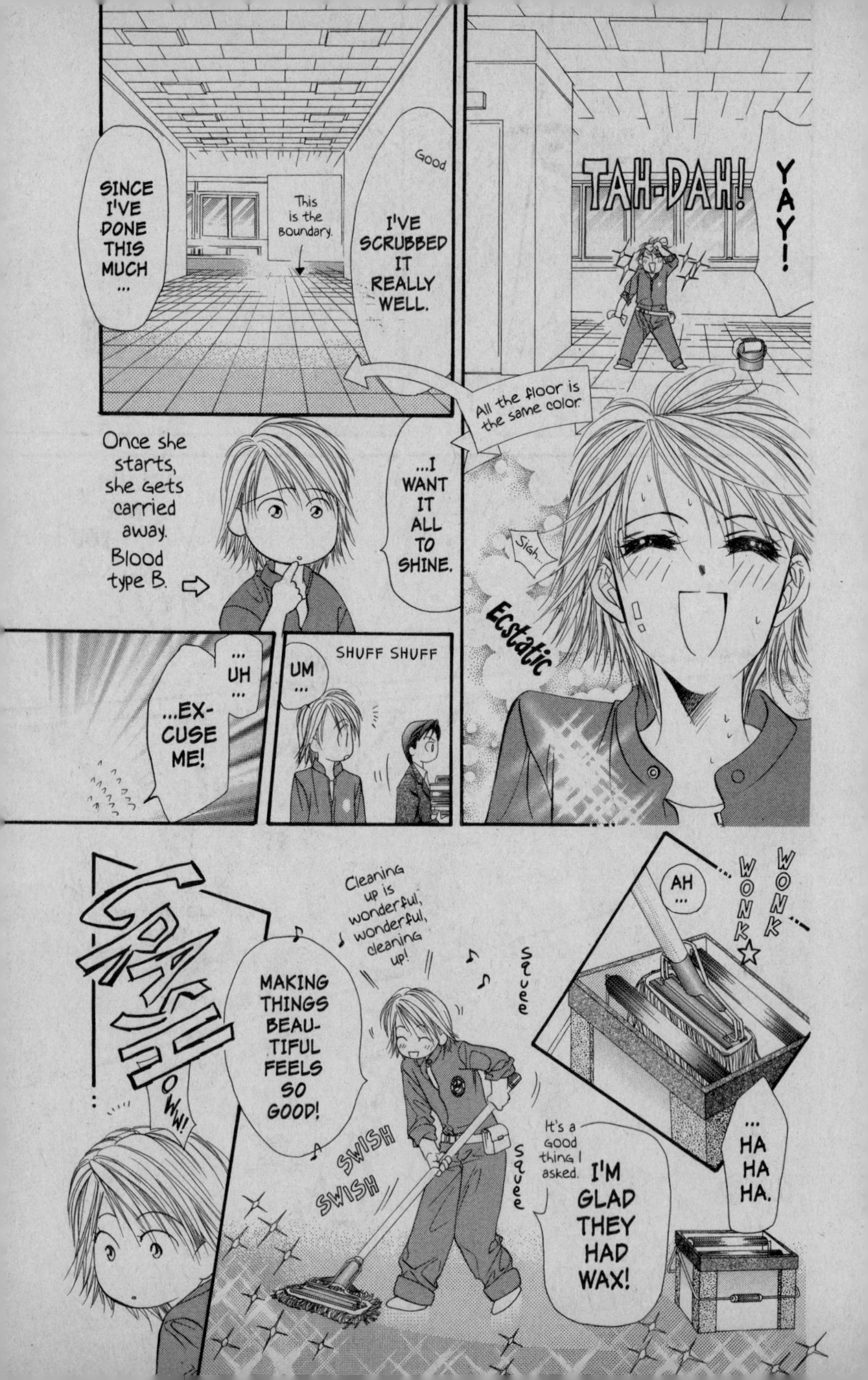
TAH-DAH!
YAY!
Good.
I'VE SCRUBBED IT REALLY WELL.
This is the boundary.
SINCE I'VE DONE THIS MUCH...
All the floor is the same color.
Sigh...
Ecstatic
...I WANT IT ALL TO SHINE.
Once she starts, she gets carried away. Blood type B.
SHUFF SHUFF
UM...
...UH...
...EX-CUSE ME!
WONK WONK☆
AH...
...HA HA HA.
It's a good thing I asked.
I'M GLAD THEY HAD WAX!
Squee
Squee
Cleaning up is wonderful, wonderful, cleaning up!
MAKING THINGS BEAU-TIFUL FEELS SO GOOD!
SWISH
SWISH
SPLASH
OWW!

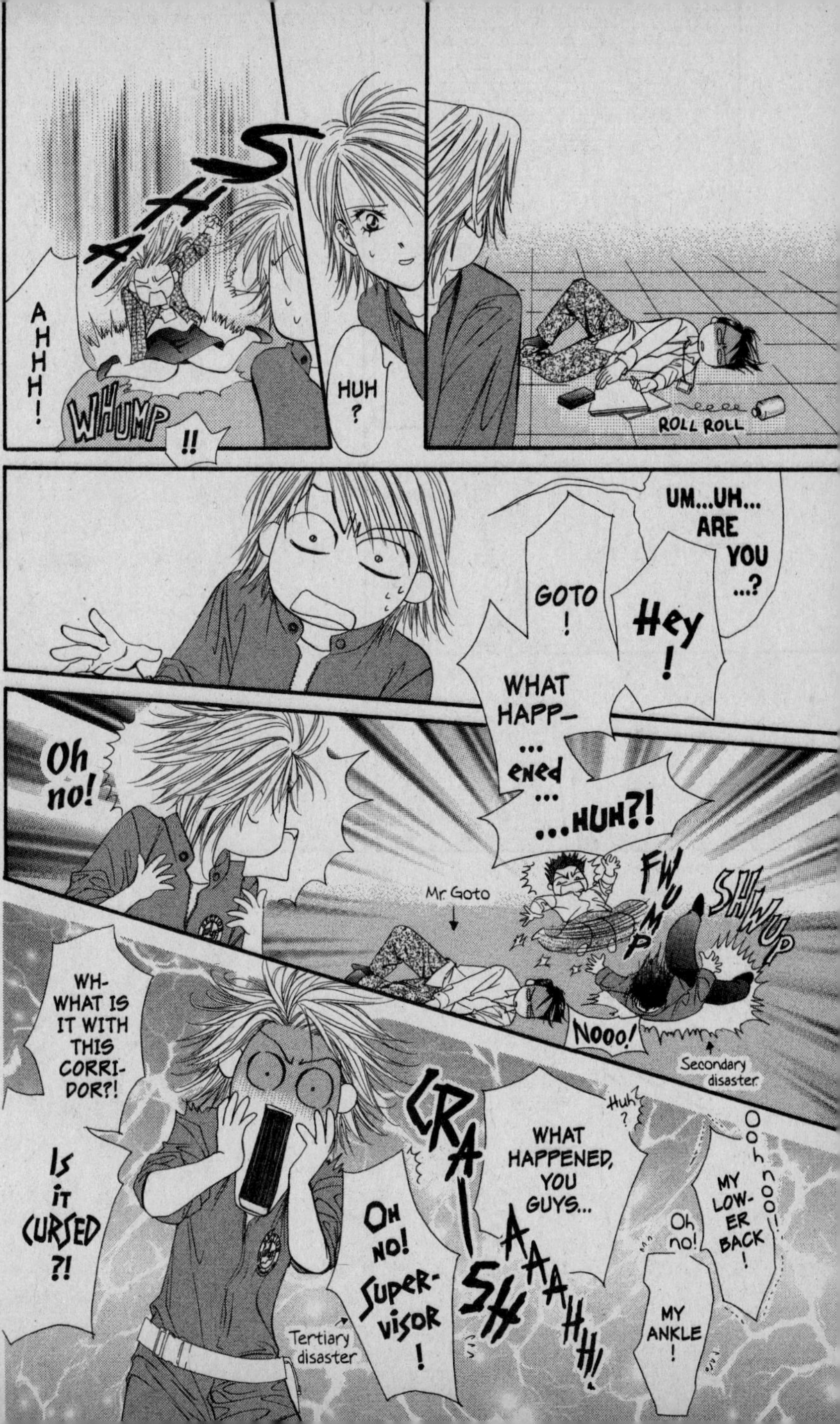
ROLL ROLL
HUH?
SHHA
AHHH!
WHUMP
!!
UM...UH... ARE YOU ...?
Hey!
GOTO!
WHAT HAPP— ... ened ... ...HUH?!
SHWUP
FWUMP
Nooo!
Secondary disaster.
Mr. Goto
Oh no!
Ooh nooo!
MY LOWER BACK!
Huh?
Oh no!
MY ANKLE!
WHAT HAPPENED, YOU GUYS...
CRASH
AAAHHH!
OH NO! SUPERVISOR!
Tertiary disaster
WH-WHAT IS IT WITH THIS CORRIDOR?!
Is it CURSED?!

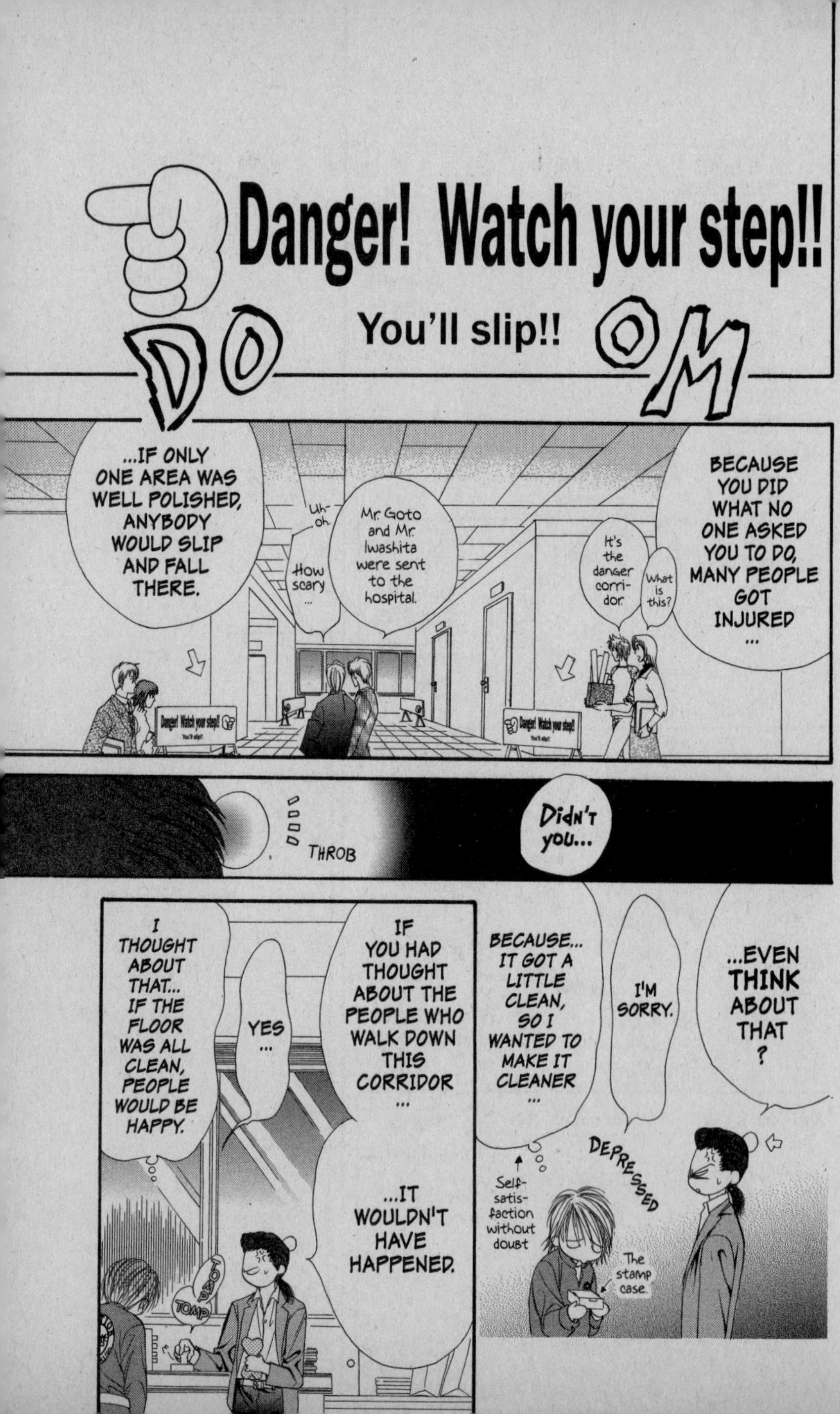
Danger! Watch your step!!
You'll slip!!
DOOM
BECAUSE YOU DID WHAT NO ONE ASKED YOU TO DO, MANY PEOPLE GOT INJURED...
What is this?
It's the danger corridor.
Mr. Goto and Mr. Iwashita were sent to the hospital.
Uh-oh.
How scary...
...IF ONLY ONE AREA WAS WELL POLISHED, ANYBODY WOULD SLIP AND FALL THERE.
Didn't you...
THROB
...EVEN THINK ABOUT THAT?
I'M SORRY.
BECAUSE... IT GOT A LITTLE CLEAN, SO I WANTED TO MAKE IT CLEANER...
DEPRESSED
Self-satisfaction without doubt
The stamp case.
IF YOU HAD THOUGHT ABOUT THE PEOPLE WHO WALK DOWN THIS CORRIDOR...
...IT WOULDN'T HAVE HAPPENED.
YES...
I THOUGHT ABOUT THAT... IF THE FLOOR WAS ALL CLEAN, PEOPLE WOULD BE HAPPY.
TOMP
TOMP

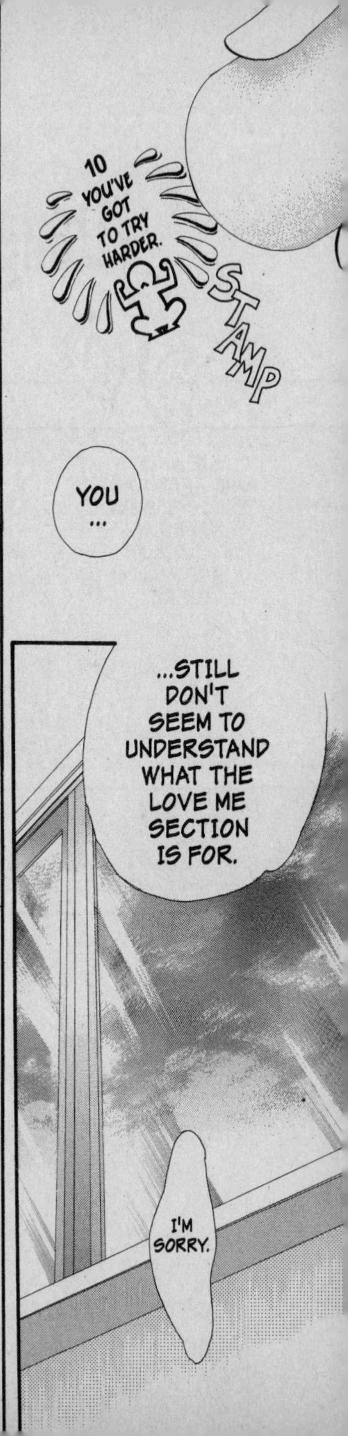
10 YOU'VE GOT TO TRY HARDER.
STAMP
YOU ...
...STILL DON'T SEEM TO UNDERSTAND WHAT THE LOVE ME SECTION IS FOR.
I'M SORRY.

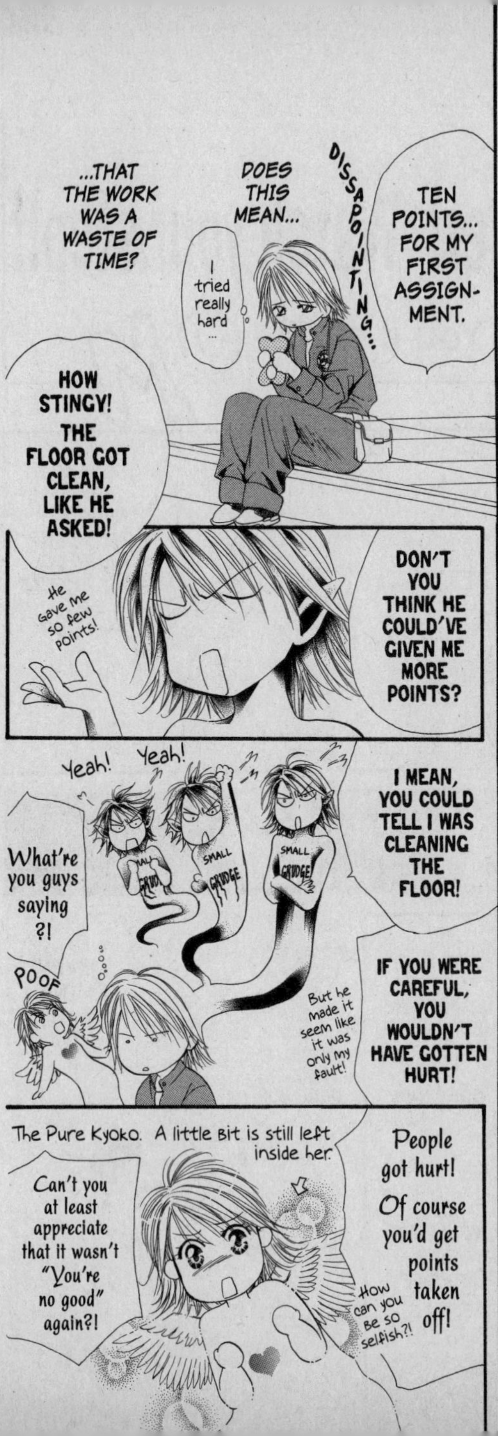
TEN POINTS... FOR MY FIRST ASSIGNMENT.
DISSAPOINTING...
DOES THIS MEAN...
...THAT THE WORK WAS A WASTE OF TIME?
I tried really hard...
HOW STINGY! THE FLOOR GOT CLEAN, LIKE HE ASKED!
DON'T YOU THINK HE COULD'VE GIVEN ME MORE POINTS?
He gave me so few points!
I MEAN, YOU COULD TELL I WAS CLEANING THE FLOOR!
Yeah!
Yeah!
SMALL GRUDGE
SMALL GRUDGE
What're you guys saying?!
IF YOU WERE CAREFUL, YOU WOULDN'T HAVE GOTTEN HURT!
But he made it seem like it was only my fault!
POOF
People got hurt! Of course you'd get points taken off!
How can you be so selfish?!
The Pure Kyoko. A little bit is still left inside her.
Can't you at least appreciate that it wasn't "You're no good" again?!

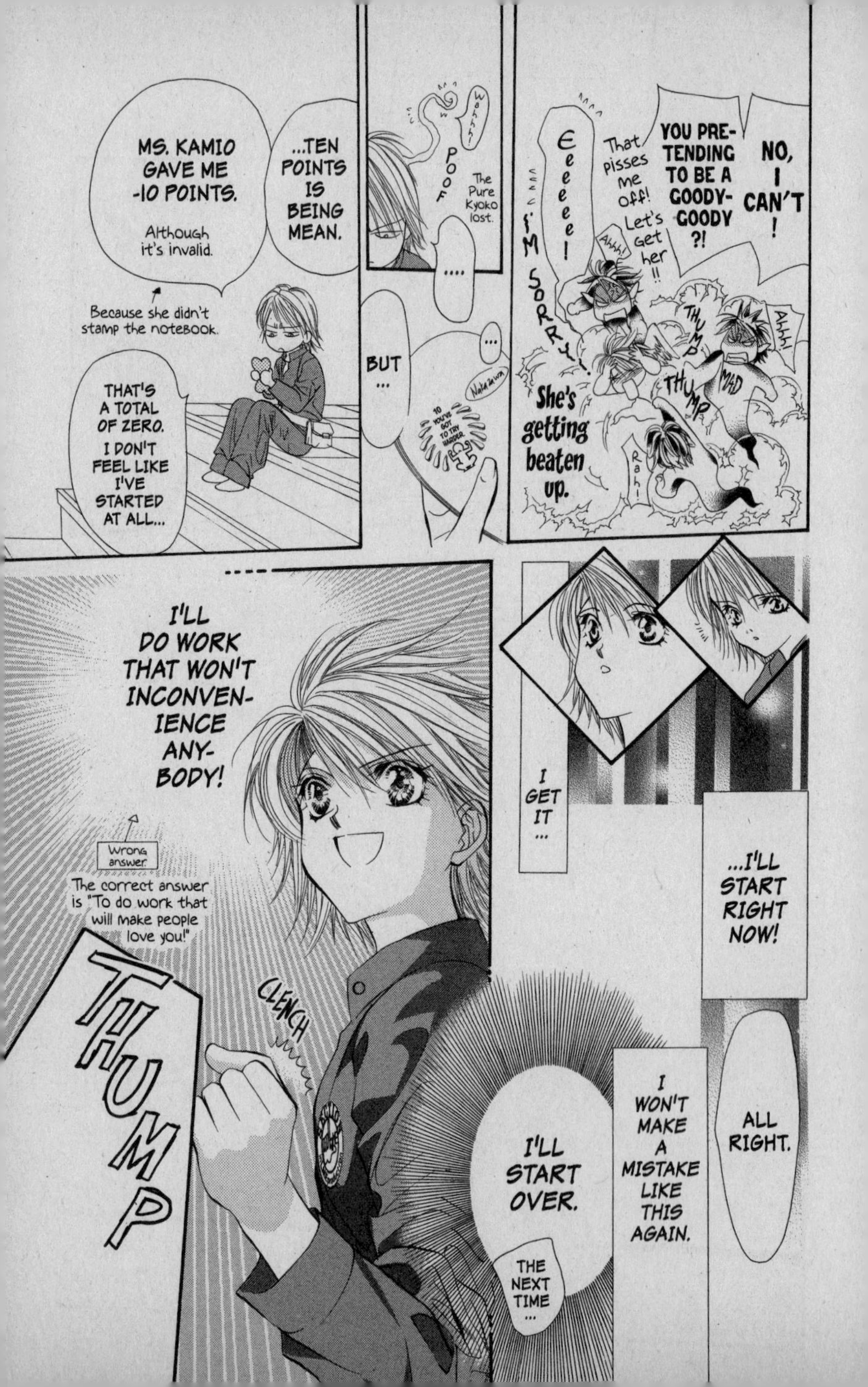
NO, I CAN'T!
YOU PRETENDING TO BE A GOODY-GOODY?!
That pisses me off! Let's get her!!
Eeeeee!
I'M SORRY!
Ahh!
Ahh!
THUMP
THUMP
MAD
Rah!
She's getting beaten up.
Wahhh!
POOF
The Pure Kyoko lost.
....
...
BUT ...
Nakazawa
YOU'VE GOT TO TRY HARDER.
...TEN POINTS IS BEING MEAN.
MS. KAMIO GAVE ME -10 POINTS.
Although it's invalid.
Because she didn't stamp the notebook.
THAT'S A TOTAL OF ZERO. I DON'T FEEL LIKE I'VE STARTED AT ALL...
I GET IT ...
...I'LL START RIGHT NOW!
ALL RIGHT.
I WON'T MAKE A MISTAKE LIKE THIS AGAIN.
THE NEXT TIME ...
I'LL START OVER.

I'LL DO WORK THAT WON'T INCONVEN-IENCE ANY-BODY!
Wrong answer
The correct answer is "To do work that will make people love you!"
CLENCH
THUMP

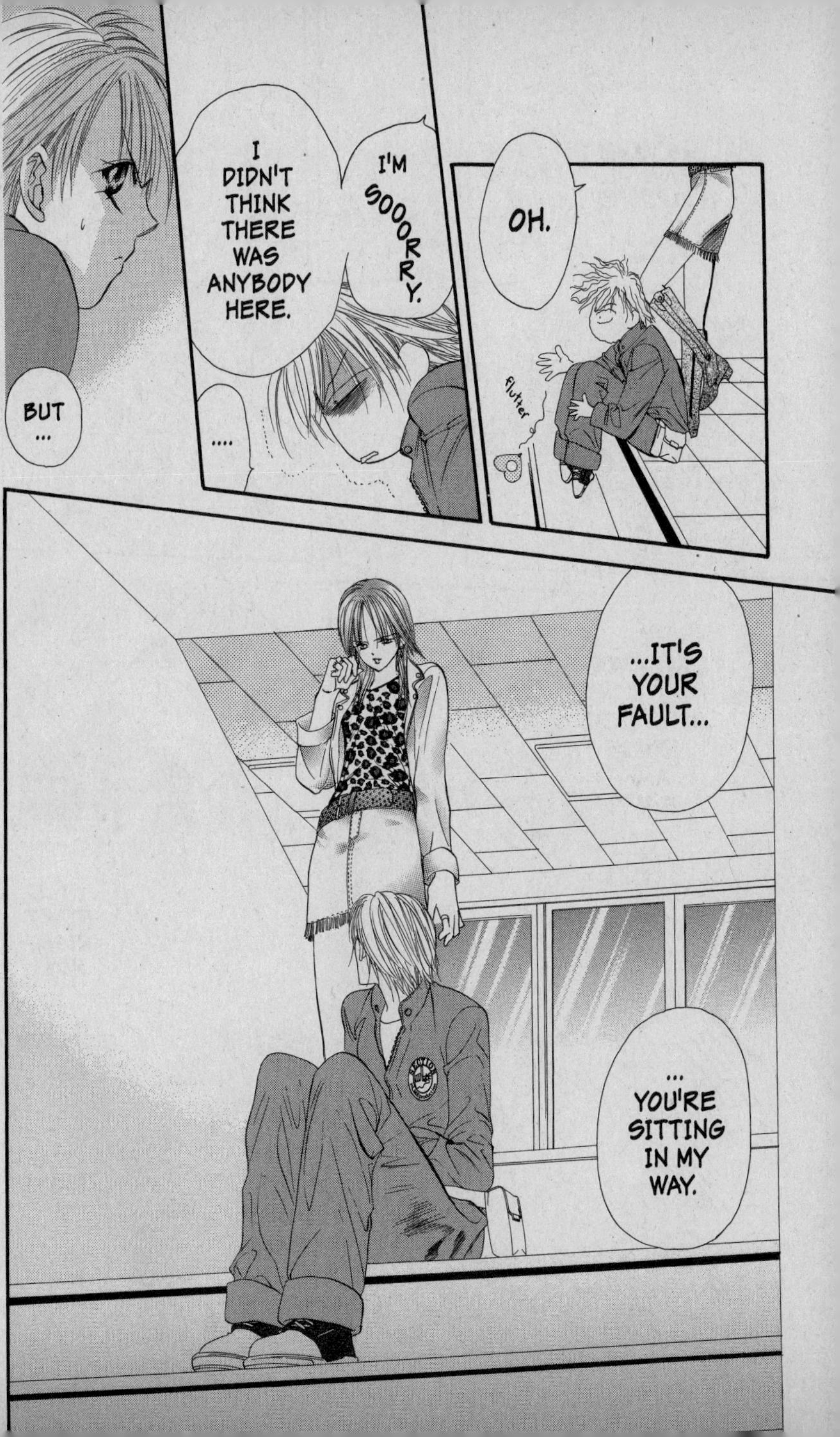
OH.
flutter
I'M SOOORRY.
I DIDN'T THINK THERE WAS ANYBODY HERE.
....
BUT ...
...IT'S YOUR FAULT...
... YOU'RE SITTING IN MY WAY.

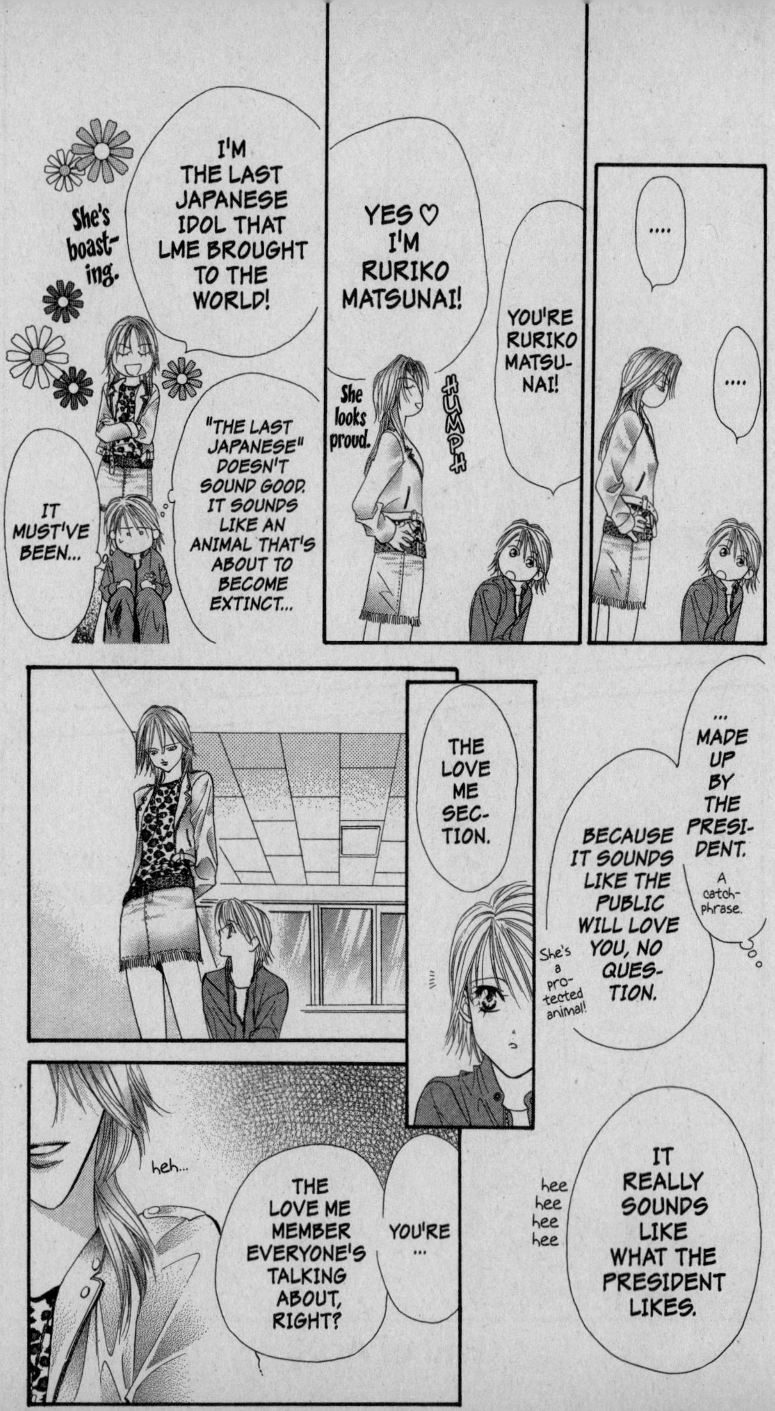
....
....
YOU'RE RURIKO MATSUNAI!
YES ♡ I'M RURIKO MATSUNAI!
HUMPH
She looks proud.
I'M THE LAST JAPANESE IDOL THAT LME BROUGHT TO THE WORLD!
She's boasting.
"THE LAST JAPANESE" DOESN'T SOUND GOOD. IT SOUNDS LIKE AN ANIMAL THAT'S ABOUT TO BECOME EXTINCT...
IT MUST'VE BEEN...
... MADE UP BY THE PRESIDENT.
A catch-phrase.
BECAUSE IT SOUNDS LIKE THE PUBLIC WILL LOVE YOU, NO QUESTION.
She's a protected animal!
THE LOVE ME SECTION.
IT REALLY SOUNDS LIKE WHAT THE PRESIDENT LIKES.
hee hee hee hee
YOU'RE ...
THE LOVE ME MEMBER EVERYONE'S TALKING ABOUT, RIGHT?
heh...

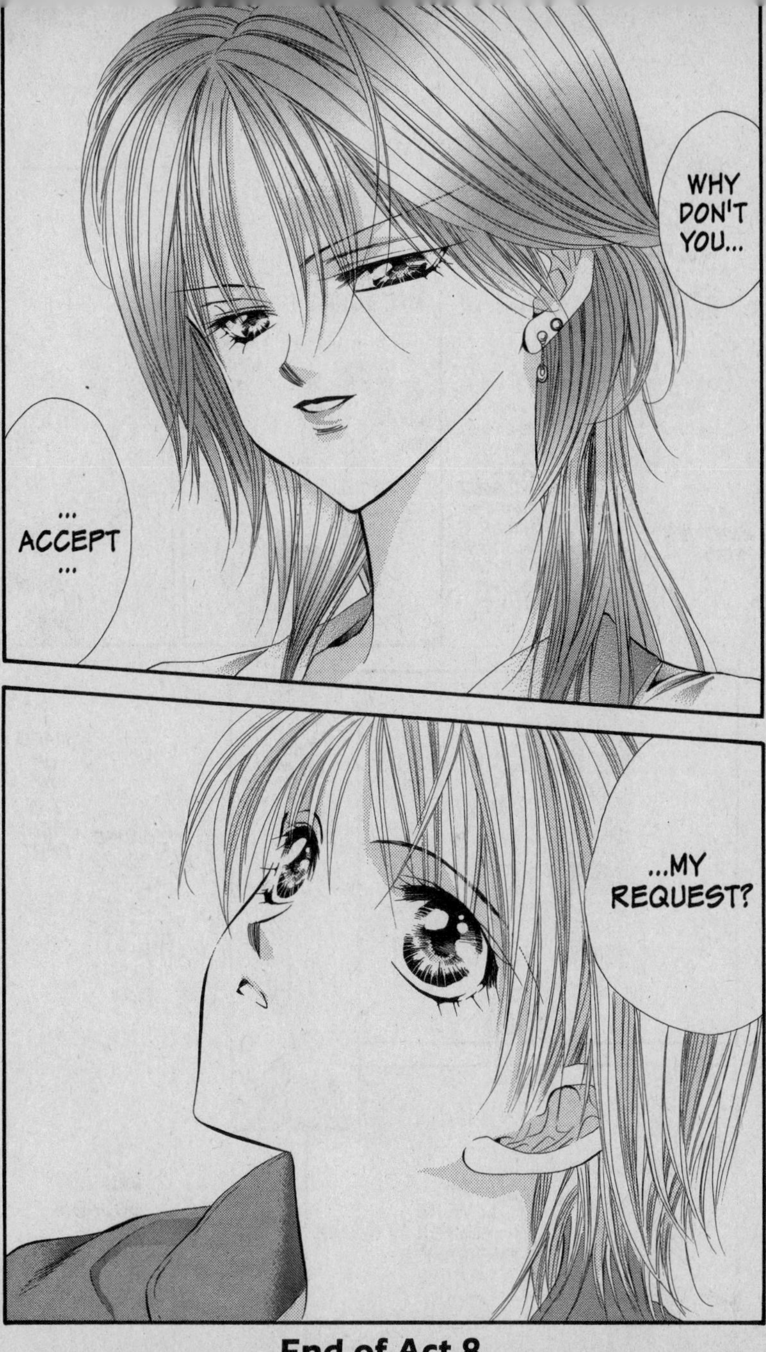
WHY DON'T YOU...
... ACCEPT ...
...MY REQUEST?

End of Act 8

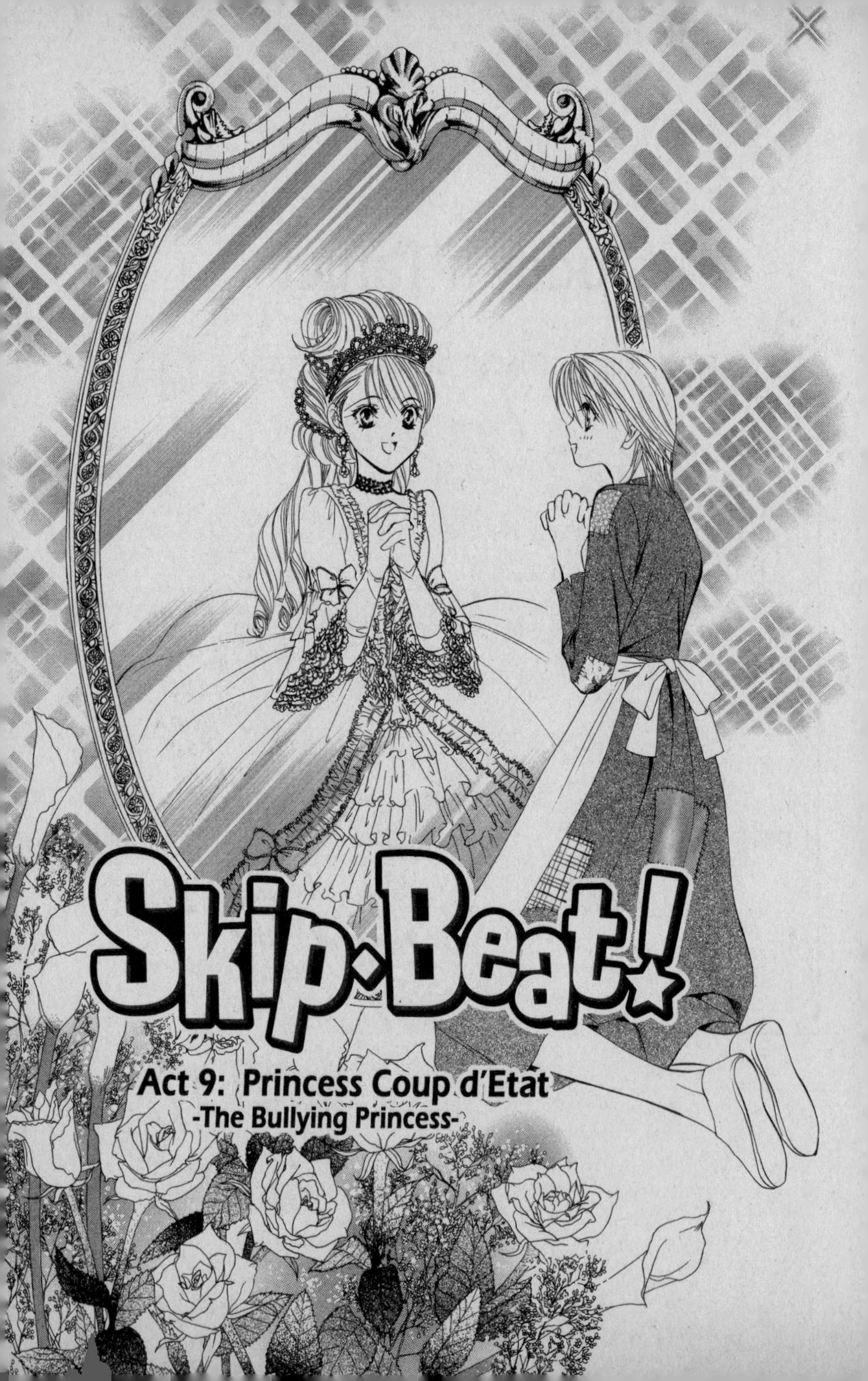
Skip·Beat!
Act 9: Princess Coup d'Etat
-The Bullying Princess-

Today's Target

Ruriko Matsunai (Idol Singer)

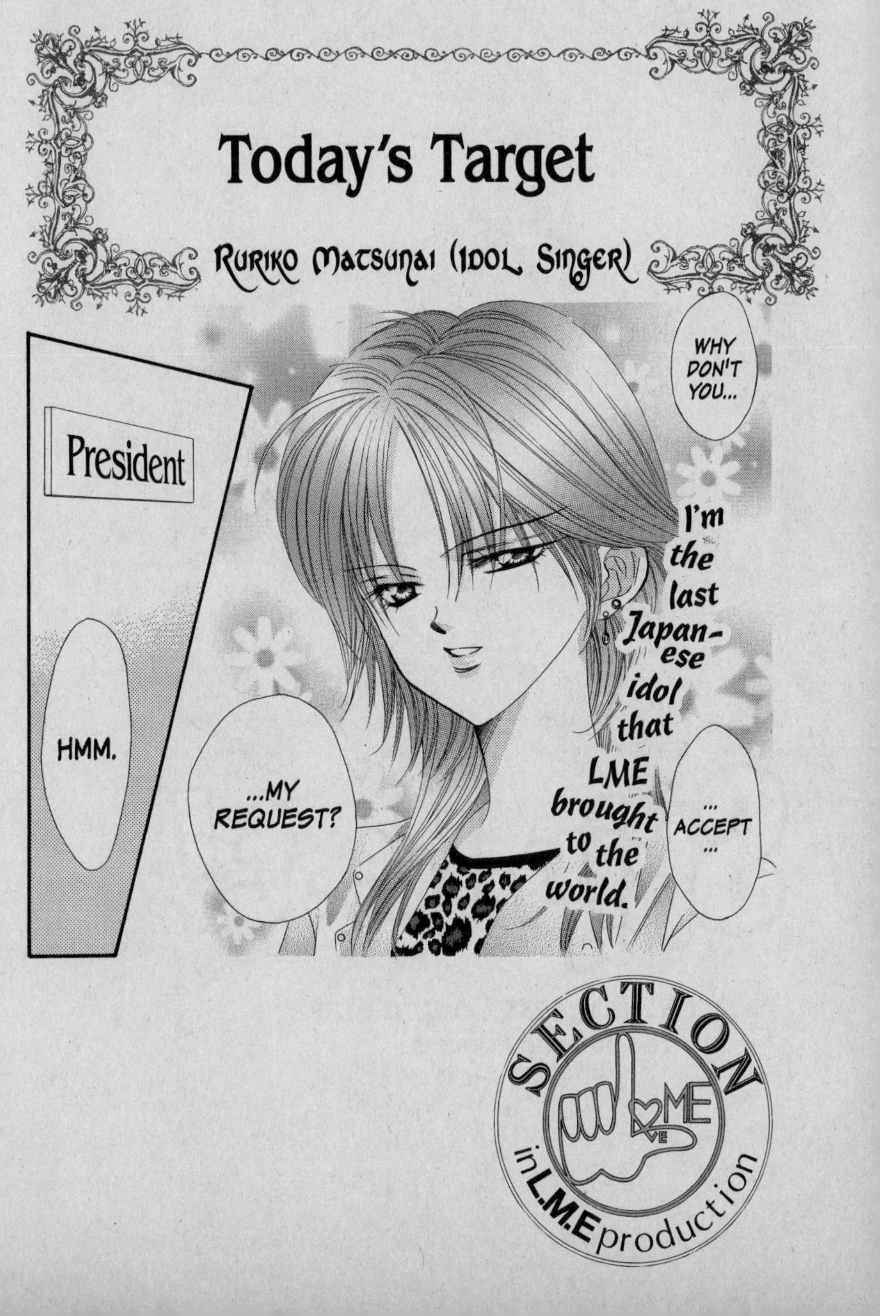

WHY DON'T YOU...
... ACCEPT ...
...MY REQUEST?
I'm the last Japanese idol that LME brought to the world.
President
HMM.

SECTION in L.M.E production

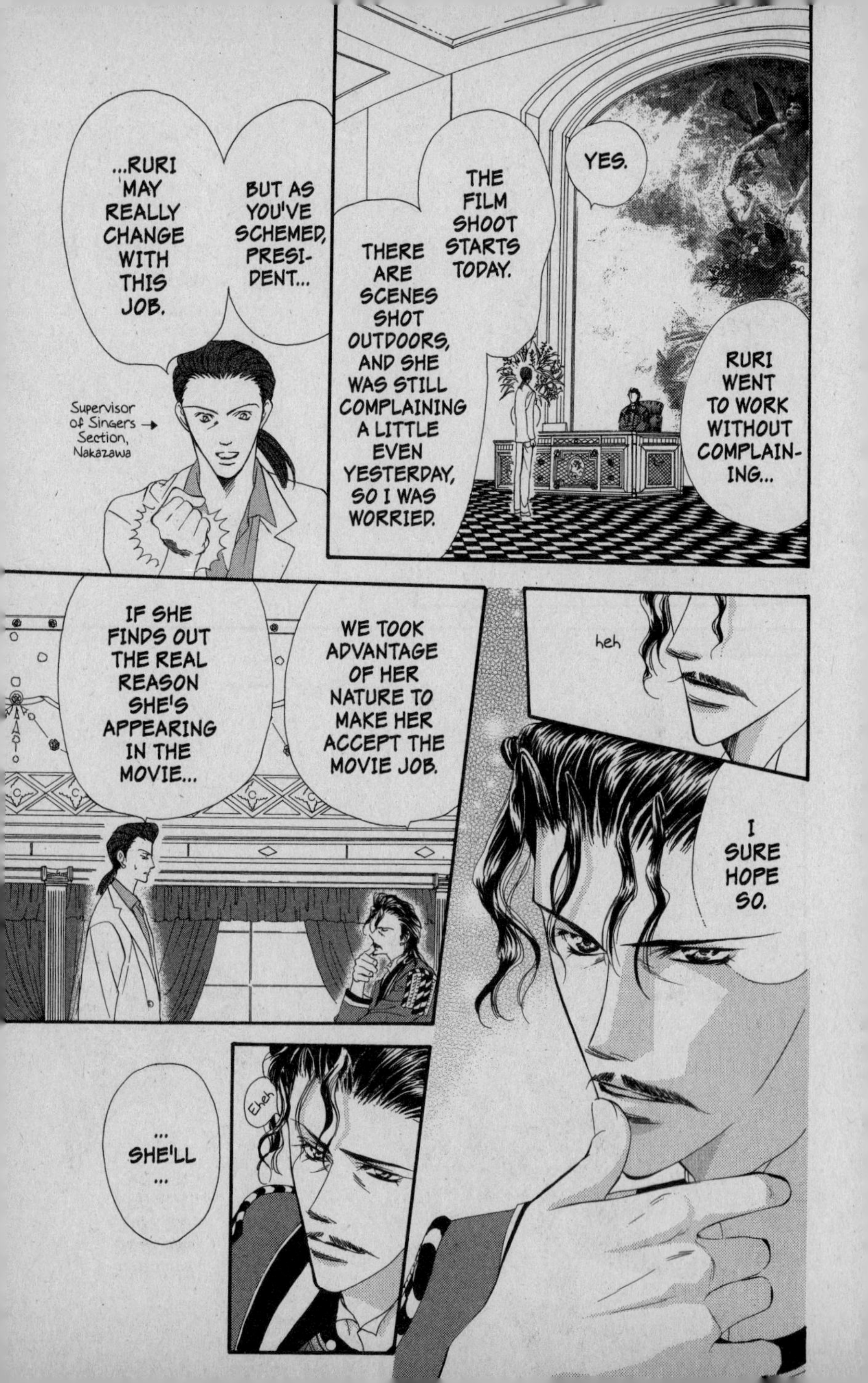

YES.
THE FILM SHOOT STARTS TODAY.
RURI WENT TO WORK WITHOUT COMPLAINING...
THERE ARE SCENES SHOT OUTDOORS, AND SHE WAS STILL COMPLAINING A LITTLE EVEN YESTERDAY, SO I WAS WORRIED.
BUT AS YOU'VE SCHEMED, PRESIDENT...
...RURI MAY REALLY CHANGE WITH THIS JOB.
Supervisor of Singers Section, Nakazawa
heh
I SURE HOPE SO.
WE TOOK ADVANTAGE OF HER NATURE TO MAKE HER ACCEPT THE MOVIE JOB.
IF SHE FINDS OUT THE REAL REASON SHE'S APPEARING IN THE MOVIE...
Eheh
... SHE'LL ...

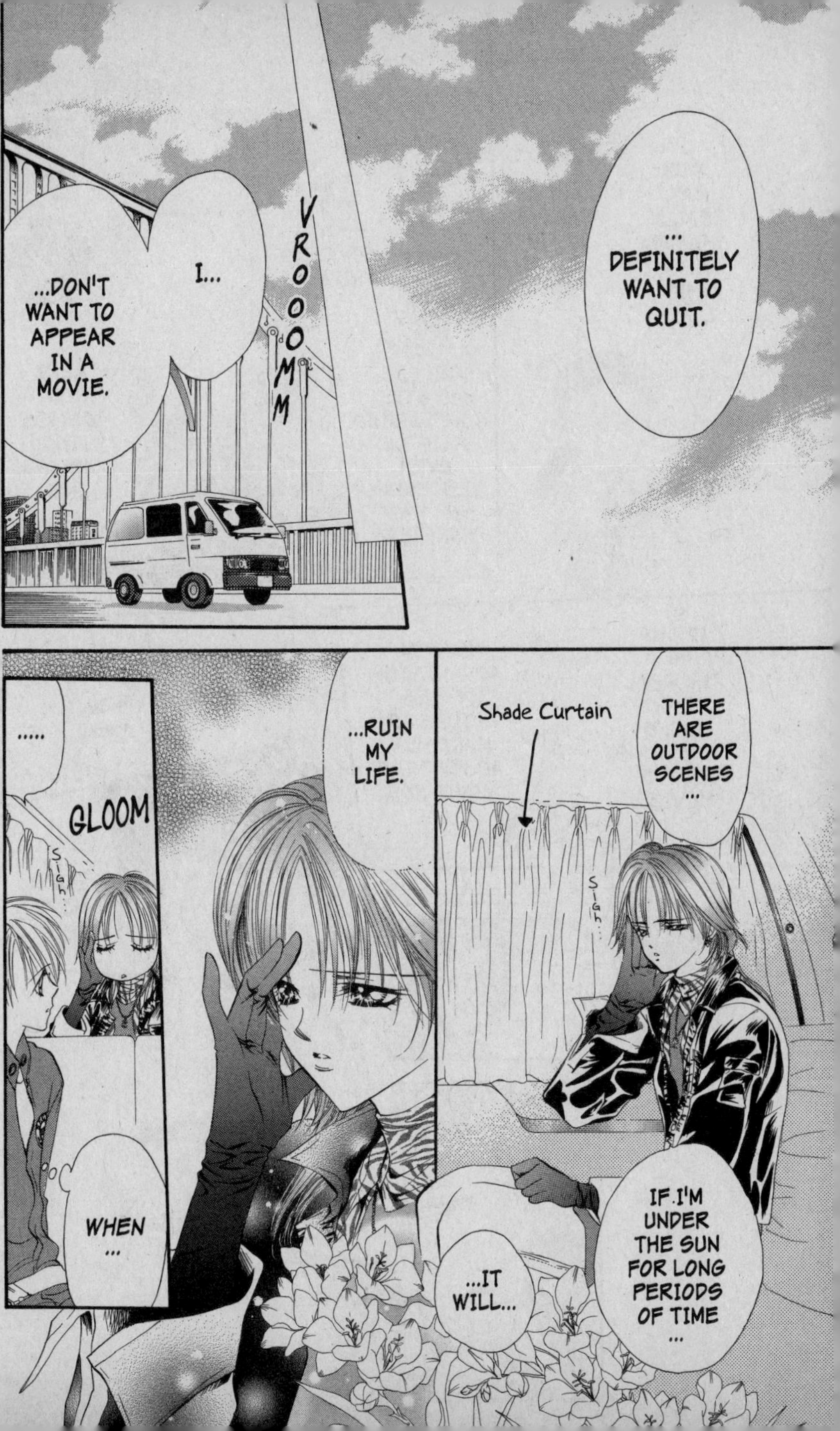

... DEFINITELY WANT TO QUIT.
VROOOMM
I...
...DON'T WANT TO APPEAR IN A MOVIE.
THERE ARE OUTDOOR SCENES ...
Shade Curtain
Sigh...
IF I'M UNDER THE SUN FOR LONG PERIODS OF TIME ...
...IT WILL...
...RUIN MY LIFE.
.....
GLOOM
Sigh...
WHEN ...

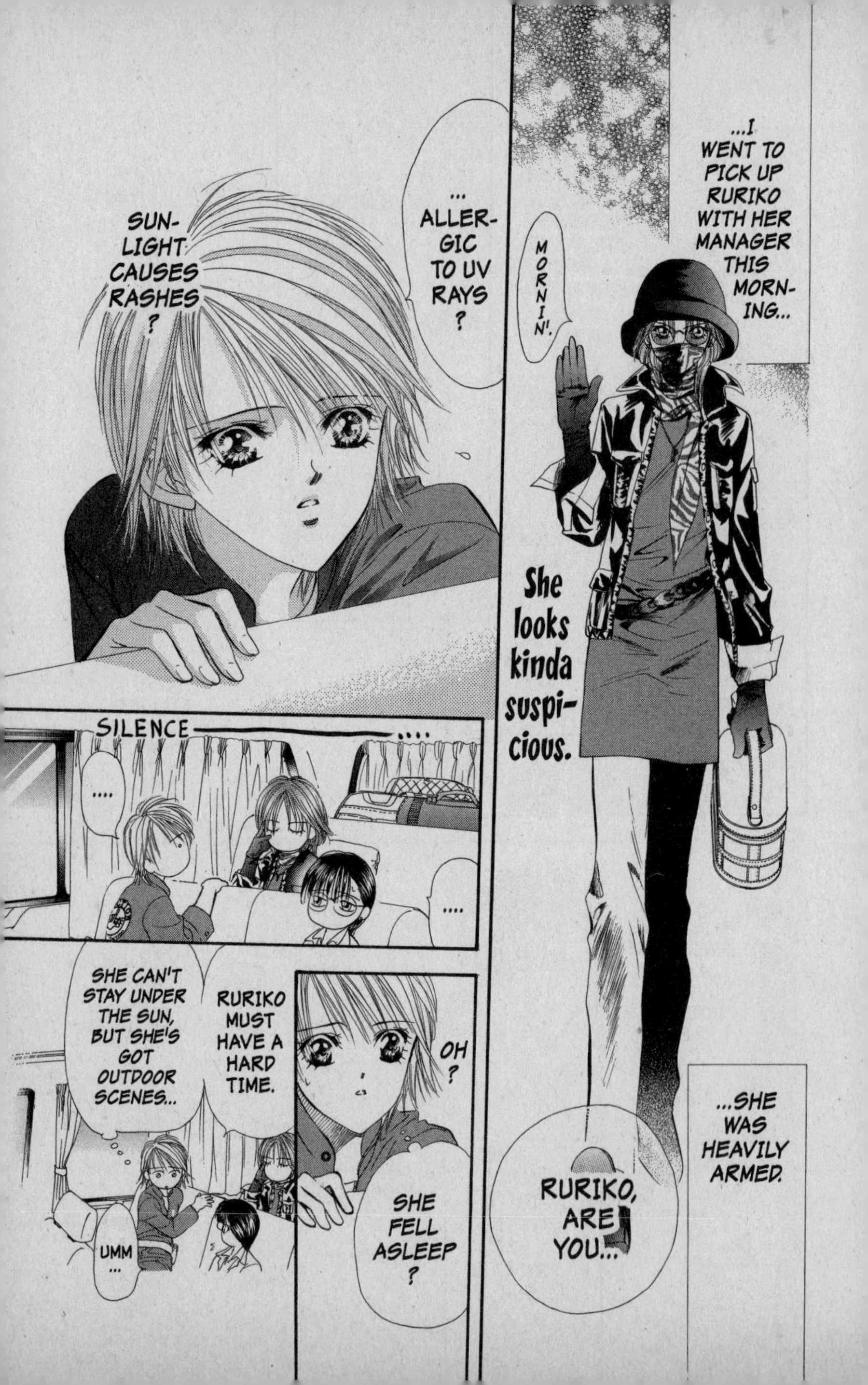
...I WENT TO PICK UP RURIKO WITH HER MANAGER THIS MORNING...
MORNIN'.
She looks kinda suspicious.
...SHE WAS HEAVILY ARMED.
RURIKO, ARE YOU...
...ALLERGIC TO UV RAYS?
SUNLIGHT CAUSES RASHES?
SILENCE....
....
....
OH?
SHE FELL ASLEEP?
RURIKO MUST HAVE A HARD TIME.
SHE CAN'T STAY UNDER THE SUN, BUT SHE'S GOT OUTDOOR SCENES...
UMM...

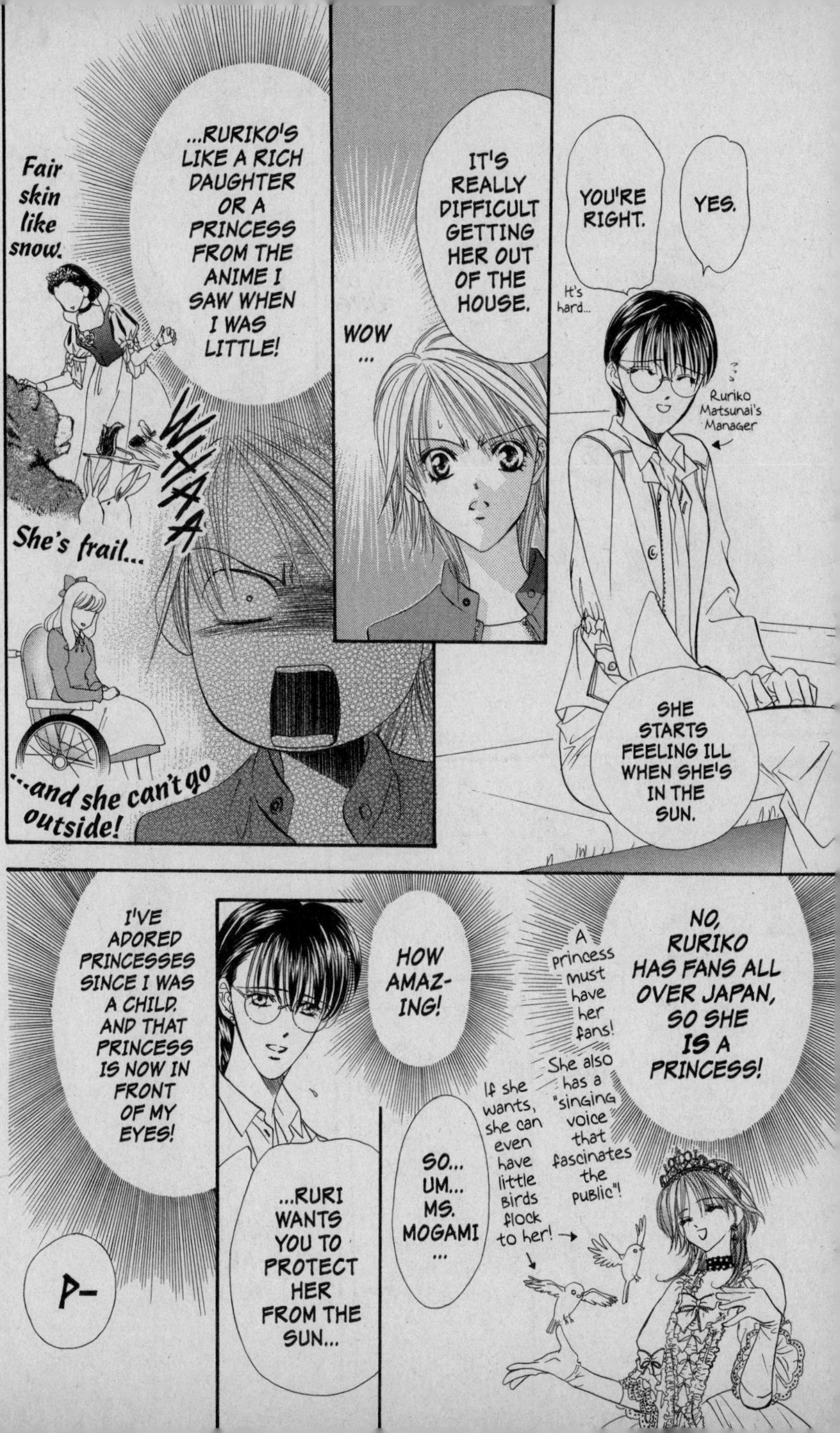
YES.
YOU'RE RIGHT.
It's hard...
Ruriko Matsunai's Manager
SHE STARTS FEELING ILL WHEN SHE'S IN THE SUN.
IT'S REALLY DIFFICULT GETTING HER OUT OF THE HOUSE.
WOW ...
...RURIKO'S LIKE A RICH DAUGHTER OR A PRINCESS FROM THE ANIME I SAW WHEN I WAS LITTLE!
WHAAA
Fair skin like snow.
She's frail...
...and she can't go outside!
NO, RURIKO HAS FANS ALL OVER JAPAN, SO SHE IS A PRINCESS!
A princess must have her fans!
She also has a "singing voice that fascinates the public"!
If she wants, she can even have little birds flock to her!
HOW AMAZ-ING!
SO... UM... MS. MOGAMI ...
...RURI WANTS YOU TO PROTECT HER FROM THE SUN...
I'VE ADORED PRINCESSES SINCE I WAS A CHILD. AND THAT PRINCESS IS NOW IN FRONT OF MY EYES!
P-

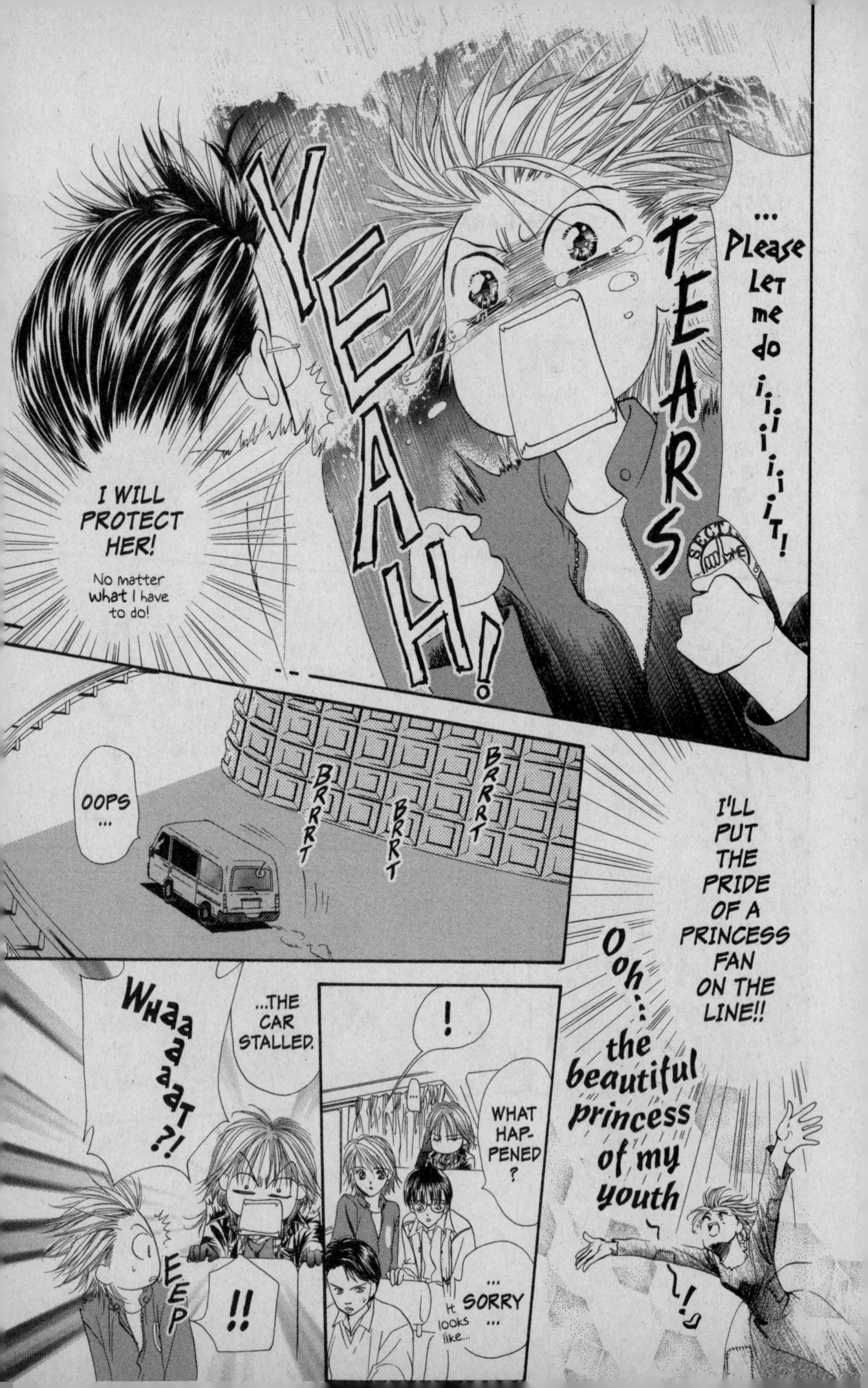
...Please let me do iiiiiiit!
TEARS
YEAH!
I WILL PROTECT HER!
No matter what I have to do!
BRRRT
BRRT
BRRRT
OOPS ...
I'LL PUT THE PRIDE OF A PRINCESS FAN ON THE LINE!!
Ooh... the beautiful princess of my youth ~ ~!
!
...
WHAT HAP-PENED ?
... SORRY ...
It looks like...
...THE CAR STALLED.
Whaaaaaat ?!
EEP
!!

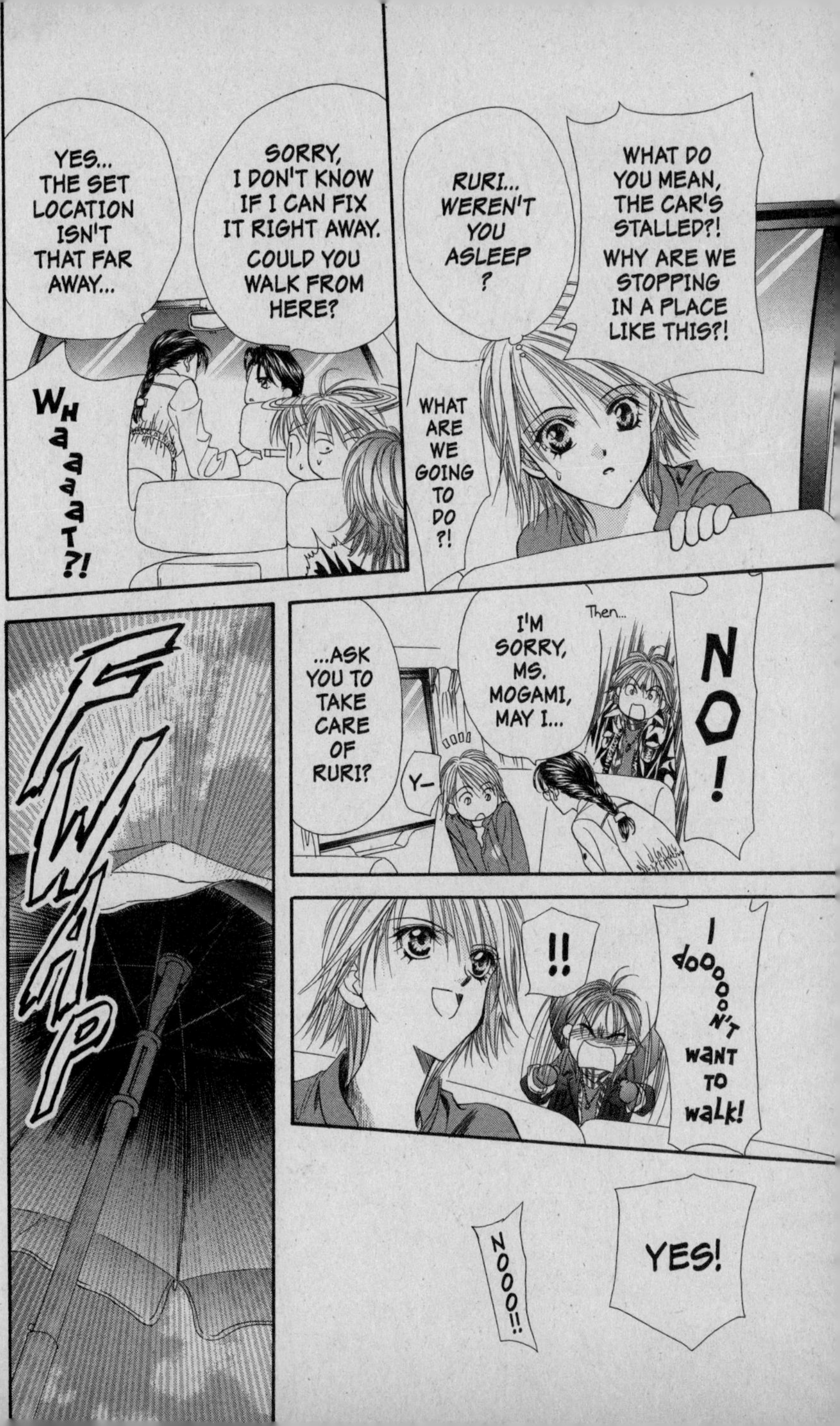
WHAT DO YOU MEAN, THE CAR'S STALLED?!
WHY ARE WE STOPPING IN A PLACE LIKE THIS?!
RURI... WEREN'T YOU ASLEEP?
WHAT ARE WE GOING TO DO?!
SORRY, I DON'T KNOW IF I CAN FIX IT RIGHT AWAY.
COULD YOU WALK FROM HERE?
YES... THE SET LOCATION ISN'T THAT FAR AWAY...
WHaaaaaT?!
NO!
Then...
I'M SORRY, MS. MOGAMI, MAY I...
...ASK YOU TO TAKE CARE OF RURI?
Y–
I dooooooon't want to walk!
!!
YES!
NOOOO!!
FWAP

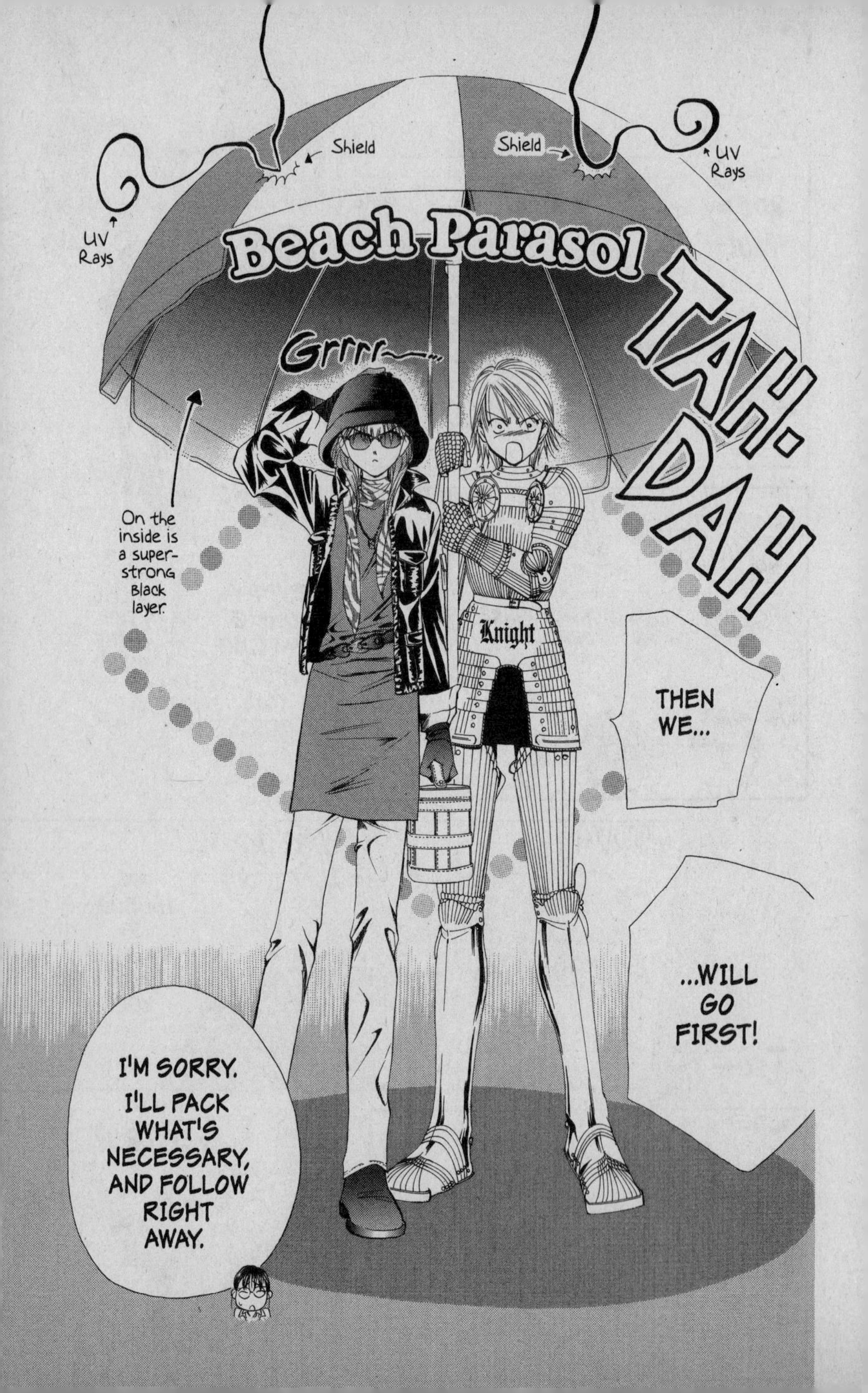
UV Rays
Shield
Shield
UV Rays
Beach Parasol
TAH-DAH
Grrrr...
On the inside is a super-strong Black layer.
Knight
THEN WE...
...WILL GO FIRST!
I'M SORRY. I'LL PACK WHAT'S NECESSARY, AND FOLLOW RIGHT AWAY.

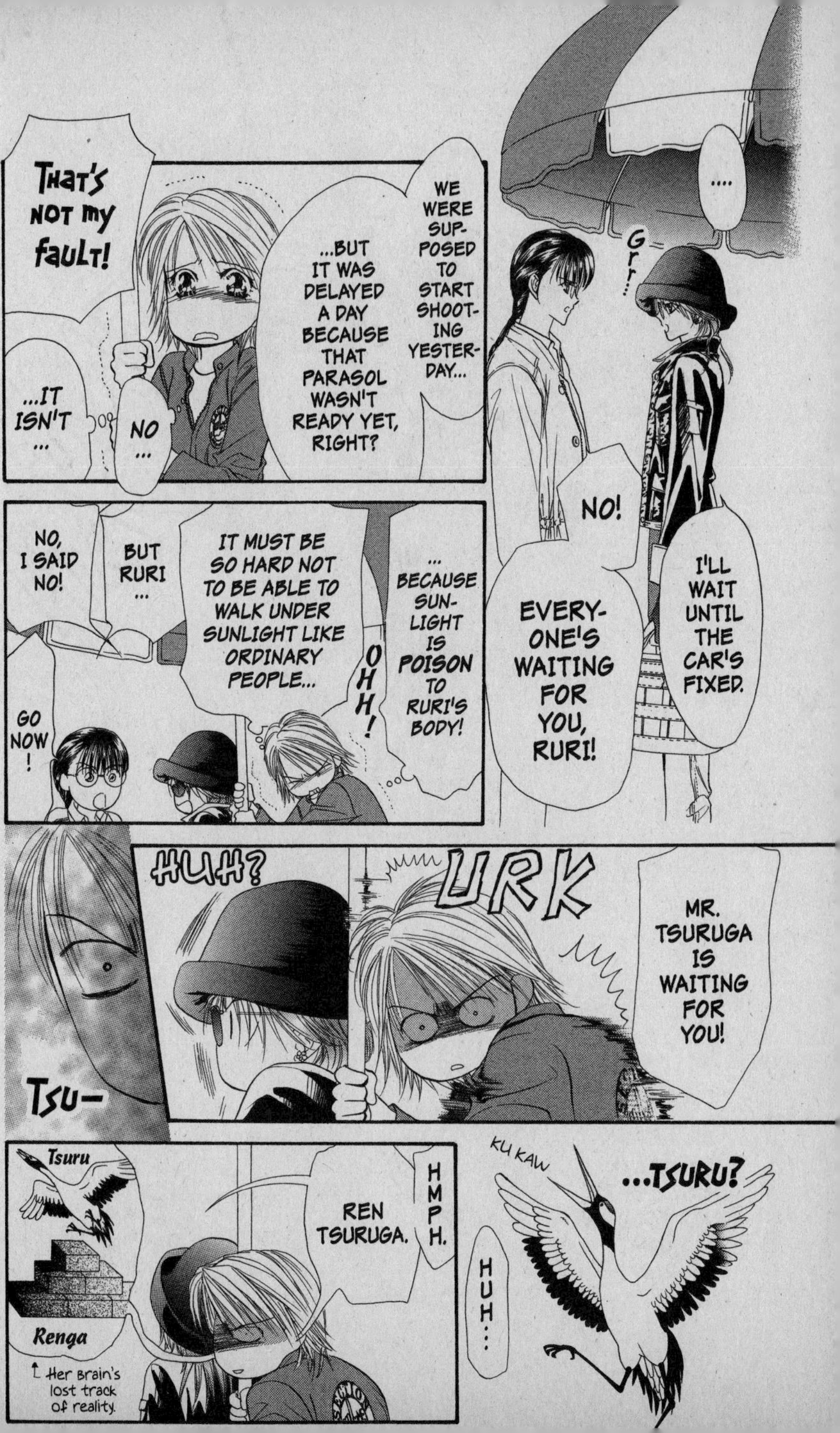
....
Grr...
I'LL WAIT UNTIL THE CAR'S FIXED.
NO!
EVERYONE'S WAITING FOR YOU, RURI!
WE WERE SUPPOSED TO START SHOOTING YESTERDAY...
...BUT IT WAS DELAYED A DAY BECAUSE THAT PARASOL WASN'T READY YET, RIGHT?
THAT'S NOT MY FAULT!
NO...
...IT ISN'T...
...BECAUSE SUNLIGHT IS POISON TO RURI'S BODY!
OHH!
IT MUST BE SO HARD NOT TO BE ABLE TO WALK UNDER SUNLIGHT LIKE ORDINARY PEOPLE...
BUT RURI...
NO, I SAID NO!
GO NOW!
MR. TSURUGA IS WAITING FOR YOU!
URK
HUH?
TSU-
...TSURU?
KU KAW
HUH...
HMPH.
REN TSURUGA.
Tsuru
Renga
↑ Her brain's lost track of reality.

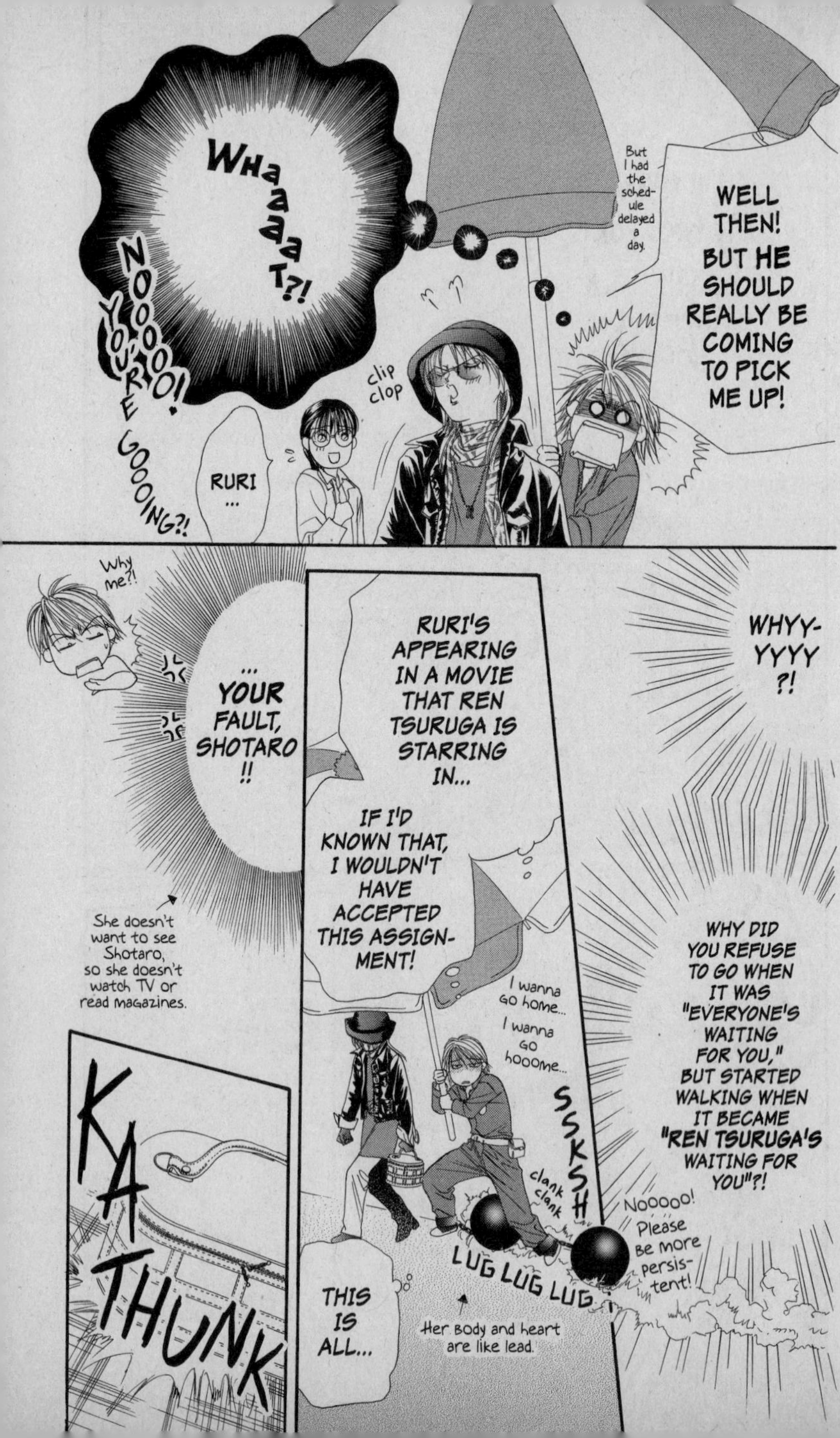
WELL THEN! BUT HE SHOULD REALLY BE COMING TO PICK ME UP!
But I had the sched-ule delayed a day.
WHaaaaT?!
clip clop
NOOOOOO! YOU'RE GOOOOING?!
RURI ...
WHYY-YYYY?!
WHY DID YOU REFUSE TO GO WHEN IT WAS "EVERYONE'S WAITING FOR YOU," BUT STARTED WALKING WHEN IT BECAME "REN TSURUGA'S WAITING FOR YOU"?!
Nooooo! Please be more persis-tent!
RURI'S APPEARING IN A MOVIE THAT REN TSURUGA IS STARRING IN...
IF I'D KNOWN THAT, I WOULDN'T HAVE ACCEPTED THIS ASSIGN-MENT!
I wanna go home...
I wanna go hooome...
SSKSH
clank clank
LUG LUG LUG
THIS IS ALL...
Her body and heart are like lead.
Why me?!
... YOUR FAULT, SHOTARO !!
She doesn't want to see Shotaro, so she doesn't watch TV or read magazines.
KA THUNK

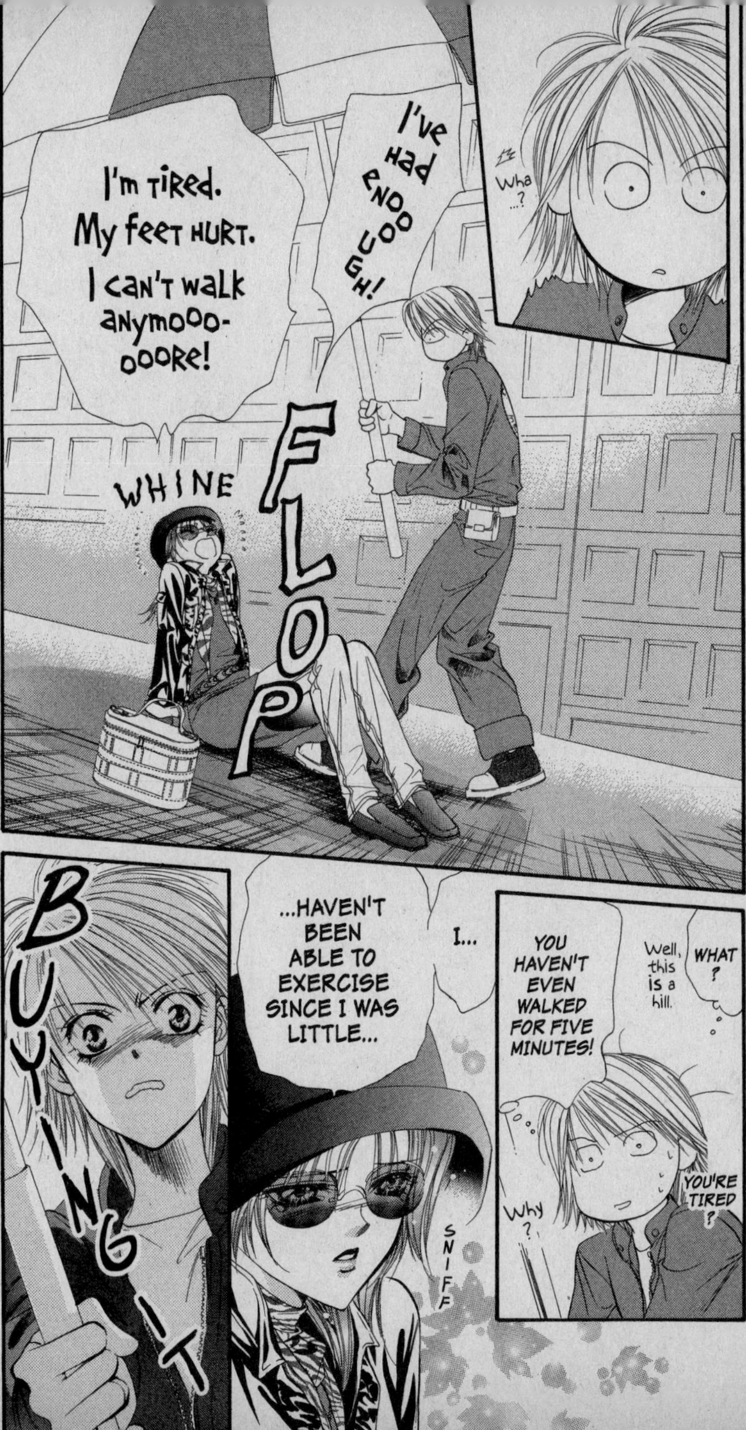
Wha...?
I've had eNOOOOUGH!
I'm tired. My feet HURT. I can't walk anymoooooore!
WHINE
FLOP
WHAT?
Well, this is a hill.
YOU HAVEN'T EVEN WALKED FOR FIVE MINUTES!
YOU'RE TIRED?
Why?
I...
...HAVEN'T BEEN ABLE TO EXERCISE SINCE I WAS LITTLE...
SNIFF
BUYING IT

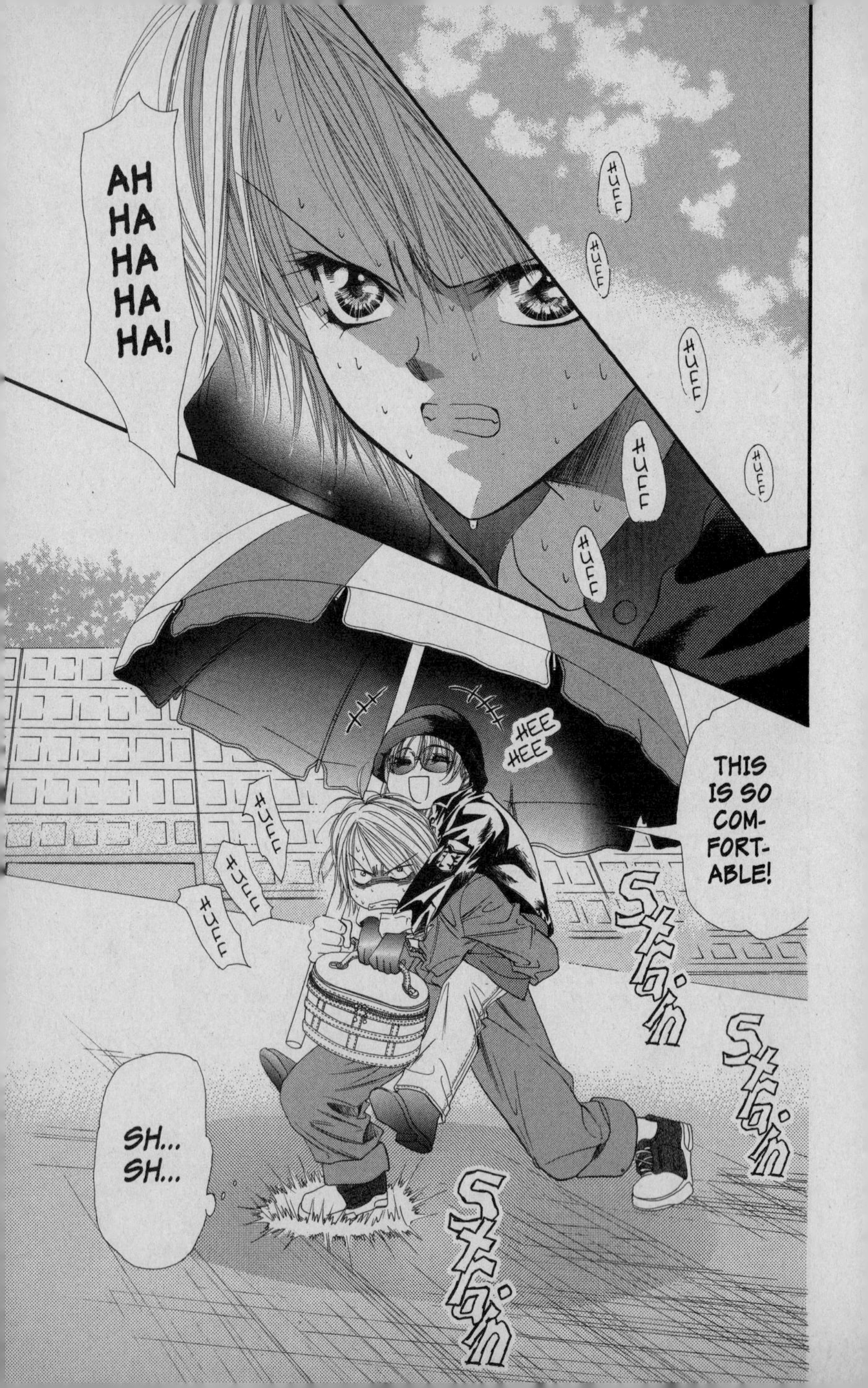
HUFF
HUFF
HUFF
HUFF
HUFF
HUFF
AH HA HA HA HA!
THIS IS SO COM-FORT-ABLE!
HEE HEE
Stain
Stain
HUFF
HUFF
HUFF
Stain
SH... SH...

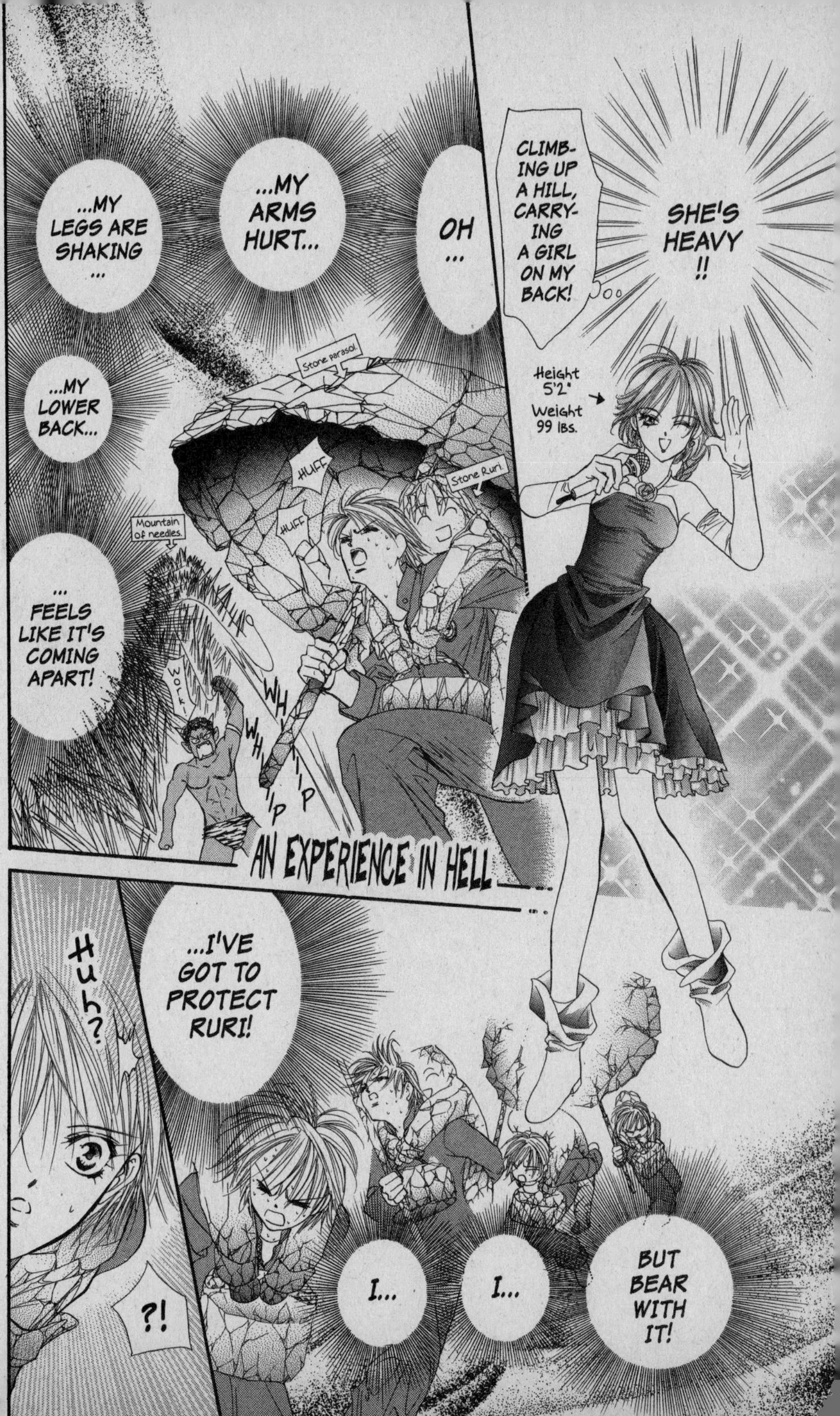
CLIMB-ING UP A HILL, CARRY-ING A GIRL ON MY BACK!
SHE'S HEAVY !!
Height 5'2" Weight 99 lbs.
OH ...
...MY ARMS HURT...
...MY LEGS ARE SHAKING ...
...MY LOWER BACK...
Stone parasol.
Stone Ruri.
HUFF
HUFF
Mountain of needles.
... FEELS LIKE IT'S COMING APART!
Work!
WHIP
WHIP
AN EXPERIENCE IN HELL
BUT BEAR WITH IT!
I...
I...
...I'VE GOT TO PROTECT RURI!
Huh?
?!

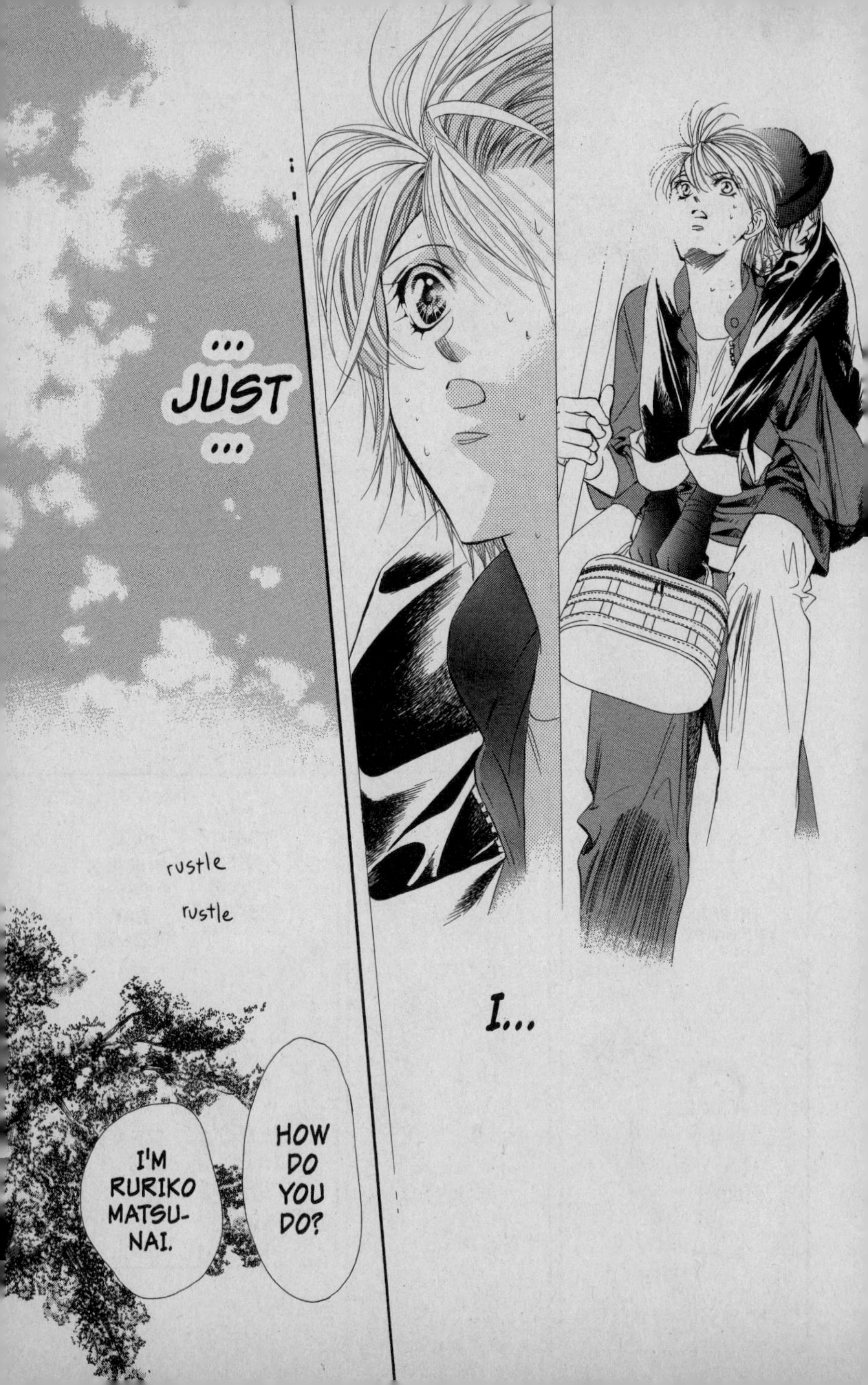

I...
... JUST ...
rustle
rustle
HOW DO YOU DO?
I'M RURIKO MATSUNAI.

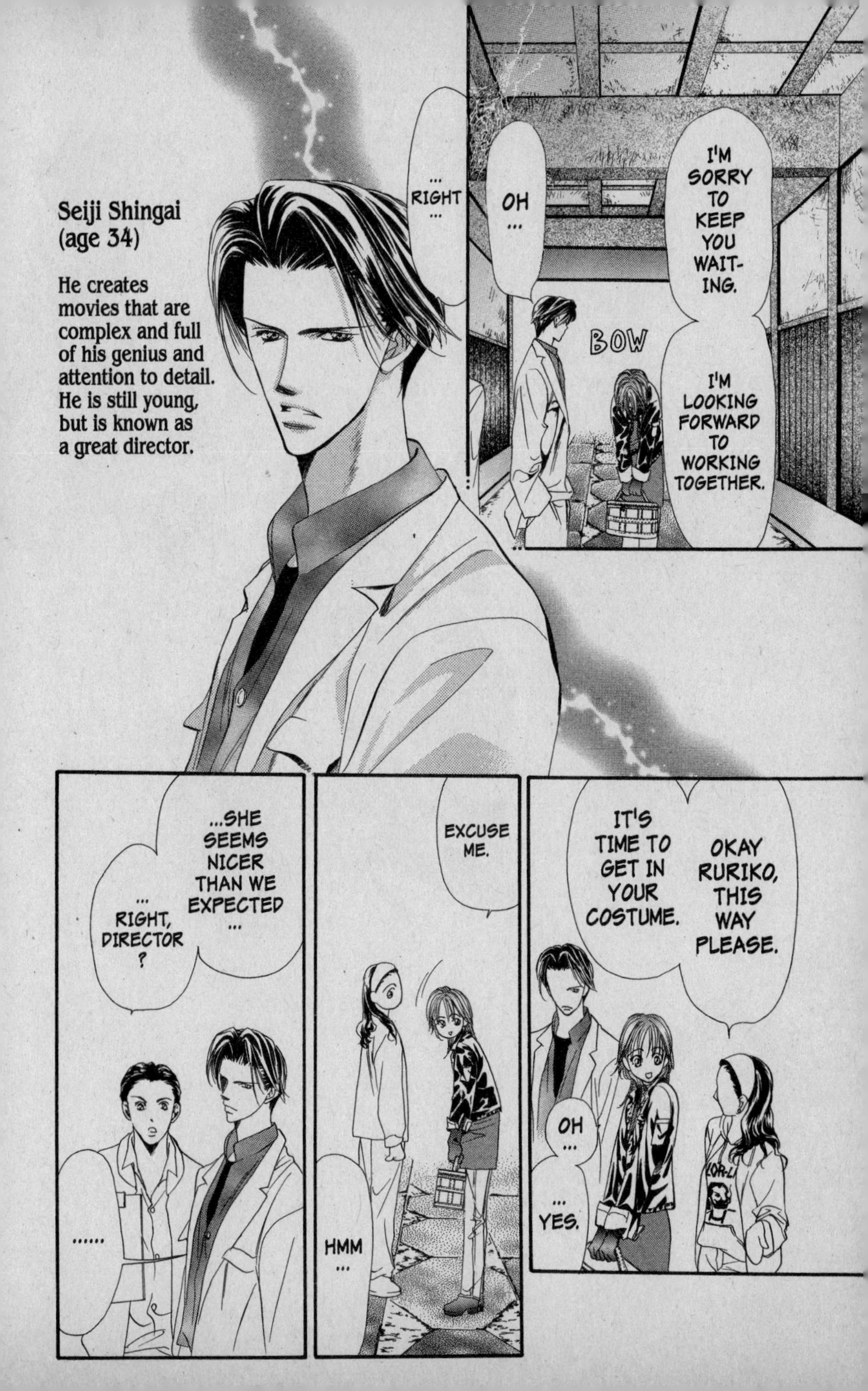
I'M SORRY TO KEEP YOU WAIT-ING.
I'M LOOKING FORWARD TO WORKING TOGETHER.
BOW
OH ...
... RIGHT ...
Seiji Shingai (age 34)
He creates movies that are complex and full of his genius and attention to detail. He is still young, but is known as a great director.
OKAY RURIKO, THIS WAY PLEASE.
IT'S TIME TO GET IN YOUR COSTUME.
OH ...
... YES.
EXCUSE ME.
HMM ...
...SHE SEEMS NICER THAN WE EXPECTED ...
... RIGHT, DIRECTOR ?
......

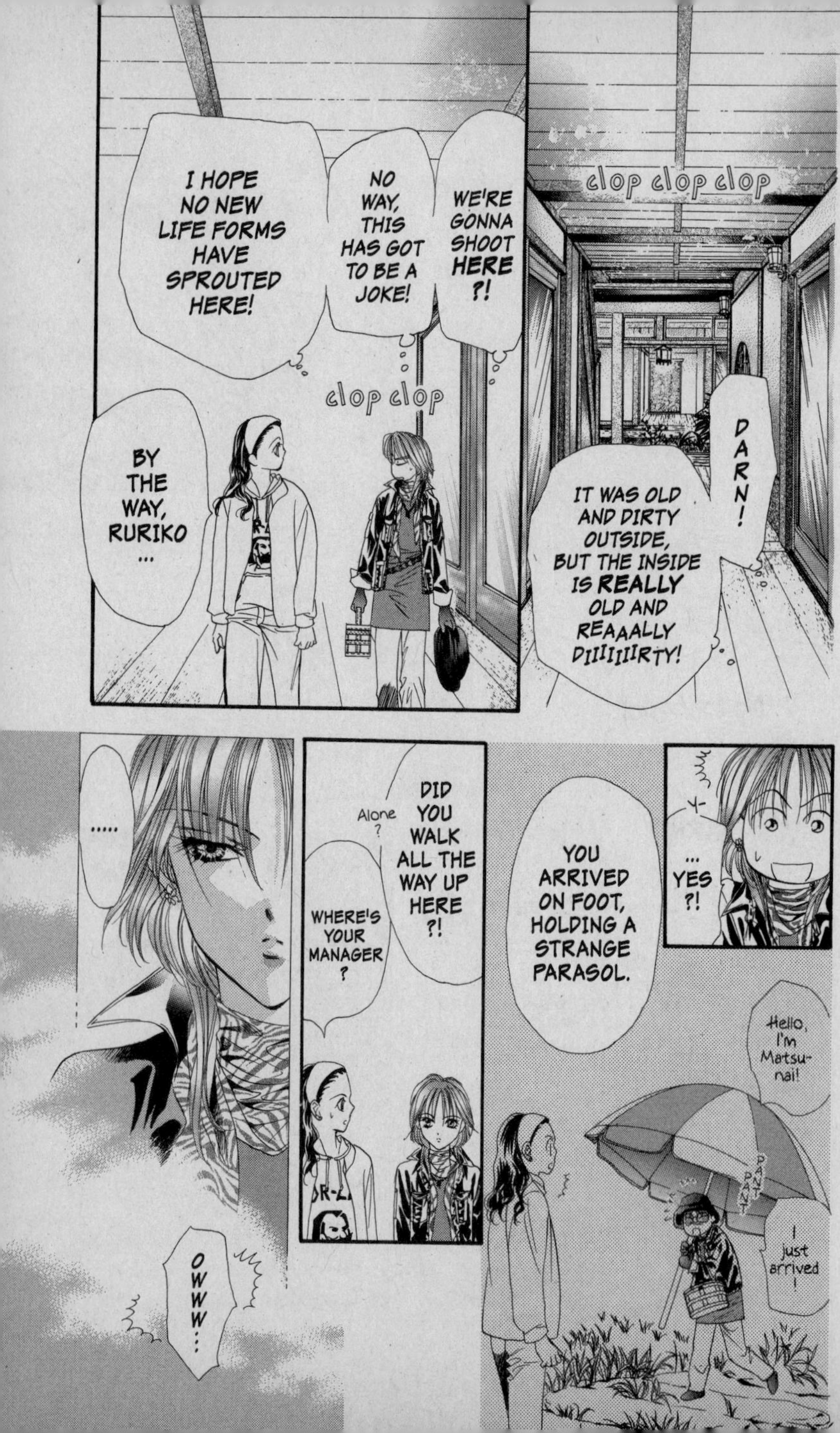
clop clop clop
DARN!
IT WAS OLD AND DIRTY OUTSIDE, BUT THE INSIDE IS REALLY OLD AND REAAALLY DIIIIIIIRTY!
WE'RE GONNA SHOOT HERE?!
NO WAY, THIS HAS GOT TO BE A JOKE!
I HOPE NO NEW LIFE FORMS HAVE SPROUTED HERE!
clop clop
BY THE WAY, RURIKO...
...YES?!
YOU ARRIVED ON FOOT, HOLDING A STRANGE PARASOL.
Hello, I'm Matsunai!
PANT PANT
I just arrived!
DID YOU WALK ALL THE WAY UP HERE?!
Alone?
WHERE'S YOUR MANAGER?
.....
OWWW...

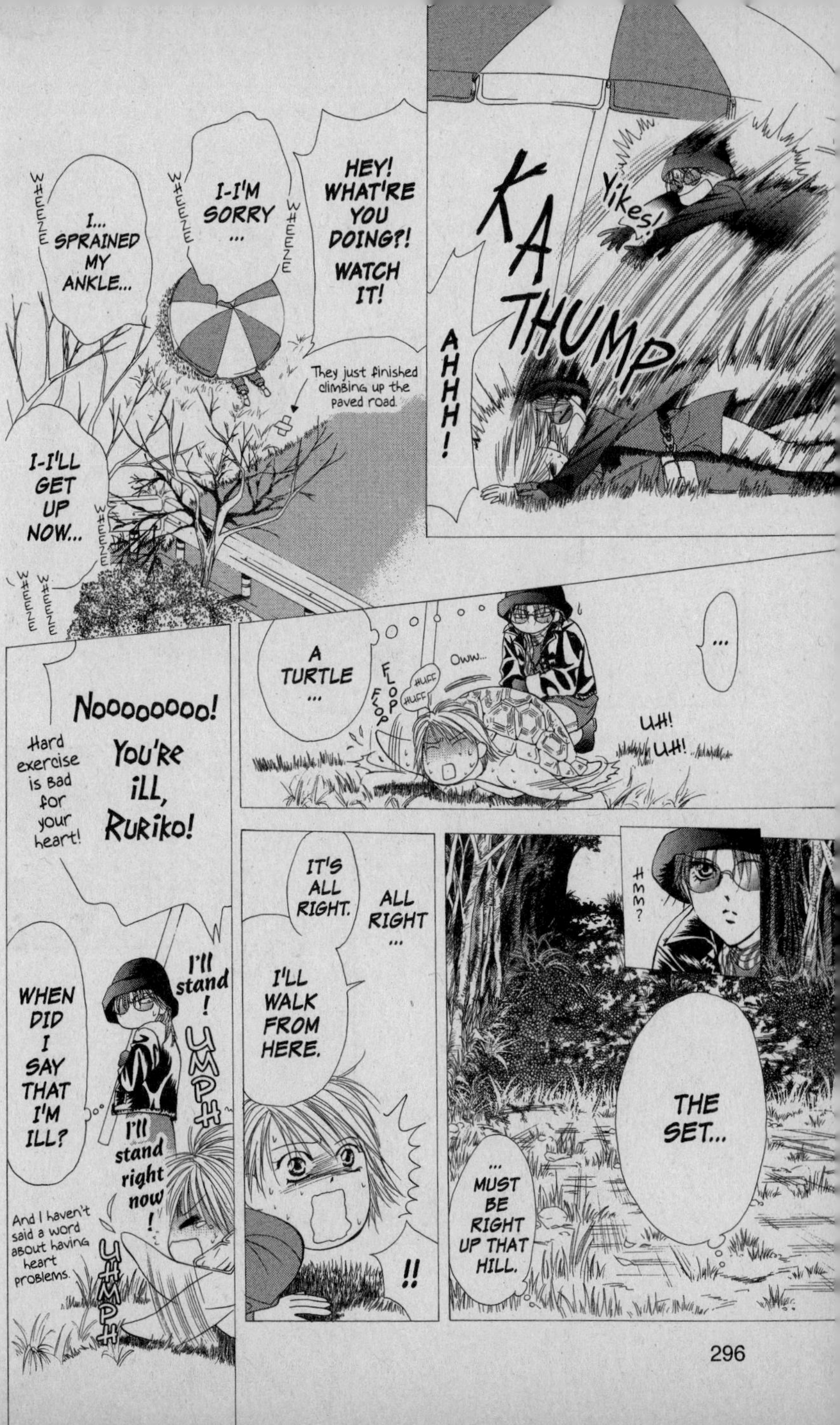
Yikes!
KA THUMP
AHHH!
HEY! WHAT'RE YOU DOING?! WATCH IT!
WHEEZE
I-I'M SORRY...
WHEEZE
I... SPRAINED MY ANKLE...
WHEEZE
They just finished climbing up the paved road.
I-I'LL GET UP NOW...
WHEEZE
WHEEZE
WHEEZE
...
UH! UH!
Oww...
HUFF HUFF
FLOP FLOP
A TURTLE...
HMM?
THE SET...
... MUST BE RIGHT UP THAT HILL.
IT'S ALL RIGHT.
ALL RIGHT...
I'LL WALK FROM HERE.
!!
Noooooooo!
You're ill, Ruriko!
Hard exercise is bad for your heart!
WHEN DID I SAY THAT I'M ILL?
I'll stand!
UMPH
I'll stand right now!
And I haven't said a word about having heart problems.
UMPH

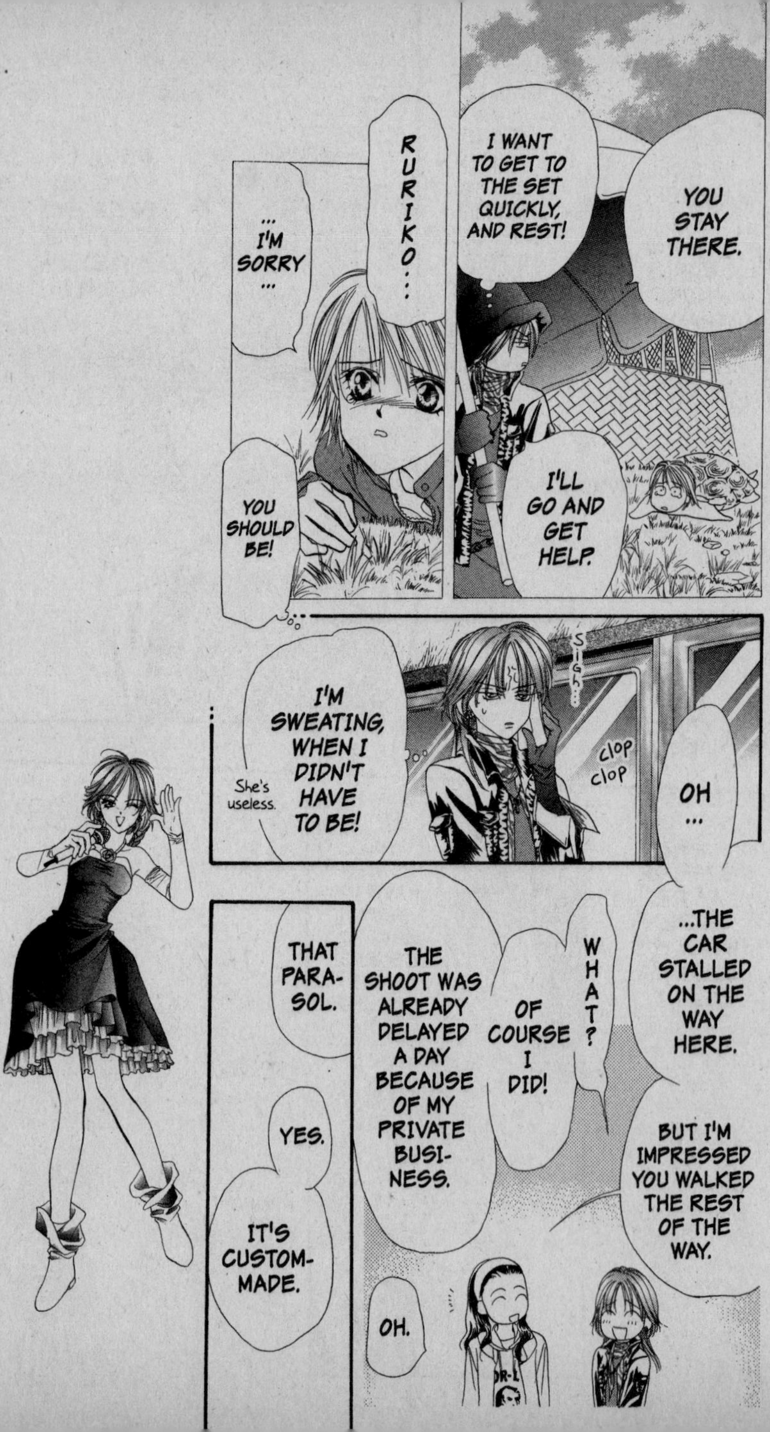
YOU STAY THERE.
I WANT TO GET TO THE SET QUICKLY, AND REST!
I'LL GO AND GET HELP.
RURIKO...
...I'M SORRY...
YOU SHOULD BE!
Sigh...
clop clop
I'M SWEATING, WHEN I DIDN'T HAVE TO BE!
She's useless.
OH...
...THE CAR STALLED ON THE WAY HERE.
BUT I'M IMPRESSED YOU WALKED THE REST OF THE WAY.
WHAT?
OF COURSE I DID!
THE SHOOT WAS ALREADY DELAYED A DAY BECAUSE OF MY PRIVATE BUSINESS.
OH.
THAT PARASOL.
YES.
IT'S CUSTOM-MADE.

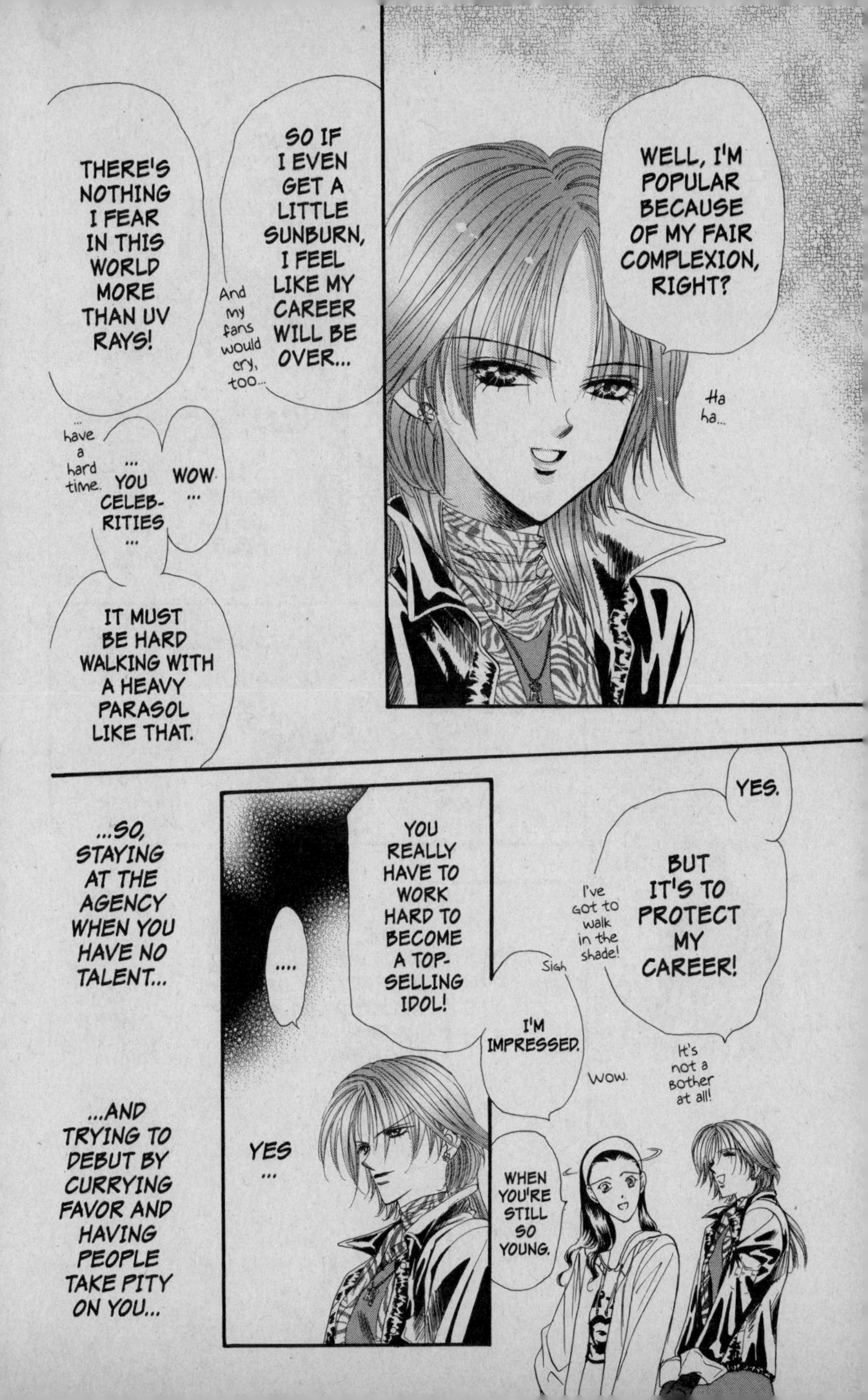
WELL, I'M POPULAR BECAUSE OF MY FAIR COMPLEXION, RIGHT?
Ha ha...
SO IF I EVEN GET A LITTLE SUNBURN, I FEEL LIKE MY CAREER WILL BE OVER...
And my fans would cry, too...
THERE'S NOTHING I FEAR IN THIS WORLD MORE THAN UV RAYS!
WOW...
...YOU CELEBRITIES...
...have a hard time.
IT MUST BE HARD WALKING WITH A HEAVY PARASOL LIKE THAT.
YES.
BUT IT'S TO PROTECT MY CAREER!
I've got to walk in the shade!
Sigh
I'M IMPRESSED.
Wow.
It's not a bother at all!
WHEN YOU'RE STILL SO YOUNG.
YOU REALLY HAVE TO WORK HARD TO BECOME A TOP-SELLING IDOL!
....
YES...
...SO, STAYING AT THE AGENCY WHEN YOU HAVE NO TALENT...
...AND TRYING TO DEBUT BY CURRYING FAVOR AND HAVING PEOPLE TAKE PITY ON YOU...

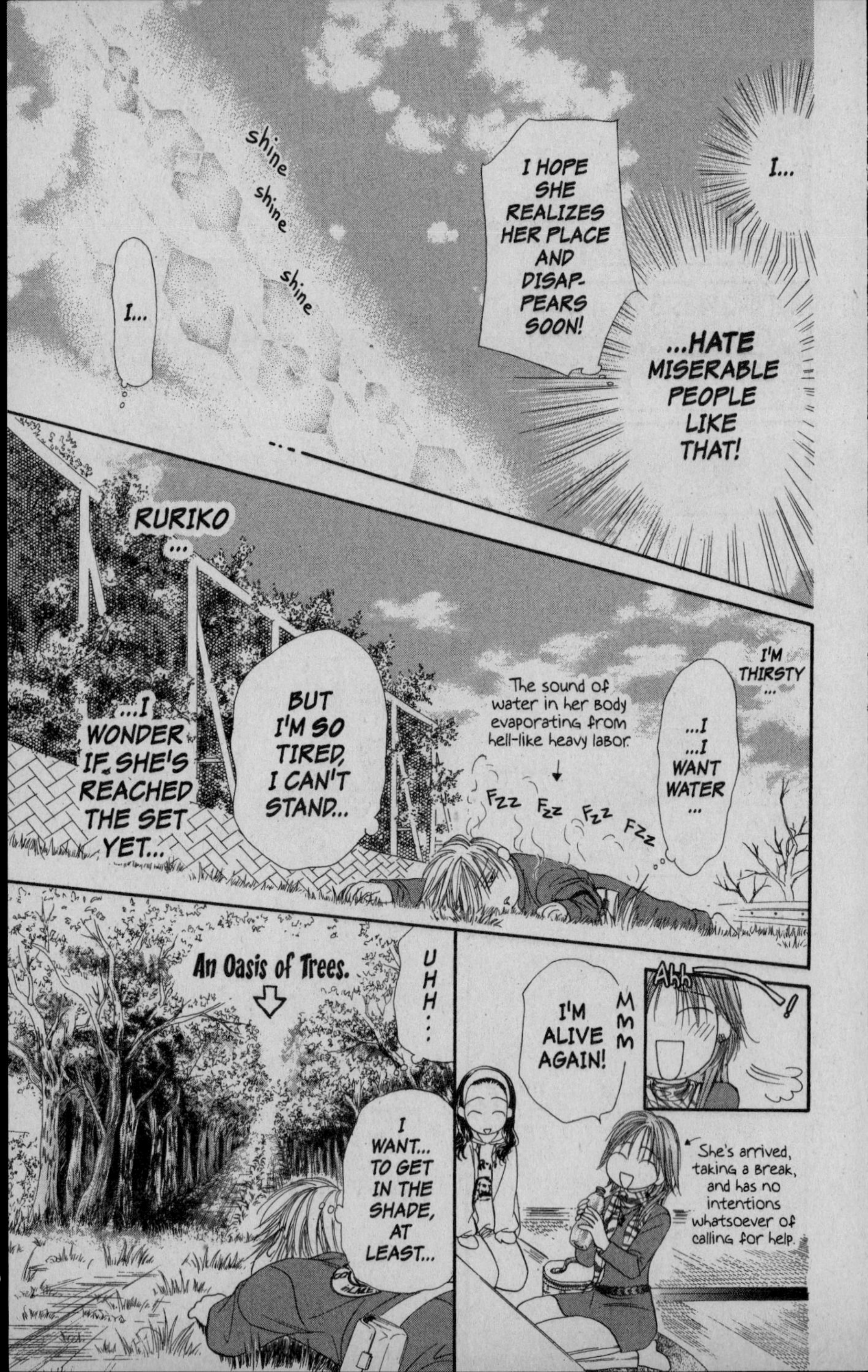
I...
I HOPE SHE REALIZES HER PLACE AND DISAP-PEARS SOON!
...HATE MISERABLE PEOPLE LIKE THAT!
shine
shine
shine
I...
I'M THIRSTY ...
...I ...I WANT WATER ...
The sound of water in her body evaporating from hell-like heavy labor.
Fzz Fzz Fzz Fzz
BUT I'M SO TIRED, I CAN'T STAND...
RURIKO ...
...I WONDER IF SHE'S REACHED THE SET YET...
Ahh
!
MMM
I'M ALIVE AGAIN!
She's arrived, taking a break, and has no intentions whatsoever of calling for help.
UHH...
An Oasis of Trees.
I WANT... TO GET IN THE SHADE, AT LEAST...

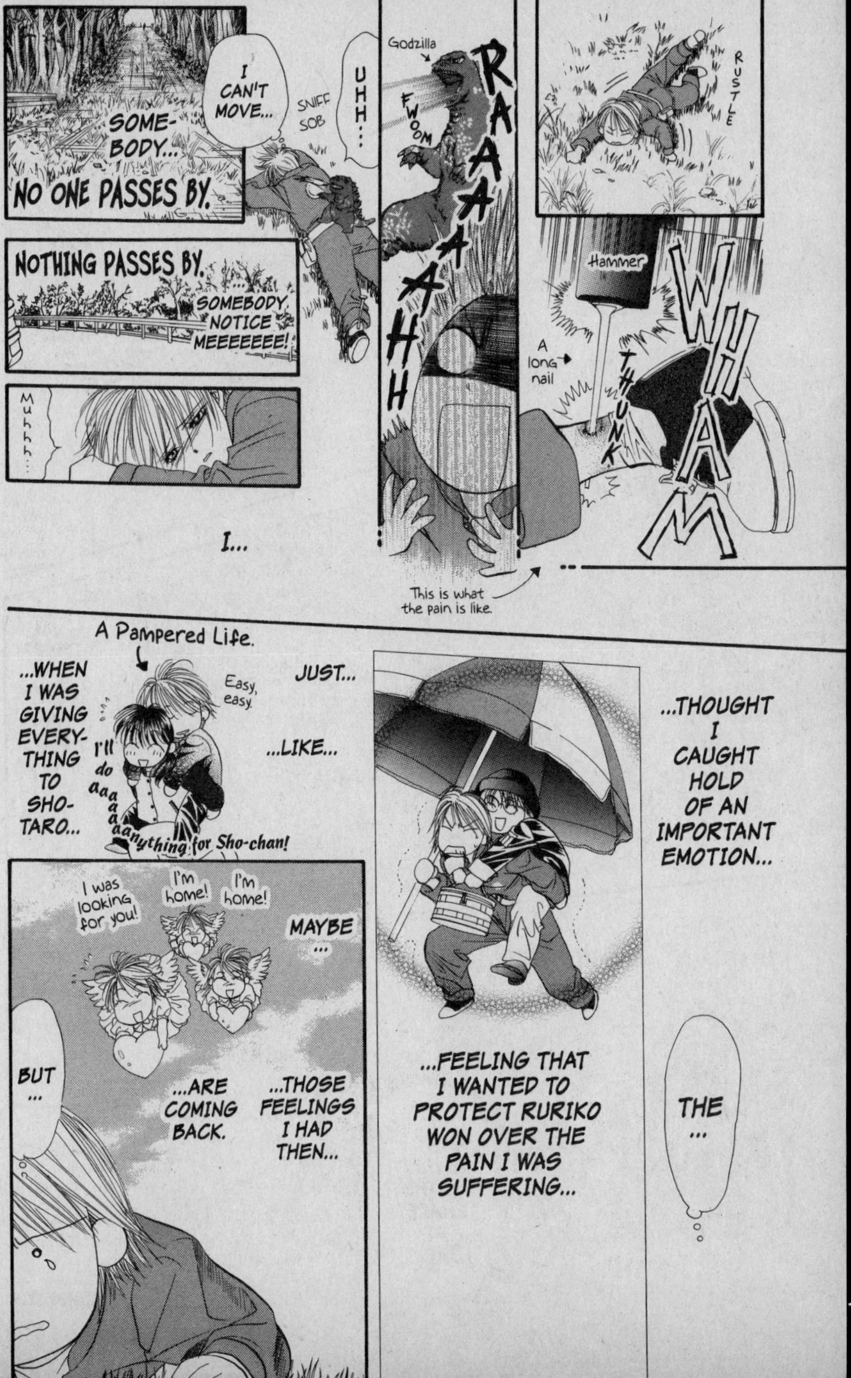

RUSTLE
Hammer
WHAM
THUNK
A long nail
Godzilla
FWOOM
RAAAAAHH
UHH...
SNIFF SOB
I CAN'T MOVE...
SOMEBODY...
NO ONE PASSES BY.
NOTHING PASSES BY.
...SOMEBODY NOTICE MEEEEEEE!
Muhhh...
I...
This is what the pain is like.
...THOUGHT I CAUGHT HOLD OF AN IMPORTANT EMOTION...
...FEELING THAT I WANTED TO PROTECT RURIKO WON OVER THE PAIN I WAS SUFFERING...
THE...
JUST...
...LIKE...
...WHEN I WAS GIVING EVERYTHING TO SHOTARO...
A Pampered Life.
Easy, easy.
I'll do aaaaaaanything for Sho-chan!
MAYBE...
I'm home!
I'm home!
I was looking for you!
...THOSE FEELINGS I HAD THEN...
...ARE COMING BACK.
BUT...

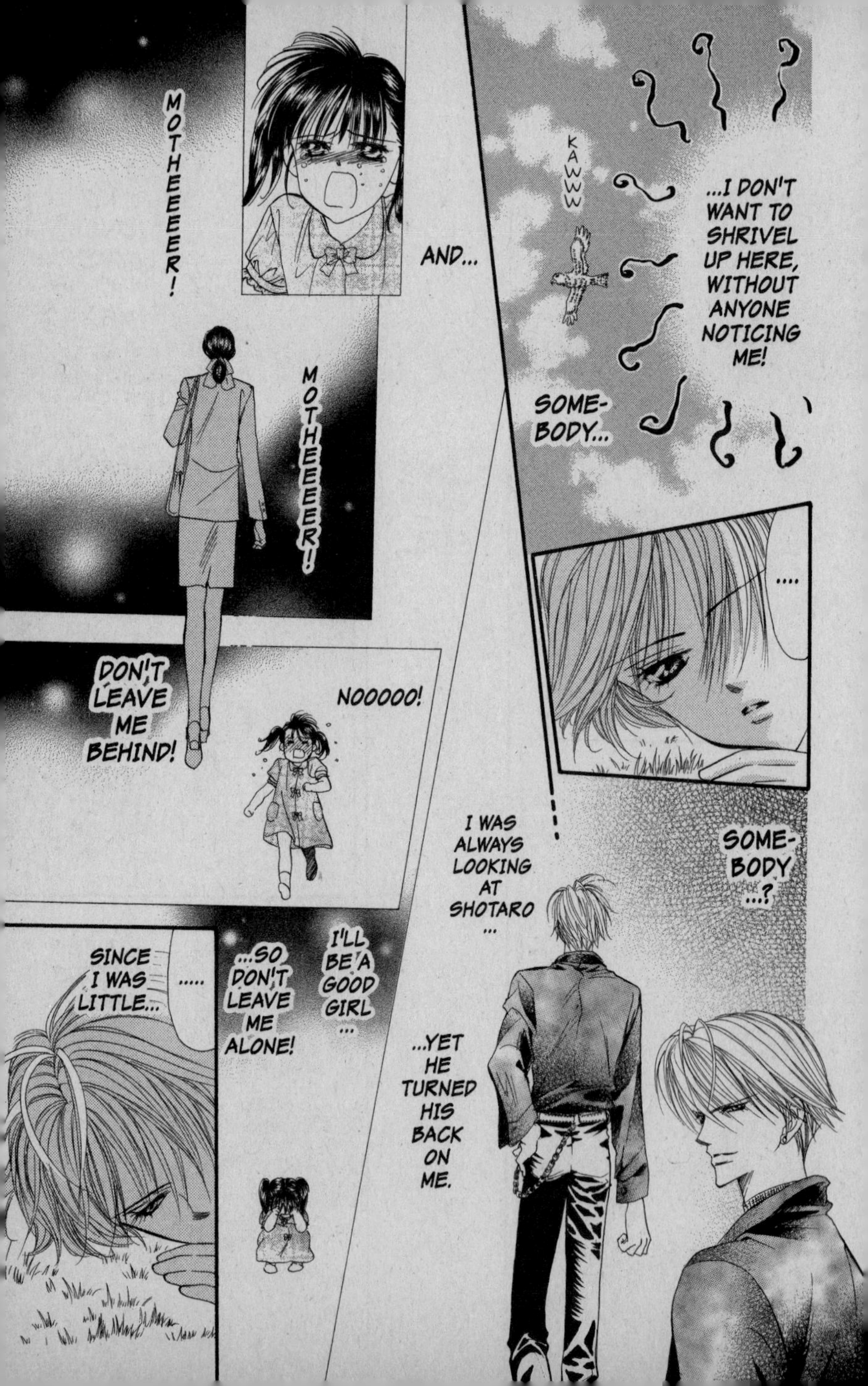

...I DON'T WANT TO SHRIVEL UP HERE, WITHOUT ANYONE NOTICING ME!
KAWWW
SOME-BODY...
AND...
....
SOME-BODY ...?
I WAS ALWAYS LOOKING AT SHOTARO ...
...YET HE TURNED HIS BACK ON ME.
MOTHEEEER!
MOTHEEEEER!
NOOOOO!
DON'T LEAVE ME BEHIND!
I'LL BE A GOOD GIRL ...
...SO DON'T LEAVE ME ALONE!
.....
SINCE I WAS LITTLE...

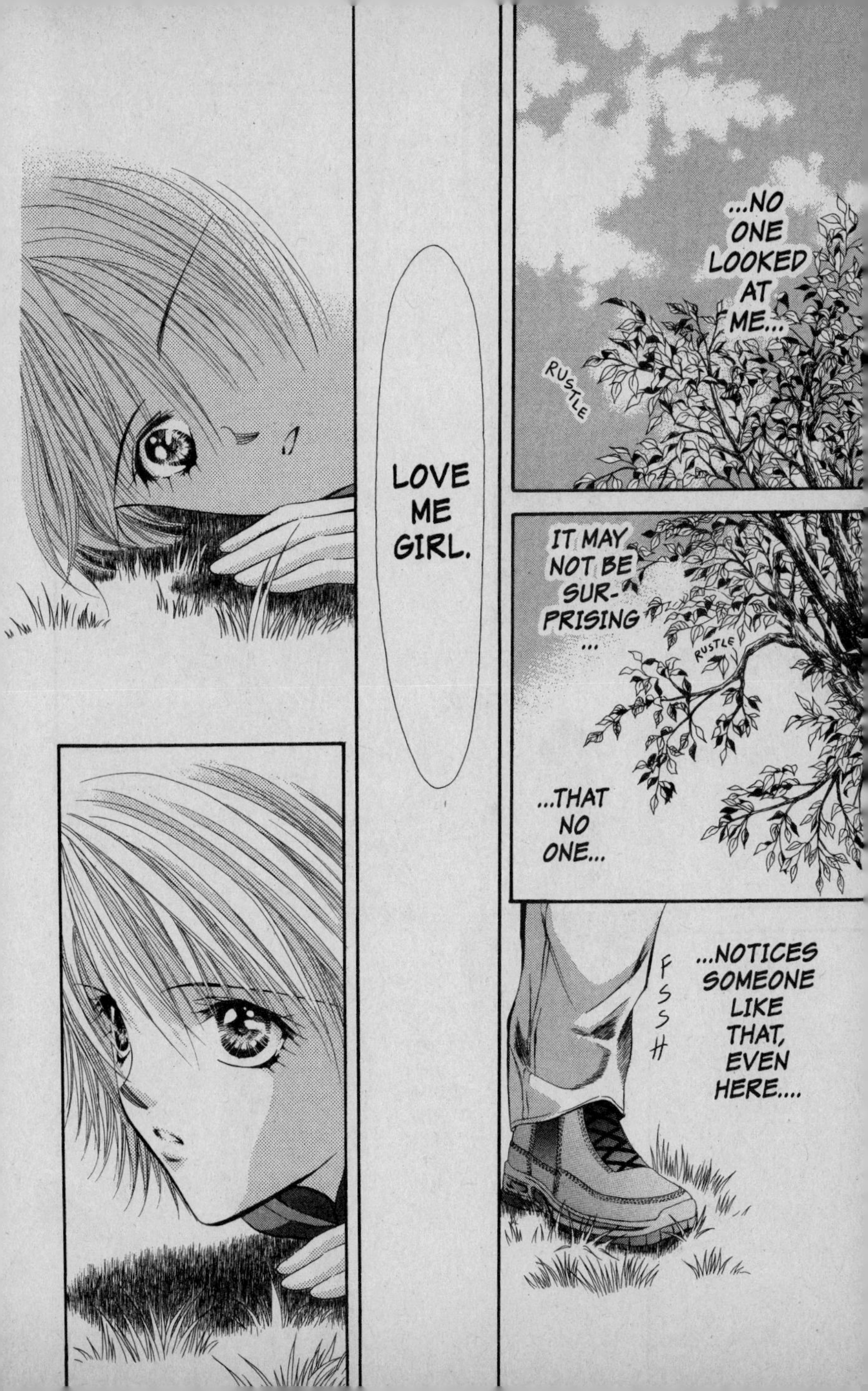
...NO ONE LOOKED AT ME...
RUSTLE
IT MAY NOT BE SUR-PRISING...
RUSTLE
...THAT NO ONE...
FSSH
...NOTICES SOMEONE LIKE THAT, EVEN HERE....
LOVE ME GIRL.

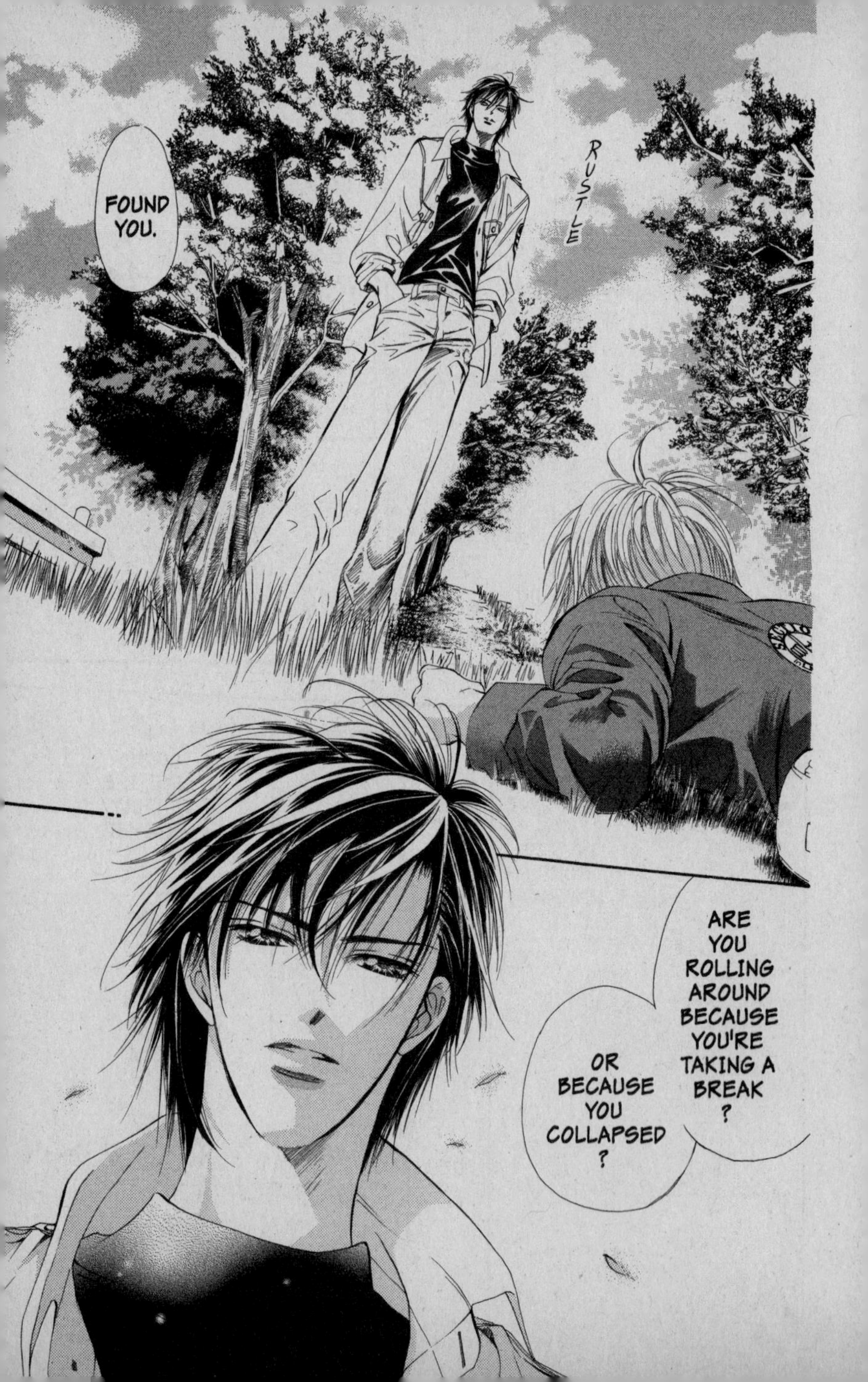
RUSTLE
FOUND YOU.
ARE YOU ROLLING AROUND BECAUSE YOU'RE TAKING A BREAK?
OR BECAUSE YOU COLLAPSED?

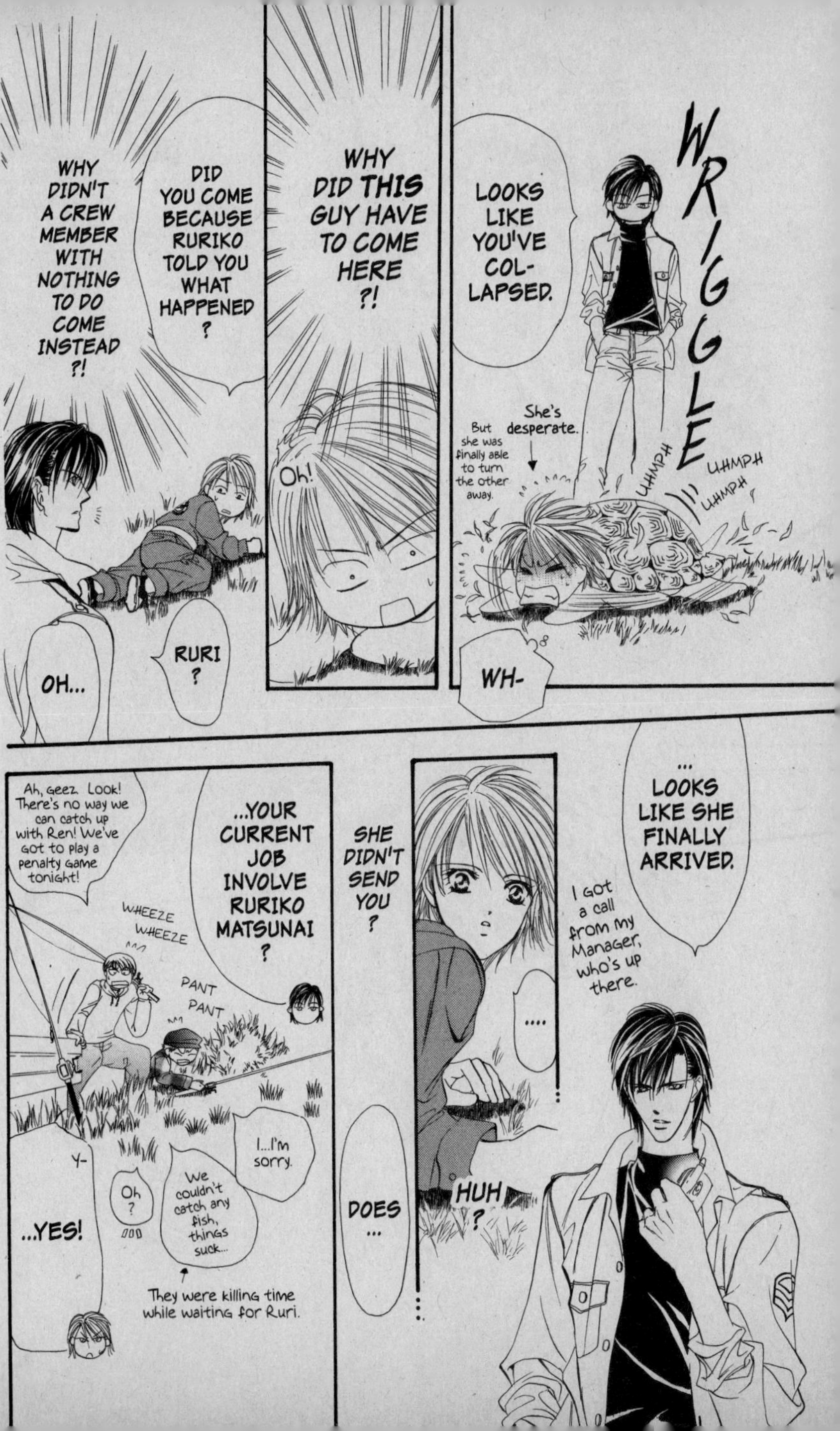
WRIGGLE
LOOKS LIKE YOU'VE COL-LAPSED.
She's desperate.
But she was finally able to turn the other away.
UHMPH UHMPH UHMPH
WH-
WHY DID THIS GUY HAVE TO COME HERE ?!
Oh!
DID YOU COME BECAUSE RURIKO TOLD YOU WHAT HAPPENED ?
WHY DIDN'T A CREW MEMBER WITH NOTHING TO DO COME INSTEAD ?!
RURI ?
OH...
... LOOKS LIKE SHE FINALLY ARRIVED.
I got a call from my Manager, who's up there.
....
SHE DIDN'T SEND YOU ?
HUH ?
DOES ...
...YOUR CURRENT JOB INVOLVE RURIKO MATSUNAI ?
Ah, Geez. Look! There's no way we can catch up with Ren! We've got to play a penalty game tonight!
WHEEZE WHEEZE
PANT PANT
I...I'm sorry.
We couldn't catch any fish, things suck...
They were killing time while waiting for Ruri.
Oh ?
Y-
...YES!

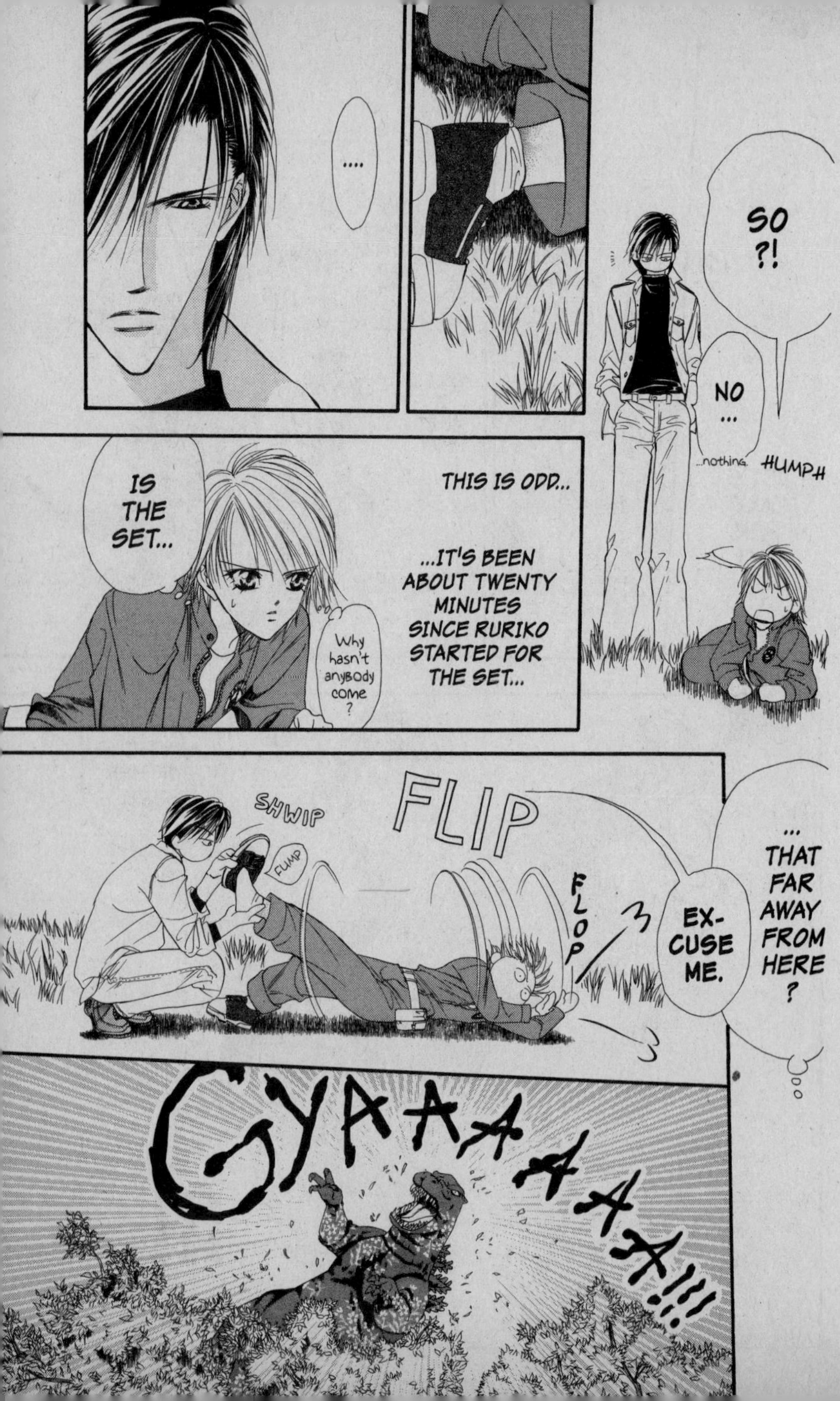
SO ?!
NO ...
...nothing.
HUMPH
....
THIS IS ODD...
...IT'S BEEN ABOUT TWENTY MINUTES SINCE RURIKO STARTED FOR THE SET...
Why hasn't anybody come ?
IS THE SET...
... THAT FAR AWAY FROM HERE ?
EX-CUSE ME.
FLIP
FLOP
SHWIP
FLUMP
GYAAAAAA!!!

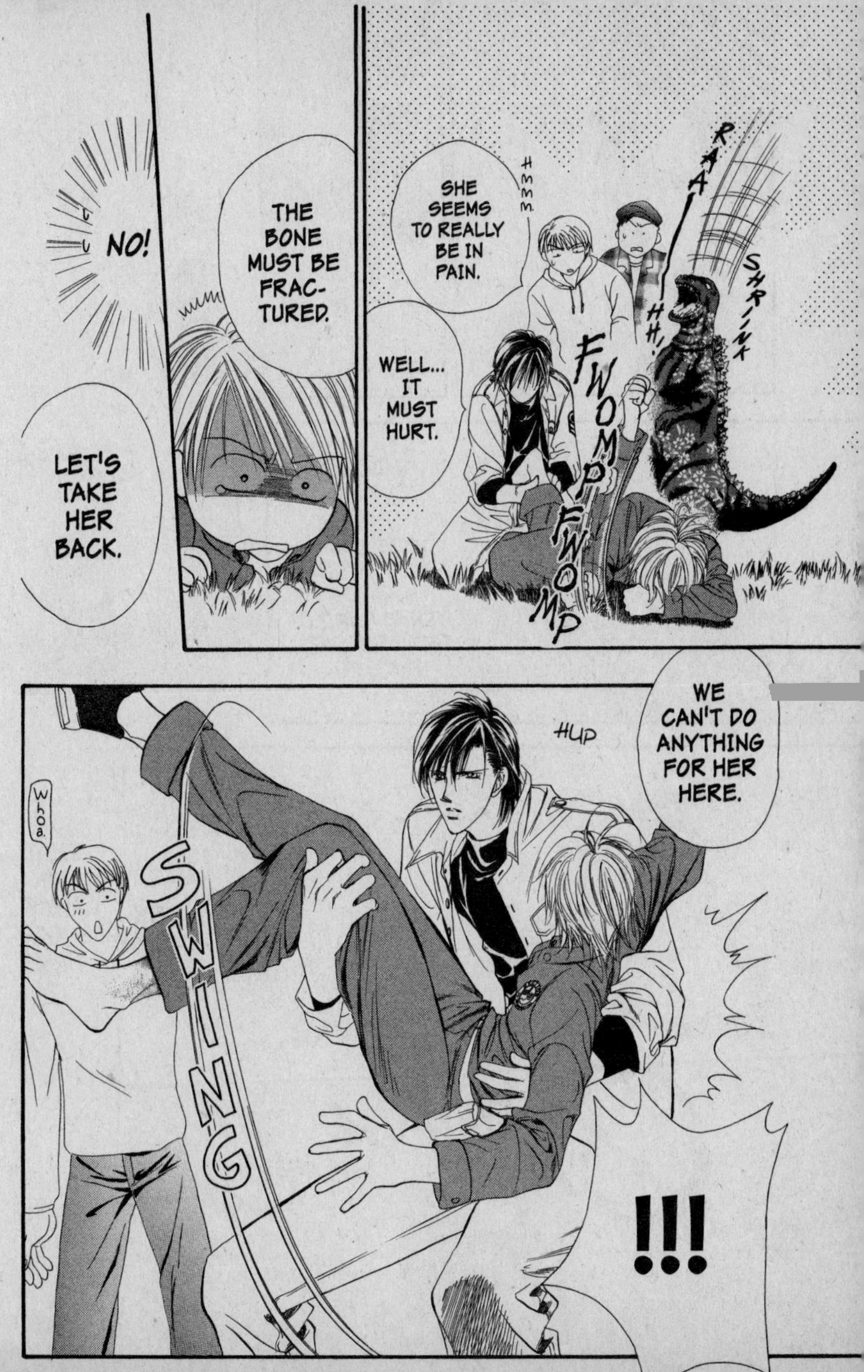
RAAHH!
SHRINK
HMMM.
SHE SEEMS TO REALLY BE IN PAIN.
WELL... IT MUST HURT.
FWOMP FWOMP
THE BONE MUST BE FRAC-TURED.
NO!
LET'S TAKE HER BACK.
WE CAN'T DO ANYTHING FOR HER HERE.
HUP
Whoa.
SWING
!!!

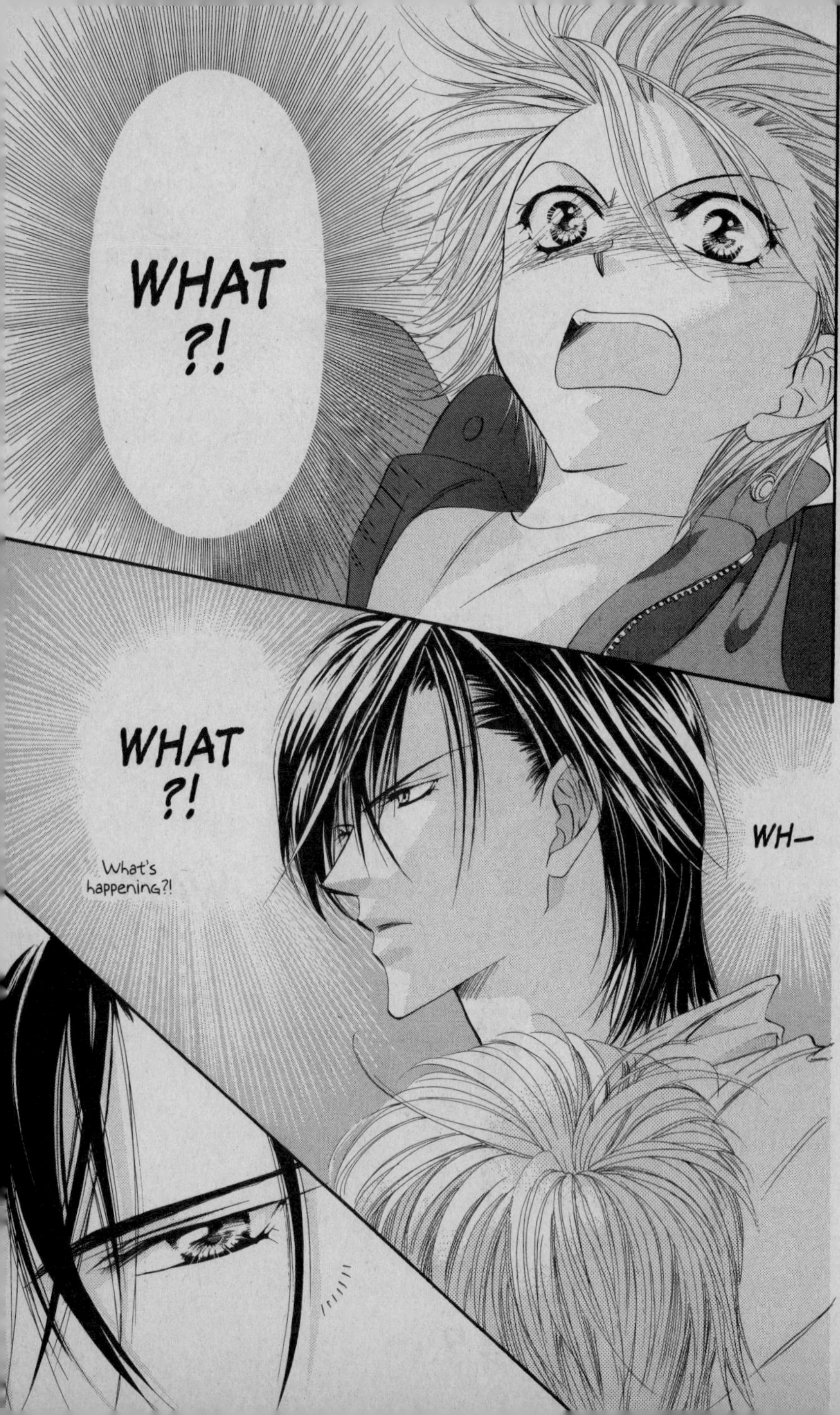
WHAT ?!
WH—
WHAT ?!
What's happening?!

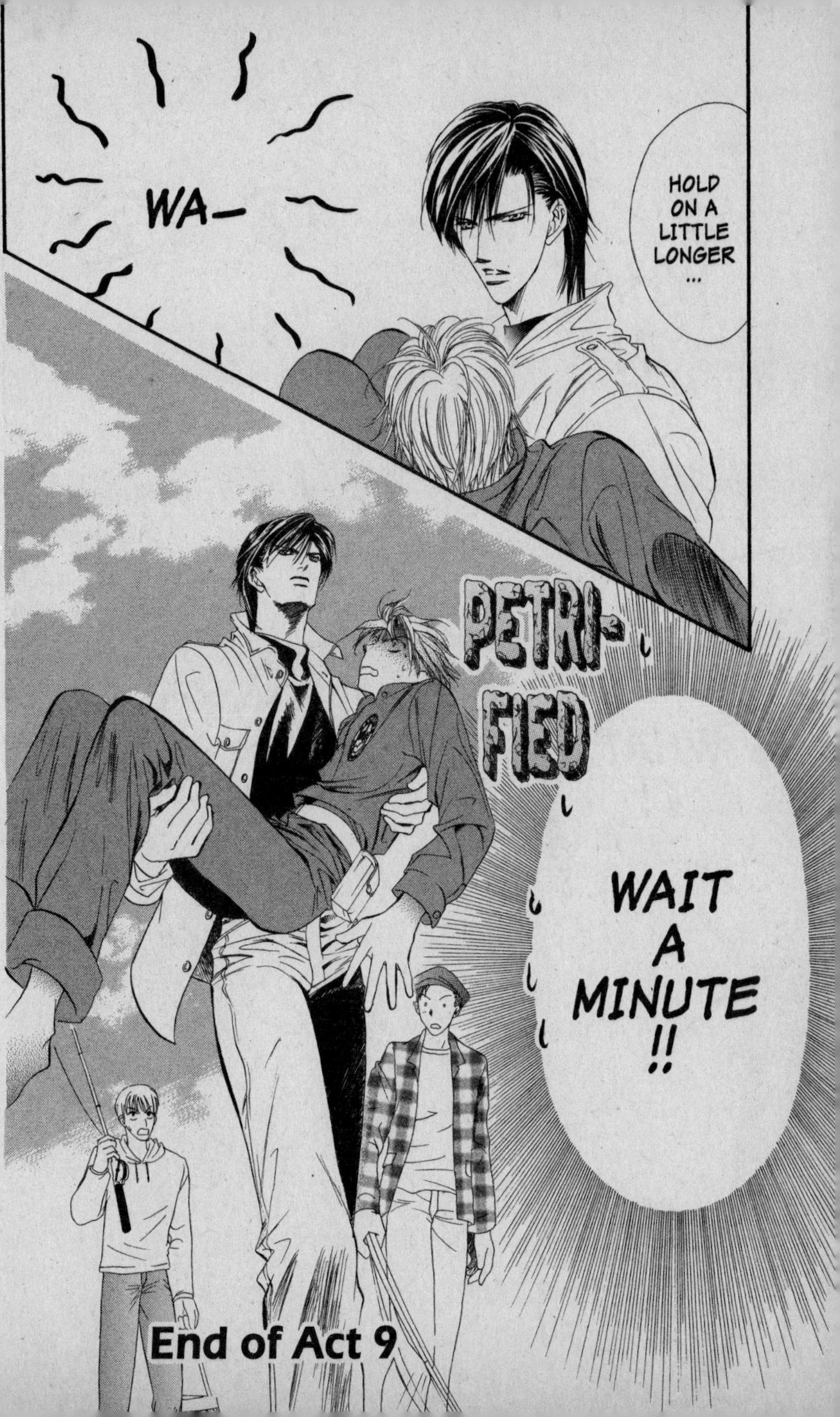
HOLD ON A LITTLE LONGER ...
WA—
PETRI-FIED
WAIT A MINUTE !!

End of Act 9

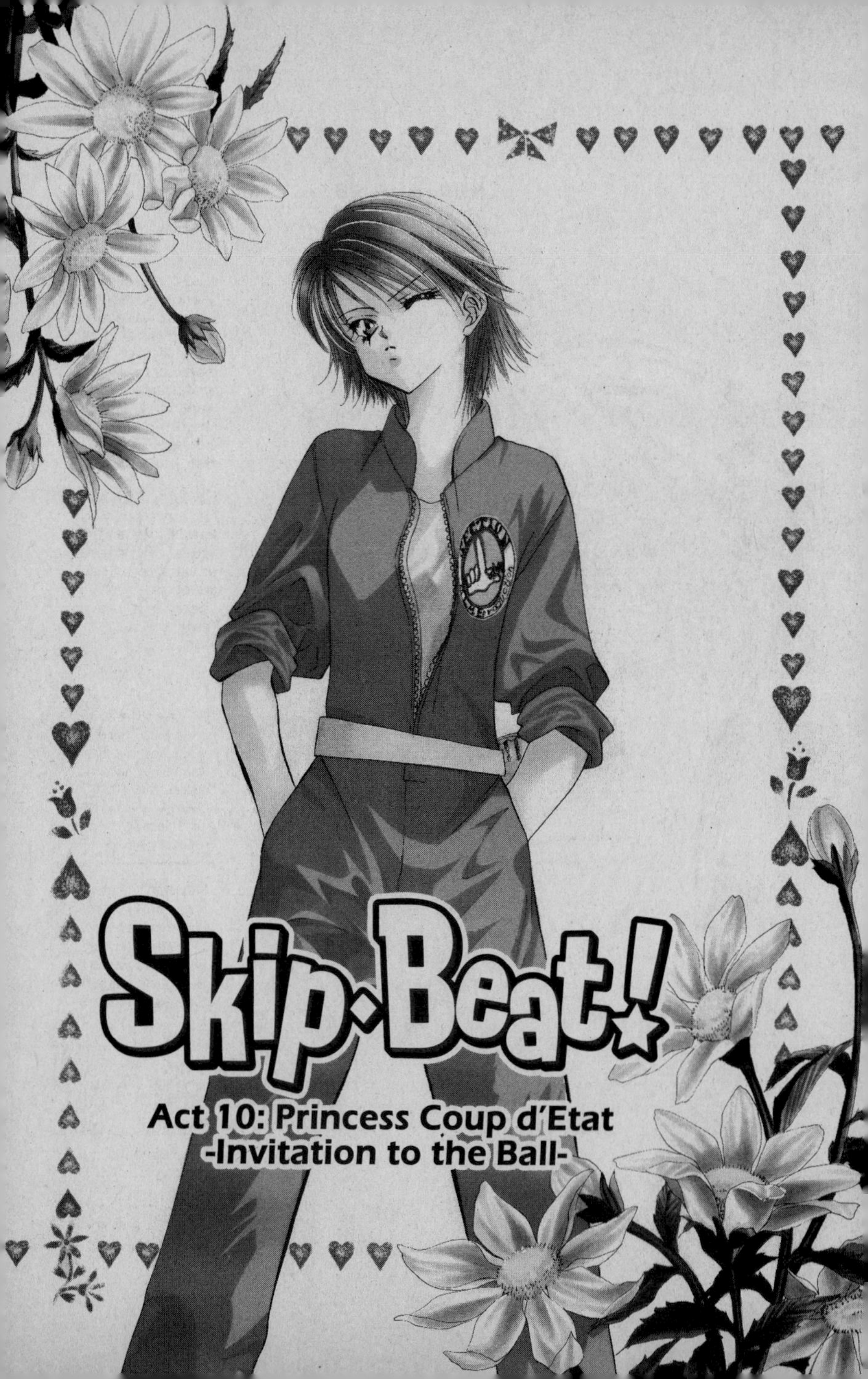
Skip·Beat!
Act 10: Princess Coup d'Etat
-Invitation to the Ball-

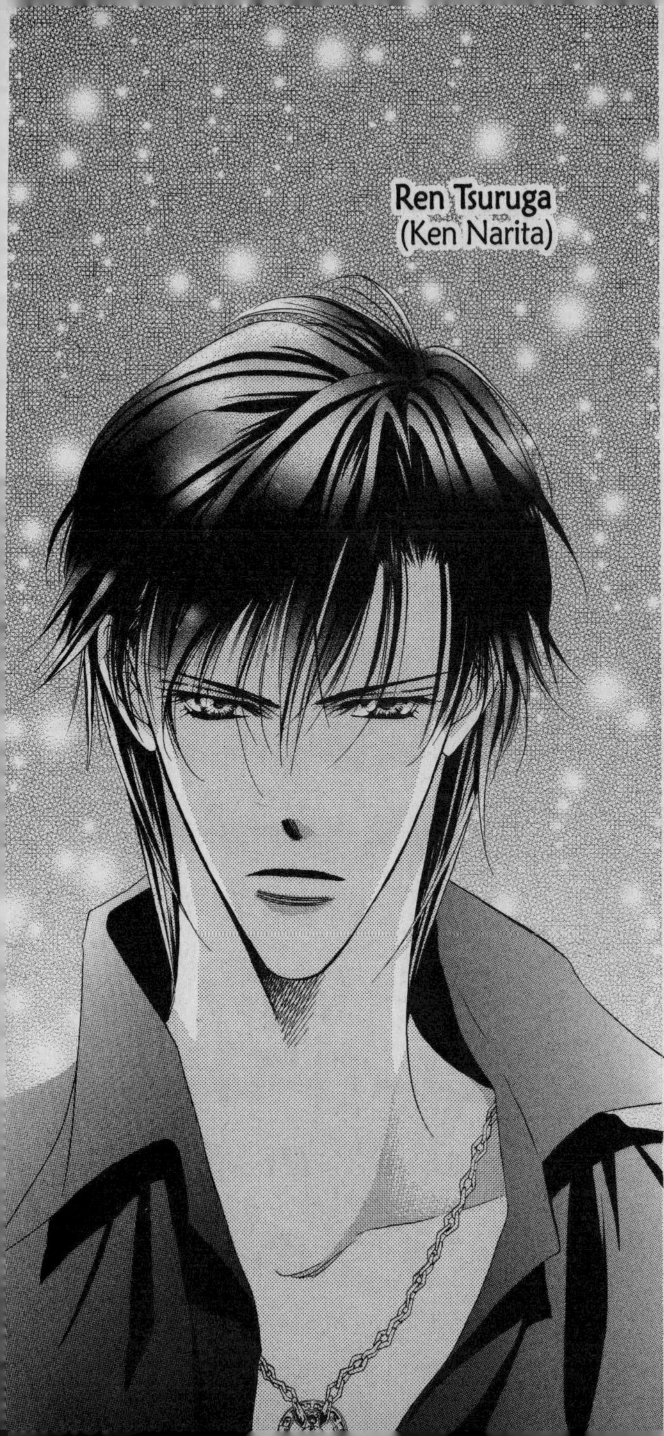
Ren Tsuruga
(Ken Narita)

So, when the last CD was made, I couldn't watch the post-recording, but I was able to watch it this time for *Skip Beat!*. The way everyone in the cast was acting, doing their best to get a feel for their characters, was really professional. There were many retakes, but they didn't make any faces. They did their work sincerely.

Especially when Miki Nagasawa-san, who played Kyoko, was acting, I was praying at her back and kept apologizing...
...Because...it was really really hard work...

Oh...

She played the ordinary Kyoko, the Pure Kyoko, and the Evil Kyoko all by herself. Besides, the first rehearsal she did to get a feel for the character was...

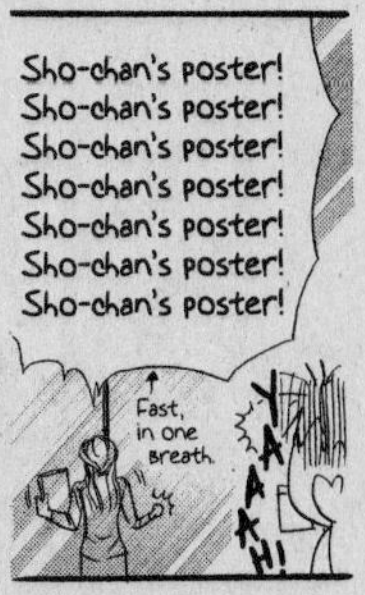
Sho-chan's poster!
Sho-chan's poster!
Sho-chan's poster!
Sho-chan's poster!
Sho-chan's poster!
Sho-chan's poster!
Sho-chan's poster!
Fast, in one breath.
YAAAH!

Before she's even begun, she's out of breath...

Uhh... I'm really sorry... Nagasawa-san...

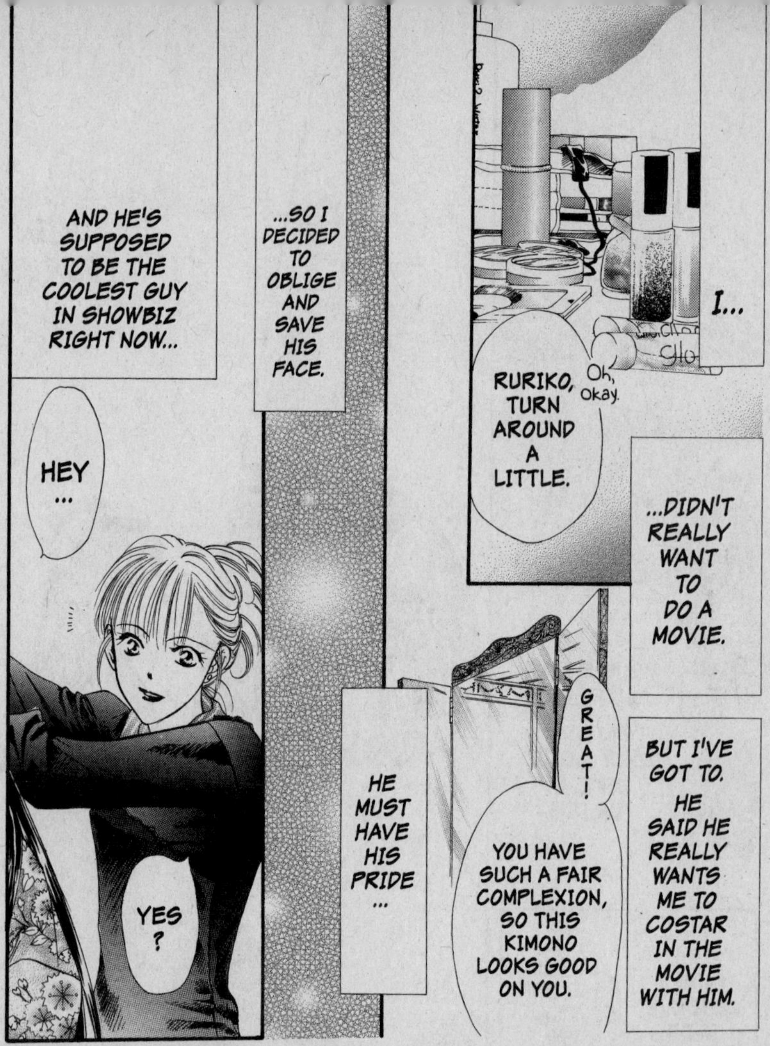
I...
RURIKO, TURN AROUND A LITTLE.
Oh, okay.
...DIDN'T REALLY WANT TO DO A MOVIE.
BUT I'VE GOT TO.
HE SAID HE REALLY WANTS ME TO COSTAR IN THE MOVIE WITH HIM.
GREAT!
YOU HAVE SUCH A FAIR COMPLEXION, SO THIS KIMONO LOOKS GOOD ON YOU.
HE MUST HAVE HIS PRIDE...
...SO I DECIDED TO OBLIGE AND SAVE HIS FACE.
AND HE'S SUPPOSED TO BE THE COOLEST GUY IN SHOWBIZ RIGHT NOW...
HEY...
YES?

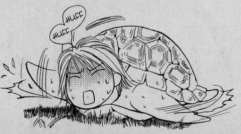

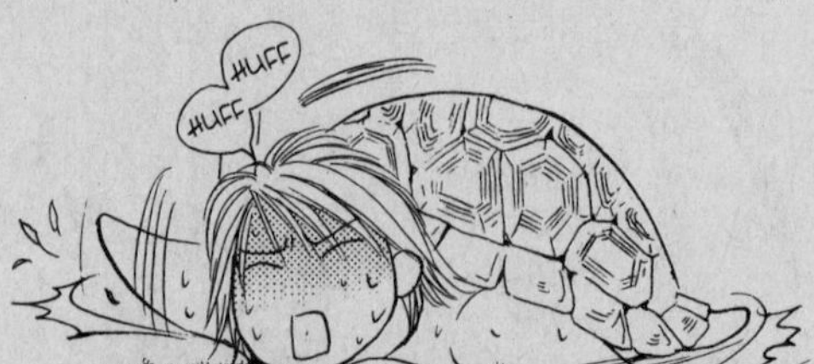
HUFF
HUFF

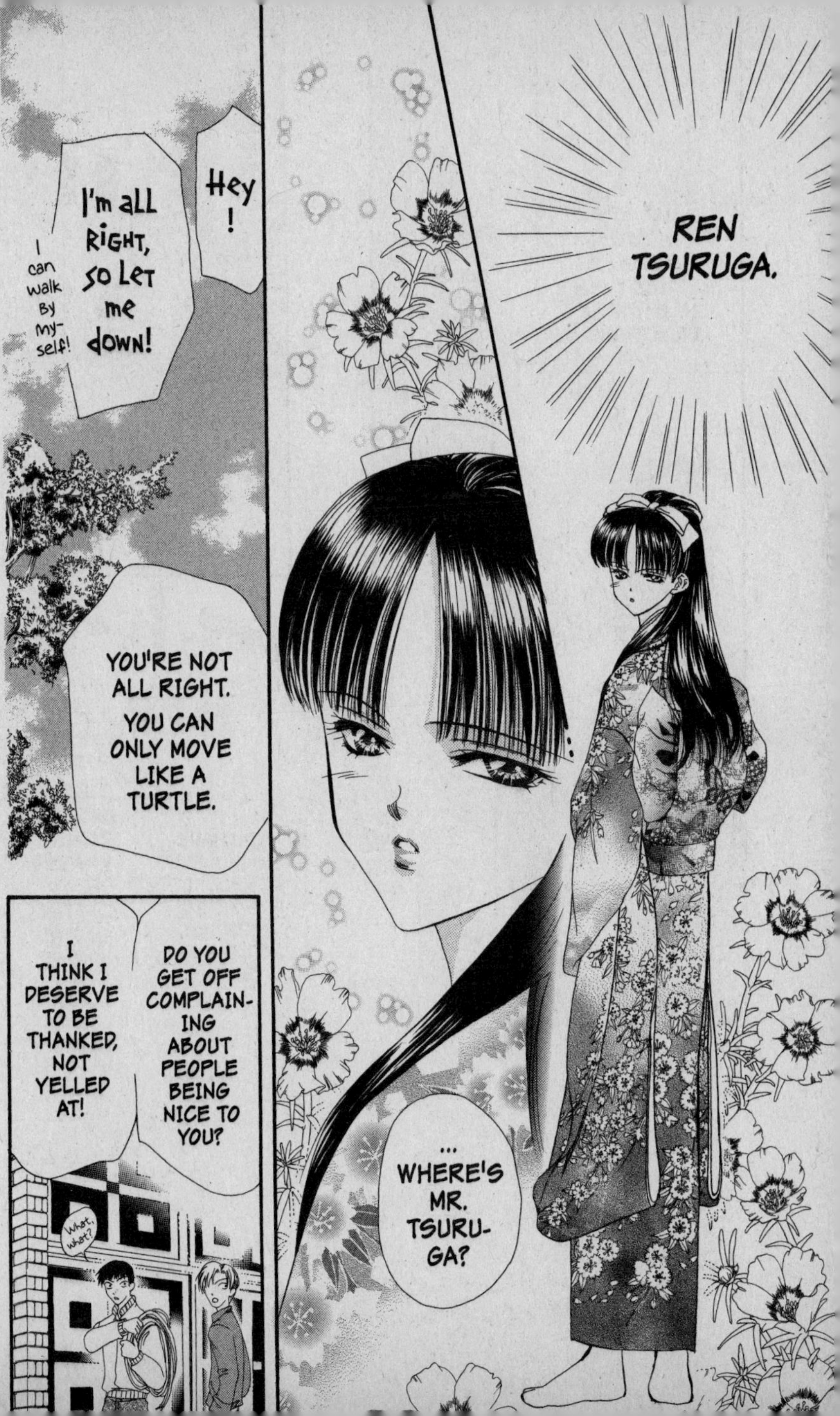
REN TSURUGA.
... WHERE'S MR. TSURU-GA?
Hey!
I'm all right, so let me down!
I can walk by my-self!
YOU'RE NOT ALL RIGHT. YOU CAN ONLY MOVE LIKE A TURTLE.
DO YOU GET OFF COMPLAIN-ING ABOUT PEOPLE BEING NICE TO YOU?
I THINK I DESERVE TO BE THANKED, NOT YELLED AT!
What, what?

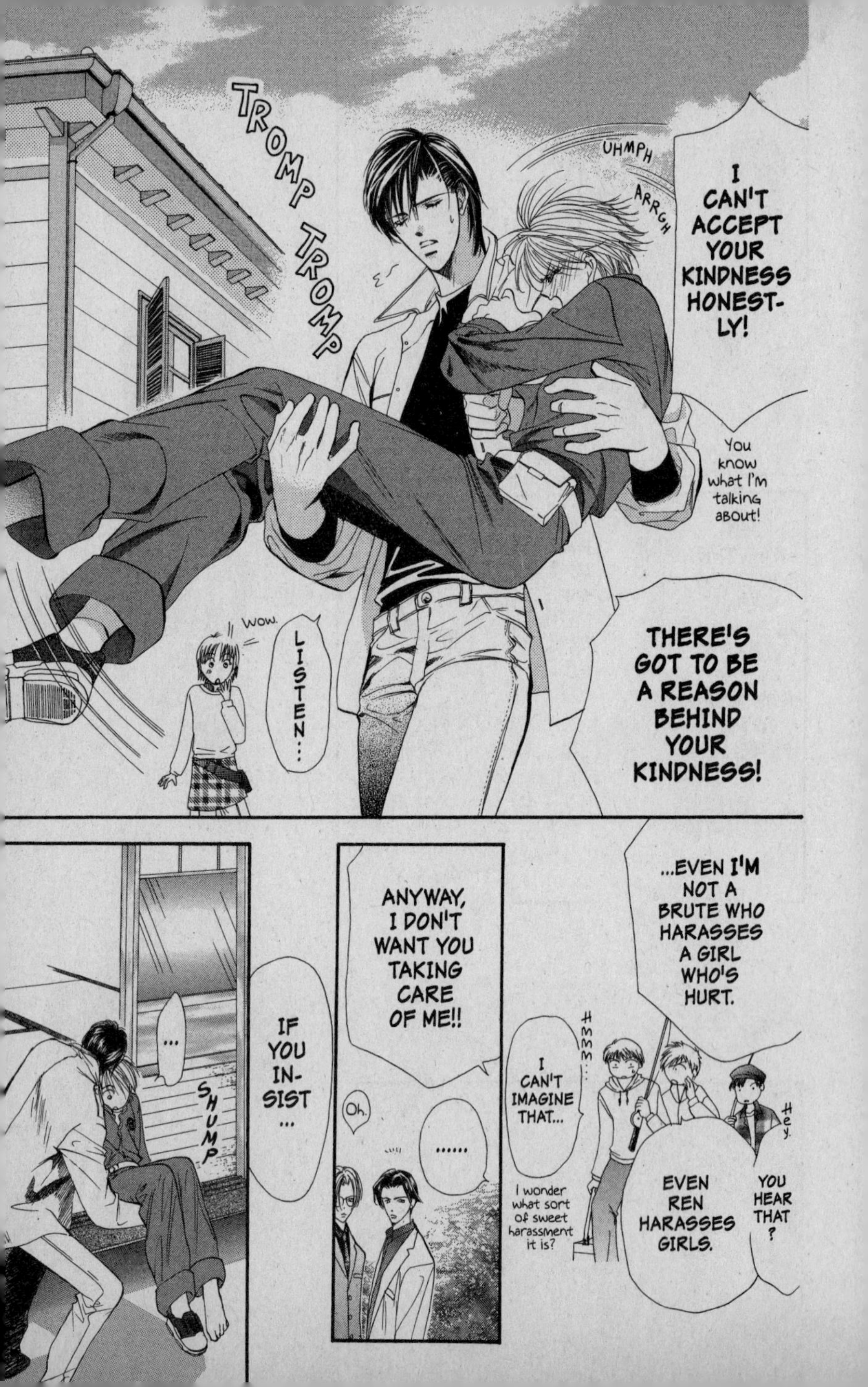
I CAN'T ACCEPT YOUR KINDNESS HONESTLY!
UHMPH
ARRGH
TROMP TROMP TROMP
You know what I'm talking about!
THERE'S GOT TO BE A REASON BEHIND YOUR KINDNESS!
LISTEN...
WOW.
...EVEN I'M NOT A BRUTE WHO HARASSES A GIRL WHO'S HURT.
HMMM...
I CAN'T IMAGINE THAT...
Hey.
YOU HEAR THAT?
EVEN REN HARASSES GIRLS.
I wonder what sort of sweet harassment it is?
ANYWAY, I DON'T WANT YOU TAKING CARE OF ME!!
Oh.
......
IF YOU INSIST...
...
SHUMP

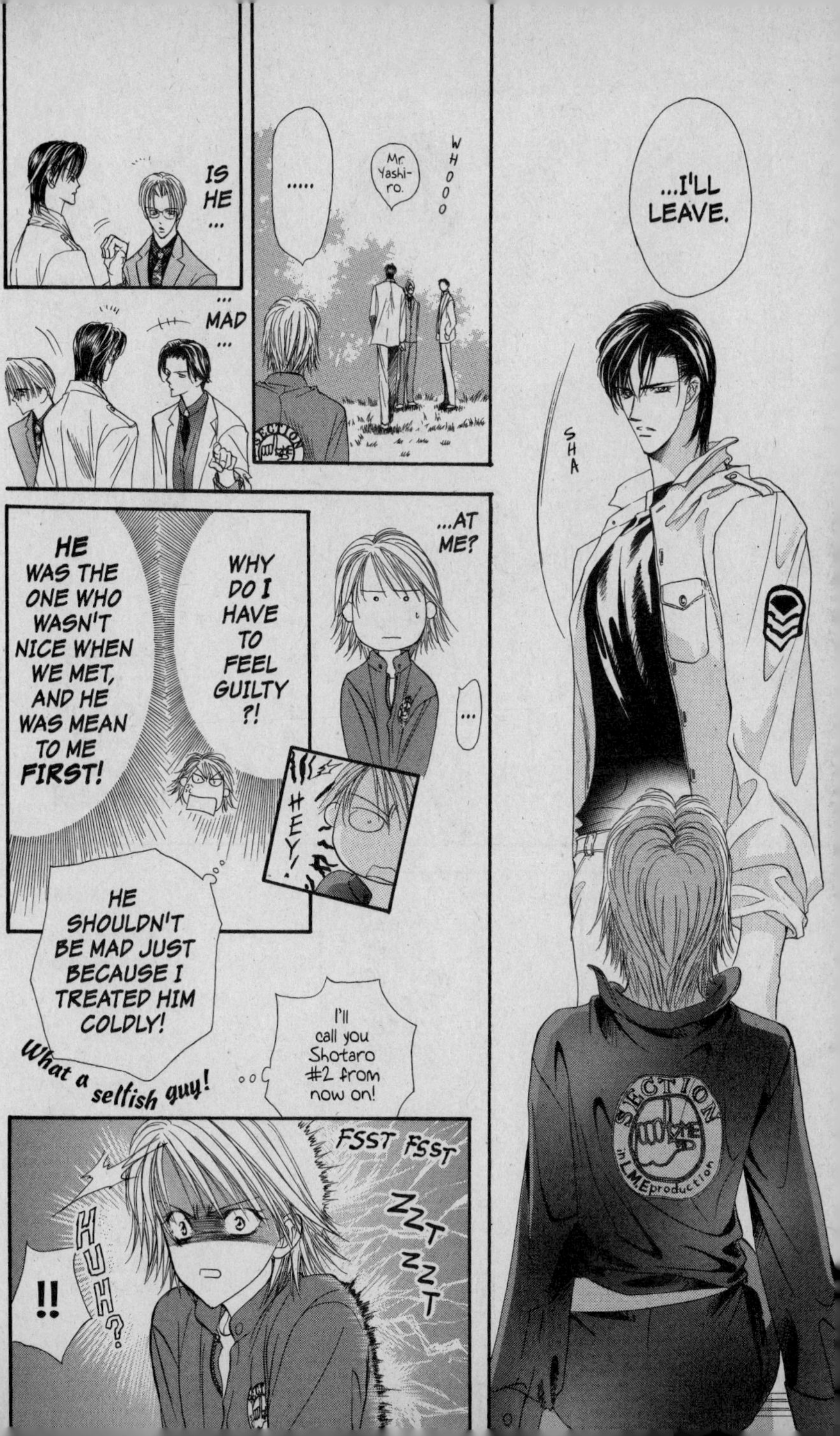
...I'LL LEAVE.
SHA
.....
Mr. Yashiro.
WHOOO
IS HE ...
... MAD ...
...AT ME?
...
WHY DO I HAVE TO FEEL GUILTY ?!
HEY!
HE WAS THE ONE WHO WASN'T NICE WHEN WE MET, AND HE WAS MEAN TO ME FIRST!
HE SHOULDN'T BE MAD JUST BECAUSE I TREATED HIM COLDLY!
I'll call you Shotaro #2 from now on!
What a selfish guy!
FSST FSST
ZZT ZZT
HUH?
!!

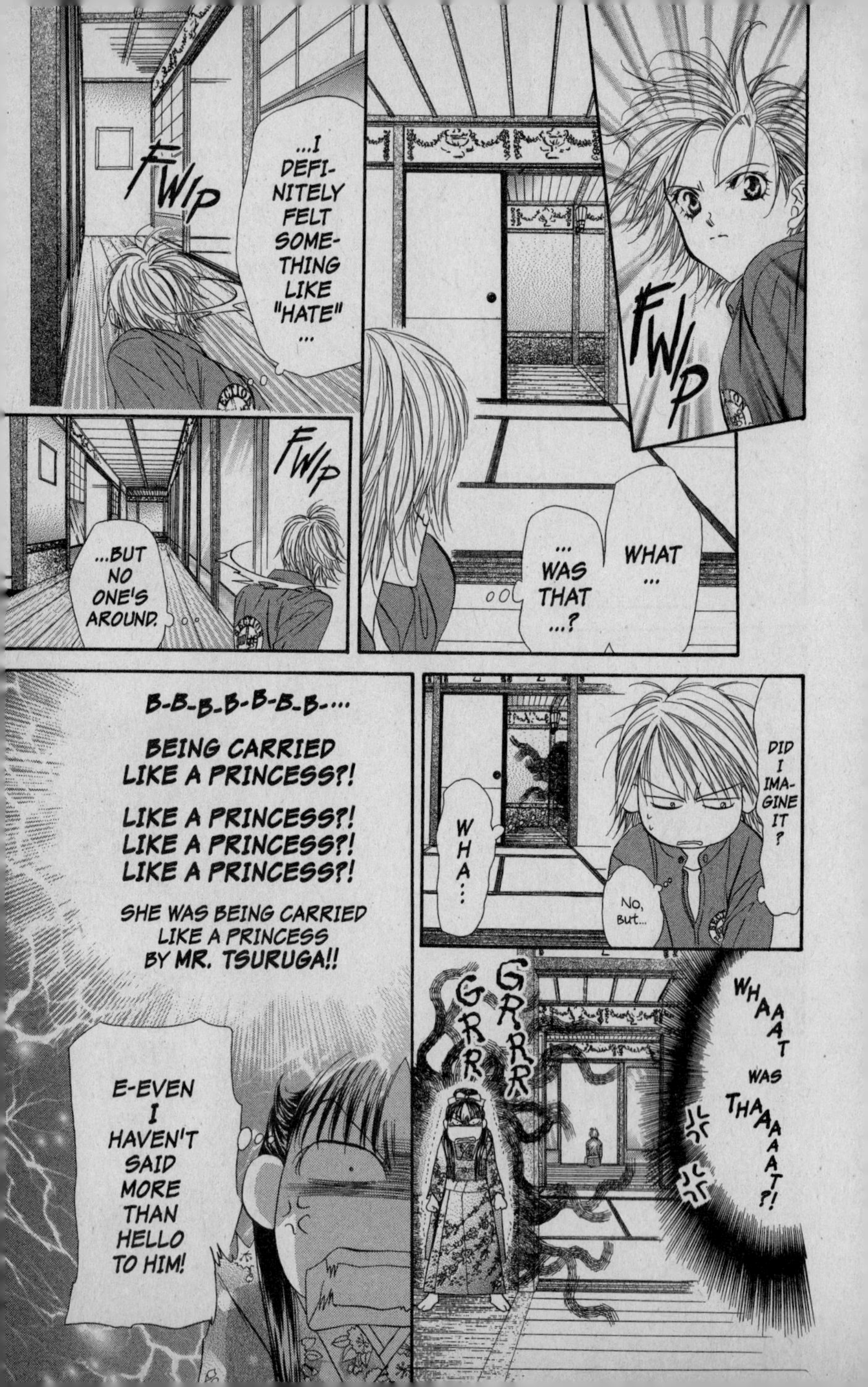
FWIP
WHAT ...
... WAS THAT ...?
FWIP
...I DEFINITELY FELT SOMETHING LIKE "HATE" ...
FWIP
...BUT NO ONE'S AROUND.
DID I IMAGINE IT?
No, but...
WHA...
G-GRRR GRRR
WHAAAT WAS THAAAAAT?!
B-B-B-B-B-B-B-....
BEING CARRIED LIKE A PRINCESS?!
LIKE A PRINCESS?! LIKE A PRINCESS?! LIKE A PRINCESS?!
SHE WAS BEING CARRIED LIKE A PRINCESS BY MR. TSURUGA!!
E-EVEN I HAVEN'T SAID MORE THAN HELLO TO HIM!

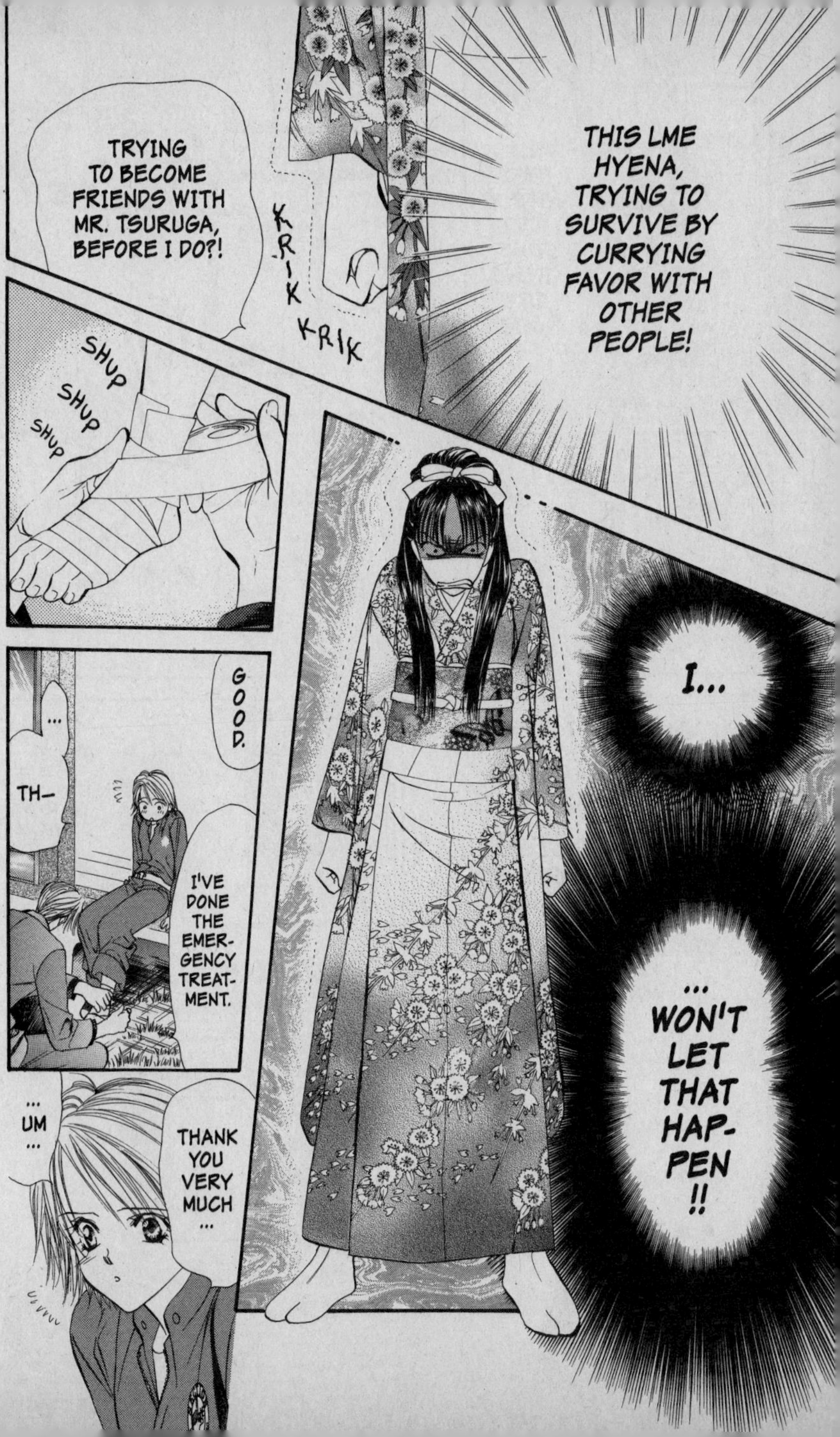
THIS LME HYENA, TRYING TO SURVIVE BY CURRYING FAVOR WITH OTHER PEOPLE!
KRIK KRIK
TRYING TO BECOME FRIENDS WITH MR. TSURUGA, BEFORE I DO?!
I...
...WON'T LET THAT HAP-PEN!!
SHUP SHUP SHUP
GOOD.
...
TH—
I'VE DONE THE EMER-GENCY TREAT-MENT.
THANK YOU VERY MUCH...
...UM...

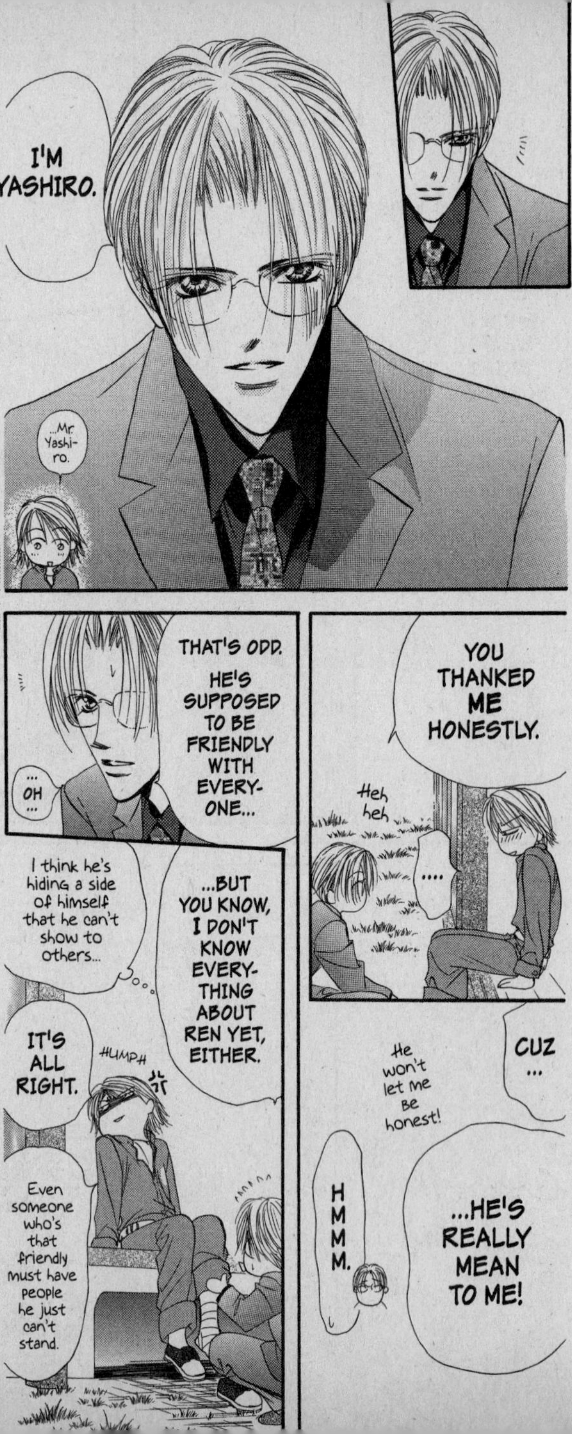
I'M YASHIRO.
...Mr. Yashiro.
YOU THANKED ME HONESTLY.
Heh heh
....
THAT'S ODD.
HE'S SUPPOSED TO BE FRIENDLY WITH EVERYONE...
...OH...
CUZ...
He won't let me be honest!
...HE'S REALLY MEAN TO ME!
HMMM.
...BUT YOU KNOW, I DON'T KNOW EVERYTHING ABOUT REN YET, EITHER.
I think he's hiding a side of himself that he can't show to others...
IT'S ALL RIGHT.
HUMPH
Even someone who's that friendly must have people he just can't stand.

When I had my previous work Kurepara turned into a CD, I apparently made the voice actress who did the main character, Tsukasa, really tired...

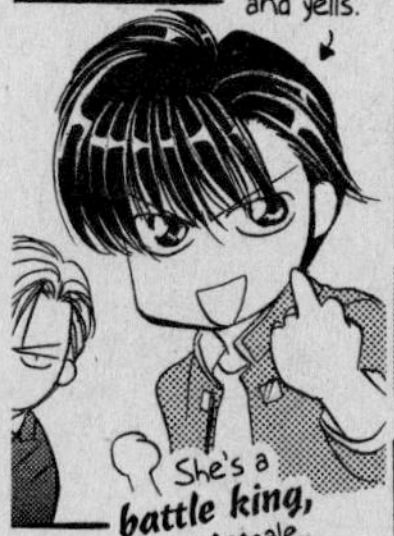
Because she's violent and yells.
She's a **battle king,** but female.

...and I felt really sorry then. Compared to Tsukasa, Kyoko is more girlish, and so it won't be as tiring as last time...that's what I was thinking, anyway. But it was a big mistake... It looks like the main characters I draw are all ones who are exhausting to portray...

But they're easy to draw...

However...!! The CD, which sucked the cast's blood and sweat and tears and souls, and stole (maybe) the staff's sleep and breaks, turned out wonderful, and my worries were kicked away.

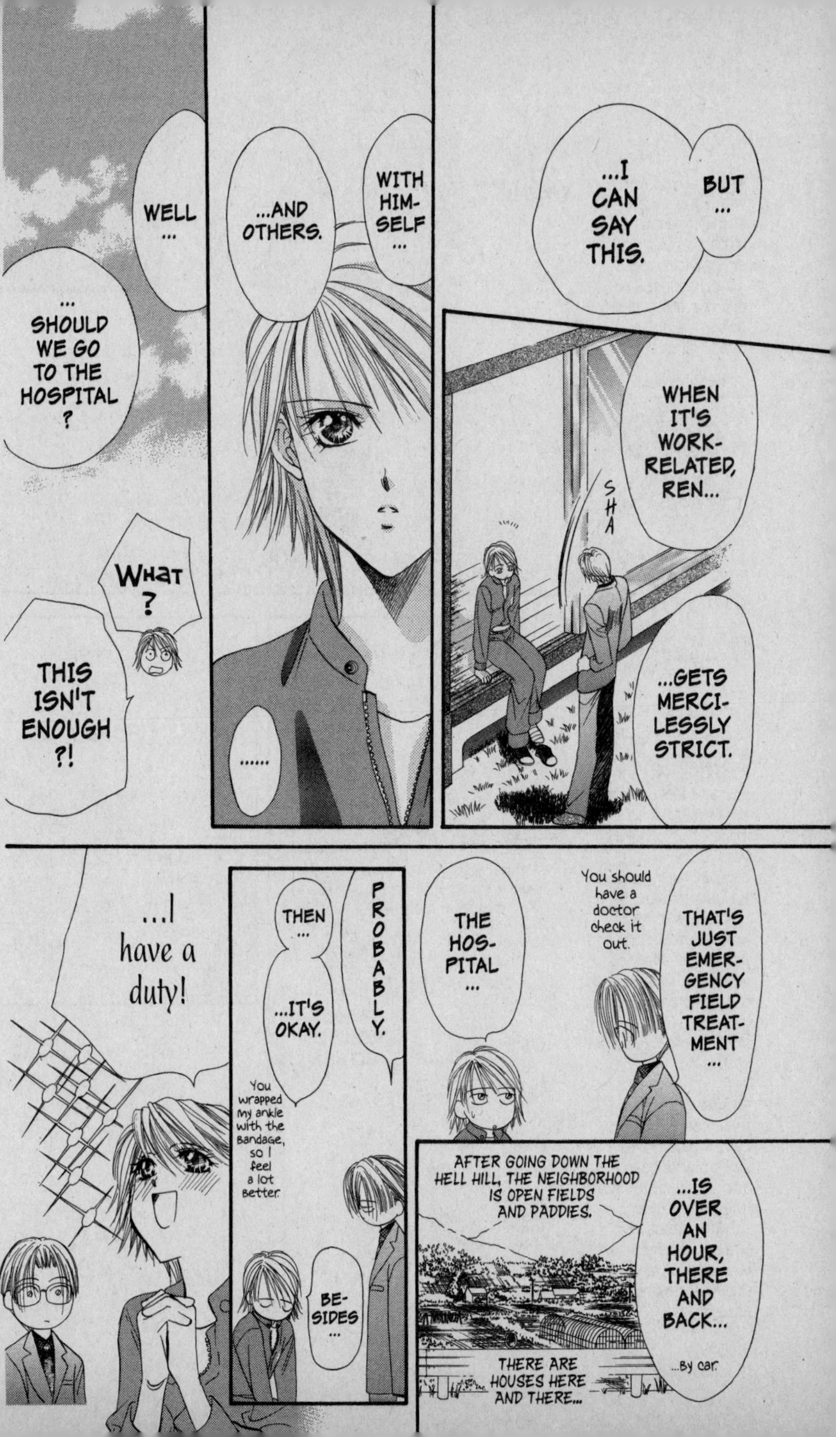
BUT ...
...I CAN SAY THIS.
WHEN IT'S WORK-RELATED, REN...
SHA
...GETS MERCILESSLY STRICT.
WITH HIMSELF ...
...AND OTHERS.
......
WELL ...
... SHOULD WE GO TO THE HOSPITAL ?
WHAT ?
THIS ISN'T ENOUGH ?!
THAT'S JUST EMERGENCY FIELD TREATMENT ...
You should have a doctor check it out.
THE HOSPITAL ...
...IS OVER AN HOUR, THERE AND BACK...
...By car.
AFTER GOING DOWN THE HELL HILL, THE NEIGHBORHOOD IS OPEN FIELDS AND PADDIES.
THERE ARE HOUSES HERE AND THERE...
PROBABLY.
THEN ...
...IT'S OKAY.
You wrapped my ankle with the bandage, so I feel a lot better.
BESIDES ...
...I have a duty!

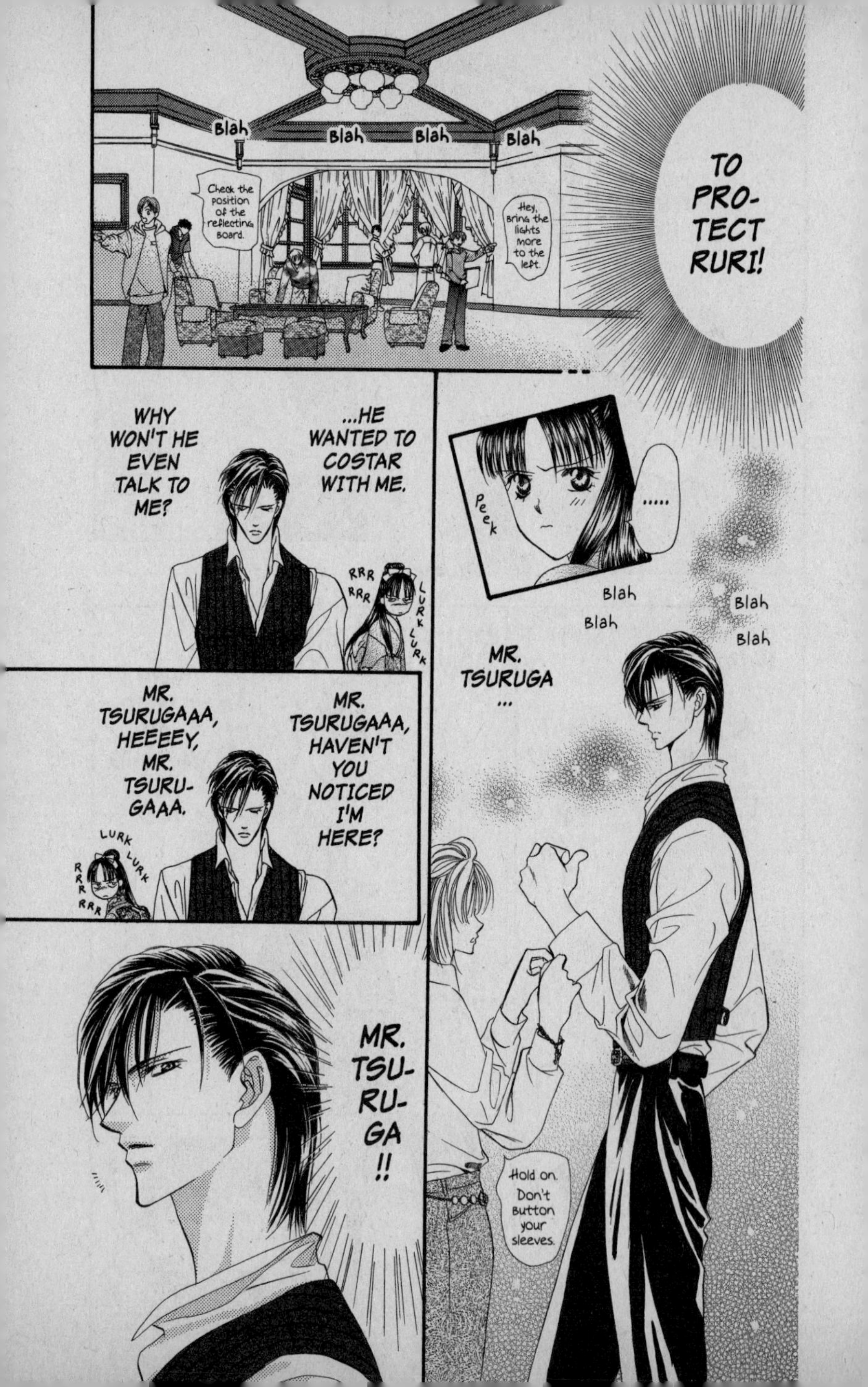
TO PRO-TECT RURI!
Blah
Blah
Blah
Blah
Hey, Bring the lights more to the left.
Check the position of the reflecting Board.
.....
Peek
Blah
Blah
Blah
Blah
MR. TSURUGA ...
Hold on. Don't button your sleeves.
...HE WANTED TO COSTAR WITH ME.
WHY WON'T HE EVEN TALK TO ME?
RRR RRR
LURK LURK
MR. TSURUGAAA, HAVEN'T YOU NOTICED I'M HERE?
MR. TSURUGAAA, HEEEEY, MR. TSURU-GAAA.
LURK LURK
RRR RRR
MR. TSU-RU-GA!!

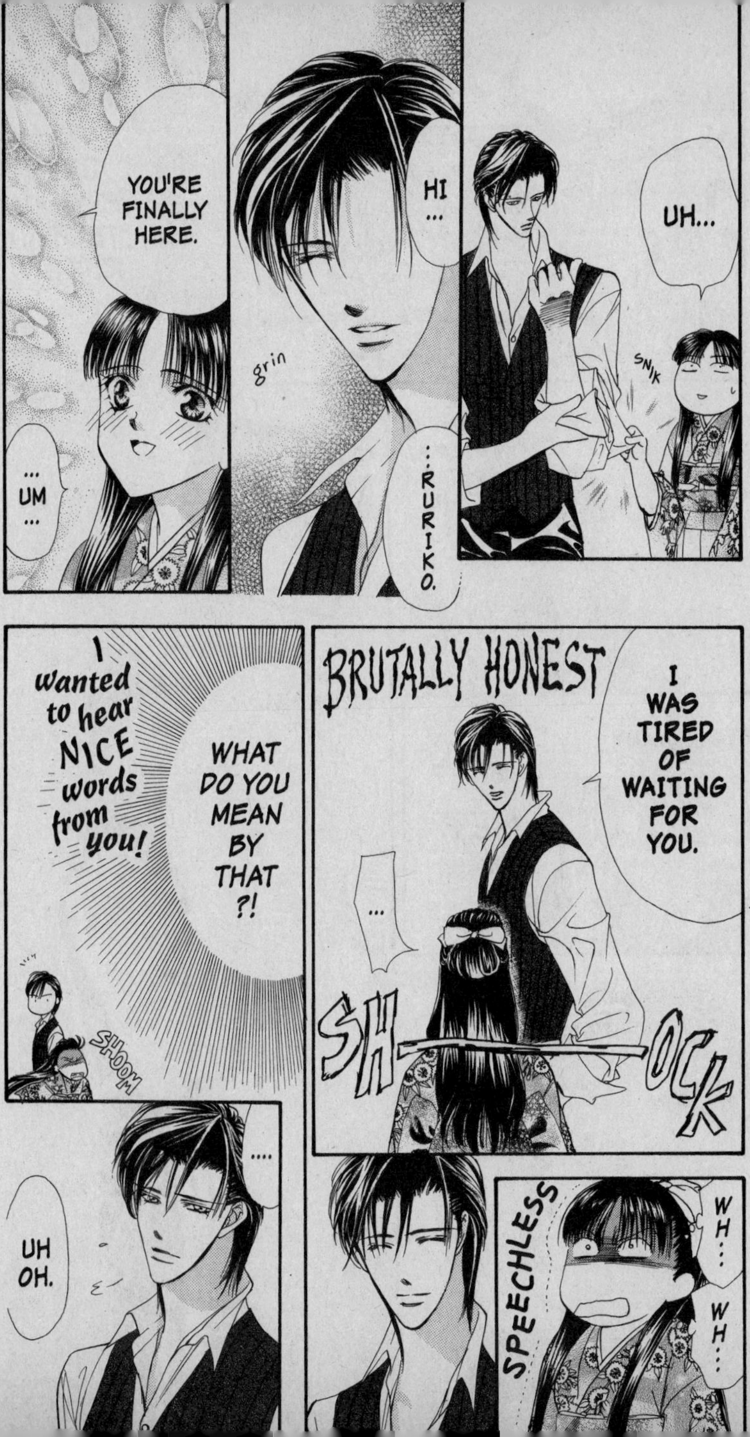
UH...
SNIK
HI ...
...RURIKO.
grin
YOU'RE FINALLY HERE.
... UM ...
BRUTALLY HONEST
I WAS TIRED OF WAITING FOR YOU.
...
SH-OCK
WHAT DO YOU MEAN BY THAT?!
I wanted to hear NICE words from you!
WHOOSH
WH...
WH...
SPEECHLESS
....
UH OH.

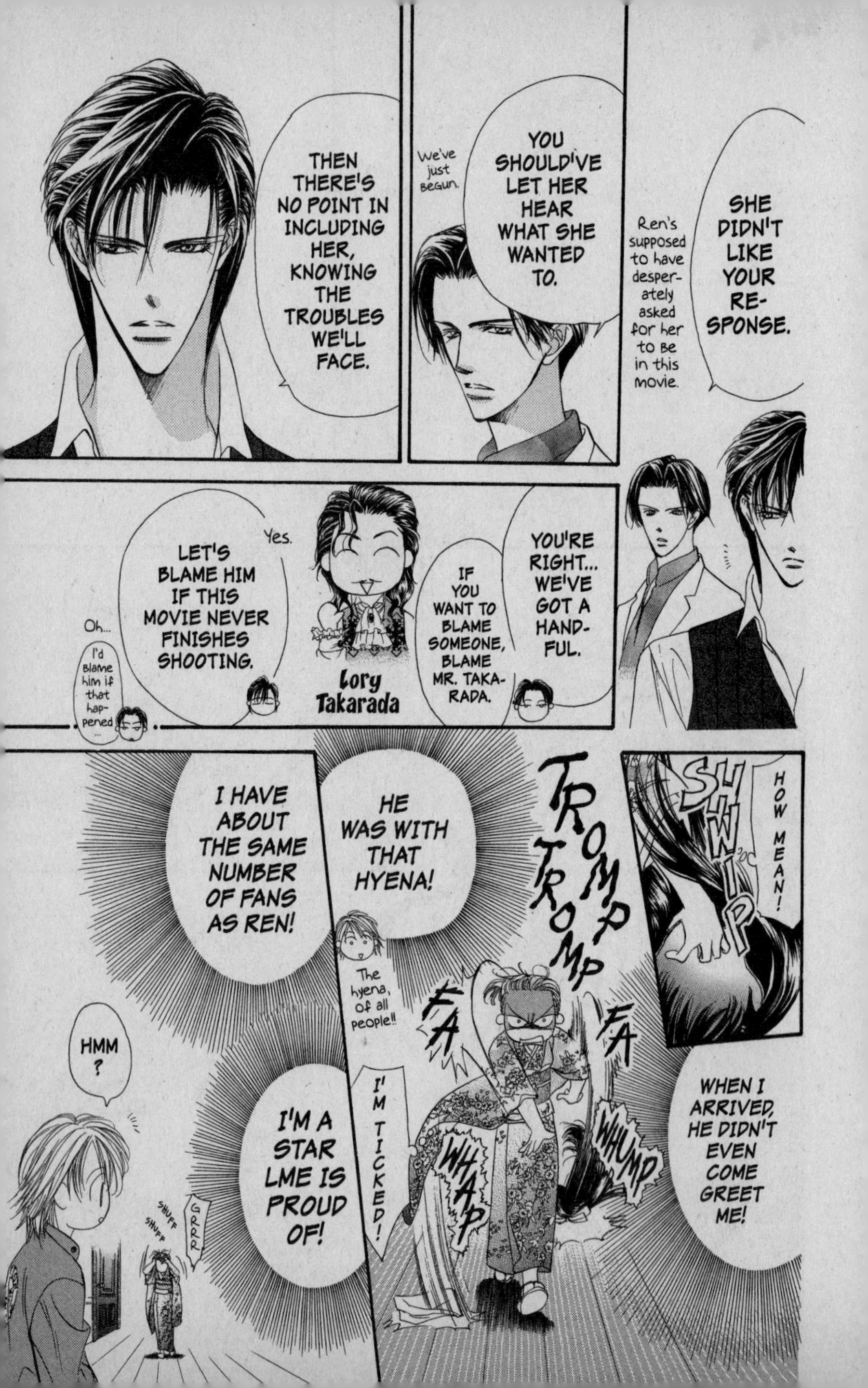
SHE DIDN'T LIKE YOUR RE-SPONSE.
Ren's supposed to have desperately asked for her to be in this movie.
We've just begun.
YOU SHOULD'VE LET HER HEAR WHAT SHE WANTED TO.
THEN THERE'S NO POINT IN INCLUDING HER, KNOWING THE TROUBLES WE'LL FACE.
YOU'RE RIGHT... WE'VE GOT A HANDFUL.
IF YOU WANT TO BLAME SOMEONE, BLAME MR. TAKARADA.
Lory Takarada
Yes.
LET'S BLAME HIM IF THIS MOVIE NEVER FINISHES SHOOTING.
Oh...
I'd blame him if that happened...
SHWIP
HOW MEAN!
TROMP TROMP TROMP
WHEN I ARRIVED, HE DIDN'T EVEN COME GREET ME!
FA
FA
WHUMP
WHAP
I'M TICKED!
HE WAS WITH THAT HYENA!
The hyena, of all people!!
I HAVE ABOUT THE SAME NUMBER OF FANS AS REN!
I'M A STAR LME IS PROUD OF!
HMM?
GRRR
SHUFF SHUFF

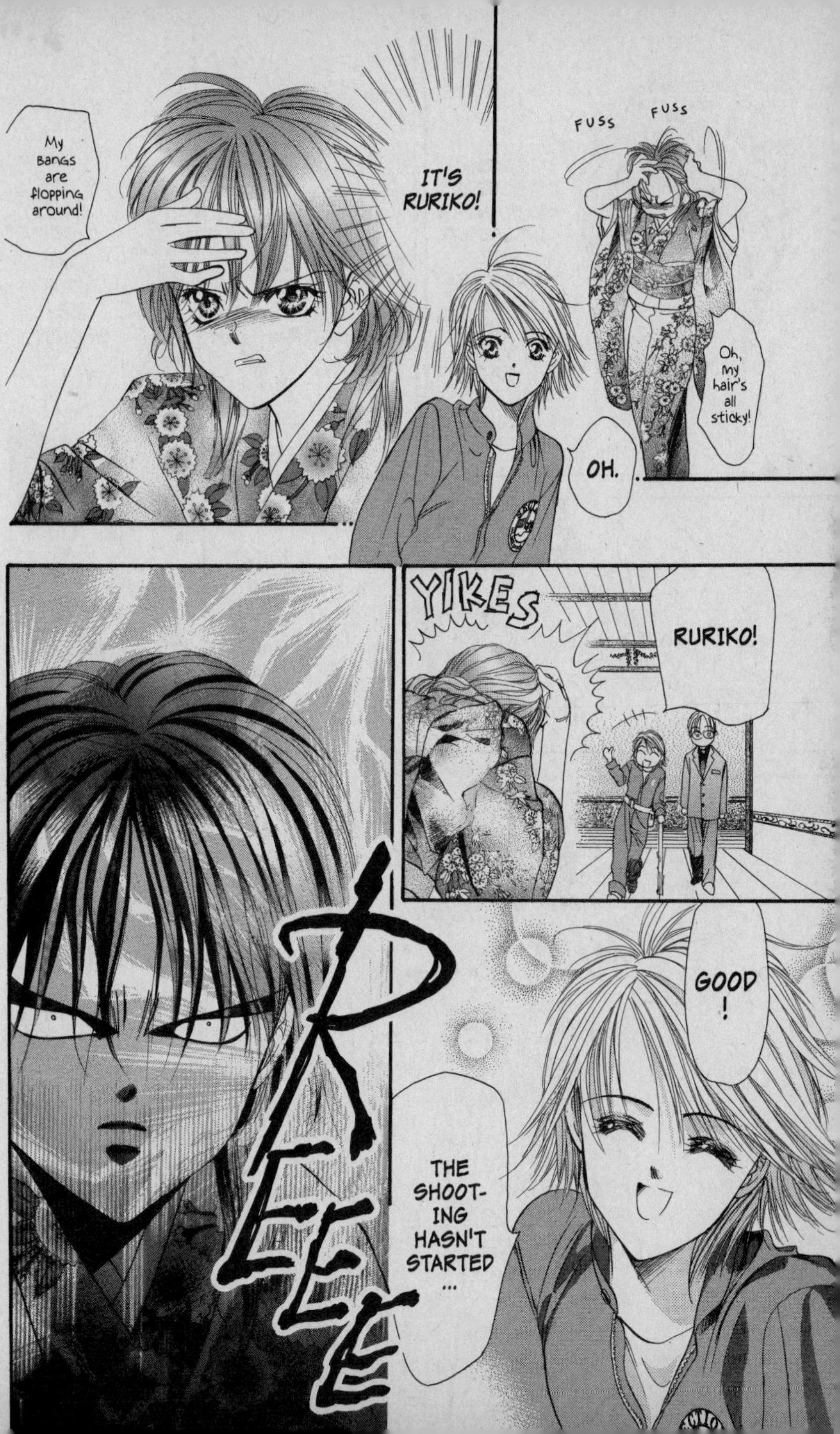
FUSS FUSS
Oh, my hair's all sticky!
OH.
IT'S RURIKO!
My bangs are flopping around!
RURIKO!
YIKES
GOOD!
THE SHOOT-ING HASN'T STARTED ...
REEE

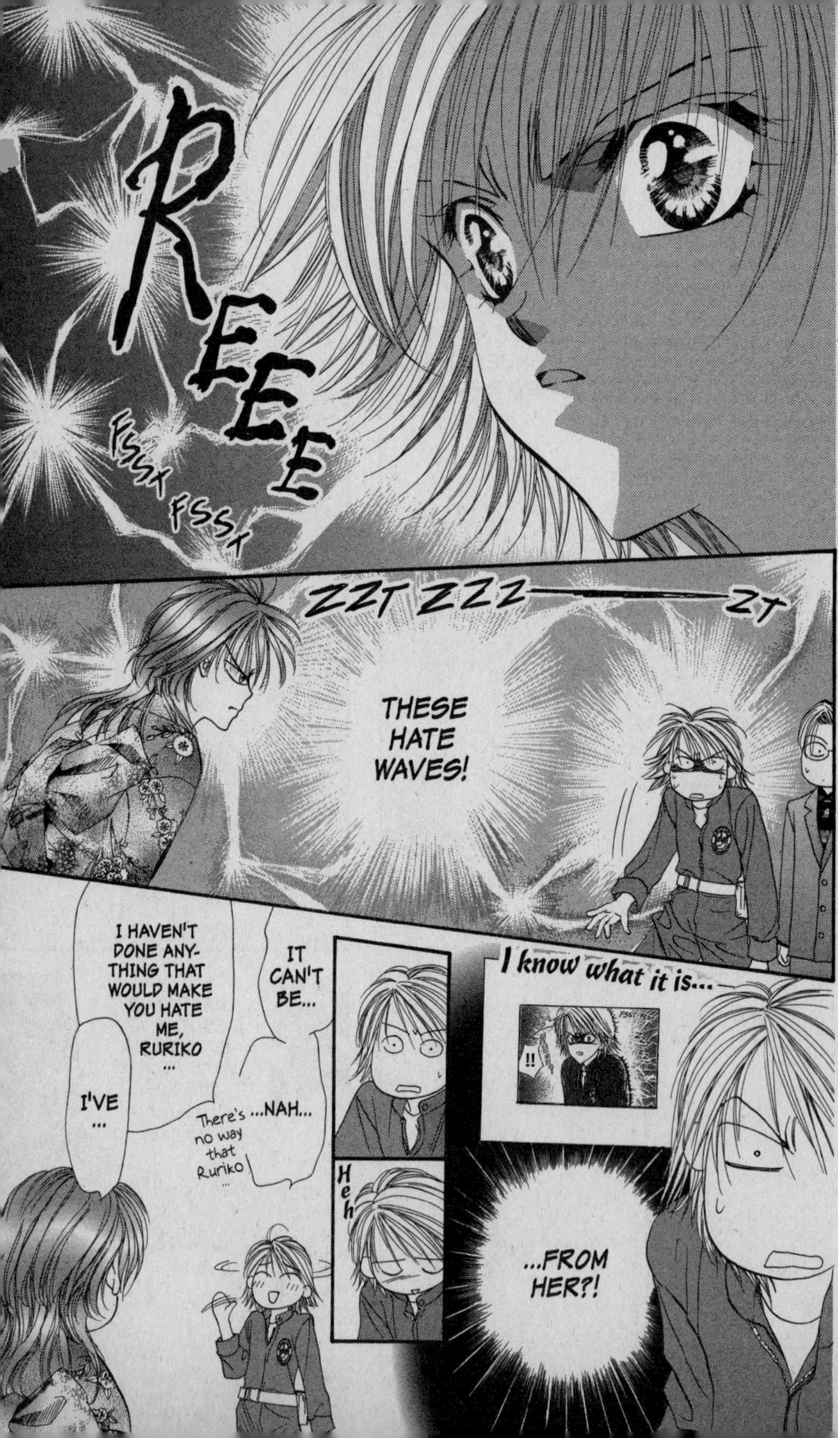
REEE
FSST FSST
ZZT ZZZ——ZT
THESE HATE WAVES!
I know what it is...
!!
...FROM HER?!
IT CAN'T BE...
...NAH...
There's no way that Ruriko...
Heh
I HAVEN'T DONE ANYTHING THAT WOULD MAKE YOU HATE ME, RURIKO...
I'VE...

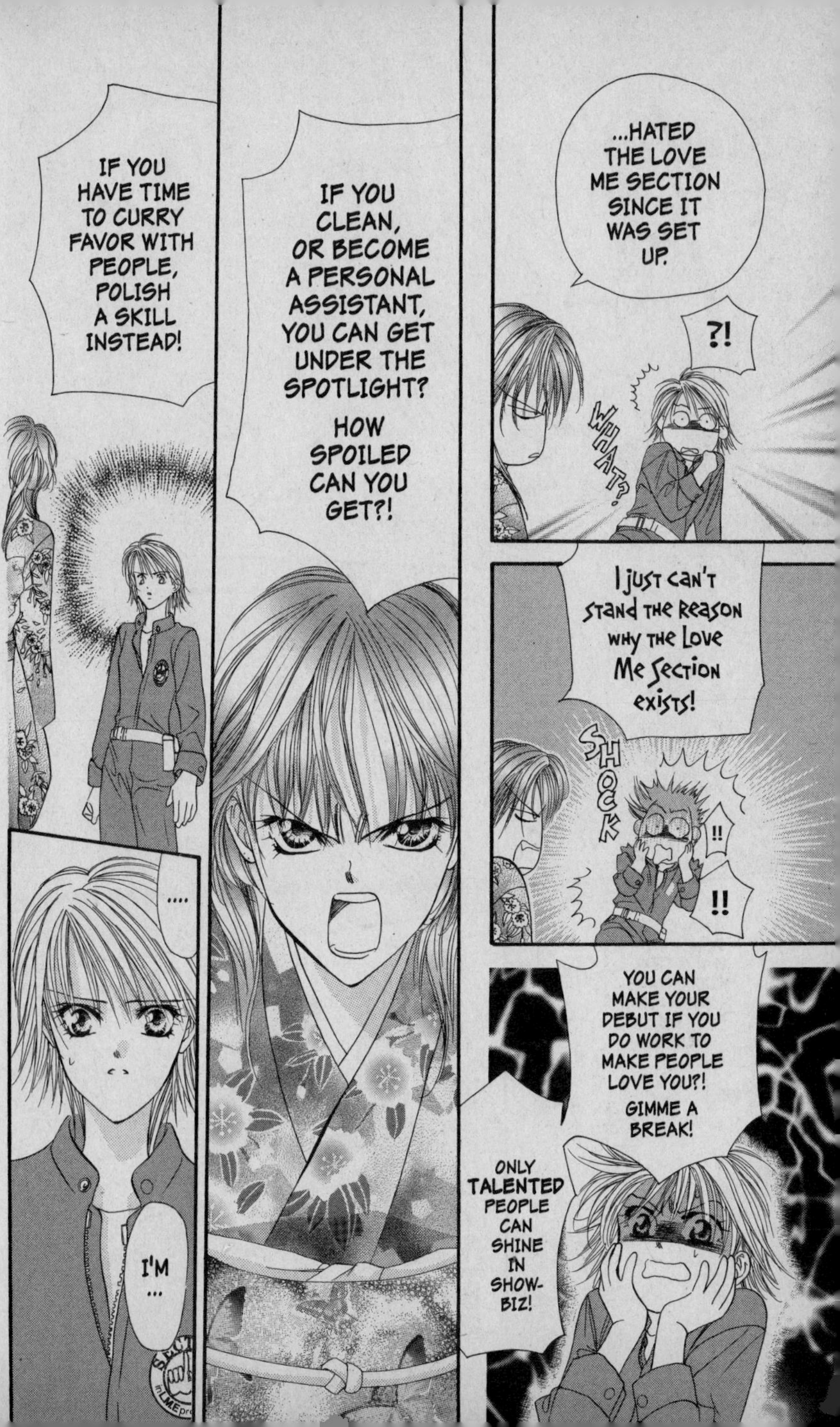
...HATED THE LOVE ME SECTION SINCE IT WAS SET UP.
?!
WHAT?
I just can't stand the reason why the Love Me Section exists!
SHOCK
!!
!!
YOU CAN MAKE YOUR DEBUT IF YOU DO WORK TO MAKE PEOPLE LOVE YOU?!
GIMME A BREAK!
ONLY TALENTED PEOPLE CAN SHINE IN SHOW-BIZ!
IF YOU CLEAN, OR BECOME A PERSONAL ASSISTANT, YOU CAN GET UNDER THE SPOTLIGHT?
HOW SPOILED CAN YOU GET?!
IF YOU HAVE TIME TO CURRY FAVOR WITH PEOPLE, POLISH A SKILL INSTEAD!
....
I'M ...

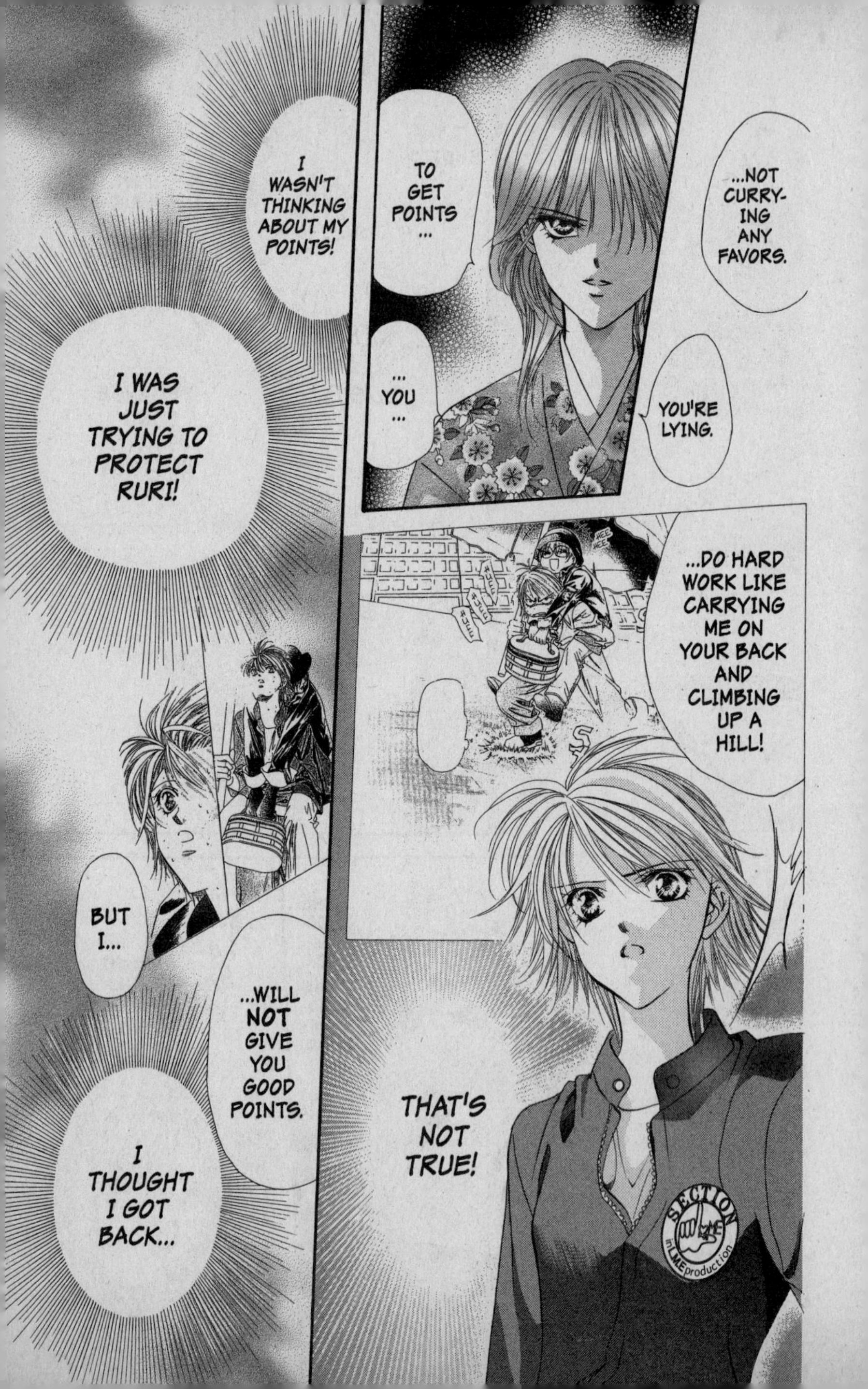
...NOT CURRYING ANY FAVORS.
TO GET POINTS ...
YOU'RE LYING.
... YOU ...
I WASN'T THINKING ABOUT MY POINTS!
I WAS JUST TRYING TO PROTECT RURI!
...DO HARD WORK LIKE CARRYING ME ON YOUR BACK AND CLIMBING UP A HILL!
BUT I...
THAT'S NOT TRUE!
...WILL NOT GIVE YOU GOOD POINTS.
I THOUGHT I GOT BACK...
SECTION
in LME production

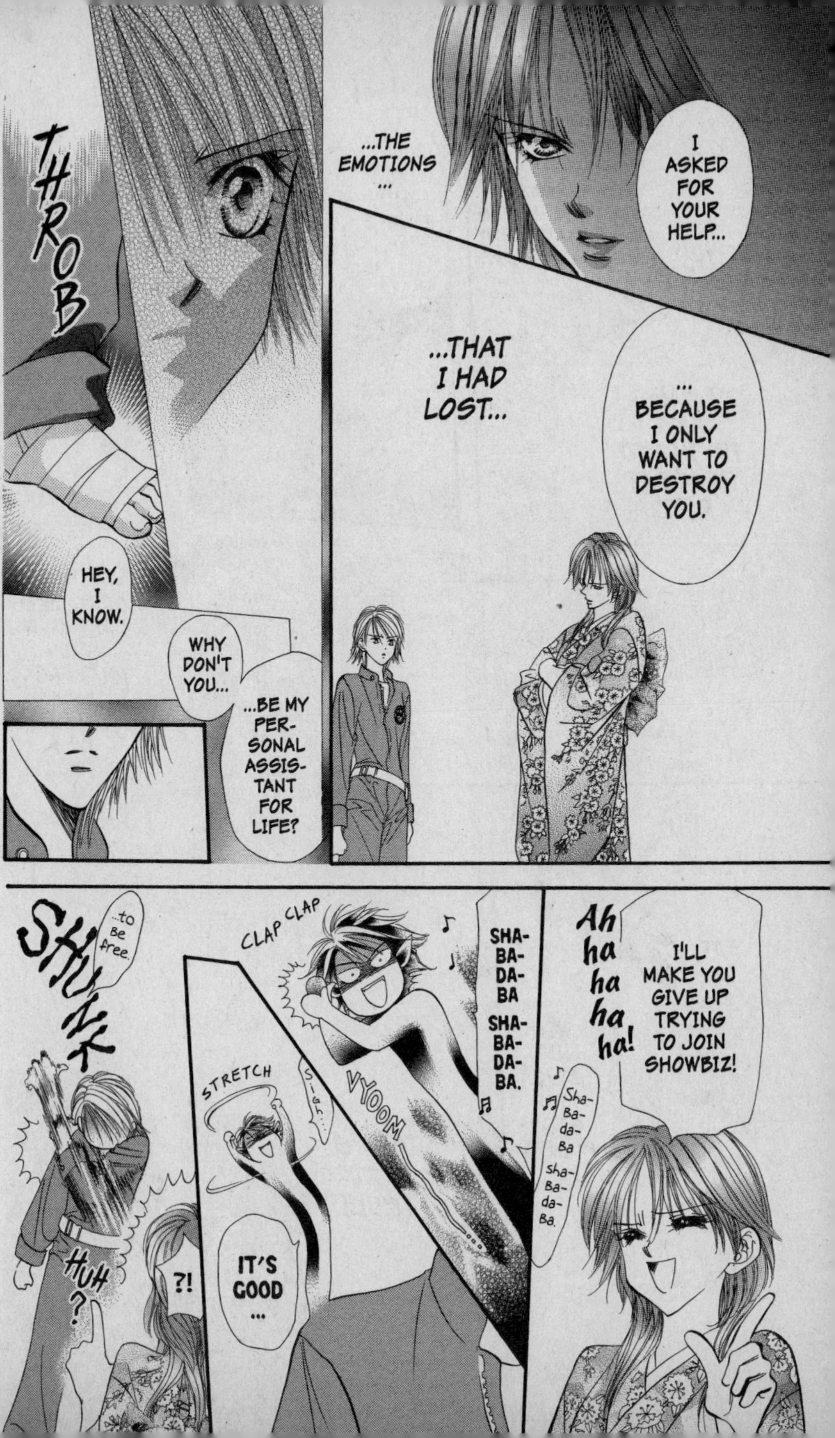
I ASKED FOR YOUR HELP...
...THE EMOTIONS...
...BECAUSE I ONLY WANT TO DESTROY YOU.
...THAT I HAD LOST...
THROB
HEY, I KNOW.
WHY DON'T YOU...
...BE MY PERSONAL ASSISTANT FOR LIFE?
Ah ha ha ha ha!
I'LL MAKE YOU GIVE UP TRYING TO JOIN SHOWBIZ!
Sha-Ba-da-Ba sha-Ba-da-Ba.
SHA-BA-DA-BA SHA-BA-DA-BA.
CLAP CLAP
VYOOM
STRETCH
Sigh...
IT'S GOOD...
...to be free.
SHUNK
HUH?
?!

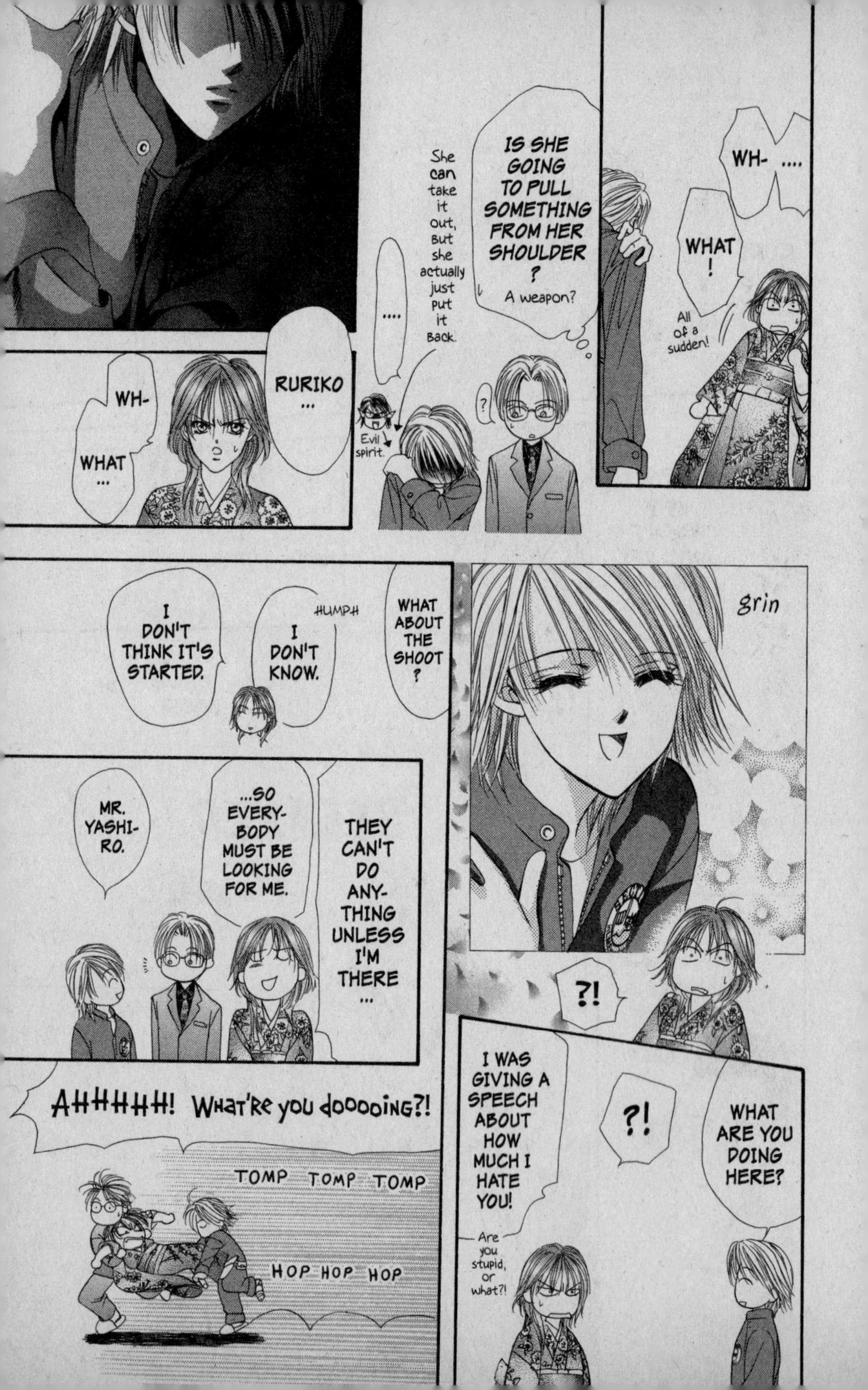

WH- ....
WHAT!
All of a sudden!
IS SHE GOING TO PULL SOMETHING FROM HER SHOULDER? A weapon?
She can take it out, But she actually just put it Back.
....
?
Evil spirit.
RURIKO ...
WH- WHAT ...
grin
?!
WHAT ABOUT THE SHOOT?
I DON'T KNOW.
HUMPH
I DON'T THINK IT'S STARTED.
THEY CAN'T DO ANY-THING UNLESS I'M THERE ...
...SO EVERY-BODY MUST BE LOOKING FOR ME.
MR. YASHI-RO.
WHAT ARE YOU DOING HERE?
?!
I WAS GIVING A SPEECH ABOUT HOW MUCH I HATE YOU!
Are you stupid, or what?!
AHHHHH! What're you doooing?!
TOMP TOMP TOMP
HOP HOP HOP

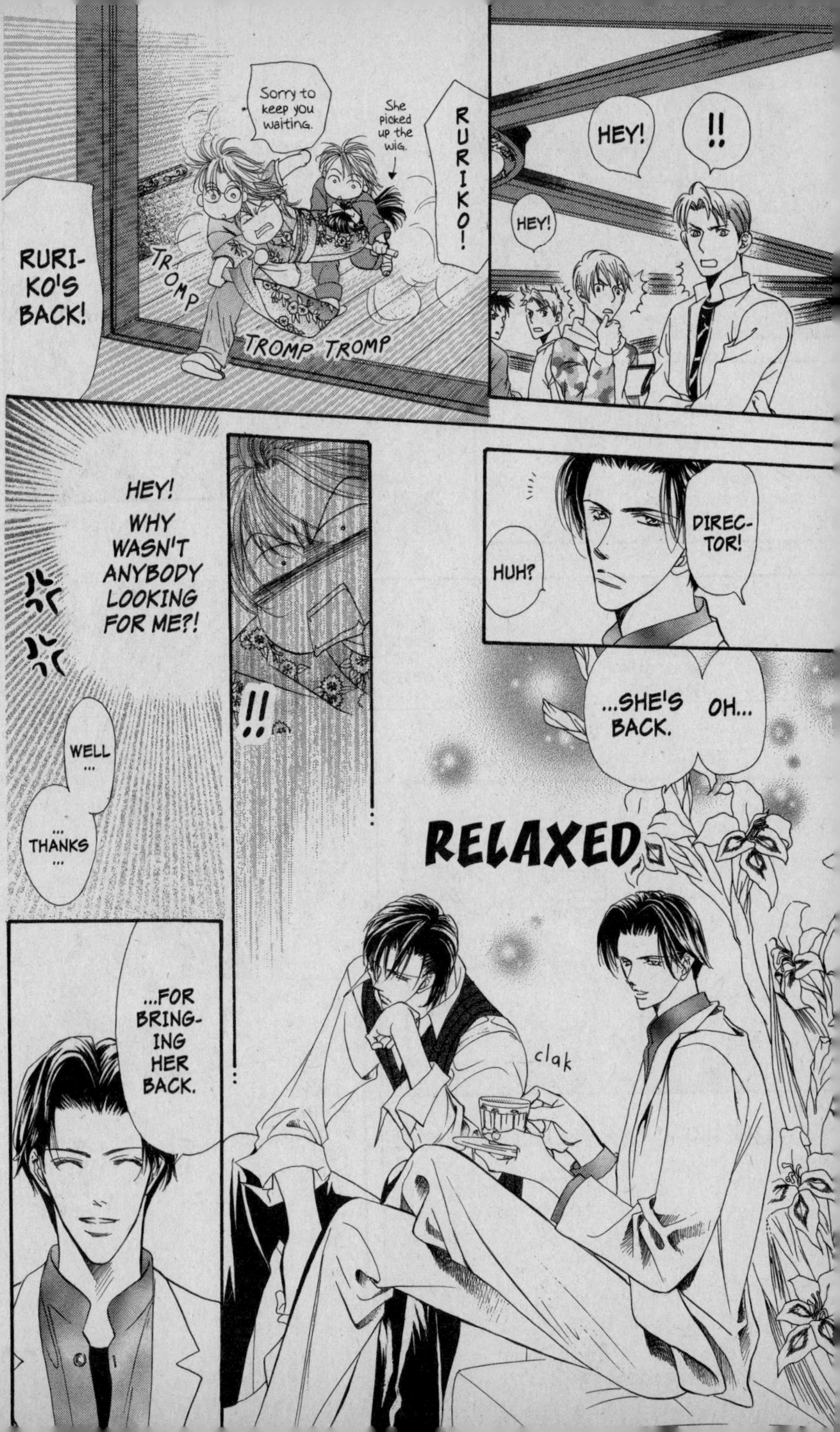
!!
HEY!
HEY!
RURIKO!
She picked up the wig.
Sorry to keep you waiting.
TROMP
TROMP TROMP
RURI-KO'S BACK!
DIREC-TOR!
HUH?
!!
HEY! WHY WASN'T ANYBODY LOOKING FOR ME?!
WELL...
...THANKS...
OH...
...SHE'S BACK.
RELAXED
clak
...FOR BRING-ING HER BACK.

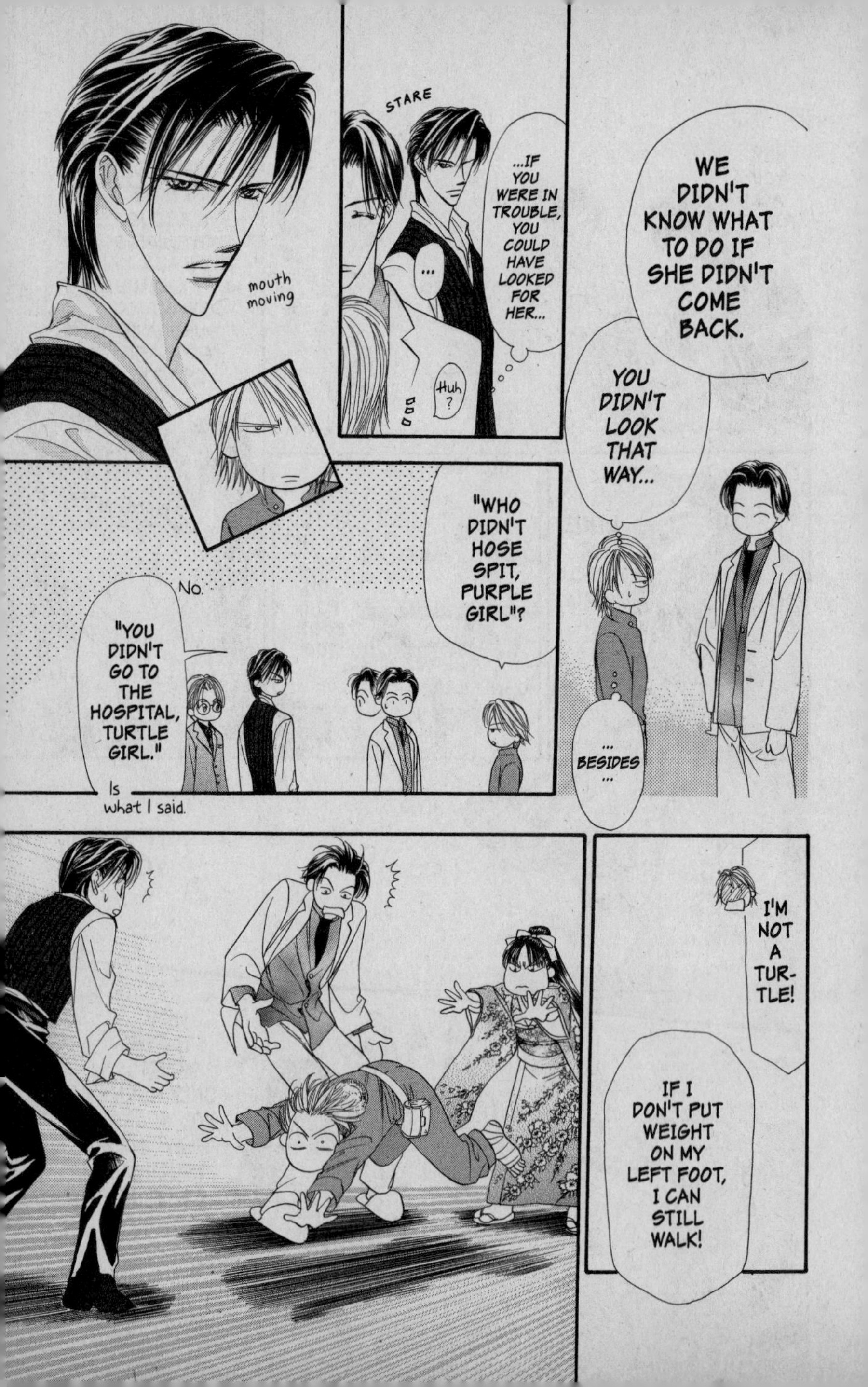
WE DIDN'T KNOW WHAT TO DO IF SHE DIDN'T COME BACK.
YOU DIDN'T LOOK THAT WAY...
...BESIDES...
STARE
...IF YOU WERE IN TROUBLE, YOU COULD HAVE LOOKED FOR HER...
...
Huh?
mouth moving
"WHO DIDN'T HOSE SPIT, PURPLE GIRL"?
No.
"YOU DIDN'T GO TO THE HOSPITAL, TURTLE GIRL."
Is what I said.
I'M NOT A TURTLE!
IF I DON'T PUT WEIGHT ON MY LEFT FOOT, I CAN STILL WALK!

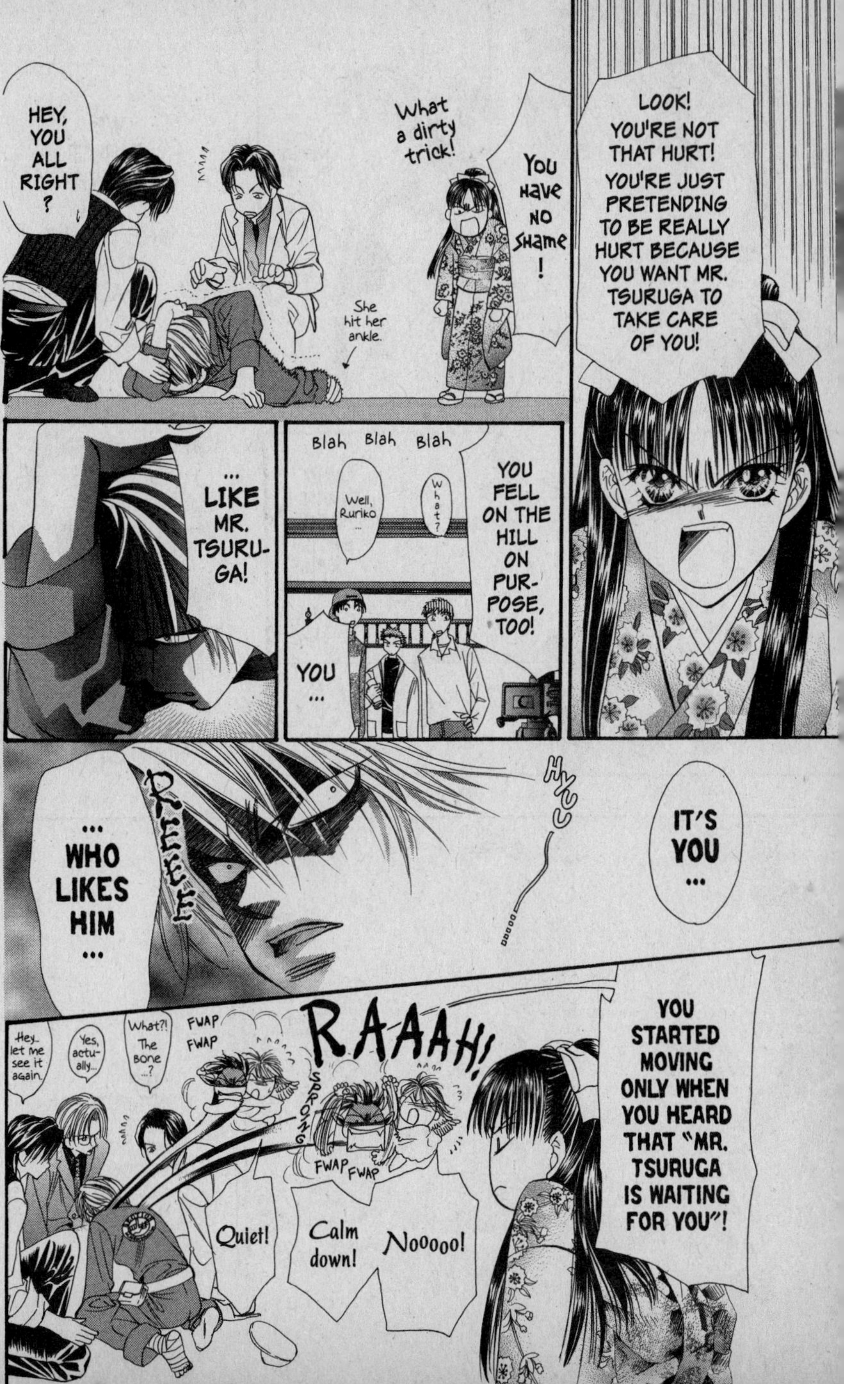
LOOK! YOU'RE NOT THAT HURT! YOU'RE JUST PRETENDING TO BE REALLY HURT BECAUSE YOU WANT MR. TSURUGA TO TAKE CARE OF YOU!
You have no shame!
What a dirty trick!
She hit her ankle.
HEY, YOU ALL RIGHT?
YOU FELL ON THE HILL ON PURPOSE, TOO!
Blah Blah Blah
What?
Well, Ruriko...
YOU ...
... LIKE MR. TSURUGA!
IT'S YOU ...
HYUU
... WHO LIKES HIM ...
REEEE
YOU STARTED MOVING ONLY WHEN YOU HEARD THAT "MR. TSURUGA IS WAITING FOR YOU"!
RAAAH!
SPROING
FWAP FWAP
FWAP FWAP
Nooooo!
Calm down!
Quiet!
What?! The bone ...?
Yes, actually...
Hey.. let me see it again.

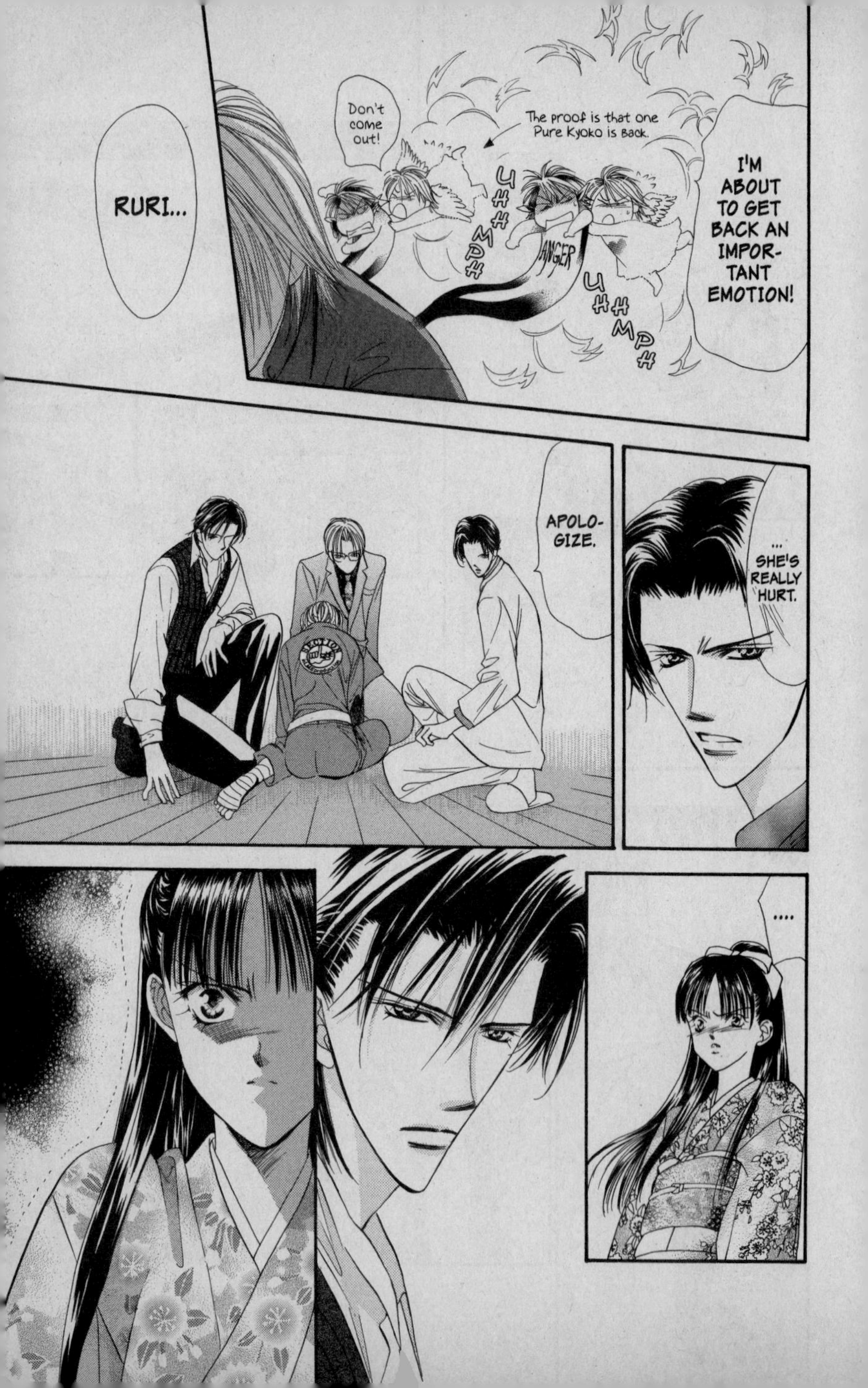
I'M ABOUT TO GET BACK AN IMPOR-TANT EMOTION!
The proof is that one Pure Kyoko is back.
Don't come out!
UHHMPH
ANGER
UHHMPH
RURI...
... SHE'S REALLY HURT.
APOLO-GIZE.
....

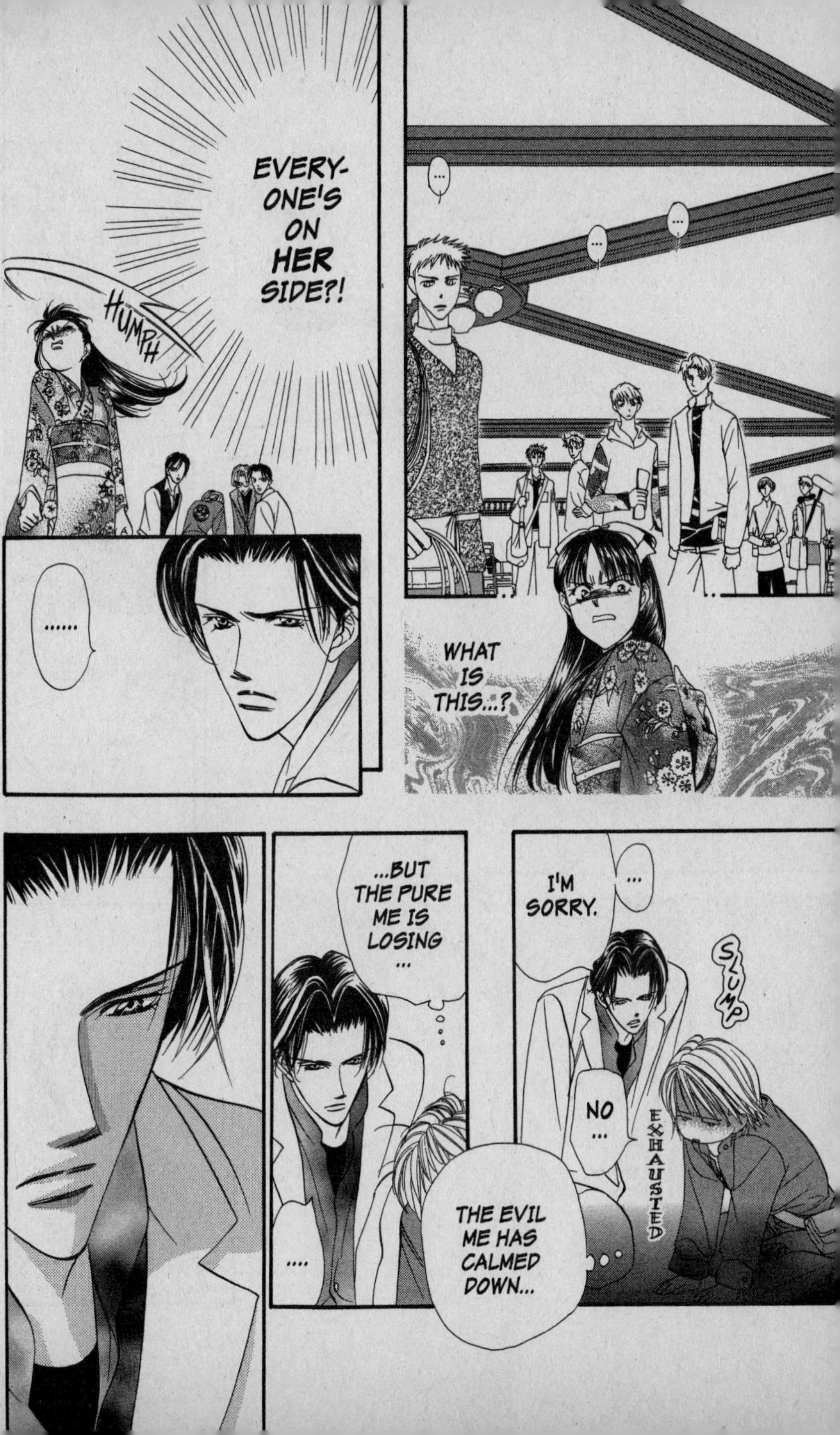
...
...
...
WHAT IS THIS...?
EVERY-ONE'S ON HER SIDE?!
HUMPH
......
...
I'M SORRY.
SLUMP
NO ...
EXHAUSTED
...BUT THE PURE ME IS LOSING ...
THE EVIL ME HAS CALMED DOWN...
....

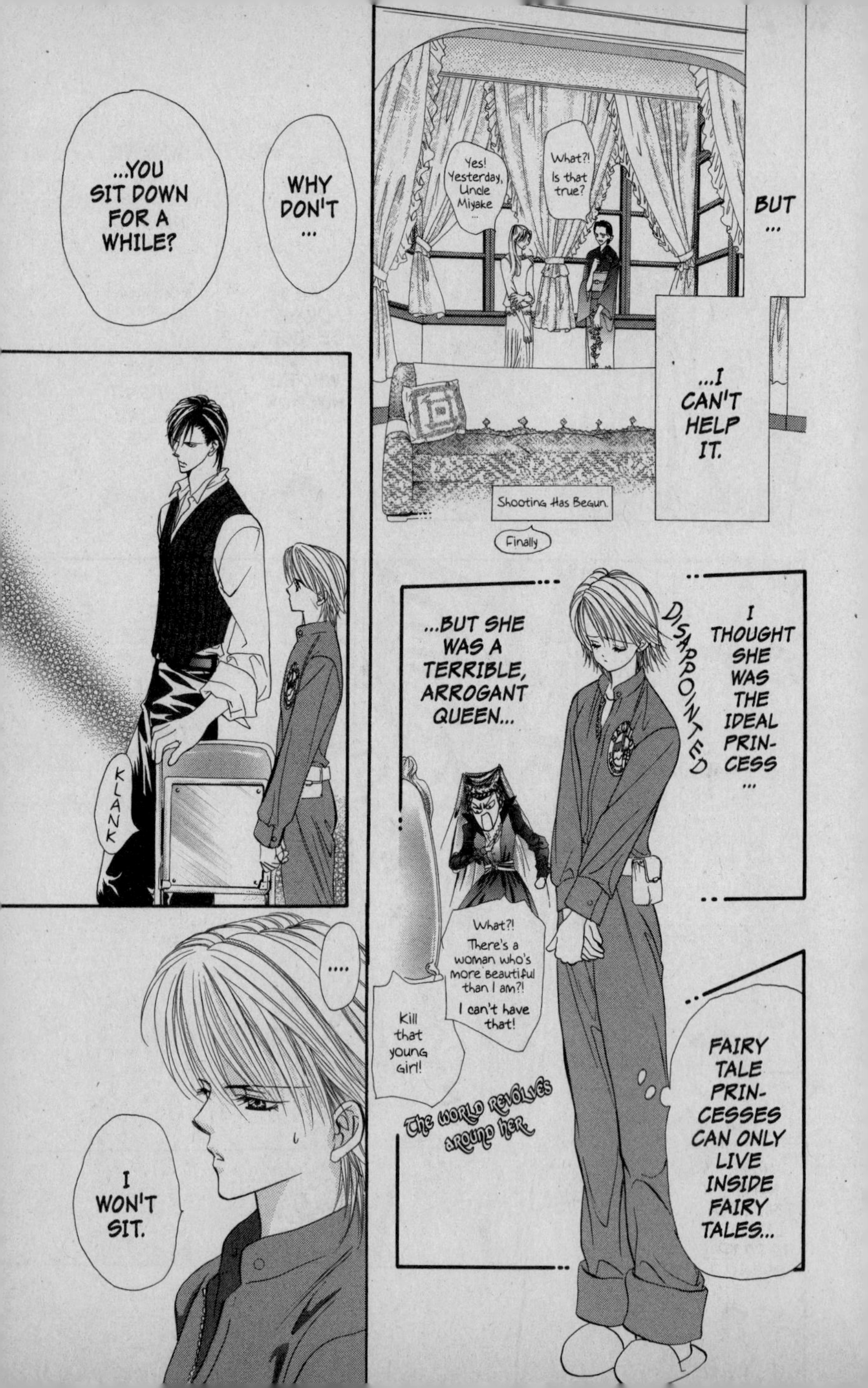
BUT ...
What?! Is that true?
Yes! Yesterday, Uncle Miyake ...
...I CAN'T HELP IT.
Shooting Has Begun.
Finally
I THOUGHT SHE WAS THE IDEAL PRIN- CESS ...
DISAPPOINTED
...BUT SHE WAS A TERRIBLE, ARROGANT QUEEN...
What?! There's a woman who's more beautiful than I am?! I can't have that!
Kill that young girl!
FAIRY TALE PRIN- CESSES CAN ONLY LIVE INSIDE FAIRY TALES...
The world revolves around her.
WHY DON'T ...
...YOU SIT DOWN FOR A WHILE?
KLANK
....
I WON'T SIT.

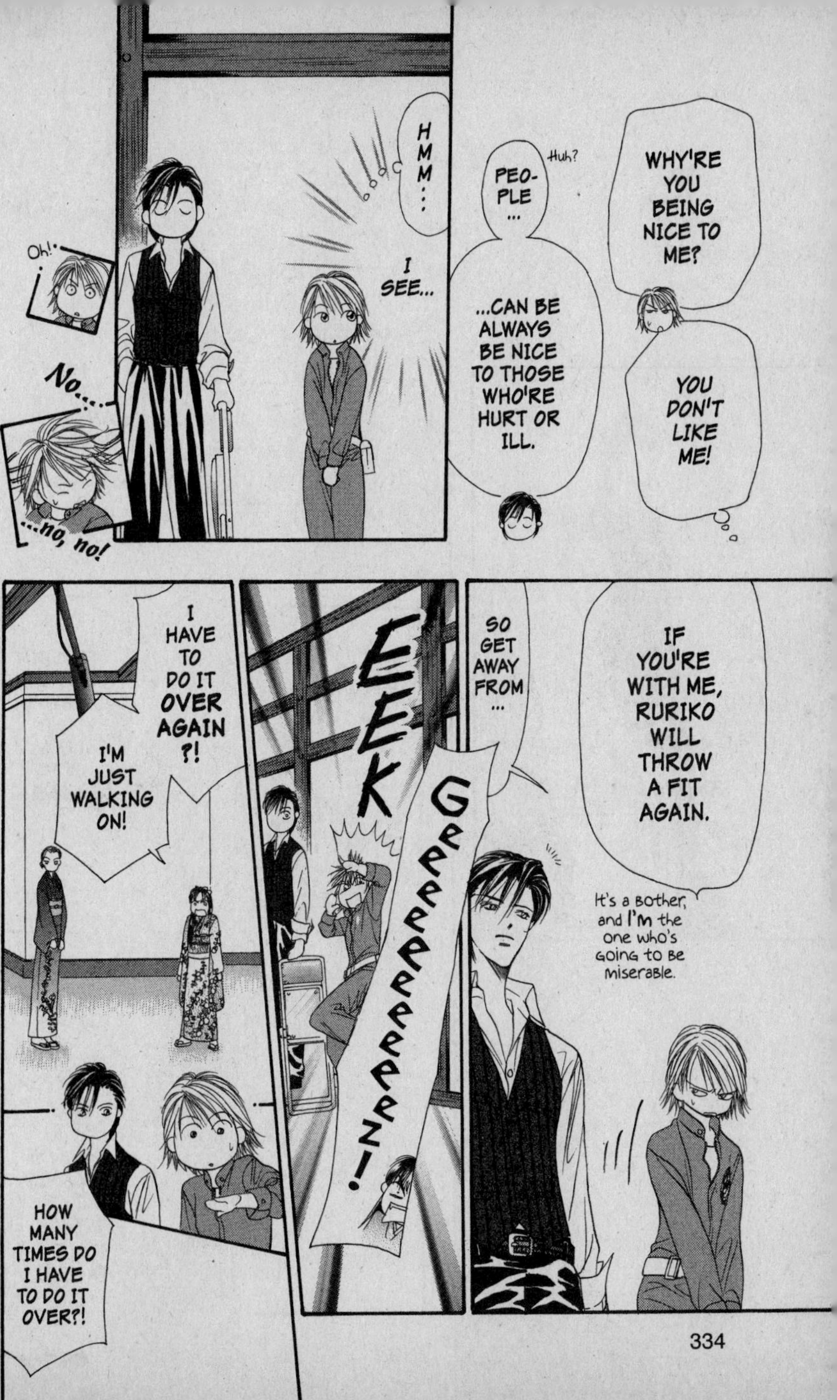
WHY'RE YOU BEING NICE TO ME?
YOU DON'T LIKE ME!
Huh?
PEO-PLE...
...CAN BE ALWAYS BE NICE TO THOSE WHO'RE HURT OR ILL.
HMM...
I SEE...
Oh!
No......
...no, no!
IF YOU'RE WITH ME, RURIKO WILL THROW A FIT AGAIN.
SO GET AWAY FROM...
It's a bother, and I'm the one who's going to be miserable.
EEK
Geeeeeeeeez!
I HAVE TO DO IT OVER AGAIN?!
I'M JUST WALKING ON!
HOW MANY TIMES DO I HAVE TO DO IT OVER?!

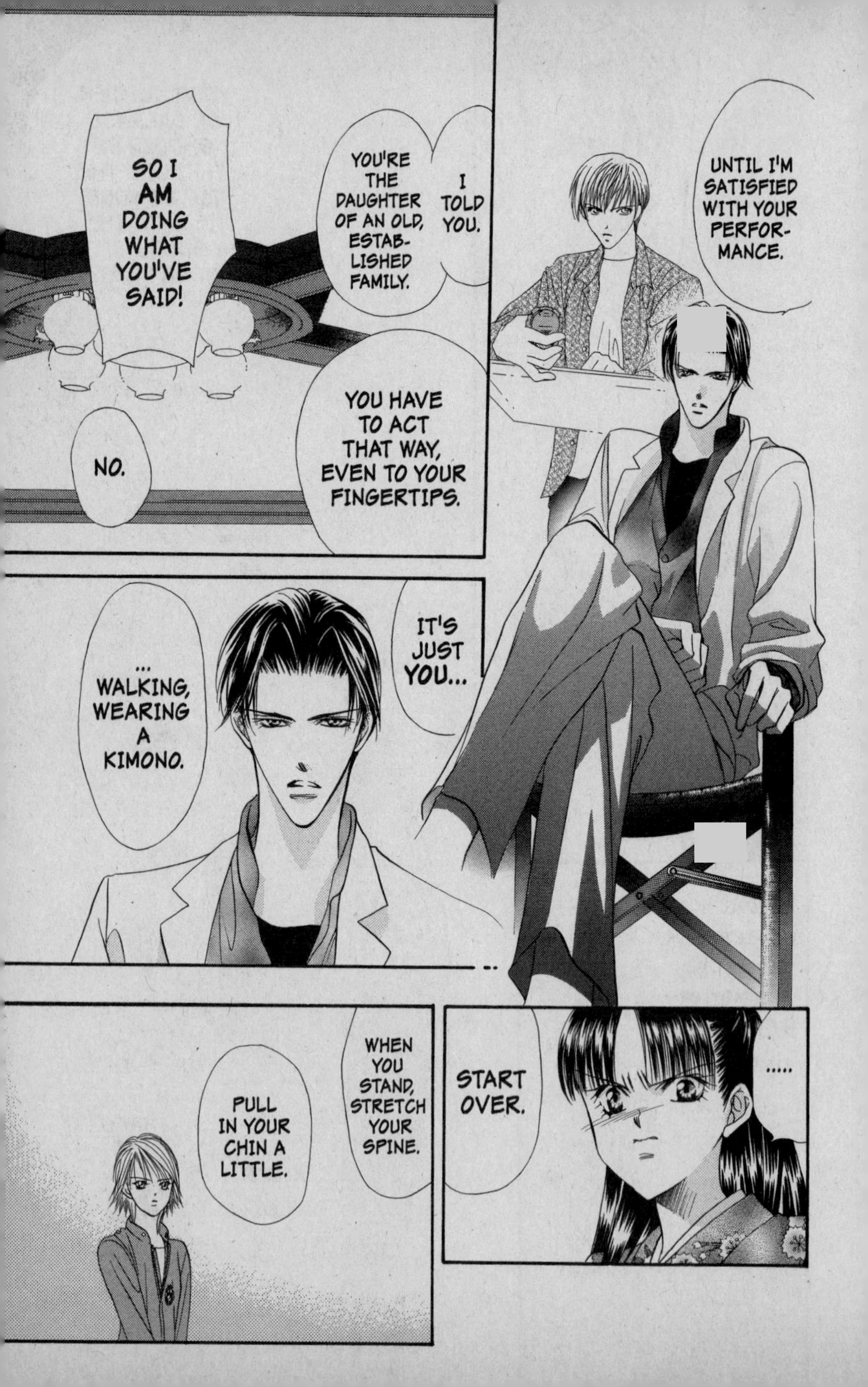
UNTIL I'M SATISFIED WITH YOUR PERFORMANCE.
I TOLD YOU.
YOU'RE THE DAUGHTER OF AN OLD, ESTABLISHED FAMILY.
YOU HAVE TO ACT THAT WAY, EVEN TO YOUR FINGERTIPS.
SO I AM DOING WHAT YOU'VE SAID!
NO.
IT'S JUST YOU...
...WALKING, WEARING A KIMONO.
.....
START OVER.
WHEN YOU STAND, STRETCH YOUR SPINE.
PULL IN YOUR CHIN A LITTLE.

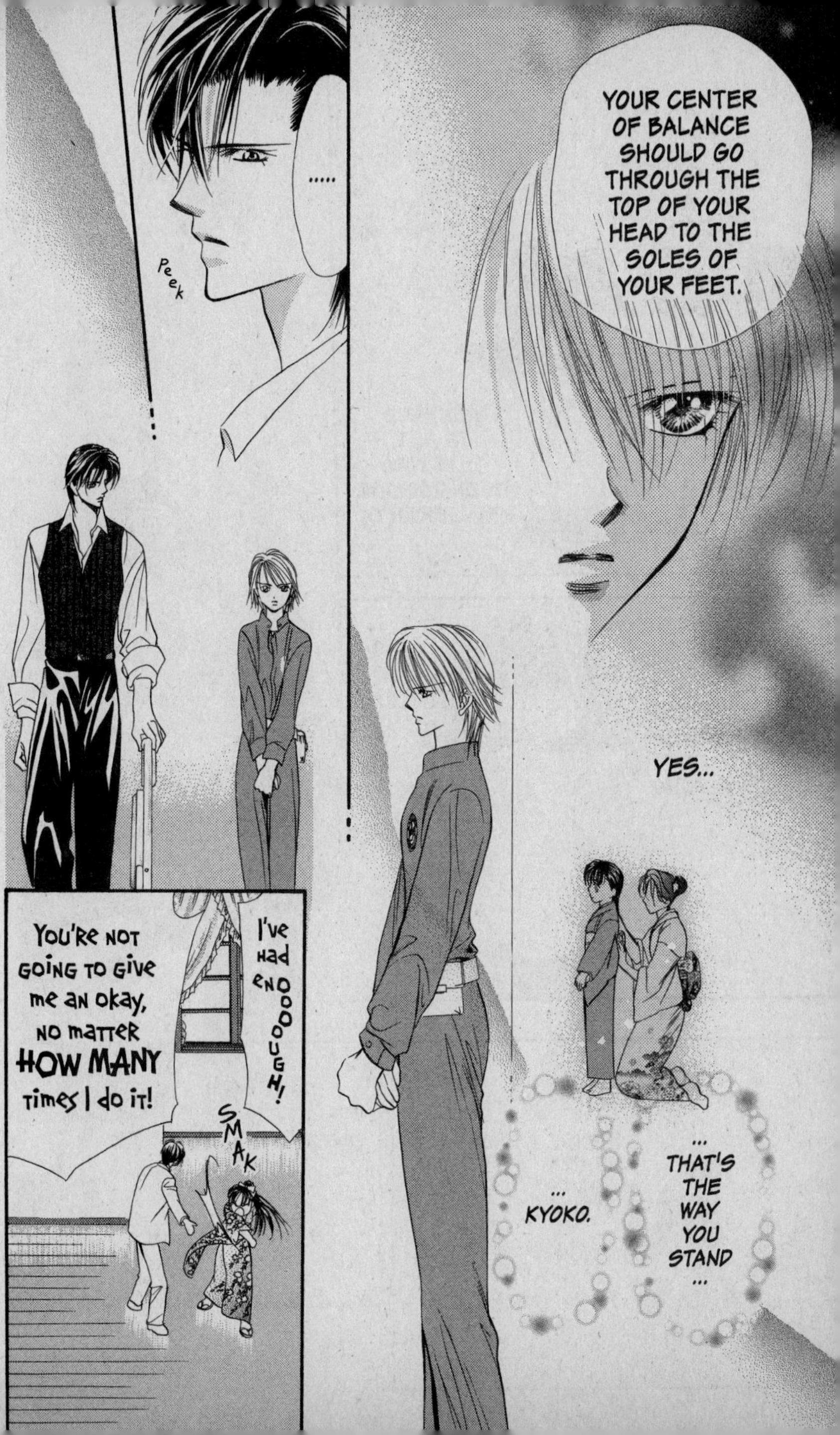
YOUR CENTER OF BALANCE SHOULD GO THROUGH THE TOP OF YOUR HEAD TO THE SOLES OF YOUR FEET.
YES...
...THAT'S THE WAY YOU STAND...
...KYOKO.
.....
Peek
I've had enoooough!
You're not going to give me an okay, no matter HOW MANY times I do it!
SMAK

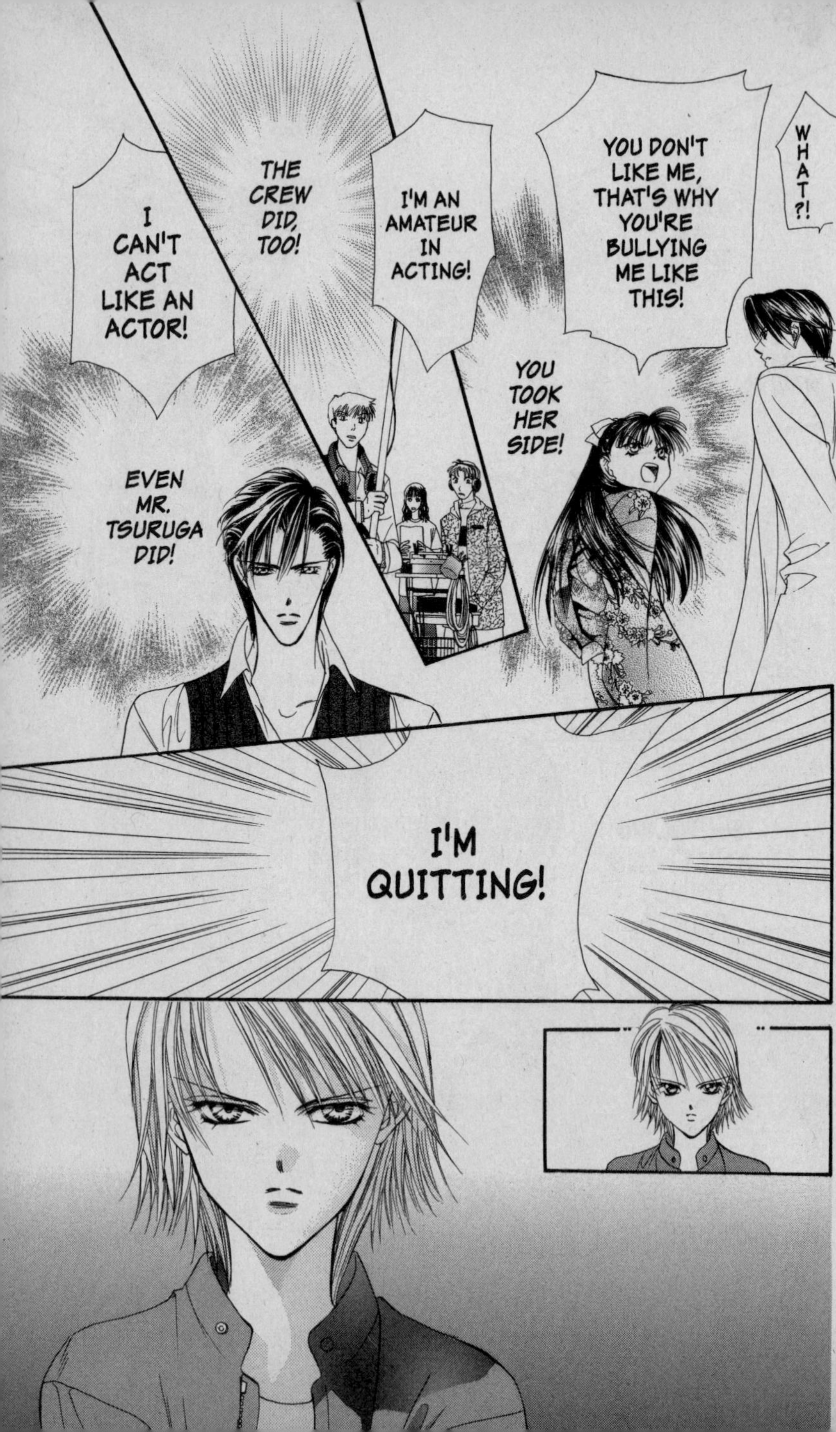
WHAT?!
YOU DON'T LIKE ME, THAT'S WHY YOU'RE BULLYING ME LIKE THIS!
YOU TOOK HER SIDE!
THE CREW DID, TOO!
EVEN MR. TSURUGA DID!
I'M AN AMATEUR IN ACTING!
I CAN'T ACT LIKE AN ACTOR!
I'M QUITTING!

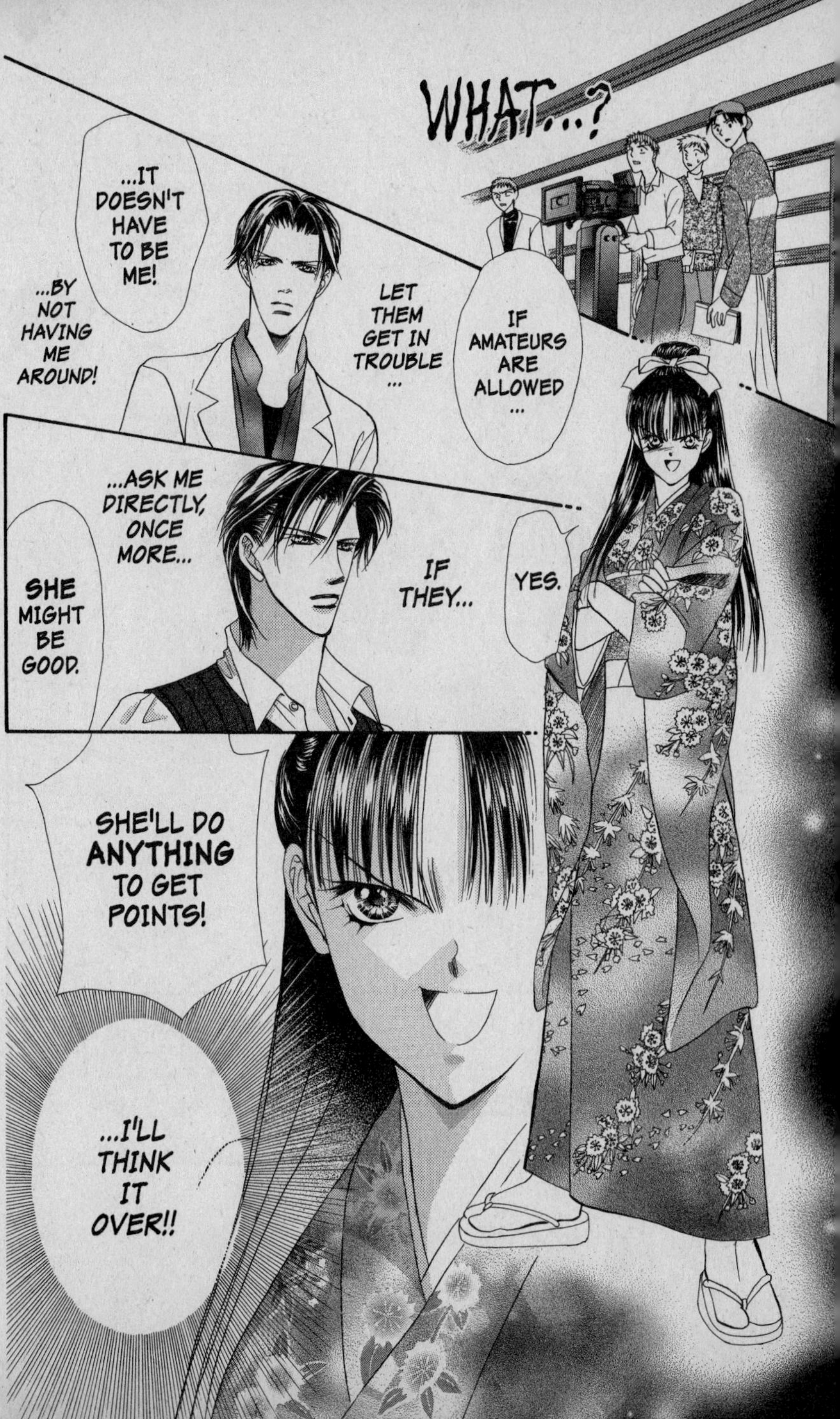
WHAT...?
IF AMATEURS ARE ALLOWED...
LET THEM GET IN TROUBLE...
...IT DOESN'T HAVE TO BE ME!
...BY NOT HAVING ME AROUND!
YES.
IF THEY...
...ASK ME DIRECTLY, ONCE MORE...
SHE MIGHT BE GOOD.
SHE'LL DO ANYTHING TO GET POINTS!
...I'LL THINK IT OVER!!

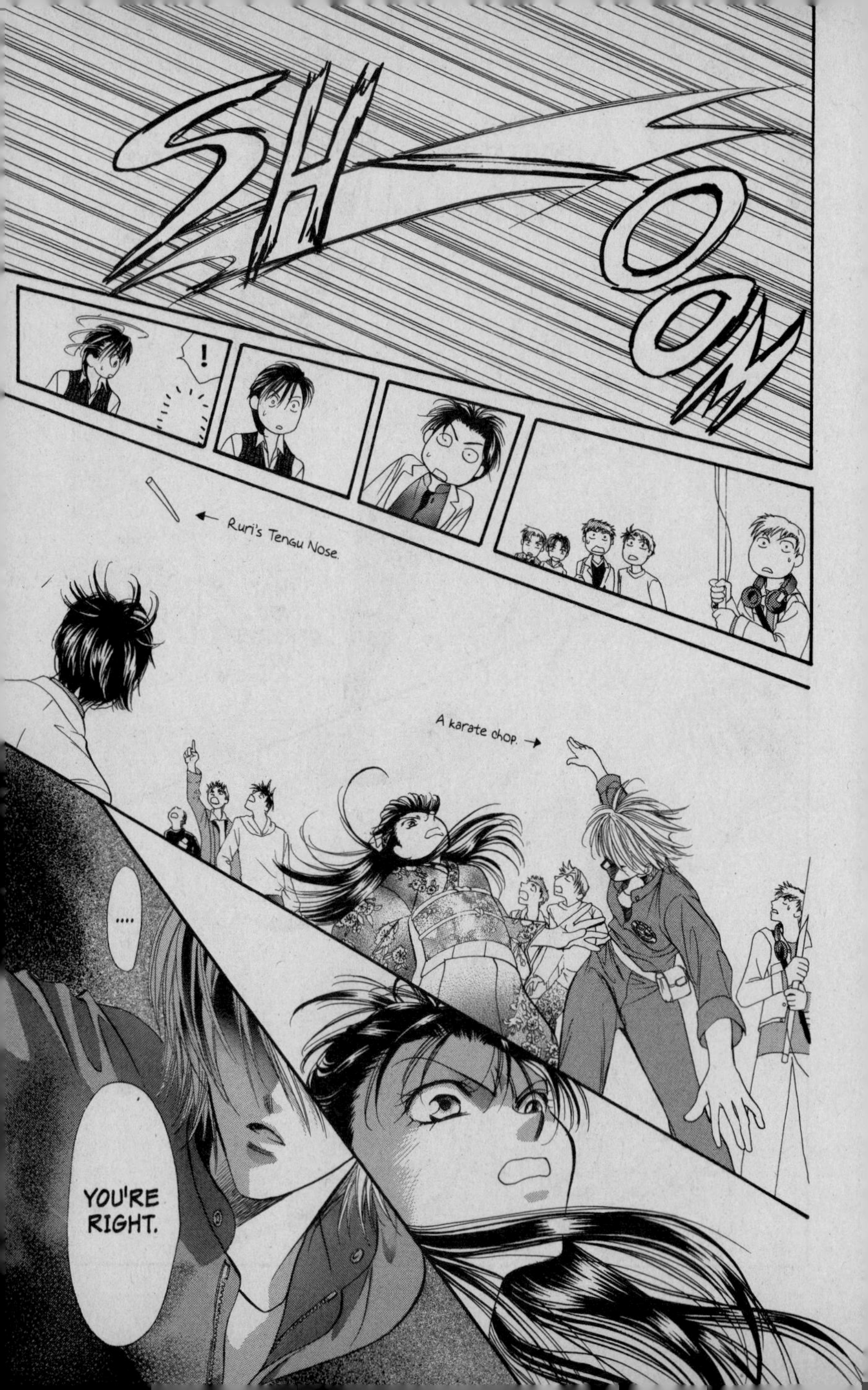
SH—OOM
!
← Ruri's Tengu Nose.
A karate chop. →
....
YOU'RE RIGHT.

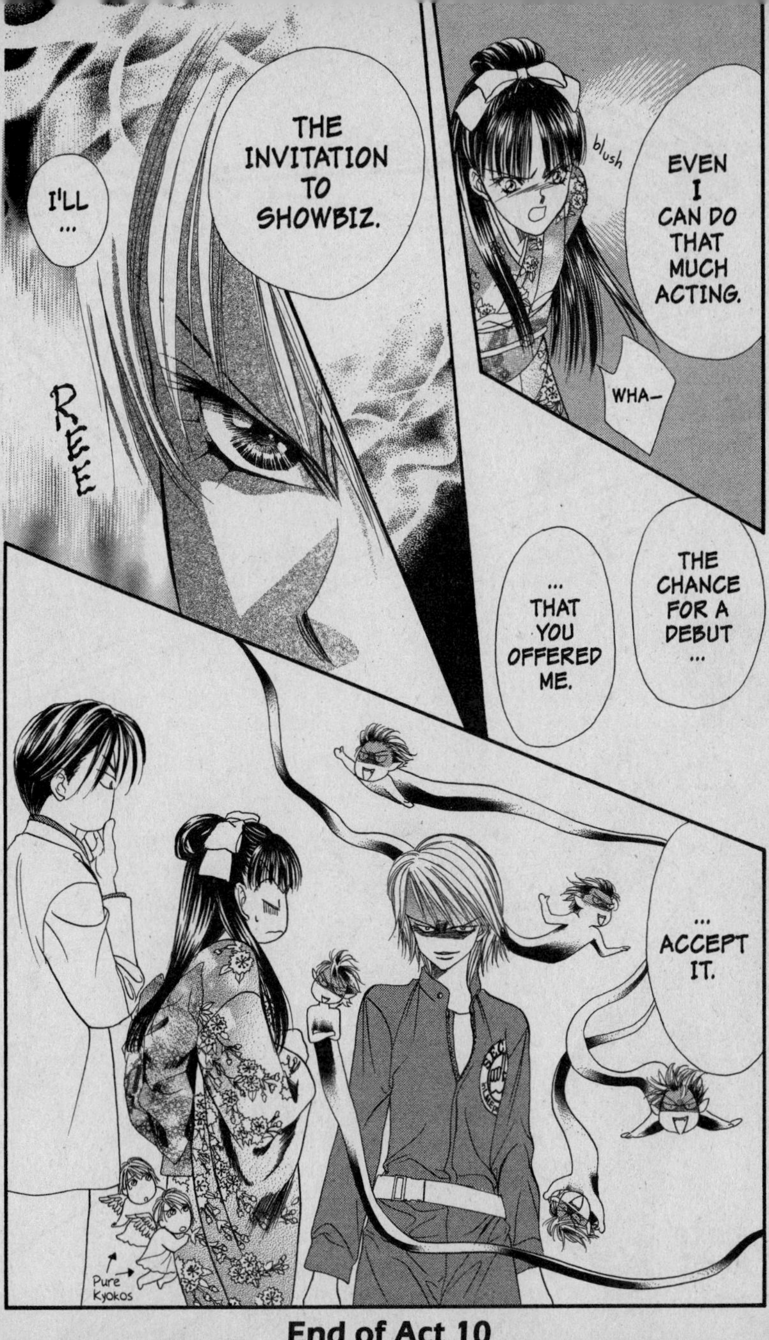
blush
EVEN I CAN DO THAT MUCH ACTING.
WHA-
THE CHANCE FOR A DEBUT ...
... THAT YOU OFFERED ME.
THE INVITATION TO SHOWBIZ.
I'LL ...
REEE
... ACCEPT IT.
Pure Kyokos

End of Act 10

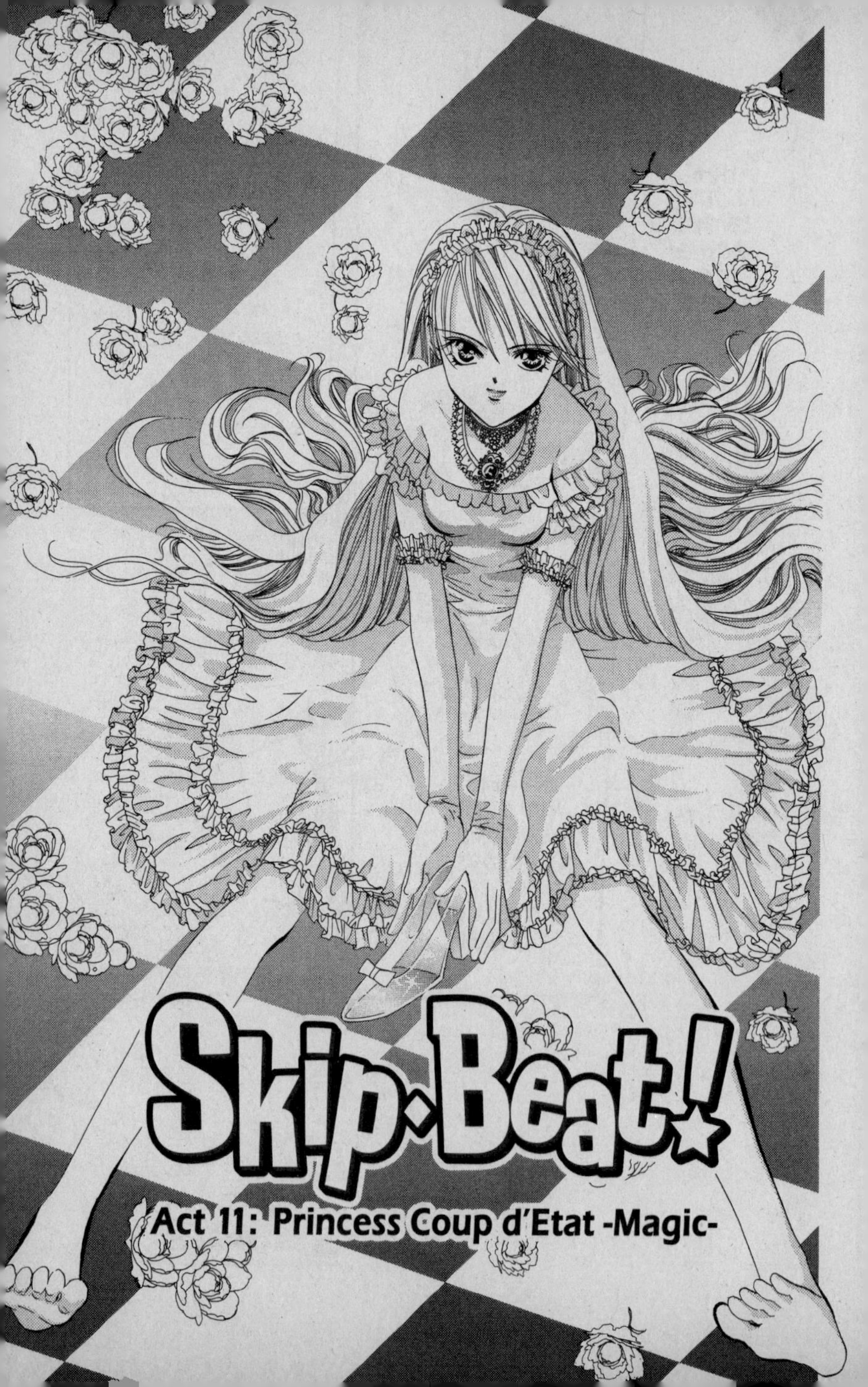
Skip·Beat!
Act 11: Princess Coup d'Etat -Magic-

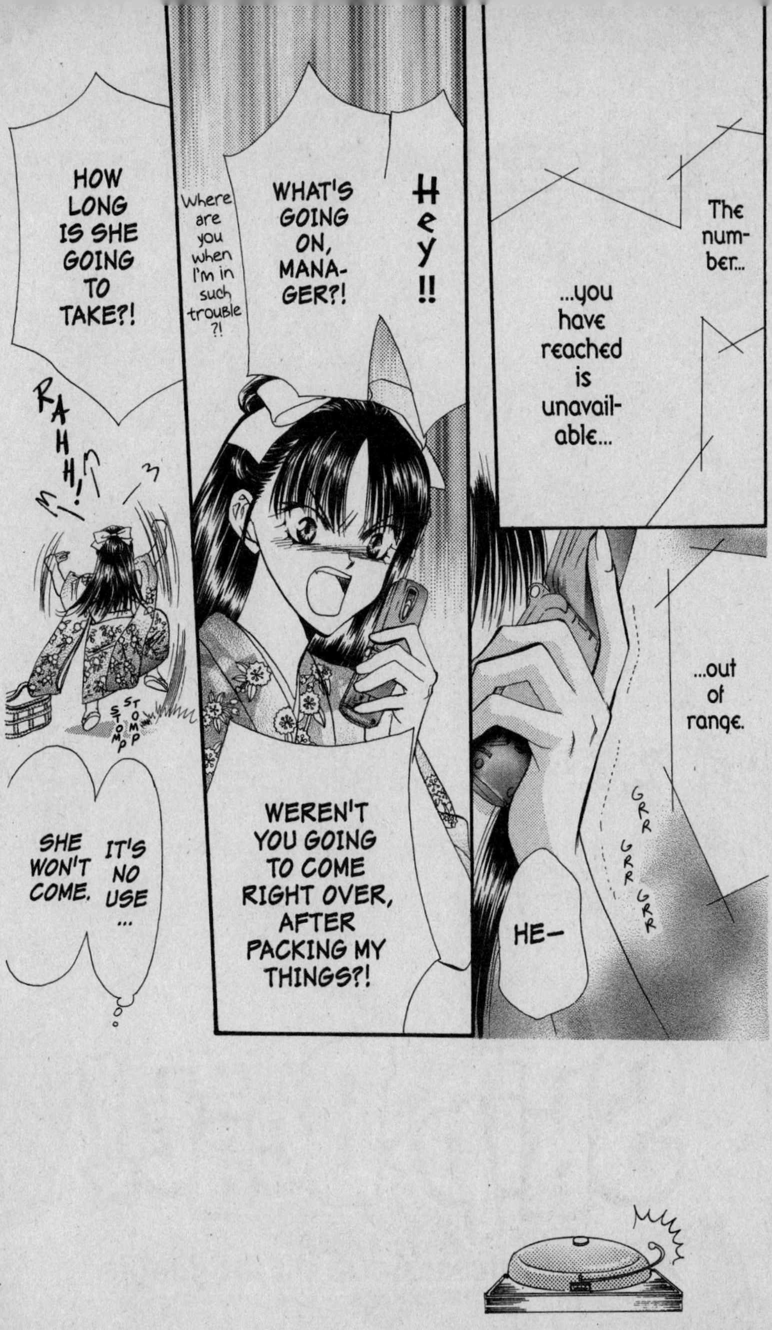
The number...
...you have reached is unavailable...
...out of range.
GRR GRR GRR
HE—
Hey!!
WHAT'S GOING ON, MANAGER?!
Where are you when I'm in such trouble?!
WEREN'T YOU GOING TO COME RIGHT OVER, AFTER PACKING MY THINGS?!
HOW LONG IS SHE GOING TO TAKE?!
RAHH!
STOMP STOMP
IT'S NO USE...
SHE WON'T COME.

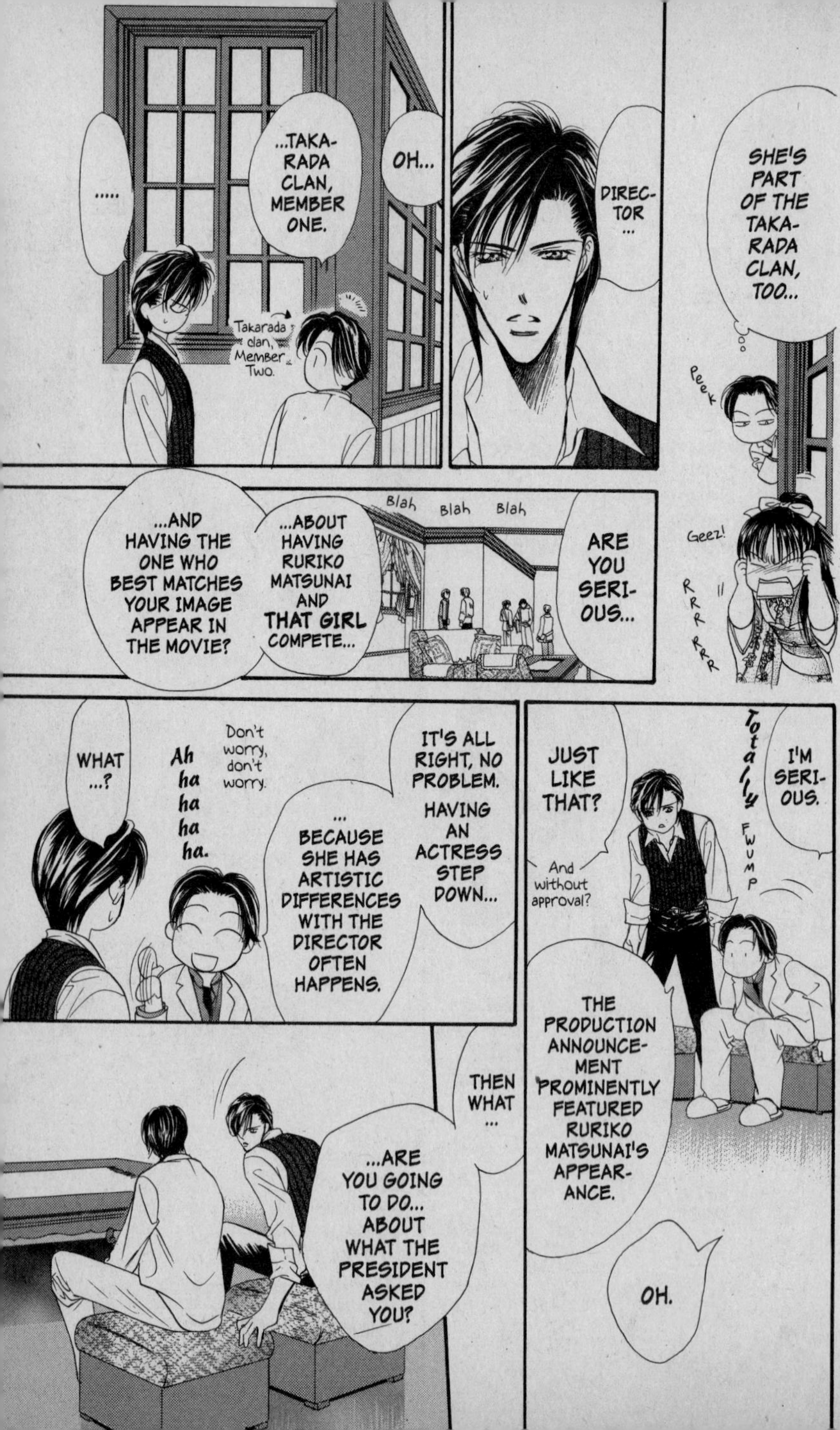
SHE'S PART OF THE TAKARADA CLAN, TOO...
Peek
Geez!
RRRRRR
DIRECTOR...
OH...
...TAKARADA CLAN, MEMBER ONE.
Takarada clan, Member Two.
.....
ARE YOU SERIOUS...
Blah Blah Blah
...ABOUT HAVING RURIKO MATSUNAI AND THAT GIRL COMPETE...
...AND HAVING THE ONE WHO BEST MATCHES YOUR IMAGE APPEAR IN THE MOVIE?
I'M SERIOUS.
Totally
FWUMP
JUST LIKE THAT?
And without approval?
THE PRODUCTION ANNOUNCEMENT PROMINENTLY FEATURED RURIKO MATSUNAI'S APPEARANCE.
OH.
IT'S ALL RIGHT, NO PROBLEM.
HAVING AN ACTRESS STEP DOWN...
...BECAUSE SHE HAS ARTISTIC DIFFERENCES WITH THE DIRECTOR OFTEN HAPPENS.
Don't worry, don't worry.
Ah ha ha ha ha.
WHAT...?
THEN WHAT...
...ARE YOU GOING TO DO... ABOUT WHAT THE PRESIDENT ASKED YOU?

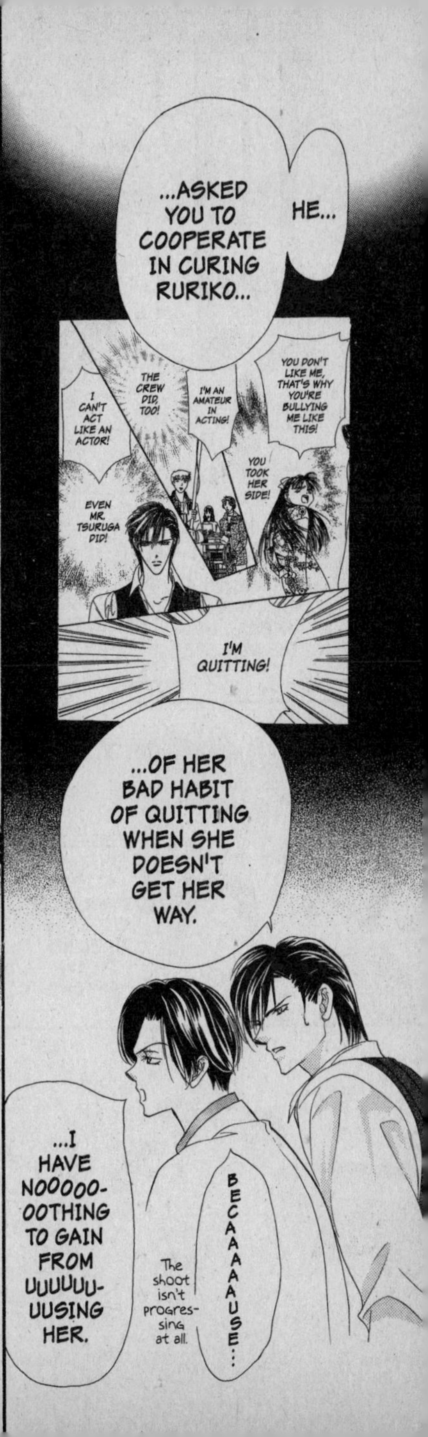
HE...
...ASKED YOU TO COOPERATE IN CURING RURIKO...
YOU DON'T LIKE ME, THAT'S WHY YOU'RE BULLYING ME LIKE THIS!
YOU TOOK HER SIDE!
I'M AN AMATEUR IN ACTING!
THE CREW DID, TOO!
I CAN'T ACT LIKE AN ACTOR!
EVEN MR. TSURUGA DID!
I'M QUITTING!
...OF HER BAD HABIT OF QUITTING WHEN SHE DOESN'T GET HER WAY.
BECAAAAAUSE...
The shoot isn't progressing at all.
...I HAVE NOOOOO-OOTHING TO GAIN FROM UUUUUU-UUSING HER.
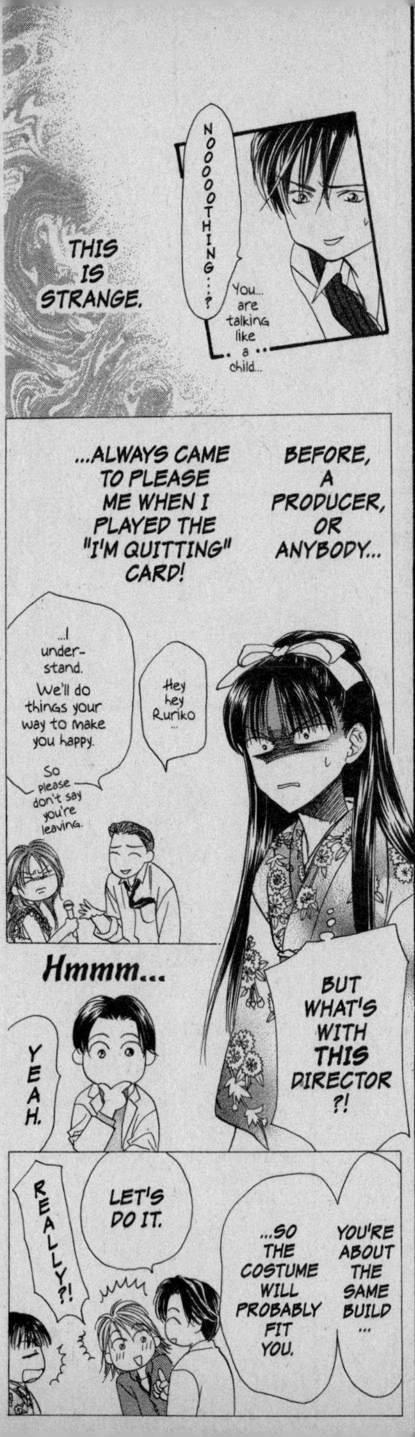
NOOOOOOTHING...?
You... are talking like a child...
THIS IS STRANGE.
BEFORE, A PRODUCER, OR ANYBODY...
...ALWAYS CAME TO PLEASE ME WHEN I PLAYED THE "I'M QUITTING" CARD!
Hey hey Ruriko ...
...I understand. We'll do things your way to make you happy.
So please don't say you're leaving.
BUT WHAT'S WITH THIS DIRECTOR?!
Hmmm...
YEAH.
YOU'RE ABOUT THE SAME BUILD ...
...SO THE COSTUME WILL PROBABLY FIT YOU.
LET'S DO IT.
REALLY?!

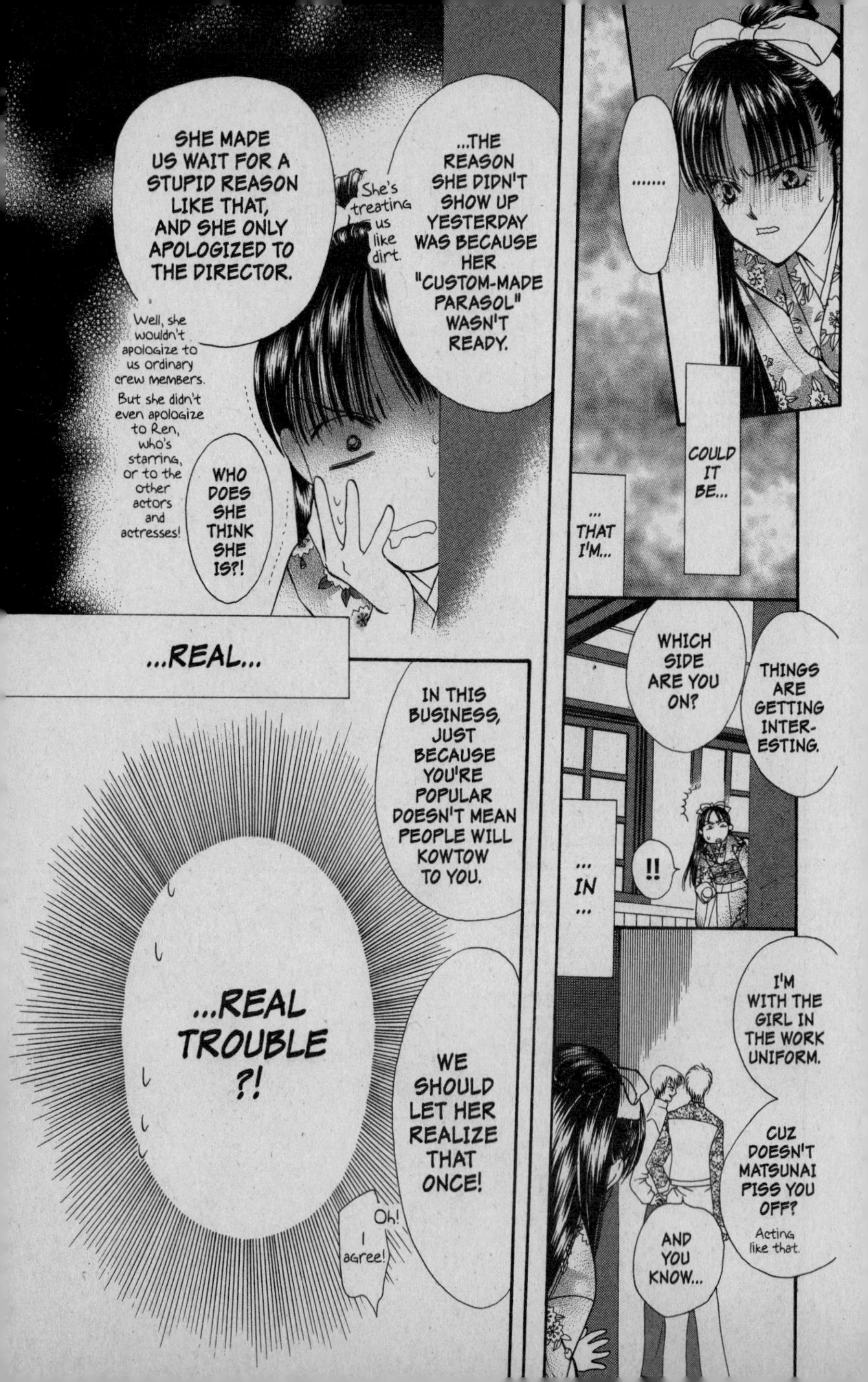

....
COULD IT BE...
...THAT I'M...
THINGS ARE GETTING INTER-ESTING.
WHICH SIDE ARE YOU ON?
!!
...IN...
I'M WITH THE GIRL IN THE WORK UNIFORM.
CUZ DOESN'T MATSUNAI PISS YOU OFF?
Acting like that.
AND YOU KNOW...
...THE REASON SHE DIDN'T SHOW UP YESTERDAY WAS BECAUSE HER "CUSTOM-MADE PARASOL" WASN'T READY.
She's treating us like dirt.
SHE MADE US WAIT FOR A STUPID REASON LIKE THAT, AND SHE ONLY APOLOGIZED TO THE DIRECTOR.
Well, she wouldn't apologize to us ordinary crew members. But she didn't even apologize to Ren, who's starring, or to the other actors and actresses!
WHO DOES SHE THINK SHE IS?!
...REAL...
IN THIS BUSINESS, JUST BECAUSE YOU'RE POPULAR DOESN'T MEAN PEOPLE WILL KOWTOW TO YOU.
WE SHOULD LET HER REALIZE THAT ONCE!
Oh! I agree!
...REAL TROUBLE?!

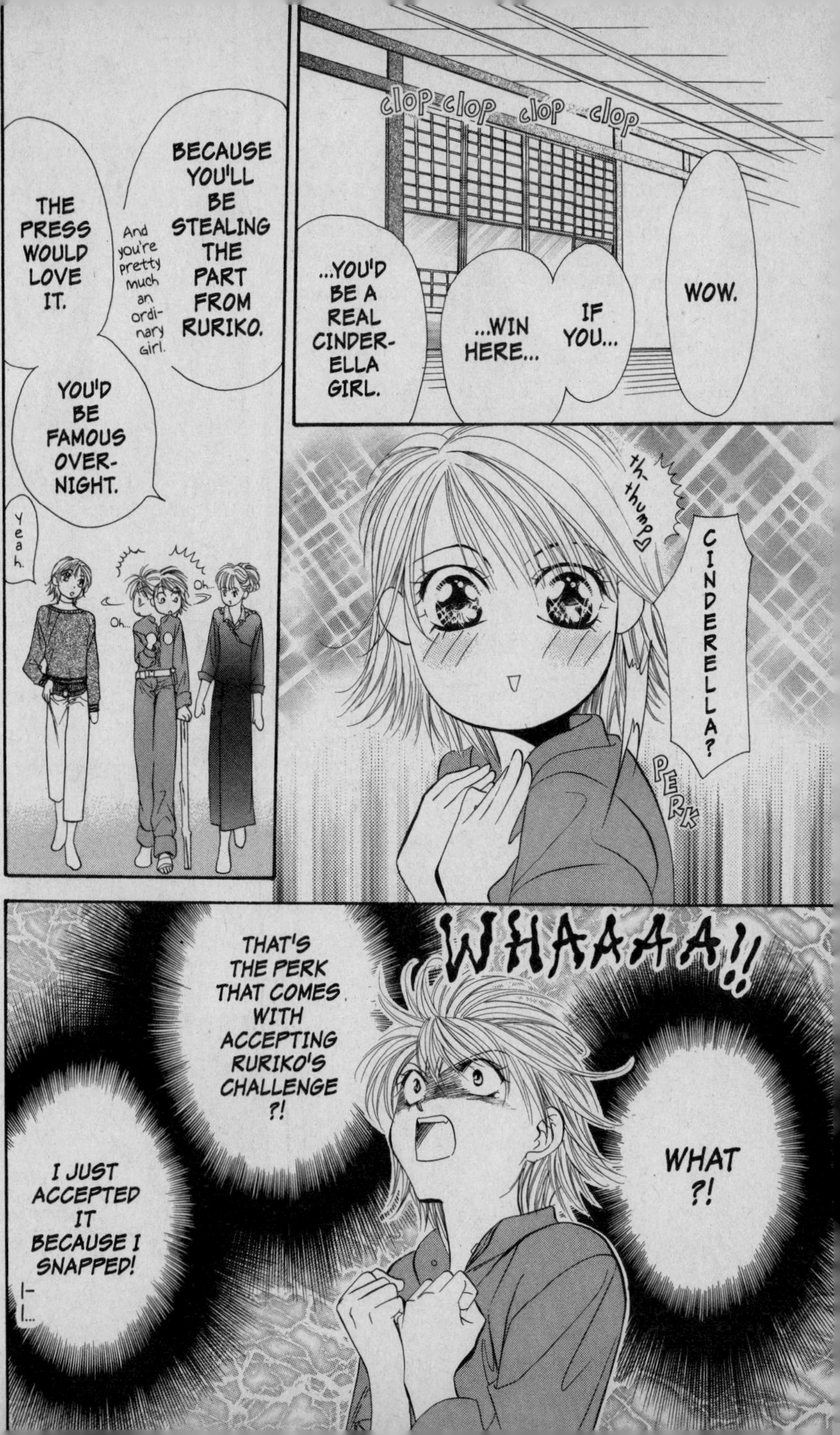
clop clop clop clop
WOW.
IF YOU...
...WIN HERE...
...YOU'D BE A REAL CINDER-ELLA GIRL.
th-thump♡
CINDERELLA?
PERK
BECAUSE YOU'LL BE STEALING THE PART FROM RURIKO.
And you're pretty much an ordinary girl.
THE PRESS WOULD LOVE IT.
YOU'D BE FAMOUS OVER-NIGHT.
Yeah.
Oh...
Oh...
WHAAAA!!
WHAT?!
THAT'S THE PERK THAT COMES WITH ACCEPTING RURIKO'S CHALLENGE?!
I JUST ACCEPTED IT BECAUSE I SNAPPED!
I—
I...

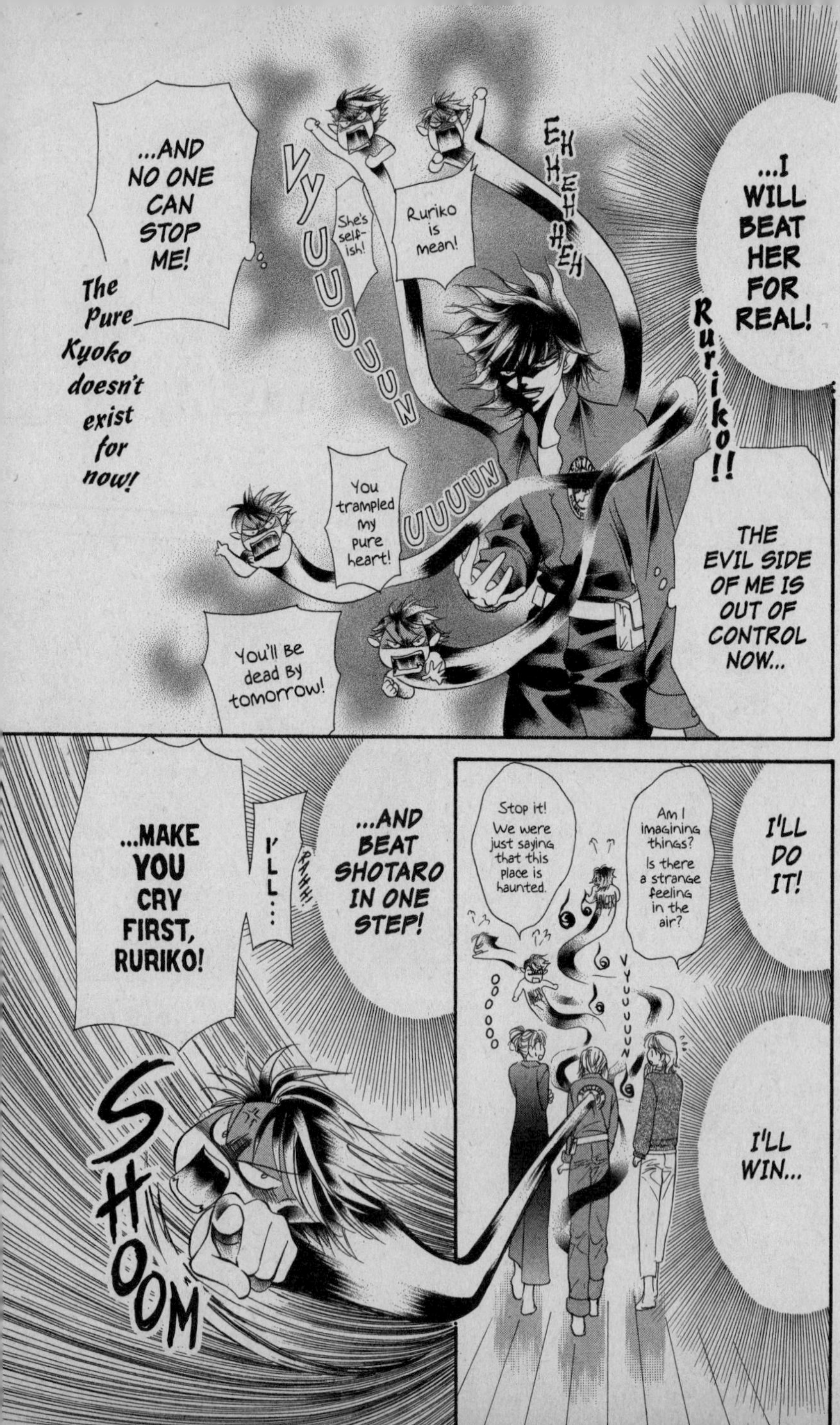
...I WILL BEAT HER FOR REAL!
Ruriko!!
EH HEH HEH HEH
Ruriko is mean!
She's self-ish!
VYUUUUUUN
...AND NO ONE CAN STOP ME!
The Pure Kyoko doesn't exist for now!
THE EVIL SIDE OF ME IS OUT OF CONTROL NOW...
UUUUN
You trampled my pure heart!
You'll be dead by tomorrow!
I'LL DO IT!
Am I imagining things? Is there a strange feeling in the air?
Stop it! We were just saying that this place is haunted.
VYUUUUUN
I'LL WIN...
...AND BEAT SHOTARO IN ONE STEP!
I'LL...
...MAKE YOU CRY FIRST, RURIKO!
SHOOM

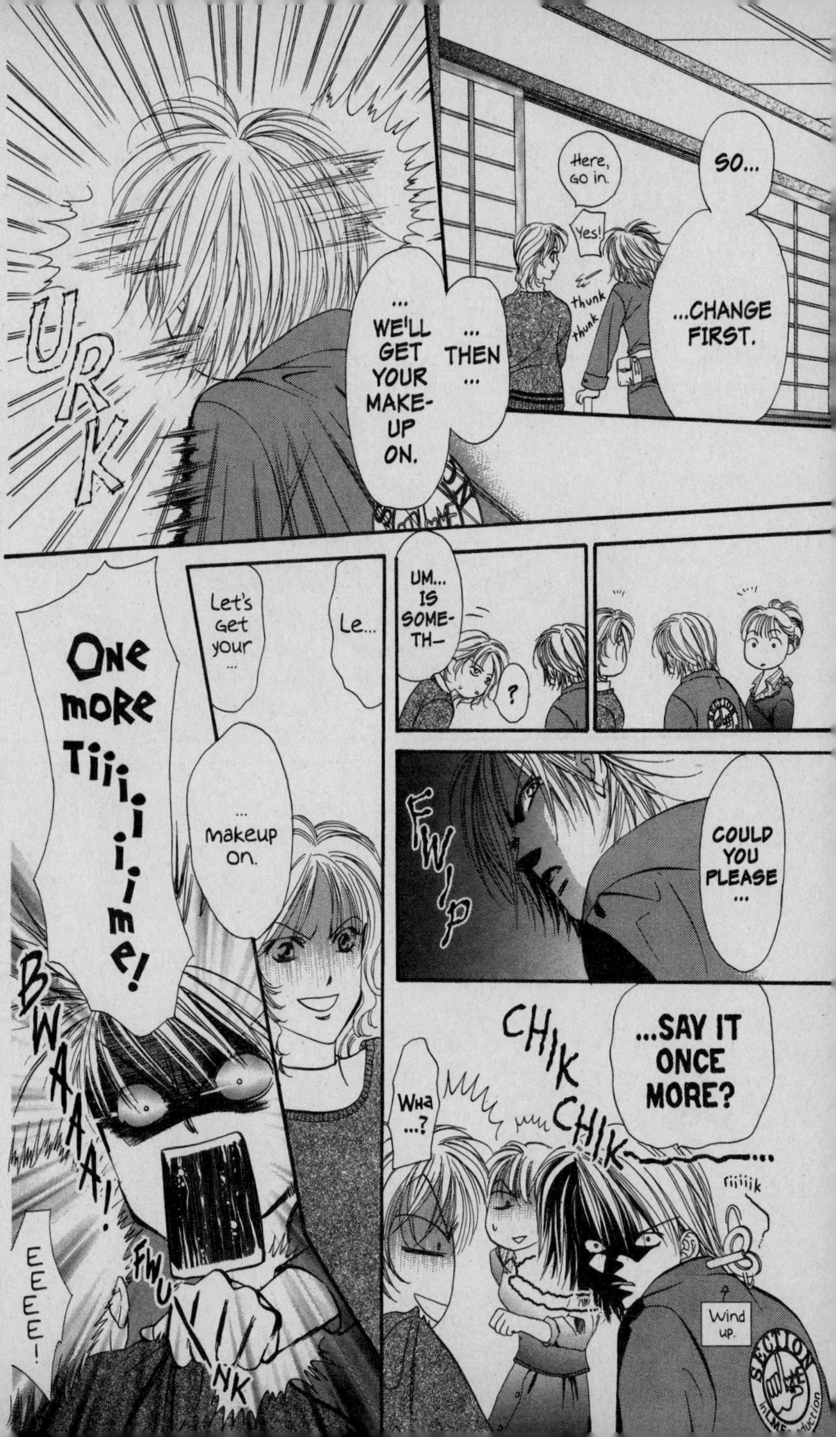
SO...
...CHANGE FIRST.
Here, Go in.
Yes!
thunk thunk
...THEN...
...WE'LL GET YOUR MAKE-UP ON.
URK
UM... IS SOMETH—
?
FWIP
COULD YOU PLEASE...
...SAY IT ONCE MORE?
CHIK CHIK
Wha ...?
riiiiik
Wind up.
Le...
Let's get your ...
... makeup on.
One more Tiiiiiiime!
BWAAAA!
FWUNK
EEEE!

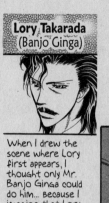

Lory Takarada
(Banjo Ginga)

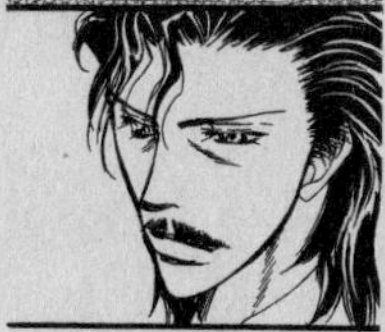

When I drew the scene where Lory first appears, I thought only Mr. Banjo Ginga could do him... Because I imagine that Lory has a really low voice that echoes in your stomach... Oh...but... I wrote "really low voice" in the FX once...

Takenori Sawara
(Tomoyuki Kono)

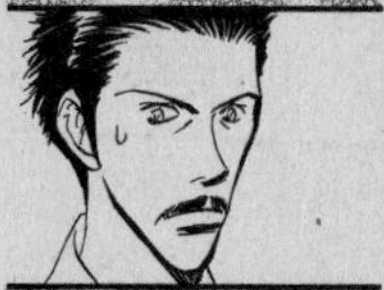

Kanae Kotonami
(Yukiko Tagami)

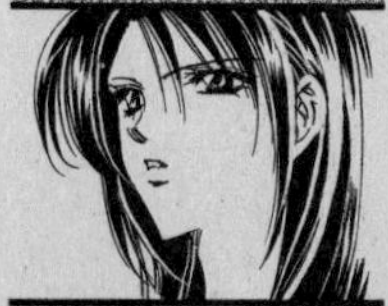

Darumaya Owners
(Masami Iwasaki)
(Mariko Nagahama)

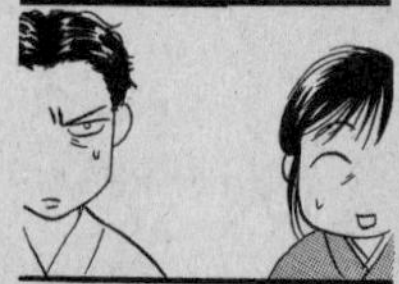

These are all the main cast. Thank you so much!!

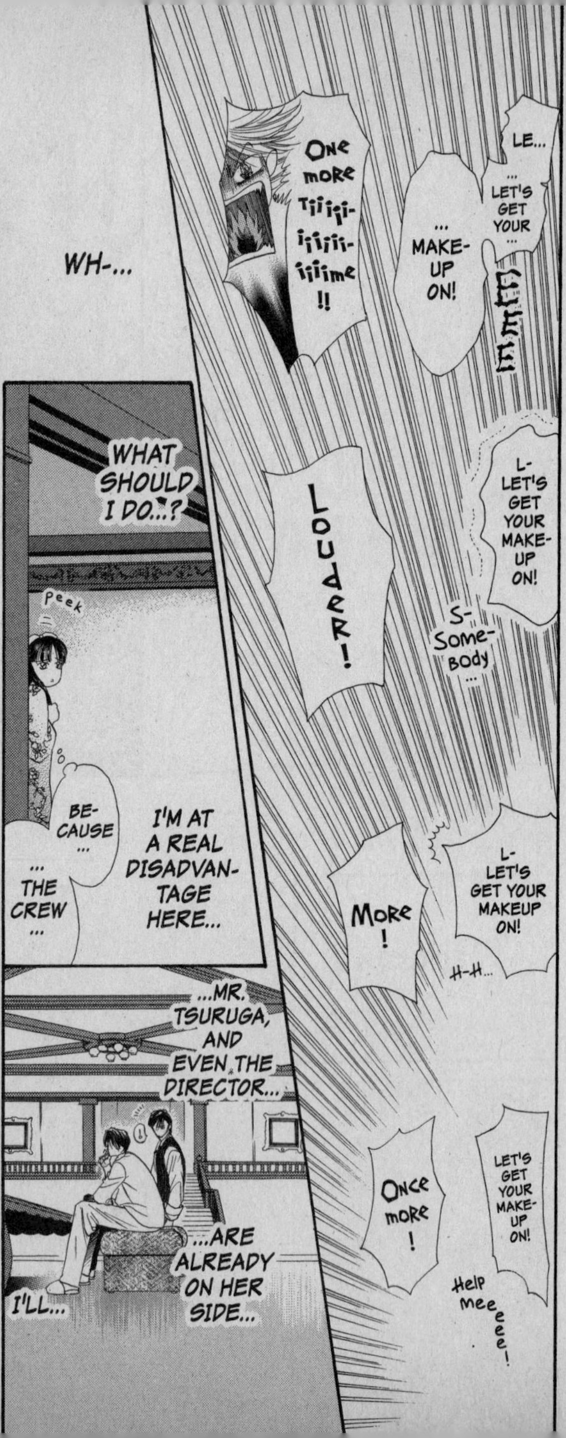
LE...
... LET'S GET YOUR ...
... MAKE-UP ON!
One more Tiiiiiiiiiiiiiiime!!
WH-...
L- LET'S GET YOUR MAKE-UP ON!
S-Some-body...
Louder!
WHAT SHOULD I DO...?
Peek
I'M AT A REAL DISADVANTAGE HERE...
BECAUSE... ...THE CREW...
L- LET'S GET YOUR MAKEUP ON!
H-H...
More!
...MR. TSURUGA, AND EVEN THE DIRECTOR...
...ARE ALREADY ON HER SIDE...
I'LL...
LET'S GET YOUR MAKE-UP ON!
Help meeeeee!
Once more!

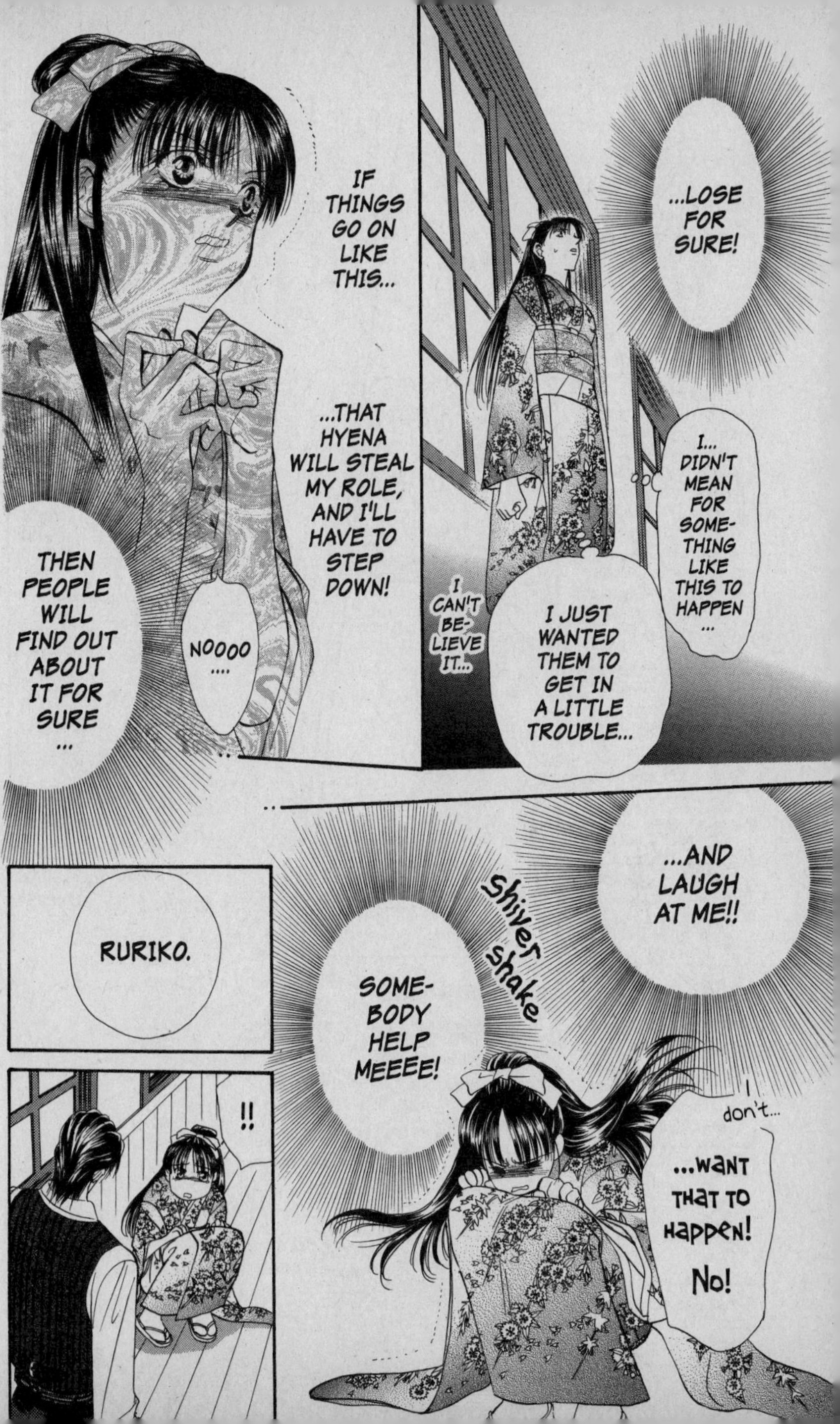
...LOSE FOR SURE!
I... DIDN'T MEAN FOR SOME-THING LIKE THIS TO HAPPEN...
I JUST WANTED THEM TO GET IN A LITTLE TROUBLE...
I CAN'T BE-LIEVE IT...
IF THINGS GO ON LIKE THIS...
...THAT HYENA WILL STEAL MY ROLE, AND I'LL HAVE TO STEP DOWN!
NOOOO....
THEN PEOPLE WILL FIND OUT ABOUT IT FOR SURE...
...AND LAUGH AT ME!!
Shiver shake
SOME-BODY HELP MEEEE!
I don't...
...WANT THAT TO HAPPEN!
No!
RURIKO.
!!

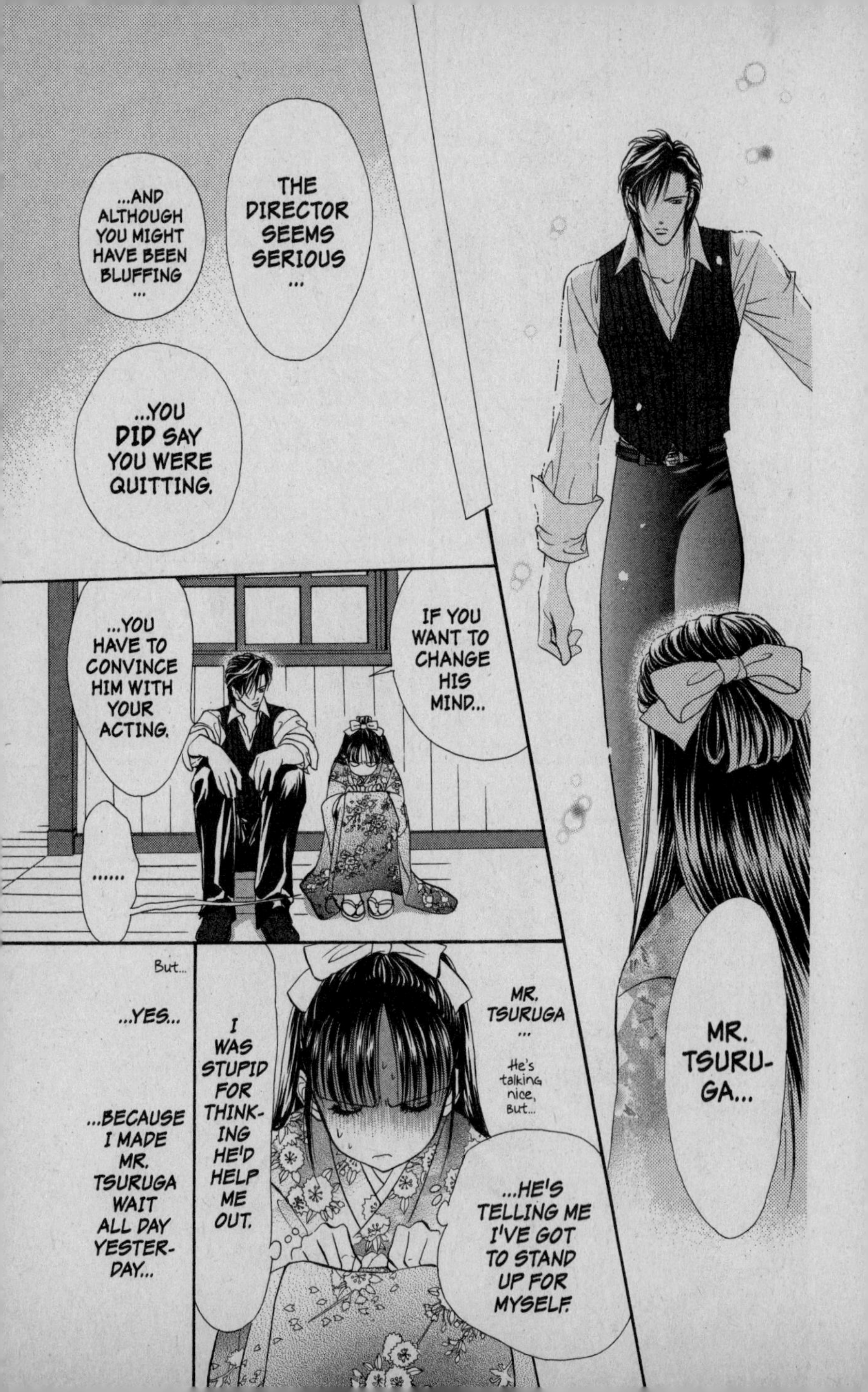
MR. TSURUGA...
THE DIRECTOR SEEMS SERIOUS...
...AND ALTHOUGH YOU MIGHT HAVE BEEN BLUFFING...
...YOU DID SAY YOU WERE QUITTING.
IF YOU WANT TO CHANGE HIS MIND...
...YOU HAVE TO CONVINCE HIM WITH YOUR ACTING.
......
MR. TSURUGA...
He's talking nice, but...
...HE'S TELLING ME I'VE GOT TO STAND UP FOR MYSELF.
I WAS STUPID FOR THINKING HE'D HELP ME OUT.
...BECAUSE I MADE MR. TSURUGA WAIT ALL DAY YESTERDAY...
...YES...
But...

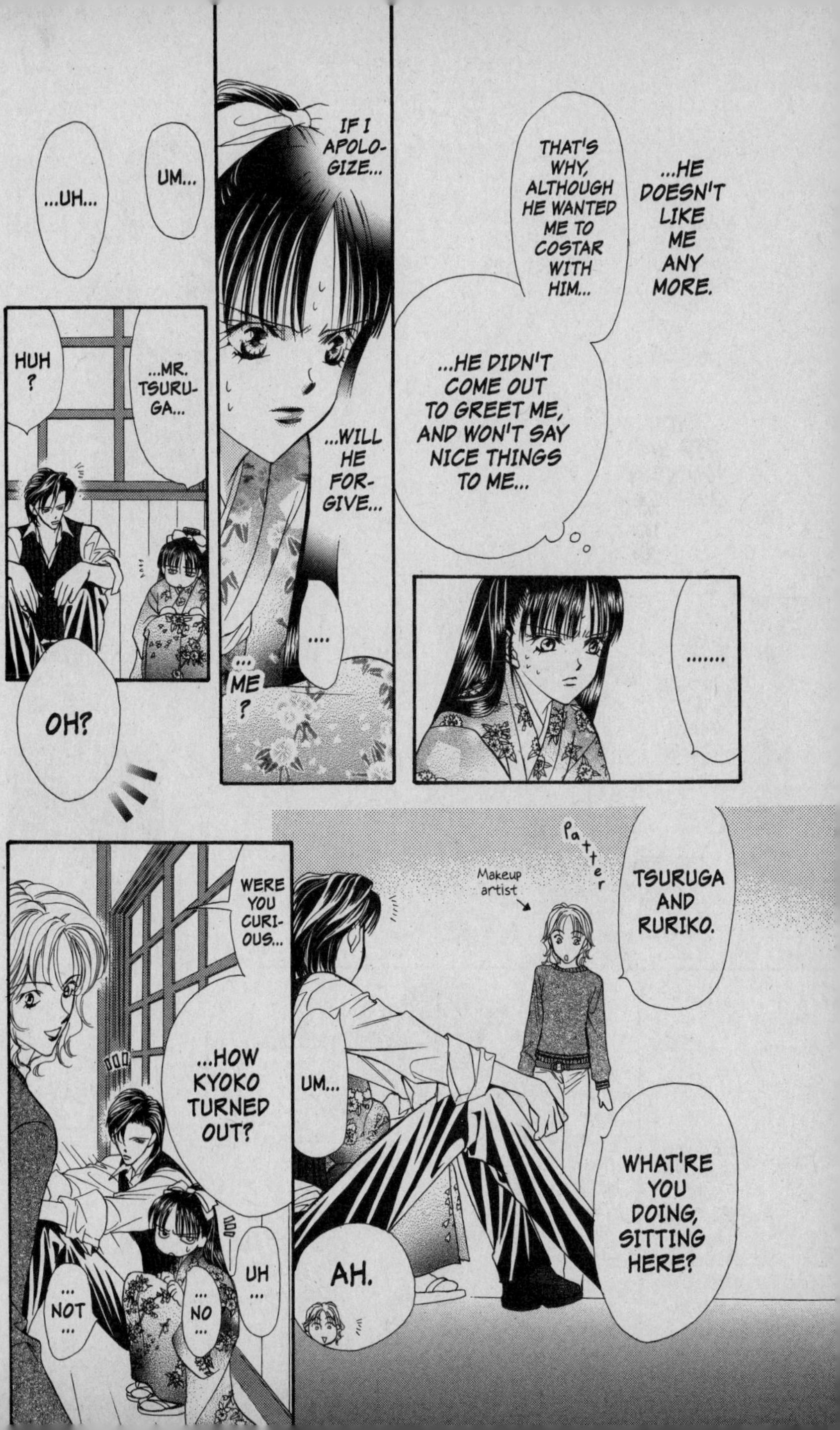
...HE DOESN'T LIKE ME ANY MORE.
THAT'S WHY, ALTHOUGH HE WANTED ME TO COSTAR WITH HIM...
...HE DIDN'T COME OUT TO GREET ME, AND WON'T SAY NICE THINGS TO ME...
....
IF I APOLOGIZE...
...WILL HE FORGIVE...
....
...ME?
UM...
...UH...
...MR. TSURUGA...
HUH?
OH?
Patter
Makeup artist
TSURUGA AND RURIKO.
WHAT'RE YOU DOING, SITTING HERE?
UM...
AH.
WERE YOU CURIOUS...
...HOW KYOKO TURNED OUT?
UH...
...NO...
...NOT...

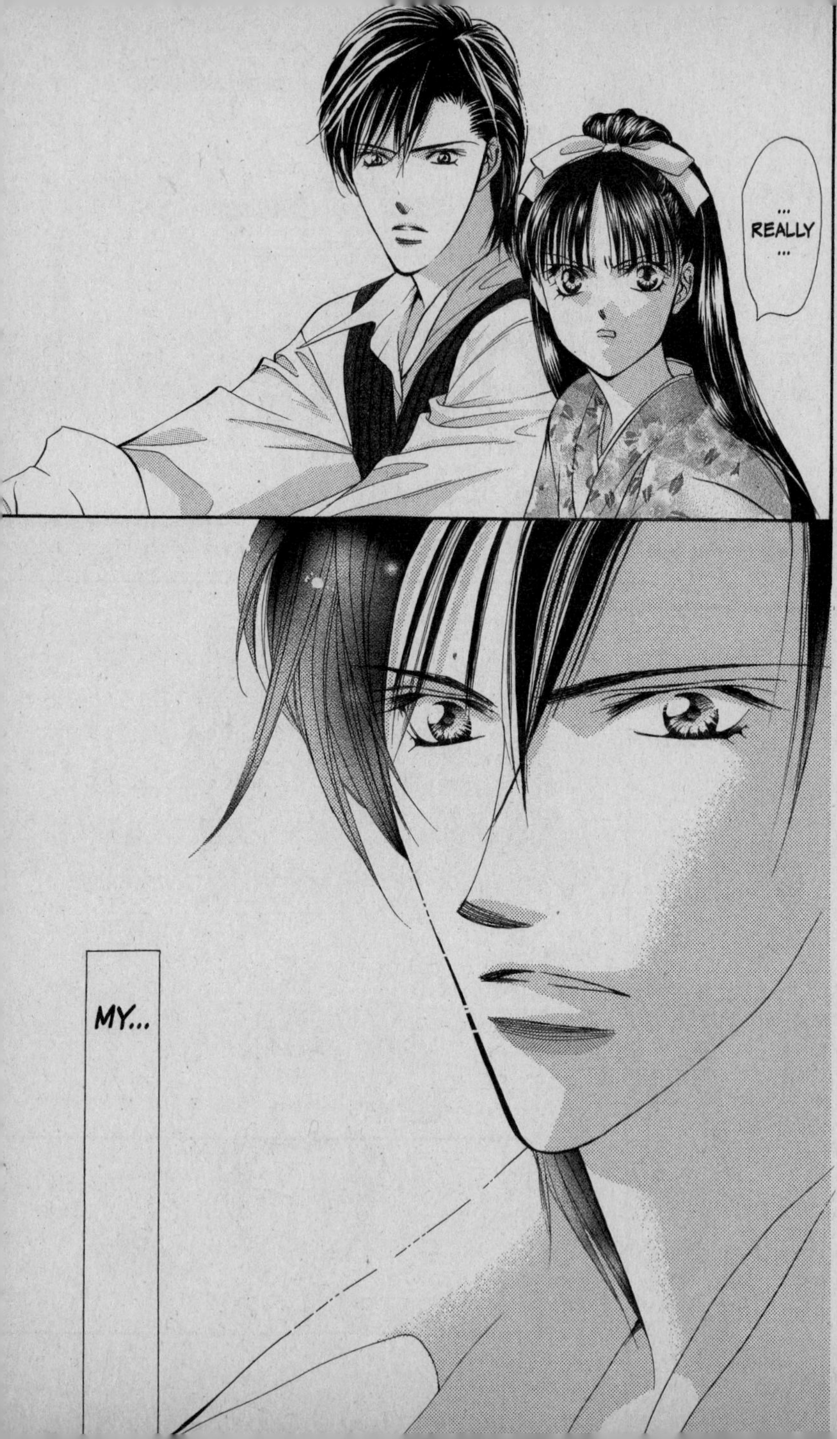
... REALLY ...
MY...

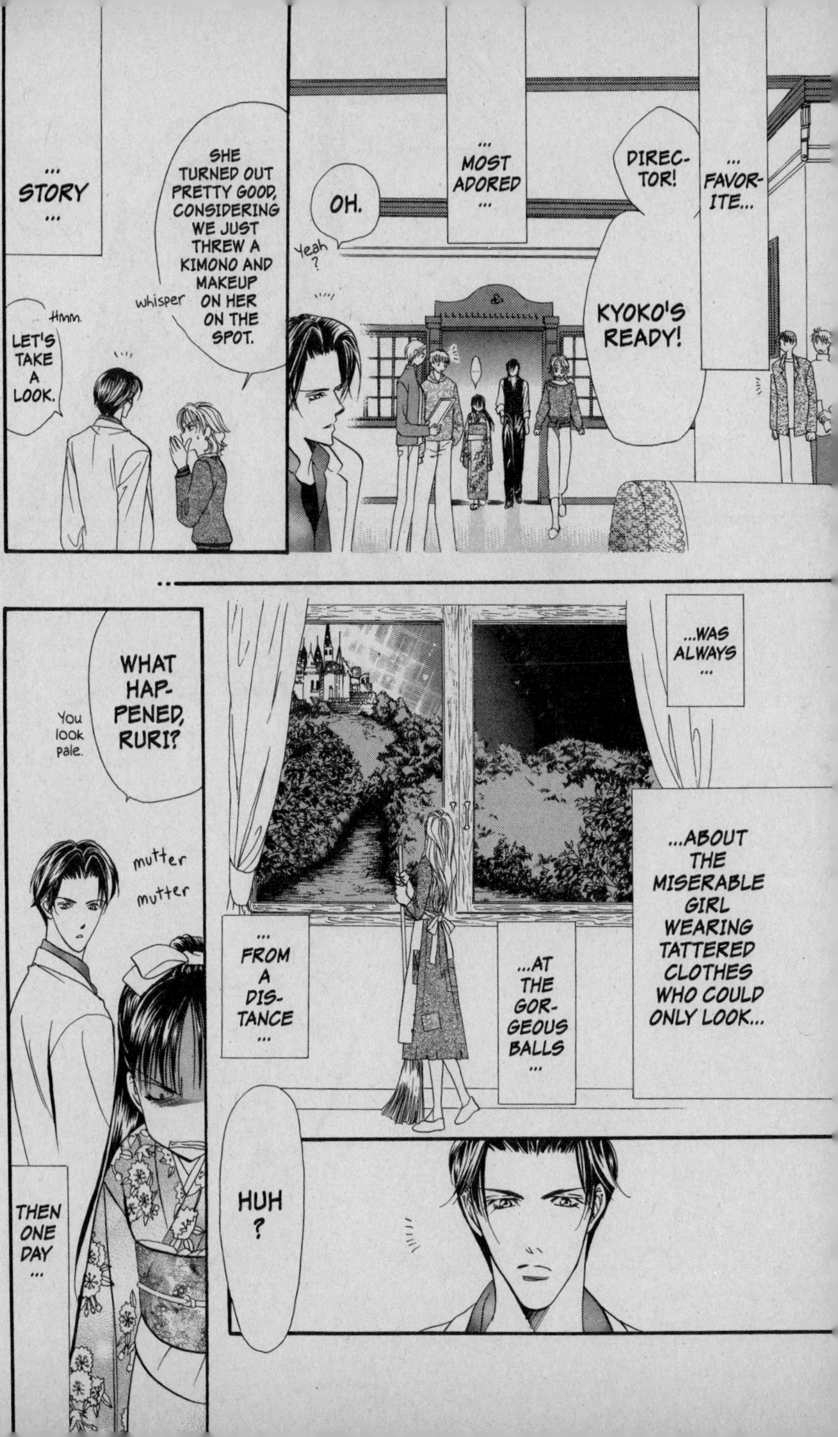
... FAVOR-ITE...
DIREC-TOR!
KYOKO'S READY!
... MOST ADORED ...
OH.
Yeah?
SHE TURNED OUT PRETTY GOOD, CONSIDERING WE JUST THREW A KIMONO AND MAKEUP ON HER ON THE SPOT.
whisper
... STORY ...
Hmm.
LET'S TAKE A LOOK.
...WAS ALWAYS...
...ABOUT THE MISERABLE GIRL WEARING TATTERED CLOTHES WHO COULD ONLY LOOK...
...AT THE GORGEOUS BALLS...
... FROM A DISTANCE ...
HUH?
WHAT HAPPENED, RURI?
You look pale.
mutter mutter
THEN ONE DAY ...

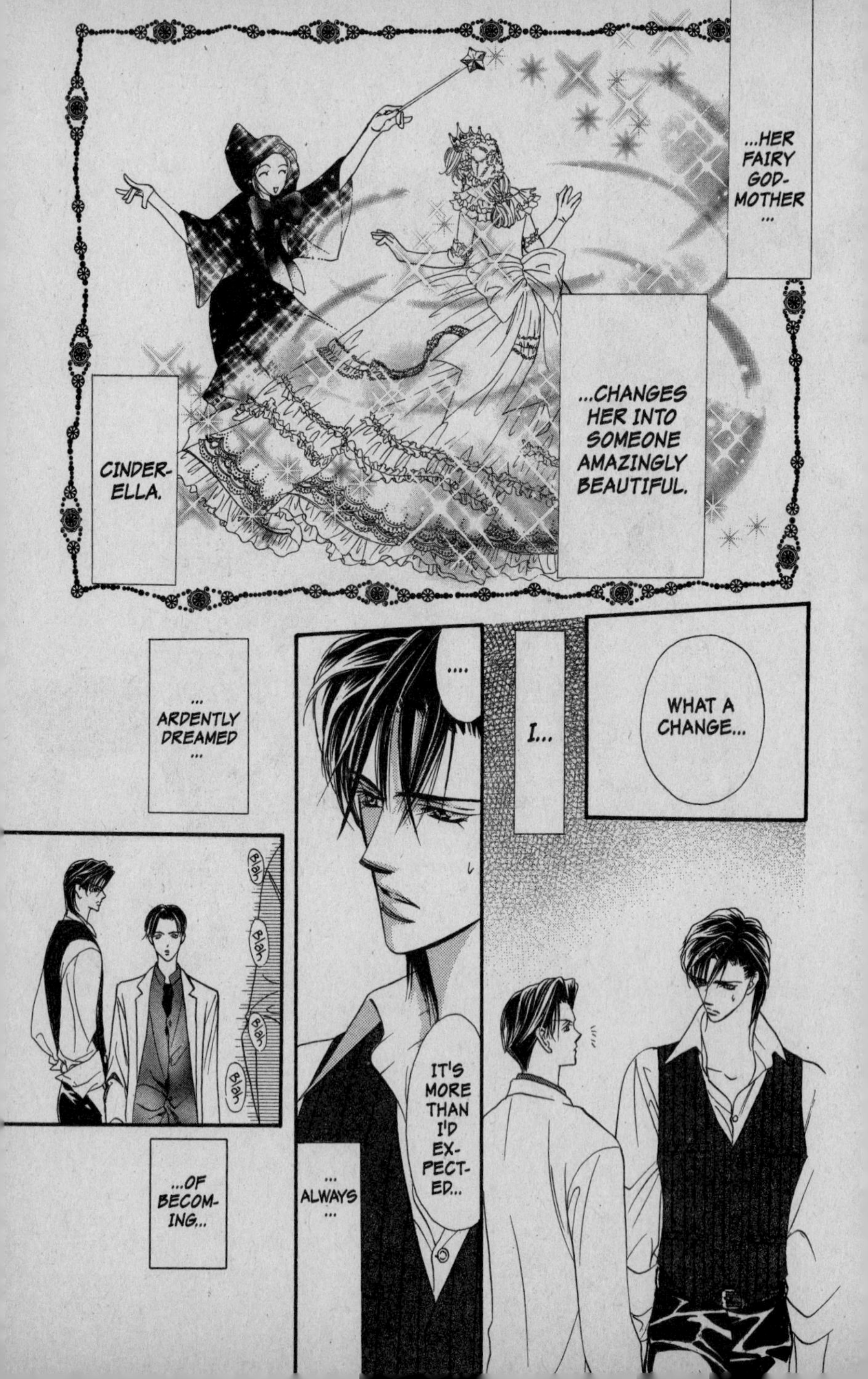
...HER FAIRY GOD-MOTHER ...
...CHANGES HER INTO SOMEONE AMAZINGLY BEAUTIFUL.
CINDER-ELLA.
WHAT A CHANGE...
I...
....
... ARDENTLY DREAMED ...
Blah
Blah
Blah
Blah
IT'S MORE THAN I'D EX-PECT-ED...
... ALWAYS ...
...OF BECOM-ING...

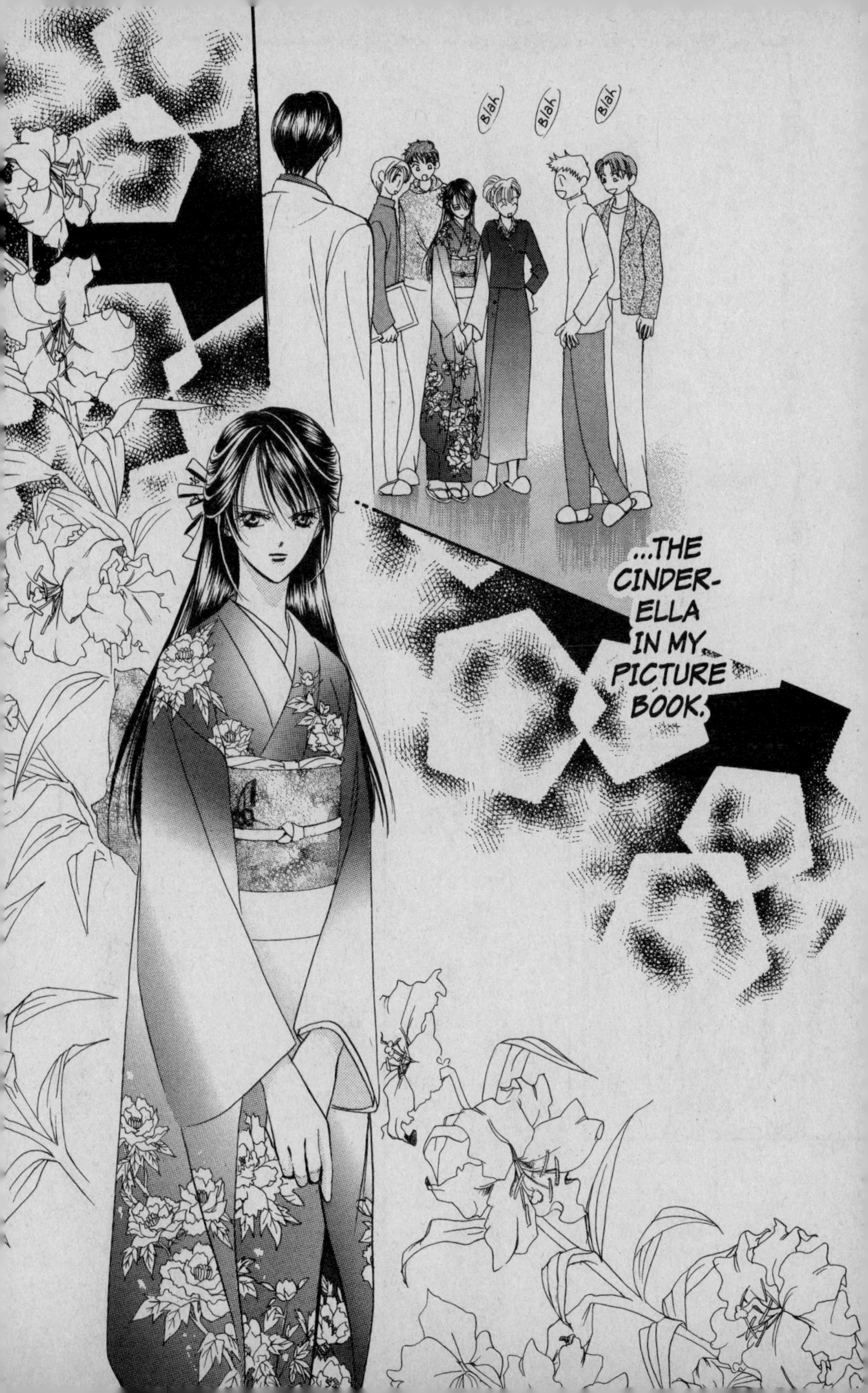
Blah
Blah
Blah
...THE CINDER-ELLA IN MY PICTURE BOOK.

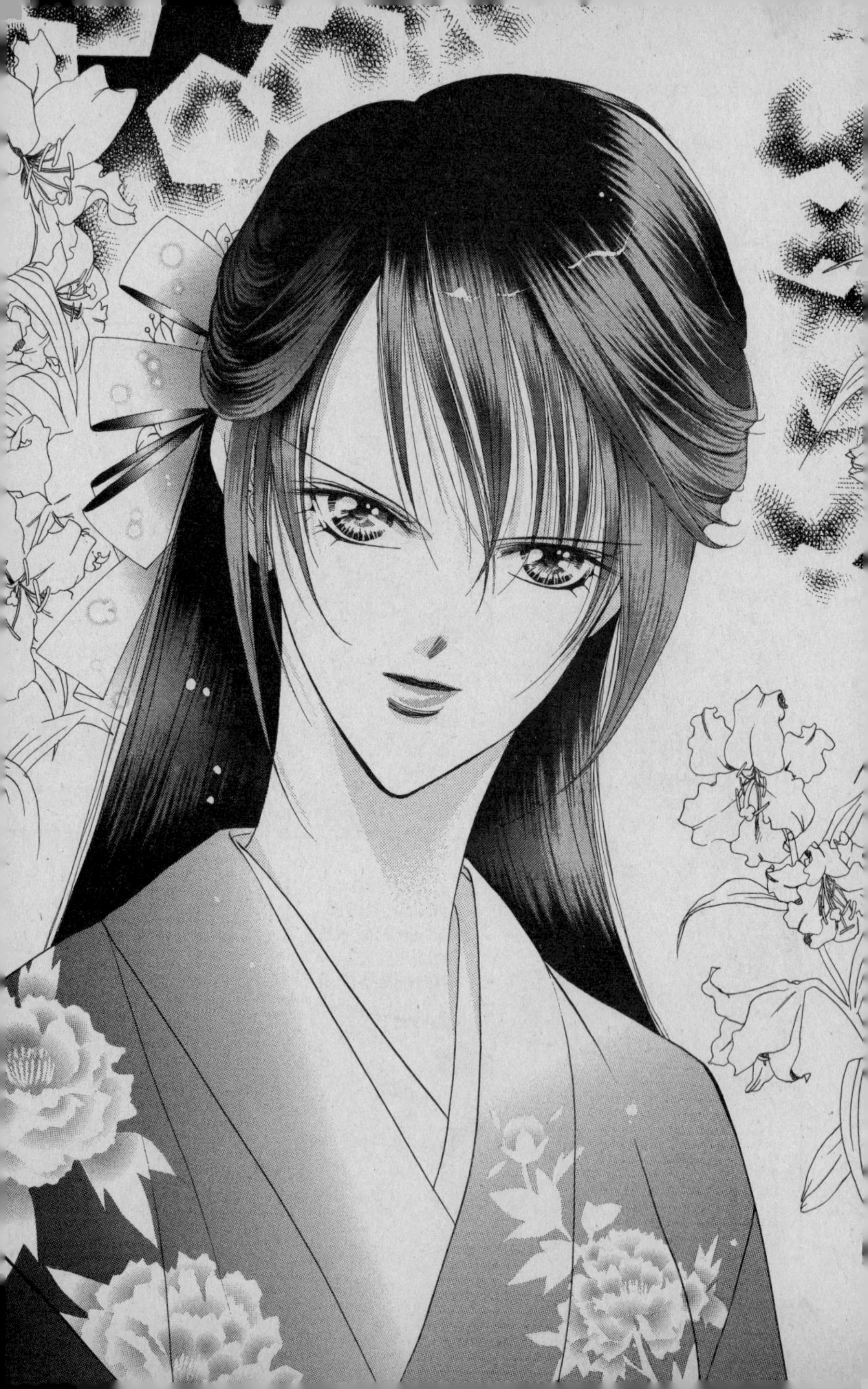

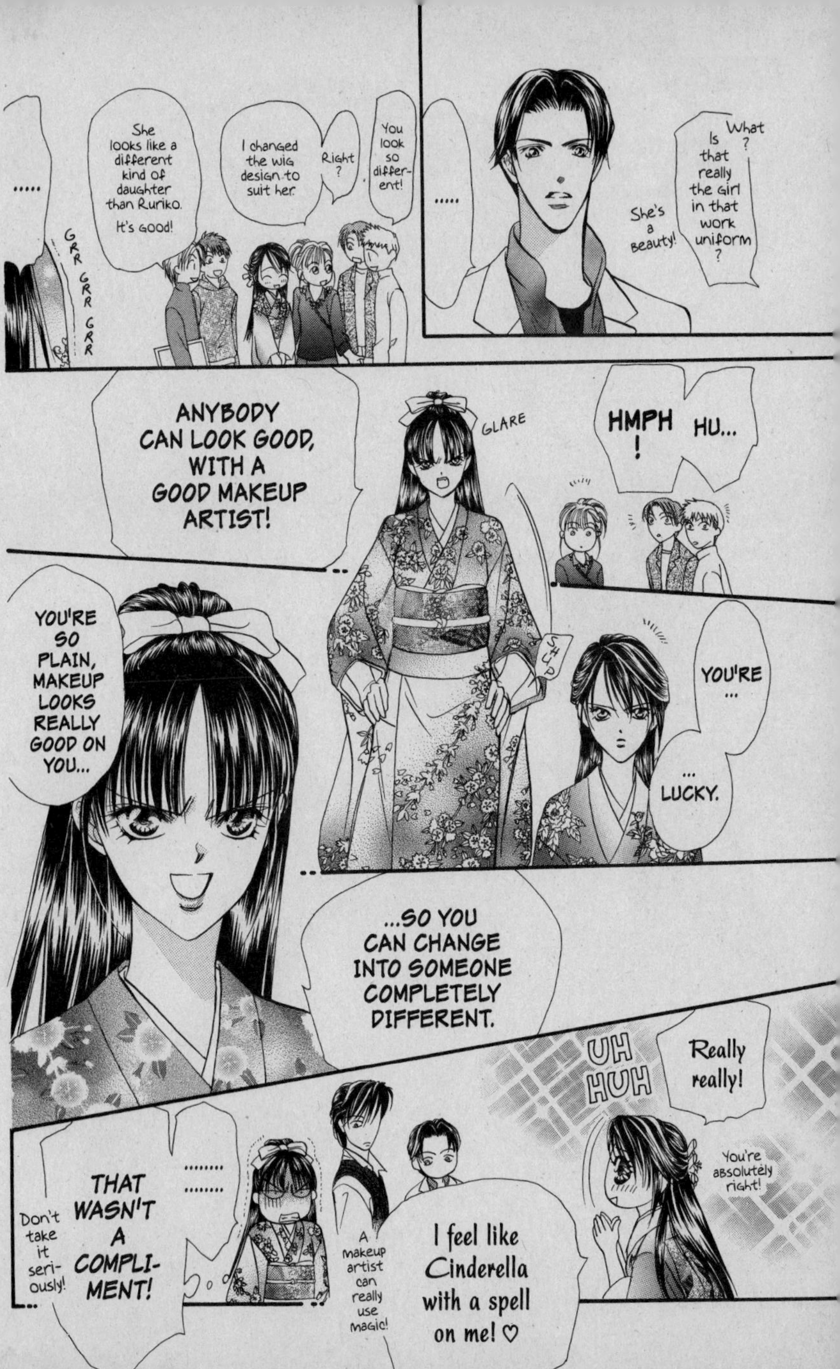
What? Is that really the girl in that work uniform?
She's a beauty!
.....
You look so different!
Right?
I changed the wig design to suit her.
She looks like a different kind of daughter than Ruriko. It's good!
.....
GRR GRR GRR
HMPH! HU...
GLARE
ANYBODY CAN LOOK GOOD, WITH A GOOD MAKEUP ARTIST!
YOU'RE ...
... LUCKY.
SHUP
YOU'RE SO PLAIN, MAKEUP LOOKS REALLY GOOD ON YOU...
...SO YOU CAN CHANGE INTO SOMEONE COMPLETELY DIFFERENT.
UH HUH
Really really!
You're absolutely right!
I feel like Cinderella with a spell on me! ♡
A makeup artist can really use magic!
....
THAT WASN'T A COMPLIMENT!
Don't take it seriously!

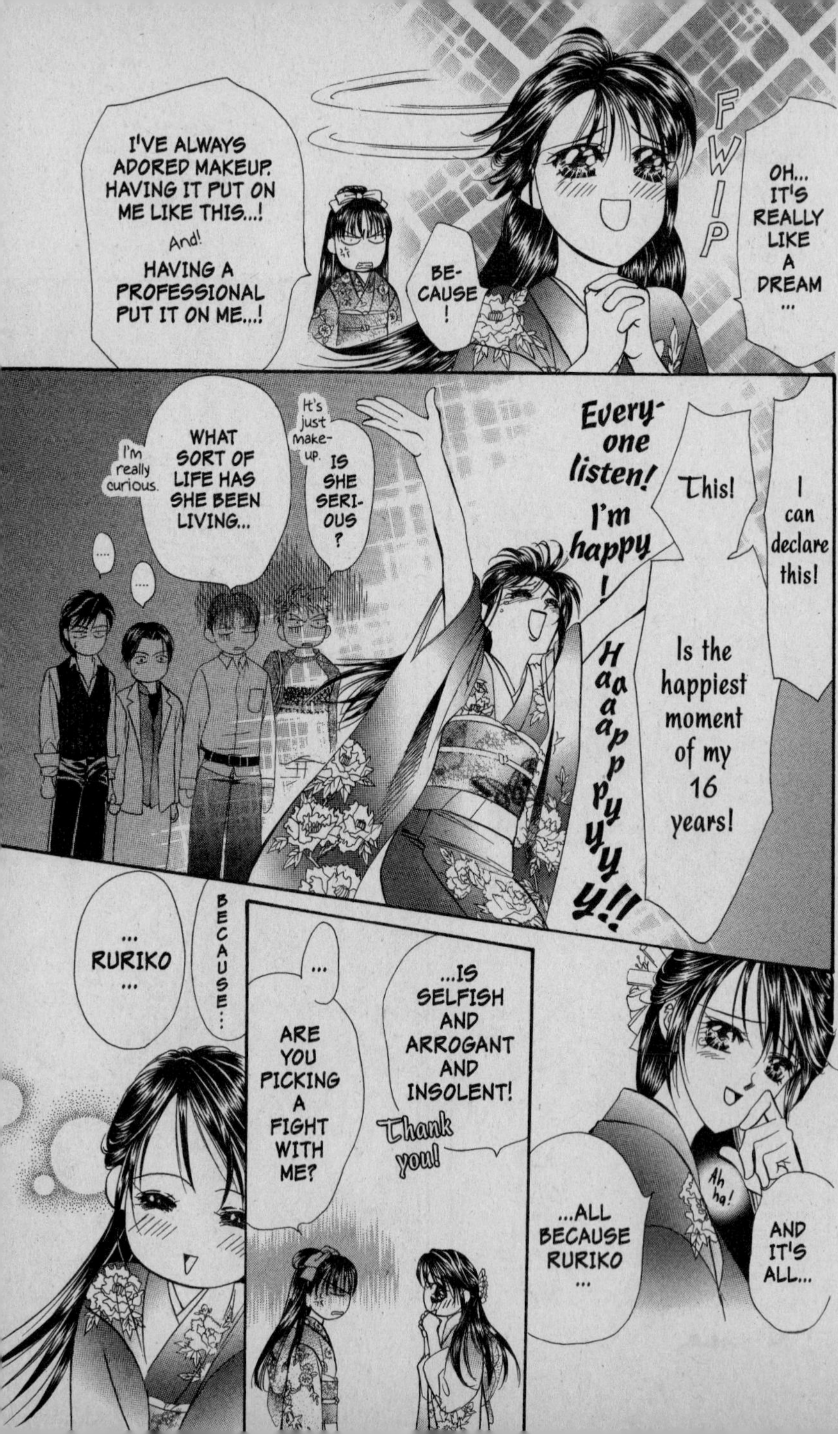
OH... IT'S REALLY LIKE A DREAM...
FWIP
BE-CAUSE!
I'VE ALWAYS ADORED MAKEUP. HAVING IT PUT ON ME LIKE THIS...! And! HAVING A PROFESSIONAL PUT IT ON ME...!
I can declare this!
This!
Is the happiest moment of my 16 years!
Every-one listen! I'm happy!
Haaappyyyy!!
It's just make-up.
IS SHE SERI-OUS?
WHAT SORT OF LIFE HAS SHE BEEN LIVING...
I'm really curious.
....
....
AND IT'S ALL...
Ah ha!
...ALL BECAUSE RURIKO...
...IS SELFISH AND ARROGANT AND INSOLENT!
Thank you!
ARE YOU PICKING A FIGHT WITH ME?
...
BECAUSE...
... RURIKO ...

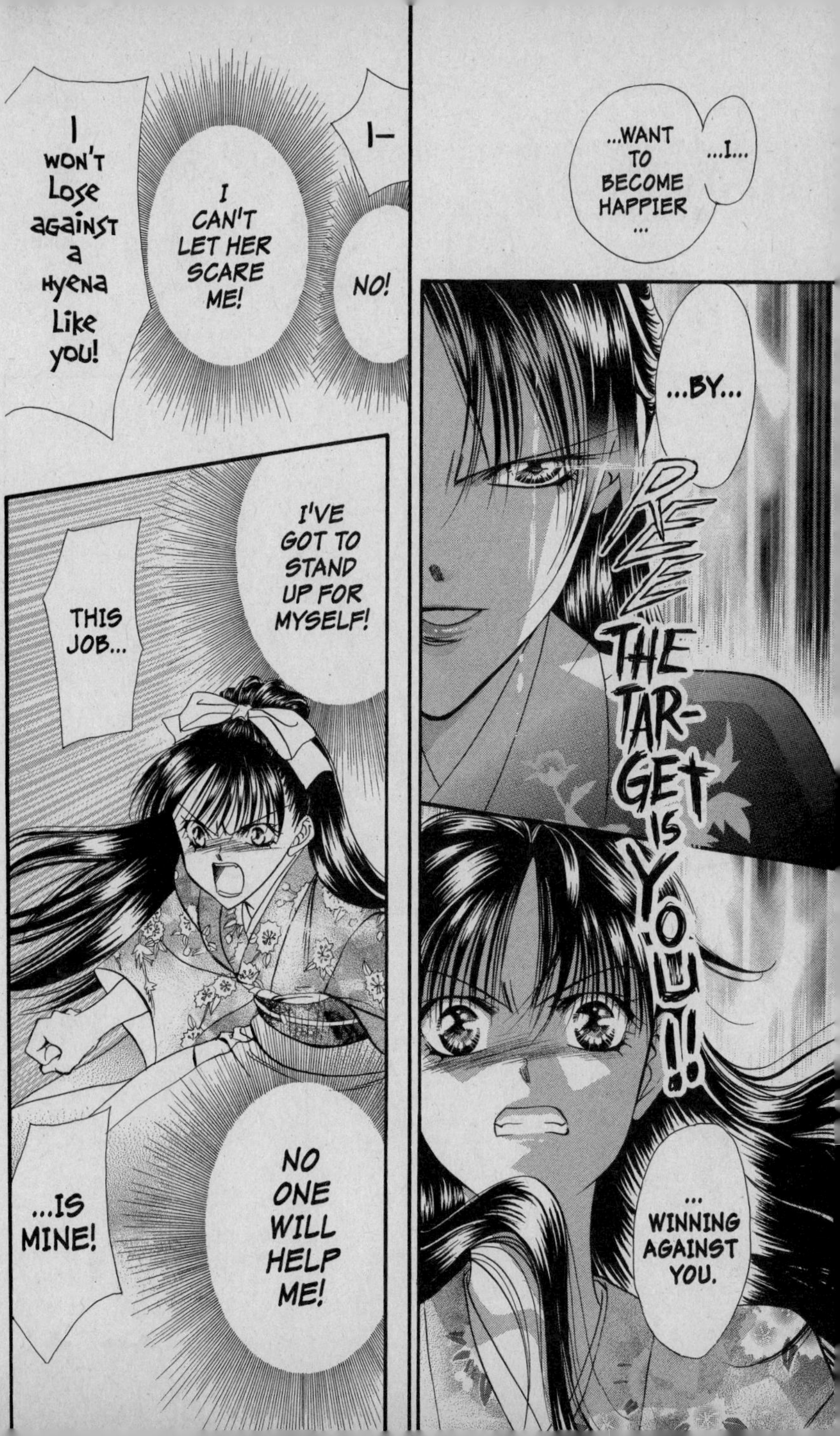
...I...
...WANT TO BECOME HAPPIER ...
...BY...
REE
THE TAR-GET IS YOU!!
...WINNING AGAINST YOU.
I—
NO!
I CAN'T LET HER SCARE ME!
I WON'T LOSE AGAINST A HYENA LIKE YOU!
I'VE GOT TO STAND UP FOR MYSELF!
THIS JOB...
NO ONE WILL HELP ME!
...IS MINE!

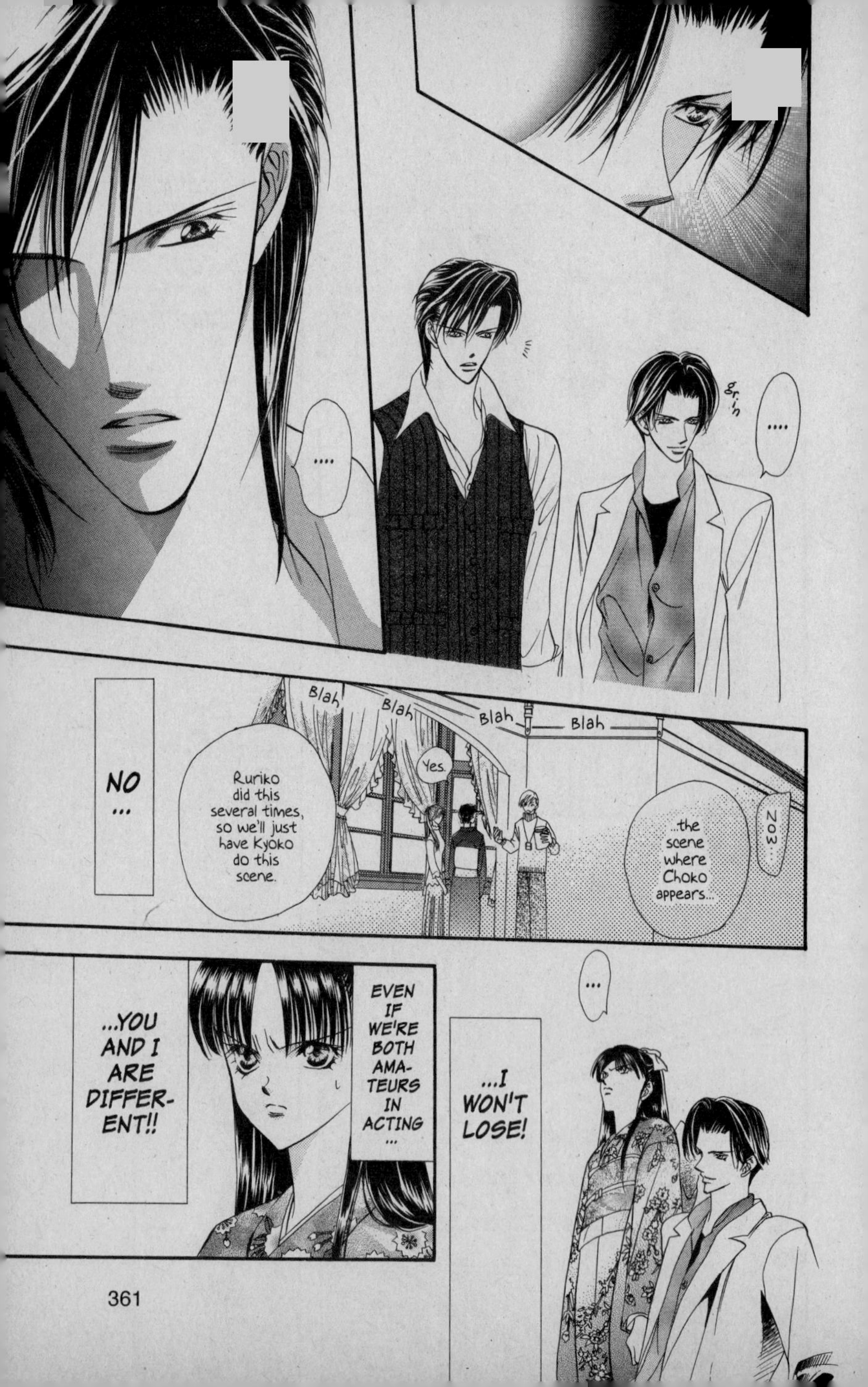
grin
....
....
Blah Blah Blah Blah
Now...
...the scene where Choko appears...
Yes.
Ruriko did this several times, so we'll just have Kyoko do this scene.
NO ...
...
...I WON'T LOSE!
EVEN IF WE'RE BOTH AMATEURS IN ACTING ...
...YOU AND I ARE DIFFERENT!!

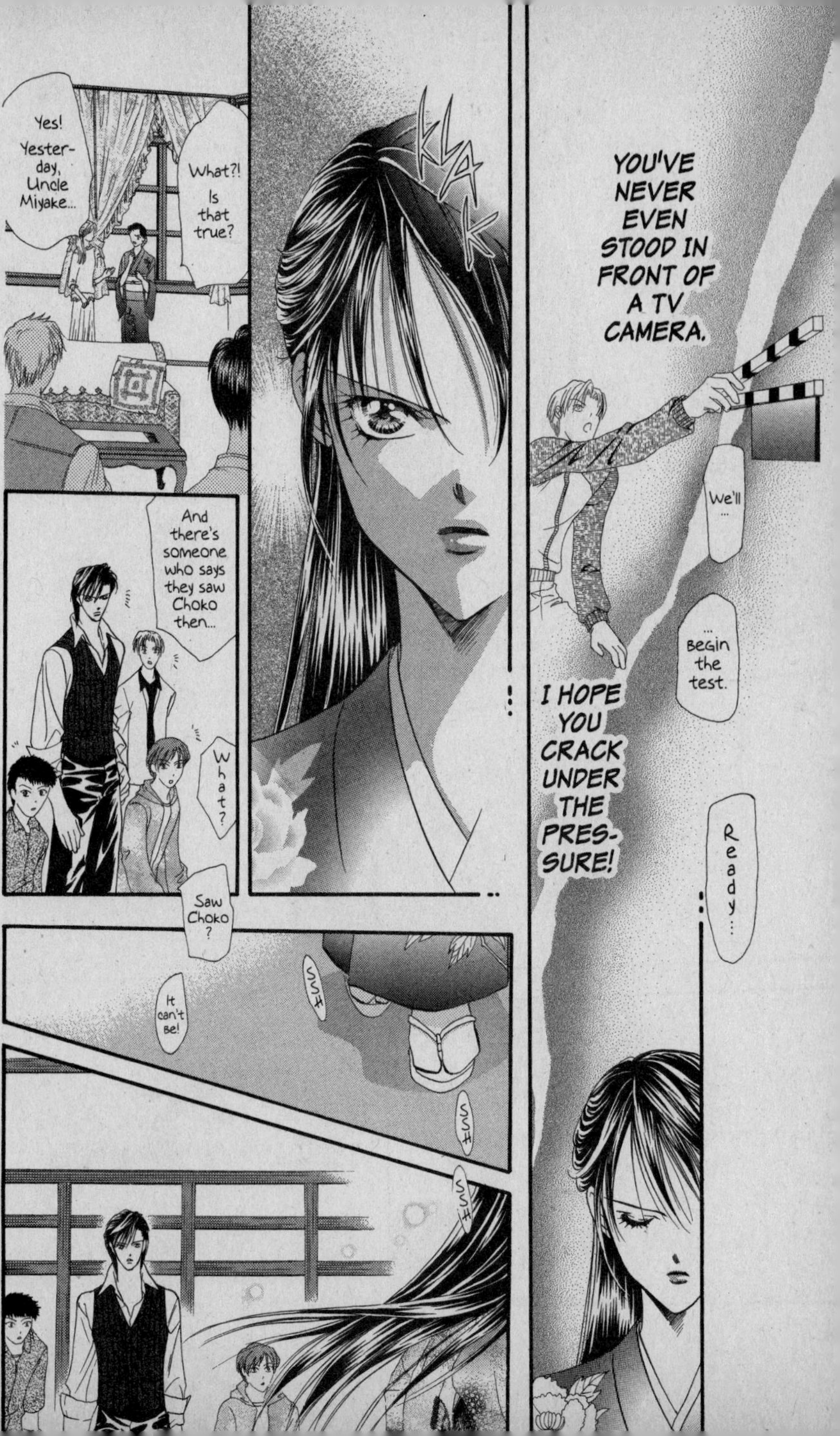
YOU'VE NEVER EVEN STOOD IN FRONT OF A TV CAMERA.
We'll...
...Begin the test.
I HOPE YOU CRACK UNDER THE PRESSURE!
Ready...
KLAK
What?! Is that true?
Yes! Yesterday, Uncle Miyake...
And there's someone who says they saw Choko then...
What?
Saw Choko?
SSH
It can't be!
SSH
SSH

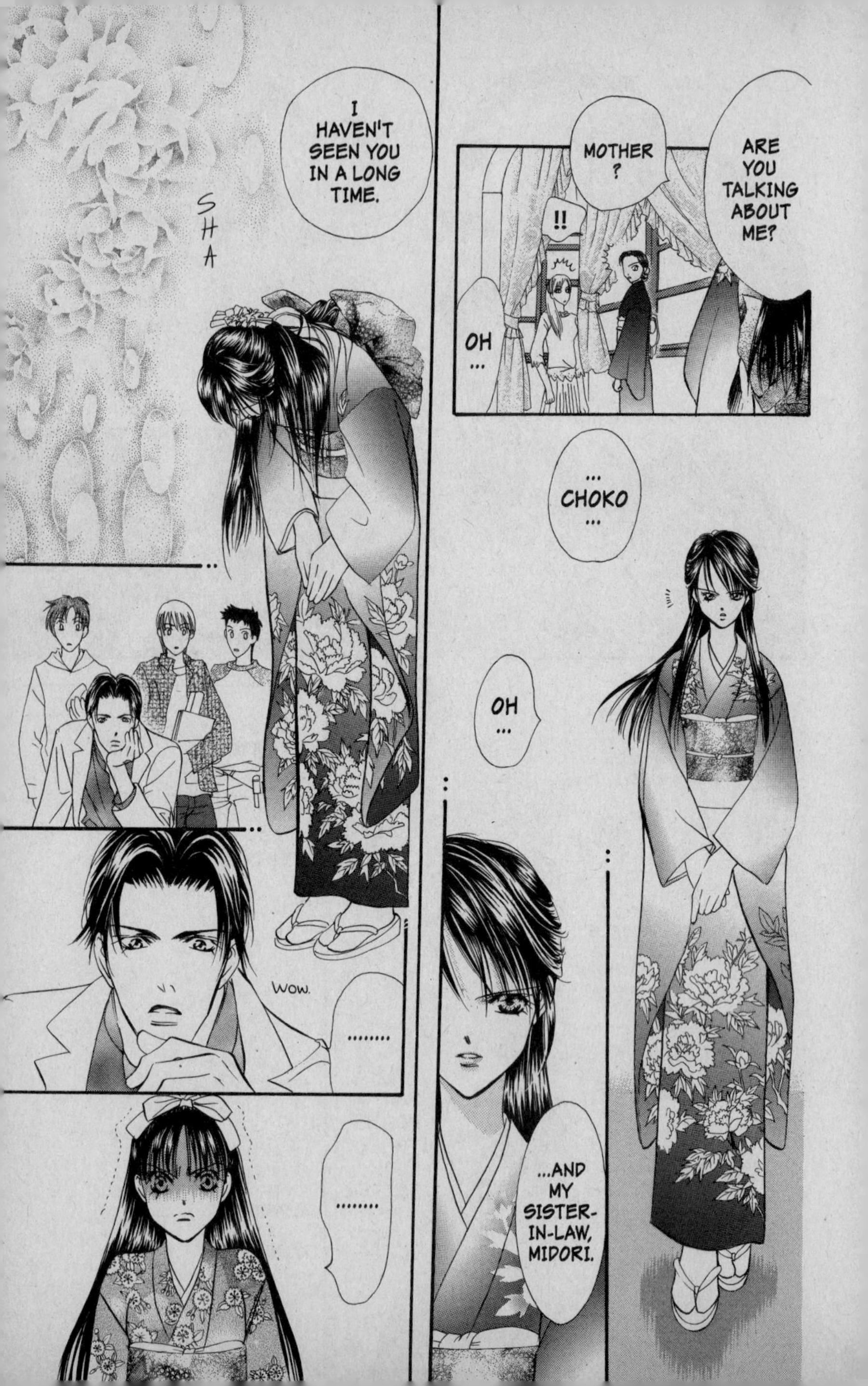
ARE YOU TALKING ABOUT ME?
MOTHER?
!!
OH ...
... CHOKO ...
OH ...
...AND MY SISTER-IN-LAW, MIDORI.
I HAVEN'T SEEN YOU IN A LONG TIME.
SHA
....
WOW.
....

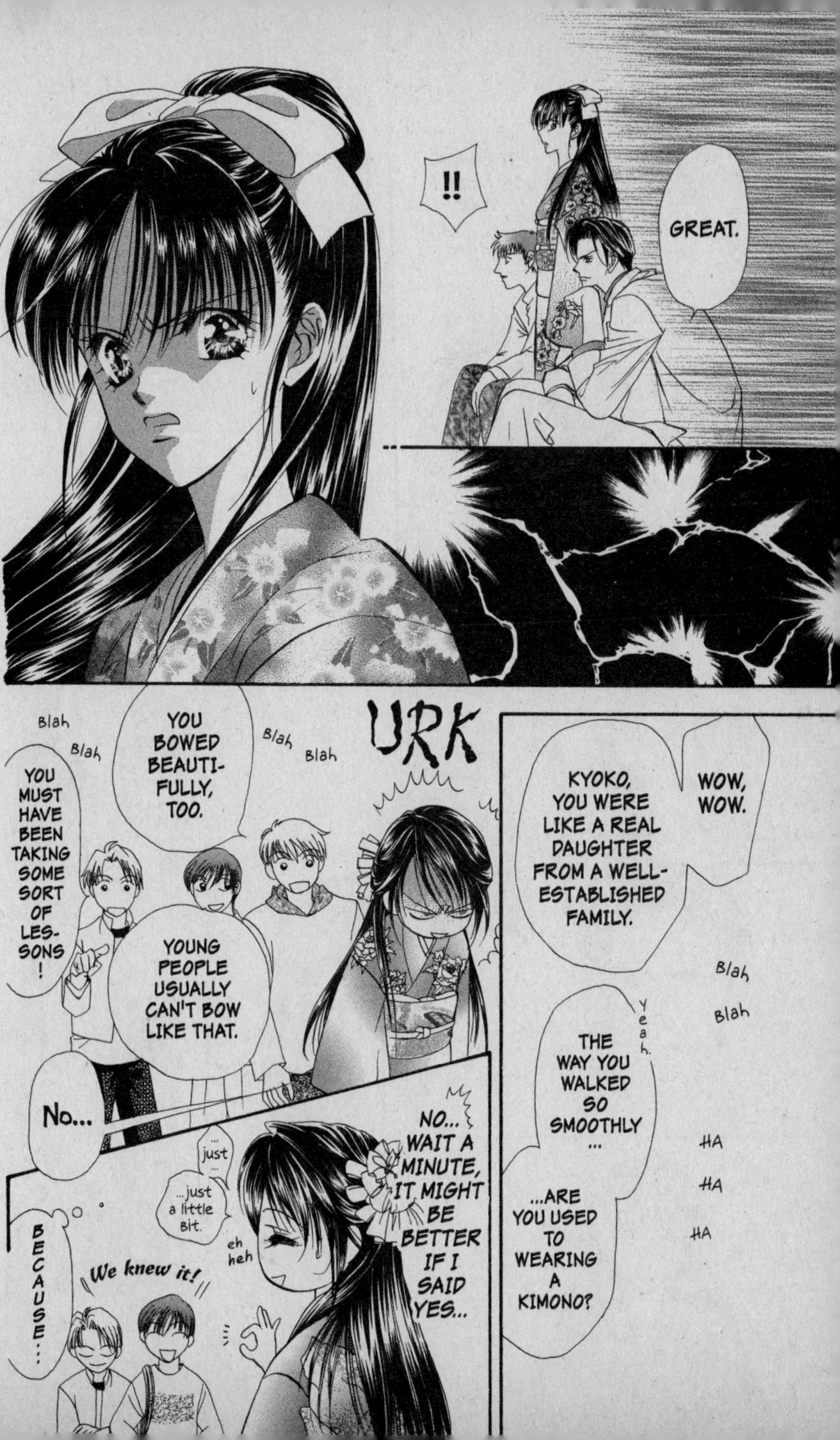
GREAT.
!!
WOW, WOW.
KYOKO, YOU WERE LIKE A REAL DAUGHTER FROM A WELL-ESTABLISHED FAMILY.
Blah
Blah
THE WAY YOU WALKED SO SMOOTHLY ...
Yeah.
...ARE YOU USED TO WEARING A KIMONO?
HA
HA
HA
URK
YOU BOWED BEAUTIFULLY, TOO.
Blah
Blah
Blah
Blah
YOU MUST HAVE BEEN TAKING SOME SORT OF LESSONS!
YOUNG PEOPLE USUALLY CAN'T BOW LIKE THAT.
No...
NO... WAIT A MINUTE, IT MIGHT BE BETTER IF I SAID YES...
...just...
...just a little bit.
eh heh
We knew it!
BECAUSE...

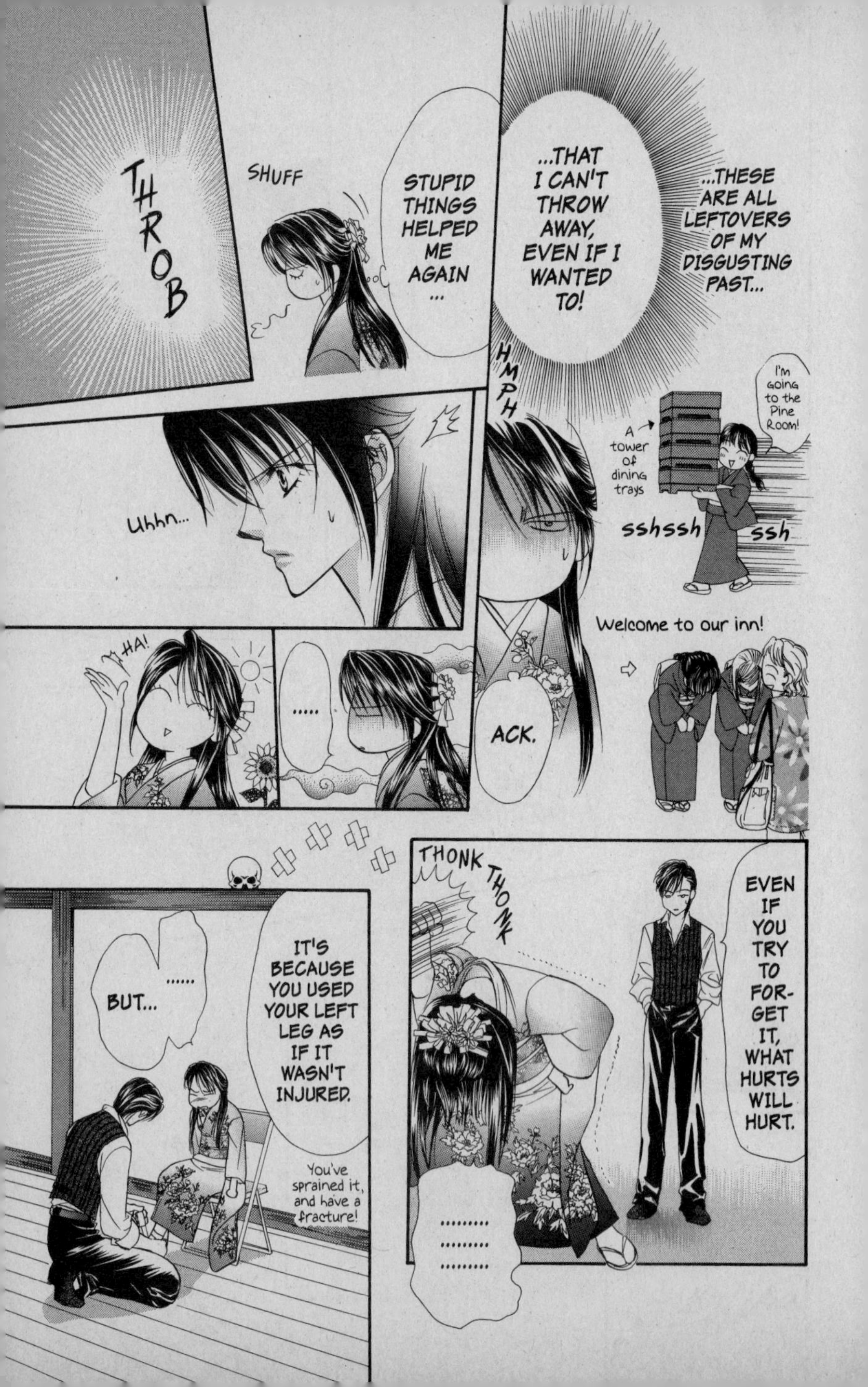
...THESE ARE ALL LEFTOVERS OF MY DISGUSTING PAST...
...THAT I CAN'T THROW AWAY, EVEN IF I WANTED TO!
HMPH
I'm going to the Pine Room!
A tower of dining trays
sshsshssh
ACK.
Welcome to our inn!
STUPID THINGS HELPED ME AGAIN...
SHUFF
THROB
Uhhn...
......
HA!
EVEN IF YOU TRY TO FORGET IT, WHAT HURTS WILL HURT.
THONK THONK
....
....
....
IT'S BECAUSE YOU USED YOUR LEFT LEG AS IF IT WASN'T INJURED.
......
BUT...
You've sprained it, and have a fracture!

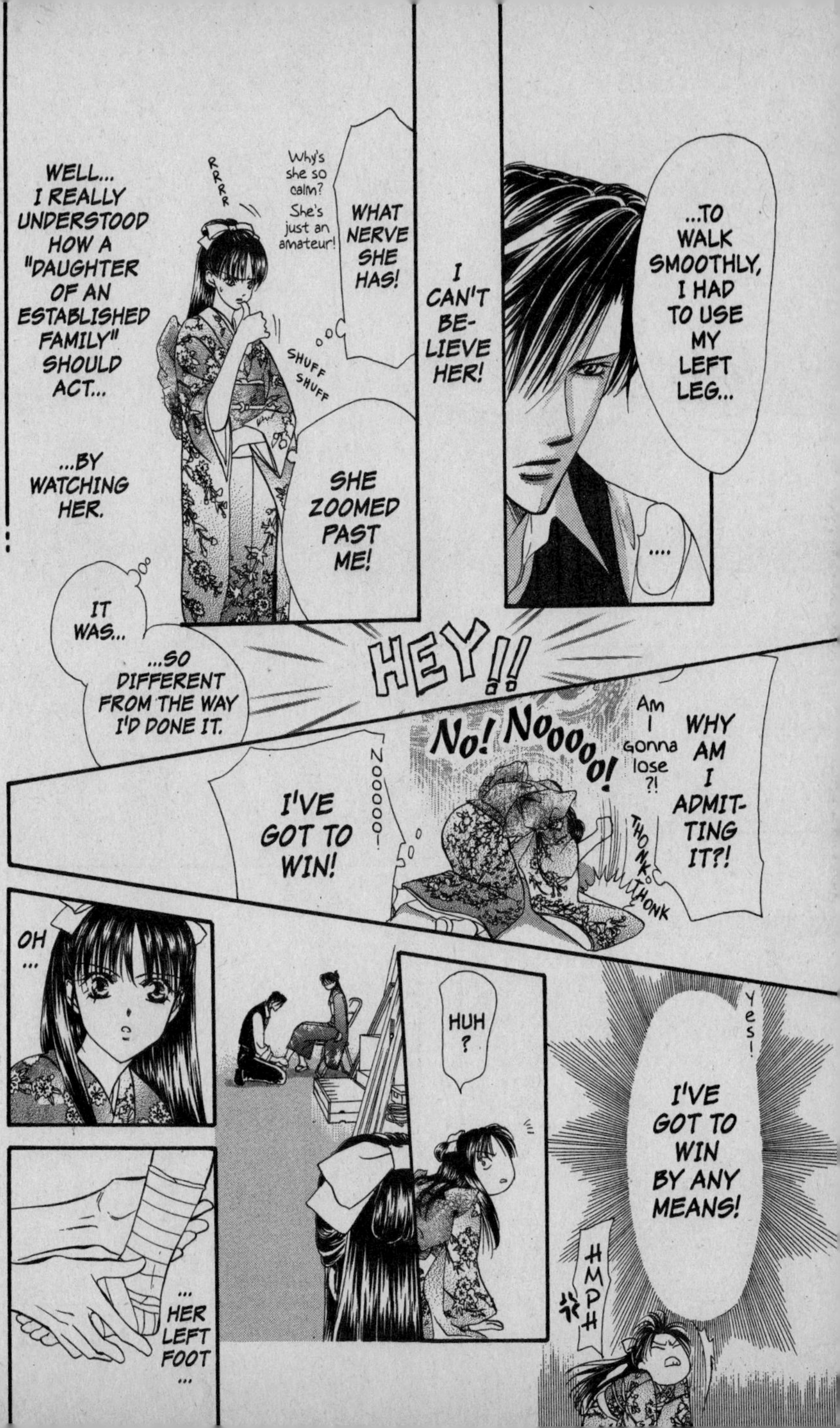
...TO WALK SMOOTHLY, I HAD TO USE MY LEFT LEG...
....
I CAN'T BE-LIEVE HER!
WHAT NERVE SHE HAS!
Why's she so calm? She's just an amateur!
RRRR
SHUFF SHUFF
SHE ZOOMED PAST ME!
WELL... I REALLY UNDERSTOOD HOW A "DAUGHTER OF AN ESTABLISHED FAMILY" SHOULD ACT...
...BY WATCHING HER.
IT WAS...
...SO DIFFERENT FROM THE WAY I'D DONE IT.
HEY!!
WHY AM I ADMIT-TING IT?!
Am I gonna lose?!
No! Nooooo!
THONK THONK
Nooooo!
I'VE GOT TO WIN!
Yes!
I'VE GOT TO WIN BY ANY MEANS!
HMPH
HUH?
OH...
...HER LEFT FOOT...

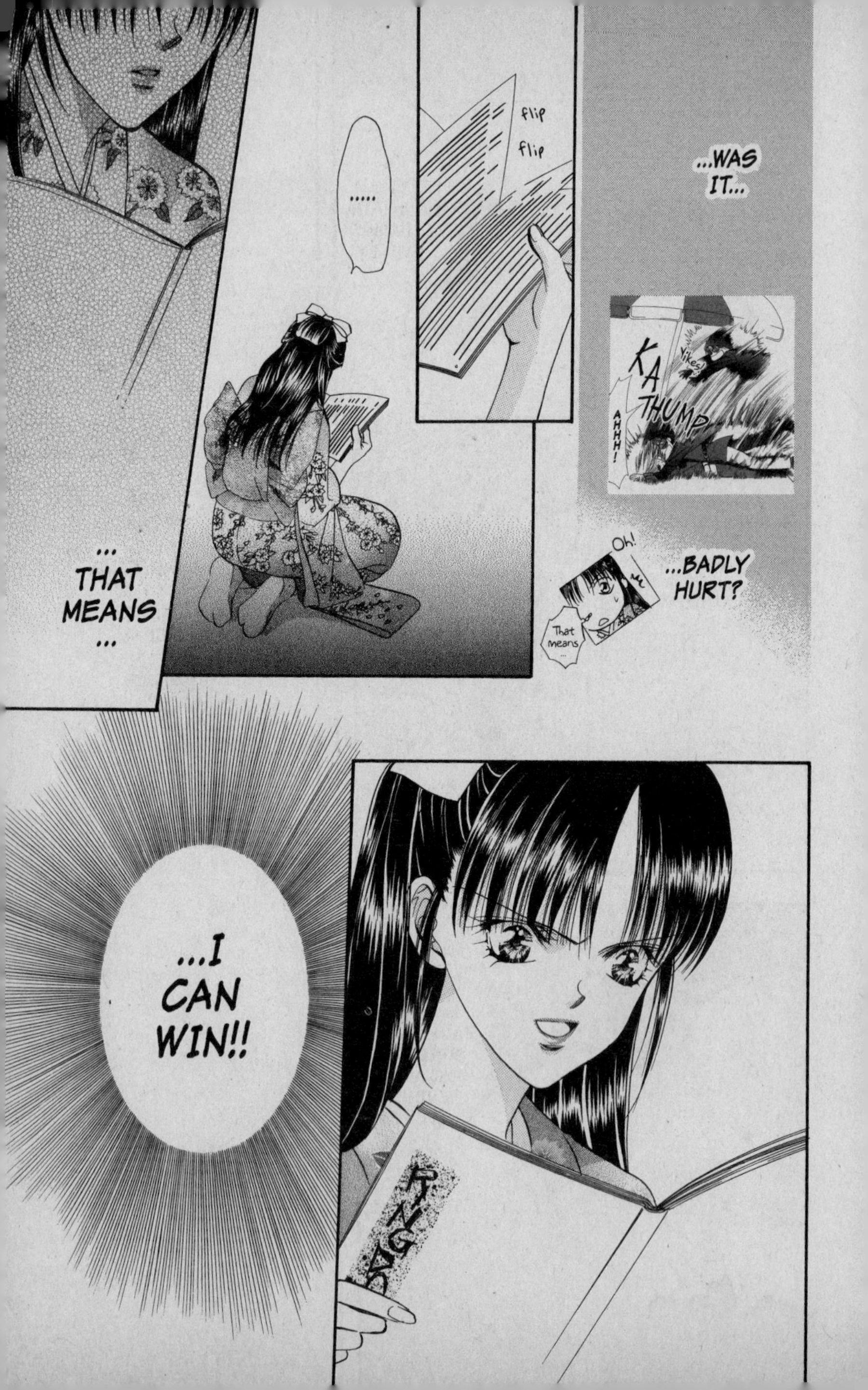
...WAS IT...
KA THUMP
Yikes!
AHHH!
Oh!
That means ...
...BADLY HURT?
flip
flip
.....
... THAT MEANS ...
...I CAN WIN!!

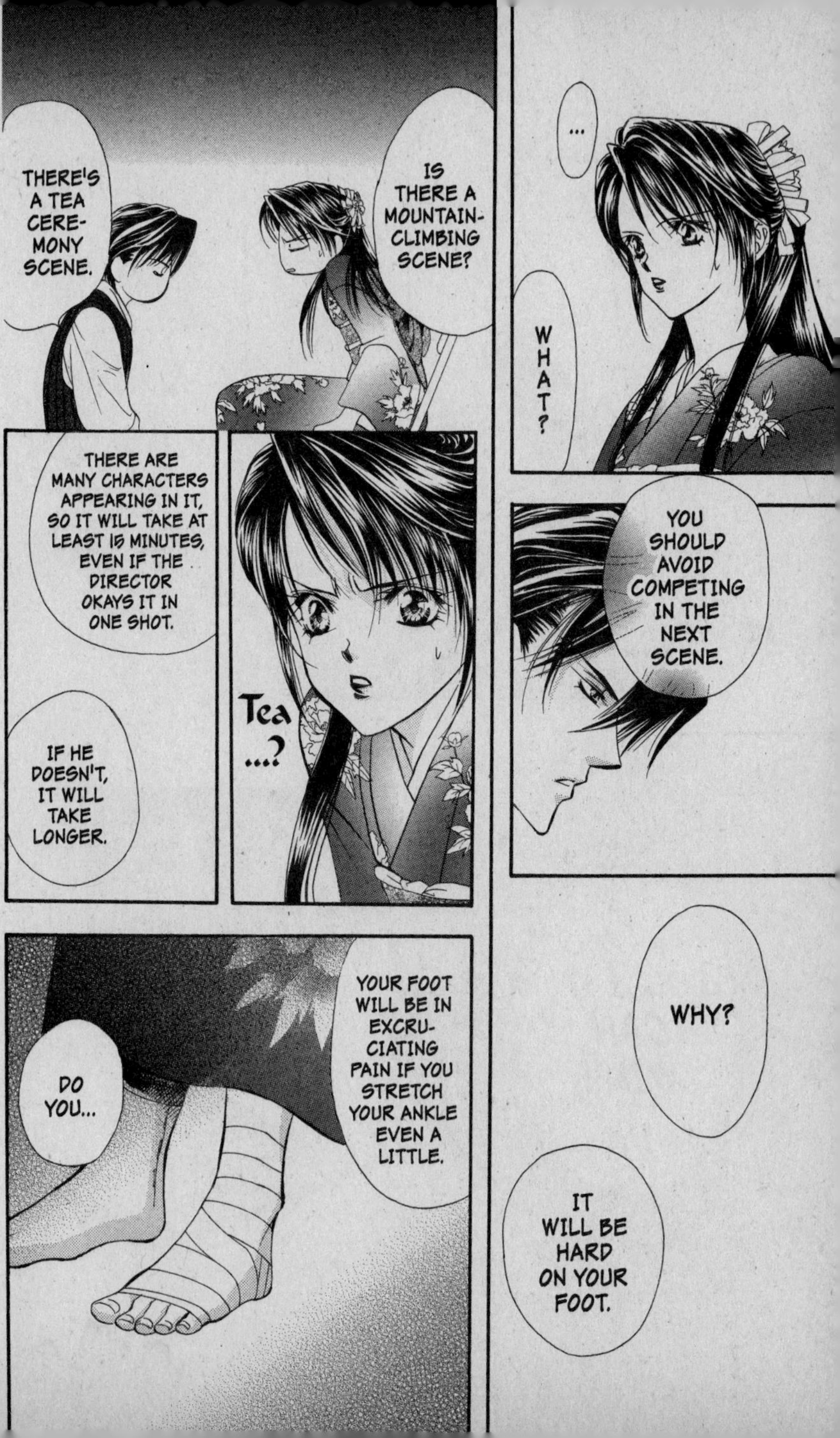
...
WHAT?
YOU SHOULD AVOID COMPETING IN THE NEXT SCENE.
WHY?
IT WILL BE HARD ON YOUR FOOT.
IS THERE A MOUNTAIN-CLIMBING SCENE?
THERE'S A TEA CERE-MONY SCENE.
Tea ...?
THERE ARE MANY CHARACTERS APPEARING IN IT, SO IT WILL TAKE AT LEAST 15 MINUTES, EVEN IF THE DIRECTOR OKAYS IT IN ONE SHOT.
IF HE DOESN'T, IT WILL TAKE LONGER.
YOUR FOOT WILL BE IN EXCRU-CIATING PAIN IF YOU STRETCH YOUR ANKLE EVEN A LITTLE.
DO YOU...

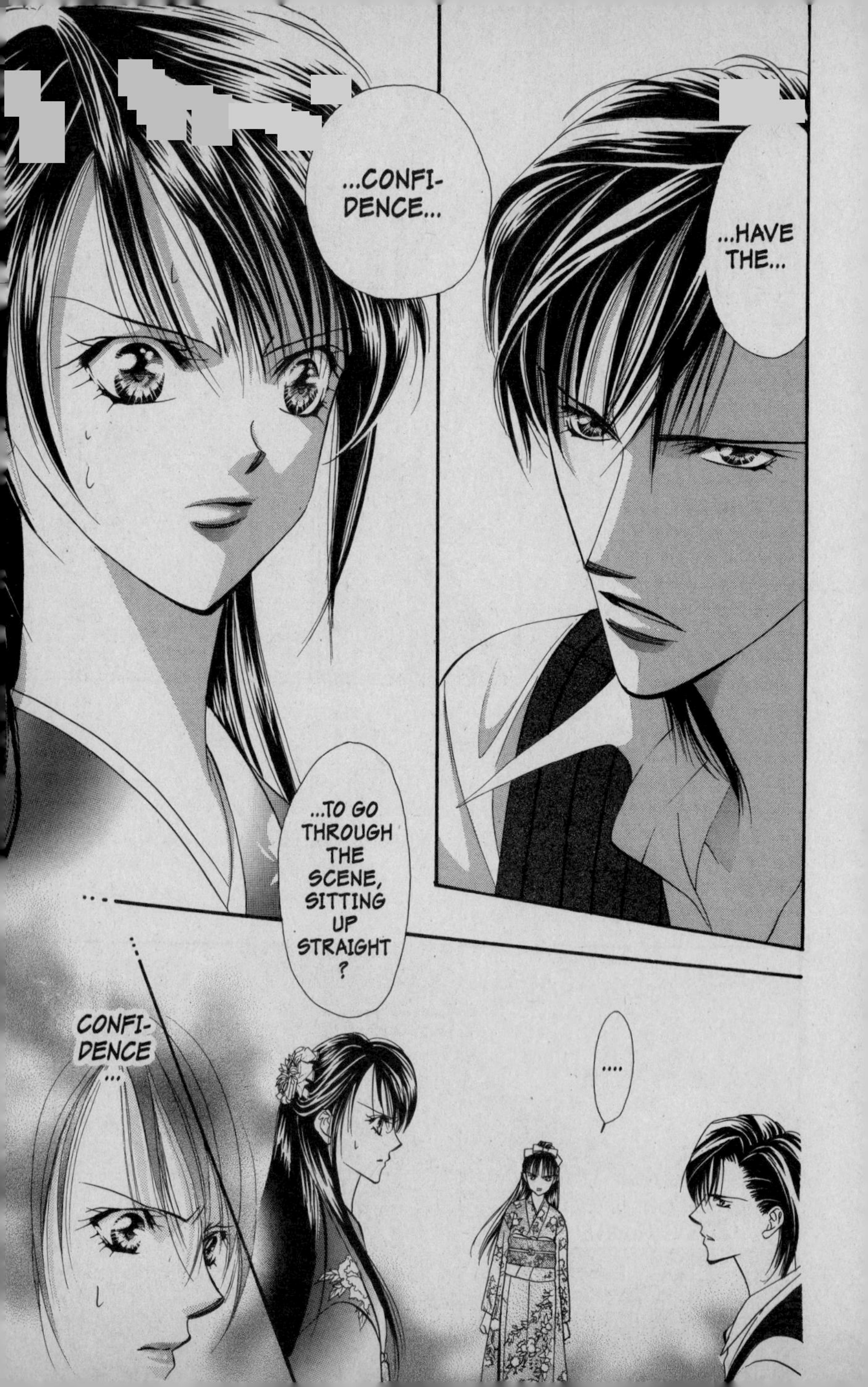
...HAVE THE...
...CONFIDENCE...
...TO GO THROUGH THE SCENE, SITTING UP STRAIGHT?
....
CONFIDENCE...

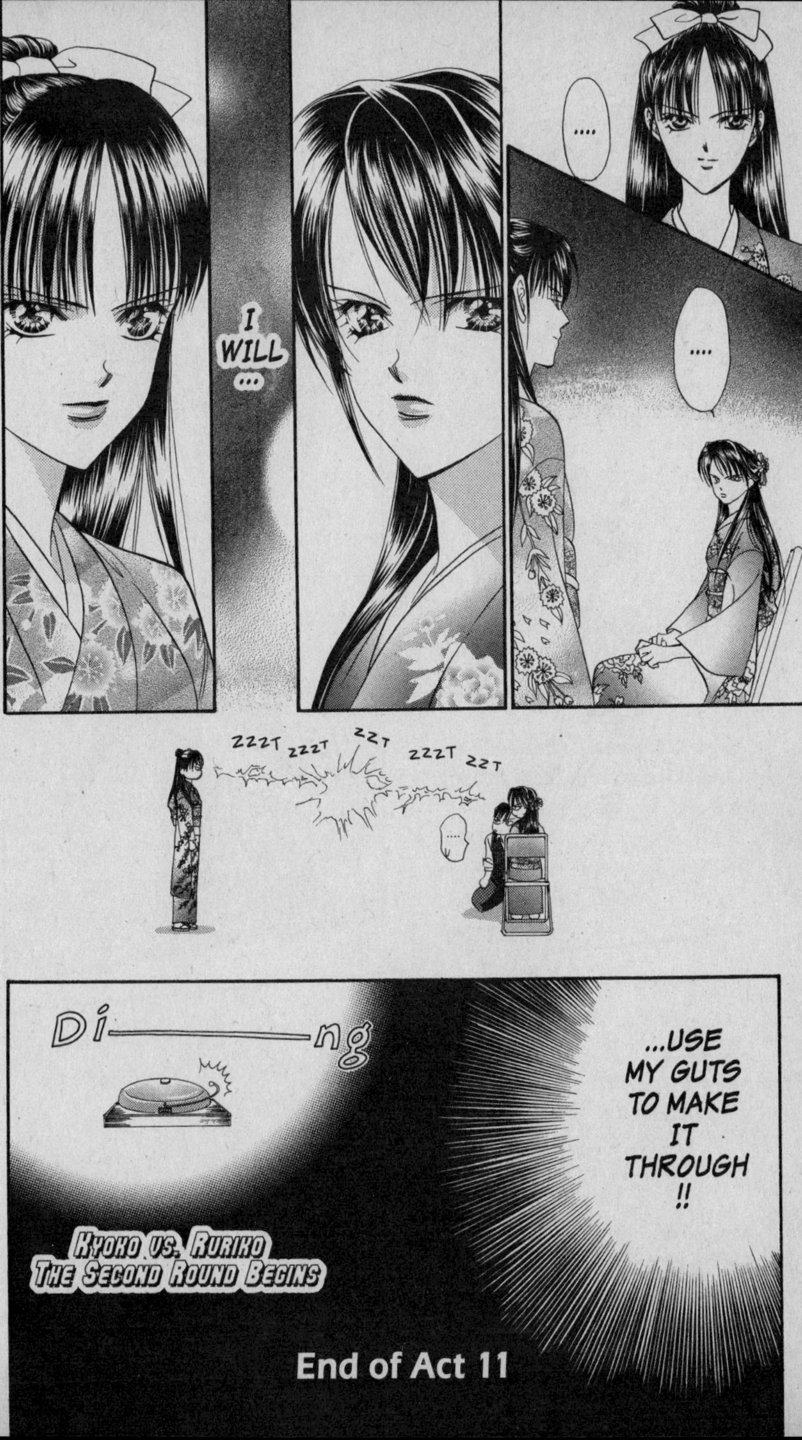
....
....
I WILL ...
ZZZT ZZZT ZZT ZZZT ZZT
....
...USE MY GUTS TO MAKE IT THROUGH!!
Di——ng
Kyoko vs. Ruriko
The Second Round Begins
End of Act 11

Skip·Beat! End Notes
Everyone knows how to be a fan, but sometimes cool things
from other cultures need a little help crossing the language barrier.

Page 220, panel 3: Draw an eye on the daruma
People draw an eye on a daruma (usually the left eye) when they have a major
goal or wish they want to achieve. The other eye is added when they reach
their goal, and the daruma is placed in a shrine as a thank-you. At election
time, many politicians can be seen drawing on the second eye when they win.

Page 222, panel 1: Tsuzumi
Hand drums used in traditional Japanese court music, Noh, and kabuki.
Kotsuzumi are played on the shoulder, while *otsuzumi* are played at the hip.
Both drums are played with the hand instead of sticks.

Page 222, panel 2: Pon
One of the sounds from the kotsuzumi, produced by hitting
the center of the drumhead.

Page 288, panel 7: Tsuru
This is a play on *Tsuruga. Tsuru* can mean "crane," but it is spelled with
a different kanji than Ren's last name.

Page 288, panel 7: Renga
Renga means "bricks." In her shock, Kyoko has temporarily gone batty and is
mixing up Ren's name…much to her own confusion.

Page 326, panel 8: Shabadaba
This isn't just a snappy tune, it's a play on words using yakuza slang. The way
shaba is spelled in the original Japanese means "the world outside prison."

Page 339, panel 6: Tengu Nose
Tengu are mountain spirits with wings and long noses. People who are being
vain and boastful are often described as tengu. Kyoko had a tengu nose herself,
back on page 11 of volume 1.

Shojo Beat

Skip·Beat!

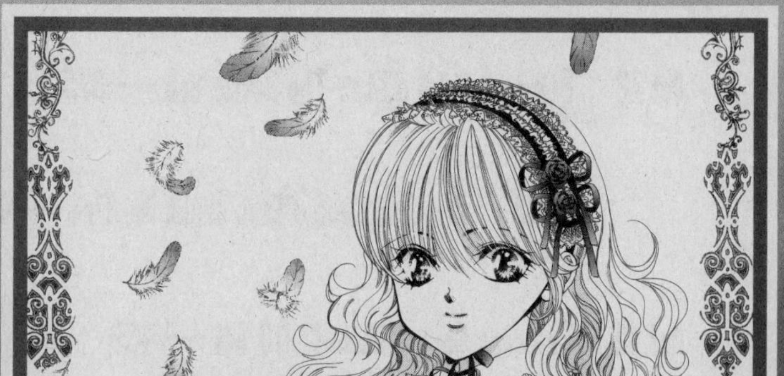

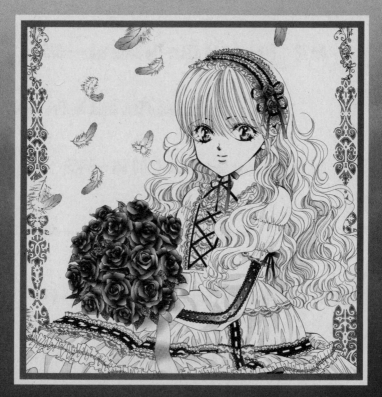

Vol. 3

Story & Art by Yoshiki Nakamura

Skip·Beat!

Volume 3

CONTENTS

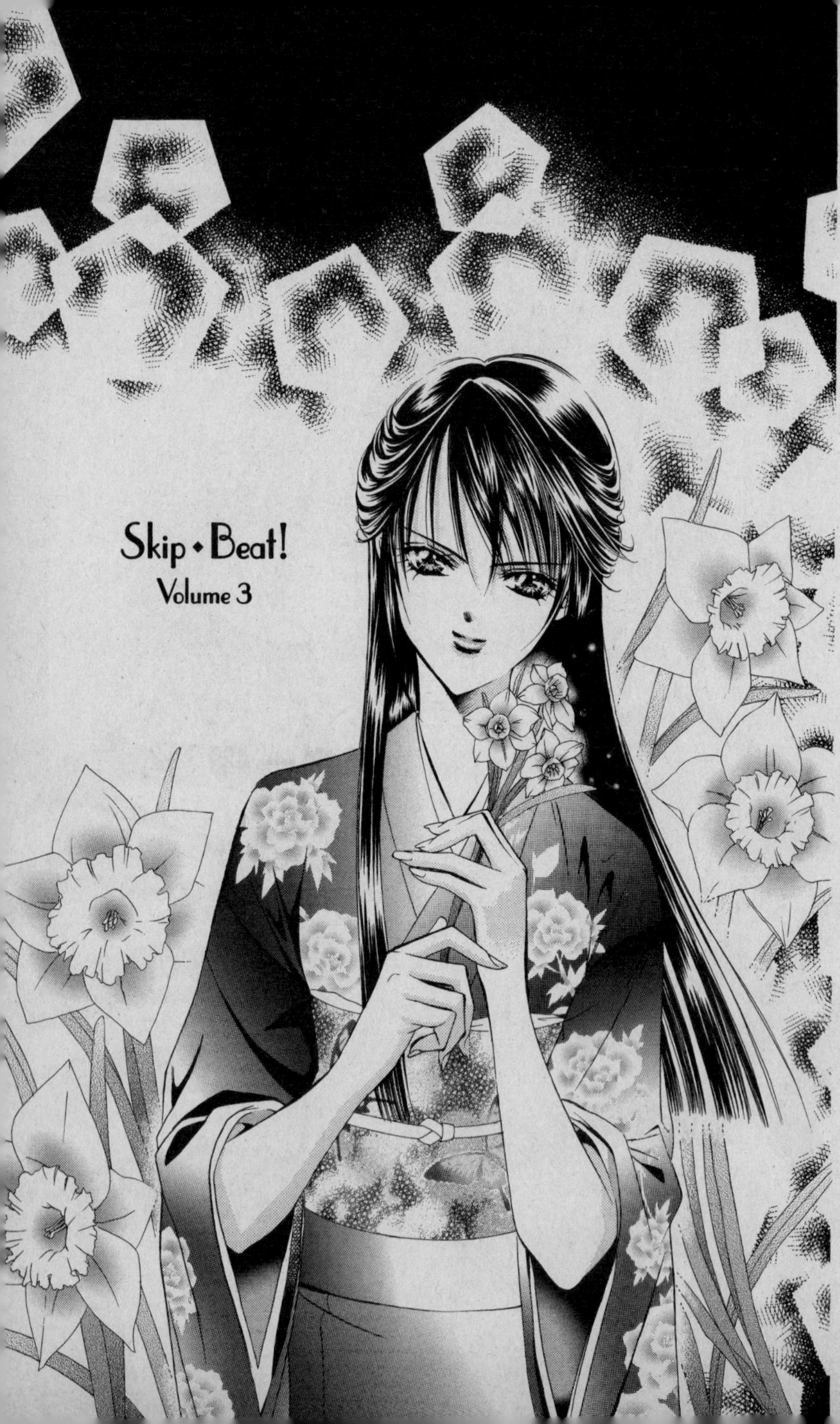
Skip • Beat!
Volume 3

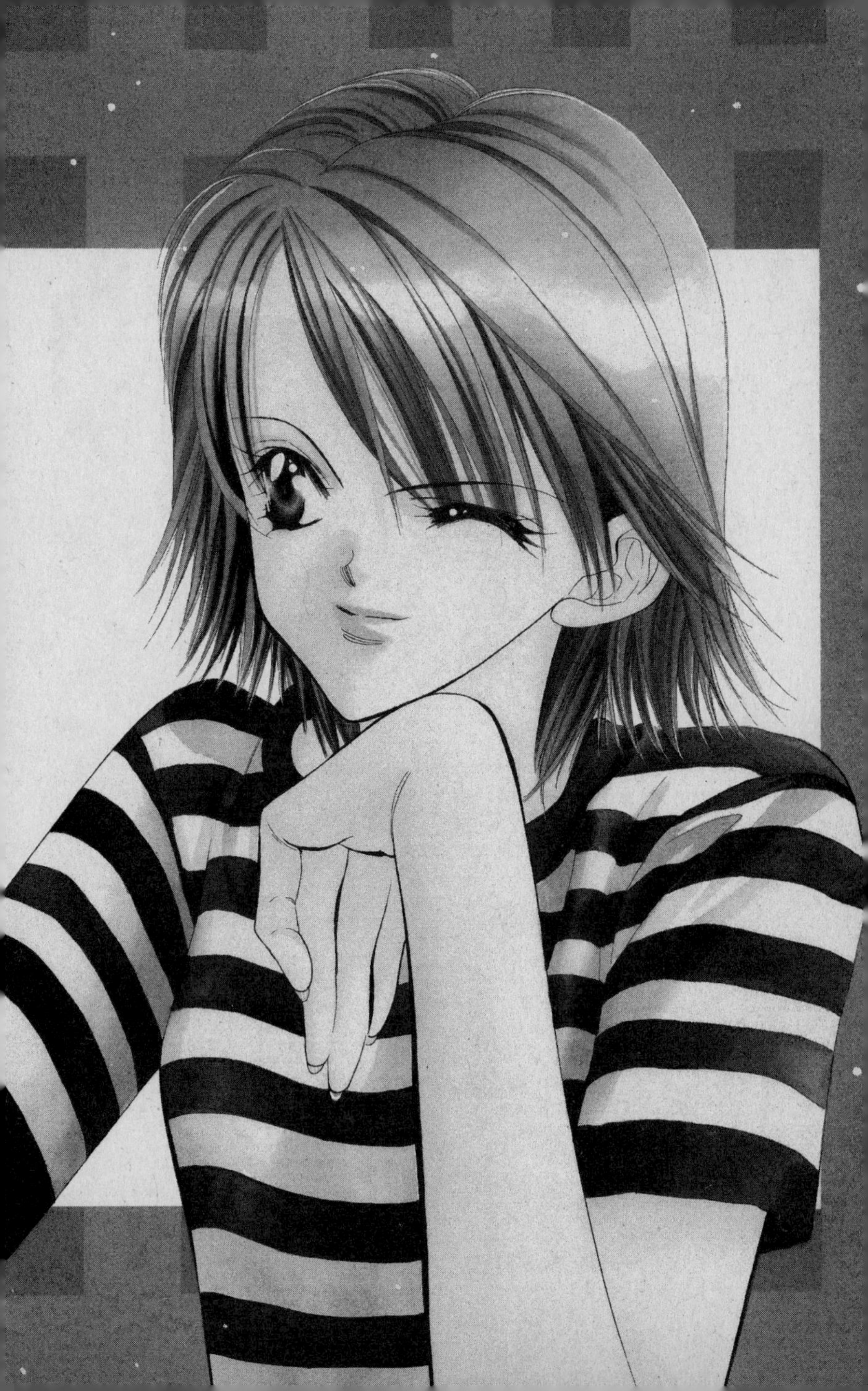

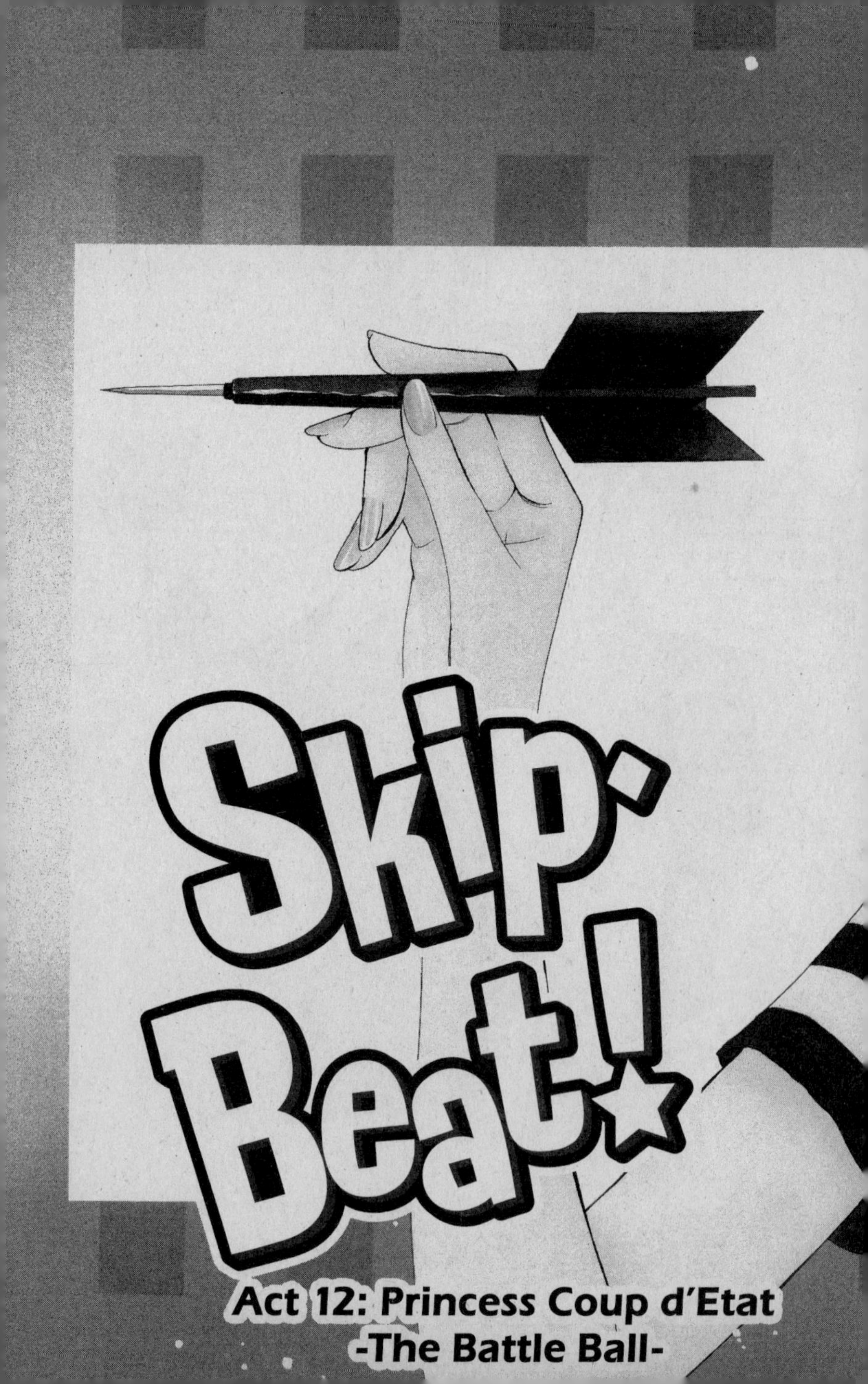
Skip·Beat!
Act 12: Princess Coup d'Etat
-The Battle Ball-

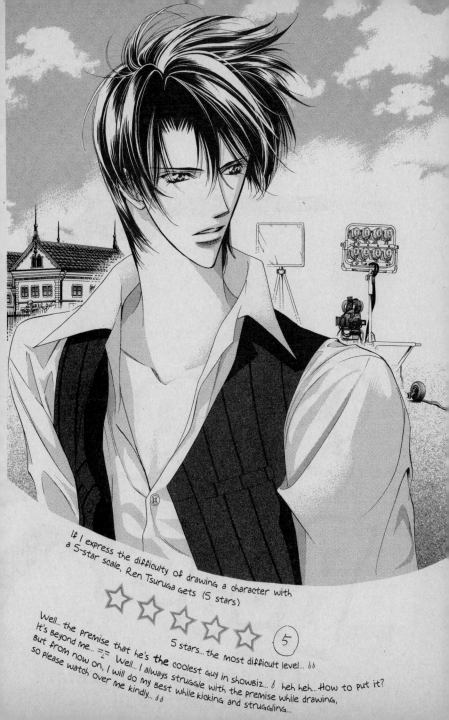

If I express the difficulty of drawing a character with a 5-star scale, Ren Tsuruga gets (5 stars)

☆☆☆☆☆ ⑤

5 stars... the most difficult level... ♪♪

Well... the premise that he's **the** coolest guy in showbiz... ♪ heh heh...How to put it?
It's beyond me... ≒= Well... I always struggle with the premise while drawing,
but from now on, I will do my best while kicking and struggling...
so please watch over me kindly... ♪♪

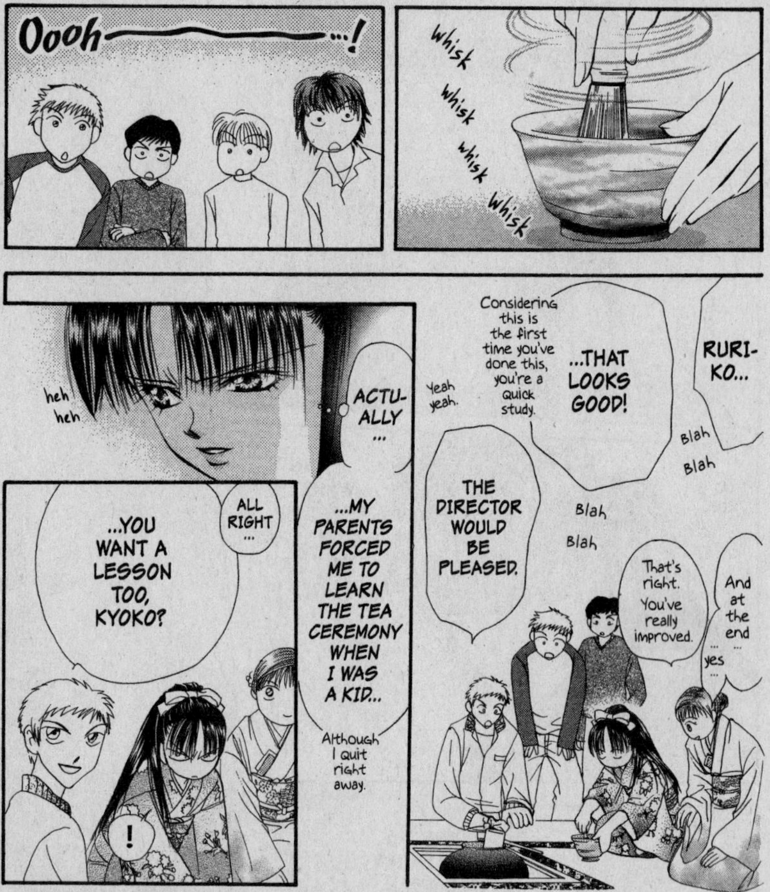
whisk
whisk
whisk
whisk
Oooh———...!
RURI-KO...
...THAT LOOKS GOOD!
Considering this is the first time you've done this, you're a quick study.
Yeah yeah.
Blah
Blah
THE DIRECTOR WOULD BE PLEASED.
Blah
Blah
And at the end...
...yes...
That's right. You've really improved.
ACTU-ALLY...
heh heh
...MY PARENTS FORCED ME TO LEARN THE TEA CEREMONY WHEN I WAS A KID...
Although I quit right away.
ALL RIGHT...
...YOU WANT A LESSON TOO, KYOKO?
!

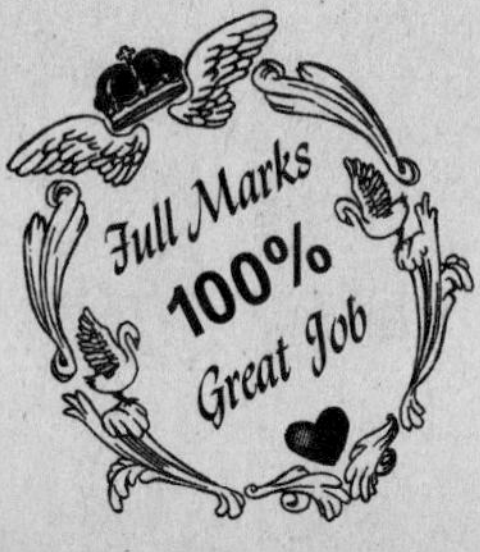
Full Marks
100%
Great Job

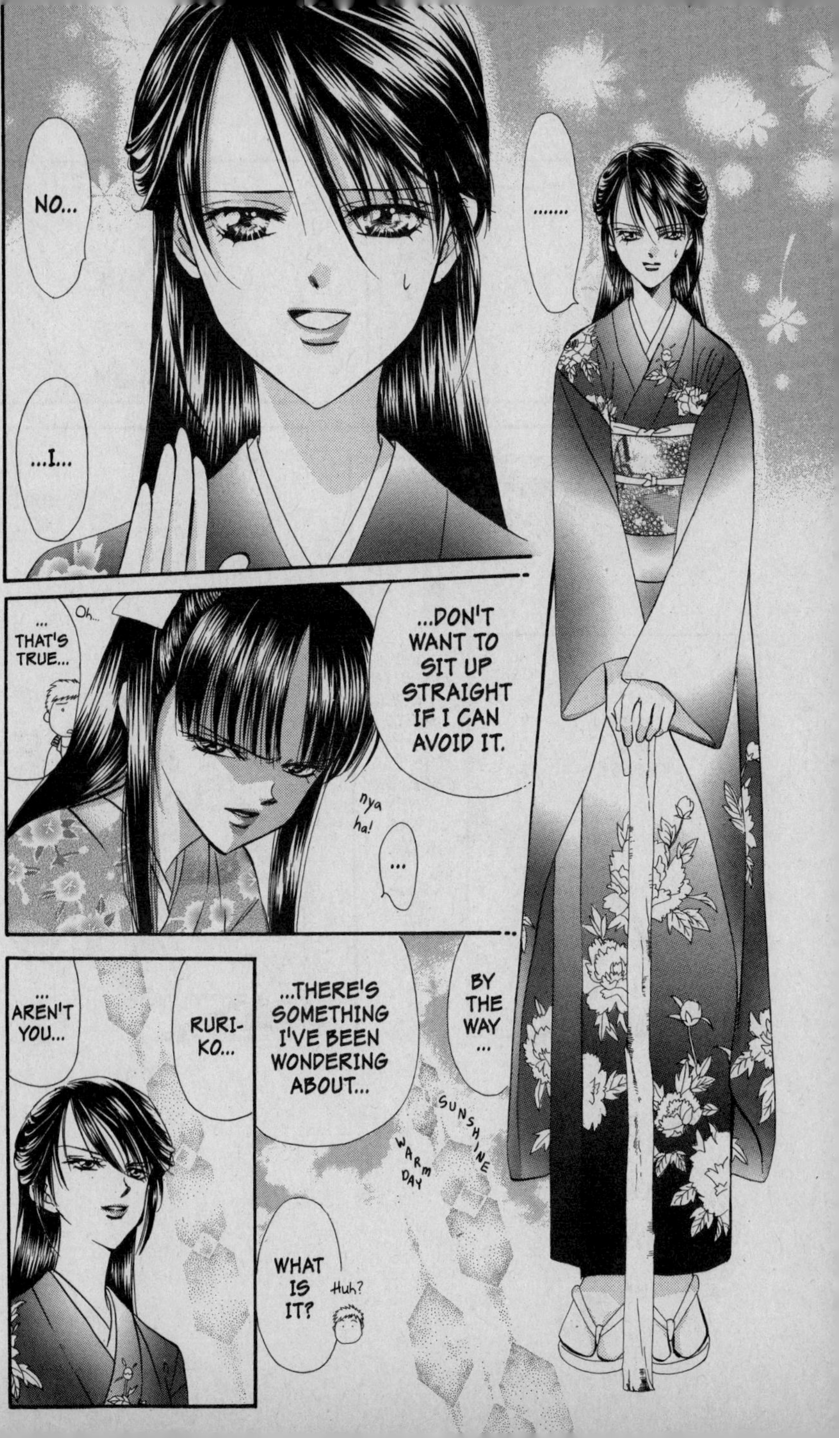
....
NO...
...I...
...DON'T WANT TO SIT UP STRAIGHT IF I CAN AVOID IT.
Oh...
...THAT'S TRUE...
nya ha!
...
BY THE WAY...
...THERE'S SOMETHING I'VE BEEN WONDERING ABOUT...
RURI-KO...
...AREN'T YOU...
SUNSHINE
WARM DAY
WHAT IS IT?
Huh?

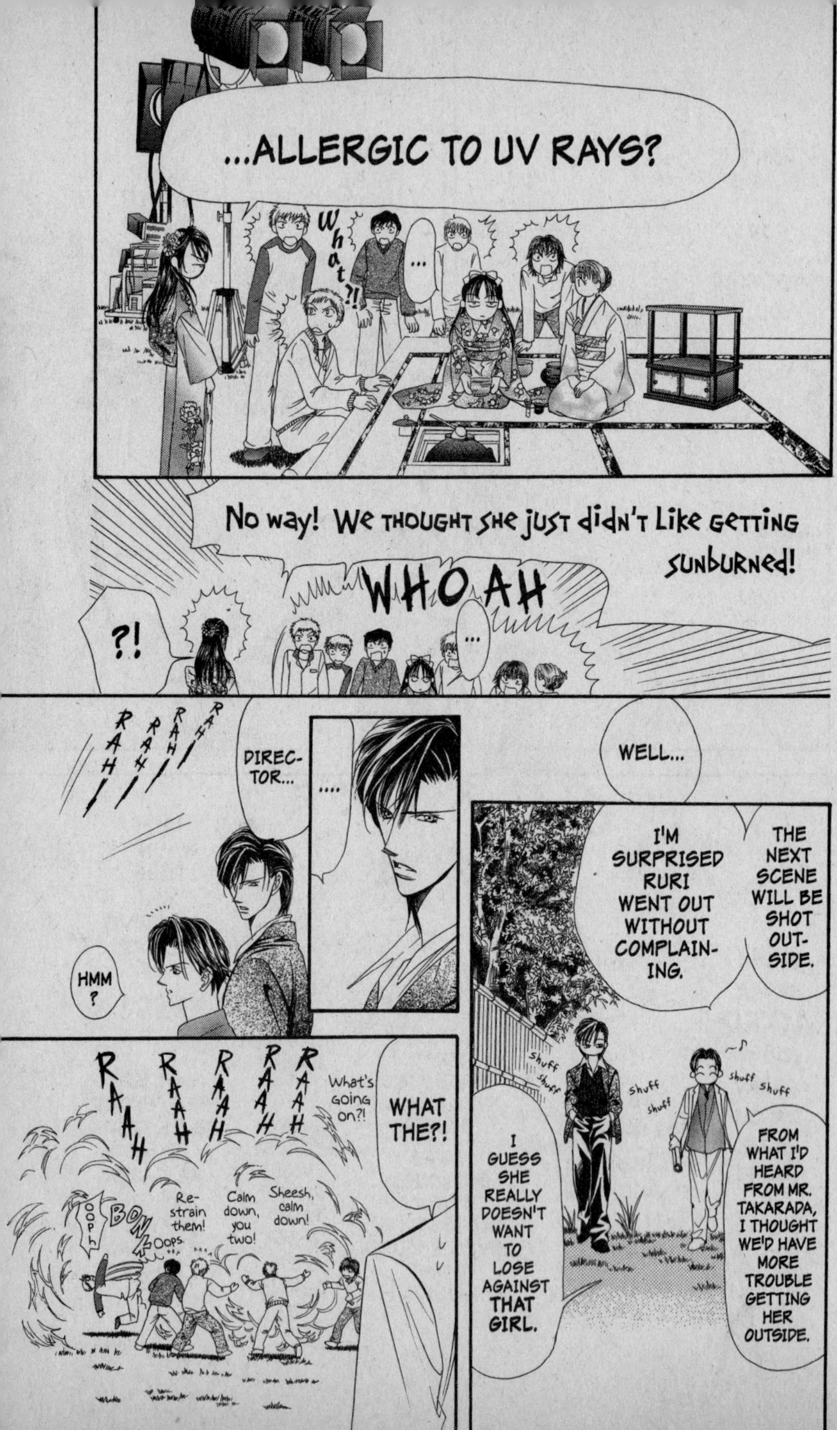
...ALLERGIC TO UV RAYS?
What?!
...
No way! We thought she just didn't like getting sunburned!
WHOAH
...
?!
WELL...
THE NEXT SCENE WILL BE SHOT OUTSIDE.
I'M SURPRISED RURI WENT OUT WITHOUT COMPLAINING.
~♪
FROM WHAT I'D HEARD FROM MR. TAKARADA, I THOUGHT WE'D HAVE MORE TROUBLE GETTING HER OUTSIDE.
shuff shuff
shuff shuff
I GUESS SHE REALLY DOESN'T WANT TO LOSE AGAINST THAT GIRL.
DIREC-TOR...
....
RAH RAH RAH RAH
HMM?
WHAT THE?!
What's going on?!
RAAH RAAAH RAAAH RAAAH RAAAH
Sheesh, calm down!
Calm down, you two!
Re-strain them!
BONK
OOPS
OOPh

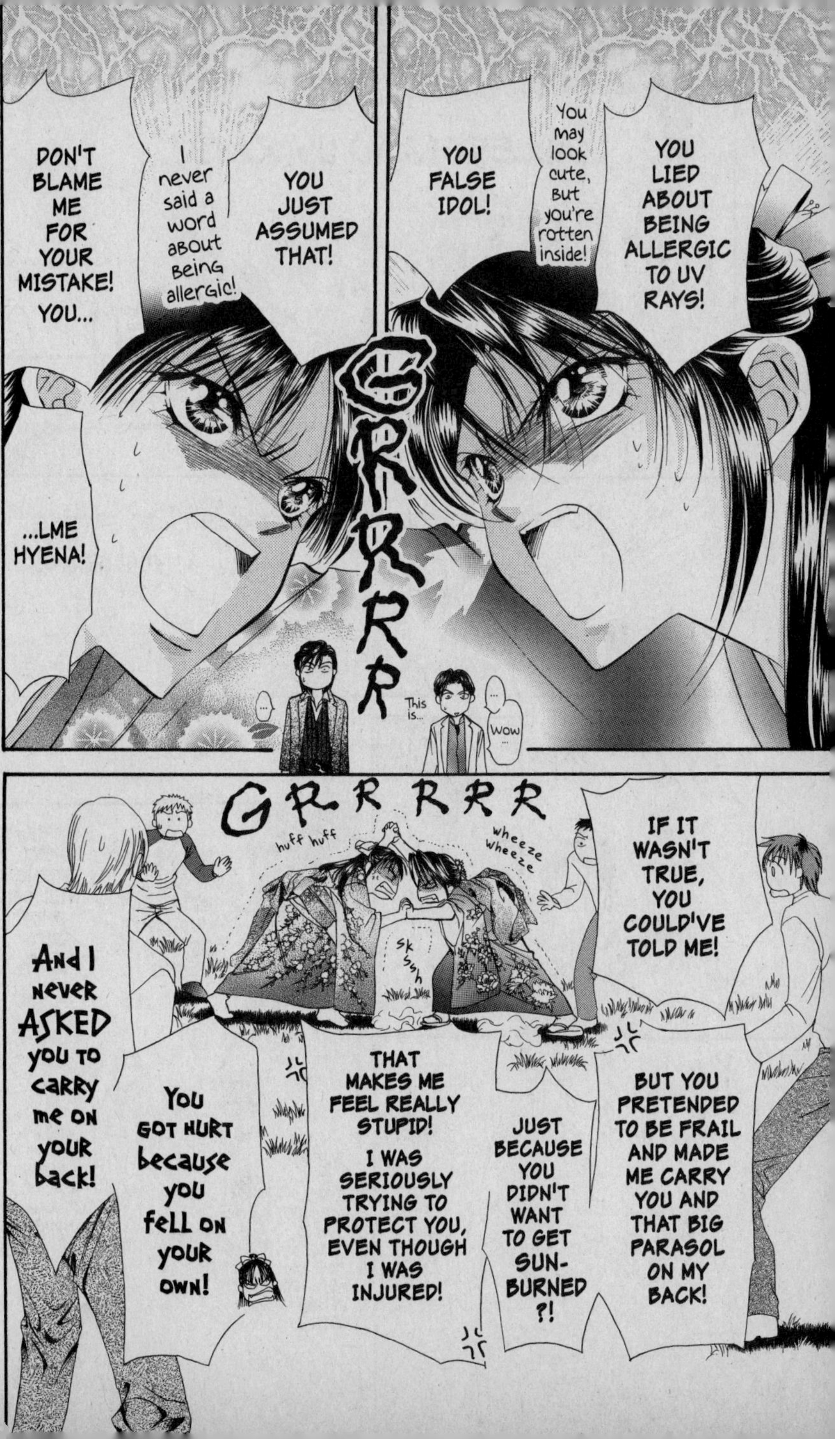
YOU LIED ABOUT BEING ALLERGIC TO UV RAYS!
You may look cute, but you're rotten inside!
YOU FALSE IDOL!
YOU JUST ASSUMED THAT!
I never said a word about being allergic!
DON'T BLAME ME FOR YOUR MISTAKE! YOU...
GRRRR
...LME HYENA!
...
Wow...
This is...
...
IF IT WASN'T TRUE, YOU COULD'VE TOLD ME!
wheeze wheeze
GRRRRR
huff huff
sk ssh
And I never ASKED you to carry me on your back!
BUT YOU PRETENDED TO BE FRAIL AND MADE ME CARRY YOU AND THAT BIG PARASOL ON MY BACK!
JUST BECAUSE YOU DIDN'T WANT TO GET SUN-BURNED?!
THAT MAKES ME FEEL REALLY STUPID!
I WAS SERIOUSLY TRYING TO PROTECT YOU, EVEN THOUGH I WAS INJURED!
You got hurt because you fell on your own!

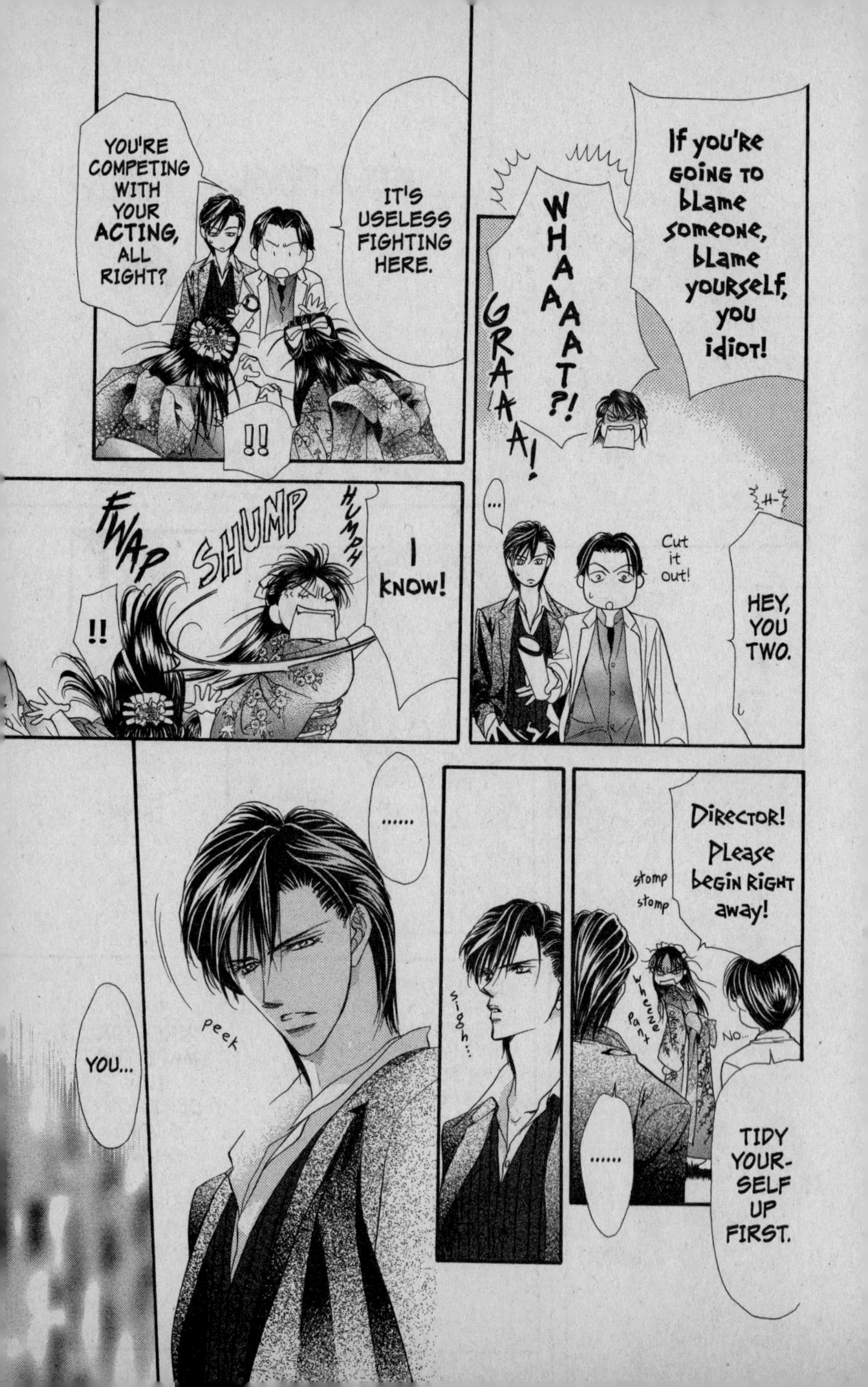
If you're going to blame someone, blame yourself, you idiot!
WHAAAAAT?!
GRAAAA!
H-
HEY, YOU TWO.
Cut it out!
...
IT'S USELESS FIGHTING HERE.
YOU'RE COMPETING WITH YOUR ACTING, ALL RIGHT?
!!
HUMPH
I KNOW!
SHUMP
FWAP
!!
Director! Please begin right away!
stomp stomp
wheeze pant
No...
TIDY YOURSELF UP FIRST.
......
sigh...
......
peek
YOU...

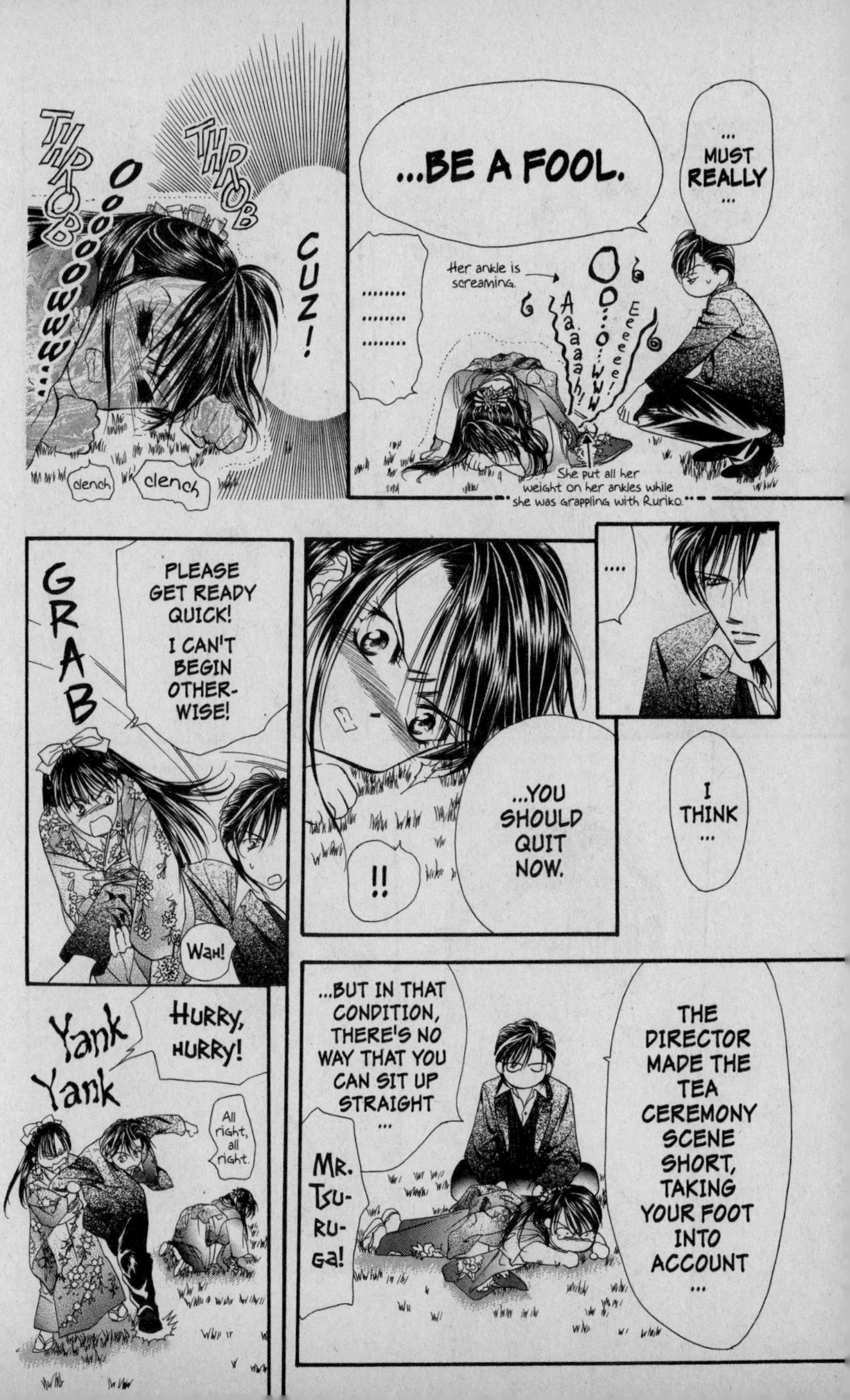

... MUST REALLY ...
...BE A FOOL.
....
....
....
Her ankle is screaming.
Aaaaah!
O... O... www
Eeeeee!
She put all her weight on her ankles while she was grappling with Ruriko.
THROB
THROB
Ooooowww...
CUZ!
clench
clench
....
I THINK ...
...YOU SHOULD QUIT NOW.
!!
PLEASE GET READY QUICK!
I CAN'T BEGIN OTHER-WISE!
GRAB
Wah!
THE DIRECTOR MADE THE TEA CEREMONY SCENE SHORT, TAKING YOUR FOOT INTO ACCOUNT ...
...BUT IN THAT CONDITION, THERE'S NO WAY THAT YOU CAN SIT UP STRAIGHT ...
MR. TSU-RU-GA!
HURRY, HURRY!
Yank
Yank
All right, all right.

Greetings

Hello. I'm Nakamura. Thank you for reading Skip•Beat! this time around, too. It happens with me often, but I redrew some of the panels that I wasn't satisfied with for the manga volume (sometimes I redraw the same panel about five times...)

My drawing ability isn't enough to satisfy my ideals. I've been a mangaka for at least ten years. It's pitiful...

...so...it took more time to fix things for the manga volume than I thought it would... Especially with Ren and Lory... If other people looked at it, I don't believe they'd think there's been much of a change...the change is veeeery subtle... probably...heh...

But...(and this happens every time) Ren always makes me cry...why? Somehow the Ren that I draw doesn't look like he's good-looking... It's because the type of male characters that I like are well-built, have single eyelids, look super evil, kind of like a savage (?!)...(The assistants who know what I like sometimes say "Nakamura-san...please don't go after dangerous-looking guys"...)

I won't go... yeah... I think... so...for sure...

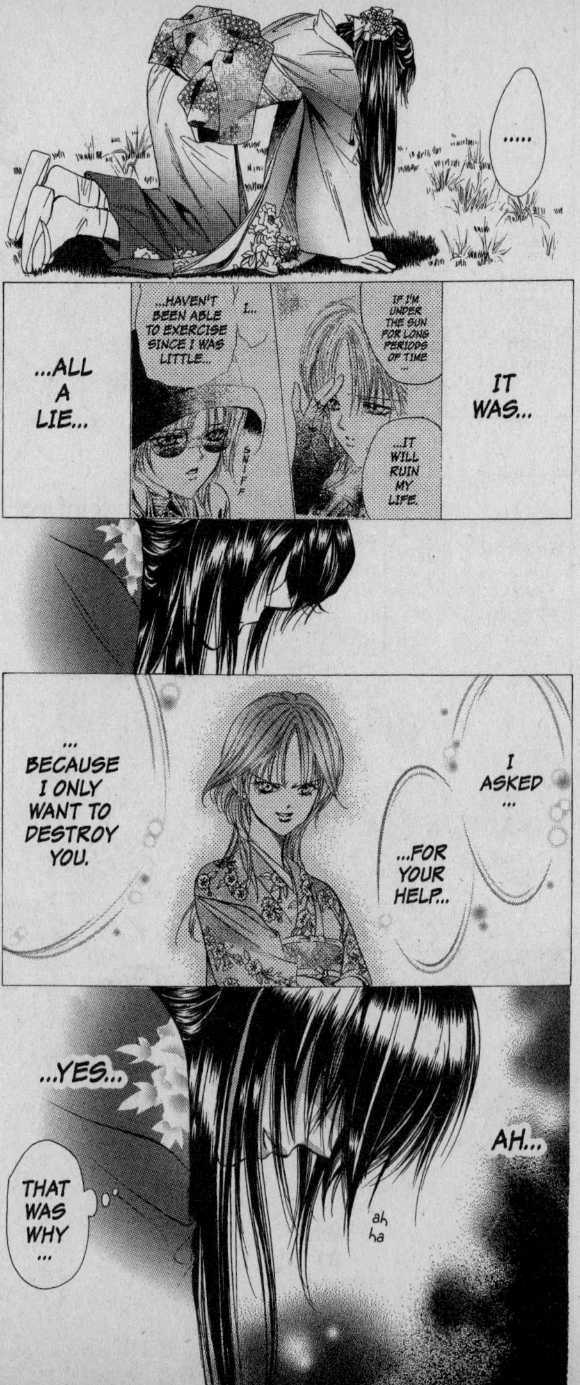
.....
IT WAS...
IF I'M UNDER THE SUN FOR LONG PERIODS OF TIME...
...IT WILL RUIN MY LIFE.
I...
...HAVEN'T BEEN ABLE TO EXERCISE SINCE I WAS LITTLE...
SNIFF
...ALL A LIE...
I ASKED...
...FOR YOUR HELP...
...BECAUSE I ONLY WANT TO DESTROY YOU.
AH...
ah ha
...YES...
THAT WAS WHY...

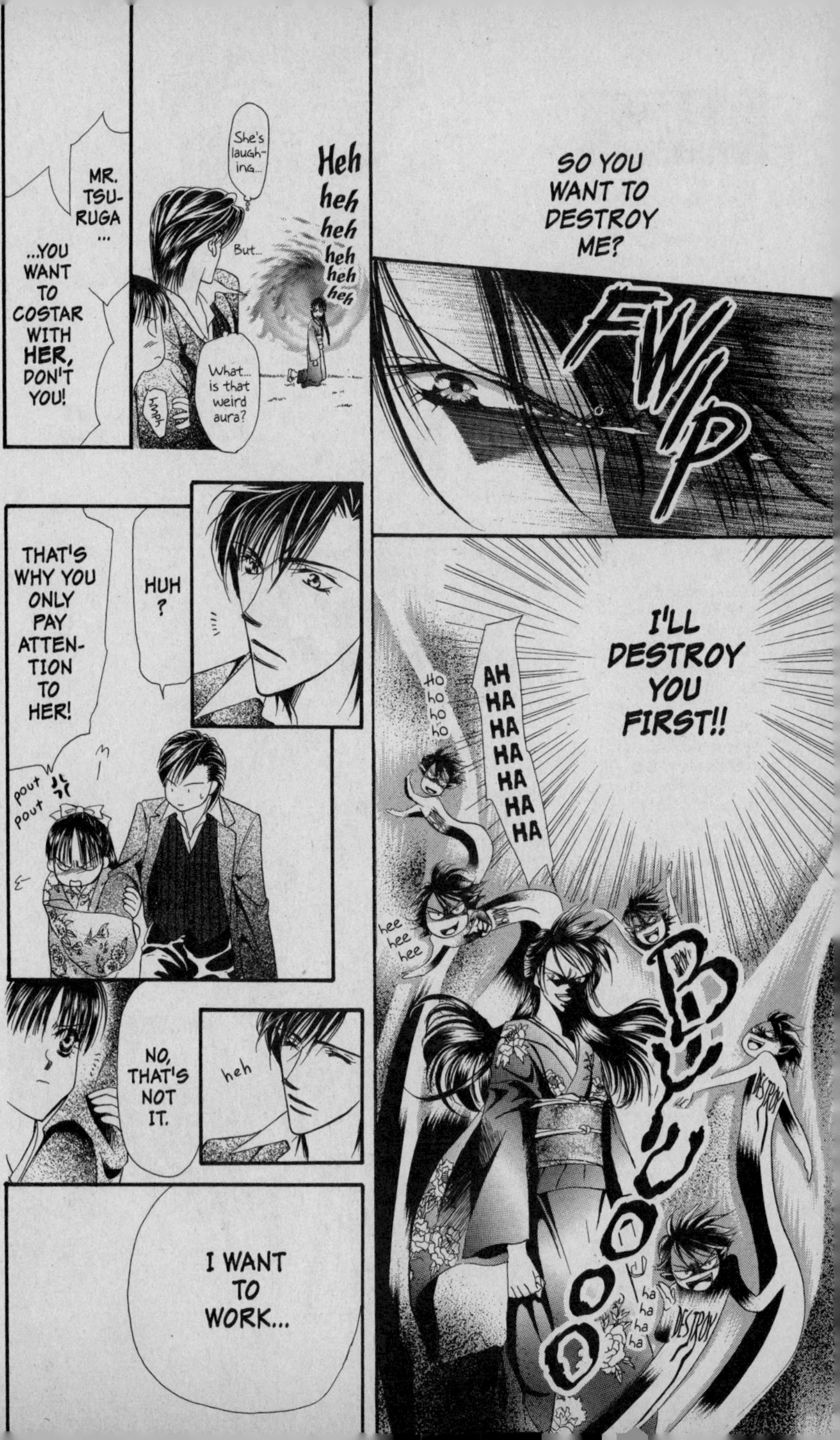
SO YOU WANT TO DESTROY ME?
FWIP
I'LL DESTROY YOU FIRST!!
AH HA HA HA HA HA HA HA
Ho ho ho ho
hee hee hee
BUWOOOOO
ha ha ha ha
DESTROY
DESTROY
DESTROY
MR. TSURUGA...
...YOU WANT TO COSTAR WITH HER, DON'T YOU!
Heh heh heh heh heh heh
She's laughing...
But...
What... is that weird aura?
hmph
HUH?
THAT'S WHY YOU ONLY PAY ATTENTION TO HER!
pout pout
NO, THAT'S NOT IT.
heh
I WANT TO WORK...

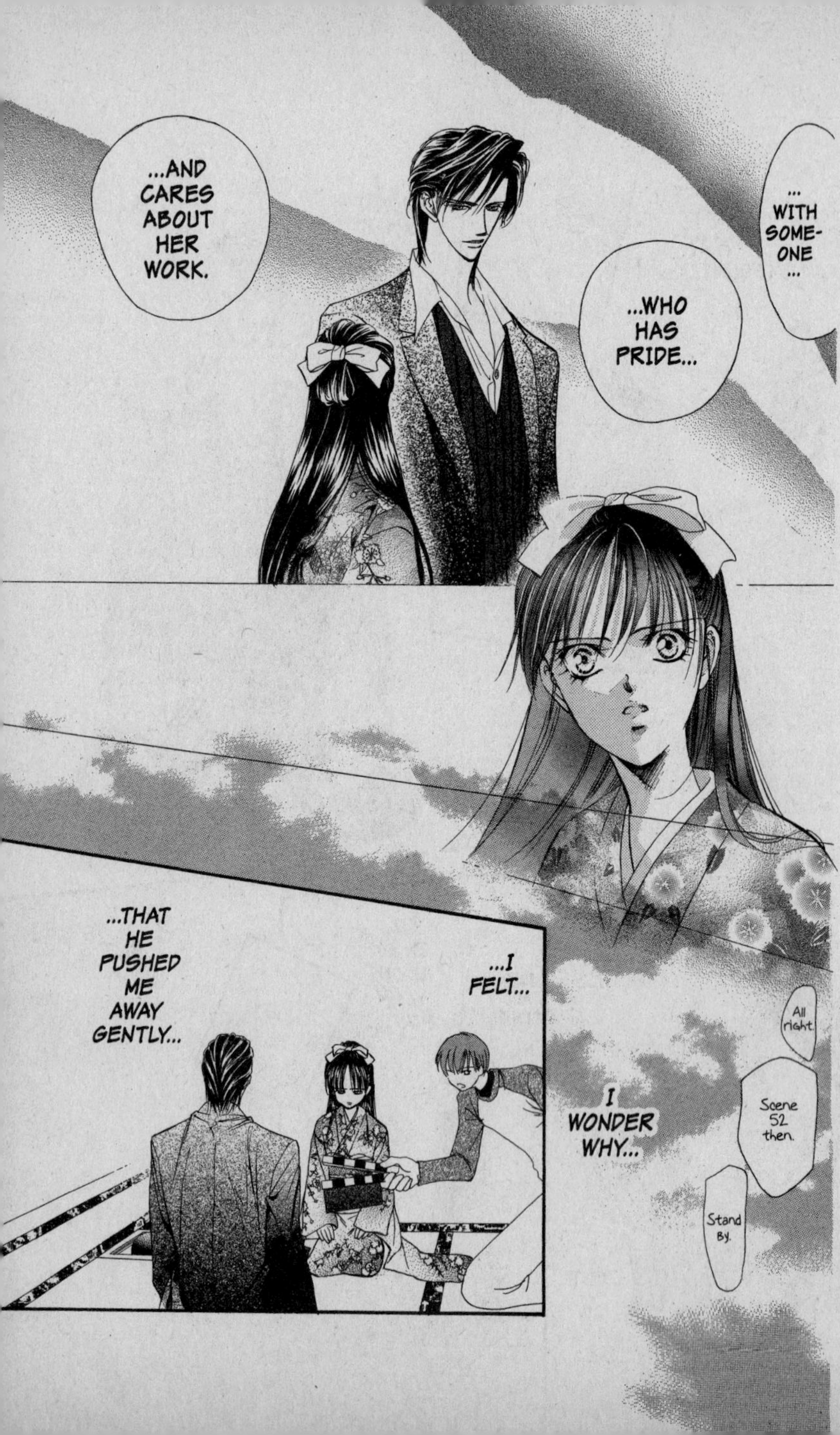
... WITH SOME-ONE ...
...WHO HAS PRIDE...
...AND CARES ABOUT HER WORK.
All right.
Scene 52 then.
Stand By.
I WONDER WHY...
...I FELT...
...THAT HE PUSHED ME AWAY GENTLY...

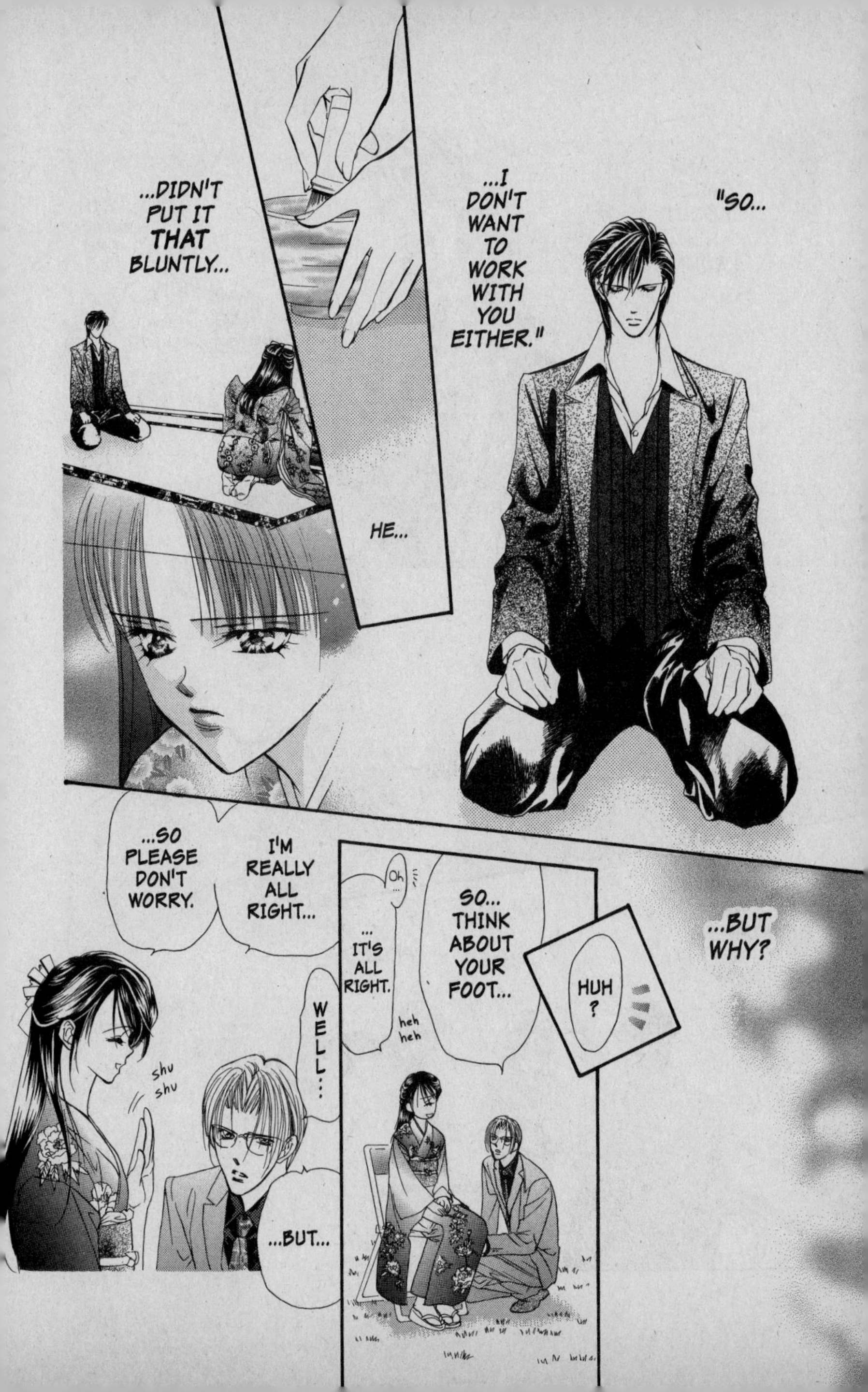
"SO...
...I DON'T WANT TO WORK WITH YOU EITHER."
HE...
...DIDN'T PUT IT THAT BLUNTLY...
...BUT WHY?
HUH?
SO... THINK ABOUT YOUR FOOT...
Oh...
...IT'S ALL RIGHT.
heh heh
I'M REALLY ALL RIGHT...
...SO PLEASE DON'T WORRY.
shu shu
WELL...
...BUT...

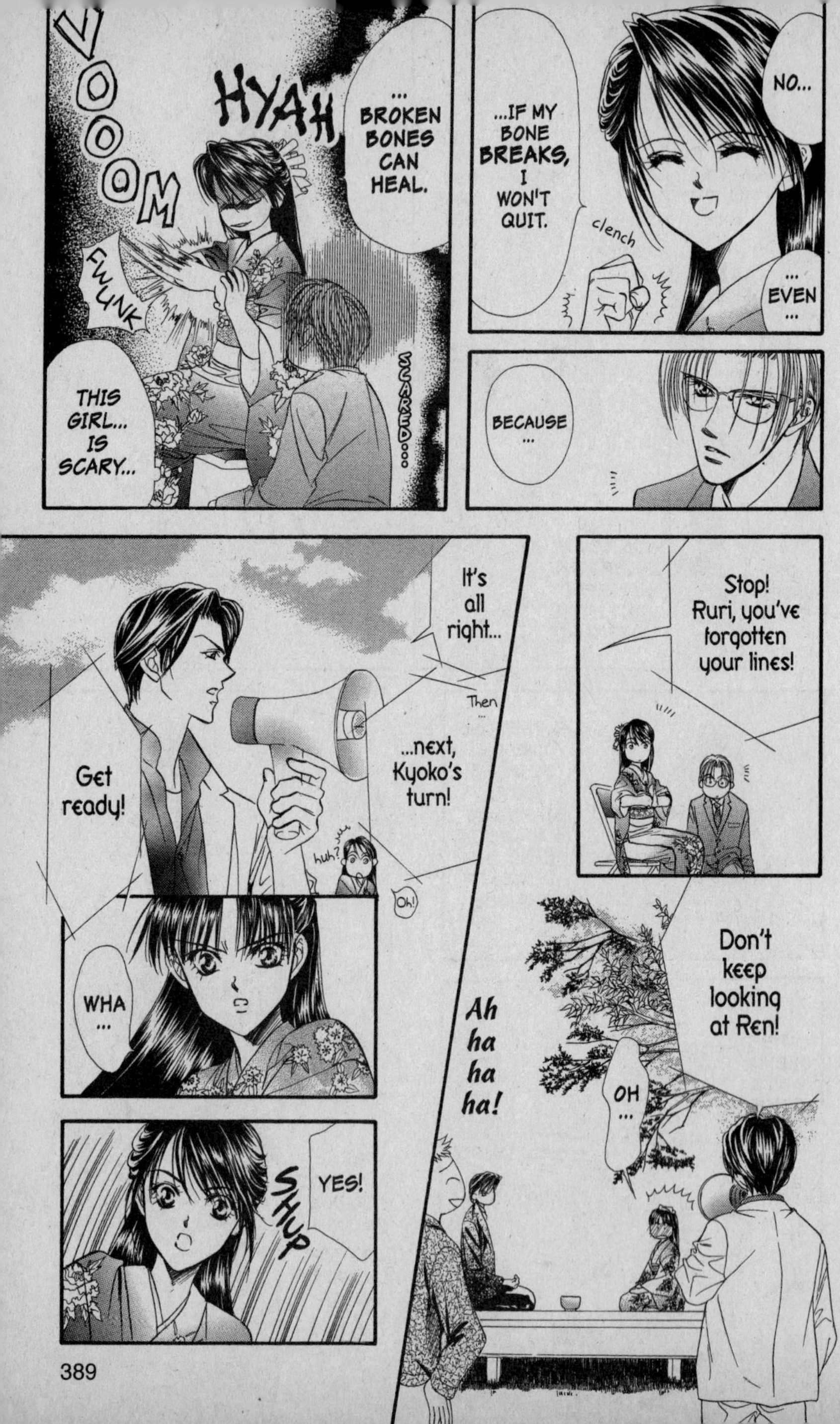
NO...
...EVEN...
...IF MY BONE BREAKS, I WON'T QUIT.
clench
BECAUSE...
...BROKEN BONES CAN HEAL.
HYAH
VOOOM
FWUNK
SCARED...
THIS GIRL... IS SCARY...
Stop! Ruri, you've forgotten your lines!
Don't keep looking at Ren!
Ah ha ha ha!
OH...
It's all right...
Then...
...next, Kyoko's turn!
huh?
Oh!
Get ready!
WHA...
YES!
SHUP

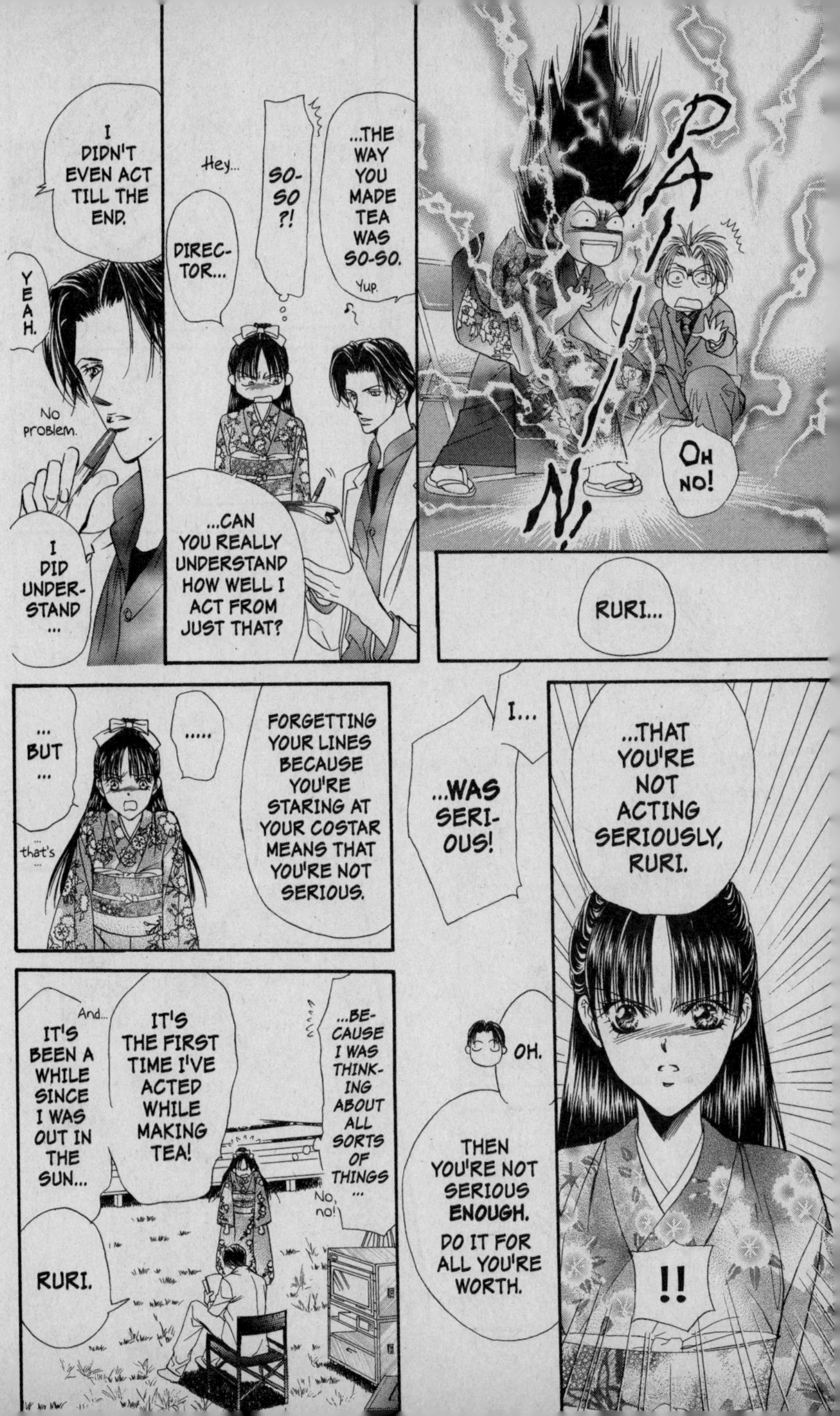

PA-I-I-N!
OH NO!
RURI...
...THE WAY YOU MADE TEA WAS SO-SO.
Yup.
SO-SO ?!
Hey...
DIREC-TOR...
...CAN YOU REALLY UNDERSTAND HOW WELL I ACT FROM JUST THAT?
I DIDN'T EVEN ACT TILL THE END.
YEAH.
No problem.
I DID UNDER-STAND ...
...THAT YOU'RE NOT ACTING SERIOUSLY, RURI.
!!
I...
...WAS SERI-OUS!
OH.
THEN YOU'RE NOT SERIOUS ENOUGH.
DO IT FOR ALL YOU'RE WORTH.
FORGETTING YOUR LINES BECAUSE YOU'RE STARING AT YOUR COSTAR MEANS THAT YOU'RE NOT SERIOUS.
.....
... BUT ...
... that's ...
...BE-CAUSE I WAS THINK-ING ABOUT ALL SORTS OF THINGS ...
No, no!
IT'S THE FIRST TIME I'VE ACTED WHILE MAKING TEA!
And...
IT'S BEEN A WHILE SINCE I WAS OUT IN THE SUN...
RURI.

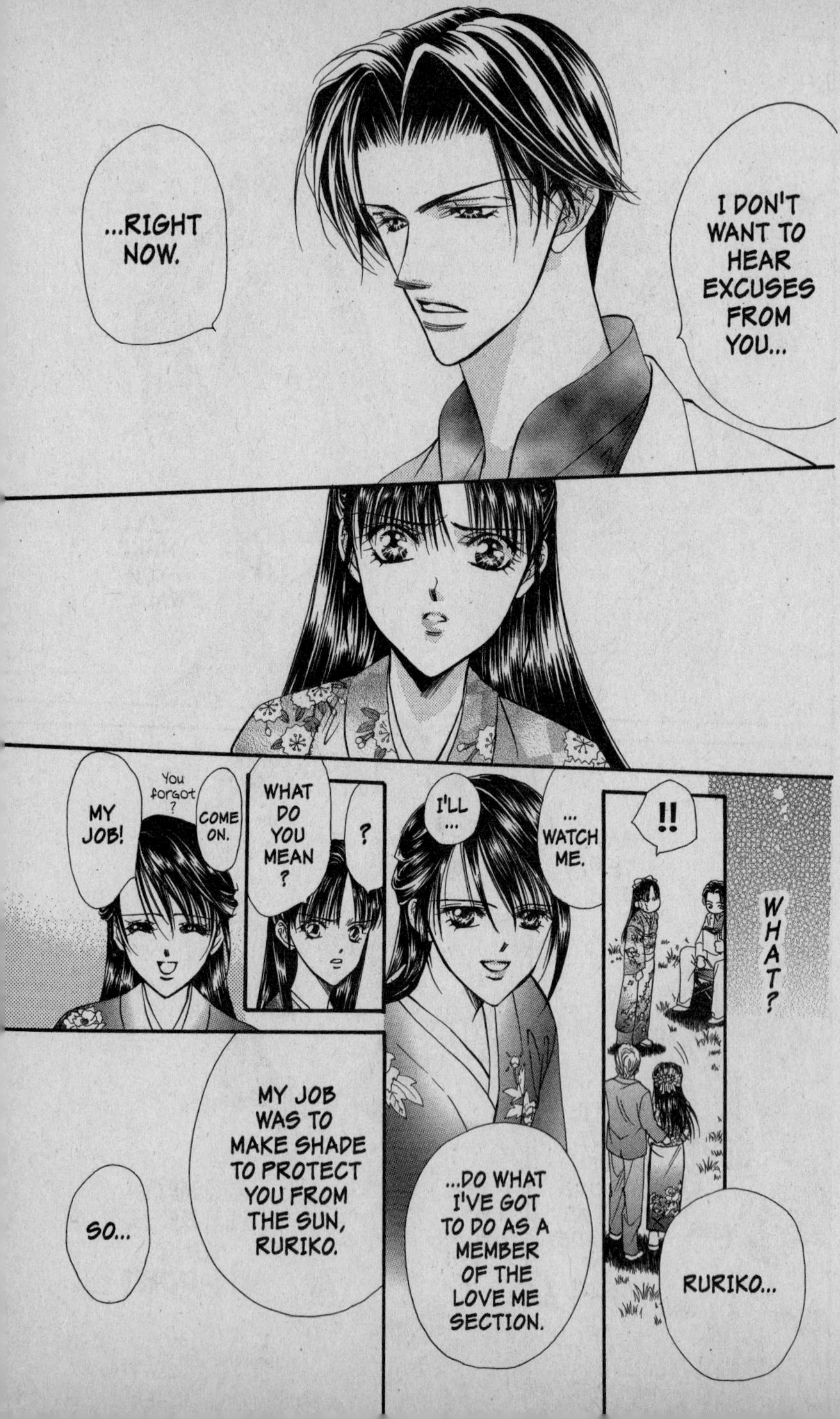
I DON'T WANT TO HEAR EXCUSES FROM YOU...
...RIGHT NOW.
!!
WHAT?
RURIKO...
...WATCH ME.
I'LL...
...DO WHAT I'VE GOT TO DO AS A MEMBER OF THE LOVE ME SECTION.
?
WHAT DO YOU MEAN?
COME ON.
You forgot?
MY JOB!
MY JOB WAS TO MAKE SHADE TO PROTECT YOU FROM THE SUN, RURIKO.
SO...

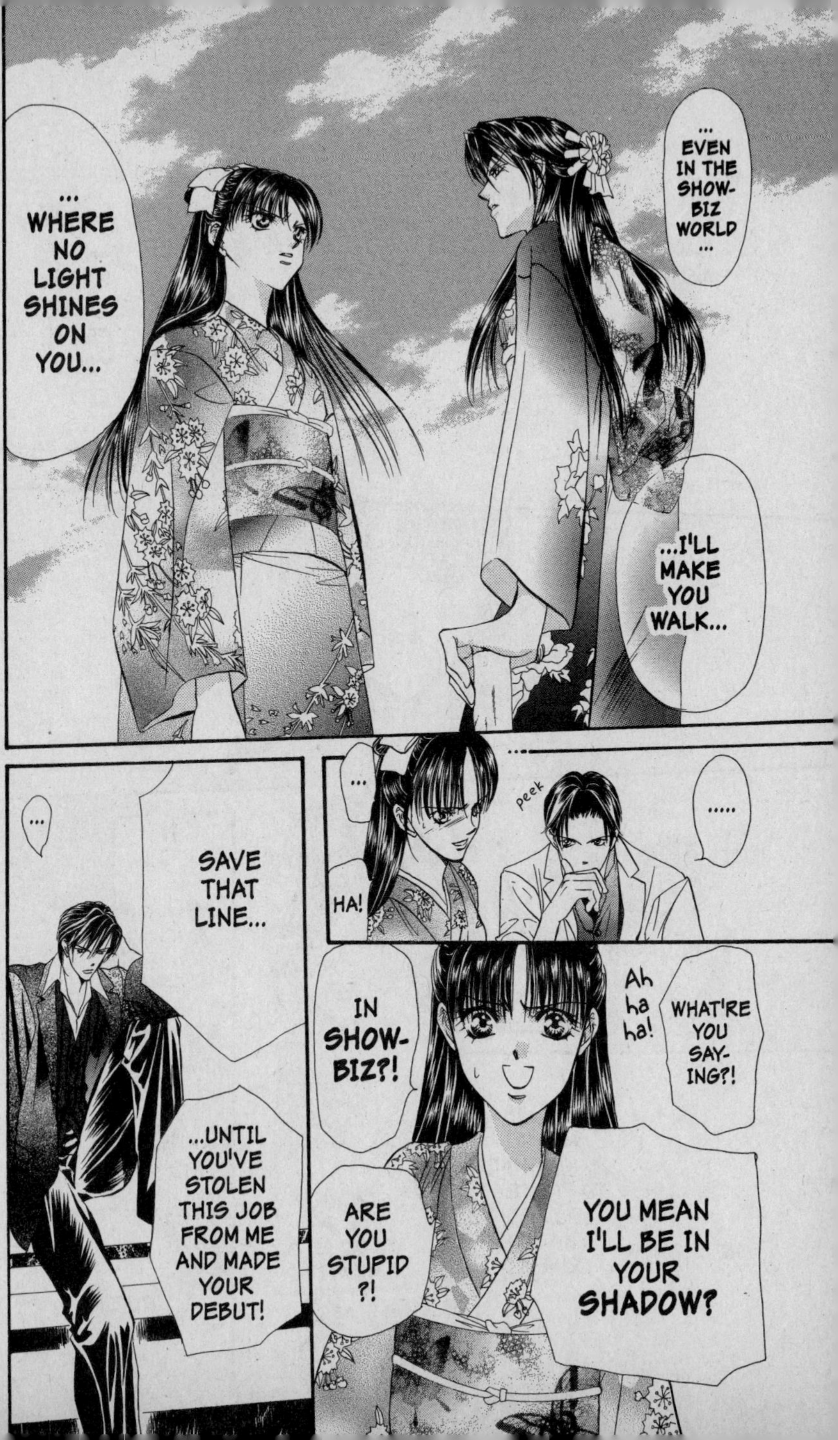
... EVEN IN THE SHOW-BIZ WORLD ...
...I'LL MAKE YOU WALK...
... WHERE NO LIGHT SHINES ON YOU...
.....
peek
...
HA!
WHAT'RE YOU SAYING?!
Ah ha ha!
IN SHOW-BIZ?!
YOU MEAN I'LL BE IN YOUR SHADOW?
ARE YOU STUPID ?!
...
SAVE THAT LINE...
...UNTIL YOU'VE STOLEN THIS JOB FROM ME AND MADE YOUR DEBUT!

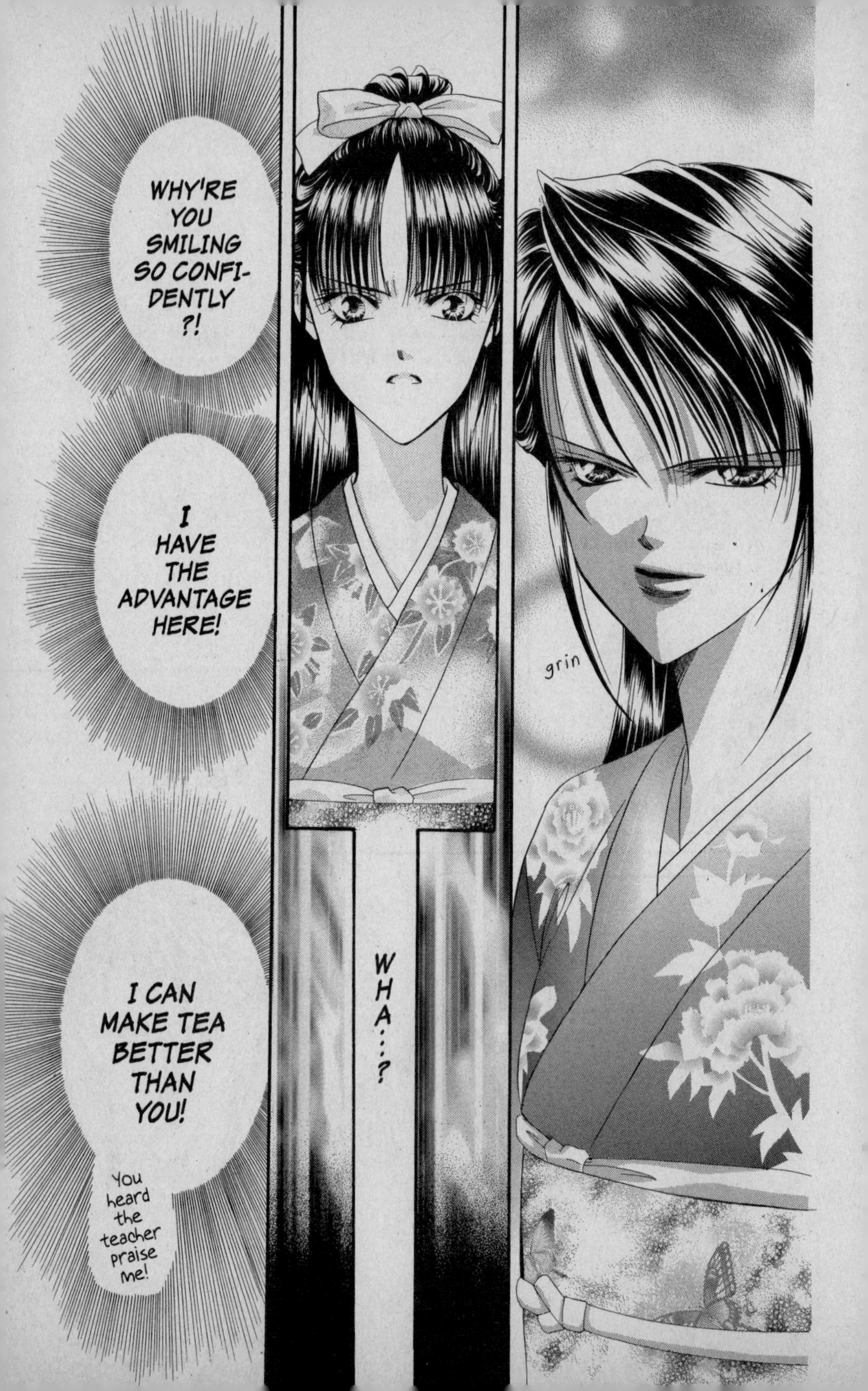
grin
WHA...?
WHY'RE YOU SMILING SO CONFIDENTLY?!
I HAVE THE ADVANTAGE HERE!
I CAN MAKE TEA BETTER THAN YOU!
You heard the teacher praise me!

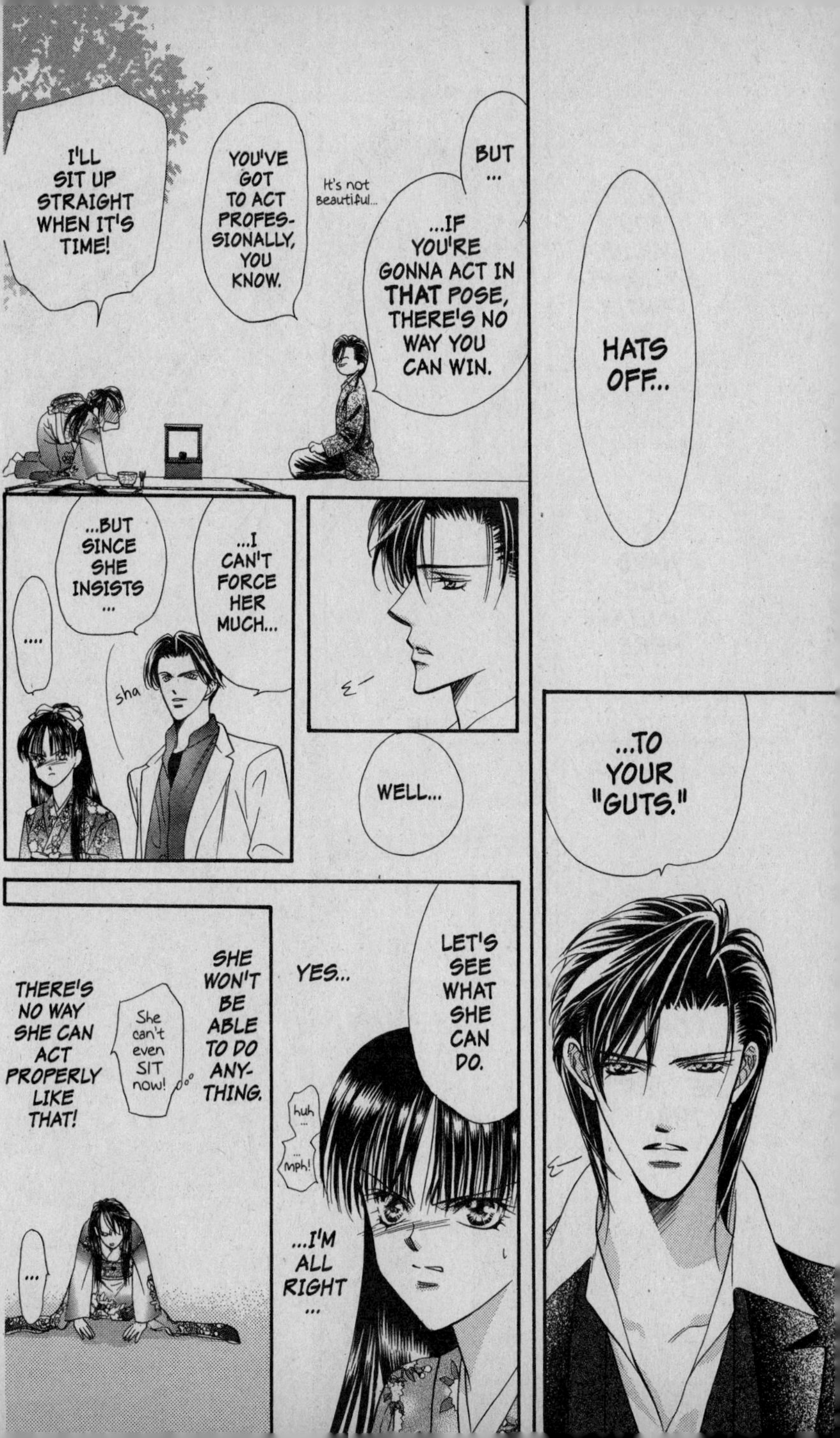
HATS OFF...
...TO YOUR "GUTS."
BUT ...
...IF YOU'RE GONNA ACT IN THAT POSE, THERE'S NO WAY YOU CAN WIN.
It's not Beautiful...
YOU'VE GOT TO ACT PROFES-SIONALLY, YOU KNOW.
I'LL SIT UP STRAIGHT WHEN IT'S TIME!
WELL...
...I CAN'T FORCE HER MUCH...
...BUT SINCE SHE INSISTS ...
sha
....
LET'S SEE WHAT SHE CAN DO.
YES...
SHE WON'T BE ABLE TO DO ANY-THING.
She can't even SIT now!
THERE'S NO WAY SHE CAN ACT PROPERLY LIKE THAT!
huh ...
... mph!
...I'M ALL RIGHT ...
...

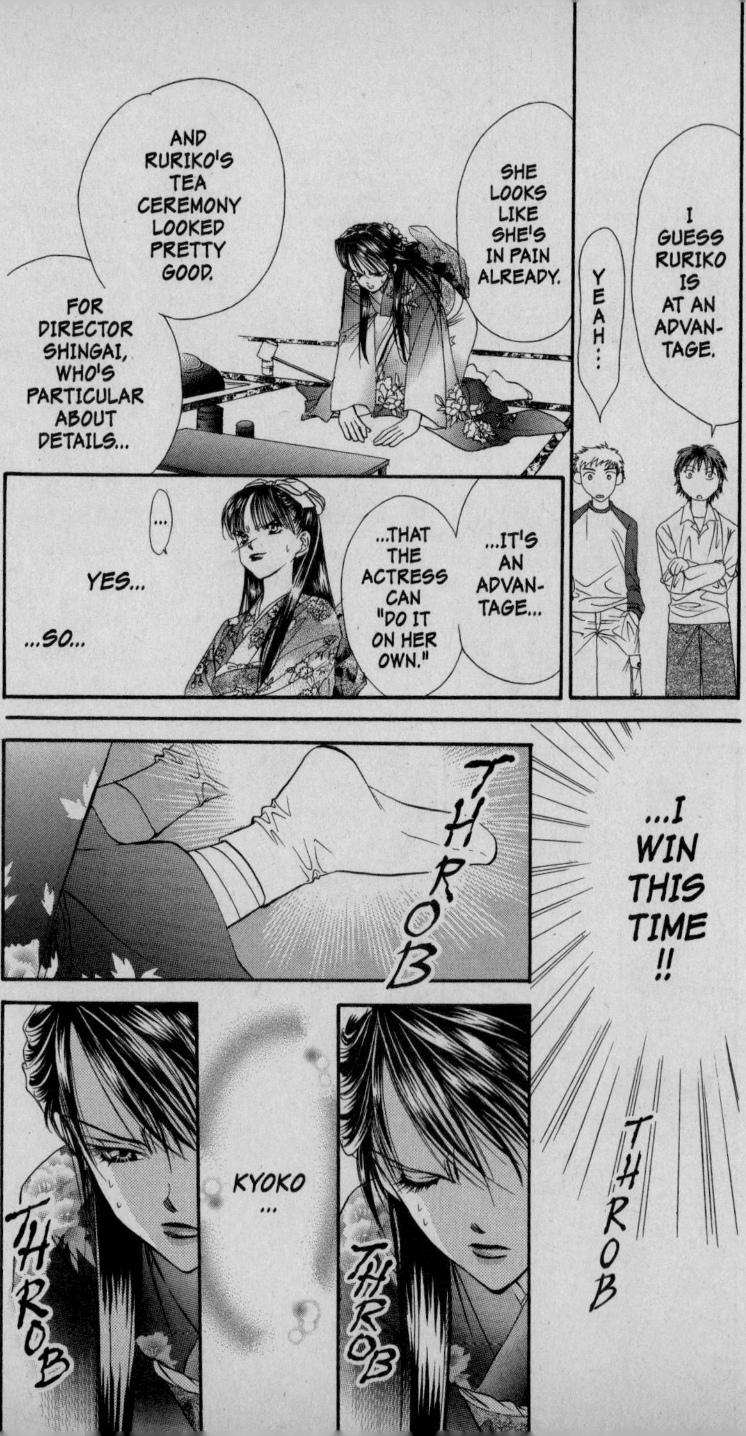
I GUESS RURIKO IS AT AN ADVANTAGE.
YEAH...
SHE LOOKS LIKE SHE'S IN PAIN ALREADY.
AND RURIKO'S TEA CEREMONY LOOKED PRETTY GOOD.
FOR DIRECTOR SHINGAI, WHO'S PARTICULAR ABOUT DETAILS...
...IT'S AN ADVANTAGE...
...THAT THE ACTRESS CAN "DO IT ON HER OWN."
...
YES...
...SO...
...I WIN THIS TIME!!
THROB
THROB
THROB
KYOKO...
THROB

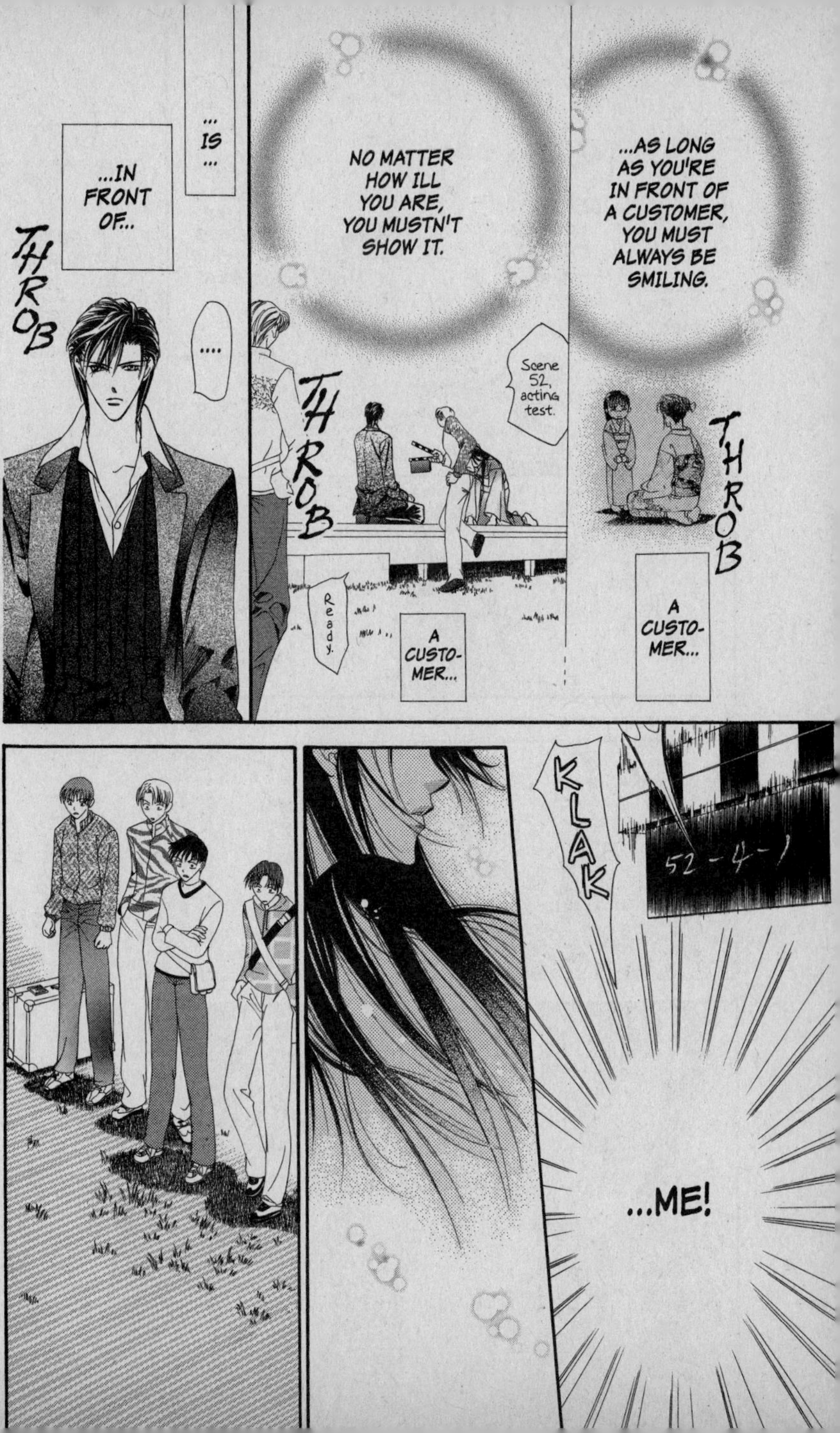
...AS LONG AS YOU'RE IN FRONT OF A CUSTOMER, YOU MUST ALWAYS BE SMILING.
THROB
A CUSTO-MER...
NO MATTER HOW ILL YOU ARE, YOU MUSTN'T SHOW IT.
Scene 52, acting test.
THROB
A CUSTO-MER...
Ready.
... IS ...
...IN FRONT OF...
THROB
....
KLAK
52-4-1
...ME!

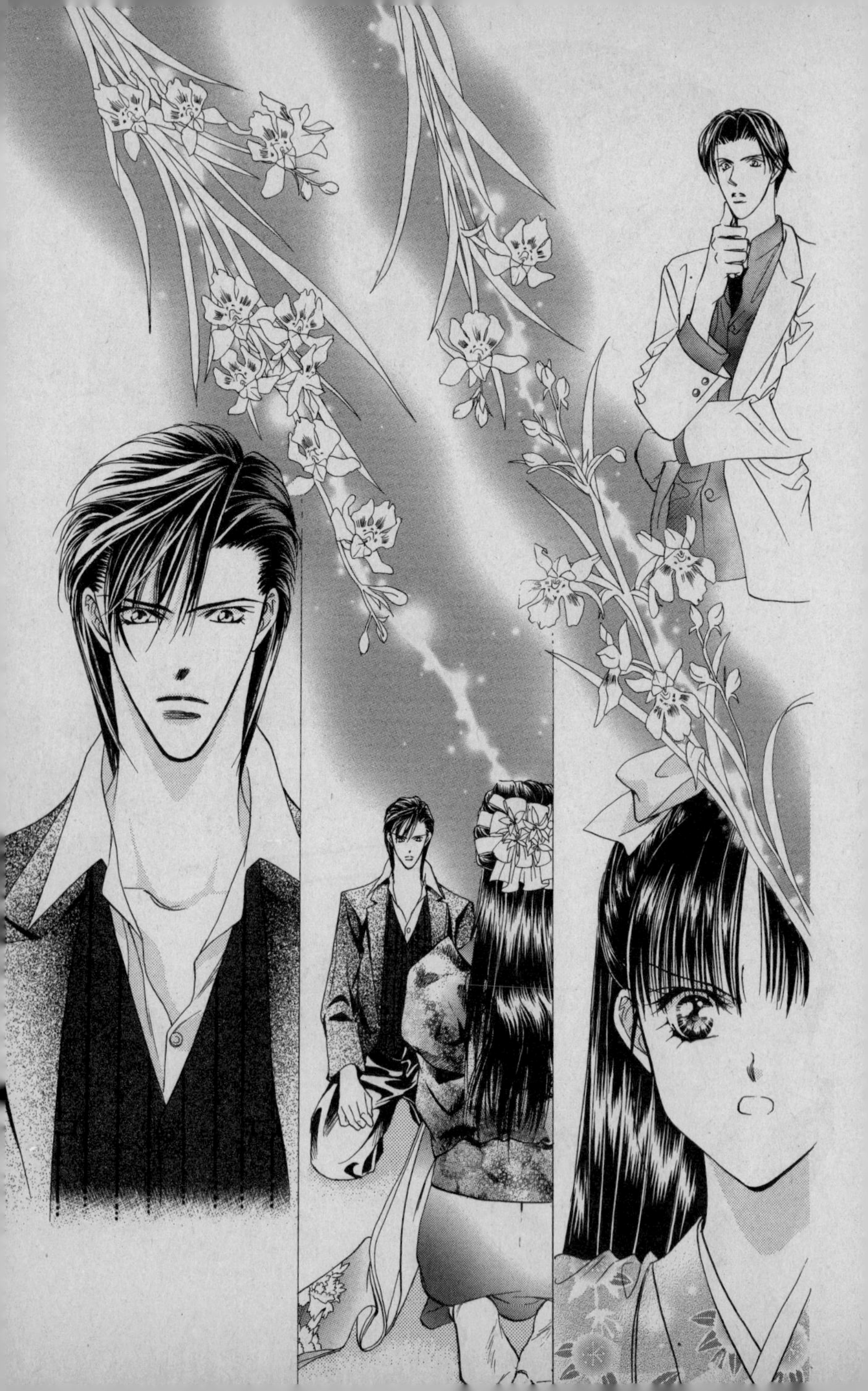

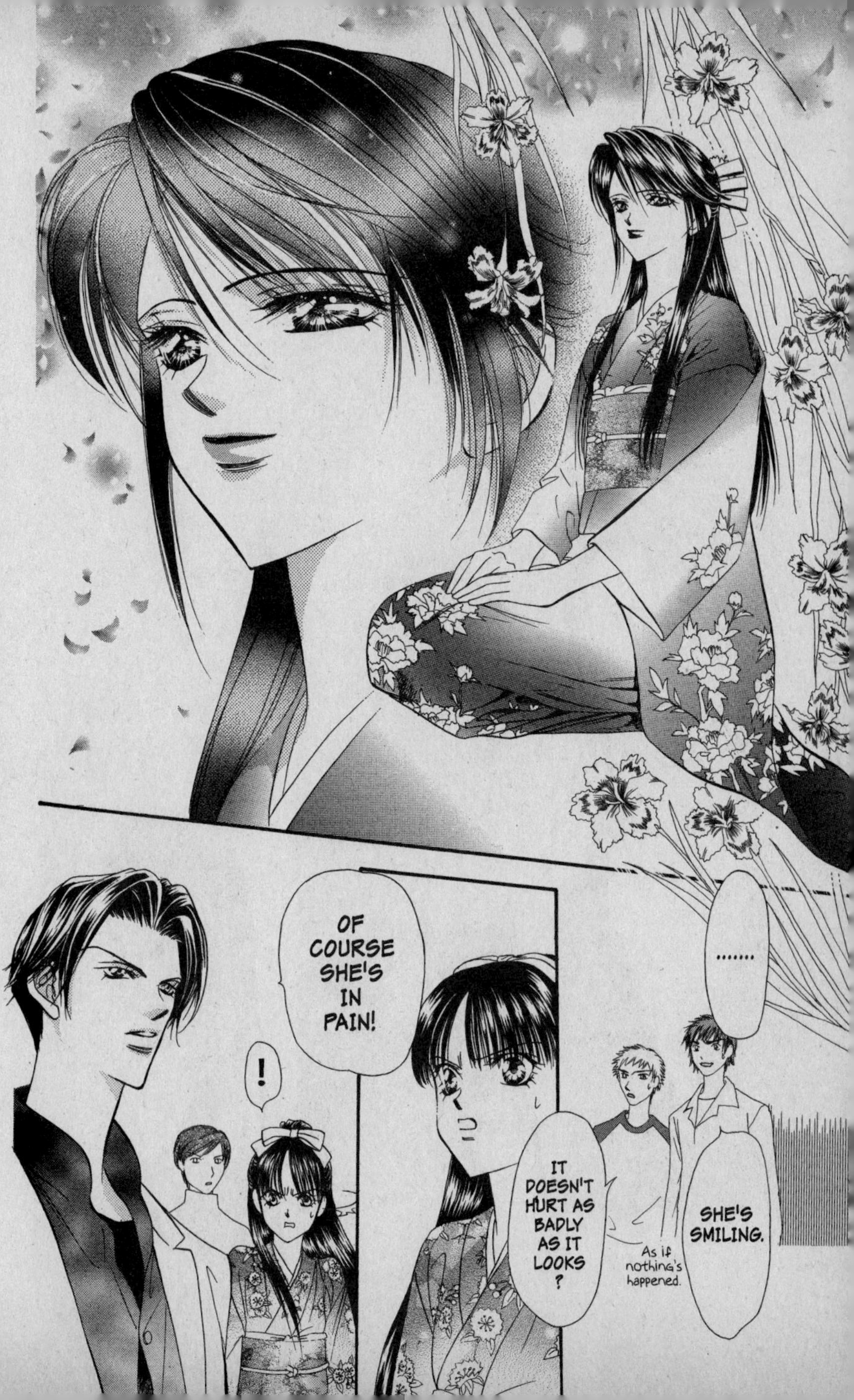

......
SHE'S SMILING.
As if nothing's happened.
IT DOESN'T HURT AS BADLY AS IT LOOKS?
OF COURSE SHE'S IN PAIN!
!

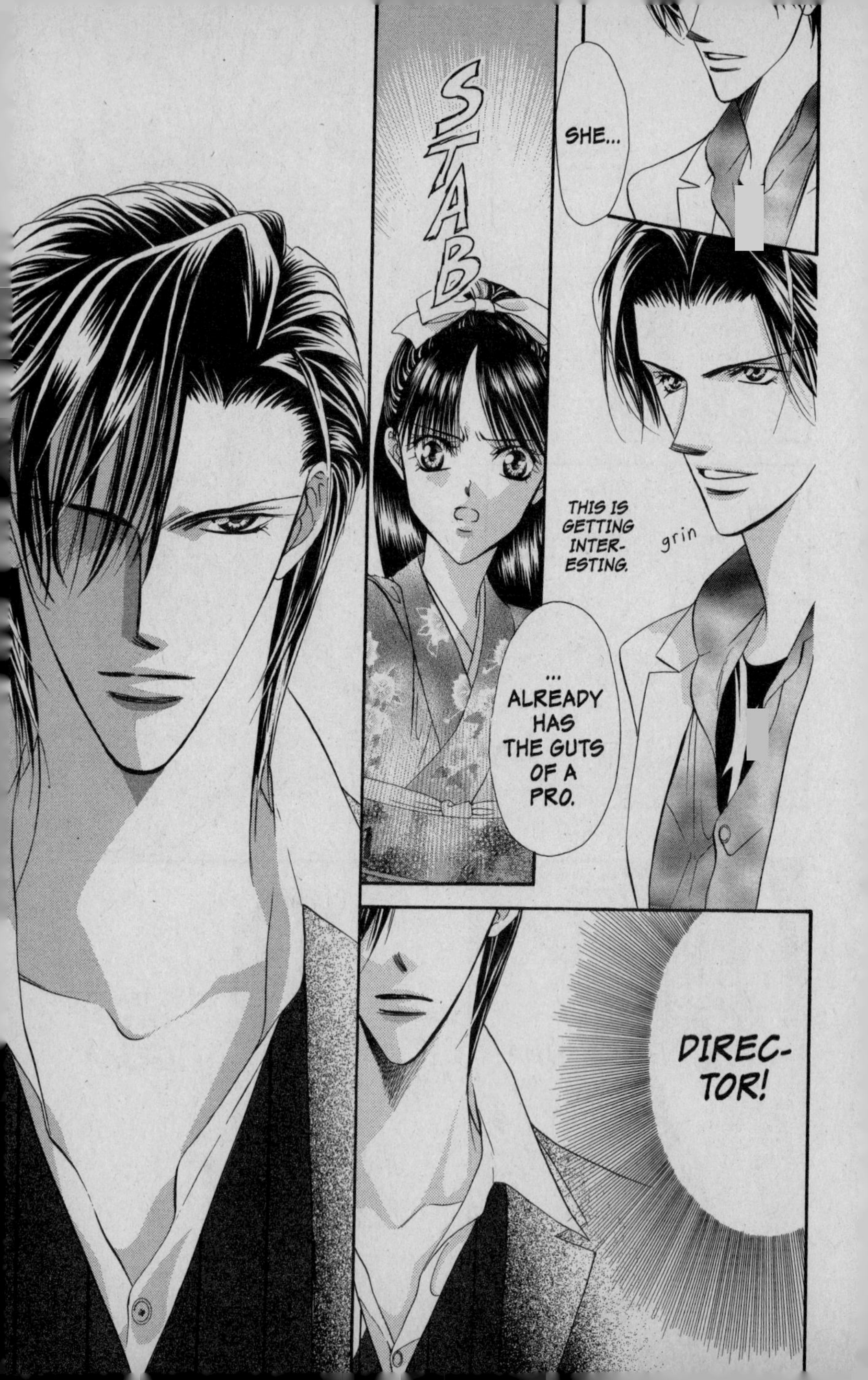
SHE...
THIS IS GETTING INTER-ESTING.
grin
...ALREADY HAS THE GUTS OF A PRO.
STAB
DIREC-TOR!

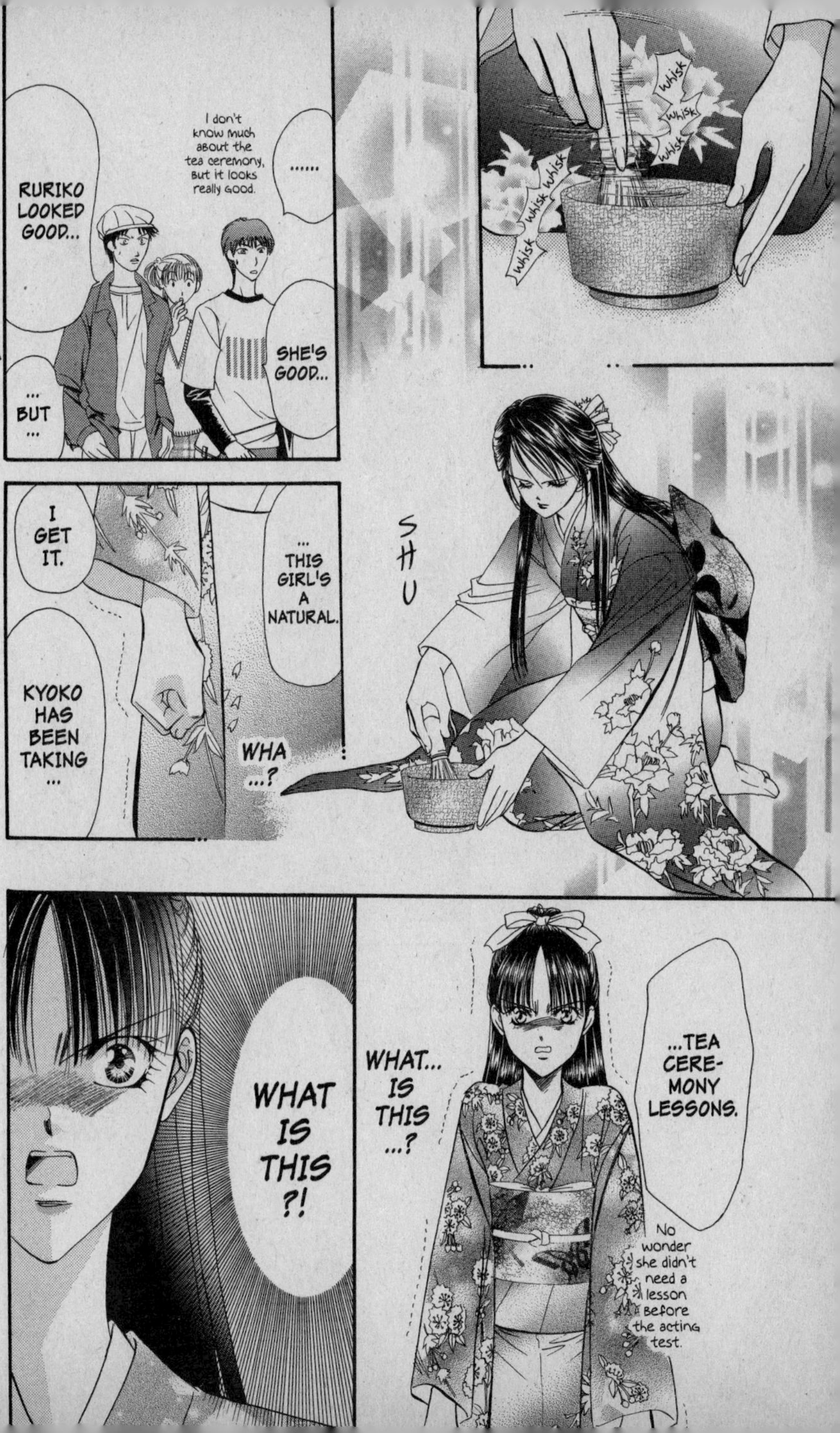

whisk
whisk
whisk
whisk whisk whisk whisk
......
I don't know much about the tea ceremony, but it looks really good.
RURIKO LOOKED GOOD...
SHE'S GOOD...
... BUT ...
SHU
... THIS GIRL'S A NATURAL.
I GET IT.
WHA ...?
KYOKO HAS BEEN TAKING ...
...TEA CEREMONY LESSONS.
WHAT... IS THIS ...?
No wonder she didn't need a lesson before the acting test.
WHAT IS THIS ?!

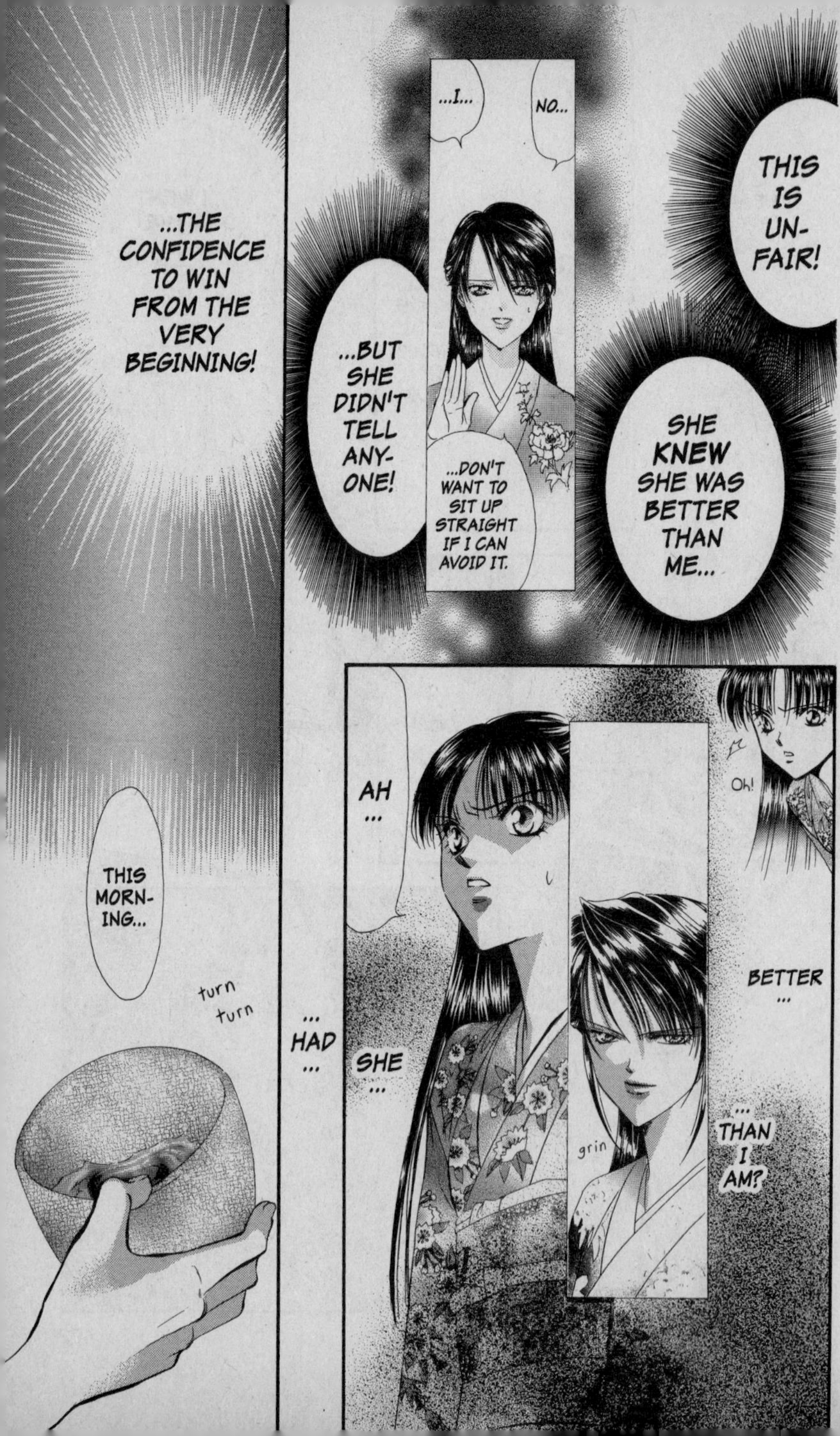
THIS IS UN-FAIR!
SHE KNEW SHE WAS BETTER THAN ME...
NO...
...I...
...DON'T WANT TO SIT UP STRAIGHT IF I CAN AVOID IT.
...BUT SHE DIDN'T TELL ANYONE!
Oh!
AH ...
BETTER ...
grin
... THAN I AM?
SHE ...
... HAD ...
...THE CONFIDENCE TO WIN FROM THE VERY BEGINNING!
THIS MORNING...
turn turn

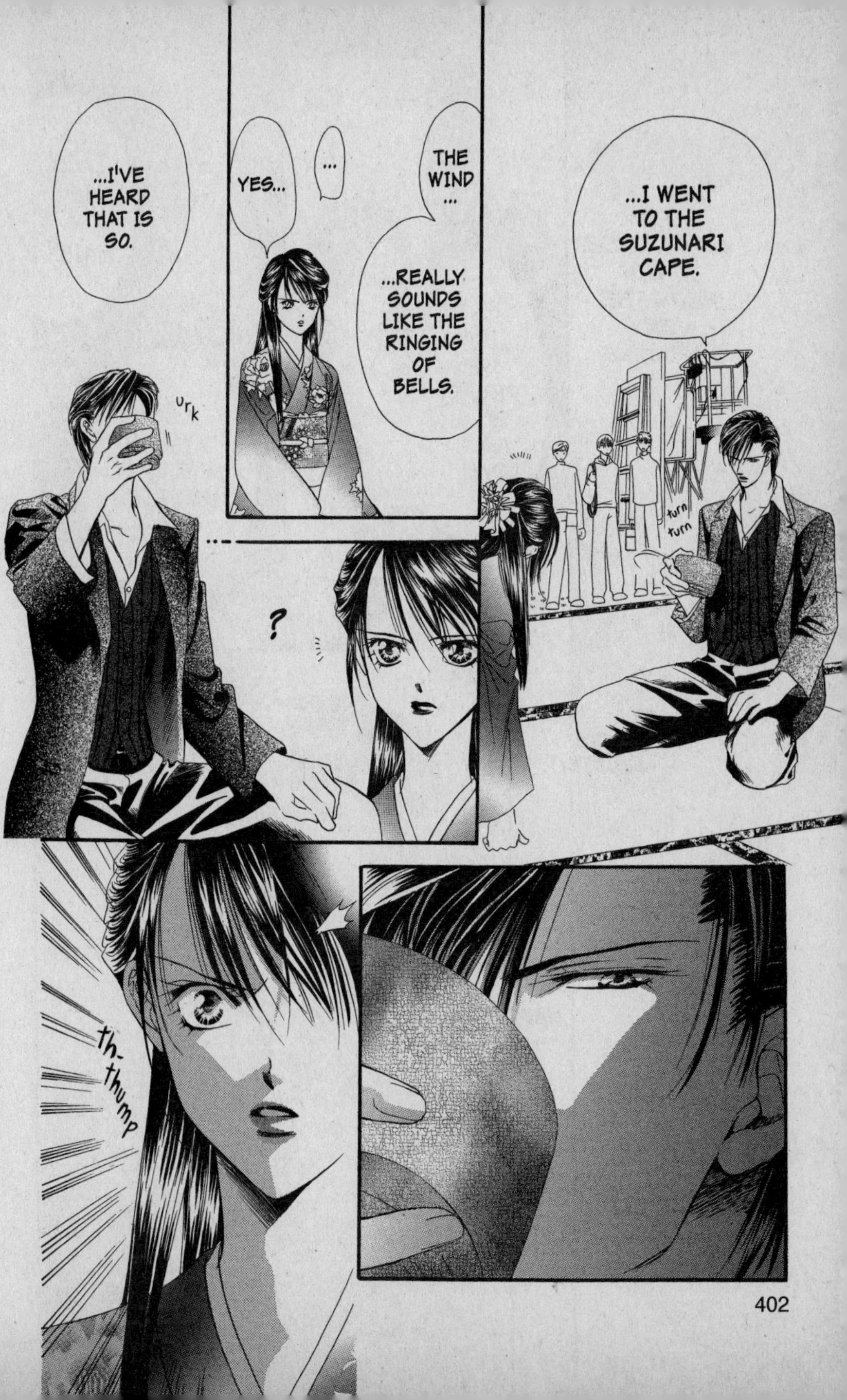
...I WENT TO THE SUZUNARI CAPE.
turn turn
THE WIND ...
...REALLY SOUNDS LIKE THE RINGING OF BELLS.
...
YES...
...–
?
...I'VE HEARD THAT IS SO.
urk
th-thump

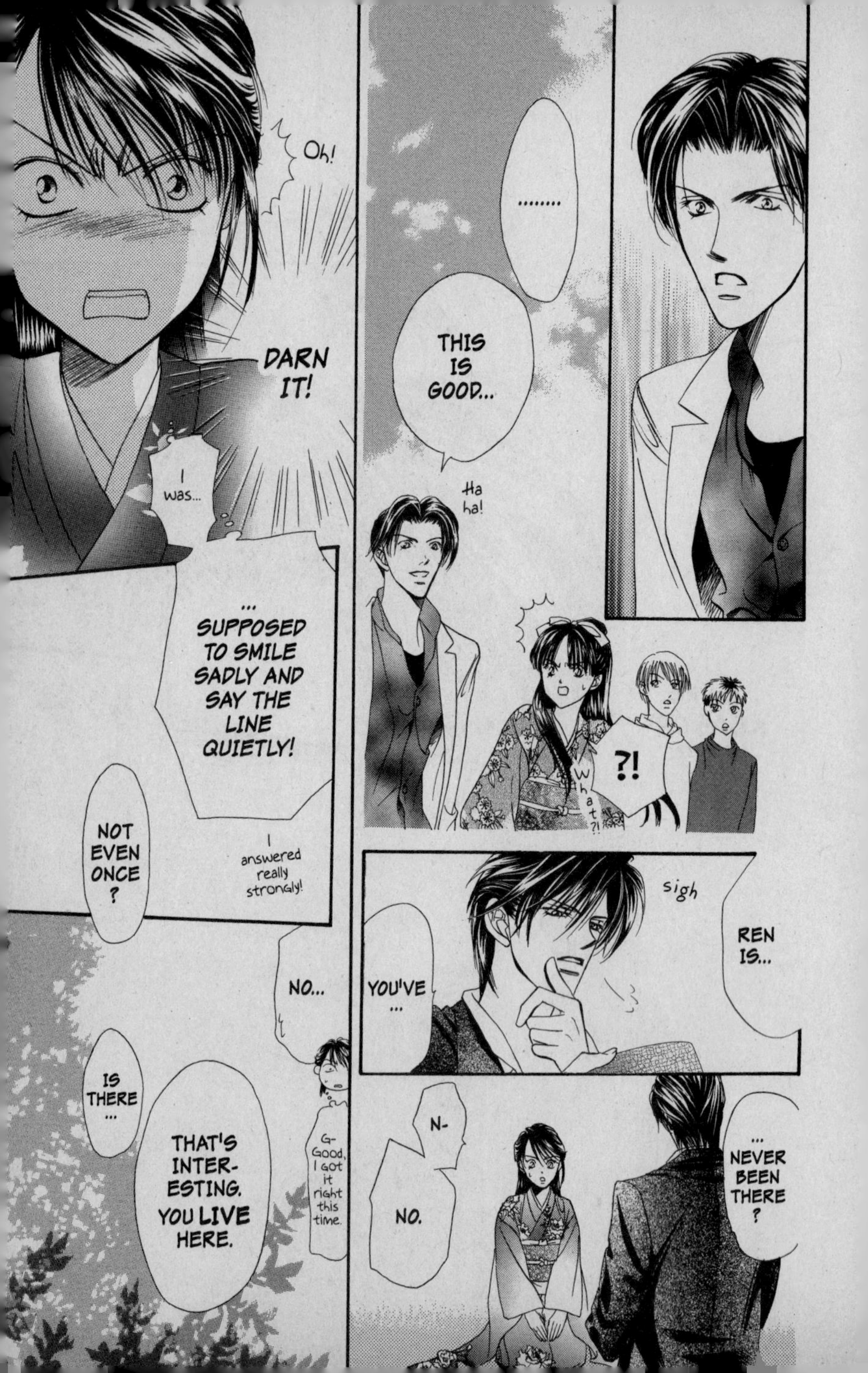
....
THIS IS GOOD...
Ha ha!
?!
What?!
sigh
REN IS...
YOU'VE...
...NEVER BEEN THERE?
N-
NO.
Oh!
DARN IT!
I was...
...SUPPOSED TO SMILE SADLY AND SAY THE LINE QUIETLY!
I answered really strongly!
NOT EVEN ONCE?
NO...
G-Good, I got it right this time.
IS THERE...
THAT'S INTERESTING. YOU LIVE HERE.

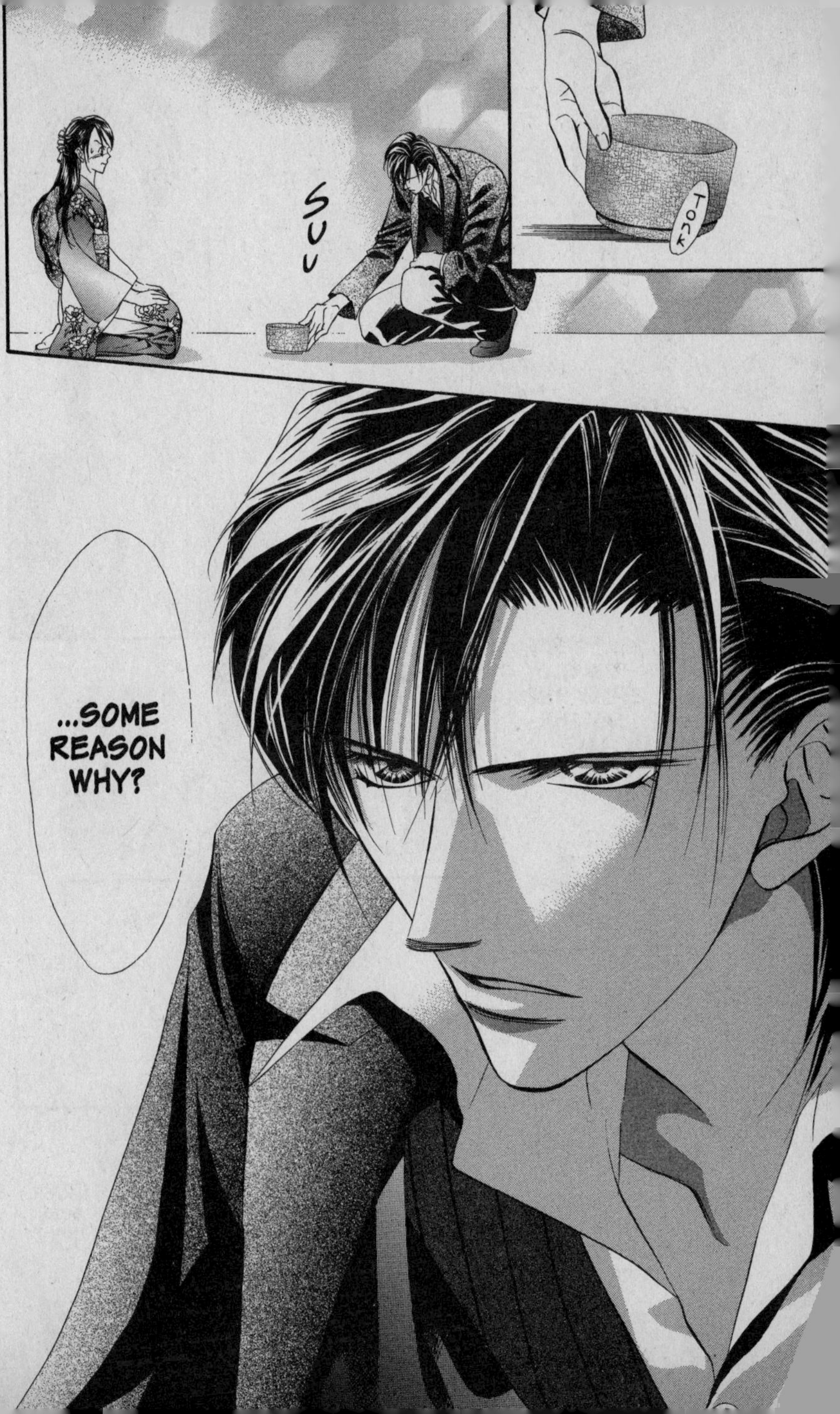
Tonk
SUU
...SOME REASON WHY?

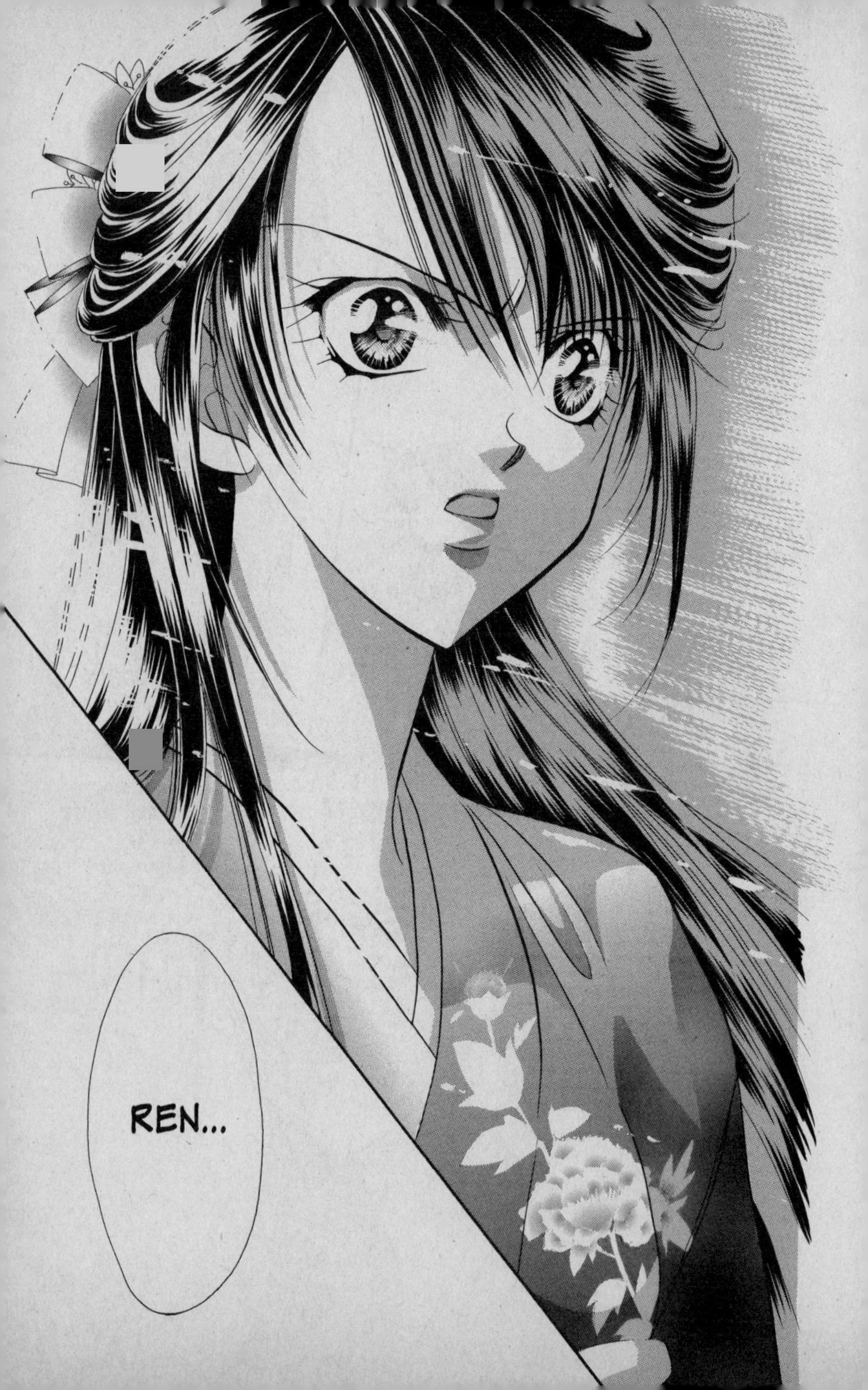
REN...

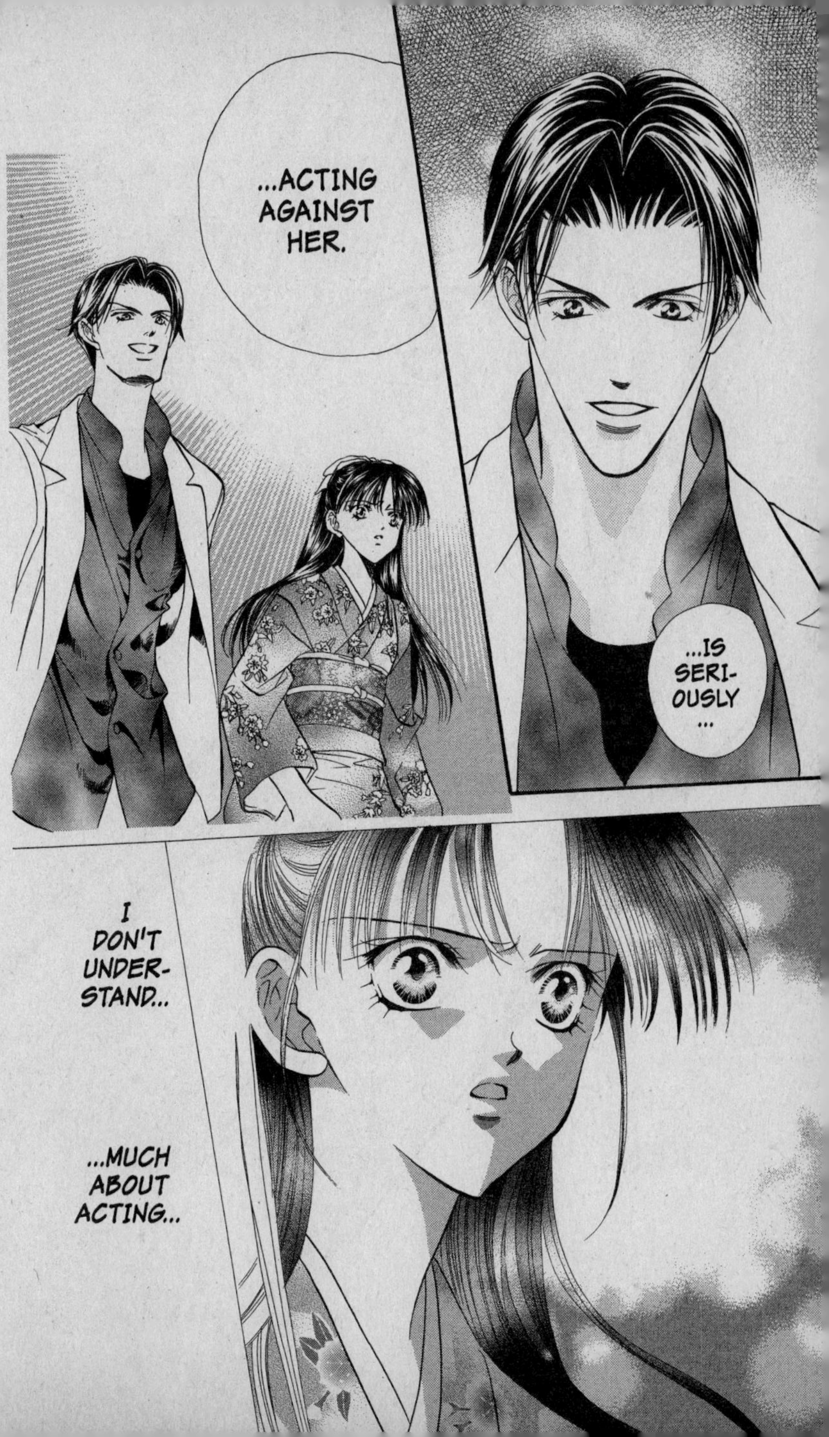
...IS SERI-OUSLY ...
...ACTING AGAINST HER.
I DON'T UNDER-STAND...
...MUCH ABOUT ACTING...

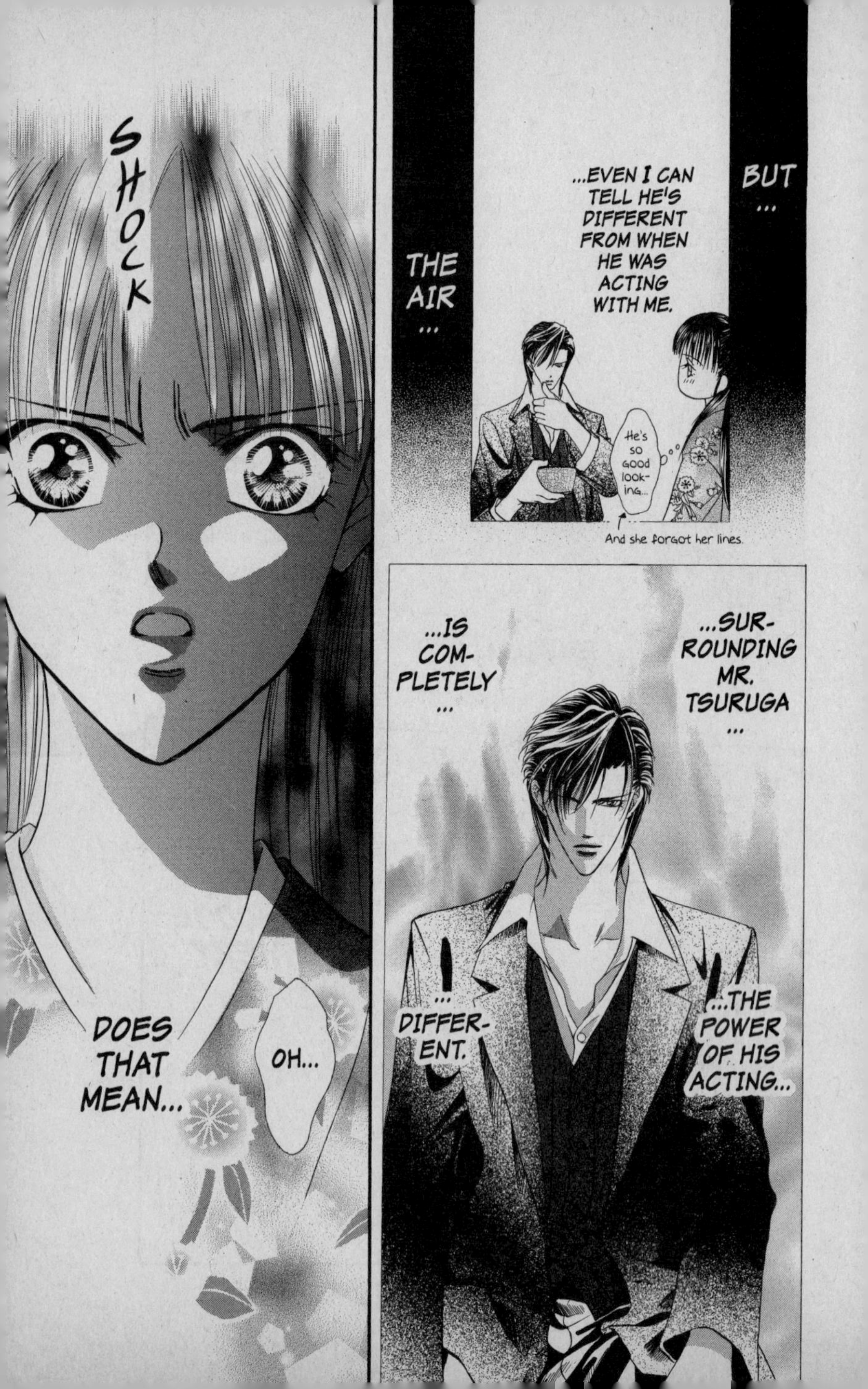
BUT...
...EVEN I CAN TELL HE'S DIFFERENT FROM WHEN HE WAS ACTING WITH ME.
THE AIR...
He's so good looking...
And she forgot her lines.
...SURROUNDING MR. TSURUGA...
...IS COMPLETELY...
...THE POWER OF HIS ACTING...
...DIFFERENT.
SHOCK
OH...
DOES THAT MEAN...

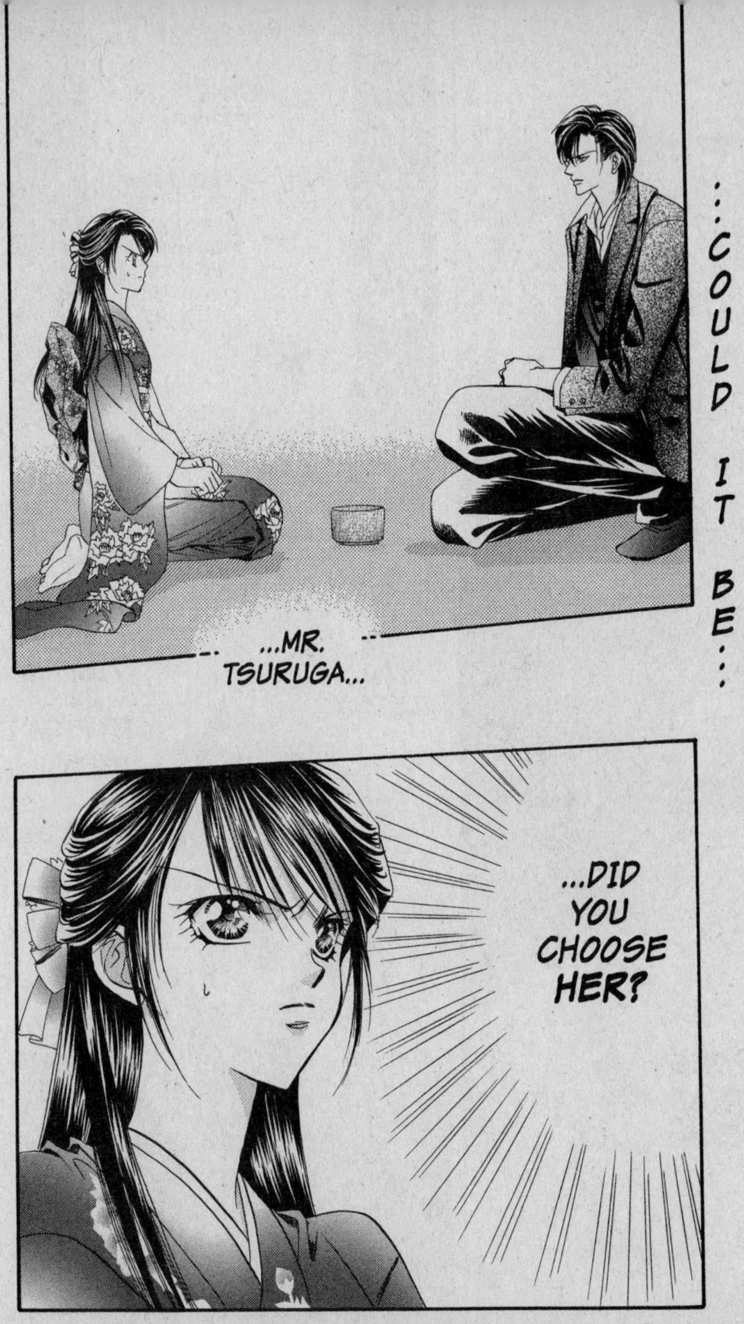

...COULD IT BE...
...MR. TSURUGA...
...DID YOU CHOOSE HER?

End of Act 12

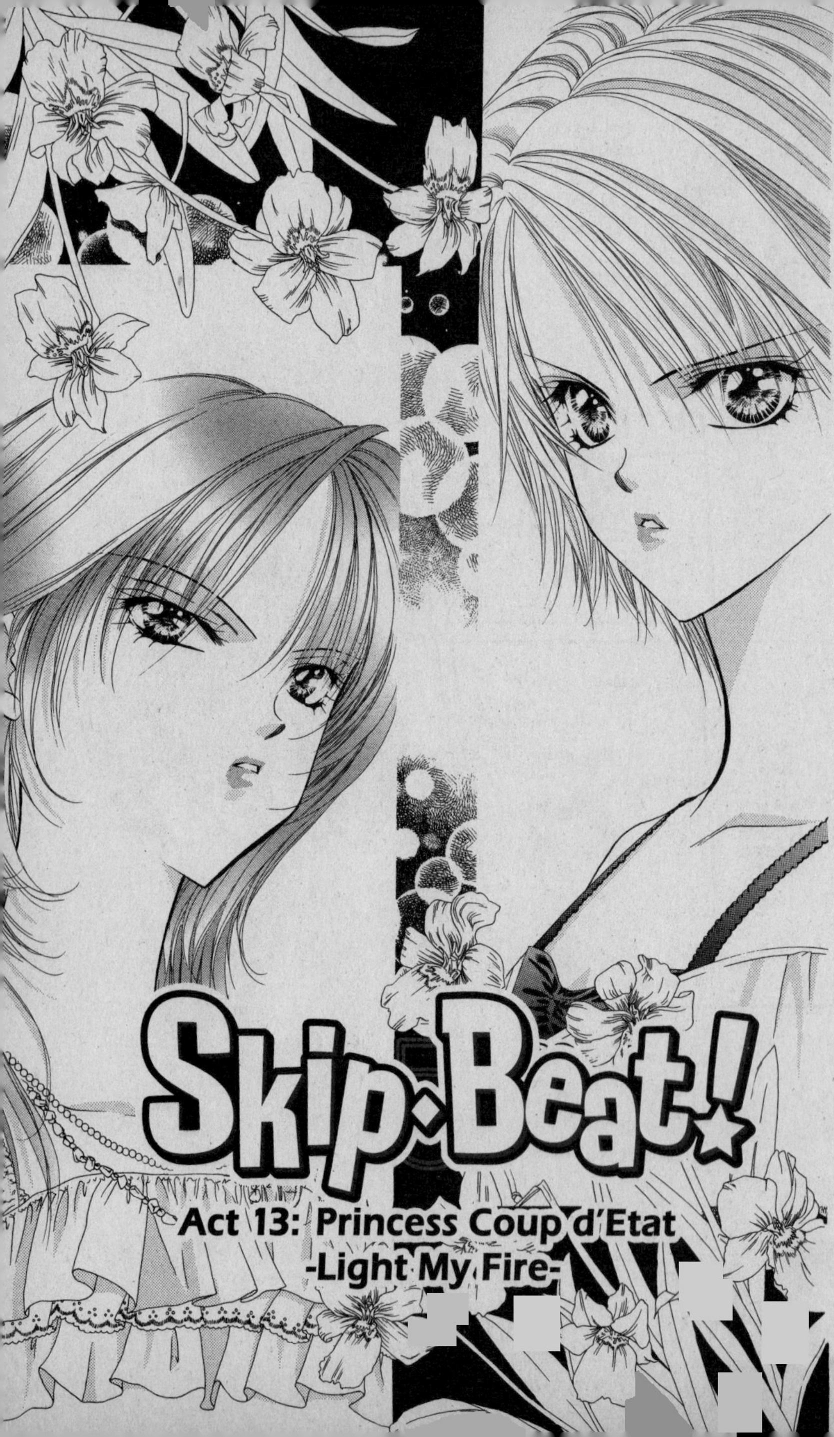
Skip·Beat!
Act 13: Princess Coup d'Etat
-Light My Fire-

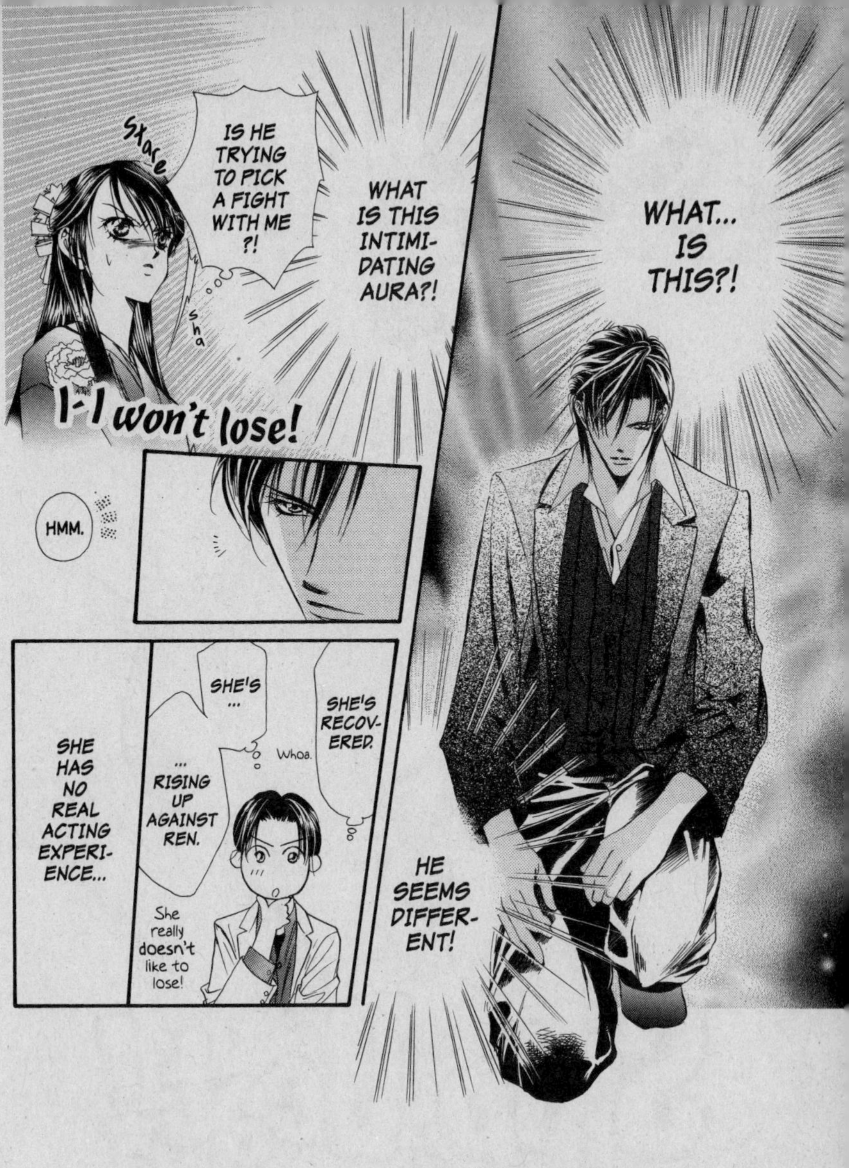
WHAT... IS THIS?!
HE SEEMS DIFFERENT!
WHAT IS THIS INTIMIDATING AURA?!
Stare
IS HE TRYING TO PICK A FIGHT WITH ME ?!
sha
I-I won't lose!
HMM.
SHE'S RECOVERED.
SHE'S ...
Whoa.
... RISING UP AGAINST REN.
She really doesn't like to lose!
SHE HAS NO REAL ACTING EXPERIENCE...

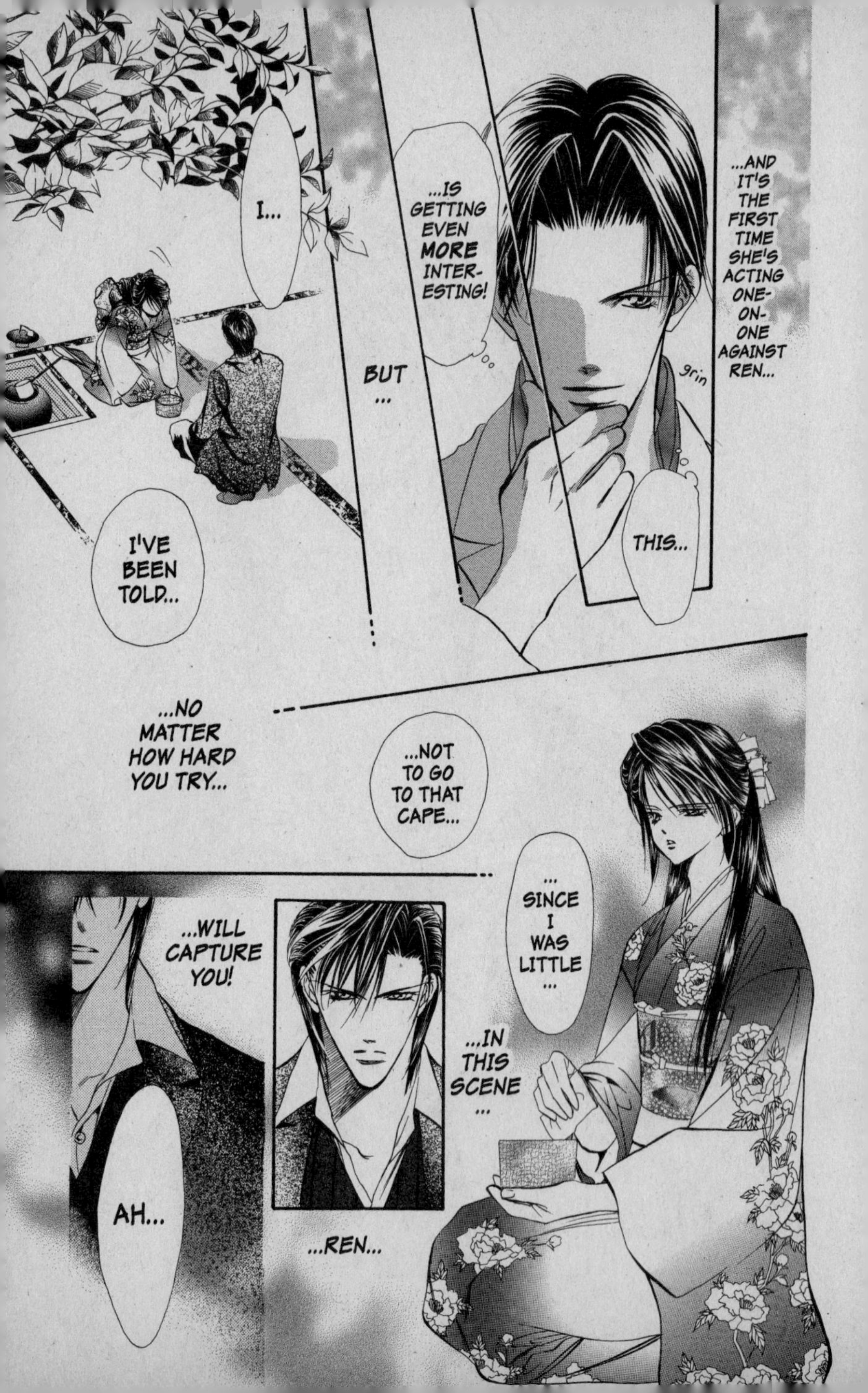
...AND IT'S THE FIRST TIME SHE'S ACTING ONE-ON-ONE AGAINST REN...
grin
THIS...
...IS GETTING EVEN MORE INTERESTING!
BUT ...
I...
I'VE BEEN TOLD...
...NOT TO GO TO THAT CAPE...
...NO MATTER HOW HARD YOU TRY...
... SINCE I WAS LITTLE ...
...IN THIS SCENE ...
...REN...
...WILL CAPTURE YOU!
AH...

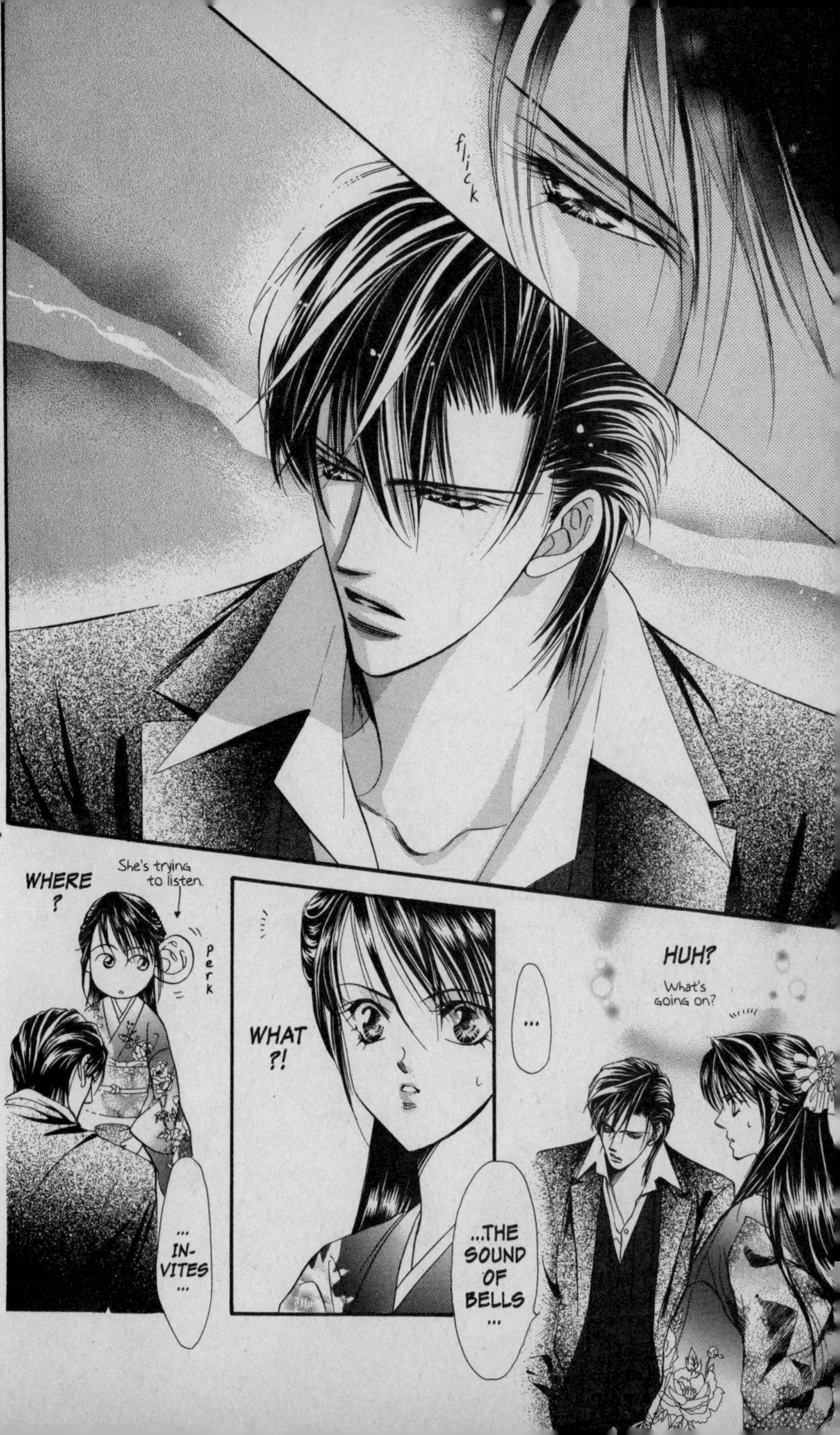
flick
HUH?
What's going on?
...
...THE SOUND OF BELLS ...
WHAT ?!
WHERE ?
She's trying to listen.
perk
... IN-VITES ...

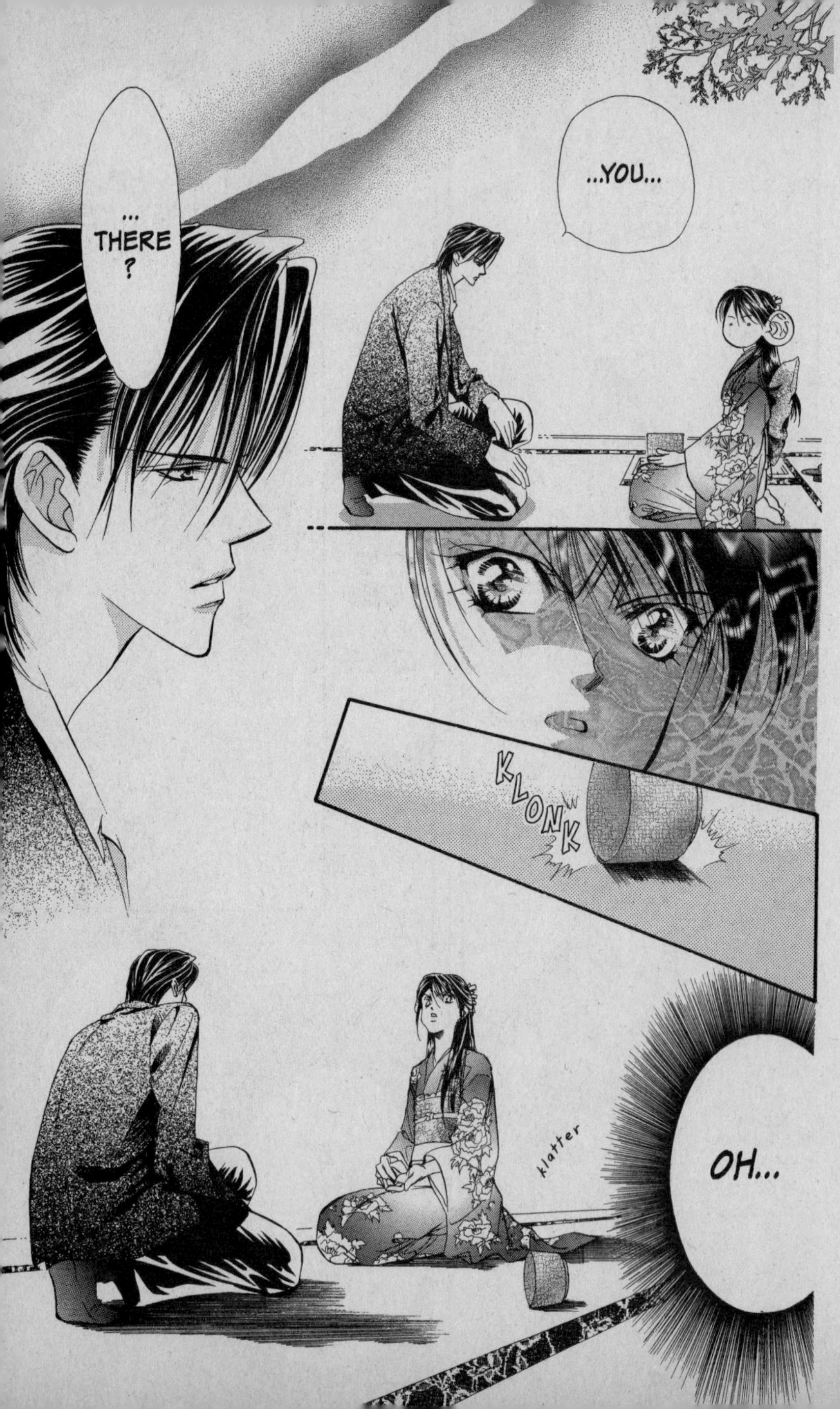
...YOU...
KLONK
... THERE ?
OH...
klatter

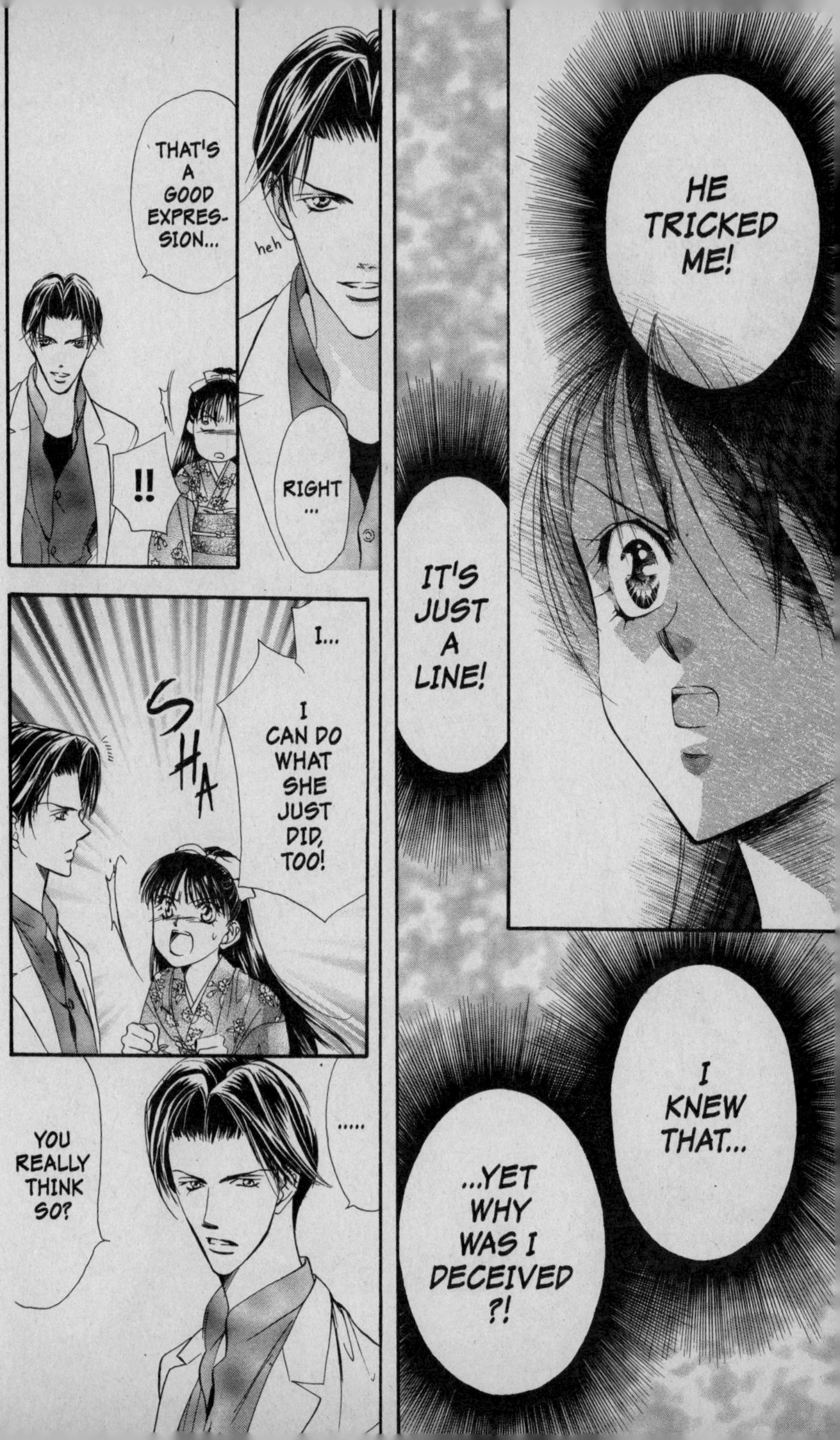
HE TRICKED ME!
IT'S JUST A LINE!
I KNEW THAT...
...YET WHY WAS I DECEIVED ?!
THAT'S A GOOD EXPRES-SION...
heh
RIGHT ...
!!
I...
I CAN DO WHAT SHE JUST DID, TOO!
SHA
.....
YOU REALLY THINK SO?

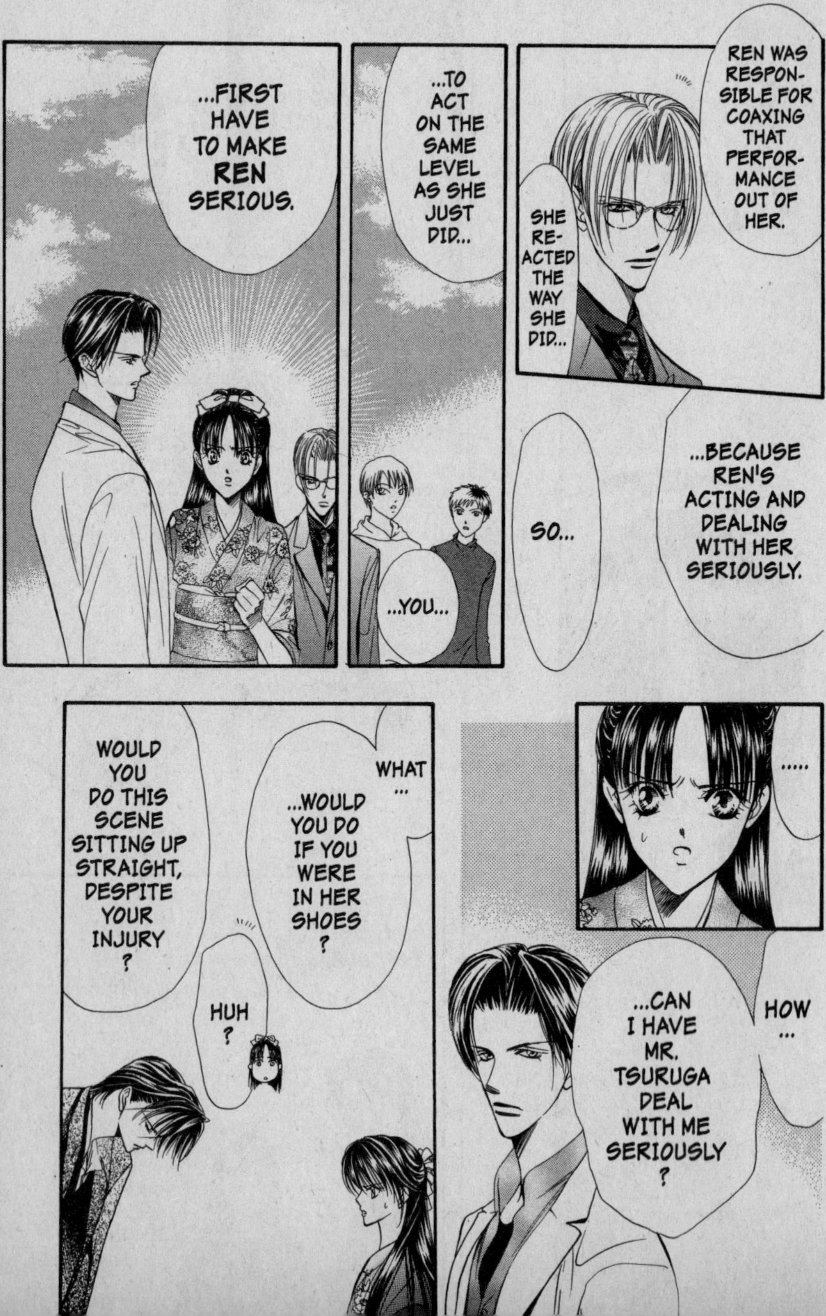
REN WAS RESPONSIBLE FOR COAXING THAT PERFORMANCE OUT OF HER.
SHE RE-ACTED THE WAY SHE DID...
...BECAUSE REN'S ACTING AND DEALING WITH HER SERIOUSLY.
SO...
...TO ACT ON THE SAME LEVEL AS SHE JUST DID...
...YOU...
...FIRST HAVE TO MAKE REN SERIOUS.
.....
HOW...
...CAN I HAVE MR. TSURUGA DEAL WITH ME SERIOUSLY?
WHAT...
...WOULD YOU DO IF YOU WERE IN HER SHOES?
WOULD YOU DO THIS SCENE SITTING UP STRAIGHT, DESPITE YOUR INJURY?
HUH?

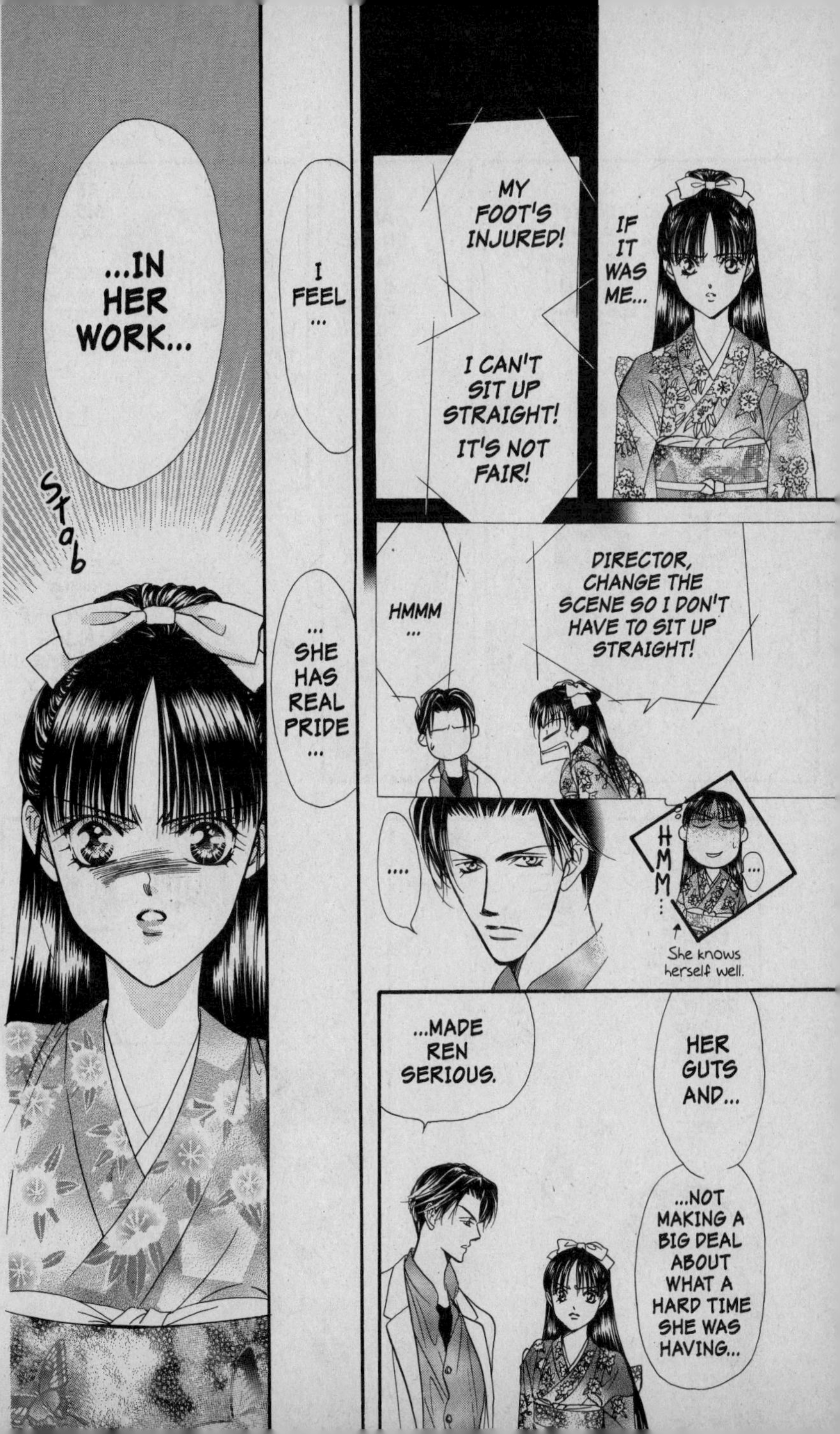
IF IT WAS ME...
MY FOOT'S INJURED!
I CAN'T SIT UP STRAIGHT!
IT'S NOT FAIR!
DIRECTOR, CHANGE THE SCENE SO I DON'T HAVE TO SIT UP STRAIGHT!
HMMM...
HMM...
...
She knows herself well.
....
HER GUTS AND...
...NOT MAKING A BIG DEAL ABOUT WHAT A HARD TIME SHE WAS HAVING...
...MADE REN SERIOUS.
I FEEL...
...SHE HAS REAL PRIDE...
...IN HER WORK...
Stab

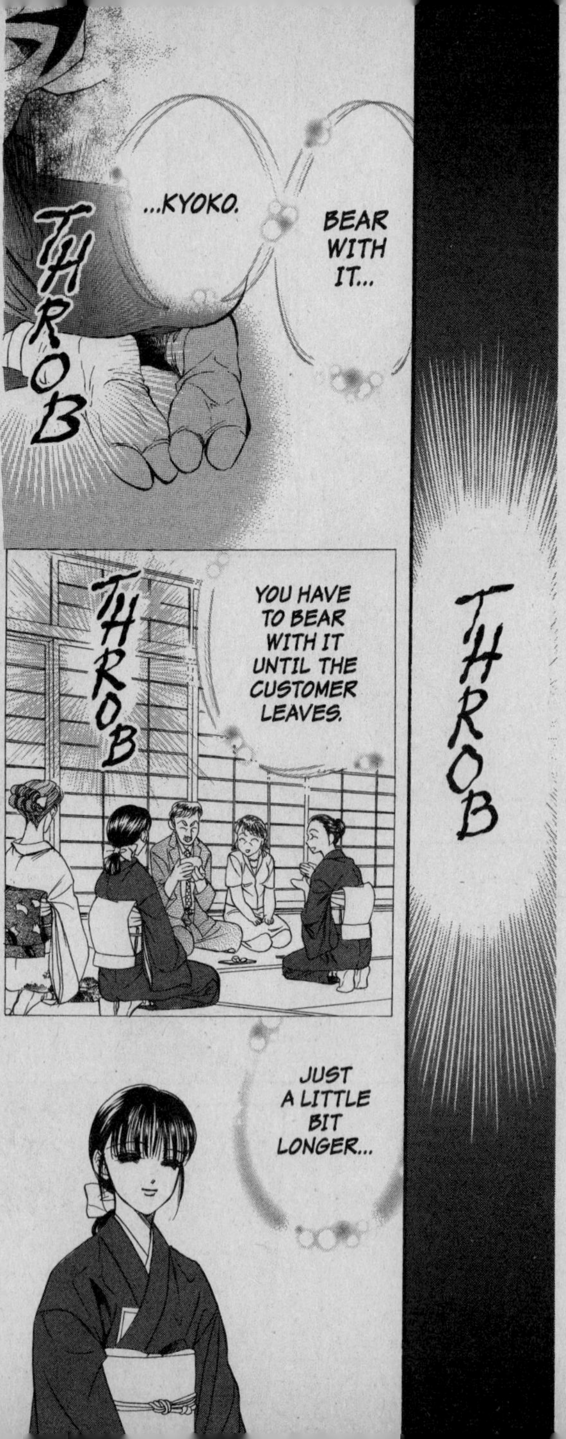
THROB
BEAR WITH IT...
...KYOKO.
THROB
YOU HAVE TO BEAR WITH IT UNTIL THE CUSTOMER LEAVES.
THROB
JUST A LITTLE BIT LONGER...

Ruriko Matsunai

Difficulty level

☆ ☆ ②

The thing that was difficult with Ruri was expressing how her fair skin is beautiful and white like snow...

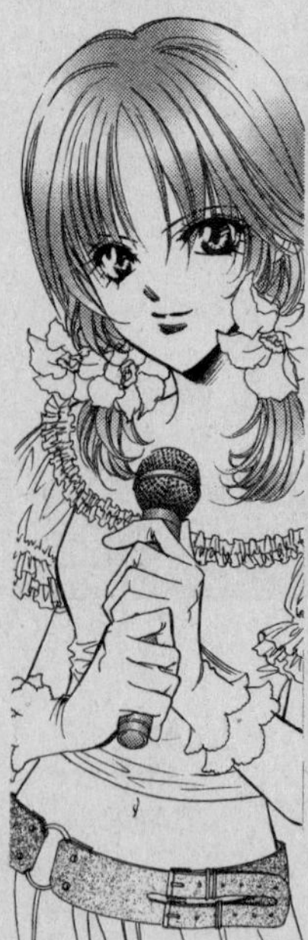

That's impossible to do in black-and-white... I have to have the dear readers imagine this... ♦

Anyway, she has fair skin that all women would be envious of... ♦♦

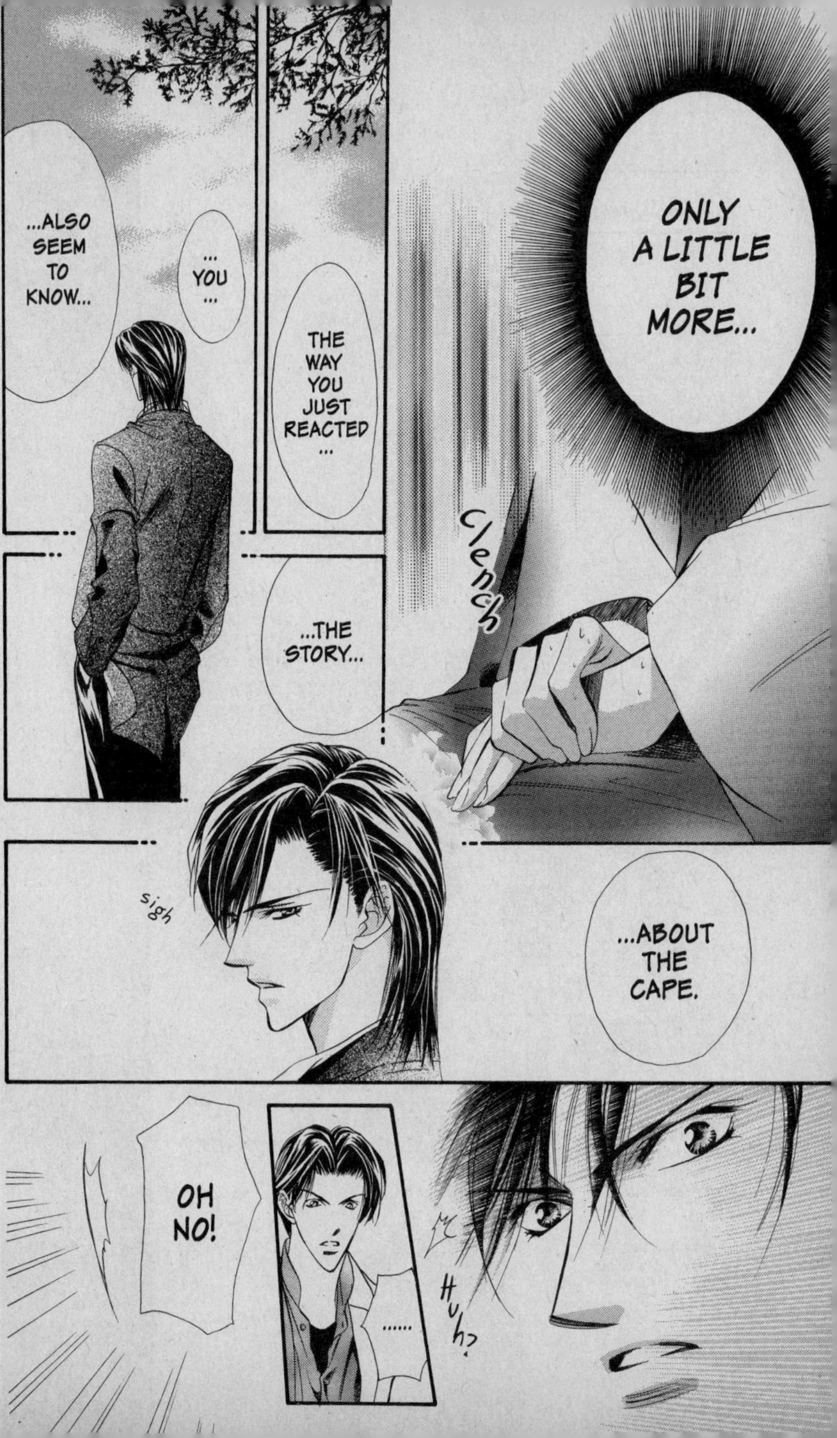
ONLY A LITTLE BIT MORE...
Clench
THE WAY YOU JUST REACTED...
...YOU...
...ALSO SEEM TO KNOW...
...THE STORY...
...ABOUT THE CAPE.
sigh
Huh?
......
OH NO!

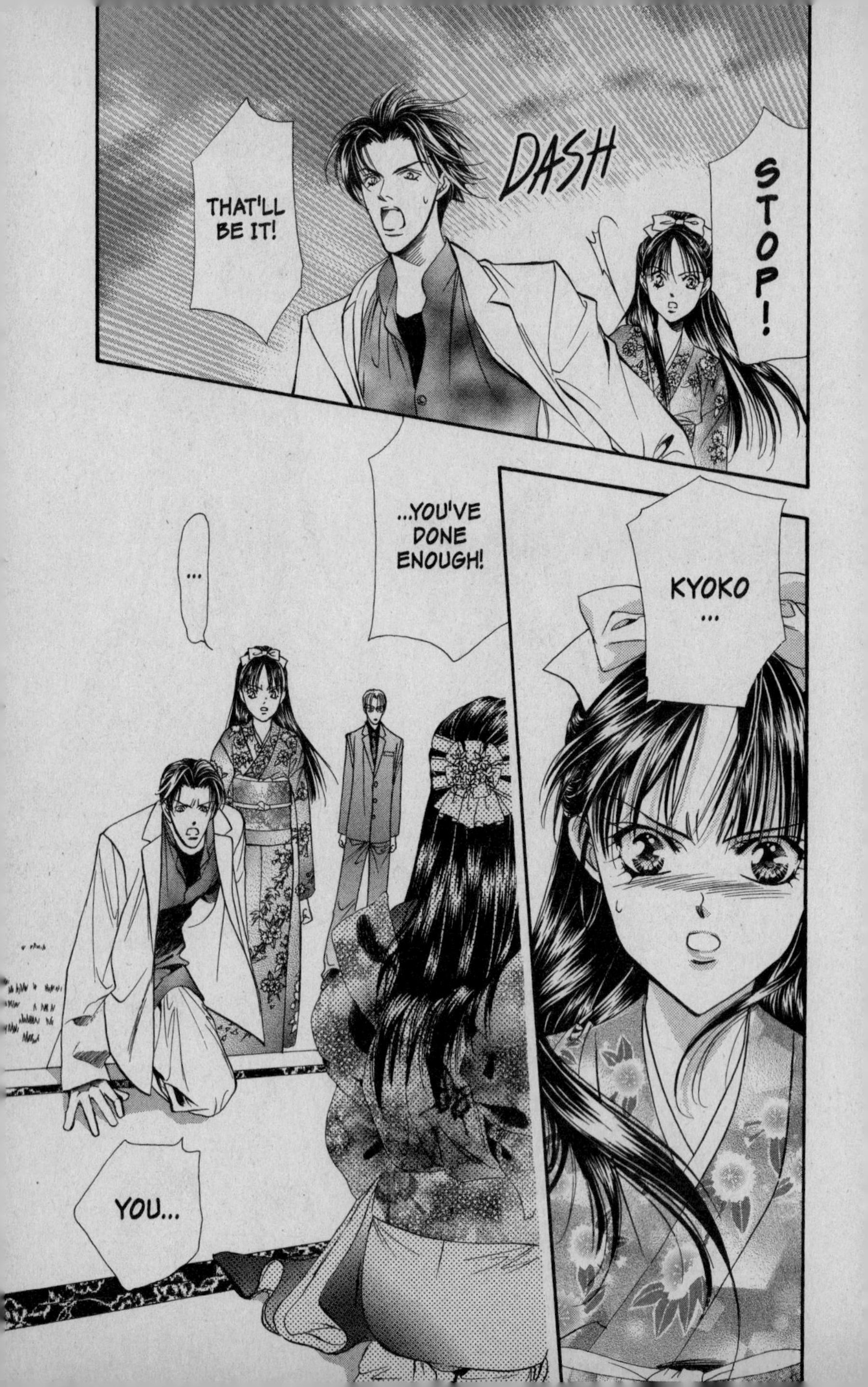
STOP!
DASH
THAT'LL BE IT!
KYOKO ...
...YOU'VE DONE ENOUGH!
...
YOU...

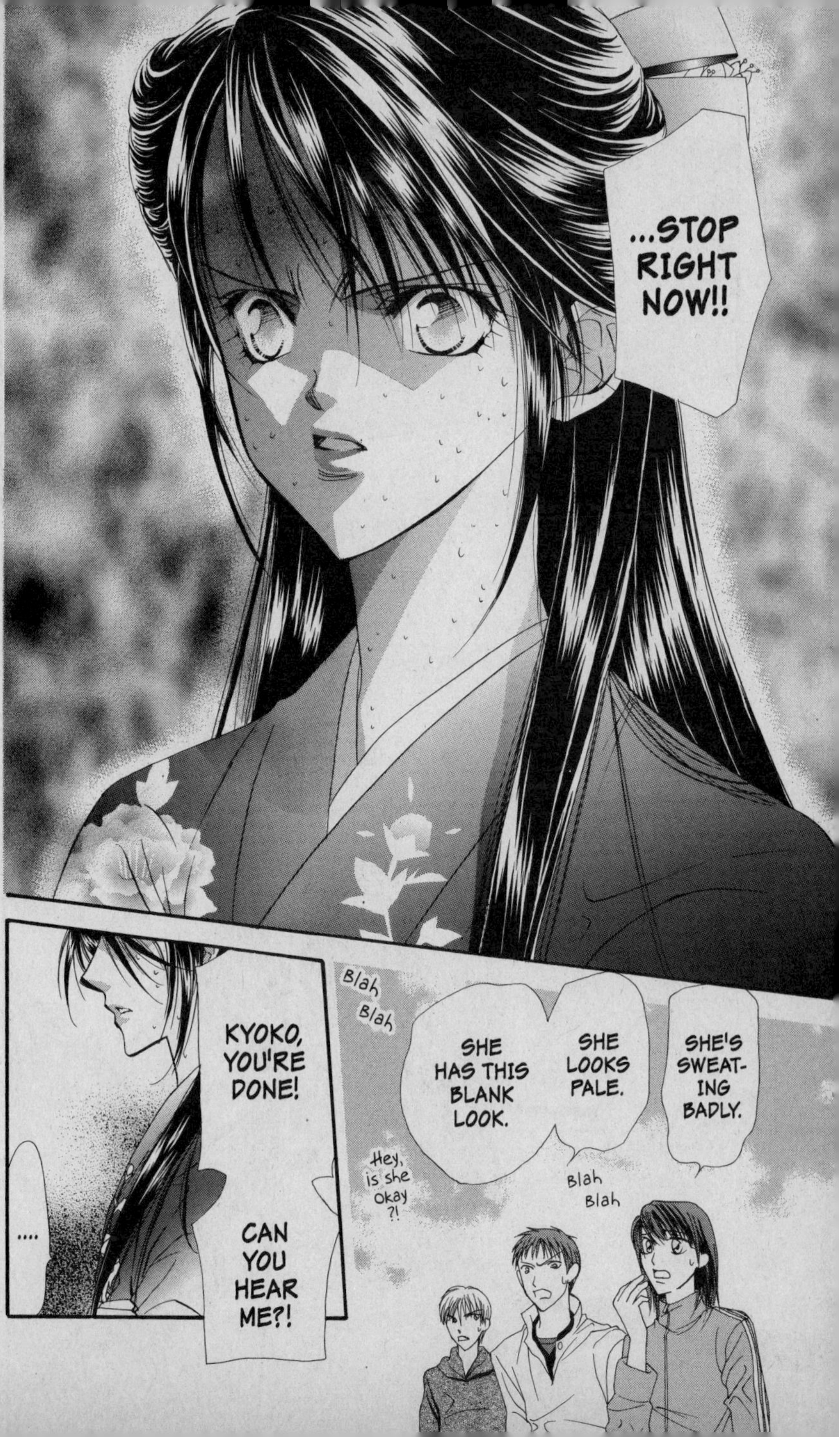
...STOP RIGHT NOW!!
SHE'S SWEAT-ING BADLY.
SHE LOOKS PALE.
SHE HAS THIS BLANK LOOK.
Blah Blah
Blah Blah
Hey, is she okay ?!
KYOKO, YOU'RE DONE!
CAN YOU HEAR ME?!
....

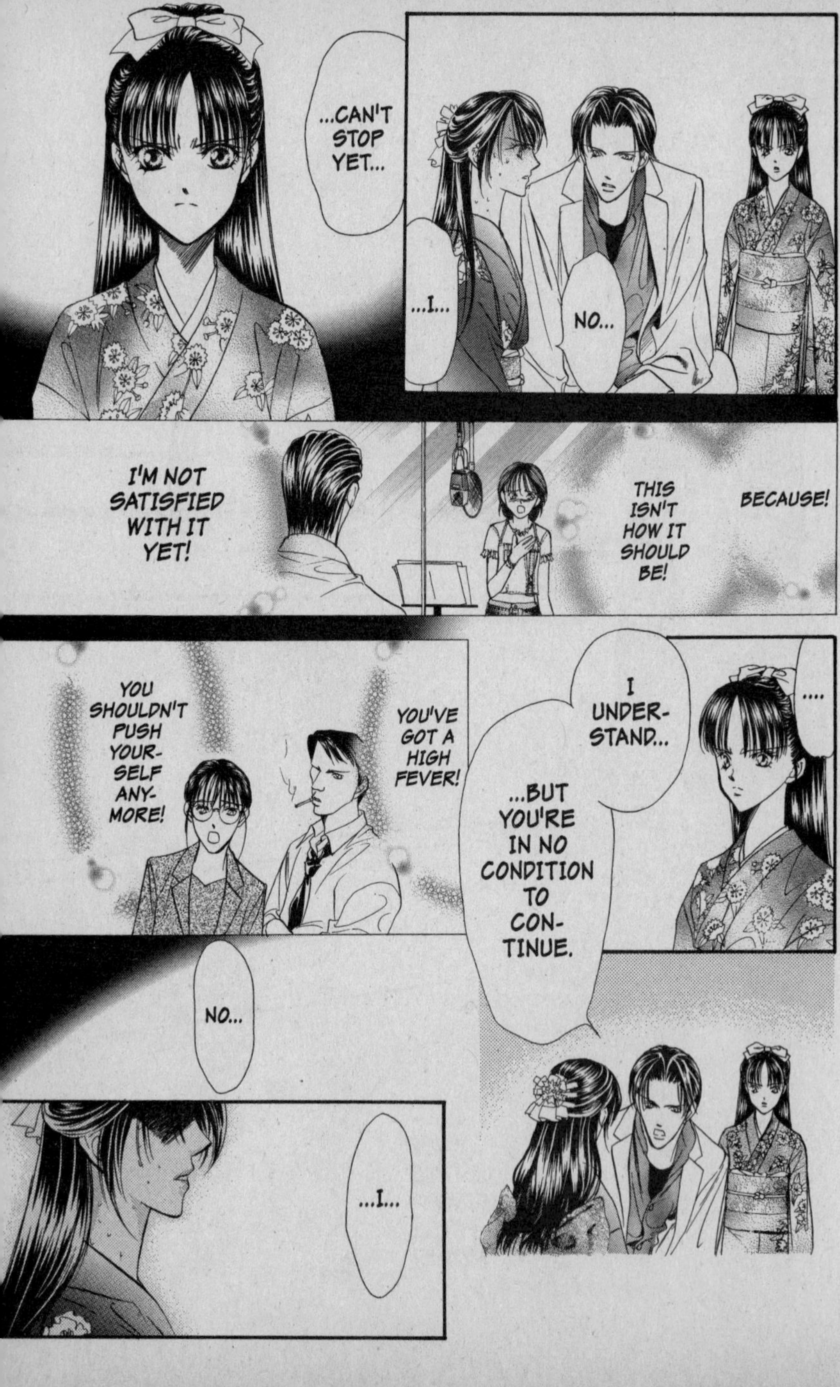
NO...
...I...
...CAN'T STOP YET...
BECAUSE!
THIS ISN'T HOW IT SHOULD BE!
I'M NOT SATISFIED WITH IT YET!
....
I UNDER-STAND...
...BUT YOU'RE IN NO CONDITION TO CON-TINUE.
YOU'VE GOT A HIGH FEVER!
YOU SHOULDN'T PUSH YOUR-SELF ANY-MORE!
NO...
...I...

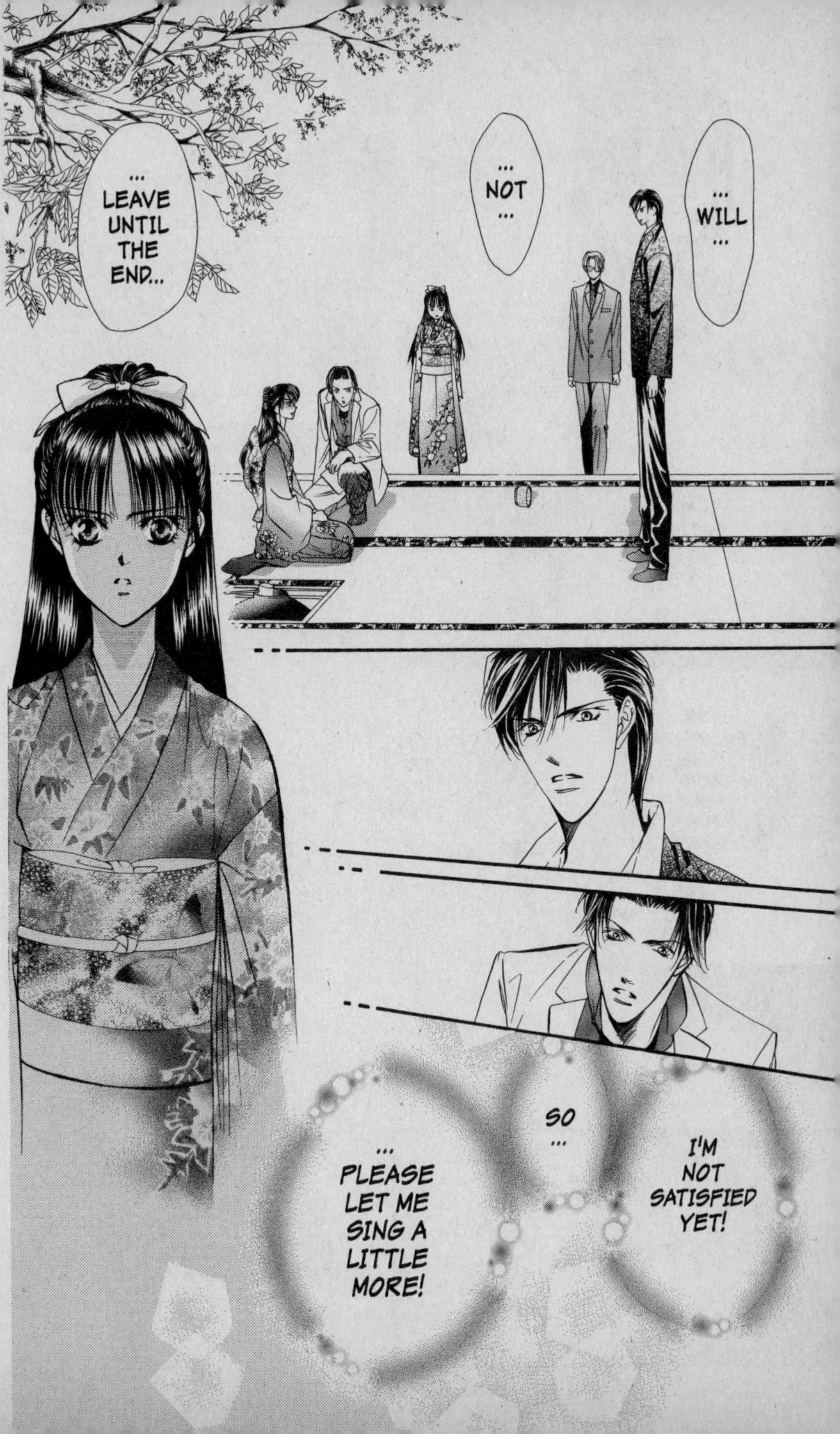

... WILL ...
... NOT ...
... LEAVE UNTIL THE END...
I'M NOT SATISFIED YET!
SO ...
... PLEASE LET ME SING A LITTLE MORE!

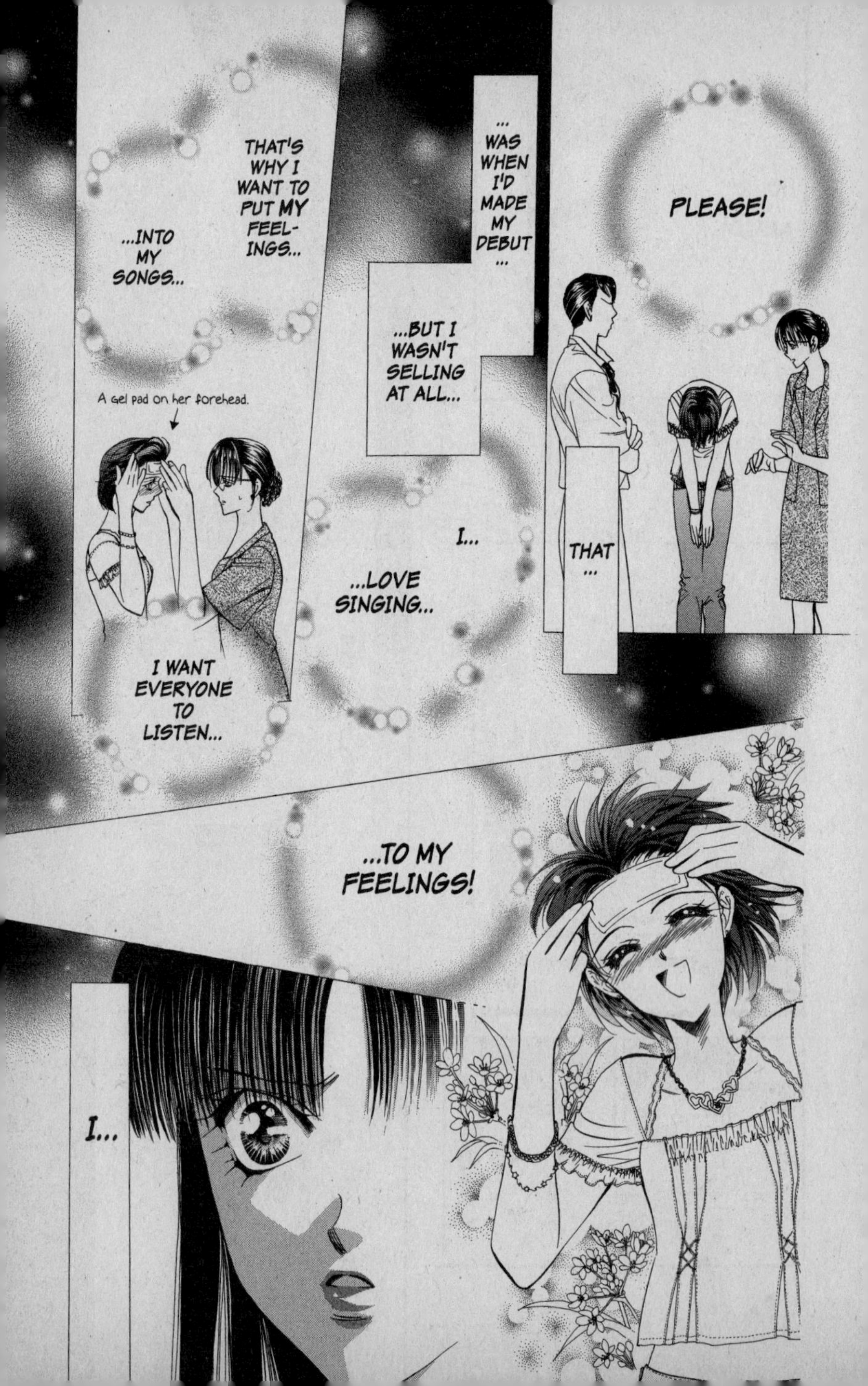
PLEASE!
THAT...
...WAS WHEN I'D MADE MY DEBUT...
...BUT I WASN'T SELLING AT ALL...
I...
...LOVE SINGING...
THAT'S WHY I WANT TO PUT MY FEEL-INGS...
...INTO MY SONGS...
A gel pad on her forehead.
I WANT EVERYONE TO LISTEN...
...TO MY FEELINGS!
I...

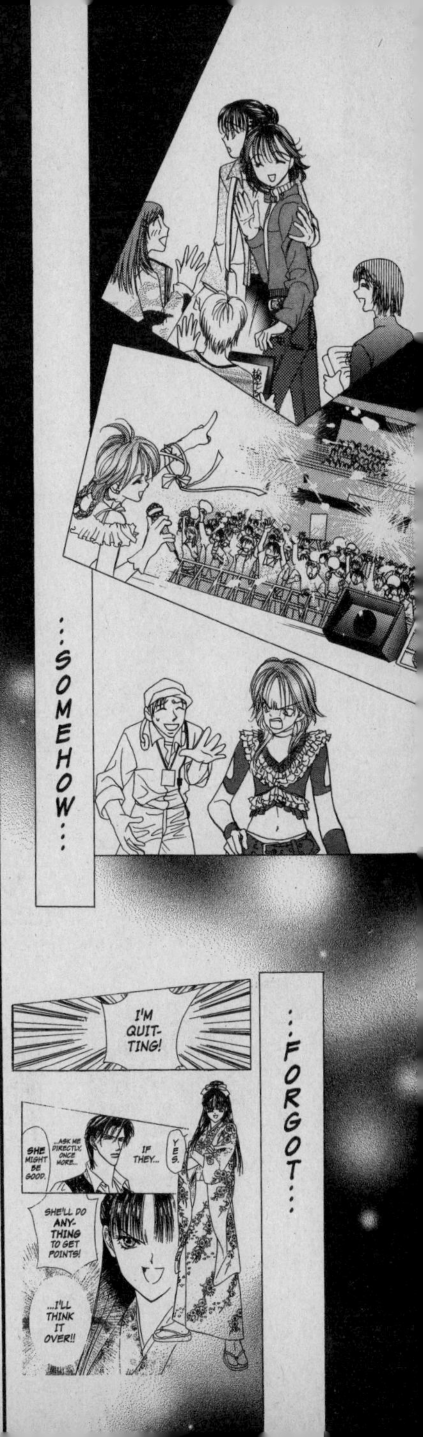
...SOMEHOW...
I'M QUITTING!
...FORGOT...
YES.
IF THEY...
...ASK ME DIRECTLY, ONCE MORE...
SHE MIGHT BE GOOD.
SHE'LL DO ANYTHING TO GET POINTS!
...I'LL THINK IT OVER!!

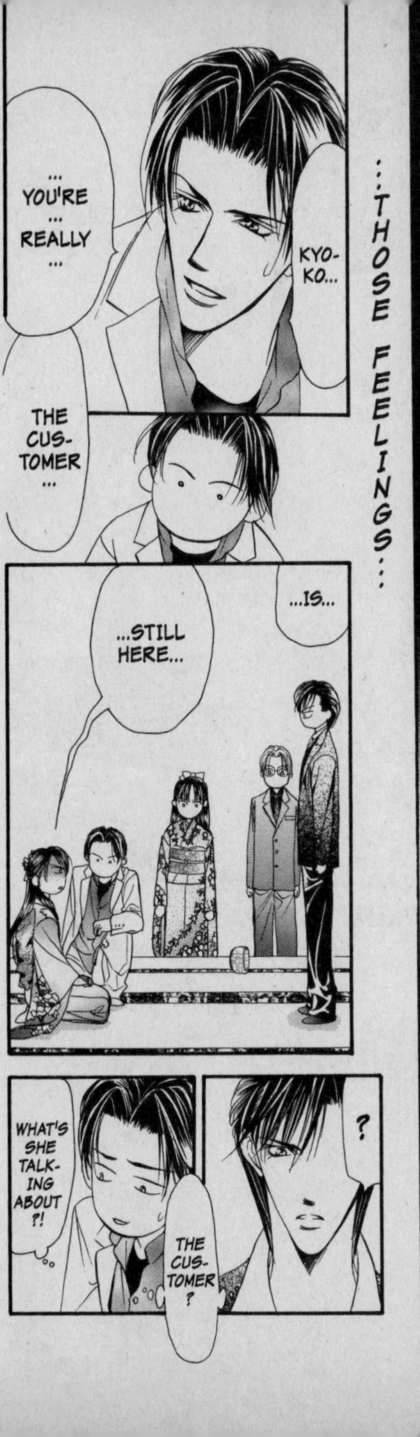
...THOSE FEELINGS...
KYO-KO...
...YOU'RE ...REALLY...
THE CUS-TOMER...
...IS...
...STILL HERE...
?
THE CUS-TOMER?
WHAT'S SHE TALKING ABOUT?!

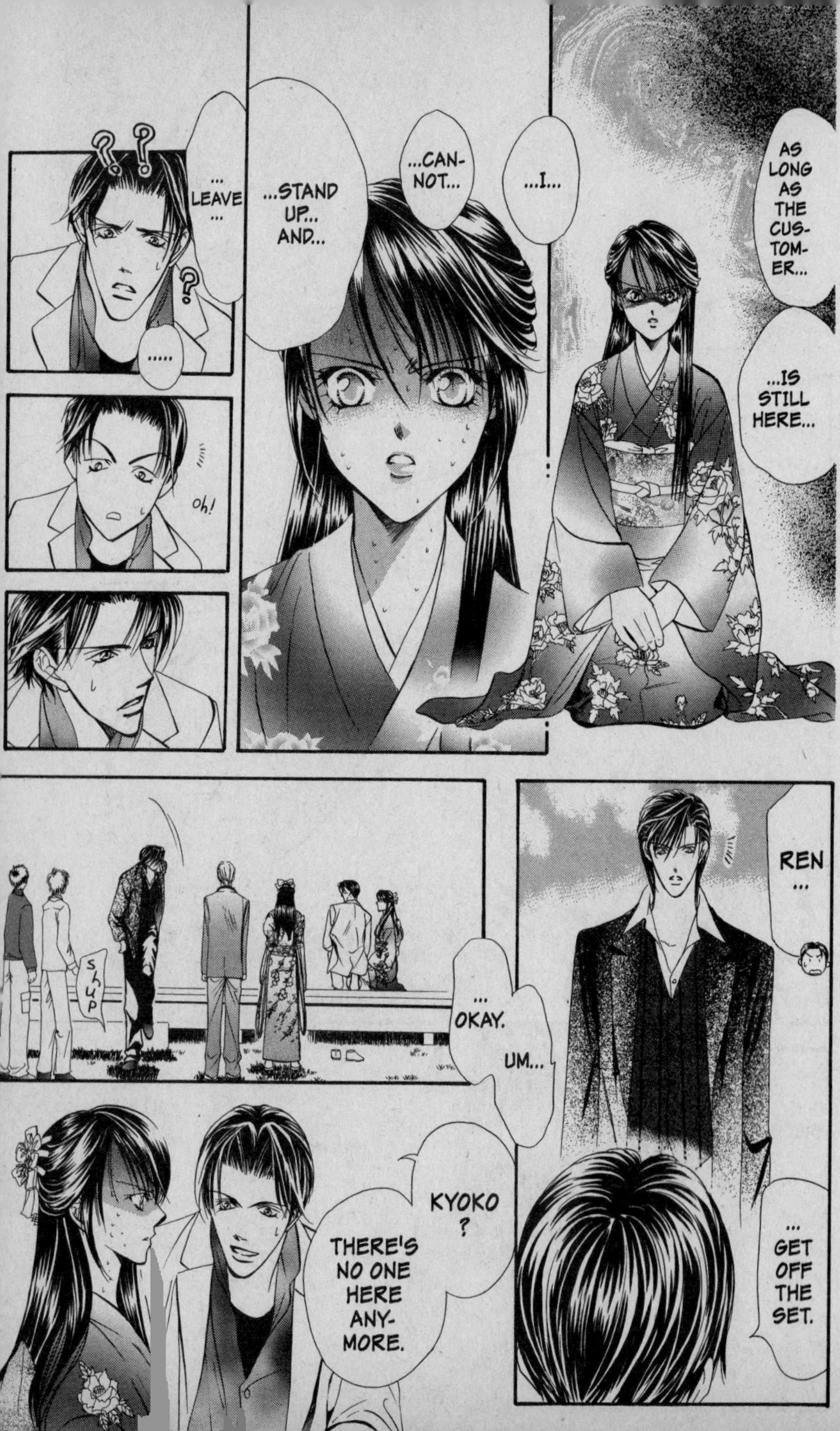
AS LONG AS THE CUSTOMER...
...IS STILL HERE...
...I...
...CANNOT...
...STAND UP... AND...
... LEAVE ...
?? ?
.....
oh!
REN ...
... GET OFF THE SET.
... OKAY.
UM...
SHUP
KYOKO ?
THERE'S NO ONE HERE ANYMORE.

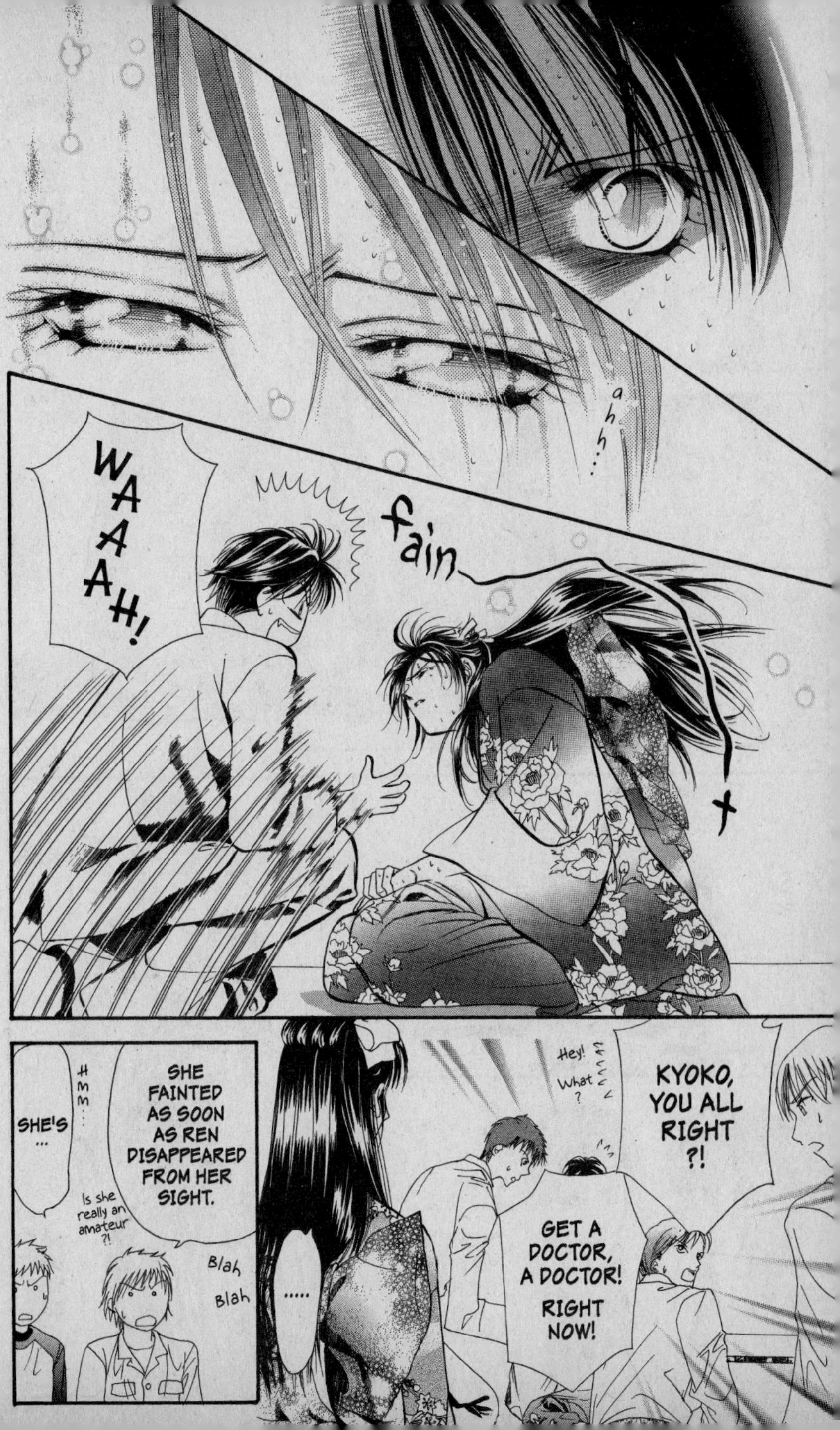
ahh...
fain-t
WAAAAH!
KYOKO, YOU ALL RIGHT?!
Hey! What?
GET A DOCTOR, A DOCTOR! RIGHT NOW!
.....
SHE FAINTED AS SOON AS REN DISAPPEARED FROM HER SIGHT.
Hmm...
SHE'S ...
Is she really an amateur?!
Blah
Blah

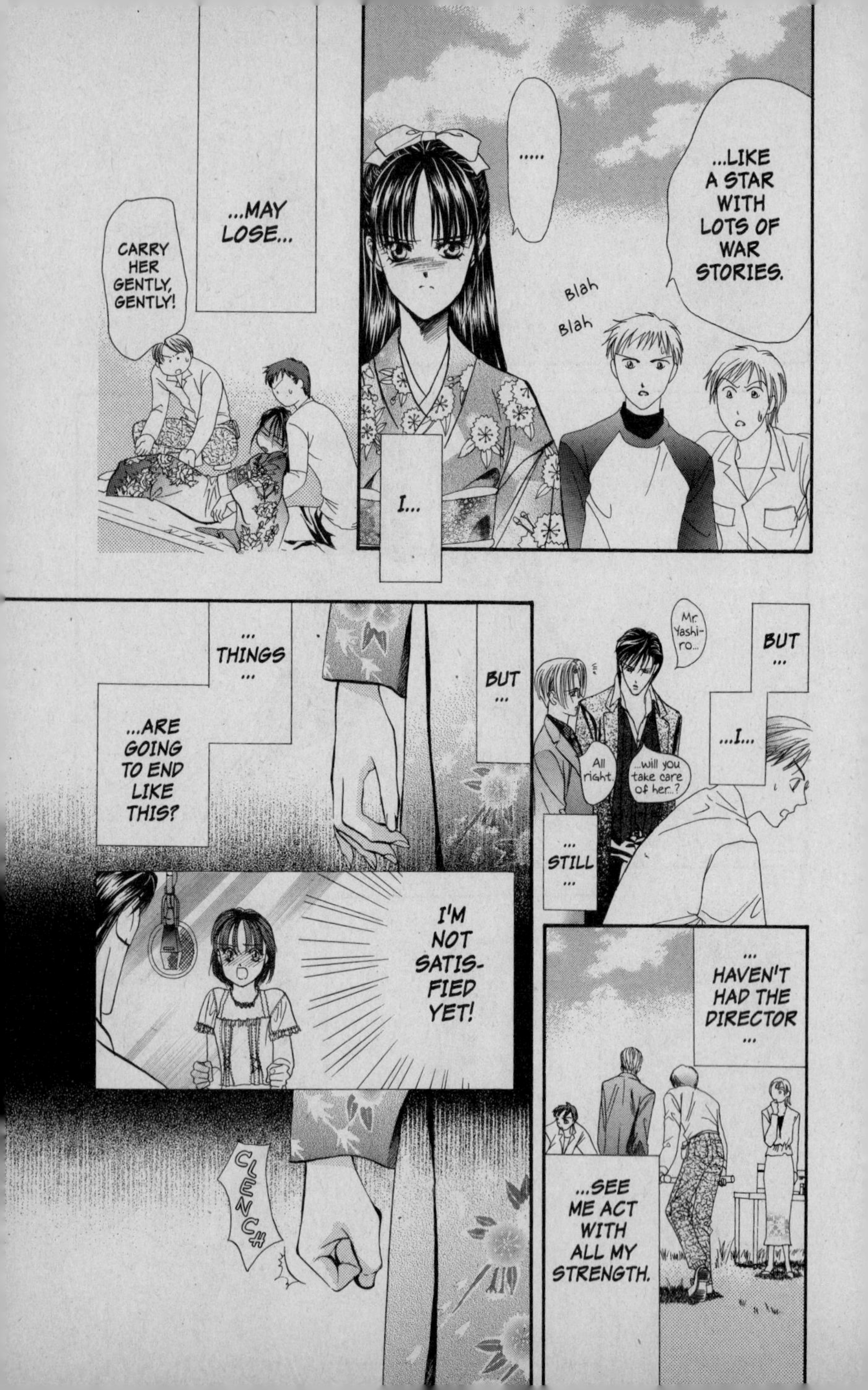
...LIKE A STAR WITH LOTS OF WAR STORIES.
Blah
Blah
.....
I...
...MAY LOSE...
CARRY HER GENTLY, GENTLY!
BUT ...
Mr. Yashiro...
...I...
...will you take care of her..?
All right.
... STILL ...
... HAVEN'T HAD THE DIRECTOR ...
...SEE ME ACT WITH ALL MY STRENGTH.
BUT ...
... THINGS ...
...ARE GOING TO END LIKE THIS?
I'M NOT SATIS-FIED YET!
CLENCH

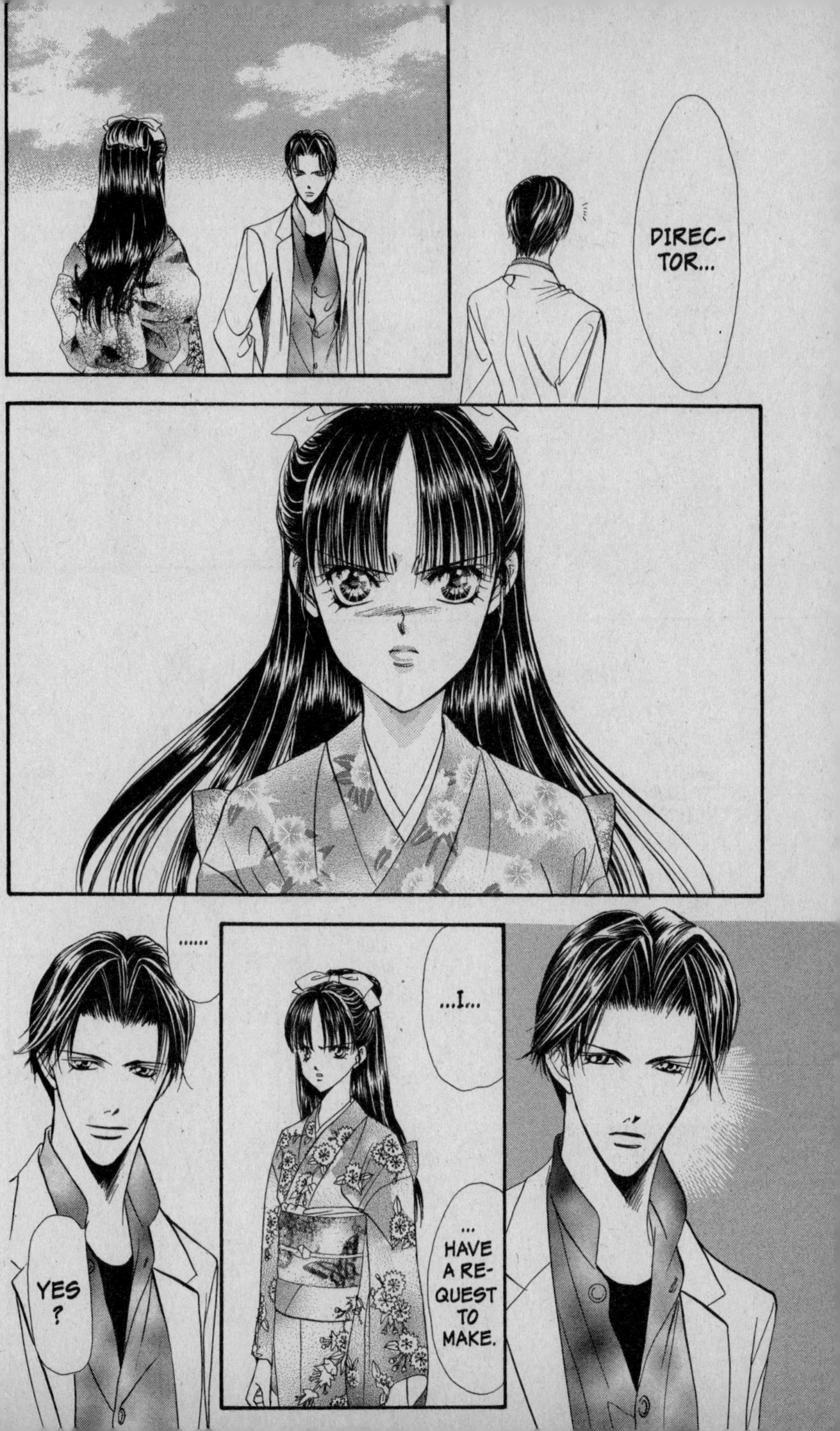
DIREC-TOR...
......
...I...
...HAVE A RE-QUEST TO MAKE.
YES?

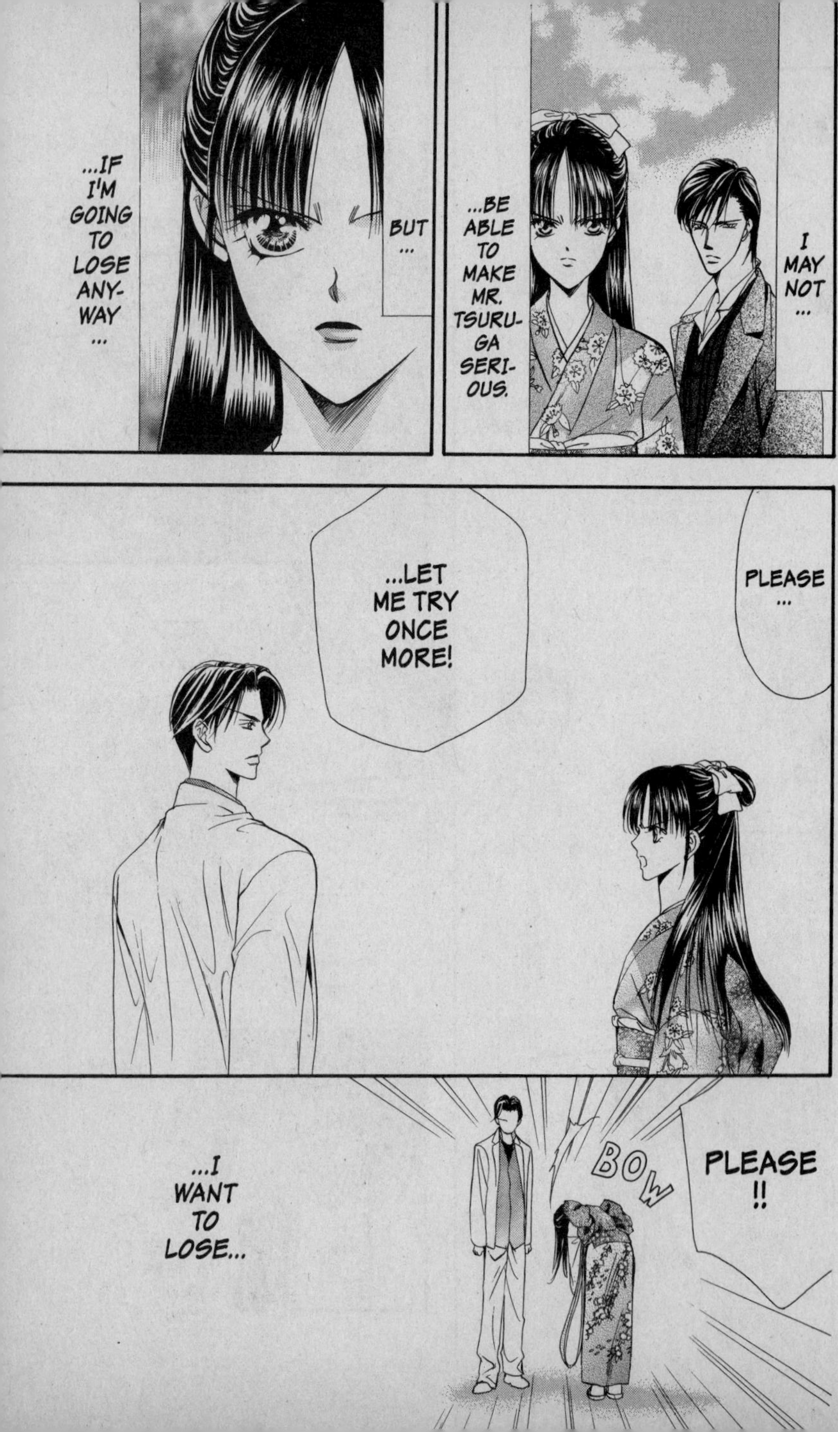
I MAY NOT...
...BE ABLE TO MAKE MR. TSURUGA SERIOUS.
BUT...
...IF I'M GOING TO LOSE ANYWAY...
PLEASE...
...LET ME TRY ONCE MORE!
PLEASE!!
BOW
...I WANT TO LOSE...

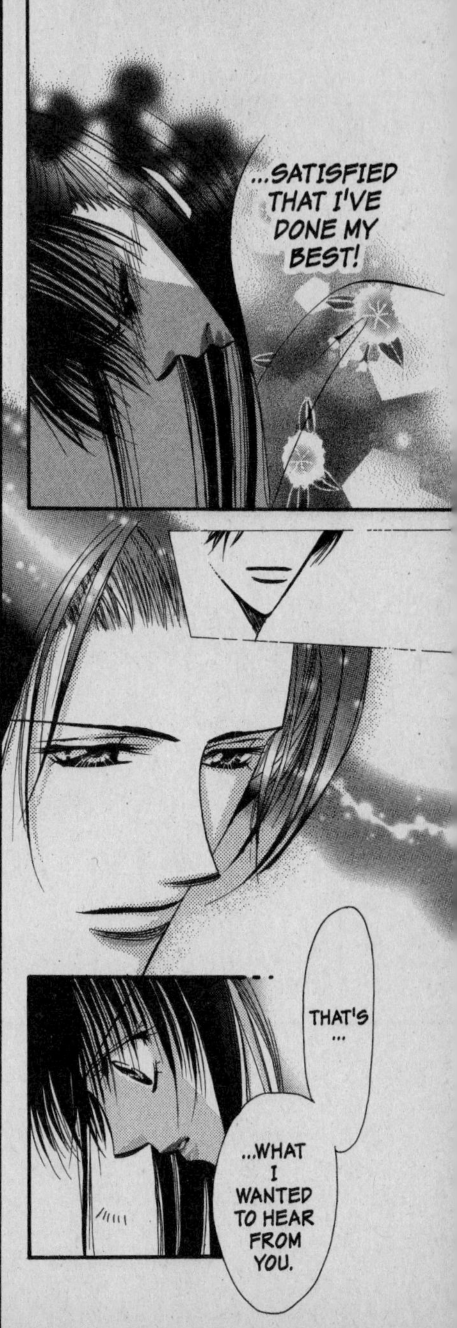
...SATISFIED THAT I'VE DONE MY BEST!
THAT'S ...
...WHAT I WANTED TO HEAR FROM YOU.

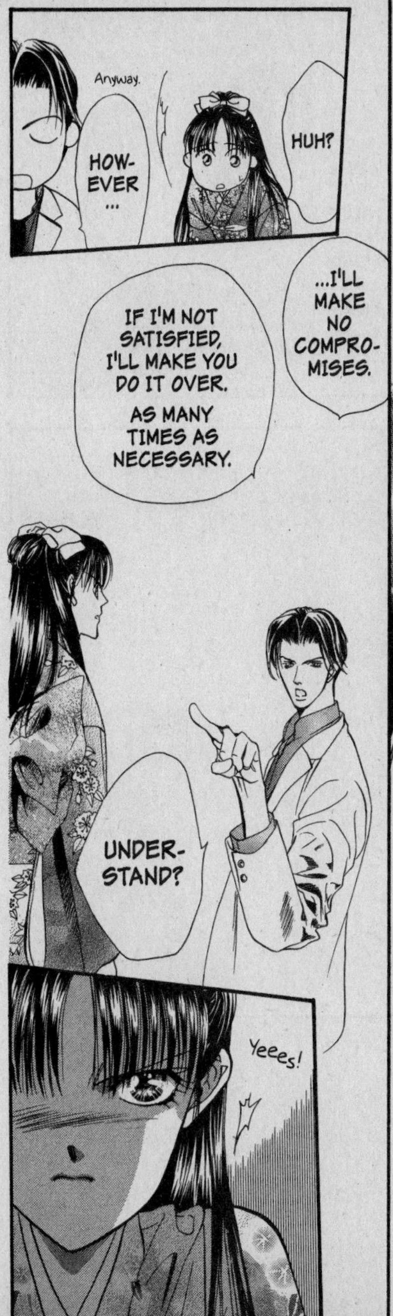
HUH?
Anyway.
HOW-EVER ...
...I'LL MAKE NO COMPROMISES.
IF I'M NOT SATISFIED, I'LL MAKE YOU DO IT OVER.
AS MANY TIMES AS NECESSARY.
UNDER-STAND?
Yeees!

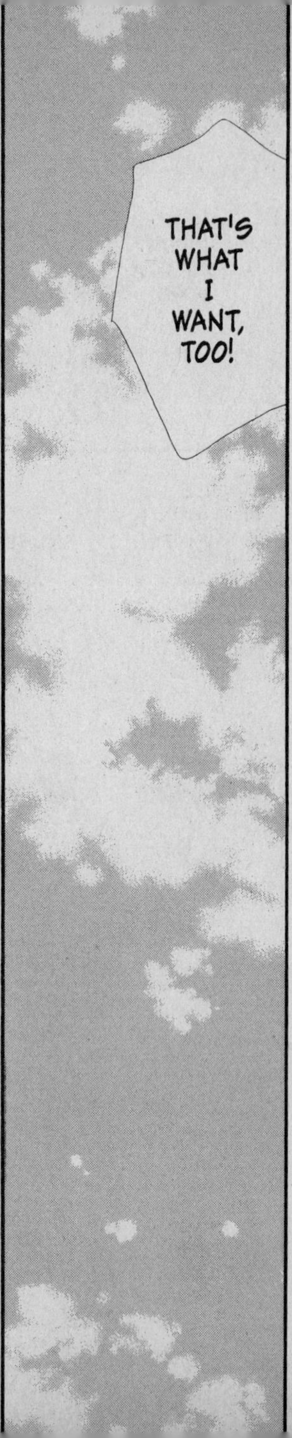
THAT'S WHAT I WANT, TOO!

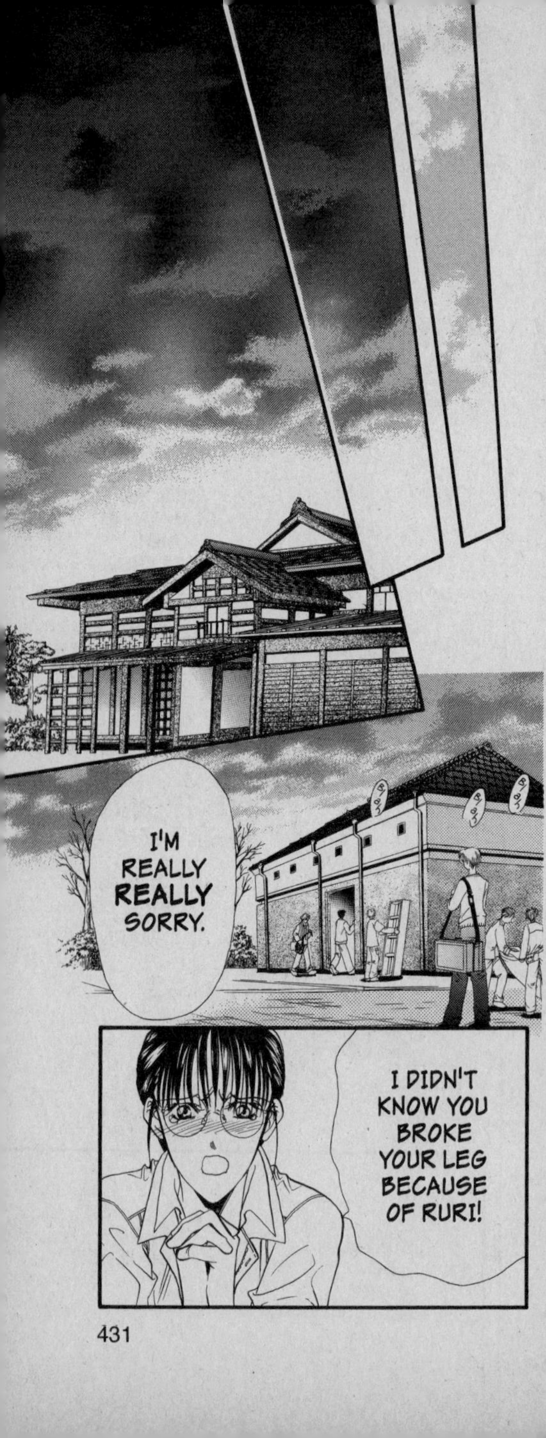
I'M REALLY REALLY SORRY.
I DIDN'T KNOW YOU BROKE YOUR LEG BECAUSE OF RURI!

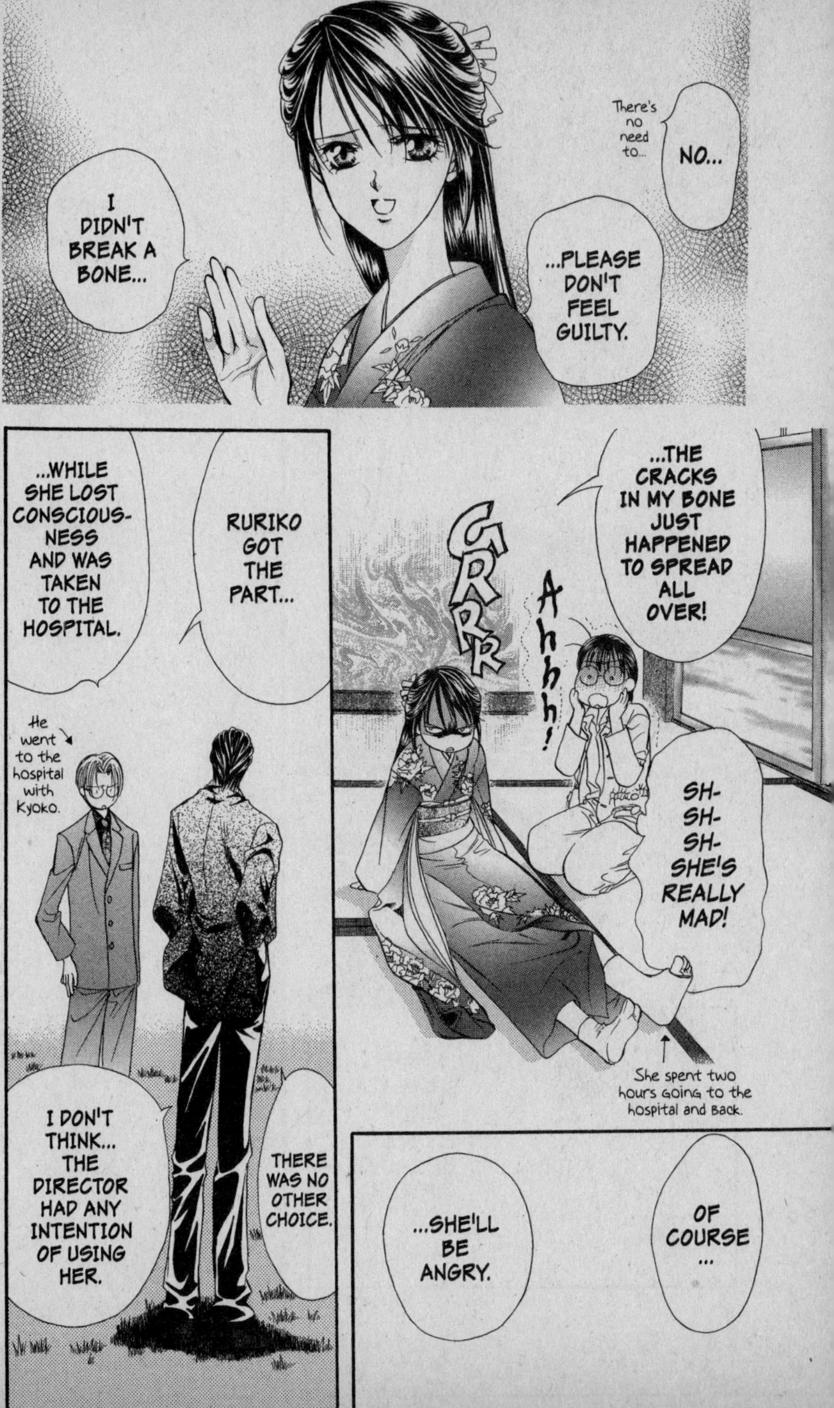
There's no need to...
NO...
...PLEASE DON'T FEEL GUILTY.
I DIDN'T BREAK A BONE...
...THE CRACKS IN MY BONE JUST HAPPENED TO SPREAD ALL OVER!
GRRR
Ahhh!
SH-SH-SH-SHE'S REALLY MAD!
She spent two hours going to the hospital and back.
OF COURSE...
...SHE'LL BE ANGRY.
RURIKO GOT THE PART...
...WHILE SHE LOST CONSCIOUSNESS AND WAS TAKEN TO THE HOSPITAL.
He went to the hospital with Kyoko.
THERE WAS NO OTHER CHOICE.
I DON'T THINK... THE DIRECTOR HAD ANY INTENTION OF USING HER.

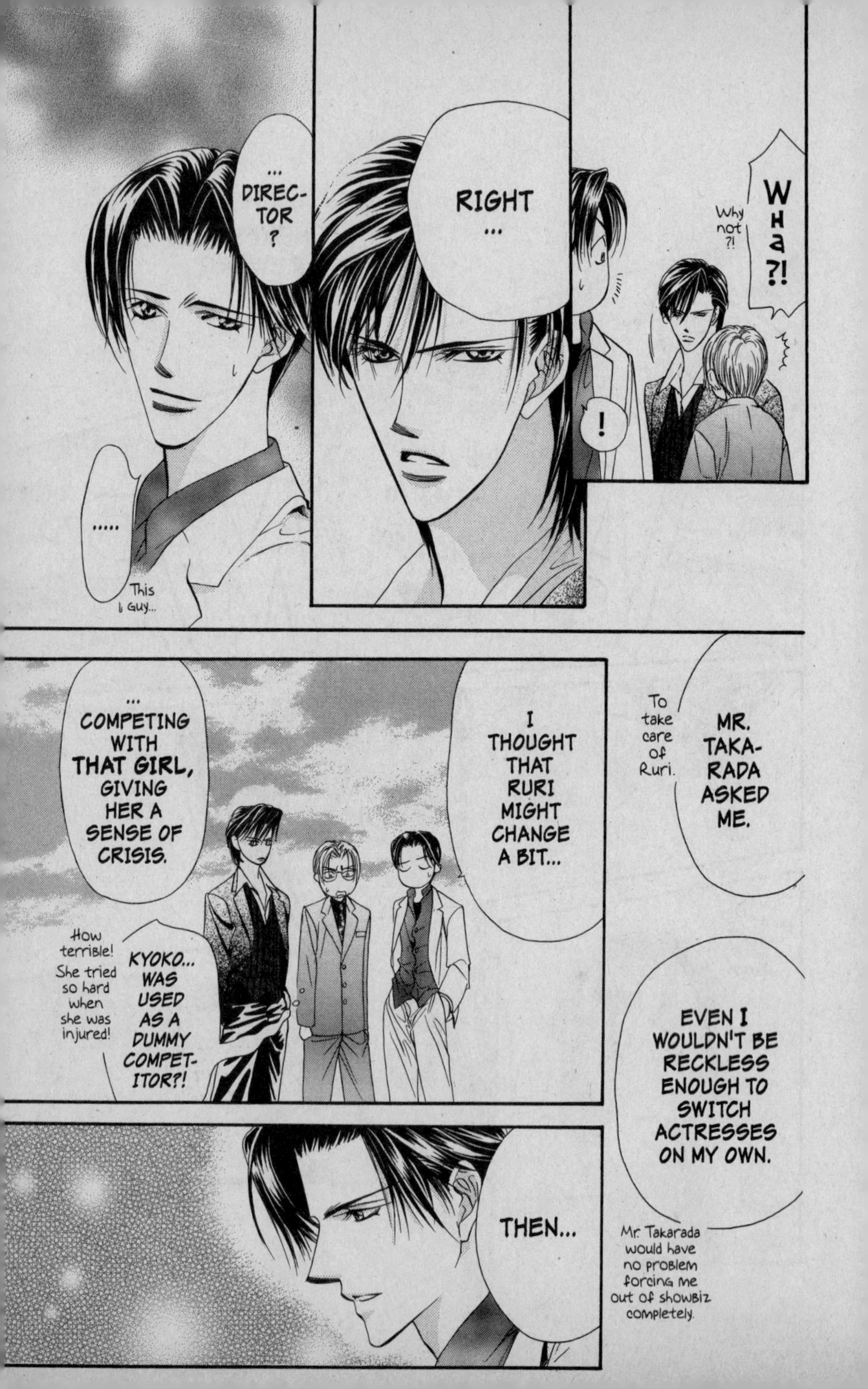
Wha?!
Why not?!
!
RIGHT...
...DIREC-TOR?
.....
This guy...
MR. TAKA-RADA ASKED ME.
To take care of Ruri.
I THOUGHT THAT RURI MIGHT CHANGE A BIT...
...COMPETING WITH THAT GIRL, GIVING HER A SENSE OF CRISIS.
KYOKO... WAS USED AS A DUMMY COMPET-ITOR?!
How terrible! She tried so hard when she was injured!
EVEN I WOULDN'T BE RECKLESS ENOUGH TO SWITCH ACTRESSES ON MY OWN.
Mr. Takarada would have no problem forcing me out of showbiz completely.
THEN...

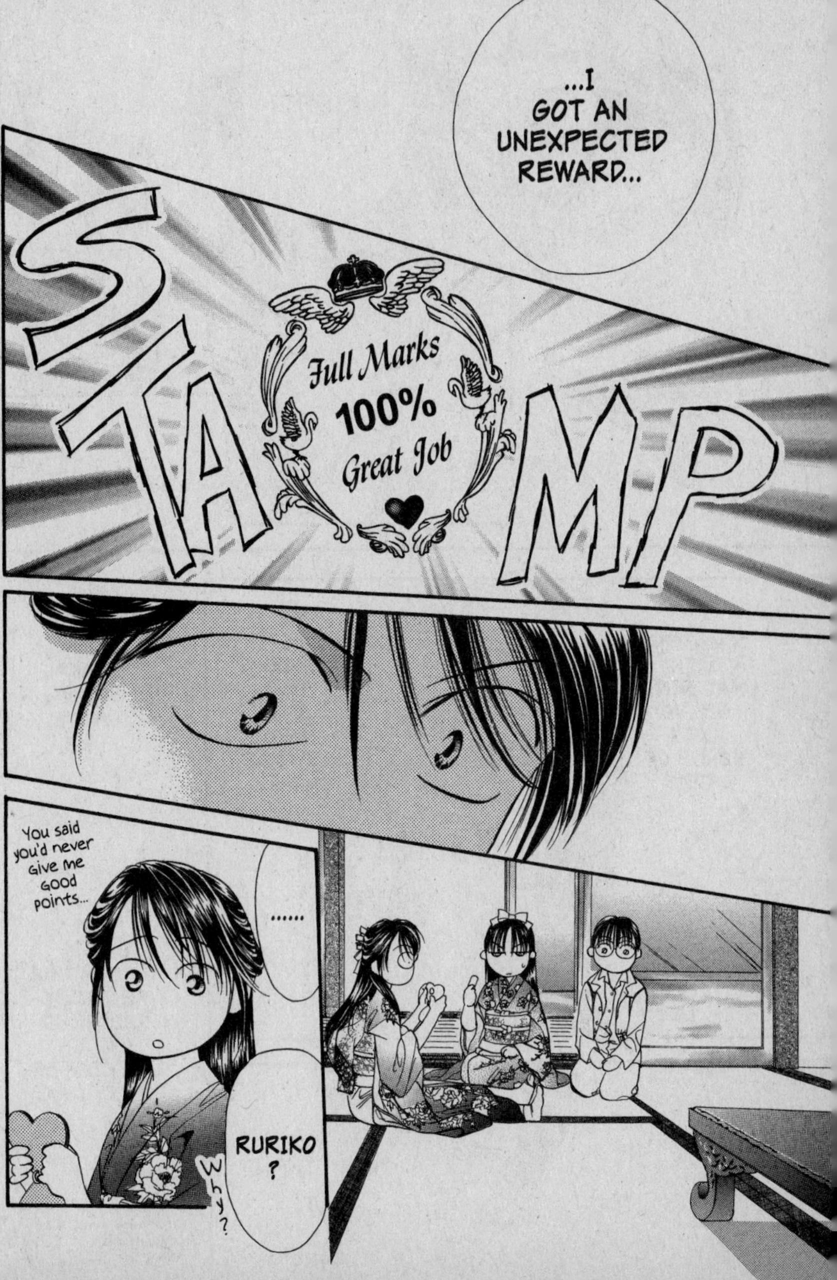

...I GOT AN UNEXPECTED REWARD...
STAMP
Full Marks
100%
Great Job
RURIKO?
......
You said you'd never give me good points...
Why?

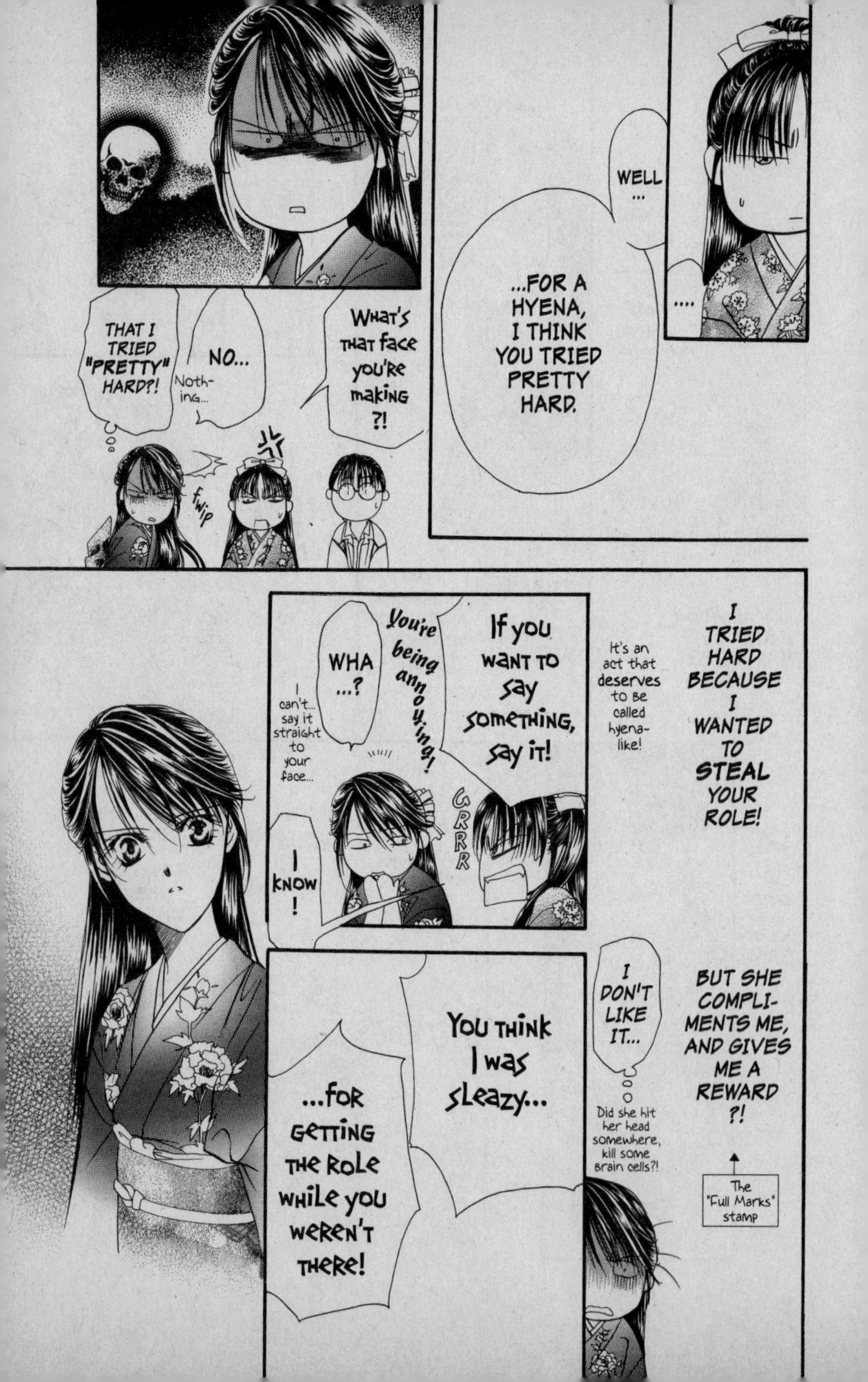
WELL ...
....
...FOR A HYENA, I THINK YOU TRIED PRETTY HARD.
WHAT'S THAT face you're making ?!
NO... Nothing...
THAT I TRIED "PRETTY" HARD?!
fwip
I TRIED HARD BECAUSE I WANTED TO STEAL YOUR ROLE!
It's an act that deserves to be called hyena-like!
If you want to say something, say it!
You're being annoying!
WHA ...?
I can't... say it straight to your face...
GRRR
I KNOW!
BUT SHE COMPLIMENTS ME, AND GIVES ME A REWARD ?!
The "Full Marks" stamp
I DON'T LIKE IT...
Did she hit her head somewhere, kill some brain cells?!
You think I was sleazy...
...for getting the role while you weren't there!

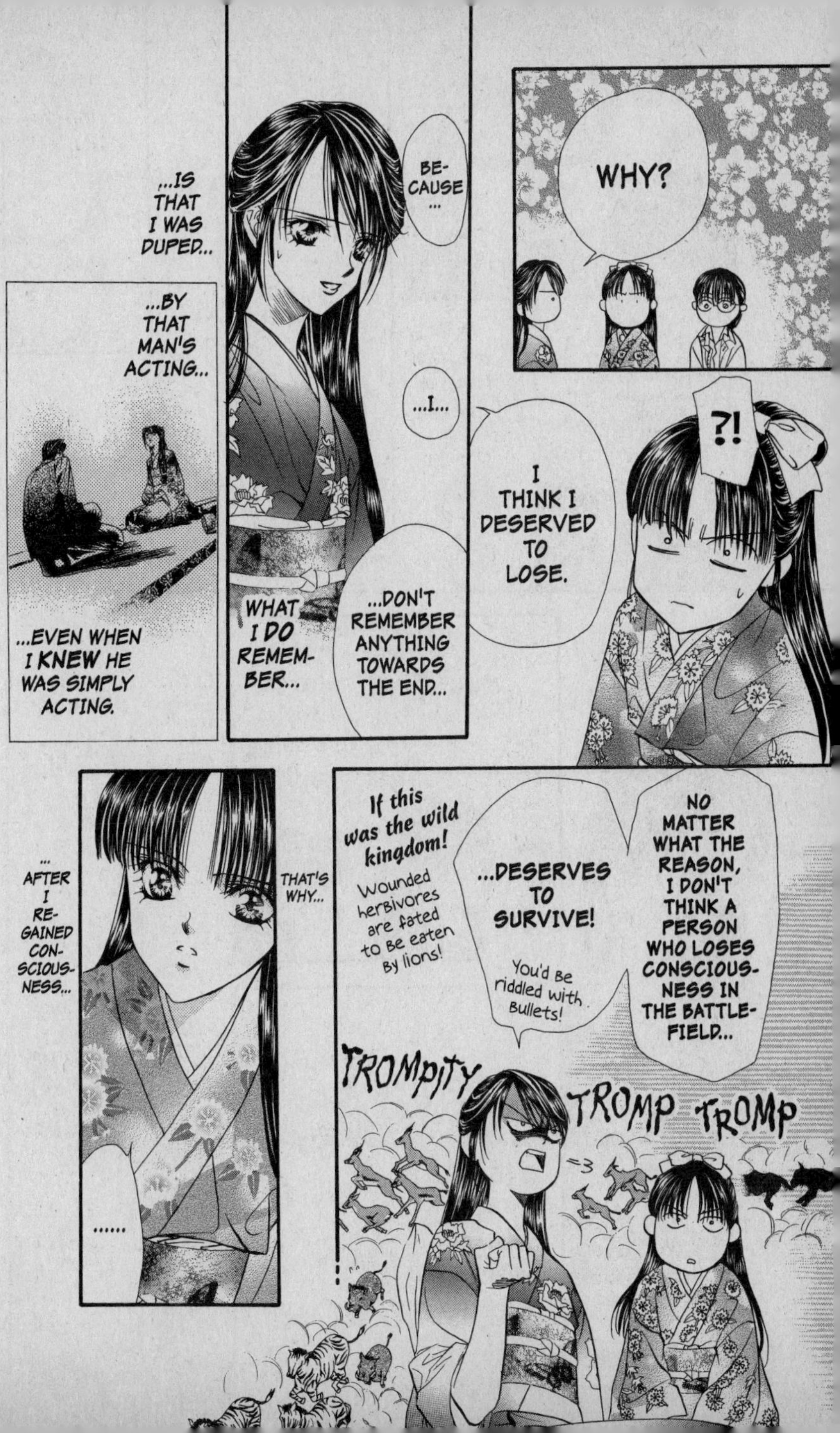
WHY?
?!
I THINK I DESERVED TO LOSE.
BE-CAUSE...
...I...
...DON'T REMEMBER ANYTHING TOWARDS THE END...
WHAT I DO REMEMBER...
...IS THAT I WAS DUPED...
...BY THAT MAN'S ACTING...
...EVEN WHEN I KNEW HE WAS SIMPLY ACTING.
NO MATTER WHAT THE REASON, I DON'T THINK A PERSON WHO LOSES CONSCIOUS-NESS IN THE BATTLE-FIELD...
...DESERVES TO SURVIVE!
You'd be riddled with bullets!
If this was the wild kingdom!
Wounded herbivores are fated to be eaten by lions!
TROMPITY
TROMP TROMP
THAT'S WHY...
...AFTER I RE-GAINED CON-SCIOUS-NESS...
......

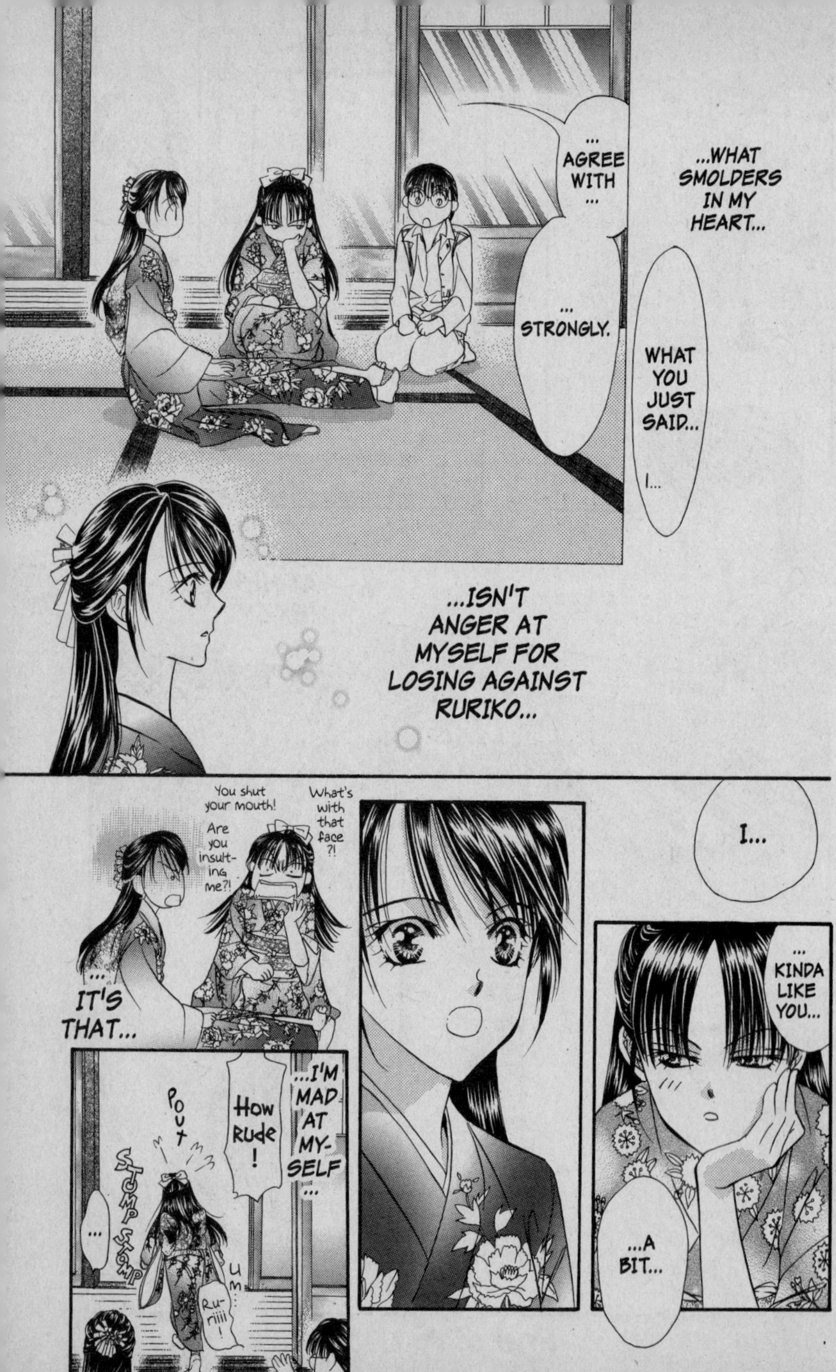
...WHAT SMOLDERS IN MY HEART...
WHAT YOU JUST SAID... I...
... AGREE WITH ...
... STRONGLY.
...ISN'T ANGER AT MYSELF FOR LOSING AGAINST RURIKO...
I...
... KINDA LIKE YOU...
...A BIT...
... IT'S THAT...
What's with that face?!
You shut your mouth! Are you insulting me?!
...I'M MAD AT MY-SELF...
How Rude!
Pout
STOMP STOMP
Um... Ru-riiii!
...

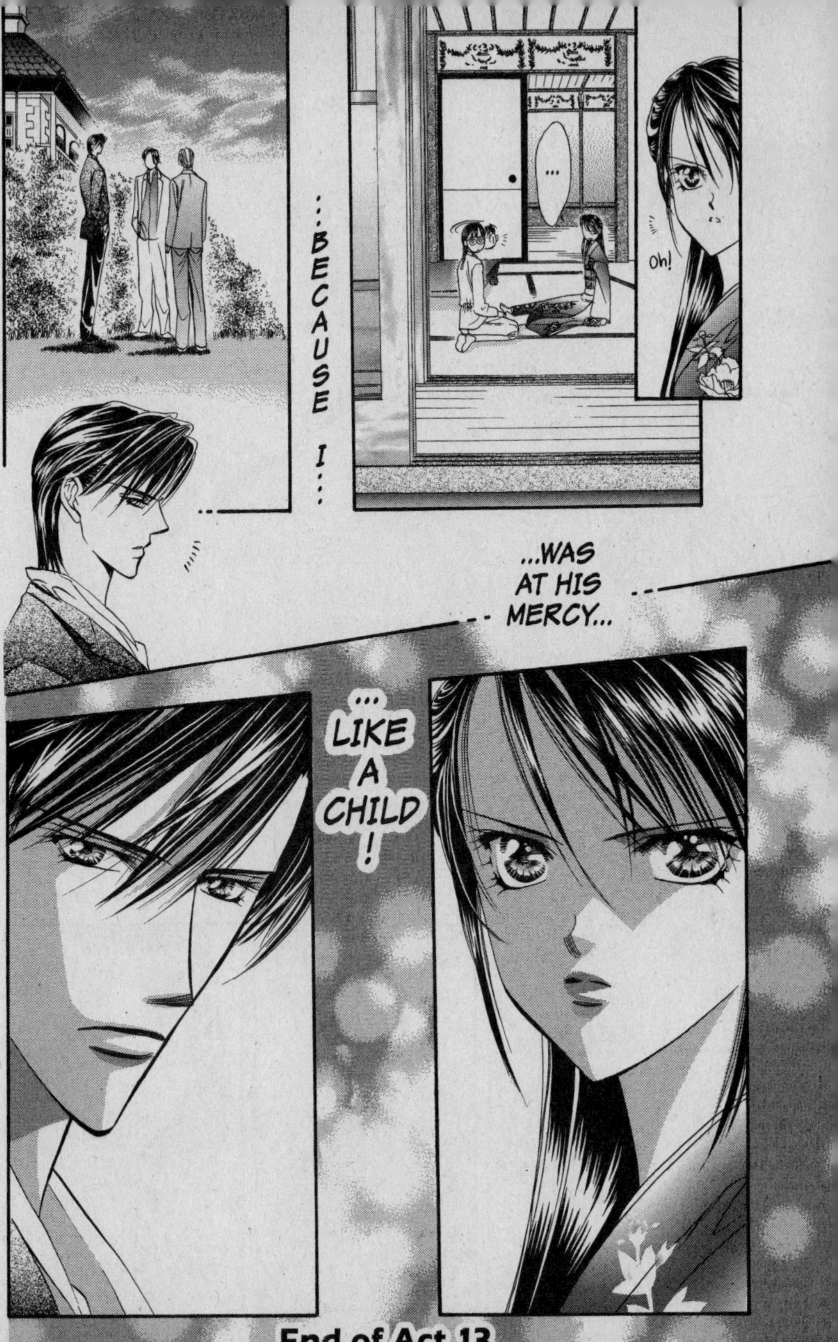
...
Oh!
...BECAUSE I...
...WAS AT HIS MERCY...
...LIKE A CHILD!

End of Act 13

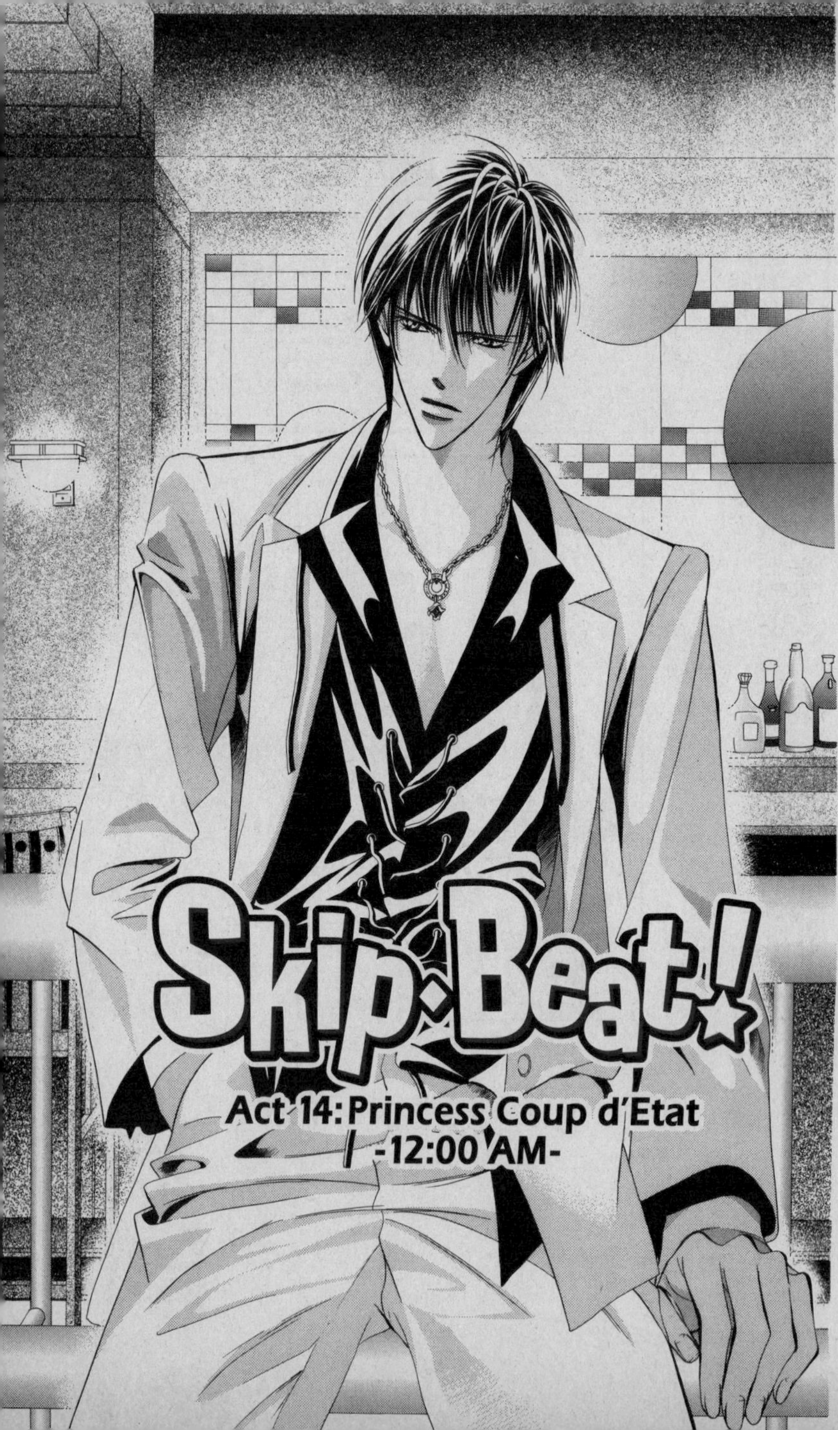
Skip·Beat!
Act 14: Princess Coup d'Etat
-12:00 AM-

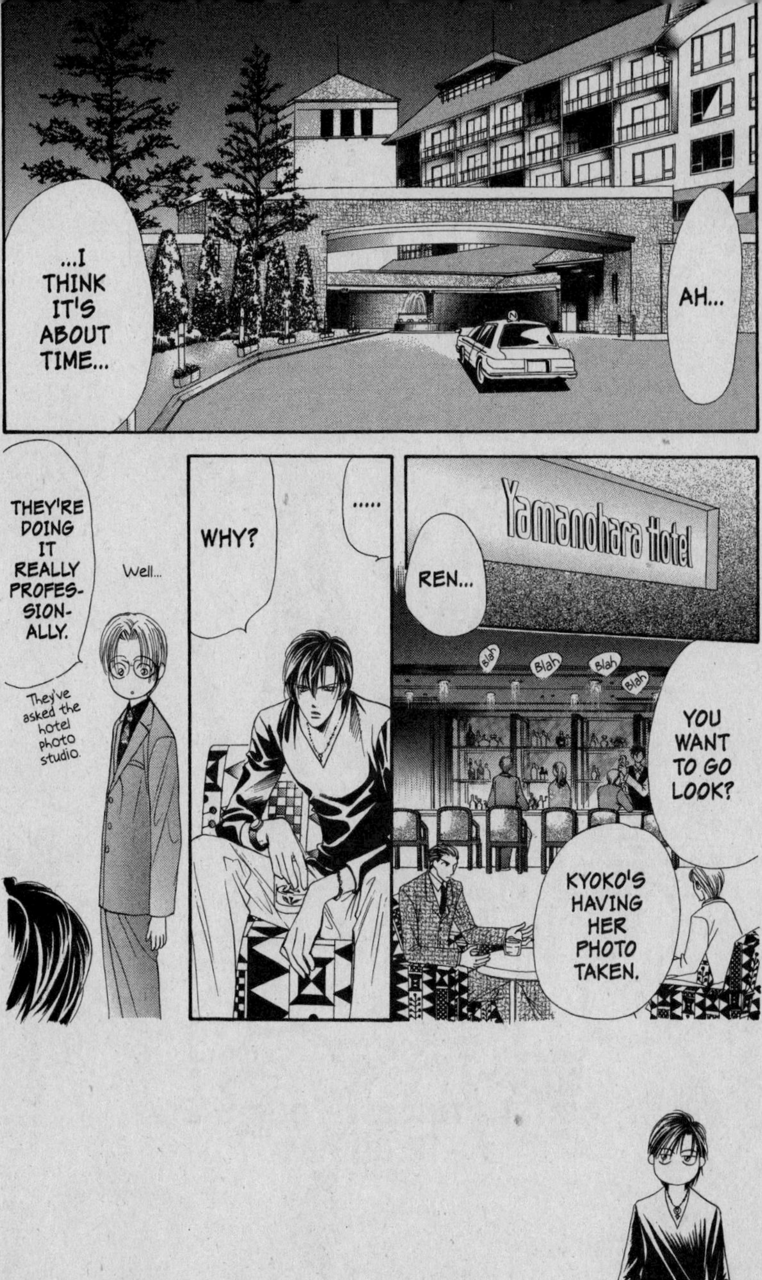
AH...
...I THINK IT'S ABOUT TIME...
Yamanohara Hotel
REN...
Blah Blah Blah Blah
YOU WANT TO GO LOOK?
KYOKO'S HAVING HER PHOTO TAKEN.
.....
WHY?
THEY'RE DOING IT REALLY PROFES-SION-ALLY.
Well...
They've asked the hotel photo studio.

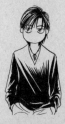

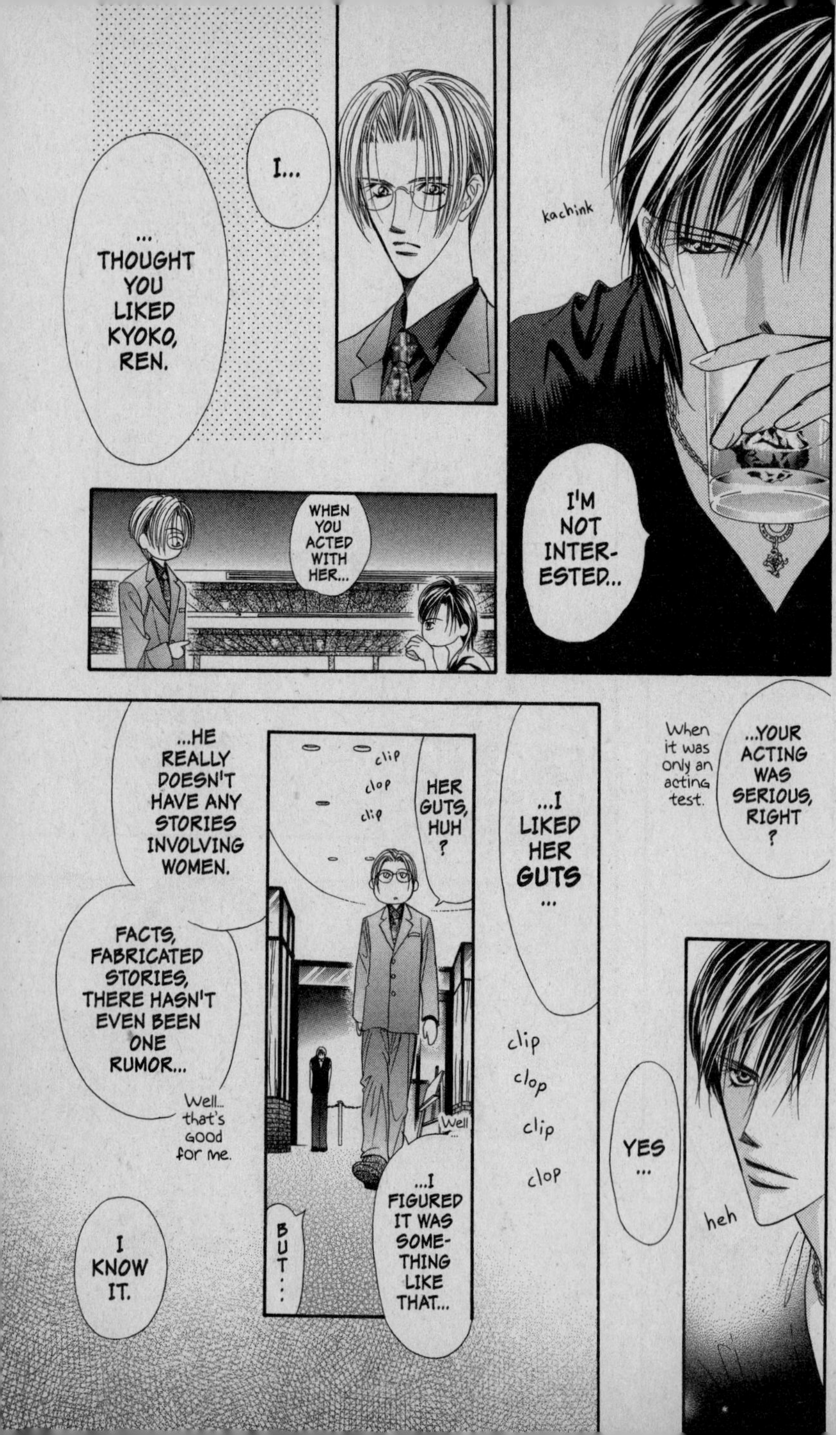
kachink
I'M NOT INTERESTED...
I...
...THOUGHT YOU LIKED KYOKO, REN.
WHEN YOU ACTED WITH HER...
...YOUR ACTING WAS SERIOUS, RIGHT?
When it was only an acting test.
YES...
heh
...I LIKED HER GUTS...
clip clop clip clop
HER GUTS, HUH?
clip clop clip
Well...
...I FIGURED IT WAS SOMETHING LIKE THAT...
BUT...
...HE REALLY DOESN'T HAVE ANY STORIES INVOLVING WOMEN.
FACTS, FABRICATED STORIES, THERE HASN'T EVEN BEEN ONE RUMOR...
Well... that's good for me.
I KNOW IT.

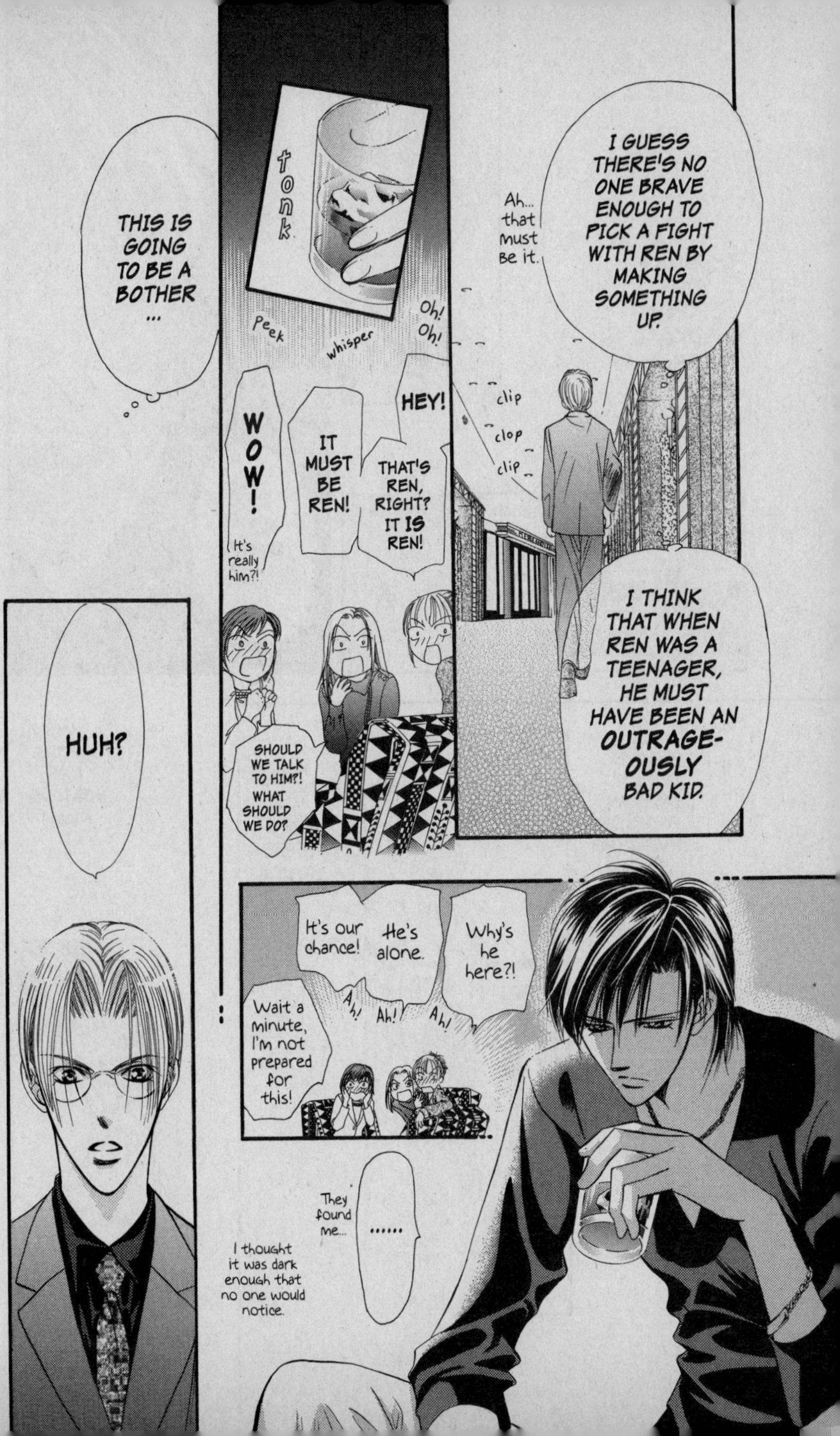
I GUESS THERE'S NO ONE BRAVE ENOUGH TO PICK A FIGHT WITH REN BY MAKING SOMETHING UP.
Ah... that must be it.
clip
clop
clip
I THINK THAT WHEN REN WAS A TEENAGER, HE MUST HAVE BEEN AN OUTRAGE-OUSLY BAD KID.
tonk
Oh! Oh!
whisper
Peek
HEY!
THAT'S REN, RIGHT? IT IS REN!
IT MUST BE REN!
WOW!
It's really him?!
SHOULD WE TALK TO HIM?! WHAT SHOULD WE DO?
THIS IS GOING TO BE A BOTHER...
Why's he here?!
He's alone.
It's our chance!
Ah! Ah! Ah!
Wait a minute, I'm not prepared for this!
......
They found me...
I thought it was dark enough that no one would notice.
HUH?

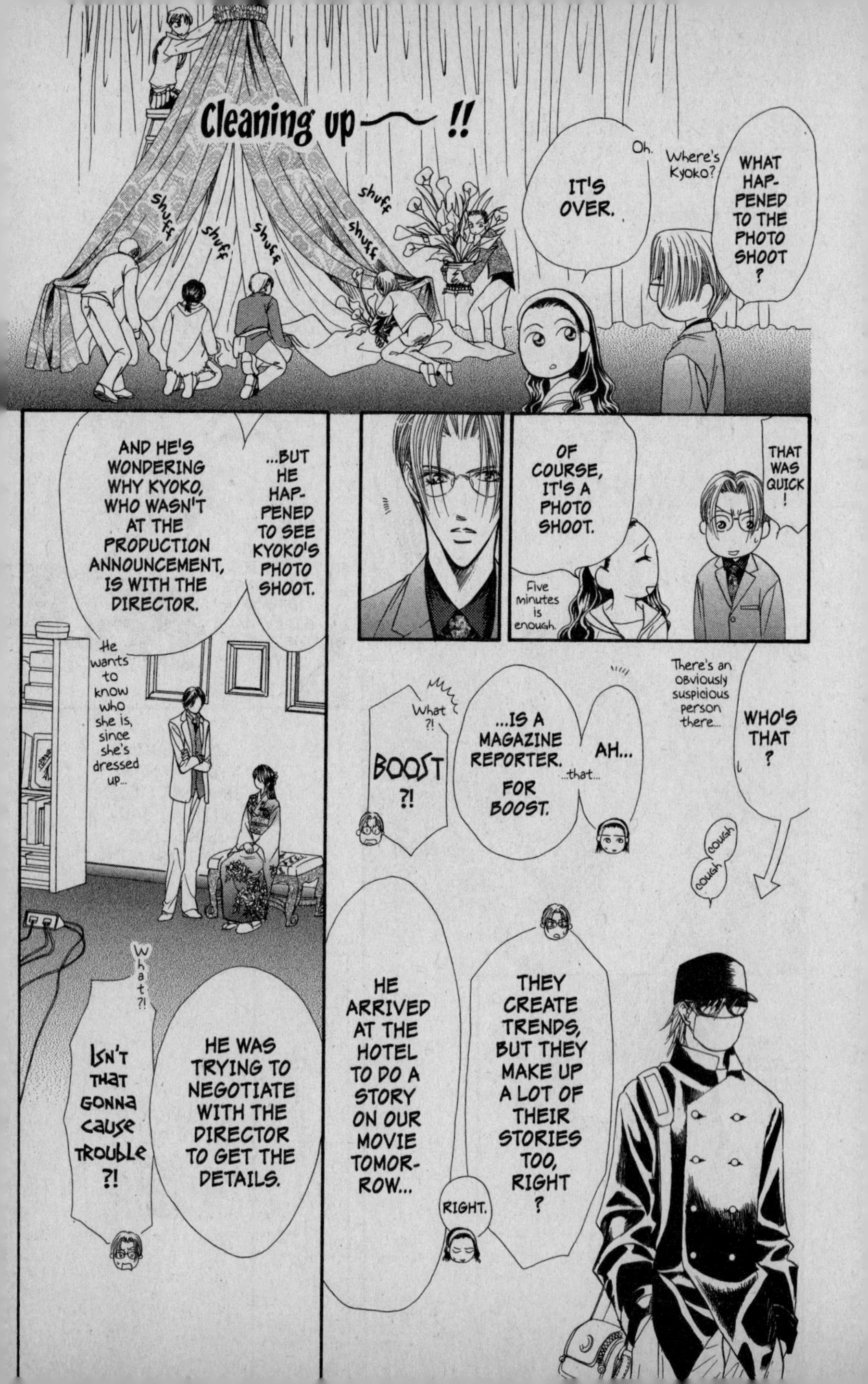
WHAT HAPPENED TO THE PHOTO SHOOT?
Where's Kyoko?
Oh.
IT'S OVER.
Cleaning up~~!!
shuff
shuff
shuff
shuff
shuff
THAT WAS QUICK!
OF COURSE, IT'S A PHOTO SHOOT.
Five minutes is enough.
WHO'S THAT?
There's an obviously suspicious person there...
cough
cough
AH...
...that...
...IS A MAGAZINE REPORTER. FOR BOOST.
What?!
BOOST?!
THEY CREATE TRENDS, BUT THEY MAKE UP A LOT OF THEIR STORIES TOO, RIGHT?
RIGHT.
HE ARRIVED AT THE HOTEL TO DO A STORY ON OUR MOVIE TOMORROW...
...BUT HE HAPPENED TO SEE KYOKO'S PHOTO SHOOT.
AND HE'S WONDERING WHY KYOKO, WHO WASN'T AT THE PRODUCTION ANNOUNCEMENT, IS WITH THE DIRECTOR.
He wants to know who she is, since she's dressed up...
HE WAS TRYING TO NEGOTIATE WITH THE DIRECTOR TO GET THE DETAILS.
What?!
ISN'T THAT GONNA CAUSE TROUBLE?!

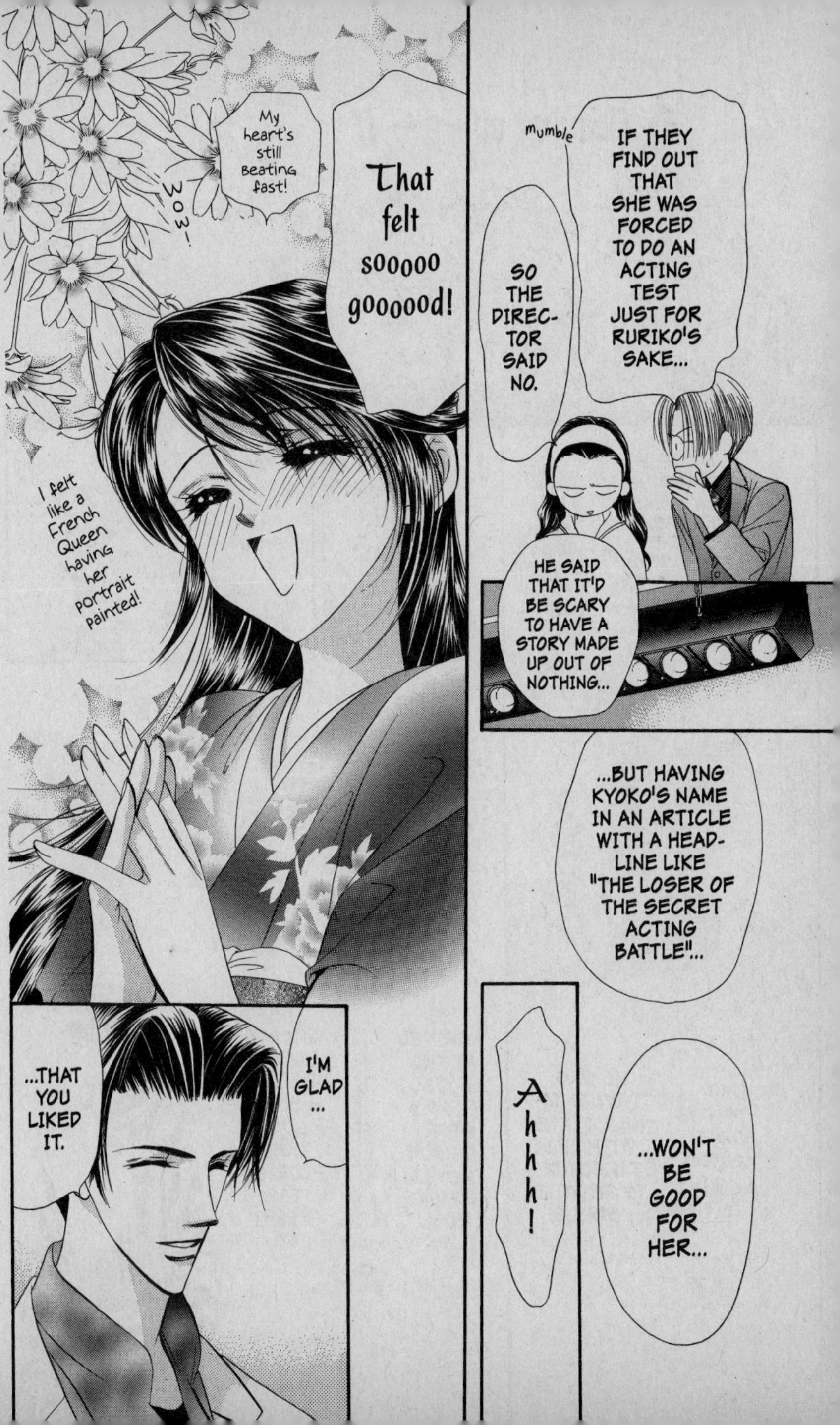
mumble
IF THEY FIND OUT THAT SHE WAS FORCED TO DO AN ACTING TEST JUST FOR RURIKO'S SAKE...
SO THE DIRECTOR SAID NO.
HE SAID THAT IT'D BE SCARY TO HAVE A STORY MADE UP OUT OF NOTHING...
...BUT HAVING KYOKO'S NAME IN AN ARTICLE WITH A HEADLINE LIKE "THE LOSER OF THE SECRET ACTING BATTLE"...
...WON'T BE GOOD FOR HER...
Ahhh!
That felt sooooo goooood!
My heart's still beating fast!
WOW!
I felt like a French Queen having her portrait painted!
I'M GLAD...
...THAT YOU LIKED IT.

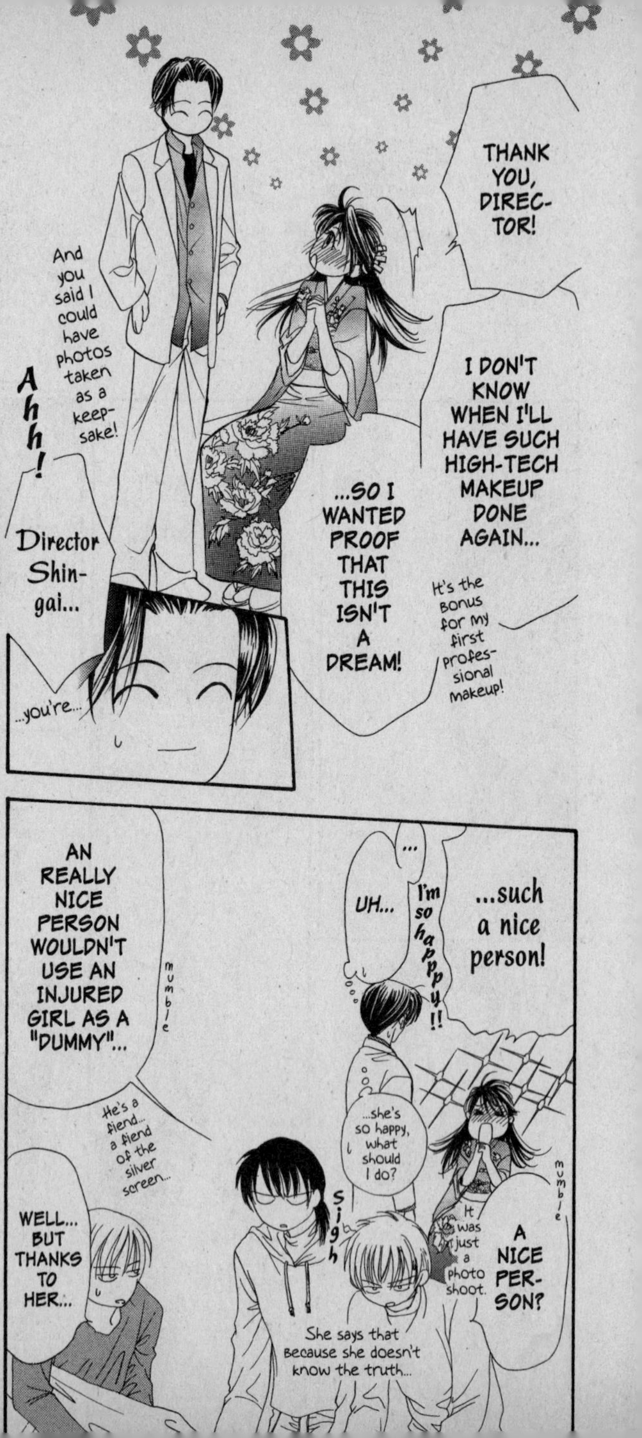
THANK YOU, DIRECTOR!
I DON'T KNOW WHEN I'LL HAVE SUCH HIGH-TECH MAKEUP DONE AGAIN...
...SO I WANTED PROOF THAT THIS ISN'T A DREAM!
It's the bonus for my first professional makeup!
And you said I could have photos taken as a keepsake!
Ahh!
Director Shingai...
...you're...
...such a nice person!
I'm so happy!!
...
UH...
AN REALLY NICE PERSON WOULDN'T USE AN INJURED GIRL AS A "DUMMY"...
mumble
A NICE PERSON?
mumble
It was just a photo shoot.
...she's so happy, what should I do?
Sigh
He's a fiend... a fiend of the silver screen...
She says that because she doesn't know the truth...
WELL... BUT THANKS TO HER...

Seiji Shingai

Difficulty level

☆☆☆ ③

He was originally a cool looking middle-aged guy, like an "amazing director must look like this"...

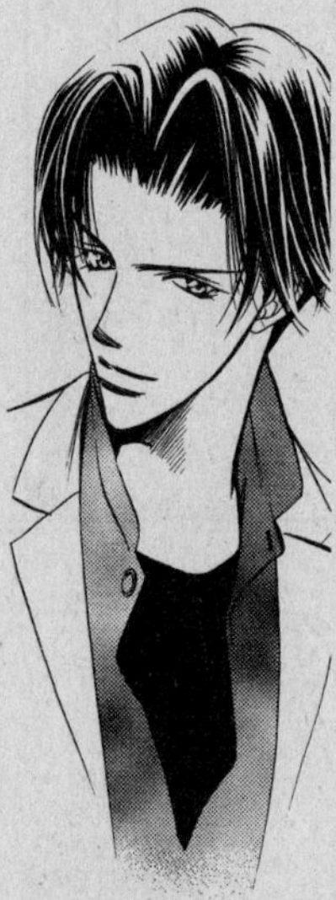

Well...because if you think about it logically, you can't be young and be well-known as a great director... that was what I'd thought... But in shojo manga, it seems to be useless to think logically like that...My editor promptly told me "Don't make him middle-aged" and his character design turned out this way...

Drooping eyes...that may be rare in a Nakamura manga...?

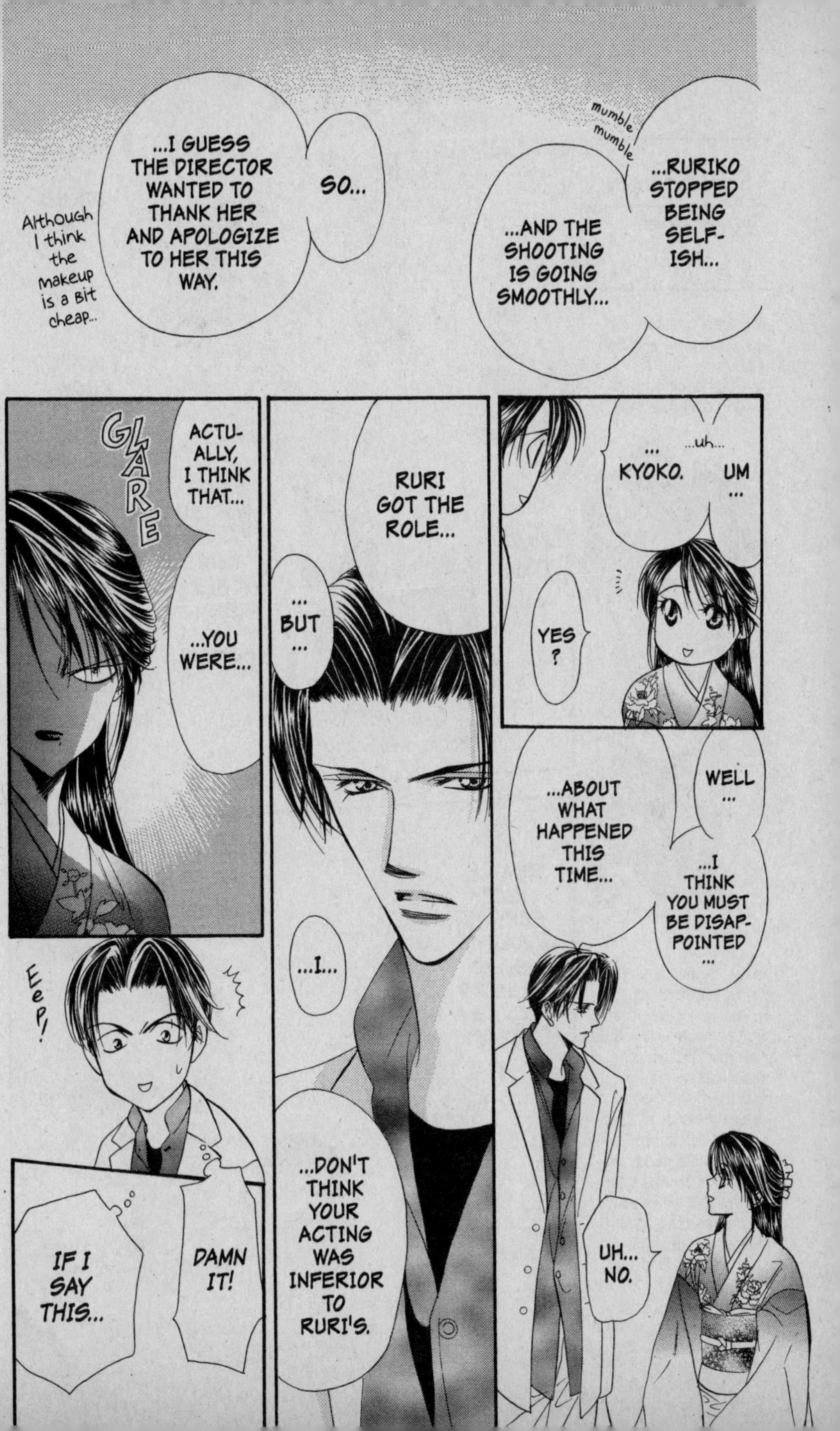
mumble mumble
...RURIKO STOPPED BEING SELF-ISH...
...AND THE SHOOTING IS GOING SMOOTHLY...
SO...
...I GUESS THE DIRECTOR WANTED TO THANK HER AND APOLOGIZE TO HER THIS WAY.
Although I think the makeup is a bit cheap...
UM ...
...uh...
... KYOKO.
YES ?
WELL ...
...ABOUT WHAT HAPPENED THIS TIME...
...I THINK YOU MUST BE DISAPPOINTED ...
UH... NO.
RURI GOT THE ROLE...
... BUT ...
...I...
...DON'T THINK YOUR ACTING WAS INFERIOR TO RURI'S.
ACTUALLY, I THINK THAT...
GLARE
...YOU WERE...
Eep!
DAMN IT!
IF I SAY THIS...

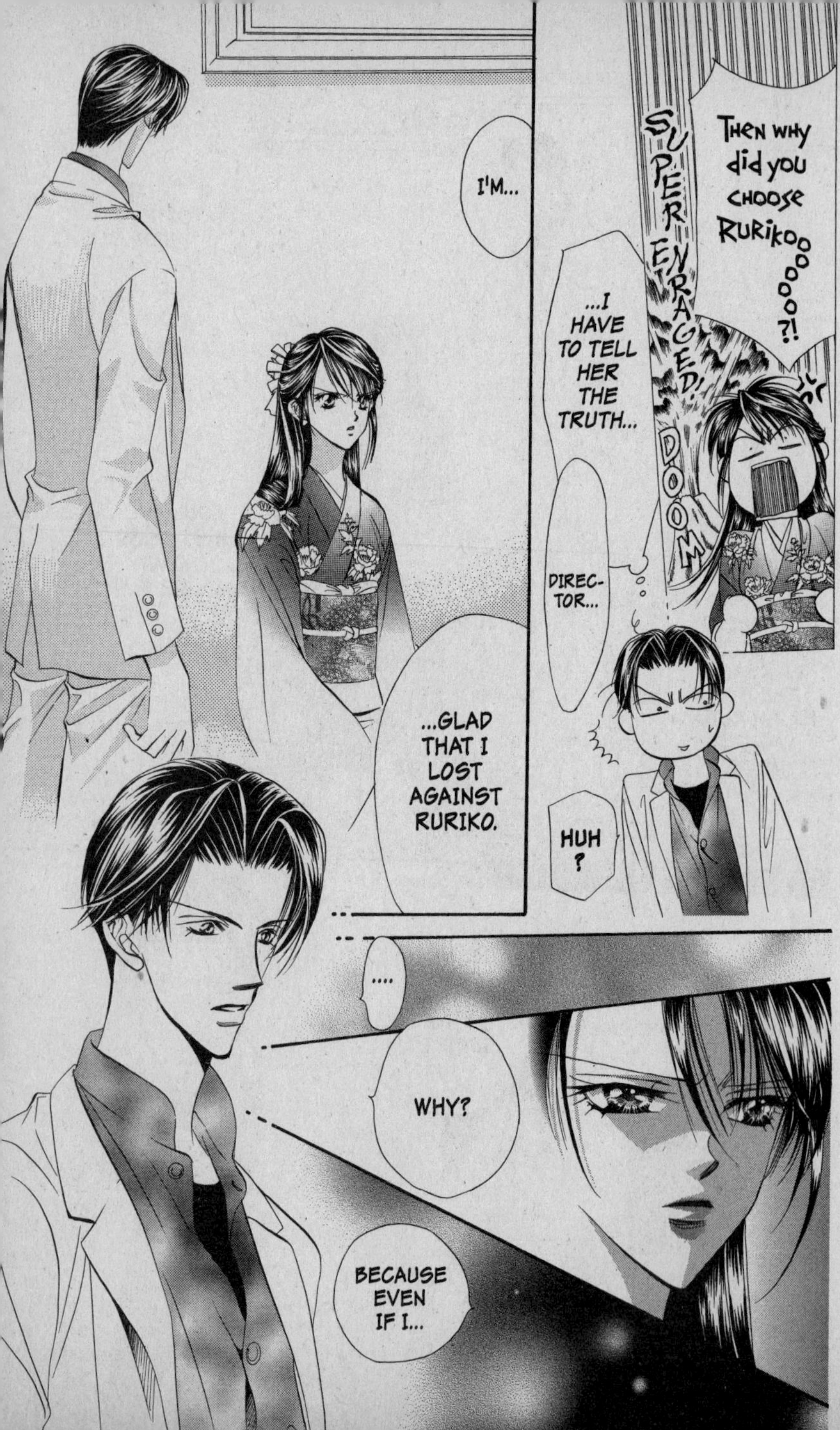
Then why did you choose Rurikooooooo?!
SUPER ENRAGED!
DOOM
...I HAVE TO TELL HER THE TRUTH...
DIREC-TOR...
HUH?
I'M...
...GLAD THAT I LOST AGAINST RURIKO.
....
WHY?
BECAUSE EVEN IF I...

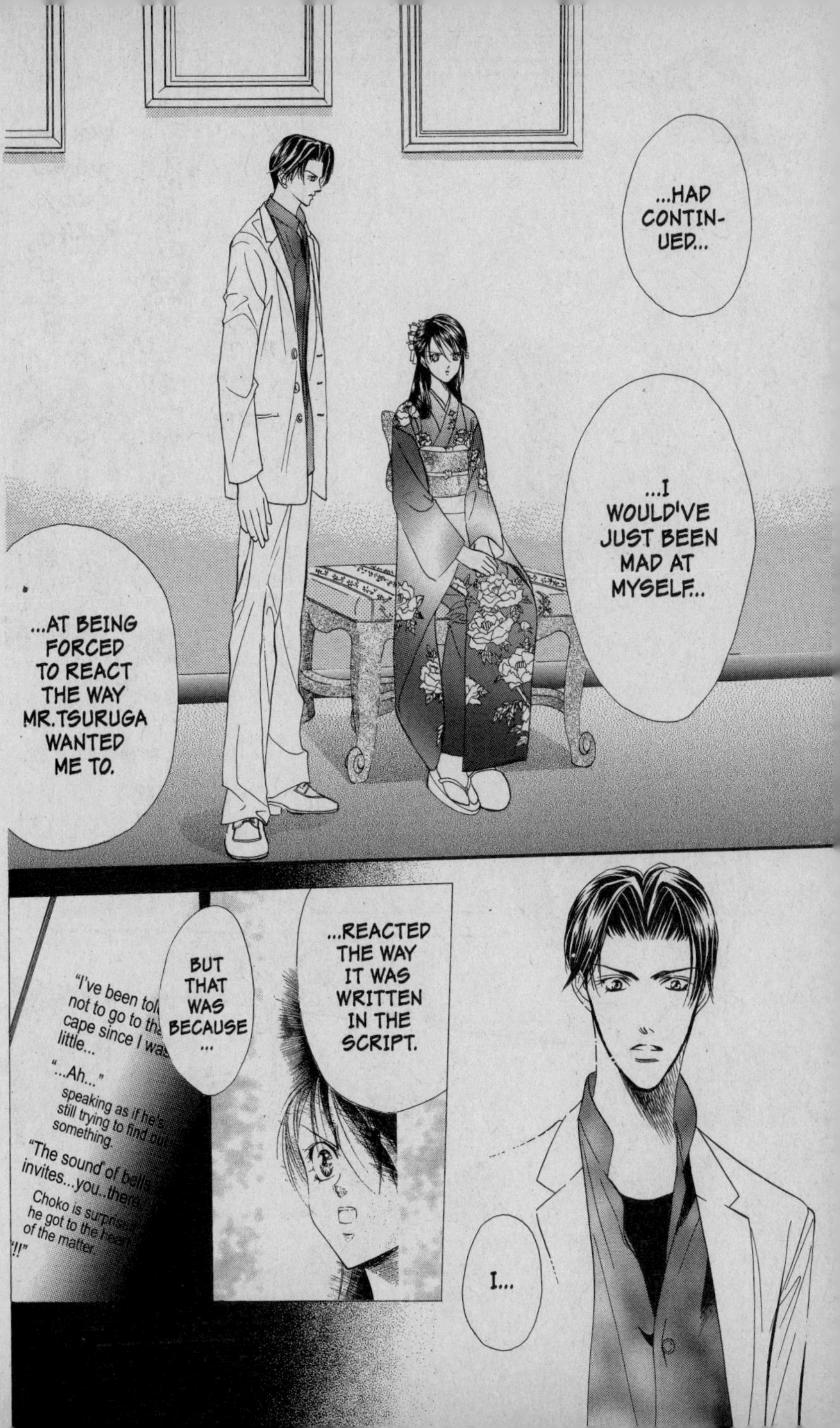
...HAD CONTIN-UED...
...I WOULD'VE JUST BEEN MAD AT MYSELF...
...AT BEING FORCED TO REACT THE WAY MR.TSURUGA WANTED ME TO.
I...
...REACTED THE WAY IT WAS WRITTEN IN THE SCRIPT.
BUT THAT WAS BECAUSE ...
“I've been tol
not to go to th
cape since I wa
little...
“...Ah...”
speaking as if he's
still trying to find ou
something.
“The sound of bell
invites...you..there
Choko is surprise
he got to the hear
of the matter.
!!”

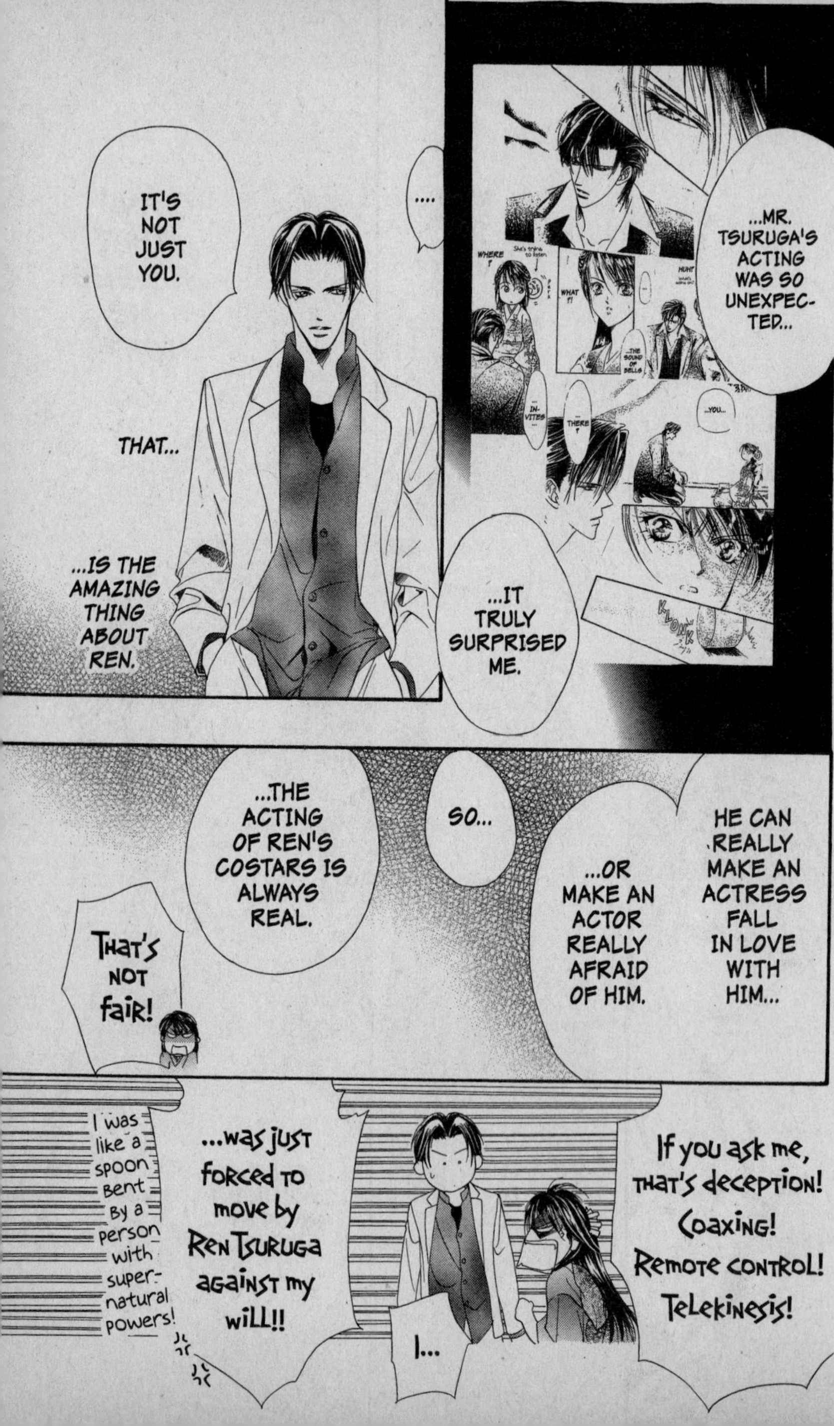
...MR. TSURUGA'S ACTING WAS SO UNEXPECTED...
HUH?
What's going on?
WHAT?!
WHERE?
She's trying to listen.
...THE SOUND OF BELLS
...INVITES...
...THERE?
...YOU...
KLONK
...IT TRULY SURPRISED ME.
....
IT'S NOT JUST YOU.
THAT...
...IS THE AMAZING THING ABOUT REN.
HE CAN REALLY MAKE AN ACTRESS FALL IN LOVE WITH HIM...
...OR MAKE AN ACTOR REALLY AFRAID OF HIM.
SO...
...THE ACTING OF REN'S COSTARS IS ALWAYS REAL.
That's not fair!
If you ask me, that's deception! Coaxing! Remote control! Telekinesis!
I...
...was just forced to move by Ren Tsuruga against my will!!
I was like a spoon bent by a person with super-natural powers!

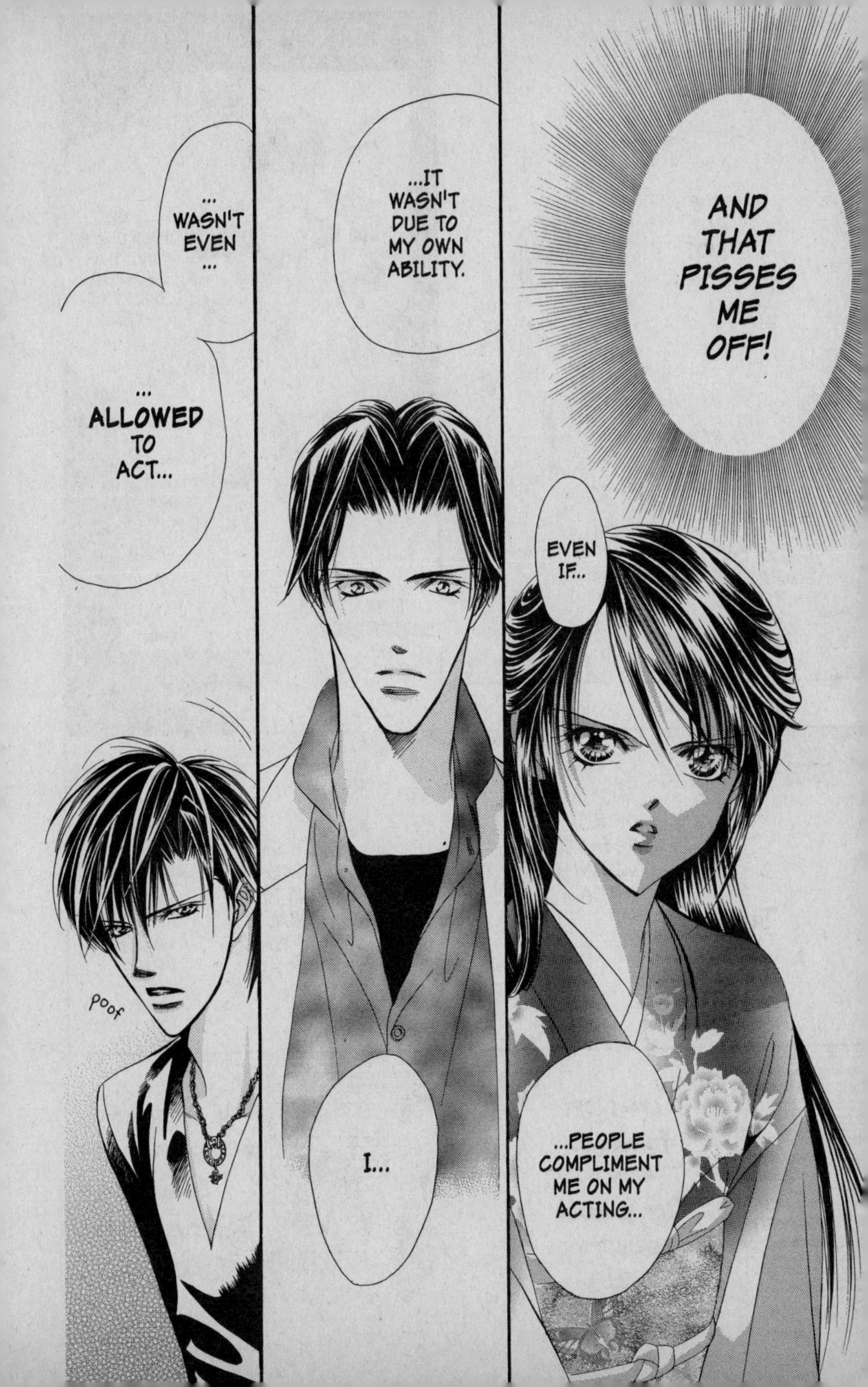
AND THAT PISSES ME OFF!
EVEN IF...
...PEOPLE COMPLIMENT ME ON MY ACTING...
...IT WASN'T DUE TO MY OWN ABILITY.
I...
... WASN'T EVEN ...
... ALLOWED TO ACT...
poof

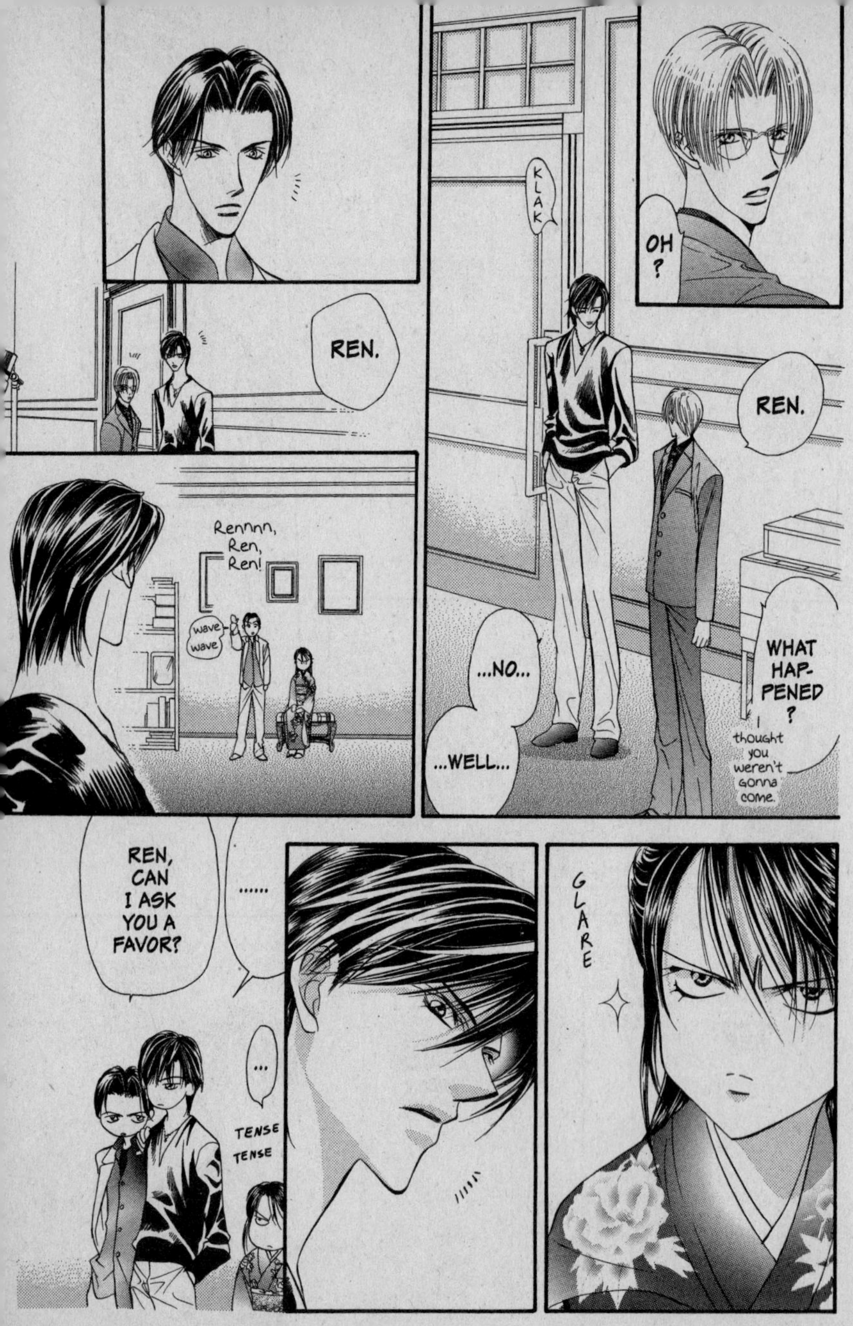
KLAK
OH?
REN.
WHAT HAPPENED?
I thought you weren't gonna come.
...NO...
...WELL...
REN.
Rennnn, Ren, Ren!
wave wave
GLARE
REN, CAN I ASK YOU A FAVOR?
......
...
TENSE TENSE

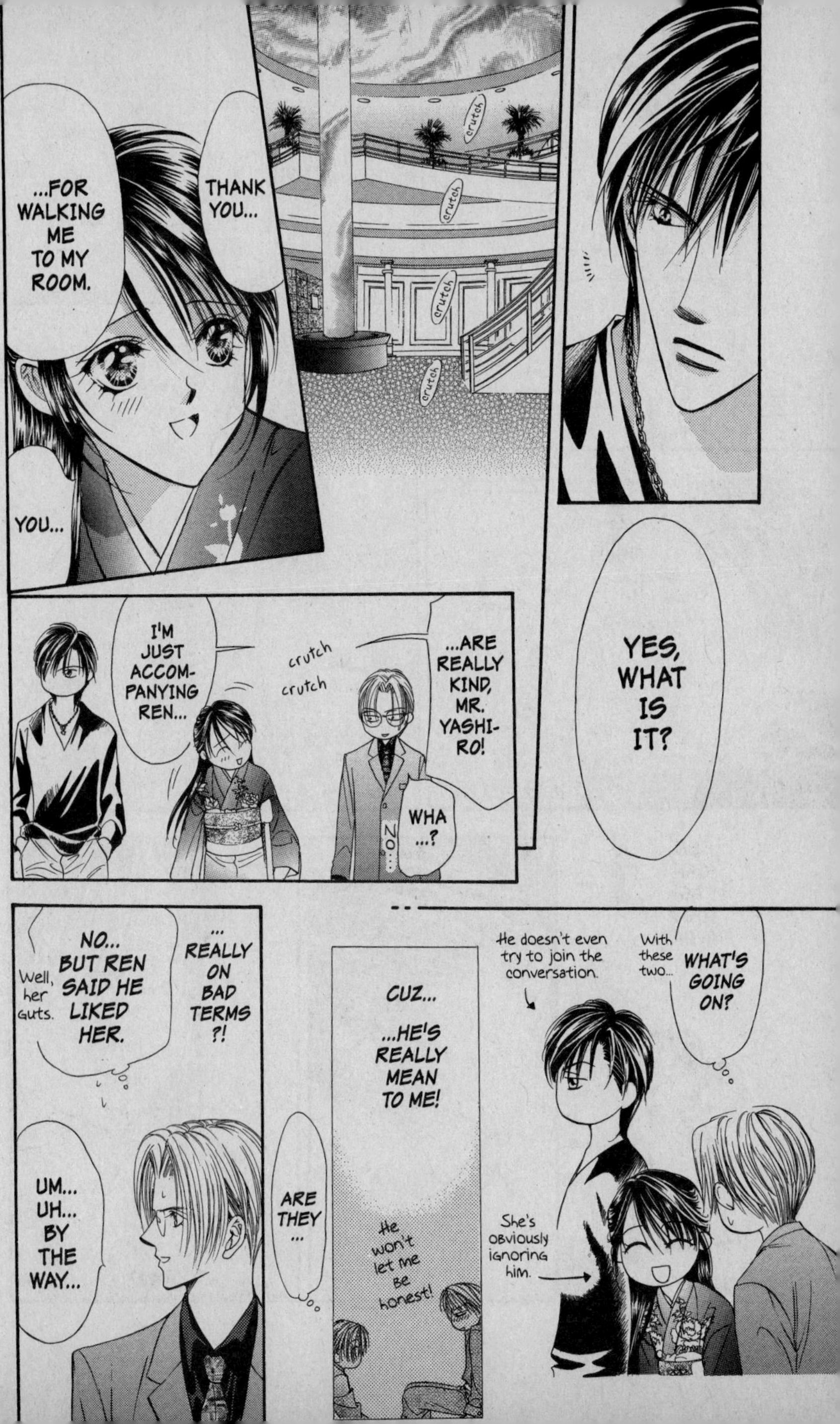
YES, WHAT IS IT?
crutch
crutch
crutch
crutch
THANK YOU...
...FOR WALKING ME TO MY ROOM.
YOU...
...ARE REALLY KIND, MR. YASHIRO!
WHA ...?
NO...
crutch
crutch
I'M JUST ACCOMPANYING REN...
WHAT'S GOING ON?
With these two...
He doesn't even try to join the conversation.
She's obviously ignoring him.
CUZ...
...HE'S REALLY MEAN TO ME!
He won't let me be honest!
ARE THEY...
...REALLY ON BAD TERMS?!
NO... BUT REN SAID HE LIKED HER.
Well, her guts.
UM... UH... BY THE WAY...

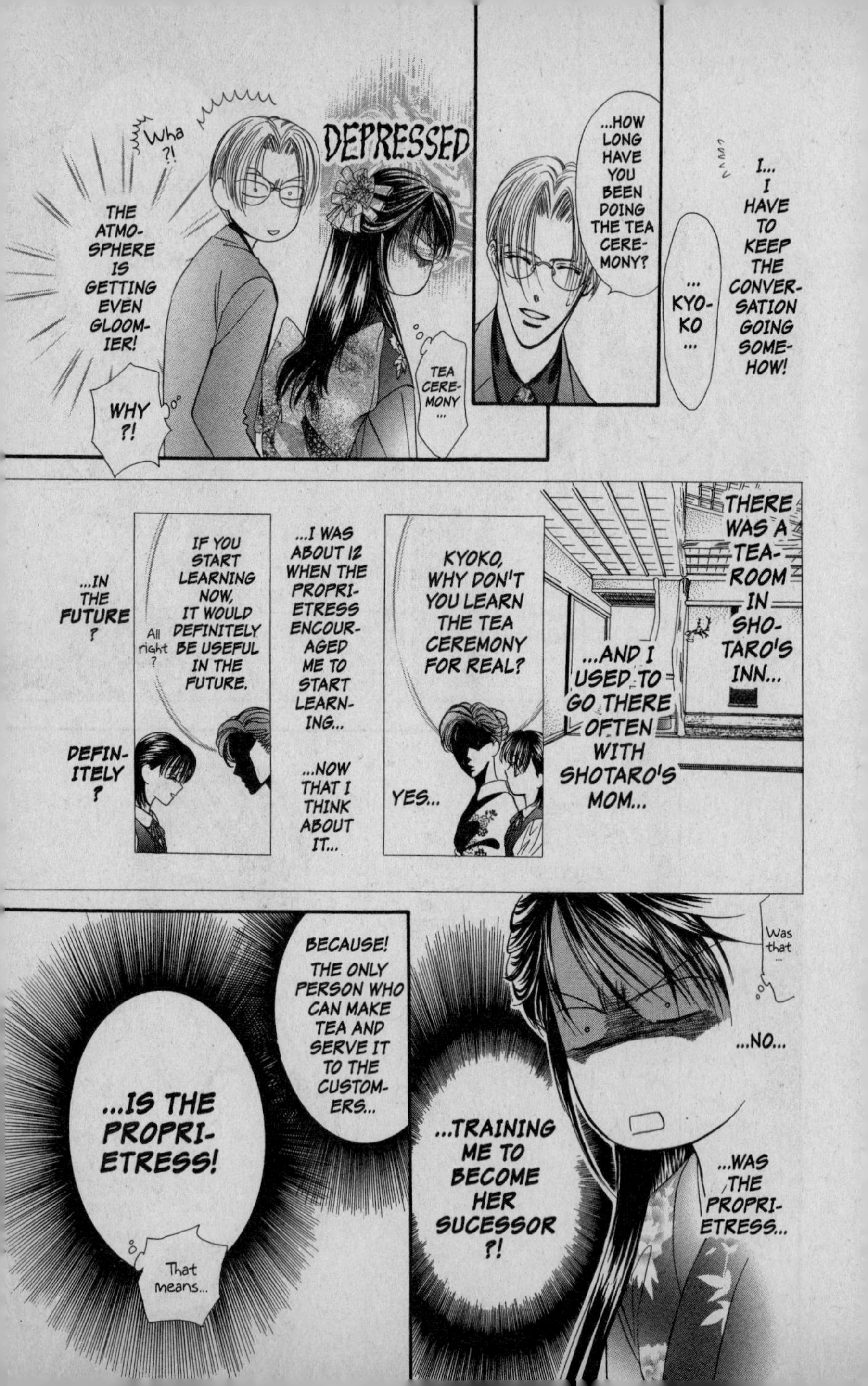
I... I HAVE TO KEEP THE CONVERSATION GOING SOMEHOW!
...KYOKO...
...HOW LONG HAVE YOU BEEN DOING THE TEA CEREMONY?
DEPRESSED
TEA CEREMONY...
Wha?!
THE ATMOSPHERE IS GETTING EVEN GLOOMIER!
WHY?!
THERE WAS A TEAROOM IN SHOTARO'S INN...
...AND I USED TO GO THERE OFTEN WITH SHOTARO'S MOM...
KYOKO, WHY DON'T YOU LEARN THE TEA CEREMONY FOR REAL?
YES...
...I WAS ABOUT 12 WHEN THE PROPRIETRESS ENCOURAGED ME TO START LEARNING...
...NOW THAT I THINK ABOUT IT...
IF YOU START LEARNING NOW, IT WOULD DEFINITELY BE USEFUL IN THE FUTURE.
All right?
...IN THE FUTURE?
DEFINITELY?
Was that...
...NO...
...WAS THE PROPRIETRESS...
...TRAINING ME TO BECOME HER SUCESSOR?!
BECAUSE! THE ONLY PERSON WHO CAN MAKE TEA AND SERVE IT TO THE CUSTOMERS...
...IS THE PROPRIETRESS!
That means...

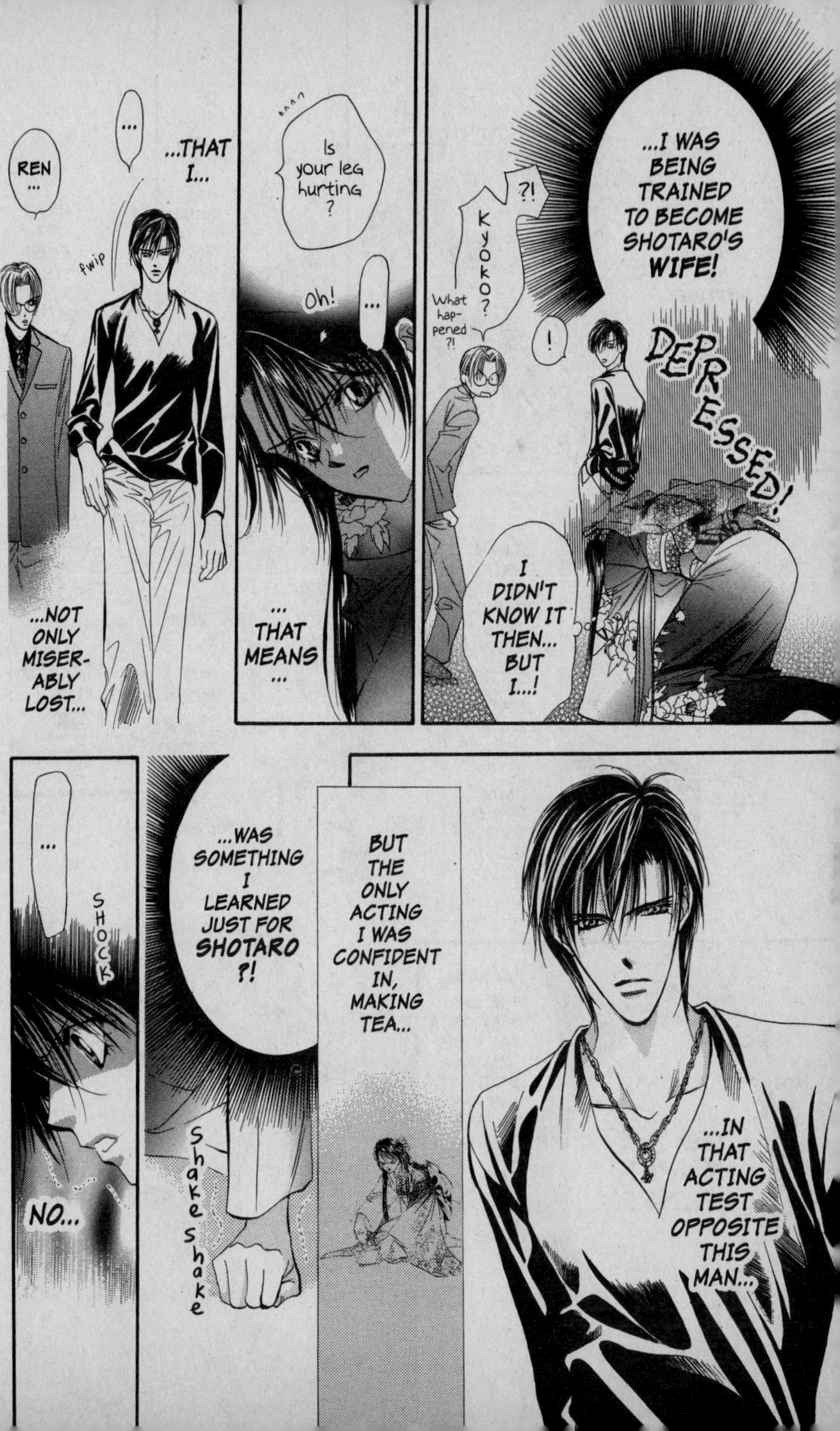
...I WAS BEING TRAINED TO BECOME SHOTARO'S WIFE!
DEPRESSED!
?!
KYOKO?
What hap-pened ?!
!
I DIDN'T KNOW IT THEN... BUT I...!
Is your leg hurting ?
Oh!
...
... THAT MEANS ...
...THAT I...
...
REN ...
fwip
...NOT ONLY MISER-ABLY LOST...
...IN THAT ACTING TEST OPPOSITE THIS MAN...
BUT THE ONLY ACTING I WAS CONFIDENT IN, MAKING TEA...
...WAS SOMETHING I LEARNED JUST FOR SHOTARO ?!
Shake Shake
...
SHOCK
NO...

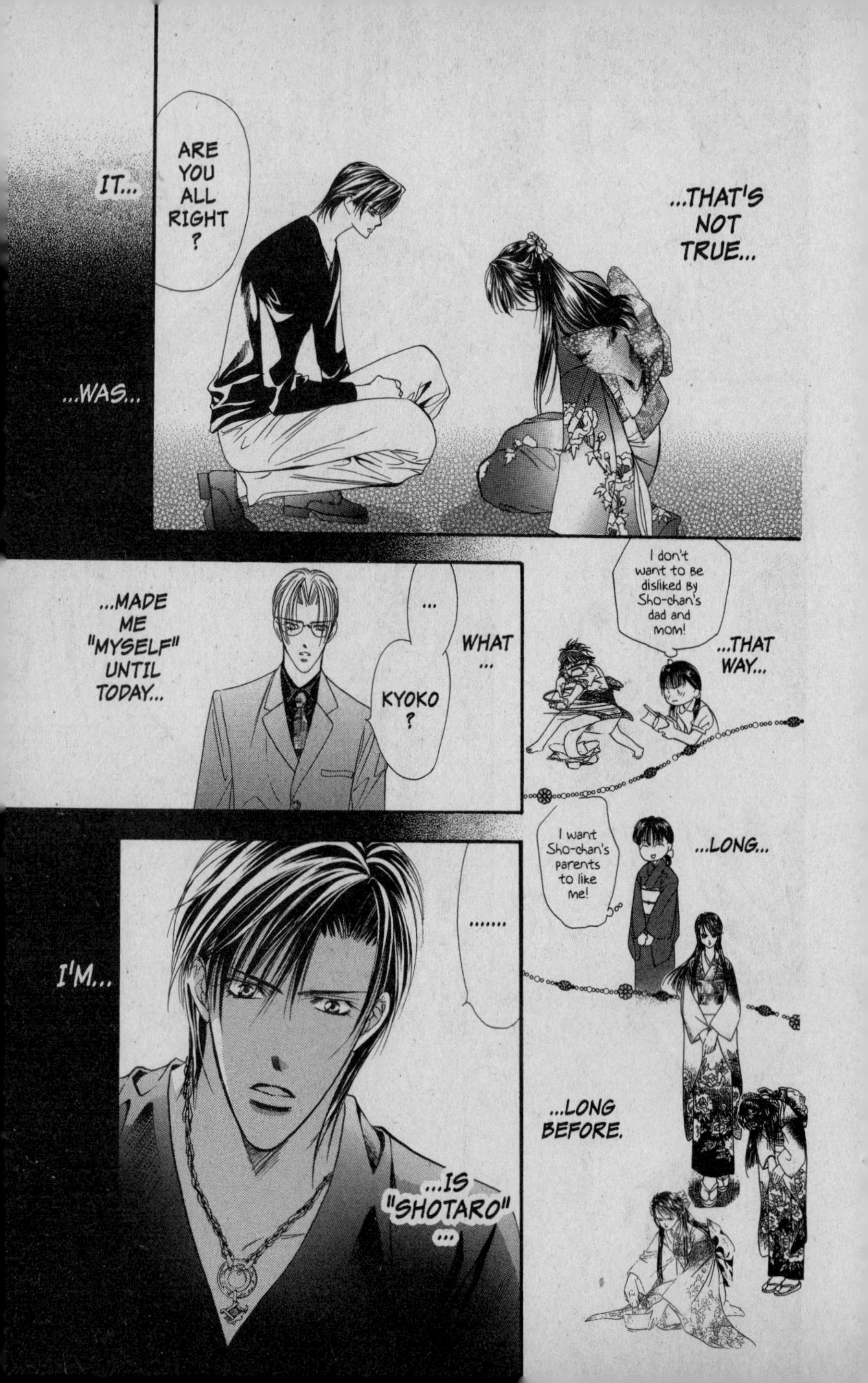
...THAT'S NOT TRUE...
ARE YOU ALL RIGHT?
IT...
...WAS...
I don't want to be disliked by Sho-chan's dad and mom!
...THAT WAY...
I want Sho-chan's parents to like me!
...LONG...
...LONG BEFORE.
WHAT... KYOKO?
...
...MADE ME "MYSELF" UNTIL TODAY...
....
I'M...
...IS "SHOTARO"...

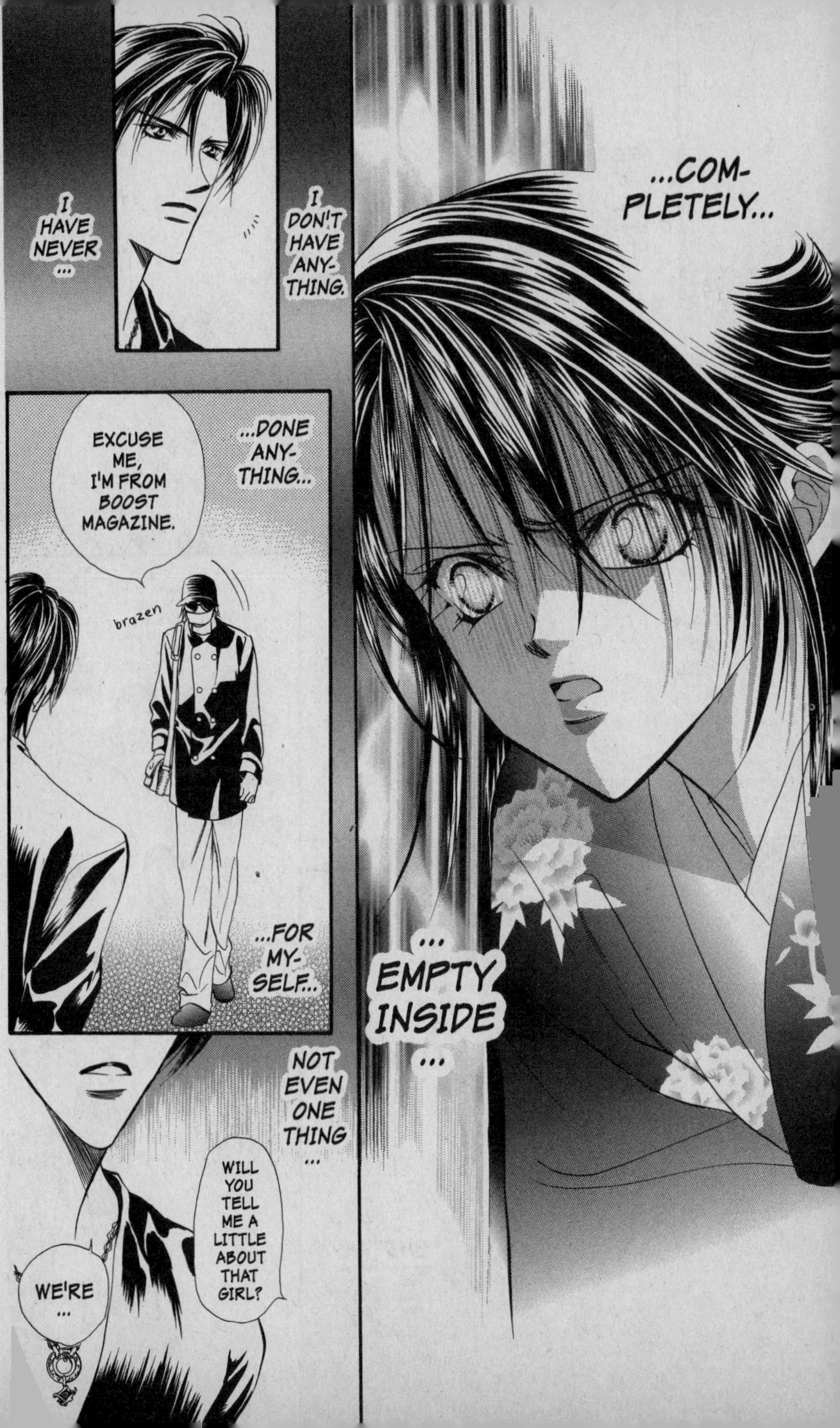
...COM-PLETELY...
... EMPTY INSIDE ...
I DON'T HAVE ANY-THING.
I HAVE NEVER ...
...DONE ANY-THING...
EXCUSE ME, I'M FROM BOOST MAGAZINE.
brazen
...FOR MY-SELF...
NOT EVEN ONE THING ...
WILL YOU TELL ME A LITTLE ABOUT THAT GIRL?
WE'RE ...

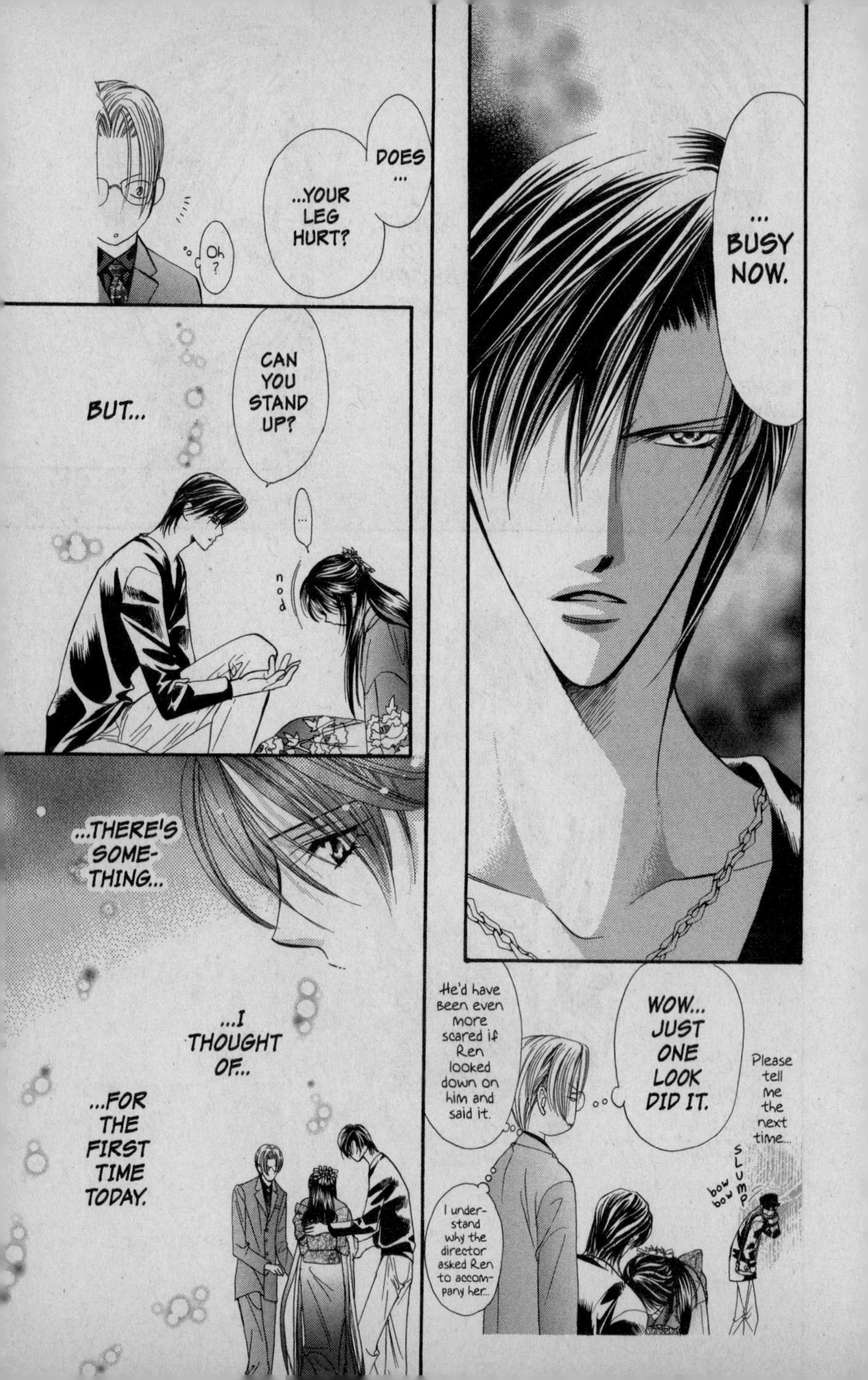
... BUSY NOW.
Please tell me the next time...
WOW... JUST ONE LOOK DID IT.
He'd have been even more scared if Ren looked down on him and said it.
SLUMP
bow bow
I under-stand why the director asked Ren to accompany her...
DOES ...
...YOUR LEG HURT?
Oh?
CAN YOU STAND UP?
BUT...
...
nod
...THERE'S SOME-THING...
...I THOUGHT OF...
...FOR THE FIRST TIME TODAY.

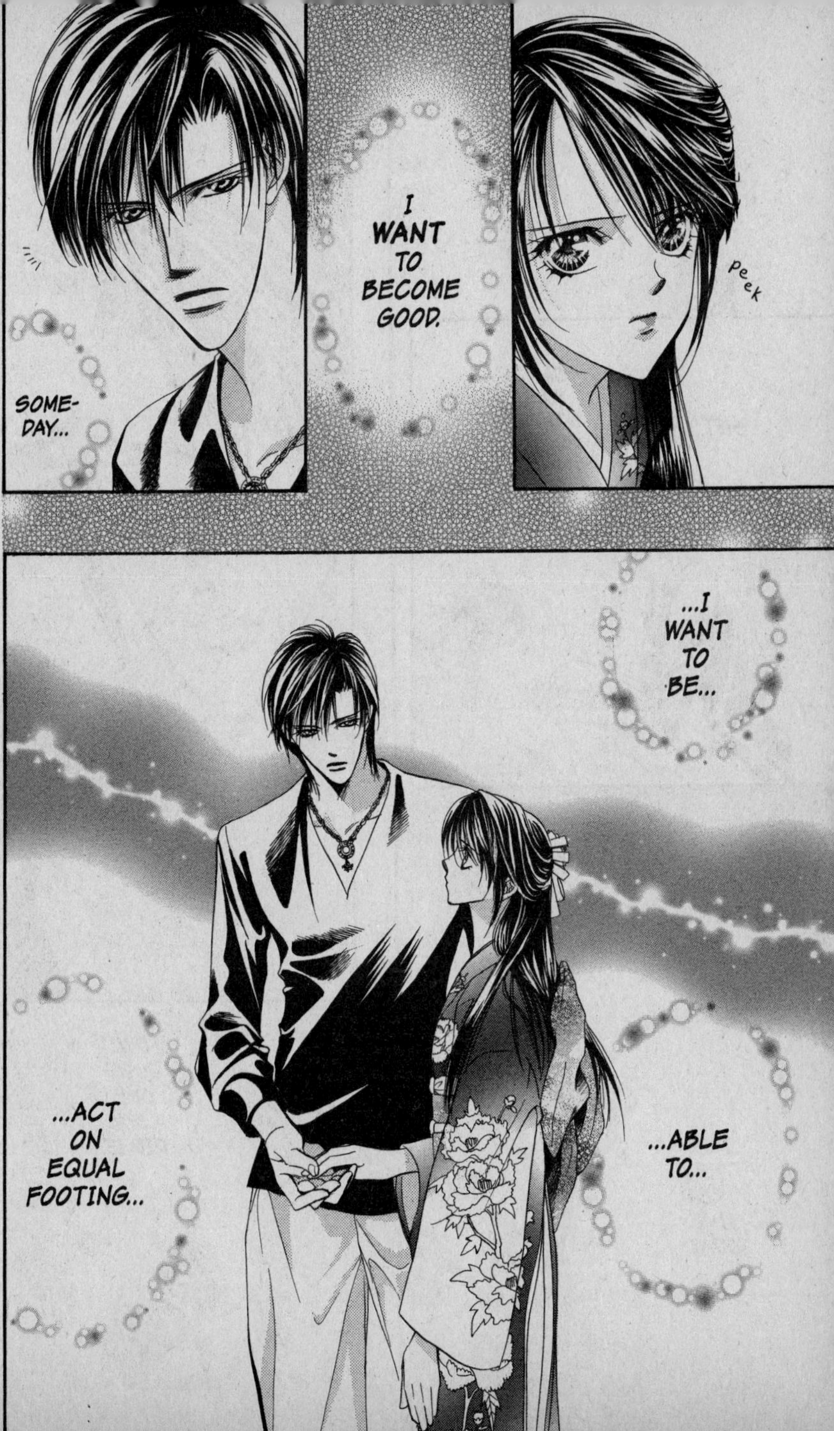
peek
I WANT TO BECOME GOOD.
SOME-DAY...
...I WANT TO BE...
...ABLE TO...
...ACT ON EQUAL FOOTING...

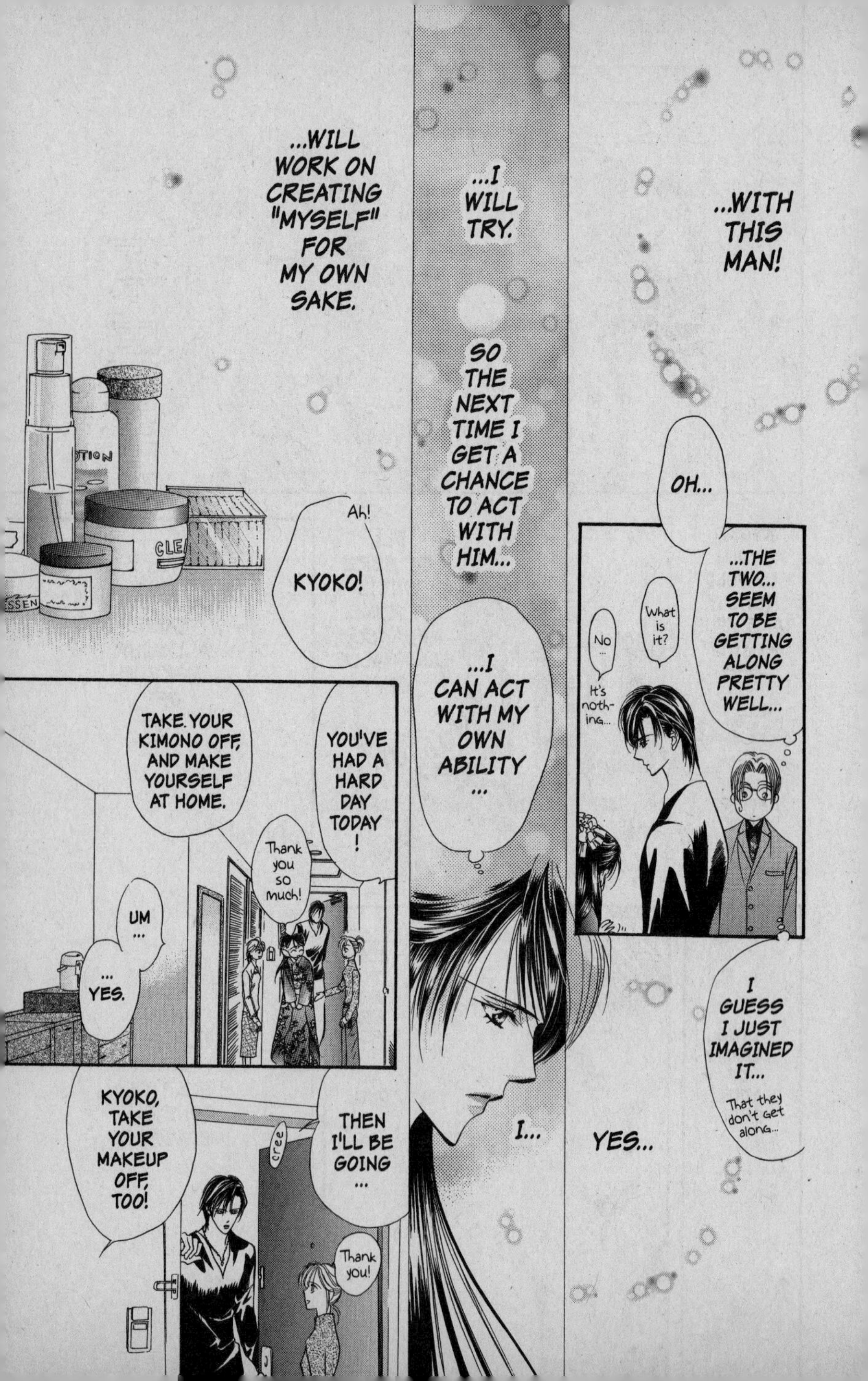
...WITH THIS MAN!
OH...
...THE TWO... SEEM TO BE GETTING ALONG PRETTY WELL...
What is it?
No... It's nothing...
I GUESS I JUST IMAGINED IT...
That they don't get along...
YES...
...I WILL TRY.
SO THE NEXT TIME I GET A CHANCE TO ACT WITH HIM...
...I CAN ACT WITH MY OWN ABILITY...
I...
...WILL WORK ON CREATING "MYSELF" FOR MY OWN SAKE.
Ah!
KYOKO!
YOU'VE HAD A HARD DAY TODAY!
TAKE YOUR KIMONO OFF, AND MAKE YOURSELF AT HOME.
Thank you so much!
UM...
...YES.
THEN I'LL BE GOING...
cree
KYOKO, TAKE YOUR MAKEUP OFF, TOO!
Thank you!

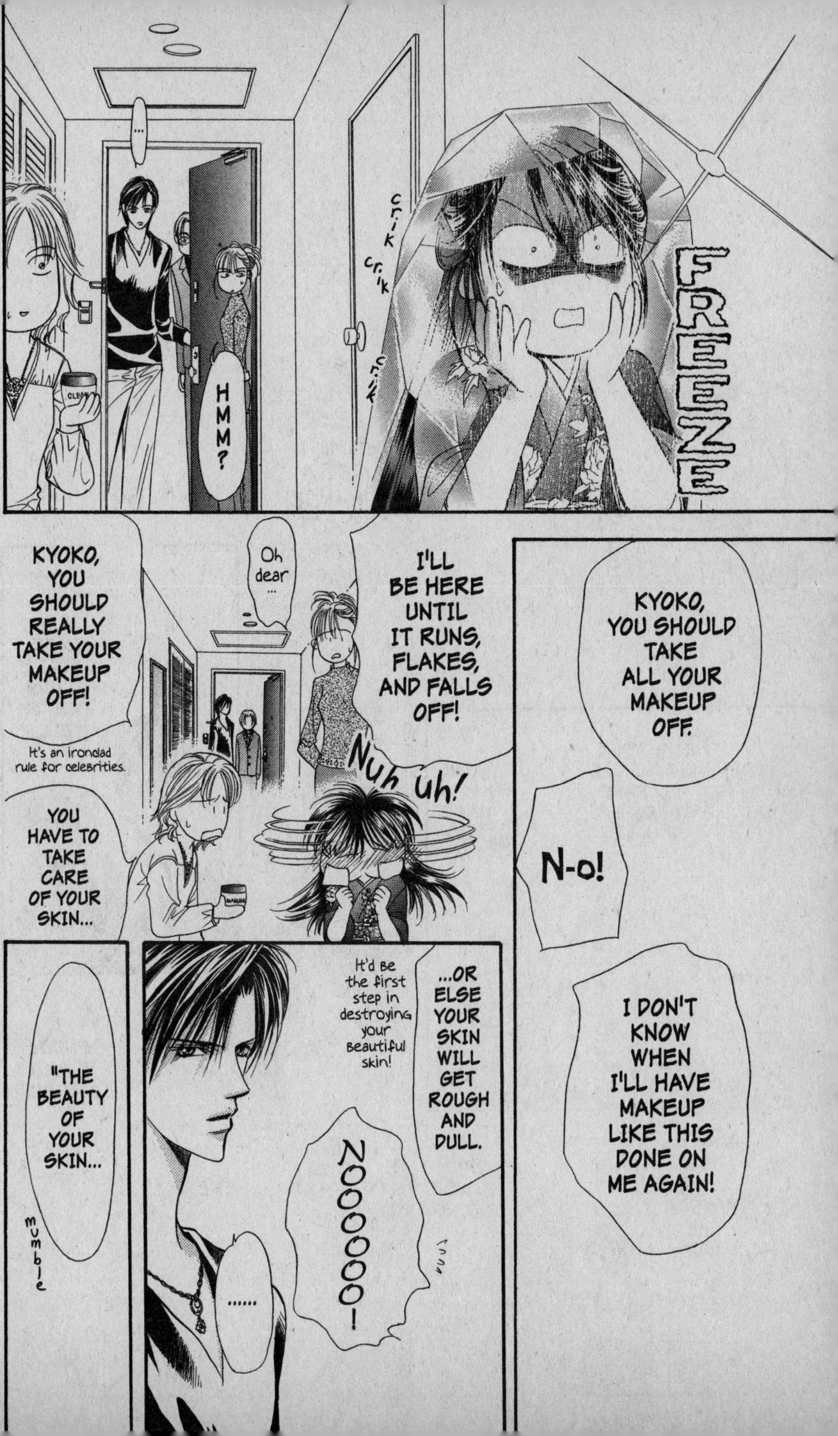
crik
crik
crik
FREEZE
...
HMM?
KYOKO, YOU SHOULD TAKE ALL YOUR MAKEUP OFF.
N-o!
I DON'T KNOW WHEN I'LL HAVE MAKEUP LIKE THIS DONE ON ME AGAIN!
I'LL BE HERE UNTIL IT RUNS, FLAKES, AND FALLS OFF!
Oh dear...
Nuh uh!
KYOKO, YOU SHOULD REALLY TAKE YOUR MAKEUP OFF!
It's an ironclad rule for celebrities.
YOU HAVE TO TAKE CARE OF YOUR SKIN...
...OR ELSE YOUR SKIN WILL GET ROUGH AND DULL.
It'd be the first step in destroying your beautiful skin!
NOOOOOOO!
......
"THE BEAUTY OF YOUR SKIN...
mumble

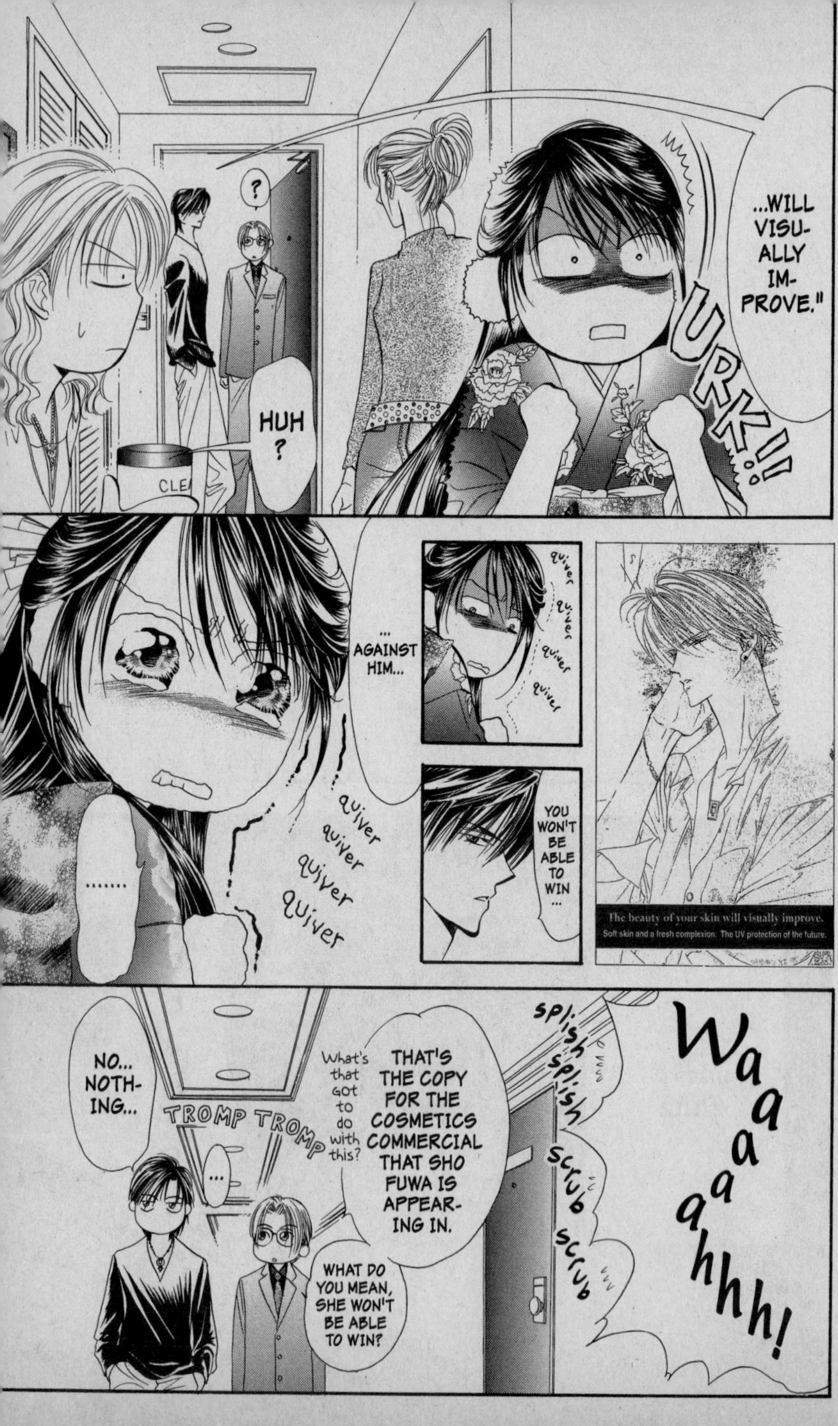
...WILL VISUALLY IMPROVE."
URK!!
?
HUH?
The beauty of your skin will visually improve.
Soft skin and a fresh complexion. The UV protection of the future.
quiver quiver quiver quiver
YOU WON'T BE ABLE TO WIN...
...AGAINST HIM...
quiver quiver quiver quiver
....
Waaaaaahhhh!
splish splish
scrub scrub
THAT'S THE COPY FOR THE COSMETICS COMMERCIAL THAT SHO FUWA IS APPEARING IN.
What's that got to do with this?
NO... NOTHING...
TROMP TROMP
...
WHAT DO YOU MEAN, SHE WON'T BE ABLE TO WIN?

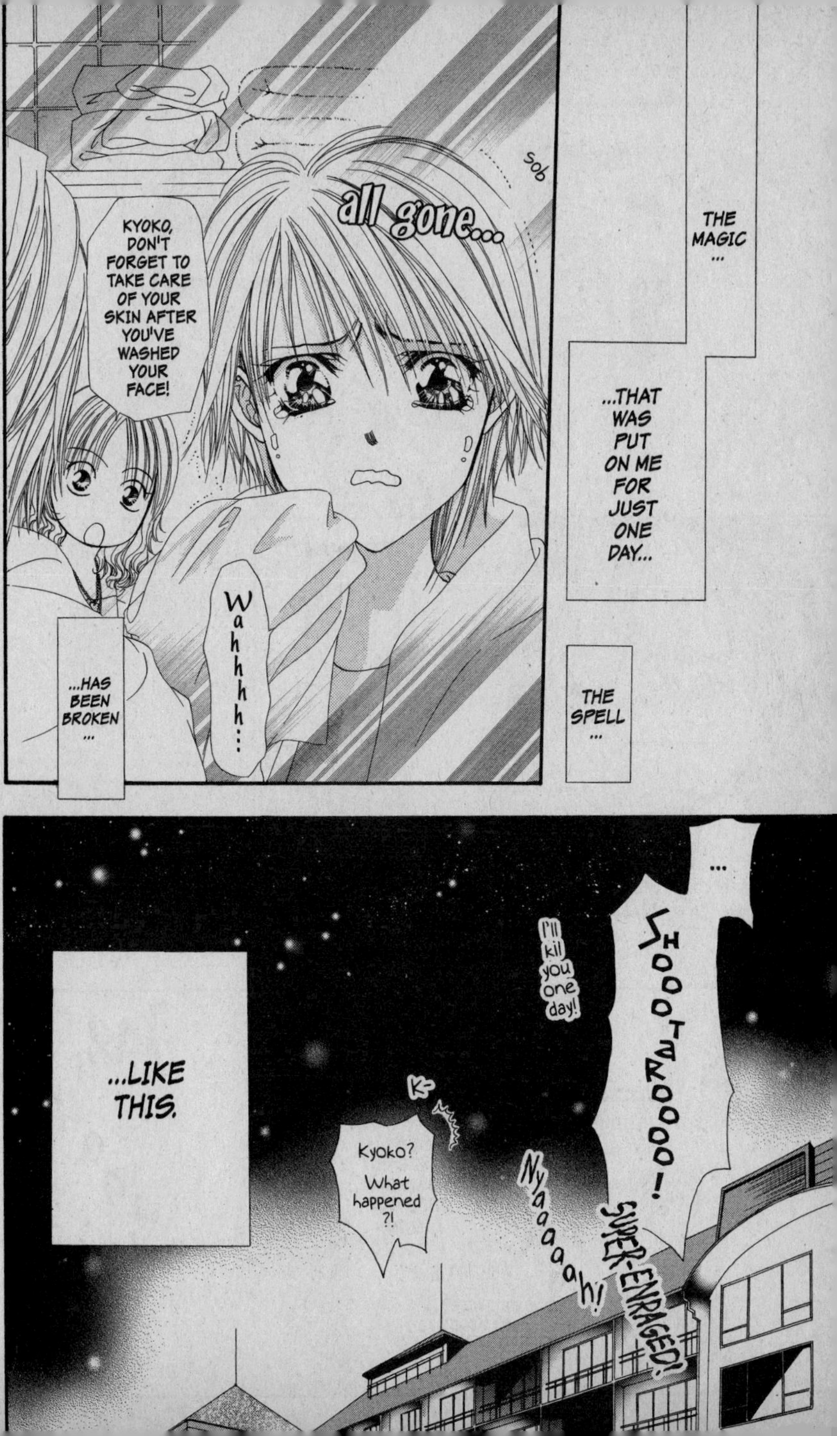
THE MAGIC...
...THAT WAS PUT ON ME FOR JUST ONE DAY...
sob
all gone...
KYOKO, DON'T FORGET TO TAKE CARE OF YOUR SKIN AFTER YOU'VE WASHED YOUR FACE!
THE SPELL...
Wahhhh...
...HAS BEEN BROKEN...
...
SHOOOTAROOOOO!
SUPER-ENRAGED!
I'll kil you one day!
Nyaaaaah!
K-
Kyoko? What happened?!
...LIKE THIS.

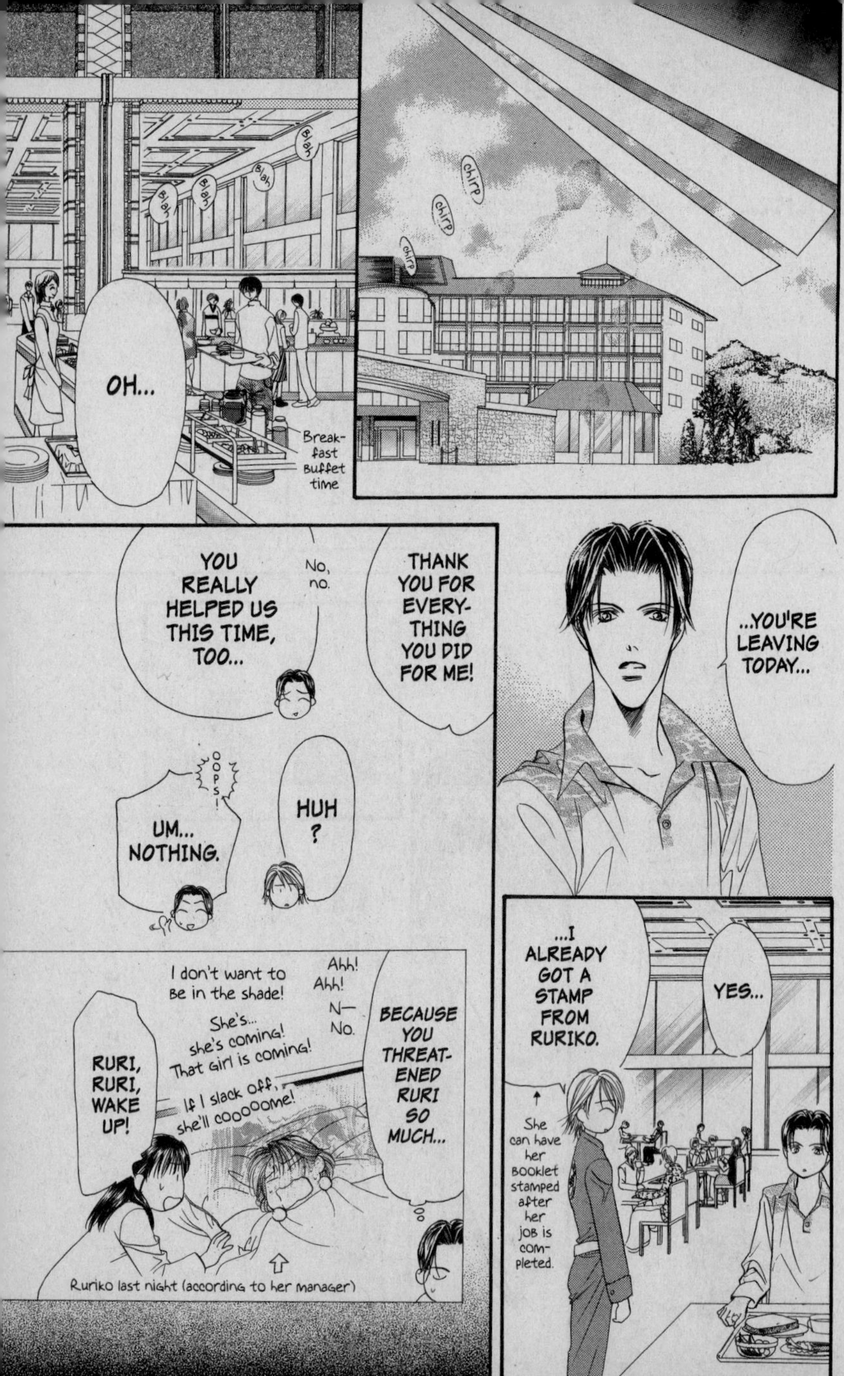
chirp
chirp
chirp
Blah
Blah
Blah
Blah
OH...
Break-fast Buffet time
...YOU'RE LEAVING TODAY...
THANK YOU FOR EVERY-THING YOU DID FOR ME!
No, no.
YOU REALLY HELPED US THIS TIME, TOO...
HUH?
OOPS!
UM... NOTHING.
YES...
...I ALREADY GOT A STAMP FROM RURIKO.
She can have her booklet stamped after her job is com-pleted.
BECAUSE YOU THREAT-ENED RURI SO MUCH...
Ahh! Ahh! N— No.
I don't want to be in the shade!
She's... she's coming! That girl is coming!
If I slack off, she'll cooooome!
RURI, RURI, WAKE UP!
Ruriko last night (according to her manager)

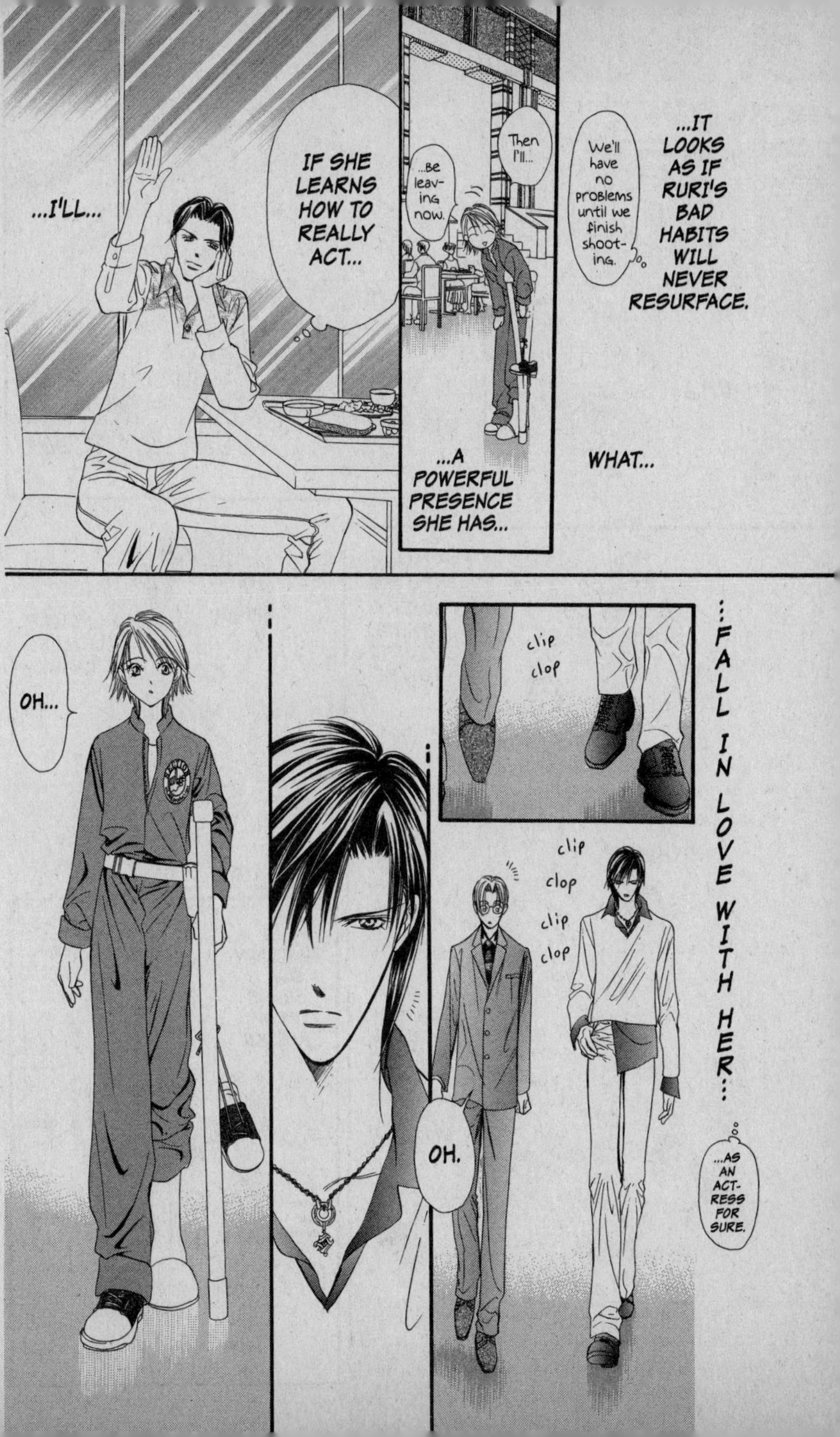
...IT LOOKS AS IF RURI'S BAD HABITS WILL NEVER RESURFACE.
We'll have no problems until we finish shoot-ing.
Then I'll...
...Be leav-ing now.
WHAT...
...A POWERFUL PRESENCE SHE HAS...
IF SHE LEARNS HOW TO REALLY ACT...
...I'LL...
...FALL IN LOVE WITH HER...
...AS AN ACT-RESS FOR SURE.
clip clop
clip clop clip clop
OH.
OH...

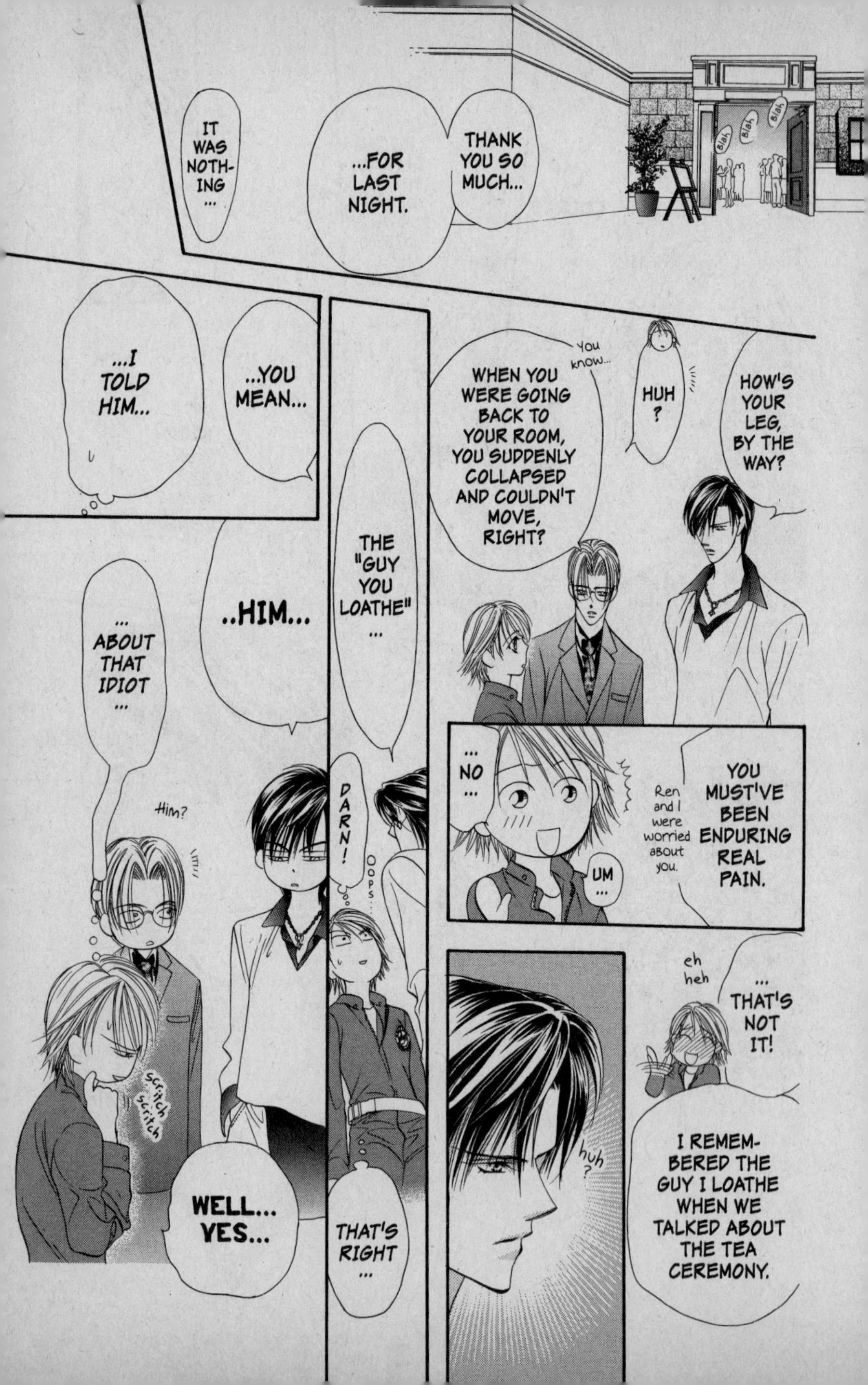
Blah
Blah
Blah
THANK YOU SO MUCH...
...FOR LAST NIGHT.
IT WAS NOTHING...
HOW'S YOUR LEG, BY THE WAY?
HUH?
You know...
WHEN YOU WERE GOING BACK TO YOUR ROOM, YOU SUDDENLY COLLAPSED AND COULDN'T MOVE, RIGHT?
YOU MUST'VE BEEN ENDURING REAL PAIN.
Ren and I were worried about you.
UM...
...NO...
...THAT'S NOT IT!
eh heh
I REMEMBERED THE GUY I LOATHE WHEN WE TALKED ABOUT THE TEA CEREMONY.
huh?
THE "GUY YOU LOATHE"...
DARN!
Oops...
THAT'S RIGHT...
...YOU MEAN...
...I TOLD HIM...
..HIM...
...ABOUT THAT IDIOT...
Him?
WELL... YES...
scritch scritch

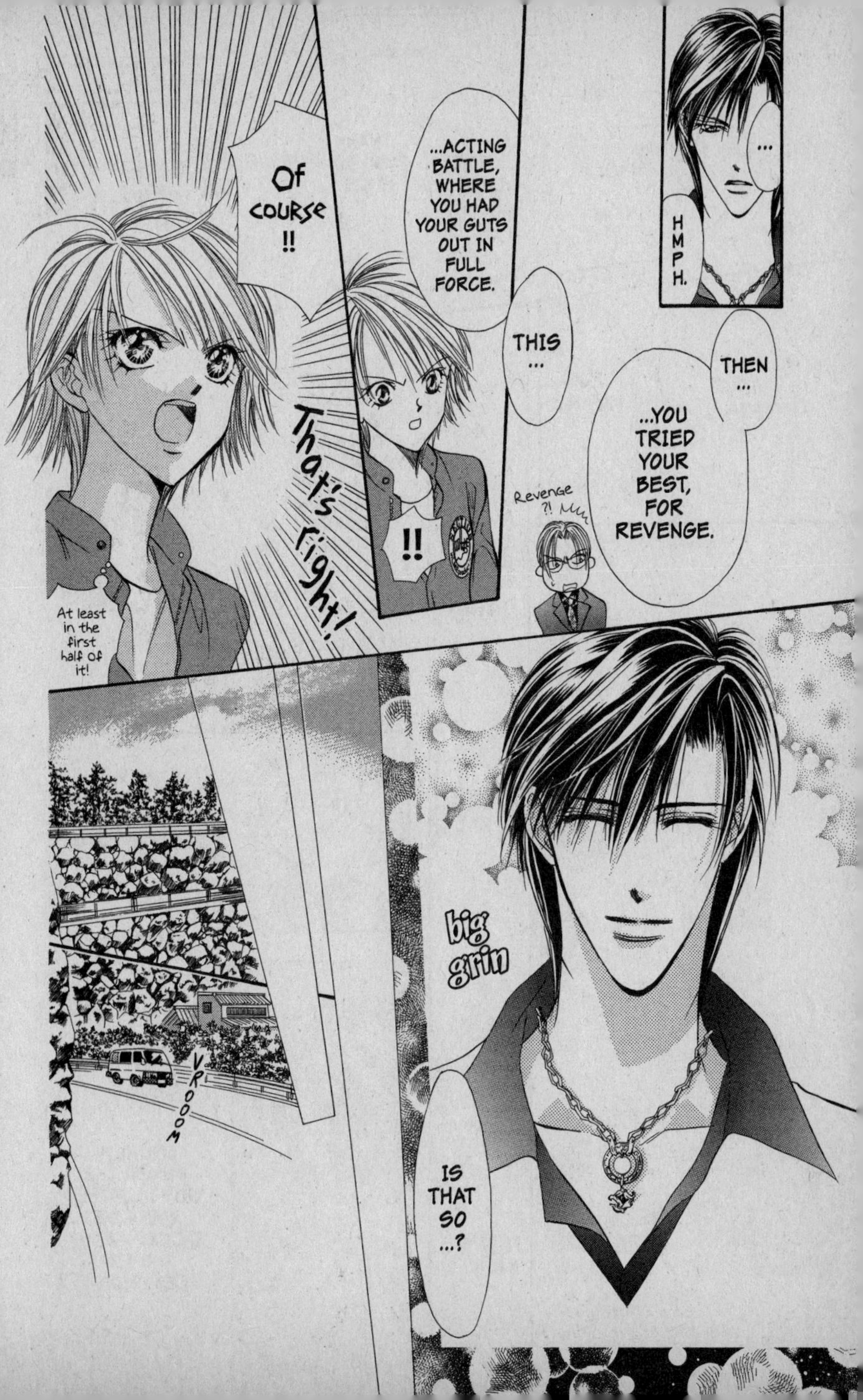
...
HMPH.
THEN ...
...YOU TRIED YOUR BEST, FOR REVENGE.
Revenge ?!
THIS ...
...ACTING BATTLE, WHERE YOU HAD YOUR GUTS OUT IN FULL FORCE.
!!
Of course !!
That's right!
At least in the first half of it!
big grin
IS THAT SO ...?
VROOOOM

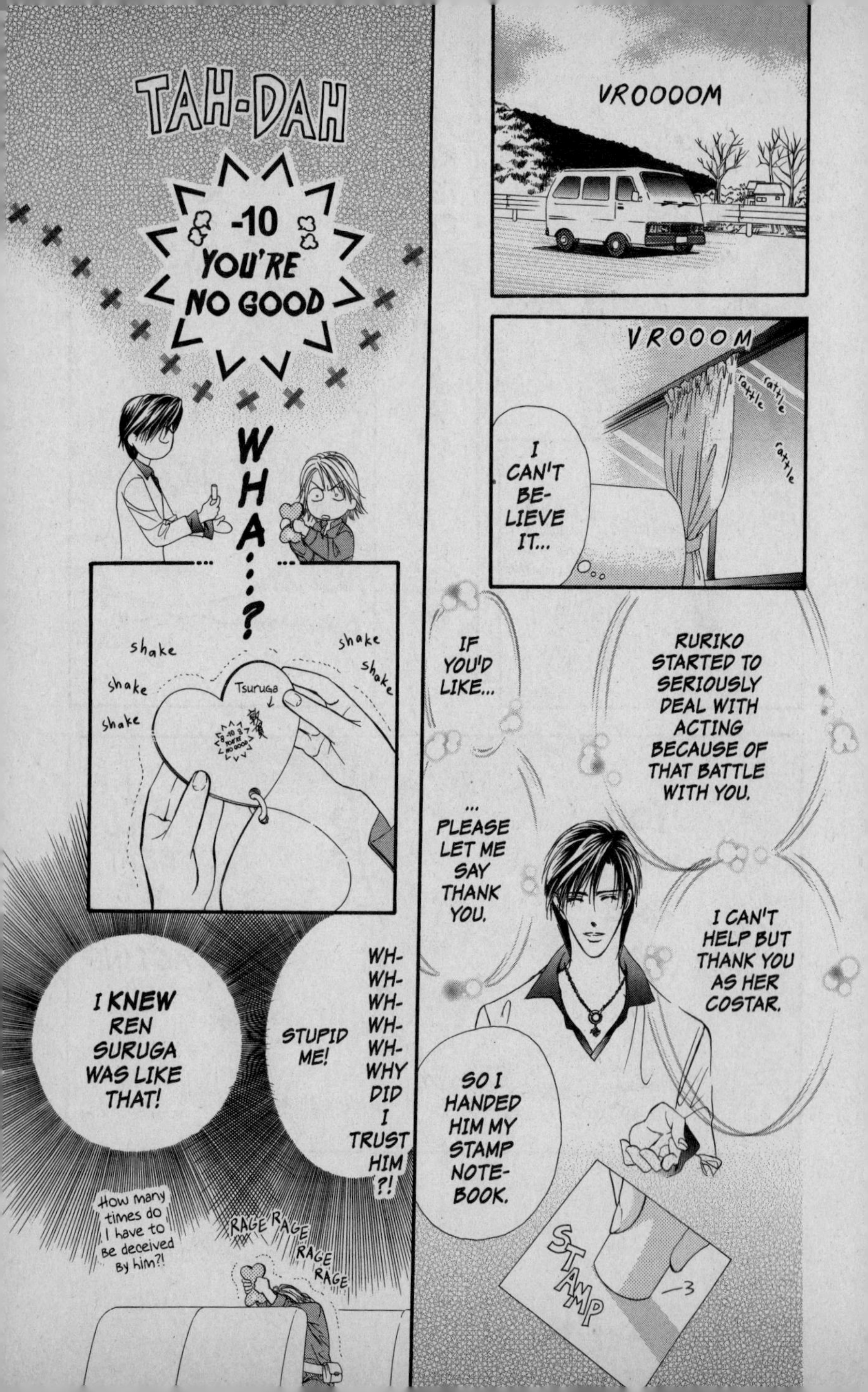
VROOOOM
VROOOM
rattle rattle
rattle
I CAN'T BE-LIEVE IT...
RURIKO STARTED TO SERIOUSLY DEAL WITH ACTING BECAUSE OF THAT BATTLE WITH YOU.
I CAN'T HELP BUT THANK YOU AS HER COSTAR.
IF YOU'D LIKE...
...PLEASE LET ME SAY THANK YOU.
SO I HANDED HIM MY STAMP NOTE-BOOK.
STAMP
TAH-DAH
-10 YOU'RE NO GOOD
WHA...?
shake
shake
shake
shake
shake
Tsuruga
WH-WH-WH-WH-WH-WHY DID I TRUST HIM?!
STUPID ME!
I KNEW REN SURUGA WAS LIKE THAT!
How many times do I have to be deceived by him?!
RAGE RAGE RAGE RAGE

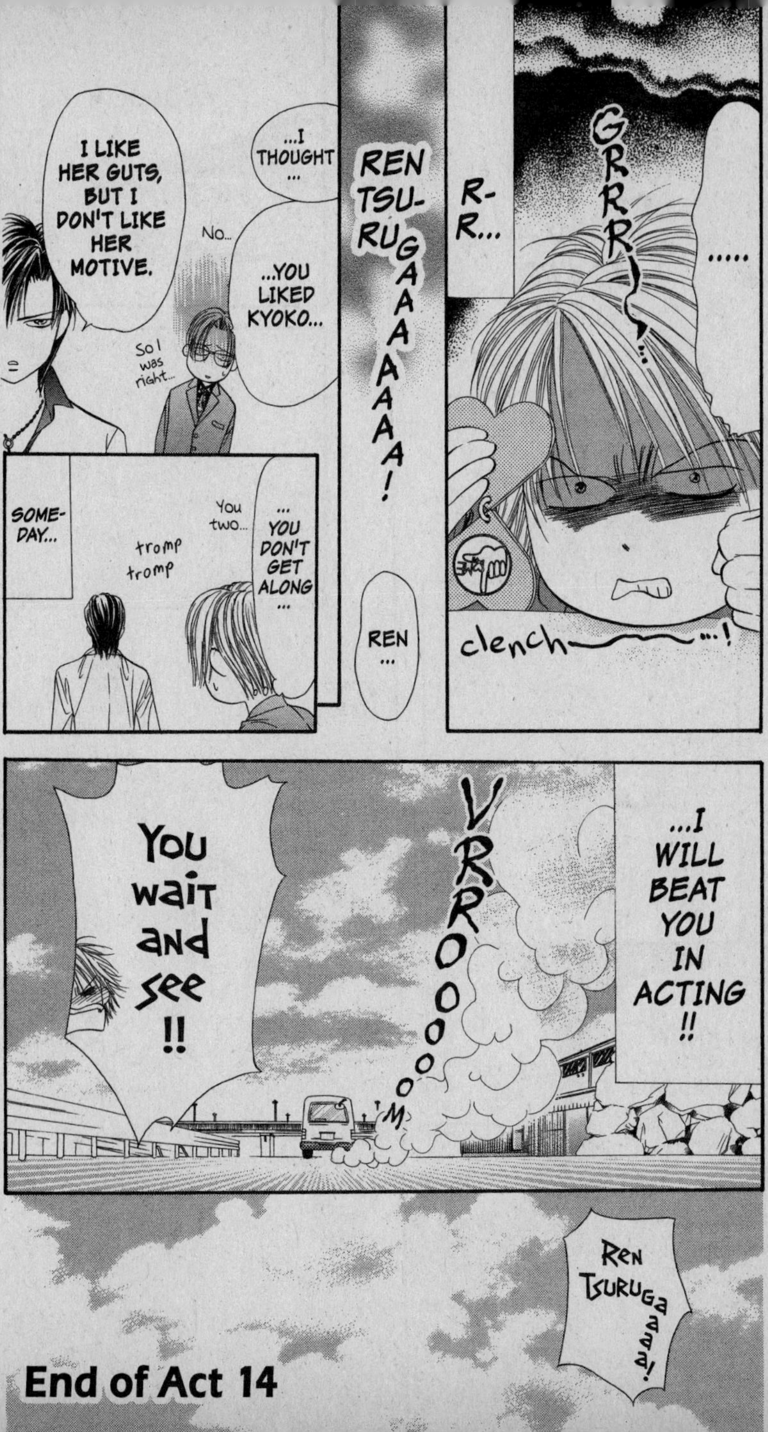
GRRRR...
.....
clench...!
R-R...
REN TSURUGAAAAAAAA!
REN ...
...I THOUGHT ...
No...
...YOU LIKED KYOKO...
I LIKE HER GUTS, BUT I DON'T LIKE HER MOTIVE.
So I was right...
... YOU DON'T GET ALONG ...
You two...
tromp tromp
SOME-DAY...
...I WILL BEAT YOU IN ACTING !!
VRROOOOOOM
You wait and see !!
Ren Tsurugaaaaa!

End of Act 14

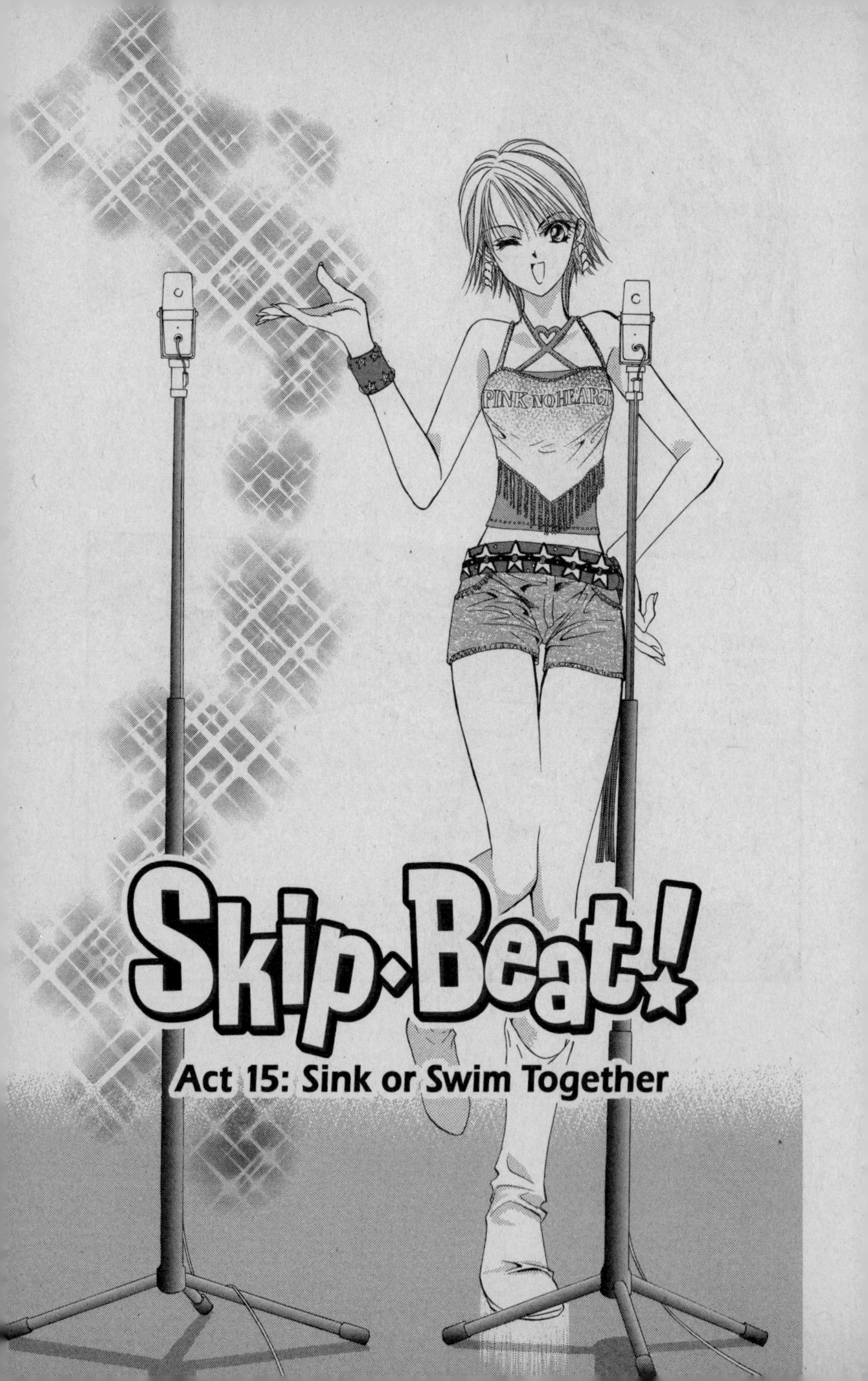
PINK NO HEART
Skip·Beat!
Act 15: Sink or Swim Together

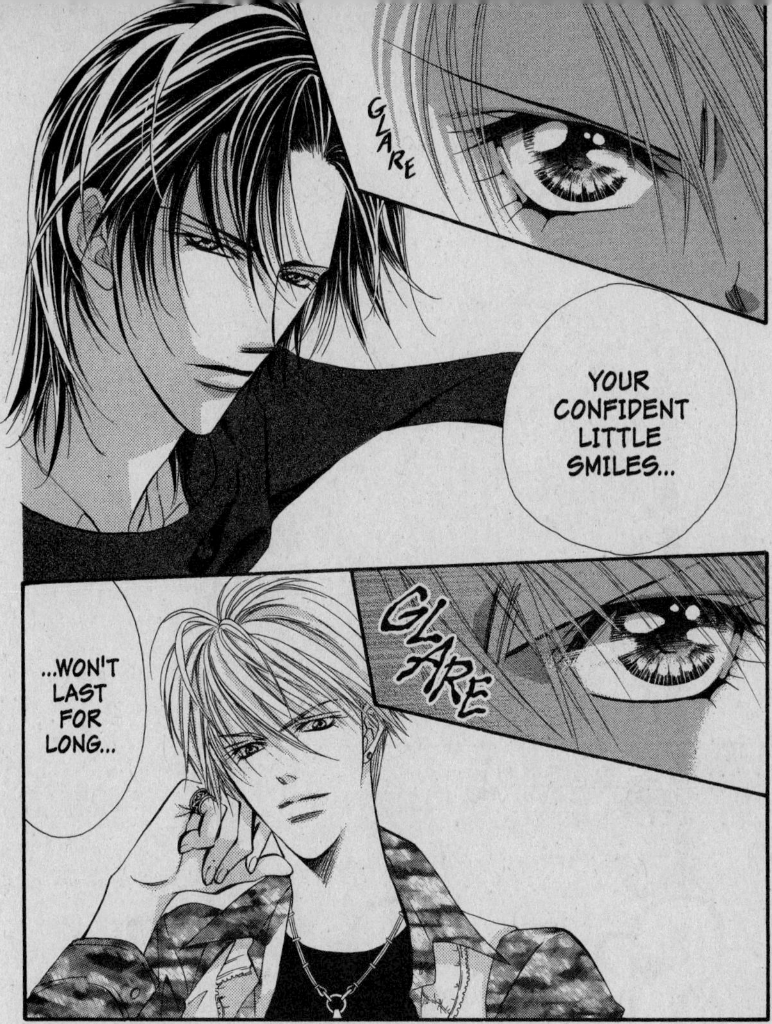
GLARE
YOUR CONFIDENT LITTLE SMILES...
GLARE
...WON'T LAST FOR LONG...

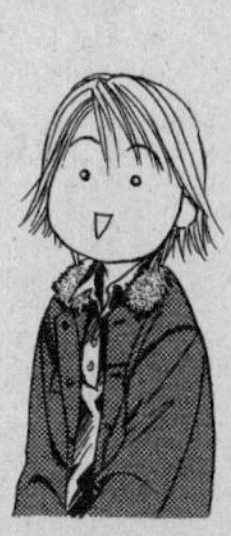

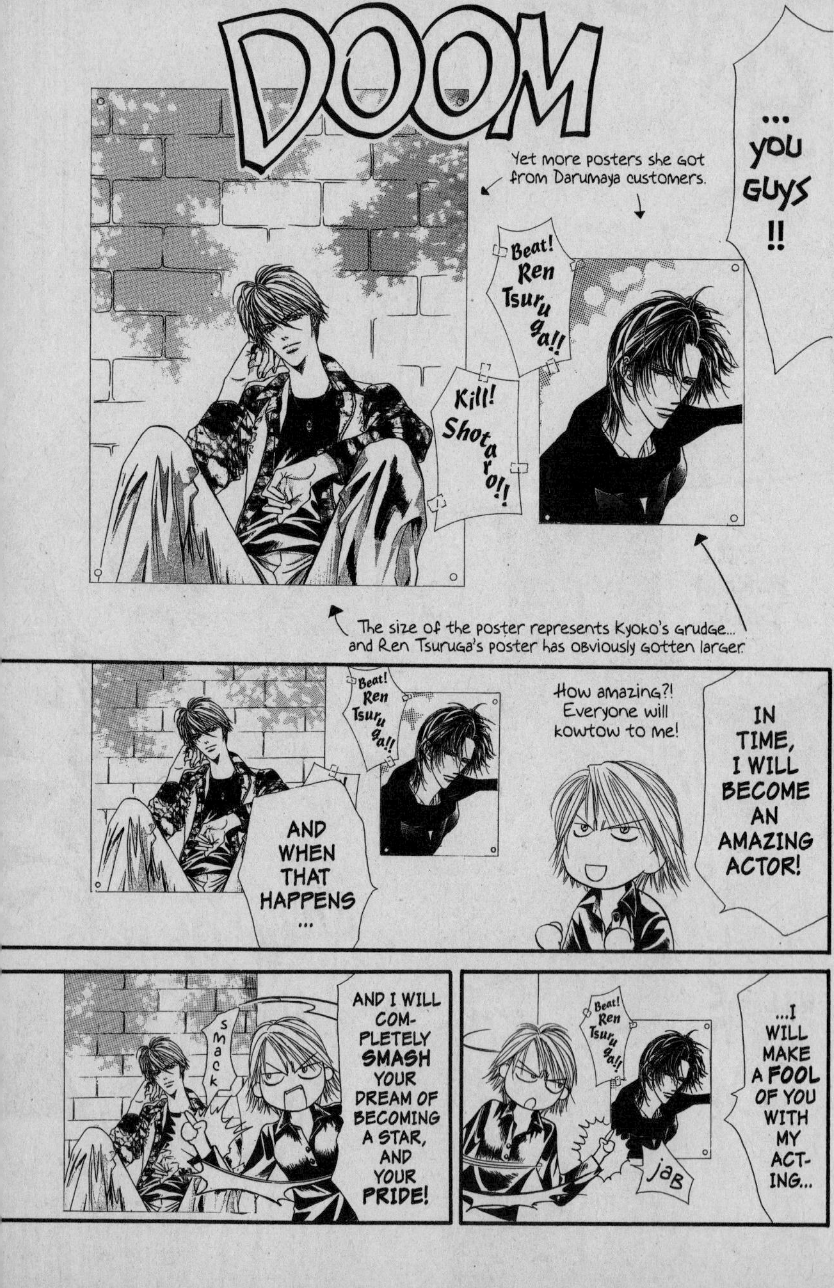
... YOU GUYS !!
DOOM
Yet more posters she got from Darumaya customers.
Beat! Ren Tsuruga!!
Kill! Shotaro!!
The size of the poster represents Kyoko's grudge... and Ren Tsuruga's poster has obviously gotten larger.
IN TIME, I WILL BECOME AN AMAZING ACTOR!
How amazing?! Everyone will kowtow to me!
AND WHEN THAT HAPPENS...
Beat! Ren Tsuruga!!
...I WILL MAKE A FOOL OF YOU WITH MY ACTING...
Beat! Ren Tsuruga!!
jab
AND I WILL COMPLETELY SMASH YOUR DREAM OF BECOMING A STAR, AND YOUR PRIDE!
smack

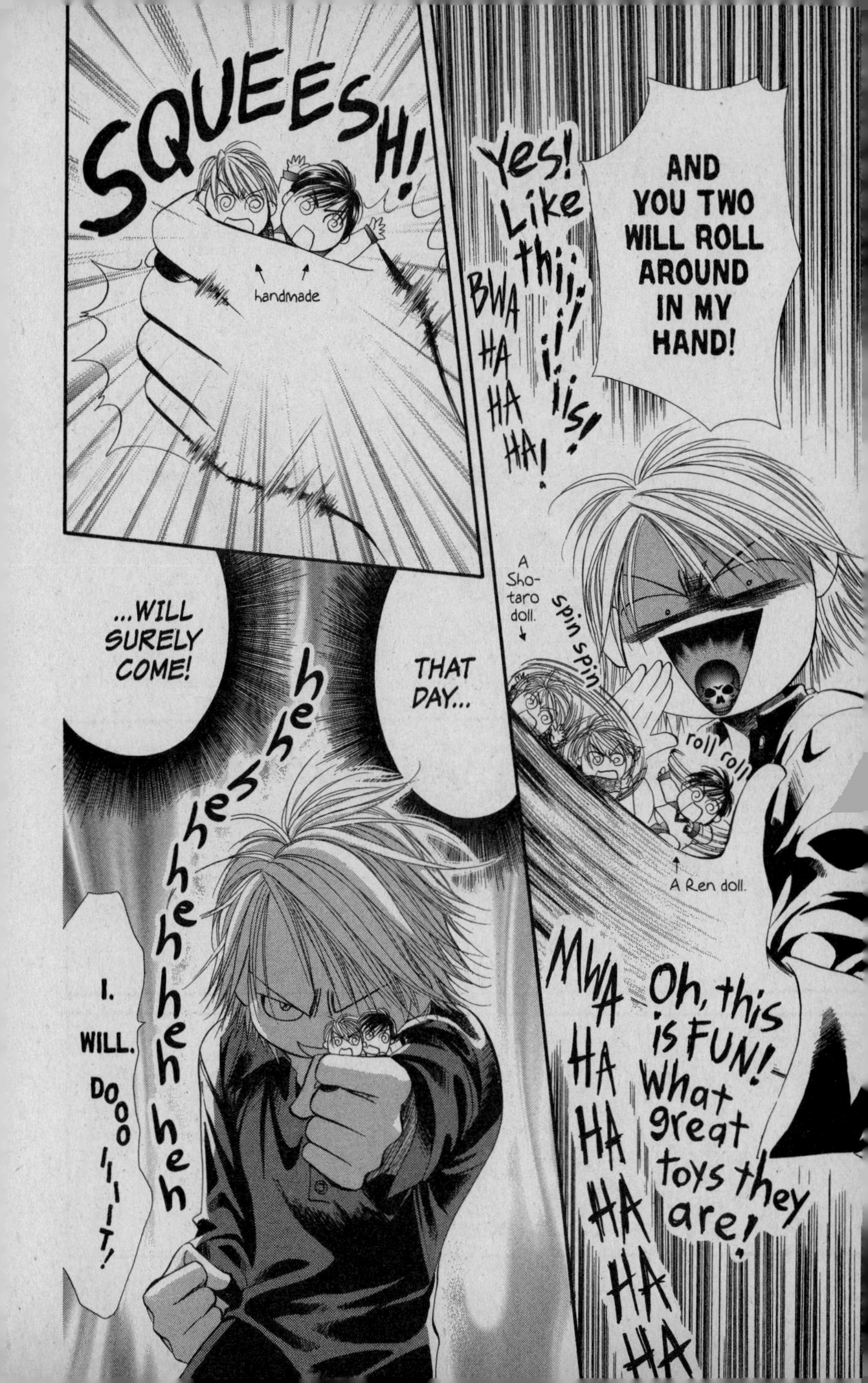
AND YOU TWO WILL ROLL AROUND IN MY HAND!
Yes! Like thiiiiiiis!
BWA HA HA HA HA!
A Shotaro doll.
spin spin
roll roll
A Ren doll.
MWA HA HA HA HA HA HA HA
Oh, this is FUN! What great toys they are!
SQUEESH!
handmade
THAT DAY...
...WILL SURELY COME!
heh heh heh heh heh heh
I. WILL. DOOOIIIIT!

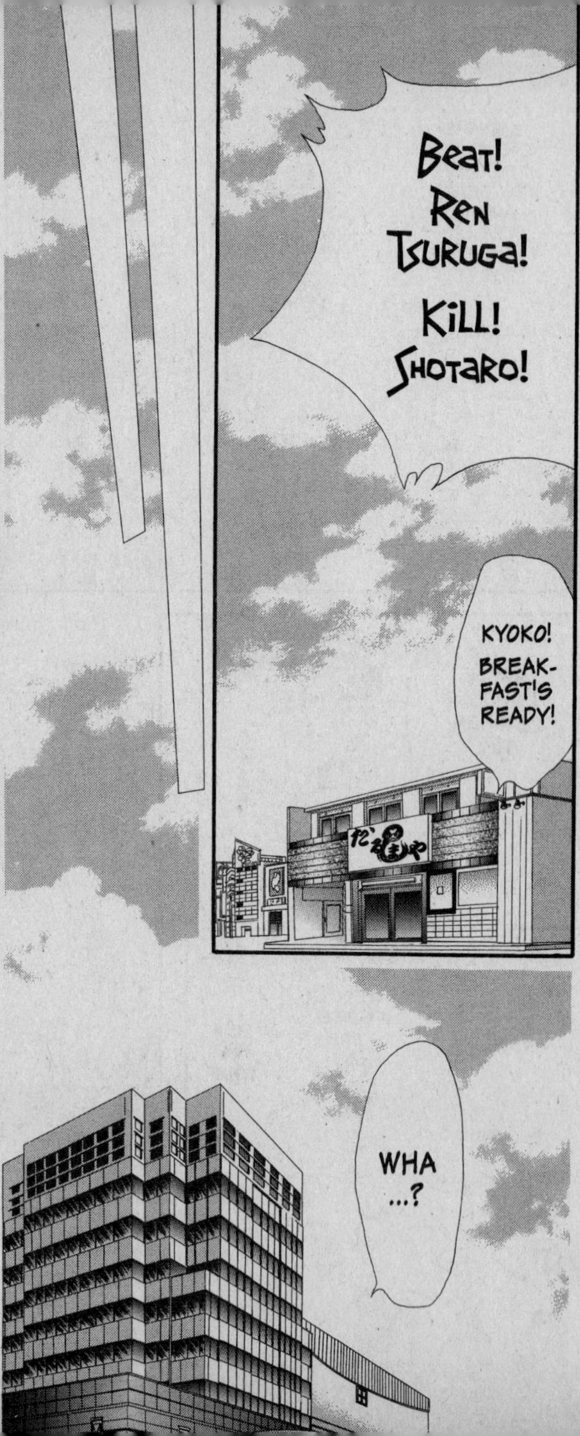
Beat! Ren Tsuruga!
Kill! Shotaro!
KYOKO! BREAK-FAST'S READY!
WHA ...?

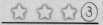

Kanae Kotonami

Difficulty level

☆☆☆ ③

When Kanae appeared, she was close to Kyoko's age, but she looked more mature than Kyoko.

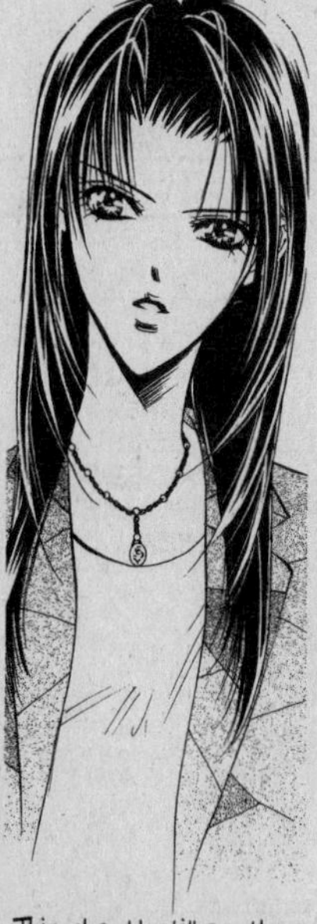

This should still be the case, but the more she appears, the more her face kinda looks younger. She's becoming the easiest girl to draw, and that's not good... When I draw Kanae, I should pay more attention to making her look **mature**... especially when she's with Kyoko. I've got to be careful from now on, too...

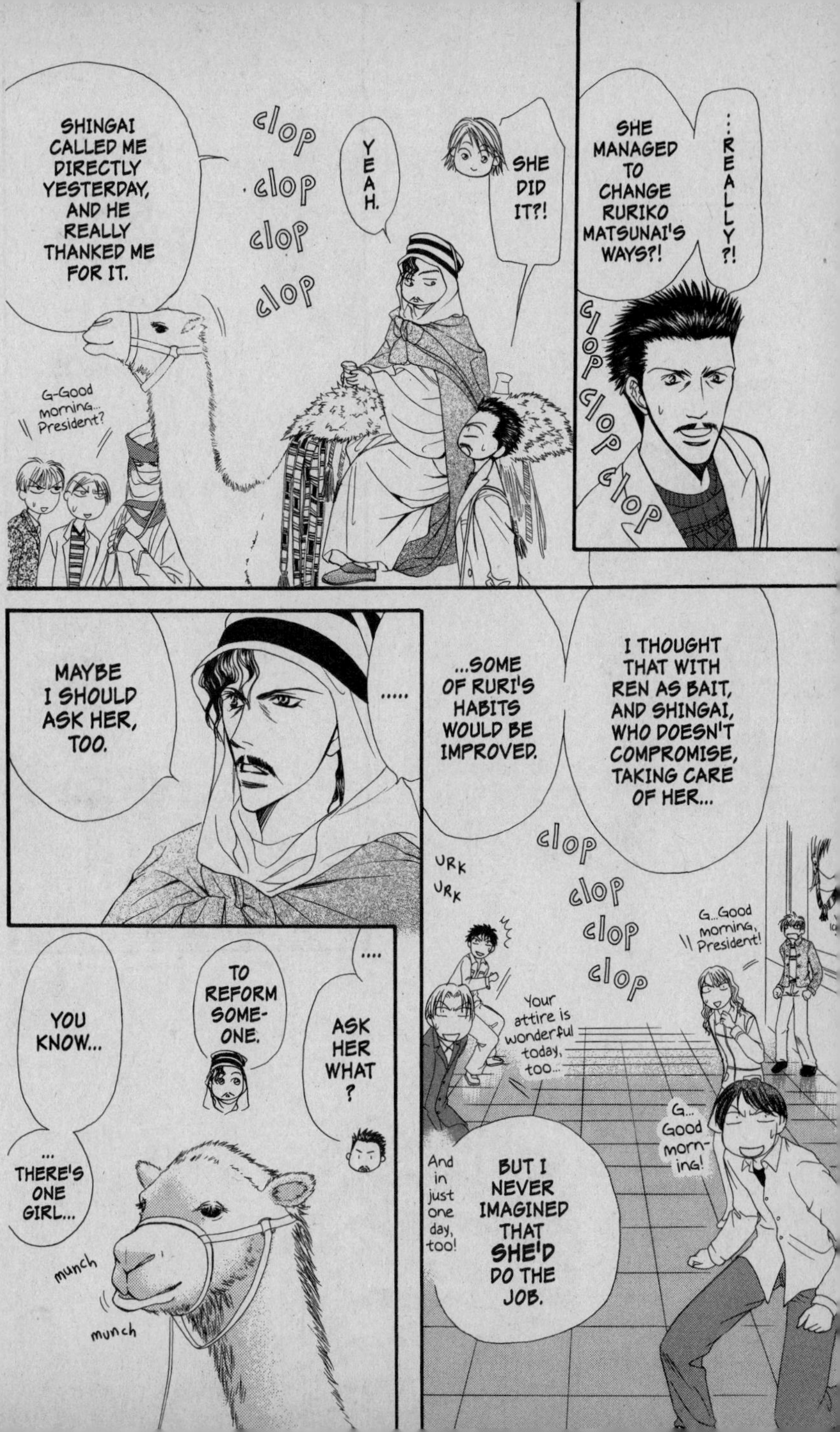

...REALLY?!
SHE MANAGED TO CHANGE RURIKO MATSUNAI'S WAYS?!
clop clop clop
SHE DID IT?!
YEAH.
clop clop clop clop
SHINGAI CALLED ME DIRECTLY YESTERDAY, AND HE REALLY THANKED ME FOR IT.
G-Good morning... President?
I THOUGHT THAT WITH REN AS BAIT, AND SHINGAI, WHO DOESN'T COMPROMISE, TAKING CARE OF HER...
...SOME OF RURI'S HABITS WOULD BE IMPROVED.
clop clop clop clop
URK URK
G...Good morning, President!
Your attire is wonderful today, too...
G... Good morn-ing!
BUT I NEVER IMAGINED THAT SHE'D DO THE JOB.
And in just one day, too!
.....
MAYBE I SHOULD ASK HER, TOO.
....
ASK HER WHAT?
TO REFORM SOME-ONE.
YOU KNOW...
...THERE'S ONE GIRL...
munch
munch

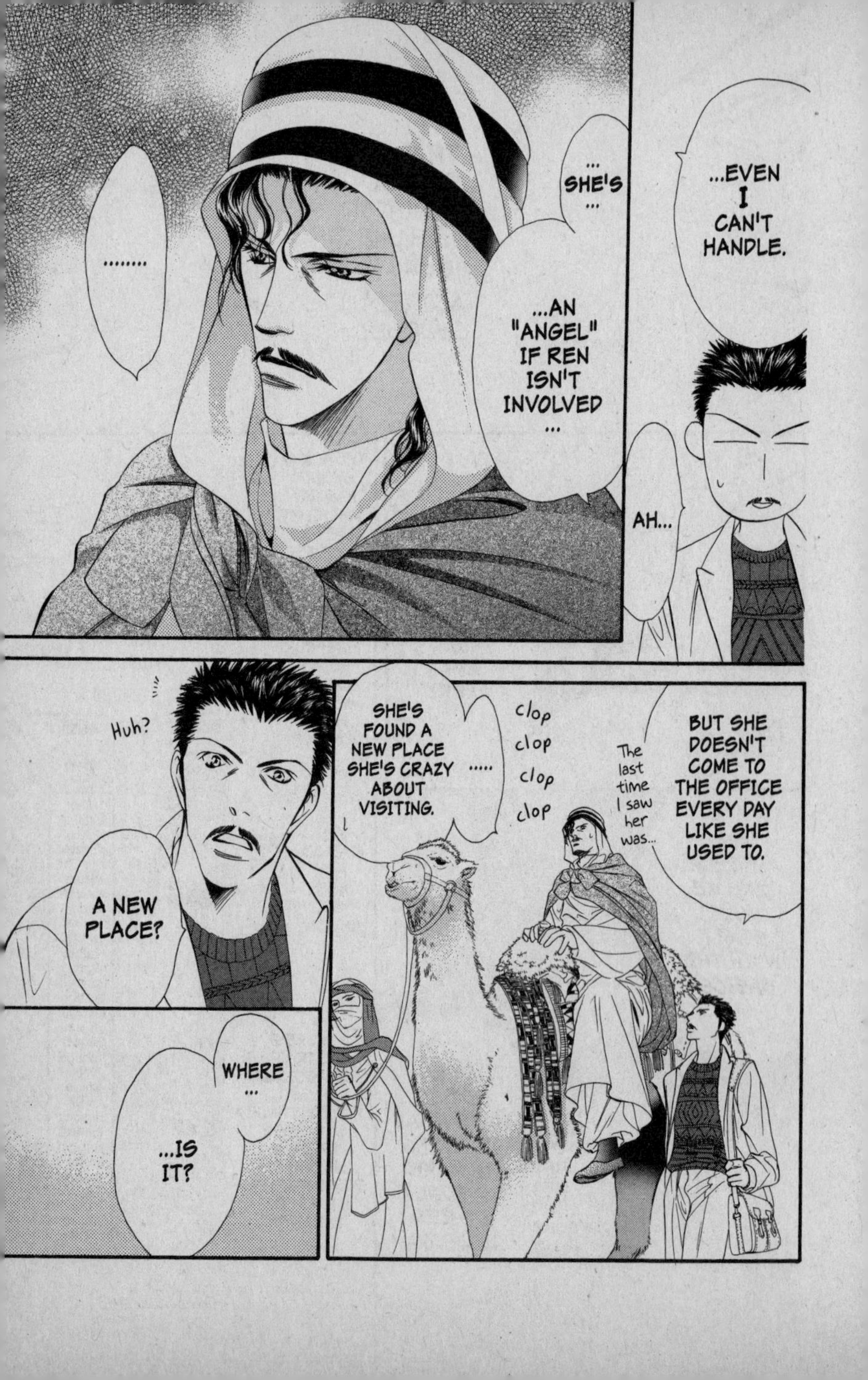
...EVEN I CAN'T HANDLE.
AH...
... SHE'S ...
...AN "ANGEL" IF REN ISN'T INVOLVED ...
....
BUT SHE DOESN'T COME TO THE OFFICE EVERY DAY LIKE SHE USED TO.
The last time I saw her was...
clop clop clop clop
SHE'S FOUND A NEW PLACE SHE'S CRAZY ABOUT VISITING.
.....
Huh?
A NEW PLACE?
WHERE ...
...IS IT?

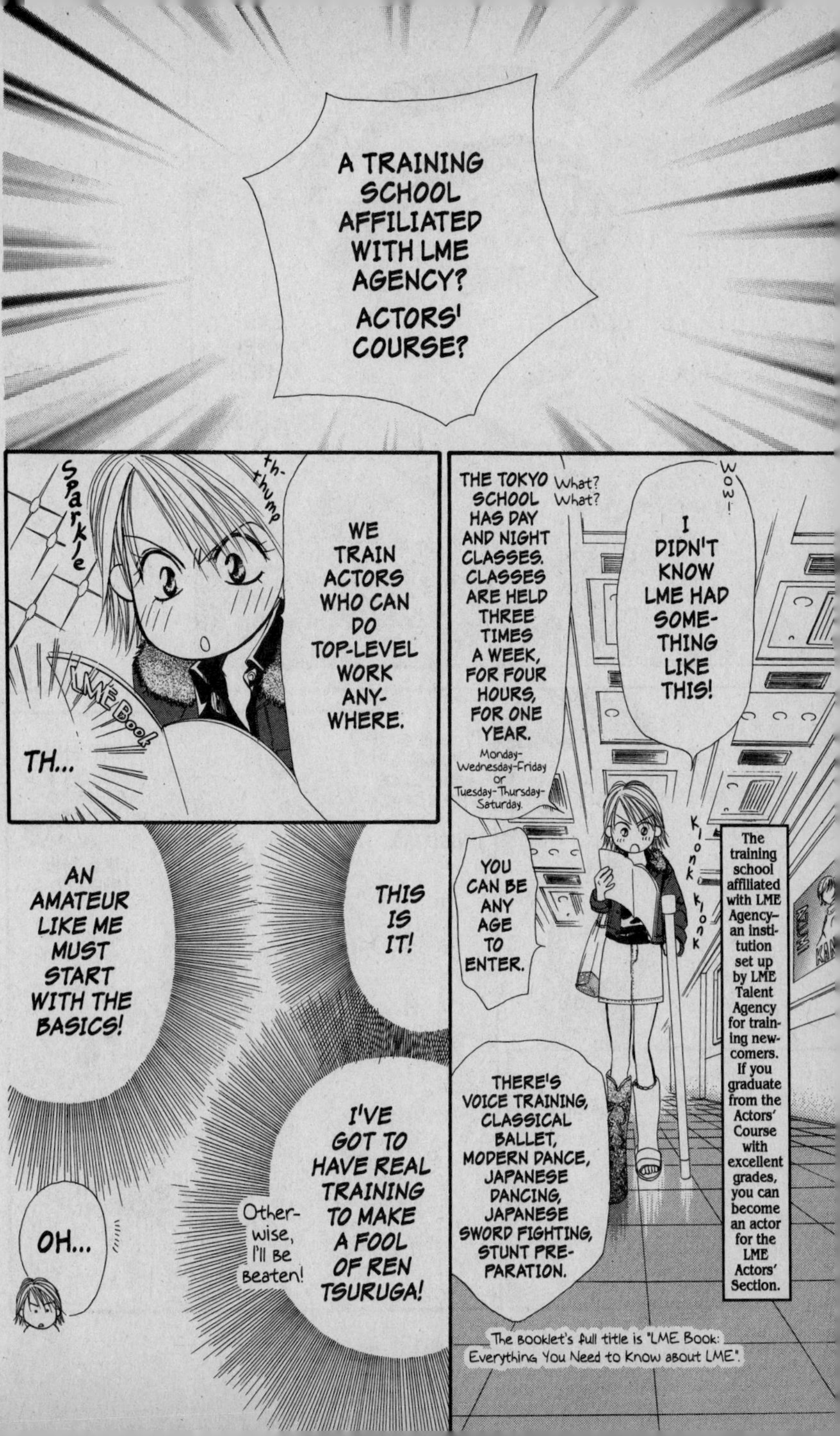
A TRAINING SCHOOL AFFILIATED WITH LME AGENCY?
ACTORS' COURSE?
WOW!
I DIDN'T KNOW LME HAD SOMETHING LIKE THIS!
What? What?
THE TOKYO SCHOOL HAS DAY AND NIGHT CLASSES. CLASSES ARE HELD THREE TIMES A WEEK, FOR FOUR HOURS, FOR ONE YEAR.
Monday-Wednesday-Friday or Tuesday-Thursday-Saturday.
Klonk klonk
The training school affiliated with LME Agency—an institution set up by LME Talent Agency for training newcomers. If you graduate from the Actors' Course with excellent grades, you can become an actor for the LME Actors' Section.
YOU CAN BE ANY AGE TO ENTER.
THERE'S VOICE TRAINING, CLASSICAL BALLET, MODERN DANCE, JAPANESE DANCING, JAPANESE SWORD FIGHTING, STUNT PREPARATION.
The booklet's full title is "LME Book: Everything You Need to Know about LME".
th-thump
WE TRAIN ACTORS WHO CAN DO TOP-LEVEL WORK ANYWHERE.
Sparkle
LME Book
TH...
THIS IS IT!
AN AMATEUR LIKE ME MUST START WITH THE BASICS!
I'VE GOT TO HAVE REAL TRAINING TO MAKE A FOOL OF REN TSURUGA!
Otherwise, I'll be beaten!
OH...

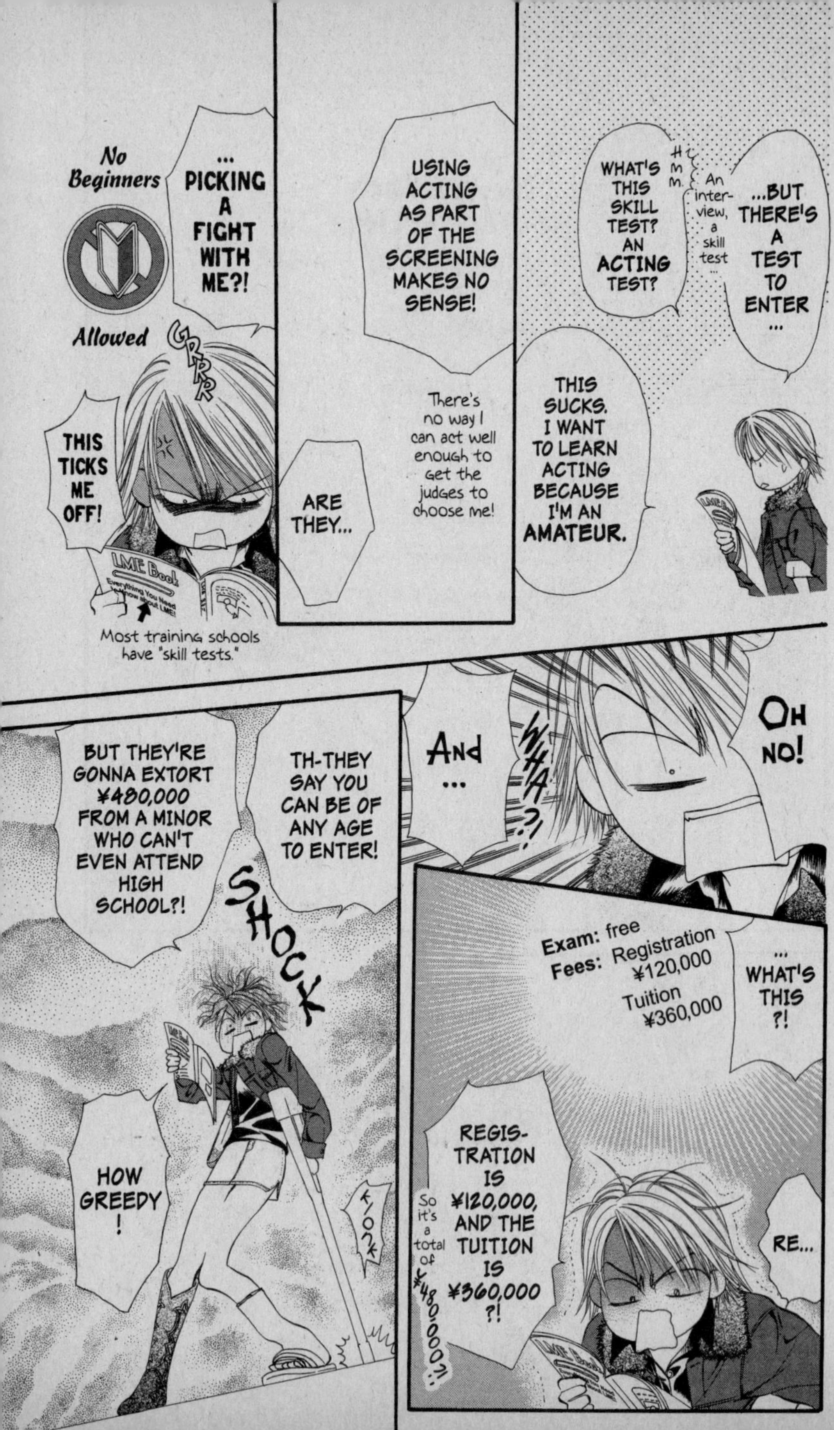
...BUT THERE'S A TEST TO ENTER...
An interview, a skill test...
HMM.
WHAT'S THIS SKILL TEST? AN ACTING TEST?
THIS SUCKS. I WANT TO LEARN ACTING BECAUSE I'M AN AMATEUR.
USING ACTING AS PART OF THE SCREENING MAKES NO SENSE!
There's no way I can act well enough to get the judges to choose me!
ARE THEY...
...PICKING A FIGHT WITH ME?!
No Beginners Allowed
GRRR
THIS TICKS ME OFF!
LME Book
Most training schools have "skill tests."
OH NO!
WHA?!
And...
...WHAT'S THIS?!
Exam: free
Fees: Registration ¥120,000
Tuition ¥360,000
RE...
REGISTRATION IS ¥120,000, AND THE TUITION IS ¥360,000?!
So it's a total of ¥480,000?!
TH-THEY SAY YOU CAN BE OF ANY AGE TO ENTER!
BUT THEY'RE GONNA EXTORT ¥480,000 FROM A MINOR WHO CAN'T EVEN ATTEND HIGH SCHOOL?!
SHOCK
HOW GREEDY!
KLONK

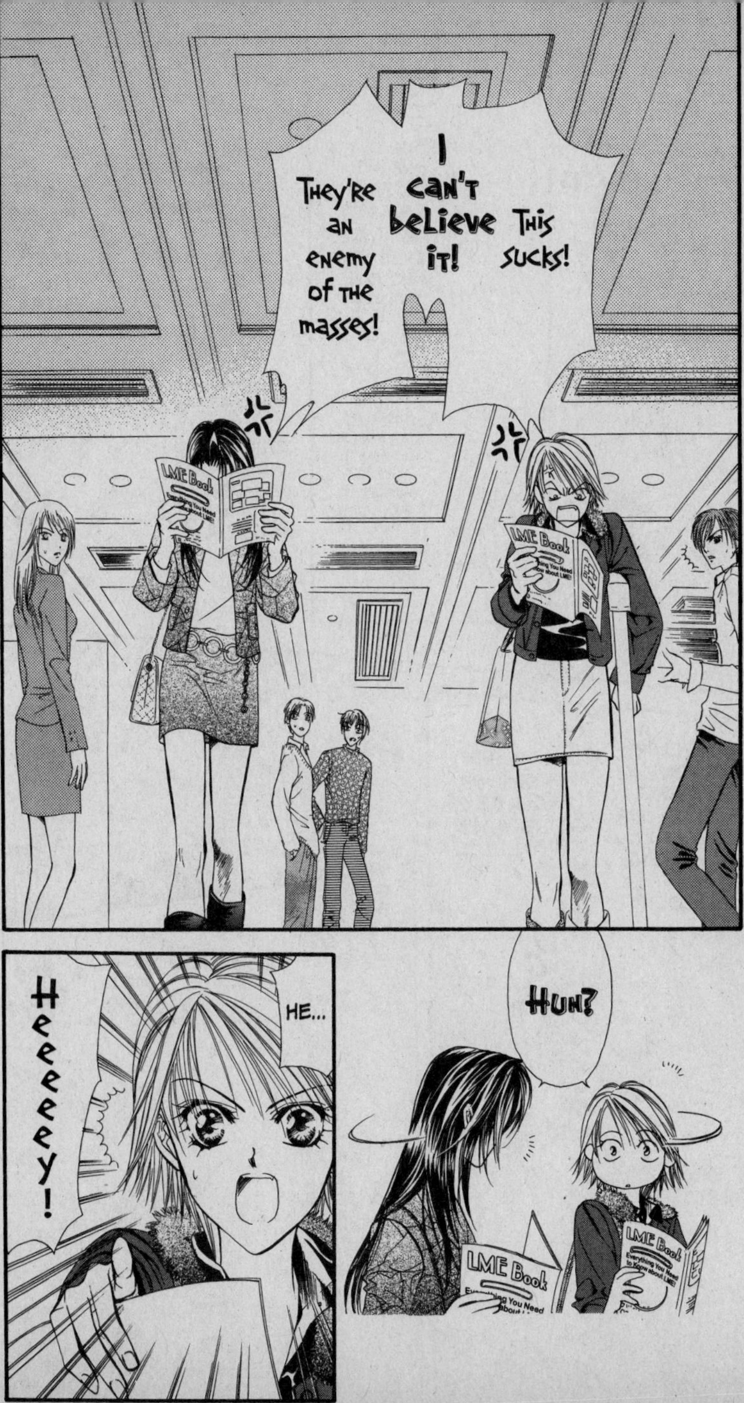
This sucks!
I can't believe it!
They're an enemy of the masses!
LME Book
LME Book
Hun?
LME Book
LME Book
Everything You Need to Know about LME!
He...
Heeeeey!

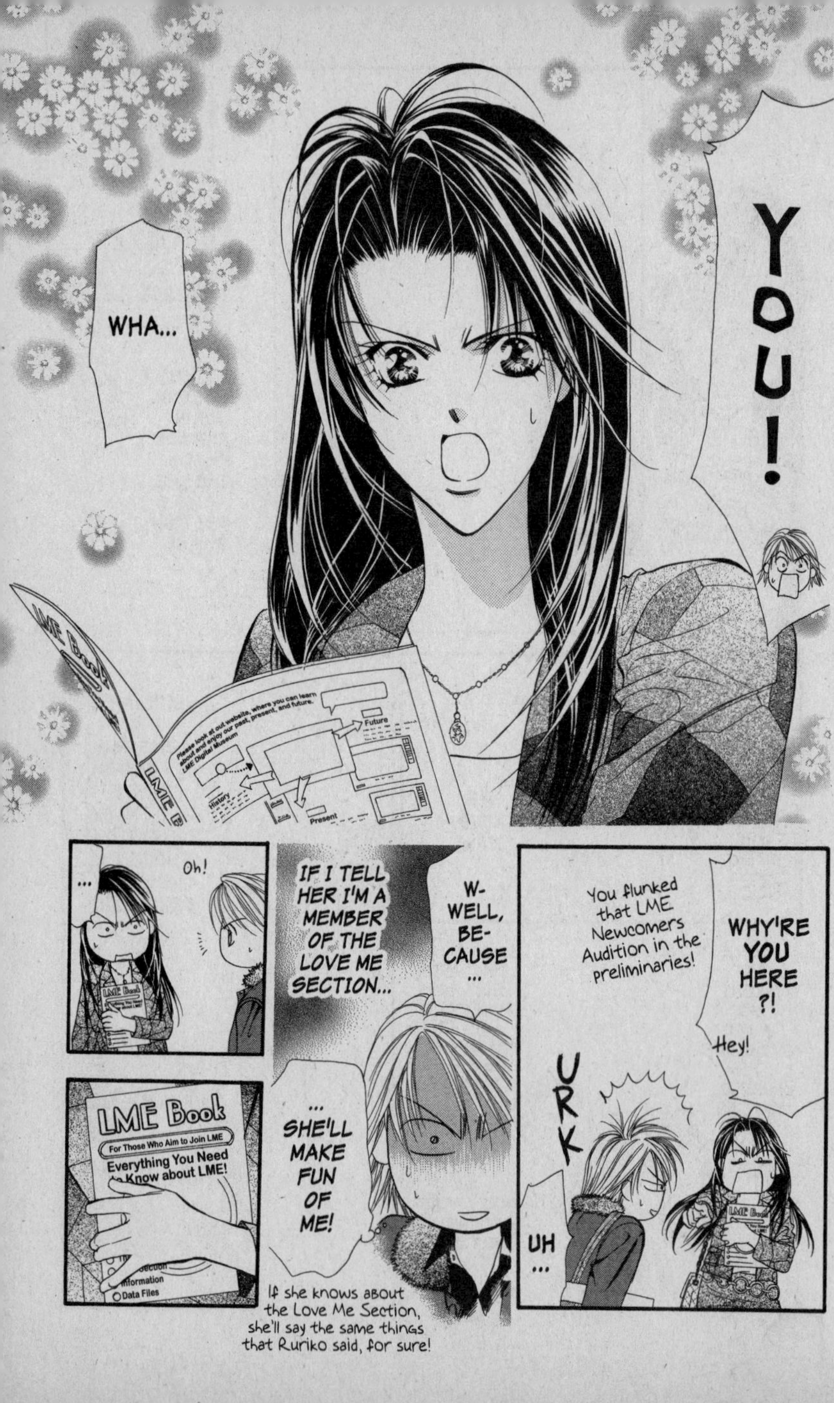
YOU!
WHA...
Please look at out website, where you can learn about and enjoy our past, present, and future.
LME Digital Museum
Future
History
Present
WHY'RE YOU HERE?!
You flunked that LME Newcomers Audition in the preliminaries!
Hey!
URK
UH ...
W-WELL, BE-CAUSE ...
IF I TELL HER I'M A MEMBER OF THE LOVE ME SECTION...
... SHE'LL MAKE FUN OF ME!
If she knows about the Love Me Section, she'll say the same things that Ruriko said, for sure!
Oh!
...
LME Book
For Those Who Aim to Join LME
Everything You Need
Know about LME!
Information
Data Files

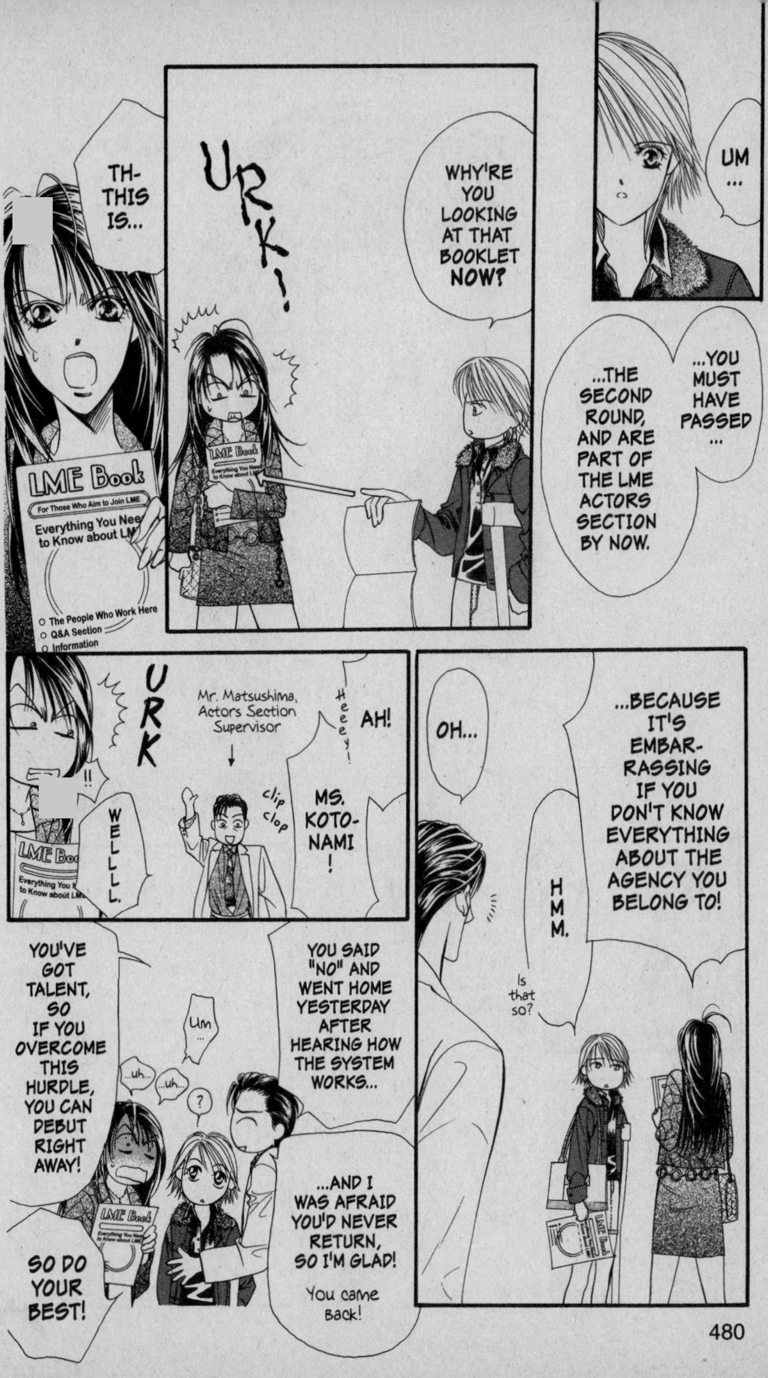
UM ...
...YOU MUST HAVE PASSED ...
...THE SECOND ROUND, AND ARE PART OF THE LME ACTORS SECTION BY NOW.
WHY'RE YOU LOOKING AT THAT BOOKLET NOW?
URK!
TH- THIS IS...
LME Book
For Those Who Aim to Join LME
The People Who Work Here
Q&A Section
Information
...BECAUSE IT'S EMBARRASSING IF YOU DON'T KNOW EVERYTHING ABOUT THE AGENCY YOU BELONG TO!
OH...
HMM.
Is that so?
AH!
Heeey!
MS. KOTONAMI!
Mr. Matsushima, Actors Section Supervisor
clip clop
URK
!!
WELLLL.
LME Book
YOU SAID "NO" AND WENT HOME YESTERDAY AFTER HEARING HOW THE SYSTEM WORKS...
...AND I WAS AFRAID YOU'D NEVER RETURN, SO I'M GLAD!
You came back!
YOU'VE GOT TALENT, SO IF YOU OVERCOME THIS HURDLE, YOU CAN DEBUT RIGHT AWAY!
SO DO YOUR BEST!
Um ...
...uh...
...uh...
?
LME Book

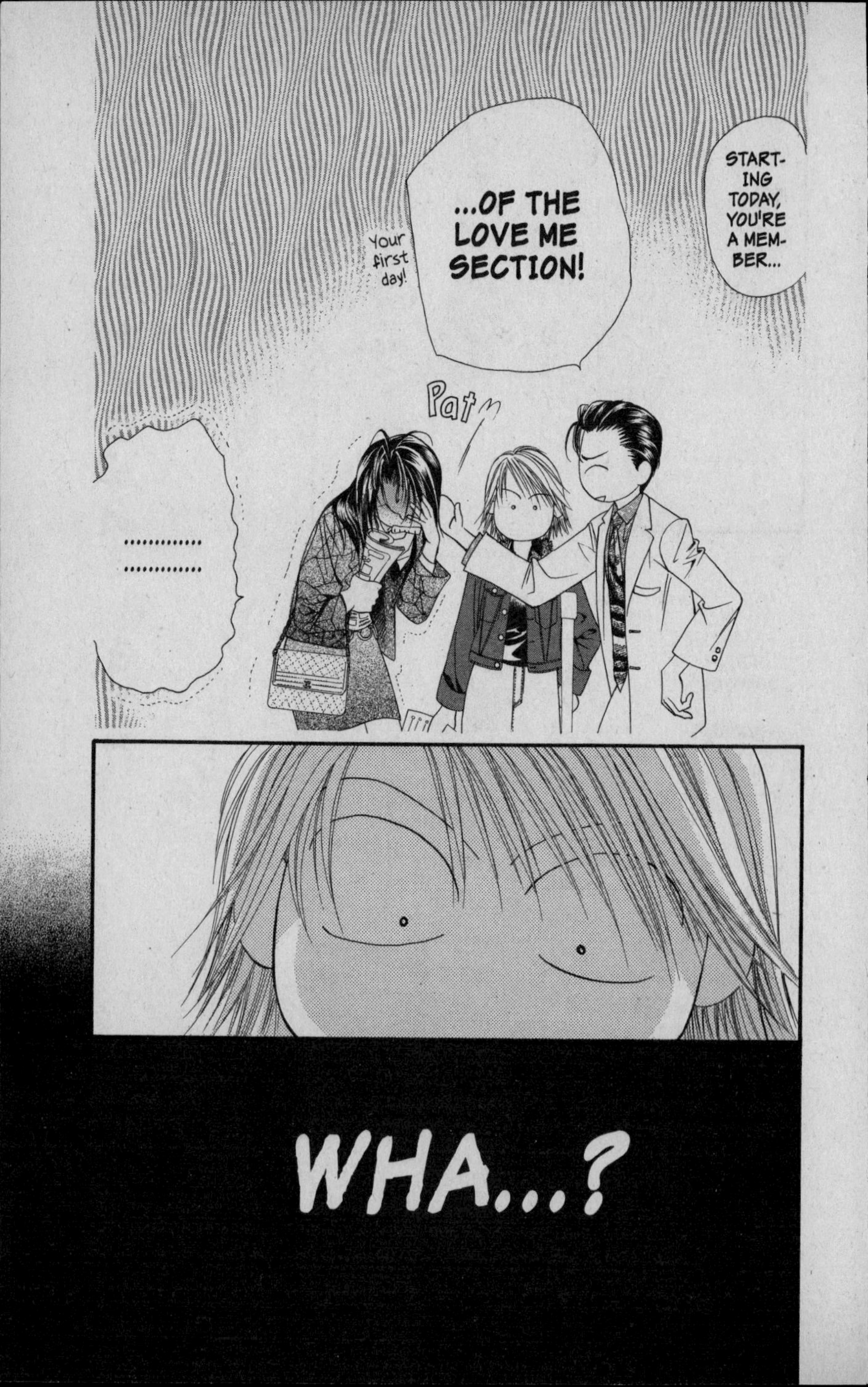
STARTING TODAY, YOU'RE A MEMBER...
...OF THE LOVE ME SECTION!
Your first day!
Pat
....
....
WHA...?

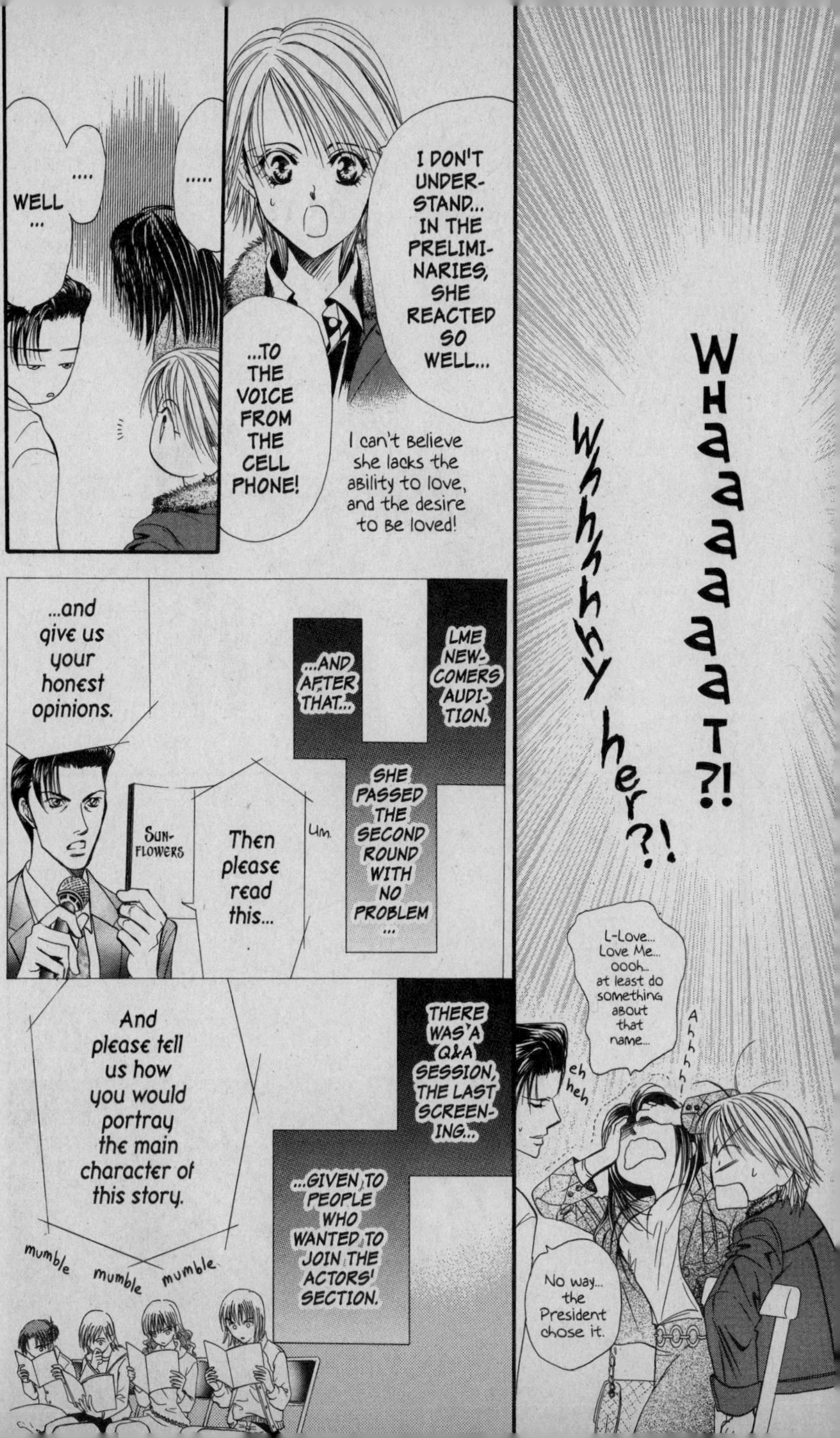
WHaaaaaaT?!
Whhhhhy her?!
L-Love... Love Me... oooh... at least do something about that name...
Ahhhh!
eh heh
No way... the President chose it.
I DON'T UNDER-STAND... IN THE PRELIMI-NARIES, SHE REACTED SO WELL...
...TO THE VOICE FROM THE CELL PHONE!
I can't believe she lacks the ability to love, and the desire to be loved!
.....
.... WELL ...
LME NEW-COMERS AUDI-TION.
...AND AFTER THAT...
SHE PASSED THE SECOND ROUND WITH NO PROBLEM ...
Um.
Then please read this...
SUN-FLOWERS
...and give us your honest opinions.
THERE WAS A Q&A SESSION, THE LAST SCREEN-ING...
...GIVEN TO PEOPLE WHO WANTED TO JOIN THE ACTORS' SECTION.
And please tell us how you would portray the main character of this story.
mumble mumble mumble

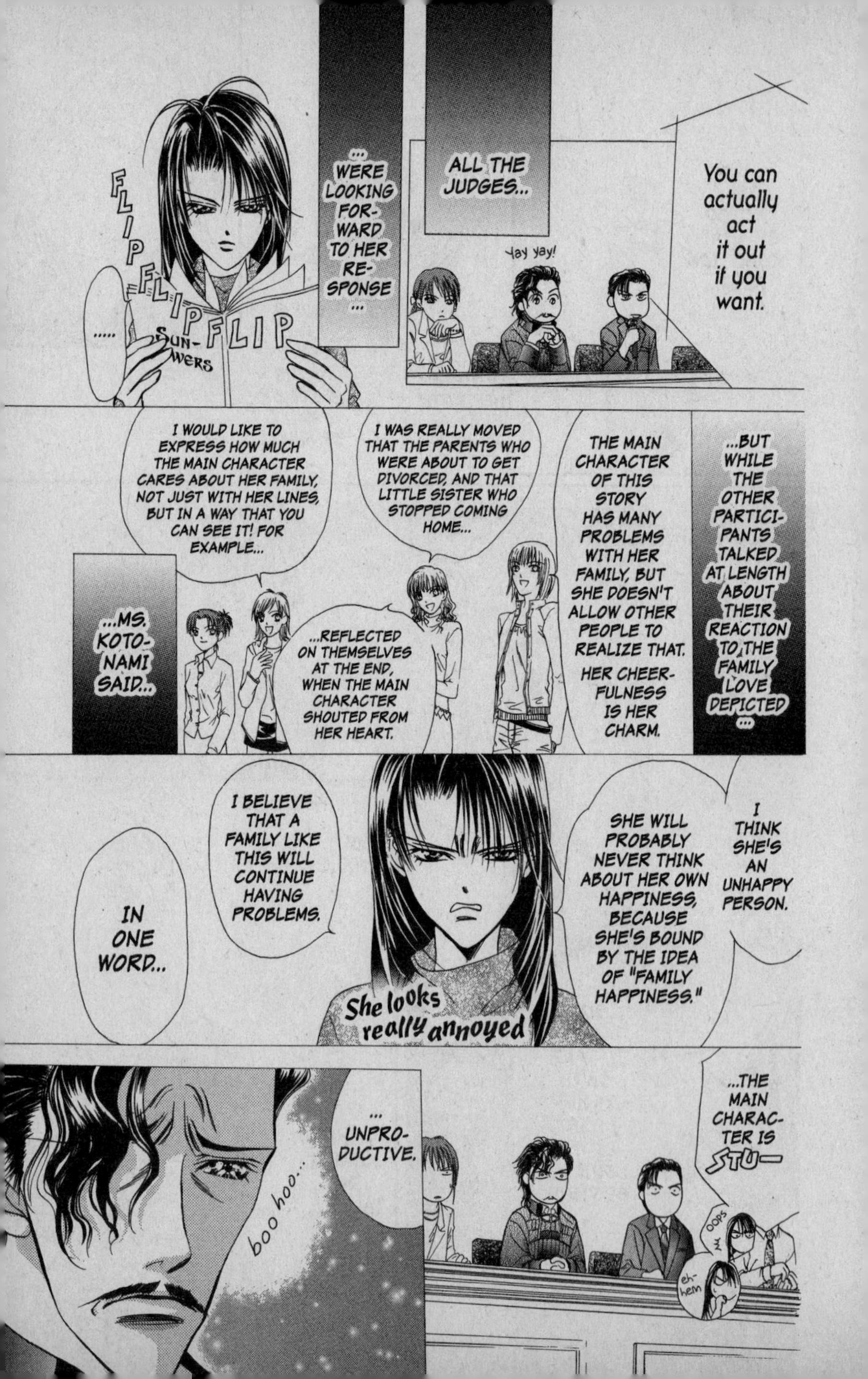
You can actually act it out if you want.
ALL THE JUDGES...
Yay yay!
...WERE LOOKING FORWARD TO HER RESPONSE...
FLIP FLIP FLIP FLIP
SUN-WERS
.....
...BUT WHILE THE OTHER PARTICIPANTS TALKED AT LENGTH ABOUT THEIR REACTION TO THE FAMILY LOVE DEPICTED...
THE MAIN CHARACTER OF THIS STORY HAS MANY PROBLEMS WITH HER FAMILY, BUT SHE DOESN'T ALLOW OTHER PEOPLE TO REALIZE THAT. HER CHEERFULNESS IS HER CHARM.
I WAS REALLY MOVED THAT THE PARENTS WHO WERE ABOUT TO GET DIVORCED, AND THAT LITTLE SISTER WHO STOPPED COMING HOME...
...REFLECTED ON THEMSELVES AT THE END, WHEN THE MAIN CHARACTER SHOUTED FROM HER HEART.
I WOULD LIKE TO EXPRESS HOW MUCH THE MAIN CHARACTER CARES ABOUT HER FAMILY, NOT JUST WITH HER LINES, BUT IN A WAY THAT YOU CAN SEE IT! FOR EXAMPLE...
...MS. KOTONAMI SAID...
I THINK SHE'S AN UNHAPPY PERSON.
SHE WILL PROBABLY NEVER THINK ABOUT HER OWN HAPPINESS, BECAUSE SHE'S BOUND BY THE IDEA OF "FAMILY HAPPINESS."
She looks really annoyed
I BELIEVE THAT A FAMILY LIKE THIS WILL CONTINUE HAVING PROBLEMS.
IN ONE WORD...
...THE MAIN CHARACTER IS STU—
OOPS
eh-hem
...UNPRODUCTIVE.
boo hoo...

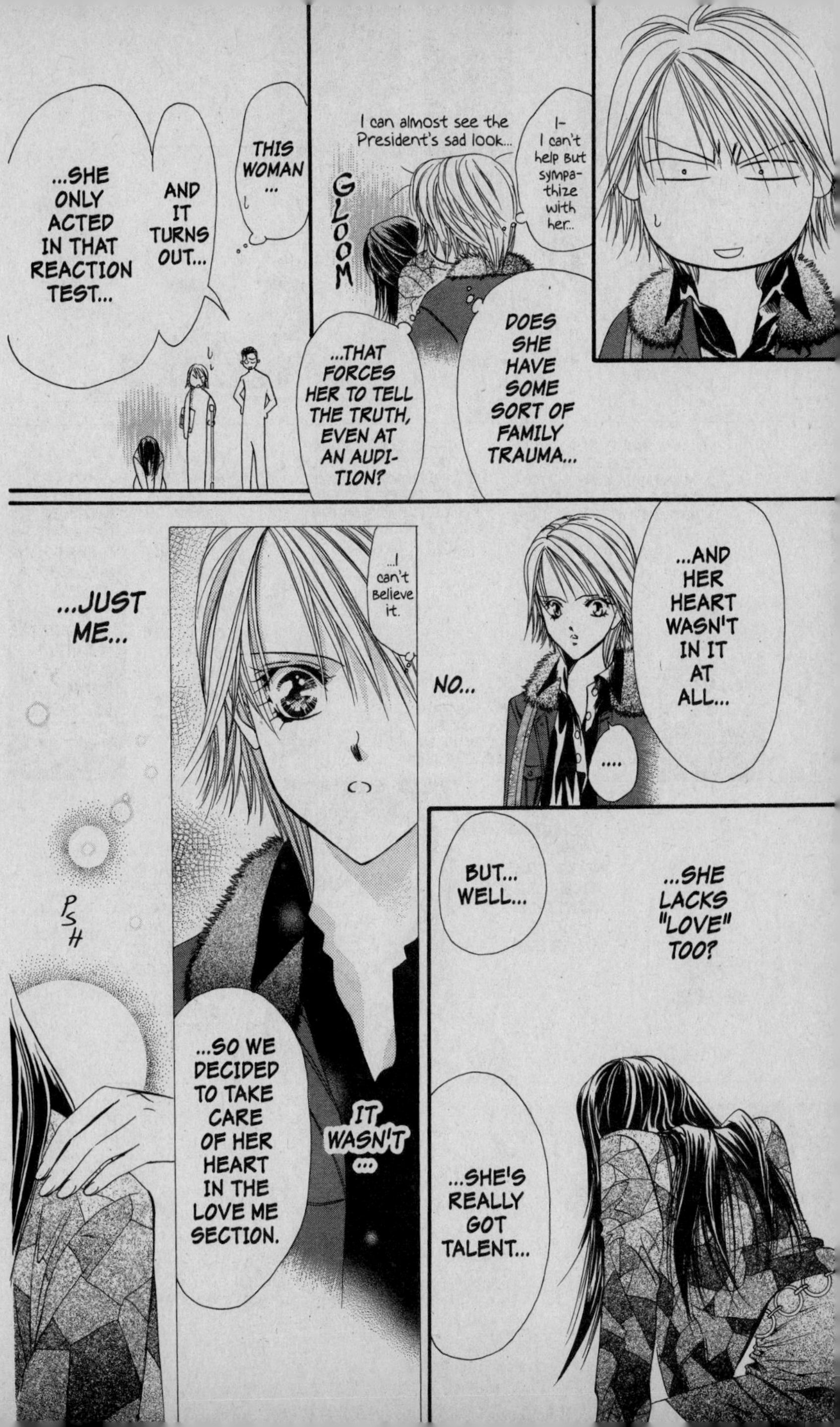
I- I can't help but sympathize with her...
I can almost see the President's sad look...
GLOOM
DOES SHE HAVE SOME SORT OF FAMILY TRAUMA...
...THAT FORCES HER TO TELL THE TRUTH, EVEN AT AN AUDITION?
THIS WOMAN...
AND IT TURNS OUT...
...SHE ONLY ACTED IN THAT REACTION TEST...
...AND HER HEART WASN'T IN IT AT ALL...
....
NO...
...SHE LACKS "LOVE" TOO?
BUT... WELL...
...SHE'S REALLY GOT TALENT...
...I can't believe it.
IT WASN'T...
...SO WE DECIDED TO TAKE CARE OF HER HEART IN THE LOVE ME SECTION.
...JUST ME...
PSH

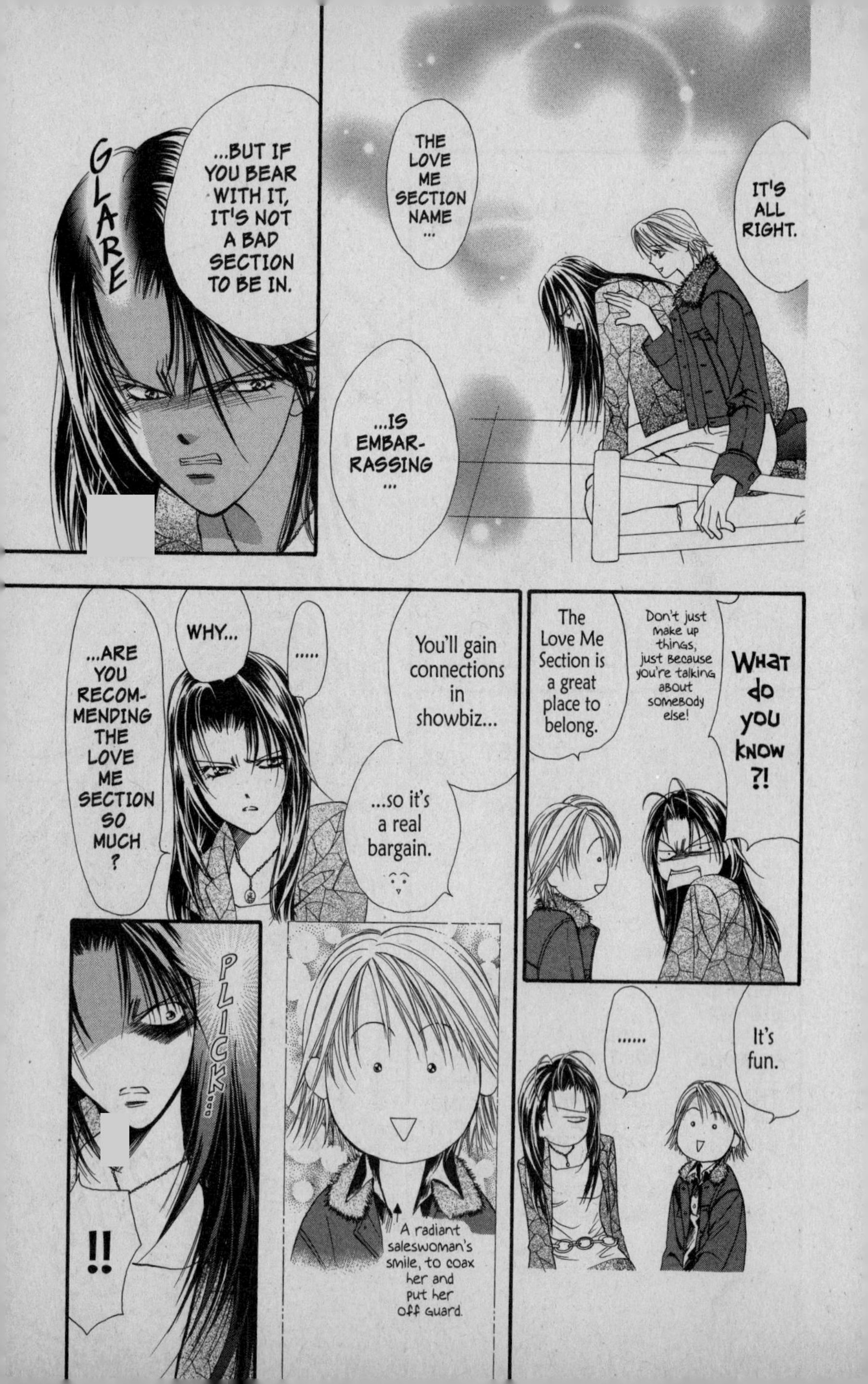
IT'S ALL RIGHT.
THE LOVE ME SECTION NAME...
...IS EMBARRASSING...
...BUT IF YOU BEAR WITH IT, IT'S NOT A BAD SECTION TO BE IN.
GLARE
What do you know?!
Don't just make up things, just because you're talking about somebody else!
The Love Me Section is a great place to belong.
You'll gain connections in showbiz...
...so it's a real bargain.
.....
WHY...
...ARE YOU RECOMMENDING THE LOVE ME SECTION SO MUCH?
It's fun.
......
A radiant saleswoman's smile, to coax her and put her off guard.
PLICK...
!!

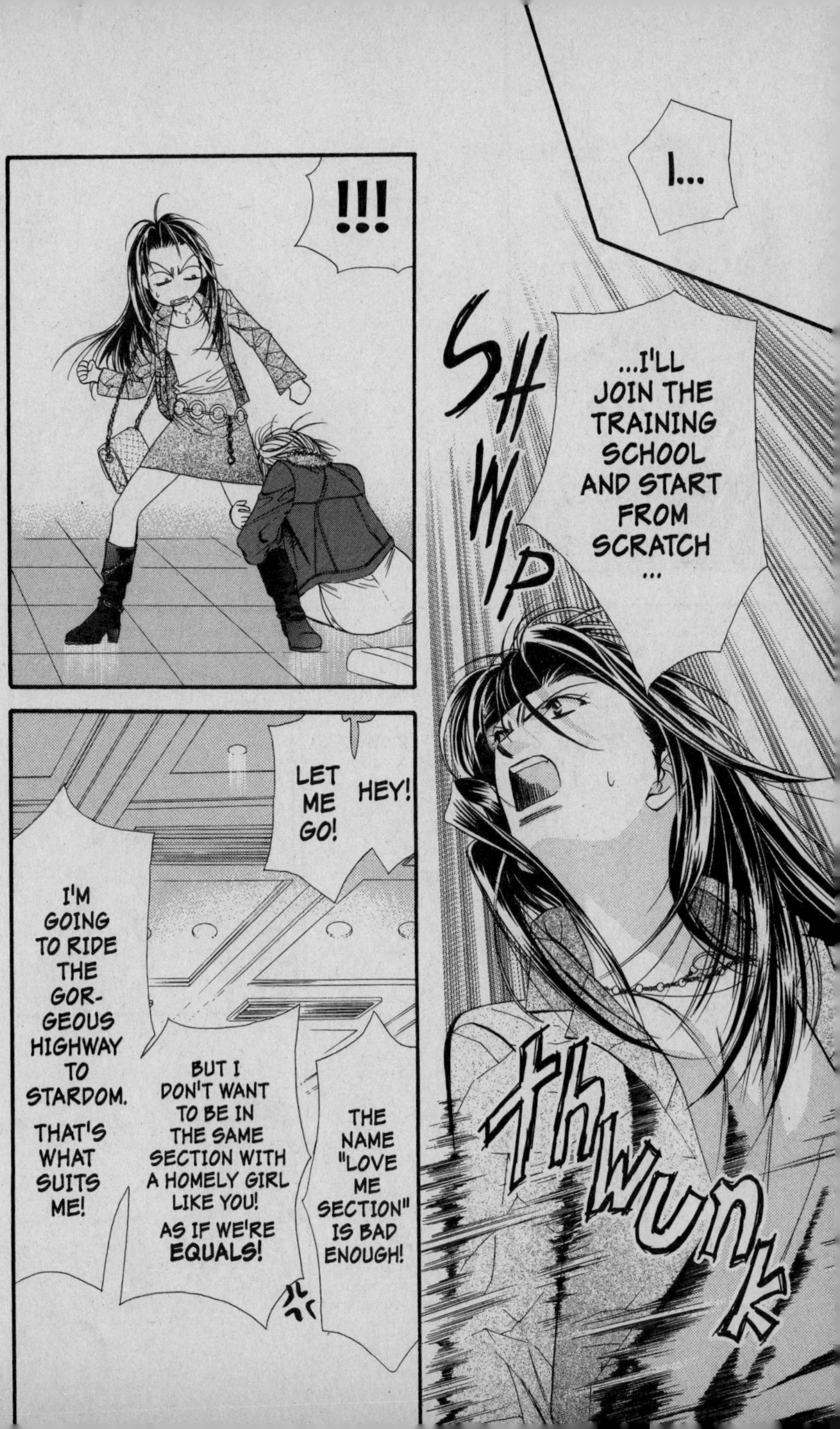
I...
...I'LL JOIN THE TRAINING SCHOOL AND START FROM SCRATCH ...
SHWIP
thwunk
!!!
HEY!
LET ME GO!
THE NAME "LOVE ME SECTION" IS BAD ENOUGH!
BUT I DON'T WANT TO BE IN THE SAME SECTION WITH A HOMELY GIRL LIKE YOU!
AS IF WE'RE EQUALS!
I'M GOING TO RIDE THE GOR-GEOUS HIGHWAY TO STARDOM.
THAT'S WHAT SUITS ME!

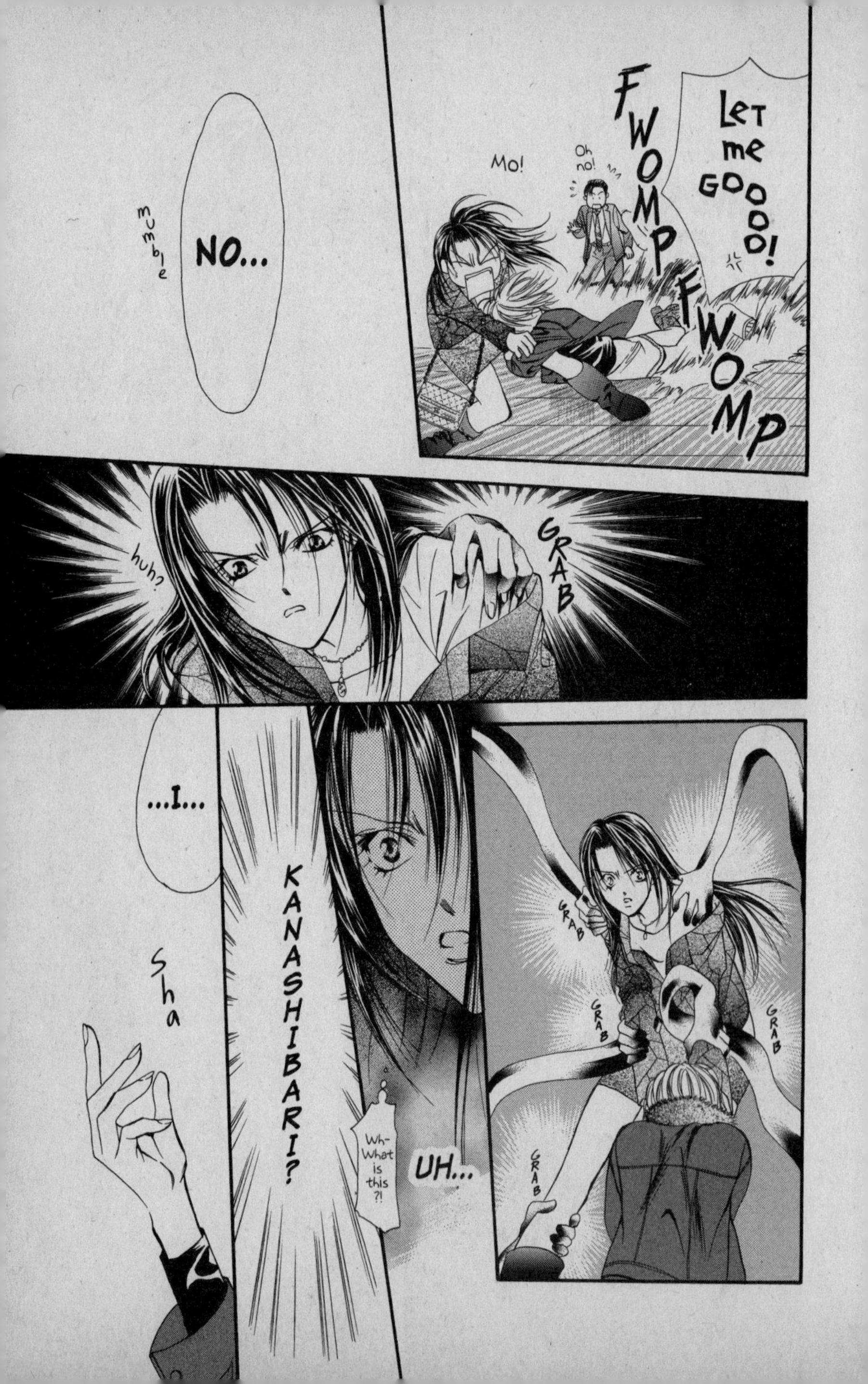
Let me GOOOO!
FWOMP
FWOMP
Oh no!
Mo!
NO...
mumble
GRAB
huh?
GRAB
GRAB
GRAB
GRAB
KANASHIBARI?
Wh-What is this?!
UH...
...I...
Sha

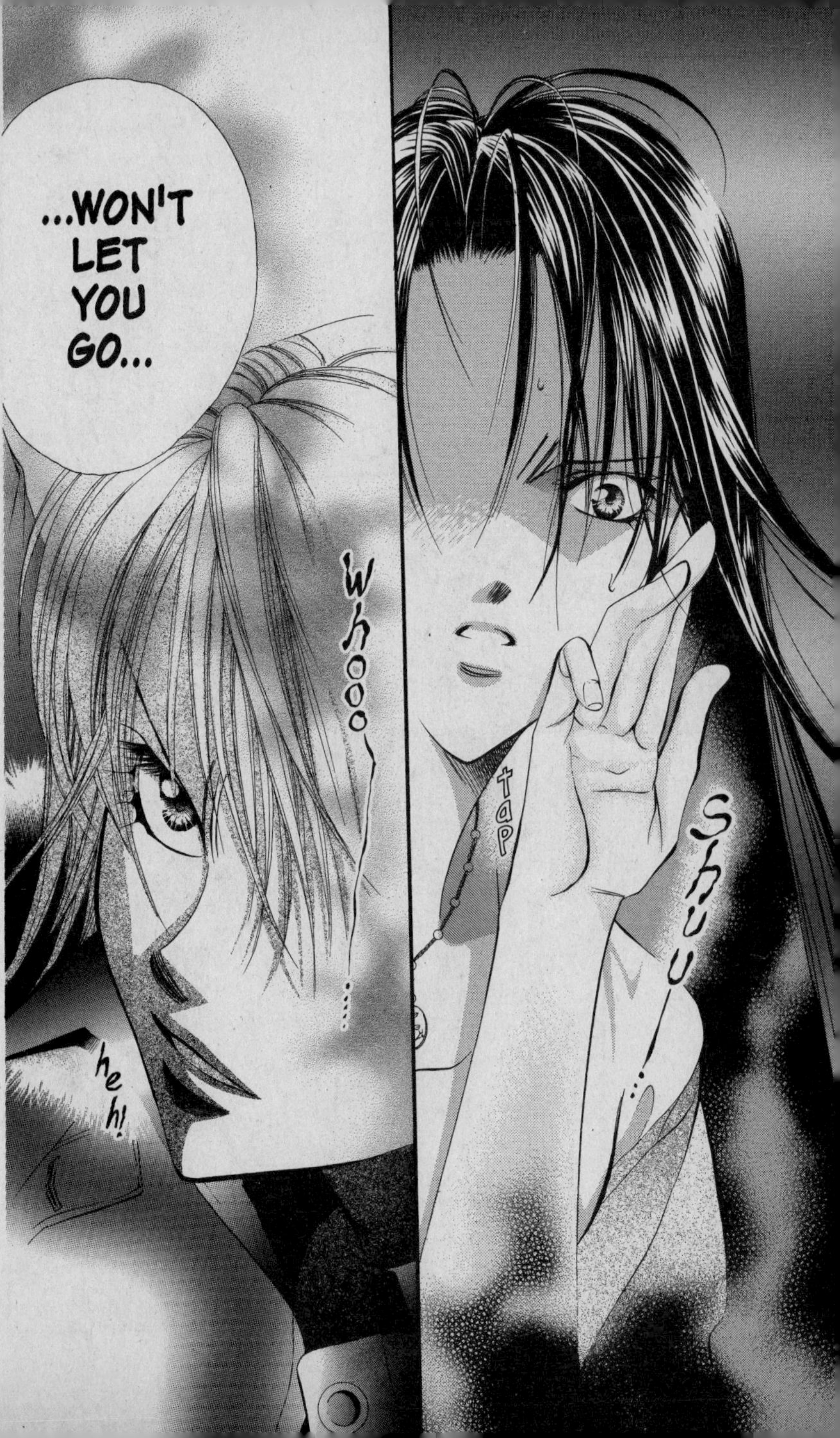
tap
Shuu...
...WON'T LET YOU GO...
Whooo...
heh!

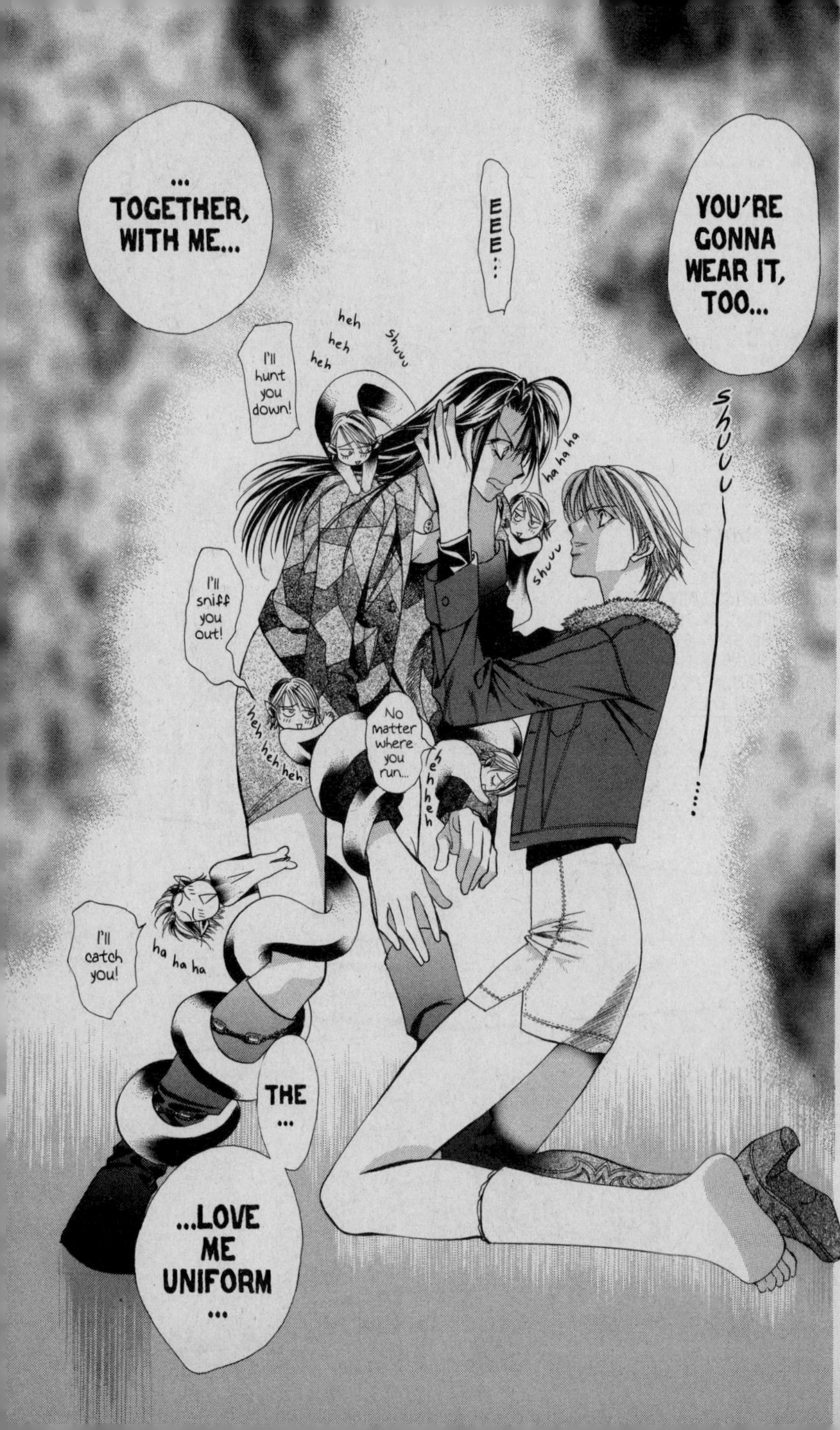
YOU'RE GONNA WEAR IT, TOO...
SHUUU......
EEE...
...TOGETHER, WITH ME...
heh heh heh
shuuu
I'll hunt you down!
ha ha ha
shuuu
I'll sniff you out!
No matter where you run...
heh heh heh
heh heh heh
I'll catch you!
ha ha ha
THE...
...LOVE ME UNIFORM...

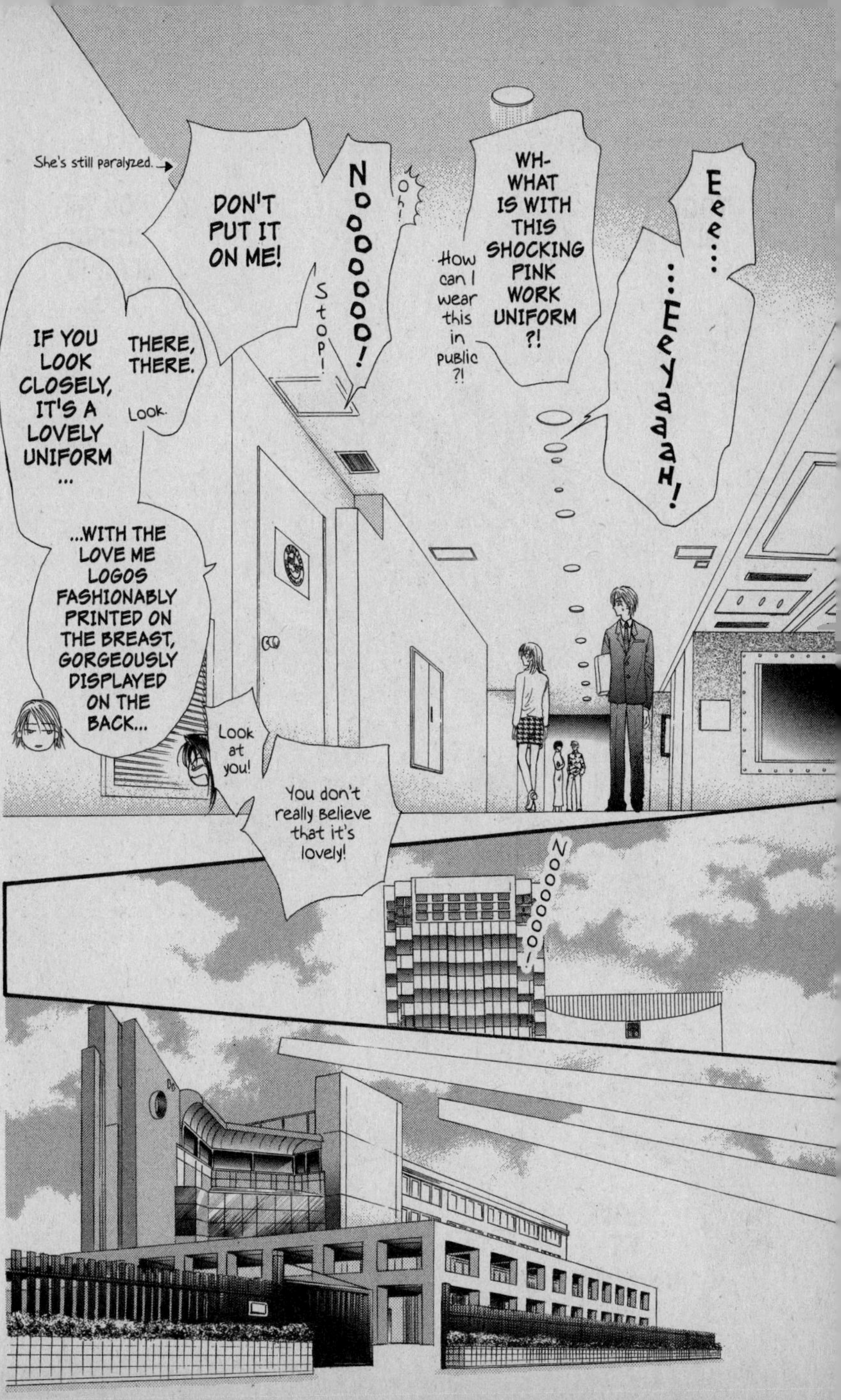
Eee...
...Eeyaaah!
WH-WHAT IS WITH THIS SHOCKING PINK WORK UNIFORM?!
How can I wear this in public?!
NOOOOOOO!
Oh!
Stop!
DON'T PUT IT ON ME!
She's still paralyzed.
THERE, THERE.
Look.
IF YOU LOOK CLOSELY, IT'S A LOVELY UNIFORM...
...WITH THE LOVE ME LOGOS FASHIONABLY PRINTED ON THE BREAST, GORGEOUSLY DISPLAYED ON THE BACK...
Look at you!
You don't really believe that it's lovely!
Nooooooo!

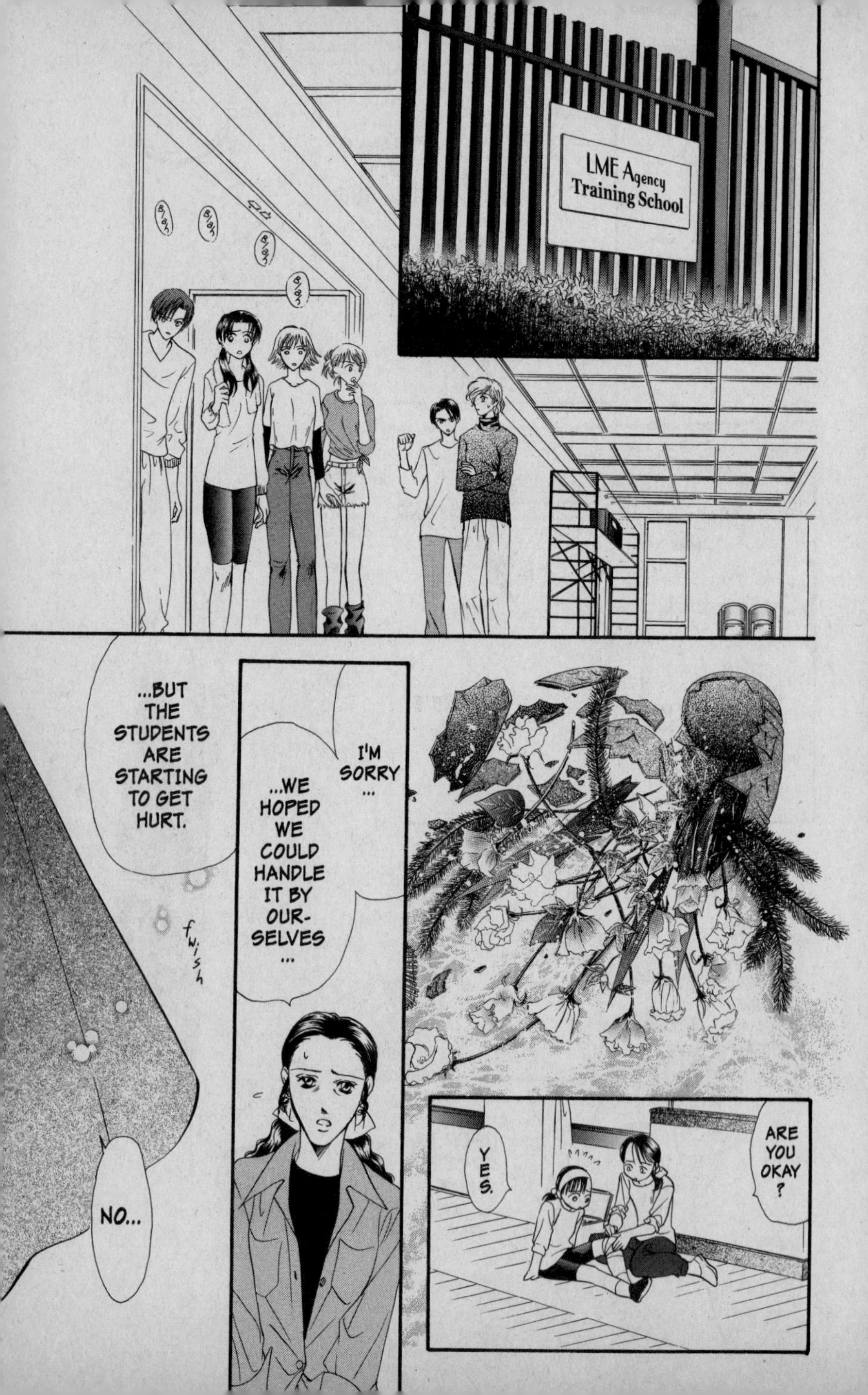
LME Agency Training School
I'M SORRY...
...WE HOPED WE COULD HANDLE IT BY OURSELVES...
...BUT THE STUDENTS ARE STARTING TO GET HURT.
ARE YOU OKAY?
YES.
fwish
NO...

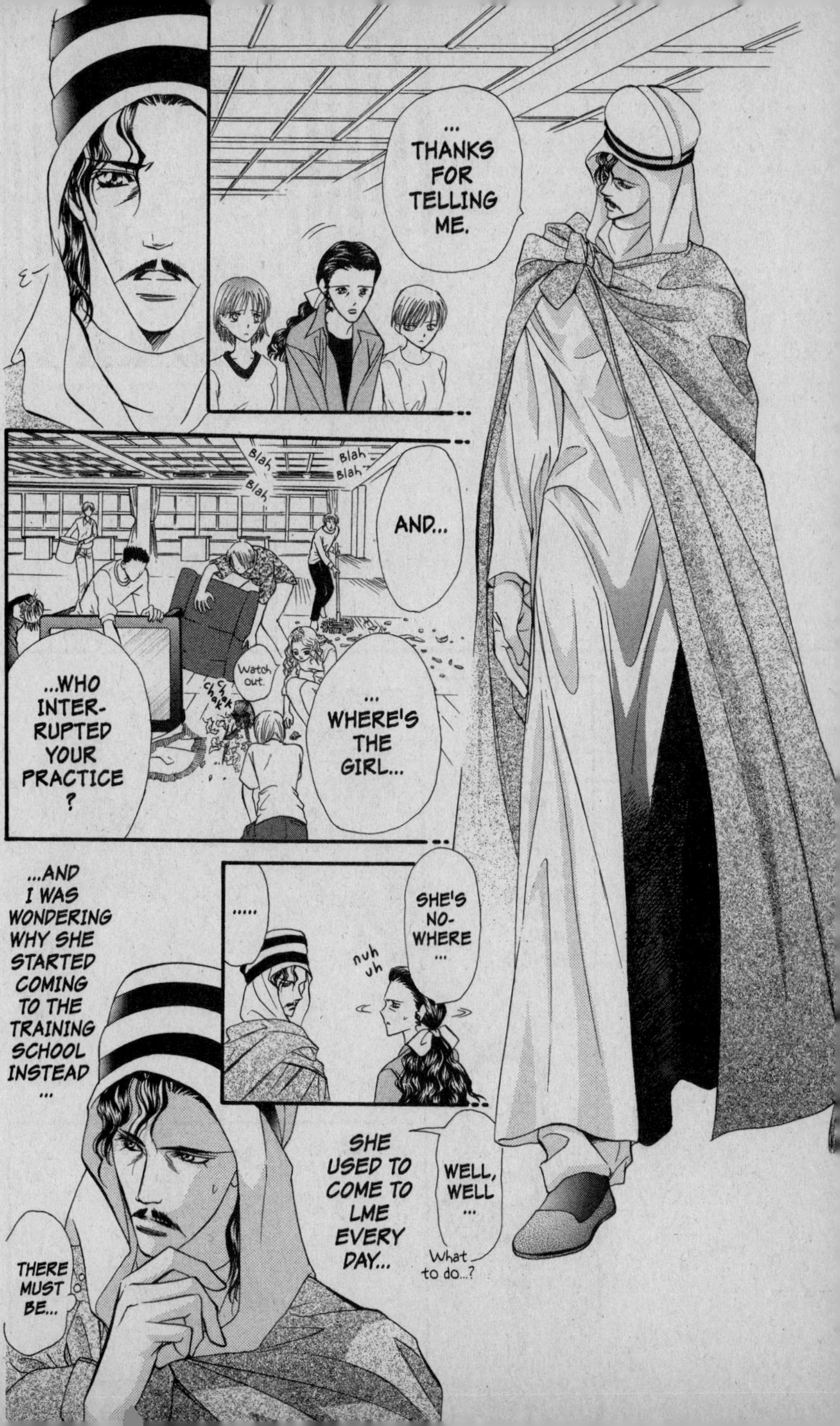

... THANKS FOR TELLING ME.
Blah Blah
Blah Blah
AND...
... WHERE'S THE GIRL...
Watch out.
Chak chak
...WHO INTER-RUPTED YOUR PRACTICE ?
SHE'S NO-WHERE ...
.....
nuh uh
WELL, WELL ...
What to do...?
SHE USED TO COME TO LME EVERY DAY...
...AND I WAS WONDERING WHY SHE STARTED COMING TO THE TRAINING SCHOOL INSTEAD ...
THERE MUST BE...

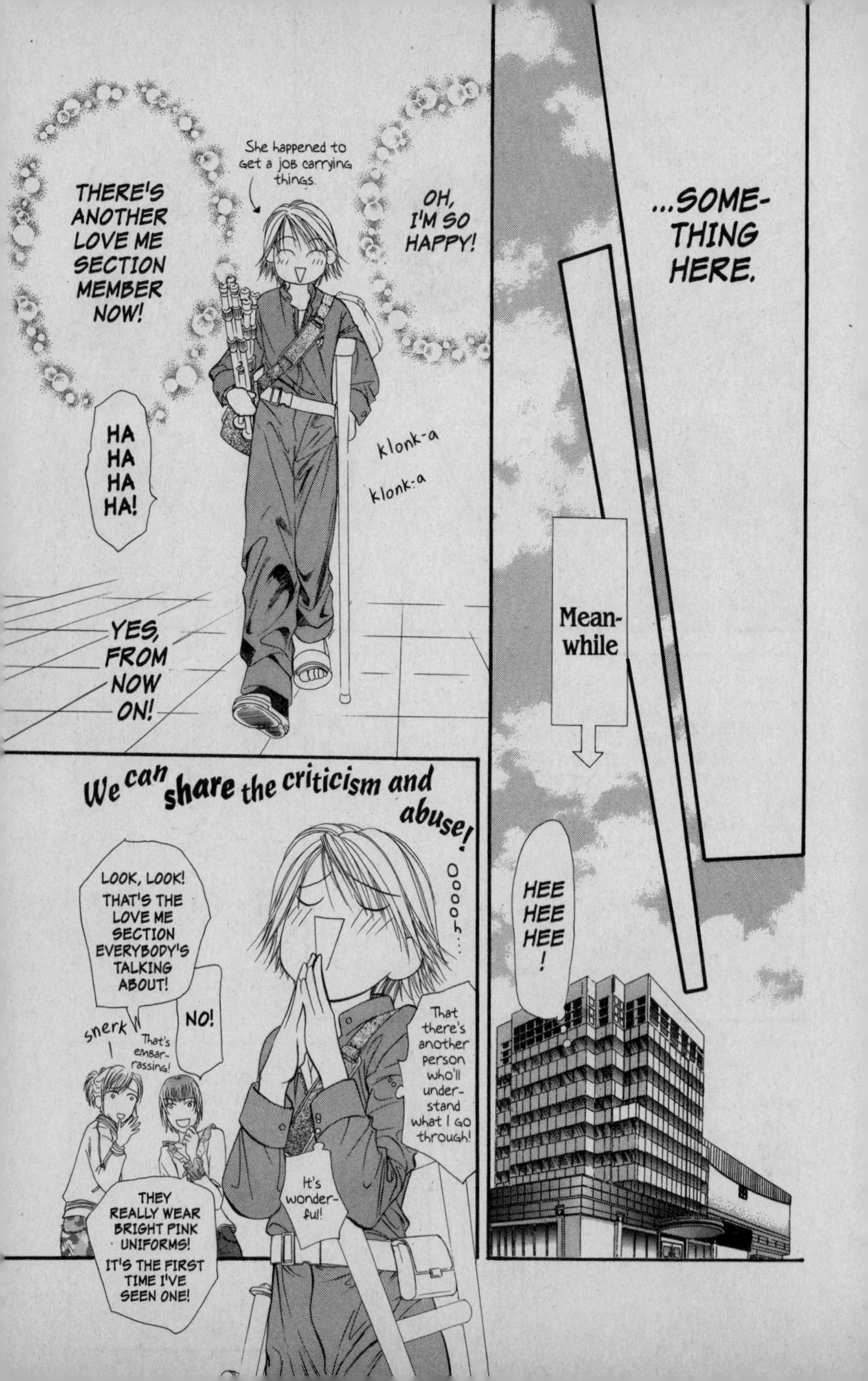
...SOME-THING HERE.
Mean-while
HEE HEE HEE!
OH, I'M SO HAPPY!
She happened to get a job carrying things.
THERE'S ANOTHER LOVE ME SECTION MEMBER NOW!
klonk-a
klonk-a
HA HA HA HA!
YES, FROM NOW ON!
We can share the criticism and abuse!
Ooooh...
That there's another person who'll under-stand what I go through!
It's wonder-ful!
LOOK, LOOK! THAT'S THE LOVE ME SECTION EVERYBODY'S TALKING ABOUT!
NO!
That's embar-rassing!
snerk
THEY REALLY WEAR BRIGHT PINK UNIFORMS! IT'S THE FIRST TIME I'VE SEEN ONE!

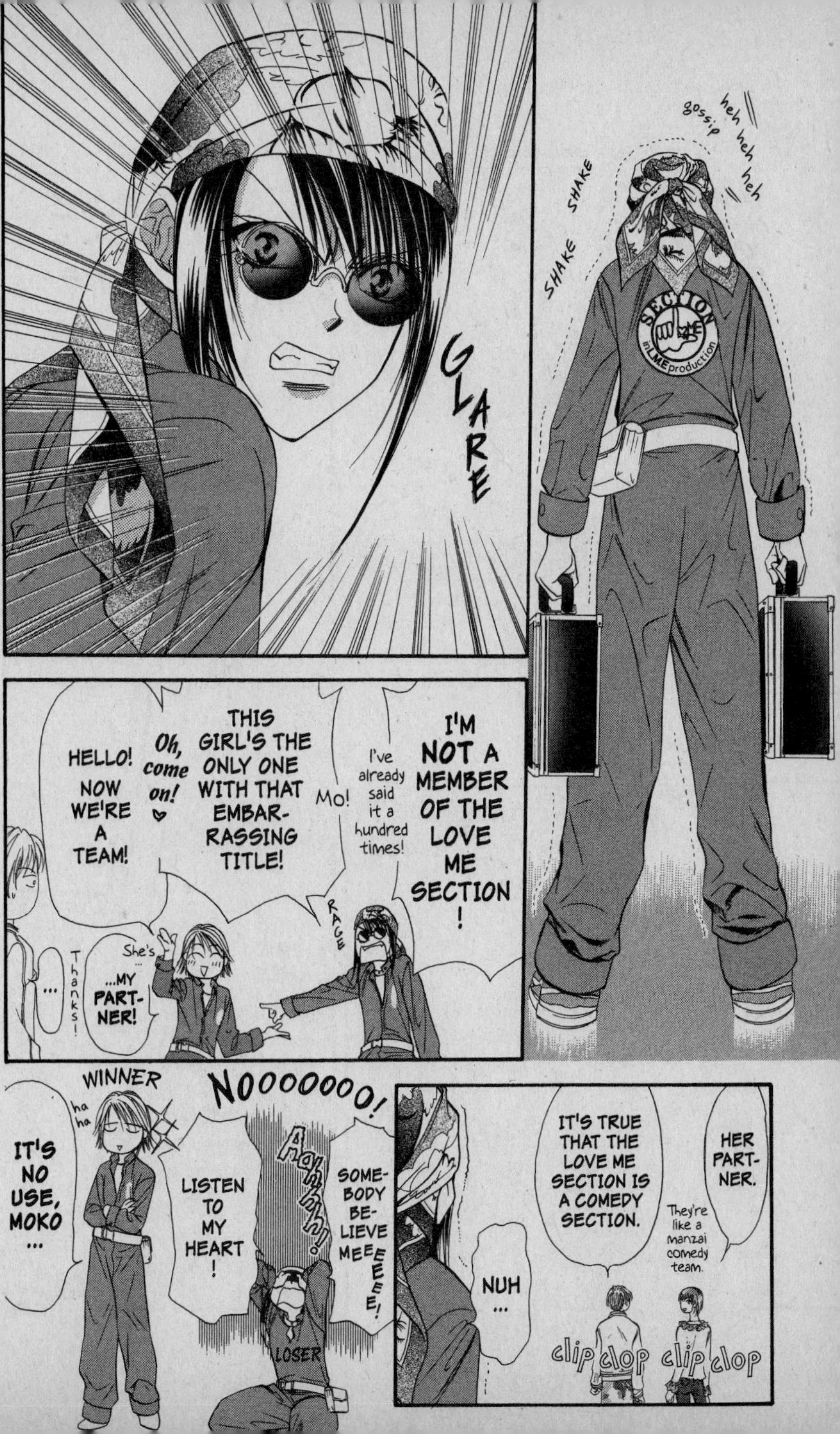
heh heh heh
gossip
SHAKE SHAKE
SECTION
LME
in LME production
GLARE
I'M NOT A MEMBER OF THE LOVE ME SECTION!
Mo! I've already said it a hundred times!
THIS GIRL'S THE ONLY ONE WITH THAT EMBARRASSING TITLE!
Oh, come on! ♥
HELLO! NOW WE'RE A TEAM!
RAGE
She's... ...MY PARTNER!
Thanks!
...
HER PARTNER.
They're like a manzai comedy team.
IT'S TRUE THAT THE LOVE ME SECTION IS A COMEDY SECTION.
NUH...
clip clop clip clop
NOOOOOOO!
SOMEBODY BELIEVE MEEEEEE!
Aahhh!
LISTEN TO MY HEART!
LOSER
WINNER
ha ha
IT'S NO USE, MOKO...

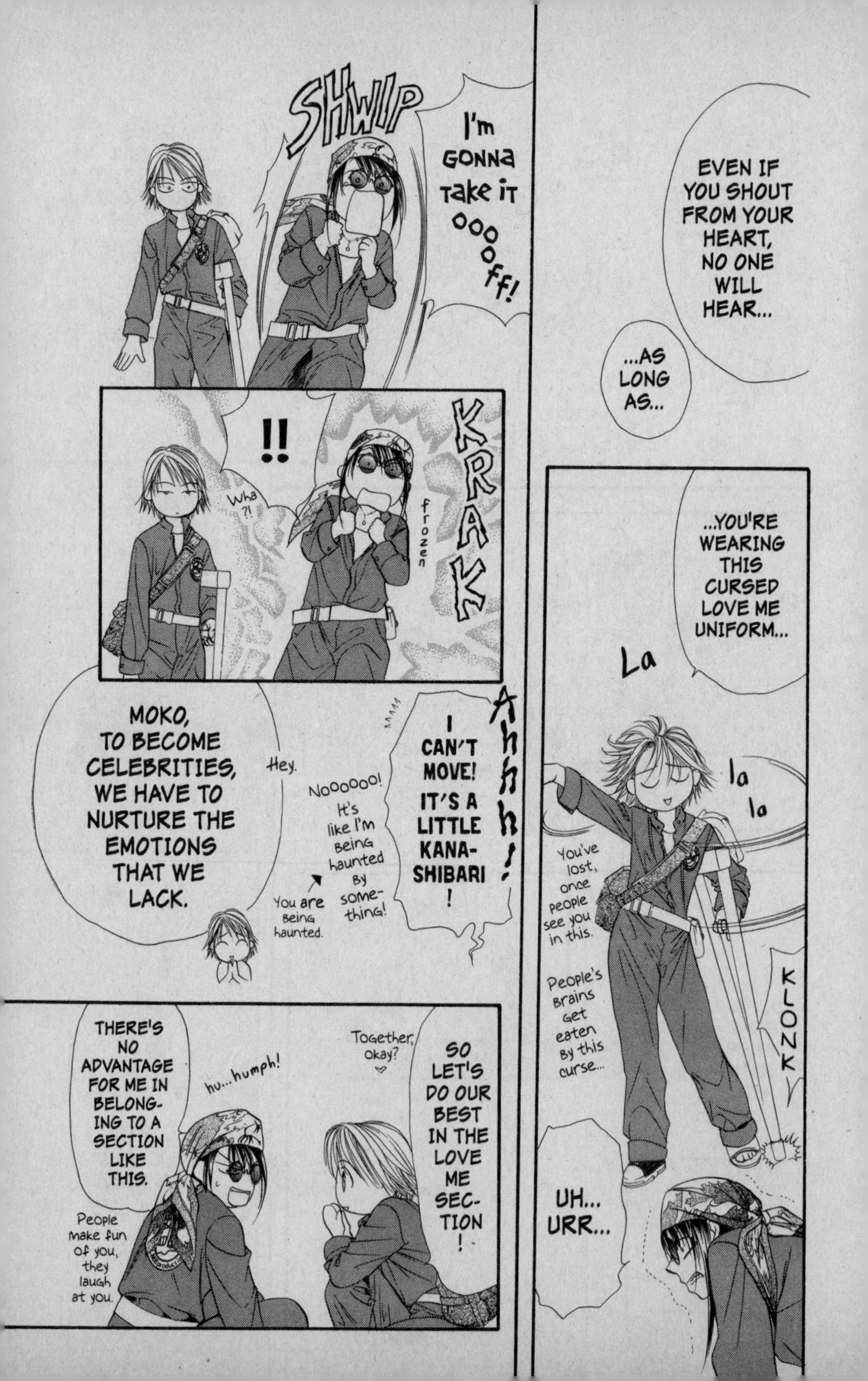
EVEN IF YOU SHOUT FROM YOUR HEART, NO ONE WILL HEAR...
...AS LONG AS...
...YOU'RE WEARING THIS CURSED LOVE ME UNIFORM...
La
la
la
You've lost, once people see you in this.
People's brains get eaten by this curse...
KLONK
UH... URR...
SHWIP
I'm GONNA take IT ooooff!
KRAK
!!
Wha?!
frozen
Ahhh!
I CAN'T MOVE! IT'S A LITTLE KANA-SHIBARI!
Noooooo! It's like I'm being haunted by something!
You are being haunted.
Hey.
MOKO, TO BECOME CELEBRITIES, WE HAVE TO NURTURE THE EMOTIONS THAT WE LACK.
SO LET'S DO OUR BEST IN THE LOVE ME SECTION!
Together, okay?
hu...humph!
THERE'S NO ADVANTAGE FOR ME IN BELONGING TO A SECTION LIKE THIS.
People make fun of you, they laugh at you.

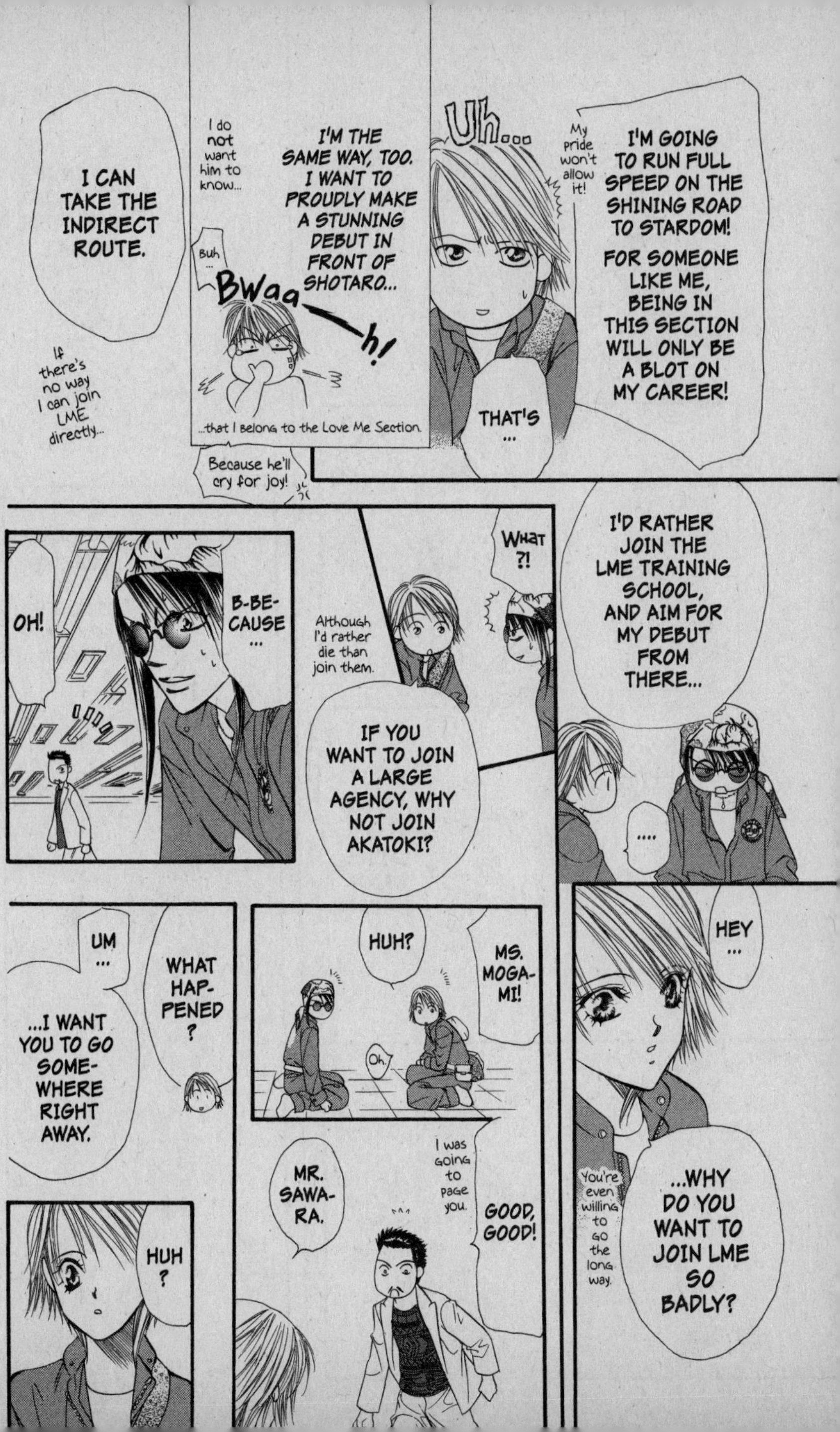
I'M GOING TO RUN FULL SPEED ON THE SHINING ROAD TO STARDOM!
FOR SOMEONE LIKE ME, BEING IN THIS SECTION WILL ONLY BE A BLOT ON MY CAREER!
My pride won't allow it!
Uh...
THAT'S...
I'M THE SAME WAY, TOO. I WANT TO PROUDLY MAKE A STUNNING DEBUT IN FRONT OF SHOTARO...
I do not want him to know...
Buh...
BWaa—h!
...that I belong to the Love Me Section.
Because he'll cry for joy!
I CAN TAKE THE INDIRECT ROUTE.
If there's no way I can join LME directly...
I'D RATHER JOIN THE LME TRAINING SCHOOL, AND AIM FOR MY DEBUT FROM THERE...
....
WHAT?!
Although I'd rather die than join them.
IF YOU WANT TO JOIN A LARGE AGENCY, WHY NOT JOIN AKATOKI?
B-BE-CAUSE...
OH!
HEY...
You're even willing to go the long way.
...WHY DO YOU WANT TO JOIN LME SO BADLY?
MS. MOGA-MI!
HUH?
Oh.
MR. SAWA-RA.
GOOD, GOOD!
I was going to page you.
WHAT HAP-PENED?
UM...
...I WANT YOU TO GO SOMEWHERE RIGHT AWAY.
HUH?

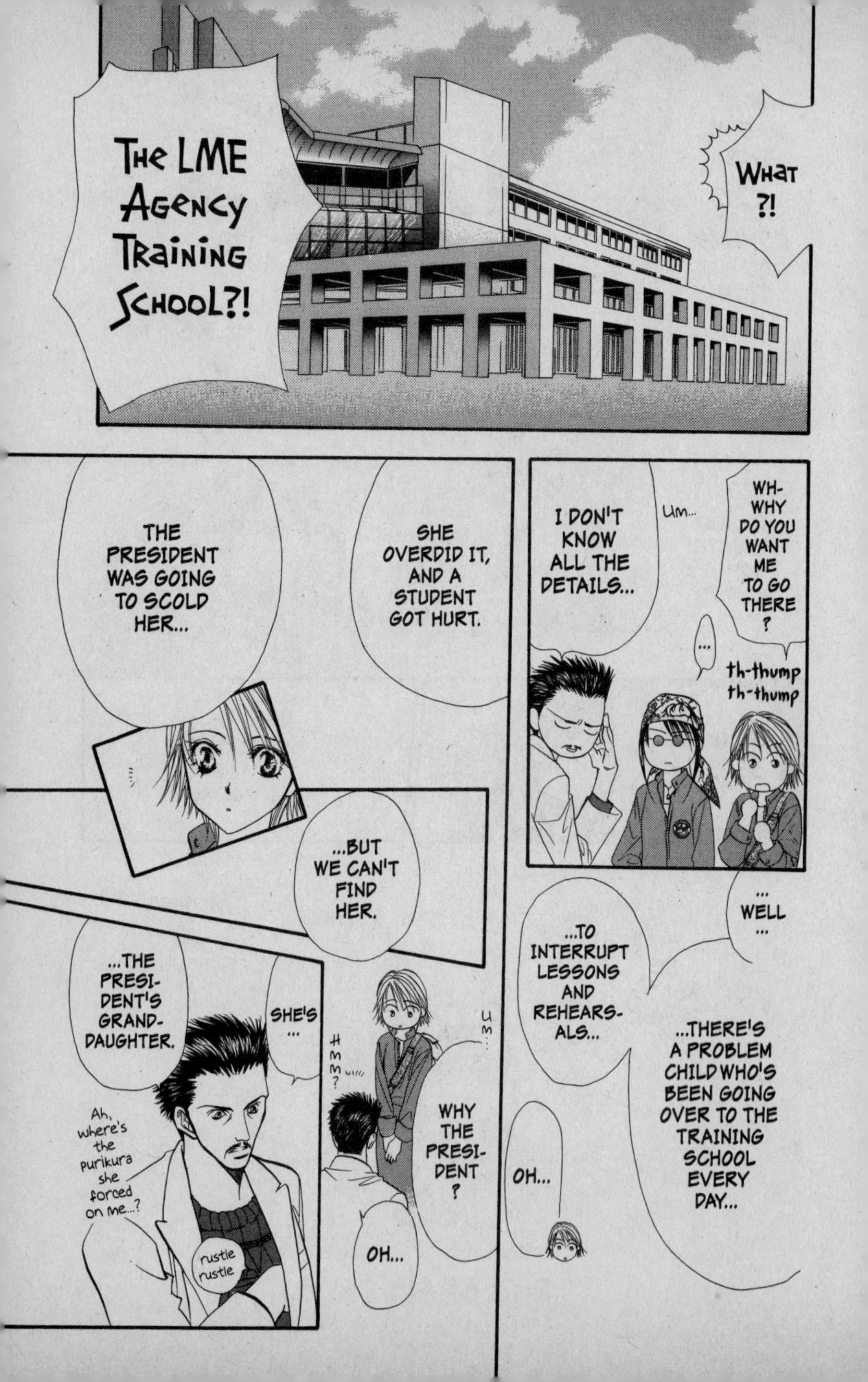
What ?!
The LME Agency Training School?!
WH-WHY DO YOU WANT ME TO GO THERE?
...
th-thump th-thump
Um...
I DON'T KNOW ALL THE DETAILS...
... WELL ...
...THERE'S A PROBLEM CHILD WHO'S BEEN GOING OVER TO THE TRAINING SCHOOL EVERY DAY...
...TO INTERRUPT LESSONS AND REHEARSALS...
OH...
SHE OVERDID IT, AND A STUDENT GOT HURT.
THE PRESIDENT WAS GOING TO SCOLD HER...
...BUT WE CAN'T FIND HER.
Um...
Hmm?
WHY THE PRESIDENT?
OH...
SHE'S ...
...THE PRESIDENT'S GRANDDAUGHTER.
Ah, where's the purikura she forced on me...?
rustle rustle

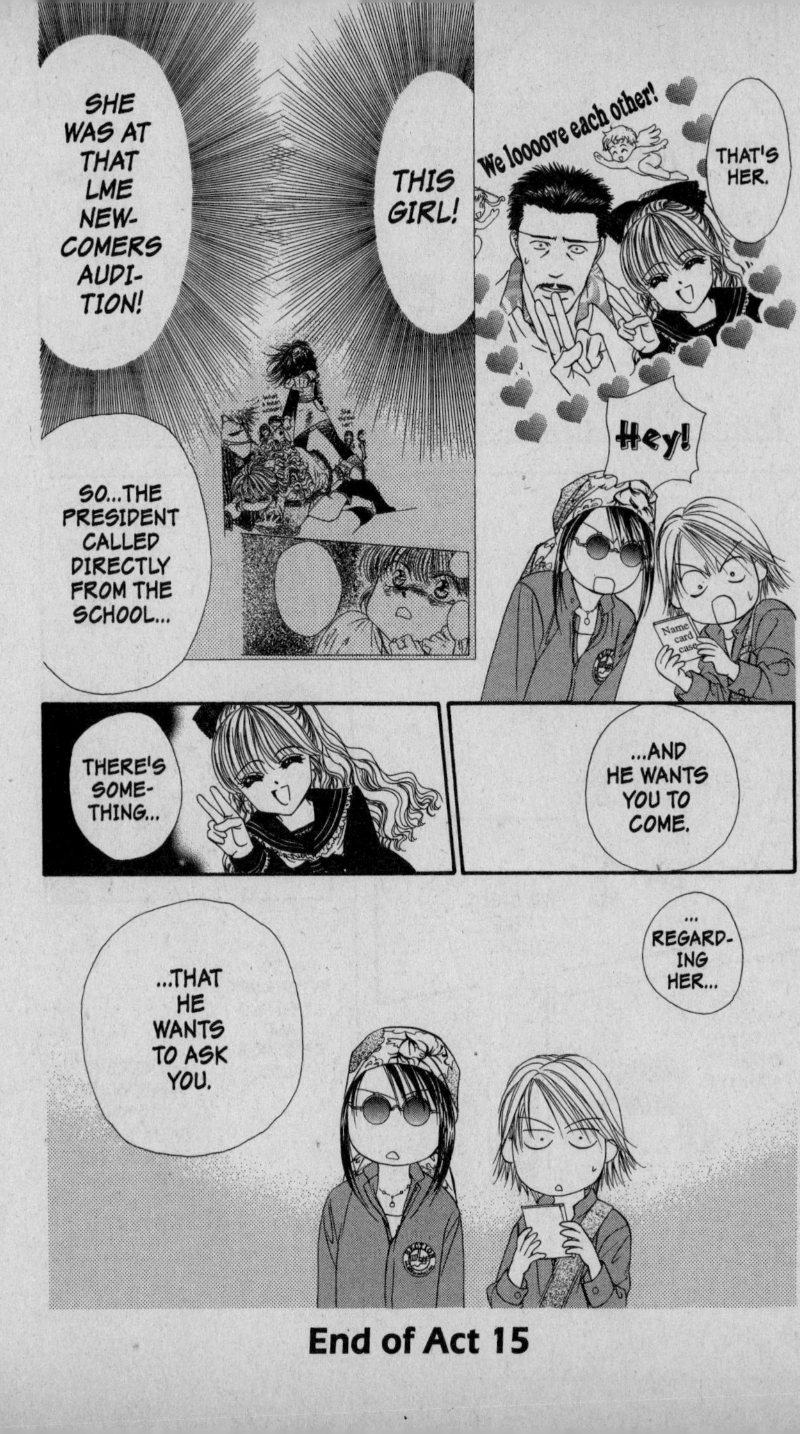
THAT'S HER.
We loooove each other!
Hey!
Name card case
THIS GIRL!
SHE WAS AT THAT LME NEW-COMERS AUDI-TION!
SO...THE PRESIDENT CALLED DIRECTLY FROM THE SCHOOL...
...AND HE WANTS YOU TO COME.
THERE'S SOME-THING...
...REGARD-ING HER...
...THAT HE WANTS TO ASK YOU.

End of Act 15

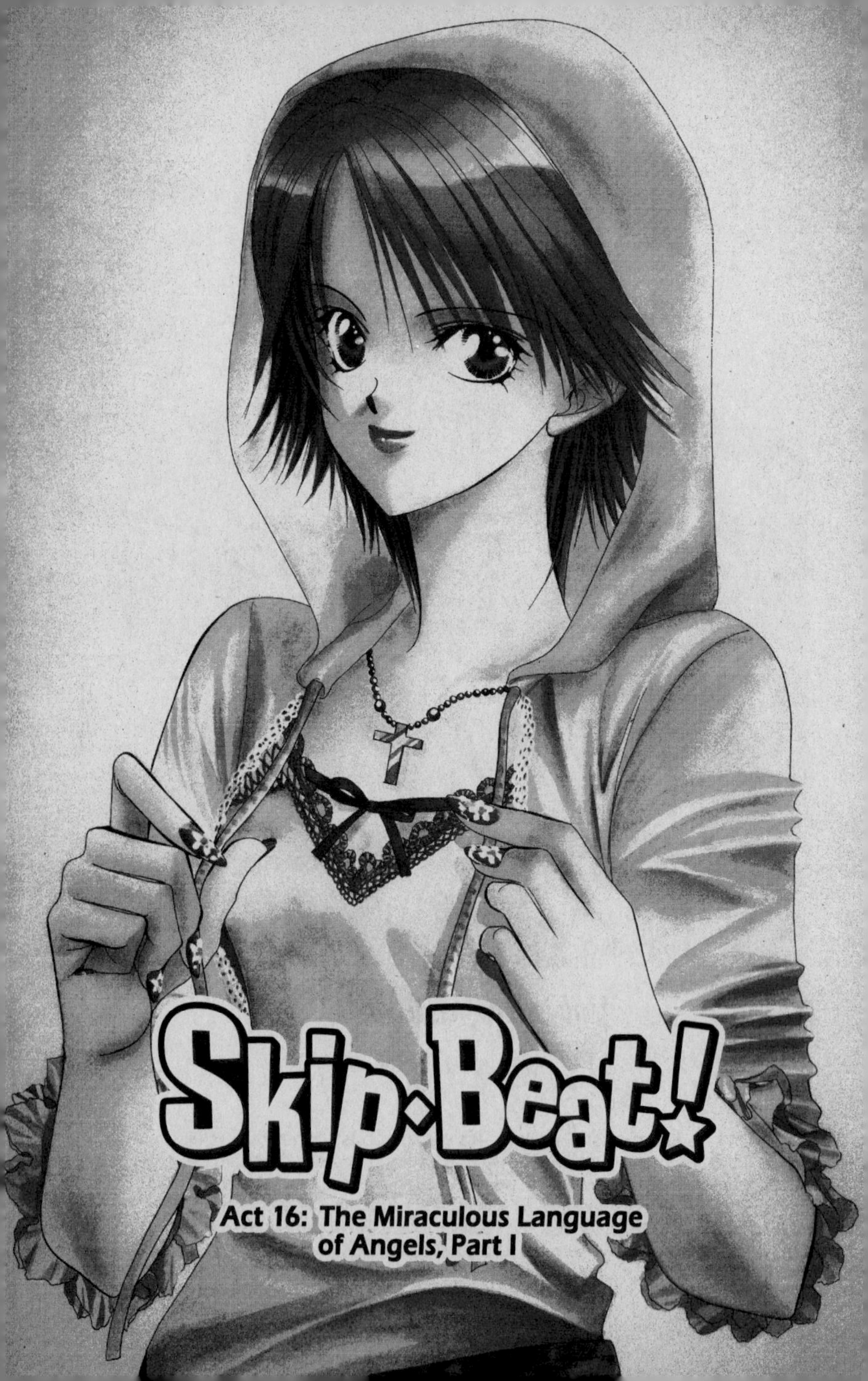
Skip·Beat!
Act 16: The Miraculous Language of Angels, Part I

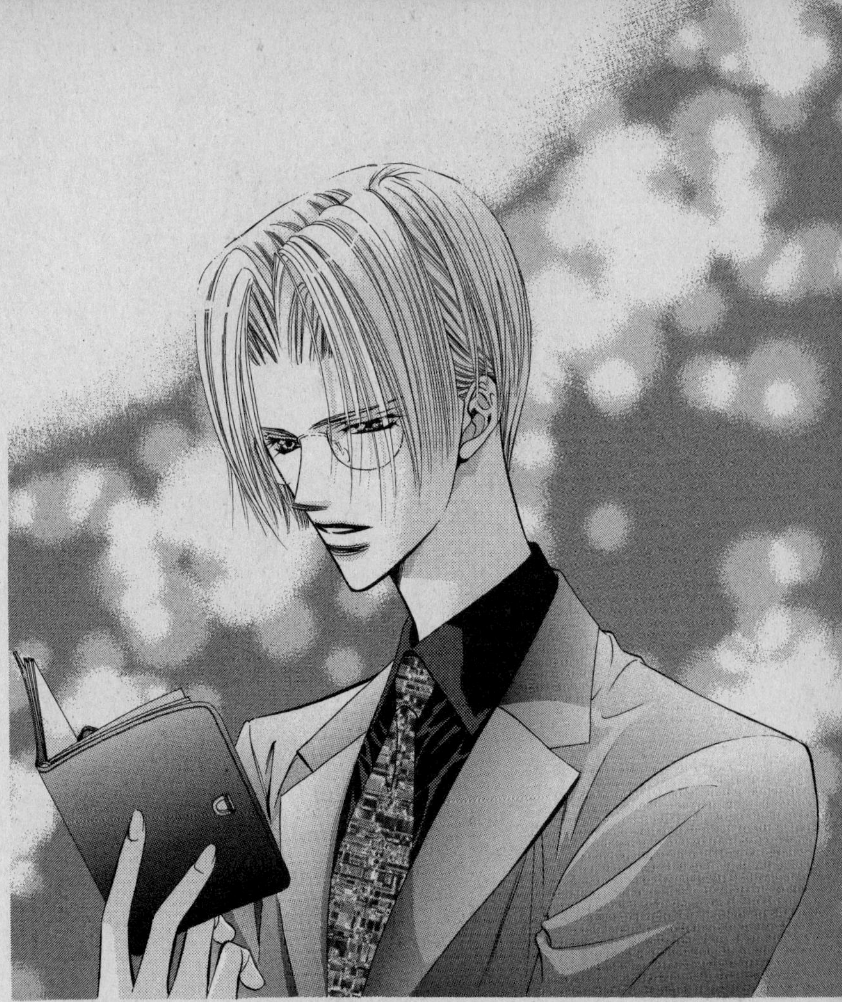

Yukihito Yashiro

Difficulty level ☆☆☆☆ (4)

It's his hair that's difficult... His expression is softer than it was in the beginning, and I'm not sure whether that's good or bad. I feel that the blurry image of Yashiro I had in my head has changed a little bit... But this Yashiro...he hasn't really done anything conspicuous, but somehow, secretly, the readers love him and I'm surprised...does that mean girls love guys who wear glasses...?

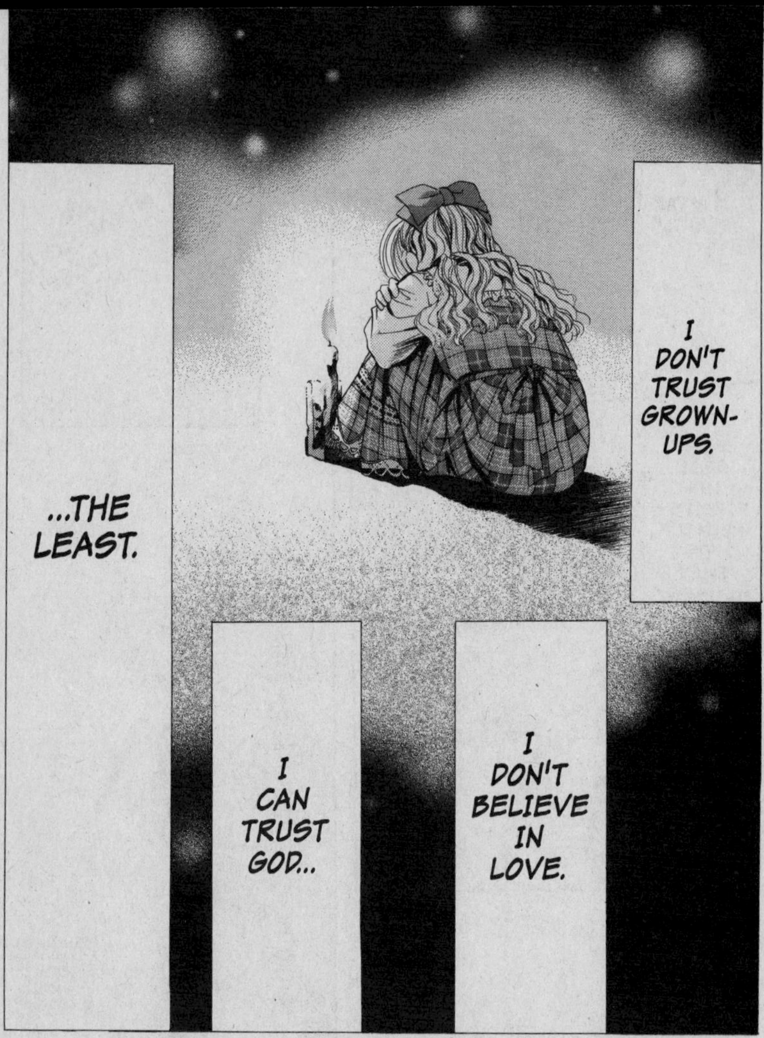
I DON'T TRUST GROWN-UPS.
I DON'T BELIEVE IN LOVE.
I CAN TRUST GOD...
...THE LEAST.

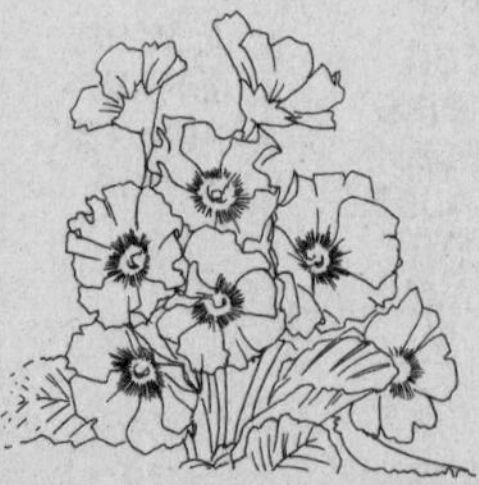

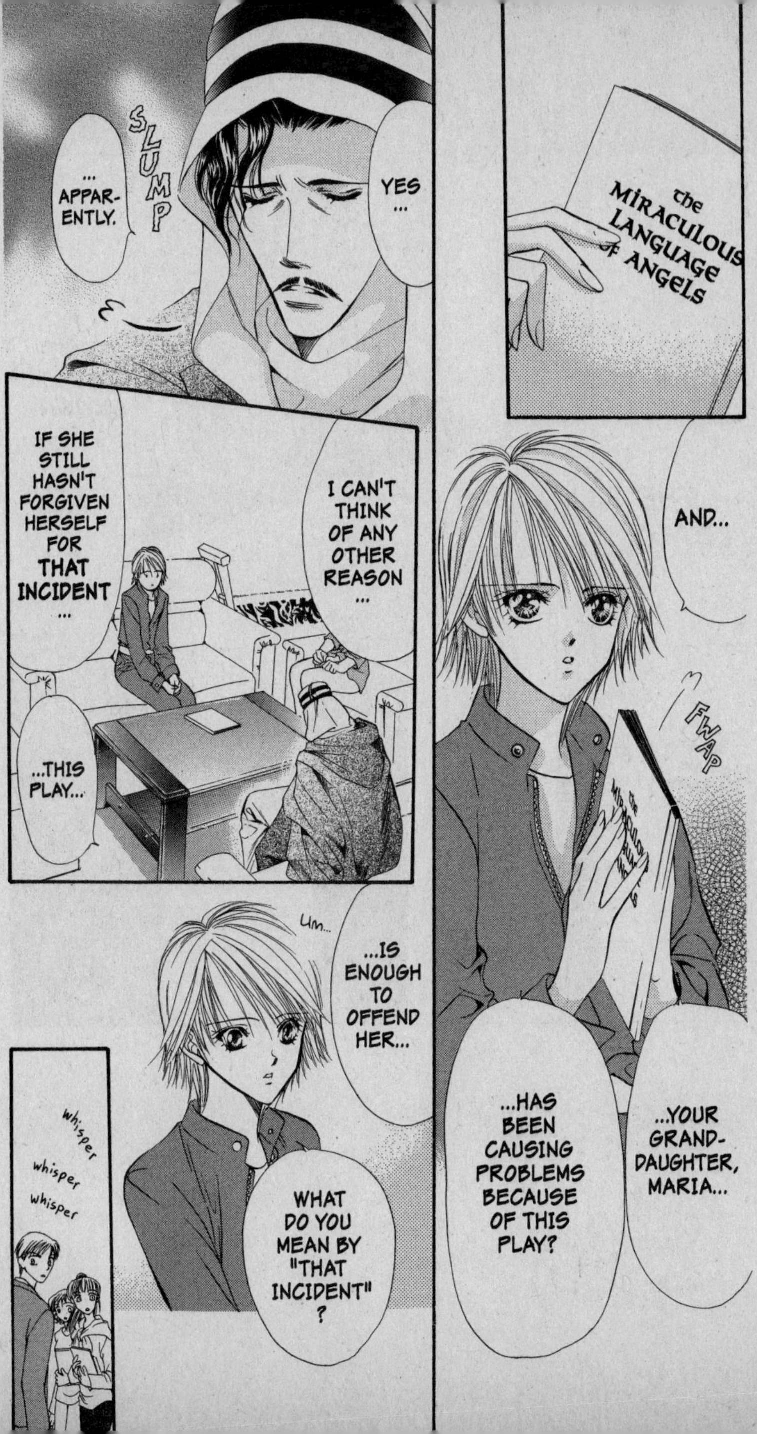
the MIRACULOUS LANGUAGE of ANGELS
AND...
FWAP
...YOUR GRAND-DAUGHTER, MARIA...
...HAS BEEN CAUSING PROBLEMS BECAUSE OF THIS PLAY?
YES...
SLUMP
...APPARENTLY.
I CAN'T THINK OF ANY OTHER REASON...
IF SHE STILL HASN'T FORGIVEN HERSELF FOR THAT INCIDENT...
...THIS PLAY...
...IS ENOUGH TO OFFEND HER...
Um...
WHAT DO YOU MEAN BY "THAT INCIDENT"?
whisper
whisper
whisper

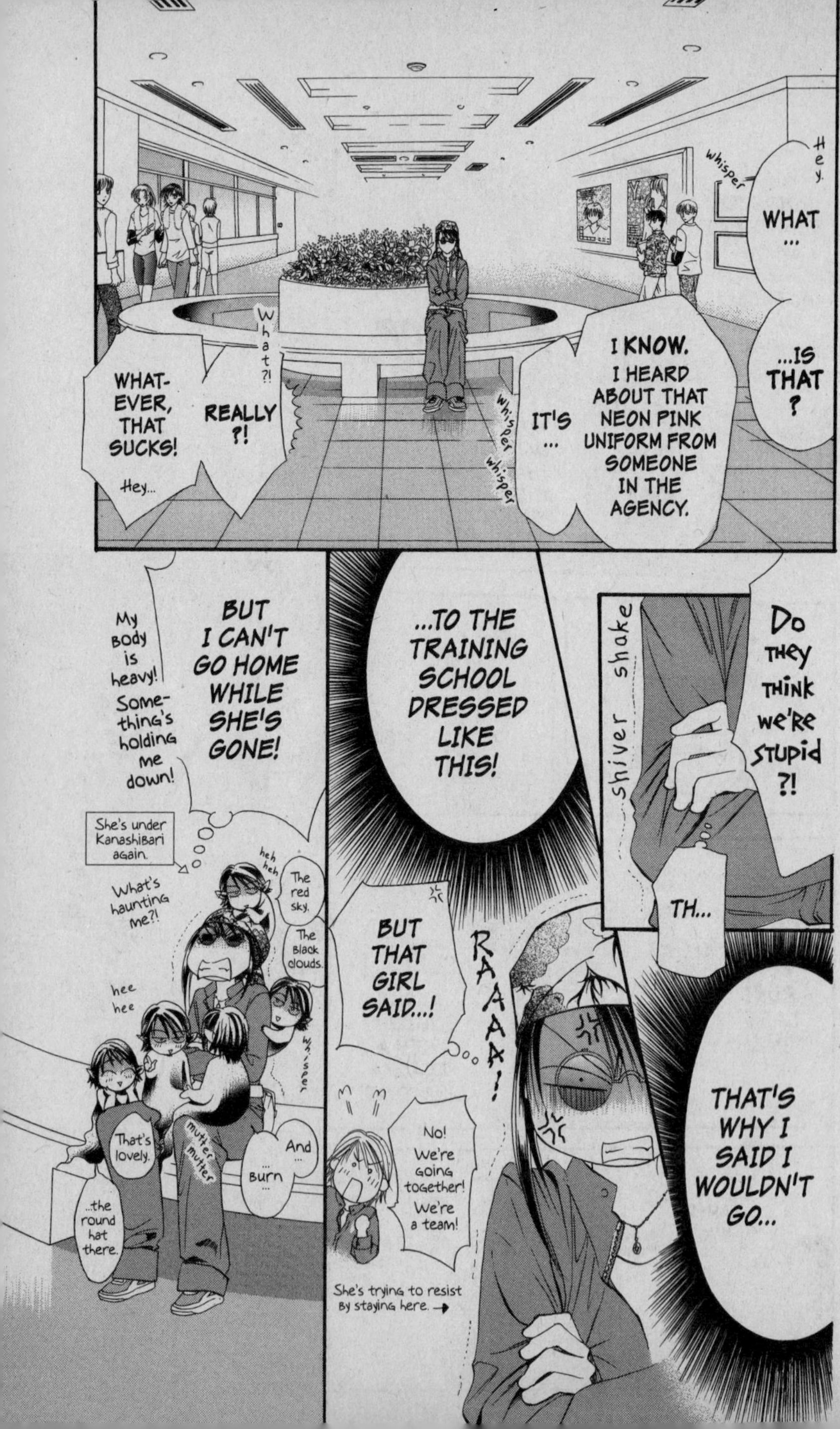
Hey.
whisper
WHAT ...
...IS THAT?
I KNOW. I HEARD ABOUT THAT NEON PINK UNIFORM FROM SOMEONE IN THE AGENCY.
IT'S ...
whisper whisper
What?!
REALLY?!
WHAT-EVER, THAT SUCKS!
Hey...
Do they think we're stupid?!
shiver shake
TH...
...TO THE TRAINING SCHOOL DRESSED LIKE THIS!
THAT'S WHY I SAID I WOULDN'T GO...
RAAAA!
BUT THAT GIRL SAID...!
No! We're going together! We're a team!
She's trying to resist by staying here. →
BUT I CAN'T GO HOME WHILE SHE'S GONE!
My body is heavy! Some-thing's holding me down!
She's under Kanashibari again.
What's haunting me?!
heh heh
The red sky.
The black clouds.
hee hee
whisper
And ...
... Burn ...
mutter mutter
That's lovely.
...the round hat there.

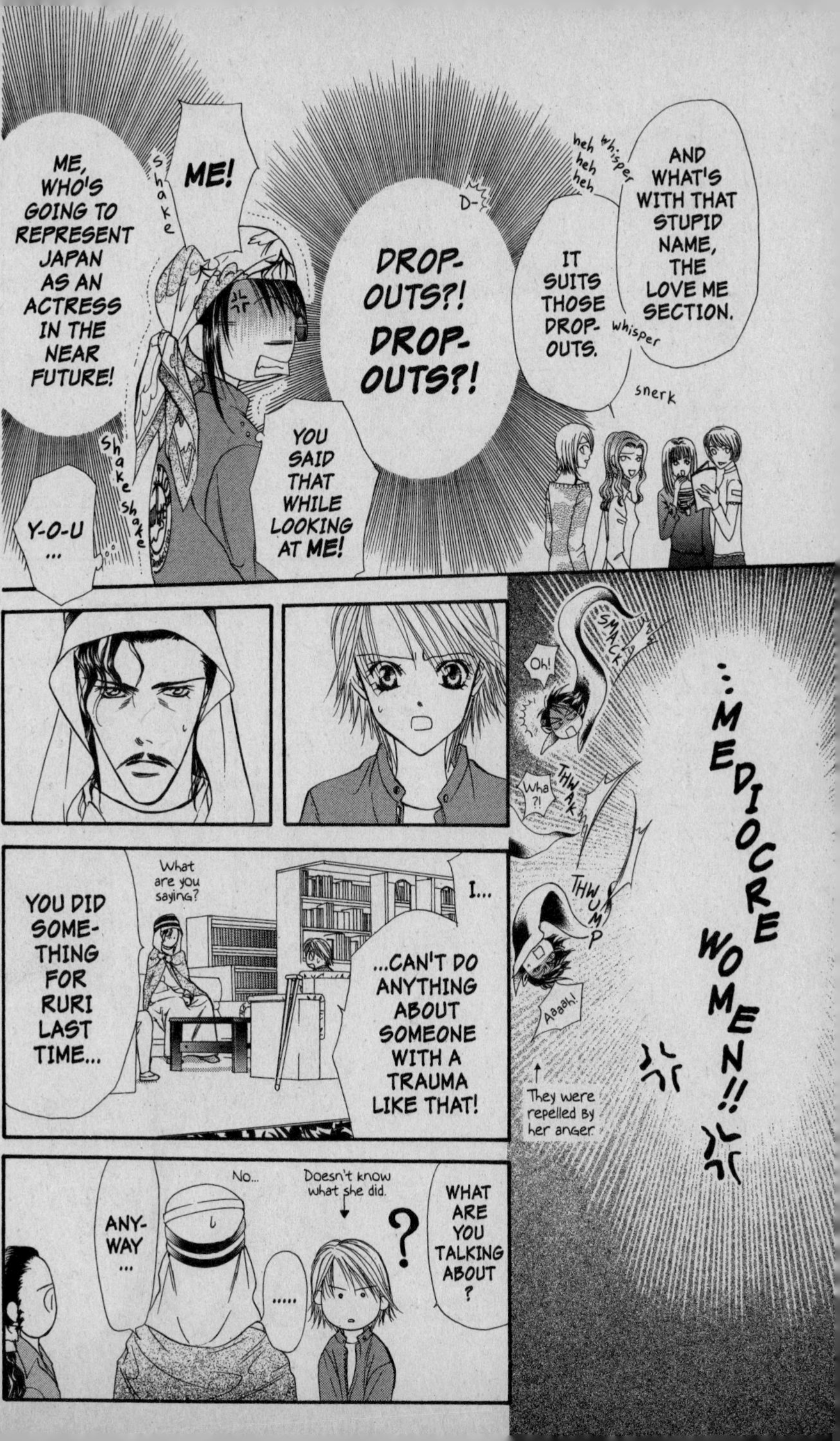

AND WHAT'S WITH THAT STUPID NAME, THE LOVE ME SECTION.
whisper
heh heh heh
IT SUITS THOSE DROP-OUTS.
whisper
snerk
D-
DROP-OUTS?! DROP-OUTS?!
YOU SAID THAT WHILE LOOKING AT ME!
ME!
shake
ME, WHO'S GOING TO REPRESENT JAPAN AS AN ACTRESS IN THE NEAR FUTURE!
shake shake
Y-O-U ...
...MEDIOCRE WOMEN!!
SMACK
Oh!
THWAK
Wha ?!
THWUMP
Aaaah!
They were repelled by her anger.
I...
...CAN'T DO ANYTHING ABOUT SOMEONE WITH A TRAUMA LIKE THAT!
What are you saying?
YOU DID SOMETHING FOR RURI LAST TIME...
WHAT ARE YOU TALKING ABOUT?
?
Doesn't know what she did.
No...
.....
ANY-WAY ...

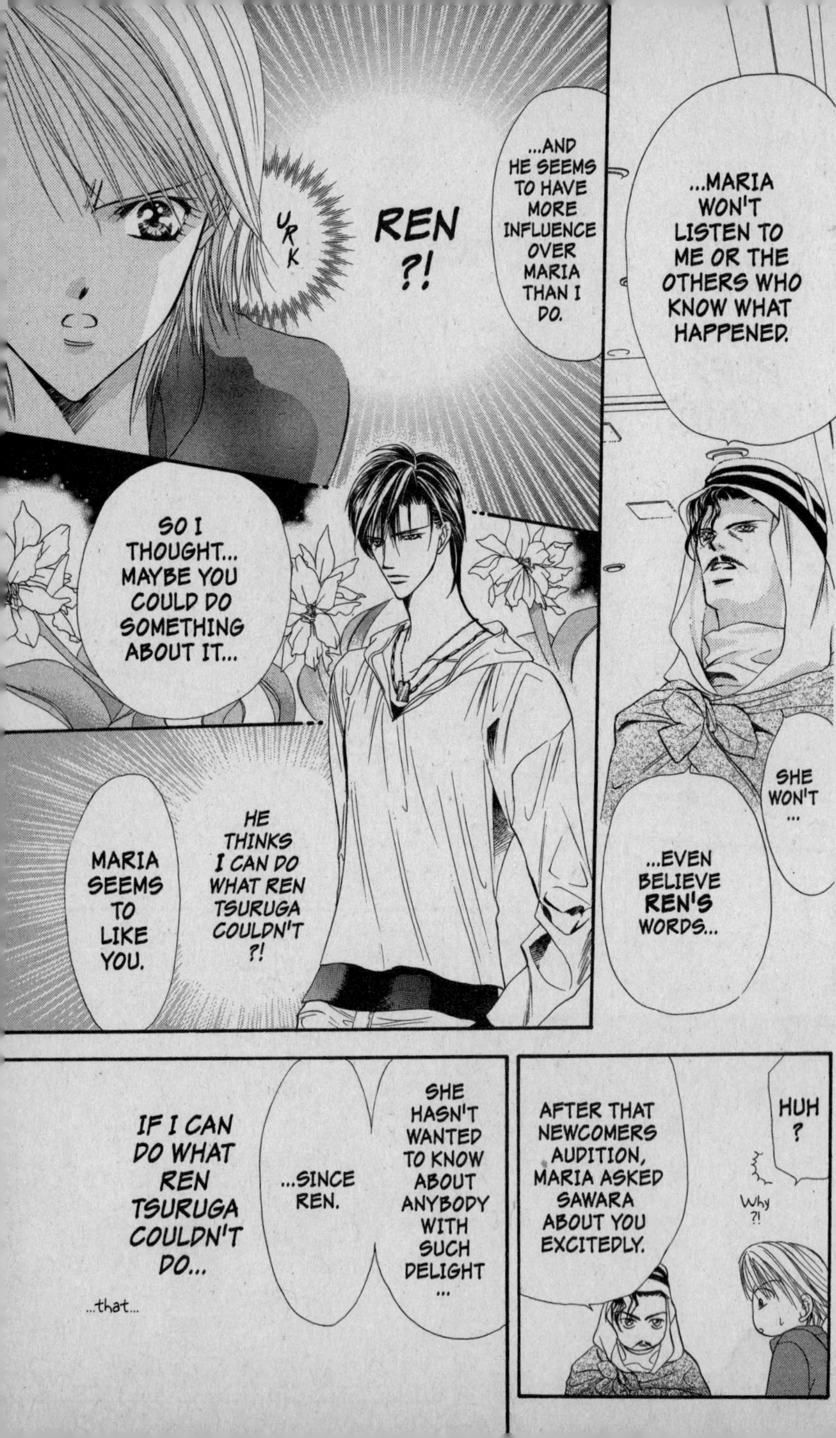
...MARIA WON'T LISTEN TO ME OR THE OTHERS WHO KNOW WHAT HAPPENED.
...AND HE SEEMS TO HAVE MORE INFLUENCE OVER MARIA THAN I DO.
REN ?!
URK
SHE WON'T ...
...EVEN BELIEVE REN'S WORDS...
SO I THOUGHT... MAYBE YOU COULD DO SOMETHING ABOUT IT...
HE THINKS I CAN DO WHAT REN TSURUGA COULDN'T ?!
MARIA SEEMS TO LIKE YOU.
HUH ?
Why ?!
AFTER THAT NEWCOMERS AUDITION, MARIA ASKED SAWARA ABOUT YOU EXCITEDLY.
SHE HASN'T WANTED TO KNOW ABOUT ANYBODY WITH SUCH DELIGHT ...
...SINCE REN.
IF I CAN DO WHAT REN TSURUGA COULDN'T DO...
...that...

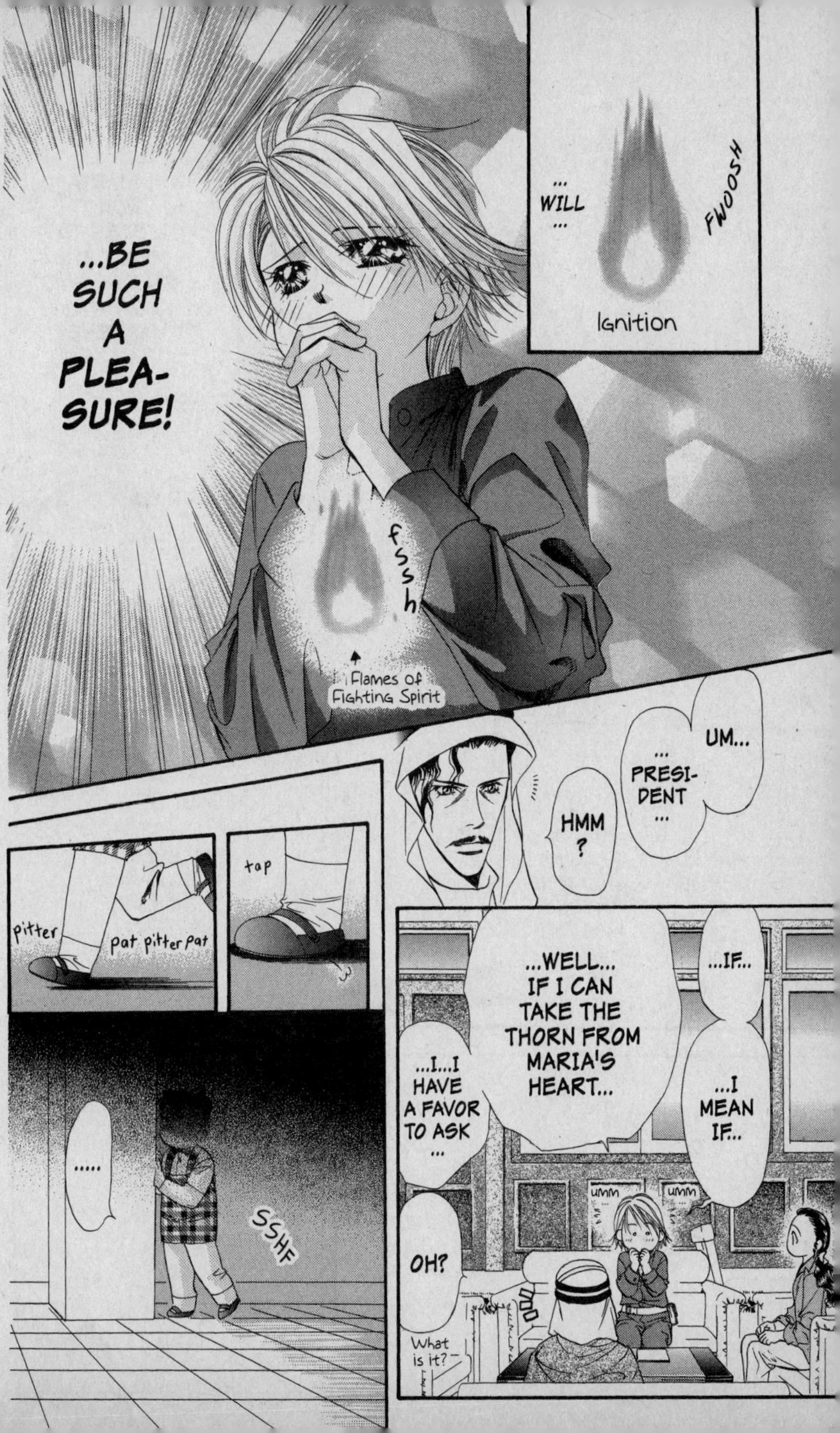

...WILL...
FWOOSH
Ignition
...BE SUCH A PLEA-SURE!
fssh
Flames of Fighting Spirit
UM...
...PRESI-DENT...
HMM?
tap
pitter
pat pitter pat
...IF...
...I MEAN IF..
...WELL... IF I CAN TAKE THE THORN FROM MARIA'S HEART...
...I...I HAVE A FAVOR TO ASK...
umm
umm
OH?
What is it?
.....
SSHF

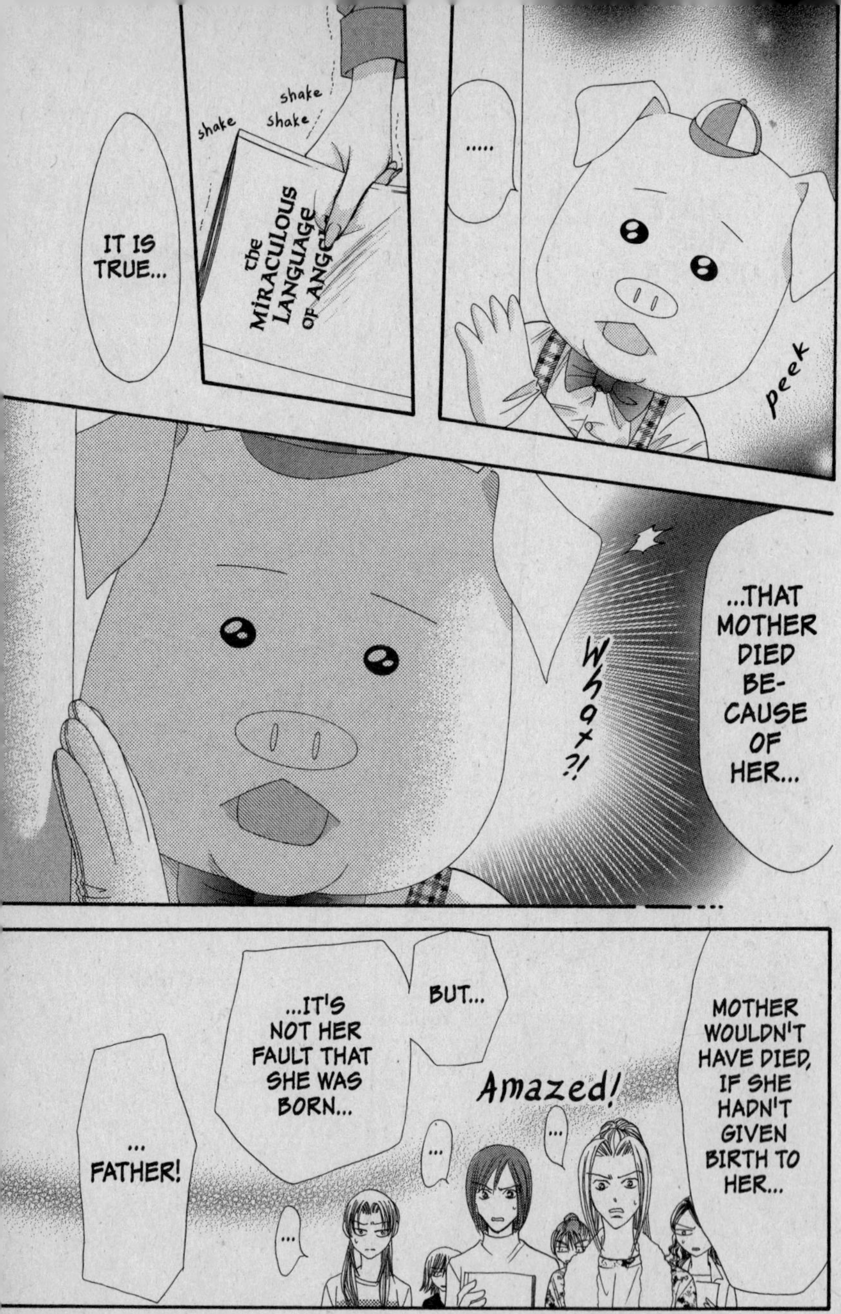
.....
peek
shake
shake
shake
the MIRACULOUS LANGUAGE OF ANGE
IT IS TRUE...
...THAT MOTHER DIED BE-CAUSE OF HER...
What?!
MOTHER WOULDN'T HAVE DIED, IF SHE HADN'T GIVEN BIRTH TO HER...
BUT...
...IT'S NOT HER FAULT THAT SHE WAS BORN...
Amazed!
...
...
...
... FATHER!

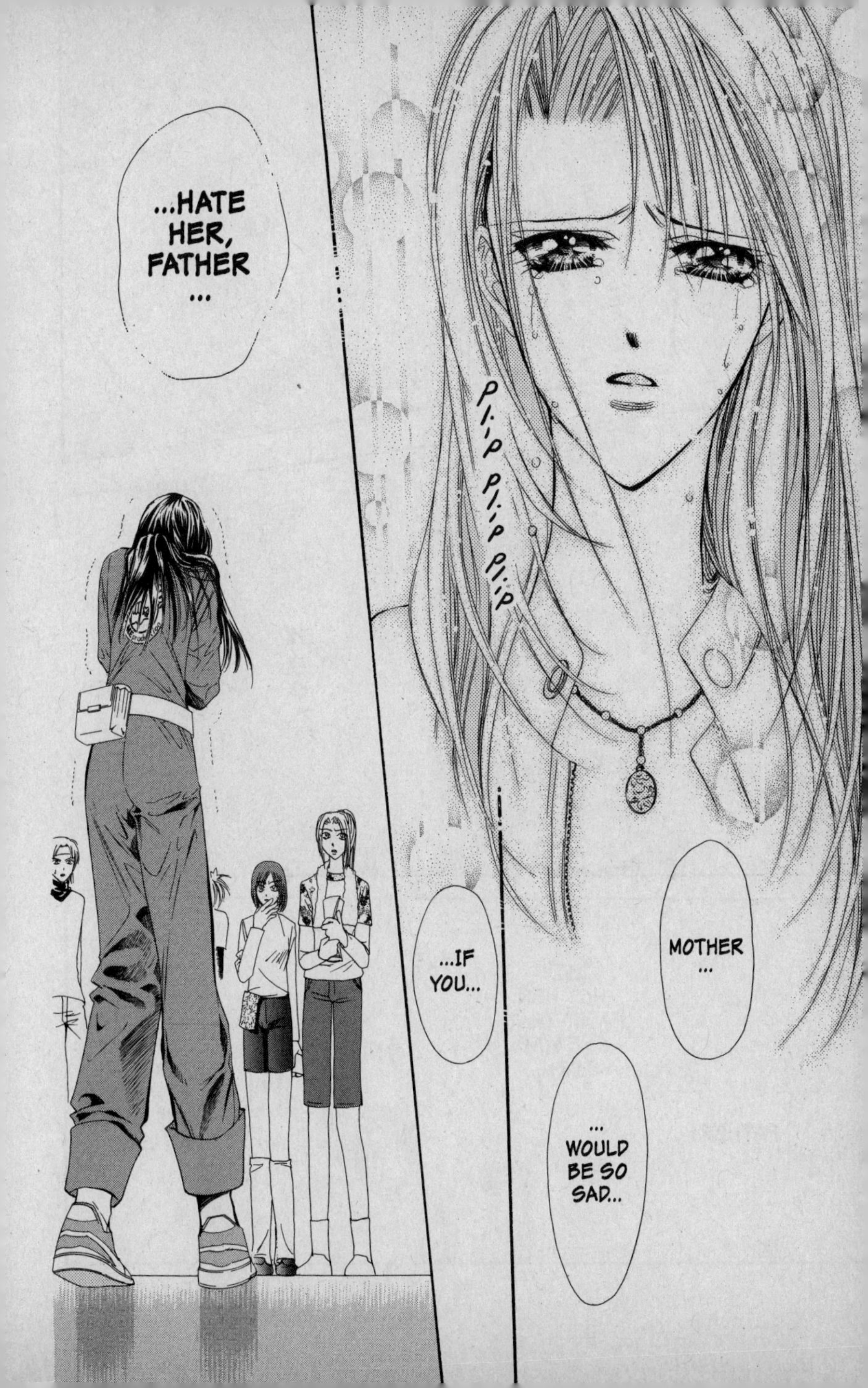
PLIP PLIP PLIP
MOTHER...
...WOULD BE SO SAD...
...IF YOU...
...HATE HER, FATHER...

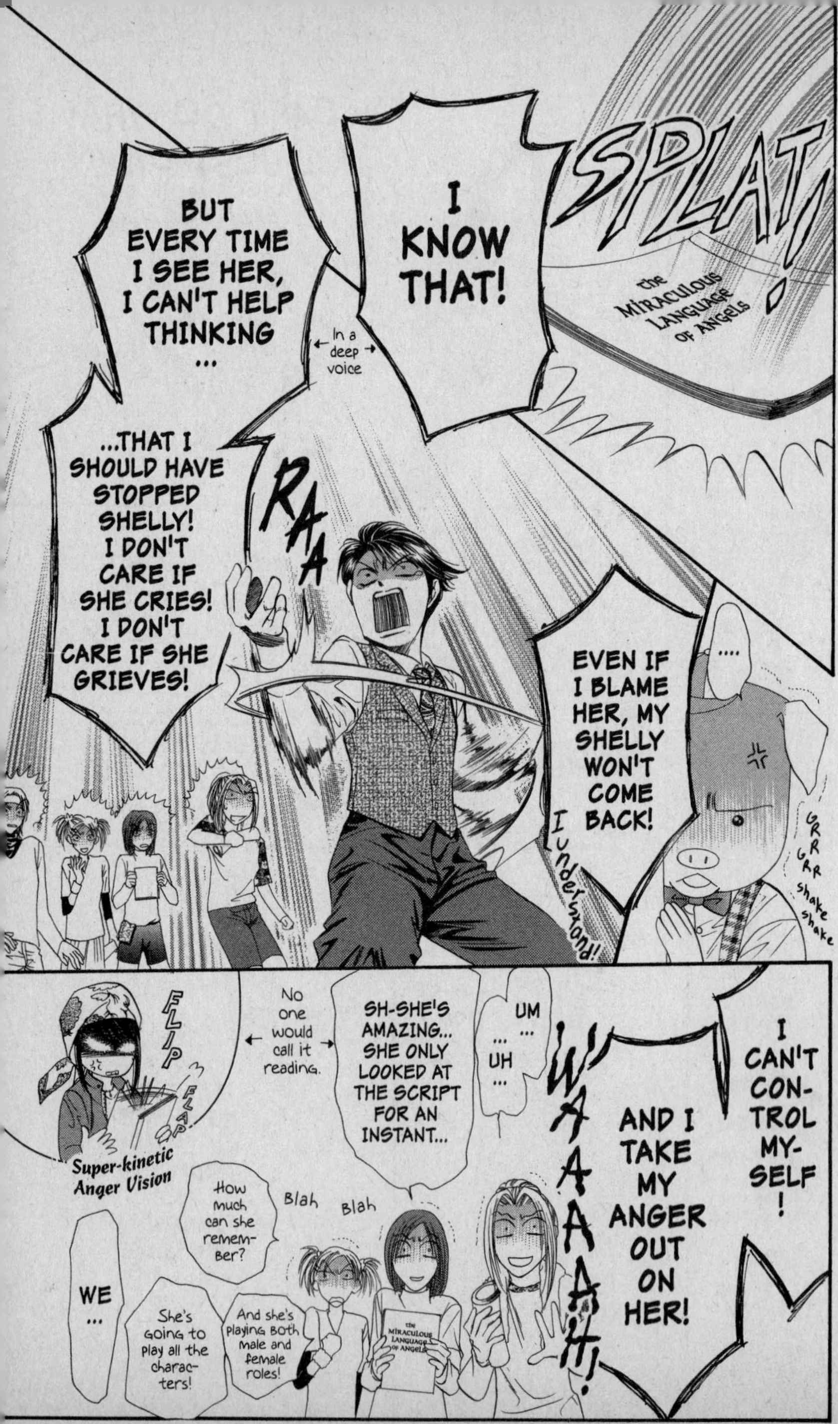
SPLAT!
the MIRACULOUS LANGUAGE OF ANGELS
I KNOW THAT!
In a deep voice
BUT EVERY TIME I SEE HER, I CAN'T HELP THINKING...
...THAT I SHOULD HAVE STOPPED SHELLY! I DON'T CARE IF SHE CRIES! I DON'T CARE IF SHE GRIEVES!
RAA
....
EVEN IF I BLAME HER, MY SHELLY WON'T COME BACK!
I understand!
GRR GRR
shake shake
I CAN'T CONTROL MY-SELF!
AND I TAKE MY ANGER OUT ON HER!
WAAAAAH!
UM... ...UH...
SH-SHE'S AMAZING... SHE ONLY LOOKED AT THE SCRIPT FOR AN INSTANT...
No one would call it reading.
FLIP
FLAP
Super-kinetic Anger Vision
Blah Blah
How much can she remem-ber?
THE MIRACULOUS LANGUAGE OF ANGELS
And she's playing both male and female roles!
She's going to play all the charac-ters!
WE...

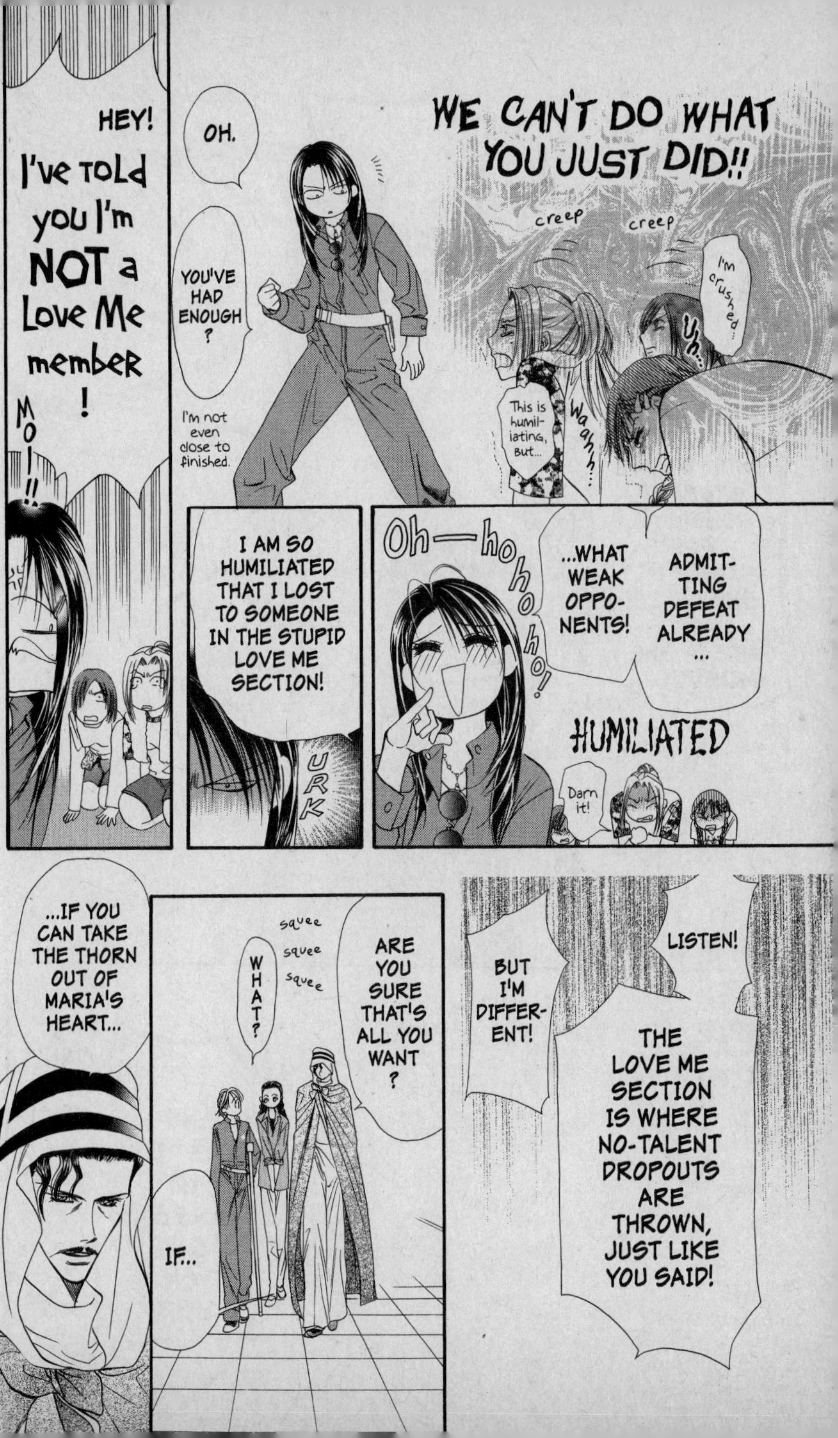
WE CAN'T DO WHAT YOU JUST DID!!
creep
creep
I'm crushed...
Uh...
Waahh...
This is humiliating, but...
OH.
YOU'VE HAD ENOUGH?
I'm not even close to finished.
ADMITTING DEFEAT ALREADY...
Oh—hohohoho!
...WHAT WEAK OPPONENTS!
HUMILIATED
Darn it!
I AM SO HUMILIATED THAT I LOST TO SOMEONE IN THE STUPID LOVE ME SECTION!
URK
HEY!
I've told you I'm NOT a Love Me member!
MOO!!
LISTEN!
BUT I'M DIFFERENT!
THE LOVE ME SECTION IS WHERE NO-TALENT DROPOUTS ARE THROWN, JUST LIKE YOU SAID!
ARE YOU SURE THAT'S ALL YOU WANT?
squee
squee
squee
WHAT?
IF...
...IF YOU CAN TAKE THE THORN OUT OF MARIA'S HEART...

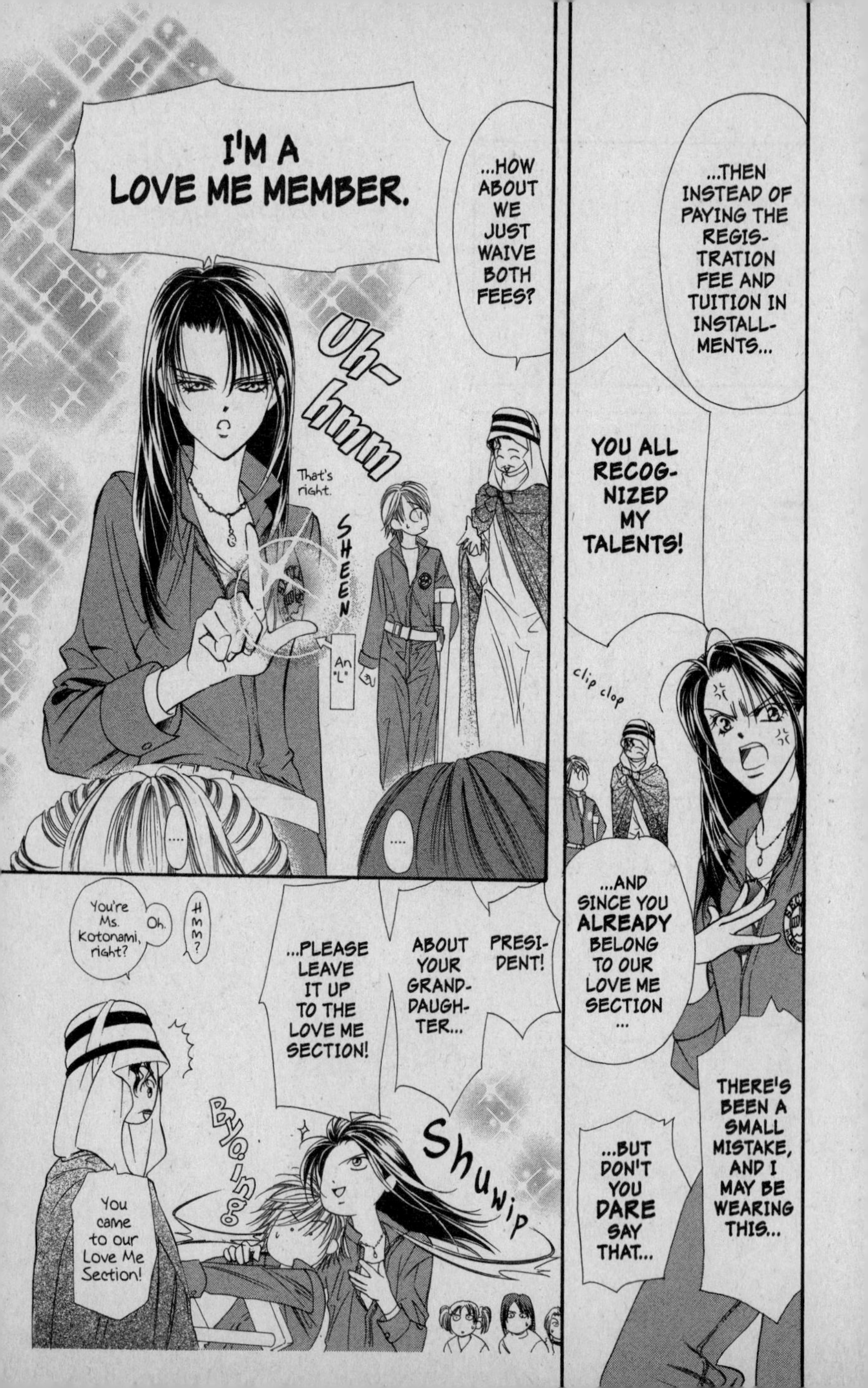
...THEN INSTEAD OF PAYING THE REGISTRATION FEE AND TUITION IN INSTALLMENTS...
YOU ALL RECOGNIZED MY TALENTS!
clip clop
...AND SINCE YOU ALREADY BELONG TO OUR LOVE ME SECTION ...
THERE'S BEEN A SMALL MISTAKE, AND I MAY BE WEARING THIS...
...BUT DON'T YOU DARE SAY THAT...
...HOW ABOUT WE JUST WAIVE BOTH FEES?
I'M A LOVE ME MEMBER.
Uh-hmm
That's right.
SHEEN
An "L"
....
....
PRESIDENT!
ABOUT YOUR GRANDDAUGHTER...
...PLEASE LEAVE IT UP TO THE LOVE ME SECTION!
Hmm?
Oh.
You're Ms. Kotonami, right?
Shuwip
Byoing
You came to our Love Me Section!

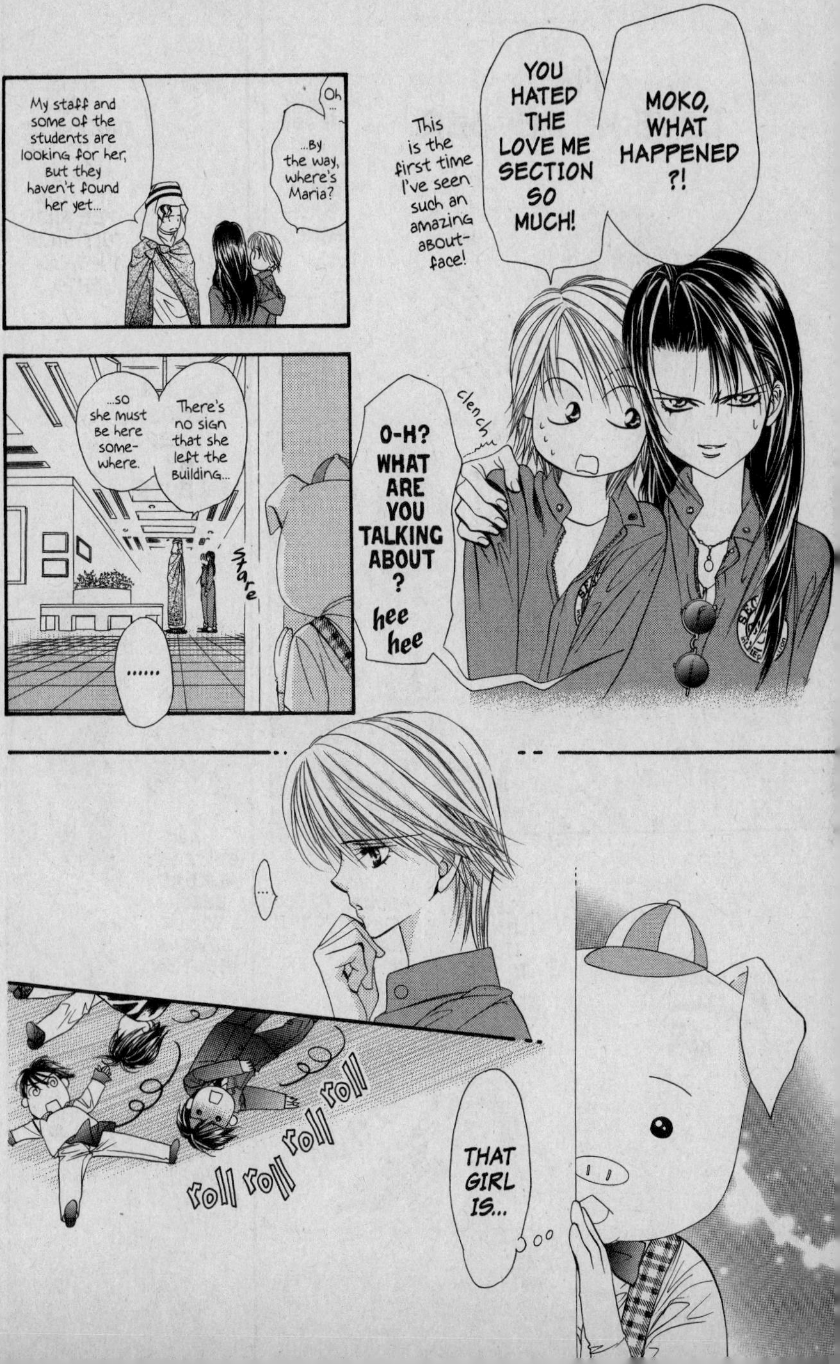
MOKO, WHAT HAPPENED ?!
YOU HATED THE LOVE ME SECTION SO MUCH!
This is the first time I've seen such an amazing about-face!
clench
O-H? WHAT ARE YOU TALKING ABOUT? hee hee
Oh...
...By the way, where's Maria?
My staff and some of the students are looking for her, but they haven't found her yet...
There's no sign that she left the building...
...so she must be here some-where.
stare
......
...
THAT GIRL IS...
roll roll roll roll

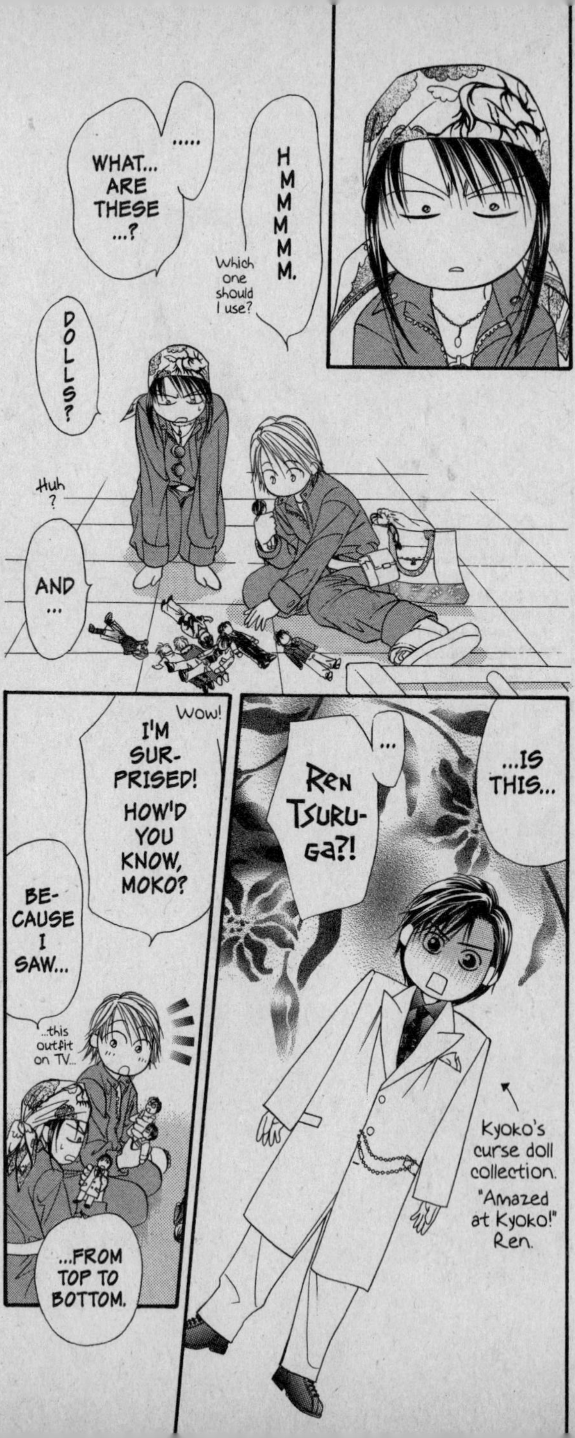
HMMMMM.
Which one should I use?
.....
WHAT... ARE THESE ...?
DOLLS?
Huh?
AND ...
...IS THIS...
...
Ren Tsuruga?!
Kyoko's curse doll collection. "Amazed at Kyoko!" Ren.
Wow!
I'M SURPRISED! HOW'D YOU KNOW, MOKO?
BE-CAUSE I SAW...
...this outfit on TV...
...FROM TOP TO BOTTOM.

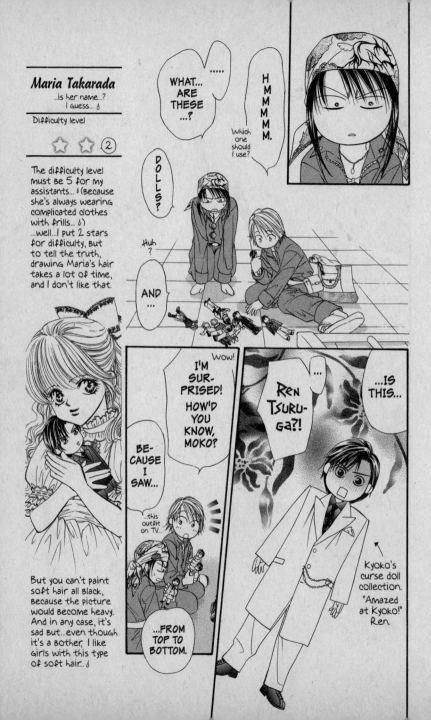

Maria Takarada

...is her name...? I guess... ♪

Difficulty level

☆ ☆ ②

The difficulty level must be 5 for my assistants... ♪ (Because she's always wearing complicated clothes with frills... ♪) ...well...I put 2 stars for difficulty, but to tell the truth, drawing Maria's hair takes a lot of time, and I don't like that.

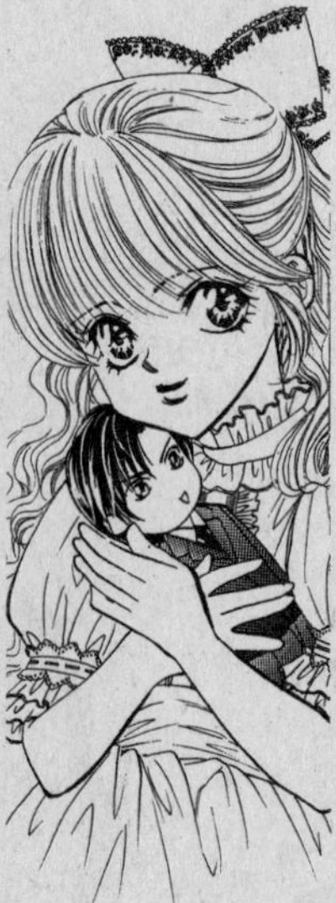

But you can't paint soft hair all black, because the picture would become heavy. And in any case, it's sad but...even though it's a bother, I like girls with this type of soft hair... ♪

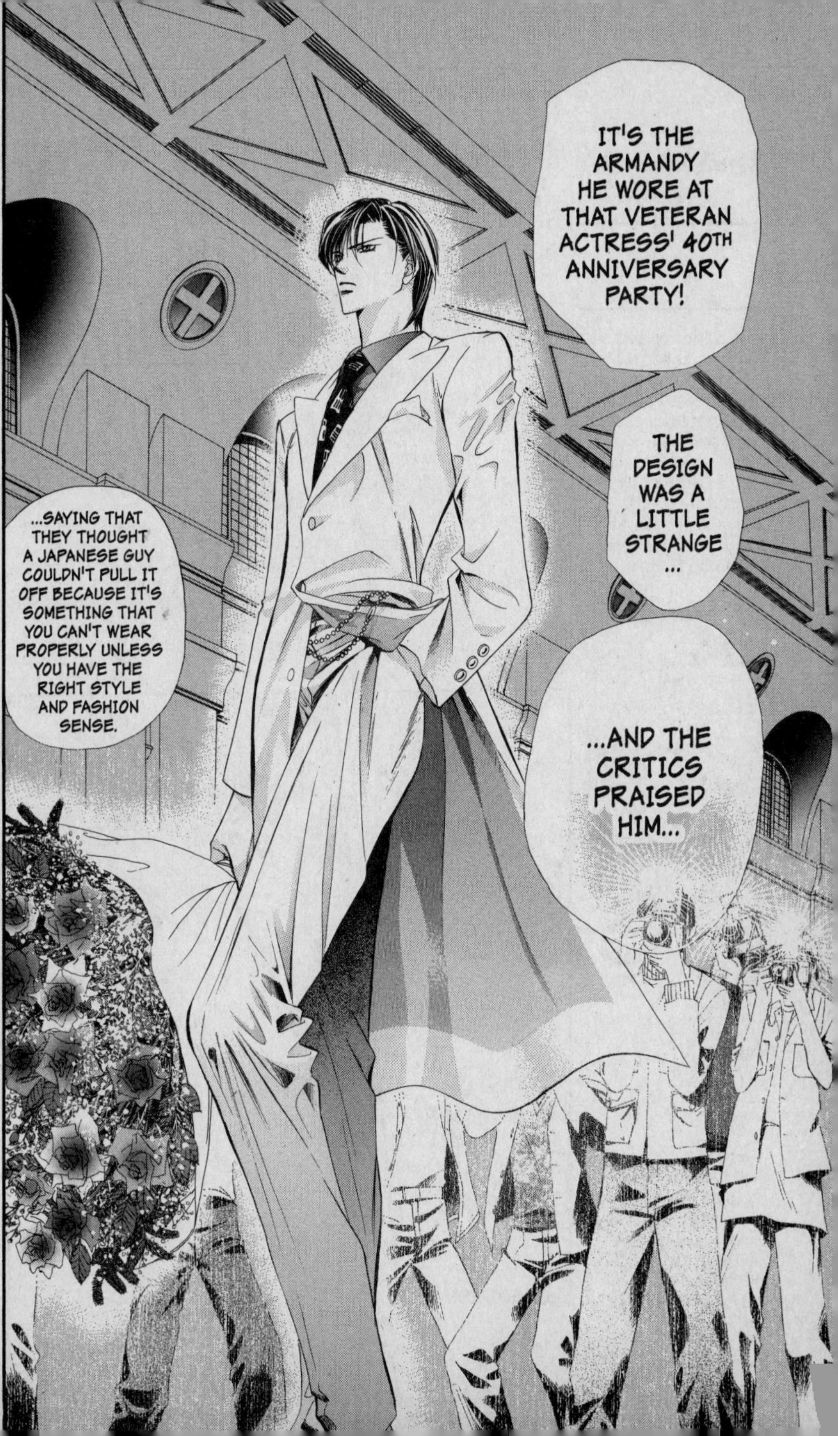
IT'S THE ARMANDY HE WORE AT THAT VETERAN ACTRESS' 40TH ANNIVERSARY PARTY!
THE DESIGN WAS A LITTLE STRANGE ...
...AND THE CRITICS PRAISED HIM...
...SAYING THAT THEY THOUGHT A JAPANESE GUY COULDN'T PULL IT OFF BECAUSE IT'S SOMETHING THAT YOU CAN'T WEAR PROPERLY UNLESS YOU HAVE THE RIGHT STYLE AND FASHION SENSE.

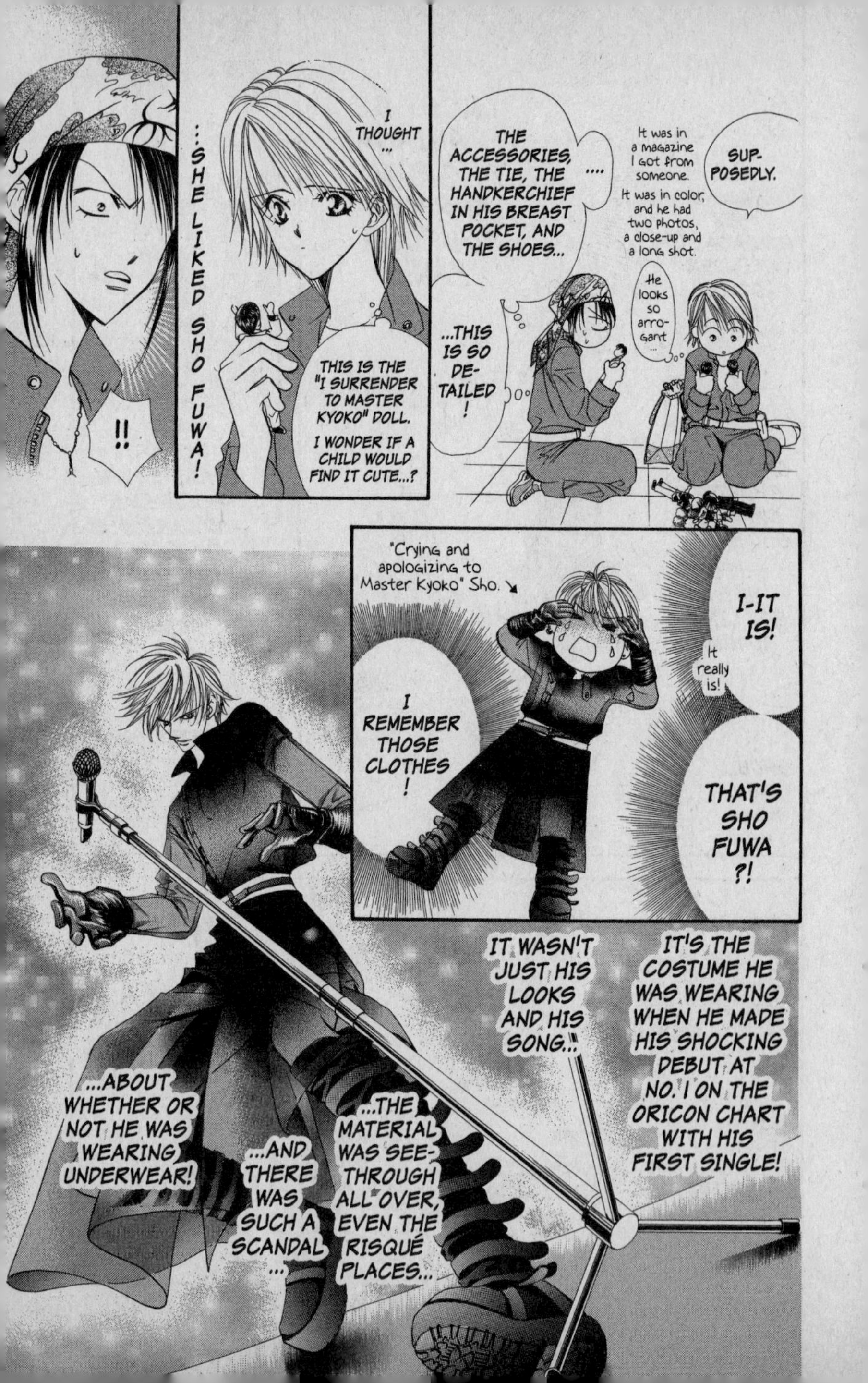
SUP-POSEDLY.
It was in a magazine I got from someone.
It was in color, and he had two photos, a close-up and a long shot.
THE ACCESSORIES, THE TIE, THE HANDKERCHIEF IN HIS BREAST POCKET, AND THE SHOES...
....
He looks so arro-gant...
...THIS IS SO DE-TAILED!
I THOUGHT...
THIS IS THE "I SURRENDER TO MASTER KYOKO" DOLL.
I WONDER IF A CHILD WOULD FIND IT CUTE...?
...SHE LIKED SHO FUWA!
!!
I-IT IS!
It really is!
"Crying and apologizing to Master Kyoko" Sho.
I REMEMBER THOSE CLOTHES!
THAT'S SHO FUWA?!
IT'S THE COSTUME HE WAS WEARING WHEN HE MADE HIS SHOCKING DEBUT AT NO. 1 ON THE ORICON CHART WITH HIS FIRST SINGLE!
IT WASN'T JUST HIS LOOKS AND HIS SONG...
...THE MATERIAL WAS SEE-THROUGH ALL OVER, EVEN THE RISQUÉ PLACES...
...AND THERE WAS SUCH A SCANDAL...
...ABOUT WHETHER OR NOT HE WAS WEARING UNDERWEAR!

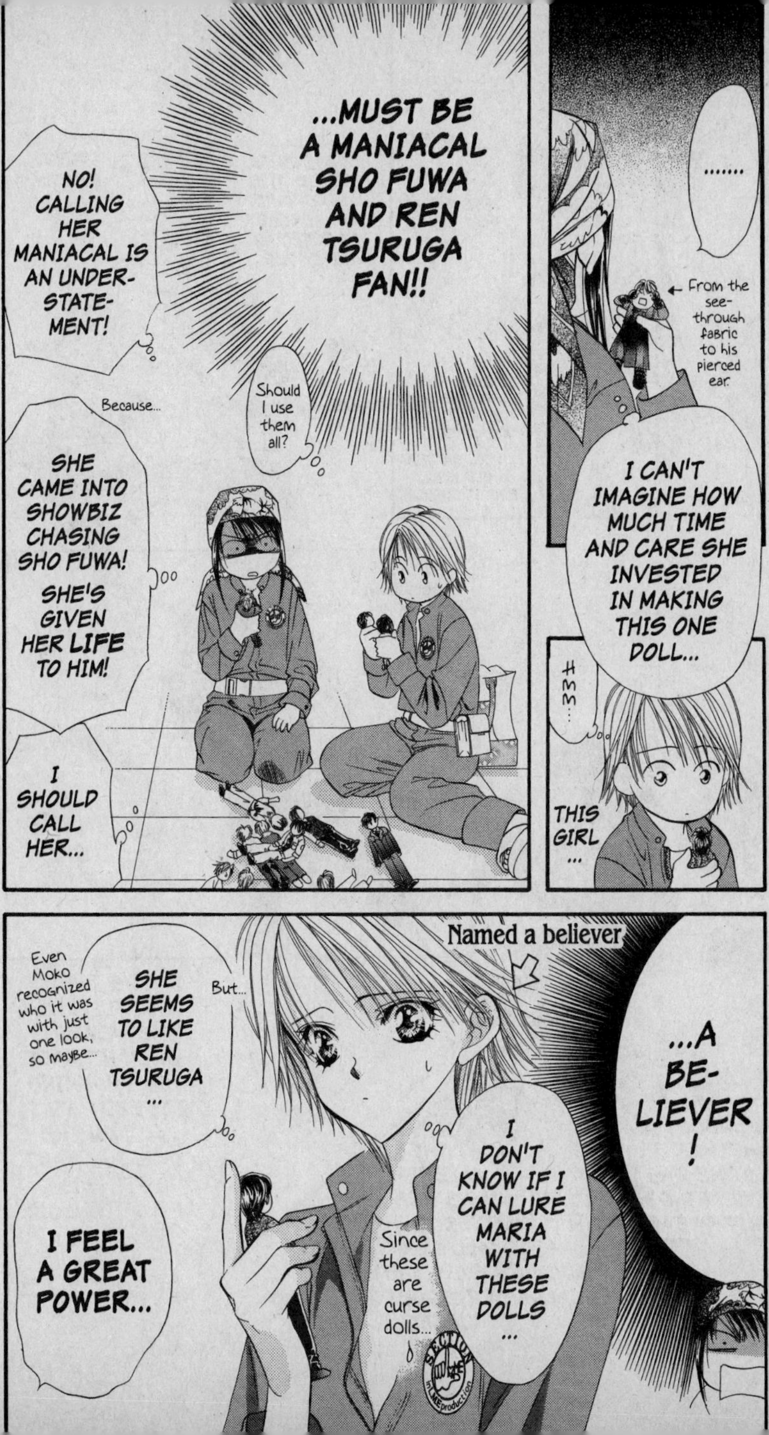
....
From the see-through fabric to his pierced ear.
I CAN'T IMAGINE HOW MUCH TIME AND CARE SHE INVESTED IN MAKING THIS ONE DOLL...
Hmm...
THIS GIRL...
...MUST BE A MANIACAL SHO FUWA AND REN TSURUGA FAN!!
NO! CALLING HER MANIACAL IS AN UNDER-STATE-MENT!
Should I use them all?
Because...
SHE CAME INTO SHOWBIZ CHASING SHO FUWA! SHE'S GIVEN HER LIFE TO HIM!
I SHOULD CALL HER...
...A BE-LIEVER!
Named a believer
But...
SHE SEEMS TO LIKE REN TSURUGA...
Even Moko recognized who it was with just one look, so maybe...
I DON'T KNOW IF I CAN LURE MARIA WITH THESE DOLLS...
Since these are curse dolls...
I FEEL A GREAT POWER...

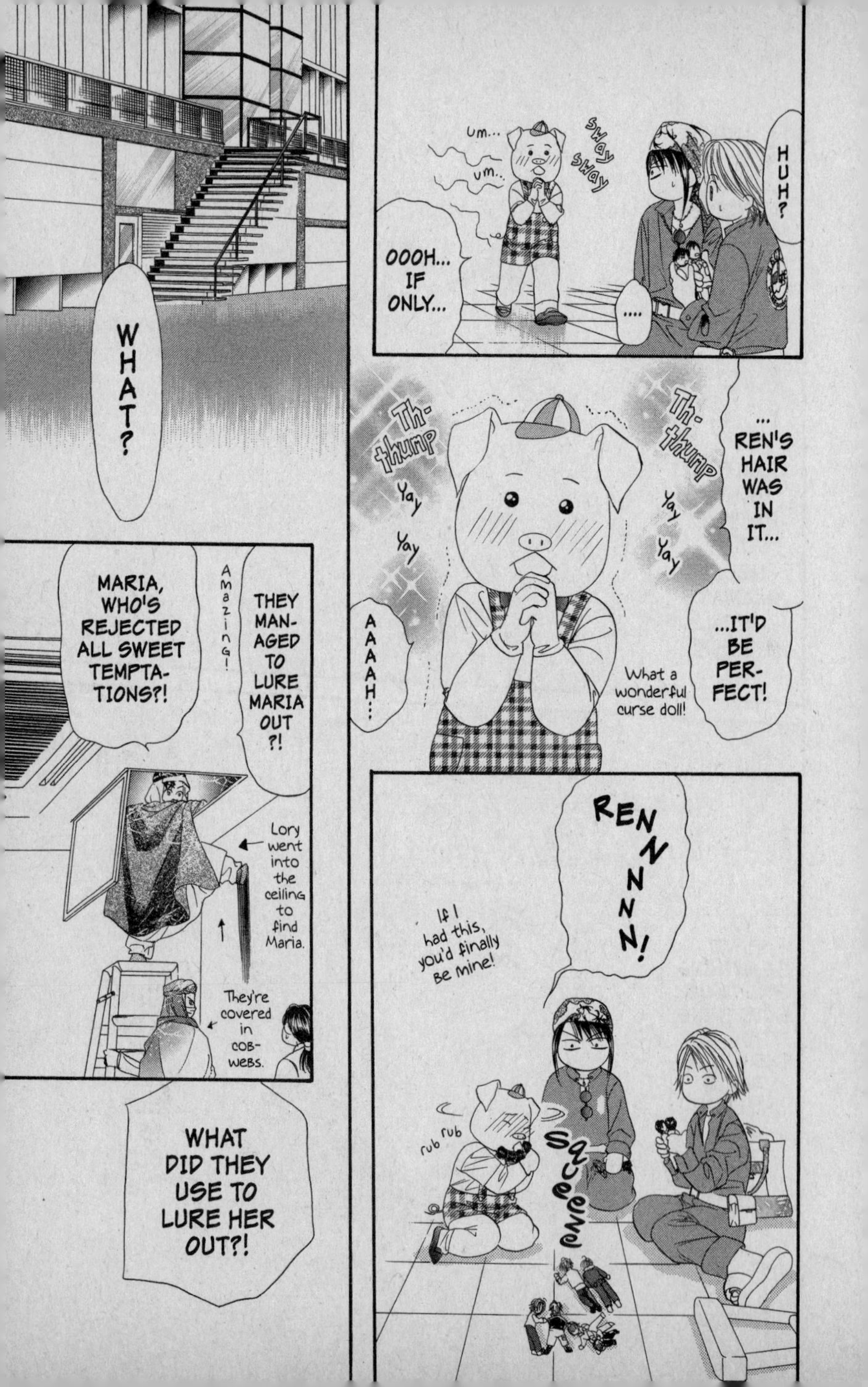
HUH?
um...
um...
SWAY SWAY
OOOH... IF ONLY...
....
... REN'S HAIR WAS IN IT...
Th-thump
Th-thump
Yay
Yay
Yay
Yay
...IT'D BE PER-FECT!
What a wonderful curse doll!
AAAAAH...
RENNNNN!
If I had this, you'd finally be mine!
rub rub
Squeeze
WHAT?
THEY MAN-AGED TO LURE MARIA OUT?!
Amazing!
MARIA, WHO'S REJECTED ALL SWEET TEMPTA-TIONS?!
Lory went into the ceiling to find Maria.
They're covered in COB-WEBS.
WHAT DID THEY USE TO LURE HER OUT?!

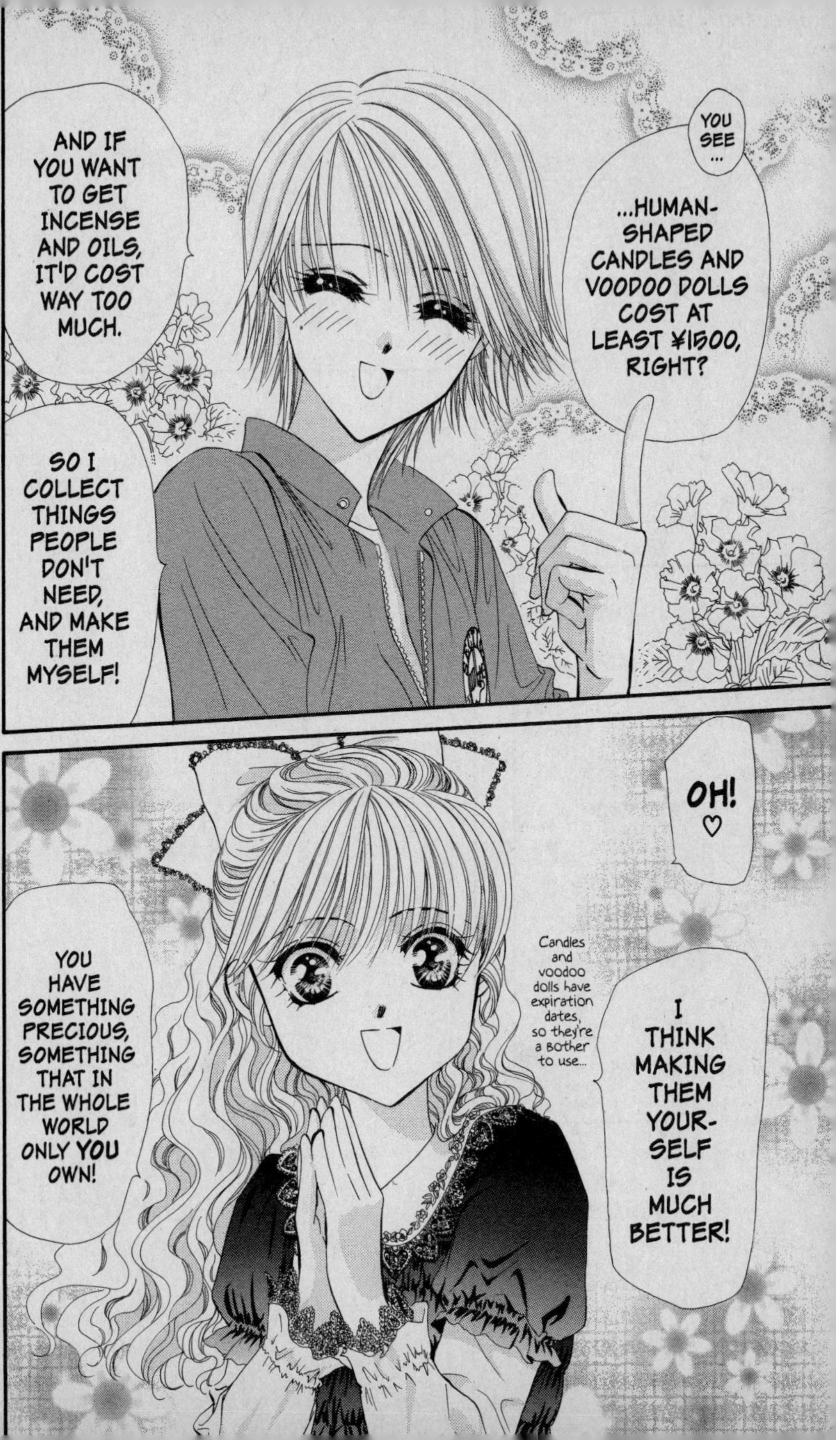
YOU SEE ...
...HUMAN-SHAPED CANDLES AND VOODOO DOLLS COST AT LEAST ¥1500, RIGHT?
AND IF YOU WANT TO GET INCENSE AND OILS, IT'D COST WAY TOO MUCH.
SO I COLLECT THINGS PEOPLE DON'T NEED, AND MAKE THEM MYSELF!
OH! ♡
I THINK MAKING THEM YOURSELF IS MUCH BETTER!
Candles and voodoo dolls have expiration dates, so they're a bother to use...
YOU HAVE SOMETHING PRECIOUS, SOMETHING THAT IN THE WHOLE WORLD ONLY YOU OWN!

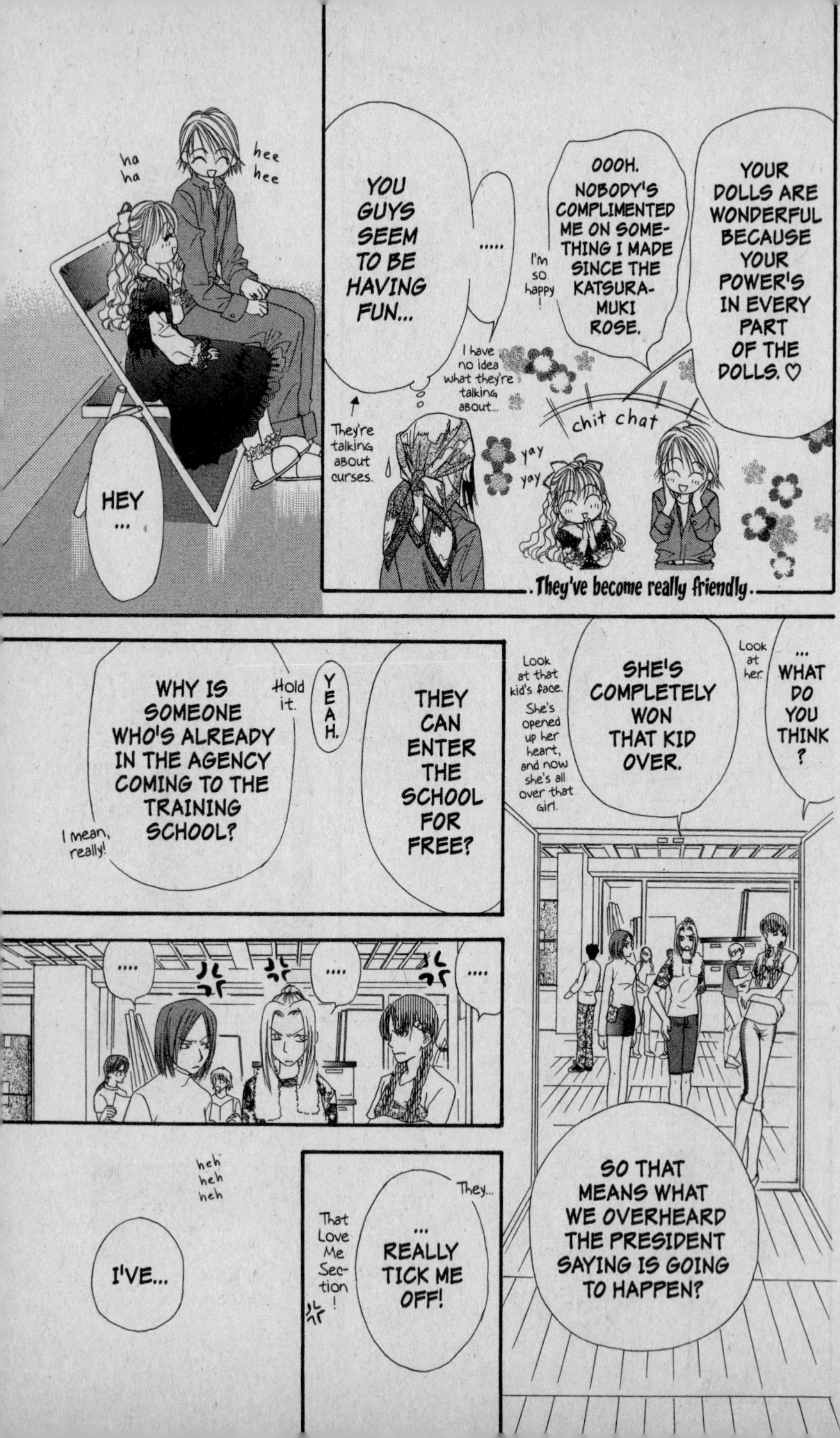
YOUR DOLLS ARE WONDERFUL BECAUSE YOUR POWER'S IN EVERY PART OF THE DOLLS. ♡
OOOH. NOBODY'S COMPLIMENTED ME ON SOME-THING I MADE SINCE THE KATSURA-MUKI ROSE.
I'm so happy!
YOU GUYS SEEM TO BE HAVING FUN...
.....
I have no idea what they're talking about...
They're talking about curses.
chit chat
yay yay
They've become really friendly.
hee hee
ha ha
HEY ...
...WHAT DO YOU THINK?
Look at her.
SHE'S COMPLETELY WON THAT KID OVER.
Look at that kid's face. She's opened up her heart, and now she's all over that girl.
SO THAT MEANS WHAT WE OVERHEARD THE PRESIDENT SAYING IS GOING TO HAPPEN?
THEY CAN ENTER THE SCHOOL FOR FREE?
YEAH.
Hold it.
WHY IS SOMEONE WHO'S ALREADY IN THE AGENCY COMING TO THE TRAINING SCHOOL?
I mean, really!
....
....
....
They...
...REALLY TICK ME OFF!
That Love Me Sec-tion!
heh heh heh
I'VE...

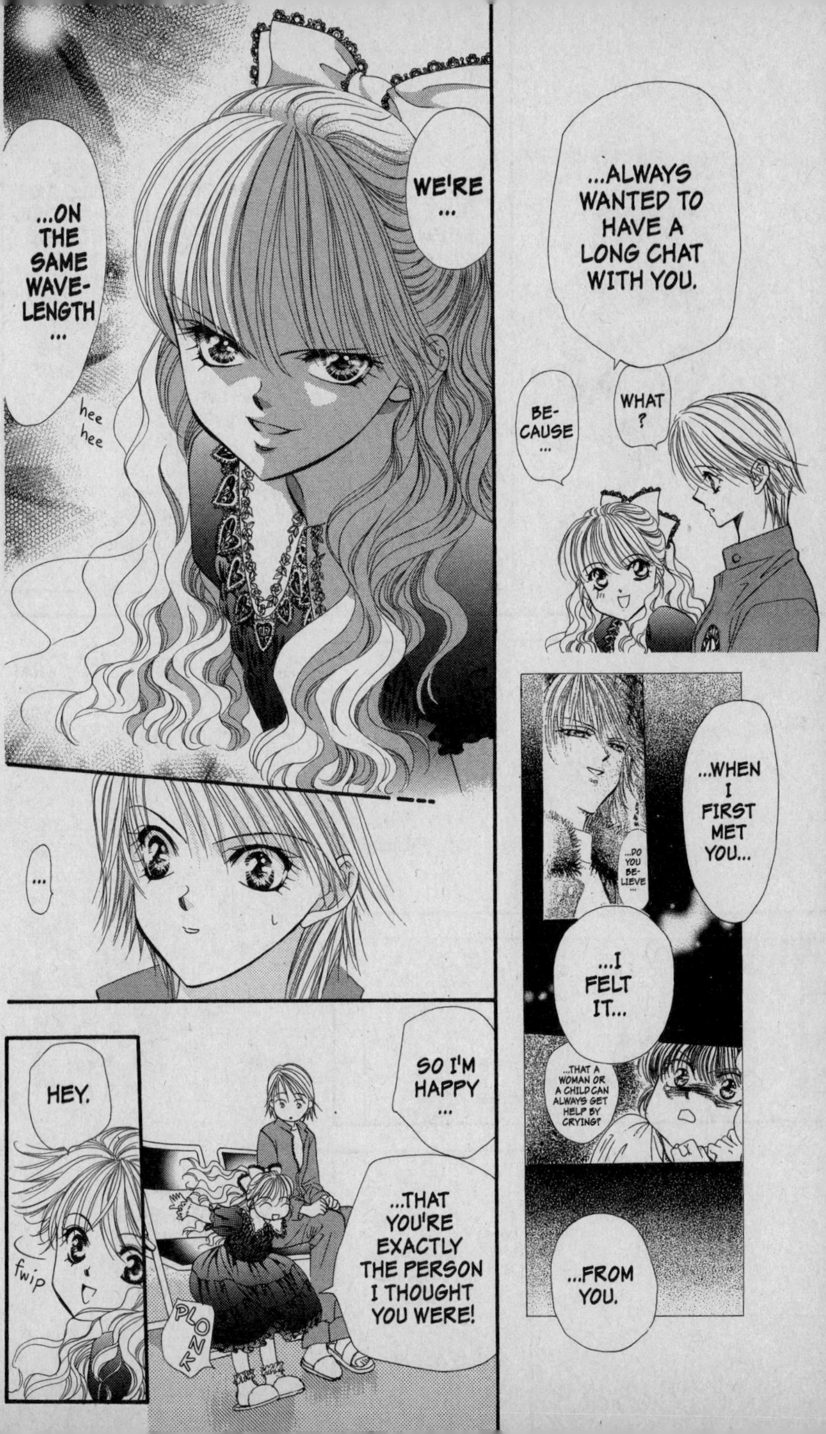
...ALWAYS WANTED TO HAVE A LONG CHAT WITH YOU.
WHAT?
BE-CAUSE...
...WHEN I FIRST MET YOU...
...DO YOU BE-LIEVE...
...I FELT IT...
...THAT A WOMAN OR A CHILD CAN ALWAYS GET HELP BY CRYING?
...FROM YOU.
WE'RE...
...ON THE SAME WAVE-LENGTH...
hee hee
...
SO I'M HAPPY...
...THAT YOU'RE EXACTLY THE PERSON I THOUGHT YOU WERE!
PLONK
HEY.
fwip

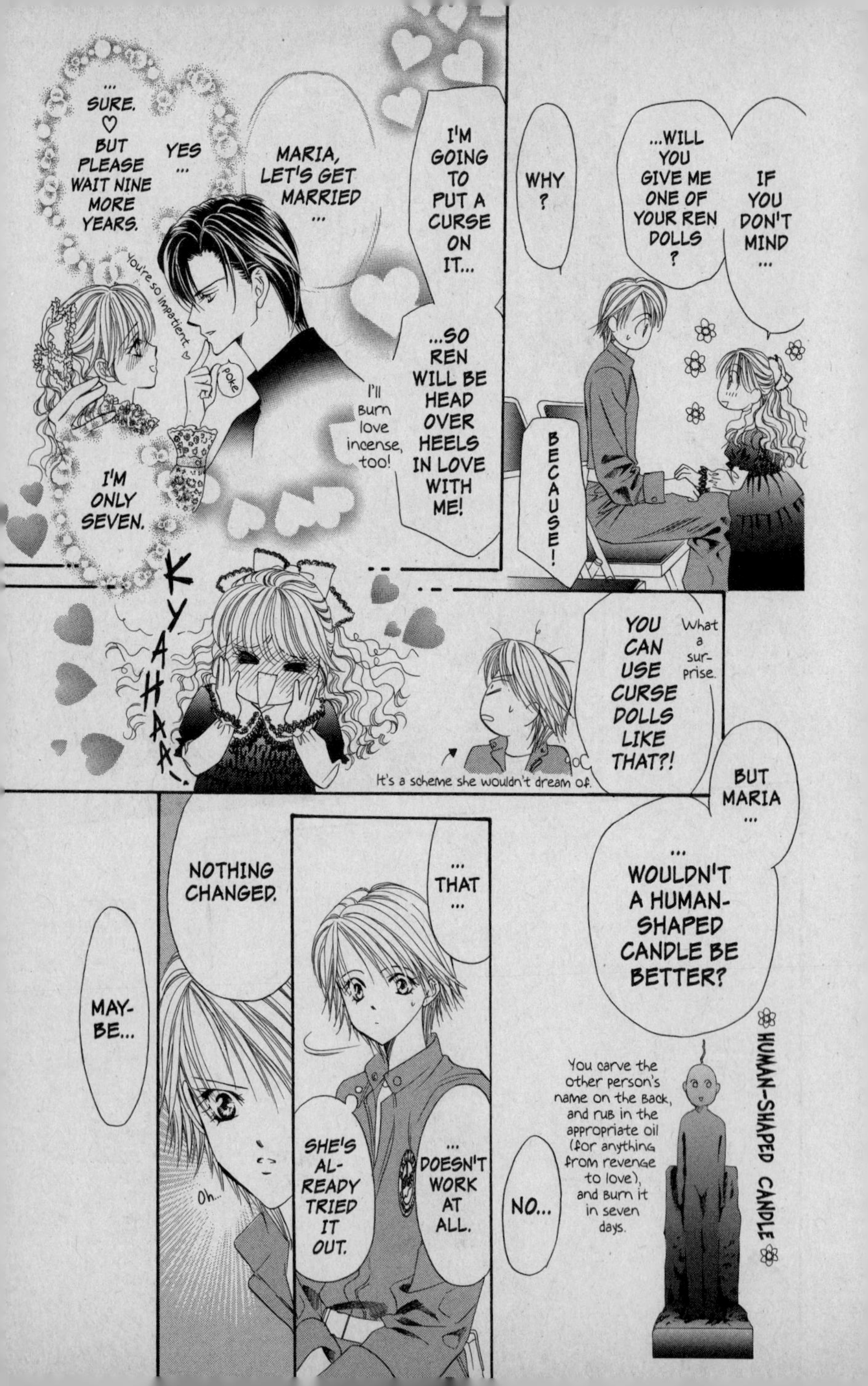
IF YOU DON'T MIND...
...WILL YOU GIVE ME ONE OF YOUR REN DOLLS?
WHY?
BECAUSE!
I'M GOING TO PUT A CURSE ON IT...
...SO REN WILL BE HEAD OVER HEELS IN LOVE WITH ME!
I'll burn love incense, too!
MARIA, LET'S GET MARRIED...
YES...
...SURE. ♡ BUT PLEASE WAIT NINE MORE YEARS.
You're so impatient. ♡
poke
I'M ONLY SEVEN.
What a surprise.
YOU CAN USE CURSE DOLLS LIKE THAT?!
It's a scheme she wouldn't dream of.
KYAHAAA!
BUT MARIA...
...WOULDN'T A HUMAN-SHAPED CANDLE BE BETTER?
HUMAN-SHAPED CANDLE
You carve the other person's name on the back, and rub in the appropriate oil (for anything from revenge to love), and burn it in seven days.
NO...
...THAT...
...DOESN'T WORK AT ALL.
SHE'S AL-READY TRIED IT OUT.
NOTHING CHANGED.
MAY-BE...
Oh...

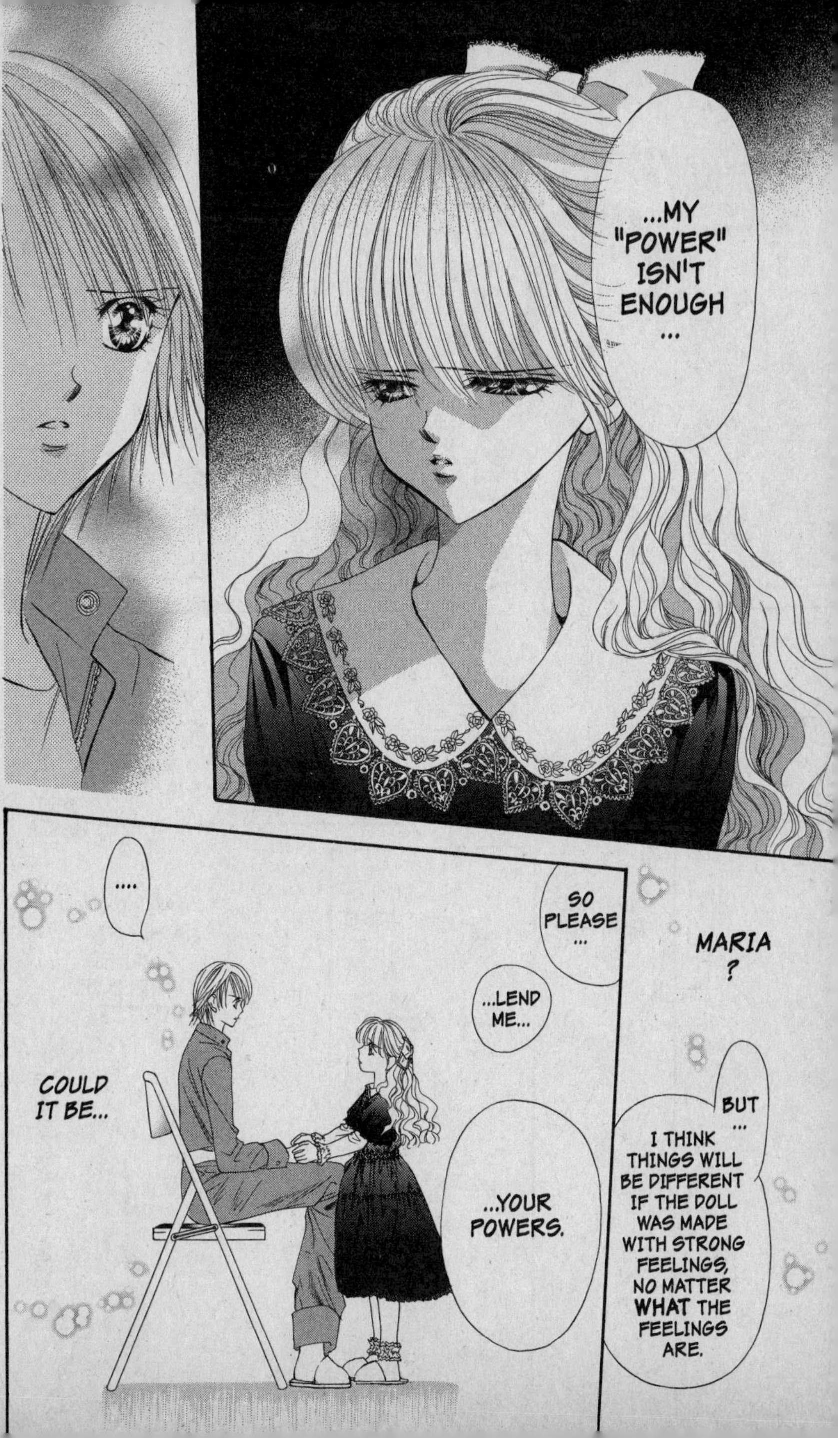

...MY "POWER" ISN'T ENOUGH ...
MARIA ?
BUT ...
I THINK THINGS WILL BE DIFFERENT IF THE DOLL WAS MADE WITH STRONG FEELINGS, NO MATTER WHAT THE FEELINGS ARE.
SO PLEASE ...
...LEND ME...
...YOUR POWERS.
....
COULD IT BE...

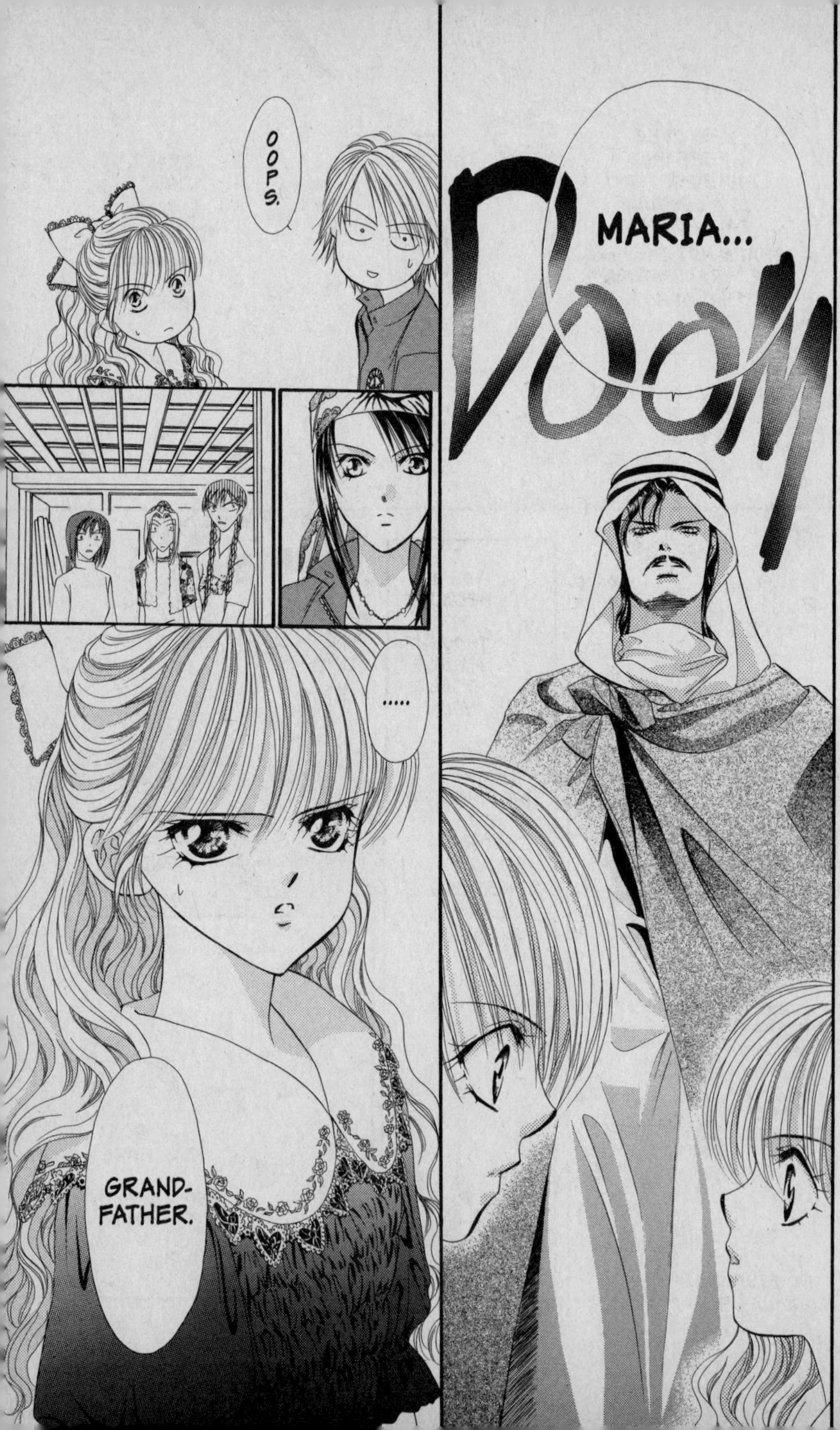
MARIA...
DOOM
OOPS.
.....
GRAND-
FATHER.

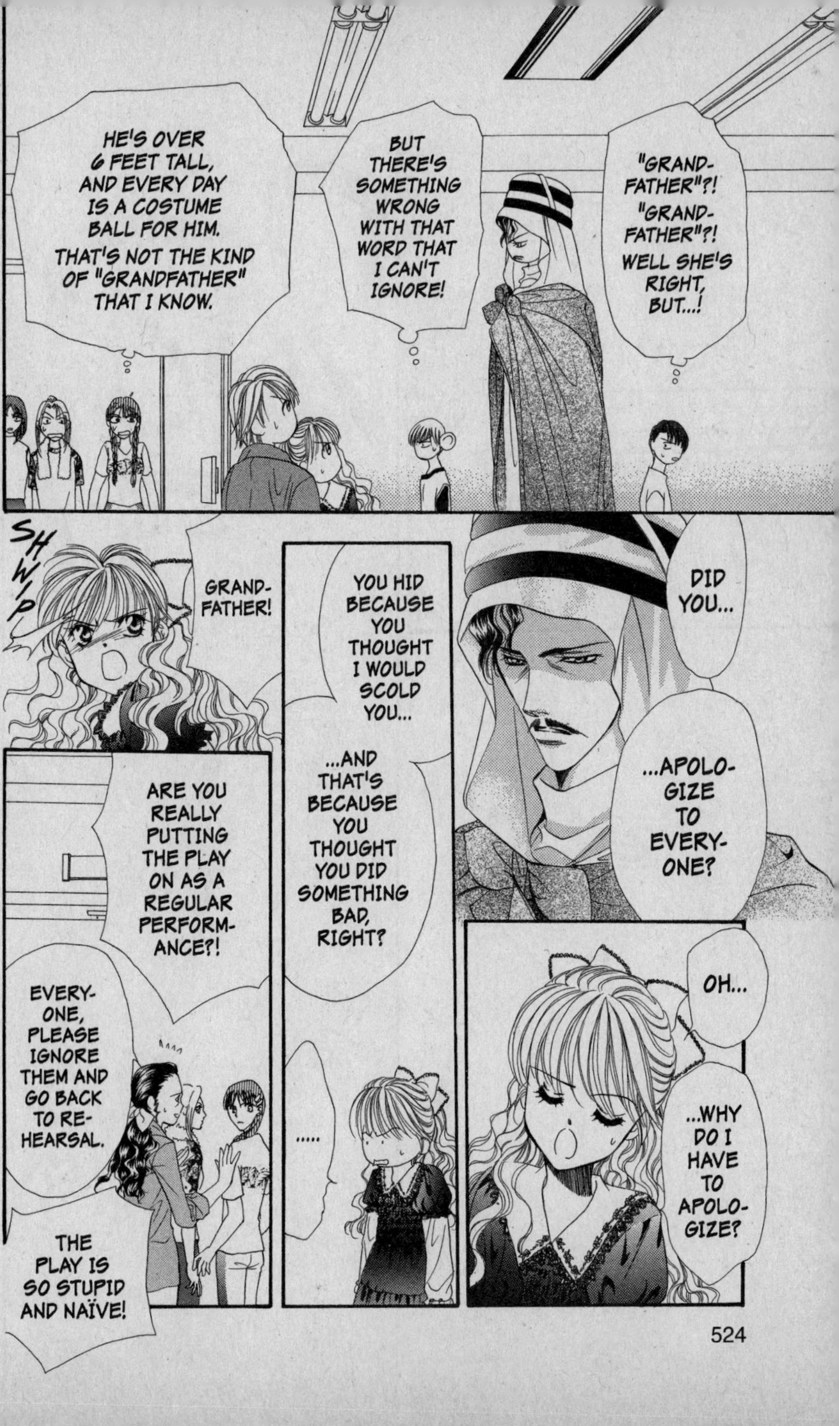
"GRAND-FATHER"?! "GRAND-FATHER"?! WELL SHE'S RIGHT, BUT...!
BUT THERE'S SOMETHING WRONG WITH THAT WORD THAT I CAN'T IGNORE!
HE'S OVER 6 FEET TALL, AND EVERY DAY IS A COSTUME BALL FOR HIM. THAT'S NOT THE KIND OF "GRANDFATHER" THAT I KNOW.
DID YOU...
...APOLOGIZE TO EVERYONE?
OH...
...WHY DO I HAVE TO APOLOGIZE?
YOU HID BECAUSE YOU THOUGHT I WOULD SCOLD YOU...
...AND THAT'S BECAUSE YOU THOUGHT YOU DID SOMETHING BAD, RIGHT?
.....
SHWIP
GRAND-FATHER!
ARE YOU REALLY PUTTING THE PLAY ON AS A REGULAR PERFORM-ANCE?!
EVERY-ONE, PLEASE IGNORE THEM AND GO BACK TO RE-HEARSAL.
THE PLAY IS SO STUPID AND NAÏVE!

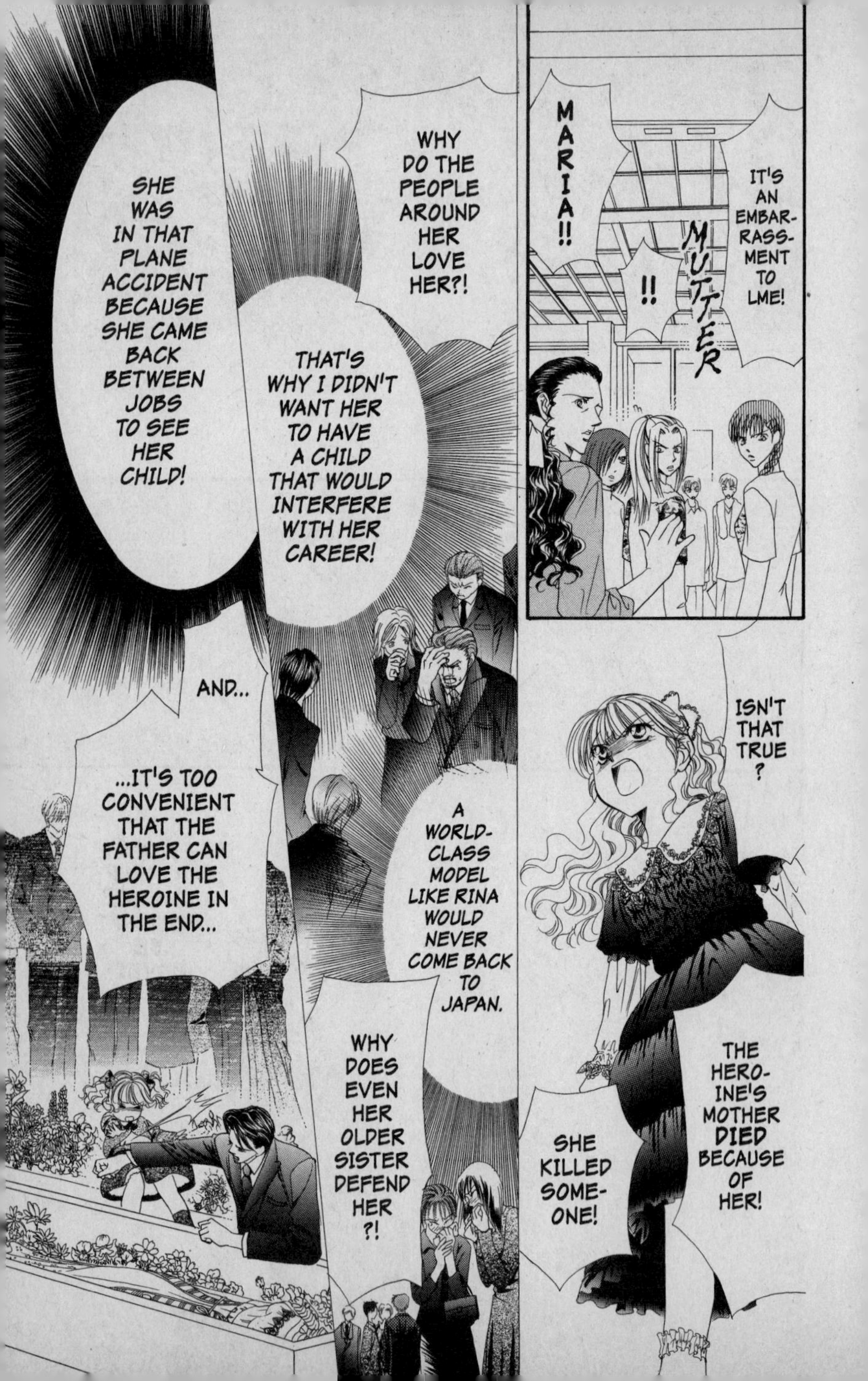

IT'S AN EMBARRASSMENT TO LME!
MUTTER
!!
MARIA!!
ISN'T THAT TRUE?
THE HEROINE'S MOTHER DIED BECAUSE OF HER!
SHE KILLED SOMEONE!
WHY DO THE PEOPLE AROUND HER LOVE HER?!
THAT'S WHY I DIDN'T WANT HER TO HAVE A CHILD THAT WOULD INTERFERE WITH HER CAREER!
A WORLD-CLASS MODEL LIKE RINA WOULD NEVER COME BACK TO JAPAN.
WHY DOES EVEN HER OLDER SISTER DEFEND HER?!
SHE WAS IN THAT PLANE ACCIDENT BECAUSE SHE CAME BACK BETWEEN JOBS TO SEE HER CHILD!
AND...
...IT'S TOO CONVENIENT THAT THE FATHER CAN LOVE THE HEROINE IN THE END...

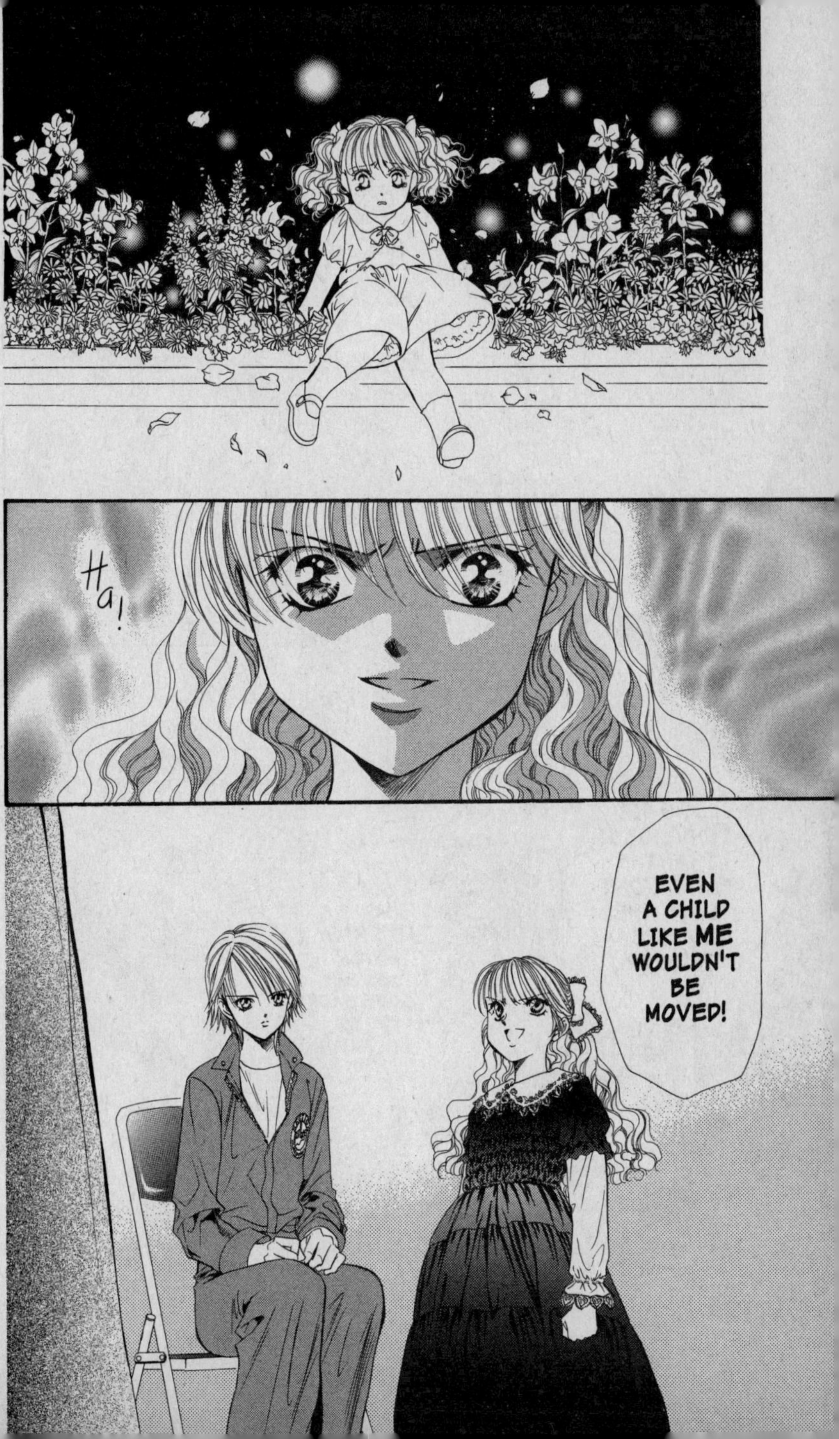
Ha!
EVEN A CHILD LIKE ME WOULDN'T BE MOVED!

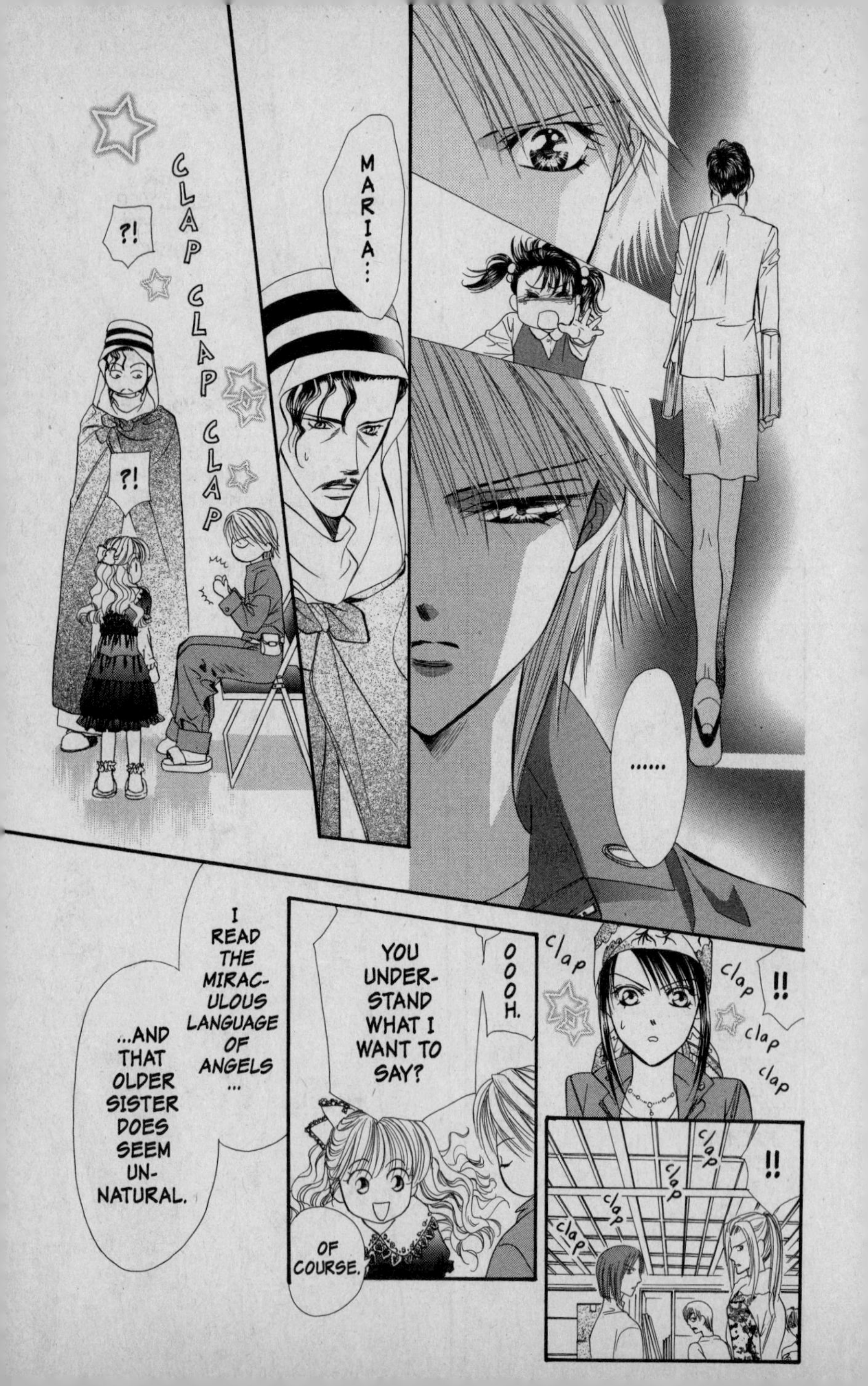
......
MARIA...
?!
CLAP CLAP CLAP CLAP
?!
clap clap clap clap
!!
clap clap clap clap
!!
OOOOH.
YOU UNDERSTAND WHAT I WANT TO SAY?
OF COURSE.
I READ THE MIRACULOUS LANGUAGE OF ANGELS...
...AND THAT OLDER SISTER DOES SEEM UNNATURAL.

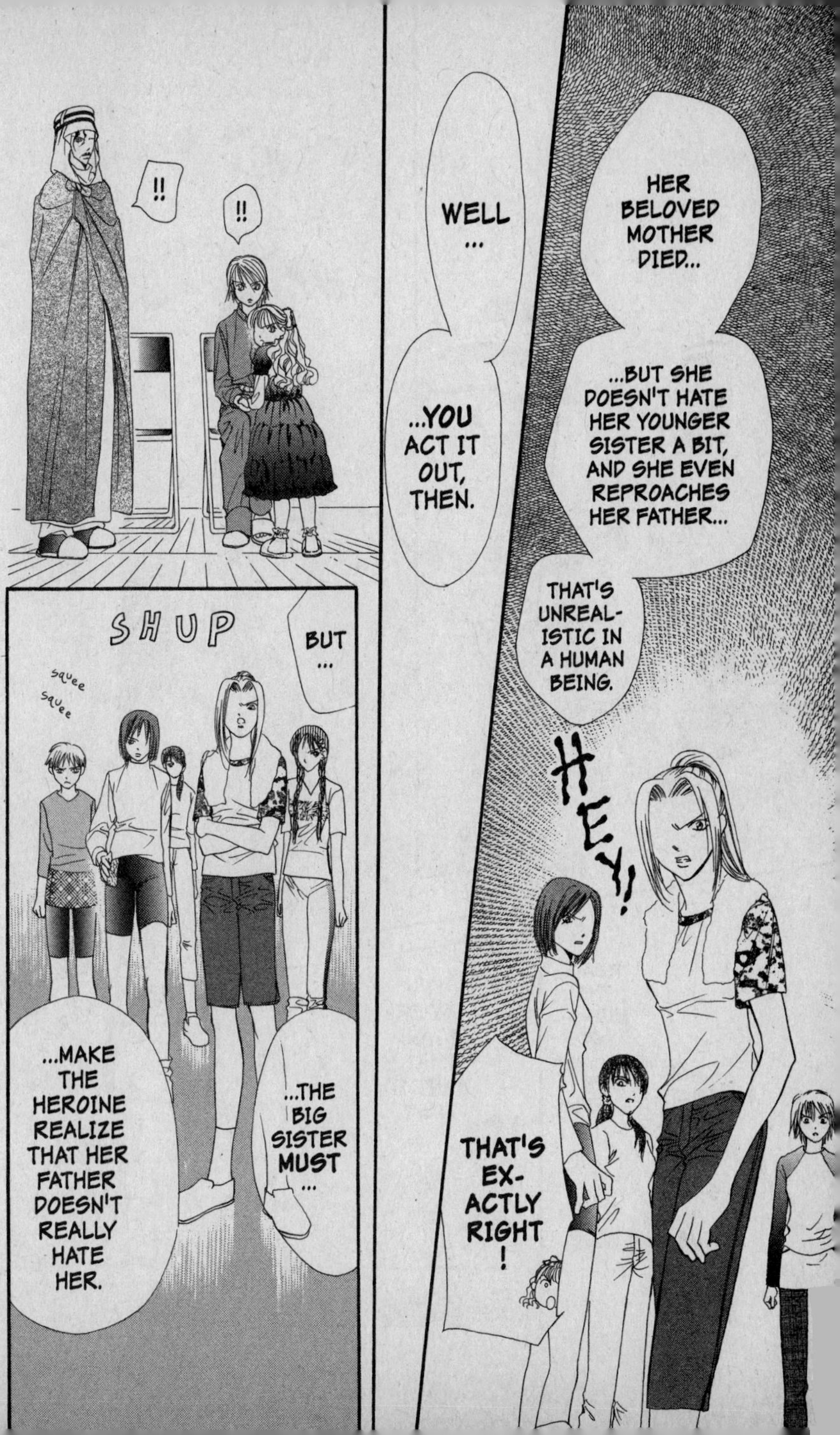
HER BELOVED MOTHER DIED...
...BUT SHE DOESN'T HATE HER YOUNGER SISTER A BIT, AND SHE EVEN REPROACHES HER FATHER...
THAT'S UNREAL-ISTIC IN A HUMAN BEING.
HEY!
THAT'S EX-ACTLY RIGHT!
WELL...
...YOU ACT IT OUT, THEN.
!!
!!
SHUP
BUT...
squee squee
...THE BIG SISTER MUST...
...MAKE THE HEROINE REALIZE THAT HER FATHER DOESN'T REALLY HATE HER.

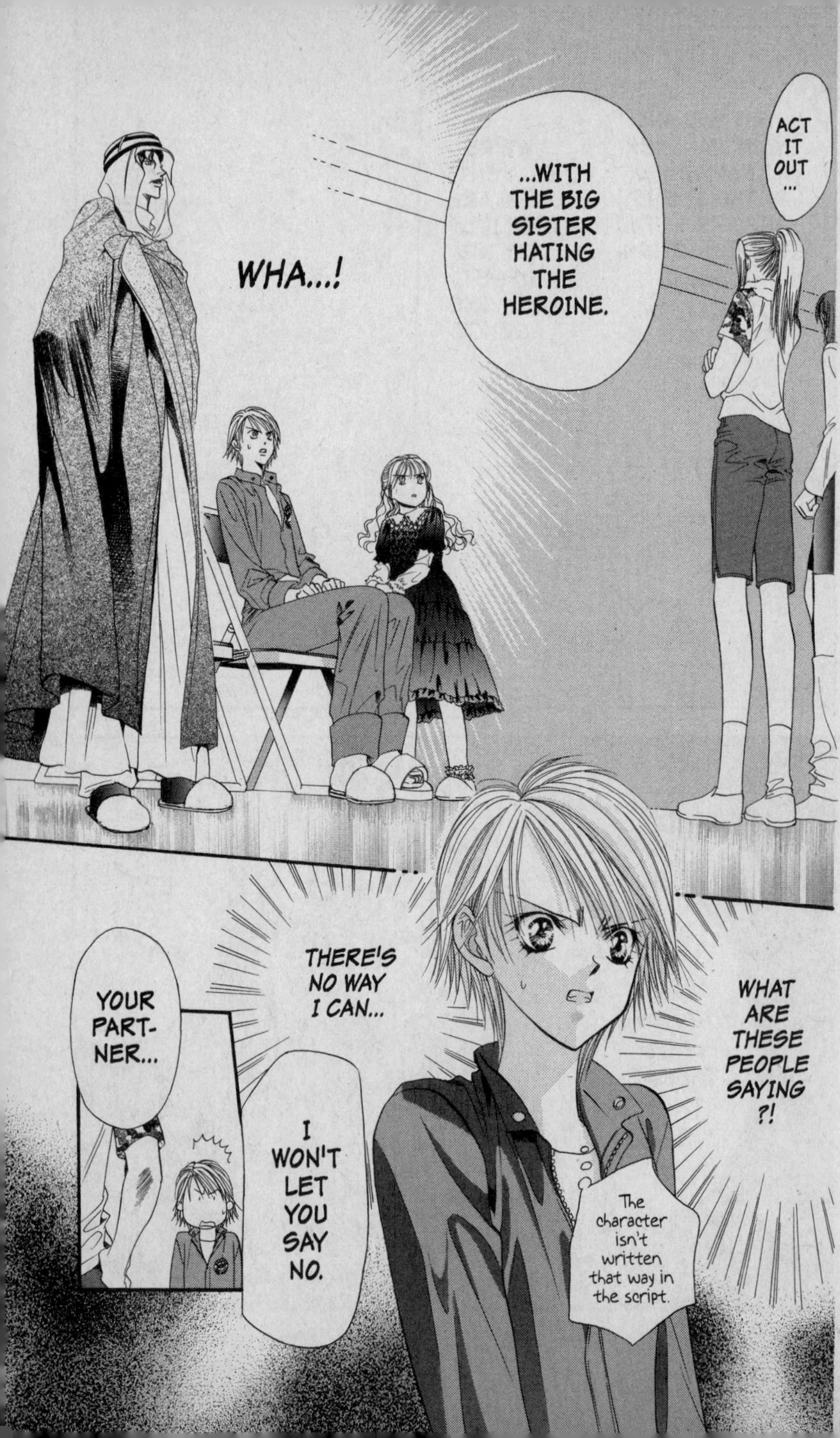
ACT IT OUT...
...WITH THE BIG SISTER HATING THE HEROINE.
WHA...!
WHAT ARE THESE PEOPLE SAYING?!
THERE'S NO WAY I CAN...
The character isn't written that way in the script.
YOUR PART-NER...
I WON'T LET YOU SAY NO.

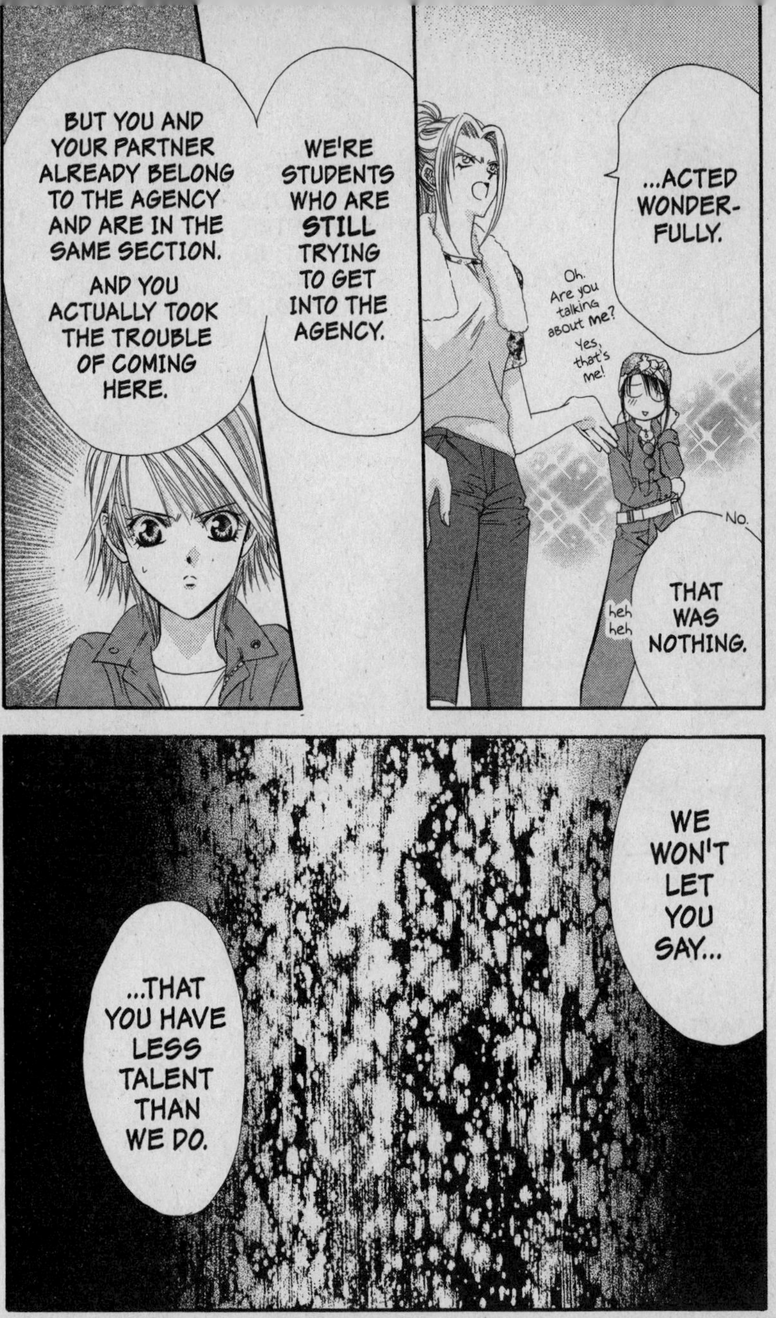
...ACTED WONDER-FULLY.
Oh. Are you talking about me? Yes, that's me!
No.
THAT WAS NOTHING.
heh heh
WE'RE STUDENTS WHO ARE STILL TRYING TO GET INTO THE AGENCY.
BUT YOU AND YOUR PARTNER ALREADY BELONG TO THE AGENCY AND ARE IN THE SAME SECTION.
AND YOU ACTUALLY TOOK THE TROUBLE OF COMING HERE.
WE WON'T LET YOU SAY...
...THAT YOU HAVE LESS TALENT THAN WE DO.

End of Act 16

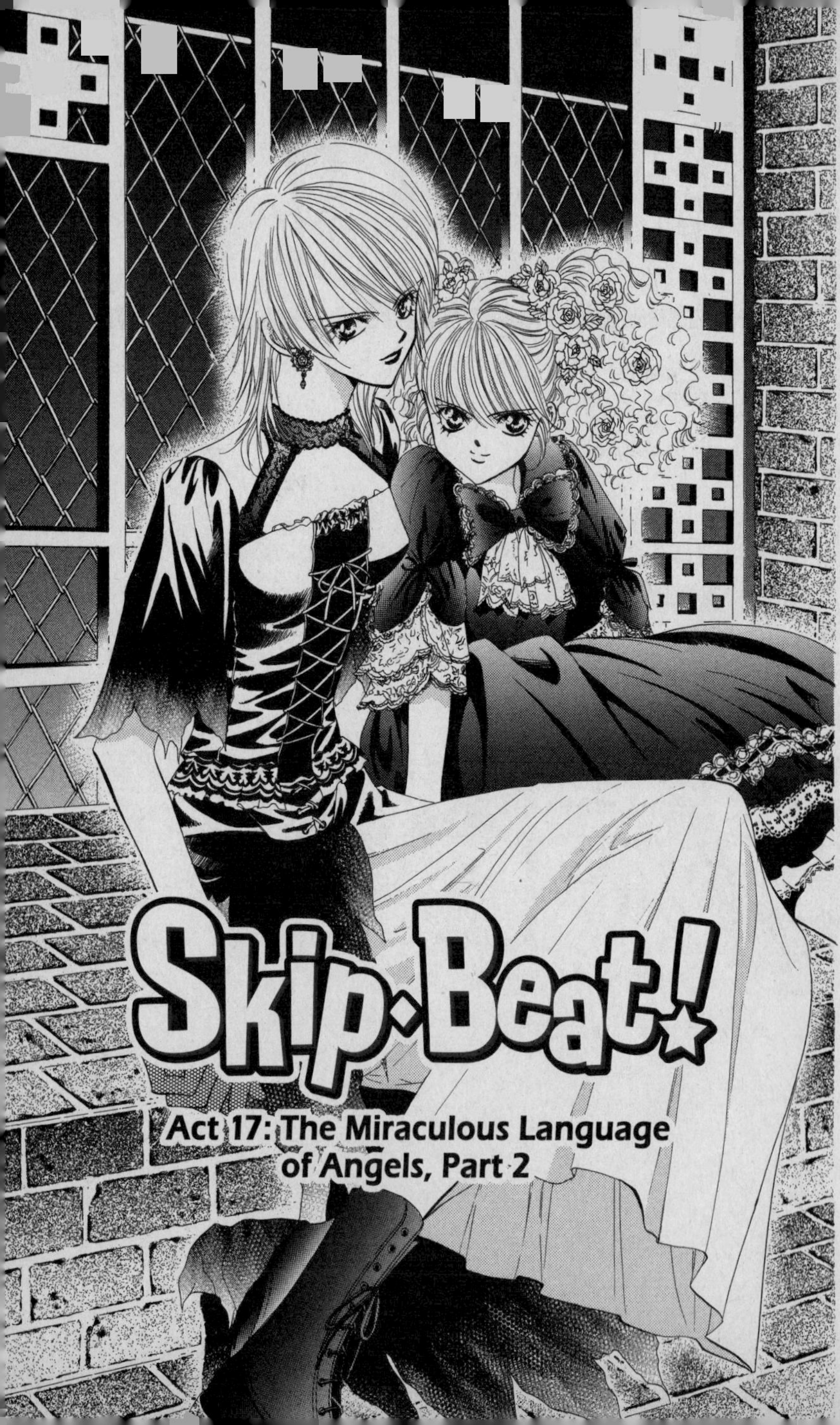
Skip·Beat!
Act 17: The Miraculous Language of Angels, Part 2

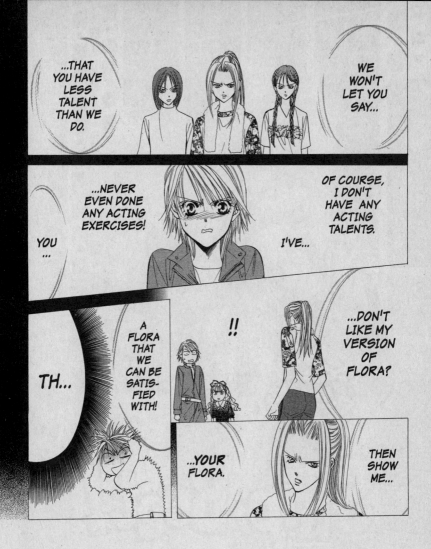

WE WON'T LET YOU SAY...
...THAT YOU HAVE LESS TALENT THAN WE DO.
OF COURSE, I DON'T HAVE ANY ACTING TALENTS.
I'VE...
...NEVER EVEN DONE ANY ACTING EXERCISES!
YOU ...
...DON'T LIKE MY VERSION OF FLORA?
!!
THEN SHOW ME...
...YOUR FLORA.
A FLORA THAT WE CAN BE SATISFIED WITH!
TH...

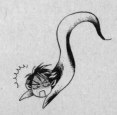

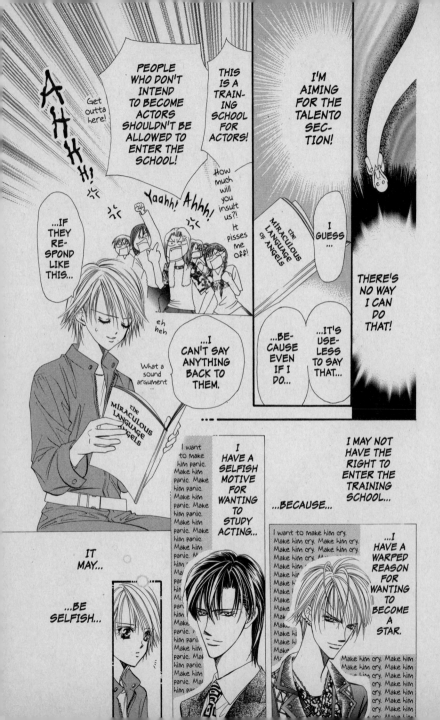

AHHH!

Get outta here!

PEOPLE WHO DON'T INTEND TO BECOME ACTORS SHOULDN'T BE ALLOWED TO ENTER THE SCHOOL!

THIS IS A TRAINING SCHOOL FOR ACTORS!

I'M AIMING FOR THE TALENTO SECTION!

How much will you insult us?! It pisses me off!

Yaahh! Ahhh!

...IF THEY RESPOND LIKE THIS...

eh heh

What a sound argument...

...I CAN'T SAY ANYTHING BACK TO THEM.

the MIRACULOUS LANGUAGE OF ANGELS

I GUESS...

...BECAUSE EVEN IF I DO...

...IT'S USELESS TO SAY THAT...

THERE'S NO WAY I CAN DO THAT!

the MIRACULOUS LANGUAGE OF ANGELS

I want to make him panic. Make him panic. Make him panic. Make him panic. Make him panic. Make him panic. Make him panic. Make him panic...

I HAVE A SELFISH MOTIVE FOR WANTING TO STUDY ACTING...

...BECAUSE...

I MAY NOT HAVE THE RIGHT TO ENTER THE TRAINING SCHOOL...

IT MAY...

...BE SELFISH...

I want to make him cry. Make him cry. Make him cry. Make him cry. Make him cry. Make him cry. Make him cry. Make him cry. Make him cry. Make him cry. Make him cry. Make him cry. Make him cry. Make him cry. Make him cry. Make him cry. Make him cry.

...I HAVE A WARPED REASON FOR WANTING TO BECOME A STAR.

Make him cry. Make him cry. Make him cry. Make him cry. Make him cry. Make him cry.

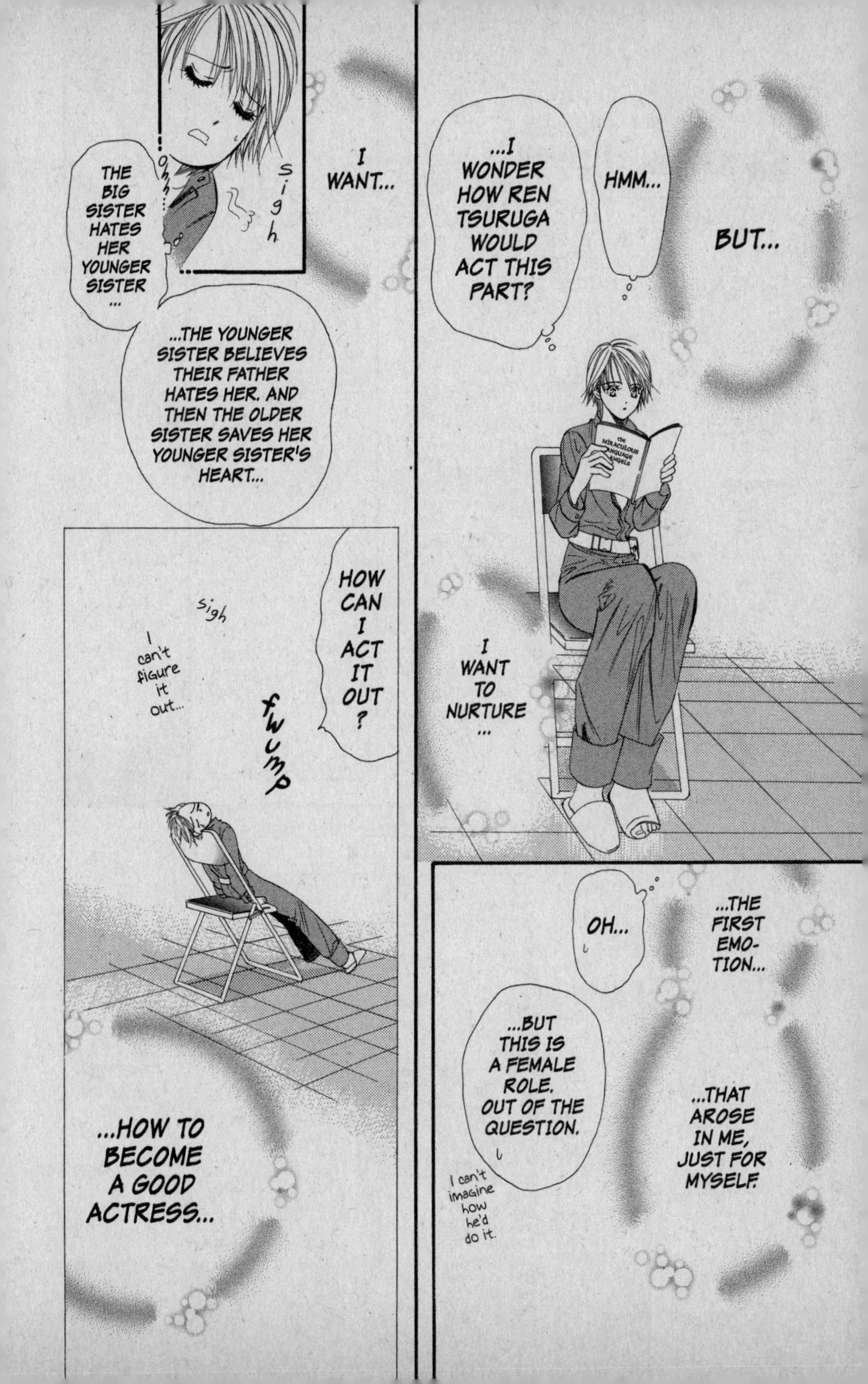
HMM...
...I WONDER HOW REN TSURUGA WOULD ACT THIS PART?
BUT...
I WANT TO NURTURE...
...THE FIRST EMOTION...
OH...
...BUT THIS IS A FEMALE ROLE. OUT OF THE QUESTION.
I can't imagine how he'd do it.
...THAT AROSE IN ME, JUST FOR MYSELF.
I WANT...
sigh
Ohh...
THE BIG SISTER HATES HER YOUNGER SISTER...
...THE YOUNGER SISTER BELIEVES THEIR FATHER HATES HER. AND THEN THE OLDER SISTER SAVES HER YOUNGER SISTER'S HEART...
HOW CAN I ACT IT OUT?
fwump
sigh
I can't figure it out...
...HOW TO BECOME A GOOD ACTRESS...

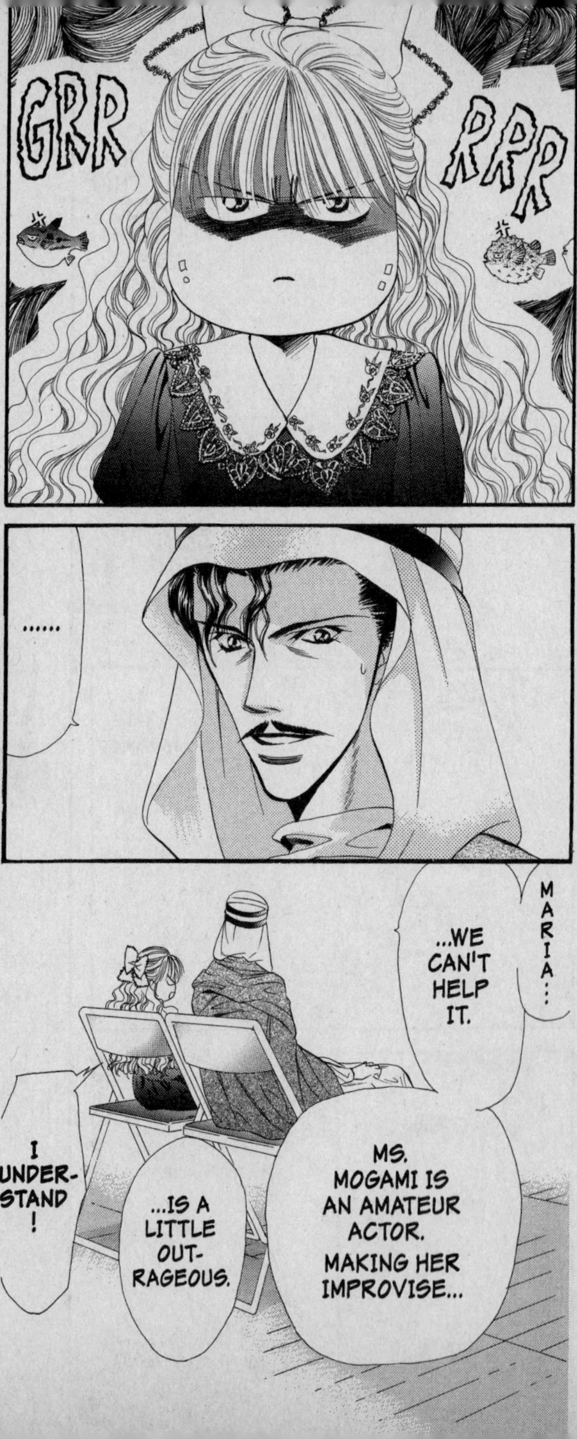
GRR
RRR
......
MARIA...
...WE CAN'T HELP IT.
MS. MOGAMI IS AN AMATEUR ACTOR. MAKING HER IMPROVISE...
...IS A LITTLE OUT-RAGEOUS.
I UNDER-STAND!

Lory Takarada

Difficulty level

☆ ☆ ②

The difficulty for my assistants must be a 4... (Because he's always wearing ethnic costumes that aren't coordinated at all...) Moreover, he sometimes comes with dancers or a camel...

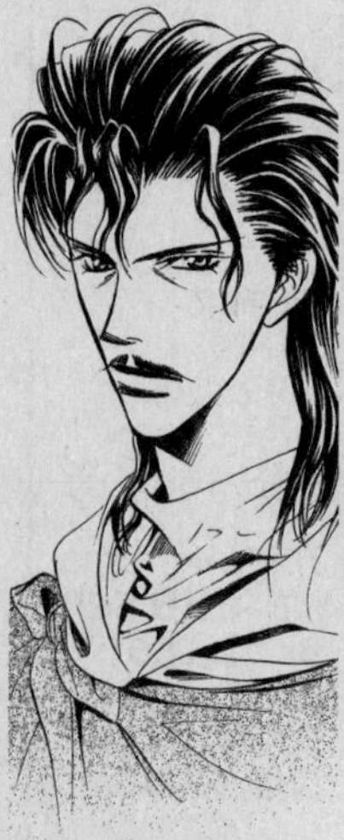

Lory should be a character that I draw without thinking, but there were lots of faces in the pages of this volume that I didn't like, and I didn't know what to do...

There is a reason Lory's name is spelled in Japanese with a small "i" at the end instead of with a dash. It is because...well...I'll talk about it...sometime in the future...so...that's it...

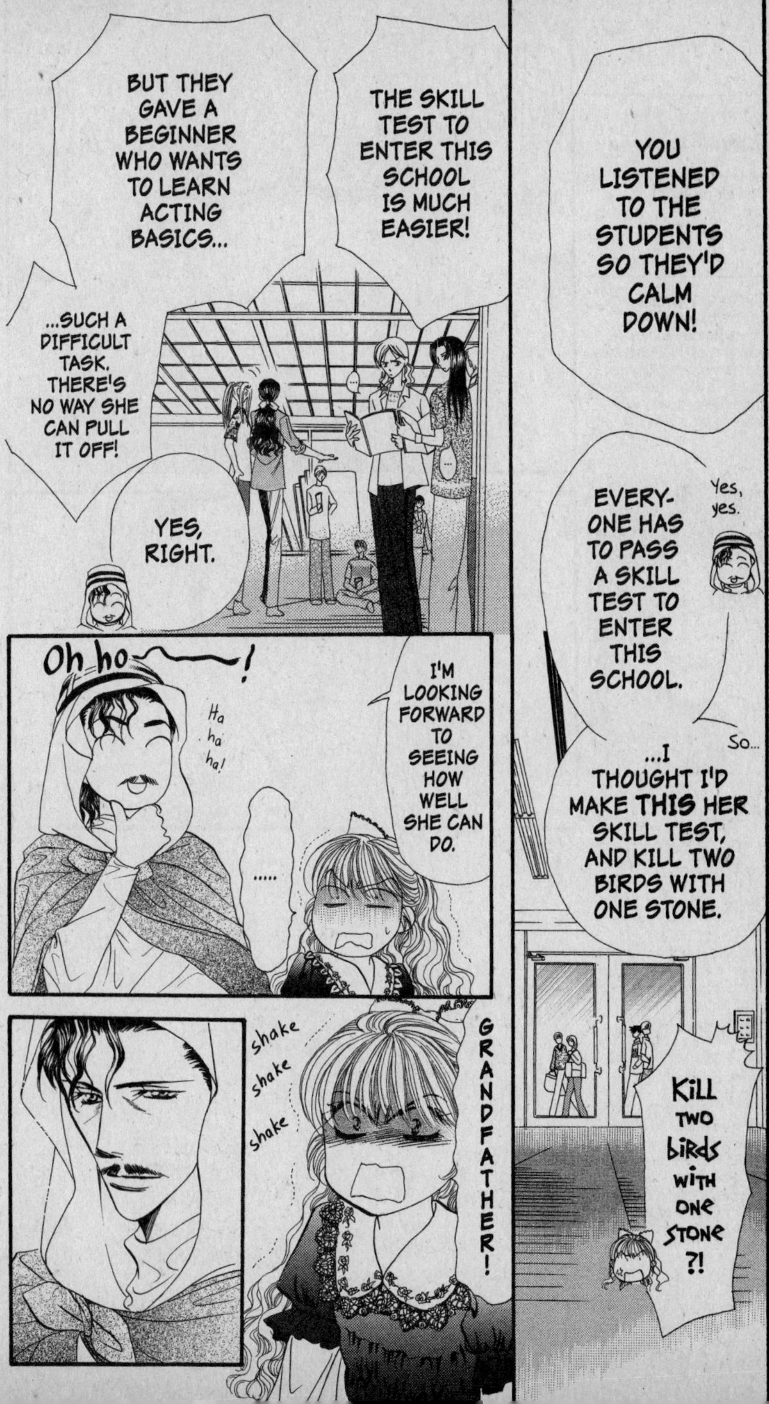
YOU LISTENED TO THE STUDENTS SO THEY'D CALM DOWN!
Yes, yes.
EVERY-ONE HAS TO PASS A SKILL TEST TO ENTER THIS SCHOOL.
So...
...I THOUGHT I'D MAKE THIS HER SKILL TEST, AND KILL TWO BIRDS WITH ONE STONE.
Kill two birds with one stone?!
THE SKILL TEST TO ENTER THIS SCHOOL IS MUCH EASIER!
BUT THEY GAVE A BEGINNER WHO WANTS TO LEARN ACTING BASICS...
...SUCH A DIFFICULT TASK. THERE'S NO WAY SHE CAN PULL IT OFF!
...
...
YES, RIGHT.
I'M LOOKING FORWARD TO SEEING HOW WELL SHE CAN DO.
Ha ha ha!
Oh ho—!
.....
GRANDFATHER!
shake shake shake

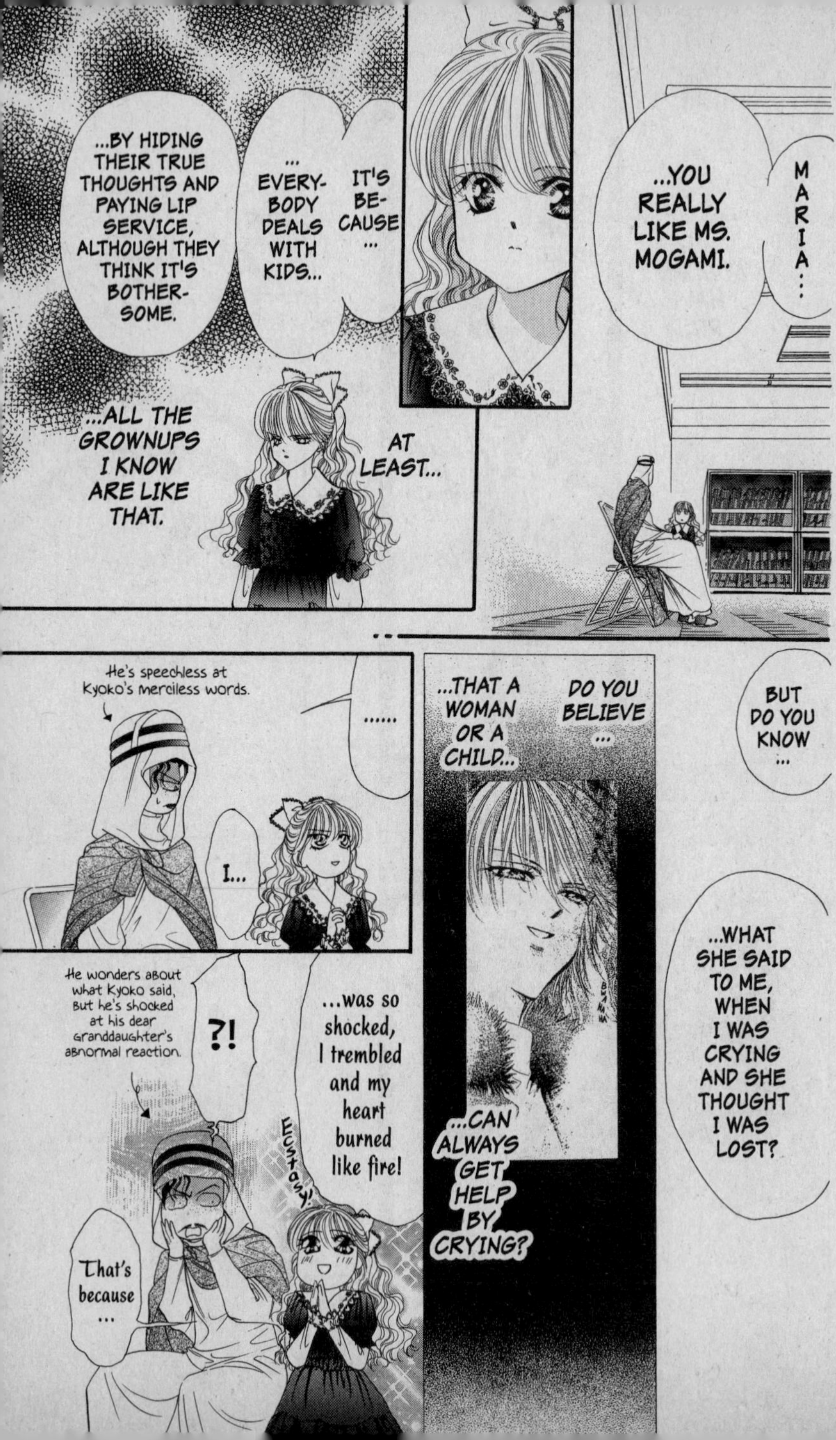
MARIA...
...YOU REALLY LIKE MS. MOGAMI.
IT'S BECAUSE...
...EVERYBODY DEALS WITH KIDS...
...BY HIDING THEIR TRUE THOUGHTS AND PAYING LIP SERVICE, ALTHOUGH THEY THINK IT'S BOTHERSOME.
AT LEAST...
...ALL THE GROWNUPS I KNOW ARE LIKE THAT.
BUT DO YOU KNOW...
...WHAT SHE SAID TO ME, WHEN I WAS CRYING AND SHE THOUGHT I WAS LOST?
DO YOU BELIEVE...
...THAT A WOMAN OR A CHILD...
...CAN ALWAYS GET HELP BY CRYING?
......
I...
He's speechless at Kyoko's merciless words.
...was so shocked, I trembled and my heart burned like fire!
?!
He wonders about what Kyoko said, but he's shocked at his dear Granddaughter's abnormal reaction.
Ecstasy!
That's because...

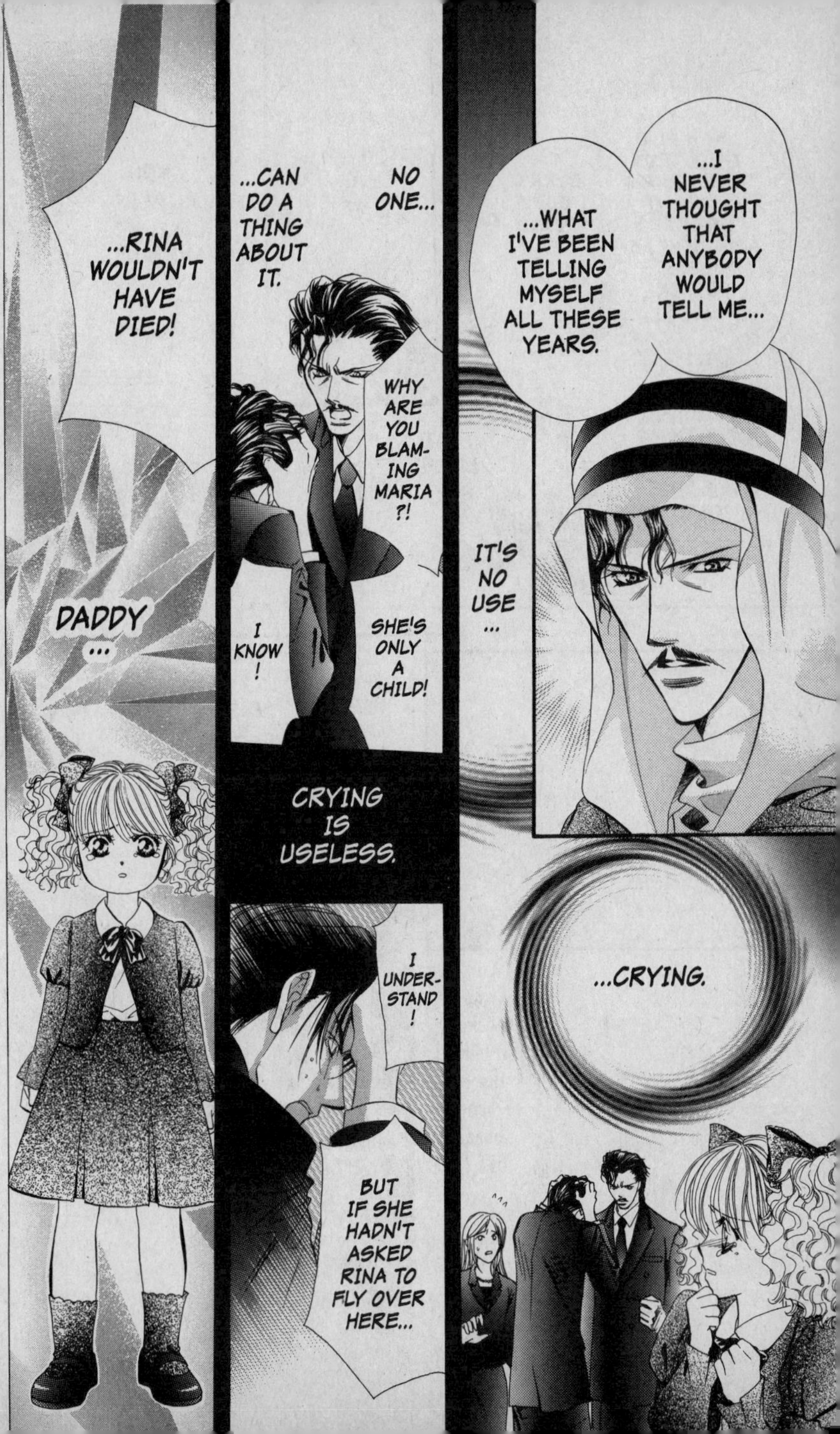
...I NEVER THOUGHT THAT ANYBODY WOULD TELL ME...
...WHAT I'VE BEEN TELLING MYSELF ALL THESE YEARS.
IT'S NO USE...
...CRYING.
NO ONE...
...CAN DO A THING ABOUT IT.
WHY ARE YOU BLAMING MARIA?!
SHE'S ONLY A CHILD!
I KNOW!
CRYING IS USELESS.
I UNDERSTAND!
BUT IF SHE HADN'T ASKED RINA TO FLY OVER HERE...
...RINA WOULDN'T HAVE DIED!
DADDY...

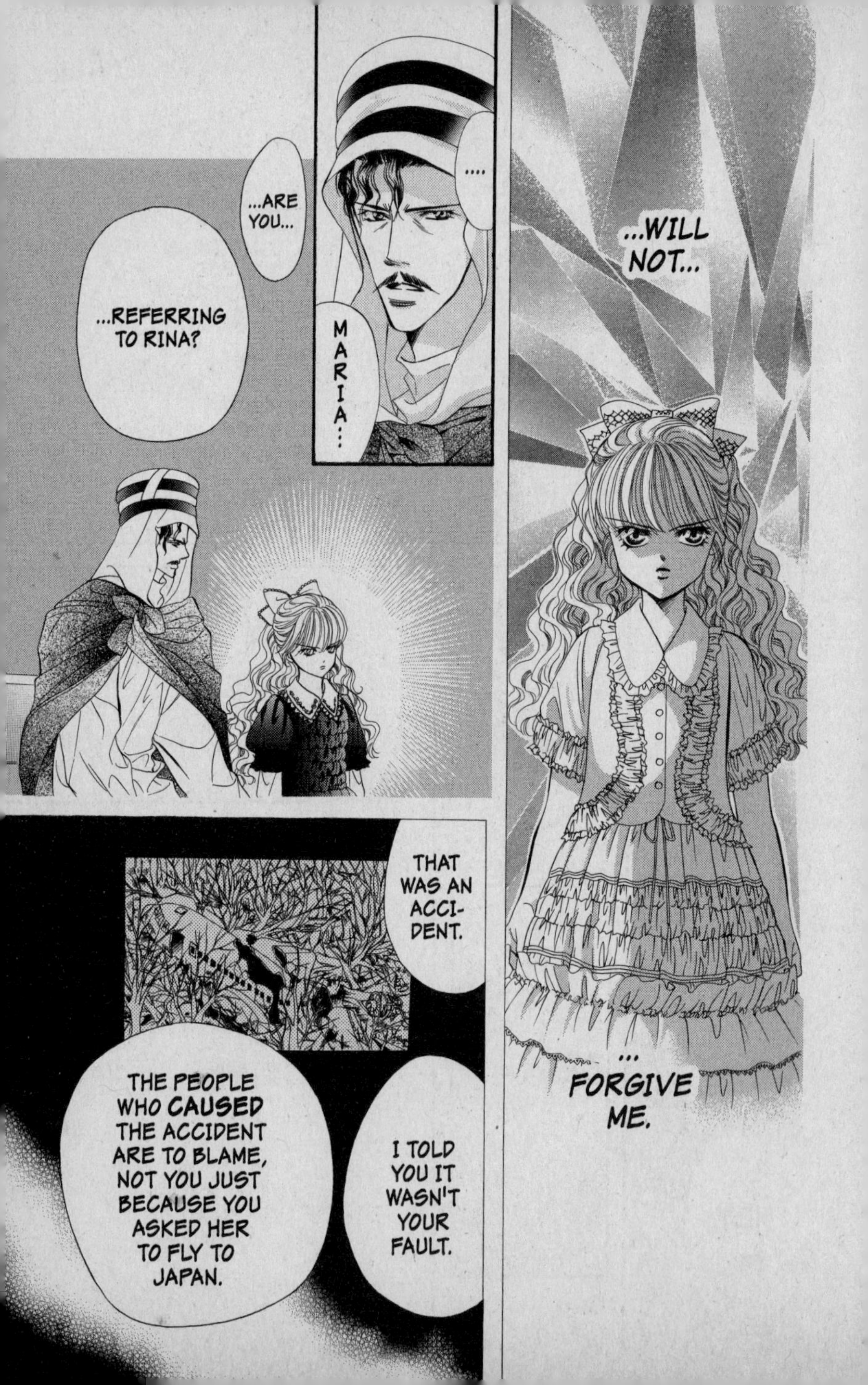
...WILL NOT...
... FORGIVE ME.
....
MARIA...
...ARE YOU...
...REFERRING TO RINA?
THAT WAS AN ACCI-DENT.
I TOLD YOU IT WASN'T YOUR FAULT.
THE PEOPLE WHO **CAUSED** THE ACCIDENT ARE TO BLAME, NOT YOU JUST BECAUSE YOU ASKED HER TO FLY TO JAPAN.

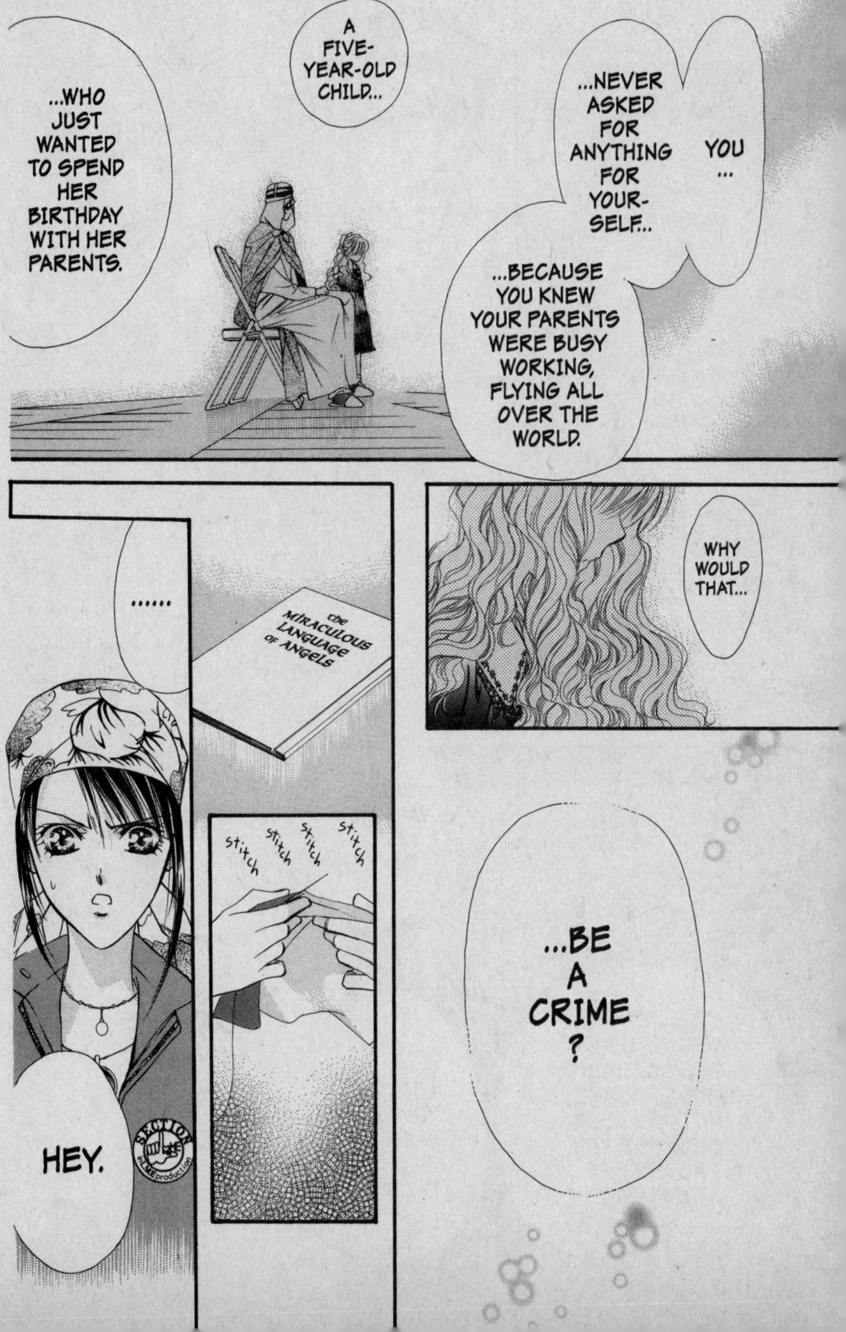
YOU...
...NEVER ASKED FOR ANYTHING FOR YOURSELF...
...BECAUSE YOU KNEW YOUR PARENTS WERE BUSY WORKING, FLYING ALL OVER THE WORLD.
A FIVE-YEAR-OLD CHILD...
...WHO JUST WANTED TO SPEND HER BIRTHDAY WITH HER PARENTS.
WHY WOULD THAT...
...BE A CRIME?
the MIRACULOUS LANGUAGE of ANGELS
stitch stitch stitch stitch
......
SECTION
HEY.

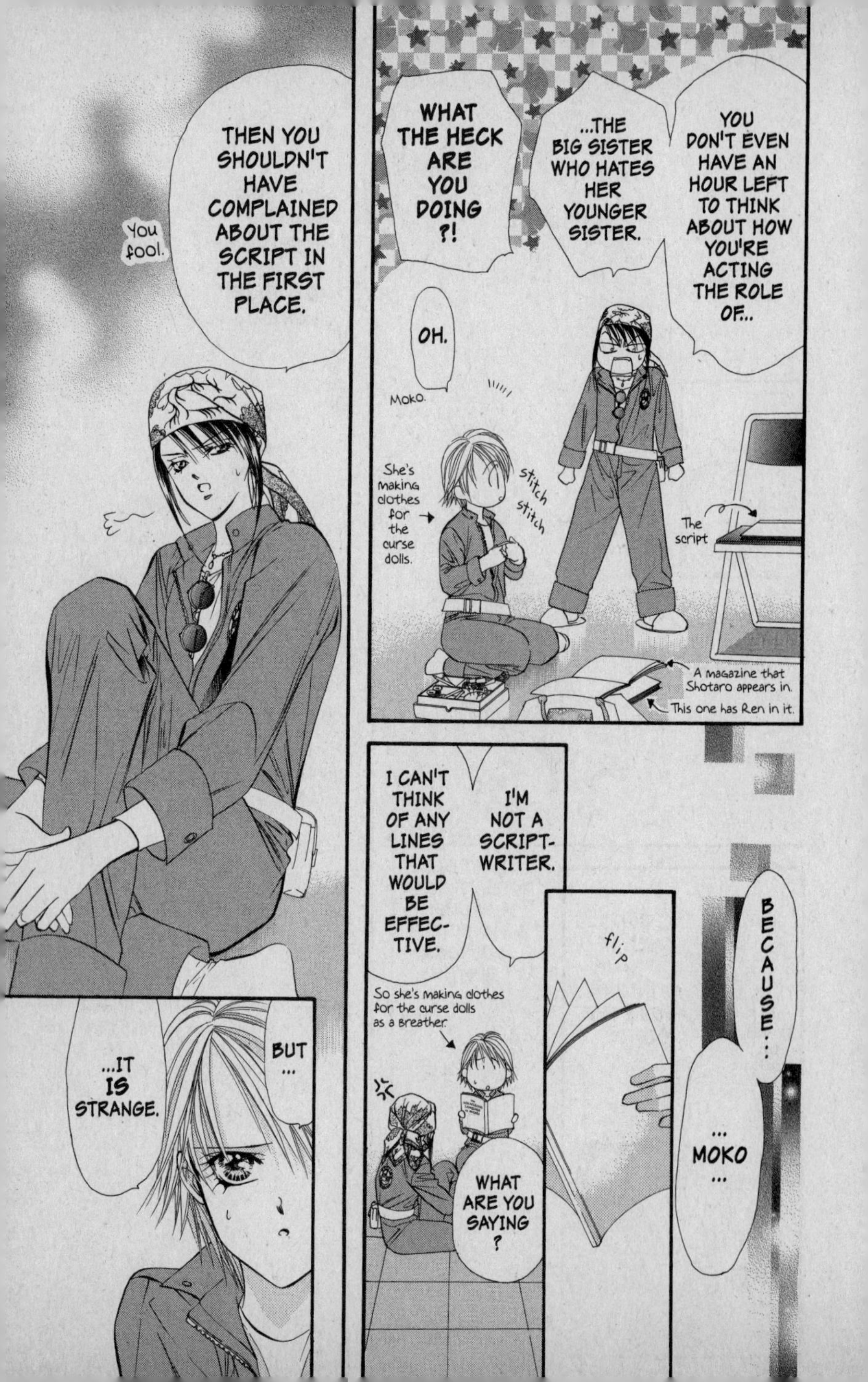
YOU DON'T EVEN HAVE AN HOUR LEFT TO THINK ABOUT HOW YOU'RE ACTING THE ROLE OF...
...THE BIG SISTER WHO HATES HER YOUNGER SISTER.
WHAT THE HECK ARE YOU DOING?!
OH.
MOKO.
She's making clothes for the curse dolls.
stitch stitch
The script
A magazine that Shotaro appears in.
This one has Ren in it.
THEN YOU SHOULDN'T HAVE COMPLAINED ABOUT THE SCRIPT IN THE FIRST PLACE.
You fool.
BECAUSE...
...MOKO...
flip
I'M NOT A SCRIPTWRITER.
I CAN'T THINK OF ANY LINES THAT WOULD BE EFFECTIVE.
So she's making clothes for the curse dolls as a breather.
WHAT ARE YOU SAYING?
BUT...
...IT IS STRANGE.

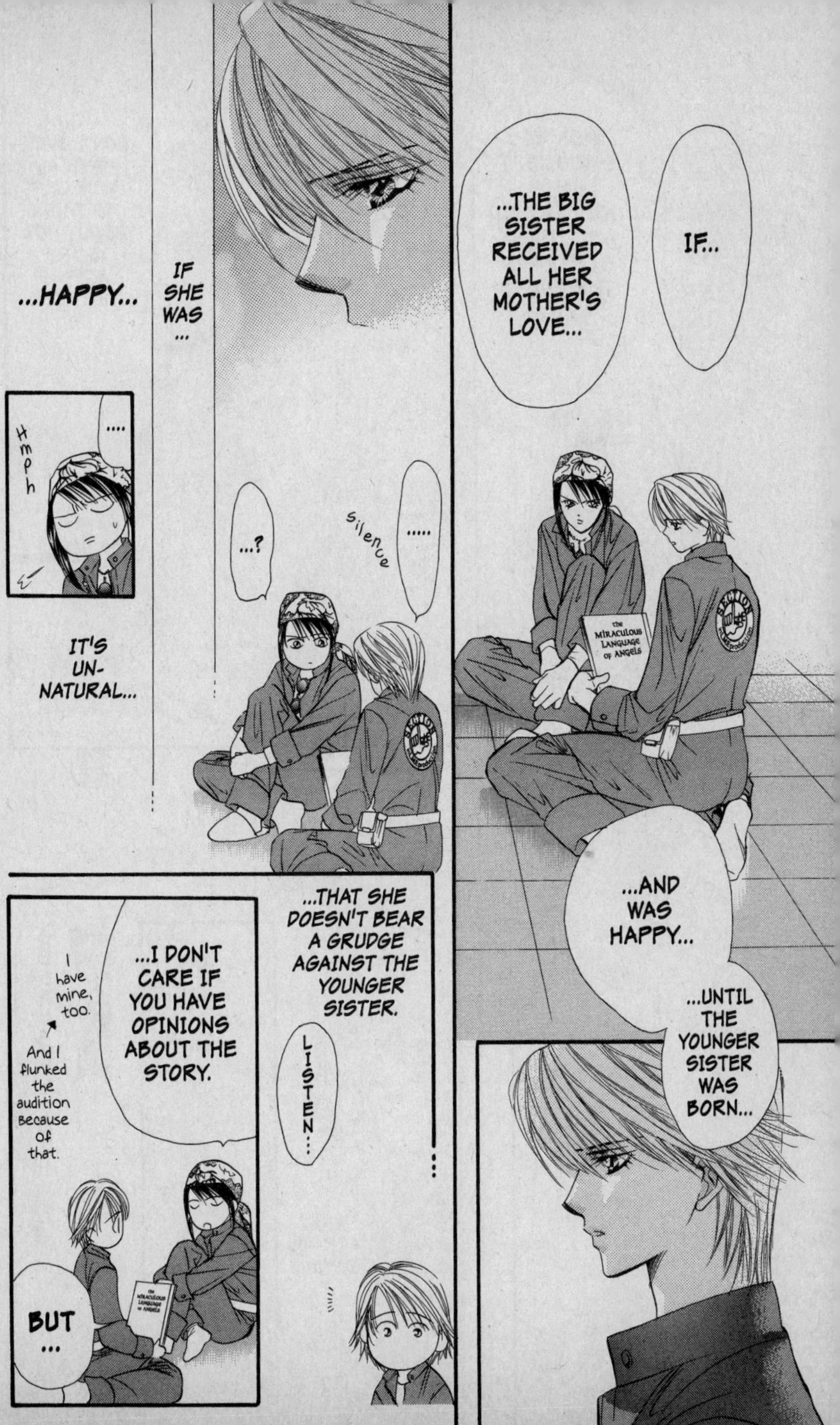
IF...
...THE BIG SISTER RECEIVED ALL HER MOTHER'S LOVE...
THE MIRACULOUS LANGUAGE OF ANGELS
...AND WAS HAPPY...
...UNTIL THE YOUNGER SISTER WAS BORN...
IF SHE WAS ...
...HAPPY...
Silence
.....
...?
....
Hmph
IT'S UN-NATURAL...
...THAT SHE DOESN'T BEAR A GRUDGE AGAINST THE YOUNGER SISTER.
LISTEN...
...I DON'T CARE IF YOU HAVE OPINIONS ABOUT THE STORY.
I have mine, too.
And I flunked the audition because of that.
BUT ...

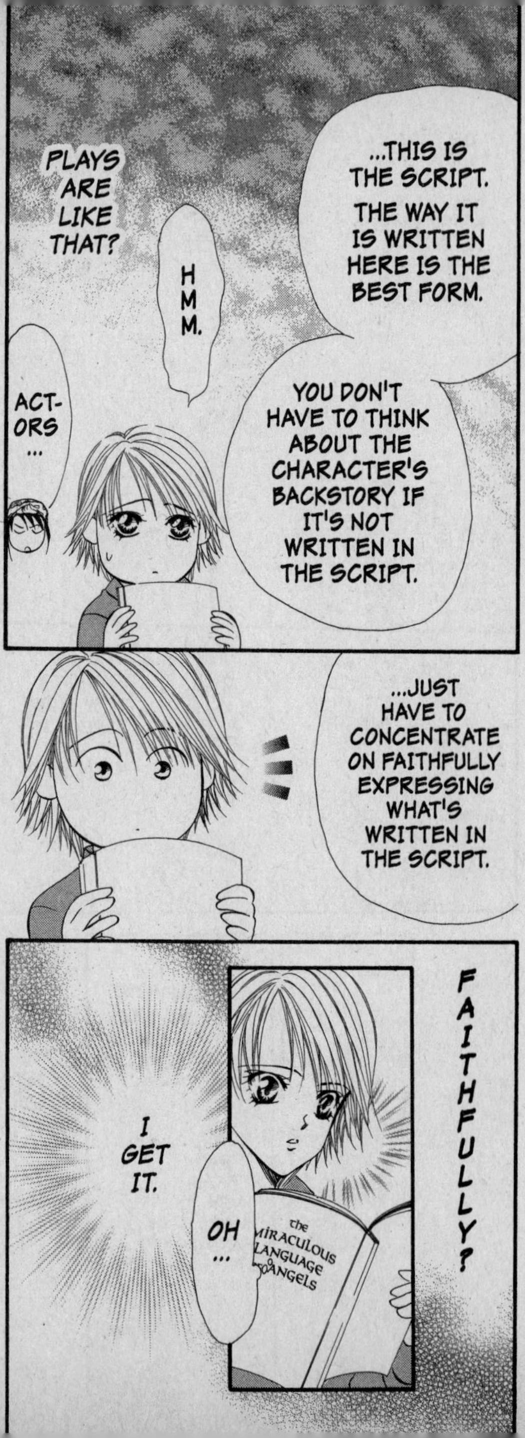
...THIS IS THE SCRIPT.
THE WAY IT IS WRITTEN HERE IS THE BEST FORM.
PLAYS ARE LIKE THAT?
HMM.
YOU DON'T HAVE TO THINK ABOUT THE CHARACTER'S BACKSTORY IF IT'S NOT WRITTEN IN THE SCRIPT.
ACT-ORS...
...JUST HAVE TO CONCENTRATE ON FAITHFULLY EXPRESSING WHAT'S WRITTEN IN THE SCRIPT.
FAITHFULLY?
I GET IT.
OH...
The MIRACULOUS LANGUAGE of ANGELS
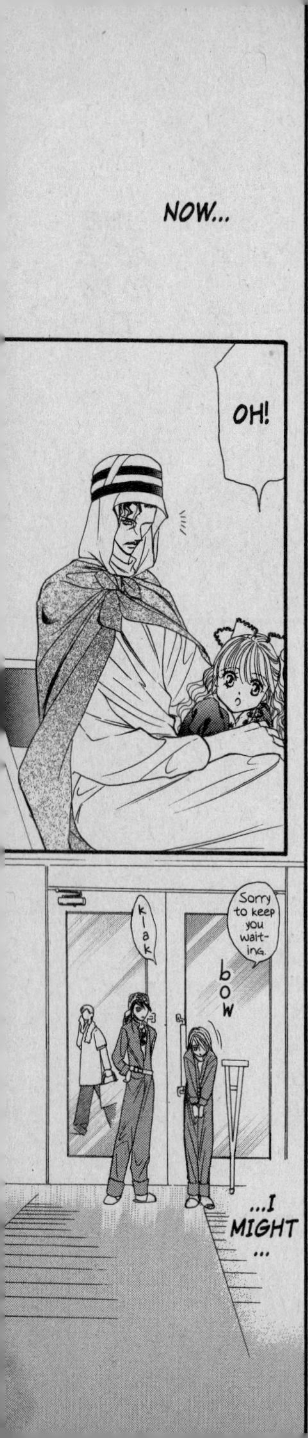
NOW...
OH!
Sorry to keep you waiting.
klak
bow
...I MIGHT...

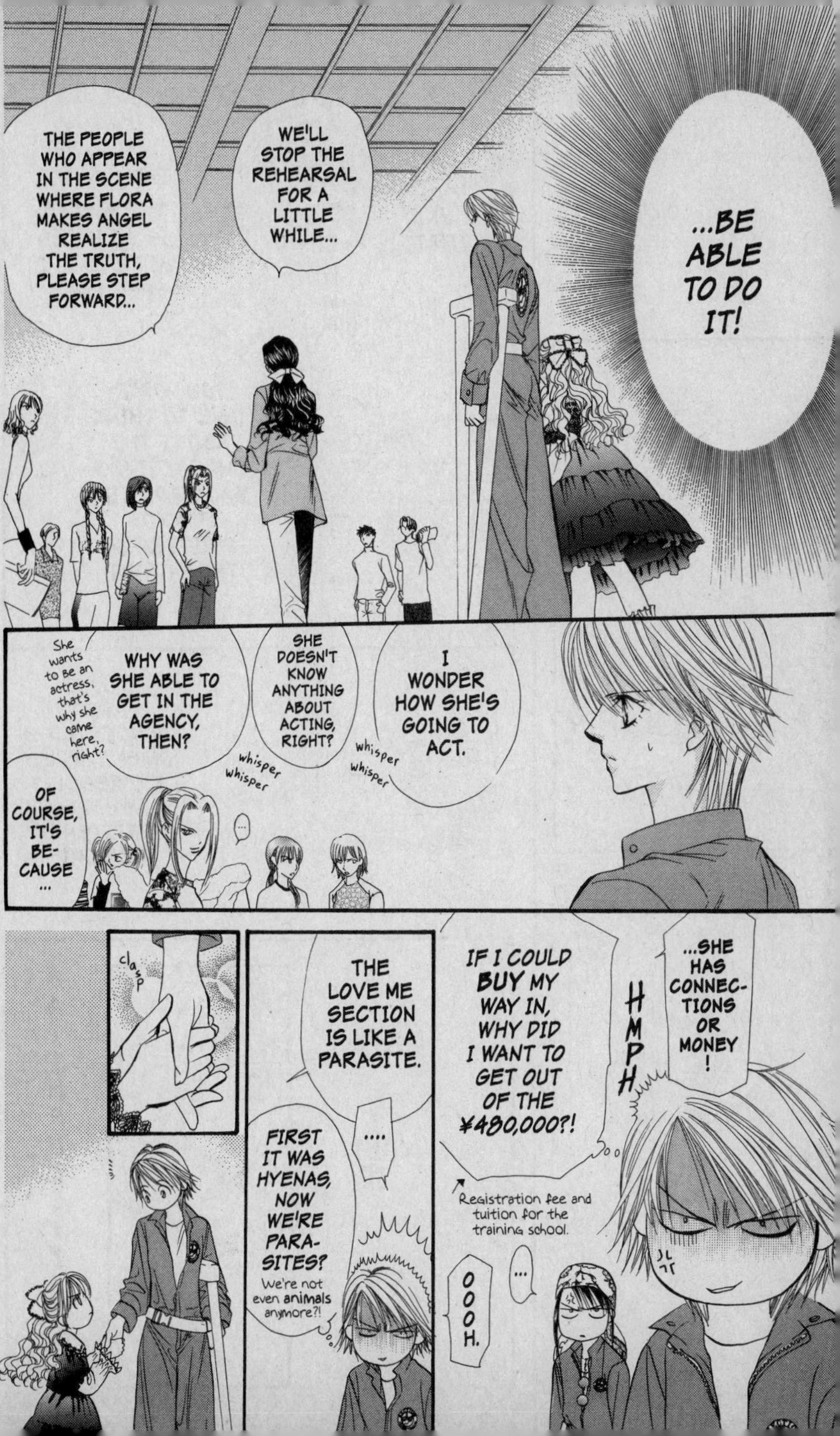

...BE ABLE TO DO IT!
WE'LL STOP THE REHEARSAL FOR A LITTLE WHILE...
THE PEOPLE WHO APPEAR IN THE SCENE WHERE FLORA MAKES ANGEL REALIZE THE TRUTH, PLEASE STEP FORWARD...
I WONDER HOW SHE'S GOING TO ACT.
whisper whisper
SHE DOESN'T KNOW ANYTHING ABOUT ACTING, RIGHT?
whisper whisper
WHY WAS SHE ABLE TO GET IN THE AGENCY, THEN?
She wants to be an actress, that's why she came here, right?
OF COURSE, IT'S BE- CAUSE ...
...
...SHE HAS CONNEC- TIONS OR MONEY!
HMPH
IF I COULD BUY MY WAY IN, WHY DID I WANT TO GET OUT OF THE ¥480,000?!
Registration fee and tuition for the training school.
OOOH.
...
THE LOVE ME SECTION IS LIKE A PARASITE.
....
FIRST IT WAS HYENAS, NOW WE'RE PARA- SITES?
We're not even animals anymore?!
clasp

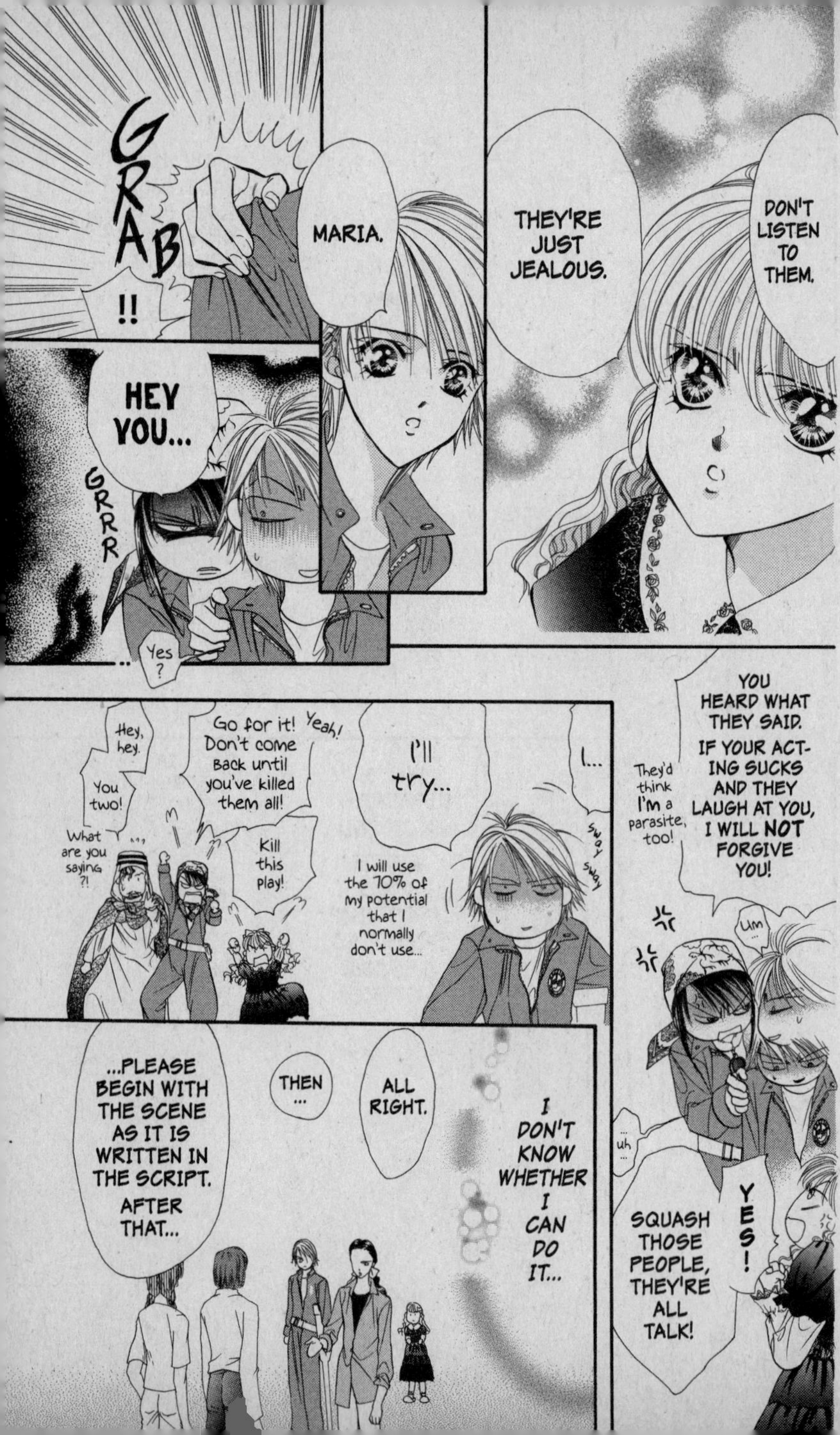
DON'T LISTEN TO THEM.
THEY'RE JUST JEALOUS.
MARIA.
GRAB!!
HEY YOU...
GRRR
...Yes?
YOU HEARD WHAT THEY SAID.
IF YOUR ACTING SUCKS AND THEY LAUGH AT YOU, I WILL NOT FORGIVE YOU!
They'd think I'm a parasite, too!
Um...
YES!
SQUASH THOSE PEOPLE, THEY'RE ALL TALK!
...uh...
I...
I'll try...
sway sway
I will use the 70% of my potential that I normally don't use...
Yeah!
Go for it! Don't come back until you've killed them all!
Kill this play!
Hey, hey.
You two!
What are you saying?!
I DON'T KNOW WHETHER I CAN DO IT...
ALL RIGHT.
THEN...
...PLEASE BEGIN WITH THE SCENE AS IT IS WRITTEN IN THE SCRIPT.
AFTER THAT...

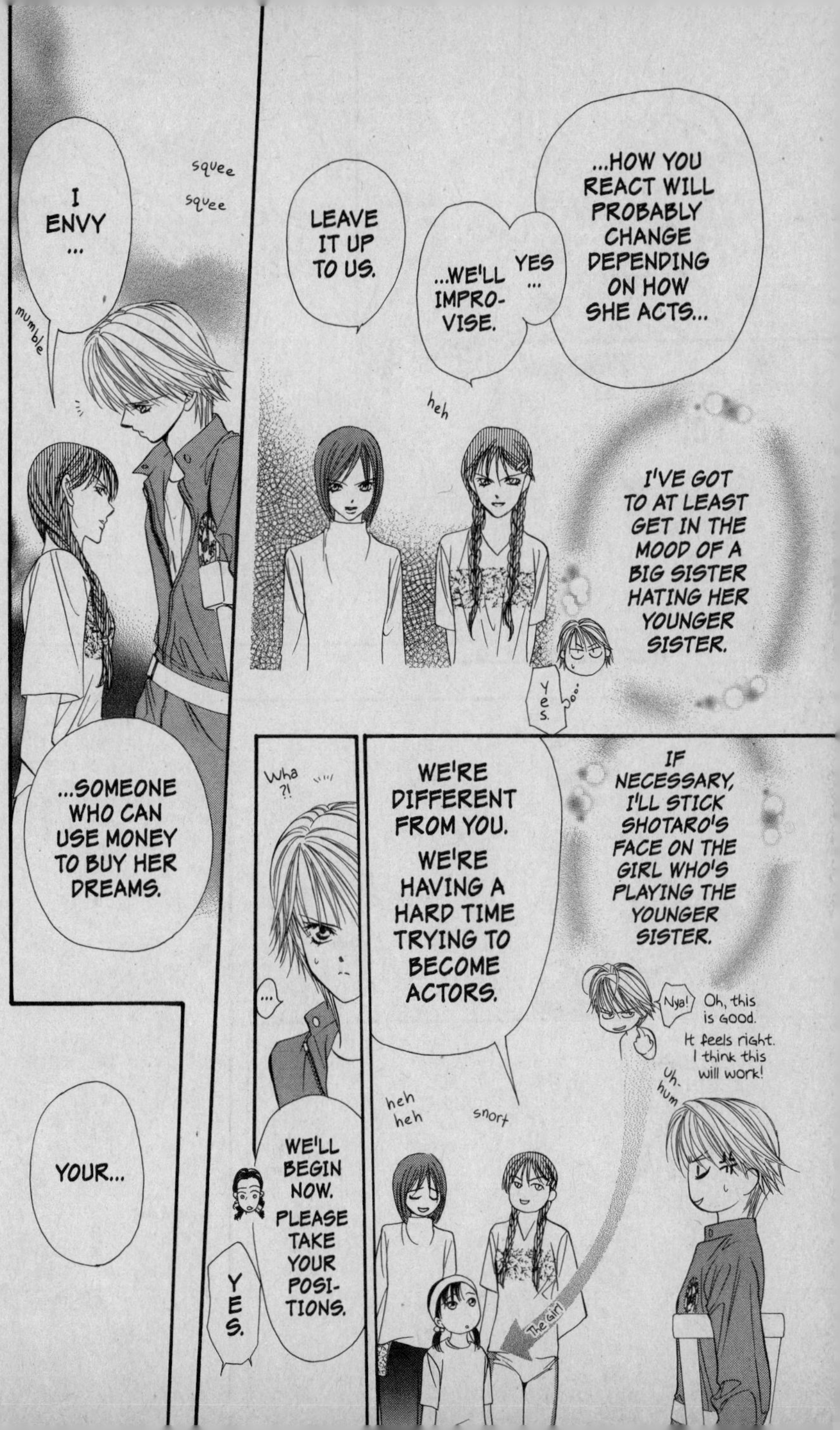
...HOW YOU REACT WILL PROBABLY CHANGE DEPENDING ON HOW SHE ACTS...
YES...
...WE'LL IMPROVISE.
LEAVE IT UP TO US.
heh
I'VE GOT TO AT LEAST GET IN THE MOOD OF A BIG SISTER HATING HER YOUNGER SISTER.
Yes.
IF NECESSARY, I'LL STICK SHOTARO'S FACE ON THE GIRL WHO'S PLAYING THE YOUNGER SISTER.
Nya!
Oh, this is good.
It feels right. I think this will work!
Uh-hum
WE'RE DIFFERENT FROM YOU.
WE'RE HAVING A HARD TIME TRYING TO BECOME ACTORS.
snort
heh heh
The Girl
WE'LL BEGIN NOW. PLEASE TAKE YOUR POSITIONS.
YES.
Wha?!
...
I ENVY...
squee
squee
mumble
...SOMEONE WHO CAN USE MONEY TO BUY HER DREAMS.
YOUR...

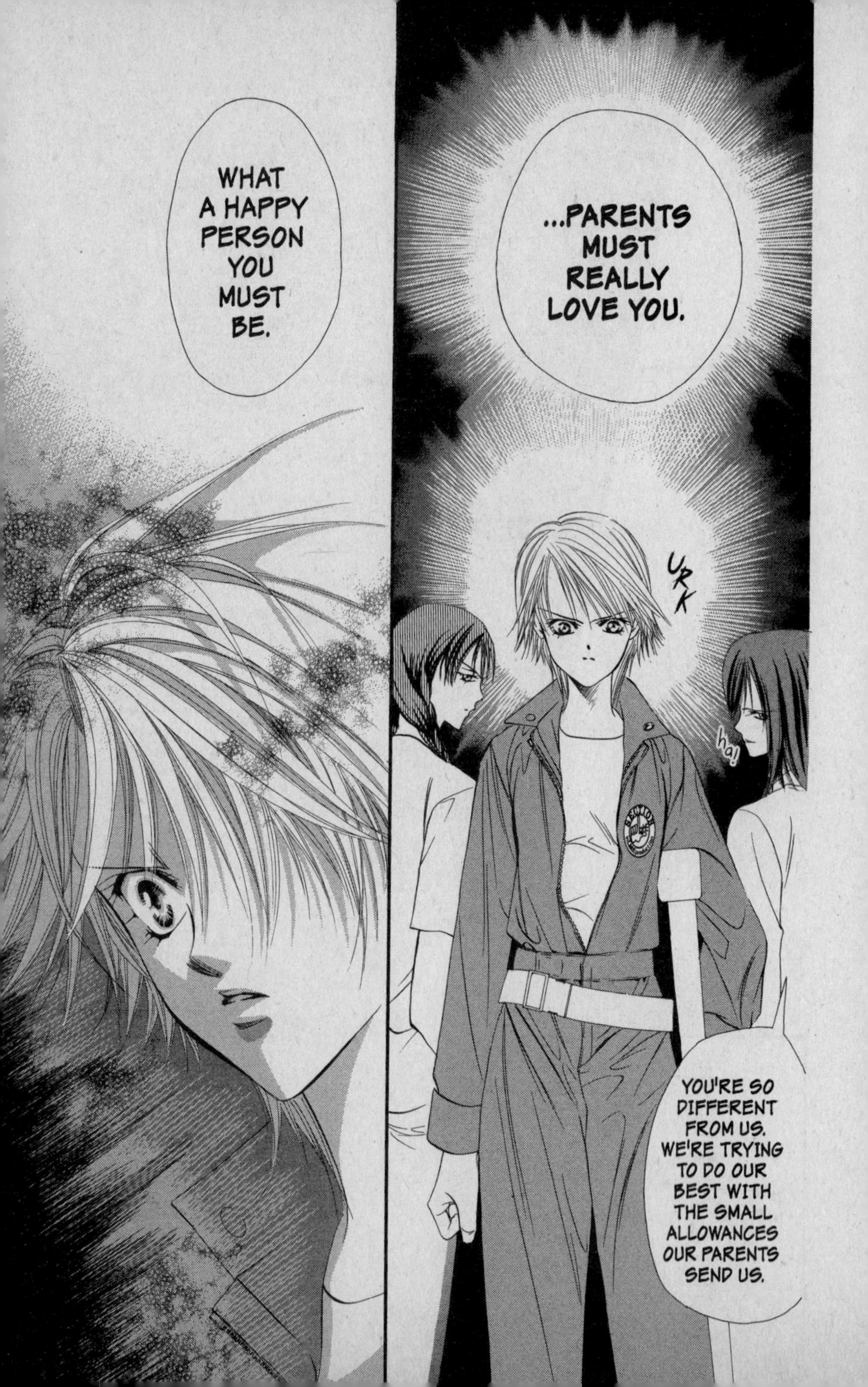
...PARENTS MUST REALLY LOVE YOU.
URK
ha!
YOU'RE SO DIFFERENT FROM US. WE'RE TRYING TO DO OUR BEST WITH THE SMALL ALLOWANCES OUR PARENTS SEND US.
WHAT A HAPPY PERSON YOU MUST BE.

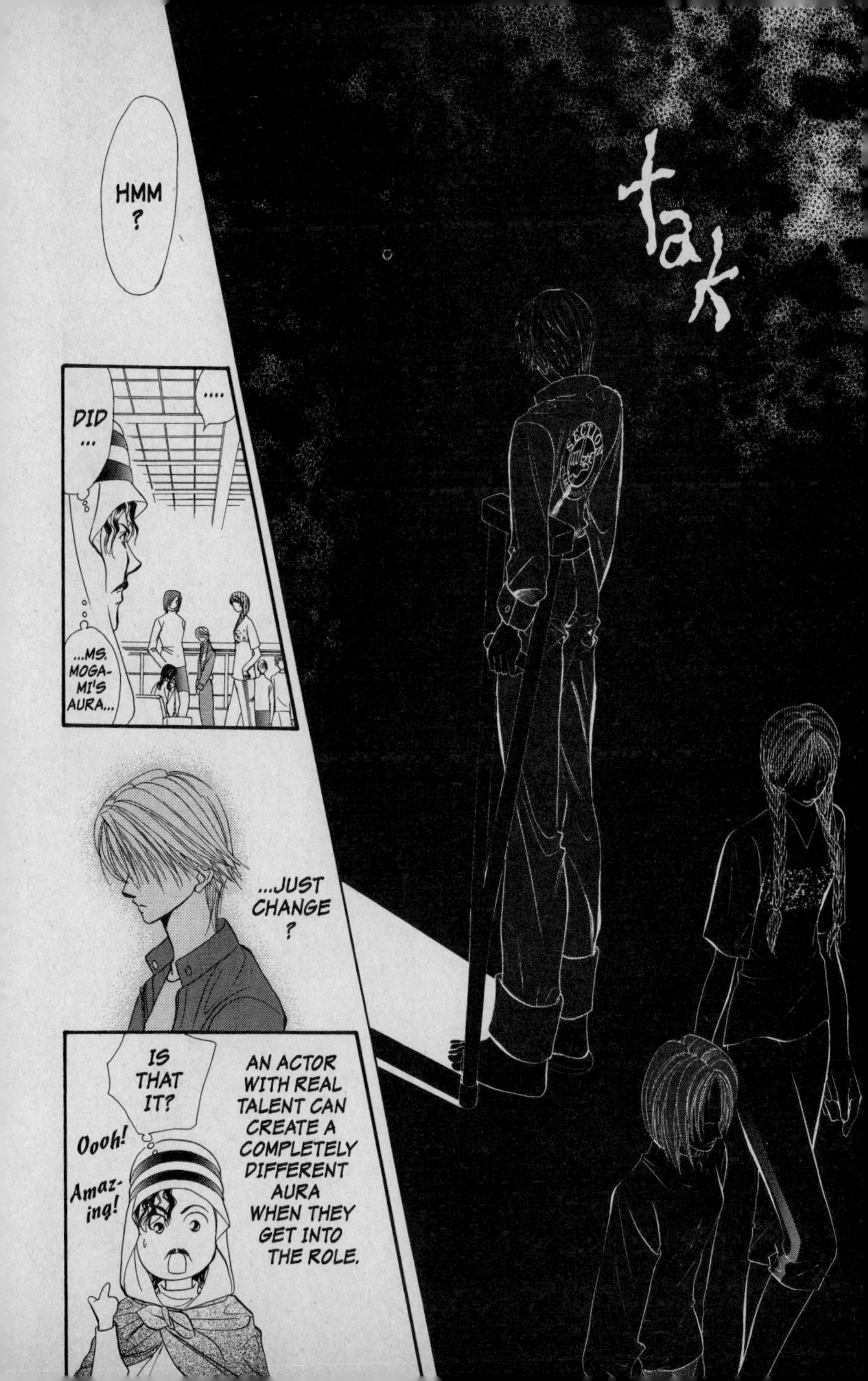
tak
HMM ?
....
DID ...
...MS. MOGA-MI'S AURA...
...JUST CHANGE ?
IS THAT IT?
Oooh!
Amaz-ing!
AN ACTOR WITH REAL TALENT CAN CREATE A COMPLETELY DIFFERENT AURA WHEN THEY GET INTO THE ROLE.

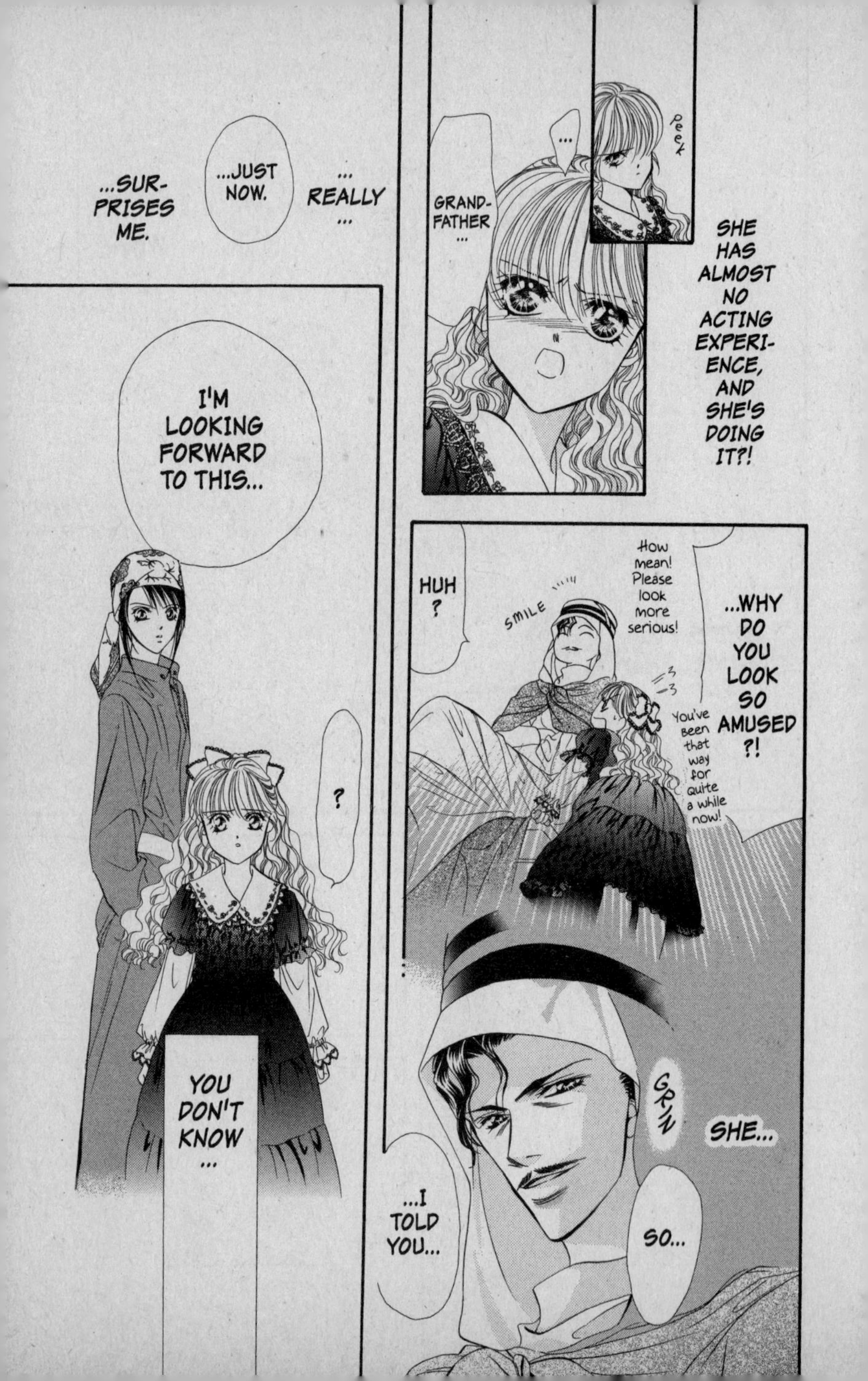

Peek
...
SHE HAS ALMOST NO ACTING EXPERI-ENCE, AND SHE'S DOING IT?!
GRAND-FATHER...
...WHY DO YOU LOOK SO AMUSED?!
You've Been that way for quite a while now!
How mean! Please look more serious!
SMILE
HUH?
GRIN
SHE...
SO...
...I TOLD YOU...
... REALLY ...
...JUST NOW.
...SUR-PRISES ME.
I'M LOOKING FORWARD TO THIS...
?
YOU DON'T KNOW ...

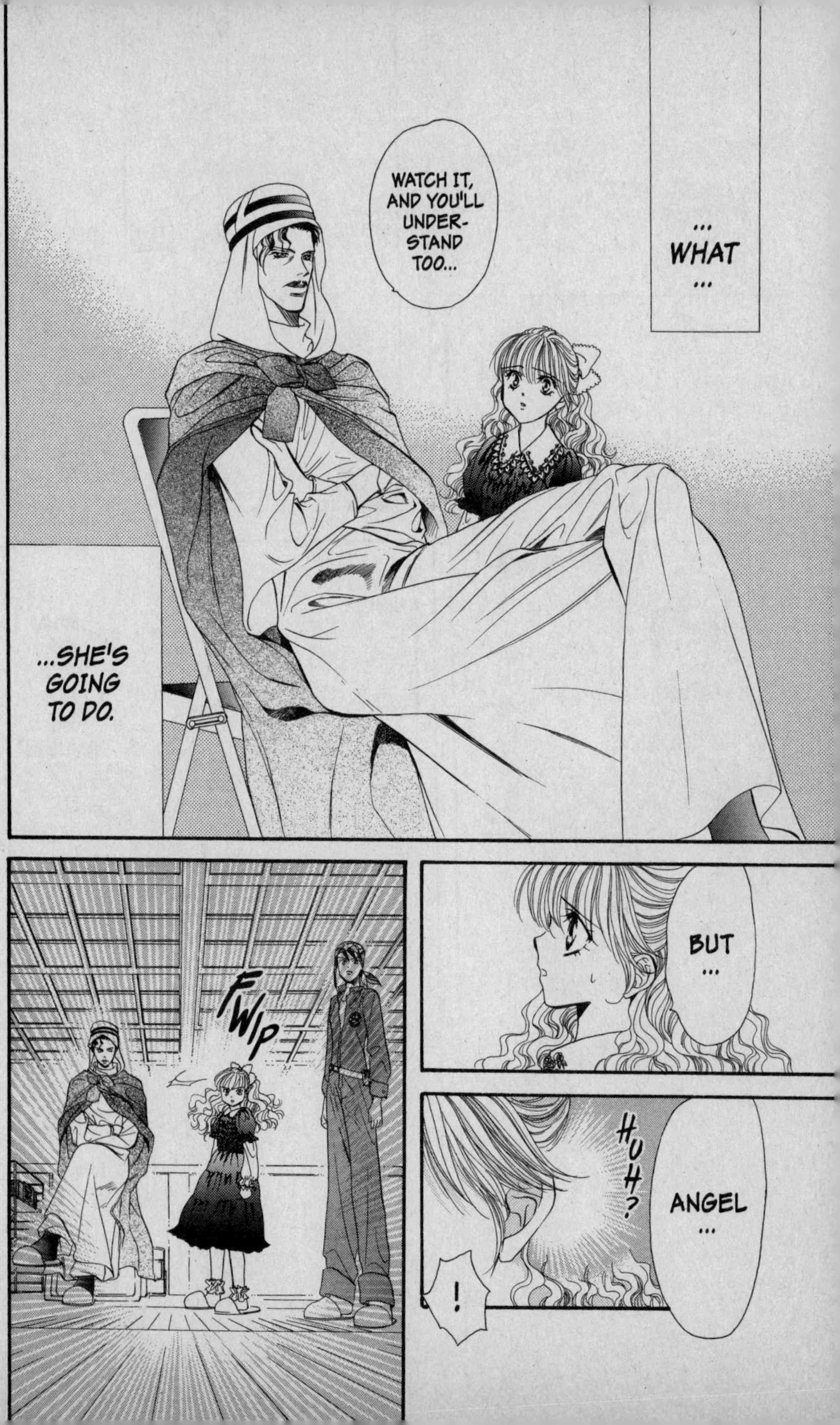
... WHAT ...
WATCH IT, AND YOU'LL UNDER-STAND TOO...
...SHE'S GOING TO DO.
BUT ...
ANGEL ...
HUH?
!
FWIP

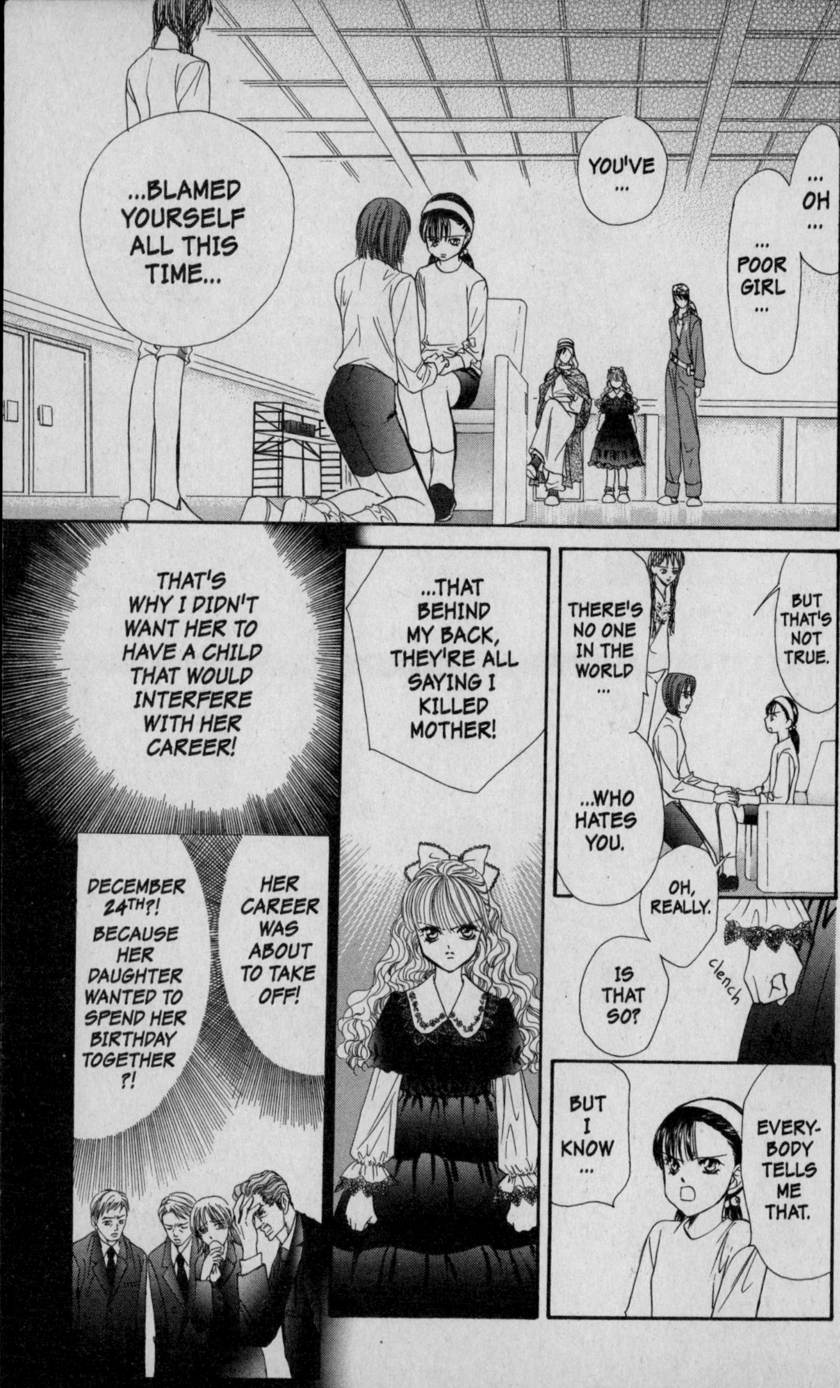
... OH ... ... POOR GIRL ...
YOU'VE ...
...BLAMED YOURSELF ALL THIS TIME...
BUT THAT'S NOT TRUE.
THERE'S NO ONE IN THE WORLD ...
...WHO HATES YOU.
OH, REALLY.
IS THAT SO?
clench
EVERY-BODY TELLS ME THAT.
BUT I KNOW ...
...THAT BEHIND MY BACK, THEY'RE ALL SAYING I KILLED MOTHER!
THAT'S WHY I DIDN'T WANT HER TO HAVE A CHILD THAT WOULD INTERFERE WITH HER CAREER!
HER CAREER WAS ABOUT TO TAKE OFF!
DECEMBER 24TH?! BECAUSE HER DAUGHTER WANTED TO SPEND HER BIRTHDAY TOGETHER?!

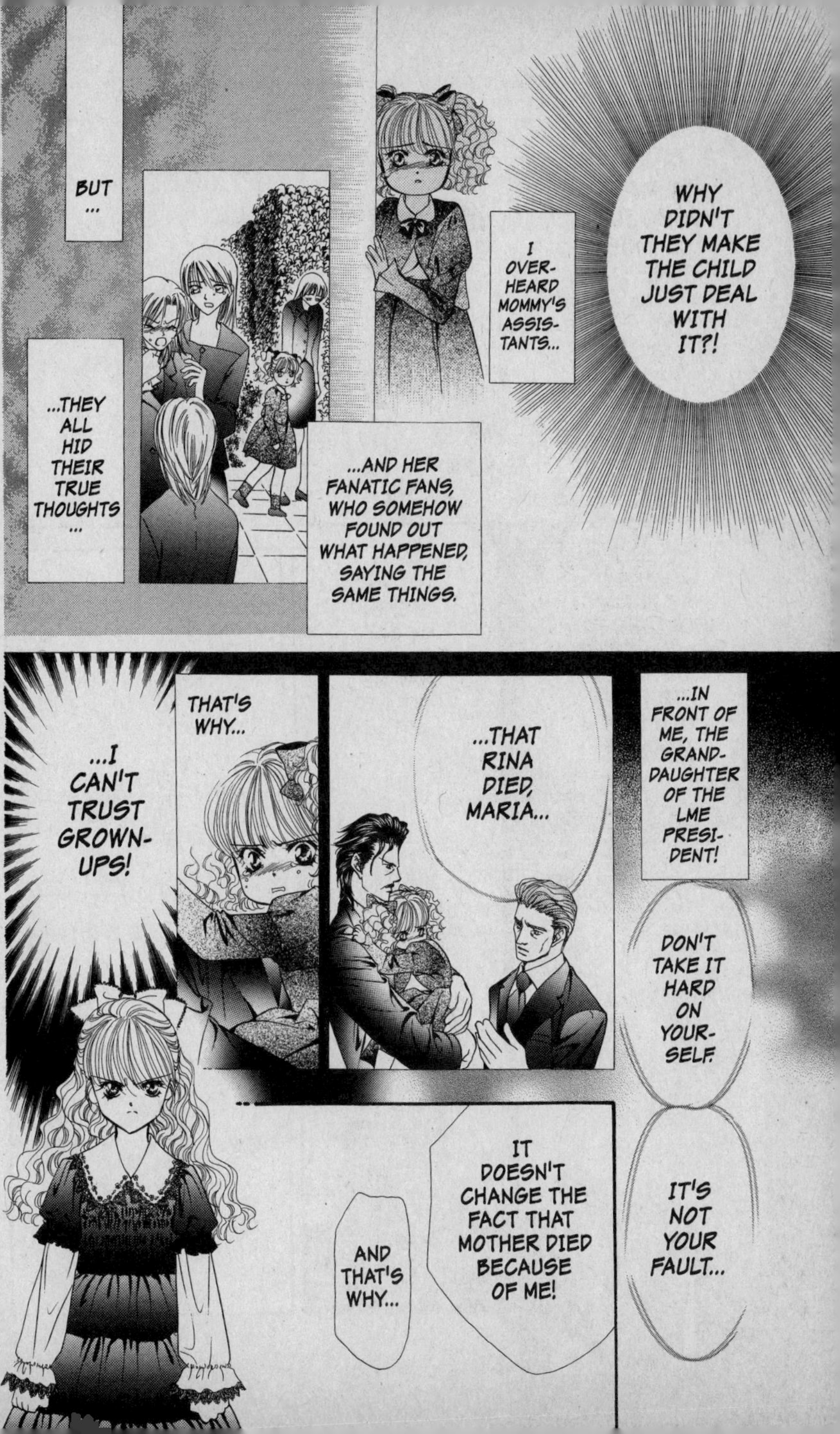
WHY DIDN'T THEY MAKE THE CHILD JUST DEAL WITH IT?!
I OVERHEARD MOMMY'S ASSISTANTS...
...AND HER FANATIC FANS, WHO SOMEHOW FOUND OUT WHAT HAPPENED, SAYING THE SAME THINGS.
BUT ...
...THEY ALL HID THEIR TRUE THOUGHTS ...
...IN FRONT OF ME, THE GRANDDAUGHTER OF THE LME PRESIDENT!
DON'T TAKE IT HARD ON YOURSELF.
IT'S NOT YOUR FAULT...
...THAT RINA DIED, MARIA...
THAT'S WHY...
IT DOESN'T CHANGE THE FACT THAT MOTHER DIED BECAUSE OF ME!
AND THAT'S WHY...
...I CAN'T TRUST GROWN-UPS!

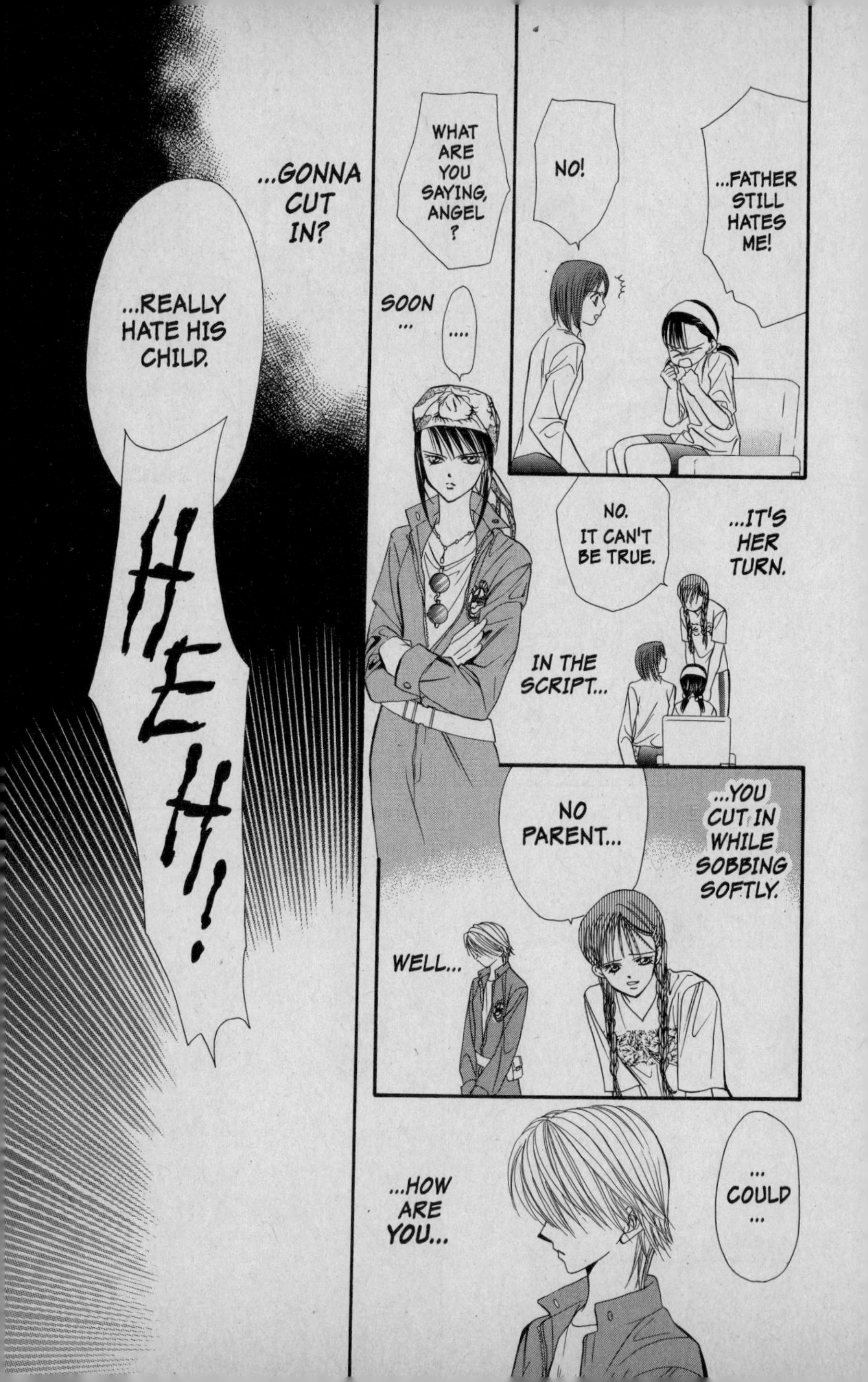
...FATHER STILL HATES ME!
NO!
WHAT ARE YOU SAYING, ANGEL?
...IT'S HER TURN.
NO. IT CAN'T BE TRUE.
IN THE SCRIPT...
...YOU CUT IN WHILE SOBBING SOFTLY.
NO PARENT...
WELL...
...COULD...
...HOW ARE YOU...
...GONNA CUT IN?
SOON...
....
...REALLY HATE HIS CHILD.
HEH!

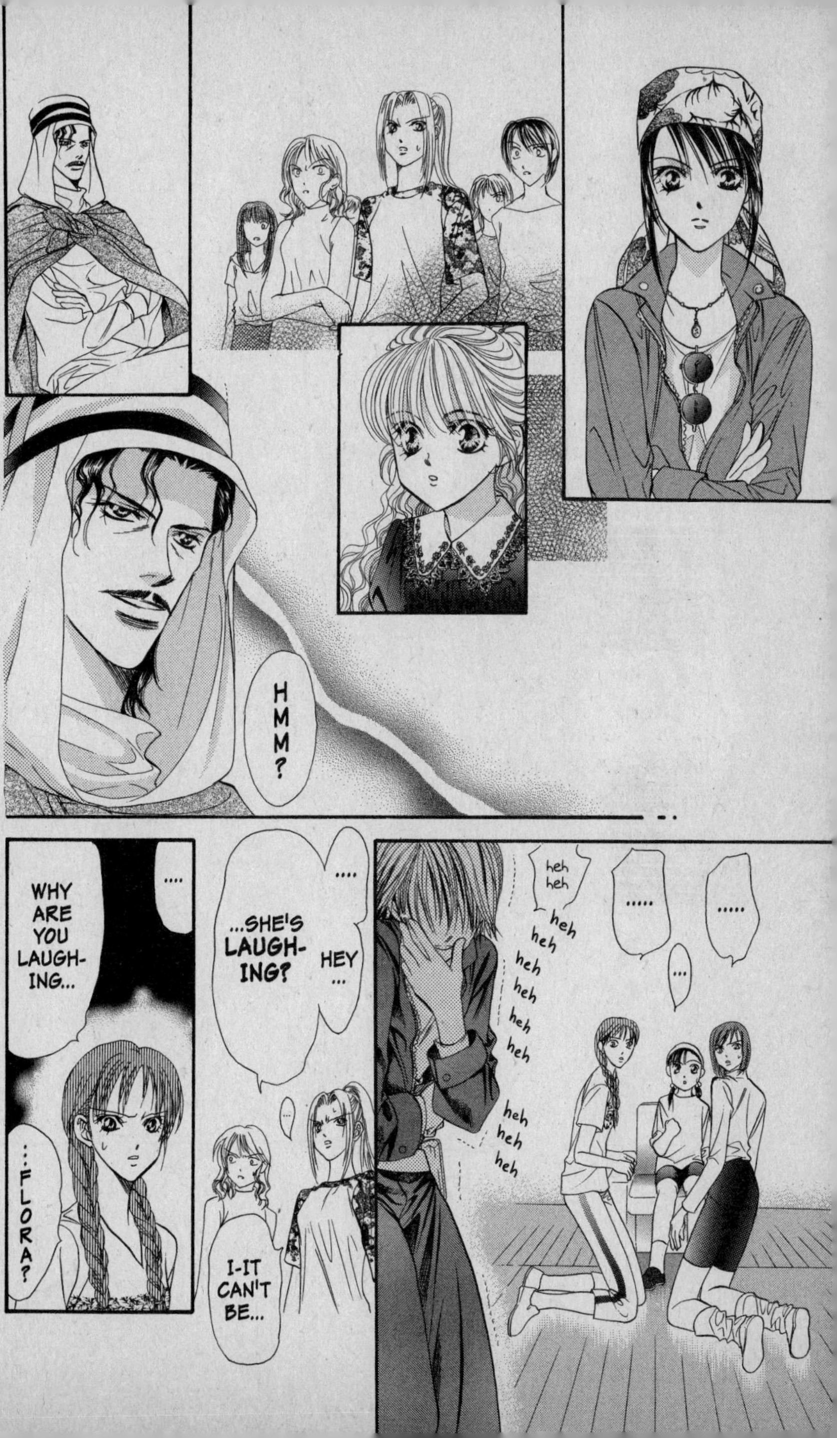
HMM?
.....
.....
...
heh heh
heh heh heh heh heh heh
heh heh heh
....
HEY ...
...SHE'S LAUGHING?
...
I-IT CAN'T BE...
....
WHY ARE YOU LAUGHING...
...FLORA?

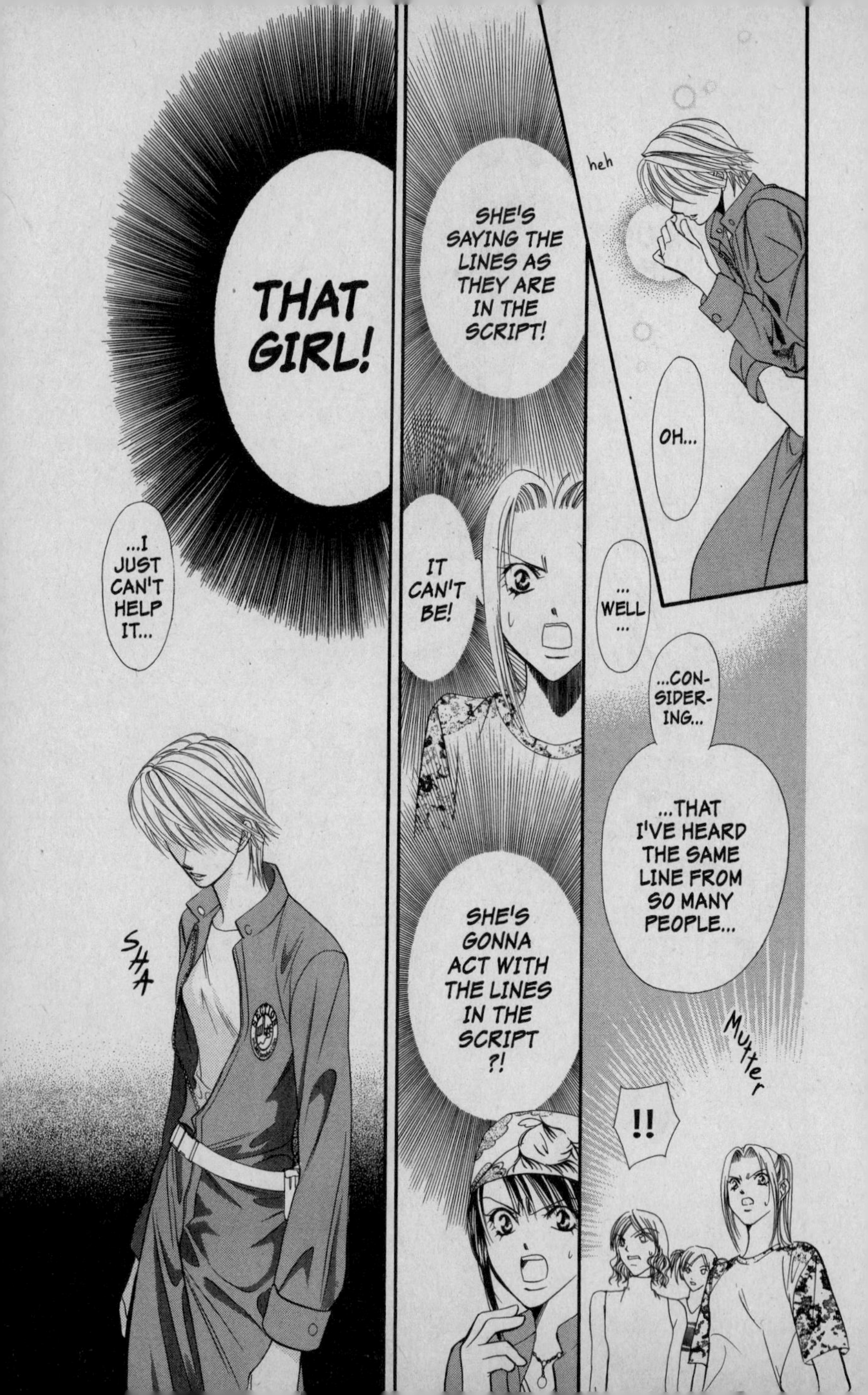
heh
OH...
...WELL...
...CONSIDERING...
...THAT I'VE HEARD THE SAME LINE FROM SO MANY PEOPLE...
Mutter
!!
SHE'S SAYING THE LINES AS THEY ARE IN THE SCRIPT!
IT CAN'T BE!
SHE'S GONNA ACT WITH THE LINES IN THE SCRIPT?!
THAT GIRL!
...I JUST CAN'T HELP IT...
SHA

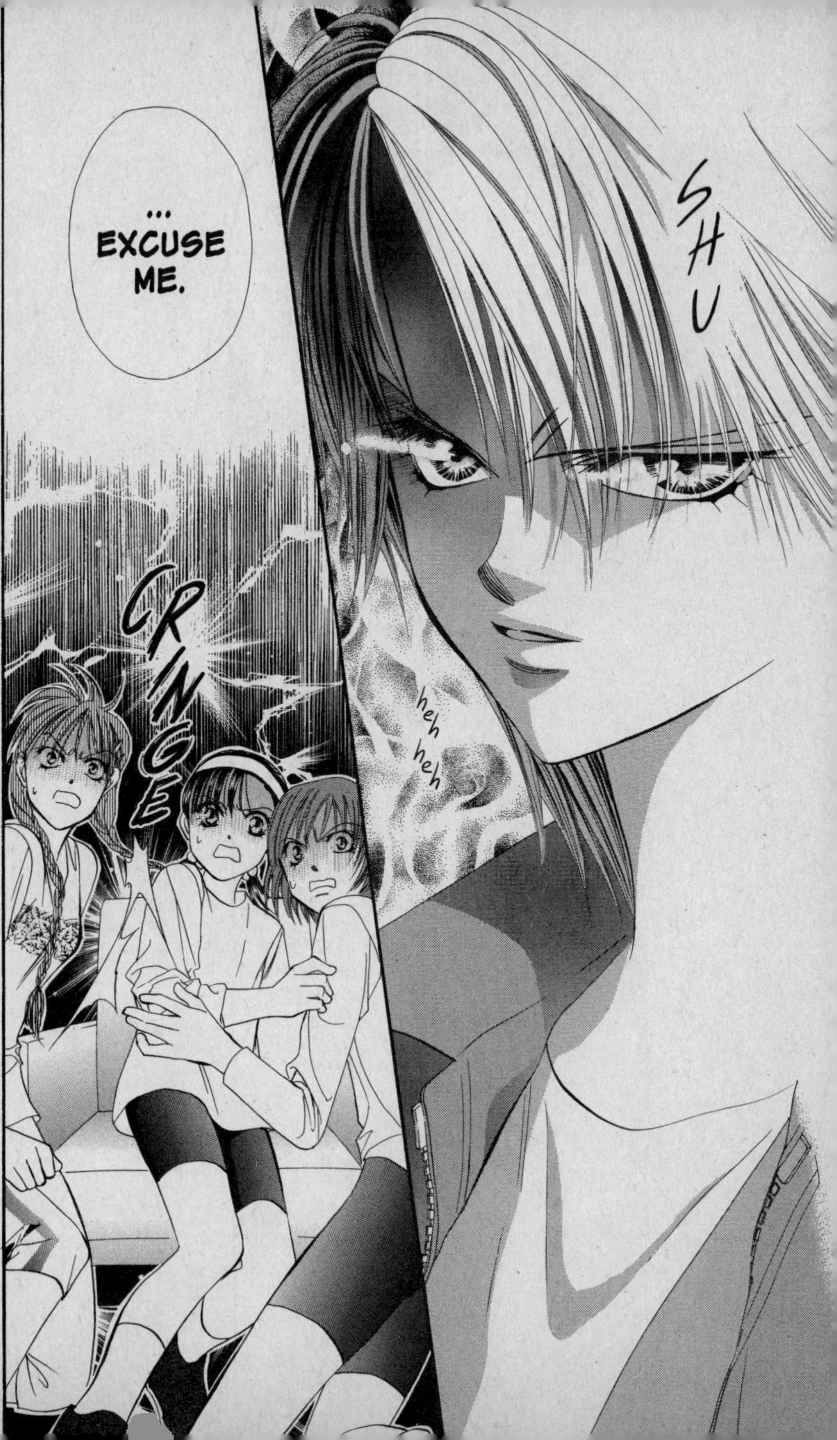
SHU
heh heh
... EXCUSE ME.
CRINGE

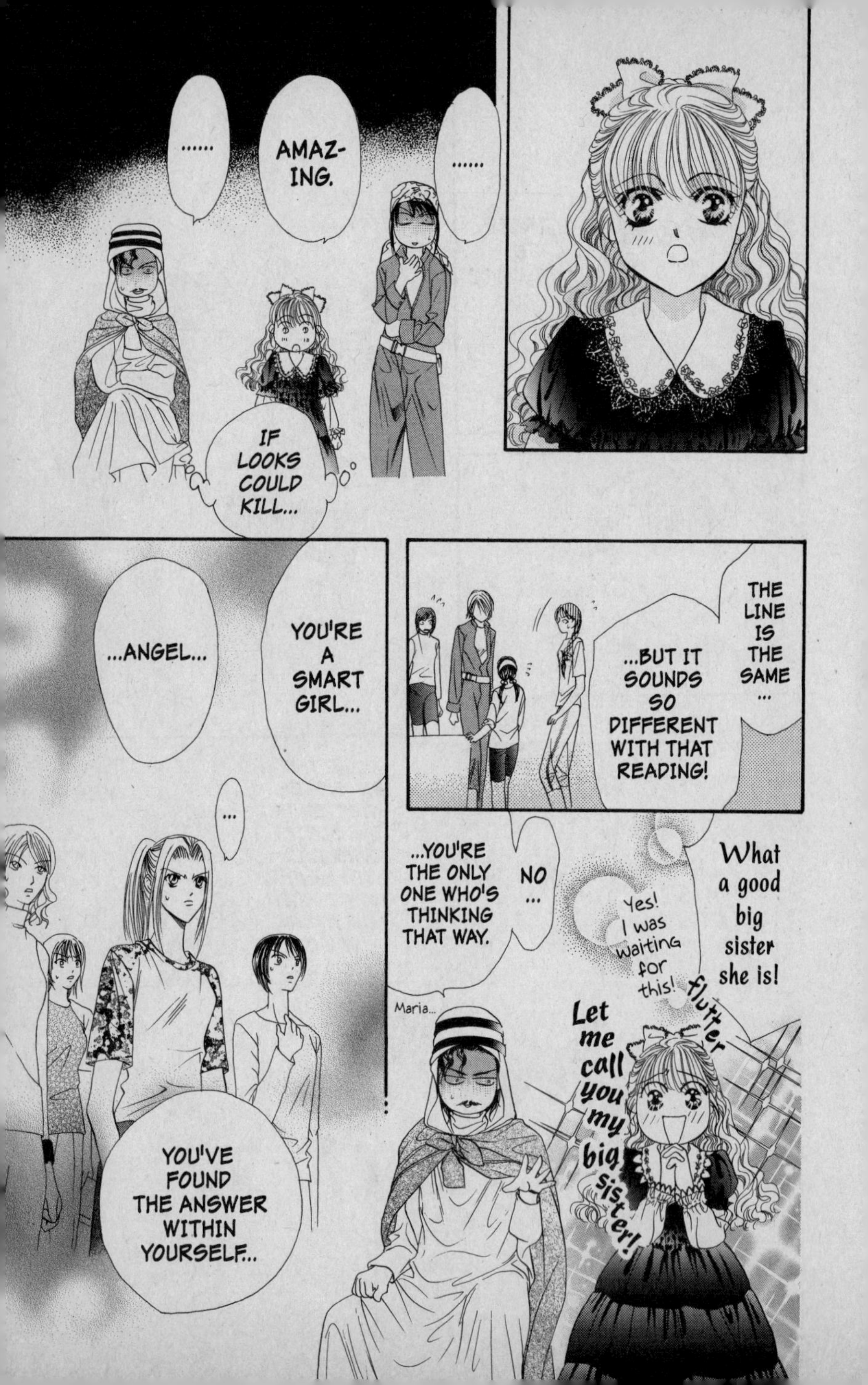
......
AMAZ-ING.
......
IF LOOKS COULD KILL...
THE LINE IS THE SAME ...
...BUT IT SOUNDS SO DIFFERENT WITH THAT READING!
YOU'RE A SMART GIRL...
...ANGEL...
What a good big sister she is!
Yes! I was waiting for this!
flutter
Let me call you my big sister!
NO ...
...YOU'RE THE ONLY ONE WHO'S THINKING THAT WAY.
Maria...
...
YOU'VE FOUND THE ANSWER WITHIN YOURSELF...

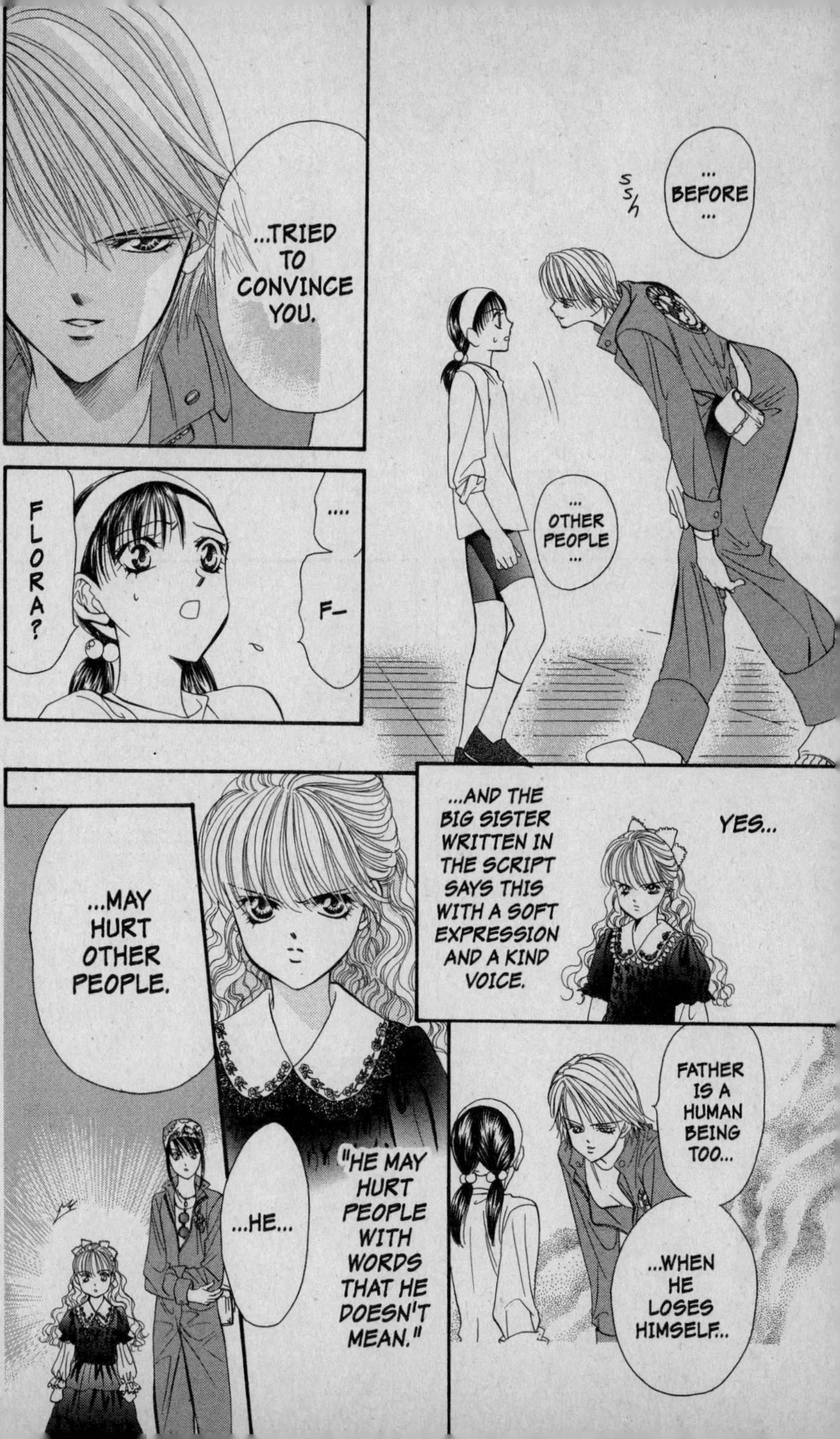

...BEFORE...
SSH
...OTHER PEOPLE...
...TRIED TO CONVINCE YOU.
....
F—
FLORA?
YES...
...AND THE BIG SISTER WRITTEN IN THE SCRIPT SAYS THIS WITH A SOFT EXPRESSION AND A KIND VOICE.
FATHER IS A HUMAN BEING TOO...
...WHEN HE LOSES HIMSELF..
...MAY HURT OTHER PEOPLE.
"HE MAY HURT PEOPLE WITH WORDS THAT HE DOESN'T MEAN."
...HE...

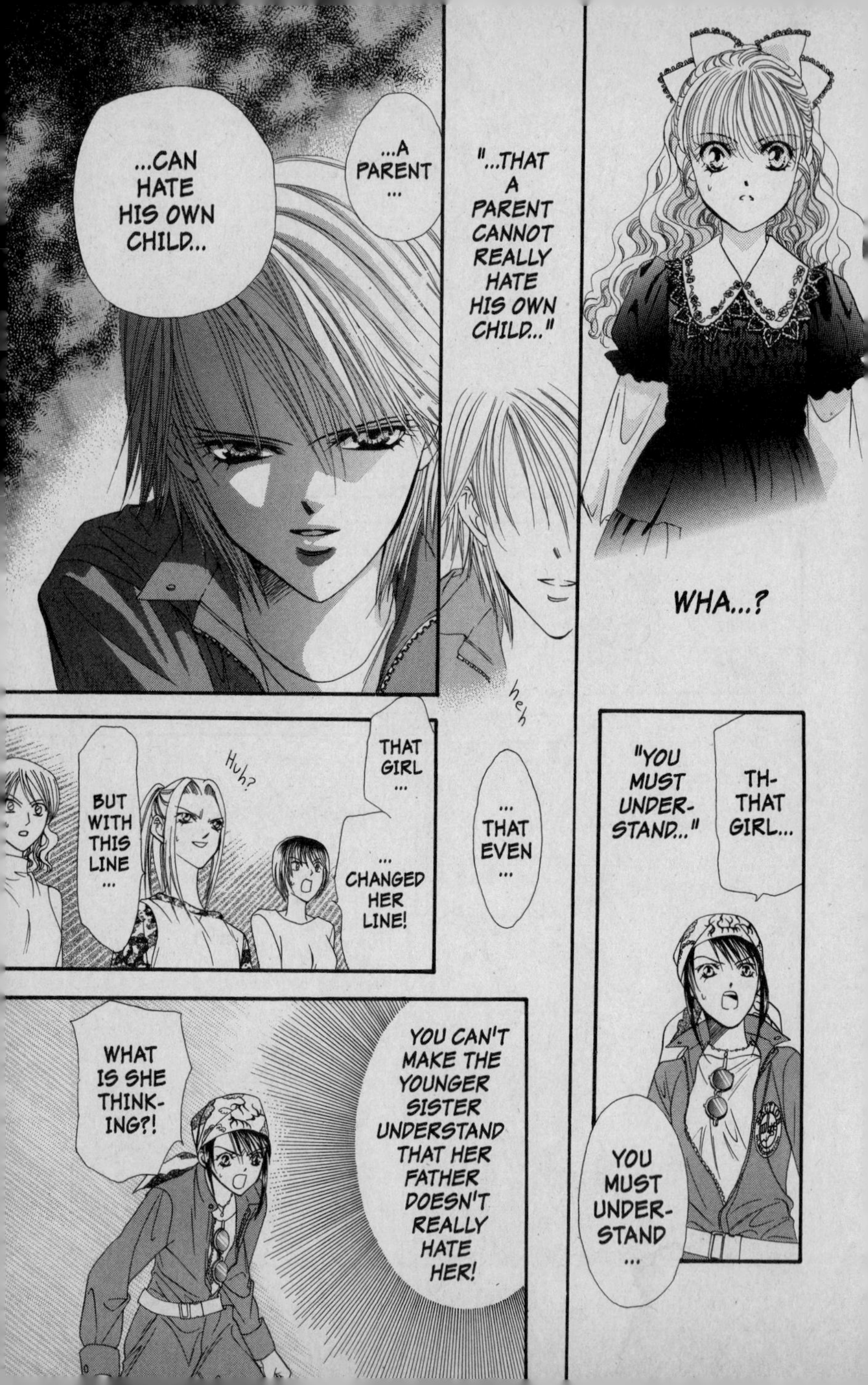
WHA...?
TH-THAT GIRL...
"YOU MUST UNDERSTAND..."
YOU MUST UNDERSTAND...
"...THAT A PARENT CANNOT REALLY HATE HIS OWN CHILD..."
...A PARENT...
...CAN HATE HIS OWN CHILD...
heh
...THAT EVEN...
THAT GIRL...
...CHANGED HER LINE!
Huh?
BUT WITH THIS LINE...
YOU CAN'T MAKE THE YOUNGER SISTER UNDERSTAND THAT HER FATHER DOESN'T REALLY HATE HER!
WHAT IS SHE THINKING?!

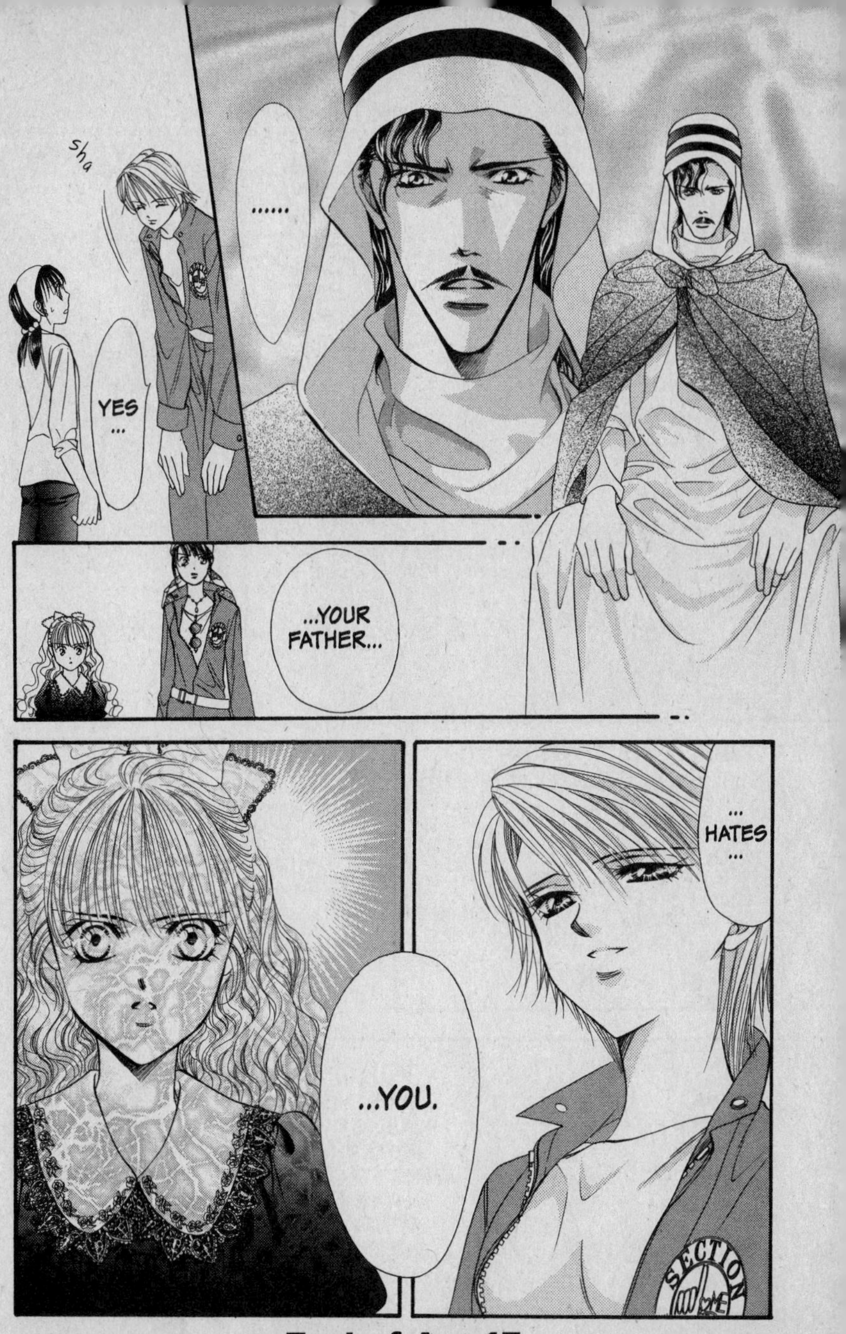
......
sha
YES ...
...YOUR FATHER...
... HATES ...
...YOU.

End of Act 17

Skip-Beat! End Notes
Everyone knows how to be a fan, but sometimes cool things
from other cultures need a little help crossing the language barrier.

Page 384, panel 6: Tea ceremony
The Japanese tea ceremony is a ritual stemming from Zen Buddhism, where
the powdered green tea, called *matcha*, is prepared and served in a serene
setting. *Cha no yu* refers to the ritual itself, while *chado* or *sado* refer to the
study of the tea ceremony. Practitioners of the tea ceremony must know
about calligraphy, flower arrangement, ceramics, incense, kimono, and other
traditional arts, along with the tenets of the particular teachings of her or his
school. It takes many years to become masterful at the tea ceremony.

Page 402, panel 1: Suzunari coast
Suzunari means "where the bell tolls."

Page 423, panel 3: Gel pad
In Japanese, these are called *hiepita*. They are disposable pads filled with a
cooling gel that you stick on your forehead when you have a fever.

Page 487, panel 6: Kanashibari
The Japanese term for a form of paralysis that occurs due to the presence of
a ghost or evil spirit. Most often occurs just after waking.

Page 494, panel 4: Manzai
This is a form of Japanese stand-up comedy involving a straight man and a
funny man. The jokes usually revolve around misunderstandings, puns, and
other verbal gags. The term was first used in 1933, in Osaka.

Page 497, panel 8: Purikura
This is a contraction of the Japanese pronunciation of "print club," and refers
to the photo booths found in arcades and game centers and the photos they
dispense.

Page 519, panel 1: Katsura-muki rose
This was Kyoko's skill in the preliminary auditions in volume 1. She carved a
rose from a daikon radish using a unique Japanese chef technique.

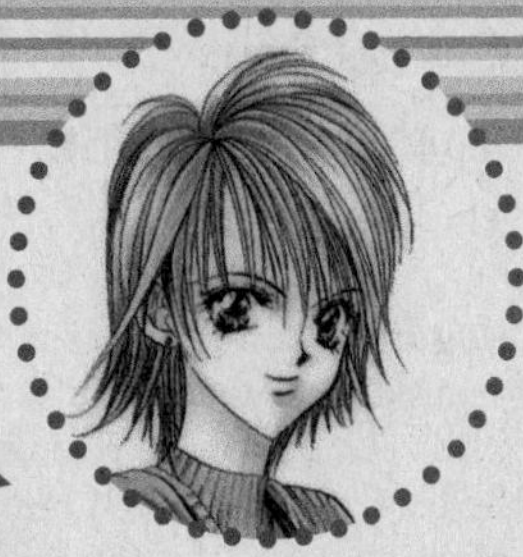

Yoshiki Nakamura is
originally from Tokushima Prefecture.
She started drawing manga in elementary
school, which eventually led to her 1993 debut of
Yume de Au yori Suteki (Better than Seeing in
a Dream) in *Hana to Yume* magazine. Her other
works include the basketball series *Saint Love,*
MVP wa Yuzurenai (Can't Give Up MVP),
Blue Wars, and *Tokyo Crazy Paradise,* a
series about a female bodyguard
in 2020 Tokyo.

SKIP·BEAT!
3-in-1 Edition
Vol. 1
A compilation of graphic novel volumes 1-3

STORY AND ART BY YOSHIKI NAKAMURA

English Translation & Adaptation/Tomo Kimura
Touch-up Art & Lettering/Sabrina Heep
Design/Yukiko Whitley
Editor/Pancha Diaz

Printed in the U.S.A.

Published by VIZ Media, LLC
P.O. Box 77010
San Francisco, CA 94107

10 9 8 7 6 5 4 3 2 1
3-in-1 edition first printing, March 2012

www.viz.com www.shojobeat.com

PARENTAL ADVISORY
SKIP BEAT! is rated T for Teen and is recommended for ages 13 and up.
This volume contains a grudge.
ratings.viz.com

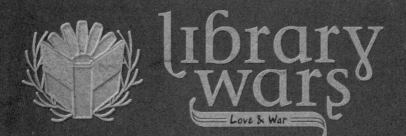
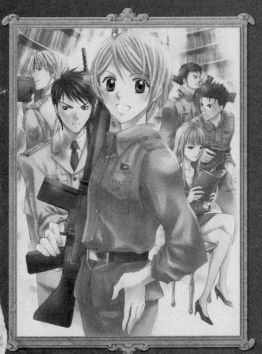
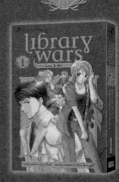

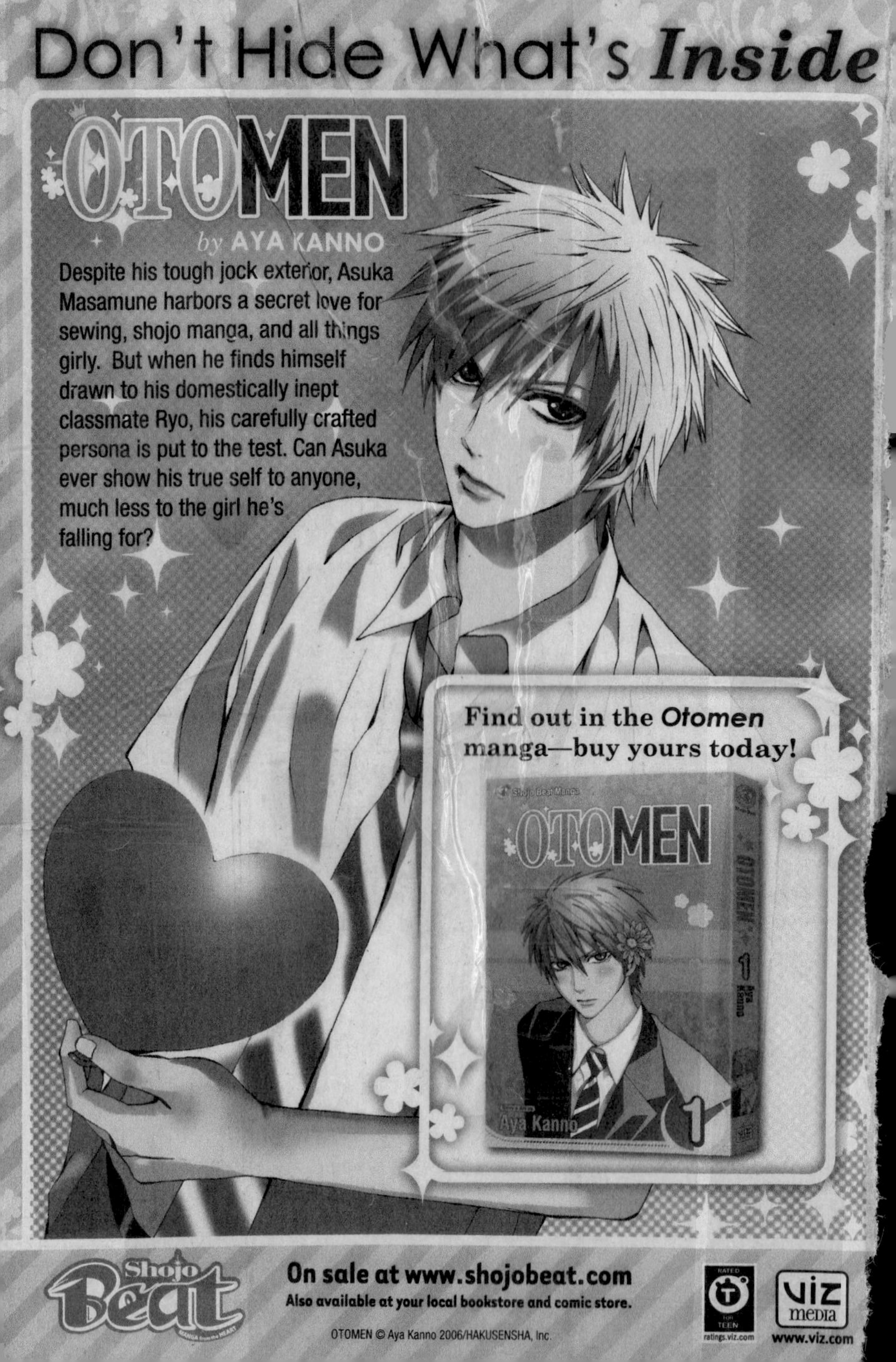
Don't Hide What's Inside
OTOMEN
by AYA KANNO
Despite his tough jock exterior, Asuka Masamune harbors a secret love for sewing, shojo manga, and all things girly. But when he finds himself drawn to his domestically inept classmate Ryo, his carefully crafted persona is put to the test. Can Asuka ever show his true self to anyone, much less to the girl he's falling for?
Find out in the Otomen manga—buy yours today!
Shojo Beat Manga
OTOMEN
Aya Kanno
1
Shojo Beat
On sale at www.shojobeat.com
Also available at your local bookstore and comic store.
OTOMEN © Aya Kanno 2006/HAKUSENSHA, Inc.
RATED T FOR TEEN
ratings.viz.com
VIZ MEDIA
www.viz.com

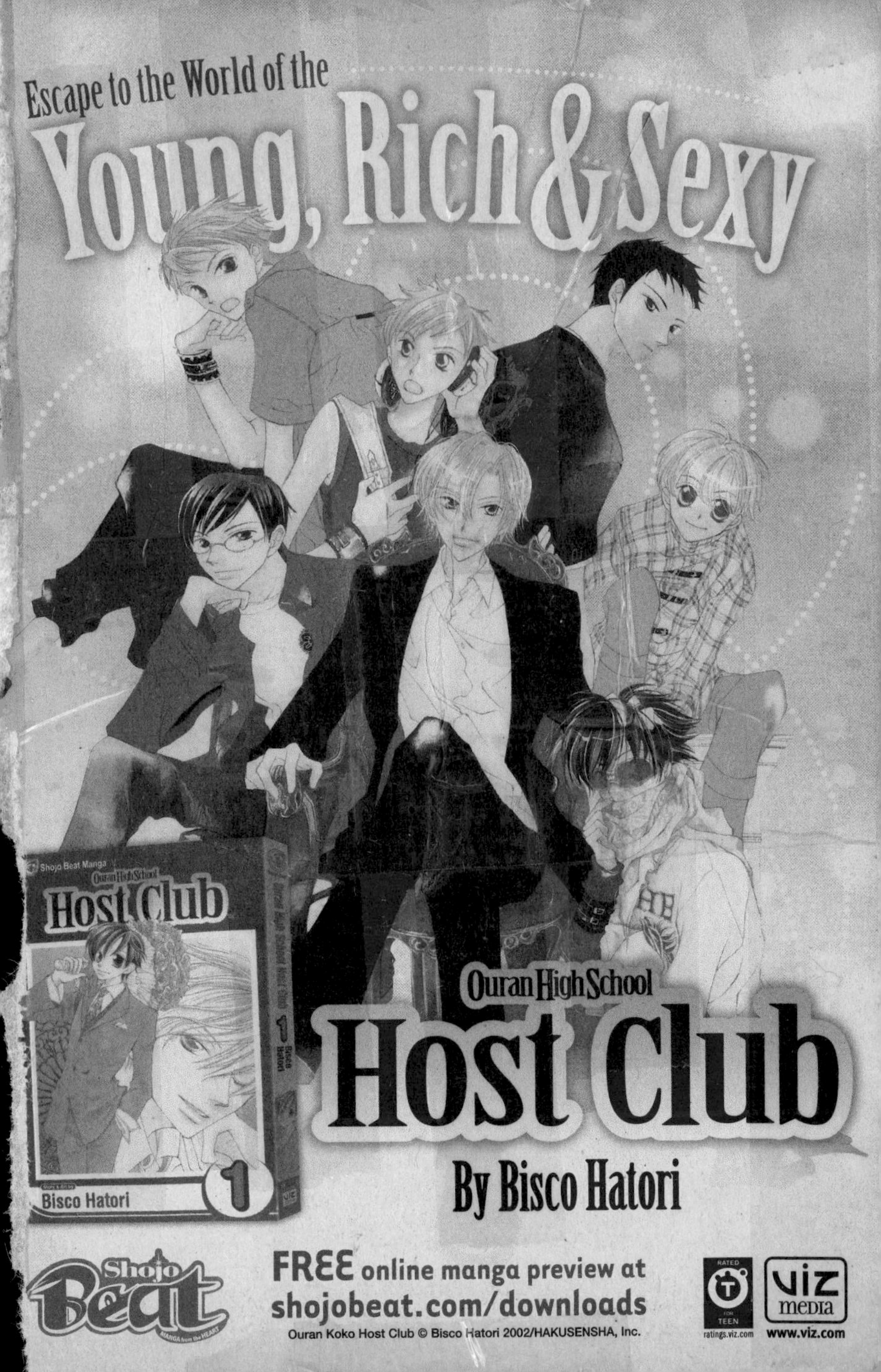
Escape to the World of the
Young, Rich & Sexy
Shojo Beat Manga
Ouran High School
Host Club
1
Bisco Hatori
Ouran High School
Host Club
By Bisco Hatori
Shojo Beat
MANGA from the HEART
FREE online manga preview at
shojobeat.com/downloads
Ouran Koko Host Club © Bisco Hatori 2002/HAKUSENSHA, Inc.
RATED T FOR TEEN
ratings.viz.com
VIZ media
www.viz.com

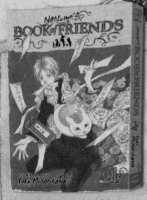

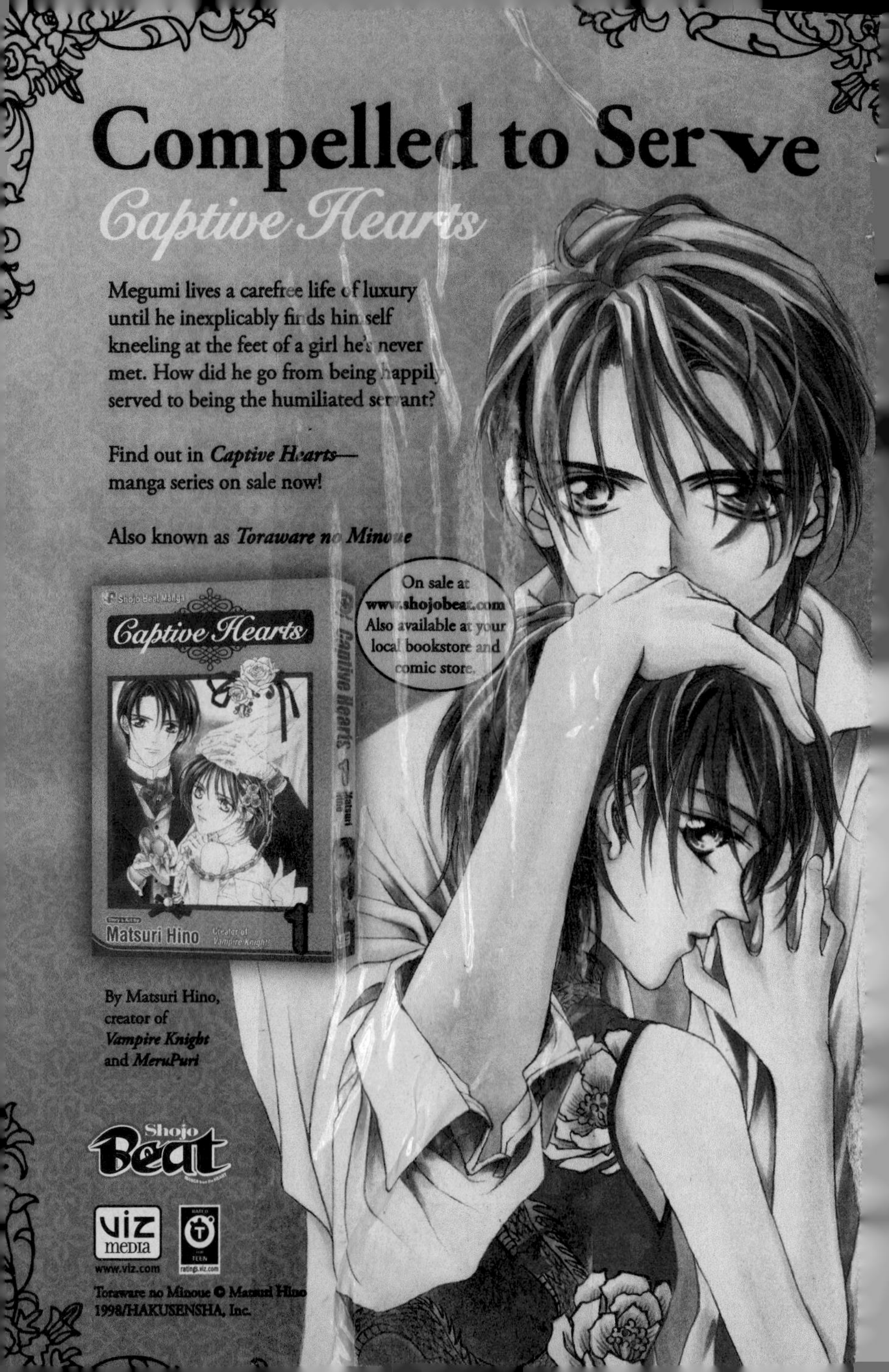
Compelled to Serve
Captive Hearts
Megumi lives a carefree life of luxury until he inexplicably finds himself kneeling at the feet of a girl he's never met. How did he go from being happily served to being the humiliated servant?
Find out in Captive Hearts— manga series on sale now!
Also known as Toraware no Minoue
On sale at www.shojobeat.com Also available at your local bookstore and comic store.
Shojo Beat Manga
Captive Hearts
Matsuri Hino
By Matsuri Hino, creator of Vampire Knight and MeruPuri
Shojo Beat
viz media
www.viz.com
ratings.viz.com
Toraware no Minoue © Matsuri Hino 1998/HAKUSENSHA, Inc.

SURPRISE!

You may be reading the wrong way!

It's true: In keeping with the original Japanese comic format, this book reads from right to left—so action, sound effects, and word balloons are completely reversed. This preserves the orientation of the original artwork—plus, it's fun! Check out the diagram shown here to get the hang of things, and then turn to the other side of the book to get started!

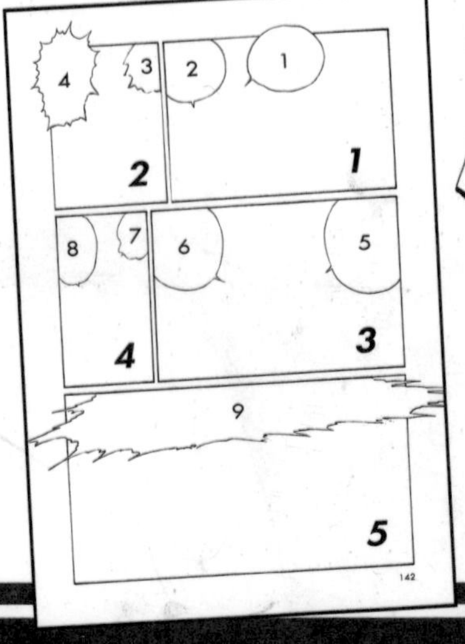

1
2
1
3
4
2
5
6
3
7
8
4
9
5
142

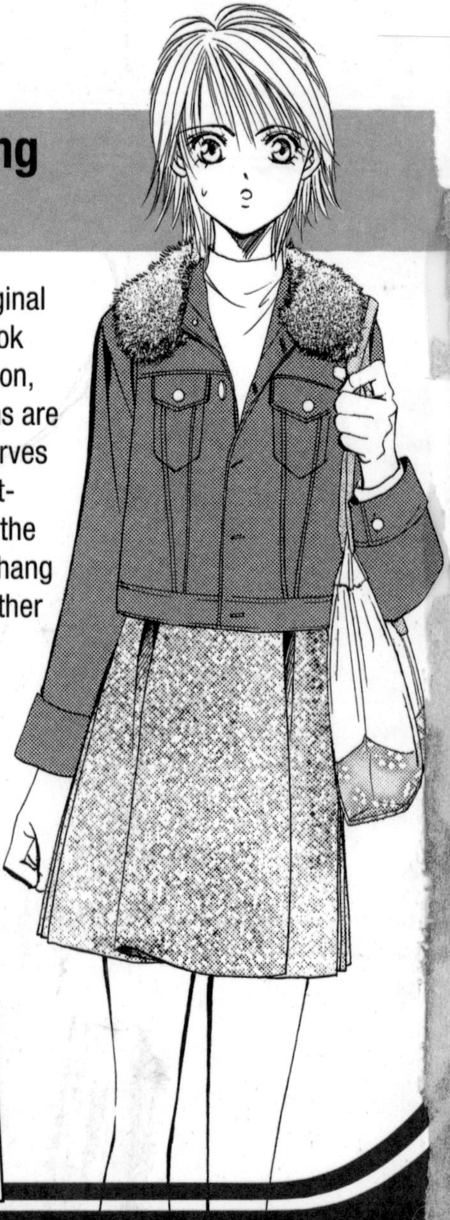

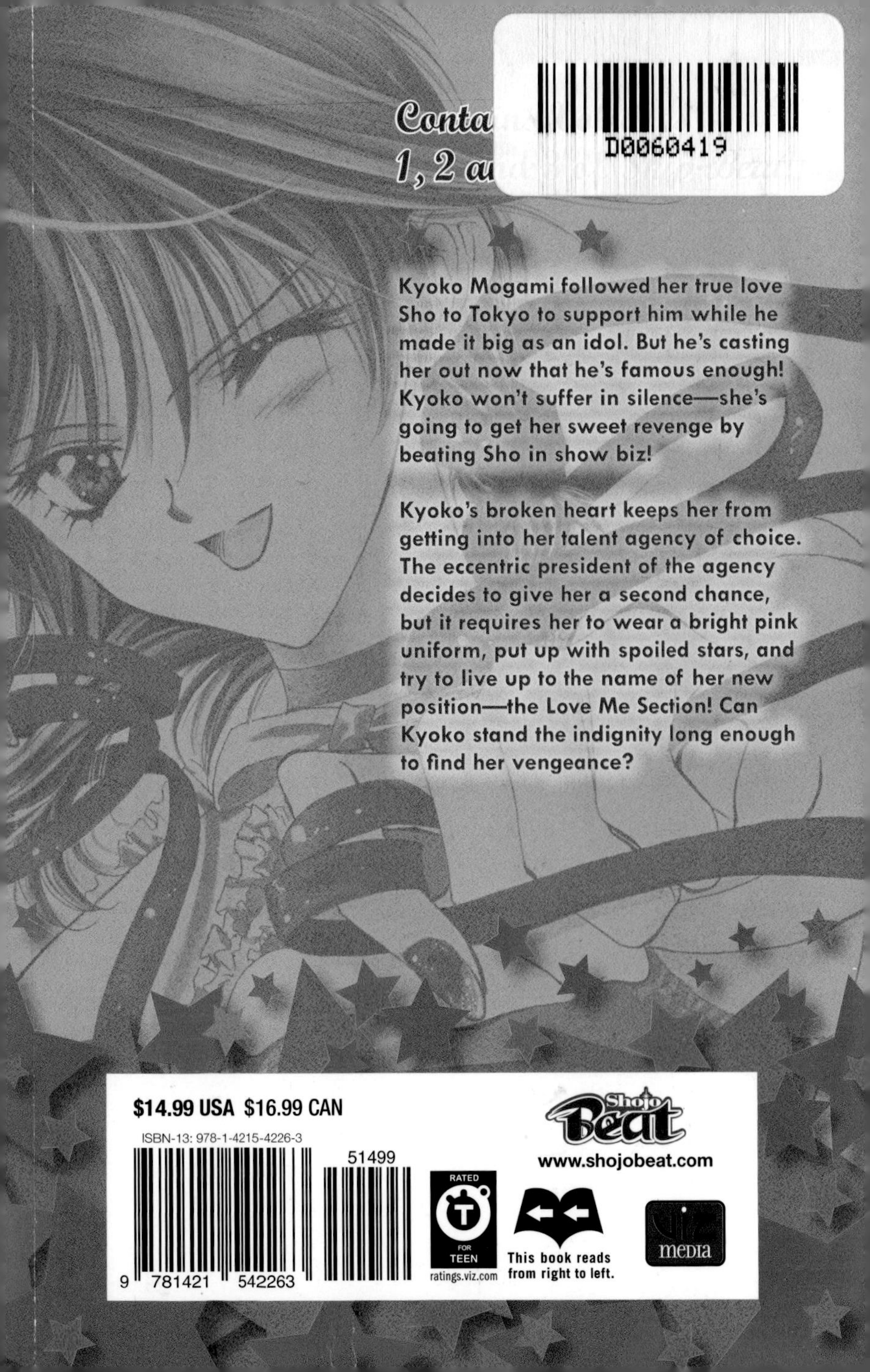

Conta
1, 2 a

Kyoko Mogami followed her true love Sho to Tokyo to support him while he made it big as an idol. But he's casting her out now that he's famous enough! Kyoko won't suffer in silence—she's going to get her sweet revenge by beating Sho in show biz!

Kyoko's broken heart keeps her from getting into her talent agency of choice. The eccentric president of the agency decides to give her a second chance, but it requires her to wear a bright pink uniform, put up with spoiled stars, and try to live up to the name of her new position—the Love Me Section! Can Kyoko stand the indignity long enough to find her vengeance?

$14.99 USA $16.99 CAN

ISBN-13: 978-1-4215-4226-3

9 781421 542263

51499

Shojo Beat

www.shojobeat.com

RATED T FOR TEEN
ratings.viz.com

This book reads from right to left.

VIZ media